Horror Film Directors, 1931–1990

Horror Film Directors, 1931–1990

Dennis Fischer

McFarland & Company, Inc., Publishers
Jefferson, North Carolina, and London

Frontispiece art by Allen Koszowski.

British Library Cataloguing-in-Publication data available

Library of Congress Cataloguing-in-Publication Data

Fischer, Dennis.
    Horror film directors : 1931–1990 / Dennis Fischer.
      p. cm.
    Includes bibliographical references and index.
    ISBN 0-89950-609-7 (lib. bdg. : 40# alk. paper) ∞
    1. Horror films – Production and direction. 2. Horror films –
History and criticism. I. Title.
    PN1995.9.H6F5 1991
    791.43′616 – dc 20   91-52510
                                                CIP

Printed in the United States of America

McFarland & Company, Inc., Publishers
  Box 611, Jefferson, North Carolina

To Horror Fans Everywhere,
but most especially to those writers
who caused me to check out many of these
films on my own and see them in a new way

Table of Contents

II. The Hopeless and the Hopeful: Promising Directors, Obscurities, and Horror Hacks   757

Acknowledgments

A book of this type builds from a number of sources without which it would not have been possible. It involved seeing literally thousands of horror movies, often going far afield to see the rarer or more obscure ones. I am particularly indebted to the Academy of Science Fiction, Horror & Fantasy Films, the Landmark Theater Corporation, and the UCLA Film Archives for making a number of rarely screened films accessible. I am also indebted to the home video explosion, which has been a mixed blessing, resurrecting a tremendous number of worthwhile and worthless films and making them available to the general public.

Portions of this book have been published in different forms in various magazines, and I am indebted to writers and editors in the cinematic journalism field who have had an influence on this book. These include Forrest J Ackerman (editor, *Famous Monsters of Filmland* and *Monsterland*), Fred Clarke (*Cinefantastique*), Bill Connolly (for information on Italian films and directors and for *Spaghetti Cinema*), David Everitt (*Fangoria*); Donald Farmer, Bill George, Kris Gilprin, Dick Klemensen (for info on British films and filmmakers and for *Little Shoppe of Horrors*); Craig Ledbetter (*Hi-Tech Terror*), Dave McDonnell (*Starlog*), Jeff Smith (*Wet Paint*), Bob Strauss, Gary Svehla (*Midnight Marquee*), Randall Larson (*Cinefan*), James Van Hise (*SF Movieland*), and Ron Borst.

I would also like to acknowledge the contributions of a number of people who have worked or are working in the film industry who gave of their time to be interviewed for this book: Dario Argento (writer/director); John Beuchler (makeup effects artist/director); Robert Bloch (screenwriter); Rob Bottin (makeup effects artist); John Carpenter (writer/director); John Carradine (actor); L. M. "Kit" Carson (writer/actor); Mae Clarke (actress); Robert Clarke (actor/director); Larry Cohen (writer/director/producer); Chris Columbus (writer/director); Roger Corman (producer/director); Wes Craven (writer/director); Joe Dante, Jr. (director/editor); Beach Dickerson (actor); Mike Finnell (producer); Larry Franco (producer); Stuart Gordon (director); Charles B. Griffith (writer/director/producer); Curtis Harrington (director); Jonathan Haze (actor); Debra Hill (producer); Tobe Hooper (director); Jackie Joseph (actress); Reginald LeBorg (director); Christopher Lee (actor); Dick Miller (actor); Dan O'Bannon (screenwriter/director);

Acknowledgments   x

George A. Romero (writer/director); Tom Savini (makeup effects artist); Curt Siodmak (writer/director); Milton Subotsky (writer/producer); Shirley Ulmer (script girl); Mel Welles (writer/actor/director); Brian Yuzna (producer).

Introduction

The oldest and strongest emotion of mankind is fear, and the oldest and strongest kind of fear is fear of the unknown.

Howard Phillips Lovecraft

The remarkable thing about horror films is you can do anything you want with that format, from making a piece of crud to making something that can express a profound element of your world view. They are one of the modern myths, sort of like Joseph Campbell on acid.

Wes Craven

This book comes from a couple of decades of viewing horror films and a decade spent partially in talking to the directors who have made them. I'm convinced that no other genre has produced more genuinely execrable films than the horror genre, a reason that many critics treat it as anathema, but it is also true that no other genre has produced more mediocre films with brief flashes of genius, of art, of the unforgettable. While many great films are viewed only once, there is something about horror films that impels viewers to see them again and again, even with better films available. There is no question they touch some nerve deep inside ourselves.

Unlike westerns or detective mysteries, which have flashes of popularity and then disappear again, horror films have been almost consistently popular over the years. There has almost always been an audience for horror films. Even if it was not always a large mainstream audience, there have been a sizeable number of devotees ready to line up for the next terror opus, however good or bad. As a result, horror has not only been one of the most durable genres, it has also been one of the most profitable, though it has undergone a number of profound changes.

Before we continue, I think it best to do what no other book on the subject has really done – that is, provide a definition of the horror film. According to the precepts of this work, a film is a horror film if one of the following is true about it:

A) It deals with a supernatural subject.
B) It has a monster.
C) It promotes an atmosphere of horror and fear.

Hence, Shakespeare's *Julius Caesar, Hamlet,* and *Macbeth,* each with their ghosts and other elements of the supernatural or horror and fear, are all horror tales, some of the finest in the English language. So too is *Horror of Party Beach* or *Make Them Die Slowly,* to go from the pinnacle of the genre to the nadir.

Sometimes the lines can get blurred, and we have to rely on distinctions dictated by convention. If a maniac comes after someone with a knife, with its implicit threat of mutilation, that is called a horror film, whereas if the same maniac were armed with a gun, the same film would be called a suspense thriller. If someone dies and becomes a ghost, which has the potential to haunt and frighten, then that is a horror film even if the ghost is friendly and the film is funny; but if the person dies and becomes an angel, which offers no threat and is associated only with good, then the film must be classified as a fantasy.

Perhaps the trickiest distinction is between the horror genre and its sister genre, science fiction. During the 1950s these genres were closely allied, but this tome covers only horror directors; SF directors are omitted. Science fiction films sometimes have monsters, but the difference is that in science fiction, these creations are given semiplausible or at least pseudo-scientific explanations for existence (e.g. the monster is an alien life form from another planet, or was created by radiation). In horror films, the monsters come from within or have a mystical or supernatural origin – some curse or fate that may represent cosmic retribution or the embodiment of evil forces at work in our world.

There's much more to say about horror films, but before we continue, let's define the other half of the title – the director. What precisely is the job of the film director? This seemingly simple question can become quite difficult when the specifics of the job can change from person to person. Originally, directors were hired as decision-makers, to be responsible for getting a production on film. It was their job to get the required performances out of the actors and to retain an overall cinematic conception that would unify the disparate pieces of a production. In filmmaking even into the early 1930s, directors of photography would sometimes control all aspects relating to the camera while the director concerned himself with coaching the actors; however, this began to change, and directors were required to tell the d.p. or cinematographer just what was to be filmed, selecting the camera angles from which a scene would be shot.

According to director Richard L. Bare in *The Film Director*:

> The director's function is unique and all embracing. He preconceives a motion picture as it will appear in its entirety and vitally participates in all phases of its preparation and execution. Since he is also in command of others, he must know something of their functions. He must

know the rudiments of acting, writing, and photography. He should be able physically to edit films. He should have a working knowledge of architecture, of costume design, of makeup, of music, else how can he communicate with those whose job it is to provide these ingredients? Above all, he must indelibly stamp his own personality, his style, his *touch* on the film he creates, and the measure of his success is the extent to which he enlightens, uplifts, and gives pleasure to the audience.

Additionally, a director must work as a psychologist, motivating the various members of a production to give their best. He must prepare very carefully for shooting to eliminate as many problems as possible in advance. He must know how to communicate with the actors and shape their performances. He must understand how his scenes should cut together and how to develop movement and pace via editing. He must know how to tell a story visually and how to use the camera to get the effects he intends. He must use the money the producer has entrusted him with wisely. Finally, he must tell a *story* with honesty and integrity while at the same time amusing and entertaining his audience.

As you realize, the director doesn't do all this by himself. Film is ultimately a collaborative medium and involves the talents of a great many people. The director is the middle man in all of this. He must take the creation of the writer and bring it to life using the talents of his actors to portray the characters and his crew to get it all on film. The editing process allows for some important refinements in pacing and emphasis, eliminating portions that don't work or that hinder the story, and scoring the film gives various scenes an emotional context. Eliminate any portion of this process and you don't have a complete movie.

However, with the growth of the *auteur* theory of filmmaking, directors have been given an increasingly larger share of the credit so that sometimes the contributions of others are unfortunately obscured. What the *auteur* theory says, in essence, is that the director is the author of the film, that his is the most vital creative contribution.

Now there are a group of directors about whom this is inarguably so. Most are writer-directors, directors who write their own screenplays, tailoring them to their needs, and it should come as no surprise that the most highly regarded *auteur* directors fall into this category. There are also directors like Alfred Hitchcock and Howard Hawks who are very intimately involved in the screenwriting process with the scenarist and who tell particular and specific types of stories. These may safely be classified as *auteurs* as well.

However, there are other directors who, while they may bring a vision and a style to their films, are not genuine *auteurs*. This is by no means to belittle their very real contributions to their films, but simply to make a clear distinction between those who cinematically conceive the stories and creative essence of their films and those who use their talents to bring life to someone else's words and concepts. To proclaim a director who had no choice in the project he was directing an *auteur* is ridiculous.

Of those directors working or specializing in the horror genre, some are *auteurs* and some are not, but they have all brought something different to the films that they make. The purpose of this book is to draw attention to the work of these artisans and show that many of them have achieved a significant body of work in an often neglected and reviled genre. To qualify for inclusion in the main section, a director must have directed no fewer than three horror films. Most of the great horror films have been directed by these specialists in the horror genre (but see Appendix), and so this book is also a survey of significant films in the horror genre.

Certain directors have been omitted because their work is what I would principally consider to be science fiction rather than horror, though some directors like Roger Corman, Edgar G. Ulmer, and Robert Wise who have produced notable work in both genres are included. For the record, those directors who have been omitted include Robert Altman (*Countdown; Brewster McCloud; Three Women; Quintet*); Jack Arnold (*Creature from the Black Lagoon; It Came from Outer Space; Tarantula; The Incredible Shrinking Man*); Irwin Allen (*The Lost World; Voyage to the Bottom of the Sea*); Michael Anderson (*1984; Logan's Run; Millenium*); Edward Bernds (*World Without End; Queen of Outer Space; Return of the Fly; Valley of the Dragons*); John "Bud" Cardos (*Kingdom of the Spiders; Mutant; The Day Time Ended*); James Cameron (*Piranha II: The Spawning; Terminator; Aliens; The Abyss*); Luigi Cozzi (*Alien Contamination; Hercules; Starcrash*); William Dear (*Timerider; Harry and the Hendersons*); Edward L. Cahn (*The Creature with the Atom Brain; The She-Creature; The Four Skulls of Jonathan Drake*); Gene Fowler, Jr. (*I Was a Teenage Werewolf; I Married a Monster from Outer Space*); Richard Fleisher (*Twenty Thousand Leagues Under the Sea; Fantastic Voyage; Soylent Green*); Val Guest (*The Creeping Unknown; Enemy from Space; Casino Royale; The Day the Earth Caught Fire*); Bert I. Gordon (*The Amazing Colossal Man; Attack of the Puppet People; Village of the Giants; Food of the Gods; Empire of the Ants; Necromancy*); Byron Haskin (*War of the Worlds; Conquest of Space; From Earth to the Moon; Robinson Crusoe on Mars; The Power*); Stephen Herek (*Critters; Bill & Ted's Excellent Adventure*); Nathan Juran (*20 Million Miles to Earth; The Deadly Mantis; Attack of the 50 Foot Woman; Brain from Planet Arous; First Men in the Moon; 7th Voyage of Sinbad*); Eugene Lourié (*Beast from 20,000 Fathoms; Colossus of New York; The Giant Behemoth* with Doug Hickox; *Gorgo*); Ib Melchior (*Angry Red Planet; The Time Travelers*); William Cameron Menzies (*Chandu the Magician: Things to Come; The Whip Hand; Invaders from Mars; The Maze*); Nicholas Meyer (*Time After Time; Star Trek: The Wrath of Kahn*); George Lucas (*THX 1138;*

Star Wars); Stanley Kubrick (*Dr. Strangelove, or How I Learned to Stop Worrying and Love the Bomb; 2001: A Space Odyssey; A Clockwork Orange*); Kurt Neumann (*Rocketship X-M; She Devil; Kronos; The Fly*); Doug Trumbull (*Silent Running; Brainstorm*); Paul Verhoeven (*The Fourth Man; Robocop; Total Recall*); and Robert Zemeckis (*Back to the Future*, parts 1–3; *Who Framed Roger Rabbit*).

I have also omitted the wonderful films of Wilhelm Dieterle (*A Midsummer Night's Dream; Six Hours to Live; The Hunchback of Notre Dame; All That Money Can Buy*, aka *The Devil and Daniel Webster;* and *Portrait of Jennie*) simply because his approach to the supernatural was one of gentle fantasy, and though all these films deserve to be considered classics, they are more classic fantasies than horror films. The same goes for the not-so-gentle, prehistoric fantasies of Ernest Schoedsack (*The Most Dangerous Game; King Kong; Son of Kong; Dr. Cyclops;* and *Mighty Joe Young*).

In reading the stories of the films and filmmakers that have been included, the reader will notice that each decade the horror genre goes through some profound changes. I do not deal with the earliest horror films, the silents, for a number of reasons. First, many of these films are lost or nigh impossible to see. Second, the silent cinema was in fact a different art form than sound cinema and requires a different aesthetic – the style of acting and presentation were naturally quite different. Finally, these scattered early entries were just that – scattered. Horror was never really defined as a film genre until after the release of Tod Browning's *Dracula*, itself initially billed as the "Strangest Love Story of All Time."

The earliest important silent horror films came from Germany, and so the interested reader is directed to Lotte Eisner's excellent study *The Haunted Screen* for information about the formative films of F. W. Murnau (*Nosferatu; Faust; Der Januskopf*); Paul Wegener (*Der Golem*); Paul Leni (*Waxworks; The Man Who Laughs; The Cat and the Canary*); Henrik Galeen (*Der Student Von Prague; Alarune*); and Robert Wiene (*The Cabinet of Dr. Caligari*). Apart from these, the most important silent work in the horror field was the early films of Lon Chaney, especially those with Tod Browning (who is included in this book), though Chaney's best horror film of the period is the beautiful silent *The Phantom of the Opera* directed by Rupert Julian (there are rumors that Chaney directed his own scenes). The recent Andrew Lloyd Webber musical borrowed very heavily from the silent film's wondrous imagery, with the Phantom appearing as Charon on the River Styx or as the Red Death in an early two-color technicolor scene of the masque made especially for the film.

The question of why horror is popular has been dealt with many times in the past, but most of the answers proposed seem at best oversimplified. No one answer tells the complete story, but there is a kernel of truth to all of them. Perhaps one generality worth stating is that the golden age of horror is 12. What I mean is that the period where one enters adolescence is the period when one is most receptive to horror films and is capable of making them a lifelong passion.

Why is that? It could be for a number of reasons. At the age of 12, a person's rational faculties are finally all falling into place and he begins to take on an "adult" view of the world. The wonders and surprises of the child's world, with its fresh experiences, begin to fade into the commonplace. One of the joys of horror films is that they present wonders that our jaded eyes have not seen. With their bent reality, they provide one way of restoring that childish awe that is within us all and puts us in touch with our willingness to believe the incredible.

Also, it is frequently forgotten that childhood is not the safe and reassuring period that many adults assume it to be. When we are children, we are basically small, helpless, surrounded by giants who have absolute power over us and are capable of completely inexplicable commands and demands. Adults have a secret knowledge. Certain things are forbidden, and therefore alluring, but they are kept from our grasp.

Part of the appeal of horror films is that they play into power fantasies, to which children are particularly receptive. That is why there can be heavy identification with monsters or even knife-wielding maniacs. It's not that the child wants to be a terrible person, but he would like to have that terrible person's power – maybe then he could get some respect, some peace and quiet, some feeling of superiority. Children don't really want to be doomed vampires, but they feel it's "neat" to pretend they have a vampire's powers – to change shape at will, to fly, to stay up all night long, to enter the adult world, to see things and do things that are forbidden. Or have a monster's brute strength to wreak havoc, in comparison to their own pitiful weakness. It's a way of using imagination to assert themselves.

One shouldn't forget the unacknowledged sexual subject, especially for boys. Adolescence is a period of awkward changes; the body transforms and grows hairy, just as a werewolf's does. Soon the boy will be a man, and he would like to have the same mastery over women that Dracula does, making them swoon, seeing them eager for his kisses and caresses. The penetration of the fangs has obvious sexual implications as well.

What child growing up does not feel as gangly and awkward as the lumbering Frankenstein's monster? The monster wants to be loved, but everyone spurns its attempts for affection, simply because of its looks. Adolescence ravages the faces of many youngsters and they can readily identify with the idea of a repellent complexion. Certainly the adolescent emphathizes, knowing that it cannot help its ugliness and is only looking for a little compassion.

Another reason horror films have maintained their popularity – among all ages – is that they help one come to terms with death and mortality.

These are indeed frightening issues and more easily dealt with in the obviously unreal context that a horror film provides. In horror films, we can see that death occurs and can be frighteningly random, but that life continues. There is also a great identification with survivors, whether heroes who defeat menaces with their wits, or with monsters who despite their filmic demises will return again in some other film. Horror films even offer the hope of resurrection, which is basically the task to which Dr. Frankenstein was devoted.

Of course, it might be the simple fact that audiences love to be scared. The films that have the most meaning for us are the ones that move us in some way. They can move us to think, but film is more a medium for the emotions. Some of the strongest emotions are love, hate, humor, and fear, and a horror film can provide all of these. When the blood is running on the screen, it is often coursing quickly through the viewer's body as well. If the film is a good one, suspense will increase, tension will build, and the viewer will be excited, moved, thrilled. Afterwards comes the relief that the characters hurt onscreen were just make-believe and that it was all just a movie. The audience smiles at its willing suspension of disbelief and at the ability of the director and his crew to fool us into momentarily accepting what we know to be unreal, or even outrageous.

As a result, most horror films do not engage the higher brain functions but work universally on a very visceral level, a gut-level response. Magazine editor and horror film commentator Gary Svehla once broke down the basic approaches to creating *frisson* in horror films into 11 categories. There is the "cheap shock," where something unexpected "jumps out" at the audience, catching them off guard; there is "gore galore," where the audience is grossed out by a graphically violent sequence which answers some prurient "what if this happened to the human body?" question; there is "subjective horror and its sister category It Hurts Me Too [empathy] horror," in which close audience identification with the main characters results in a feeling of discomfort because the audience feels as if what is happening to the character is happening to them as well; there is "body out of control," a type that director David Cronenberg specializes in, where a character's body betrays him or won't respond at a crucial moment; there is "perversions of horror," in which the horror takes an unexpectedly perverted or kinky twist and ventures on the taboo; there are "extraterrestrial frights" and "nature runs amok," which propose the horrible consequences of some fantastic situations, a sort of "what if?" horror; there is "dream [is it real?]/ illusion" in which audiences lose their sense of security as the filmmaker manipulates reality and throws them off balance – the rubber reality movies of the 1980s such as the *Nightmare on Elm Street* films and Wes Craven's other dream sequences are pretty good examples of this type of horror, not to mention Paul Verhoeven's chilling *The Fourth Man,* which cannily uses a variety of images known to disgust or upset people; there is "Boogey Man Creeps," the feeling of being helpless while some relentless, implacable enemy is slowly stalking you, which is the basis for most psycho-killer movies; and finally the hardest and most delicate fright to pull off, the "atmospheric fright" in which a general atmosphere of unease is built up until it becomes almost unbearable, something that suggests dark forces at work or something jarringly wrong and menacing.

The horror genre can be broken down into seven basic subgenres, as director Michael Armstrong (*Mark of the Devil*) did in an article for *Films and Filming*. Armstrong's categories were the horror of insanity, where an insane person goes on a killing rampage, a type of horror film that had a popular vogue both in the early '60s and the early '80s; the horror of the undead, your basic supernatural horrors pioneered in the '30s; monsters created by madmen such as the Frankenstein films and their many spin-offs; things from this planet, where science or aliens enter the picture and present a problem that mankind has never had to deal with before; the horror of the occult, which had its greatest vogue in the years following *The Exorcist;* and finally the horror of metamorphosis, the idea that we can change into something horrible, like a werewolf or a maniac.

Part of what gives the horror film its power is that it shows people dealing with that most powerful of fears – the fear of the unknown. When in life we have to deal with something terrible but do not know just how terrible, it can be frightening. One of the most effective illustrations of this principle comes from a non-horror movie – *She's Having a Baby,* directed by John Hughes. Inside this manic comedy is a perfect horror scene: Elizabeth McGovern is pregnant and in labor, and Kevin Bacon is her nervous husband. Suddenly, Hughes shows us a single drop of blood, telling us that something is wrong, but we don't know what. Bacon tries to find out, but all the doctors will tell him is that he must leave, refusing to relieve his (and our) anxiety and making him increasingly frantic. With the proper context and a simple drop of blood, Hughes has created a scene more horrifying than any blood-drenched splatter opus can boast because it plays so expertly on our fears that something unknown and unutterably terrible has happened.

Of course, part of what makes such a scene effective is that while it plays on our fear of the unknown, it is also connected to what we do know. There can also be a tremendous fear stirred up by the horrors that we know, especially if they are put in the right context. A good example of this comes from John Schlesinger's 1976 film *Marathon Man* in which Laurence Olivier uses a dentist's drill to extract information from Dustin Hoffman. We have all been uncomfortable in a dentist's chair and know how painful it can be even when the dentist is being benign and not trying to hurt us. The scene speaks to the core of our fears because we can relate to being in such a horrible situation without ever having fully experienced it ourselves.

Noticeably, this brings up the question of the age-old horror debate: Is it better to show or not to show the violence on the screen? The fact that a good case can be made for either side of the proposition tells us that the answer is situational. There have been a few tremendously scary films that have shown nothing horrible or horrifying on the screen, but there are times when not showing anything just becomes a kind of frustrating coyness. A film like *Jaws* postponed showing us the great white shark and what it could do, though the examination of the remains at the morgue vividly hinted at the shark's power. Still, it would have been a cheat and ineffective if the film had continued in that vein indefinitely. A good filmmaker can scare us with simply what's in our imaginations, and that is much harder to do than hiring a good special effects crew to create some stomach-turning special effects; but then the imagination can be hazy and undefined where a superbly brought-off special effects sequence can show the audience the true horror involved in some horrific action. Atmosphere thrives more on not showing – witness the Val Lewton films or John Carpenter's original *Halloween,* which showed very little – but thrills tend to come more from the spectacle of something that we've never seen before, part of the promise that horror films use to lure us into the theater.

We ask to be entertained, to be taken to a magical world where the supernatural is real, to be astounded – and the best horror films do that for us. They bring us head-on with society's worst nightmares, though there isn't always the clear-cut relationship between the horrors on the screen and society's fears that some would have us believe. Filmmaking is a business and is far more manipulated by what has been successful (financially) in the past.

I would not dispute that seeing violence on the screen has an effect on an audience, but to blame violence in movies for society's ills is ill-considered and unrealistic. Horror films are not made as tracts on how to commit mayhem, and horror fans include some of the gentlest and most violence-abhorring people I know. Horror films have brought them face-to-face with the horrible consequences of violent action, and they have no wish to see such things in real life.

Aristotle spoke of a cathartic effect in art, and I believe that a good horror film, and perhaps even a mediocre one, can serve as a catharsis, a way of releasing repressed tensions and emotions, violent feelings and tendencies safely by jointly experiencing a violent fantasy with an audience of like-minded individuals. Yes, there are violent individuals who have doted on the repulsive images of some artless and violent horror movies, but there is no evidence to suggest that these films "made" them that way, while there *is* evidence that such inclinations have caused these individuals to seek out the unsavory in films. And who knows – perhaps such films have a cathartic effect on them that temporarily lessens their violent tendencies by giving them a socially acceptable outlet. Movies tend to respond to trends, not create them, though it is true that they can advertise a particular point of view or conception. Movies, even horror movies, like other art, are created out of a reaction to something that is already there, be it a fear, an idea, a way of looking at things, an injustice, or whatever. So let us not be so unwise as to blame the messenger for the message, as some have done.

Horror movies, with their fantasy basis, are less likely to convince you of a lie than a more realistic and mainstream film. For the most part, they do not tout, for example, that allowing people to have civil rights is simply a way to allow criminals to "get away" with their crimes. They do not tend to espouse any particular political point of view. And like all art, they should be filtered through a person's sensibility as to what is acceptable and what isn't. If a horror film is not to your personal taste, it's simple to turn off the video or leave the theater and forswear subjecting yourself to it again. There is no reasonable basis for censoring horror films, though obviously what a parent allows a child to see or experience should be selectively limited and discussed. But it is the parents' responsibility to monitor what their children are watching, and not society's. Assuredly, because filmmaking is primarily a business, if there is no market for certain types of horror films, they will die out and no one will have to see them. Meanwhile, neophytes can rely on books like this one to decide for themselves whether a particular film sounds as if it will appeal to them and so pick and choose what they will be exposed to.

Tales that arouse pity and fear date back as far as *Gilgamesh* and *Beowulf.* Mankind has long been fascinated by violence and monsters. They crop up again and again in myth after myth, fairy tale after fairy tale. These are subjects that are inexhaustibly interesting, and horror films have created a kind of modern mythology that has become part of our ordering of the world.

In examining the work of the directors covered in this book, I have not used any of the fashionable new critical school approaches, though there are no doubt some rich readings which might be derived from doing so. Horror films do conform to some basic structures, allowing for a structuralist reading. They abound in archetypes, so archetypal criticism is possible as well as a formalist approach. It can also be argued convincingly that sometimes horror films convey things they don't intend to, allowing for a deconstructionist look at the genre. (I have even seen an interesting Marxist reading of the James Whale version of *Frankenstein* which interpreted the monster as representing the proletariat immigrant work force that came to the New World, was assembled from a multiplicity of parts, and then wasn't allowed to fit in.) There are numerous psychological symbols in horror, dealing as it does with two primal human experiences – sexuality and death, often perversely linking the two. It can also be shown that as the culture has changed, so has the horror film, allowing the basis for a reader-response look at the genre (e.g. it was once expected that good would triumph in the end of a horror film, but this has changed so that for the past two decades, evil has been far more likely to emerge triumphant, confirming an audience's bleak and fearful perception of the world around them).

There is also room for a semiotic look at the horror film (as per Peter Wollen's work *Signs and Meaning in the Cinema*), since the horror genre abounds in icons that can be variously interpreted. In fact, some of these icons, such as the proper deterrents for a vampire, are either strictly adhered to lest the fans and filmgoers become upset, or violated for the purpose of providing an additional shock. To the horror connoisseur, Frankenstein refers to the creator, not his creation. Vampires should cast no reflection in mirrors or shadows, cannot cross running water or bear the sight of the cross, and must be killed by sunlight, by a stake through the heart, or by beheading, methods which allow the undead finally to achieve their eternal rest. Items such as hawthorne bushes, garlic, water (especially Holy Water), wolfsbane, wooden stakes, silver, electricity, full moons, heavy fog, blood, crucifixes, mirrors, villagers carrying flambeaux, old castles, pentagrams, hairy palms, elongated incisors, bloodshot eyes, grey pallor, etc., have a special significance in the horror genre and are staples of it.

I intend to concentrate on plot and theme. Aristotle considered plot to be the most important element in drama, and it certainly is in the horror film, where part of the central appeal comes from the storytelling nature – the illustration of an incredible yarn – and part of the joy lies in recognizing the fantastic things the audience is asked to accept as real, as well as the surprise of something that is beyond their usual ken.

Thematically, the effects of paranoia and fear can be just as legitimate a subject for art as anything else. In examining the works of some horror directors, certain themes do tend to recur, and recognition of this thematic interest can enrich one's perceptions of the work. Some directors emphasize style over content or have narrative obsessions such as the use of two different murderers as a plot twist in the films of Dario Argento.

In the main, I have tried to give an impression of the work that these men have done and sometimes the difficulties they faced in trying to achieve it. There are many fascinating and funny tales concerning how low-budget films get made, and horror movies have by and large always been low-budget, meaning that directors often have had to use imagination to get out of difficulties rather than simply buying their way out.

The unfortunate trend in recent horror films has been increasing emphasis on spectacle (particularly gory makeup effects) at the expense of plot and characters. While monsters and mayhem have also been part of the genre's appeal, many modern horror films have almost forsaken telling a story and even providing much of a context for their spectacle. More and more, modern filmmakers have bent the rules of reality for the sake of additional shock effects, moving a menace without rhyme or reason to wherever it would provide the greatest shock. Perhaps the most daring trend of all has been the total fracturing of reality in some movies (the "Freddy Krueger" *Nightmare* films or the Sean Cunningham–produced *House* and *House II: The Second Story,* as well as the *Poltergeist* series), suggesting that horrors are lurking in an alternate dimension right in our own neighborhoods and can break through and wreak havoc at any time. These films have the illogic of a dream and are inspired by dream fantasies such as Don Coscarelli's *Phantasm* (1979), leading a viewer to expect only the unexpected. However, what is gained in special effects is sometimes lost in coherence and interest and the film becomes increasingly dependent on the visual skills of a director and his effects team.

For the reader who is new to the horror genre, I hope you have a good time discovering films to check out. Since the video revolution, a number of once obscure and hard-to-see horror films are now easily available. (I still have memories of spending long hours driving to obscure theaters and university screenings to catch rare horror films I'd only heard about.) There is something about the nature of these films that invites people to rent them and watch them in their own homes. Perhaps because many were cheaply made, watching them on a television screen does not detract so much from the quality as it does for some films. Also, even mediocre horror films have a quirky, offbeat nature that invites repeat viewings and adds an element of interest that might not otherwise be there.

For the experienced horror film watcher, I hope that I have illuminated some new and interesting aspects about some old favorites, put various careers in the genre into perspective, and perhaps even presented some new films for you to seek out and enjoy. In Russian, *horosho* (pronounced "horrorshow") means good, and I wish you all many hours of some really horrorshow viewing.

Dennis K. Fischer

A Brief History of Horror Films

The horror genre, like the gangster genre, did not really become defined until sound came in, though there had been plenty of filmed adaptations of Broadway fright plays in which visitors would become trapped in
some old dark house with family secrets, sliding panels, and a murderer on
the loose. *Dracula* (1931) changed all that by bringing the supernatural
clearly into the story, and by bringing Old World terrors into what apparently was supposed to be modern-day London.

The "old style" horror film could be seen on view the previous year in
The Bat Whispers, shot in both a 35mm (by Ray June) and a 65mm (by
Robert Planck) version for special engagements. The widescreen format of
the film was quickly abandoned by anxious theater owners who had just
recently updated their equipment for sound and weren't up to revising their
systems once again, which delayed the real breakthrough in widescreen until the '50s when films had to compete with television. But the type of horror
represented by *The Bat Whispers* was also abandoned as supernatural
monsters began to dominate.

Though it had some definite competition from Paramount, MGM and
Warner Bros. (the Michael Curtiz horror films), Universal dominated the
horror field in the '30s and produced the largest number of unforgettable
classics. Dracula, Frankenstein's monster, and the Mummy all shambled
forth from the same studio. There was even an abortive attempt to introduce werewolves, Stuart Walker's misshapen *WereWolf of London* with
Henry Hull as its distinguished lycanthrope (who picks up the disease from
Warner Oland, best known of the screen's many Charlie Chans). Universal
also had the best horror actor, Boris Karloff, under contract and made some
of Bela Lugosi's best-loved horror pictures.

Warner Bros. and First National's horror films (*Doctor X; Mystery of the
Wax Museum; The Walking Dead*) were all directed by Michael Curtiz,
whose directorial strengths lay in other areas. They were all more mysteries than true horror films. MGM's horror films include two of the best-
shot black and white horror films – *Mad Love* (Karl Freund) and *Mark of the
Vampire* (Tod Browning) – as well as the most unusual film of the period

1

(Browning's *Freaks*), but that studio didn't really have a taste for horror and was soon concentrating on color musicals and prestige dramas. Paramount produced some excellent horror films (Mamoulian's *Dr. Jekyll and Mr. Hyde;* Kenton's *Island of Lost Souls;* Edward Sutherland's *Murders in the Zoo*), but soon the bottom fell out of the horror market.

Midway through the '30s, the public seemed to feel it was inundated with enough terrible things thanks to the Great Depression, and attendance at horror films fell off dramatically, with the result that none were released in 1937 or 1938. However, Rowland V. Lee rescued the horror genre by producing such money-making films as *Son of Frankenstein* (the production of which was prompted by the incredible success of a reissue double bill of the original *Frankenstein* and *Dracula*) and *Tower of London*. Lee was far from a horror specialist, but he had an excellent eye for composition and a good sense for developing atmosphere. Having resuscitated the horror genre, he left it, never to return.

Meanwhile, Paramount had a hit with a horror-comedy starring Bob Hope, *The Cat and the Canary;* Fox experimented with horror elements in Allan Dwan's remake of *The Gorilla* with the Ritz Brothers, Bela Lugosi and Lionel Atwill, and in Sidney Lanfield's classic version of Arthur Conan Doyle's *The Hound of the Baskervilles* (which typed Basil Rathbone as Sherlock Holmes for most of the rest of his life); and finally, Warner Bros. punished a recalcitrant Humphrey Bogart by forcing him to play a vampire in the awful *The Return of Dr. X,* Vincent Sherman's directorial debut (and not a sequel to the Curtiz film as might be expected).

Horror returned from the grave in the '40s, a decade principally represented by two very different approaches to horror filmmaking. On one side of the coin were the excellent, atmospheric, low-budget horror films produced by Val Lewton at RKO (see chapters on Jacques Tourneur, Mark Robson and Robert Wise); and on the other were the hefty group of sequels to previous horror hits over at Universal, which brought back Frankenstein, Dracula, the Mummy and with George Waggner's film *The Wolf Man* had a permanent lycanthrope thrown into the bargain as well. The Universal films experimented with follow-ups and matchups, eventually cramming as many different monsters as possible into each film in an effort to attract an audience. The Lewton films, on the other hand are distinguished by the very literary intelligence of their producer, who secretly served as a scriptwriter as well on many of his endeavors. These films hold their own with the finest efforts of the '40s.

Additionally, poverty row studios started getting more into the act, turning out cheaper versions of the studios' already low-budget B films. Monogram and Producers Releasing Corporation made horror part of their staple output along with westerns and crime films. Columbia, having gotten a gem out of Roy William Neill's *The Black Room* starring Boris Karloff, hired Karloff when he was free from his Universal contract to do a series of Mad Doctor films (*Before I Hang; The Man They Could Not Hang;* and *The Man with Nine Lives*).

Universal also launched a brief and forgettable series about a *Captive Wild Woman* and started the ultra-low-budget *Inner Sanctum* series, which provided Reginald LeBorg some of his best horror work.

If the '40s were a hodgepodge of combining and recombining familiar horror elements from the past, the '50s brought something new. As if in a delayed reaction to the dropping of the atomic bomb as well as numerous reported sightings of flying saucers, the decade began a frenzy for science fiction–flavored horrors. People worried about what terrors outer space could bring or what horrible things science might have wrought. With the secret of nuclear energy in Soviet hands and the Cold War heating up, fear and paranoia ran high and were reflected in the films of the period.

Meanwhile, horror filmmaking began to take hold in Italy, beginning with *I Vampiri,* aka *The Devil's Commandment,* directed by Richard Freda and photographed by future horror director Mario Bava. It was a mediocre movie, but it caught on anyway and inspired others, eventually launching Bava's career, which in turn launched the careers of many other Italian horror directors.

In Mexico, Fernando Mendez switched from melodramas to horror films with *El Vampiro* and kicked off a horror cycle there, largely influenced by the poetic and atmospheric horror films of the '30s. Rafael Portillo got into the act with a trilogy about an Aztec Mummy (*The Aztec Mummy,* aka *Attack of the Mayan Mummy; The Robot vs. the Aztec Mummy;* and *Curse of the Aztec Mummy*). Later the character was brought back during Mexican film's wrestling craze for Rene Cardona's ludicrous *Wrestling Women vs. the Aztec Mummy* (1965).

Over in Japan, Inoshiro Honda began a series of films about giant monsters with *Godzilla, King of Monsters.* More importantly, in 1953 Kenji Mizoguchi produced one of the horror genre's few enduring masterpieces with *Ugetsu Monogatari* (see Appendix) and launched a vogue for ghostly tales as well. The horror film was beginning to spread internationally.

Finally, the most important new contributor to the horror genre was a British company by the name of Hammer. Hammer hit upon the idea of remaking the old horror classics in color, and giving them what their '30s counterparts lacked – namely a certain amount of gore and sex. The result thrilled audiences worldwide and launched the company as a mini-major in England with distribution deals via various major companies all over the world. Said films launched the horror careers of actors Christopher Lee and Peter Cushing and gave a major boost to the directorial career of Terence Fisher, who became Hammer's number one horror specialist.

Also, the '50s are remembered as the decade of gimmicks. They gave us the best 3-D horror films: Andre de Toth's *House of Wax,* which turned leading man Vincent Price's career in the direction of horror, and Jack Arnold's evocative *Creature from the Black Lagoon,* the last classic Universal monster creation, as well as Arnold's science fiction–flavored *It Came from Outer Space* with its poetic script by Ray Bradbury and Harry Essex. William Castle, king of the gimmicks, launched his extensive horror career during this decade.

As television took away more and more viewers, theater owners found it hard to book films that could compete – until the independents, specifically American International, found that they could make low-budget pictures for a specific but major portion of the filmgoing audience which hadn't been previously served. What AIP discovered – changing filmmaking forever – was the teenage market. Back in the '50s, the concept of teenagers was still a fairly new one; not much special attention was paid to the adolescent years until after the Second World War. Now the independent studios, realizing there were millions of teenagers who didn't want to hang around the house watching television with their folks, began to make movies specifically for them with titles like *I Was a Teenage Werewolf* (Gene Fowler, Jr.) and *I Was a Teenage Frankenstein* (Herbert L. Strock). These movies and others like them launched the careers of producers Samuel Arkoff, James Nicholson, Herman Cohen, and most famous of all, Roger Corman who also doubled as director.

While such fare was initially only a marginal portion of the market, the youthful audiences proved so reliable that today all major studio releases are geared towards an audience 18 to 25 years old who are single and have the freedom to go to movies on dates. Older moviegoers sadly watch the number of adult-oriented films dwindle in comparison.

The last significant item of the '50s was the development by Forrest J Ackerman of *Famous Monsters of Filmland,* the first magazine entirely devoted to the horror genre. It helped codify what the horror genre was and what it was made up of. It is also significant that the late '50s saw the release of the *Shock Theater* package of old horror films, which played on television and helped to infect a new generation of horror fans and converts. Previously, old horror films were seldom revived and thus seldom seen, but now they could be caught for free in one's own living room.

As horror came into the homes of America, so too did it spread out all over the world, as the 1960s marked a worldwide horror explosion. The cycles that began around 1957 were in full flower during the '60s as new monsters and new sequels were churned out by Hammer and by Spanish filmmakers. Two prolific cycles were started: Jacinto Molina's Spanish "Hombre Lobo" series, in which he launched himself as a horror actor under the name of Paul Naschy, and the Santo and Blue Demon wrestlers-versus-the-monsters series.

A Polish immigrant, Roman Polanski, would bring new sophistication to the horror film with movies like *Repulsion* and *Rosemary's Baby.* In France, Jean Rollin clumsily combined horror and eroticism in a series of sex-vampire movies. In Spain, the superprolific Jesus Franco began his seemingly endless career. In Italy, there developed a vogue for *giallo* films, named after the yellow covers of crime thrillers being sold at the time. With the smash success of Hitchcock's *Psycho,* the time for madmen was at hand, and that classic film spawned countless imitators. Robert Aldrich showed that mad women could have an equal attraction for audiences with *What Ever Happened to Baby Jane?* and *Hush... Hush, Sweet Charlotte.*

Meanwhile, in the American South, Herschell Gordon Lewis was churning out a series of horror films featuring gore for gore's sake. Most people called them trash, but some now insist that Gordon was simply a man ahead of his time. With the advent of Roger Corman's Edgar Allan Poe series, gothic horror made a return, and studios started spending more money on horror productions.

Where previously most horror films had been monster movies (which, if made cheaply enough, rarely lost money), starting with the '60s there began to be a regular focus on the horror of personality, in which man himself became the biggest monster as aberrant personalities wreaked havoc upon society. Also, the horror films of the '60s hinted at fears that the world might be coming to an end, playing on the fear of armageddon – that the animals would revolt, à la *Willard* or *The Birds,* or the dead would come back to life to consume the living as in Romero's *Night of the Living Dead.* These two trends were to last all the way through the 1980s as more and more films featured people, or a world, going mad.

The 1970s saw a breakthrough for horror films in the form of William Friedkin's *The Exorcist.* Previously, there had been some horror films which were hugely successful financially. Back in the '30s there were *Frankenstein* and *King Kong;* in the '60s, *Psycho* and *Rosemary's Baby.* But none of them matched the enormous success of *The Exorcist* and later *Jaws,* which showed that horror films could be mainstream successes as well, not to mention all-time blockbuster champions. Suddenly, the horror genre seemed like a wise thing to invest in.

While many people did not recognize that *Jaws* was a horror film (despite the Great White's monstrous intelligence and capability for destruction), there was no doubting that *The Exorcist* was a good, old-fashioned horror romp, well-orchestrated to capture fears of the times (i.e., why were all these young people starting to grow their hair long, look strange, use foul language – maybe the devil made them do it!) and to astound audiences ("Did you see the film where this young girl masturbates with a crucifix, turns her head about 360 degrees and has furniture flying all over the room?"). While *The Exorcist* was not the most original horror film ever made, and certainly was not profound by any stretch of the imagination, it was a very cannily crafted film, well designed to heighten tension and capture the public's fancy. Naturally, it spawned a horde of imitators, bringing on a deluge of films with a demonic theme. Richard Donner's *The Omen,* a mere three years later, was by far the most successful of these, tying in once more to the cultural myths of Biblical prophecy.

The '70s constituted an eclectic decade that featured some very good, quirky, and unusual films (e.g. Robin Hardy's *The Wicker Man;* David Lynch's *Eraserhead;* Paul Bartel's *Private Parts;* Richard Mulligan's *The Other*); launched several major horror film careers; and was padded out with endless pieces of cinematic mediocrity. It was also the last decade in which horror actors played a major role.

In the '80s, horror producers took a look at films like 1968's *Night of the Living Dead,* 1974's *The Texas Chain Saw Massacre* and 1978's *Halloween* and realized that these low-budget efforts, which featured no name actors, proved to be immense box office successes simply by selling the public on sensation. If expensive name talent was not needed to be a major horror box office draw, then why not dispense with it?

The result is that the '80s became a decade in which amateurs and unknowns took over the lead in horror films, which were increasingly written to formula based on the last major success. After *Halloween* collected a $30 million take at the box office, theaters were chock-a-block with all kinds of opuses about knife-wielding maniacs, so many that a separate subgenre was created and named variously knife-kill flicks, dead-teenager movies, and splatter films. The audiences responded to makeup and special effects, and so those became the things which received the most money, imagination, and attention in these low-budget movies. *Night of the Living Dead* had broken convention by daring to end on a downbeat note, but after *Carrie,* it became de rigueur to end a horror film on a shock and a downbeat note. Not surprisingly, the effectiveness of such a once-novel approach was quickly muted.

Monsters and the supernatural went from being staples of the horror film to being fairly rare. Gone were the icons of the Frankenstein monster, the vampire, and the wolf man. Instead, the '80s horror icons were Michael Myers, the masked boogeyman killer from *Halloween;* Freddy Krueger, the nightmarish dream killer from *A Nightmare on Elm Street;* and Jason, the maniac from the successful *Friday the 13th* series of films. These were the monsters who defined what a horror film should be for a new generation of fans. (A case can also be made for Leatherface and his family of the *Texas Chain Saw Massacre,* though his film saga spans a film for each decade – the '70s, '80s and '90s.)

Poetic curses, doomed men suffering under an ill-fated moon, and literary prettiness all but disappeared after the initial batch of Universal horror films and the Val Lewton–produced films of the '40s. The atmospheric films of the '50s and '60s (*Curse of the Demon; The Haunting*) were made by directors who had won their wings under Lewton. Occasionally, an atmospheric production would still come through – Herk Harvey's haunting one-shot *Carnival of Souls* immediately comes to mind – but most '60s films were into shock and sensation, and these elements simply increased in explicitness as the '70s and '80s came along.

Sometimes the explicitness was used for laughs, as in Douglas Hickox's brilliant *Theater of Blood* (which featured a very literate script by Anthony Greville-Bell and one of Vincent Price's best hammy performances) and Sam Raimi's *Evil Dead* films (which were truly wonky). More often, the explicitness was used to disgust the audience or manipulate them, as in Romero's *Dawn of the Dead* and *Day of the Dead*. Sadly, what the horror film has gained in spectacle, it has lost in other areas.

A major signpost of the '70s and '80s was the fact that a major releasing company like Paramount would distribute a film like *Friday the 13th*, the kind of a film a major company would previously have shunned as being out of keeping with its image or in bad taste. Suddenly, box office success guaranteed that films have no flavor when it comes to satisfying stockholders, and the majors entered into an arena heretofore held only by independents, pushing many of the independents out when it came to competing for screen space.

Another phenomenon of the '80s was the rise of horror as a literary genre, due largely to the success of Stephen King. King's works began to top the bestseller list regularly, and naturally enough Hollywood quickly began to pay attention and option each work as soon as it became available. While this led to a string of largely uninteresting and unsuccessful films, it also gave us such great works as De Palma's *Carrie*, Kubrick's *The Shining*, Cronenberg's *The Dead Zone*, and even Rob Reiner's *Stand by Me* based on the King novella *The Body*, a film about what it means to grow up, change, be brave, and confront death, all in the guise of a simple tale of traveling to see the dead body of another kid.

Horror comedy tried to defuse the disgust most people were beginning to feel with the explicitness of modern horror, and there were two tremendous successes: Ivan Reitman's *Ghostbusters* and Tim Burton's *Beetle Juice*, both of which matched their wild senses of humor with even wilder, inventive visuals. However, there was a much larger group of horror spoofs that failed both as horror films and as comedies, ranging from *Student Bodies* to *Transylvania 6-5000*. A couple were significant despite their ineptitude: *Teen Wolf*, which was a freak success due to being Michael J. Fox's first film after the supersuccess of *Back to the Future*, and Michael Herz's over-the-top *The Toxic Avenger* in which toxic waste transforms a nerd into a super-heroic monster given to gory feats of strength.

Finally, the other significant trend of the '80s was the tremendous inroads the VCR made in the entertainment industry. It greatly increased the demand for videocassette titles, and a number of marginally profitable films became worthwhile when revenues from videocassettes were considered. In fact, some box office flops even merited sequels based on how many units of the videocassette original had sold. Additionally, some distributors began to formulate a market for made-for-video horror films. Figuring into the appeal of such ventures was the promise they offered of an end-run around the restrictions placed by the MPAA, which with the success of *Friday the 13th* began to tighten its guidelines to combat charges that it was letting too much violence get through under an R rating. There are some filmmakers, like former fans Fred Olen Ray, Don Dohler and Donald Farmer, whose films rarely see theatrical distribution at all. Still, the most successful horror videocassettes start off as theatrical releases.

The availability of films in the home may be one reason that horror movies, which have always appealed to adolescents, now seem to be geared to an even earlier age level. When children are very young, they don't spend time discussing the plot of a film. Instead they focus on its emotional moments when the action was at its peak. They grow impatient with connecting material – and quickly learn how to fast-forward through it on the VCR, looking instead for the next effect, the next scare, the next thrill. Given this sort of childhood experience, just what that next thrill might require by the time this audience comes of age is hard to imagine.

However, there is an indication that the limits of extremity have been reached and rejected in the death of the Italian cannibal subgenre. In the early '80s, Ruggero Deodata (*Cannibal Holocaust*) and Umberto Lenzi (*Make Them Die Slowly*) pushed the boundaries by serving up films that were nonstop human and animal mutilations as "entertainment." These films proved so disgusting that attendance at Italian horror films began to fall off drastically and by the end of the '80s, this particular subgenre was dead.

Major directors such as Francis Coppola (*Dementia 13*) and Oliver Stone (*Seizure: The Hand*) began their careers directing horror films because they can be done cheaply and have a built-in audience, and many others have tried to do the same. Horror remains a commercial and popular genre, one that reflects contemporaneous anxieties and mythologizes them as monsters and figures of fright.

Old style horror is not dead as evidenced by the resurrection of Dan Curtis' *Dark Shadows* as a prime time series in the '90s and Coppola's plan to make a definitive *Dracula* movie. These myths have become part of our collective psyche, never giving up the ghost and always returning from the grave, they are as undying as man's hopes and fears.

I
The Major Directors

Dario Argento (1940–   )

The Bird with the Crystal Plumage (1969); *Cat o' Nine Tails* (1970); *Four Flies on Grey Velvet* (1971); *Five Days of Milan* (aka *Le Cinque Giornate*) (1973); *Deep Red* (1975); *Suspiria* (1976); *Inferno* (1979); *Tenebrae* (aka *Sotto gli Occhi dell' Assassino; Unsane*) (1982); *Phenomena* (aka *Creepers*) (1985); *Opera* (1988); *Two Evil Eyes* (aka *Due Occhi Diabolici*) (codirected with George Romero, 1990)
TELEVISION: *The Tram; Eye Witness* (TV movies)

Dario Argento was born in September 1940, the son of motion picture executive Salvatore Argento. At a young age, he became interested in film and worked as a film reviewer for one of Rome's daily papers. Determined to break into the film industry, he was given his first big break when Sergio Leone, Italy's greatest director of spaghetti westerns, commissioned Argento and Bernardo Bertolucci to storyboard his next epic, *Once Upon a Time in the West,* a highly stylish and stylized western that remains Leone's best film.

Given this credit, Argento was able to find work writing scripts for movies, including a couple of westerns (*Today It's Me, Tomorrow You* and *Five Man Army*), a couple of war films (*Battle of the Commandos, Probability Zero*), a "pornographic epic" (*La Rivoluzione Sessuale*), and others (*Metti, una Sera a Cena,* for example).

One day Bertolucci loaned Argento a copy of Fredric Brown's book *The Screaming Mimi* to get Argento's opinion of it. (Bertolucci was considering adapting the book into a film.) Argento liked what he read and saw some possibilities in some of the ideas. Earlier, he had been struck by Mario Bava's classic *giallo* thriller *The Girl Who Knew Too Much* (aka *The Evil Eye*) in which a young American tourist witnesses a brutal murder attempt but is not certain she can recognize the killer (the murderer has apparently struck four times before). She is nagged by something she might have missed. (See the chapter on Bava for more about the film.)

Argento decided to take this basic idea and change the sex of the witness, coming up with *The Bird with the Crystal Plumage,* a suitably intriguing title. He made a deal with producer Goffredo Lombardo to be allowed to direct the film from his screenplay. (Argento had previously taken the script away from Euro Films because they had insisted that it be directed by Terence Young, fresh from his success on *Wait Until Dark.*)

11

However, midway into filming, Lombardo was not happy with the dailies and sought to replace Argento with Ferdinando Salvatore. Argento pointed out the clause in his contract that stipulated only Dario Argento be allowed to shoot a film from a script by himself. . . it was him or no film at all. Lombardo relented, and *The Bird with the Crystal Plumage* went on to become an unexpectedly big hit.

Tony Musante plays Sam Delmas, an American tourist who happens to catch a murder attempt through the glass window of an art gallery. He bravely attempts to come to the rescue but winds up trapped inside a glass anteroom in the gallery, where he impotently pounds on the glass doors. However, that is sufficient to stop the attack, and a figure in black darts away. This opening is the most memorable part of the film and serves as a metaphor for Sam's character. He is trapped out in the open where he can become a target for a killer that he can't get at.

The woman who was attacked, Monica (Eva Renzi), survives and recovers in the hospital. Meanwhile, Sam becomes more and more obsessed with piecing the mystery together, much to the distress of his girlfriend, Julia (Suzy Kendall). There are some very clever sequences, including Sam chasing a figure who resembles the killer into a convention where everyone is dressed the same as the killer. Sam and Julia begin to get threatening calls from the killer with the sounds of a bird in the background (the source of the elegant title). There is a chilling scene where the killer turns out the lights at the top of a long set of stairs, a change which escapes the attention of a young woman climbing to the top, who lights a match.

More shocking than suspenseful are the attack on Julia in which the killer hacks through the closed doors behind which Julia barricades herself, and the final attack on Sam in which the police arrive in the nick of time to shoot the killer and reveal her to be Monica. It is then that Sam recalls what he actually saw: Monica trying to murder her husband, rather than the reverse. Although the editing is jarring, *The Bird with the Crystal Plumage* greatly benefits from the work of Italy's top cinematographer, Vittorio Storaro (*Apocalypse Now, Reds, Ladyhawke*), and top film composer, Ennio Morricone.

It was an auspicious debut, and Argento soon began working on his second film, *Cat o' Nine Tails*. The distributors wanted American actors in the lead roles to help sell the film overseas so the leads went to Karl Malden and James Franciscus. The plot centers around the belief that an extra "Y" chromosome causes some men to be killers (first espoused in *Twisted Nerve*).

Malden has a particularly strange role as Franco Arno, an ex-reporter who is now blind yet manages to create crossword puzzles (Argento delights in showing us how he manages that trick). Arno is walking home one night with his niece when he happens to overhear a conversation between a man who had stolen some important papers from a center of genetic research and a blackmailer. He teams with Carlo Giordani (James Franciscus), a reporter, and together they begin to unravel the mystery with all the clues pointing to Anna Terzi (Catherine Spaak), the daughter of the institute's chief. (Terzi seems unemotional but looks stunning in a series of kinky outfits.)

The opening shot over which the credits run is a subjective camera shot of the murderer-thief prowling the rooftop of the Terzi Institute, an homage to Orson Welles' *Touch of Evil.* Argento was to use this technique effectively throughout this and subsequent films, presaging John Carpenter's use of the device to open *Halloween* and countless other "slasher film" directors' employment of the same "audience as killer" technique. (In the '30s and '40s, when the director wanted to conceal the identity of a killer, he usually showed just the killer's feet. However, in 1946 Robert Montgomery experimented with making an entire film, *Lady in the Lake,* in the subjective technique, and the results were unique to say the least.)

Cat o' Nine Tails marks the beginning of Argento's obsession with eyes and blades. He presages each of the murders with a close shot of one of the killer's eyes. The killer, for example, rids himself of the blackmailer by pushing him in front of an oncoming train. We are alerted to his presence by a close-up of his eye intercut with the crowd at the station.

Unfortunately, the revelation of the killer as Dr. Casoni (Aldo Reggiani) comes out of left field, with his motive of wanting the knowledge that he possesses an extra "Y" chromosome being a particularly weak one. But plot does not concern Argento as much as style does, and he does provide a bravura finish in which Casoni falls through a skylight. He grabs at a rope to break his fall, but his hands shred to pulp on the rope and he plummets to his death in an elevator shaft. Strangely enough, as we look down on the killer's body, we hear the voice of Lori (Cinzia De Carolis), Arno's niece, whom the killer claimed to have killed, though we never see her. Was she really dead or was she rescued? Argento doesn't seem too interested in indicating just how the story wraps up – perhaps, as Riccardo Menello suggests in his article on the director's work in *Photon,* to keep from letting up on the action, which would relieve the tension or provide the audience an emotional outlet from the stunning climax. All we are left with is a memory of the violence that has occurred, without a sigh of relief or a cathartic happy ending.

Cat o' Nine Tails did not prove as successful as *The Bird with the Crystal Plumage,* though there were definite indications that Argento was refining on and improving his technique, which many people mistakenly assumed as Hitchcockian. Argento and fellow Italian director Luigi Cozzi (*Alien Contamination, Starcrash*) collaborated together to script a follow-up film. Originally, the story was to have involved a seance where a medium predicts that her seven guests will all be killed; however, a similar story aired on

Italian TV as they were working on the script so that approach was abandoned. Argento then proposed a story about a murderer who finds he has been observed by someone he knows. He methodically starts doing away with his friends, only to discover that the witness was his loyal wife, who would not have said anything to the police. That approach was abandoned when it was decided it would make the hero too unsympathetic.

However, thought Argento, what if the hero merely *thought* he had killed someone and was not the killer at all? Argento came up with the evocative title *Four Flies on Grey Velvet,* and he and Cozzi completed the script. There was, unfortunately, one drawback: There was nothing about flies on velvet in the picture. So a killer wearing a pendant with a fly on it was added along with the hoary and wholly inaccurate idea that the last thing a murder victim would see would somehow become photographically imprinted on his or her retina. (The same idea appeared, for example in Lambert Hillyer's *Invisible Ray,* 1936.) Because the pendant is swinging, the single fly becomes four on the victim's eye.

Casting the film proved difficult. In an article for *Photon,* Cozzi recalled the parade of actors and actresses that passed by before leads were finally chosen. Actresses under consideration included Florinda Bolkan, Carla Gravina, Stefania Sandrelli, Lisa Gastoni, Catherine Spaak, and Claudia Cardinale, until at last Argento "sort of stumbled onto Mimsy Farmer, who turned out very well." The male lead was even harder to cast. Among those considered, and the reasons for their not being cast, were Tony Musant of *The Bird with the Crystal Plumage* (requested too much money); Terence Stamp (requested changes in the character, which Argento refused to make); Tom Courtenay (vetoed by Paramount); John Lennon or Ringo Starr (offered by Paramount, vetoed by Argento); Jean-Luis Trintignant (other commitments); James Taylor (another Paramount suggestion – evidently they thought a pop singer was just what the film needed – also vetoed by Argento); and Michael York (who was signed for the role but developed a scheduling conflict with his film *Zeppelin*). At last Argento signed the young actor Michael Brandon, whom he had seen in *Lovers and Other Strangers,* though Cozzi recalled that "nobody (including Dario) was ecstatic about the choice."

In *Four Flies on Grey Velvet,* Roberto (Michael Brandon) is a jazz drummer who notices that someone has been following him. He decides to confront the stranger in a darkened and deserted theater and in the ensuing scuffle, believes that he has killed the man. Just then, a bizarre masked figure snaps a picture from one of the theater's balconies and suddenly disappears. Roberto tries to forget about what happened, but then he finds a photo that the figure took in his house. Paranoid and frightened, he confesses everything to his wife (Mimsy Farmer).

To make matters worse, those close to Robert are being threatened and eventually his maid is murdered. There's a great eerie sequence where the maid is sitting in a brightly lit park filled with happy children, but as she is absorbed in her thoughts, time passes quickly. The children seem to vanish, the sun rapidly sets and the moon literally springs up into the sky (accomplished via time-lapse photography). Darkness falls on us all and death is proclaimed "a commerical necessity" by one of the more philosophizing characters in the film (a man named Godfrey who is wryly referred to as God and is played with amusing gusto by Bud Spencer).

Seeking help, Roberto goes to a spectacularly unsuccessful gay detective (Jean-Pierre Marielle) who manages to solve the case only, ironically, to get murdered for his pains.

Concerned that his wife might be next, Roberto sends her packing for the country. Meanwile, he begins an extramarital dalliance with his wife's cousin (Francine Racitte) who becomes the killer's next target. There is a suspenseful scene where she hides out in a cupboard while the killer passes by. Figuring she has eluded the killer, she slips out only to have the killer jump out at her from the shadows. (Carpenter also had a shot like this at the end of *Halloween.* Argento and Carpenter share a number of stylistic devices and both are more concerned with the style of their films than with the content or narrative qualities of their stories.)

It's at this point that Roberto's wife returns, and we discover that she was the one who bludgeoned the man Roberto thought he killed. It was part of an elaborate revenge-on-men scheme fostered by her father having cruelly treated her and raising her as a boy. (The maid was killed for attempting to blackmail her; the detective because he discovered her secret; and the cousin for having the audacity to "seduce" her husband.) She shoots her husband, but Roberto's life is saved by the timely arrival of "God" (a sly bit of Argento humor). The wife takes off and is killed when she smashes into the rear end of a truck.

Argento took a break from horror thrillers to direct *The Five Days of Milan,* which Cozzi describes as "a comic venture set during a revolution that took place in 1848." It does not appear to have been released in the United States. Afterwards, Argento produced four thrillers for Italian TV, two of which, *The Tram* and *Eye Witness,* he directed. The other two were *The Puppet,* directed by Mario Foglieti, and *Il Vicino di Casa (The Man Upstairs)* directed by Luigi Cozzi.

When Argento returned to feature thrillers, he came up with his best film in the genre yet with *Deep Red* (aka *Profondo Rosso, The Hatchet Murders*).

Deep Red opens with a halcyon Christmas scene into which Argento quickly inserts sinister overtones as the shadows on the wall indicate that one person is stabbing another. The bloody knife that has done the deed falls to the floor by the stockinged feet of a young child who apparently observed the entire thing. This is a typical Argento teaser. The events have no apparent relation to the plot that is soon to follow, but Argento is a careful enough craftsman to have this setup pay off later when he wants the audience to have a clearer idea of what was happening in that opening scene.

The scene also introduces the child's theme, which becomes a motif heard during the murders. A psychologist later theorizes that the killer uses the music to get into the proper frame of mind for murder. Then as counterpoint, Argento starts a rock theme by the Goblins, whose work became a trademark in his subsequent films.

The Italian version is slightly longer than the American/British one and differs principally in showing the hero, Marcus Daly (David Hemming), as a jazz pianist in rehearsal. The other trims are three silly dialogue scenes with Gianna Brezzi (played by Daria Nicolodi, for a time, Argento's common-law wife), a short sequence in which Daly plays in a club with his lower-class and lower-paid friend Carlo (Gabriele Lavia), and minor trims of the violence.

Argento shows off his fancy camera work right from the beginning. After the Christmas scene, the camera opens the story at a lecture at the Rome Institute of Parapsychology, where Helga (Macho Meri), a Lithuanian psychic (who speaks German in the Italian version), is delivering a lecture and demonstrating her powers. Suddenly she picks up emanations of evil that send her reeling. The source of these psychic impressions gets up in a standard point-of-view shot and leaves, setting up a definite connection between Helga and the killer. Argento even teases the audience to the point of having the killer enter a unisex bathroom and look in a mirror that is too scratched to give off a reflection.

Immediately Argento sets up what will be the visual and aural motif before each killing: the camera pans past various toys and the killer zipping up his or her gloves and applying eyebrow pencil (once more the fascination with eyes). Knowing that Helga knows his or her identity, the killer seeks her out. When Helga senses the killer just outside her door, the killer forces the door open and swings a meat cleaver twice at the victim, but this does not prove enough to kill her. She crawls to a large window pane and screams for help, only to have another blow propel her face through the window and slit her throat, ending her screams. (Argento would use shots of women being forced through panes of glass at the openings of both *Suspiria* and *Phenomena*, so he was evidently pleased with the effect.)

Helga was the upstairs neighbor of Daly, who happens to be the crime's only witness. He was in the village square down below talking to a drunken Carlo, who, when he hears the screams, jokes that they must emanate from some raped virgin and offers her a toast. While Carlo is in no shape to do anything, Daly acts quickly and dashes up to Helga's flat, running down a long corridor past paintings of blank-eyed faces. Argento inserts an almost subliminal shot of a woman standing by a curtain, an important if easily overlooked clue. By the time Daly can pull Helga from the window, he sees a figure that might be the killer dash away down the street.

While Daly is undergoing questioning from the police, Brezzi breezes in and takes a picture of him, which is then printed in the newspaper, alerting the killer to the existence of an "eyewitness." Argento uses the Brezzi character to take the press to task for irresponsibility, but he obviously has affection for the character as well. The film was made in the early '70s when women's lib was still considered something new and untrustworthy in Italy, and Daly evinces a typical disregard for it. There is a cute scene where Brezzi challenges Daly to arm wrestle and beats him, though each time he offers an excuse and then refuses to play along anymore lest his ego become bruised.

Daly is a typical Argento hero in that having observed the crime, he cannot let it go. Instead he is haunted in his mind by the feeling he overlooked something important. After retracing his steps through the hallway, he thinks that a picture might be missing, but why would a murderer, after committing the deed, take time to steal a picture? He talks it over with Carlo, who suggests that it could have been something important. That idea bothers Daly so much that he goes to great pains to try to seek Carlo out again.

First he has to come across Carlo's exceedingly eccentric mother, Martha (Clara Calamai), who can't shake the mistaken idea that Daly is an engineer. After much persuading in a semicomic scene, he gets an address for Carlo and finds himself at a gay residence. He almost gives up when Carlo, having sobered up, says he can't remember what he told Daly and advises him to drop the case. That night while Daly is writing music, the killer prowls around Daly's apartment and advises him likewise, but in so doing provides Daly with another clue via a children's recording that the killer is playing in the background (another sound motif as in *Crystal Plumage*).

Daly becomes more and more obsessed, tracking down the recording, and his obsession begins to infect others, including Calcabrini (Eros Pagni), who was also present at Helga's lecture. Calcabrini suggests that the song may be "the *leitmotif* of the crime" and dubs the killer a paranoid schizophrenic who uses the music to trigger "himself into a state of madness." The music reminds another participant of a famous "haunted" house known for the sound of children singing that could be heard from within.

Tracking down a book of local legends, Daly comes across a description of the legend and a picture of the house. Perhaps the author of the book, Amanda Righetti, knows more and could tell him where the house is, so he resolves to seek her out. A montage of children's toys and a close-up of an eye encircled by eyebrow pencil indicates that the killer is ready to strike again, apparently aware of the threat Righetti might pose.

Argento builds up tension in the scene by showing Amanda discovering a baby doll hanging from a noose in her living room. When she touches this talisman, the doll's head falls off. When the lights snap off, we know that Amanda is not alone. The frightened woman picks up a knitting needle to defend herself, only to have one of her own birds fly into the needle's point and impale itself on it. This distracts Amanda, and us, allowing the killer to club her over the head and drag her to the bathroom, where the tub is filled with scaldingly hot water. Methodically, the killer slams Amanda's head against the wall and then drowns her in the tub, though she lives long enough to etch a message in the mist-shrouded glass. However, an open window blows in cool air, which cleverly obscures Amanda's dying missive.

Daly finds Amanda's place too late, but does tell Calcabrini about it before tracking down the mysterious haunted house in the photograph which he is able to detect via the unusual foliage in front of it. The house itself is in decay, but as it is for sale, Daly persuades the realtor to let him in.

Argento adds an odd touch via the realtor's daughter. The realtor appears to slap his daughter for no apparent reason until Argento swings his camera down and shows us the squirming lizards she has been impaling with long needles. The character seems to represent cruel fate, spitefully spearing her helpless victims. In the house Daly uncovers a picture behind the plaster in the old house, evidently drawn by some demented child. It is of a grinning boy holding a bloody blade standing over a stabbed adult. However, Daly leaves before another piece of plaster falls off, revealing there is more to the story.

Meanwhile, Calcabrini goes to Righetti's house and questions the housekeeper, who fortuitously turns on the hot water to clean up the blood after the police have completed their investigation and unknowingly reveals Amanda's message in the steam. Calcabrini sees the message but leaves without contacting the police, desperately seeking to contact Daly first. As he waits for Marcus to reach him, he suddenly becomes aware that the killer is in the house with him. In a memorably surreal scene a mannikin of a child laughs and runs through the door towards him, and Calcabrini splits its skull and laughs at the absurdity of it. However, this distraction is just what the killer intended. The killer attacks from behind and sadistically slams Calcabrini's mouth several times on the ends of the bookcase and his desk before stabbing him with a large knife.

While Daly is seeking Carlo again, he notices that one of the windows appearing in the photo of the old house had apparently been walled over. Determined to discover what could be concealed, he attacks the walled-over section from the outside but almost loses his life when a ledge gives way.

Tackling the problem from the inside, he uncovers a hidden room that contains a cobwebby corpse. Suddenly, he is attacked and knocked out. When he wakes up, Brezzi has pulled him from the house, which is going up in flames, its secrets safe forever. The realtor, naturally, would like to know what's going on, but as Daly talks to him, he notices that the realtor's daughter has a picture which is identical to the childish murder scene he uncovered. From her he extracts the information that she based her drawing on one she saw in the archives of the Leonardo da Vinci school.

Daly and Brezzi find the picture at the school, but someone else finds them there as well. Daly has discovered that Carlo drew the original, and Carlo, after stabbing Brezzi, tries to kill him to cover that knowledge up, but the police arrive in time to shoot first. Carlo jumps the schoolyard fence but is hit by a truck, which knocks him right in the path of an oncoming car. (The final "coup de gross" of Carlo's head being squashed like a melon is missing from many prints of the film.)

Suddenly, Daly realizes that Carlo could not have killed Helga, and in going back to Helga's apartment, he realizes what he saw was not a painting but a mirror. The difference he noted was that he had seen the killer's face in the mirror within the reflection of the blank, staring, pupil-less eyes of the faces in the paintings in the hallway. In a quick flashback Argento finally shows what Daly saw. The killer is Martha. She promptly appears and explains that her husband was planning on returning her to the mental hospital so she stabbed him, and young Carlo (the child whose feet we saw at the beginning) picked up the crimsoned knife and drew pictures about it. Martha then attacks Daly, but gets her chain caught in the elevator grill. Thinking quickly, Marcus pushes the button for the elevator, which forces the chain through Martha's neck (a close-up of which is frequently omitted), decapitating her. The bleak, final shot is of Marcus reflected in the deep red blood of the killer.

The screenplay by Argento and Bernardino Zapponi is the best and most tightly plotted of any of Argento's films. Unfortunately, the film was frequently trimmed when distributed, and scenes which would help the viewer understand the plot were often removed, giving Argento an unfair reputation for being incomprehensible. The plot relies heavily on "doubles": there are two killers (Carlo kills Brezzi to cover up for his mother Martha); it takes two attacks to kill Helga; a bird is killed before Amanda can be; Calcabrini "kills" the mannikin before he is dispatched; we see Marcus' trip through Helga's apartment twice via the telltale flashback (though Argento "cheats" in the sense of not providing the audience with the visual clue the first time through); and there are two endings, in both of which the killers lose their heads. There are also two sequences where the camera alerts us to the killer's oncoming madness (showing the children's toys and the made-up eye).

Argento must have become quite enamored of the double killer plot twist, as he would use it frequently thereafter. Like his inspiration, Mario Bava, Argento likes to play with uncertainty, lulling the audience into a false sense of security by providing them with misleading clues as to what is going on before pulling out the rug from under the expectations and giving them a novel surprise.

His themes center around the horror created by random violence – meaningless violence being more frightening than the supposedly more rationally motivated kind – and the extent people will go to when driven to extremes. His films are like beautiful descents into worlds of madness. His technique includes assured and elaborate camera movements coupled with extreme close-ups for punctuation, as well as skillful use of the soundtrack to heighten tension or counterpoint innocence with evil. His central concept was summed up by a line from his next, best-known film, *Suspiria*: "Bad luck isn't brought by broken mirrors but by broken minds."

Argento makes good use of elaborate tracking shots and extreme close-ups in his films, achieving a peculiar rhythm by alternating them. The music by Giorgio Gaslini and the Goblins helps wind the characters tighter than a watch spring and then suggests the energy released when there is an attack. Argento is constantly propelling his story forward, but these shifts in pace help keep it from becoming predictable. The pace quickens as the story heads towards its climax, though this pacing is altered in many domestic prints because of minor cuts. (In *Deep Red*, Daly's journey inside the house was originally much longer; a shot of a window mysteriously slamming itself shut was deleted. Later, when Carlo is killed, the scene of the truck dragging him through the streets of Rome was initially quite prolonged before the oncoming car squashed his head. The only other significant cut was a brief shot of Martha's necklace being pulled through a dummy neck while white fluid seeped from the mouth. There was not an elaborate decapitation scene as some have insisted.)

Deep Red represents an important, transitional film for Argento as he moved away from the thriller mode and more into splatter, though it has a much stronger story than his later epics. He shows himself very adept at using cinematic techniques to hook an audience's interest. He is able to mystify us without producing the confusion that typically results when similar techniques are in less talented hands, though sometimes censorship has rendered even Argento's films incomprehensible. Such being the case, I have decided to go into great detail on those films that originally had clear linear plots since many readers have seen only highly trimmed versions.

Suspiria was the film that really caught the attention of horror fans worldwide. It was much more original in 1977 than it seems today when so many others have followed similar footsteps. It made a striking contrast to the relatively genteel pabulum that studios like AIP were dishing out at the time with its striking color schemes and intense, often very gory, violence. The film was shot on the last of the IB Technicolor stock in Italy, marking a farewell to the rich hues (particularly the sumptuous blues) that the process provides. Coupled with its almost overbearing Dolby stereo soundtrack of Goblin music and intense colors, this highly stylized feature gave the horror fan of the time what amounted to sensory overload.

The American distributor was 20th Century–Fox, who, apparently embarrassed by the film, released it under a made-up subsidiary name, International Classics, adding a shot of breathing, flesh-like title letters and trimming some of the more intense violence, perhaps to keep an R rating. I originally caught up with the film in Switzerland, where it was shown in its uncut glory, and I was shocked. In that pre–*Dawn of the Dead* time, I had never seen a horror film that went so far as to show not only a killer repeatedly stabbing his victim, but that victim's still-beating heart being exposed and then stabbed twice again.

Suspiria is still infamous for its opening, in which Susy Banyon (Jessica Harper) comes up to the Dance Academy in Freibourg and espies a terrified girl talking to someone and then running away into the woods. The only words she can make out of the conversation are "secret" and "irises." She tries to gain entry but is turned away by a voice on the intercom until morning.

Immediately, Argento sets up a sinister if childlike musical theme. These opening scenes give a feeling of disorientation as we follow Susy on her adventure. Argento even manages to make the mechanical doors at the airport seem threatening. The stylized lighting (e.g. different colored lights play on Banyon's face as she is being driven to the academy) add to the air of menace and unreality.

However, what really makes the opening memorable is when Argento picks up the story of the girl who ran into the rain. She arrives at a friend's house, seeking refuge and obviously terrified for her life. As she enters a scarlet art deco apartment, the shrieks on the soundtrack let us know she is not safe, even though the predominate color changes to blue and the music stops as she takes a shower. The fugitive refuses to tell her friend why she is so upset. The window bangs open and sinister sounds start again. Peering into the inky black night, she spies a pair of inhuman eyes staring right back at her. Before she can move away, an arm bursts through the other window and pulls her into and then through a pane of glass.

Whereas other directors would leave it at that, Argento doesn't let up but continues the scene. The girl, Pat, continues to be attacked and stabbed by an unseen attacker with hairy arms. Her body is then laid on a colorful skylight which breaks, leaving her eviscerated body hanging by a rope. The shards of glass fall down and impale the head and heart of her erstwhile friend.

Since this is the beginning of the film, and these practically the only characters familiar to us, there is an immediate sense of connection between these hapless individuals. The director is obviously pulling no punches. If this sequence had appeared later in the film, we would feel justified in wanting to know more about these people in order to identify with them. Instead, the intensity almost sets the film off balance as it never manages to top its opening in sheer horror and excess.

Suzy returns to the academy the next day and is allowed to enter. Academy head Madame Blank (Joan Bennett, deliberately made up to resemble how she looked in Fritz Lang's films) informs her that the chaos is partly due to the fact that a student who was just expelled has been found murdered. Banyon admits to seeing her leave the night before. The other members of the academy do not seem a friendly lot to the American stranger, though Suzy does end up rooming with one of them in town when accommodations haven't been made.

Jessica Harper has a great "little girl lost" quality that is perfect for this role, as if she is struggling to do her best given the overwhelming circumstances. She had made an impressive debut in De Palma's *Phantom of the Paradise,* and while she is not as impressive here, she makes a more than capable lead.

The basic structure of *Suspiria* is more along the lines of a *My Name Is Julia Ross* or a *Rebecca* – a young woman is introduced to a strange and somehow threatening environment, manipulated by the people who claim that they wish to protect her – than the Edgar Wallace thrillers that Argento had imitated in the past. The academy is a colorful, large and yet sinister location with unfriendly faces in nearly every occupied room.

Madame Tanner (Alida Valli) is a severe and repressive taskmaster, a virtual Nazi overlord of the ballet floor, pushing Suzy to exhaustion. Is it part of a plot or is she just upset over the recent events? Suzy faints and Argento tantalizes us with possibilities. A Prof. Verdegast (Udo Kier in a *Black Cat* tribute perhaps?) gives her an injection and prescribes bland food and a "drop of *vin rouge* after each meal" to restore the blood. Mysteriously, Suzy is moved directly into the institute and is no longer permitted to live in the village with Olga.

Argento's garish lighting scheme, based on using bright, primary colors for horror scenes, derives from Mario Bava, who used a similar scheme in *Black Sabbath.* Argento regarded Bava as the master of the macabre and something of a mentor. However, Argento has a knack for coming up with things to make an audience uneasy that even such a horror maestro as Bava would have had a hard time improving on. He makes the art deco environment even more threatening by having the floor where the girls sleep become infested with maggots (evidenced initially by a girl discovering maggots in her comb and then looking up at a ceiling full of them).

Everyone is bedded down in a dance gym, where a mysterious figure resides in a bed behind a sheet. The teachers at the school leave every night, supposedly to go to town, but from their location Suzy and Sara, an inquisitive student who befriends Suzy, notice that their footsteps turn the wrong way for them to be leaving the building. What could they be doing?

Mystery is piled upon mystery, but Argento knows that is not enough to hold an audience, so he includes a minor subplot in which the school's blind pianist, Daniel (Flavio Bucci), is accused of having his seeing-eye dog bite a child. Madame Tanner yells at him as if he were deaf, not blind, and scornfully throws his coat and cane into the center of the room where he must stumble across them to retrieve them. Later, after drinking beer, he is crossing the Koenigplatz, site of many Nazi rallies, when his dog becomes entranced and attacks him. Argento pushes the limits of graphic depictions for the time by adding scenes of the dog tearing at raw meat which is supposedly what's left of Daniel's throat, a grisly touch if there ever was one.

Sara and Suzy go for a swim together, and Sara reveals that she was the one on the intercom who had told Suzy to go away. She and Pat had been friends and Pat had discovered something about the school that had terrified her, something to do with witches. Suzy becomes groggy after dinner and cannot stay awake, while Sara is chased by something or someone. She barricades herself in a closet, but a knife comes through the crack and tries to raise the jamb. Crawling through a window in the closet, she is finally driven into a pit full of steel mesh of razor sharpness. The more she tries to climb out, the more the steel bites into her flesh until it cuts her to ribbons and her throat is cut by an unseen assailant, thankfully without the explicitness of the earlier murders.

Going outside to Pat's old boyfriend, Suzy is introduced to an expert on witchcraft, who informs her that the school's building was once the headquarters of a powerful woman who was reputed to have been a witch. He also tells her that a coven of witches is like a snake: Without the head, it is helpless.

Suzy resolves not to drink the drugged wine, and she follows the footsteps of the school's teachers to their hidden lair, located behind a secret door that is opened by manipulating an iris on the wall. Once inside, she spots the Black Widow (as she is called here—later to be designated as the Mother of Whispers in the Three Mothers trilogy, about which more later). A warlock comes to kill Suzy while the Black Widow, having turned herself invisible, laughs. However, as lightning flashes, Suzy can just make out the Black Widow's outline.

Taking a crystal feather from a bird with crystal plumage (a neat bit of self-homage), Suzy manages to skewer the dreaded witch in the neck,

Jessica Harper stabs the "Black Widow" witch with a bit of crystal plumage in the climax of Dario Argento's Suspiria, *which took the screen to new heights of goriness for the time. (Photo courtesy of Donald Farmer.)*

rendering all her followers powerless. She flees the academy as it is purged of its evil by a cleansing fire, the traditional agent in a horror film. A title card informs us that we have been witnessing *Suspiria*, an indication that the film was something new and different, and for its time it was.

Suspiria is still an impressive and often intense film today, though the coven of witches does not prove a very resourceful enemy by the end, and the extremes of the film have been matched by many '80s films. Nonetheless, the film does show more style and finesse than most of its descendants and is a notable achievement in horror, both as a stylistic milestone and a gruesome yet still entertaining film. It exists not for any deep messages or enlightenment that its story might offer, but purely to shock and thrill, which it does, sometimes admirably.

As influential and successful as *Suspiria* was, it was quickly overshadowed by the next project that Argento found himself involved in, albeit in only a minor capacity. Argento served as the producer for George Romero's *Dawn of the Dead* and oversaw the release of the Italian version known as *Zombi* in Europe, which spanned countless imitation films about cannabalistic, flesh-eating zombies and featuring ultra-graphic and gory violence. He also oversaw the production of a score by his old friends the Goblins. *Zombi* was a huge European hit and helped usher in the era of splatter in the '80s. (For more on *Dawn of the Dead*, see the chapter on George Romero.)

Because *Suspiria* proved to be such a success, Argento decided to make it the first film in a trilogy, each of which would feature a witch. Said Argento in an interview with Alan Jones, in *Starburst*, "It all stemmed from a book called *The Confessions of an Opium-Eater* by De Quincey. In it he said he wanted to write a book about The Three Mothers. Well, he never got around to it – so I did it instead!"

But writing the sequel, *Inferno,* proved difficult. Argento suffered from writer's block and had difficulty coming up with a storyline. Additionally, he alienated many of his friends in the effort to get the film made.

Suspiria dealt with the subject of sorcery; Argento decided that *Inferno* should deal with alchemy. While it in no way matches the visceral power and shock of *Suspiria*, it is a more atmospheric and often more intriguing film. A woman (Irene Miracle) discovers a book by an alchemist/architect on *The Three Mothers*, evil witches who send out sorrow, tears, and darkness into the world. The woman learns that the Mothers are located in Freibourg, Germany; New York, New York; and Rome, Italy, and that there are three keys to their identity.

One is that the places they inhabit reek horribly. Two is that hidden in the cellar of each mother's dwelling place is the picture and name (in Latin) of each. The third key is "under the soles of your shoes." Naturally, we are meant to wonder if this is a riddle or a prophecy.

Investigating an old building's cellar, the woman discovers a submerged room which has Tenebrium (Darkness) emblazoned over an underwater fireplace. A floating corpse scares her into leaving. The scene has a haunting and eerie beauty all is own.

She writes her brother Mark (Leigh McCloskey), who is studying music in Rome (and unbeknownst to him, the Mother of Tears is in the same class). A classmate of Mark's finds the letter and begins an investigation of her own, which results in her demise and the disappearance of one of the rare remaining volumes of *The Three Mothers*. Back in New York, the Mother of Darkness is also searching for and destroying copies of the book and dispatching their owners. When Mark's sister disappears, Mark comes to New York to investigate, little expecting what he finds.

The film has a mysterious and even haunting aura about it, but the plot mainly becomes punctuated with the deaths of the incidental characters. There's a macabre scene where the antique dealer who had the book is murdered by rats while drowning cats, and another where Daria Nicolodi finds doors locking themselves as she tries to escape, but Mark's final confrontation with the Mother of Darkness and Shadows is ultimately disappointing. The Mother comes forward and appears as a skeleton with a woman's hands (the hands at least still have flesh on them).

The score, a combination of Keith Emerson and Verdi, is largely effective. The film employs a slow build, but perhaps because it is the middle film of a trilogy, the payoff is not all it could have been. The film received only a very limited release in Great Britian and the United States, and was trimmed from 107 minutes to 83 minutes, though the eventual videocassette did restore the absent footage. The film is notable for being the last film featuring work by Mario Bava, who did some of the effects, while Bava's son Lamberto was the assistant director. (Argento would later produce *Demons* and *Demons 2* for Lamberto Bava.)

The inspiration for Argento's next film, *Tenebrae,* came when a man got ahold of Argento's number while he was in Los Angeles and began making vague threats on his life. Argento has always been both fascinated and appalled by apparently senseless violence, and he decided to make that the subject of his film.

Despite the title, which would suggest that *Tenebrae* is the third segment of the Three Mothers trilogy (still, as yet, uncompleted), *Tenebrae* is more of a return to the *giallo* film. Like *Inferno, Tenebrae* opens with someone reading a book, only this time the person reading is a maniac and the book he is reading is called *Tenebrae* by American writer Peter Neal (Tony Franciosa in a part originally written for Christopher Walker, who was deemed too young). The maniac reads: "He realized every human obstacle, every humiliation could be swept aside by this simple act of annihilation: Murder." He throws the book into a fire.

Meanwhile, Neal, whose book has become an Italian best-seller, is on his way from New York to Rome. Upon arrival, he is greeted with an anonymous threatening phone call, followed by a visit from Inspector Germani (Guiliano Gemma), who informs him that a young shoplifter (Ania Peroni, who played the Mother of Tears in a brief bit in *Inferno*) has been found with her throat slashed and pages from Neal's book stuffed into her mouth. Next thing Neal knows, he, his press agent (John Saxon), and his secretary (Daria Nicolodi) are caught in a web of senseless murders.

The twist-laden plot has plenty of references to Argento's past work, including an apparently meaningless flashback, a black-gloved killer and two murderers (à la *Deep Red*). This time it's Neal himself faking his own suicide and picking up where the original murderer, a mad TV personality (John Steiner), left off because of his secret and intense feelings of misogyny.

Misogyny has been a charge frequently laid at Argento's door. Women often turn out to be the murderers in his films, and the victims are frequently female. Argento claims that he just feels he works better with women. He went on to feature a scene in *Tenebrae* where a lesbian journalist (Mirella D'Angelo) quizzes Neal about his sexism and the violence against women in his books. Argento himself explains the charge much more simply and directly when he said in an interview with Alan Jones in *Starburst,* "I like women, especially beautiful ones. If they have a good face and figure, I would much prefer to watch them being murdered than an ugly girl or man."

The film does have some rather inventive camera work, particularly in one scene where the camera crawls all over a large apartment building, peering in empty windows, climbing across the roof, before finally revealing the murderer breaking in through a window. The cinematography by Luciano Tovoli (who also shot *Suspiria*) is exquisitely sharp and detailed, and the score is by former Goblin members Simonetti, Pignatelli and Morante. Still, it is little more than a high-class slasher film with a frustrating ending in which the killer kills himself by knocking over a steel sculpture which impales him.

Argento was offered to direct an adaptation of Stephen King's *The Stand* but turned it down. He worked on trying to make a film on H. P. Lovecraft's Cthulhu mythos but could not come to grips with it. Producer Dino De Laurentiis offered to let him direct one of 27 Agatha Christie novels, but again Argento declined. He's one horror director who takes his time between projects.

Argento's next directorial effort, *Phenomena*, suffered when it was trimmed by 25 minutes and retitled *Creepers* by its American distributors, New Line. Jennifer Connolly (who played the young Maureen McGovern in *Once Upon a Time in America*) gives a sympathetic performance as Jennifer Corvino, an American girl sent to Switzerland to the Richard Wagner School for Girls (shades of *Suspiria*). She has the power to control insects. When a maniac starts beheading young girls and making off with their bodies, wheelchair-bound entomologist John McGregor realizes that Corvino's ability could potentially help solve the murders with the help of a "sarcophagus fly." Donald Pleasence seems to be having a ball in the role of McGregor, giving his character a Scottish accent and a sense of pathos. It is a delightfully off-key performance.

Argento has McGregor note that one of the names for the devil is Beelzebub, or literally "Lord of the Flies." (Given other ties between them, it's interesting to note that Carpenter's film *Prince of Darkness* is about the devil who partly manifests himself by controlling large quantites of insects.) Argento cowrote the film with Franco Ferrini, and it is finely photographed by Romano Albani.

Luckily, *Phenomena* is available via import from Japan in English with Japanese sidetitles so that one may judge the film in the form that Argento intended it to be presented. Though it is not his best work or his most visually inventive or assaultive, it does incorporate a number of his typical touches. To begin with, the photography is far superior to the standard Italian shocker. The film opens with a poor girl who misses her bus and happens to call at the wrong house; the sequence ends with her head smashing through some glass, reminiscent of the openings of both *Deep Red* and *Suspiria*.

In that isolated Swiss chalet, we only see that something successfully pulls free from the chains that bind it to the wall. The girl is first stabbed in the hand with a pair of scissors, but she pulls them out and flees outside, only to be pursued by the unseen killer (another typical Argento touch) who has the knife. The scenery is quite beautiful and lush, with a nature trail winding up the side of a lush waterfall, but the audience is more concerned with the victim and her plight than the scenery. She is stabbed in the abdomen, and in slow motion her skull smashes through a pane of glass designed to shield spectators from the cascading water. In a long shot, something falls into the water, and it's not difficult to figure out that the girl has lost her head – permanently.

Jennifer arrives at the Wagner school, but she begins having a strange dream in which oddly angled doors fly past her down a long corridor, which Argento uses as a visual signal that she is about to begin sleepwalking. She ends up on a ledge outside a window where the killer is claiming another victim by shoving a steel spike through her throat and out her mouth. This shocking sight begins snapping Jennifer out of her trance, but a portion of the ledge she's on gives way (as it did for Marcus in *Deep Red*), and only by a miracle does she make it safely to the ground, where she is picked up by two puzzled Swiss youths. They are even more surprised when suddenly she flings herself out of their speeding cars and rolls down a hill, where she meets with McGregor and his trained chimp. (The chimp is trained to fetch anything that McGregor designates using a red laser. Romero used the same gimmick in *Monkey Shines*.)

Jennifer's father, a movie star, is working on a movie in the Philippines beyond the reach of any telephone. Jennifer finds the head mistresses of her school rather oppressive, and the other girls begin to taunt her about her sleepwalking, causing her to bring down a swarm of insects on the school to command some at least momentary respect. The only other sympathetic student is the French schoolgirl she initially bunks with who is a great fan of her father's acting (and body). Unfortunately, this friend relinquishes her responsibility for keeping an eye on Jennifer's sleepwalking when she goes outside for a brief tryst with her boyfriend, who has to leave to rejoin his Swiss army platoon. Unfortunately, this attracts the attention of the killer, who, because the girl has borrowed Jennifer's outfit and has similarly colored hair, mistakes her for Jennifer (a potential witness) and kills her. Jennifer wakes and is guided by a firefly to her roommate's body, where she discovers an important clue: a torn portion of the killer's glove with maggots in it that give her psychic impressions of the murder.

McGregor and Jennifer share a kinship now that each of them has lost someone to the killer (McGregor had a secretary disappear whom he's convinced that the killer got) and each has shown a fascination with insects. (Earlier there was a macabre scene where McGregor explains to a pair of policemen how he can pinpoint the date of death of the first victim by studying the development of insect larvae on her decaying skull and applying a little common logic.)

McGregor explains how the "sarcophagus fly" thrives solely on dead human flesh and will become agitated when it approaches the place where the killer is hiding the bodies. (The maggots on the glove indicate that the killer is maintaining some kind of physical contact with his dead victims.) So, trapping one in a box, he gives it to Jennifer, who takes it on a scenic bus ride past where the victims are believed to have disappeared. Eventually she comes across the chalet we saw at the beginning. (A police inspector hovers in the background as an added red herring, plus there's the unexpected appearance of a realtor trying to sell the house, whom Argento uses to keep the audience on edge and off balance.)

When she gets back, however, she discovers that the killer has dispatched McGregor, leaving only his insects and his chimp. She wisely decides that the best thing would be to get out of the country as quickly as possible. She manages to reach her father, but then one of the headmistresses (Daria Nicoldi) arrives for her, explaining that she will be given money and a ticket to leave in the morning. After the unpleasant experience at the school, Jennifer doesn't want to go back there, so the woman takes her to her home, a large mansion filled with mirrors, all of which are covered because of her son's illness. The woman insists that Jennifer take some medicine, and after swallowing it, Jennifer begins to fear that she has been poisoned. She forces herself to vomit up the pill, but finds herself trapped in the house while the woman meets with the police inspector outside.

The pieces suddenly start falling into place as we learn that the woman had been raped and scarred many years ago, and the product was her diseased son. After that experience, she apparently is none too mentally stable herself. She leads the inspector away. We hear a scream.

Jennifer desperately contrives a way to reach the telephone in the locked room next door using what utensils she has at hand. Unfortunately, the telephone slips down a deep hole under the house. Jennifer crawls after it and is just about to call the police when the phone rings (a nice bit by which Argento manages to heighten the tension). It's her father's friend, who had already come to Switzerland looking to bring her back after her frantic phone call.

However, before she can respond, she is pulled into the next room and sent ass-over-teakettle into a foul pit full of putrefying corpses. Chained to the wall, covered with blood, is the still-living inspector. The mad woman comes down to gloat and prevent Jennifer from escaping the maggot-infested pit. (Jennifer may love insects, but there's a limit for everyone.)

Here things really start getting bizarre. The inspector smashes his thumb, breaking it so that he can escape from his handcuffs, and starts beating on the killer. Jennifer gets the hell out of there but is stopped by the sound of sobbing. The woman's little boy is crying, face to the wall. When Jennifer goes to help the lad, she turns him around and sees a monstrous face and malformed, beast-like mouth. Once more, Argento has two killers; this time a mother is covering up for her bestial son, rather than the reverse.

Jennifer runs down to the dock and jumps in a boat, but, bladed instrument in hand, the boys follows her and succeeds in puncturing the gas tank. Jennifer calls on a swarm of bees to attack and they drive the fiendish child into the water. Then the gas ignites and the boat explodes. Underwater, Jennifer is attacked again (the ol' "it's not over yet"), but she surfaces beyond the flames while the boy is consumed. On shore, her father's friend arrives to take her to safety. . . .

. . . And has his head knocked off by the still-living mother with a sheet of steel. The mother prepares to saw Jennifer's head off with it, daring her to call on her insect friends, when Argento pulls a ludicrous but highly amusing topper. McGregor's chimp suddenly knocks the woman down and stabs her to death with a scalpel, avenging the death of its master. Original, but far beyond the bounds of plausibility.

Fitting this description even better is *Demons*, which Argento produced with Lamberto Bava directing. While it features some arresting images and elaborate makeups as people are lured into a cinema and turned into demons while watching a horror movie, Lamberto Bava lacks the style of either Argento or his father, and the technical qualities are far below the standard that Argento set with his previous films. Nonetheless, the film proved a hefty hit in Europe and spawned two official sequels. In the first, monsters come from television rather than a cinema screen with people trapped inside an apartment complex (as in David Cronenberg's *They Came from Within*) rather than inside a theater.

As an addendum to Argento's career, home video distributor Vidmark has released a cassette called *Dario Argento's World of Horror*, which contains several scenes that have been chopped from film and video releases of Argento's other feature films. The video is directed by Argento associate Michele Soavi.

Perhaps what is most disturbing about Argento is that as Italy's top horror stylist, he seems increasingly to prefer the disgusting to the frightening. Where once his films built mood, they now spill gallons of beautifully photographed blood. Nevertheless, his films are definitely a notch or two above most others in the fright film field and demonstrate a lively cinematic imagination. We can only hope that he will make his final *Three Mothers* film and that it will live up to his promise of being "the most sensational and spectacular" film he's done yet.

After a long absence from directing, Argento returned with *Opera*, another bravura exercise in style, but one which found the horror market had dwindled even in his native Italy. The film opens with scenes of an opera being reflected in the eye of a raven, another piece of Argento cinematic daring. The opera being performed is *Macbeth* by Verdi, long regarded as a cursed production. The prima donna singing complains about the noises caused by onstage ravens, and after leaving in a huff, she meets with a car accident outside the opera house which temporarily disables her. (Once again, Argento strikes his theme of the randomness of violence in the modern world.)

We then focus on Betty (Cristina Marsillach), the young understudy, who hears a mysterious voice tell her that she will make her debut as Lady Macbeth. When her agent calls to confirm, Betty voices her anxieties that she is too young and that she is insecure about her voice. Meanwhile, a mysterious someone watches her through a grill in her apartment.

Argento hides the identity of the killer once more by taking the killer's point of view as he visits the opera, sitting in a box seat. There is a flashback of a previous victim, part of a typical Argentian puzzle. When an attendant finds the killer, he knocks over a light and impales the attendant on a coat hook while Betty finishes her aria.

In the film, Argento uses the opera director, Mark (Ian Charleson), as something of a stand-in for himself. Mark is a horror director trying his hand at directing an opera, but he faces prejudice because of his background and resistance to his daring staging. After Mark has congratulated Betty, Alan (Urbano Barberini), a police inspector posing as a fan, presents Betty with a rose. The prima donna expresses her feelings by sending over some foul-smelling perfume with the message, "Good luck, little snake."

The cinematography, which like that of most Argento films, is quite good, and is by Ronnie Taylor, B.S.C. Argento wrote the screenplay in collaboration with Franco Ferrini. One of the film's most peculiar aspects is its visual motif of a twitching human brain which presages the killer's reappearance, like the eye motif in *Deep Red*.

The killer seems obsessed with the Lady Macbeth costume for some reason, and steals into the opera's wardrobe department to shred the garment. However, the ravens are also stored in this area, and they become quite agitated in the killer's presence, escaping from their enormous cage and swooping down on him. In retaliation, he swipes at and kills several birds with his butcher knife, but when someone else comes down, the intruder flees.

Betty is in love with the stage manager but can't bring herself to make love to him, instead offering him jasmine or mint tea. As she goes to fetch it, the killer grabs her, tapes her mouth shut, ties her to a post, and inserts needles next to her eyes to force them to stay open (if she tries to close them, her eyes will be shredded). When the young stage manager comes through the door, Betty vainly tries to warn him, and in one of the film's most visceral moments, Argento shows the killer's knife inside the stage manager's screaming mouth (this grisly effect courtesy of Sergio Stivaletti). Though the violence may be deemed gratuitous, there is no denying its impact or power to startle.

Murdering the stage manager seems to turn the killer on; he feels Betty's breasts, telling her, "It's not true you're frigid, you're a bitch in heat." Then, instead of killing her, the killer lets her go running off into the rainy night. The distraught singer phones an anonymous tip about the homicide to the police.

One of the motifs of the film is sex myths. Betty had heard that singers shouldn't make love before they go on stage as it will take energy away from their performance. After the killing, she runs across Mark who boasts, "I always jerk off before I shoot a scene," equating creative energy with sexual energy. Betty tells Mark about the murder and about a recurring nightmare she's having in which she's a young girl who sees a man in a black hood hurting a woman. Tonight, she says, the killer was wearing the same black hood that appeared in her dream.

Alan investigates the murder and discovers that the stage manager had left a cast party with Betty. He consults with Mark, asking his advice. The horror director says very pointedly, "I think it's unwise to use movies as a guide to reality, don't you, Inspector?" This seems to be Argento's defense against taking the thrills too seriously, relying on the old saw that it's only make-believe. Mark in turn harshly criticizes the costumes to the wardrobe mistress, prompting his girlfriend to call him a sadist, adding, "Everyone I know who knows you says the same thing."

"That must be very boring for you," Mark laconically returns, indicating that he, like Argento himself is unconcerned with the criticism against him.

Julia, the wardrobe mistress, notices that Lady Macbeth's costume has been torn. Argento augurs more violence with shots of sharp objects: scissors falling from a table; Julia cutting at the costume with a razor. While doing so, she sees a gold bracelet that doesn't belong on the costume. A quick shot of a pulsating brain, and the killer strikes again as Julia examines the bracelet. Julia sees Betty tied up as before, but the killer distracts her attention by throwing an iron at her, causing her to throw away the bracelet. While the killer goes to retrieve it, Julia knocks him out with the iron. She hesitates between freeing Betty and pulling off the killer's mask. When she goes to do the latter, the killer strangles her and stabs her with the scissors, redonning his disguise. However, his bracelet has fallen into Julia's mouth and he must pry the mouth open with a pair of scissors to retrieve it. When that doesn't prove sufficient, the killer cuts up Julia like a chicken until he's successful. Then he threatens Betty that he can take her wherever and whenever he wants before he frees her.

Betty goes to Alan, who notices the rope burns on her hands and wants to know why she didn't tell the police that she was an eyewitness to the murder. Betty explains that she just wanted to forget everything, that it was worse than he could have imagined. Concerned for her safety, Inspector Alan instructs her to lock herself in her apartment and await the arrival of his assistant.

A man knocks just as Betty has put some eyedrops in, so she can't see him very clearly. Betty's agent Myra (Daria Nicolodi) drops by and comments that the officer *downstairs* was keeping an eye on things. Then who's in the apartment? The women go look, but then the lights go out. Which is the real police officer – the one in the apartment or the one outside?

To protect themselves (Argento's women are typically more than screaming victims, strong but still very vulnerable), the pair go into the kitchen to get some knives. There is a phone call, and the man in the apartment leaves. He comes back to the door and demands to be let in. Myra demands to see his I.D. through the keyhole. Then, in one of the film's most audacious shots, we see a bullet traveling through the keyhole and then a master shot of it going out the back of Myra's head.

Betty tries to cope with the stress by putting on a relaxation tape and sends her feather pillow out the window, scattering feathers everywhere. The killer gets through the door and Betty seeks a place to hide, coming across the body of a man stabbed with a switchblade – the real police officer. Taking his gun, Betty shoots at the masked murderer and flees to her bedroom. There a little girl opens the grill and helps her escape down a ventilation shaft.

The girl, Alma, has long been spying on Betty to hear her practice her singing. Together, they manage to evade the killer and get back to Alma's apartment, where Alma's suspicious mother gives them an unfriendly welcome and refuses to call the police despite Betty's pleas. Betty flees back to the opera house – it's the only place where she feels safe.

While reality may not conform to movie conventions, movie reality does, and so Mark springs a plan whereby he hopes to reveal the killer. Recalling the trainer's claim that ravens remember, he arranges for the ravens to be released during an aria. One of the most magnificent shots in the film is a raven's-eye-view of flying through the grand opera house while a terrified audience ducks away from the swooping claws and beaks. Sure enough, a raven plucks out Inspector Alan's eye and swallows it. Alan manages to grab ahold of Betty and take her away to a secret niche, telling her she's "just like [her] mother."

Once more Betty is trussed up, only this time she's blindfolded. Alan explains that it would be better if he were to die while he splashes gasoline around the musical scores stored in the room. "No one must ever find me; I want to disappear," he tells Betty before giving her his gun and telling her

where to shoot. When Betty doesn't seem able to bring herself to do it, Alan tells her he strangled her mother. She shoots, causing him to drop a match, and the gas goes up in flames. Betty frees herself from the chair she's tied in, but can't open the room's locked door. The key to the lock is next to the burnt body, and Betty manages to tear her dress and handle the hot key only to have it break off in the lock. Having stretched suspense to the breaking point, Argento has Mark break open the door just in time.

The next scenes, set in the countryside of Switzerland, make a dramatic contrast to the enclosed spaces of the story's previous settings. There Mark and Betty are on holiday, and he discusses the possiblity of having her play in a production of *La Traviata*. In the background, a TV show imparts the information that the burnt body found at the opera was merely a mannequin. Mark sees that the maid has been stabbed and yells for Betty to run.

This sets up the climactic chase where Alan chases Betty over the scenic countryside with Mark in hot pursuit. Mark manages to tackle Alan but gets stabbed by him for his pains. Hoping to placate Alan, Betty tells him, "I am like my mother – I wanted you to win, to kill him. Come, we must get away." Momentarily duped, Alan is distracted until Betty clubs him on the head with a handy rock. Betty realizes her dreams were of her mother being a sadist, but she has freed herself from her troubled past. The police and a crowd, led by some German shepherds, have tracked Alan down and restrain him. Betty smiles – she's not like her mother, she loves nature, and she delights in the splendor of the grass. Argento leaves it ambiguous whether his ending is meant to be upbeat or whether past events have simply driven Betty bonkers.

Argento's most recent movie, *Two Evil Eyes*, a portmanteau of a film with two Edgar Allan Poe stories, "The Black Cat" directed by Argento and "The Strange Case of M. Valdemar" directed by George A. Romero, at least received distribution in the United States, which was more than *Opera* was accorded, albeit through a minor distributor. Argento's sequence is the superior of the two, showcasing once more his elaborate camera work and presenting a rather grisly story that bears little relation to Poe's original work (Romero's work in the film, a tepid story of a man returning from the dead, is rather moribund); however, it is far from the major horror opus that Argento is capable of. The time where horror films could distinguish

Opposite top: *The heroine of* Opera *has to undergo a particularly nasty form of torture: The unknown killer has taped needles to her face which will shred her eyeballs if she tries to close her eyes, forcing her to witness every moment of his killings.* Opposite bottom: *Dario Argento setting up a close-up shot of some grass for* Opera. *While Orion Pictures picked up the rights for a United States release in 1987, they elected not to distribute this thriller domestically.*

themselves by developing a distinctive look seems to have passed, and that is Argento's primary asset. Nevertheless, he has already accrued quite a legacy and his stylish efforts have influenced several modern horror directors.

Operatic seems the best description of Argento's gifts – he is to the horror genre what Sergio Leone was to the western. Argento makes films that are larger than life, inflates the violence and thrills, displays a scene-stealing sense of design and style. His voluptuous fulminations on violence still resonate with audiences who have seen and remember them.

Roy Ward Baker (1916–   )

The October Man (1947); *The Weaker Sex* (1948); *Paper Orchid* (1949); *Morning Departure* (aka *Operation Disaster*); *Highly Dangerous* (1950); *The House in the Square* (aka *I'll Never Forget You*) (1951); *Don't Bother to Knock; Night Without Sleep* (1952); *Inferno* (1953); *Passage Home* (1955); *Jacqueline; Tiger in Smoke* (1956); *The One That Got Away* (1957); *A Night to Remember* (1958); *The Singer Not the Song; Flame in the Streets* (1961); *The Valiant* (codir. with Giorgio Capitani, 1962); *Two Left Feet* (1963); *Five Million Years to Earth* (aka *Quatermass and the Pit*, 1967); *The Anniversary* (1968); *Moon Zero Two* (1969); *The Vampire Lovers; The Scars of Dracula* (1970); *Dr. Jekyll and Sister Hyde* (1971); *Asylum; Vault of Horror* (1972); *And Now the Screaming Starts; Legend of the Seven Golden Vampires* (1973); *The Monster Club* (1980).

TELEVISION: "The Tower of No Return," "Two's a Crowd," "Too Many Christmas Trees," "Silent Dust," "Room Without a View," "The Girl from Auntie," "The 13th Hole," "Split," *The Avengers; The Spy Killer* (1969); *Foreign Exchange* (1970); *Flame Trees of Thika* (1980); *The Masks of Death* (1984); *Fairly Secret Army II; The Irish R.M. II* (1985); *Minder IV* (1988); (TV movies); Episodes of *The Saint, The Human Jungle, Gideon's Way, The Baron, The Champions, Department S.,* and *The Persuaders.*

Roy Ward Baker was born in London in 1916. He entered the British film industry in 1934 as an assistant director. While serving in World War II, he got the opportunity to direct documentaries, honing his skills and finally being signed as a director for the British outfit Two Cities.

He had an excellent debut with his film *The October Man,* written by top mystery writer Eric Ambler. It is the mystery of a man with amnesia who has a history of mental disturbance and is now accused of murder. The film stars John and Juliet Mills and the ever wonderful Joan Greenwood.

Baker followed this initial success with *The Weaker Sex,* a weaker production centering around Ursula Jeans as a housewife who demonstrates her patriotic zest during World War II, and *Paper Orchid.* Baker then demonstrated that suspense was his forte with *Morning Departure* in which a submarine on a routine cruise hits a mine left over from the war and John Mills and 11 other men become trapped inside as the sub sinks to the bottom. It's a tense story of rescue and survival.

Highly Dangerous, a spy thriller with Dane Clark as an American reporter behind the Iron Curtain, followed. Next came *I'll Never Forget*

37

You; a remake of *Berkeley Square,* it was Baker's first foray into fantasy. In this delightful story, Tyrone Power is transported back to the eighteenth century, where he falls in love with Ann Blyth. The film offers able support from such stalwarts of British acting as Michael Rennie, Dennis Price, and Beatrice Campbell. This is one film deserving rediscovery. (It was also known as *The House in the Square.*)

I'll Never Forget You was a British-American coproduction and led to Baker going to Hollywood for a few years. His first film there, *Don't Bother to Knock,* offered a young Marilyn Monroe her first dramatic lead. She played a mentally disturbed babysitter in a big hotel. Said Baker about his star in an interview with Sam Irvin in *Bizarre #3,* "She was an extraordinary girl; not like anyone else. I don't think she was entirely sane. She was somewhere in the middle and this made her fascinating. This is what made her the sex symbol that she was. Marilyn Monroe was unlike anything any man had ever taken on a date, taken to bed, or whatever."

Night Without Sleep has yet another mentally disturbed man, this time one who is convinced he's committed a murder. (Dario Argento would play with this idea more effectively in *Four Flies on Grey Velvet.*) It's a tightly constructed little drama, but one which won't deprive the audience of a good night's sleep.

The 3-D craze was on, and Baker's contribution, *Inferno,* was actually one of the better films in the cycle, holding up well even without the 3-D. Robert Ryan stars as a millionaire who is stranded in the desert by his scheming wife and her lover. As in Jack Arnold's famous desert films, the desert takes on an impressive and oppressive mood. Ryan's attempts at survival and the heat and other elements that constantly plague him make for another suspenseful drama. The 3-D works well on the desert vistas and isn't gimmicked up until the finale, which features a fight between the principals with plenty of things being thrown, including an oil lantern which burns down a poor desert rat's place.

Baker booked a passage home and returned to England to make *Passage Home* and *Jacqueline,* the latter a heart-warming drama about a young Irish girl trying to help her alcoholic father. *The One That Got Away* has an excellent performance by Hardy Kruger as a Nazi who is captured in Great Britain but is determined to escape and return to Germany.

Baker followed this with one of his best-remembered and just downright best films, *A Night to Remember,* a dramatization of Walter Lord's book on the sinking of the *Titanic.* Eric Ambler provided the stirring script, giving a good cross section of characters and plenty of examples of grace under pressure. Among the leads are a young David McCallum and Honor Blackman. The result is definitely an unforgettable film with Baker beautifully capturing the horror and confusion of the sinking with documentary-like precision.

With the undistinguished *The Singer Not the Song*, Baker also ventured into producing as well as directing. He served in both capacities on *Flame in the Streets* and *Two Left Feet*, but judging from the results, Baker overtaxed himself, as the films are not as tight as his previous efforts, nor are their scripts as polished.

Baker became involved in television production, eventually directing the season opener for the 1965–66 season of *The Avengers*. Significantly, this was the episode that established the popular character of Mrs. Peel, seductively played by Diana Rigg in outfits especially designed for her by John Bates. Baker directed several episodes of the highly regarded British spy series that often had a wild touch of science fiction thrown in.

Then one day Hammer Films rang Baker up and asked him what he was doing. "My immediate thought was that they wanted me to do a horror film like the Draculas or Frankensteins," Baker recalled in *Bizarre #3*. "Well, I knew nothing about this and I did not want to get into something which I did not understand. Then they told me that they wanted me to do science fiction: *Quatermass and the Pit*. . . . So I said, 'Well, I see, let's talk about this!' I looked at the script and became very excited."

Quatermass and the Pit was the third serial in the famous Quatermass series created by Britain's top science fiction screenwriter, Nigel Kneale. The Quatermass films each started as a television serial and then Hammer Films bought the rights and made movies out of them. The first two, *The Creeping Unknown* (aka *The Quatermass Experiment**) and *Enemy from Space* (aka *Quatermass 2*), were filmed by Val Guest and starred American actor Brian Donlevy, much to the dismay of Quatermass creator Kneale, who had specifically envisioned Quatermass as a forceful British scientist.

The third series came about when Kneale suggested to producer Rudolph Cartier, "Suppose a building contractor was excavating a site for a big office block and going really deep, and suddenly came across what looked like a spaceship—" "Let's do it," Cartier immediately returned, and thus *Quatermass and the Pit* was born. Each film dealt with contact with an alien race, but whereas the first one begins when an astronaut becomes infected and mutates into an alien life form, and the second one deals with an invasion that has been under way for a year (aliens control the bodies and minds of some British workers in an effort to take over the earth), the third would set the contact almost immeasurably back in time to keep the series from seeming to repeat itself.

Wrote Kneale in his introduction to the printed scenario, "The intrusion would have come five million years in the past, when no resistance was possible, so that it succeeded wholly and built certain undesirable

---

*Posters for the film read *The Quatermass X-Periment* in a effort to capitalize on the British "X" rating which restricted the audience for the film to adults.

characteristics into Earth's future population. Quatermass would be fighting his own heredity."

The result was one of the most brilliantly and intelligently written science fiction screenplays ever. The original production was largely broadcast live on the BBC from December 1958 to January 1959 and starred veteran actor Andre Morell as the ever questing Quatermass.

Five Million Years to Earth is simply one of the finest science fiction films ever made, and one that packs a horrifying punch to boot. Long before Von Däniken, Nigel Kneale hit upon a scientific explanation for man's evil – his bigotry, violence, and racism. Along the way in his cleverly concocted story, Kneale provides explanations for ghosts, the devil, telekinesis, and other odd phenomena, all in a tightly compacted script with nary a wasted moment. Kneale himself brilliantly condensed the six-hour television original into an eventful 98 minutes for the film version.

The film opens with the credits printed next to a human skull with what appear to be flames printed over it, and then the camera zooms into the darkness of one of the eye sockets. (The credits of John Carpenter's *Halloween* are very reminiscent of this opening only with a Jack o'Lantern instead of a skull). The darkness is pulled aside to reveal a London bobby making his rounds. In a closed subway terminal, some men are excavating for a new line and in the process unexpectedly unearth some skeletons.

The skeletons are revealed to be an anthropological find of some significance, and Dr. Matthew Roney (James Donald) holds a press conference at the excavation. He knows that there will be pressure for the government-funded subway project to start up again, so he eloquently tries to persuade the press to emphasize that his team needs time to excavate and evaluate the find.

Baker emphasizes some nice human touches, such as Roney's difficulty in making himself heard over the subway noises. Donald does a beautiful job playing the intelligent but enthusastic scientist who is not so caught up in his field that he doesn't understand how the outside world works. Roney is a practical and concerned individual. He also knows how to play to the press, revealing a fascinating sculpture that represents what the fossils they've discovered might have once looked like.

One worker discovers a "pipe" where there shouldn't be one – could it be an unexploded V-2 bomb? The bomb squad quickly arrives but makes the startling discovery that the surface of the object is non-metallic.

Meanwhile, in another part of town, Professor Bernard Quatermass (Andrew Keir), head of Britain's Rocket Group, argues that said group is intended purely for peaceful purposes. He fears that a change in government policy will cause the military to take over, an idea that disgusts Quatermass because he'd hoped that as mankind explored space, he would leave his vices behind him. Colonel James Breen (Julian Glover) emphasizes the military importance of establishing a base on the moon and is assigned to Quatermass' Rocket Group over Quatermass' objections.

Abruptly, the message comes through about the discovery at Hobbs End. Breen, a former head of a detonation squad, agrees to investigate, and Quatermass tags along.

Arriving, the pair find that the "missile" has mostly been excavated. However, a peculiar discovery is made – an unbroken skull is found *inside* a hollow of the ship. Roney is absolutely ecstatic over the find; however, the significance of finding a delicate 5 million-year-old fossil unbroken dawns on him. That ship was no German bomb.

Quatermass and Roney's assistant Barbara (Barbara Shelley) follow a bobby outside when he tells them that the local area has long been abandoned and has a bad reputation. The bobby used to live in the area when he was a "nipper" and recalls stories about "noises, bumps, even things being seen," but he discounts them. However, inside one of the abandoned houses are strange scratches on the wall. The bobby becomes increasingly nervous and cannot remain inside.

Outside, Quatermass and Barbara notice that the name for the area has been changed. The new name is Hobbs End, but an old sign indicates it used to be called Hob's Lane with only one "b." Barbara goes on to note that Hob was an old nickname for the devil.

Quatermass visits Roney to discover whether the skeletons found were "of this earth." Roney assures him that they were, though they do have unaccountably enlarged skulls. Barbara shows up with clippings that indicate the area had experienced some trouble when the subway was first built in the '20s, but Quatermass dismisses them.

Back at Hobbs End, a blowtorch fails even to make the surface of the craft warm. It has been noticed that touching the surface for a long period of time leads to frostbite, though the surface isn't even cold, so those operating on or near the craft are issued gloves. (This is a rather subtle way of indicating that the ship absorbs energy.) The surface has been discovered to be harder than diamond, yet Quatermass discovers some concentric circles forming a pentacle have been etched into the surface. "Resistant to heat of 3000°; harder than diamond – that's the material every rocket engineer's been looking for," he exasperatedly exclaims to the unimaginative Colonel Breen. Obviously, whatever it is, the Germans couldn't have made it. Quatermass suggests that a Borazon drill be employed.

Just then a scream emerges from the hollow. West (Hugh Futcher) is led outside, babbling about seeing a horrible little figure that came through the wall, matching a description in one of Barbara's clippings.

Quatermass and Barbara are able to track down reports of strange phenomena in the area back to 1341. Quatermass is astounded by the possibilities of what he's learned. "I suppose it's possible for ... ghosts –

let's use the word – to be phenomena that were badly observed and wrongly explained," he speculates.

Returning to Hobbs End, Quatermass begs Colonel Breen to put off using the Borazon drill, but Breen has brought in an outside specialist, Sladden (Duncan Lamont), and insists on proceeding. The drill doesn't work. Instead, the whole ship begins to vibrate and issue a painful, high-pitched sound. (Baker's direction of the actors' reaction shots expertly conveys almost unbearable pain.)

Roney drops by, and when he looks inside the ship, the wall over the ship's opening suddenly begins melting and disintegrating in a beautiful shot that resembles that of the *Andromeda Strain* growing in Robert Wise's film. Inside are revealed four green locust-like space travelers, which quickly start decomposing and give off a horrible stench. Roney and Barbara have to work fast to preserve them as they start falling apart and dripping green ichor. The figures are classified as three-legged arthropods which, with their pointy antennae and bulging eyes, resemble ancient ritual masks and gargoyles in several cultures. (The triangular head and horns are also meant to suggest drawings of the devil.) From their physical makeup, Roney deduces that they must be from a planet with a thin atmosphere and a low-gravity environment. Quatermass theorizes that the planet Mars, which has those conditions, might have once been inhabited by creatures such as these and that the bodies they have found could be those of Martians. The press clamors for details, so Quatermass decides to release a few.

He is then summoned by the Minister of Defense, who is furious with him for having talked without first getting authority. Quatermass, a private citizen as well as a public servant, is puzzled at the suggestion that he would need to get authority. The minister's mood isn't helped by the constantly ringing phones, including calls from the Home Secretary and the private secretary of the Prime Minister. Quatermass relates the astounding implications that he mentioned briefly to the press. It is his theory that Martians, learning that their planet was doomed and knowing they could not live in Earth's atmosphere, took apes and mutated them, giving them new faculties such as intelligence and possibly something else. In essence, they would colonize Earth by proxy.

Colonel Breen has another theory more to the minister's liking. He insists that the ship was merely a Nazi propaganda hoax stuffed with fake aliens and designed to create panic. The ship is declared safe, and a press conference is announced over Quatermass's objections and pleas that they listen to expert testimony. Their minds are made up and not even the facts can change them.

Sladden comes back after a tea break and discovers the army pulling out (and, in an amusing touch, taking Sladden's toolbox with them). When he goes inside the craft to retrieve his drill, he touches his steel wrench to the surface of the ship. A strange sound is suddenly emitted, and the objects within Sladden's vicinity begin to float wildly in the air. Sladden tries to flee, fighting some invisible force, and wherever he goes, objects begin to fly up and swirl around. Barbara notices what is happening and chases after him. Finally, Sladden collapses in a cemetery, where even the ground under him begins to undulate, rippling up and down.

Quatermass and Barbara locate Sladden after he has taken sanctuary in a church. Describing what happened, Sladden relates a "racial memory"; however, the race involved is Martian. He saw himself as part of a great, leaping crowd of alien locusts under a purple sky. The telekinesis begins again inside the church as Sladden gets more agitated.

Back at the lab, Quatermass calls everyone, and they try hooking Roney's brainwave-measuring device to a visual output device of one of Quatermass's associates. They initially hook up the apparatus to Roney and succeed at getting a look at Roney's unconscious images, but they fail to tap into the racial memories they hope to find.

Quatermass decides to duplicate Sladden's experience as closely as possible and brings all the brainwave apparatus to Hobbs End, wearing the device himself. Once more he touches the steel wrench to the side of the ship and objects start moving, but Quatermass receives no visual impressions – Barbara does. Barbara dons the headgear and the videotape machine begins recording what she is "seeing." Meanwhile, the whole excavation site becomes agitated with mud oozing through the floorboards and tiles falling off the walls. On the video monitor, we see stick figure locusts in action, moving in great masses and apparently killing each other. Finally, the effect subsides. As directed by Baker, this is a particularly intense and engrossing scene. Despite the inadequacies of the effects representing the Martian hive, Baker wonderfully orchestrates a feeling of immense power unleashed and threatening to pull the place apart. The small details on which he focuses are telling and effective in suggesting that everything has gone haywire.

Quatermass shows the video to the Department of Defense, interpreting the images to represent the Martians engaged in ritual slaughter for the purpose of preserving a fixed society. That is the way they lived, and even more importantly, that is the way they intended for *humans* to live – to seek out and destroy those elements which do not conform to the norm. The minister doesn't go along with Quatermass's interpretation and decides to go ahead with the press conference.

Great power is funneled into the excavation to provide light for the television cameras. One power cable is taken inside the ship itself to light the inside, but a worker slips on the smooth surface and is electrocuted. Barbara senses that the ship is coming alive and is starting to glow. There is another short and the effect begins again. The crowd panics and rushes to get out while the dark blue ship begins to give off a white glow. Earthquakes begin to shake the area. Colonel Breen is transfixed by the sight. He approaches the ship and has all of his life energy sucked out.

Quatermass is swept along with the crowd, but Roney stops him and pulls him out. Quatermass is susceptible to the Martian influence and can only overcome it with thought and determination. Luckily, Roney and a few others are immune; however, their very immunity makes them different, and those who are immune become targets of the unthinking crowds. Fires begin to break out. It is chaos outside. The sounds of screams can be heard – the crowd is killing animals, but not only animals. They move in on an unaffected man, and huge rocks start to pummel the individual.

The huge figure of a Martian rises from the pit and towers over the houses of London. It is the focus of all the unleashed energy, appearing like an evil devil who gloats on the damage he was wrought. Roney seizes on the idea that iron was considered an effective weapon against the devil. If they can ground the energy, they can destroy the Martian influence. Quatermass and Roney start to move on a giant steel crane to maneuver it into the Martian apparition, but a possessed Barbara sees them. Roney dispatches Quatermass to stop her while he ascends the tower himself. As he climbs out to the end of the crane, an earthquake causes the crane to lurch forward and swing into the energy itself. Roney is killed, but the plan works. Quatermass and Barbara are moved by the death of their colleague, who sacrificed himself to save humanity, but they cannot bring themselves to say anything to each other. Meanwhile, the sounds of dogs and fire engines indicate that the madness is over and that efforts to stop the chaos have begun.

It's a very somber ending, reflecting the drained feeling that the audience should have at the close. Baker builds the intensity of the film beautifully, and his efforts at depicting a full-fledged disaster on a limited budget are admirable, even when the model work is not convincing. However, the ending does lack the summation of the story's themes that was presented at the end of the teleplay.

In that ending, Kneale has Quatermass on a television addressing the audience about what has happened and saying, "That is the full account. Matthew Roney was a brave man and a friend. Much more – it is with his kind that hope lies. For they have outgrown the Martian in us. If another of these things should ever be found, we are armed with knowledge. But we also have knowledge of ourselves ... of the ancient, destructive urges in us, that grow more deadly as our populations approach in size and complexity those of ancient Mars. Every war crisis, witch hunt, race riot, and purge ... is a reminder and a warning. We are the Martians. If we cannot control the inheritance within us ... this will be their second dead planet!"

Kneale portrays the will to conform and the fear and loathing of people who are in some way different as alien drives that were imposed on mankind in its formation. He points out that these drives make sense when applied to insects who weed out mutants to preserve the basic colony, but have been artificially and inappropriately imposed on mammals, thus creating evil. The drives that cause hatred and persecution are alien to us, Kneale indicates, and can be overcome with reason and willpower until all mankind becomes immune to their nefarious influence. But we must never forget that that potential for evil is within us and the blame is not to be shifted onto innocent, nonconforming outsiders. Buried in this often overlooked science fiction classic is an apt metaphor for the sources and reasons for man's inhumanity.

Science fiction is the literature of ideas, but rarely do science fiction films have so many ideas contained in them. Kneale indicates that as mankind evolves, he often unthinkingly takes patterns of behavior with him as part of his cultural heritage, but the reasons for those patterns get lost in mysticism that replaces knowledge.

Five Million Years to Earth came out just before *2001: A Space Odyssey*, and it was lost in the excitement surrounding Kubrick's masterpiece, though it has managed to build up a following and some recognition in the ensuing years. It obviously provided some of the inspiration for Tobe Hooper's film *Lifeforce*, but it far surpasses Hooper's film in terms of depth and verisimilitude, as well as in the performances of the cast.

Keir makes an excellent Quatermass, suggesting an open-minded intelligence and an impatience with tomfoolery. With his forceful personality and determination, we can see why he would make a good leader and be assigned the head of the Rocket Group even though he occasionally lacks tact. Unfortunately, Hammer seemed to consider Keir as a substitute for Peter Cushing and would rarely assign him comparable roles.

Julian Glover captures the officiousness of Colonel Breen perfectly. Breen is not a bad chap – despite Quatermass' obvious dislike of him, he continues to make peaceful overtures – but he is unimaginative and singleminded in his purpose. James Donald likewise conveys intelligence and enthusiasm as Roney, and notably it is he who, being immune to the Martian influence, sees what must be done and sees it through at the cost of his life. He's devoted to the cause of knowledge, but he's no starry-eyed dreamer. His demise is truly heroic, the giving of his life to successfully destroy the source of evil.

The attractive Barbara Shelley well fills out the important role of Barbara, an intelligent, no-nonsense heroine with a dedication to knowledge that matches Quatermass' and Roney's. Her role is given less characterization, but I like how Shelley conveys her admiration and possibly even love for Roney without there being so much as a word in the script to indicate such feeling. It's all in how Shelley looks at Donald – her body language. Commented Baker in the *Bizarre* interview, "I was mad about Barbara Shelley who was in the picture – mad in the sense of love. We used to waltz around the set together; a great love affair. It puzzles me about her. She should be much bigger than she is, but I don't think she really cares whether she is a star or not. She can act; God can she ever act!"

Duncan Lamont gives a wonderful performance as Sladden, at first a cheerful, open bloke. Sladden tries to comfort Quatermass with talk about insurance when he prepares to drill what he thinks might be a bomb. He even makes jokes to himself as he works. This contrasts sharply to the later Sladen, who appears to have lost control of his own body and has been scared to his wits' end by the peculiar phenomenon that follows him.

Producer Anthony Nelson-Keys was responsible for selecting Baker to head *Five Million Years to Earth*. He explained in an interview in *Little Shoppe of Horrors* magazine that he decided not to use Terence Fisher because "I didn't see Terry in this atmosphere of things out of space. And with all the special effects we had, I wanted a director who had a very great deal of technical know-how." Knowing that Baker was familiar with effects from working on *A Night to Remember*, Nelson-Keys called Baker up and told him, "This is a technical picture – this is what we've got to spend on it. Regarding special effects, we've got to spend that amount and that amount only. I must say, he was absolutely marvelous. He worked out, went away, came back and sat down with the special effects bloke and myself and had, already, himself, worked out all these things."

Like most Hammer films, *Five Million Years to Earth* looks much better than similarly budgeted American films. If the Martians are never quite convincing, the physical effects are superbly done and some of the other effects are pulled off marvelously. The blue spaceship of the Martians has a unique and interesting look to it, even more so when it starts glowing white with blue veins at the end. Moreover, the film aptly demonstrates that the best science fiction films don't depend on effects so much as they do on good and imaginative storytelling, something that *Five Million Years to Earth* has in abundance.

Hammer was so pleased with the final result that they offered to allow Baker to take over direction of the troubled *The Anniversary* from Alvin Rakoff. Baker had known Bette Davis from his days back in Hollywood and the two were good friends, so he agreed. Baker explained what happened in *Little Shoppe of Horrors #4*: "They began the picture at Hammer with Bette [Davis]. She pointed out to them that the play was the mother in the centre with the children all 'round, and she analysed the play and said, 'What this play is doing is that the mother is setting up the jokes for other characters to crack and they are getting all the laughs. . . . Well, that is absolutely fine, but for that picture you don't want me.'" Davis wanted changes, but since most of the cast had appeared in the play, her request caused some friction with those who did not want their parts changed. Baker was called in to manage the conflict. "I didn't alter the script," Baker said, "but I did say to them, there's going to be a few changes . . . [and] they all had to bloody well put up with it."

Davis plays the one-eyed Mrs. Taggart, a monstrous mother with three almost equally monstrous children: Terry (Jack Hedley), who is married to an obnoxious wife, Karen (Sheila Hancock); Henry (James Cossins), a misogynist transvestite; and Tom (Christian Roberts), who has knocked up his finacée, Shirley (Elaine Blair). Davis is in fine fettle in this tale of family fealty gone hideously awry, with its melodramatic revelations promoting laughter rather than shock.

Mrs. Taggart celebrates her wedding anniversary every year, though her husband died ten years ago. She's very insistent that her sons attend the celebration. When Terry and his wife tell her they plan to move to Canada, she retaliates by telling them that their children were in an accident with Henry, who was bringing them home, but this turns out not to be true. Later it's revealed that they have five children because Mrs. Taggert has been paying Jack to have children, hoping that Karen will suffer a heart attack before delivery.

Tom plans to gently break the news that he is marrying Shirley, but Mrs. Taggert discovers that Shirley wears her hair long to cover her deformed ears and taunts her unmercifully. Meanwhile, she had been encouraging Henry to wear women's clothes to tie him to her, but Henry was almost caught stealing lingerie and left Terry's car at the scene of the crime. Mrs. Taggert agrees to get Terry off the hook if he will pay her back the 5,000 pounds she's given him to have their children. Terry gives her an I.O.U. and heads off with Karen to Canada.

However, Mama is not going to be foiled so easily. She calls up emigration and lets them know that Terry and Karen owe her a good deal of money. She also arranges to give Shirley a large amount of money as a wedding present, expecting that she will proceed to make Tom's life miserable. The rebellion has been quelled, and she looks forward to spending her anniversary with her children again next year.

The Anniversary delights with its hammy performances, particularly those of Davis and Cossins, and with its black comedy. The film is perhaps the best screen presentation of Philip Wylie's theory of "Momism" taken to absurd extremes. The horror lies not so much in an old dark house with skeletons in its closets as in the extremes to which manipulative personalities will go in order to have their way.

Since he had tackled one effects-laden project successfully, Hammer next assigned Baker to the disastrous *Moon Zero Two*. The film does have some adherents in the bad film set, and there is admittedly some perverse looniness in making the world's first space western (with an incredibly cornball script courtesy of Hammer producer Michael Carreras), but even its director admits it was a mistake and a disappointment.

The plot has Bill Kemp (James Olson), a space cowboy, entering under the employ of the villainous J. J. Hubbard (Warren Mitchell) and assisting him in a search for a 6,000-ton sapphire asteroid that will make Hubbard the richest man in the solar system. However, Clementine (Catherine von Schell) convinces Kemp that Hubbard cheated her out of her inheritance and asks him to thwart Hubbard's dastardly plans.

Coming on the heels of the first American moon landing, the film seemed particularly unconvincing. Baker hoped to create the wildest western gunfight ever with cowboys being propelled backwards every time they fired their guns, but the budget would not allow for it. The film became a bottomless pit into which money was thrown, and the returns at the box office headed off at the pass any possibility of a sequel.

In 1970, the vampire genre suffered from rather tired blood. Producer Harry Fine came across a copy of the story "Carmilla" by Sheridan Le Fanu and decided that it would make a good basis for a vampire film. Together with coproducer Michael Style and scriptwriter Tudor Gates, they created an outline and sent it to James Carreras, head of Hammer Films, who immediately contacted American International Pictures to cofinance the film and release it in America. (AIP put up $400,000 towards the film's budget and Hammer guaranteed any overbudget expenses.) Roy Ward Baker was then suggested as the director.

As Baker recalled to Sam Irvin (*Bizarre #3*),

> Hammer rang me up and said, "We're thinking of doing a horror picture." ... I said to myself, "Oh. Here we go. I knew it was coming sooner or later." Then they asked me if I had ever read the book "Carmilla" by Joseph Sheridan Le Fanu. I said I had read it and liked it very much. In fact the first time I read it was when I was 14 years old. So I became more interested. They said, "We've developed it into a script. We feel that there are lesbian undertones and we have brought those out." From the industrial side, it was thought, "Well, we've done everything with vampires that the mind of man could possibly imagine, so let's have a woman and let's have lesbianism, ha ha ha."

Baker decided that if he was stuck with the film, he would at least try to preserve Le Fanu's dignity. With the sole support of star Ingrid Pitt, he made the film "straight," avoiding the campy or silly, toning down the lesbian angle where possible and treating the story seriously. He explained his philosophy as follows:

> One thing I insist upon constantly is the old, old principle laid down in *King Kong* – even if your hero is a monster, he has still got to be

understandable if not sympathetic. I refuse to make a villain out of anyone. He may be destructive and have to be killed to prevent more havoc, but at least he is understandable and perhaps pitiable.

The Vampire Lovers became the fourth film adaptation of "Carmilla." The first was Carl Dreyer's *Vampyr*, which did little more than borrow the idea of having a female vampire. In 1960 Roger Vadim did *Blood and Roses*, a pretty but dull film clearly inspired by the Le Fanu story. Two years after that, Christopher Lee starred as Count Karnstein in *Terror in the Crypt*, which adapted the Le Fanu story but removed the vampire elements.

The Vampire Lovers opens in the graveyard of the Karnstein estate, where Baron Joachim Von Hartog (Douglas Wilmer) searches out and decapitates a vampire while a freeze frame of spurting blood heralds the coming credits. The story picks up with a Countess (Dawn Addams) who drops off her daughter Marcilla (Ingrid Pitt) at the home of General Von Spielsdorf (Peter Cushing) while she leaves to visit a dying friend. Not long after the start of Marcilla's visit, the general's daughter, Laura (Pippa Steel), starts having nightmares, becomes ill and dies.

Next we see the Countess stopping off at the home of Roger Morton (George Cole), leaving behind her niece Carmilla (also Pitt). It's not long before Carmilla starts vamping Morton's daughter Emma (Madeleine Smith) and it seems like the pattern is going to repeat itself. Renton (Harvey Hall) becomes alarmed at Carmilla's influence and alerts the local physician (Ferdy Mayne) to the possiblity of vampirism, but it isn't long before Carmilla claims the good doctor as a victim.

Morton dashes off to enlist the aid of General Von Spielsdorf and Baron Von Hartog in an effort to save Emma. With the help of Carl Eberhardt (Jon Finch), Emma's puzzled sweetheart, the men go to Karnstein Castle where Von Hartog relates the history of the Karnstein family, noting how he killed all of them but one many years ago. That one, Mircalla, has a portrait that both Morton and the general recognize as their daughters' companion. Carl then rushes homeward to save Emma.

Meanwhile, Carmilla has taken the opportunity of Morton's absence to decimate the household and is planning to abscond with Emma when Carl arrives. Abruptly, Carmilla disappears, reappearing back at the Karnstein cemetery where the general is ready for her, sword in hand. A quick swing puts an end to the curse of the Karnsteins.

As Baker promised, the lesbian overtones and nudity were handled tastefully. *The Vampire Lovers* became the first horror film to receive an R rating in the United States. (Previously, horror was considered a genre for kids, so even as bloody a film as *Dracula Has Risen from the Grave* was given a G rating). The success of *The Vampire Lovers* proved that there was an adult audience for horror films out there.

Roy Ward Baker with star Ingrid Pitt on the set of The Vampire Lovers, *a Hammer-AIP co-production which exploited lesbian vampires for the first time on screen. (Photo courtesy of Bill George.)*

The Vampire Lovers also dared to play with the traditional elements of vampirism. These vampires can only be killed by cutting off their heads – no stake through the heart for them. Carmilla indicates she prefers to stay out of the sun, but it does not faze her, much less disintegrate her. In fact, when Laura dies, it is Carmilla who suggests that Cushing open the drapes and let the light in. Rather than a bat, Carmilla turns into a grey cat, a more feminine creature. However, she has also been granted the power of teleporting back to her gravesite. None of her victims come back from the dead to spread the plague of vampirism.

Unfortunately, while the production values were better than in other Hammer films of this period, the script is repetitive and features some rather dull dialogue. The film loses its momentum about a third of the way through and never quite recovers. Additionally, the character of the Countess is simply forgotten about (what exactly is her role in all this?) while an additional character of a man or vampire on horseback (John Forbes-Robertson) wanders around the background being mysterious and never getting directly involved in the action. The film ends with him riding off into the night while laughter is heard on the soundtrack (Herzog's remake of *Nosferatu* has a surprisingly similar ending). Is he meant to represent the omnipresence of evil, a vampire Von Hartog overlooked, fate? We're never clued in.

Ingrid Pitt makes the most she can of her first starring role. (She had previously had a bit in *Where Eagles Dare*.) She has an odd foreign accent which gives her an exotic flavor plus an attractive, amply bosomed body which made her a favorite pinup of many horror fans. She demonstrates more acting ability than most Hammer actresses (many of whom were obviously picked only for their looks) and can add a nice purr to any suggestive lines. Sadly, most of her material was rather limply written.

The rest of the cast gives at least able support, with Jon Finch making his debut of particular note. Finch went on to star in Polanski's *Macbeth*, Fuest's *Last Day of Man on Earth* (aka *The Final Programme*), and Hitchcock's *Frenzy*, giving excellent performances in each, though here he is little more than a typical Hammer hero. Douglas Wilmer and Ferdy Mayne (*Fearless Vampire Killers*) add color to their limited roles, and Peter Cushing is always welcome.

The film did indicate a new direction and look for Hammer and is fairly handsomely mounted. Unfortunately, there simply wasn't time to polish the screenplay, which keeps *The Vampire Lovers* from being any kind of classic. The death of Laura, the presumed heroine of the film, a third of the way through was meant to be a shock, echoing *Psycho*, but it is obvious what is going to happen to her so there is no sudden shock and the whole episode seems like a lengthy prologue to the rest of the film. Perhaps if Carmilla had alternated between the two daughters it would have been more interesting (is her fondness for the women genuine or manipulative? would they become jealous if they knew of each other?), but they went ahead with the hastily contrived script instead.

Having tackled one film with vampirism as its subject, Hammer assigned Baker to helm *Scars of Dracula*, which was intended as a new start for the Dracula series starring Christopher Lee as the sanguinary count. Unlike previous entries, *Scars of Dracula* does not pick up where the previous film, in this case Peter Sasdy's *Taste the Blood of Dracula*, left off. Lee's Dracula is revived by blood dripping off a giant vampire bat (unfortunately, a very unconvincing one). Meanwhile, the villagers of Kleinenburg, fearing that Dracula has returned, storm the castle with torches and set it aflame. Dracula's servant Klove (Patrick Troughton) cannot stop them, but when the villagers return to the church where their loved ones were meant to wait in safety, they find them all dead, victims of the giant bat.

From here we pick up the dull story of Paul Carlson (Christopher Matthews), who has seduced the daughter of the burgomaster of a neighboring village and must flee to Kleinenburg for safety. Finding the villagers there frightened and unfriendly, he pays a call on Castle Dracula, where he is greeted by Tania (Anoushka Hempel) and her master, Count Dracula. Tania greets Paul with open arms – a bit too open for her master's taste as he breaks into Paul's bedroom just as she prepares to put the bite on him. Enraged, Dracula stabs her and sucks her wound dry.

Scars of Dracula returns to Bram Stoker's novel for inspiration, retelling the story of Jonathan Harker with Carlson taking Harker's place. However, as an added inspiration, Dracula has been reinterpreted along the lines of Vlad Tepes, the cruel warlord on whom Stoker based the character of Dracula. Here Dracula is not only a vampire, but a sadistic nobleman ready to torture insubordinate servants.

Poor Paul wakes up to find himself trapped in his room, the only egress a window that overlooks a steep cliff. He resolves to tie his bedsheets together and make it to a window below and perhaps escape. He no sooner reaches the window than Klove pulls up the sheets, leaving Paul in the same chamber as Dracula's coffin.

At this climactic point, the film switches to Paul's brother Simon (Dennis Waterman), who is concerned about Paul's disappearance. With Paul's friend Sarah (Jenny Hanley), he journeys to Kleinenburg, and like Paul, they are forced to spend the night at the castle. That night, Dracula makes his move on Sarah but is repelled by the cross she wears around her neck. Undaunted, he orders Klove to remove it, but Klove is attracted to Sarah and instead helps her and Simon escape during the daylight. When Dracula rises, he tortures Klove for disobeying by burning him with a red-hot sword blade, another indication of how Baker emphasized Dracula's sadism.

Simon decides he must know what happened to his brother and resolves to return to the castle after leaving Sarah in the care of the local priest. Gaining entrance to Dracula's secret chamber, he prepares to stake the dread menace when the vampire's eyes seem to blaze through his eyelids and hypnotize him. Saving Simon for later, Dracula takes off, sending his bat to kill the priest. Simon wakes to find the bloody remains of Paul.

Sarah flees, heading for the castle in search of Simon. There Dracula prepares to induct her into the ranks of the undead. Klove and Simon rush up, but Dracula smiles and throws the meddlesome Klove over the side of the cliff. Simon hurls a steel pike javelin-style into Dracula's side, but the Count merely pulls it out and brandishes it. Just then the pike acts as a lightning rod, and the stricken vampire bursts into flames and topples to his final rest.

In terms of centering the story around Dracula and giving Lee more screentime than the immediate predecessors in the series, *Scars of Dracula* is an improvement. Unfortunately, it was shot on a limited budget, which shows in the dull art direction and tacky sets as well as in some poorly executed special effects. There is some attempt at revitalization going on, but the lovers' subplot is uninteresting and the film doesn't do much in the way of establishing an overall mood or tone.

One positive thing it does do is go back to the book. It presents some dialogue from Stoker's original, and in one of the more interesting scenes, it gives the first visual depiction of Dracula crawling down the wall of his castle as he does in the book. Baker is also careful not to have Dracula open any doors. The doors open by themselves or he simply appears, a subtle suggestion of supernatural powers. Also, when he burns Klove, we see a mad, gleeful expression on his face, an indication of his cruel and sadistic predilections. Sadly, John Elder's script does not keep up a high level of invention. The result is a tepid Dracula film with some interesting moments.

Dr. Jekyll and Sister Hyde is a better film largely because it has a better script, courtesy of Brian Clemens, the man behind many clever *Avengers* episodes and director of the lively and inventive horror film *Captain Kronos Vampire Hunter*. Taking the old and tired Dr. Jekyll theme, Clemens manages to inject some new life into the story by having Dr. Jekyll (Ralph Bates) experiment with female hormones and become a woman (Martine Beswick).

Dr. Jekyll starts out experimenting on flies and hopes his secret serum will lead to prolonging people's lifespans. When he moves into human experimentation, he initially gets his raw materials from the morgue, but when they are no longer able to supply him, he turns to Burke (Ivor Dean) and Hare (Tony Calvin) (real-life grave robbers who actually died quite some time previous to the Victorian setting of this tale) until the resurrectionists are caught by an angry crowd which lynches Burke and blinds Hare.

As the influence of Sister Hyde gets stronger, Jekyll is forced to kill prostitutes to continue his experiments, thus giving rise to the legend of Jack the Ripper! (The recent Anthony Perkins film *Edge of Sanity* borrowed this plot device.) Complicating things is that while Jekyll is falling in love with his neighbor's sister Susan (Susan Brodrick), Sister Hyde falls for the neighbor himself, Howard (Lewis Fiander). Jekyll's identity becomes so confused that he accidentally makes a pass at Howard, who naturally fobids Susan to see him.

Finally, Hare betrays Jekyll to the constabulary, who pursue him along the rooftops. Jekyll slips and hangs on for dear life but finds himself unable to prevent himself from changing into his feminine personality, whose weaker hands lose their hold. He hits pavement and dies a hermaphrodite, part man, part woman.

Baker makes the most of the Victorian setting, adding colorful details and the effects of Jekyll/Hyde's personality on Victorian mores. In addition to featuring one of the strangest love triangles ever, the film also benefits from dollops of cheeky humor, but not at the expense of the characters or plot.

The film also benefits from the fact that Bates and Beswick have a similar facial structure, though this fact was apparently not noticed until partway into production when it was too late to do more with it. Baker would like to have had a scene of the two halves confronting each other, but Clemens stuck to the integrity of his story, which requires that, being one person, Jekyll and Hyde can never be seen together.

Unfortunately, this clever film was given the standard exploitation treatment when it was released by AIP in America, with ads promising, "Warning! The sexual transformation of a man into a woman will actually take place before your eyes!" and "Parents: Be sure your children are sufficiently mature to witness the intimate details of this frank and revealing film." Naturally, there were no "frank and revealing" details, and in the words of an AIP advertising executive, the kids just had to be mature enough to experience a dissolve (the fading of one image into another).

Baker's next film, *Asylum*, also benefited from a strong screenplay, this time by horror veteran Robert Bloch, who concocted an anthology of his own stories. The result was the best horror anthology film since *Dead of Night*, which *Asylum* appears to be patterned after. Both films feature an intriguing framing story which does more than string the stories together, unlike the tepid framing stories in most anthology films. The classic *Dead of Night* had five episodes, including one humorous episode, while *Asylum* has four – a humorous fifth segment was trimmed before filming. Both films build slowly in terms of mood and intensity, though this effect was altered in *Asylum* when the producers shuffled the order of the stories around.

Asylum starts off as a mystery. A young psychiatrist comes to a mental sanitarium to meet with the head of the institution, Dr. B. Starr. He is met instead by Dr. Rutherford (Patrick Magee), who informs him that Dr. Starr is now one of the inmates – having gone mad himself. Rutherford challenges the young man to guess which of four inmates is Dr. Starr, thereby testing his qualifications for employment. The doctor agrees and asks to meet with the patients, each of whom tells him about the events leading to their commitment. This effectively hooks the audience, challenging them to match wits and discover the secret for themselves.

The first story is told by Bonnie (Barbara Parkins) and is based on Bloch's story "Frozen Fear." Bonnie conspires with her lover, Walter (Richard Todd), to do away with his wife. Walter chops the woman into pieces, wraps them in butcher paper, and stores them in a large freezer in the basement.

While Bonnie heads over to meet Walter, the pieces come alive and strangle him in a sequence that is genuinely unnerving without ever really showing anything horrible. We see only moving packages of paper, but the realization of what they contain and the sight of them squirming across the floor with heavy crinkling sounds make this segment an outstanding bit of screen horror, far more effective than, say, the crawling hand story in Freddie Francis' *Dr. Terror's House of Horrors*.

In contrast, "The Weird Tailor" is merely *outré*. Peter Cushing plays a man who entreats an impoverished tailor (Barry Morse) to make a magical suit which will, he hopes, bring his dead son back to life. When the tailor finds out that Cushing doesn't have the money to pay for the suit, Cushing tries to take it away at gunpoint. In the ensuing struggle, Cushing is shot and killed, and the frightened tailor leaves with the suit, planning to burn it.

However, his wife puts the suit on their window mannequin instead. The tailor becomes enraged when he discovers this and starts beating his wife – only to be strangled to death by the mannequin which has been brought to live by the magical suit. (A better and far scarier version was done on Karloff's TV show *Thriller*.)

Despite a pair of fine actresses, "Lucy Comes to Stay" is the most expendable of the four tales. Charlotte Rampling has a companion named Lucy, played by Britt Ekland. Unfortunately, Charlotte is psychotic, and when James Valliers tries to explain that Lucy does not exist, he gets stabbed to death with a pair of scissors for his pains. (Bloch's original story preceded his handling of a dual-personality psychotic in *Psycho*.)

"Mannikins of Horror" is reminiscent of the Tod Browning classic *The Devil-Doll*. This final tale ties in with the framing story in a clever way. The last patient to be seen is Dr. Byron (Herbert Lom), who believes he can will life into toy-like dolls he fashions in the image of real people. When the young doctor returns to discuss his conclusion with Dr. Rutherford, Byron puts his will into a doll-like replica of himself, which he sends to kill Rutherford for imprisoning him.

The doll succeeds, only to be crushed by the young doctor. (The tubes that appear from the crushed mannequin resemble entrails, a nicely macabre touch.) Downstairs, Dr. Byron's body is found crushed and mangled like that of the mannequin. The young doctor is left in a quandary – how can he rationally account for the deaths, especially to the police?

There is a final twist in store which brings the story full circle, revealing at last Dr. Starr's identity and setting up for the next unwary but cocksure psychiatrist to apply for a job at this particular asylum. (Hint: the twist is similar to that in Edgar Allan Poe's classic horror story "The System of Dr. Tarr and Prof. Fether.")

Baker does an able job handling the directorial chores on the film, keeping the pacing from sagging the way it does in most anthology films and setting up each new situation deftly and swiftly. Bloch, who has been dissatisfied with most film adaptations of his work, was pleased that Baker filmed the "Frozen Fear" episode pretty much as written, and it is indeed the best sequence in the film. Years later, *Asylum* was rereleased under the title *House of Crazies* with a few minutes of footage trimmed.

Amicus, the company that produced *Asylum*, was pleased with Baker's work and set him up to direct the follow-up to their hit *Tales from the Crypt*, namely *The Vault of Horror* (which has also shown up on cable television under the title *Tales from the Crypt II*). Unfortunately, despite a good cast, the script, an adaptation of various E. C. Comics horror stories, just didn't work, and Baker does not get too visually inventive with his material. He shoots it in a yeoman, straightforward manner which benefited his more somber projects but fails to generate any excitement in *Vault*.

The stories ran the gamut of horror: A man murders his sister only to discover that she and her friends are vampires and the drinks literally are on him. A fussbudget of a man with a passion for neatness drives his wife to madness and murder, but neatness has become so ingrained that she gives herself away by neatly bottling the various components of his remains in appropriately labeled bottles. A humiliated Indian fakir uses the rope trick to get his revenge on an obnoxious and scoffing Englishman. A man is prematurely buried and then, just when he hopes to be rescued by the timely arrival of some grave robbers, he is killed. Finally, a painter who uses voodoo and his paintings to revenge himself on snobbish critics gets his comeuppance when he does a self-portrait.

Moving from anthology films, Amicus put Baker on *And Now the Screaming Starts*. (The title was originally announced as *I Have No Mouth and I Must Scream*, the title of a famous Harlan Ellison story. Ellison's agent sold producer Milton Subotsky the title without Ellison's knowledge or permission. The matter was cleared up and the film then became *Fengriffen* after the David Case book on which it is based, but was changed one last time to its present title.) *Screaming* is a well-mounted but dull story of a family curse, scripted by Roger Marshall.

Charles Fengriffen (Ian Ogilvy) takes his virginal bride, Catherine (Stephanie Beacham), to his ancestral home. Once there, Catherine is haunted by horrible visions, most notably a severed hand which springs from a painting and a woodsman (Geoffrey Whitehead) with a strange birthmark who sometimes appears sans an arm and with his eyes shot out.

Everyone Catherine turns to for help – the housekeeper (Rosalie Crutchkey), a doctor (Patrick Magee), a lawyer (Guy Rolfe, who starred in *Mr. Sardonicus*) and Catherine's chaperone (Gillian Lind) – is killed before he or she can be of assistance.

Finally, Dr. Pope (Peter Cushing) is sent for. Pope uncovers that the Fengriffin family is under a curse because Charles' grandfather Henry (Herbert Lom) ravaged the wife of Silas the woodsman on her wedding night. When Silas tried to prevent him, Henry chopped off his hand. "The evil that you did this day," intones Silas, "will be avenged. The next virgin bride to come to the House of Fengriffen will be violated. But then shall come the true vengeance of the House of Fengriffen. And death shall befall anyone who tries to prevent it."

Since Charles' father married a widow, that makes Catherine the first virgin bride. Catherine bears a son, and when Charles sees it, he shoots out the eyes of the woodsman and desecrates Henry's tomb. What drove him to this? Catherine looks at her child and sees that it has only one arm, the other ending in a stump.

While Tony Curtis' sets do have a sumptuous look about them and the cast features many fine performers, most in bit parts, Baker's direction cannot do much to enliven a ho-hum story. The filmmakers apparently hoped to hold audience interest by withholding the backstory until the film is almost over, so that they'd be kept wondering what Catherine's visions are supposed to mean. However, those visions simply are not that interesting, and the deaths of those who plan to help her are handled perfunctorily. In all, a disappointment.

Then Baker was sent to Hong Kong to make *The Legend of the 7 Golden Vampires* as part of a collaboration between Hammer Films and the Shaw Bros., specialists in kung fu movies. The result was the first kung fu vampire movie. However, when Baker and his crew arrived in Hong Kong, the difficulties began to mount. First of all, the Chinese there shot their movies without sound, so the soundstages were not soundproofed. Additionally, the Shaw Bros. planned to have one of their own directors direct the fight scenes in the film, but Baker was adamantly against it, insisting that there was to be only one director on the film. They could choreograph the fight scenes, but he would direct them. Finally, the Chinese demanded that Dracula make an appearance in the picture as Dracula pictures had done well in Hong Kong, so a prologue and epilogue featuring John Forbes-Robertson as Dracula were added to the general mishmash.

For some reason, an old shaman comes to a pagoda and Dracula is there. The spirit of Dracula takes over the shaman's body and calls forth some zombie-like Chinese vampires, who then ride forth into town and wreak havoc. These scenes are atmospherically shot with a minimum of dialogue and some slow motion shots of the undead riding and running toward their prey. The exotic location gives these scenes a look far different from most western horror films and are a definite part of the film's appeal.

The story moves forward to the turn of the century. Professor Van Helsing (Peter Cushing, naturally) is one a tour of China lecturing about vampires. He is accompanied by his son Leyland (Robin Stewart), who doesn't have much to do, and Julie Ege, who also doesn't have to do much except be voluptuous and fall for Hsi Ching, the leader of a family of kung fu fighters whose village is being terrorized by vampires. The story is largely built around three major fight scenes in which the eight kung fu fighters (they have a talented sister) demonstrate their prowess.

In between these, Baker adds some nice touches. There is an eerie scene where the sound of the wind is transformed into the screams of female victims who are being bled by the Chinese vampires in a pagoda. Instead of the cross, these vampires react to the images of Buddha. There's also a memorable film quote when Forbes-Robertson springs up stiff as a board from his coffin in imitation of the vampire from *Nosferatu*. Overall, the film manages to be good lightweight entertainment, far better crafted than most kung fu films, but falling short of the quality of, say, the average samurai movie.

The film had troubles even after it was made, partly due to its appearing on the tail end of Hammer's film efforts and partly because a distribution deal with Warner Bros. ended up with Warners shelving the film in the United States. AIP picked up and then dropped the option. The film was finally picked up by Max Rosenberg's Dynamite Films after Rosenberg split from Amicus. It was trimmed to 83 minutes and released as *The Seven Brothers Meet Dracula*. (In the Far East it had been released uncut as *Dracula and the 7 Golden Vampires*.) Rosenberg not only recut the film, removing large sections, but he duped and inserted the same shot of vampires coming out of the ground several times.

The Legend of the 7 Golden Vampires was Baker's last film for some time. Milton Subotsky wooed him back in 1980 for the execrable *The Monster Club*. On paper it must have sounded good. Subotsky planned to combine all the greatest living horror actors in one film but Christopher Lee, Peter Cushing, and Klaus Kinski all declined to participate. The script was based on the stories of veteran horror writer R. Chetwynd-Haynes, but the script by Edward and Valerie Abraham is uninspired and sometimes downright lame.

Vincent Price in his first appearance as a vampire puts the bite on writer Chetwynd-Haynes (played by John Carradine) and then confesses that he is a fan of Chetwynd-Haynes' work. Eramus (Price) is the head of the Monster Club, a nightclub for monsters, or at least people in cheap monster masks, where the "entertainment" is provided by such rock 'n' roll acts as B. A. Robertson, Night, The Pretty Things, The Viewers and The Expressos, whose work makes up the awful rock 'n' roll soundtrack. (If Subotsky wanted to attract a rock audience for his film, he failed miserably.) Eramus sits in the club and tells stories about various Chetwynd-Haynes creations in an elaborate family tree of monsters.

The first is about a Shadmock, a "monster" designed to look like Erik, the famous Lon Chaney *Phantom of the Opera*, who possesses a killer "whistle" which can fry his victims when used. Barbara Kellerman comes to his house and overreacts to his appearance, but eventually the tender-hearted Raven (Simon Ward), as the Shadmock is called, falls in love with her and invites her to meet his relatives at a masked ball. (They all wear masks similar to Lon Chaney's in *Phantom of the Opera*.) Instead, her boyfriend instructs her to steal from Raven's safe. When Raven finds out, he lets go a devastating whistle (the effect of Ward's pursed lips is particularly ridiculous with the camera angle and lens that Baker has chosen, exaggerating the idiotic effect.)

The second section is supposedly an autobiographical film-within-a-film about producer Lintom Busotsky (perhaps the unsubtlest anagram since Count Alucard). It relates how young Busotsky's father was a vampire who lived in fear of a vampire squad and their leader, the Bleeny (Donald Pleasence). The Blood Squad searches out innocent vampires and dispatches them with stakes concealed in violin cases. Busotsky's father outwits them by faking his own demise and vamping the Bleeny. It is an extended one-joke routine that isn't very inventive to begin with.

The final segment is a bit better, with much of the decor recalling the Subotsky-produced *Horror Hotel* (aka *City of the Dead*). In it, a film director named Sam (Stuart Whitman) is looking for rest and a new location to film his next horror movie. He turns off the main road, passes through some mysterious fog (shades of *Brigadoon*) and enters a run-down town, only to discover the town is filled with ghouls (shades of *2000 Maniacs*). For once the ghouls are depicted as they are in supernatural folklore – not as grave robbers like Burke and Hare nor as zombies, but as corpse-eating creatures with supernatural powers.

The leader of the ghouls is played by Patrick Magee in what probably was his last film role. Unfortunately, it's not much of a part for the actor who had appeared so memorably in *Marat/Sade* and *A Clockwork Orange* as well as numerous horror films. Sam takes a room in town and discovers the dimwitted Luna (Lesley Dunlop), who reveals herself to be a "humegoo," that is, half-human, half-ghoul. (R. Chetwynd-Hayes appears to have made some particularly unfortunate choices in naming his monsters.) Sam attempts to rescue her and soon has half the town's population on his heels. The ghouls cannot pass through a barrier on the edge of town, so they throw rocks and kill Luna. Sam is picked up by the police, who promptly take him back to the town of the ghouls in the final twist.

The framing story ends with Eramus nominating Chetwynd-Hayes for membership in the Monster Club, proclaiming man, who has exterminated over 150 million of his own kind within the past 60 years, the greatest monster of them all. His membership is gleefully accepted and everyone gets up to dance.

A second unit director badly filmed the club sequences in the worst *Ready Steady Go* rock style with flashing lights and the camera zooming in and out in annoying and pointless fashion. With its weak script, *The Monster Club* is a waste of Baker's skills; indeed, he does not appear to have made much of an effort to use them apart from some tributes to some cinematic classics.

Baker's career has concentrated on television, particularly after his highly regarded miniseries *Flame Trees of Thika* which chronicles Elspeth Huxley's early years in Africa. The miniseries was shown in the United States on *Masterpiece Theatre* where it gained a wide and enthusiastic audience.

Sadly, many of his later projects, particulary as he entered his main horror period, were saddled with inadequate budgets and scripts, though Baker has managed a few wonders on limited funds. His best horror films are the thoughtful and thought-provoking *Five Million Years to Earth*, the clever *Dr. Jekyll and Sister Hyde* (Hammer's best treatment of the Jekyll and Hyde theme), the multistoried *Asylum* and the blackly amusing histrionics of *The Anniversary*. His tasteful handling of *The Vampire Lovers* and the better-than-average performances he directed from Ingrid Pitt and Stephanie Beacham are not to be sneered at either, particularly in this day when many horror films feature performances which can barely be termed as adequate. Though Baker is now in his seventies, some smart producer may yet take advantage of his expertise and provide him with a suitable showcase for his talents. Few directors can match his ability of taking sensational subjects and making them straightforward, believable and gripping. His best work is memorable without calling attention to itself, sublime rather than flashy. In essence, Baker has proved himself a worthy successor to Terence Fisher.

Mario Bava (1914–1980)

Black Sunday; Erik the Conqueror (aka *Fury of the Vikings; Gli Invasori*); *Hercules in the Haunted World* (1961); *The Wonders of Aladdin* (2nd unit only, 1962); *The Girl Who Knew Too Much* (aka *The Evil Eye*); *What!* (aka *Night Is the Phantom*); *Black Sabbath* (1963); *Blood and Black Lace* (1964); *The Road to Fort Alamo; Planet of the Vampires* (aka *The Demon Planet; Terror in Outer Space; Planet of Blood*) (1965); *Kill Baby Kill; Dr. Goldfoot and the Girl Bombs* (1966); *Knives of the Avenger* (1967); *Danger: Diabolik* (1968); *Hatchet for a Honeymoon; Five Dolls for the August Moon; Roy Colt e Winchester Jack* (1969); *Four Times This Night* (1970); *Twitch of the Death Nerve* (aka *Carnage; Bay of Blood*) (1971); *Baron Blood; Lisa and the Devil* (aka *House of Exorcism*) (1972); *Shock* (aka *Beyond the Door 2*) (1977).

UNRELEASED: *Wild Dogs* (1974)

TELEVISION: "Venus of the Isle" *Il Giornale del Diavolo (The Devil's Notebook)* (1978, codirected with Lamberto Bava)

Mario Bava was one of Italy's finest visual stylists, unfortunately something which was known only to horror fans. With his background as a cinematographer, Bava brought a shrewd eye to his film projects, many of which were regrettably saddled with underdeveloped screenplays. Bava produced one horror masterpiece–remarkably enough, his debut film, *Black Sunday*–and added colorfully to several other genre projects. He has proven an influential figure in Italian exploitation cinema, particularly for such Italian horror and *giallo* directors as Dario Argento, Lucio Fulci, and even his own son, Lamberto Bava, who followed in his father's footsteps.

Bava was born in 1914 in San Remo, Italy, the son of the great silent cameraman and sculptor Eugenio Bava. Bava began working as a camera assistant in the '30s, getting his first director of photography credit in 1943 on *L'Avventura di Annabella*. He worked under many fine directors and developed a reputation for his facility in handling trick photography.

Bava finally got his chance to try his hand at directing by handling the second unit photography on the classic Italian musclemen films *Hercules* and *Hercules Unchained* with Steve Reeves. When Jacques Tourneur left the production of *The Giant of Marathon* before the battle scenes had been shot, Bava was called in to fill the breach.

Apparently such events were not uncommon in the Italian film industry

61

as Bava also filled in for two days when director Riccardo Freda left the filming of *I Vampiri* (aka *The Devil's Commandment; Lust of the Vampire*) after a dispute with the producers. *I Vampiri* is a vampire film in name only. It was actually concerned with a mad doctor who injected blood into a woman to restore her youth, but the picture is significant as it led to the development of the Italian horror genre.

Bava worked with Freda again on *Caltiki, the Immortal Monster*, which concerns a group of scientists who discover the remains of a Mayan god in a cave. Bava officially handled the photography and the special effects for the film, but according to Freda, he also handled much of the direction as another argument with a producer caused Freda to be absent for two weeks of the film's shooting.

Bava himself described the film as a parody of *The Creeping Unknown*, the first of the Quatermass films written by Nigel Kneale and known in England as *The Quatermass Experiment*. The monster itself is nothing more than a pile of cow intestines made ambulatory by a poor man in a raincoat underneath, but it certainly has a unique appearance.

Bava's abilities did not go unnoticed. According to Tim Lucas' excellent article on the director in *Fangoria*, Nello Santi of Galatea Film was so impressed with Bava's rescue efforts on *The Giant of Marathon* that he offered to produce a Bava-directed film. Though a bit reluctant to make the leap from cameraman to director, Bava did think of a project that might be fun. Lucas quotes Bava:

> Because, at that time, the [Hammer] *Dracula* film had been released, I thought I might do a horror film. Years earlier, I had read "The Vij" by Gogol – a stupendous story! Before we had television, I used to read it to my children and, scared to death, they slept together in the middle of the bed.

Bava and screenwriter Ennio De Concini padded the classic Russian ghost story until "our genius saw that absolutely *nothing* remained of it."

The result was *Black Sunday*, one of horror's few authentic masterpieces. The film, cophotographed by Bava and Ubaldo Terzano, employs a striking visual style, abetted by a restless, moving camera that travels through atmospherically drenched landscapes filled with twilight lighting, shadows, fog, cobwebs, and crawling insects. In the film, dream and reality seem to merge. The landscapes suggest pestilence and decay; leafless trees seem ever ready to reach out and snare unwary travelers. The interiors are the most atmospheric and suggestive since the classic Universal horror films of the '30s, thanks to the art direction by Giorgio Giovannini and, once again, Bava. The settings of a baroque castle, a cobwebby mausoleum, and a sleepy peasant village seem like perfected ideals from hundreds of other, inferior horror films. All this is enhanced by the carefully shaded monochromatic black-and-white cinematography, evidence of Bava's long years as a cinematographer.

Not only is the film constantly inventive visually, it also uses sound to good effect. Early in the film we have the eerie sound of wind going through the broken pipes of an abandoned church organ, appropriately setting the mood; frequently we hear the wind blowing and dogs howling, adding to the unease; and in one superb sequence, the complete absence of sound where there should be some creates a haunting and beautiful, nightmarish image of a ghostly coach that veers out of the mist in slow motion, travels at high speed around a corner and vanishes into the mist again. You may have seen scenes like it dozens of times, but this one is truly unforgettable.

Finally, the film crystalizes what seems to be the central theme in Bava's work: uncertainty. The characters in Bava's films almost always must come to terms with some uncertainty, using their wits and perspicacity.

"One day in each century, it is said that Satan walks among us," begins *Black Sunday.* "To the God-fearing, this day is known as Black Sunday." The film immediately gains our attention with the final moments of an inquisition in which Princess Asa (Barbara Steele) and her lover Javuto have been convicted of witchcraft and sorcery and are to be put to death at the stake. But first, a spiked mask of the devil's face is hammered into their faces. While *Black Sunday* has the technical virtues of the Universal classics, it also contains shocking material such as the preceding, which helped mark it as a transition into the type of horror films that would dominate the '60s and '70s. (The film was considered so shocking that it wasn't released in Britain until 1968 as *The Revenge of the Vampire.* The original title was *La Maschera del Demonio [Mask of the Demon].*)

Two hundred years later, in 1830, Dr. Choma Kruvajan (Andrea Checchi) and his young assistant, Dr. Andrej Gorobek (John Richardson), are traveling across the Moldavian countryside when their coach throws a wheel. Dr. Kruvajan notes that the coachman seems in an unseemly hurry, but attributes it to the anticipation of a tip rather than a rush to reach the village by sundown.

Stopping to investigate the countryside and a strange noise, the two men enter a ruined courtyard, where their attention is attracted by a banging door. Entering the door, they descend a staircase to a mausoleum, which has a unique coffin set off in one alcove. Going to investigate, Dr. Kruvajan is attacked by a bat. He shoots it with his gun and smashes it with his cane, also smashing a cross on the coffin—which is that of Princess Asa—and breaking a pane of glass that was meant to allow the witch to see the cross, and therefore be unable to rise, should she awake once every century on Black Sunday. Dr. Kruvajan cuts his hand on the glass when he decides to remove the devil's mask from the corpse's face, revealing a pock-marked (where the spikes of the mask had gone in) eyeless visage, crawling with insects and maggots.

Departing, the doctors are surprised by the sight of a young woman with a face almost identical to that of the corpse they left behind in the tomb. The woman is holding onto two huge mastiffs and seems like an apparition out of a dream, but it is only Princess Katia (Barbara Steele again), the daughter of Prince Vaida (Ivo Garrani), taking the dogs out for a walk. Dr. Gorobek is struck by her strange beauty and boldly suggests that he hopes they shall meet again, but meanwhile they must make for the inn.

In another of the film's classic shots that is at once beautiful and horrifying, Dr. Kruvajan's blood drips onto Asa's remains. Suddenly, something resembling a poached egg begins to fill the darkened eye sockets. The witch is coming back to life. Dr. Kruvajan has unwittingly supplied the blood, destroyed the cross, and taken the religious icon that held her powerless in her tomb.

Meanwhile, back at the castle, Prince Vaida is concerned and disturbed. Today is Black Sunday and he fears the effects of the family curse, as he confides to Ivan, the loyal family servant. A century ago, Princess Marcia was mysteriously murdered at the age of 20, the same age as Katia is now. Marcia and Katia not only share ages, they also have an identical resemblance to the painting of Vaida's ancestor Asa. Says Vaida, "It's as if the witch granted her own beauty to her victims before killing them." Ivan returns that the cross will protect them. Reassured, the prince drinks some wine, only to see a reflection of the devil's mask in his drink.

At the inn, all is gaiety, with both doctors drinking heavily and Dr. Gorobek expressing his wishes to see Katia again. The innkeeper's daughter expresses her reluctance to milk the cow because it's late and the cow is "very near the old haunted cemetery," but her mother insists that she go anyway.

Bava here shows his ability to build a sequence, skillfully combining sight and sound. (Unfortunately, the dubbing job on the film is terrible, but the best sequences play beautifully without any dialogue.) While Bava shows the girl timidly going through the misty night, through the forest to the cowshed, the sounds of the inn's band fade into the background while the chirruping of frogs and crickets gets louder, signifying the girl's increasing fright. The leaves rustle and the girl sprints off in terror, running suddenly into branches – startling her and us as well. Finally, she reaches the safety of the cowshed and the audience is allowed to breathe a sigh of relief. Meanwhile, Dr. Kruvajan decides to take in the night air for his evening's constitutional.

Back in the ruined crypt, Asa commands Javuto to rise, and Javuto turns over in his grave and pushes on the door of his coffin, causing the earth atop it to fall aside. Bava makes this one of the most memorable resurrections

Two views of the seldom photographed Mario Bava, the top one taken in 1960 and the bottom from 1975. Bava confessed that he made most of his films out of dire financial need, despite their ludicrous stories. "I've shot some incredibly stupid movies. . . . I couldn't refuse them and didn't have time to rewrite them. One of my big faults is that I try too hard to please the producer and then, in the end, they turn against me," he was quoted as saying in Photon *magazine. Despite his film's shortcomings, he's still acclaimed as a master stylist.*

from the grave in horror film history. While lightning flashes fiercely, we see Javuto's slime-covered hands clawing through the dirt until he can pull himself out. Bava reminds us that the girl and the cowshed are nearby. Will Javuto attack them? No, he wanders off, removing his devil's mask.

In the castle, a secret passageway opens behind the fireplace and the wind coming in fans the flames, knocks over a candlestand and the music on the piano, rustles the curtains, and finally knocks over three suits of armor and a pair of chairs. Is it really the wind, or the invisible spirit of Javuto? The already nervous Vaida is startled by these sounds. Then his door opens and there is Javuto, who moves implacably toward him until Vaida holds up a Russian Orthodox cross and drives Javuto off.

Katia and her brother Constantin (Enrico Olivieri) dash in to see what is the matter with their father. They find him acting feverish. Katia recalls that there are two doctors staying at the inn and Boris, a servant, is sent to fetch one to help the prince.

However, Javuto arrives to pick up Dr. Kruvajan instead in the marvelously ghostly coach mentioned earlier. He takes the doctor to the castle, but then proceeds to lead him through the secret passageways back to the crypt. The doctor notices Javuto getting ahead of him and tries to catch up, but when he reaches the lighted lantern, all he sees is the lantern itself hanging in midair. A door creaks open and the doctor goes inside, only to have the door close shut behind him. It's the crypt where he first saw Asa, and now he looks on her once again. He is momentarily distracted by some noise, but when he turns to look again, Asa's eyes are open, blazing into his. He tries to escape but cannot get the door open. Asa's stone coffin rocks and finally explodes, leaving Asa, her chest heaving, lying on the remnants, smiling while she hypnotizes the doctor.

"Just a few drops of your blood brought me to life," she says. "All of it will give me the strength to accomplish my vengeance.... Come on, embrace me. You will die, but I can bring you pleasures mortals cannot know. Let all your blood course through my veins so that I may live again and you will be one with me. You will live by night and die in each dawning. You shall bring *her* to me and through her blood I shall live forever." Kruvajan finds himself unable to resist her deadly embrace.

Prince Vaida is still in torment. "The devil is waiting," he cries. Constantin thinks his father is delirious. Just then Dr. Kruvajan enters the door and approaches Vaida, causing him to fall asleep. Constantin picks up the cross and explains what happened, but he doesn't notice that Kruvajan turns from the cross. The doctor orders that the cross be taken away and promises to stay with the prince while the others go to sleep.

The next morning Ivan finds no sign of Kruvajan and discovers Vaida dead with strange markings on his neck. Dr. Gorobek cannot find Kruvajan either, but hears from the innkeeper that the doctor was called to the castle

in the middle of the night. Borrowing a horse, he gets directions to the castle from a young girl doing her wash. Some children knock a piece of her
laundry into the river, and in recovering it, she comes across the body of
Boris the coachman.

Dr. Gorobek arrives at the castle to be confronted by Constantin, who
is upset over the disappearnce of Dr. Krujavan and holds him responsible
for his father's death. Gorobek is bewildered by the description of Kruvajan's behavior and relates that Kruvajan did not return to the inn either. He
goes to examine the prince's body and discovers a hole in his neck. Katia
faints in his arms and he takes her into the next room. Unbuttoning her
blouse so she can breathe easier, he notices she wears a diamond cross.

Upset villagers come to the castle with news of Boris' death. The innkeeper's daughter is among them, and she identifies the painting of Javuto
as the man who picked Dr. Kruvajan up to take him to the castle. Katia,
awakened, overhears this and becomes upset. Nonsense, she cries, that man
has been dead 200 years, stop this or she'll go mad.

Gorobek realizes that something unnatural is going on and decides to
consult with the village priest, telling him that Boris and the prince both
died in the same way. The priest becomes alarmed when he learns that the
girl identified Javuto's portrait as the coachman. That night, Kruvajan
visits Gorobek at the castle and warns him to leave. Gorobek is oblivious to
any changes in his former colleague and is about to show him the religious
icon from Asa's grave, the markings on which he intends to have translated
but Kruvajan flees at the sight of it. Following him, Gorobek comes upon
the dying forms of Katia's dogs, whose throats have been torn open.

The next day, the tapestry by the fireplace accidentally catches fire and
Ivan beats it down trying to put it out, accidentally slashing Javuto's portrait. He calls Constantin, who calls on Gorobek to join him. A secret passageway is revealed behind the painting. Constantin and Gorobek open the
passageway behind the fireplace and go inside to investigate, leaving Ivan
to stand guard. Inside, they discover a nude portrait of Asa behind which
is another passageway, which they also investigate.

The fireplace door closes and Ivan is strangled from behind by Javuto.
Meanwhile, Gorobek and Constantin discover Asa's body and notice that it's
breathing. Gorobek sends Constantin back to protect Katia while he goes
to the priest to figure out how to combat this unearthly menace. Constantin
finds the fireplace passageway closed. Javuto materializes, smiling, before
him and the pair fight furiously. A trap door opens up behind Constantin
and he falls into a pit.

The priest and Gorobek resolve to track down Javuto's grave. They
discover the devil's mask Javuto discarded and, noticing some loosely turned
earth, surmise they have found his grave. However, much to Gorobek's
shock, inside the coffin they find the sleeping form of Kruvajan. The priest

has deciphered the Cyrillic message on the icon and knows what to do. He puts a cross on Kruvajan's forehead, which burns him. Knowing him to be one of the undead and an emissary of the devil, the priest puts his soul to rest – in this version, not by the traditional stake through the heart, but with a stake through the eye. The change is significant in the greater sense of discomfort it engenders. (Mercifully, Bava only shows us the blood squirting up on the priest's black smock.) The priest vows to exorcise Boris while Gorobek heads back to the castle to take care of the prince.

Katia prays and holds vigil over her father's corpse, only to have the prince rise up and inform her that now he is a vampire and wants some of her blood. Since this would be contrary to his mistress' plans, Javuto intervenes by throwing Vaida into the fireplace, where he is consumed. Katia faints and Javuto sweeps her up and takes her to Asa.

In the crypt, Asa begins draining the life from Katia, which Bava shows by the sudden appearance of eyebrow-penciled wrinkles on Katia's face while the same kind of wrinkles disappear from Asa's. (This was accomplished without dissolves by using a filter the same color as the penciled-in wrinkles, making them seem to disappear once the face is a uniform color. Steele's acting helps this sequence: Katia gets more agitated as the wrinkles appear, and Asa grows calmer with their disappearance.)

However, Asa cannot complete her plans for Katia because Katia is still wearing her cross. Meanwhile, Gorobek has arrived and Javuto goes to meet him. The two engage in a tremendous struggle and Gorobek is almost thrust down the same pit as Constantin when unexpectedly Constantin's arms reach up and pull Javuto to his death down in the pit. Constantin, however, has been fatally wounded and can only gasp out his wish that Gorobek protect his sister before he too expires.

Gorobek rushes into what he assumes to be his young love's arms and prepares to put a stake in the eye of the one whom he assumes to be Asa when he notices Katia's cross around her neck. Removing the cross, he tries to put it on Asa, who exposes her decayed innards and tries to hypnotize him like she did Kruvajan. Fortunately, the cavalry, in the form of the angry villagers led by the priest, arrives and Gorobek denounces Asa as the witch.

The villagers overwhelm her and take her away to be burned at the stake. Katia, however, does not revive, and so Gorobek and the priest pray for her. As Asa burns, she begins to grow older again, and when she dies, Katia revives. Gorobek and Katia embrace; evil has been vanquished.

Bava's camera work was never better than in this film. He is constantly dollying and panning; there are none of those annoying zooms that he was forced to use later in his career for budgetary reasons. To set up the crypt, Bava uses a complete 360° pan that wonderfully evokes the right atmosphere and mood. The camera is always carefully directing our attention to those points most crucial to the story, increasing our fascination with each new revelation. It would be difficult to find a film richer in evocative horror imagery.

Bava is quoted in Lucas' article as saying:

> It was the only one of my films which was really well-done, all shot with a dolly which, because of the time and money involved, isn't used (on Italian productions) anymore. I did the photography myself; I was very fast. At most, it would take me seven minutes to set up the lights, maybe 12 for an entire room. The photography in a horror film is 70% of its effectiveness; it creates all the atmosphere.

The film is also notable for launching the career of Barbara Steele as a horror star, a kind of typecasting she was later to regret. Steele has a wide, interesting face which can be very expressive. She does make Asa and Katia seem like two very different personalities who happen to share the same body; whereas Katia is sweet and open, with just a touch of shyness and reticence, Asa is cruel and brazen, and smiles in a completely different way. She has a mysterious quality which gives her presence and attracts the camera to her high-cheekboned features and raven-dark hair.

Bava's mastery of the horror elements in the film is superb and promised great things to come. While it was given scant critical attention when it reached the United States in 1961, it was a very successful moneymaker the world over. The American version, in addition to being dubbed, included a new score by Les Baxter, which is a bit bombastic but not annoying, augmenting the mood of the film. However, what really makes *Black Sunday* a masterpiece is its visual poetry, which seldom has been equaled and never surpassed.

Bava took time out to direct the second unit and special effects on Henry Levin's *The Wonders of Aladdin*, with the great Italian director Vittorio de Sica (*Shoeshine, The Bicycle Thieves, Miracle in Milan, Garden of the Finzi-Continis*) playing the genie. He also tried his hand at producing and came up with the abominable *Atom Age Vampire*, a pathetic retelling of Georges Franju's *Eyes Without a Face*. In this one, a mad doctor tries to restore the face of his beloved by removing the flesh of other, still-living women. To get away with his crimes, he injects himself with his serum, which temporarily changes him into a hairy monster; however, like Dr. Jekyll, he ends up unable to control his transformations. The film was flatly directed by Anton Giulio Majanno, whose name was transformed to "Richard McNamara" in the American credits.

After helping out on previous Hercules films, Bava was finally given one of his own to direct. The result was *Hercules in the Haunted World* (aka *Ercole al Centro della Terra; Hercules at the Centre of the Earth; Hercules vs. the Vampires*). In this tale, Hercules (Reg Park) must fetch a golden apple from the island of Hesperides and a magic stone from Hades to cure an insane princess, who is under the influence of Lico, the king of the dead (played by Christopher Lee). There is even an appearance by Procrustes, who either stretched his guests or chopped off their limbs to make them fit his bed. There's also an appearance by the goddess of Hades and some vampires, though Lee does not play a vampire as some ads suggest.

Bava served as director, cocinematographer (with Ubaldo Tezzano) and coscreenwriter (with Allesandro Contineza, Franco Prosperi, and Duccio Tessari, who went on to become the director of many spaghetti westerns). He used vivid, even garish colors with bright reds, green and blues adding to the fantasy setting – indeed, it was the most fantasy-oriented of the many Hercules films until the Luigi Cozzi versions of the '80s.

Lee, who described Bava as "one of Italy's greatest cameramen," related the following anecdote in *The Films of Christopher Lee*:

> The Hercules was played by a former Mr. Universe – Reg Park, a most delightful man. I'm afraid we completely disgraced ourselves by giggling in certain scenes. It was the idea of me, who was very thin and strong, literally throwing a man like Reg Park aside with a mere flick of my wrist because I'm not of human blood and have supernatural strength – this enormous man with muscles the like of which you've never seen. It struck us both as so completely ludicrous, we just couldn't stop laughing. It was very naughty of us, and Mario Bava was rapidly losing his patience. But he forgave us.

Next Bava tackled *Erik the Conqueror*, a Viking film starring Cameron Mitchell. Mitchell plays a Viking named Iron who is forced to fight his brother, Erik (Giorgio Giovannini).

The Girl Who Knew Too Much (aka *La Ragazza Che Sapeva Troppo; The Evil Eye*), Bava's next film, is indeed a neat twist on Hitchcock's classic *The Man Who Knew Too Much*. Leticia Rawson plays Nora Drowson, an American tourist who witnesses a brutal murder attempt. Rome is being terrorized by an "alphabet murderer" who has already killed women whose last names end with A, B and C. Nora is haunted by the idea that there is some detail that she has overlooked and she is not quite certain she will be able to identify the killer, should she see him again.

Her paranoia begins to mount and she soon convinces herself that she has been targeted as the killer's next victim, but only her Italian boyfriend, Dr. Marcello Bassi (John Saxon), shares her conviction.

You see, she has been admitted to a hospital for chronic alcoholism and her story is dismissed as a case of the d.t.'s. In the hospital, she meets with the woman who was almost stabbed to death, and she decides to visit her after her release. Far from being friendly, her surroundings begin to be perceived as constantly concealing a possible threat. When a man follows her, she thinks it must be the killer, though it turns out he only wants to proposition her. Another time, she tries to trip up the killer but only succeeds in almost breaking Dr. Bassi's neck.

In the end, the attack victim's husband is revealed as the killer, but afterward Nora remembers that what she actually saw was the victim trying to kill her husband. Marcello insists that she forget all about the murders, so when they happen to observe a jealous husband killing his wife and her lover aboard a cable car, Nora refuses to admit seeing anything.

The final twist possibly inspired Brian De Palma's ending for *Sisters*, while the basic plot provided the inspiration for Dario Argento's *Four Flies on Grey Velvet*. The film is also important as a precursor to the Italian *giallo* (yellow) films, so named after a series of mystery thriller books which all had yellow covers. The film, significantly, was also the last to make use of Bava's excellent sense for achieving atmosphere in black and white.

Next came *What!* (aka *The Whip and the Body; Night Is the Phantom; La Frustra e il Corpo*), the rather perverse story of a woman, Nevenka (Daliah Lavi), who can't say no. She is married to Christian (Tony Kendall) while at the same time being mistress to Christian's father, Count Vladimir (Gustavo de Nardo performing under the name Dean Ardow). Things really begin to get complicated when Christian's brother Kurt (Christopehr Lee) returns, though his father still has not forgiven him for driving a servant girl to suicide.

Kurt develops an interest in his sister-in-law, and when she goes out riding one day, he follows her and begins making advances, which she resists. Enraged, he takes his whip to her and beats her. Nevenka goes mad and returns to the castle, killing Kurt with the very dagger that the girl he'd driven to suicide had used to kill herself. However, she secretly harbors masochistic tendencies and thinks she can see Kurt coming back for her; she actually experiences welts from an imagined whipping. She feels she is possessed by Kurt's spirit and kills the Count. Christian comes upon her trying to attack her hallucination of Kurt, and finally she stabs herself with the same dagger as before.

Bava deliberately leaves it ambiguous whether the spirit of Kurt exists or is all in Nevenka's mind. In this film, Bava began using the zoom lens more extensively to shift from the overall tableau to a particularly telling reaction (such as Nevenka's mixture of pain and pleasure at being whipped). With the exception of the innocent Christian, everyone in the film ends up using or trying to use someone else as an instrument to his own ends. It was a rather daring film for its time, and as a result has often been censored, cut or mutilated beyond comprehension. Nonetheless, it manages to be an adult film without pandering and fits neatly into Bava's overall theme of uncertainty – Nevenka is uncertain of her true feelings and finally of her own identity.

The title of *Black Sabbath* was obviously chosen by its American distributor, AIP, to recall *Black Sunday*, though the original Italian title was *I Tre Volte della Paura (The Three Faces of Fear)*. The script, by Bava, Alberto Bevilacqua and Marcello Fondata, adapts three classic horror stories: Anton Chekov's "The Drop of Water," F. G. Snyder's "The Telephone" and Ivan Tolstoi's "The Wurdalak." The film opens in the manner of the old *Thriller* series with the face of Boris Karloff, alternately lit by various colored gels, intoning, "Ladies and gentlemen, how do you do? This is *Black Sabbath*. You are about to see three tales of terror and the supernatural. I so hope you haven't come alone." He expresses the hope that the person sitting behind "you" in the theater isn't a wurdalak or blood-drinker. After this sanguine thought, he proceeds to introduce the first of the three tales, "The Drop of Water."

A nurse (Jacqueline Soussard acting under the name Jacqueline Pierreux) is called in by a housekeeper because her mistress, a medium, has just died while in a trance. The nurse prepares the body but covets a ring the medium is wearing and decides to steal it. Once more Bava creatively uses sound effects (particularly waterdrops) and selecting lighting (flickering firelight) to create an atmospehre of unease. The nurse closes the medium's eyelids, but when she turns around, they are open again and the corpse bears a sneering expression. (The corpse was actually sculpted out of wax by Bava's father.)

Back at home, the nurse admires her ring, but is startled by the apparition of the dead medium coming for her. Her hands reach up to ward off the medium's clutching hands, but the nurse only ends up strangling herself. When the police find her body behind the locked door of her apartment, they notice a bruise where the ring used to be, but the ring itself is gone.

In the second story, Rosy (Michele Mercier) is being terrorized by a series of phone calls purporting to be from her long-dead boyfriend, Frank. She even receives a note from him which chillingly writes itself. She calls Frank's previous ex, Mary (Lydia Alfonsi) about the phone calls, and Mary volunteers to stay over and spend the night with her. Rosy goes to bed and Mary stays up. A man breaks into the apartment and strangles Mary. Rosy wakes up and sees Frank coming for her. Thinking quickly, she takes a knife which Mary instructed her to put under her pillow and stabs him. However, from the telephone, we hear the boyfriend's voice again, promising never to let her alone. Was the man just a prowler and Frank all in her mind, or has her boyfriend really come back from the grave to haunt her?

According to Lucas, the original Italian version featured a twist which was dubbed out of existence. In it, Lucas claims, it is revealed that Mary was the one who was making the phone calls to talk herself into Rosy's bed, so the appearance of the dead boyfriend becomes an additional surprise. (Actually, there is a hint that Mary plans to revenge herself on Rosy for stealing Frank from her by sending her to a psychiatrist because of her "delusions.")

The final episode is geneally regarded as the best, and despite the film's low budget, has the best production values. Like the other tales in the film, it is suggestive rather than explicit. A nobleman named Vladimir D'Urfe (Mark Damon, hero of Corman's *House of Usher*) is riding through the countryside when he spots a decapitated man with a dagger in his back. Putting the body across the man's horse, he rides until he comes to a farmhouse. Inside, he spots a place on the wall which matches the general shape and configuration of the dagger he found.

The family comes out and identifies the dagger as their father's and the body as that of Alibek, a Turkish bandit who had terrorized the neighboring region. Their father, Gorca (Karloff) had left to hunt down this bandit five days ago. There were rumors that Alibek was a wurdalak, a vampire, and Gorca left instructions that if he did not return in exactly five days, they were to drive a stake through his heart when he did. Scant moments after the hour has rung, Gorca comes limping up, but the fearful family is uncertain whether or not he has become a wurdalak. He is gruff, but shows a human side in wanting to fondle his favorite grandchild, which they reluctantly let him do. He brags about killing Alibek and carries the robber's head which he wants fastened to a post outside, but is disturbed when his dog howls and does not appear to know him. He orders one of his sons to kill it, a command which the son reluctantly obeys.

Meanwhile, D'Urfe becomes increasingly enamoured of Gorca's beautiful daughter Sdenka (Susy Andersen), begging her to come away with him. Gorca sucks his grandson's blood and disappears. The child comes back from the grave a wurdalak and the boy's mother cannot help letting him in. Soon, with the exception of Sdenka, the family become wurdalaks.

Sdenka and D'Urfe stop off at an old ruin to spend the night. Sdenka's family show up and beg her to join them, and she finally complies, leaving her would-be lover behind. (Bava uses some very vivid tints in these scenes, casting the sky in a bright, unreal blue and employing red lights for contrast.) D'Urfe rides back to the farmhouse and finds Sdenka there. He makes the mistake of proclaiming that he'd rather die than leave her, so she puts the bite on him while the rest of her wurdalak family looks on through the frosty windows. D'Urfe's horse has the sense to turn and flee into the night.

According to Lucas' article, Bava was told to lighten the tone of the film shortly before its completion, and so he concocted a shot so outrageous it was omitted from American prints. From a tight closeup of Gorca fleeing on horseback with his grandson in tow, the camera pulled back to show how the illusions of the shot were created: "Technicians passing branches in front of the camera, a revolving background with paper clouds to provide the sensation of speed, and the two actors astride a large, rocking *hobby horse!*"

Bava is quoted as saying that he found Karloff's reaction both surprising and touching: "Karloff embraced me and said that, in front of those huge fans, he would surely catch pneumonia . . . that he might even die . . . but that he didn't care, because it was the first time in his career he had enjoyed himself so much."

Karloff does what he can with the part of Gorca, which is only lightly sketched in by the scriptwriters. For example, he gives a marvelously sinister smile when, after he rebukes his family for their cold greeting, he says, "I'm hungry," suggesting evil desires, something that is confirmed when he rejects the roast lamb he is offered, claiming not to be hungry because the cold is choking him. Karloff's makeup and the lighting give his skin a ghastly pallor that suggests he might not be among the living and contrasts nicely to the orange glow cast on most of the other characters until they too become infected. Sadly, Karloff did catch pneumonia, and his participation in this film may have hastened his demise.

Bava's next film, *Blood and Black Lace* (aka *Sei Donne per l'Assassino*), set the trend for future films featuring a faceless killer who takes out his aggression on beautiful fashion models. It is a '60s-style "shocker," with the shocks involving the sudden deaths of women or the discovery of their bodies.

The film opens with an almost avant-garde title sequence combining a mannequin with a death's head and garishly lit lace which is nonetheless beautiful. Clearly, Bava's eye for imagery is as good as ever.

The plot centers around the murder of a woman named Nicole who was blackmailing someone and kept a diary with embarrassing secrets about other people who worked in the same beauty salon, run by Eva Bartok. One murder leads to another as women are drowned, have their faces and hands burned on a hot stove in a particularly unpleasant sequence, or have their faces gouged by a steel glove (a forerunner of Freddy Krueger in *Nightmare on Elm Street*?).

The killer turns out to be Cameron Mitchell, but Bartok also manages to get her licks in. Unfortunately, the plot is weak and the characters uninteresting compared to Bava's previous thrillers.

Bava than worked on a western, *The Road to Fort Alamo*, followed by *Planet of the Vampires* (aka *Demon Planet; Terror in Outer Space; Planet of Blood; Terrore nello Spazio*), which is most famous for inspiring the scene in Ridley Scott's *Alien* where the crew members find the giant skeleton of an alien being on another planet. However, apart from this great shot, which Scott pulled off better thanks to the incredible designs of Swiss artist H. R. Giger, *Planet of the Vampires* is pretty dull going. For his alien planet, Bava was given nothing more than a couple of rocks, so he made heavy use of a fog machine to bathe the soundstage floors in a creepy mist, which does add to the atmosphere of the film.

Based on Renato Pestriniero's "One Night of 21 Hours," the American version was scripted during its shooting by Ib Melchior (*Angry Red Planet, The Time Travellers, Journey to the Seventh Planet, Robinson Crusoe on Mars*), never the most able of science fiction writers as his films often featured dull plots, duller dialogue, and even worse science.

The spaceship Argos lands on an unexplored planet, Aura, looking for its sister ship the Galliot. Captain Mark Markary (Barry Sullivan) and his assistant (Norma Bengel) come to the conclusion that the planet is deserted, but invisible aliens begin to take over the bodies of the Argos crew. The final twist is that the crew members are revealed not to be humans as we were led to assume and that their next target is a little planet known as the earth.

With its painfully bad attempts at comedy, Bava's next film, *Dr. Goldfoot and the Girl Bombs*, proved to be even worse. Part of the problem is that the film was intended to be a sequel to two different films: the American-made *Dr. Goldfoot and the Bikini Machine* and the Italian-made *Two Mafia Guys vs. Goldginger*, which featured two bumbling Italians who inadvertently foil spy schemes.

The film was given appropriately ridiculous advertising copy: "Meet the girls with the thermo-nuclear navels! . . . That cruel, evil, grasping Dr. Goldfoot is back with a brand new hysterical harem of honeys, and he's heck bent to hurl the world into a howling holocaust of hilarity." (Gee, doesn't that make you want to rush out and see it?)

The plot has the Red China–backed Dr. Goldfoot (Vincent Price) planning to instigate World War III by knocking off top NATO generals with his robotic girl bombs (who have fuses planted in their navels which are designed to ignite during lovemaking with the NATO officers that they seduce). Then he'll bombard Moscow, hoping that the Russians will assume that the United States is responsible and will retaliate. Luckily, Bill Dexter (Fabian Forte) and, of course, the two bumblers (Franco Franchi, Ciccio Ingrassia) are able to foil his fiendish formula for destruction and frame the unfortunate Goldfoot.

In this film Bava made his only cameo appearance in his own work, playing an angel on a cloud. The film came at an unfortunate time for Bava as his father had just died. The fact that his producer cowrote the screenplay probably also meant that there was little he could do to change the abysmal material he had to work with.

Knives of the Avenger became Bava's second Viking epic followed by *Kill Baby Kill!* (aka *Operation: Fear; Curse of the Living Dead; Operazione: Puara*). Dr. Eswai (Giacomo Rossi-Stuart) and his assistant, Monica (Enrica Bianchi Colombatto acting under the *nom de thesp* of Erica Blanc), visit a small Italian town which lies under a strange curse. Years before, feasting villagers let a young girl bleed to death after running her over, and now her lacy, petite, sweetly innocent figure has come back from the dead to goad them into destroying themselves. An aged baroness and the local witch (Fabienne Dali) are also involved in the plot. Dr. Eswai does his best to uncover the secrets and exorcise the spirit.

It's a dandy little horror film, one of the last gasps of the gothic cinema that was soon to give way to more graphic bloodletting. Once more Bava carefully builds the atmosphere of the creepy town, but he gets his best effects by inverting the symbolism of good and evil (the malefic, giggling, ghostly child) and from counterpointing gaiety with the grim goings-on (the laughter of children and the tolling of bells create fear in the villagers instead of joy). Best moments come with such simple gimmicks as the mysterious appearance of a child's handprint on a pane of glass and a small, bouncing ball appearing where there shouldn't be one, signaling the proximity of the sinister spirit. (Interestingly enough, the film apparently influenced Fellini in his depiction of the devil as a small golden-haired girl with a bouncing ball in his brilliant "Toby Dammit" section of *Spirits of the Dead*.)

Danger: Diabolik was budgeted by producer Dino de Laurentiis at $3,000,000, but Bava used his special effects and miniature know-how to bring the film in for a mere $400,000. Diabolik is a master criminal (played by John Phillip Law, fresh from playing an angel in *Barbarella*) who delights in pulling off elaborate capers and foiling the plans of the government to capture him. For the most part it is good comic book fun; particularly delightful is a scene where Terry-Thomas as the Minister of Finance goes on TV to beg that people pay their taxes because Diabolik has blown up all the tax records and the government doesn't know how much anyone owes. Again and again, Diabolik escapes certain death, ending the film encased in a gold statue but winking to his female accomplice.

Bava found that, unfortunately, with bigger budgets comes more front office interference. He'd been used to being left alone on his films and found de Laurentiis' restrictions particularly irritating, which led to him refusing to film a sequel. None was ever made.

He next tackled the special effects for a TV miniseries based on Homer's *The Odyssey*, which was ultimately released as *The Adventures of Ulysses* in a condensed feature version (not to be confused with the 1955 *Ulysses* starring Kirk Douglas).

Hatchet for a Honeymoon combines elements of *Blood and Black Lace* and *What!* In it, John Harrington (Stephen Forsyth) tries to prove one character's assertion that "reality is more horrible than fiction." He is haunted by a childhood memory, more of which comes back to him when he kills a model on her wedding night, incited into a homicidal rage by her wedding dress. Meanwhile, at home he is impotent with his shrewish wife, Mildred (Laura Betti), who matches taunt for taunt but makes the mistake of responding, "Give you a divorce? Never! It is 'til death do us part!" John gets over the problem of how to get himself in the mood by donning the wedding dress himself, and he gets his "divorce," but the pair are not parted even then. His wife's spirit comes back to haunt him and taunt him into further killings.

The Harringtons' salon scenes were shot at the villa of Generalissimo Francisco Franco, who was concerned that no blood be spilled there. Bava gets some mileage out of a creepy room where he has a collection of dummies dressed in marital finery, but his overuse of the zoom does become annoying and the overall execution makes this film only average for the genre, though it does benefit from Bava's special visual touches and a puckish sense of humor.

Early on, John says of himself, "No one would think to look at me that I am completely insane," and the entire force of his character hinges on his Oedipal obsessions. Finally, when he goes to attack Dagmar Lassander, he finally remembers what the audience has suspected all along: That he was the one who killed his mother on her wedding night. Once more, traditional symbols of innocence such as a music box and toys are given a sinister significance because of Harrington's deranged and uncertain mind.

Roy Colt e [and] Winchester Jack is a western comedy which I have not seen, while *Four Times That Night* (aka *Quattro Volte Quella Notte*) is said to be a variation of Kurosawa's classic *Rashomon*. Bava next worked on *Five Dolls for an August Moon (Cinque Bambole per la Luna d'Agosto)* which is based on the Agatha Christie classic *Ten Little Indians* (aka *And Then There Were None*), which Rene Clair did an excellent job of adapting back in 1945. (It was remade in '65, '75 and '89, each version weaker than the last.)

Bava never liked Mario di Nardo's script for the film and reports are that it is far from his best work. As yet, the film has not been released in the United States.

The same cannot be said of Bava's next film, *Ecologia del Delitto*, which has appeared under numerous titles including *Twitch of the Death Nerve, Carnage, Bloodbath, Last House on the Left Part 2, Bay of Blood, Antefatto, Reazione a Catena, The Ecology of a Crime* and *Before the Act*. The film is an important precursor to many of the '80s slaughterfests where a lone psycho stalks young teens around some scenic real estate, but in terms of style and black humor, it remains head and shoulders above any of them.

Bava abandoned his color gels for a more realistic and crystal-clear photographic look appropriate to this story's outdoor setting. He not only directed, but also shot the film and cowrote the story.

Bava is constantly confounding expectations with this film. Everything revolves around who will own the property that surrounds a scenic bay. Every time you think that the story has established a hero, he or she turns out to be another victim or killer. The story starts off with the murder of an old lady in her wheelchair and then her murderer is quickly disposed of, establishing that there is a maniac loose in the vicinity.

Into this idyllic scene come some young hippies who decide to invade an uninhabited house and go for a swim. A killer begins to make short work of these trespassers. The climax of a very effective and gruesome chase scene has the killer getting his curved machete in front of a running girl and slitting her throat in a full body shot that defies detection of the special effects technique employed.

All in all, 13 of the bay's inhabitants meet their deaths, usually by some extremely unpleasant means including an axe in the face, a spear plunged through a pair of lovers at the climax of lovemaking (Steve Miner copied this form of murder for *Friday the 13th Part 2*), and a knife in the belly. In the last outrageous twist, the final pair of murderers are shotgunned by their own children. The film has no heroes and the murderers are constantly getting murdered themselves. Except for the trespassing teenagers, most of the victims seem to deserve their fates. While not unusually explicit by today's standards, it certainly was for 1971 when it was first filmed, and subsequently has often suffered from a series of cuts, though the most gruesome scene in my opinion is nothing more than the discovery of a live octopus on the face of one of the victims. With tongue firmly in cheek, Bava managed to make the film exciting and suspenseful without grossing out the audience with the carnage.

From this high point, *Baron Blood* (aka *Gli Orrori del Castello di Norimberga*) is quite a disappointment. Once more the audience suffers through overused zoom shots and a dull script, though Bava does use his Austrian locations to some good effect. Peter von Kleist (Antonio Cantafora) and his girl friend Eva (Elke Sommer) accidentally resuscitate Baron Otto von Kleist, who died in the sixteenth century under the curse of a witch whom he tortured and burned at the stake. The Baron was apparently quite into torture as an amusing pastime, and his villagers finally rebelled and overthrew him.

Revived, he takes the form of Alfred Becker (Joseph Cotten), a wheelchair-bound gentleman who plans to buy the Baron's castle and turn it into a resort. Soon the torture chamber is being cranked up again and several nosy onlookers meet their untimely doom. Eva and Peter are saved by a magic amulet that revives the Baron's victims, who rise from their graves and wreak their vengeance on him.

Baron Blood's producer, Alfred Leone, was pleased with the results and gave Bava carte blanche to make his next project any kind of horror film he wanted. The result was *Lisa and the Devil*, which starred Telly Savalas and Elke Sommer. Unfortunately, the film had a difficult time getting sold at the international film markets. The film was subsequently recut with additional scenes filmed by both Bava and Leone and was finally released as *The House of Exorcism* (aka *The Devil in the House of Exorcism*) which lists a pseudonymous "Mickey Lion" as its director. Thanks to William Connolly, I can give you a rundown on the seldom seen original version of Bava's film, which did finally achieve a very limited release and has appeared on television in some places.

Lisa (Elke Sommer) is a very young tourist who is attracted to a fresco of the devil, that resembles Telly Savalas. Leaving her tour group, she espies a bald man (Savalas) in a curio shop working with a life-sized puppet. She leaves, gets lost, and comes across the strange puppeteer again.

Heading off, she encounters Carlo (Espartaco Santoni), who resembles the puppet. He makes advances to her, calling her Elena. Lisa breaks away and flees. She hitches a ride with three Italians but their car breaks down, and the omnipresent bald man pops his head out from behind a gate, frightening Lisa. A handsome stranger named Max (Alessio Orano) comes up and persuades her to stay at the residence until their car is repaired.

Things begin to get complicated as the wife of one Italian goes to bed with her chauffeur. The chauffeur is later killed and his body brought into the house of a rich man, named Leandro (Savalas). Max is attracted to Lisa, but has a strange obsession regarding a shadowy figure in the attic, who later turns out to be the corpse of his first wife, Elena (Sommer in different makeup), who is the spitting image of Lisa. Meanwhile Carlo makes a reappearance as does the puppet which resembles him.

The adulterous wife and her husband argue and she ends up running over him, several times, which Leandro silently observes. Lisa has fainted in all the confusion and Carlo tries to revive her, but is clubbed to death. When the wife observes this, she too is clubbed by Max. Max goes now to the thoroughly confused Lisa and takes her upstairs to his secret room, where he chloroforms her and tries to make love to her next to the corpse of Elena. Max's mother comes in and reveals Max's history of insanity, all stemming from Max's desire to keep Elena to himself. When she urges that he kill Lisa, he in turns disposes of her.

Looking for Leandro, he comes into a room containing all the corpses of his former victims sitting around a dining table. When his mother comes in, Max backs out a second story window and becomes impaled on an iron fence below. Leandro comes in and reveals that the "corpses" are just some more of his life-sized puppets.

The next morning, Lisa wakes up and finds the house deserted except for the puppets, including one of Max. As she leaves, some children taunt her, calling her a "ghost" and saying that no one has lived in that house for 100 years. Lisa gets back to her tour group and manages to get on a plane headed for home. Naturally, the plane is filled with those sinister puppets and the pilot turns out to be none other than Leandro, and on his command, Lisa crumbles, nothing but a puppet herself.

Fantasy and reality are indistinguishable in this dream-like film. It is decidedly an odd tale, but it is not without its poetic touches. It must be presumed that Leandro is in fact the devil, though this is never clearly stated. In fact, to maintain a high level of uncertainty, nothing is clearly stated in this often bewildering film, though the metaphor of the devil as a jeering puppeteer manipulating his charges seems an apt one at times. It was in this film that Savalas developed his trademark lollipop-sucking that became an integral part of his Kojak character on American TV.

House of Exorcism uses material from *Lisa and the Devil* for a series of dreams or flashbacks, it's unclear which. Lisa is taken to the hospital. There Father Michael (Robert Alda, who did not apear in the original film) diagnoses her as being possessed and in the climax of the film tries to exorcise the spirit only to be struck by a lightning bolt. These scenes represent a totally different story which has been grafted onto the original and they badly break up the latter's dream-like pacing, adding scenes of Lisa vomiting up pea soup and frogs and Father Michael ranting and raving to no apparent good purpose.

After the disastrous recutting of *Lisa and the Devil*, Bava had even more problems with his gangster drama, tentatively titled *Wild Dogs*. Because the producer of the film owed a lot of money, the film was confiscated by his creditors just before completion and has never been released. Bava's son, Lamberto, has tried to buy it back, but to no avail. Bava went into a kind of semiretirement.

Bava's last film was *Shock* (aka *Beyond the Door II; Transfer Suspense Hypnos; All 33 di Via Orologio fa Sempre Freddo*), which Bava produced, secretly letting his son Lamberto handle much of the direction. (Lamberto had been his father's assistant since *Planet of the Vampires*, though he was not credited on *Shock* as the codirector.) This may explain why the beginning and the end of the film, with their restless camera, resemble the old Bava while the rest of the film seems flat and without the ironic touches that Bava had been employing in his work for the last decade.

Dora Baldini (Daria Nicolodi) moves into a new house with her young son Marco (David Colin, Jr.), who resents his stepfather, Bruno (John Steiner). The boy behaves very strangely, at one time falling on his mother and thrusting his hips in and out, at another swearing to kill her for marrying Bruno. Dora becomes convinced that the boy has become possessed by the spirit of his father, a drug addict whom Dora killed and Bruno walled up in the basement of their house.

In one of the film's creepiest scenes, the boy shares his mother's bed while Bruno is away, and when his hand begins exploring her sleeping figure, it transforms into the rotting hand of her former husband. When Bruno comes back in the next scene, his question, "Been taking care of your mother for me?" takes on a chilling new meaning in the context. The rotting hand begins to haunt the mother, and the couple finally die in a horrible bloodbath in a basement.

From the beginning we know that Dora isn't in a stable mental condition, and her health is not improved by her son sending her roses with cards signed by her dead hsuband or putting razor blades between the piano keys or porcelain fingers poking through the sofa cushions. Is Marco himself driving her mad or is he possessed, guided by the vengeful spirit of his dead father whose tomb in the basement he embraces?

Shock does have some flashes of merit, but it is a disappointing last film for a former master. It was retitled *Beyond the Door II* by American distributor Film Ventures to cash in on the success of *Beyond the Door*, an *Exorcist* rip-off starring Juliet Mills. The only thing the two films have in common, apart from the title, is that both feature Colin, Jr., and have something to do with possession, though in the case of *Beyond II*, not demonic possession.

Bava did codirect an episode of the television show *Il Giorno dei Diavolo (The Devil's Notebook)* entitled *La Venere d'Ille* ("Venus of Ille") about a statue of Venus that comes to life when a man places a wedding ring on her finger; she enters his marital bed and crushes him to death in her embrace. Bava also worked on the special effects for the TV miniseries *Moses: The Lawgiver* starring Burt Lancaster and directed by Gianfranco De Bosin. His last film work was some uncredited special effects on Dario Argento's little-seen *Inferno*, on which Lamberto Bava also served as assistant director. At the age of 65, Mario Bava suffered a fatal heart attack. Italy lost its greatest horror stylist.

While his plots were usually not very strong and the characterization in his films was often weak to nonexistent, Bava had a great visual eye, and film is primarily a visual medium. Thus Bava was able to leave an indelible impression on a generation of filmgoers and is still much revered by fans today. Few can match his ability to create an atmosphere of terror with only a few deftly placed lights, an appropriate camera movement, and some unsettling sound such as a door banging in the wind. It is for his ability, and not the often gratuitous violence that marred his later work, that Bava will be most remembered.

John Brahm (1893–1982)

Broken Blossoms (1936); *Counsel for Crime* (1937); *Penitentiary; Girls' School* (1938); *Let Us Live; Rio* (1939); *Escape to Glory* (1940); *Wild Geese Calling* (1941); *The Undying Monster* (1942); *Tonight We Raid Calais; Wintertime* (1943); *The Lodger, Guest in the House* (uncred. codir. Lewis Milestone, Andre De Toth); *Hangover Square* (1945); *The Locket* (1946); *The Brasher Doubloon; Singapore* (1947); *Il Ladro di Venezia* (aka *The Thief of Venice*, 1950); *The Miracle of Our Lady of Fatima; Face to Face* ("The Secret Sharer" episode); *The Diamond Queen* (1953); *The Mad Magician; Die Goldene Pest* (aka *The Golden Plague*, 1954); *Von Himmel Gefallen* (aka *Special Delivery*); *Bengazi* (1955); *Hot Rods to Hell* (1967).

TELEVISION: *Medic; Screen Director's Playhouse; General Electric Theatre; Studio 57; Johnny Staccato; Video Theater; M Squad; Cimarron City;* "A Night with the Boys," "Dry Run," "Insomnia," "Pen Pals," "Touché," "The Five Forty-Eight," "The Throwback," "The Hero," *Alfred Hitchcock Presents; The Deputy; Riverboat;* "Time Enough at Last," "Judgment Night," "The Four of Us Are Dying," "A Nice Place to Visit," "Mr. Dingle the Strong," "Shadow Play," "Person or Persons Unknown," "Young Man's Fancy," "The Next Exhibit," "You Drive," "Queen of the Nile," "Mirror Image," *Twilight Zone;* "The Watcher," "The Prediction," "The Cheaters," "The Merriweather File," "A Good Imagination," "Dark Legacy," "The Remarkable Mrs. Hawks," "An Attractive Family," "Waxworks," "A Wig for Miss Devore," "Cousin Tandifer," "Flowers of Evil," *Thriller; The Defenders; Naked City;* "Don't Look Behind You," "Death and the Joyful Woman," "Murder Case," "The Trap," "The Final Performance," *Alfred Hitchcock Hour; Alcoa Premiere; The Virginian; Arrest and Trial;* "Zzzzz," "The Bellero Shield," *The Outer Limits;* "The City Beneath the Sea," "Hot Line," *Voyage to the Bottom of the Sea;* "Terror Island," *Bob Hope Chrysler Theater; Dr. Kildare;* "The Waverly Ring Affair," "The Napoleon's Tomb Affair," "The Maze Affair," "The Pieces of Fate Affair," *The Man from U.N.C.L.E.;* "The Horns of a Dilemma Affair," "The Montori Device Affair," "The Jewels of Topango Affair," "The Lethal Eagle Affair," "The Double-O-Nothing Affair," "The Furnace Flats Affair," *The Girl from U.N.C.L.E.*

John Brahm is most acclaimed for *The Lodger* and *Hangover Square*, two baroquely filmed thrillers featuring a psychotic Laird Cregar, but these are not the only notable or worthwhile efforts in Brahm's often overlooked filmography. Brahm had a flair for orchestrating lights and shadows in black-and-white cinematography and for stylish direction far above the average B film director, yet he never garnered a big hit or graduated to full-fledged A films. Brahm instead went into televison, where his fine work has almost been totally forgotten.

Brahm was born and raised in Hamburg, Germany, where he wanted to become an actor like his father, Ludwig Brahm. Under his real name of Hans, he began work as a stage director in Vienna, Berlin and Paris. In 1934, he became a dialogue director and film editor at Paris' Terra Film. Moving on to Twickenham Studios, he wrote the script for and supervised the production of that ghostly classic *Scrooge*, with Sir Seymour Hicks playing the title role and cowriting the script based on Dickens' *A Christmas Carol*.

Hans Brahm's big break came when an English producer planned a remake of *Broken Blossoms* as a comeback film for D. W. Griffith. Emlyn Williams wrote the script and the film was to star Dolly Haas, who was Brahm's wife. However, Griffith objected to both the script and the star and returned to the United States. Brahm was then assigned to take over and so made his debut, which resulted in Myron Selznick signing Brahm to a four-year contract as a director at Columbia.

Assigned to the B film unit, Hans' name was changed to John. His first film for Columbia, *Counsel for Crime*, was a moderately entertaining B movie with Otto Kruger playing a ruthless lawyer. *Penitentiary* was a thinly disguised retelling of Howard Hawks' *The Criminal Code*, while *Let Us Live* was a variation on Fritz Lang's *You Only Live Once* with an innocent Henry Fonda again convicted of murder while Maureen O'Sullivan tries to clear him. *Rio* has a fine Basil Rathbone performance as he rots in prison and worries about his wife possibly being unfaithful. *Escape to Glory*, the story of a British ship attacked by a German sub, gives some hint of Brahm's ability to handle atmosphere and lighting. *Wild Geese Calling* featured Henry Fonda in the Yukon.

The Undying Monster (British title: *The Hammond Mystery*) was 20th Century–Fox's attempt to cash in on George Waggner's unexpected success with Universal's *The Wolf Man*. While it doesn't match Waggner's film, it is one of the better horror films of the '40s *not* made by Val Lewton's RKO group. The reason for this largely lay in Brahm's atmospheric direction and a young Lucien Ballard's cinematography. (Ballard started his career working for Joseph von Sternberg and had previously worked for Brahm on *Penitentiary, Let Us Live, Wild Geese Calling* and in an uncredited sequence in *Orchestra Wives*.) The film was based on a novel of the same name by Jessie Douglas Kerruish and was picked up by producer Bryan Foy because it could serve as a low-budget follow-up to the Universal horror hit.

The story centers around the Hammond family in Cornwall. Kate O'Malley, who works as a servant for the Hammonds, is found in a coma along with an unconscious Oliver Hammond (John Howard) near the mangled remains of the family dog. Oliver's sister Helga (Heather Angel) gets help and brings them back to Hammond Hall, where Oliver wakes and tells Helga and Dr. Geoff Cobert (Bramwell Fletcher, the guy who goes mad at the beginning of Karl Freund's *The Mummy*) his story:

> Suddenly I felt something coming at us from all sides! Then it closed in on me, like a blast from a furnace, only it wasn't hot, it was . . . it was simply horrible! Kate screamed, and I was fighting it . . . fighting it in a darkness that went all red . . . all dark red . . . till a splash of fire split it up and put it out! I awoke in the light and saw Helga. . . .

Kate dies, and Scotland Yard is called in in the form of Inspector Robert Curtis (James Ellison), who learns from Helga that her grandfather had commited suicide several years ago after seeing "it." There is apparently a curse on the Hammond family because a member of their family had sold his soul to the devil and is reputedly still living (hence the title), venturing forth to claim another victim to prolong his life. The butler, Walton (Halliwell Hobbes, who was also the butler in Mammoulian's *Dr. Jekyll and Mr. Hyde*), lumbers around suspiciously.

Down in the crypt, the tomb of Reginald Hammond is found next to a statue of a large wolf and the strange inscription, frequently repeated by the butler, "When stars are bright on a frosty night/Beware thy bane, on the rocky lane." Examination of a hair found at the scene of the crime reveals it to be the hair of a wolf, which miraculously disappears when light touches it.

Inspector Curtis takes a sample of Kate's blood and is surprised to discover it contains traces of cobra venom. Later, he finds vials of cobra venom in Dr. Corbet's lab, and he accuses the doctor of injecting the girl with the serum to prevent her from ever regaining consciousness. An unearthly howl is heard, and the Hammond monster enters Helga's bedroom and carries her off.

Brahm elected to keep his monster mysterious, having it stalk through the shadows of the house, keeping the audience from getting too good a look at it. In discussing the film in *Photon*, Paul Mandell noted:

> For the establishing shot at the start of the story, the camera pans mysteriously around the Hammond mansion revealing odd statues of crusaders lit by firelight in a truly gothic atmosphere. From the outset, Brahm asserts his somber visual style. When the main characters congregate in the Hammond crypt, Oliver's great dane jumps out of the shadows in a jolting, but harmless display of affection for his master. Later on, the camera slinks through the shadows of Helga's bedroom as a hand is chillingly revealed from behind a curtain, eerily illuminated by the moonlight spilling in from the window. Such foreboding visuals were sadly lacking in most horror efforts of the forties. . . .

Finally we are able to dimly see the monster, a werewolf, as his shadowy figure absconds with Helga, climbing down from the balcony. The monster moves over some rocks with supernatural speed (jerkily conveyed by
a slowed-down camera) until he is stopped by a policeman's bullet. In perhaps the most interesting shot in the film, we see the werewolf transform
back into his human form via a traveling matte – rather than use the lap
dissolves of Universal's Wolf Man pictures, Brahm chose to have his monster change while staring directly into the camera. The dying figure reveals
itself as Oliver Hammond, who was apparently unaware of his alternate existence as the not-so-immortal Hammond monster.

The film, at least, was not a straight copycat version of *The Wolf Man*,
though its corny "When stars are bright" refrain was obviously meant to
echo the "Even a man who is pure of heart" poem from the earlier film. Instead, *The Undying Monster* is played as a mystery for most of its length,
though the sense of unease that is essential to atmospheric horror is
definitely present in Brahm's careful direction. The final film also benefits
from an effective score by Emil Newman with additional music by David
Raksin.

Brahm returned to the horror genre with his most critically praised
film, *The Lodger*. Hulking through the streets of London, shrouded in the
fog, is a figure who kills actresses (censors would not allow the script to use
"prostitutes") out of a twisted sense of moral righteousness. Yet Laird
Cregar, who had played a number of "heavies," plays the obsessed man
almost against type. Rather than accentuate Jack the Ripper's menacing
qualities, he portrays him as polite, shy, and even uncertain.

Brahm's cinematographer, Lucien Ballard, wanted *The Lodger* to have
a special look, and Brahm gave him his head. Said Ballard in Leonard Mal-
tin's book *Behind the Camera*:

> I'd always wanted to do fog the way I did it in *The Lodger*. Before
> then it was always a gray haze. I did it with the fog in spots, with black
> and white definition still coming through. And when they ran the
> rushes I got hell for it; the producer said, "I've lived in London, and the
> fog doesn't look like that." I said, "You may have lived in London, and
> the fog doesn't look like that – but that's how it *should* look.

The Lodger has a very handsome look, even for a 20th Century–Fox B
movie. In addition to the eerie and beautiful photography of the fog, Brahm
links the film together with water imagery. At the beginning of the film, the
blind man asks a large, mustachioed gentleman with a doctor's bag to read
a notice to him. The notice calls for vigilantes to take over if the police don't
identify and capture Jack the Ripper. Meanwhile, a streetwalker leaves a
merry pub heading down the foggy streets to her home. When a bobby

offers to help, she demurs, but not long after she leaves the frame, we hear a scream and know her fate is sealed. Her body is discovered beside a gutter which has brackish water running through it.

Later, we will see Cregar washing his hands, reflecting on the peacefulness of the Thames ("Deep water is dark and restful and full of peace"; "I take my problems to the river"), presaging his final demise by throwing himself into the river. The fog, itself made out of water, is like the perspiration the uneasy environment gives off.

Belloc-Lowndes' novel was previously adapted into a film by Alfred Hitchcock in which the mysterious lodger proved not to be Jack the Ripper afterall. The strange thing about Brahm's remake is that after a while, it seems so obvious that the lodger is the Ripper that by the conventions of the mystery genre, he almost has to be a red herring. Instead, Brahm gives us a chance to see how a disturbed figure can enter a normal household and go unsuspected precisely because to believe that he could be a mass murderer would just seem too incredible.

The lodger gives his name as "Slade," obviously taking it from a street sign he passes on the way there. The family consists of Robert Burton (Cedric Hardwicke), his wife, Ellen (Sara Allgood), and their niece Kitty (Merle Oberon). They are impressed by their lodger, though they notice he has eccentricities. These include turning all pictures of famous actresses in his upstairs room to the wall, and saying, "Mine too are the problems of life and death" when he sees the record of births and deaths in the family Bible, but such actions merely causes Robert to conclude that their lodger is a "curious fellow." When "Slade" burns his black bag, Robert suggests that it would be sensible for any man who owned one to do so, given the environment of fear that the Ripper has generated. After all, a crowd might "mistake" him for the Ripper and lynch him.

Apparently, being obtuse runs in the family. When Kitty asks "Slade" to observe her performance at the Whitechapel Palace of Varieties, he states that he disapproves of theaters and can't come. She decides to follow him on his way to work, but he discovers her. He acknowledges that his actions arouse curiosity. Her suspicions are allayed and do not return even when the lodger burns a bloody overcoat, which he "contaminated in an experiment," or when he quotes Solomon at her: "A strange woman lieth in wait for her prey. She increases transgressions among men."

The lodger goes on to explain, "It was the evil of woman that led my brother to his destruction. There is evil in beauty, but if the evil is cut out of a beautiful thing, then only the beauty remains." Despite this tip-off that the mysterious lodger is the Ripper, all a visibly shaken Kitty tells her aunt is that "Mr. Slade is quite a philosopher."

Meanwhile, Inspector Garrick (George Sanders in a rare heroic role) sees a pattern beginning to emerge, noting Slade's antipathy towards "actresses." In an anachronistic bit, he tries to track down the Ripper by his fingerprints a good decade before the sytem was accepted by law enforcement officers; however, the prints on the hand don't match the Scotland Yard's as the Ripper had used his other hand.

Still, the police know who the Ripper is and they begin searching the theater where Kitty is giving her performance for him. Slade is in the audience, visibly disturbed by Kitty's sexual attractiveness, but the police disrupt the performance. He attacks Kitty in her dressing room, but a copper shoots and wounds him, causing him to hide in the theater. The police put Kitty in the middle of the stage for her protection, but in a memorably creepy moment, the Ripper creeps across a catwalk to try to crush her beneath a sandbag which he unleashes. (Ballard's camera work on Cregar's face as the shadows of the catwalk's latices slip by and he comes ever closer to the camera is exquisite.)

However, the Ripper is spotted in time to yell a warning, and the sandbag falls harmlessly to one side. The police corner him in Kitty's dressing room, and the desperate figure seeks a final refuge by diving into the deep, dark water of the Thames, bringing to a close the water motif threaded throughout the film and suggesting a final cleansing.

While parts of Brahm's film are highly predictable, it is very well-made and even beautiful in spots. It not only established Brahm as a craftsman, it made a star at last out of the third-billed Cregar. Cregar had memorably played an insane cop in *I Wake Up Screaming* (aka *The Hot Spot*), a pirate in *The Black Swan*, and a smooth and charming devil in Lubitsch's delightful comedy *Heaven Can Wait*. He hoped to be recognized for his talents and become a conventional leading man; however, his bulky 328 pounds led to his mainly being cast as "heavies." During the filming of *The Lodger*, he trimmed down to 252 pounds and was cast as Waldo Lydecker (the part which revived Clifton Webb's career) in *Laura*, which was to be his next film. Unfortunately, for Cregar, producer-director Otto Preminger, who took over production of the film from Rouben Mamoulian, objected to Cregar's casting, feeling that his identification as a heavy would tip off the audience too soon. Preminger recast the part with Clifton Webb, who walked away with the acting honors on the film and revitalized his film career.

Cregar looked for something else he could do and came across a novel by Patrick Hamilton, the author of *Gaslight*. The novel, *Hangover Square*, was about a sensitive young man who suffers from schizophrenia. Here at last was the romantic role that Cregar had been seeking – or so he thought when Fox acquired it for him.

However, scriptwriter Barre Lyndon saw it as an opportunity to reprise a previous success, and turned the story into a virtual remake of *The Lodger*, changing the setting to the past and having the schizoid pianist

George Harvey Bone commit arson and murder whenever triggered by discordant sounds. Cregar was angry over the changes and refused to accept the part bought specifically for him. He was placed on suspension for two weeks until he relented.

John Brahm was once more assigned to direct Cregar, but this time instead of an enthusiastic star who contributed a great deal (Cregar gave the Ripper in *The Lodger* homosexual overtones to imply the source of the character's misogyny), he found himself confronted by a belligerent and uncooperative star who resented the film he was being forced to make. Additionally, the emotionally troubled Cregar was attempting his first heterosexual romance, and was also severely dieting to lose the pounds that he felt were restricting him to particular kinds of roles. He had lost 80 pounds previous to undertaking the role, but he unwisely continued to diet and took dangerous drugs. Finally, just after production halted, Cregar underwent an abdominal operation to correct a hernia and control his food intake. It proved the last straw, and the actor had two heart attacks in quick succession, dying on December 9, 1944, at the age of 31. Cregar never lived to see the release of *Hangover Square*, the only film on which he received top billing.

Gregory Mank in his excellent survey of Hollywood heavies, *The Hollywood Hissables*, relates the following anecdote about the notoriously uncooperative George Sanders. During the crucial and expensive burning scene, Sanders announced that he didn't like a particular line of dialogue he'd been given and refused to say it when his cue was given. Infuriated, producer Robert Bassler chewed Sanders out and was promptly punched by the burly actor. Bassler had to apologize for calling Sanders a "son-of-a-bitch" before a compromise was reached and the line uttered. Amazingly, throughout all this Brahm held his temper and achieved his shot. On the last day of shooting, Cregar told off Brahm, which caused further problems when David Zanuck ordered the film back into production for additional retakes. The crew of the film supported Brahm, and the unruffled director finished his film.

Fortunately, the acrimony on the set does not appear to have affected *Hangover Square* adversely, and Cregar was able to deliver the kind of performance that conveyed his character's pathos and loneliness. Cregar's weight loss is quite evident in the film, though he still looks more like a football player than a pianist.

Whereas Brahm used water as a recurring visual theme in *The Lodger*, for *Hangover Square* he used fire. The film opens with a bravura pan across a pawnbroker's shop after it has been set ablaze while the camera pulls out the window to survey the ever-building blaze from the street. A weary and disoriented Bone comes home and continues to work on his concerto. Bone's fiancée, Barbara (Faye Marlowe), and her father (Alan Napier) pay him a

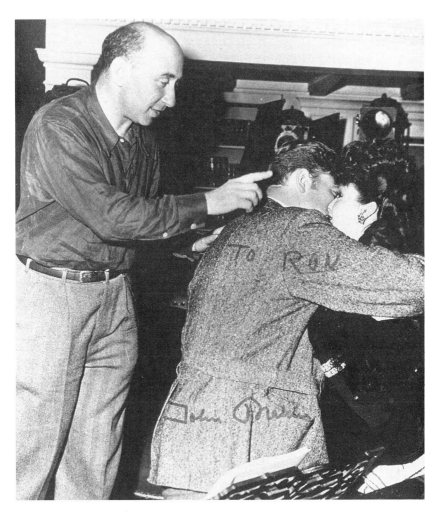

A rare photo of John Brahm on the set of Hangover Square *directing Laird Cregar and Linda Darnall in a love scene.*

visit. Observing how haggard he looks, they express concern about his health. Eventually, the father offers Bone a chance to perform his concerto publicly once he finishes it.

As in *The Lodger*, there is no mystery as to who the maniac is. An off-pitch sound causes Bone to take down the curtain sash and almost strangle Barbara, but he remains pitiable as he is obviously in the throes of a problem he cannot control.

Seeking solace, Bone stops off in a music hall and falls in love with a manipulative singer named Netta (Linda Darnell), who sidetracks him into writing some music hall songs for her instead of finishing his concerto. When she has what she wants, she heartlessly dumps him. Outside, some falling pipes set the otherwise gentle Bone off and he returns to strangle Netti, covering her head and disposing of her body atop a Guy Fawkes Day bonfire. Brahm demanded so many retakes of this scene that Cregar was almost burned. The pair had disagreed over the scene where Bone strangles Darnell, with Cregar insisting that it not be shown while Brahm considered its depiction essential.

Once more George Sanders plays a character whose shrewd psychology uncovers what the main character has been hiding from himself. By talking with him, Sanders' character causes Bone to realize what has been happening during his mental blackouts. Bone decides to give himself up, but insists that he be given the chance to play his beloved concerto first. He locks Sanders up and starts performing at the concert when some more noise disrupts his thinking pattern and he is unable to continue. A female pianist continues the piece for him as the police arrive and confront him in a side room. There Bone throws a lantern and sets the concert hall on fire. As the crowd rushes out, he resumes his place at the piano and finishes his concerto, expiating his guilt with his own fiery immolation that ends his torment forever.

Brahm's direction is notable not only for Cregar's sensitive performance but also for his interesting use of camera angles, subtly suggesting a world and a mind out of kilter. He tended to position his camera above or below the characters rather than shooting them directly on. Joseph La Shelle did an excellent job with the cinematography, matching the quality of Ballard's work on *The Lodger* (ironically, LaShelle also replaced Ballard on *Laura* when Preminger took over the direction of that film).

Both *The Lodger* and *Hangover Square* are aptly aided by beautiful musical scores, with Bernard Herrmann's "Concerto Macabre for Piano and Orchestra" being particularly notable as it combines all the themes Herrmann had used earlier in the film, suggesting that Bone's experiences had contributed to creating his final masterpiece and because it is perhaps the only piano concerto to end with the soloist sans orchestra.

Though less frequently discussed, *Hangover Square* matches the high quality of *The Lodger* while surpassing it in making the agonized killer a sympathetic character, though it does lack the superb suspense sequences of *The Lodger*. Both films are far above the average horror film in quality, making it curious that Brahm's work is not better known.

After *Hangover Square*, Brahm worked on *The Locket*, another portrait of mental illness. In this one, Laraine Day plays a kleptomaniac whose past finally catches up with her when, prior to her wedding, her fiancé presents her with a locket she had previously stolen. Not a horror film, *The Locket* is nonetheless notable for its complex story structure, which contains flashbacks within flashbacks within flashbacks without losing the thread of the story. It is also interesting to note the dichotomy between what we see (Day as sweet, lovely, and an ideal bride) and what we are told (she is a habitual liar and thief, has killed one person and driven another to suicide and almost causes her fiancé to lose his sanity until she finally "escapes" into madness herself).

Thanks to Nicholas Musuraca's excellent cinematography, *The Locket* has the look of a top-grade RKO B film, à la the Val Lewton works. It has a good film noir look to it as many key scenes take place in near darkness; a very dramatic scene between Day and Robert Mitchum, playing a former husband, is illuminated only by flickering firelight.

This was followed by the unjustly maligned *The Brasher Doubloon,* an adaptation of Raymond Chandler's *The High Window* (which had previously been filmed as *Time to Kill* in 1942 as part of the Michael Shayne series). While George Montgomery is far from the best actor to play Chandler's detective Philip Marlowe, he does an adequate job and was unjustly criticized for being miscast due to his popular association with western films. (Not having seen many of Montgomery's exploits as a cowboy, I had no such associations.)

The mystery is both convoluted and engrossing with a number of memorably grotesque characters to make things interesting along the way. Mrs. Murdock (Florence Bates) wants the stolen doubloon back and hires Marlowe to do it. However, Marlowe soon realizes there is more to the case than a simple robbery, particularly when he is beaten by the vicious Vannier (Fritz Kortner in a particularly creepy performance). There's also Mrs. Murdock's mentally disturbed secretary, Merle Davis (Nancy Guild), who is involved in a blackmail scheme. Finally, the mystery comes full circle, leading back to Mrs. Murdock who had hired Marlowe in the first place. In all this, Brahm manages to be stylish without being overstated and offers a few memorably moody scenes. Unfortunately, the overall production lacks a certain *frisson* which might have helped make it a classic noir film. Nonetheless, it does serve as an absorbing story and good entertainment.

I haven't seen Brahm's next film, *Singapore,* in which Ava Gardner suffers from amnesia and remarried, much to the consternation of husband Fred MacMurray. Brahm did become one of several uncredited directors on Gregg R. Tallas' absolutely abysmal *Siren of Atlantis* (the others were Arthur Ripley and Douglas Sirk), an awful adventure film in which Dennis O'Keefe and Jean-Pierre Aumont stumble upon Maria Montez and the fabled Lost Continent. (Poor Henry Daniell has to stumble through a role here as well.)

That assignment was said to have led to Brahm's helming *Il Ladro di Venezia (The Thief of Venice)* in Italy with Maria Montez on sets leftover from Orson Welles' *Othello*. Brahm fared better under old friend Bryan Foy on *The Miracle of Our Lady of Fatima* (aka *Miracle of Fatima*) in which three Portuguese children see the Virgin Mary and miracles begin to happen. It's a religious picture that manages to be charming rather than embarrassing, but it still doesn't seem an appropriate choice for someone of Brahm's talents. For the prestigious anthology film *Face to Face*, Brahm filmed a faithful adaptation of Joseph Conrad's classic story "The Secret Sharer" with James Mason as the captain and Michael Pate as the fugitive, but the story works better on paper than it does on film. (The other half of the film consisted of famed film critic James Agee's adaptation of Stephen Crane's "Bride Comes to Yellow Sky," directed by Bretaigne Windust.)

Brahm returned to the horror genre with a follow-up to the greatest 3-D horror film yet made, Andre De Toth's *House of Wax*. The follow-up featured the same star (Vincent Price), the same producer (Bryan Foy), and the same screenwriter (Crane Wilbur, who later directed the lukewarm *The Bat*) and was called *The Mad Magician*. However, this Columbia production, coming at the tail end of the 3-D craze and being a virtual remake of *House of Wax*, has been rather neglected, not entirely without reason.

Rather than in full Warnercolor, *The Mad Magician* was filmed in black-and-white and featured Price as The Great Gallico. Gallico is the number one inventor of clever gadgets for prestidigitators and illusionists to use. However, he is himself prevented from acting as a magician by Ross Ormand (Donald Randolph), his former employer, who has secured an injunction preventing Gallico from performing, claiming to hold all rights to any illusions Gallico invents by a previous contract. Gallico assumes the guise of fellow magician Rinaldi and takes Rinaldi's place after disposing of Ormand. Brahm even resurrects the Guy Fawkes bonfire body disposal method from *Hangover Square*. Finally, Gallico is incinerated in one of his own devices as novelist Alice Prentice (Lenita Lane) figures out what exactly is going on.

The film isn't bad, just unmemorable. As an attempt to make lightning strike in the same place, it failed, though the film is entertaining and, like most of Brahm's films, well made. It might also be noted that *The Mad Magician* became the first feature-length film to be broadcast on television in 3-D in the Los Angeles area when it appeared on Elvira's *Movie Macabre*. (A special pair of video 3-D glasses had to be purchased at participating 7-Eleven stores.)

If the rest of Brahm's feature films are not particularly interesting or distinguished, the same cannot be said of his television work, much of which was excellent. He was even reunited with scripter Barre Lyndon for one episode of *The Alfred Hitchcock Hour*, "Don't Look Behind You," about a psychotic music professor (director Alf Kjellin) who murders two female co-eds before getting caught and who in turn inspires a psychology professor

(Jeffrey Hunter) to attack his fiancée (Vera Miles). Brahm directed several memorable *Alfred Hitchcock Presents, Twilight Zone* and *Thriller* episodes, which represent his best television work. His *Thriller*s were among the best for that series and he directed 12 episodes of the *Twilight Zone*, more than any other director who worked for the show.

Among his most memorable *Twilight Zone* episodes were "Time Enough at Last," in which Burgess Meredith plays a persecuted book lover who accidentally survives World War III only to lose his glasses; "Shadow Play," in which Dennis Weaver has a recurring nightmare in which he is sentenced to die, a uniquely somber and moody piece for television; "Person or Persons Unknown," in which Richard Long wakes up to find that no one knows him; and "You Drive," in which Edward Andrews is involved in a hit-and-run accidental killing of a boy on a bicycle. When another man is mistakenly identified as the driver, Andrews feels he is off the hook, but his *car* has other ideas, honking its horn, driving by itself, chasing Andrews down, and almost running over him. Brahm's direction makes this the best "haunted car" story ever, turning a simple automobile into an unnervingly creepy device of guilt and conscience.

Brahm's best television work shared much in common with his best theatrical work. He seems to have loved dealing with obsessive, psychologically disturbed characters, and delighted in creating shadowy environments which occasionally illuminate their tormented psyches. He had a fine grasp of black-and-white camera effects and creating atmosphere and moods. His stylish shots are effective without seeming out of place by calling too much attention to themselves. Unfortunately, as television switched over to color and the shuddery anthology series died out, Brahm was stranded without a medium in which to create his best work. Nonetheless, his sure and capable hand has elevated a handful of shockers into classy, carefully crafted films notable for their fine photography and performances.

Tod Browning (1882-1962)

The Lucky Transfer, The Highbinders, The Living Death, The Burn Hand, The Woman From Warren's, Little Marie (1915); *Puppets, Everybody's Doing It, The Deadly Glass of Beer* (1916); *Jim Bludso, A Love Sublime, Hands Up!, Peggy, The Will O' The Wisp, The Jury of Fate* (1917); *The Eyes of Mystery, Revenge, Which Woman?, The Deciding Kiss, Set Free* (1918); *The Wicked Darling, The Exquisite Thief, The Unpainted Woman, The Petal on the Current, Bonnie, Bonnie Lassie* (1919); *The Virgin of Stamboul* (1920); *Outside the Law, No Woman Knows* (1921); *The Wise Kid, The Man Under Cover, Under Two Flags* (1922); *Drifting, White Tiger, The Day of Faith* (1923); *The Dangerous Flirt, Silk Stocking Sal* (1924); *The Unholy Three, Dollar Down, The Mystic* (1925); *The Blackbird, The Road to Mandalay* (1926); *The Show, The Unknown, London After Midnight* (1927); *The Big City, West of Zanzibar* (1928); *Where East Is East, The Thirteenth Chair* (1929); *Outside the Law* (1930); *Dracula, Iron Man* (1931); *Fast Workers, Freaks* (1932); *Mark of the Vampire* (1935); *The Devil-Doll* (1936); *Miracles for Sale* (1939).

Tod Browning was born Charles Albert Browning on July 12, 1882, in Louisville, Kentucky. During 1898, he ran away from home to join a carnival as a contortionist and a clown. He eventually drifted into vaudeville, working in various acts. In 1913, he acted in two films for Biograph, *Scenting a Terrible Crime* and *A Fallen Hero*. In 1914, he left Biograph to join Komic, where he performed in several one-reel films. His last acting job was as a car owner in the modern segment of D. W. Griffith's *Intolerance*, on which he was also an assistant director for the crowd scenes.

Browning was, by all accounts, a quiet and gentle person who nonetheless worked his actors very hard. He was also known for his sardonic humor, which he used to ward off interference from the front office. He wrote most of his films, making him a genuine *auteur*. Browning believed that plots were secondary to characterization, which helps explain why so many of his films feature very memorable characterizations but fizzled, unexciting endings.

Most of Browning's silent career was made up of melodramas and falls outside the scope of this study anyway. Browning's first directorial job was *The Lucky Transfer* in 1915. In addition to directing a number of two-reel films, he also wrote such films as *The Queen of the Band, Sunshine Dad, The Mystery of the Leaping Fish* and *Atta Boy's Last Race* (remade as *The Old*

Age Handicap) for other directors. Of these, *The Mystery of the Leaping Fish* has achieved some notoriety and has been revived on some college campuses. The ludicrous plot involves Douglas Fairbanks as private detective Coke Ennyday, who shoots cocaine into his palm periodically to assist him in solving a case involving opium smugglers. Browning's first fantasy was *Puppets* (working title *The Mummy*), which was done in *Commedia dell'Arte* style. (Despite the working title, no mummies are featured.)

His first feature-length film was *Jim Bludso* (1917), codirected with Wilfred Lucas, who also starred as the title character. The pair's next film, *A Love Sublime*, was based on Samuel Hopkins Adams' story "Orpheus," a modern retelling of the classic Greek fable. This film introduced Browning to Alice Wilson, who was to become his wife. Browning made one more film with Lucas, *Hands Up!* for Griffith's Triangle film organization, before leaving for Metro Pictures. For them, in New York, he made *Peggy, The Will o' the Wisp, The Jury of Fate,* and *The Eyes of Mystery*, which featured many of the standard gimmicks of "haunted" house pictures (e.g. sliding doors, secret stairways, portraits with eyes behind them).

For *The Legion of Death*, Browning and his cast and crew relocated to California for Metro's first West Coast–produced feature. After doing *Revenge*, Browning was lured away to Universal to take over *Which Woman* from an ailing Harry A. Pollard, and that became the director's new studio. There, in 1919, Browning made his first film with Lon Chaney, *The Wicked Darling*, a standard metropolitan melodrama. Later, their joint films at MGM would make them famous.

Unfortunately, Browning became an alcoholic, a problem which for a time led to his work becoming sporadic, though he was still entrusted with his first epic, *The Virgin of Stamboul*, which was released with great success in 1920. His next film, *Outside the Law*, brought him back together with Lon Chaney, who essayed a double role as "Black Mike" Silva and Ah Wing. As a gimmick, Wing kills Silva at the finale, so Browning shows Chaney killing himself. (Wing was coyly billed as "Guess Who.") Browning remade the film in 1930 as his second sound film with Edward G. Robinson taking the Chaney gangster role. The film was remade a final time with the story rewritten almost beyond recognition as *Inside Job* by Jean Yarbrough. Browning got story credit for that one, making it his last credit on a feature film.

Browning left Universal after *White Tiger* in 1923. His alcoholism had gotten so extreme that he was no longer considered dependable and his wife had left him. He was able to get a one-picture contract with Goldwyn, where he made *The Day of Faith*, a film espousing the notion that faith could cure anything. It was considered a mess and received scathing reviews.

Browning decided to climb on the wagon, and there he stayed. He succeeded in making *The Dangerous Flirt* for Gothic Pictures, a film which has a surprisingly frank approach to sex for a 1924 picture. (Evelyn Brent starred as a prudish woman whose timidity comes across as disgust to her husband on their wedding night, so he leaves her and heads for South America. She chases after him and reconciles.)

Seeing that her husband made good on his resolve, Alice Wilson Browning came back and received a part in Browning's next picture, *Silk Stocking Sal*, a dramatic story about jewel thieves. His next film after this would also concern some jewelry robbers, but would become far more famous.

Browning returned to Metro-Goldwyn-Mayer at Lon Chaney's insistence to make that film, a silent version of *The Unholy Three*. In it, Browning made very effective use of dissolves to tell the story of a jewelry gang that uses a ventriloquist dressed as a kindly old lady to sell "talking" parrots to rich families and then invades their houses when the birds mysteriously stop talking. It was the beginning of a Browning-Chaney association that would produce some of the best films in either's career including *The Blackbird, The Road to Mandalay, The Unknown, London After Midnight, The Big City, West of Zanzibar* and *Where East Is East*.

In these films, certain Browning themes emerge. As in *The Unholy Three*, the main characters are often not as they seem. This is particularly apparent in the memorable *The Unknown*. Not only does this film contain an element of deception, but with its castration symbolism, it evokes psychosexual undertones of great significance. Chaney plays Alonzo the "Armless Wonder," who throws knives with his feet. Alonzo does have arms, but he's so adept at using his feet that, as his dwarfish assistant observes, he forgets sometimes. Cojo, the assistant, is the only one who knows his master's secret.

Alonzo has fallen in love with Estrellita, the circus owner's daughter, played by a very young Joan Crawford. Estrellita has a neurotic aversion to being held by men. One night she witnesses a man with two thumbs strangling her father. That man is Alonzo, but she doesn't recognize him and doesn't even know he has arms. Alonzo decides to go ahead and marry Estrellita, but to keep her from discovering his secret, he has his arms amputated.

While he's in the hospital recovering from the operation, Estrellita recovers from her phobia and falls in love with Malabar the Strongman (Norman Kerry). Alonzo plots to have Malabar's arms torn from his body by a team of horses going in opposite directions, but is trampled to death before he can succeed.

Circuses and sexual undertones will prove prime elements of one of Browning's greatest works, *Freaks*, which we will look at in depth presently. As for deception and illusion, the "vampire" in *London After Midnight* (alas, a lost film, though there are constant rumors about it being found) turns out to be a detective on a case; the crippled minister in *The Blackbird* is actually a criminal mastermind; and "Dead Legs" Flint's stock in trade in *West of Zanzibar* is illusion.

Most of these heroes are deformed or have suffered horribly at the hands of another. Revenge is a dominant motivation, though Browning is also sharp enough to include at least brief moments of humanity in even his cruelest characters (e.g. Flint's encounter with the chimp and his final self-sacrifice in *West of Zanzibar*). They also tend to have a dramatic conflict between the better and worse sides of their natures which are often split into two identities. However, Browning frequently confounds their obsessional certainties with surprise revelations, such as when Professor Phorso is about to kill his own daughter in *Zanzibar*, or when Singapore Joe tries to protect his in *The Road to Mandalay*.

While Browning's silents often deal with the macabre and the horrible, they are not really horror films, except for the lost *London After Midnight*, where there is a deliberate effort to present a monster and to scare the audience before pulling back the curtain to unveil that it was all a trick. (Some scholars and critics have stated that it was assumed "sophisticated" audiences would not accept mysterious occurrences as actually being caused by supernatural means. While many people look back on the pre–Depression era as being more "innocent," it certainly wasn't that; however, if the supposition that a vampire is stalking victims is what drew people to the film in the first place, it strikes me as peculair to think that audiences would *prefer* that the vampire be explained away or would scoff if it was not.) Chaney would create some classic monster characterizations, especially Erik the Phantom of the Opera and the Hunchback of Notre Dame, but these were not supernatural and were for other directors.

Browning's first sound film was *The Thirteenth Chair*, which was also his first film with Bela Lugosi, who appeared as Inspector Delzante in this tale of seances and murders. However, the pair would really make their splash when Browning collaborated with Garrett E. Fort (who scripted the sound remake of *Outside the Law* for Browning) on a screen adaptation of Bram Stoker's classic horror novel *Dracula*. (This adaptation was based, not directly on the novel, but on the stage play by Hamilton Deane and John Lloyd Balderston.)

Many, many commentators have taken Browning's *Dracula* to task for being "stagey." There is no doubt that it could have been more lively and cinematic and that it does not hold up as well as James Whale's *Frankenstein*, which was made in the same year, but nevertheless this classic does have much to recommend it and is an important horror film – in fact, it's the film that virtually created horror as a genre.

While such films as *The Terror* (1928), *The Ghost Talks* (1929) and *The Cat Creeps* (1930) were also sound films which could be classified as horror, *Dracula* was, as Ron Borst has pointed out, the first horror film of the sound era that did not explain away its supernatural content. Furthermore, it introduced what has come to be known as one of the classic horror monsters – Count Dracula, the vampire. It was not the earliest vampire film (so far, the earliest title discovered is a reference to *Vampires of the Coast* in the January 1909 issue of *The Film Index*; many silents were released with vampire in the title, though most of these meant it in the sense of a "vamp," or woman who seduces young men). Nor is it the first adaptation of Stoker's novel – Friedrich Murnau's *Nosferatu* was an unauthorized adaptation that was the subject of a successful lawsuit brought by Stoker's widow. However, literally hundreds of horror films owe their ancestry to the Browning version, and many people received their first exposure to horror and vampires via this film.

Interestingly enough, as mentioned in *Famous Monsters of Filmland* #22, Lugosi was not Browning's first choice to play Dracula despite having essayed the role on the New York stage. Browning was hired because of his affinity with the proposed star of *Dracula*, Lon Chaney, who died of throat cancer shortly after completing his first and only talkie, a remake of Browning's *The Unholy Three*. The Laemmles then considered such people as Conrad Veidt, star of *The Cabinet of Dr. Caligari, Der Januskopf, The Hands of Orlac*, and *The Man Who Laughs*; Paul Muni of *Scarface* and *I Was a Fugitive from a Chain Gang* fame; Ian Keith of *The Big Trail* and *Nightmare Alley*; and William Courtenay. Chester Morris, who starred in *The Bat Whispers*, turned the role down.* Meanwhile, Lugosi campaigned vigorously for the role, cluing the impoverished studio that he was desperate for the part and that they could have his services fairly cheaply. Lugosi had not as yet mastered the English language and knew that the number of parts open to him would be limited.

Writers Garrett Fort, Louis Bromfield, and Dudley Murphy all took a crack at writing a script for the film. Eventually, Browning himself took a hand to comply with the studio's wishes that *Dracula* be made less costly, and so several of the most cinematic sequences were cut in the scripting stage. Universal offered Lugosi a mere $3,500 to play the part, but, desperate to become established, he accepted. (David Manners, who played Harker, the nominal hero in the film, received $2,000 a week over the seven-week production.)

The production cost a grand total of $441,984.90, much of that cost going into the magnificent sets of Castle Dracula, constructed under the supervision of art director Charles D. Hall from designs by Hermann Rosse

---

*Ron Borst, in doing research for Scott MacQueen's career article on director Roland West found a memo from Universal associate producer E. M. Asher asking if Chester Morris would be interested in playing Dracula starting in only two weeks! Acting on Morris' behalf, West declined.

and John Ivan Hoffman. To extend their dimensions, matte paintings on glass were mounted in front of the camera to give Dracula's lair an even more spacious look. The cinematographer was the great Karl Freund, later to be a director himself. What atmosphere the film possesses is largely due to Freund's photography and those early cobwebby sets.

Unfortunately, Browning and Freund were both working on increasingly severe budget constraints as Universal tried to tighten its belt during the Depression. Freund was forced to shoot the film in sequence, and Browning cut many of the reaction shots and special effects that would have added to the film's effectiveness. There is a story that Freund became so fed up that he once started a camera and let it run unattended. It is true that one master shot runs for three full minutes without a single cut or reaction shot even though it is apparent that there should be one – especially when Chandler tells Manners not to look at her like that when Manners retains the same bland expression he's kept throughout the scene.

Manners himself is quoted in *Hollywood Gothic*, David J. Skal's excellent history of how *Dracula* made the transition from print to screen, as saying, "Tod Browning was always off to the side somewhere. I remember being directed by Karl Freund, the photographer who came from Germany and had a great sense for film. I believe that he is the one who is mainly responsible for *Dracula* being watchable today." Skal also quotes Lugosi as saying, "The studios were hell-bent on saving money – they even cut rubber erasers in offices in half – everything that Tod Browning wanted to do was queried. Couldn't it be done cheaper? Wouldn't it be just as effective if. . .? That sort of thing. It was most dispiriting."

An indication of how effective *Dracula* could have been is given by a Spanish version starring Carlos Villarias and directed by George Melford, who directed Valentino in *The Sheik*, which was filmed evenings on the same sets by cinematographer George Robinson (who would later film *Dracula's Daughter, Son of Frankenstein* and *Abbott and Costello Meet Frankenstein*). The Spanish version, long thought lost until recently unearthed, was made for Spanish-language markets before techniques for film dubbing had been developed. It proves to be a far more fluid, atmospheric, and eerily beautiful film, and it suffered far less from studio interference. However, what it lacks, apart from a missing reel of the American print, is a presence as distinctive and memorable as Lugosi for Dracula and a Van Helsing as authoritatively commanding as Edward Van Sloan, who had played the same part opposite Lugosi in New York.

When Universal released *Dracula* on February 12, 1931 (Browning did not want to open on Friday the 13th), they billed it as "The Strangest Love Story Ever Told." Later it was billed as a horror film, and the idea of a horror genre was born. *Dracula* is no more, and in some places no less, primitive than most films released in the early sound period, but unlike many of its competitors, it has weathered the test of time and been released and shown again and again. Part of this is due to Lugosi's wonderful performance, which etches itself indelibly on the mind so that for many people the two were inextricably linked – much to Lugosi's eventual misfortune.

What is easy to overlook today is that the suave Hungarian fitted neatly into the concept of a sex symbol for the time. The character he played was titled, exotic, and mysterious. He seemed to have a strange power over women, who swooned over his mere presence. In terms of popularity, Lugosi became the object of a mini–Valentino phenomenon, receiving hundreds of letters from female fans all across the country.

But it is unfair to credit only Lugosi for *Dracula*'s success. The final film was the product of input from many talented people under the guiding hand of Browning. It stands today as a classic fairy tale, set in a Transylvania and a fog-shrouded London that never were.

After the famous "Swan Lake" theme opening, the film begins with Englishman Renfield (Dwight Frye) aboard a coach headed for the inner Balkans. Browning and Fort do what they can to build an air of expectation and dread by adding such details as cries in the background as the coach moves over the hill at sunset, a peasant mentioning that it is Walpurgis Night, and a peasant woman crossing herself at the very mention of the name Count Dracula.

Further mystery is built up by keeping the coachman who meets Renfield (actually Dracula who is supposed to be disguised but Lugosi refused to conceal his distinctive features) mute, answering Renfield's queries only with gestures. We hear wolves howling and see a bat flying over the horses' heads, apparently guiding them and cluing us that we have entered the land of the uncanny.

Charles Hall's set of Dracula's castle is magnificent, and one of the most atmospheric ever created. In fact, it so overshadows the later sets in the film, even the excellent one of Carfax Abbey, that many commentators divide the film in half, calling the castle scenes atmospheric while laying the "staginess" appellation on the rest of the film. These critics credit the relative success of the first half of Karl Freund's moody cinematography. A close look at the film reveals that Freund's cinematography is consistent throughout, that the camera is frequently static rather than dynamic, and that the so-called "stagey" portions of the film actually have more changes of scenery than the earlier section, largely played on a few vast though quite atmospheric soundstages.

There is no doubt that Browning added some peculiar touches, especially the shots of armadillos and opossums crawling around Castle Dracula, though these animals are far from native to the region. (Perhaps he expected audiences would be unfamiliar with them and suppose them to be unearthly creatures of the undead.)

Browning did not want audiences seeing vampires clambering out of their graves, so when Dracula makes his first appearance in the film, he shows Dracula's fingers emerging from the coffin lid, then discreetly pans away, returning to show the great vampire in all his evening finery. As a droll touch, he even parodies this action with a shot of a bug climbing out of its own miniature coffin, which establishes a kinship between Dracula and other creatures of the night.*

Once Renfield is inside the castle, Dracula gets to make another grand entrance, this time coming down an enormous staircase, candelabra in hand, and intoning in his unforgettable drawn-out Hungarian accent, "I am ... Dracula ... I bid you welcome." Relieved that he is in the right place, Renfield follows him up the stairs, mysteriously having to brush aside a gigantic cobweb that Dracula apparently walked right through. "The spider spinning his web for the unwary fly," observes Dracula. "The blood is the life, Mr. Renfield," he says, metaphorically spelling out the situation and providing the proper portents of doom.

Frye was often acclaimed for his portrayal of madmen and lunatics, and indeed his creepy "Heh-heh-heh" chuckle has never been equaled and he does an excellent job as a madman later in the story, but *Dracula*'s early scenes show that he was more skilled than many '30s stars in portraying normal people in dubious circumstances. You see him noticing the strangeness of the events, his surroundings, and particularly his host, but he nevertheless is there on business and does his best not to offend the Count. His reactions to things like his supposedly rich host playing servant to him or reacting peculiarly to a small cut on his finger are vivid without being overplayed. However, Frye gave himself so fully in playing his later mad scenes, a flashier kind of role, that he was forever typed and ended up struggling to get even small parts.

Browning has Lugosi pace himself very slowly, approaching with menace and confident that his prey will not get away. These slow, deliberate movements are great for creating anticipation – we clearly can see what the character intends to do, yet we continue to fear his actually doing it. The same dream-like movements also are present with the appearance of the three vampire brides, who close in on a fainting Renfield only to be gestured away by their master. But Lugosi gives Dracula a human side as well, having him delight in telling Renfield, "I never drink ... wine," or simply smile with pride at how well he's able to bid Renfield good night in his newly acquired language of English.

The trip across the channel is largely presented with stock footage from

*Ron Borst believes that this potato bug was meant to be taken as a giant bug, making *Dracula* the grandaddy of all later "big bug" films by being the first to have a "giant bug" crawling out of a supposedly "full-sized coffin."

a silent Universal film plus a few shots of a now-mad Renfield telling a wooden box, "Master, the sun is gone," or "We're here!" Still, the shot of the shadow of the dead captain tied to his wheel, followed by the discovery of Renfield with madness positively shining out of his eyes, speaks volumes.

Dracula is introduced in his new environment by showing him pausing to take refreshment from a hapless flower girl. (She disappears from the frame into the fog, screaming over some violation that the viewer is invited to imagine.) He then attends the opera, where we meet the nominal hero, John Harker (David Manners); his fiancée, Mina Seward (Helen Chandler); her father, Dr. Seward (Herbert Bunston), owner of the asylum which now houses the fly-eating Renfield; and her friend Lucy Weston (Frances Dade), who takes the occasion to recite a portion of a poem about the dead. "To die, to be really dead," Dracula responds, "that must be glorious."

"Why, Count Dracula...," responds a surprised Mina.

"There are far worse things awaiting man than death," answers the Count. This exchange does give Dracula some classical tragic overtones, implying that he too is a victim of vampirism and seeks release, though for most of the film he is simply evil incarnate hidden by a facade of high breeding and good manners. Just before this scene, we also see a demonstration of Dracula's power of hypnotism. He hasn't selected these people at random, but deliberately sends an usherette to pick out Dr. Seward and call him away.

While Mina initially stays faithful to John, Lucy is quite taken with the Count. One night he enters her bedroom. The very next shot has her dying on the operating table from a loss of blood. Meanwhile, the deterioration of Mina's relationship with Harker helps chart the prograss of her increasingly falling under the spell of her other "lover," Dracula.

By now the audience needs someone who can explain what we are dealing with, and Edward Van Sloan's Dr. Van Helsing, a Dutch professor well versed in the ways of the supernatural, is just the man to do it. After analyzing a sample of Renfield's blood, he boldly proclaims, "Gentlemen, we are dealing with the undead. Nosferatu ... I may be able to bring you proof that the superstition of yesterday can become the scientific reality of today." Renfield comes in and, after being exposed to wolfbane (no garlic here), is finally led to exclaim, "You know too much to live, Van Helsing!"

Mina is visited by Dracula and the next evening relates a dream she had about a stranger who was drawing ever nearer. Professor Van Helsing notices that she is covering her neck; exposing it, he sees two telltale tiny marks. Harker's line, "What could have caused them, Professor?" is juxtaposed with the maid announcing, "Count Dracula," negating Van Helsing's need for a response. Van Helsing is so distinguished that upon introduction, even Dracula knows of his reputation.

In most respects, the drawing room scene is like something out of the play, but in the midst of it, Browning adds something that is purely cinematic – namely, Van Helsing's discovery that Dracula casts no reflection in the mirror of a cigarette case that Harker opens. Browning has Van Helsing check this several times, continually cutting from Dracula giving his lines to a shot in the mirror where a person responds to the empty air, a purely cinematic device which obviously could not work in a play.*

Browning plays upon this by having Van Helsing invite Dracula to see something "very interesting," and then showing him the mirror. Dracula instantly reacts by smashing the case to the floor and glowering at Van Helsing; then, realizing where he is, he turns to Seward and Harker and says, "Dr. Seward, my humble apologies. I dislike mirrors. Van Helsing will explain." He turns to leave and pauses to deliver a message directly to Van Helsing: "For one who has not lived even a single lifetime, you are a wise man, Van Helsing," a nice indication that Dracula has lived for an unnaturally long span.

Naturally, Seward and Harker find Van Helsing's explanation incredible (later even Renfield will get into the act, claiming that they are participating in crazy talk for supposedly sane men), but Van Helsing points out, "The strength of the vampire is that people will not believe in him." The line hints at why it would be hard to get outside help as well as why Dracula decided to come to London in the first place. The villagers back in Transylvania were all too aware of what a vampire is and does, living fearfully in the castle's shadow.

Renfield somehow escapes his cell and comes into the drawing room while, unbeknownst to the gentlemen, Mina meets with Dracula out on the lawn. Renfield is about to warn them, having obviously become quite taken with "Miss Mina" as he calls her, when a large bat flies outside the window. Van Helsing realizes that Renfield is clamming up and tries to pressure him into revealing what he has to say by telling him, "You will die in torment if you die with innocent blood on your soul," but Renfield believes that God will have mercy on the weak-minded.

Due to cuts in the film after its preview, during which it ran 84 minutes, it seems as if Renfield might be stalking the maid in order to rape her; however, in a sequence which was cut from the film, it was made clear that he only wanted a fly on her blouse. Nine whole minutes were excised from the film in an attempt to speed up Browning's deliberate funereal pacing, and as a result various discrepancies and continuity problems cropped up. One instance of this is the subplot about Lucy.

There is a brief shot of Lucy walking through a park as well as a

---

*The original trailer has a different version of this scene that was actually done like the stage version at the time!

newspaper headline to indicate that Lucy has become a vampire, a woman in white who preys upon young children. Van Helsing's dialogues with Mina become weighted with significance, like the odd line, "And when was the next time you saw Miss Lucy *after she was buried?*" The problem with the latter half of the film is that Browning decides to have his characters relate horrifying experiences rather than show them, inevitably leading to a sense of disappointment, though it must be admitted that effects and what audiences were prepared to accept were both somewhat limited in 1931. The destruction of Lucy as a vampire is only briefly hinted at as a job that Van Helsing must do before she is simply forgotten about like those other loose threads, Dracula's three silent brides.

According to the film, a person becomes a vampire under one of two conditions. If Mina dies by day, Van Helsing thinks she will be safe, but Dracula informs him that he will make sure she dies by night and becomes a vampire. However, this is something of a dodge. Mina confides that Dracula has slit his arm and forced her to drink his blood. With their blood intermingled, Mina begins taking on vampiric aspects. She can understand when a bat squeaks to her on the terrace. She focuses on John's neck with almost a sexual hunger, her animalistic desires all too apparent in her eyes. Mina begs John to take the crucifix from the professor and then closes in on him as he cries, "Your eyes, they look at me so strangely. Mina? No, Mina, no!" However, before we can discover what terrible thing Mina is trying to do (presumably bite his neck, though other sexual connotations are possible in this unusually suggestive scene for the time), Van Helsing springs in and holds the cross up to her, causing her to recoil in terror.

The scene is disrupted by a gunshot. Martin (Charles Gerrard), the comic asylum caretaker, has tried to shoot the giant bat, but Van Helsing informs him that bullets will not work. "They're quazy," Martin says wonderingly to his female partner. "They're *all* quazy except me and you, and sometimes I'm not so certain about you," to which the woman agrees, much to Martin's exaggerated disbelief.

Meanwhile, Dracula has taken advantage of the disturbance to hypnotize the nurse (Josephine Velez) into removing the wolfbane and opening the door. He enters and then exits with Mina.

Van Helsing and Seward see that Renfield has escaped once more and follow him into Carfax Abbey. Peering through a window, they see him ascending a great staircase as Dracula and Mina, moving as they were sleepwalkers, descend. Noting that Renfield has led Van Helsing and Seward to his lair, Dracula kills the unfortunate Renfield.

We are now building to the climax of the film, but unfortunately, *Dracula* was made in the days prior to the scoring of sound films. The scenes of Dracula approaching his female victims in utter silence are made more effective by the absence of musical scoring, but the lack of a musical underpinning makes the climax come off as flat just when the film should be at its most rousing.

Dracula sweeps Mina off her feet and takes her into the catacombs of the abbey where his coffin lies. The sun has risen before he could finish draining Mina of her blood and so convert her fully into one of the undead. John is sent to look for her while Van Helsing breaks apart the top of Dracula's coffin to fashion a stake.

Dracula's death is limply conveyed by an off-screen groan (the original screams having been edited out) while Mina reacts to an imagined stake entering her chest, followed by a look of relief and normalcy. John and Mina ascend the stairs, heading into the light out of the darkness to the sound of church bells, a symbol of their marrying and living happily ever after.

While there is no question that the film is dated, *Dracula* has a quaint charm to it and is far better than its immediate successors. Not only does it feature Lugosi's memorable and classic performance, but it is a moody production that fills audiences in on plenty of arcane vampire lore, has enjoyably ominous dialogue full of double meanings, and has helped shape in some way every vampire movie made since.

Universal copyrighted their version of Count Dracula, with the consequence that subsequent vampires either were called Count Dracula but looked different, or aped Lugosi's look in the film but were given different names.

Perhaps the fairest method of assessing the original Browning *Dracula* is not to compare it with more modern films but to contrast it with the George Melford Spanish version. In comparing the two, it is easy to see that Melford's version has more atmospheric photography and he shows off those magnificent Universal sets to better advantage than in the Browning version, giving more of an impression of their breadth and scope. Like the Browning version though, the film suffers in the later scenes from the same stage play–inspired script filled with talky scenes. What keeps the Browning version the definitive one is that Carlos Villarias simply does not have the same presence as Lugosi, and with Edward Van Sloan, Dwight Frye, and the amusing Charles Gerrard as the Cockney asylum attendant, the Browning version features finer and more memorable performance than the rarely screened Spanish edition.

Universal made two official sequels to the film: *Dracula's Daughter*, in which Gloria Holden also vampirizes a female victim, giving rise to a notion that it has lesbian undertones, and *Son of Dracula*, in which the new count Dracula, played by Lon Chaney, Jr., comes to the United States under the alias Count Alucard. While Dracula appeared in other Universal productions (*House of Frankenstein, House of Dracula, Abbott and Costello Meet Frankenstein*), these were not ostensibly sequels to Browning's original but merely resurrections of the character in another form. Only *Dracula's*

Daughter is directly a sequel, picking up right where *Dracula* left off, though it makes the strange mistake of changing Van Helsing's name to *Von* Helsing (who is once more played by the dependable Edward Van Sloan).

Browning followed *Dracula* with *Iron Man*, a boxing drama starring Lew Ayres (who had wanted to play Renfield, but Universal would not let him) as a prizefighter who isn't able to see through his gold-digging wife, played by Jean Harlow. The film was remade in 1937 as *Some Blondes Are Dangerous* and in 1951 under its original title. The film is based on a novel by W. R. Burnett, whose novels provided the basis for a number of top Hollywood crime films such as *Little Caesar, High Sierra* and *The Asphalt Jungle*.

Browning's friend Harry Eales, the midget who had played the baby in both versions of *The Unholy Three*, brought the story "Spurs" by Clarence Aaron "Tod" Robbins to Browning's attention as a possible vehicle. Browning in turn brought it to the attention of Irving Thalberg at MGM. Interestingly, Thalberg relates a different version: According to Bob Thomas' biography, Thalberg ordered coscreenwriter Willis Goldbeck to give him something more horrible than *Frankenstein*, which Goldbeck did by writing *Freaks* from the Robbins story. Thalberg (again according to the Thomas biography) then selected Browning as the man to helm the project. However, given Browning's background in the circus, and his previous circus pictures, including *The Unknown* and *The Show*, as well as his writing background, it seems more likely that the project originated with Browning. Additionally, a rejected makeup of a carnival sham, a chicken-man, which was to have appeared in *West of Zanzibar* on Professor Phroso, was resurrected in *Freaks*, which also features a clown named Phroso.

The original Robbins story concerns a midget who inherits a large sum of money and is married to a bareback rider, who has a lover on the side and expects the midget to die soon. Unfortunately, she makes the mistake of humiliating the midget at their wedding by claiming that she could carry her husband on her shoulders from one end of France to the other. Her new husband, with the help of a huge, vicious dog, turns her jest into something of a reality by forcing her to carry him the prescribed number of miles, goaded on by tiny spurs which he wears. Her former lover tries to rescue her but is killed by the dog. An ironic twist is added at the end where an observer misinterprets the scene of the bareback rider carrying her husband as her continuing to needle him after their marriage.

The production caused quite a stir and a lot of opposition on the MGM lot during production, largely from studio people who objected to sharing the commisary with the genuine freaks that were employed in the film. The film was completed in nine weeks and then previewed. The film caused such a stir and sense of shock in the audience that it was drastically trimmed and an additional "happy ending" was tacked to the end of the film.

The film has had a mixed history and was largely reviled upon release. It was later acquired by Dwain Esper, the producer-director of the genuinely bizarre horror film *Maniac* (1934), which combined equal parts madness, Mary Shelley's *Frankenstein*, Edgar Allan Poe's "The Black Cat" and stock footage from *Witchcraft Through the Ages* to make one of the most unusual exploitation films ever. Esper, who was also responsible for such films as *Marihuana, Weed with Roots in Hell* and *How to Undress in Front of Your Husband*, would "four-wall" his films – that is, rent the theaters he showed them in and take all the box office receipts, bypassing the regular channels of film distribution. At various times he retitled *Freaks* under such titles as *Nature's Mistakes, The Monster Show* and *Forbidden Love*, all designed to attract a rube audience for a supposedly informative lecture and film. For a long time, the film seemed to vanish, and it was banned in Great Britain until 1963. Because of these circumstances, many have chosen – rather romantically, I might add – to see *Freaks* as causing the destruction of Browning's career, though he made three more major films before embarking on a comfortable retirement.

Most prints today seem to be struck from Esper's *Nature's Mistakes* version, to which Esper added a title crawl informing the audience that "History and Religion, Folklore and Legend abound in tales of misshapen misfits who have altered the world's course. Goliath, Caliban, Frankenstein, Gloucester, Tom Thumb and Kaiser Wilhelm [a snide joke] are just a few. . . ." It continues, ending on an upbeat note that "never again will such a story be filmed, as modern science and teratology is rapidly eliminating such blunders of nature from the world."

The actual story begins with a carnival barker setting up the story by informing us, "We didn't lie to you folks. We told you we have living, breathing monstrosities! But for an accident of birth, you might be as they are. They did not ask to be brought into this world. Their code is a law unto themselves. Offend one – and you offend them all."

Carnival barkers are notorious for shams and tall tales, allowing the audience to accept or reject as much of what follows as they want. The barker directs the crowd's attention to a particular exhibit, which we do not see, explaining that "she was once a beautiful woman. A royal prince shot himself for love of her. She was once known as the Peacock of the Air."

The scene then dissolves to Cleopatra on a flying trapeze being admired from below by Hans (Harry Earles), a midget at the circus. The shot serves as a visual metaphor for how she is far beyond Hans' reach, despite the adoring look on his upturned face.

The part of Cleopatra was played by Olga Baclanova after both Myrna Loy and Jean Harlow backed out. (The Russian actress previously had important parts in *Street of Sin* and *The Man Who Laughs*, played on Broadway, and had a noted radio program in the late '30s.)

Director Tod Browning stands in the midst of some of the cast for Freaks. *To the immediate left of Browning is the legless Johnny Eck. To the right are Pete Robinson, the Living Skeleton; Josephine-Joseph, the Half Woman-Half Man; Olga Roderick, the Bearded Lady. Seated are Koo Koo, the Bird Girl, and the Snow Twins Elvira and Jennie Lee. Embracing Browning is Schlitzie. Unidentified: dwarf in suspenders.*

Despite the film's reputation as a shocker, Browning constantly confounds the audience's expectations. The first half of the film is not a horror film at all, but a slice-of-life circus portrait with the addition of some melodrama. Despite the sensationalistic opening, Browning films the freaks matter-of-factly, deliberately inviting us to accept them as less fortunate brothers or children playing in the sun, to be admired for how well they cope with their handicaps and keep each other's spirits up. (This truly is an ensemble film, though each performer is given a chance to shine.)

On the other hand, Cleopatra and her lover, the strong man Hercules (Henry Victor), are clearly the "monsters" of the piece. (As a tonic, there are also two nice normal people, Phroso the Clown [Wallace Ford] and Venus [Leila Hyams], who accept the freaks and are meant to help with the audience's own acceptance of them.) From the start, Cleopatra seems to delight in humiliating Hans, as when she lets her cape slip and he tries to place it on her shoulders but cannot reach that far.

"Are you laughing at me?" asks Hans. "Most big people do. They don't realize I'm a man with the same feelings they have." From the start, Browning is emphasizing acceptance and respect for those who are different. Hans' fiancée, Frieda (Daisy Earles, Harry's sister), sees Cleopatra's cruelty but realizes that her love is falling under the spell of the trapeze artist.

Next we are presented with a caretaker leading a landowner to where he saw "horrible, twisted things . . . crawling, whining, laughing," but once we come upon the freaks themselves, cavorting in the sun with Madame Tetrallini (Rose Dione), they are far from menacing; rather they hide in fear from the strangers behind Tetrallini, who pleads her "children's" plight to the landlord. The landlord relents.

Next we see the various freaks leading nearly normal lives, showing how they have adjusted to their deformities. Pete Robinson, the living skeleton, is having a baby with the bearded lady (Olga Roderick); Prince Randian is both armless and legless but can roll and light his own cigarette; Johnny Eck's body cuts off below the rib cage, but he gets about quite handily on his hands and is even amazingly agile; Schlitzie, Elvira and Jennie Snow are pinheads; Martha Morris bills herself as the Armless Wonder, Frances O'Connor as the Turtle Girl, and Koo Koo as the Bird Girl.

Truly surprising for the time are the rather sophisticated jokes and sexual overtones, supposedly supplied by additional dialogue writers Edgar Allan Woolf and Al Boasberg. For example, the audience is left to conjecture about the sleeping arrangements between the Siamese Twins, Daisy and Violet Hilton, as one is married to a man the other cannot stand, while the other has a fiancé. (We also see that the kiss one gets is enjoyed by the other.) Josephine-Joseph, the Half Man-Half Woman, finds his female half attracted to Hercules, while the male half cannot stand him.

These overtones are not only sensed among the freaks, but extend to the others in the film as well. When Venus tells Phroso, "You're a pretty good kid," he replies enigmatically, "You're darn right I am, and you should have caught me before my operation." There is even a scene where we are led to believe that she is talking to him while he is in a bathtub, until Browning reveals that the tub is a prop Phroso is carrying around with him. It's also plain that Venus lived with Hercules in the past and now does not like him.

Cleopatra gets pretty steamy when, after asking Hercules how many eggs he would like, she takes off her bathrobe, flaunting her figure in a black nightie, and asks, "How do you like them?" Hercules answers "Not bad," obviously not in response to the question about the eggs.

Obviously jealous and upset, Frieda tries to confront Cleopatra over her toying with Hans, who has bought her expensive gifts, including a platinum necklace. Unfortunately, she lets slip that Hans has inherited a fortune, and so Cleopatra schemes to marry him, chillingly pointing out, "Midgets are not strong . . . they could grow sick. . . ."

This is followed by the famous wedding feast scene in which the freaks gather together to celebrate Hans' wedding and accept Cleopatra as one of them. "We accept her / One of us / One of us / One of us / Gooble, gabble / One of us," they chant over and over again. Meanwhile, Cleopatra clearly has had too much champagne to drink and kisses Hercules, much to her new husband's obvious displeasure. She secretly pours the contents of a small phial into Hans' champagne bottle. Except for Frieda, the freaks are boisterous and oblivious. A dwarf (Angelo Rosstitto, who went on to appear in such films as *The Corpse Vanishes, Scared to Death, Daughter of Horror, Dracula vs. Frankenstein* and *Mad Max – Beyond Thunderdome*) fills up a large cup and passes it from one freak to the next, each one taking a sip. When he presents it to Cleopatra, she loses control, yelling "Freaks! Freaks!" at the wedding guests, and then showering them with the remaining contents of the goblet.

Hans grows weaker and weaker as Cleopatra starts poisoning him. We now see the freaks from a different light as they emerge from various locations, keeping an eye on the treacherous Cleopatra. The freaks keep her under constant watch, and Hans secretly begins to spit out the medicine she gives him. "*Tonight,*" he whispers to one of his diminutive friends.

That night the carnival packs up and begins to move away to their next destination. Browning makes the scene more interesting by now adopting the freaks' point of view as Johnny hops along, looking for shelter from the breaking storm. Inside Hans' wagon, Cleo is trying to give him more medicine, but he insists on seeing the bottle she has poured from. She turns and sees various little people holding weapons at her and flees into the woods.

Hercules decides to quiet Venus permanently, and Phroso comes to her rescue. The pair have a tremendous brawl, resulting in Venus' carriage crashing. Hercules and Phroso tumble out and as Hercules prepares to finish Phroso, the freaks come to his rescue by throwing a knife into Hercules. Phroso takes Venus and scrams while the assorted freaks close in on Hercules for their revenge, flashing knives.

What follows is one of the most disturbing and memorable sequences in the Browning canon. As Hercules slips in the mud, lightning flashes reveal the little people squirming towards him, each with a weapon in hand or mouth. Hercules moans and tries to get away. Cleopatra has continued running but stops to look back. In a lightning flash, she sees that crawling freaks are close behind, and she screams.

This sequence is very brief but powerful. It marks the one time in the film when the freaks do not seem human or sympathetic, when common fears about creeping, menacing things in the dark seem to come true – though unquestionably Cleopatra and Hercules remain the villains of the piece. The way the film is presently cut, we assume that the freaks murdered

Hercules, but the original cut of the film had a brief epilogue in "Tetrallini's Freaks and Music Hall" in which the mighty strong man now sings in falsetto, indicating that the freaks emasculated him.

The present cut does take us back to the hall we saw at the beginning, where the Barker now shows us his highly unusual attraction – Cleopatra, now a quadruple amputee with only one good eye, in a feathered suit, playing a "chicken woman." She cannot talk so much as squawk, indicating that her tongue may have been cut out as well. Was the barker telling a true story?

Finally, there is a very brief coda in which Phroso and Venus come smiling to visit Hans at his estate. They bring Frieda with them, and Hans and Frieda hug each other with tears in their eyes and smile back at their friends, a sentimental upshot that does nothing to diminish the power of the previous scenes.

Modern prints run about 64 minutes, but the original film was longer. It is doubtful that the missing scenes will ever be found or restored. The film was rarely screened, and only recently shown on Ted Turner's TNT cable channel, its first televised appearance.

Despite the strong horrific punch of the finale, *Freaks* stands more as a touching and occasionally artfully humorous plea for understanding, for the need to treat those different from ourselves with dignity and respect and not to demean or underestimate them as Cleopatra and Hercules do. That Browning succeeds in this intention with most audiences is indeed a sincere tribute to his artistry, though the negative reception the film received may have discouraged filmmakers from using or exploiting deformities apart from dwarves or a few made-up hunchbacks in horror films (overlooking the acromegalic Rando Hatton's "Creeper" films) for many years to come. The Hilton sisters did prove adept enough at comedy that in 1950 they were starred in an exploitation film known as *Chained for Life*, which supposedly had a sequel, *Torn by the Knife*.

Most people are repelled by deformities and have no interest in seeing genuinely deformed persons on the screen. A monster in a monster movie is unreal and temporarily deformed by makeup, rather than being genuinely afflicted. Still, deformities were to appear in such films as *House of the Damned* (1961), *She-Freak* (an uncredited, semi-remake of the Browning classic), *Mutations* (1972, directed by famed color cinematographer Jack Cardiff), Michael Winner's *The Sentinel*, and David Lynch's *The Elephant Man*.

Following *Freaks*, Browning produced and directed *Fast Workers*, also for MGM, which I have not seen. Stuart Rosenthal describes the plot as "a construction worker tries to prove to his pal that the girl he plans to marry is a gold-digger."

It was a couple of years before Browning embarked on his next project, tentatively titled *Vampires of Prague* with a screenplay by Guy Endore (writer of *Werewolf of Paris*) and Bernard Schubert. The film, eventually released as *Mark of the Vampire*, was an unofficial remake of Browning's earlier *London After Midnight*. Sadly, it is a tired script bereft of the inventive ideas and dialogue of the original *Dracula*, though lighting cameraman James Wong Howe does a superior job of photographing the film and many of the sets and costumes are of a high order as might be expected from an MGM production.

The story begins in the Czechoslovakian village of Visoka, where Sir Karell Borotyn (Holmes Herbert) has been found murdered, his body drained of blood. Naturally, rumors of vampires start spreading throughout the superstitious village; however, police inspector Neumann (Lionel Atwill) can find no clues. Irene Borotyn (Elizabeth Allan), Sir Karell's daughter, is understandably distraught, a situation which is not helped by a visit from Baron Otto (Jean Hersholt) and her fiancé, Fedor (Henry Wadsworth), who postulates that Sir Karell became a victim of Count Mora (Bela Lugosi) and his daughter Luna (Carol Borland), vampires suspected of inhabiting an abandoned castle on the edge of town.

When Luna makes a surprise appearance in Irene's house, a specialist, Dr. Zelen (Lionel Barrymore) is called in. He, too, professes to believe that vampires are responsible. Dr. Zelen and Baron Otto make a trip to Sir Karell's crypt, but his body is no longer there! Perhaps he too has become one of the undead. They resolve to search the spooky castle.

Joined by Fedor, they discover Sir Karell's body in an old chest. Otto argues for destroying the vampire at once, but Zelen dissuades him, insisting that will only bring the wrath of the other vampires down on their heads. Especially memorable is a moment when they catch a glimpse of Luna, with giant batwings, flying across the castle.

At this point, *Mark of the Vampire* becomes a completely different movie. Dr. Zelen reveals that the vampires were an elaborate ruse to try to get Otto to confess to the murder of Sir Karell, but since that has failed he will resort to plan B, which is to hypnotize him and recreate the scene of the crime.

An actor is hired to play Irene's father and after greeting Otto, Irene leaves. Otto pleads for the hand of Irene but is refused. He then mimes pouring something into his host's drink, waiting until the draught has taken its effect, and then reenters and mimes draining the blood from "Sir Karell's" body with a hypodermic needle so that his death can be attributed to vampires. Naturally, Dr. Zelen unhypnotizes him and leads him away to be taken into custody. We see the "vampires" once more, removing their makeup. Lugosi, who contributes a silent, menacing presence to his brief role as Count Mora, which mostly consists of him walking through atmospheric sets, gives his only lines in the film: "This vampire business has given me a great idea for a new act. Did you watch me? I gave all of me. I was greater than any real vampire!"

This ending has led many horror fans to cry cheat. It makes them feel that a wonderful film has been ruined. Sad to say, apart from its excellent technical values, *Mark of the Vampire* was not a wonderful film even before its twist ending. Compared to earlier excursions into the subject, it seems rather dull, parodying the very idea of vampires.

An interesting bit that was cut from the film involved a depiction of the vampires' background in which Count Mora supposedly kills his daughter/ lover Luna before committing suicide himself. While the explanation was cut, Mora does walk throughout the film with a bullet hole in his right temple.

The largely excellent cast unfortunately gives uniformly lackluster performances, with an especially disappointing performance by the usually fine Lionel Barrymore in the lead.

Ace makeup man William Tuttle, who won a special Oscar for his work in George Pal's *The Seven Faces of Dr. Lao*, worked on the film as an apprentice to makeup man Jack Dawn. In *The Films of Bela Lugosi* by Richard Bojarksi, he has this to say about Browning and the films:

> The crew and I didn't like to work for director Tod Browning. We would try to escape being assigned one of his productions because he would overwork us until we were ready to drop from exhaustion. As far as Browning was concerned, he was ruthless. He was determined to get everything he could on film. If the crew didn't do something right, Browning would grumble: "Mr. Chaney would have done it better." He was hard to please. I remember he gave the special effects men a hard time because they weren't working the mechanical bats properly. Though he didn't drive his actors as hard, he gave Lionel Barrymore a difficult time during a scene. Lugosi's performance, however, satisfied Browning. . . . Lugosi did his own makeup for the film. I added the bullet hole wound in his head.

Forrest J Ackerman interviewed Carroll Borland in *Famous Monsters of Filmland #59*, where she revealed that she had toured with Lugosi as Lucy in the stage play of *Dracula,** which led to her being auditioned for the part of Luna. Ackerman asked her about what sort of director Browning was, to which she replied:

> He was very easy to work with. He was used to working with pros, and these were the days right after – I'm not going to date myself that way and say right after talkies came in – but near enough to the time when the majority of actors in Hollywood were theater trained. And all of the people in the picture knew their business, and he would tell them

*This claim is somewhat questionable given Borland's age and experience during her brief association with Lugosi as a friend.

what he wanted [snapping her fingers] and they'd give it to him. Jimmy Howe, the photographer, was, you know, almost a genius. I loved working with him. . . . We would work late at nite, but he mostly had his difficulties with the young lovers.

Along with *The Mask of Fu Manchu* and Rouben Mammoulian's classic version of *Dr. Jekyll and Mr. Hyde*, *Mark of the Vampire* has been a rarely screened MGM film, running a scant 60 minutes, until they all turned up on TNT in recent years. Metro-Goldwyn-Mayer did not find the horror field as lucrative as they had hoped and quickly abandoned it, though they made one more attempt with Browning in the form of *The Devil-Doll*, based on the novel *Burn Witch Burn* by Abraham Merritt (not to be confused with the film *Burn Witch Burn* aka *Night of the Eagle* based on Fritz Leiber's classic horror novel *Conjure Wife*, which had previously been filmed as *Weird Woman* by Reginald LeBorg. For more on that film, see chapter on LeBorg.)

Browning came up with the screen story for *The Devil-Doll*, which was then turned into a screenplay by Guy Endore, Garrett Fort and Erich von Stroheim. Once more Browning turned to Lionel Barrymore to star. Barrymore played Paul Lavond, a man framed by his three business partners who escapes from prison along with a man named Marcel (Henry B. Walthall).

The film opens with the police searching for them along a bayou, but the pair make it to Marcel's wife's hut, where she and a half-wit female servant have been continuing Marcel's "humanitarian" work of devising a way to shrink human beings to the size of dolls, requiring less food and thereby solving the problem of world hunger. Before he was put into jail, Marcel's experiments were only partially successful. He was able to shrink test animals down, but the process would destroy the animals' brains, leaving them stiff and frozen until animated by the will of a human being. While in prison, Marcel thinks he has discovered the solution to his problem which will allow the shrunken beings to retain their intelligence.

While an amazed Lavond gets a demonstration of the results, he is interested in only one thing—revenge. Waking up late at night, he discovers that the couple have shrunken down their half-wit servant, but before the process can be completed, the excitement becomes too much and Marcel suffers a fatal heart attack. His crippled wife then turns to Lavond to help her continue her husband's work, and Lavond decides that the amazing process might well be useful in his scheme of revenge.

Back in Paris, Lavond's three wealthy business associates hear of his escape and, fearing reprisal, offer first a 50,000-franc and then a 100,000-franc reward for his capture. Lavond comes to Paris anyway, disguised as an old woman, and with Marcel's widow opens a doll shop. He discovers that his mother is an invalid, his wife committed suicide, and his daughter, Lorraine (Maureen O'Sullivan), doesn't believe in his innocence and hates him bitterly for bringing shame to the family and leaving them in poverty. Her loathing is so intense, she cannot even accept her boyfriend's offer of marriage because of the stain on her family name.

Lavond is touched by her plight and pained that her feelings mean that he must remain estranged from her. He proceeds to ruthlessly pursue and exact his revenge by shrinking one ex-partner and paralyzing another. He threatens the third with death unless he confesses. Trimming the demand for a confession from the death threat, the remaining partner goes to the police and demands protection. Just as the time is up, and both a "devil-doll" (one of the shrunken figures animated by Lavond's will with a miniature stiletto dipped in a paralyzing fluid) and the clock are about to strike, the man breaks down and confesses to framing Lavond, clearing his name.

Satisfied now that his revenge is complete, Lavond realizes that his genuine guilt in revenging himself on his partners precludes a reunion with Lorraine and decides to flee. However, he makes the mistake of telling Marcel's crippled widow that he doesn't plan to continue Marcel's work and plans to destroy the equipment. She retaliates by animating a doll against him; when that fails, she attempts to blow up the both of them, succeeding in destroying herself and the equipment in the doll shop.

The film ends with Lavond pretending to be a friend of Lorraine's father and passing along a message of comfort to her on the Eiffel Tower, giving his blessings on her forthcoming marriage to her boyfriend now that Lavond's name has been cleared. While she and the boyfriend are left in joy in the clouds at the top of the tower, Lavond descends in the elevator, a symbol of his descent from grace.

The film is less stagey and more cinematic than most of Browning's other sound films. The special effects are very well done for the time and rather cleverly executed, often "sandwiched" between a normal-sized foreground figure and a standard set background. Browning's eye for effective angles and interesting images is demonstrated to good effect. There are also the Browning story staples of the bizarre, the crippled character, the deep desire for revenge and the painful realization that in pursuing that desire, the hero has in turn cut himself off from society. Often overlooked in favor of Ernest Schoedsack's *Dr. Cyclops*, an early color horror film about a mad scientist (Albert Dekker) shrinking things out in the jungle (based on a Henry Kuttner short story), *The Devil-Doll* is in most ways a better film and an obvious influence.

It was three years (1939) before Browning made his last film, *Miracles for Sale*, once more for MGM. The film is well noted for its striking opening in which a military officer orders a female spy into a child's coffin (her head and feet protrude) and she is then machine-gunned in half because her information led to the bombing of a schoolhouse. This elaborate setup is quickly revealed to be a "miracle for sale," an illusion offered by ace magician Michael Morgan (Robert Young). However, the remainder of the film is described by most contemporary commentators as a mediocre murder melodrama in the *Thirteenth Chair* mold.

Browning retired to live in Santa Monica. Five years later, *Variety* mistakenly published his obituary, though Browning was to live until 1962. He died shortly before a screening of *Freaks* at the Venice Film Festival helped to revive an interest in his work. And yet somehow it does seem appropriate that the magic-loving Browning managed to manufacture a demise, escape it, and depart quietly unnoticed in the wings, leaving behind a memorable legacy of movie miracles.

John Carpenter (1948–   )

Dark Star (1974); *Assault on Precinct 13* (1976); *Halloween* (1978); *The Fog;
Escape from New York* (1981); *The Thing* (1982); *Christine* (1983); *Starman*
(1984); *Big Trouble in Little China* (1985); *Prince of Darkness* (1987); *They Live*
(1988).
TELEVISION: *Someone Is Watching Me* (1978); *Elvis* (1979).

"I think I have always known I have wanted to direct motion pictures,"
John Carpenter wrote to *Photon* magazine in issue #24 after completing his
first feature film, *Dark Star*.
He went on:

> Sometime in 1953 in a theater in Rochester, New York, my mother
> took me to see *It Came from Outer Space* in 3D. The first shot I
> remember in the picture is a long shot of a barren desert landscape. The
> camera is panning with a meteor plunging down out of the sky toward
> earth. The second shot is of the meteor coming straight into the camera
> and exploding. In 1953 that meteor came directly out of the screen and
> blew up in my face. I deserted my mother and dashed up the aisle in
> terror. But by the time I had reached the lobby, I was in love with
> movies.

John Carpenter was born on January 15, 1948, in Bowling Green, Kentucky. When he was eight years old, his father gave him an 8mm camera
and he began experimenting with making his own fantastic films, heavy on
action and special effects. He also wrote three issues of his own fanzine,
Fantastic Films Illustrated, as well as contributing to the burgeoning fanzine movement of the sixties.
He attended USC's famous film school (though because he never fulfilled
a foreign language requirement, he never officially graduated), where he
became involved in various student productions. The most famous of these
was *The Resurrection of Bronco Billy* on which Carpenter did some second
unit work as well as cowriting, editing, and scoring. The short went on to
win an Academy Award.
Carpenter came up with the idea for a lengthy student project called
The Electric Dutchman about four men whose job it is to drop bombs on suns

117

that are about to go supernova. During one of the runs, a bomb gets stuck in the bomb bay and one of the men goes EVA and tries to loose the bomb only to accidentally detonate it. Left without a ship, he enters a planet's atmosphere and burns up à la the ending to Ray Bradbury's classic sf story "Kaleidoscope." He pitched his idea to a fellow USC student, Dan O'Bannon, who had made an impressive short known as *Bloodbath*. O'Bannon suggested making the bombs talking bombs and added the character of Commander Powell, who has died before the picture begins and was apparently the motivating force behind these men. In essence, it was O'Bannon's idea to transform it into a "Waiting for Godot" in outer space.

The result was *Dark Star*, named after the ship designed by Ron Cobb and manufactured by Greg Jein. The original short was 45 minutes long and cost a mere $6,000 to produce using the equipment at USC. This section was shot on 16mm and comprises the beginning and end of the final film. The pair designed the film as a showcase – to show what they could do and, they hoped, lead them to jobs in the film industry. Carpenter acted as producer, director, cowriter and composer on the film, while O'Bannon was cowriter, actor, editor, set builder, and special effects supervisor. Carpenter also had to replace the lackluster performance of one of the actors with his own voice, meticulously dubbing in the lines for the character of Talby. However, when the pair scouted around the major studios, no one seemed impresed. Finally, Jack Harris offered them $60,000 to pad the film out to 83 minutes and blow it up to 35mm.

Despite a good reception at Filmex, the film never took off the way its creators expected it to. O'Bannon would later cannibalize some of the ideas from *Dark Star* to script the all-time science fiction/fright classic *Alien* and finally had his film debut with the delightful *Return of the Living Dead*.

Dark Star is a quirkly little film that stands out in Carpenter's ouvre. The film is not polished, but the love and dedication lavished on it shine through its limitations. It is a very personal and personable film, highly dependent upon the establishment of the general malaise infecting the crew members of the *Dark Star* and a sardonic, sometimes frantic sense of humor. There isn't another science fiction film like it, and naturally it became a cult classic.

Dark Star does not have much in the way of horror except the horror of *ennui* and later the terror of having to deal with a mechanical being who is committed to a fatal course of action. Carpenter practices his suspense technique by cross-cutting between Doolittle (Brian Narelle) and Bomb #20 (voice by O'Bannon) and a scuffle between Pinback (O'Bannon in a fine comic performance) and Boiler (Carl Kuniholm) over what to do about it. Carpenter's favorite director is Howard Hawks, and like Hawks he insisted that the narrative be linear and straightforward. No flashy camera angles or flashbacks, just well-composed shots of group action. He even sets up his trademark prowling camera through the limited corridors of the *Dark Star*. All in all, a very impressive and promising debut.

Finding that *Dark Star* was not the success that he hoped it would be, Carpenter went back to square one and started trying to peddle scripts to the various studios. His script *Eyes* was about a woman who has a psychic experience – she sees whatever a skid row slasher sees while he is killing. At one point, she even starts envisioning a nightmare that the killer has. The script was sold to Columbia and Jon Peters as a possible vehicle for Barbra Streisand, who backed out because of the amount of violence in it. Then someone came up with the "bright" idea of making the killer someone the heroine is close to, possibly her lover, and Carpenter left in disgust. (The picture was finally made as *The Eyes of Laura Mars* starring Faye Dunaway and directed by Irvin Kershner. It failed to deliver on its promising premise.)

Carpenter sold a western, *Blood River*, to John Wayne's Batjac Productions, but that was never produced. For producer Harry Gittis, Carpenter wrote *Black Moon Rising*, a fantasy-adventure about a car-stealing ring that takes a rather special sports car and the four men who must assault a building to get it back. Years later, the script was rewritten and released by New World starring Tommy Lee Jones and directed by Harley Corkliss (*Battletruck* aka *Warriors of the 21st Century*) in January of 1986.

In an interview in *Phobos*, Carpenter explained the genesis of his next film this way:

> I was approached by a backer from Philadelphia who said, "I have money for a movie . . . what do you want to do?" And I said, "Well, that sounds great. I want to do a modern day western.". . . You can't really do a western unless you get John Wayne or Bronson and Eastwood . . . and we couldn't afford them, so we made one making the Indians the youth gangs . . . let's do a classic . . . the guys holed up inside the jail . . . like *Rio Bravo*. So we came up with this.

Originally titled *Anderson's Alamo*, it became *Siege* and was finally released by its distributor as *Assault on Precinct 13*. The film was written and directed by Carpenter, who also composed the music and coedited the film with future partner Debra Hill under the pseudonym John T. Chance, the name of Wayne's heroic character in *Rio Bravo*. The film takes the same basic situation as *Rio Bravo* (men trapped inside a jail surrounded by hostile outsiders) and plays it up for suspense and action. In my somewhat heretical opinion, he surpasses Hawks in these departments, but the film suffers from weak performances and some poorly scripted lines, and it lacks the characterization that makes the Hawks film a classic.

Here the horror is of relentless, senseless, mindless violence being unleashed. Near the beginning of the film, Carpenter breaks an unwritten taboo by having the gang gun down an innocent young girl as she complains about getting the wrong flavored ice cream cone. This scene immediately establishes the gang as having no respect for human life and being totally ruthless, but it turned many people off. Carpenter plays with the audience, setting up several prospective targets, effectively building suspense. We know these men will fire at somebody, but when? And, of course, because they *don't* fire several times, when they finally do, it comes as a surprise and a shock. Additionally, Carpenter decided to vary the typical Hollywood killing by having the gang use a silencer. Instead of reacting to a loud bang or gunshot, the victim mysteriously crumbles, seemingly hit from nowhere at random. No one is safe on these streets.

Paranoia grows as the gang assaults the almost abandoned Precinct 13 (most everyone having moved to a new building in a new location) because a fellow gang member is being held prisoner there. Inside are only a black cop, two convicts, two women, and the father of the girl who was murdered and who has killed one of the gang members in return and is seeking sanctuary. An interesting relationship of mutual respect develops under fire between Officer Leigh (Laurie Zimmer) and Napoleon Wilson (Darwin Joston), one of the cons. Leigh is intended to be a typical Hawksian heroine: cool, detached, professional, and just as capable as (maybe even more than) the men around her.

The interracially mixed gang makes for an effective horror element. They are never personalized. The most any of them says is, "For the 6," apparently referring to six comrades slain when they made a raid on an arsenal, but it could also refer to the six people trapped inside the precinct. Carpenter's approach to them has been likened to Romero's approach to the zombies in *Night of the Living Dead*. After a blood ritual in which they prepare for the assault, they are the relentless enemy, not stopping no matter what the cost. They have numerical superiority and are dedicated to achieving their goal. (The situation is somewhat analogous to that in the excellent and highly suspenseful *Zulu*.)

Though containing many standard exploitation elements, the film is definitely better crafted than most exploitation films, presenting an interesting situation in an exciting and suspenseful manner. However, despite successful runs in the inner cities, the film was mostly critically ignored and sank without a trace in the United States. In December of 1977, it played at the London Film Festival, where it garnered a tremendous response. Producer Irwin Yablans, formerly connected with Turtle Releasing, was setting up a new company called Compass International. He noted the attention Carpenter was getting from critics at the festival and contacted him about making a picture to be called *The Babysitter Murders*.

Meanwhile, Carpenter continued scripting, selling *Escape* to 20th Century–Fox and *Prey* to Warner Bros., neither of which got made. However,

Warner Bros. did contact Carpenter in 1976 to write about a woman being terrorized in a high-rise in Chicago. After writing the script, Carpenter was asked if he would like to direct it. It was shot in 18 days and Carpenter was able to keep control of it. He insisted on not providing coverage, shooting just what he needed to get the sequences to cut together. This film introduced him to his future wife, actress Adrienne Barbeau. It also finally allowed him to have a professional directing credit which would allow him to enter the Directors Guild.

The TV movie appeared as *Someone's Watching Me* (originally titled *High Rise*) and starred Lauren Hutton. Hutton plays Leigh Michaels, a woman who moves into her dream apartment only to become the object of a sadistic peeping Tom. *Someone Is Watching Me* clearly owes a debt to Hitchcock's *Rear Window*, with Carpenter doing a great twist on the scene where Grace Kelly investigated Raymond Burr's apartment by having Lauren Hutton check out the mysterious voyeur's apartment only to look back through the telescope focused on her own apartment and see her friend Sophie (Barbeau) being attacked. Carpenter is very good at providing an atmosphere of expectancy. We are constantly certain that something bad will happen at any moment, and this gives the film the needed *frisson* to succeed despite the weak dialogue and chracterizations. Another device Carpenter uses is making his killer "faceless" through most of the film. We don't see him much on camera, but rather see what he is seeing through elaborate point-of-view shots, allowing the audience to "become" the killer and see things from his perspective. This device of subjective tracking proved to be one of the key elements in Carpenter's next film, *Halloween*.

Halloween is an important horror film for a number of reasons, many of them having nothing to do with the art of making good films but everything to do with the business of making movies. Made for a mere $300,000, the film grossed $50 million, making it the most successful independent film of all time. Explains *Halloween*'s cowriter and producer Debra Hill, the decision to make a horror film was definitely a commercial one. Said Hill when I interviewed her, "The horror genre is one of the most profitable film genres and it doesn't require a big budget. . . . We decided to do a horror film because you don't need a Jane Fonda or a Robert Redford to compete in today's markets."

Not only did its huge financial success kick off Carpenter's film career in a big way, it started a trend of imitation maniac-on-the-loose films that hoped at least partially to match its phenomenal success. However, what the others largely missed was *Halloween*'s style, playfulness and restraint. Though the film generates a feeling of constant menace, its violence is brief and overall practically bloodless, Carpenter going for the Val Lewton tradition of suggestion rather than showing. (This is particularly apparent in a mini-homage to *The Leopard Man* when Laurie is being pursued by the

Shape and cannot open her own door. She is forced to wait outside and unprotected until her charge, Tommy, can come and open the door.)

Executive producer Irwin Yablans said in an article by Lou Gaul in *Midnight Marquee*: "Carpenter said he'd do the movie under three conditions:
'I want complete autonomy; I want no interference; I want to write the
music.' I said fine, and told him I only had one question, 'Can you do it for
$300,000?' "

After the titles, Carpenter started the film with a bravura opening shot,
a semi-homage to the classic opening of Welles' *Touch of Evil*. In one prolonged take, we follow a point-of-view shot as the camera approaches a
house, looks through a side window at a young girl and her boyfriend necking who then decide to go upstairs, enters the house, picks up a large, sharp
knife, and sees the boyfriend coming down the stairs and putting on his shirt
and promising to call tomorrow (many people interpret that the pair had
made love, but it could not have been much of a session, only seconds having
passed since they went upstairs). The camera goes upstairs, pausing to pick
up and put on a halloween mask, then enters a bedroom to see clothes scattered about and the young woman sitting naked at her nightstand.
"Michael!" she protests before there is the sound of a knife plunging into
her. With a side glance we see the bloodied knife swing up and down a couple of times and the camera leaves the room, goes downstairs and outside.
Police arrive and someone snatches off the mask. Finally we reach the first
cut as the murderer is revealed to be a six-year-old child in a clown outfit.
The camera tracks up and back to end the scene.

Carpenter took advantage of a new kind of gyroscopic camera, a Panaglide camera, to avoid having to lay down nearly impossible tracks for this
scene. The Panaglide has a unique floating quality that adds to the nightmarish dreaminess of the scene. Cinematographer Dean Cundey's crisp
work is of a high standard for an independent film and makes excellent use
of shadows and reflections. This film began a long association between Cundey and Carpenter.

The film then jumps ahead 15 years. Dr. Sam Loomis (Donald Pleasence) accompanies a nurse to the insane asylum in Smith's Grove on a rainy
night. Loomis explains that Michael Myers must be kept under sedation
when he is taken to see the judge, that he must never get out. However,
once they reach the asylum, it is apparent that something is wrong. There
are patients wandering about the lawn. Carpenter later added a sequence
to the television version of the film where Loomis goes to the gate, Michael
jumps on top of the station wagon the nurse waits in, pulls her out and
drives away. (Loomis' name is an in-joke reference to the John Gavin
character in Hitchcock's *Psycho*.)

Back in Haddonfield, Illinois, Laurie Strode (Jamie Lee Curtis) is instructed to leave the key under the mat at the old Meyers house – no one has

lived there since that awful night when Michael killed his sister 15 years ago. As she approaches the house, we hear breathing and glimpse a Shape (Nick Castle) inside. From here on Carpenter plays a cat-and-mouse game in which Laurie continually glimpses the Shape only to have him disappear. He establishes a connection between them when she leaves the Myers house singing, "I wish I had you all alone; just the two of us," a playful bit of fore-shadowing, just as the Shape/Michael's figure enters into the right fore-ground area.

Carpenter frequently follows the Shape in his travels around town, but always denies us a look at his face. We know he is there and he is going to kill, but when? All we know is that it is inevitable, like the "fate" that a teacher drones on about in a classroom scene as a distracted Laurie looks out the window.

One area in which the film exceeds the standards of many exploitation films is the believability of the female characters. Laurie is established as being smart but feels her intelligence is keeping her from getting dates. We sense a feeling of frustration and jealousy towards her more gregarious and outgoing friends Annie (Nancy Loomis) and Lynda (P. J. Soles). Annie is en-couraging to Laurie, but not much of a role model; she foolishly smokes pot while driving. (Her father, Sheriff Leigh Brackett, named after one of Howard Hawks' screenwriters, fails to notice the residue odor in her car – so much for confidence in the town's law enforcement.) Lynda is just looking forward to using the upstairs bedroom with her boyfriend, Bob (John Mich-ael Graham), while Annie is babysitting young Lindsey downstairs.

Early on the idea of the boogey man is raised when some of little Tommy's friends try to scare him. Tommy's favorite reading material is comic books with names like "Tarantula Man" and he begins to fear and finally see this boogey man. (While kids bump into the Shape early in the film, he never hurts them. There seems to be a strange kind of kinship, as if Michael's 21-year-old body still has a six-year-old mind.) When Tommy starts ranting about seeing the boogey man to his babysitter, Laurie, she doesn't believe him even though she's been seeing strange things herself lately.

It is Halloween. While trick-or-treating begins in daylight, Loomis dis-covers that Michael has killed a truck driver and stolen his sister's grave-stone. He warns Sheriff Brackett about the danger but insists that he keep quiet and only have his men on the lookout lest there be a panic. Loomis then spends most of the film waiting by Michael's old house, hoping and expect-ing that he will return, waiting for his confrontation with his patient whom he sees as nothing less than evil itself.

The houses are dark with the lights off because the kids (Lindsey and Tommy) are watching the horror festival on "Doctor Dementia," which in-cludes *The Thing* and *Forbidden Planet* (though one scene is shown out of sequence). Annie attracts the Shape's attention after she removes her blouse and jeans when she spills something on them. She drives herself into a panic when she accidentally locks herself in an outside washing room but is rescued by Lindsey. She then escorts the little girl over to Laurie who, ever the "girl scout," agrees to take care of her while Annie plans to drive off and pick up her grounded boyfriend.

When Annie first goes to the car, the door is locked and she has to head back into her house to get the keys. When she returns she fails to notice (until too late) that the door is now unlocked and that the windows of the car have been fogged from the inside. The Shape springs into action, strangling her.

Lynda and Bob arrive and, learning that Lindsey is at Laurie's, decide to go upstairs to make a little whoopie. Afterwards, Lynda sends Bob down to get her a beer, but poor Bob is impaled when the Shape springs out of the closet. In a memorably playful touch, the Shape gets a bedsheet and Bob's glasses and stands in the bedroom door, pretending to be Bob. After she fails to get a rise out of him, Lynda decides to call Laurie and ignore him, but the Shape makes his move and strangles her.

Laurie is not sure if the strange sounds she has heard are another of Lynda's gags, but she is worried enough to go and investigate. In the upper bedroom, she sees a strange tableau – Annie stretched across the bed with Judith Myers' gravestone over her head and a grinning jack o'lantern by the nightstand. Suddenly, in a cleverly orchestrated shock, Bob's body swings down and Laurie uncovers Lynda's remains. She has attracted the Shape's attention; he comes after her, and she runs back to Tommy's house.

She sends Tommy and Lindsey upstairs but somehow senses that the Shape is inside. The Shape attacks and she stabs him with a knitting needle. He drops the knife and falls to the floor. However, this resolution seems too sudden and too pat. Sure enough, as Laurie, much to the frustration of the audience, leaves the knife behind and goes upstairs to tell the children that the boogey man is dead, the Shape appears in the back of the frame behind them. Shoving the kids into one closet, Laurie hides in another behind a louvered door. The Shape attacks the secured door with his butcher knife, and Laurie fashions a weapon out of a coat hanger and stabs him, causing him to drop the knife. She then stabs him with the knife.

She lets the kids out and tells them to run for the police, which attracts the attention of Loomis, who has spotted the stolen station wagon and is looking for Michael. While Laurie looks ahead, we can see Michael sitting up again in the background. As the pair engage, Laurie stops him momentarily by pulling off the mask he has been wearing. The Shape stops his attack to put on the mask again, thus giving Loomis a clear shot at him. Loomis ends up blowing him away and sends the Shape tumbling out the second story balcony window. However, when Laurie and Loomis look down again, the Shape is gone. He really is the boogey man and is as unkillable as evil itself.

With *Halloween*, Carpenter showed himself to be more concerned with style than content. The film does not have much depth or motivation, but is extremely effective in manipulating audiences into desired responses. He has the camera glide around so much that the audience is kept off balance – are we experiencing the killer's point of view now, or just the director's? Carpenter also composed a very simple but effective score for the film, improving on his previous scores. The music establishes tense moments and seems to count the seconds until something will happen, preparing us for something but again not cluing us as to when it might happen. Its very repetitiveness also makes it the equivalent of the irritating sounds in William Castle's shock gags.

The acting on the part of the "teen" leads is quite good, perhaps because their characters are drawn from cowriter Debra Hill's background. (Then as now, there were not too many women writing exploitation scripts, and most exploitation films are utterly insensitive towards their female characters, looking to them only to provide the marketable qualities of nudity and sex). Jamie Lee Curtis makes an impressive debut which led to her being temporarily typecast as a "scream queen." Her character runs the gamut of emotions from laughter with friends to utter horror, and she carries it off well with a Bacallish husky voice and a Hawksian sense of intelligence. (Though terrorized, she nonetheless deals with Michael effectively.) P. J. Soles' Lynda seems a little bit of an airhead with her use of the word "totally" to describe almost everything, but we like her, and Nancy Loomis' Annie makes for a good average student (she is not interested in studying like Laurie) with a sense of humor and devotion to her socially reticent friend. Pleasence is also entertaining as the psychiatrist who is so obsessed with Michael Myers that he seems a little crazy himself. Unlike some other mass murder movies where the victims seem to warrant their deaths, we never root for the killer in this one. We don't want these nice people to die.

After *Halloween*, it became a cliché to have the maniac pursue and kill promiscuous teenagers, thereby linking horror and sex. When I questioned Hill on this relationship (the teenagers who have sex are always doomed), she responded:

> Aren't we most vulnerable when our clothes are off? I certainly am.... Good girls don't get it. You know, *Halloween* was sort of an autobiographical film. I grew up in Haddonfield, New Jersey, and it takes place in Haddonfield, Illinois. It's a small town. I'm from the '60s. I graduated in 1966–67 from high school, and there was the realm of the girls who did and the girls who didn't, and though that aspect was not intentional, maybe that morality was there.

In an interview in *Film Comment,* Todd McCarthy asked Carpenter about the parallel between sexual activity and horror, and Carpenter responded:

> They completely missed the boat there, I think. Because if you turn it around, the one girl who is the most sexually uptight just keeps stabbing this guy with a long knife. She's the most sexually frustrated. She's the one that's killed him. Not because she's a virgin, but because all that repressed sexual energy starts coming out. She uses all those phallic symbols on the guy.

Carpenter goes on to explain that the others weren't killed because they were having sex but because they weren't on their guard, adding, "They're interested in their boyfriends, so they're ignoring the signs. *She's* aware of it because she's more like the killer, she had problems. She's a little more uptight, a little bit rigid. She and the killer have a certain link: sexual repression. She's lonely, she doesn't have a boyfriend, so she's looking around. And she finds someone – him."

Carpenter's choice not to make the killings explicit is a very deliberate one. Carpenter is quoted in Lou Gaul's *Midnight Marquee* article as saying:

> You've got to put them [the viewers] on edge. And you can't gross them out . . . because you'll lose them. They'll sit and watch the movie, but they'll stop enjoying it. If you don't gross them out and don't show the meat when the knife goes in, don't cut to the blood going everywhere, then all of them will stay with you. If you suggest it, they'll do it right up here, in their heads. This idea, of the audience projecting their fantasies, is to me the secret of movies. And the secret for me is that I get emotionally involved with the characters I'm dealing with. How I feel about them is how I make them out on the screen, and how I want the audience to feel.

Unfortunately, Carpenter did not stick with this idea when he got around to producing and cowriting *Halloween II.* After previewing a hastily put together "director's cut," he added some violent scenes to punch up the film and make it more contemporary. The result was a far more violent but much less enjoyable movie which lacked the original's compactness. We never get to know any of its new characters for very long, and Laurie spends most of the film in a hospital under sedation. (Jamie Lee Curtis, who was tired of her scream queen roles, suggested that she be killed off early in the film, like her mother Janet Leigh in *Psycho,* but coproducer and cowriter Hill insisted that audiences would want her to survive. She survives all right, but still is not given much to do until the climax.)

After the huge success of *Halloween,* Carpenter was continually offered new scripts with maniacs on the loose. He did not want to get typed as a horror director, and when he was offered the chance to do a TV movie on Elvis Presley, he jumped at the chance. (Carpenter once stated that rock 'n' roll was as important to him as the movies he loved.) *Elvis* did show that Carpenter was improving greatly with his handling of actors and that he was capable of doing a standard dramatic film. It featured what may be Kurt Russell's best performance to date as Elvis Presley and helped revitalize Russell's flagging career.

Carpenter was not *Elvis* producer Dick Clark's first choice as a director, but he did prove to be an inspired one. The film was shot in 31 days, and as Carpenter has pointed out, that's not much time for a period film, following Elvis from the 1950s to 1971. It premiered to blockbuster ratings, unexpectedly beating out both *Gone with the Wind* and *One Flew over the Cuckoo's Nest*. In Europe it was released as a theatrical feature.

However, due to changes and compromises, the experience was not a completely happy one for Carpenter, who insisted that his cut was "tougher" than that which was finally shown and that the studio had added inappropriate music to some of the dramatic scenes, killing their impact. Carpenter's only other association with rock was coscripting 1978's made-for-TV movie *Zuma Beach*, designed to demonstrate the talents of Suzanne Somers.

Carpenter started working on *Better Late than Never*, another TV movie, but he pulled out before completion. Frustrated at the compromises he had encountered at Universal, he was delighted with Avco-Embassy's promise of autonomy and began working on his next production, *The Fog*.

The Fog is an ambitious film and represents something of a change of direction for Carpenter. He decided to dispense with the prowling camera and utilize cross-cutting more. Rather than making a scary and horrifying story about more maniacs on the loose, Carpenter concentrates on the weird and the eerie. He sets the tone beautifully for his ghost story by having John Houseman in a delightful cameo set up the background for the film as a ghost story told around a campfire just minutes before midnight, the witching hour. He follows this effectively with a series of incidents from all over town, each unexplained and unnerving. Stones fall out of walls, bottles shake, pay telephones suddenly start ringing, car horns sound, glass shatters, a gas pump starts pumping itself. What could be the explanation for all these mysterious events?

Where *Halloween* was focused on a narrow area and a small group of characters, *The Fog* covers the stories of several different groups of people and the area covers all of Antonio Bay. It is basically a tale of ghostly revenge. Through a diary that Father Malone (Hal Halbrook) uncovers, he learns that his ancestor and several men conspired to lure the ship the

Elizabeth Dane to its doom on the rocks off Arkham Point. The ship contained much gold and was intended to transport a colony of lepers to an area near where Antonio Bay was being founded. The conspirators planned to take the money and build up their town with it. Now, 100 years later, Captain Blake and his crew come out of the fog to claim revenge and reclaim their lost treasure.

However, this revenge is exacted rather indiscriminately. Inside the quick-moving fog are the shambling zombies of Blake (Rob Bottin, makeup artist on the film) and his crew. They do not seem to be after the descendants of the conspirators in particular, but rather anyone who happens to cross the fog's path. Once more Carpenter films the horror of random violence, but it does not ring true to the tenets of the ghost story genre.

The primary character in the film is a female disc jockey and radio station owner, Stevie Wayne, played by Carpenter's wife, Adrienne Barbeau. She runs radio station KAB out of a lighthouse and her husky-voiced delivery makes it very believable that she's a radio dj. She is the one who is initially alerted to the fog by weatherman Dan O'Bannon (Charles Cyphers). She realizes there must be something dangerous in the fog after it moves contrary to the prevailing winds and the crew of the *Seaview* are never heard from again after passing through it. From her vantage point, she alerts the town via the radio when the mysteriously glowing fog swirls in again. Particularly agonizing for her is when she pleads that somebody save the life of her son Andy (Ty Mitchell) when the fog surrounds the house of Mrs. Kobritz, Andy's sitter.

The other major character is Nick Castle (Tommy Atkins), who picks up a hitch-hiking art student, Elizabeth Solley (Jamie Lee Curtis), on her way to Vancouver. Almost immediately the windows in his pickup truck shatter. Castle is almost killed on the first night when the zombies come knocking at his door, but fortunately the magical hour of one o'clock strikes and the zombies and fog instantly disappear before he opens the door. Elizabeth sticks around and the pair go to look for Castle's friend aboard the *Seaview*, finding it adrift and covered with saltwater, though it had only recently been thoroughly cleaned. They also come across the corpse of one of the *Seaview*'s hapless crew and take it back to the medical examiner, who incredulously explains that the corpse appears to have been underwater for some time even though he knows that just is not possible.

Carpenter's primary concern – to do something weird or shocking rather than to have the story make sense – becomes clear in this scene, which climaxes with the corpse rising from the table and stalking Elizabeth only to fall down dead again. None of the other victims in the film are thus revived or even seen after they have been attacked. (Perhaps they become members of Blake's zombie crew, but this is pure surmise; nothing in the film indicates what becomes of them.)

Interwoven with Castle and Solley's driving all over town and Wayne at her radio station are Kathy Williams (Janet Leigh) presiding over a centennial celebration for the town and the alcoholic Father Malone's disgust and torment over what he has learned about the founding of his church. Leigh does well in her portrayal of a hard-headed woman who presents a smiling face and tries to carry on with her celebration plans despite her husband's disappearance, while Holbrook plays the tormented priest to the hilt, being best in his delivery of passages from his ancestor's diary.

While none of the characterizations are very deep nor particularly memorable, Carpenter gets good mileage out of his professional cast, and such Carpenter stalwarts as Nancy Loomis and Charles Cyphers give better performances than they have in his previous pictures.

The film climaxes as most of the major characters – except for Stevie, who is chased by zombies up to the roof of her lighthouse, which bears a strange resemblance to the top of the Empire State Building in *King Kong* – all seek refuge at the church as zombie hands begin to thrust through the stained glass windows. Father Malone uncovers a golden cross which represents the remainder of the treasure and the threat disappears even more suddenly than it appeared. The film ends with a warning from Stevie echoing the end of *The Thing* ("Watch for the fog!") plus a final twist in which the ghostly zombies decide not to let Father Malone off the hook.

There are plenty of in-joke references throughout the film with many characters being named after people Carpenter has worked with: Dan O'Bannon, Nick Castle (who played the Shape in *Halloween* and the Beachball Alien in *Dark Star* and who went on to direct *T.A.G., The Last Starfighter,* and *The Boy Who Could Fly*), and Tommy Wallace (the film's production designer and coeditor, who directed *Halloween III* for Carpenter). Also, one character is named Dr. Phibes after the Robert Fuest films and Houseman's character is called Machen, probably a reference to horror writer Arthur Machen. Carpenter himself has a cameo as the church caretaker named Ben who asks fruitlessly for his wages.

In terms of the images Carpenter presents, *The Fog* is sometimes quite stunning, benefiting from a higher budget than *Halloween* had. Dean Cundey's photography plays around strikingly with gels, giving the fog a blue glow and sometimes contrasting it with red lights that shine on characters. It is a colorful film that never becomes cartoonish or unrealistic. One subtly striking scene, for example, has the colors of the church's stained glass windows reflected off of Janet Leigh's hair. The ghostly apparition of a tattered sailing vessel is also quite attractively done. Technically, the film is an advance on *Halloween*, but it suffers in reputation because it is not nearly as intense or as frightening. The story is just too diffuse and Carpenter has a tendency to cut away from situations just as they are building in intensity, depriving the horror of momentum and failing to achieve an inexorable feel.

Carpenter must have sensed that his fairy tale was out of place in the present market as he did insert some violent scenes to build up the film's shock quotient. Explains Debra Hill:

> John and I wanted to do a ghost story, a real old-fashioned ghost story, and we shot it and we show almost all of our films to the Hollywood High School audience. We asked them about the film. And they said, we want to see more. We want to see what's in the fog. So we went out and showed what was in the fog. The major part of the film still contains none of that violence.

Carpenter explained the genesis of the film to Jordan Fox of *Cinefantastique* thusly:

> ...when I was in England, several years ago, I took a drive out to see Stonehenge. There was a tremendous mood to the countryside. I looked across, and there was this fog sitting there. It was very visual, eerie, white and ghostly. I thought, "what if some dark shape just walked out of that thing and started coming toward me?" I'd have gone through the roof of the car! ... Imagine a small town, with this fog bank drifting quietly across the road. Suddenly it surrounds your house, and you hear a knocking at the door. The things you could do with that!

Waiting for *The Fog* to come out, Carpenter made some big plans on other projects including a long-proposed western, *El Diablo*, and an adaptation of the Frank Robinson and Thomas Scortia novel *The Prometheus Crisis* about a nuclear accident, though the combination of Three Mile Island's disaster and *The China Syndrome* ended up stealing the thunder from the latter project. Carpenter even proposed doing the film as a musical, but that was hardly a concept anyone could take seriously. Carpenter also worked on an untitled project about the navy testing a radar screen back in the '40s only to have the ship disappear. Some of the crew members then find themselves in the '80s – but what would happen next? Carpenter could not figure out a good final act and let the project go into other hands. In 1984 it was finally filmed as *The Philadelphia Experiment* with Carpenter getting story and executive producer credit. However, an old script he had written in 1974 called *Escape from New York City* was taken off the shelf and with the help of Nick Castle was rewritten to become Carpenter's next feature.

Escape from New York is a great popcorn, action-adventure movie with an imaginative science fiction setting. In fact, it is so imaginative that it becomes disappointing when that imagination begins to flag about halfway through the movie and finishes up "merely" as a rousing adventure piece. *Escape from New York* was pitted against such big box office competition as *Raiders of the Lost Ark, Superman II,* and *For Your Eyes Only* when it opened in the United States hampering its box office potential. It did well in Europe and spawned a number of low-budget Italian imitations.

Costing $7 million, it was Carpenter's most lavish production at that time, but the film has a rich look to it and its complicated effects were achieved for a pittance. (Special effects head Jim Cameron went on to direct *Terminator* and *Aliens.*) St. Louis doubled fairly convincingly for New York in the film, the premise of which is that New York has become such a jungle that by 1997 it is turned into a colossal prison surrounded by a high wall and guards along the outside. No one is much concerned with how the prisoners treat each other on the inside, and there is no escape. Unfortunately, the President of the United States (a very English Donald Pleasence) is on his way to a peace summit to prevent World War III when his plane is hijacked and he is forced to bail out in an escape pod that lands – you guessed it – in the middle of the New York prison.

In a desperate move Commissioner Bob Hauk (Lee Van Cleef) decides to send in a captured felon, "Snake" Plissken (Kurt Russell), to retrieve the President and a tape cassette that is absolutely essential to prevent World War III. To motivate Plissken, Hauk has him injected with mini-explosive which will blow his head off if he does not accomplish his objective and return in 24 hours. A similar kind of cynicism runs throught the whole movie; everyone is ruthless about attaining their own ends.

Sent over by glider, Plissken lands atop the World Trade Center and now must figure out where the President is being held captive. Plissken was a Special Forces veteran who fought in Siberia and at Leningrad, and is resourceful. He manages to weave in and out of the rubbish of disaster-strewn New York and its zombie-like inhabitants, though not without cost. He hooks up with Brain (Harry Dean Stanton) and his main squeeze Maggie (Adrienne Barbeau), the brains behind the Duke (Isaac Hayes), who has the island under his subjugation.

There are plenty of colorful touches such as chandeliers mounted on the Duke's cadillac, an oil pump inside Brain's headquarters, some men in drag putting on a skit and singing "Everyone's Coming to New York," and Ernest Borgnine as a cabbie who refused to leave and still picks up fares in his old territory. There are also some in-jokes, such as a nutty punk being named Romero (after director George Romero) and another referred to as Dr. Cronenberg (after director David Cronenberg). The most extended joke is borrowed from *Big Jake* – almost everyone upon meeting Russell's character says, "Snake Plissken? I thought you were dead."

But the film becomes conventional when a captured Plissken is forced to go into the Madison Square Garden ring with a huge bald man known as Slag, using nail-spiked baseball bats as weapons. Perhaps it is an *hommage* to the gladiator films Carpenter loved as a child, but the scene fails to build any excitement as it is crosscut with Brain rescuing the President. The film finishes up with a rousing race across the 69th Street bridge, but while expertly done, it seems old hat. It bothers Plissken that the President seems primarily interested in saving his own ass, though the President does help Plissken and gets revenge on the Duke at the climax.

Regrettably, Carpenter undermines our growing respect for the Plissken character by having him peevishly replace the vital tape cassette with a cassette from Borgnine's cab because the President does not show enough gratitude for the sacrifices made on his behalf. Worse, Plissken's "fuck it" attitude causes him to destroy the real tape as he's walking away, possibly ensuring both his and the world's destruction. Carpenter seems to have been too concerned with having Plissken not be the conventional hero while doing heroic things. The pettiness of his final actions seems like a letdown after all he's been through.

Nevertheless, the film is breezy and fun and even highly engrossing for much of its length. Russell leaves the Disney image behind once and for all with his tough Plissken character, though his manner of hissing his name makes him reminiscent of Clint Eastwood's Man with No Name character from the Sergio Leone spaghetti westerns. This is reinforced by the appearance of Lee Van Cleef, who costarred in two of the best of that series with Eastwood. Van Cleef was an excellent choice for the ruthless, tough-as-nails police commissioner. Most of the rest of the actors seem to have been cast for the associations we have with them, reinforcing what are in reality minor parts, but all come through with just the right attitudes to make their parts work. Each is perfectly cast to his role and seems to be having a good time.

Joe Alves' production designs are richly detailed, and Dean Cundey's use of Ultra Speed Panatars gives the film a crisp, clear quality even in the low light levels. The ugliness of the trashed-out city is made to seem almost beautiful, even haunting, by the beautifully realized lighting scheme. The film has no high aspirations apart from being entertaining and it achieves that admirably.

Carpenter decided to make the ultimate monster movie with his next film, *The Thing*. Rather than remaking the Howard Hawks–produced classic, he decided to go back to the source, John W. Campbell's original novella "Who Goes There?" In it, an alien from another solar system comes to earth and can change into any form desired. It is capable of perfectly imitating human beings, so the people in the story cannot be certain who might be an extension of the alien until they concoct a test whereby a person's blood is checked. The alien's survival instincts are so strong that even its

John Carpenter during the filming of The Thing, *the most elaborate monster movie up to that time and still an impressive achievement today.*

blood will try to save itself if threatened, thereby exposing itself as an alien simulacrum. Scripter Bill Lancaster retained these two ideas but threw out much of Campbell's scientific extrapolation. The situation would seem to be the perfect setting for paranoia – is that person next to you your friend, or is it the Thing? However, that aspect does not successfully come across in the film. Instead we get an ever-changing monster as spectacle.

Big budget horror films are rare, and it is doubtful whether so much money and attention will be lavished on the creation of a monster ever again. The special makeup effects of Rob Bottin and his crew became the stars, overshadowing everything else. While the designs were utterly incredible, many viewers were disgusted by such conceptions as a dog which turns inside out or the thing's slimy, entrail-like look. The film cost $15 million to make and grossed about that much at the United States box office, requiring that it do well overseas and have substantial cable and video sales to recoup its cost. It was not the blockbuster that Carpenter and Universal were counting on, though it has proved an influential film, changing the look of horror monsters forever. Films as diverse as Chuck Russell's remake of *The Blob* (1988) and George Pan Cosmatos' *Leviathan* (1989) were clearly influenced by it.

Carpenter's inspiration for remaking the Chris Nyby/Howard Hawks classic came from Stuart Cohen, a fellow student at USC, who was working at Universal. Eventually, David Foster and Larry Turman took over the project as producers, and they made a deal with Tobe Hooper and Ken Hinckel, who wrote a script which was rejected. The project simmered on the back burner for a while as different people were assigned to present treatments. Carpenter was approached a couple of times, but Universal wasn't familiar with his work and had doubts about the whole thing, while Carpenter was receiving more lucrative offers elsewhere. Finally, Carpenter was offered the chance to direct it; as part of the deal, he could help develop the screenplay but would not be allowed to write it. That assignment went to Bill Lancaster, who had scripted *The Bad News Bears*, which had become a sizeable hit.

One original concept that was eventually rejected was that of starting the film *after* the story, with a rescue team discovering the survivors and asking what happened. They would finally be confronted with the problem of whether the survivors were in fact human or simply clever manifestations of the Thing.

Carpenter wisely knew that if he was going to make a monster movie in the present day, the monster would have to be pretty fabulous for the film to work. He gave makeup artist Rob Bottin plenty of freedom to explore his ideas in creating the various shapes and manifestations of the Thing, with Carpenter always insisting that it be unique and original. Effects work can be very grueling, sometimes requiring take after take to get a shot right, but Carpenter has the patience for effects work and knows precisely what image he wants the camera to capture. Unlike many directors of remakes, he does manage to put a different spin on the material.

Carpenter's respect for the original shows in some subtle *hommages* near the beginning of the film. Two Norwegians in a helicopter are tracking down a husky and trying to shoot it with a rifle. (The one with the rifle is Larry Franco, the film's associate producer and assistant director.) After the Norwegians crash and burn, Americans at an Antarctic base head for the Norwegian camp to try to find what exactly is going on. The Norwegian camp is based on the camp in the 1951 film, and a video found there replays the scene from the original where men spread themselves out in a circle around a flying saucer that is submerged in the ice. Also, significantly, there is a large block of ice that once contained something that has been partially thawed.

Carpenter assembled a talented cast for *The Thing* including Kurt Russell, Wilford Brimley, David Clennon, T. K. Carter, Richard Dysart, Charles Hallahan, Richard Masur, and Donald Moffat, but he gives them very little to do. The only characterization each of the base's 12 men is given is a particular obsession (one is obsessed with scotch, another with videotapes, another with caring for the dogs, etc). These men seem burned out, isolated for too long to begin with. Naturally, if one of them loses his humanity, it is often hard to tell the difference as there was so little of it apparent in the first place.

In contrast, the special effects are quite vivid, and it is these images that viewers take away with them: a doctor massaging the chest of a heart attack victim when the torso opens and bites the doctor's hands off, and the head wriggles off the body, sprouts six legs and two eyestalks and crawls spider-like away; a huge, awful head soaring from the body until it reaches the ceiling; the Thing whipping tentacles rapidly under the floorboards; and finally the awful and ever-changing Blairmonster, which seems to have a little bit of everything thrown into its asymmetrical design.

The film ends on an adult, downbeat note as MacReady (Kurt Russell) and another survivor, Childs (Keith David), survey the wreckage of the base. For the time being, the Thing has been prevented from leaving Antarctica and reaching civilization where it would be unstoppable; but without food or shelter, if the survivors are human, they are not going to last long. If one or both of them are the Thing, then the Thing will just have to bide its time until someone comes to rescue or investigate what happened to the base. MacReady says nothing to his companion but offers him a drink. Fade out. Did the titanic struggle we just witnessed accomplish anything, or was it for naught? Carpenter's not saying.

Commented Larry Franco:

> I think one of the problems with *The Thing* was that there were too many characters involved at the station and you never really got the chance to know a lot of those peple very well. We were obligated a lot of times to find out where this guy was and where that guy was. It got a little bit too much. If it had been six guys instead of twelve, you may have had more time to spend on the characters. . . . There were just too many people that you couldn't really get involved with any of their characters, and there were too many things happening with the thing itself.

Carpenter hoped next to get involved with adapting Stephen King's novel *Firestarter*, but that was eventually turned over to another writer and director. Hooking up with Richard Kobritz, who produced *Someone's Watching Me*, Carpenter instead got to adapt King's *Christine*, the story of a teenager who is gradually possessed by a custom car's former owner, and turned it into the best killer car movie ever made (though not the best killer truck movie, an honor which still belongs to Spielberg's *Duel*).

Christine is very slickly made and shiningly photographed by Donald M. Morgan. It gets off to an appropriate start by having Christine, the fatal Fury of the title, kill someone on the assembly line while George Thoroughgood's

"Bad to the Bone" provides rock 'n' roll exposition in the background. The opening is witty in its brevity and shows Carpenter's willingness to depart slightly from the source novel to focus on the car itself. (In the novel, there is no such scene. In fact, it is established that Christine's distinctive red and white paint job was a custom paint as the factory model did not offer those colors.)

Keith Gordon does a good job limning the archetypical high school nerd, Arnie Cunningham, who is threatened and beaten by the boys in his shop class. John Stockwell smashes certain clichés by portraying high school jock Dennis Guilder as intelligent, going against the established film grain that high schoolers could be good at sports or at studies but not both.

Arnie spots the hulk of a banged-up Plymouth Fury and it is love at first sight. He only seems to see the car it could become, and immediately he has to buy it from its creepy owner, George LeBay (Roberts Blossom). He works hard at restoring the car at Will Darnell's fix-it-yourself garage.

By the time Christine, as the Fury is called, is finally restored and driveable, Arnie has undergone a startling transformation. Arrogant where he once was timid, he leaves his nerd appearance and behavior behind along with many of his likable qualities. He is suddenly able to land the most attractive and previously unavailable girl in school, Leigh Cabot (Alexandra Paul), and his life is definitely headed in a new direction.

However, it becomes apparent that Christine, and not Arnie, is in the driver's seat, almost knocking Leigh off at the drive-in. When attacked by some of Arnie's previous tormentors, Christine miraculously repairs herself and goes off on her own to avenge the indignities she has suffered.

Carpenter has an excellent eye for imagery, and the scenes of Christine popping back out the dents she has received, shearing her sides to get at a fat kid in an alleyway, and especially vivid, flaming through a gas station like a fiery Fury from hell are all highlights. In addition, the performances are good, with Robert Prosky registering strongly as the crude Darnell.

However, one essential thing is missing that was in King's long and unwieldy novel, namely his humorous banter between the main characters. King's characters came alive because they talked and joked like real high school kids and their affection for each other is quite apparent. While Bill Phillips' screenplay does a fine job of telescoping the novel, much of the humanity and humor is lost. Carpenter's camera setups and classic '50s rock 'n' roll soundtrack (Christine's radio will play nothing but '50s tunes) keep the energy level high, but all we are really left with is a well-executed killer car movie, something that entertains but offers no resonances except, perhaps, as an oblique commentary that there are people who love their cars more than anything else and to whom their girl friends are nothing more than another kind of accessory.

It is all pretty simple once the setup has been established. Christine gets revenge on the twerps who damaged her paint job, and Dennis and Leigh figure out how to put an end to the threat of Christine in an elaborate bull-dozer-versus-killer-car climax. One can almost see a Chuck Berry–inspired Carpenter going to the star of the film and asking, "OK, what's your motor-vation?"

As if to counter all the charges that his movies did not have enough heart, Carpenter made his next film his most human, with the lead character ironically being an alien. *Starman* is a sweet love story in science fiction guise, a sugary combination of bits of *The Day the Earth Stood Still* with *It Happened One Night*. Romance is a tradition that temporarily went out of fashion in modern-day movies, but Carpenter brought it back in a decidedly odd, offbeat fashion.

Starman floundered on the shelves of Columbia for many years, causing that studio to turn down *E.T.* because it already had an "alien visits earth" story of its own. The original script was written by Bruce A. Evans and Raynold Gideon while the final drafts were done by an uncredited Dean Riesner, who receives a dedication in the film's credits. The ad campaign showed little more than a night sky with the ad line promise that "Company's coming." Thus it was impossible to tell if *Starman* might be a horror film, a mystery, or what, except that it was certainly science fiction. Without a sufficient audience hook, the film took in paltry box office receipts but garnered enough respect within the acting community to net star Jeff Bridges a Best Actor nomination.

Carpenter sees *Starman* as "the classic story of star-crossed lovers, the lovers who can't make it together but who have a bond of love, like in *Brief Encounter*," as he told Michael Dare in an interview published in *L.A. Weekly.* "It really works on that level because it touches a little thing inside of us."

Carpenter deliberately chose to de-emphasize the technology, making the Starman seem magical. The film opens with a Voyager spacecraft being absorbed by a large sphere (the Starman's mother ship). A spacecraft crash-lands in a forest and through a point-of-view shot, something comes down from the woods to check out Jenny Hayden's house. Unlike previous Carpenter point-of-view shots, this one suggests, from the way the camera explores the house, something more curious than menacing about whomever is looking around. Finally it settles on a photograph of Jeff Bridges and a lock of hair, the DNA of which it is able to encode. There is a rapid transformation shot as a fetus grows into a mature man in the space of a few seconds and suddenly Jenny (Karen Allen) is confronted with a stranger who is physically identical to her late, lamented husband. (We see that Jenny has been drinking and watching old home movies of her late mate before going to bed.)

Bridges gives an astonishing performance as an alien, hinting that there is something else controlling his body and seeming quite outside of himself. The body twitches and jerks as if the controlling intelligence has not quite figured out how to work the clutch yet, but gradually gets smoother as the film goes on. Immediately, the Starman insists that Jenny must drive him to Arizona, though we are never quite told why, and the film becomes a typical road picture as the two initially antagonistic individuals fall in love while learning to appreciate each other over the course of difficulties along the road. Carpenter brings a light, humorous touch to these scenes that propels them along nicely and helps establish the love affair believably. (Initially, the Starman is more of a terrorist than a lover, forcing Jenny to his will. Allen portrays Jenny as very vulnerable due to the death of her husband; understandably, she cannot help being somewhat attracted to this look-alike stranger.)

There are also two subplots. In one, Charles Martin Smith plays a scientist who figures out what is going on and is dying to meet the Starman (which certainly strikes a responsive chord with anyone who's daydreamed of meeting a friendly extraterrestrial). In the other, Richard Jaeckel plays a heartless bureaucrat who sees the Starman as a potential menace and would like nothing better than to vivisect him, an ugly and seemingly unfounded motivation which seems designed only to add an element of suspense (i.e., present a threat that the Starman must escape).

Basically, the movie is uplifting in that it provides hope for Jenny, who has been fruitlessly spending her time recalling the bittersweet past. By meeting the Starman, she allows herself to love again and be human. She was frustrated that she was barren and so when her husband died, nothing was left her. The Starman's magic changes all that, promising her that she will have a child who will grow up to be a great teacher, bringing peace and understanding to mankind. Such an optimistic fantasy is rare in today's films.

Some have criticized the pregnancy aspect of the film as being based on an outdated notion that a woman is incomplete until she has become a mother. Yet it seems an appropriate choice, acknowledging the character's desires and frustration and indicating that she has been changed from looking back at the past to looking ahead towards her child and their future. Meanwhile, it is apparent that the Starman does not belong in this world, and he leaves in the mothership in an ending very reminiscent of the closing of Michael Gray's low-budget science fiction effort *Wavelength*.

"There has never been a film like this before," John Carpenter promised about his next project, *Big Trouble in Little China*. "An action/adventure/comedy/Kung-Fu/ghost story/monster movie" is how he described the film for *Cinefantastique*, and the final film does in many respects live up to Carpenter's promises for it. He also injected a human touch by having the hero, Jack Burton (Kurt Russell), adopt a skeptical and disbelieving attitude towards all the wonders he is experiencing. No Indiana Jones he. In fact, he is nothing more than a rugged truck driver who is out of his league and tends to look foolish whenever he attempts anything heroic. But this approach ran counter to audience expectations and the film's wildness ended up seeming out of control. As fellow 20th Century–Fox releases *The Fly* and *Aliens* charged out into the theaters in the summer of '86, *Big Trouble* was in big trouble, left somewhere in the dust.

Originally, the film was conceived as a rather wild western by writers Gary Goldman and David Z. Weinstein. Their version featured a cowboy having incredible experiences in San Francisco's Chinatown in the 1890s. W. D. Richter decided to update the script to the present day and change the hero to a flippant truck driver.

The whole thing begins as a tall tale told by Egg Shen (Victor Wong). Shen explains how Burton helps his friend Wang Chi (Dennis Dunn) meet his green-eyed girlfriend, Miao Tin (Suzee Pai), at the airport, only for her to be kidnapped by minions of Lo Pan (James Hong). It turns out that Lo Pan is a ghost who must remain noncorporeal until he marries a green-eyed maiden. Lo Pan is a secret power in Chinatown and rules an underground fantasy kingdom full of kung fu masters and monsters. His chief instruments are Masters of Death (reminiscent of the three brothers in *Shogun Assassin*), who can fly and have magical powers.

Various elements of Chinese myths are thrown in, some of them to good effect (my favorite is a multi-eyed sphere that flies around and spies on folks looking like something from a Dungeons & Dragons game come to life), but much of the comedy misfires, and Russell's husky-voiced hero seems an affectation that fails to become credible. (Many critics accused him of imitating John Wayne unsuccessfully.) His Burton character has more bluff and bluster than ability, but in the midst of all this unreality the hero should not appear unreal as well. Dunn gives good support as Burton's friend and sidekick and then turns into a sudden kung fu master himself. The fights are nicely staged and this certainly is the glossiest and, in terms of special effects, the most elaborate kung fu film ever made, but despite the film's enjoyable aspects, one comes away with the feeling that great potential has been wasted on trivializing the story, characters and situations in an effort to be both hip and fun.

Part of the problem might have been that once more, in submitting himself to the studio system, Carpenter had to deal with executives who tried to second-guess him. He also feels that his film was promoted wrongly and suffered because of it. Due to his dissatisfaction, he returned to independent filmmaking and the kind of automony he was able to achieve under those circumstances. After the inflated budgets of his last two features (both over $20 million), he vowed that his next project would be low-budget.

That project was *Prince of Darkness*, the first of a proposed series of four works for Alive Films. It starred Donald Pleasence as a priest with doubts about his faith who discovers a canister that contains the very essence of evil. Victor Wong is a physics professor who brings his graduate students, including Dennis Dun and Lisa Blount, to study the phenomenon. The film was produced by longtime Carpenter associate Larry Franco, who also produced *Big Trouble*. Once more Carpenter returned to the terrain of horror, and the film crossed aspects of *The Exorcist* with *The Thing*, unfortunately retaining more of the faults than the strengths of both. The screenplay was attributed to "Bernard Quatermass," the scientist from Nigel Kneale's science fiction series (Carpenter approached Kneale to write the original screenplay for *Halloween III: The Season of the Witch*, which was extensively rewritten by Tommy Lee Wallace, its director). Many feel that Carpenter himself wrote the script, but Carpenter claimed it was written by a physicist as a lark.

The script does show familiarity with some fairly well known aspects of quantum physics and uses these concepts as a paradigm for the basic uncertainty of the universe, but such plot devices as video signals being picked up as dreams seem unlikely to have come from a scientist. Carpenter's Argento influence is abundantly evident, and there is a very creepy scene where bugs completely engulf and apparently devour one of the characters. Rock star Alice Cooper is effective in a creepy cameo as the leader of the street people who are under the devil's influence and barricade the graduate student heroes inside the church that contains the canister, which slowly leaks and looks like a lava lamp from hell.

However, despite the liquid evil's ability to possess anyone and take over bodies, once again Carpenter has difficulty conveying the paranoia inherent in the situation. Coworkers find they cannot trust each other as some of them might have been possessed by pea-soup-green liquid which is ingested rather than spewed. Technically, though low-budget, the film is very proficient, but the story and characters both lack substance.

Much better is Carpenter's last film of the '80s, *They Live*, a paranoid fantasy based on the idea that Yuppies are actually aliens from outer space. Carpenter has a rather Manchean view of the universe, seeing evil as an outside force (whether it be a thing, Michael Myers, green evil concentrate, or aliens) and does not seem comfortable with the view that each individual carries within him the seeds of both good and evil. Disgusted by the number of "pod people" in the world – soulless individuals who seem to make only a pretense of having emotions and feelings – he decided to make a science fiction thriller exposing the evil among us, and in the process made a sometimes subtly subversive film.

Taking the side of the down-and-out, the film stars wrestler "Rowdy" Roddy Piper as John Nada, an out-of-work laborer who comes into the big

Universal spoofed the Bentson-Quayle vice presidential debates in this droll ad that shows the true form of the yuppie aliens in Carpenter's They Live.

city looking for some construction work. Being short on cash, he is forced to take up residence in "Justiceville," an area of makeshift shacks similar to the Hoovervilles that sprang up during the Great Depression. There he is intrigued by a blind preacher (Raymond St. Jacques) who harangues a crowd about not having their minds taken over. There are also disturbing breaks in the television picture and oddball graffitti everywhere.

The curious Nada ignores the warnings from coworker Frank (Keith David) not to stick his neck out. Nada investigates and finds a mysterious underground hidden in a local church which contains broadcasting equipment and cartons full of sunglasses. Suddenly, the police raid and raze the makeshift settlement to the ground as part of planned oppression and crowd control. Nada escapes, taking a pair of the sunglasses with him.

Donning the sunglasses gives Nada a different view of things. Through the sunglasses, he sees the world in black and white. Additionally, subliminal messages to obey, multiply, consume are revealed behind headlines and billboards. What's more, every person who wears a suit and a Rolodex watch is revealed to be a hideous, skeletal alien from outer space. The aliens have already invaded and have disguised their presence by "colorizing" the world, covering up their sinister purposes.

For the first part of this film, Carpenter's conceits work. He uses Piper very effectively, and we sympathize as Nada must extensively revise his world view and come to grips with the paranoid fantasy that Carpenter is presenting. The concepts are cleverly and simply presented, and Carpenter shows us the underclass that was ignored and victimized by the "Reagan revolution," a rare occurrence in modern-day films with their emphasis on glamorous and powerful characters.

However, the plot's tightness begins to unravel as Nada kidnaps Holly Thompson (Meg Foster), an assistant programmer for a TV channel, who tries to turn this seemingly crazed psycho in. Even worse, Carpenter stops the film dead while Nada and Frank have a seven-minute knock-down, drag-out fight over whether Frank will wear the revealing sunglasses or not. The scene seems simply a poor motivation for Piper to display his wrestling prowess, paying tribute to the wrestling matches Carpenter loved as a kid.

From being rich with ideas, the rest of the film becomes simpleminded as Nada leads a revolution against the Yuppie-aliens, falls for Holly and makes the obvious mistake of trusting her, and finally knocks down the one transmitter that has been concealing the aliens' true nature so that they are finally revealed for all to see. (Why the aliens have only one transmitter and how this colorizes the whole world is never dealt with.)

Meg Foster's disturbing blue eyes make her an odd candidate for trustworthiness in any event, particularly since she has already sent Nada flying through her window and down a long hill in a titanic tumble earlier in the film. The film does reclaim a little *frisson* by revealing that some humans are already aware of the aliens' presence and have cooperated with them for the sake of success and higher profits, selling out their fellow human beings. It is also interesting to see earth viewed as a Third World country by the alien invaders who have come to exploit the local economy, causing the misery shown at the beginning of the film.

However, like *Escape from New York*, once it has mapped out its admittedly interesting territory, *They Live* falls back on conventional action film clichés for its resolution. Still, it is worthwhile for its wonderfully satirical first half.

The script for *They Live*, based on Ray Nelson's story "Eight o'Clock in the Morning," is credited to Frank Armitage. Armitage is believed to be Carpenter himself, which may explain why the story's weaknesses were not shored up.

Carpenter is comfortable working with genre films, and he knows as Hawks knew that meaningful stories could be told within the limitations of a genre format. His visual eye remains strong and his films must be seen on the wide screen to be properly appreciated (the images are not framed for their eventual video release). His best work revolves around people who pull together while struggling against outside forces, asserting their need to determine their own destinies.

William Castle (1914–1977)

The Chance of a Lifetime; Klondike Kate (1943); *The Whistler; She's a Soldier, Too; The Mark of the Whistler; When Strangers Marry* (1944); *The Crime Doctor's Warning; Voice of the Whistler* (1945); *Just Before Dawn; Mysterious Intruder; The Return of Rusty; The Crime Doctor's Manhunt* (1946); *The Crime Doctor's Gamble* (1947); *Texas, Brooklyn and Heaven; The Gentleman from Nowhere* (1948); *Johnny Stool Pigeon; Undertow* (1949); *It's a Small World* (1950); *The Fat Man; Hollywood Story; Cave of Outlaws* (1951); *Serpent of the Nile; Fort Ti; Conquest of Cochise; Slaves of Babylon* (1953); *Drums of Tahiti; Charge of the Lancers; Battle of Rogue River; Jesse James vs. the Daltons; The Iron Glove; The Saracen Blade; The Law vs. Billy the Kid* (1954); *Masterson of Kansas; The Americano: New Orleans Uncensored; The Gun That Won the West; Duel on the Mississippi* (1955); *The Houston Story; Uranium Boom* (1956); *Macabre* (1958); *House on Haunted Hill; The Tingler* (1959); *13 Ghosts* (1960); *Homicidal; Mr. Sardonicus* (1961); *Zotz!* (1962); *The Old Dark House; 13 Frightened Girls* (1963); *Strait-Jacket* (1964); *The Night Walker; I Saw What You Did* (1965); *Let's Kill Uncle* (1966); *The Busy Body; The Spirit Is Willing* (1967); *Project X* (1968); *Shanks* (1974).

William Castle has been called "the poor man's Hitchcock" and "the King of Gimmicks." Castle himself was under no illusions, admitting, "I have modeled my career on Barnum rather than Hitchcock," though Hitchcock certainly was one of his influences, especially when it came to self-promotion. Beginning with *Macabre* in 1958, he did all he could to promote himself as a master showman and maker of thrillers. He developed a highly recognizable silhouette of himself sitting in a director's chair smoking a cigar that did much to fix in the audience's minds the image of the director as a showman and ringmaster of the circus that is the cinema.

Born William Schloss (German for "Castle"), Jr., in 1914, Castle went to live with his sister when his parents died early in his life. The years that followed were marked by frustration and resentment, leaving him with an immense desire to prove himself by gaining recognition and applause. In his autobiography, *Step Right Up! I'm Gonna Scare the Pants Off America*, Castle credits visiting Bela Lugosi backstage after the play *Dracula* with inspiring him to want "to scare the pants off audiences." He was 13 years old at the time. At 15, he joined Lugosi on a road company tour of *Dracula* as its assistant stage manager.

143

He continued working in the theater for several years, trying his hand at acting in such plays as *Ebb Tide, No More Frontiers* and *Oliver Twist*. Working in the Depression when there were few jobs and little money, Castle learned to get by on bluff and bravado. He landed a part in *An American Tragedy* by claiming to be Samuel Goldwyn's nephew, hinting that he would approach his "uncle" about financing the producer's next production. When asked about his name, Castle claimed he changed it to Castle because he "didn't want to trade on the Goldwyn name."

He decided to become a producer of plays when he learned that Orson Welles was about to leave the Stony Brook Theatre in Connecticut to helm *Citizen Kane* in Hollywood. Extracting Welles' phone number (again by bluff) from Everett Sloan at a party, he called Welles and pretended to be an experienced producer with plenty of money who was interested in taking over Stony Brook. Welles agreed to meet him the next day. At the same party, Castle met Ellen Schwanneke, star of *Mädchen in Uniform*, and hit upon the idea of having her star in a revival of *Seventh Heaven*. By persuading Welles that he had a great love for theater (and by leasing Stony Brook for $500 a week), Castle was able to secure Stony Brook, only to be told by Actors Equity that non–Americans could not play in summer stock unless the material was something that no American artist could perform. Seeing his only out, Castle made up a play title on the spot, *Das ist Nicht für Kinder* (That Is Not for Children), and set about writing this play over a weekend's time.

Getting approval to star Schwanneke in the play, Castle nevertheless had trouble: Namely, that the Connecticut audience, upon learning that Welles' Mercury Company had left, did not purchase the expected advance tickets. However, when Schwanneke received an invitation from Adolf Hitler to return to Germany, Castle spotted a potential publicity stunt or gimmick to attract the required audiences. He had Schwanneke cable Hitler that she refused to return to Germany; then he made copies of the request and her cable and dropped them off at all the major newspapers. A slow news day and a high amount of anti–Nazi fervor led to the story being featured prominently in several New York papers. As a final touch, Castle trashed his own theater, painting swastikas on the walls to make it appear as if some pro–Nazi group had protested Schwanneke's actions, and to top it off, he convinced the governor of Connecticut to send the state militia for protection by pretending to be Orson Welles. The resulting publicity guaranteed the play's success.

Castle also wrote and acted in radio soap operas, including *The Romance of Helen Trent*, and wrote and produced his first thriller, *This Little Piggy Had None*, as his second production for Stony Brook. Castle described it as a horror play "about the mental breakdown of a timid man who is so taunted by his facial resemblance to a pig that he finally cracks

up and becomes a murderer." During its run, he was contacted by Sam
Marks about whether he was interested in going to work at Columbia Pictures. Quickly assenting, Castle agreed to drive Marks' car back to the West
Coast even though Castle never learned how to drive. He found a driver and
started to make the trip across but was arrested at a Wyoming bordello
when he and the driver were mistaken for some holdup men. They could not
produce the registration for the car they were driving, which contained
several stage guns, a blackjack, handcuffs and counterfeit money (props for
a production of *Dead End* which never came off). After word finally reached
Marks, Castle's identity was established and he was released, finally making
it to Hollywood.

At Columbia, he was put under a six-month contract for $50 a week and
was assigned various duties including dialogue director, production assistant, film editor, and bit player. George Stevens took a liking to the brash
young Castle when Castle offered to help Stevens in his Hollywood career
without knowing who he was. As a result, Castle's first film assignment was
as dialogue director on *Penny Serenade*. He worked in a variety of minor
capacities on different films, champing at the bit to get a chance to direct.
He finally got it with 1943's *The Chance of a Lifetime*, one of the worst of
the Boston Blackie series. Castle claims that Irving Briskin would not allow
him to rewrite the script and furthermore did a drastic reediting job on the
picture. The result opened to positively scathing reviews in the trades. Castle followed this with *Klondike Kate*, a film whose major claim to fame was
that it starred Tom Neal and Ann Savage, who shone in Edgar Ulmer's noir
classic *Detour*.

Castle finally had a success with his third time at bat. *The Whistler*, based
on the old radio series, proved to be a success and spun off a successful series
(of which Castle also directed *The Mark of the Whistler*, *Voice of the Whistler* and *Mysterious Intruder*). Regarding the original film, Castle wrote in
his autobiography:

> ... Richard Dix and J. Carrol Naish, veterans of many fine movies,
> liked my originality and fresh approach and encouraged me to try out
> any new idea I came up with. I tried every effect I could dream up to
> create a mood of terror: low-key lighting, wide angle lenses to give an
> eerie feeling and a hand-held camera in many of the important scenes
> to give a sense of reality to the horror. To achieve a mood of despera-
> tion, I insisted that Dix give up smoking and go on a diet. This made
> him nervous and irritable, particularly when I gave him early-morning
> calls and kept him waiting on the set—sometimes for an entire day
> before using him in a scene. He was constantly off-center, restless,
> fidgety, and nervous as a cat. When I finally used him in a scene, I'd
> make him do it over and over until he was ready to explode. It achieved
> the desired effect—that of a man haunted by fear and trying to keep
> from being murdered.

The plot is fairly ingenious for a B movie. Dix is despondent over the disappearance and presumed death of his wife and worries that his friends believe him to be responsible. He cannot bring himself to commit suicide, so he contacts someone to have them put out a contract killing on himself. Naturally, he receives word that his wife is alive, but the man he contacted has been shot to death by the police and he has no way of reaching the professional killer to cancel the contract.

She's a Soldier Too (1944) was a minor piece starring Beulah Bondi as a cab driver helping soldier Lloyd Bridges, but *When Stranger Marry* proved to be one of Castle's best and most important films. The King Brothers, impressed with *The Whistler*, borrowed Castle for this Monogram production. According to Castle, the script originally offered him by the King Brothers was terrible, and they agreed to let him get together with Philip Yordan and come up with a new screenplay very quickly. According to the credits of the film, it was based on an unpublished story by George V. Moscov and was written by Yordan and Dennis J. Cooper.

The plot involves a man with a large sum of money who has been murdered in a hotel by a stranger. Newlywed Millie Baxter (Kim Hunter) checks into the same hotel to meet her husband, Paul (Dean Jagger), who preceded her. Instead, she meets old flame Fred Graham (Robert Mitchum), who tells her of the murder. When Paul fails to show, Fred urges Millie to contact the police. Millie is finally contacted by Paul, who acts very suspiciously and seems anxious to avoid the police. Paul admits meeting the murdered man but denies murdering him. Just as the police catch up with the couple, new evidence emerges that implicates Fred Graham, and the police arrest him as he tries to hide the money.

Castle was very definitely influenced by Val Lewton's B thrillers in *When Strangers Marry*, with Kim Hunter playing a role similar to the one she played in *The Seventh Victim*. Castle imbues the film with a kind of neorealism, shooting the dismal hotel room with dull, flat, grey lighting that accentuates the setting's oppressive atmosphere. The jazz blaring from next door and the city sounds that invade the room also help to underscore Hunter's fear and hysteria. Castle effectively uses a neon "Dancing" sign to bathe Hunter's room alternately in stark brightness and utter darkness, perhaps out of recollection of the time he spent in similar circumstances in Greenwich Village when he was a young, struggling actor. The film does have some strong, simple imagery and very fine performances by both Hunter and Mitchum. Mitchum at times reveals a chilling madness under his cool exterior. This film helped him gain recognition as an actor and brought him to the attention of many prominent critics. The scene of a young woman rushing home, haunted by faces which Castle superimposes over her fleeing figure, is an effective borrowing from Tourneur's *Cat People* and *Leopard Man* sequences. The film would later be reissued as *Betrayed*.

The film was shot in only seven days for $50,000. It contains many of the hallmarks of the better moments in Castle's later horror films: It is stark and unrelenting, builds atmosphere and suspense through the use of irritating sounds, and offers some quick cuts of grotesque and surprising images. It is also rather solid evidence that Castle was something more than the hack or gimmick-meister that his detractors maintained, though much of the promise of *When Strangers Marry* remained sadly unfulfilled.

The success of the film initially resulted in an offer for Castle to direct a play on Broadway, *Meet a Body*. Castle first directed the play through a successful Boston run before bringing it to Broadway, where it was murdered by the New York critics. Undeterred, Castle came up with the gimmick of advertising the play with a large ad in the obituary papers that ran:

> YOU ARE CORDIALLY INVITED TO ATTEND A FUNERAL AT THE FORREST THEATRE. TWO CAN BE BURIED AS CHEAPLY AS ONE. BRING A DATE AND GET HER BURIED FREE WHILE YOU ATTEND *MEET A BODY*.

While Castle was in New York, a cab driver game him a copy of *If I Die Before I Wake*, an Inner Sanctum novel by Sherwood King. He read it and bought the rights for the purpose of using it as a plot for a *Whistler* film. As it happened, Castle contacted Orson Welles again after Welles had given *When Strangers Marry* a glowing notice in the New York *Graphic*, calling it "one of the most gripping and effective pictures of the year. It is not as slick as *Double Indemnity* or as glossy as *Laura*, but it's better acted and better directed by William Castle than either." Welles suggested that the pair might make a picture together, and when *If I Die* was turned down by the Columbia story department, Castle sent it on to Welles, who decided it would be a perfect vehicle for him and his soon-to-be bride, Rita Hayworth.

Thanks to his success with *The Whistler*, Castle was assigned to work on another radio-based mystery series, the *Crime Doctor* series starring Warner Baxter. He was working on *The Crime Doctor's Warning*, about Baxter trying to find out who murdered a model, when Harry Cohn, head of Columbia, announced to Castle that Welles had selected him to be associate producer of the new film Welles was going to produce, direct, write and star in – *If I Die Before I Wake*, which Welles had sold to Columbia for $150,000 after Castle had previously picked it up for $200.

If I Die became *The Lady from Shanghai*. Along with *Rosemary's Baby*, it would prove to be the best film Castle was ever associated with, though the filming was an ordeal as weather proved fickle, Welles worked slowly, an assistant cameraman died of a coronary while aboard Errol Flynn's yacht, the *Zaca* (Flynn immediately ordered that a duffle bag be brought so they could bury him at sea), several people became sick, and Castle himself finally came down with amoebic dysentery while remaining behind to shoot second unit footage of insects, snakes and iguanas.

Finally recovering, Castle returned to Columbia with high hopes and expectations. Unfortunately, he found he was in debt to the studio due to his illness and was assigned to do more *Crime Doctors* and *Whistler*s. Or, as Castle wrote in his autobiography, "I was forced to direct films that I could do with my eyes shut." And that is just how many of them appear to have been directed. However, *Crime Doctor's Man Hunt* does have some elements which stand out. Based on a story by Eric Taylor, it was scripted by science fiction writer Leigh Brackett (who also coscripted such films as *The Big Sleep, Rio Bravo,* and *The Empire Strikes Back*). In some ways, it foreshadows Castle's *Homicidal* in its tale of a woman (Ellen Drew) with a dual personality who takes on the physical appearance of her dead sister and begins murdering people. (Interestingly enough, as often as Castle has been accused of stealing from Hitchcock, one can see minor elements of both *Psycho* and *Vertigo* in this B movie's plot.)

The film opens with Philip Armstrong (Myron Healey) wandering around a carnival in a daze, secretly followed by his fiancée, Irene (Drew). That Irene's personality is split is indicated pictorially by showing her body divided into two parts by a shop window when we first see her, an isolated bit of inventiveness. Philip consults the Crime Doctor, Dr. Robert Ordway (Warner Baxter), who investigates the vicinity that Philip is attracted to only to come upon two men trying to dispose of Philip's corpse. Philip had told Dr. Ordway that his death was foretold by a fortuneteller named Alfredi (Ivan Triesault) whom Dr. Ordway resolves to track down. Meanwhile, he learns that Irene had a troublesome twin sister named Natalie who had been thrown out of her father's house three years before. When informed of Philip's demise, Irene observes demurely, "If Natalie were here, she'd help me. Natalie always helped me."

"Natalie" makes an appearance, a blonde to Irene's brunette, and murders the two men who were discarding Philip's corpse. Dr. Ordway discovers that a blonde had paid Alfredi to give Philip that prophetic fortune, supposedly to frighten him because, the blonde had claimed, he was after Irene's money. To make matters more complicated, Dr. Ordway discovers that Natalie has been dead for two years.

Dr. Ordway takes Irene to an empty house where her family once lived. Claiming to have found some evidence, he sends Irene off to get the police. Then Natalie returns to shoot him. But it is a setup. Dr. Ordway signals the waiting police and they take Irene/Natalie into custody. Underneath the blond wig Irene and Natalie are one and the same.

Baxter lends his typical professional authority to the role of Dr. Ordway,

A jokey publicity still of William Castle indicates that he desired to have film patrons enjoy his little horror films as well as become aware of the figure behind the camera. Castle was indeed a genius in self-promotion, even if he was not similarly gifted when it came to directing.

while Ellen Drew gives a good, if obvious, performance as the twin sisters. With her distinctive looks, Drew was clearly playing both parts, diminishing what little surprise the twin sister plot might have had. But then Jean Arliss was obviously playing both brother and sister in *Homicidal*, though more of an attempt was made to disguise her than simply using a wig and glasses. The psychologically disturbed personality would prove a major plot gimmick in almost all of Castle's series of horror shockers, so *The Crime Doctor's Man Hunt* may be counted as another seminal film in his career.

Castle has tried his hands at westerns such as *The Return of Rusty* (which I have not seen) and *Texas, Brooklyn and Heaven* (a labored comedy about a cowboy falling in love with a city girl). Castle finally rebelled at having to do a seemingly endless series of B movies, refusing to do the tentatively titled *The Crime Doctor's Secret* (later released as *The Crime Doctor's Diary*), and on November 28, 1947, was placed on suspension, meaning he would not be paid and was not allowed to work anywhere else in the film industry. Going out to dinner to pick up his spirits, he was struck by the prettiness of Lowell Gilmore's date, one Ruth Falck. Complimenting her with the old line, "I wish you had a twin at home like you," Castle was surprised to discover that she did, and so set up a blind date with Ellen Falck. The two fell in love and were married. As a wedding present, Cohn, who had been charmed by Falck, took Castle off of suspension and sent the couple on a honeymoon to Paris where Castle was also to direct some second unit work. Promise of a top Columbia picture was cabled to Castle in Europe, but he then fell ill due to a kidney stone. After finally passing the stone, Castle was crestfallen to discover that the top picture was cancelled, and so he opted to try his hand over at Universal-International instead.

His first assignment there, *Johnny Stool Pigeon*, was a step up, albeit a small one. It was a competent, routine thriller about a convict released from jail so that he could lead police back to uncover a dope ring. The film proved to be one of Tony Curtis' first assignments after being signed to Universal, though he played only a minor role. The stars were Howard Duff, Dan Duryea and Shelley Winters.

This was followed by *Undertow*, an efficiently told thriller in which Scott Brady is on the run, an innocent man accused of murder which he now must prove he did not commit. Peggy Dow makes a particularly attractive love interest. Castle was then loaned out to Eagle-Lion for an obscure piece called *It's a Small World*.

Universal next assigned him yet another radio adaptation, perhaps figuring that Castle must be a specialist in them. The result was a one-shot called *The Fat Man*, from a character created by Dashiell Hammet with J. Scott Smart from the radio show. Rock Hudson appeared in a small part in both this and *Undertow*, and the famous Ringling Bros. clown Emmett Kelly appeared as the villain.

The Cave of the Outlaws, filmed in the famous Carlsbad Caverns, was an undistinguished western with a below average performance by Alexis Smith. Castle claims that he then tried to interest William Goetz in a 3-D version of Jules Verne's *From the Earth to the Moon*, anticipating both the science fiction and the 3-D trends of the 1950s, but was turned down. Instead, he was assigned to *Hollywood Story*, in which a producer hopes to solve a mystery by making a picture about it. The most unusual aspect of the film was its depiction of the silent era in black-and-white with intertitles, while the present-day portions of the film were shot in color and sound. As part of this affectionate tribute, Castle used silent stars Francis X. Bushman, Chester Conklin, Charlie Chase and several former Keystone Kops to play parts in the silent era sections of the film.

Universal offered Castle another three-year contract, but he opted to return to Columbia. There he was put under the notorious Sam Katzman, a producer of mediocre or worse films but very knowledgeable in showmanship and how to save a buck.

Castle started with *Serpent of the Nile*, starring Rhonda Fleming (who had had a bit part in *When Strangers Marry*) as Cleopatra and shot on sets left over from Rita Hayworth's *Salome*, and *Fort Ti*, in which Castle threw everything he could think of at the camera—tomahawks, balls of fire, arrows, and cannonballs. This led one wag to comment, "He may not be able to direct, but he sure can pitch." Many other films followed in rapid succession: *Conquest of Cochise; Slaves of Babylon; Drums of Tahiti; Charge of the Lancers; Battle of Rogue River; Jesse James vs. the Daltons; The Iron Glove; The Saracen Blade; The Law vs. Billy the Kid; Masterson of Kansas; The Americano* (for RKO); *New Orleans Uncensored; The Gun That Won the West; Duel on the Mississippi; The Houston Story;* and *Uranium Boom.*

Perhaps the strangest debacle of this time occurred during *The Houston Story*. Originally, Lee J. Cobb was supposed to play the lead as an unscrupulous oil man trying to take over a crime syndicate. However, partway into filming, Cobb fell sick. Because he had been mistaken for Cobb on a number of occasions, Castle doubled for Cobb in long shots. Finally, Cobb had to drop out entirely and was replaced by Gene Barry. The disparate footage was all cobbled together with Barry doing all the lines and close-ups, but with shots of both Castle and Cobb performing in many of the action shots, despite the fact that neither Cobb nor Castle bore much of a resemblance to Barry.

Denied the chance to produce at Columbia, Castle moved into television, producing two series: *Meet McGraw* and *Men of Annapolis*. On the latter series, he needed to find a writer who had had Naval Academy experience. Among the names of Naval Academy graduates he found the name of Robb White, who wound up writing most of the episodes for the series despite not belonging to the Writers Guild. A collaboration of the two, pooling talent and resources, was the true beginning of Castle's noted horror career.

According to Castle, he was inspired to make *Macabre* after seeing the long lines waiting to see Henri Georges Clouzot's classic *Diabolique*. After seeing the film, Castle decided he needed to make a movie with thrills and chills and set about looking for a similar type story (i.e., a scary story about someone trying to frighten a weak-hearted person to death). He thought he found just the right combination of elements in *The Marble Forest* by Theo

Durrant (actually, it was a round-robin mystery story written by Terry Adler, Eunice Mays Boyd, Anthony Boucher, Florence Austin Faulkner, Allen Hymson, Cary Lucas, Dana Lyon, Lenore Glen Offord, Virginia Rath, Virginia Shattuck, Darwin L. Teilhet, and William Worley). When Columbia was not interested in allowing him to produce the film, he decided to produce it himself. Castle mortgaged his house, sold his TV series, cleaned out his bank account and with partner Robb White formed a company, Susina Association, and raised the $86,000 the film cost.

The entire film took somewhere between six (according to Mark Thomas McGee in *Fangoria*) and nine (according to Castle in his autobiography) days to shoot. The McGee article quotes Castle as saying, "When I finished I looked at it and recognized that a Clouzot I ain't. I had to have a gimmick to sell that movie."

The gimmick he came up with was to insure the entire world against death by fright during the showing of *Macabre*. He was able to set up a policy through Lloyds of London for a mere $5,000. People attending screenings of *Macabre* were given copies of the policy stating that if any member of the audience died by fright, their beneficiary would receive $1,000. He first offered the film to Warner Bros., who refused to guarantee the cost of the picture and stole his insurance-against-death-by-fright idea until Castle threatened them with a plagiarism suit. Telling Allied Artists that the picture had cost $250,000 to produce, Castle sold it to them for $150,000 plus 75 percent of the profits (the film grossed about $5 million and returned profits in the neighborhood of $1,200,000).

The gimmick had proved to be an incredibly shrewd move. The picture would not have gone far on its own merits. The title was changed from *The Marble Forest* because Castle wanted a punchy one-word title like *Diabolique*. *Macabre* had an intriguing air about it, but what made customers particularly curious was the death-by-fright gimmick – people wanted to know what could be so scary that the producers would have arranged to protect themselves with "death by fright" policies.

The answer was, of course, nothing. Death by tedium would have been far more likely, as *Macabre* was more of a dull melodrama than a horror shocker. The plot centered around one Dr. Rodney Barrett (William Prince), whose wife died in childbirth and whose sister-in-law, a blind girl beloved by Sheriff Jim Tyloe (played by Jim Backus with surprisingly scuzzy undertones) he also failed to save. As a result, his practice is not going well. To make things worse, when his devoted nurse Polly Baron (Jacqueline Scott) gets home, she received an anonymous phone call which makes her scream. The caller told her that Marge, the doctor's young daughter, has been buried alive and has only five hours to live. Soon a frantic search is on at the cemetery and elsewhere in an attempt to find Marge before it is too late.

There are some tense moments in the cemetery when it appears that *all* the graves have freshly turned dirt (making it harder for anyone to locate where Marge might be). Polly and Dr. Barrett fear an unseen presence around them and have to scramble into a deep open grave. Meanwhile, the time keeps ticking away, building up a suspense element which is unfortunately undercut by the extensive flashbacks we get tracing the tragic history of Barrett's wife, Alice (Dorothy Morris), and sister-in-law, Nancy (Christine White). A big buildup comes when the searchers investigate a funeral parlor filled with coffins and suddenly notice they hear breathing, only to discover that the phenomenon is due to a mechanical pump designed to make the corpses seem more lifelike by making breathing noises. (Huh? Somehow it is hard to imagine such a device ever being much comfort to the bereaved, but it is another gimmick and no one said gimmicks had to have logical explanations.)

Everything climaxes at Nancy's funeral when a small, disfigured corpse that is presumed to be Marge is discovered in the process of burying Nancy's body. Rich old Jode Wetherby (Philip Tonge), Dr. Barrett's father-in-law and Marge's grandfather, has a weak ticker and promptly dies from shock, thereby leaving all his money to Dr. Barrett and Marge. But before the doctor can enjoy his inheritance, he is shot down by the mortician Ed Quigley (Jonathan Kidd). Quigley confesses to Sheriff Tyloe that not-so-kindly Dr. Barrett had orchestrated a mad plot to scare Wetherby to death and collect his inheritance by faking the kidnapping and slow death of Wetherby's granddaughter. Nurse Polly was so blinded by her love for Barrett that she never suspected. A dash back to the doctor's office uncovers the quite healthy Marge and the tape recording of the shocking call that Polly had received at Dr. Barrett's house.

Castle then reminds the audience that the death-by-fright policy will be in effect for just a few minutes more; however, the shocking anti-climax is nothing more than animated closing titles with hearses and caricatures of the principal players filing past under the credits.

While *Macabre* does get some mileage out of its settings, there is a rather perfunctory air about the whole project. Everyone performs competently, but the film just never comes alive. Scenarist Robb White did not much care for the book and decided he could do better doing an original. However, Allied Artists was more than pleased by the business *Macabre* was doing and encouraged Castle to begin working on another film. Castle and White decided to throw together all the haunted house clichés they could think of and came up with *House on Haunted Hill*.

House on Haunted Hill is far from a horror classic, but at least it was a definite improvement on *Macabre*. While many of the horror devices are used ineffectively and fail to frighten, the film does have some good moments and particularly benefits from Vincent Price's narration. Price plays the wealthy Frederick Loren who, on the prompting of his not-so-beloved wife, Annabelle (Carol Ohmart), has invited five guests who are hard up for money to spend the night in a haunted house, for which they will receive a prize of $10,000 if they survive. The guests are Ruth Bridgers (Julie Mitchum), a newspaperwoman with a penchant for gambling and drinking; Dr. David Trent (Alan Marshal), a suave psychiatrist in some financial difficulty; Watson Pritchard (Elisha Cook, Jr.), who previously inhabited the house during an evening when half his family killed each other off; Lance Schroeder (Richard Long), a lawyer; and Nora Manning (Carolyn Craig), a scream-prone actress.

Price gives absolutely delightful line readings discussing his wife's plans and her shortcomings. He sounds both amused and disdainful of the rather morbid proceedings, which include such elements as handing out mini-coffins with guns in them as party favors. Soon all the familiar haunted house gimmicks are trotted through their paces: clinking chandeliers, thunderstorms, disembodied heads (Price even carries one in the advertising art, though not in the film itself), organs that play themselves, etc. Perhaps the most effective shock sequence comes when Nora supposes herself alone in a small room in the wine cellar, then turns to find a white-eyed, shrewish figure extending her claws and cackling at her. (It turns out to be one of those old horror standbys, the mysterious caretaker's blind wife doing the menacing servant routine.) A rope which snakes its way into a room and around Nora's ankles, though, totally defies credibility as it is obviously being pulled via a fishing line.

Naturally, none of these occurrences have a supernatural basis. They are all part of a plot to conveniently dispose of Loren for his money on the part of his scheming wife and her lover, Dr. Trent. Dr. Trent is shoved into an acid bath by Loren offscreen. Loren has been onto them for some time and prepares the coup de grace via an acid-proof skeleton that he arranges to emerge from the bath and frighten his wife to her doom. All rather convenient – particularly for Castle's new gimmick, "Emergo." When the skeleton appeared on the film, it was arranged by some theaters to have a skeleton sail over the heads of the audience, manipulated via fishing wire by the projectionist. Reportedly, during an initial test, the skeleton broke the wire and fell on the heads of several executives. While Emergo may have proved more real than 3-D for some, mostly it proved an effective target for fun-loving youngsters.

One strange aspect of *House on Haunted Hill* was the selection of the house that was supposed to be haunted. An ultra-modern, Frank Lloyd Wright–designed residence with a large door stood in for the haunted house – hardly the type that would have collected ghosts and been passed on down through generations. The studio interiors recalled old haunted house movies and in no way reflected the exterior.

The characters were all rather bitchy, typical of Robb White's screenplays, but the frosting of cynical humor made for a fun, lightly entertaining kind of film. It remained for *The Haunting* to show what could really be done with a good haunted house movie, but *House on Haunted Hill* is full of incidents to delight horror fans and moves past the dead spaces at a good clip, clocking in at a lean 75 minutes. In typical Castle fashion, the film was given a "screamiere" instead of a premiere.

House on Haunted Hill proved another success and proved to Columbia that Castle could be entrusted with producing a picture. In John Brosnan's book *The Horror People*, he quotes Castle as saying, "The reason I became a producer as well as a director was that I *hated* producers. I hated the interference. I wanted the autonomy of creating what I wished, and in order to have that I had to become a producer myself and wear two hats. That way I got the freedom of directing the way I wanted to."

There is some reasonable speculation as to whether the infamous central gimmick of *The Tingler* might have been inspired by Harry Cohn's sense of humor. According to Hollywood legend, Cohn had a seat in his private dining room that was wired so that when he pressed a button an unwary guest would get a small electric shock. (Supposedly, the story relates, Cohn kept this up until one day he tried it on Vicki Baum without getting a reaction. She remained oblivious because an elaborate girdle insulated her from the shocks, which were administered in great doses and for longer durations by an increasingly frustrated Cohn.)

The idea that the seats actually administered shocks to movie patrons is, not surprisingly, another Hollywood legend, but one not grounded in fact. The gimmick Castle conceived for the *Tingler* involved placing small vibrating motors under every tenth seat. (It was too expensive to wire every seat, so an explanation was given that only certain people would be able to pick up the Tingler's tingle. Mostly, Castle counted on the resulting tumult in the theater to make going to see his latest epic an event.)

As outrageous as wiring up the bottoms of audiences everywhere might be, the plot of *The Tingler* is even more bizarre, straightfacedly feeding the audience a steady stream of erroneous and outrageous "facts." To a large degree, it is this serious, straightforward approach that makes the film so much fun to see today as the film is talky, flat, and does not have many thrilling scenes.

Price stars as William Chapin, a scientific researcher and part-time medical examiner. As the film opens, he is doing an autopsy on an executed convict and notes how the man's spine was crushed, apparently by his fear. The corpse's brother, silent-movie theater operator Ollie Higgins (Philip Coolidge), suggests that perhaps this mysterious spine-crushing fear might arise from the same thing that makes one's spine tingle when one is scared, so Chapin dubs it the Tingler.

Ollie invites Chapin home. He lives with his miserly wife above the theater they own and operate. His wife, Martha (Judith Evelyn), is a deaf-mute who is terrified of blood and germs or that someone might steal her money. When Dr. Chapin accidentally cuts himself, Martha collapses in terror. The conscientious doctor, not wanting to violate his ethics and make a house call (however unintentional), decides to head home himself.

Things are not going much merrier there. His ill-tempered wife, Isabel (Patricia Cutts), is aghast at the idea that her younger sister Lucy (Pamela Lincoln) wants to marry Chapin's assistant David (Darryl Hickman). (Unhappy marriages were an element both in White's life and in his screenplays, making for some amusingly bitchy exchanges.)

Chapin decides to track down and isolate the spine-breaking Tingler, even if he has to grow one inside himself. (Talk about your dedicated scientists! Actually, he first muses whether Dave might be willing to be frightened to death so that he could get his hands on a specimen; however, David, who is not that dedicated, demurs.) Price experiments with frightening himself by taking some LSD (making this, I believe, the first commercial film to make reference to this famous hallucinogen) and has a bad trip in which the walls frighten him with a ripple effect. Although Price's histrionics are far more amusing than frightening, X-rays taken during the ordeal reveal a Tingler growing and disappearing from Chapin's spine.

Back to Martha's apartment above the theater, where poor Martha has become the focus of a campaign of terror. The key elements in this campaign include a hairy arm, a hatchet, a man in a fright mask, and (most arresting of all in an otherwise black-and-white film) a bathtub filled with red blood from which a sanguinary arm arises, and faucets that run red with blood. As a capper, the medicine cabinet contains a copy of her death certificate. At last she keels over dead, her spine crushed by the Tingler.

Ollie comes home and, sensing how pleased Dr. Chapin will be, rushes his late wife's body to Chapin's office. Chapin extracts the rubbery Tingler and stuffs it into a conveniently sized box he happens to have lying around. Chapin then tells Ollie to take Martha back home, since the funeral parlor will no doubt be closed.

Chapin returns home, telling Isabel of his triumph and celebrating the occasion with drinks. Isabel has other plans and drugs Chapin's drink. She opens the Tingler's box in the hope that it will dispose of her husband for her, and indeed the plan almost seems to work, but when the Tingler attaches itself to Chapin's throat, Lucy comes in and screams, causing the curious little creature to fall off. (Earlier they explained that screaming causes Tinglers to shrink and dissipate, which is why Martha makes such a great target in that she cannot scream to rid herself of this peculiar creation; however, this Tingler conveniently fails to shrink, saving Castle from having to make subsequently smaller models of it.)

With the Tingler recaptured by Chapin, he decides that this is yet another of those things that neither man nor science should meddle in. He resolves to dispose of the Tingler by reattaching it to Martha's spinal column. He takes it back to Ollie and Martha's apartment, and the two men get into a discussion while the Tingler escapes its box and creeps downstairs. But whenever it attaches itself to a member of the audience's legs, that person screams and it drops off in fright and frustration.

Vincent Price's voice at times comes on over a black screen and advises the audience to "Scream! Scream for your very lives! The Tingler is loose in this theater!" Finally, the Tingler is captured by Chapin with a 35mm film can (how appropriate), and he replaces it inside Martha's body. Knowing that Ollie was the one who not only committed the murder his brother died for but was also responsible for frightening his wife to death, he's off to tell the authorities. Ollie seems to take this rather calmly, but the minute Chapin leaves, things really get out of hand – doors slam, windows close, and Martha's body, apparently animated by the Tingler, approaches Ollie, who is petrified and cannot scream and is growing a Tingler of his own. (Maybe this is the way Tinglers find their mates?) We know that Ollie is growing a Tingler because whenever a Tingler grows or is onscreen, Castle clues us in by adding the sound of a loud heartbeat to the film.

Much of the film goes nowhere. Isabel, for example, disappears after she attempts to dispatch her husband. Neither David nor Lucy is very important to the story. There *is* something creepy about a little, alien thing crawling around – something which was used to good effect on a few *Outer Limits* episodes – but here the story has no other purpose than to frighten and entertain. The frights are rather perfunctory, but the film does seem at times to have its tongue in its cheek, which gives it an enjoyable quality.

However, as critic Bill Warren complained in his *Keep Watching the Skies Volume II*: "[I]nstead of taking a thriller situation and finding the humor in it, [Castle and White] create such situations *to* find the humor. Castle was too conventional and unimaginative a director to make this approach consistently, and White had no affection for his material. As a result, the films [they made] seem naive and too sophisticated at once."

Once more demonstrating his knack for naming his gimmicks, Castle came up with "PerceptoVision," and dared his audience to experience it. (Typical ads ran, "Do you have the guts to sit in this chair? Can you take Percepto? Can you take it when The Tingler breaks loose?") This daring of audiences to expose themselves to such fright as the film offered became an increasingly common marketing tactic and is related to the basic appeal of horror films for many.

There are a couple of amusing stories associated with the film. In Castle's autobiography, he explains how a bored projectionist decided to test the Tingler equipment and switched it on during a screening of *The Nun's Story* attended by several elderly Bostonian ladies. Also, Robb White revealed in an interview in *Fangoria* with John Wooley that kids started packing screwdrivers to Tingler screenings and were stealing the motors under the seats.

Perhaps missing the 3-D trend at its inception rankled Castle, but it certainly proved the inspiration for his next project, *13 Ghosts*, a dismal little film that was meant to be "fun for the whole family." The gimmick this time was called "Illusion-O" and the audience was given "Ghost Viewers and Removers," red and blue strips of cellophane around a glass frame. The film was in black and white with the ghosts tinted a reddish color. Thus, if you were chicken and looked through the red side, you would see nothing, but if you looked thorough the blue tint, the red images stood out and were clearly visible. (Later prints dispensed with the gimmick by simply printing the ghost images onto black-and-white film.) Sensitive to the complaints about 3-D, Castle arranged it so that viewers would have to look through the glasses only when the characters on the screen themselves were looking through special glasses and viewing the "ghosts."

The film's nominal hero was a little boy, a member of the Zorba family. Professor Zorba inherits his uncle's house and moves there with his famly. There is a nice red herring role for Margaret Hamilton as a sinister housekeeper who Uncle Zorba insists be kept on, and there is the hoary cliché of a treasure somewhere on the premises that is being protected by ghosts.

The ghosts do not make 13 different appearances, instead frequently preferring to appear in tandem. The apparitions are clutching hands; a floating head; a flaming skeleton; a screaming woman; a man with a meat cleaver in his hand; his unfaithful wife; her lover; an executioner and a decapitated head; a hanged woman; a lion; a lion tamer without a head; and Uncle Zorba. If you have kept count, you will notice that is only 12 ghosts — the last is a vacancy that the villain of the piece, a smarmy lawyer (played by Martin Milner), fills.

Still, no amount of ghosts could enliven this deadly dull story. The cast, which includes Rosemary De Camp, Charles Herbert, Jo Morrow and Donald Woods, is competent, but the script is strictly a by-the-numbers compendium of clichés. Castle seems to have put most of his energy into perfecting his simple Illusion-O gimmick.

Luckily, Castle's next film, *Homicidal*, was a definite improvement over *13 Ghosts*. The film starts out by proclaiming that "Columbia Pictures Presents William Castle." Castle makes an amusing onscreen appearance, putting the finishing touches on an embroidery of the title and telling us, "The more adventurous among you might remember our previous excursions into the macabre — haunted houses, tinglers, ghosts. . . ." With a name before the title and an onscreen appearance, Castle was trying to establish a personality for himself in the Hitchcock manner. Hitchcock, with a television series, a series of short story collections, and a mystery magazine in addition to his movies, was the best-known director in the world, and extremely successful at peddling his brand of shock and suspense. Castle knew he did not have Hitchcock's talent, but realized that he could reap financial benefit from some of the same exploitation techniques that Hitchcock had used. He was particularly impressed by *Psycho*, a low-budget, black-and-white film which had become the sensation of 1960. One key element in its success, Castle reasoned, was Hitchcock's strictly enforced gimmick of not seating anyone after the film had begun. This meant that invariably there would be a line of people waiting to see the film, heightening the sense that it was attracting audiences and was something worth waiting in line to see.

A major story element of his new film, he decided, would be a homicidal transvestite. Initially, he auditioned young men, most of them gay, to see if they could be convincingly transformed to play the feminine role, but he decided that approach was wrong. Finally, Jerry Lauren brought him a woman named Joan Marshall who Castle thought would do. To prevent the audience from determining whether she was a man or a woman, he changed her stage name to Jean Arless. Unfortunately, one aspect of the transformation included an appliance in Marshall's mouth which prevented her lips from closing naturally. Thus through most of the picture she has an open-mouthed, stupid look on her face whenever she is playing the "Warren" role, something which is decidedly odd and a big giveaway as to the final revelation.

The film opens with a strange, short sequence in which a young boy, Warren, steals his half-sister Miriam's doll. The calendar on the wall clues the audience as to the time (1948) and the setting (Solvang). Abruptly, the time and setting switch to Ventura in the "present," as a blond woman, Emily, checks into a hotel and catches the eye of a bellboy there. The sleazy, shadowy, strident tone of the picture is quickly established, and the plot intrigues as the bellboy is offered $2,000 to marry Emily with the understanding that the marriage will be immediately annulled.

Reaching the justice of the peace's house at midnight, Emily offers extra cash to have them married right away. After a perfunctory service, Alfred Adrians, the justice of the peace, leans to kiss the bride, and she promptly stabs him repeatedly with a stiletto. The murder was shocking to 1961 audiences not only for coming so early in the film, but for being far more graphic (though far less artistically crafted) than the infamous one in *Psycho*. Emily stabs several times, and we see the blood well up under Adrians' shirt before he expires in the arms of the shocked bellboy as Emily makes her escape. She switches cars en route to Solvang, and we see that she must have planned the whole bizarre escapade – but what could have been her motivation? As she is cleaning off the stiletto, a noisy thumping behind her makes her aware of Helga (Eugenie Leontovich in a fine performance as a bitter and often frightened mute) coming up behind her in her wheelchair. Emily announces proudly that she has dispatched Adrians.

The next morning, Miriam (Patricia Breslin) comes by to look in on Emily and Helga. Emily is clearly resentful of the affection that Miriam has for Warren. (The characters all seem to wear their likes and dislikes on their shirtsleeves.) Warren is supposedly married to Emily and lives away but he comes up every Thursday. Warren and Emily and Helga have all recently returned from Denmark because Warren is nearing his twenty-first birthday, at which time he will inherit his father's fortune. It is later revealed that Warren's parents have long been dead and that Warren was an abused child. His father and mother wanted him to be "tough."

Things begin to get sticky for Warren and Emily when Miriam's boyfriend Karl (Glenn Corbett), Solvang's drugstore owner and apothecary, discovers Emily's handiwork after she has gone into Miriam's florist shop and destroyed a wedding arrangement and a picture of Warren that he signed and gave to his half-sister. Unfortunately, in the process Karl comes across some medicine that he had given Emily for Helga. When the police visit Miriam because the murderess of the justice of the peace had given Miriam's name when she was married, Karl quickly begins to fit the pieces together. (Though, strangely enough, when Warren first encounters Karl, he shows Karl the newspaper sketch of the murderess and Karl fails to find anything familiar in the picture.)

Castle plays with his audience, particularly in a sequence after Emily summons a knife sharpener to the house to put a new edge on her stiletto. She goes back inside to finish off Helga, but then the town doctor chooses now of all times to pay his long-postponed visit. Helga is naturally stressed and perturbed, but the doctor consistently fails to react to her silent histrionics. After he leaves, Emily calmly puts Helga on her stairwell escalator and rides with her to the top. Castle cuts from her swing to the sound and image of Karl's car careening around a corner, on his way to show a picture of Emily to the police and the eyewitness, the bellboy.

Back at the florist's, Miriam is waiting for word from Karl when Warren drops by. When it is confirmed that Emily is the murderess, Warren professes concern for Helga. It will take the police an hour to get to the family mansion from Ventura. Miriam insists on accompanying him, but Warren leaves her behind in the car with only the loud ticking of the car's clock to keep her company.

When Warren fails to reappear right away, Miriam decides to investigate. The house is quiet and Warren does not respond when his name is called. Then at the top of the stairs, the escalator is activated and Helga comes down. When her wheelchair reaches the bottom, we see the shadow of her head tilt forward – then impossibly forward as it falls off her shoulders (the film's most memorable macabre joke).

Emily shows up with her stiletto and pulls off her wig to reveal that she is Warren, who explains that she killed Adrians and Helga because they were the only ones who knew her secret (that she was not a boy and therefore not entitled to inherit her father's millions) and that she plans to kill Miriam and put the kibosh on "Warren's" fictitious "wife" by having "Emily" disappear for good after proclaiming her insane. However, just then, the doctor pays another of his timely visits and Warren and the doctor struggle. Miriam fires a gun in their direction, luckily hitting (and presumably killing) only Warren.

At the tag, a psychiatrist explains that Emily's father had left his first wife (Miriam's mother) because she had given him a girl instead of a boy. Therefore, Emily's mother tried to keep Emily's true sex from her father by raising her as a boy. (Obviously, this was done in the days before both parents were involved in changing diapers.) Emily sought to get rid of Miriam because she was the heiress if Emily's ruse should ever be discovered. Now she will be a rich woman. Miriam turns to Karl and says, "I hope my being rich won't make any difference." Karl brightly returns that he is sure it will – he will love her more. (A typical Robb White hero, he is even more interested in the money than in the girl.)

Castle's gimmick for the new film was a "Fright Break." Before Miriam enters the house, Castle advises the audience that they can retreat to "Coward's Corner" and get their money refunded if they are too frightened to see the last few minutes of *Homicidal.*

At a test engagement, the gimmick did not work quite as well as planned when the audience for the first showing stayed for the second showing so that they could get a full refund at the fright break. Castle solved the problem by having the exhibitors sell different colored tickets for each performance. Over America, not too many refunds were given, partly because of the demeaning things Castle set up for his audience to get one, which included the "Coward's Corner" where a loudspeaker squawked, "These cowards are too frightened to see the end of *Homicidal!* Watch them shiver in the Coward's Corner. Coward . . . coward . . . coward. . . ." Also, anyone desiring a refund had to sign a yellow card stating "I am a bona fide coward."

Despite Arless' off-kilter performance (I do not believe she ever made another film) and the bad dubbing job done on Warren's early scenes, the surprise apparently worked for many people and the film overall was a success. To the amusement and pleasure of Castle, no less than *Time* magazine proclaimed that *Homicidal* was better than *Psycho*, though this was far from a consensus among critics of the day. White reportedly saw *Psycho* after the film was made and was embarrassed by the similarities. He never worked for Castle again.

Homicidal is one of Castle's better offerings, having some atmosphere in the depressing hotel room Emily checks into and the shadowy mansion later. The first murder was indeed shocking and, H. G. Lewis aside, quite gory for its time. The whole thing moved at a good clip and the dialogue and people act so peculiarly that the result is almost dreamlike – reality is left behind. It is a fun shocker that was better than many of the other *Psycho* imitations that followed or surrounded it.

Castle found the idea for his next film in an issue of *Playboy*. He read Ray Russell's story "Sardonicus" and decided to buy the story and hire Russell to write the screenplay. It became the first period horror film that Castle attempted, and perhaps that was part of the problem.

Mr. Sardonicus seems to ape the low-budget atmosphere of such films as *The Black Sleep*. The studio sets are all very artificial and never convincing or interesting. Castle was not able to give the whole mess a period flavor, and the story itself was rather listless.

Sir Robert Cargrave (Ronald Lewis) is a doctor who has perfected a technique for relieving paralysis by massage. An old sweetheart (Audrey Dalton) sends him a message that his services are urgently needed. He is met at the train station by a skulking man named Krull (Oscar Homolka), who is the Baron Sardonicus' personal manservant. Castle makes a small attempt to imitate Corman's Poe pictures as Krull guides Cargrave past portraits of his master's ancestors.

Finally, he finds out that Maude, his former sweetheart, is now the unhappy Baron's wife. The Baron (Guy Rolfe) hides his visage behind a simple mask and eventually explains that his face became deformed when, as a young man, he won a lottery but the ticket had been left in his dead father's coat. His now deceased first wife insisted that he dig up his father's grave and retrieve the ticket, but in doing so, the shock of seeing his father's decaying corpse in its death rigor caused his own face to imitate it and remain in a hideous grin. While wealthy beyond belief, Sardonicus still lacks what he most desires: a normal face.

Cargraves' massage techniques fail to make any difference on the Baron's face, and he slowly discovers just what a cruel and evil man Sardonicus is. The whole village lives in fear of him, and he is not above torturing his own servants in his search for a cure. Desperate, Sardonicus insists that Cargrave use an experimental formula, which Cargrave is reluctant to do, and so Sardonicus threatens to kill Maude if he does not comply. Cargrave pretends to go along with the Baron's wishes and decides to use psychology instead. He arranges for the Baron to be locked in a dark room with the remains of his father in hopes of shocking him back to normalcy. When he recovers, the Baron finds his grin is gone and agrees to set the lovers free.

Just as Cargave and Maude are leaving, Krull shows up and informs the pair that while his master's face is no longer in a grin, he has a new problem. It is seemingly immobile and he cannot open his mouth even to accept food. Cargrave explains that Sardonicus' condition is purely psychological – the serum he was injected with was only water. He assumes that once Sardonicus knows that it was all in his mind, he will be normal once more.

Krull returns to the castle and informs the Baron that he was too late. The Baron has sat down to a large dinner and tries to force himself to eat but to no avail. Meanwhile, Krull starts gorging himself, enjoying his revenge on the Baron for the cruelties the Baron has inflicted upon him.

According to Castle, Columbia found his ending too bleak and insisted he reshoot a happier one, one in which the cruel Sardonicus does not appear to be doomed to die of starvation amidst plenty. Ultimately, Castle agreed and decided to have alternate endings be his next gimmick.

The gimmick was dubbed "The Punishment Poll" and involved glow-in-the-dark cards that had "thumbs up" and "thumbs down" printed on them. At a crucial moment in the film, the projectionist was supposed to stop the film, survey whether the audiences wanted Sardonicus to die or survive and put on the appropriate reel. However, there never was an alternate reel. A projectionist could not have made a selection from an audience holding cards up to "the screen" and be able to make an accurate count in a darkened theater. The whole thing was simply another gimmick.

Overall, the film is uninteresting and disappointing. The liveliness and humor that had enlivened some of Castle's other productions were largely absent except for the macabre ending. At first brief glimpse, Sardonicus' face with its terrible grin is effectively unnerving, but it becomes ludicrous as one continues looking at it. Castle kept shots of it down to a minimum, withholding it from the audience for most of the film. However, Conrad Veidt's "permanent" grin in *The Man Who Laughs* was far more effective and unnerving, possibly because it seems more natural and its consistency and inappropriateness is unnerving. Sardonicus' face is obviously just a clever special effect, one that has been aped in other films and music videos since then.

Castle decided on a change of pace, coming up with a Disneyesque comedy based on Walter Karig's novel *Zotz!* Once more, he had Ray Russell write the screenplay, this time going for laughs rather than screams. As poor as Castle was sometimes at going for screams, he was even worse at intentionally going after nothing but laughs. The whole film centers around Tom Poston as a professor who discovers that with a special Zotz coin, he can will anything to happen simply by pointing and saying "Zotz." Poston has always seemed to me to be more annoying than funny, and the screenplay fails to do anything really interesting. The closest it comes to humor and imagination is having Castle put himself in the place of the Columbia statue in the logo and go, "Zotz!"

Castle decided to use Poston again for his next film. A coproduction with the famed Hammer Studios in England, it was a remake of a James Whale classic, *The Old Dark House*. While the film does have many good things going for it, particularly the Charles Addams credits and actors like Robert Morley and Peter Bull, the film mostly falls on its face. Poston decides to visit his distant (in more ways than one) relatives, the Femms, in England. There are a pair of twins obsessed with dying, both played by Bull; Joyce Grenfell plays the mother, who is obsessed with knitting; Morley's uncle is obsessed with guns; Mervyn Johns is obsessed with building an ark; Danny Green is a puritanical father; Janette Scott (of *Day of the Triffids* fame) is obsessed with killing her family off; and Fenella Fielding is the large-breasted female that no Hammer film can do without, who somehow becomes obsessed with Posten. Strangely enough, though it was shot in color, it was released in the United States in black-and-white, then later released in Britain in 1968 in a trimmed color version which eliminated some of the supposedly humorous sequences.

In an effort to make a truly international film, Castle next came up with *13 Frightened Girls*, not a horror film but rather a spy story. It was about the daughters of 13 diplomats who, while staying in a Swiss boarding house, decide to pool information and take up spying. The film was originally titled *The Candy Web* and the leads were found via an international talent contest in 13 different countries. The winners were given first-class transportation and accommodations for themselves and a chaperone, and $300 in spending money plus expenses. Most of the actresses did not know how to speak English and had to learn their parts phonetically. The result has been described by some as a film so bad that it is good. To allow each girl to "star" in the film in her native country, the initial scene, in which the "heroine" narrates the arrival at the airport, was shot 13 times, featuring a different girl each time.

In the meantime, both *What Ever Happened to Baby Jane?* and *Hush . . . Hush, Sweet Charlotte* had proven big box office, so Castle decided he wanted to make a thriller with the star of one of those films. For the scriptwriter, he selected Robert Bloch, who in addition to writing the book on which *Psycho* was based had done the screenplays for *The Couch* and the remake of *The Cabinet of Caligari*. Bloch wrote a tidy script, and it was offered to Joan Crawford, who accepted upon the condition that she work with the writer to make a few changes. While overall a positive experience for Castle, the film was his first exposure to a major star's demands. Unlike the typical Castle film, this one included rehearsals at Crawford's insistence. In the course of those rehearsals, Crawford decided that the woman playing her daughter was inadequate. That person was replaced by Diane Baker.

Strait-Jacket is one of Castle's best and, strangely (perhaps due to the lack of gimmicks, though there were some cardboard axes with fake blood handed out), most overlooked films. The film opens strikingly with headlines proclaiming Lucy Harbin (Crawford) declared insane. This image shatters like glass. Next we see that Lucy's husband, Frank (a bit part for a very young Lee Majors, who was cast at Rock Hudson's suggestion), is stepping out with a woman named Stella. They go home together because his wife's away, but they wake up his daughter Carol.

At the same time, Lucy emerges from some smoke at the railroad station, home earlier than expected. Her character is described as "very much a woman and very much aware of the fact." When she looks in the window and sees Frank and Stella lying on the bed, she grabs an axe and decides to get into the swing of things, so to speak. In shadow we see their heads fall off. Meanwhile, we also see that young Carol has been a silent witness to the massacre. Lucy is put away, but no one seems to question whether Carol might have been affected by the tragedy.

Now it is 20 years later and Lucy is being released on a probationary status, hopeful that she is cured. Her reunion with her now grown-up daughter Carol (Diane Baker) is not particularly joyous—Carol is rather unresponsive at first, failing to return her mother's hug. This is followed by a trip through the farm that they live on, which seems designed to remind Lucy of her ordeal. She mentions hating to see the chickens or anything else caged, and Carol cheerfully adds, "Oh, that's all right, we butcher them...." As soon as Lucy sees the pigs, Carol mentions something about slaughter. The realization that Carol's boyfriend, Michael Fields (John Anthony Hayes), is coming to dinner then throws Lucy into a tizzy. She is not ready to meet anybody.

Carol shows off a bust of her mother (she has become a sculptress, mostly of animals) and Lucy swells with pride and emotion. However, the sound of jangling trinkets disturbs her. Carol is shocked when Lucy suddenly picks up a putty knife absentmindedly. Is Lucy really cured?

Michael comes by that evening, but Lucy has hidden herself away. Looking for her, Carol leads Michael into her studio where they discover that someone has cut off the heads of her father's photos in a family photo album.

The next day, Lucy and Carol go shopping and Lucy gets a wig which makes her look 20 years younger. She starts hearing young girls' voices chanting the old Lizzie Borden rhyme about her. She also is talked into buying clothes that will make her appear youthful, as if she were trying to pick up where she left off 20 years ago.

That night things get particularly bad when Lucy wakes up and sees two disembodied heads and an axe in her bed. She runs screaming from the bedroom and rouses the house, but naturally when they return, there is nothing there. If that is not disturbing enough, the next day while walking around she comes upon the farm's handyman, Leo Krause (George Kennedy), lopping the heads of chickens. Krause offers her the axe to do it herself – after all, she is an old farm girl – but she gets the shakes and cannot bring herself to do it, so Krause takes over. The sound of machinery in the barn becomes oppressive and she has to leave.

Carol goes with Michael to visit his parents, telling him, "There's a murder mystery down at the drive-in – nice and gory," along the way. (Bloch's script persistently manages to bring up those macabre topics, which is part of the film's humor.) The Fieldses are polite but are also interested in learning more about Carol's "invalid" mother's "illness." As they are very wealthy, Carol thinks they would not approve of her background if they knew. Clearly, she has no intention of losing Michael as a potential husband.

Coming back to Lucy, Castle makes it clear that she has lost all of her earlier confidence and is now particularly nervous and on edge. Strangely, though, once Michael arrives and she sees how handsome he is, Lucy starts coming on to Carol's beau, much to Carol's dismay. Far from being shy, she becomes positively kittenish, but all that changes when she gets a phone call from a "secret admirer" who says he will be right out. She becomes upset and leaves the room.

Doctor Anderson is the so-called admirer. He was heading out on a fishing trip and decided to drop by and check up on Lucy's progress on adjusting to normal life. Lucy receives him very coldly, but then tries to hide her nervousness under a festive facade. She start knitting, but talk about her daughter upsets her. When Anderson asks if she has been having any dreams, she explodes at him and stabs her needles into the floor.

Anderson seeks out Carol, who wants to know if Lucy is sane. "Sane is a relative term," he replies by way of comfort. Anderson advises taking her back to the institution. On his way across the farm, he conveniently uses the chopping block to empty his pipe against. Just then the door slams shut and an axe begins to fall.

Carol looks for Lucy and finds her needles in the floor. Lucy returns, no longer wearing the wig and the youthful dress. Noticing the doctor's car is still there, she asks Lucy where the doctor is. "The doctor's gone," is all she will say. Carol decides to hide the car in an unused barn but is noticed by Krause.

Lucy is cheerful the next morning because the absence of the doctor's car means that he is indeed gone. A phone call comes from the hospital looking for the doctor, at which point Lucy takes a knife and starts shredding paper. Carol assures her, "Don't worry mother, I won't let them take you back."

Krause claims the doctor's car for his own and begins painting it. Carol tries to fire the creepy handyman, but he will not go away. Since Michael makes an unexpected appearance, she lets the matter drop. She advises Michael not to announce their engagement. Michael assures her that his parents will accept her mother once they meet her and arranges for the parents to meet.

Meanwhile, Krause begins to get nervous. He is startled by a shirt on a line, the sleeve of which whips around him. Nervously, he investigates the farm. He bends over and finds the doctor's body in a freezer, but someone walks up from behind and chops his head off. The shot is bloodless but gruesomely explicit.

While Lucy is reluctant, Carol convinces her to have dinner with Michael's parents and wear her dress and wig. When they arrive, there is a disorienting visual "wash" after which Lucy seems to be back at the institution, trapped in a striped room. Only it is a Blochian fake-out – she's in the Fieldses' bathroom after having spilled coffee on her dress. Mrs. Fields compares the difficulty of removing coffee stains to blood stains. Lucy spills the secret of Carol and Michael's plans, to the evident displeasure of Mrs. Fields, who feels that marriage would be out of the question considering Lucy's background, which they had hired a private detective to find out about.

"I paid for anything I did – you'll never know how much I paid," Lucy tells them.

"You're insane!" Mrs. Fields tactfully returns.

"My girl is going to have what she wants out of life. I was cheated," Lucy protests and leaves, furious. Uncle Bill goes to look for her while Michael drives Carol and Aunt Emily home.

Meanwhile, Mr. Fields goes up to brush his teeth when his bathroom door mysteriously closes. He opens it up but sees nothing out of the ordinary on the other side. However, when he goes to his closet, he gets axed. Mrs. Fields goes up and see the door of the study close. Peering inside, she sees the shadow of a head, but it only turns out to be a bust. Looking in the bathroom, particularly the curtained shower, she finds nothing, but she does discover Mr. Field's body in the closet as Carol comes rushing in wearing a Lucy mask, wig and dress. While the pair struggle, Lucy bursts in and Carol throws an axe at her, hitting the doorjamb. They tussle and Lucy pulls the mask off Carol. Michael returns home and is naturally confused by the commotion. Lucy hands him Carol's mask while Carol exhorts that she and Michael can get married at last. She knew Michael's parents would object so she planned to murder them and pin the blame on her mother, whom she alternately loves and hates.

The whole thing was a carefully planned scheme, down to a tape recording of girls chanting the Lizzie Borden rhyme and Carol making busts of the murdered couple to leave in Lucy's bed. Lucy vows that while she was not around before when Carol needed her, she will be with her at the asylum because she knows better than anyone what she will go through. It is an ironic triumph of mother love. As a final joke, the Columbia statue is missing its head over the final "the end" credit.

Crawford gives a strong, controlled performance in the film. She handles well a wide emotional range and does suggest someone who has been to the edge of sanity and is trying to recover under difficult circumstances, though some of the changes called for in the script are rather abrupt. George Kennedy makes for an effectively creepy red herring, a disquieting presence on the sunny, rural farm. However, credulity is quite stretched by the bizarre time sequence in which characters travel around to make the murders happen, particularly at the end. For example, if Carol is driven home, how does she apparently get back on foot before Michael does when he is driving, and where does she have the time to change back and forth into clothes identical to her mother's? But then, that is what Hitchcock called kitchen logic, something you are not supposed to think about until you get home from the film and reach into your refrigerator. All in all, the film is well paced and has some very effective sequences, combining editing, lighting and sound effects to create tension and shock. Castle felt this film was strong enough to go out without a gimmick, and he was right.

Bloch also scripted Castle's next film, *The Night Walker*, an ambitious thriller which unfortunately fails to come off fully. It would prove to be Barbara Stanwyck's last film. Stanwyck talks in her sleep about a lover, causing her blind husband (Hayden Rourke), an electronics engineer, to accuse her of being unfaithful with Robert Taylor, his solicitor. When her husband is accidentally blown up, he haunts Stanwyck's dreams. In one particularly bizarre dream, a man (Lloyd Bocher) takes her to a chapel to get married by a wax-figure priest before wax-figure witnesses, and then she sees the figure of her husband horribly burned. It becomes difficult for her to tell what is reality and what is dream.

As usual, it all turns out to be an elaborate ruse. Her husband had hired Bochner as a detective before her husband died, and now Bochner wants to blackmail Stanwyck. Meanwhile, Taylor wants to gain her money and drive her insane by pretending to be her dead husband. He kills Bochner and is about to dispatch Stanwyck when he falls to his death. Stanwyck gives the film some credibility with her fine performance, but the dream effects and Castle's attempt to blend fantasy and reality just are not up to carrying it off. The film bombed.

Castle's next film, *I Saw What You Did*, was based on a suspense novel, *Out of the Dark* by Ursula Curtiss. It involves two teenage girls who love to make prank phone calls. Unfortunately, they have the bad luck to call John Ireland just after he has murdered his wife (Joyce Meadows) in the shower and tell him, "I saw what you did; I know who you are." Joan

Crawford has a cameo role as the amorous neighbor who realizes Ireland's true nature shortly before being dispatched herself. While routine, the picture does generate a fair amount of suspense. Castle thought of a gimmicky tie-in with the phone company, but that backfired when teenagers started making prank calls, aping the ones in the film. He settled for offering some cinemagoers seat belts to keep them in their seats during the shocks.

This was followed by *Let's Kill Uncle*, in which 12-year-old Pat Cardi and his uncle, played by Nigel Green, square off on an island over a $5 million inheritance and try to kill each other. Mary Badham is the boy's only ally as the man tries to use hypnotism, sharks, tarantulas, fire, and poison mushrooms against him.

Next were a pair of unfunny comedies with Sid Caesar, *The Busy Body* and *The Spirit Is Willing*, the first about gangsters and misplaced corpses and the second about three ghosts in a New England house. Both were box office disasters and are rarely seen. Castle's career as a director was spiraling downwards as audiences stopped coming to his films, lured away by television and higher class features. He lucked out by coming across galley proofs of Ira Levin's *Rosemary's Baby* and buying the rights and producing it for the screen. (For more on *Rosemary's Baby*, see chapter on Roman Polanski.)

Following *Rosemary's Baby*, Castle was supposed to produce Neil Simon's *The Out-of-Towners* but fell ill and was unable to take the assignment. He did direct a science fiction thriller, *Project X*, based on L. P. Davies' *The Artificial Man*. In the year 2118, secret agent Christopher George is brainwashed into thinking he is a bank robber in 1968 so as to break down his mental defenses. Trapped in his head is a secret plan that the Sino-Asians have of destroying the western world. The mind probe is accomplished by animation (courtesy of Hanna-Barbera) which is far from impressive. The big secret? That George has been infected with bubonic plague, but by isolating him, the western world is saved. The entire effort does have its intriguing aspects but is mediocre in execution.

Castle retired from directing and produced the film *Riot*, a violent prison film starring Gene Hackman and Jim Brown. Later, he got back into television, producing the series *Circle of Fear* aka *Ghost Story*.

Castle made a few brief cameo appearances, playing a Harry Cohn–like producer in *The Sex Symbol*, a director in *The Day of the Locust*, and a political supporter in *Shampoo*. Finally he became executive producer on a film called *Shanks*, which was to star Marcel Marceau – Marceau's first film since his disastrous cameo in *Barbarella*. Marceau wanted Polanski to direct, but Polanski was busy and his fees were far outside the film's modest budget. Castle suggested someone Marceau never heard of. Finally, Marceau insisted that Castle be the director. Castle agreed with reluctance, finding Marceau very demanding and unrealistic.

Shanks is probably the closest Castle got to a standard horror plot, involving as it does the reanimation of dead bodies. Marceau has a dual role as a puppeteer named Malcolm, a mute, and the elderly scientist who hires him. The scientist, Walker (Marceau in an awful old age makeup), can reanimate bodies by inserting electrodes into their joints and controlling them like puppets—hence his need for the puppeteer.

Malcolm resurrects Walker's body when he dies, and the bodies of his sister (Tsialla Chien) and her husband (Phillipe Clay) when they have an accident. When he takes the group on a walk, the results are indeed peculiar and hilarious. All three of the "corpses" are excellent mimes and bring a unique interpretation to being reanimated. Unfortunately, the rest of the film around them is not worthy of their talents, especially as things get ugly when a sadistic motorcycle gang rapes and kills a young girl who befriends Malcolm. Malcolm naturally takes his revenge using the automatons, but the film's previously sweet tone has now been utterly lost. Apart from the mimes, the film's only strong element is a good score by Alex North, father of the film's producer. (Castle was the executive producer on the film.)

Castle's final film, *Bug*, was produced by him and directed by Jeannot Szwarc (*Jaws II, Somewhere in Time, Supergirl*). It was based on Thomas Page's *The Hephaestus Plague* and involves huge, flying cockroaches that can set things on fire. It is a silly premise that makes for a silly film, but somehow it manages to be fun on a campy level, as if the makers did not know how ridiculous it was to have intelligent cockroaches group themselves into the letters "We live." Castle even came up with a new idea for a gimmick—tiny windshield wipers attached to the bottom of patrons' seats which at key moments would simulate cockroaches crawling on them. The idea was rejected by the exhibitors across America. Castle claims that he didn't pursue the subject because he guessed that in some theaters the genuine article would be present anyway. He did finally settle on another insurance gag, insuring Hercules the Cockroach, whom he took with him on a promotional jaunt across the country, for a million dollars if Hercules died a natural death during his one-month tour.

Coming out in the same summer that produced *Jaws, Earthquake*, and *The Towering Inferno, Bug* never really had much of a chance, especially since it was not much of a movie. Also, while people share a common revulsion towards cockroaches, on the surface of it, the idea of killer cockroaches can never be anything but laughable. But then, part and parcel of the Castle approach was that you could never take these things too seriously—horror was meant to be fun.

While developing *2000 Lakeview Drive*, Castle died at the age of 63 of a heart attack. His work is rarely discussed these days and his gimmicks are more often reviewed than his films. He recognized he was not the world's best filmmaker, but he knew people fondly recalled his promotions, and it was better to be remembered as King of the Gimmicks than not to be re-membered at all.

Unfortunately, much of his initial promise is whittled away by being placed in the "movie-a-month" environment of the Columbia B-unit. By the time he could approach films more leisurely, the importance of cost-cutting was ingrained in him as deeply as the need to find some clever device of at-tracting people into the theaters. Those were the areas where he concen-trated his energies rather than on his art, though here and there one can see cleverly conceived sequences that indicate he might have been capable of something more than the generally mediocre movies he typically pro-duced.

Castle seems to have shared much of Browning's view of horror, tend-ing to explain it away or go for let-down trick endings rather than taking it seriously. He was a living example of the adage, "You can make a buck if you're the first to be second" – or in other words, let someone else take the risk of being original, and if it hits, you can make money with a quick and cheap follow-up, cashing in on the trend. Castle concentrated on plots which involved scaring a character to death, but while he would give audiences the chance to have fun and scream, he never went so far that audiences would experience anything that would really frighten them. He stuck to the tried and true methods for producing his shocks and chills – hands popping up suddenly on shoulders, quick cuts to ugly images, sudden sounds. In fact, he did particularly well with using annoying sounds to build horror and sus-pense, a very effective technique often overlooked in these supposedly more sophisticated times. The world of his films was greedy and strident, but far enough removed from reality that it was never bothersome. He kept away from "monsters," showing instead people who did monstrous things, and in the early '50s, that was rather a refreshing approach.

Perhaps the main thing that Castle contributed to the horror film was clearly establishing that people went to them with an "it's all in fun" at-titude. He wanted people to enjoy being scared and as a result never pushed things to the limits. But if you bought into it, you could always just sit back and enjoy the ride. Rather than a King of Horror, Castle was a court jester, amusing audiences with simple but clever tricks, always calling attention to himself, and for that people remember him fondly.

Bob Clark (1941–   )

Deathdream; Children Shouldn't Play with Dead Things! (1972); *Black Christmas* (aka *Silent Night, Evil Night; Stranger in the House,* 1974); *Breaking Point* (1976); *Murder by Decree* (1979); *Tribute* (1980); *Porky's* (1982); *Porky's II: The Next Day; A Christmas Story* (1983); *Rhinestone* (1984); *Turk 182!* (1985); *From the Hip* (1987); *Loose Cannons* (1990).

Benjamin Bob Clark made his inauspicious directorial debut with 1972's horror camp classic *Children Shouldn't Play with Dead Things!* an attempt to emulate the staggering success of George A. Romero's *Night of the Living Dead.* The film was scripted by Clark and Alan Ormsby (who would later script *My Bodyguard* and the Paul Schrader version of *Cat People*); Clark coproduced and directed while Ormsby handled the makeup chores and played the part of Alan, a theatrical director who takes five young actors to an isolated island off of the Florida coast.

Ormsby hammed up his part of the egotistical director who calls upon his "children" to dig up a corpse and conduct a black mass for the resurrection of the dead. The group is scared by a couple of "plants" (i.e., actors) who were set up ahead of time for that purpose and laugh at Alan's practical joke.

The group having dug up a corpse, which is dubbed Orville the Awful (Seth Sklarey), make an anti-climactic attempt to revive it. The corpse is taken to a drunken bash at an abandoned house on the island. The sounds of partying prove enough to wake the dead, and soon dozens of zombies prepare to join the party, where they devour the guests in Romero zombie fashion.

The film was executed on a very low budget and was done tongue-in-cheek. The arch dialogue occasionally proves amusing, but more for laughing at than with. According to an interview conducted by Bill George with Alan Ormsby in *Black Oracle #6,* 80 percent of the script was Bob Clark's work while Ormsby contributed most of the material that took place in the house.

The film proved a small success and the pair decided to collaborate again on a film they planned to call *The Veteran* but which was actually released as *Dead of Night* or *Deathdream.* An improvement over *Children,*

Director Benjamin "Bob" Clark with script girl Sandy Ulesowitch on the set of Clark's comical horror opus Children Shouldn't Play with Dead Things. *(Photo courtesy of Bill George.)*

Deathdream chronicled the story of a veteran (Richard Backus) who returns from Vietnam and whose parents discover that he is actually a zombie. In order to survive in his undead state, the vet must have a fresh supply of blood, which he initially gets from the family doctor (Henderson Forsythe). He is driven to murder to survive, which causes his guilt-ridden father to commit suicide. The film ends with him finally deciding to rest in peace at the local cemetery. The film is particularly notable as the first makeup assignment of former Vietnam vet Tom Savini, who collaborated with

Ormsby on the makeup effects. (Later Savini would showcase his gore effects for Ormsby and Jeff Gillen's film *Deranged*, a gruesome shocker that comes closest to recreating the facts of the infamous Ed Gein case, which supplied the inspiration for both *Psycho* and *The Texas Chain Saw Massacre*.)

In 1974 Clark went to Canada to film *Black Christmas*, which was also released as *Silent Night, Evil Night* and *Stranger in the House*. The film caused a minor sensation among horror fans and is remarkably similar to the series of stalk-and-slash films that *Halloween* popularized (though Mario Bava had been doing those kinds of films in the '60s).

The setting is a sorority house in which a maniac (Keir Dullea, star of *2001*) has secreted himself. The old chestnut of terrifying phone calls that emanate from inside the house being called is dragged out, along with plenty of subjective camera shots from the killer's point of view, his identity a mystery and his reasons for killing obscure.

Clark decided to get away from horror with *Breaking Point*, a film about a man (Bo Svenson) who testified against the mafia and now has to run for his life, but the results were so atrocious that this Canadian film never went anywhere except television oblivion. The film was an overall step back in quality, featuring murky photography and a muffled sound mix.

Surprisingly, Clark's next horror film has thus far proved to be his best. *Murder by Decree* takes its cue from a BBC documentary on Jack the Ripper called *The Ripper File* and combines Saucy Jack with the most famous literary detective of the period, Arthur Conan Doyle's Sherlock Holmes (here ably played by Christopher Plummer).

The script by John Hopkins was based on the idea that the Jack the Ripper murders were committed by members of the upper class to conceal an indiscretion on the part of the Duke of Clarence, heir to the throne, known to his friends as Eddy. The film depicts how the murders of prostitutes in Whitechapel have inflamed the radical left, who use the murders to demonstrate the ruling class' apparent indifference to the sufferings of the poor and underprivileged.

Holmes heads home with Watson (James Mason, probably the ablest Watson ever depicted onscreen) after one of the murders, and he is puzzled as to why the police have not called him in to help solve the crime as they have in the past. At 221B Baker Street, their famous abode, a group of men who claim to be merchants from around the Whitechapel area beg Holmes for his assistance. Holmes recognizes that they are part of the radical movement. They hope that Holmes will uncover evidence of a cover-up that will embarrass the Old Guard currently in power.

Receiving a tip, Holmes and Watson meet a mysterious stranger by the wharf. There one of the radicals they received earlier tells them to seek out a psychic named Robert Lees* (Donald Sutherland). After Holmes and Watson leave, the man is killed by Jack the Ripper with a sword cane and left to be discovered by the police.

Lees gives them the clue that the murderer is a member of the upper class because of some psychic visions he has had. However, Sir Charles Warren (Anthony Quayle) has threatened him so that he will not reveal the name of the man he suspects. Warren does not want Holmes investigating the case and wipes out a message blaming the murders on the "Juwes." Holmes perceives correctly that Sir Charles is a Freemason, shocks Sir Charles by giving him a secret Masonic handshake, and intuits that "Juwes" refer to Masonic lore about the men who destroyed Solomon's temple. The Ripper murders in their violence echo the oaths of these "Juwes."

Watson proves an able detective himself as he tracks down prostitutes who knew the murdered women, finding a connection between them, but he ends up in jail when a tart uses her boyfriend to try to extort money from him, and failing that, accuses him of being the Ripper. Watson is released in Holmes' custody, much to the amusement of Inspector Lestrade (Frank Finlay).

Watson has discovered that a woman named Mary Kelly (Susan Clark) may have the key to the secret, and so Holmes succeeds in tracking her down when she attempts to attend the funeral of one of the murdered women. She reveals that she is in fear for her life because she is sheltering the child of Annie Crook (Genevieve Bujold). That child is the result of "Eddy's" little dalliance. Holmes and Kelly are almost run over by a mysterious man driving a coach pell-mell through the cobbled streets. They separate, and Kelly goes back into hiding.

With Watson's aid, Holmes discovers that Annie Crook has been transferred from a hospital to permanent residence in an insane asylum. Holmes gets her to speak by showing her the name of "Eddy." She begins to talk and gives him the clues to fit the pieces of the puzzle together before he is chased out by the head of the establishment.

Disgusted, Holmes confronts Inspector Foxborough (David Hemmings), who is a secret radical on the police force and has been sending Holmes anonymous tips to guide him along in his investigation. Holmes castigates Foxborough for allowing the killings to continue merely so that he and his radical friends can exploit the tragedy to gain sympathy for their anti-government position.

Inadvertently, Holmes' investigation has led the court physician (Roy Lansford) and the Ripper right to Mary Kelly's hiding place. Holmes and Watson arrive too late to save Kelly's life, with the Ripper throwing coals at Holmes and stabbing Watson in the chest with a red hot poker. The blood-

*A real person who did supposedly lead the police to the Ripper's house.

soaked physician with him seems nearly catatonic, but the Ripper attempts to escape and then to waylay Holmes as he looks for him. Holmes, who spurns the use of a gun, makes a bolo out of his muffler and finally knocks the Ripper into some netting, where his neck becomes entangled and he hangs himself.

In the film's final sequence, Holmes confronts the Prime Minister (John Gielgud) and presents what he knows about the government's complicity in the case. The Ripper was motivated out of a misguided desire to protect the heir apparent from public knowledge about his indiscretion. He was also a Freemason and as the heads of the government were Freemasons, they were sworn to protect him. Holmes makes a bargain to keep silent about what he knows, as many of the men involved in the case have already ruined themselves in the process of the cover-up, in exchange for a solemn promise that Annie Crook's daughter not be harmed. As the child has no knowledge who her father is and all others who might reveal the truth of the matter are now dead, the heads of state agree, leaving Holmes depressed about the evil in the world, though heartened by the nobility of people like Mary Kelly and his friend Dr. Watson.

Clark recreates the pre-turn-of-the-century England very well with plenty of realistic, fog-strewn sets atmospherically photographed by Reg Morris. Although some of the accents are occasionally off, he gets excellent performances from the cast, particularly Plummer and Mason. The film proceeds at an expansive, leisurely pace that provides plenty of opportunity for developing interesting and amusing character quirks which make this downbeat film endearing.

Unfortunately, the days when Sherlock Holmes was popular with moviegoers have long passed and despite its high quality, *Murder by Decree* failed at the box office. However, Clark was able to demonstrate his ability to wring sensitive performances out of his actors and so was given a chance to direct a "quality" film, *Tribute*, starring Jack Lemmon, Robbie Benson and Lee Remick. Lemmon plays a Broadway agent who is constantly joking in the face of death and is a trial to his family. It was a very basic adaptation of Bernard Slade's stage play.

Clark then hit the big time with the sleeper success of *Porky's*, a teen comedy that grossed more than $100 million at the box office. Set nostalgically in Florida of 1954, the film strings together a series of sex-related practical jokes with an awkwardly grafted-on subplot about anti–Semitism to give it "relevancy." Porky's itself is a whorehouse where the randy teen heroes are ripped off; they come back at the end of the film to get their revenge by knocking it down.

Given the film's huge success, Clark was immediately put to work on a sequel called *Porky's II: The Next Day*, but the idea of people being humiliated over their sexual peculiarities (one girl is nicknamed Lassie because she howls like a dog when she climaxes) just doesn't make these smutty comedies funny. Clark's real success as a director of comedies came with his filming of Jean Shepherd's *A Christmas Story*, the delightfully arch recounting of a young boy's quest to receive a B.B. gun for Christmas (over the oft-heard objections by adults that he will shoot his eye out). Along with *Murder by Decree*, this is Clark's best film, but MGM hadn't anticipated the film's success and gave it a scant two-week release before Christmas to theaters that were committed to exhibiting other product.

Given that Clark's subsequent comedies – the disastrous *Rhinestone*, one of Sylvester Stallone's biggest flops; *Turk 182!* and *From the Hip* – perhaps it is time that Clark either re-teamed with Shepherd or went back to making the horror films that launched his career in the first place. He has shown himself capable of handling sensitive material well; now he only has to restrain himself from his misguided attempts to be hip.

Jack Clayton (1921–   )

The Bespoke Overcoat (short, 1955); *Room at the Top* (1959); *The Innocents* (1962); *The Pumpkin Eater* (1964); *Our Mother's House* (1967); *The Great Gatsby* (1974); *Something Wicked This Way Comes* (1983); *The Lonely Passion of Judith Hearne* (1987).

While Clayton can hardly be called a horror specialist, he did craft two of the most significant, subtle horror films of all time – *The Innocents* and *Something Wicked This Way Comes*. Born in 1921 in Brighton, England, Jack Clayton got into the film industry at the early age of 14, working for London Films. He worked his way slowly up the ranks becoming by turns an assistant director, a film editor, and a production manager, the latter on Alexander Korda's adaptation of Oscar Wilde's *An Ideal Husband* with Paulette Goddard and Michael Wilding. He was the associate producer of the overlooked horror classic *Queen of Spades*, a moody ghost story based on the Pushkin classic that was directed by Thorold Dickinson. (Dickinson also directed the original version of *Gaslight*, aka *Angel Street*, another thriller with elements of the macabre that was superior to the more famed George Cukor remake.)

Clayton continued as associate producer of such films as *Flesh and Blood* (1950), *Moulin Rouge, Beat the Devil* and *I Am a Camera* before trying his hand at directing. His first short, *The Bespoke Overcoat*, became a prizewinner at the Venice Film Festival, leading the way to his feature debut, the classic *Room at the Top*, which outlined the troubles of a man torn between marrying for love or money. (In this deliberately anti-romantic story, he married for money to accomplish his social ambitions. The film starred Laurence Harvey, Simone Signoret, Hermione Baddeley, and Donald Wolfit, all of whom gave excellent performances, and the film won Oscars for Signoret and for Neil Paterson's screen adaptation of John Braine's novel.)

Clayton became known for his quality productions and the fine performances he achieved from his actors, both rare qualities in horror films. Fortunately, when he tackled the task of adapting Henry James psychosexual classic "The Turn of the Screw," one of the most famous ghost stories in all of literature, he retained just those qualities. Like almost all of James' work, the story turns on the theme of the corruption of innocence, something which the title points up nicely. The story is reliant on its ambiguities, and Clayton and the talented screenwriters, John Mortimer, Truman Capote, and William Archibald, work hard to retain those ambiguities in the film. As in the original James story, we are uncertain whether the governess has discovered the hideous truth that the children are possessed, or her misguided suppositions and neurotic drives have turned *her* into a demon who destroys them and their innocence.

The difficulty in making a film ambiguous is, of course, that things must be shown, and there is a limit as to how ambiguous something that we can actually see can be. Clayton makes certain that diametrically opposed viewpoints can both be supported by the evidence presented to retain this element of ambiguity. He is aided by the beautiful, almost ethereal photography of Freddie Francis, who provides some of his finest monochromatic work here, allowing for a hazy impreciseness to some of the imagery.

James opened up his original story with a framing device, setting up how a man comes across a governess' journal and then telling the rest of the story from her point of view with all its attendant limitations. The filmmakers wisely dispensed with this framing device; instead they inserted a scene where the governess, unnamed in the story but here given the name of Giddens (which suggests giddiness and gullibility), is interviewed by the Uncle (Michael Redgrave in an impressive cameo performance). From the performances, it is clear that the governess harbors subconscious desires for her employer, and her wish to prove worthy of his trust clouds her judgment and leads her to perceive great opportunities for heroism. She imagines herself as a savior, courageous and self-sacrificing, and shows a pronounced determination to leap to irresponsible conclusions. Thus the seeds are sown that lead us to suspect that *she*, rather than any supernatural element, may be responsible for what follows.

Right from the opening credits, Clayton begins providing us with clues. The film opens with a child singing on the soundtrack followed by the image of some praying hands, then gasps of pain and bird noises. The audience is not given a clue as to what to make of these ambiguous sounds until the end of the film, where they fit chronologically. Deborah Kerr does a superb job of playing the repressed governess, and she sets off the conflicting possibilities with her opening line: "All I want to do is save the children, not destroy them. More than anything I love the children. They need affection, love, someone who will belong to them and to whom they will belong."

These sentiments echo the desires expressed by the uncle in the opening scene, who is revealed as a selfish bachelor who has "no room mentally or emotionally" for the two orphaned children that have been entrusted to him. He wants a governess who will take complete responsibility and never trouble him. This scene establishes not only that the governess is a neo-phyte – this is her first position – but also that she is to have ultimate and total authority over her charges. It also sets up the theme of the governess' imagination when the uncle starts the interview by asking her if she has one, to which she readily admits. Ironically, the uncle sees this as a good sign, believing that imaginative people are more likely to perceive the truth of things.

Despite his admissions and his calling the children "poor brats," Giddens tries to gloss over the uncle's character by calling him "honest, not heart-less." She gives him longing, loving looks, and it is evident that she wants to please him. Her agitated manner indicates that she is strongly attracted to him. This is later confirmed when she hesitates to contact him about her suspicions about the children; she very revealingly states, "He'll think I'm insane, or he'll say it's some stupid trick to get him to notice me." If the solution is not supernatural, here we are supplied with a reason to suggest that Giddens' subconscious mind has motivations for her actions which are not wholly pure.

The interview is concluded with the uncle saying about the previous governess: "The confounded woman died. It was all very odd." Mysterious deaths are one of the conventions of the ghost story, thereby giving the supernatural interpretation credence, but it also plants suggestions in Giddens' brain that her overwrought imagination might work on.

The film continues its delicate balance between the two interpretations, the supernatural and the psychological. For example, when Giddens first comes to the manor, she hears Flora's name being called, though later Mrs. Grose (Megs Jenkins) denies that anyone had spoken it aloud in her hearing, establishing early on that Giddens is apt to hear things. Her state of mind is revealed when she tells Mrs. Grose, "To think of the qualms I had. I was so afraid," which immediately establishes that she has some secret fears and misgivings about the whole enterprise, though she proclaims herself enchanted with the house.

The theme of manipulation is introduced as Mrs. Grose acknowledges how "persuasive" the uncle can be. Furthermore, the nephew Miles (Martin Stephens) is described as being just like him, and more and more throughout the film Miles and the uncle become linked, which further underscores the ambiguous nature of Giddens' relationship with him.

There is a hint of the supernatural as Flora (Pamela Franklin) announces with absolute certainty that "Miles is coming," though she has no way of knowing. It is not long before this statement proves accurate, though the adults are apprised of the situation only a short time later when a letter is forwarded by uncle from Miles' school. (The uncle's lack of interest is further indicated by the fact that he did not even open the letter.)

A visual motif that Clayton uses throughout the film is that of white roses (a symbol of innocence) crumbling in Miss Giddens' hand. Giddens' touch destroys the flowers just as her suspicions will drive Flora (note the floral connection) to hysteria and ultimately will cost Miles his life. Significantly, each subsequent occurrence of this motif is followed by a shock of one kind or another to Miss Giddens. It is just after snipping a rose in the garden that Giddens sees a bug crawling out of a statue's mouth, with its suggestions of obscenity, and then she espies Quint (either the ghost of an evil influence or the demon figure of her imagination) for the first time. Later, after brushing some flowers in a vase and knocking the petals off while playing hide and seek, she gets her first full view of Quint outside the window. When a flower petal falls onto her Bible, she has her most hysterical night. Finally, the fatal confrontation occurs just after Giddens has it out with Miles in the greenhouse. The flowers are spread throughout the house and garden, indicating that the potential for harming innocence is everywhere.

Another theme that runs throughout the film is that of self-deception. The basis of Giddens' consuming interest in ghosts is laid when, while saying her prayers, Flora asks what happens if you die and you are not good and God does not take you to heaven? Do you just stick around? Suddenly, there is the jarring sound of an animal screeching, and Flora tells Miss Giddens to just pretend that she did not hear it, indicating that she too hears strange noises which no one else does but must pretend she does not. Increasingly, though the children appear angelic, Giddens doubts their honesty.

While most of the film is presented from the governess' point of view, Clayton does shift from that point of view upon occasion. For example, he has a scene where Flora observes the sleeping Miss Giddens, then goes to an open window and hums a tune which will be a leitmotif in the movie—it later reappears as a tune from a musicbox that Giddens associates with Miss Jessel, the previous governess. Clayton directs the child actors to act in a very adult manner, which suggests possession by adult spirits as well as a subtle, almost indefineable something wrong with them that is not immediately apparent. Flora seems a shrewd perceiver, giving a sly, enigmatic smile as she notices Giddens' pleasure in receiving a letter from her uncle and hears that Miles is indeed coming. Giddens tries to ask her about it, but she simply smiles as the music strikes an ominous chord, indicating Giddens' unease. Flora is further depicted as unnatural when she turns her attention to a spider devouring a butterfly; she describes the spiders as "lovely" while showing no concern for the butterfly. While this hints at a warped sensibility and a streak of cruelty, it could also be no more than childish curiosity.

Further unease is developed when it is revealed that Miles is returning home unexpectedly because he was expelled from school, and the only explanation given is that "...he has done injury to others." Right from the start there is a hint of something contaminated or corrupt about Miles, and all of the governess' subsequent decisions are based on the questionable assumption that Miles has in some way been corrupted.

Clayton keeps shifting the focus in the film from objectivity to subjectivity and back again. There is a kind of visual ambiguity in Giddens' first sighting of Quint, during which all outdoor sounds are mysteriously silenced while she gazes into the sun and, squinting up at the manor's tower, sees the figure of a man looking back down at her. The figure is only a dark, indistinct silhouette with the sun behind it. Following this sighting, the sounds of nature return, more acute than normal, indicating an increased sensitivity or a heightened, agitated state of mind. The sounds of birds and flies become particularly oppressive. When Giddens reaches the top of the tower, Miles denies that anyone was ever there.

In addition to shifting the point of view, Clayton and the screenwriters have departed from James' story in another way, by interpolating the scene where Giddens decides not to leave after seeing Miss Jessel crying in the schoolroom. As she reaches where Jessel was sitting, the chair is empty, but there is a mysterious drop of moisture left on the desk – could it be the tear of a ghost or simply residual moisture? Giddens takes the water to be a kind of mystical confirmation, and for those who wish, it can be seen as confirmation that there are ghosts – or is it simply a drop of water?

A recurring piece of imagery in the film is that of the hunter and the hunted. Giddens believes that Quint is stalking her; meanwhile she stalks the children, particularly Flora when she thinks Miles has created a diversion. In turn, the children imprison and dominate their pets. But who is imitating whom? Miles and Flora lure their governess outside after Miles. Miles later explains that he feared she might be beginning to find him boring and so wanted to do something bad to be "different"; however, Giddens cannot accept this explanation and keeps pressing him for the "real" one. Here Miles goes from manipulator to manipulated as Giddens becomes increasingly overbearing in her frantic effort to get the children to admit the evil she is certain is there. She believes that the souls of the lovers, Quint and Jessel, are planning to take over the bodies of the children in an effort to continue their love affair.

However, rather than being another Quint, Miles is more a stand-in for his uncle as mentioned earlier. He tends to call his governess "my dear" and condescends to her as if he were the older and more experienced one, though he is still a child. Mrs. Grose reveals that Quint was a sadist who beat the masochistic Jessel, and Giddens searches for signs of cruelty in Miles. This combination of innocence and cruelty is suggested when, visiting Miles' bedroom after hearing a cat cry, Giddens discovers a child's slingshot, and later the cat is revealed as blinded. There is something cruel in the sound of peacocks crying out in the film as well as when Miles reveals a pigeon with a broken neck under his pillow, which he caresses tenderly. (Romanticizing adults often forget or overlook the natural cruelty of children.)

Miles sees things clearly. He perceives that if he reveals why he was expelled from school, his governess might turn against him. He accurately notes that his uncle doesn't care or have much time for him and Flora.

Giddens refuses to recognize these realities despite the evidence. Her blindness is symbolically communicated when she asks Miles to trust her just as the wind slams a door shut and blows the candle out.

The topic of reliability is resurrected when Miles tells Giddens that she can "never believe Flora. She invents things, imagines them." Tellingly, Giddens indicates that the same is true about herself, though she later blinds herself to this truth with her fears and qualms. The viewer is constantly put into the position of asking whom we can trust? Is what we are being shown real or imagined?

One of the methods Clayton uses to achieve ambiguity is to utilize a soundtrack full of startling natural and unnatural sounds. The fact that some of these sounds are exaggerated or electronically created supports the idea that Giddens has a neurotic hypersensitivity and that the sounds are aural manifestations of her hallucinations. The problem with the ghosts in the film is that they are seen too clearly, and subsequently are not as frightening as mere indications of their presence. However, sounds are easily made ambiguous when we cannot see their source. The sounds used include various bird cries, screams, laughter and giggling, footsteps, the sound of a curtain ring tapping against a windowpane, and phrases such as "Softly, the children" and "love me" (which presumably emanate from the ghostly lovers, who in life were described by Mrs. Grose as "using rooms in the day as though they were dark woods.")

While Miss Jessel is never clearly shown, a curtain moving from her brushing against it is more effectively chilling than her dark figure crossing a corridor. The first glimpse we have of her is of a dark figure standing amid some stalks on the other side of a pond which has a familiar air about it, but her presence barely registers before she is gone, making her all the more eerie. One of the most effective manifestations in the film is when Giddens goes up to the attic when the children are playing hide and seek and is confronted with a clown's head rocking in the darkness, which is far more startling than the more traditional shock of Miles unexpectedly coming out from hiding and attacking her.

Part of what makes *The Innocents* such a fine fright film is that it encourages the audience to use its imagination and to feel caught up in the fear and anxiety that the governess is experiencing. Clayton even gets some *frisson* from having Miles recite an odd poem about a dead lord leaving the prison of his grave, knocking on the door and entering the home of his beloved, ending with the words "He is arisen; Welcome my Lord." Clayton projects such a feeling of intensity that we half expect to see Quint himself coming through the door as if in response to Miles' morbid poem. Miles shocks again when he gives Giddens a disturbingly adult goodnight kiss, suggestive of her repressed sexual feelings for his uncle, to which she registers her shock and surprise.

Clayton sometimes uses sexual symbolism to underscore these repressed feelings. For example, Quint is first glimpsed atop a high, phallic tower, though significantly, Giddens does not see him clearly until after she has seen a locket with his picture in it. When Mrs. Grose warns that there is "too much whispering in this house," Giddens imagines the lovers whispering sexual secrets. Giddens plunges a phallic poker into a roaring fireplace, symbol of desire, which triggers strange sounds and the haunting tune that is threaded throughout the film, here played at a piano when nobody is there. She frightens the children when in her desperation she grabs them in a passionate embrace and beseeches them to declare the truth to her. Flora cannot bear it when Giddens tries to make her see a Miss Jessel that Flora cannot see and so flees with Mrs. Grose in a highly agitated state. Giddens has failed to heed Mrs. Grose's dictum that "a body can only judge themselves." Giddens has judged the children guilty and they must suffer the consequences.

The finale is presented in an appropriately ambiguous way. Miles flees from Giddens in the greenhouse with its drops of moisture dripping down the walls like perspiration. There is a dizzying pan around the hedges, which are graced with statues at intervals; at the end of the pan we see the figure of Quint. Giddens tries to point him out, but Miles looks desperately about, not seeing the apparition. Then there is a peculiar shot from behind Quint which shows him extending his hand and figuratively seizing Miles. Miles stares off into space – has he finally seen Quint? – and then drops dead, any hold on him released. Giddens cradles his head in her lap and strokes his face the way he has stroked the dead pigeon under his pillow earlier, and then she bestows a prolonged kiss. Rather than being Miles' savior, the innocent Miss Giddens turns ironically into his tormentor; instead of saving him, she destroys him. But while Giddens' escalating anxiety which she forced on Miles has led to his demise, she remains herself innocent. One innocent is destroyed by another innocent, for Giddens is truly innocent of the knowledge that her quest to root out corruption in the children was itself abusive and the true contaminating factor. The once happy children are indeed traumatized by her insistence that they admit to being influenced by the ghosts of their past acquaintances. Like a puritan, Miss Giddens has the best of intentions but instead winds up creating greater evil or misery through her selfless desire to do good. The result here is a beautifully realized, tantalizing film and one of the few masterpieces of the horror genre.

Clayton continued specializing in literary adaptations, though he has made remarkably few films. He insists that he will only work on material he likes, and even then many of the projects he has developed have not come to fruition. However, famed fantasy author Ray Bradbury had interested him in doing an adaptation of his 1962 novel *Something Wicked This Way Comes* for quite some time.

The project originated from a short story, "Black Ferris," that Bradbury had written for the 1948 *Weird Tales* magazine. Years later, after seeing Gene Kelly's *Invitation to the Dance*, Bradbury had been excited at the idea of working with Kelly and had looked back over his material to see what he could develop. Selecting "Black Ferris," he expanded it into a 75-page treatment, but when *Invitation* failed at the box office, Kelly was not able to get financing for the new film. Bradbury then took the material and fashioned it into a novel, which he later called "a love letter to my father." Bradbury sent Clayton a copy of the manuscript after *The Innocents* came out, but nothing came of it for quite some time.

Meanwhile, years later producers Robert Chartoff and Irwin Winkler optioned the book and asked Bradbury to work on the screenplay. Bradbury suggested using Sam Peckinpah as the director, and Peckinpah was quite keen to do it. After a personnel change at 20th Century–Fox, however, the project died once more, though there was a period where Mark Rydell worked with Bradbury on it.

Meanwhile, as the option ran out, it attracted the interest of Peter Vincent Douglas, one of the sons of Kirk Douglas, who picked up the option. They met with Clayton, who expressed an interest in doing *Something Wicked*, and the whole project moved to Paramount. While Bradbury worked out yet another screenplay, one that proved overlong at 260 pages, Clayton worked with him, teaching him how to trim the script to its essentials. After six months of such work, the script was shown to Paramount chief Barry Diller, who rejected it in three hours – largely, Clayton believes, over differences that Diller was having with David Picker, one of the project's backers. Angered, Clayton threw a chair through Diller's office windows and was taken off of the project.

Douglas approached Jonathan Demme, John Carpenter, and Steven Spielberg about the project, and in fact Spielberg gave some serious consideration to following up *Close Encounters of the Third Kind* with *Something Wicked This Way Comes*, but the deal mysteriously fell through once more. With the project in turnaround, it was finally rescued from oblivion by Disney and the then current head of film production, Tom Whilhite. Tony Scott, David Lynch and Carroll Ballard were all approached to direct, but Douglas fought for asking Clayton back on the project, though Disney was concerned that Clayton's approach might be too distant or cool for a major project that was expected to attract a large audience. His last film, *The*

Jack Clayton, the British craftsman in command, directing the underrated Something Wicked This Way Comes, *a warm rendition of Ray Bradbury's novel.*

Great Gatsby, had been a resounding disappointment both artistically and financially, failing to draw an audience for Clayton's generally faithful retelling of F. Scott Fitzgerald's classic tale despite the attraction of Robert Redford and Mia Farrow as the stars. Nevertheless, Douglas persisted and Disney relented.

Clayton brought his friend John Mortimer to do a little uncredited rewriting on Bradbury's final screenplay, but no major changes were made. Unfortunately, the production itself proved rather an acrimonious affair for many of those involved. The original cinematographer, Laszlo Kovacs, left the project early on, and many of the technical people did not get along with his replacement, Stephen Burum.

Production designer Richard MacDonald did a marvelous job reconstructing a clean, turn-of-the-century country town (Green Town, Illinois) on the backlot, but the set was so solidly built that it became difficult to move things in it and to light. By contrast with the solidity of Green Town, the design of Dark's Pandemonium Carnival was far more ethereal and easy to achieve. However, an expensive special effect in which the carnival would assemble itself out of the steam of a passing locomotive failed to come off and had to be scrapped.

Many of the people working on the project found that Clayton was strongly opinionated and tended to stick to his guns when they brought in differing concepts. Initially, Clayton admitted that he was intimidated with the special effects jargon and difficulties that the film entailed. He was far more concerned with communicating the film's human element. For the key role of Charles Halloway, hero Will Halloway's troubled father, Clayton selected Jason Robards, whom Sam Peckinpah had considered for the role of Mr. Dark in his production of the film. For the key role of Mr. Dark, the film's most poetic and sinister figure, Clayton selected the then unknown Welsh actor Jonathan Pryce, who did a marvelous job of creating a mysterious figure of menace. The major roles of the two boys were performed by relative unknowns as well, Vidal Peterson essaying the role of Will Halloway while Shawn Carson played his friend Jim Nightshade. Exploitation actress Pam Grier was given the role of the Dust Witch, a sometimes bewitching temptress, but the part gave her little to do.

The film suffered a disastrous initial preview to an unenthused audience and underwent several changes. The original Georges Delerue film score was scrapped in favor of a more intrusive one by James Horner. The scenes showing the arrival and destruction of the carnival were completely changed, and several small effects shots were added throughout the film. Some scenes of character interplay were cut, while a scene of Charles Halloway overcoming his fear and rescuing his son in the Hall of Mirrors was added. After several million dollars worth of tinkering, the net change in the film was actually rather minor. (I have seen both versions.) Nevertheless, there were some small improvements – some additional autumnal scenes were shot to open the film up, make it less claustrophobic, and these add to establishing the feel of the opening. The best addition was a minor rotoscoping of pages that Mr. Dark is tearing out of a book representing Charles Halloway's life bursting into flame and ebbing away, which makes their confrontation in the library more dramatic.

A sequence where the giant hand of the Dust Witch knocks at the window of Jim and Will was ultimately scrapped and a tarantula attack was put in its place. Clayton directed this added sequence, but it is easy to tell his heart was not in it as it generates no genuine thrill or suspense and fails to engage the emotions. A narration by Arthur Hill was also added to help clarify the story for audiences, though the narration is largely intrusive and unnecessary.

Despite the problems and revamping, Ray Bradbury is very pleased with the film – and well he should be, for whatever its flaws, the film does have quite a bit going for it. However, it was family fare at a time when horror films were no longer considered family fare, and it disappointed those expecting gory thrills from horror films while failing to attract the youthful audiences who would have loved it most. The film itself is a paean to a bygone era as well as to fatherhood, circuses, magic, lost dreams, etc. The poetic language of Bradbury's script is a style that not everyone appreciates, and it does distance the film from the reality in which Clayton sought to ground it, but it also captures the excitement of certain childhood emotions.

The film is basically about temptation. An ominous lightning rod salesman named Tom Fury (Royal Dano) warns that a change in the weather will bring bad fortune, but the two young heroes can only sit back and observe the changes in their town when Dark's carnival comes to it. We see the town's Sherwood Anderson–like grotesques and their pathetic dreams, which the carnival promises to fulfill in the process of taking them under its wing, permanently. As the boys discover what is going on, Mr. Dark, the carnival's evil proprietor, comes looking for them, hoping to seduce Jim Nightshade into a partnership with him and to destroy Charles' depressed and despairing father, who at last is given the chance to prove the great love he has for his son.

It is a subtle and underappreciated film, not without its charm. The film does have an impressive aging shot where Dark is trapped on a carousel that spins him forward into old age and then oblivion, but the real dynamics are not in the unsatisfying special effects. The power lies rather in the message that despair can invade our dreams and turn them into nightmares unless we can settle back and put life into proper perspective, with all its glories and mysteries, its love and its miseries intact.

Queen of Spades, The Innocents and *Something Wicked This Way Comes* are all classy and classic horror pictures. One can only hope that Clayton will work his magic and bring his sensitivity to the field once again.

Larry Cohen (1941-   )

Bone (1972); *Black Caesar; Hell Up in Harlem* (1973); *It's Alive* (1974); *God Told Me to* (aka *Demon*, 1976); *It Lives Again; The Private Files of J. Edgar Hoover* (1978); *Full Moon High* (1981); *Q* (1982); *Special Effects; Perfect Strangers; The Stuff* (1985); *Island of the Alive; Return to Salem's Lot* (1987); *Deadly Illusion* (codirected with William Tannen, 1988); *The Wicked Stepmother; The Ambulance* (1990).
TELEVISION: *See China and Die* (1981).

Larry Cohen is a maverick, independent filmmaker, almost the horror genre's equivalent of Samuel Fuller. His films consistently receive poor distribution, and while he has had hits, none have made a tremendous amount of money (though almost all have been profitable). His filmmaking technique is often crude and his stories are exposition-heavy, but what makes him special is that he is one of the few horror filmmakers to be consistently interested in characters and ideas – his films often virtually burst with them, however crudely executed. Because of his unusual perspectives, Cohen, who frequently works as a triple-threat filmmaker – writer, director and producer – is unique, *sui generis*, in a class by himself.

Not that his originality does not occasionally flag, as in the poor sequel to *Black Caesar (Hell Up in Harlem)*, or the inferior sequels to *It's Alive (It Lives Again* and *Island of the Alive)*. Nevertheless, Cohen rarely repeats himself and keeps exploring new ideas, permutations on interesting concepts which stand out in a field known more for its empty-headed, cookie-cutter films that seek to do nothing but push the same buttons in the viewer over and over again. As a result, whatever his strengths and weaknesses, Cohen can seem like a breath of fresh air in the stagnant tomb of horror genre conventions.

Born in New York on July 15, 1941, Cohen initiated his interest in the cinema by making spy films with an 8mm camera as a child. He had a fondness for thrillers and made his first television sale as a writer by adapting an Evan Hunter novel for *The Kraft Television Theater*. He became a regular writer for such shows as *The Defenders, The Fugitive, Arrest and Trial* and *Sam Benedict*. He created and wrote for the series *Branded* and *The Invaders*.

He broke into the film business by writing the scripts for *Return of the*

Seven and *Daddy's Gone a-Hunting*, the latter directed by Mark Robson, who directed *The Seventh Victim* and *Isle of the Dead* for Val Lewton. However, Cohen was disappointed with the casting of *Daddy*, and that spurred him to produce and direct his own films from then on. His first three films, *Bone, Black Caesar,* and *Hell Up in Harlem,* were all blaxploitation films that at the same time rejected the basic rules set down for this subgenre. His black lead characters were not sympathetic, heroic, guiltless, or victorious. One of the basic tenets of Cohen's films is that there are no heroes, nobody who is wholly good and pure. Unlike most action directors, Cohen always tries to make morality central to his story, and as a result there are no clearcut definitions of good and evil in his films. The lead characters must deal with moral issues and make decisions, and they may not always be the "right" ones.

His first venture into the fantastic was "False Face," an episode of the Roald Dahl–hosted *Way Out* series on CBS. It was about an actor playing the Hunchback of Notre Dame who copies his face from an unfortunate derelict and then finds that the face will not come off. Dick Smith executed the makeup, which was an uglier version of Lon Chaney's makeup for *The Hunchback of Notre Dame.*

Cohen created *The Invaders* and wrote about 13 stories for it, but he began to be dissatisfied with it. He later recalled in an interview with this author:

> I was involved with it in its first season, and by the time the show was in its second year, almost everybody in the show had turned out to be an Invader. It was harder to find out who wasn't one. The show would have been much more fun if there had been fewer Invaders in it. It would have been fun figuring out who was who, and also I felt the stories needed to be better as it went on. I think it was a good series, and actually it would be very successful again if they reissued it now.
>
> It's funny. I was going to do a show called *The New Invaders*, which was exactly the same format as *V*, which was submitted around and it got turned down by all the networks. That was two years before *V* came on, but generally I don't do anything about those things because the idea of aliens conquering the world is not such an original idea that you start to worry that somebody stole it.

Speaking of original ideas, Cohen's first horror feature was an old horror concept – innately evil children – but he put a unique twist on it. This time the kid was an infant, a killer baby if you will. The title itself was a tribute to one of horror's most memorable moments, when Frankenstein shrieked, "It's Alive!"

It's Alive (1974) was largely buried when Warner Bros. originally released it directly to the rural drive-in circuit. The film is usually mentioned

as an early credit for makeup artist Rick Baker, who created the terrorizing
tyke, or a late film score for Bernard Hermann, who did a fine job. The film
begins simply enough with Frank and Lenore Davies (John Ryan and Sharon
Farrell) going to the hospital to have their second child. However, there appears to be some difficulty with the birth. Suddenly, the father in the waiting room sees an orderly stumble out of the delivery room and die at his feet.
Frank rushes in and finds chaos, the hospital staff dead, his wife barely conscious, and no sign of the kid. The baby proves to be a freak of nature with
razor-sharp claws and superhuman strength.

Admittedly, this is a ridiculous premise to make a film out of, though
such premises are typical of Cohen's work; however, if the audience is willing to suspend their disbelief and go along with the story, it becomes fairly
exciting and quite enjoyable. Just as the film was influenced by *Them*, with
the climax set in the Los Angeles sewers, there is a flashlight scene, the look
of which Steven Spielberg borrowed in turn for *E.T.* Because the baby
model could not be animated very well, Cohen wisely decided to show only
quick cuts so that it is barely glimpsed, which help make the scenes with it
more effective. (The unseen always holds a greater potential for terror than
the fully disclosed. Audiences tend to adjust to even a terrific monster like
Rob Bottin's in Carpenter's *The Thing* – a veritable living, breathing nightmare – by thinking, "Oh well, it's only special effects," or, "Well, that's bad,
but I was afraid it would be so much worse!") The film features many fine
supporting performances from such actors as Michael Ansara, Guy Stockwell, and Robert Emhardt, plus one of the most memorable, simultaneously
funny and horrific scenes ever, in which the baby attacks a milk truck, and
we see the milk spilling out the back slowly turn red.

It's Alive also establishes a couple of Cohen trademarks. Cohen believes
that terror begins in the home (for example, in his film *Bone*, aka *Dial Rat
for Terror* or *Beverly Hills Nightmare*, Yaphet Kotto terrorizes an upper
class household by threatening to rape and murder an executive's wife if he
does not come back with the ransom money, but the executive decides to
leave town with his lover instead). The family is a very important, central
unit in most Cohen films, but it is also the source of much anguish and terror
as the people living together expose unexpected sides of their personalities.
Another aspect of Cohen's writing is that he firmly believes a plot is more
than a collection of incidents. His characters change in the course of the
story because the events they encounter alter their viewpoints.

This is strikingly portrayed in *It's Alive*, with Frank's gradual acceptance of his new "son." Initially repulsed and seeking to kill it like everyone
else, Frank comes to accept his monstrous son and see things from the
infant's point of view. Everyone has appeared threatening to it and
large masses of armed guards are gathering together to hunt it down. While
the baby's actions have been far from sympathetic, audience empathy is

nonetheless aroused when we see that the creature is hungry, cold, and frightened. Frank accepts the responsibility and accepts the child as his own. The infant progresses from the hospital to the school of his brother, coming ever closer to the Davies' home, indicating that a family feeling is drawing him. Cohen builds suspense by having guardsmen traipsing through a darkened school, but the viewer begins to wonder why somebody does not just turn on the lights. As Cohen recalled:

> When we ran the picture at UCLA for Arthur Knight's classes, he said, "This is obviously a low budget picture because nobody ever turns the lights on." It's a big favorite for Spielberg. He's told me he loved the picture. He picked up a few elements which you see later in *E.T.* A lot of people have borrowed scenes from the picture. There's a big steal from it in a picture called *Prophecy*, about an ecological monster that was going around in the swamps. Imagine that, a good director like John Frankenheimer stealing from me?

The film ends with some officials asking Frank to drop the baby so they can shoot it. Instead, the father hurls the baby at the official he considers responsible and the kid is riddled with bullets. Said Cohen:

> I left the end the way it is because it's like when Alec Guinness falls on the plunger in *Bridge on the River Kwai.* You never know whether he fell on it on purpose or whether it was by accident. You're not sure whether he destroyed the bridge because he realized that he had done something wrong or whether he accidentally falls on the plunger.
>
> I didn't want you to be sure whether he threw the baby away from himself because of fear, because he knows the baby was going to be shot, or because the man he was throwing it at is the one who is really responsible because he was the doctor. Remember, there's a scene in *It's Alive* where they talk about the pharmaceutical guy – the guy from this pharmaceutical company is telling this doctor, "We don't want the baby captured alive, we want it destroyed so there can't ever be any affirmative decision as to what caused this." Whether it was birth control pills or some medication that the woman is taking, it would be much better if no one could ever determine what caused it.
>
> Basically, what you have there is the pharmaceutical people who are selling people potentially dangerous products. Obviously, we were way ahead of our time because it turns out that there is a famous birth control product that it has now been determined causes damage and deformities to children and cancer to mothers. There's another thing now where there's a shield and if you ever used this shield, you should go in and take a medical examination. That proved that the company knew the shield was dangerous for many, many years and still kept silent about it. So there definitely is a progression between *It's Alive* and *The Stuff*, where people are selling this killer ice cream to the public even though they know it is deadly and people buy it. [They feel] if people are buying it, that's their problem, isn't it?

However, *It's Alive* almost died aborning. Recalled Cohen:

Warner Bros. didn't have enough money in it. Usually a studio doesn't try too hard on a picture they don't have too much faith in. Actually, they'd gotten to 1974 and they had *The Exorcist* at the same time, and all their effort went into *The Exorcist*. They really didn't have any time for a smaller picture because they were making so much money with *The Exorcist*, they couldn't believe it.

So they just kind of put *It's Alive* aside, put it out on drive-ins, and forgot about it. I kept saying that the campaign was lousy. It didn't tell you what the picture was about; it didn't mention the baby or anything. They were afraid that the baby idea would turn the audience off. I said, "Well, if that's the case, we should never have made the picture. That's what the picture is about. You go out and sell the picture." You don't sell people oranges and give them apples. That never works. No matter what you got, tell them what you got. If they want to see it, they're gonna come, and if it was worth making the picture in the first place, you should be able to tell them what it's about and they should come. But you've got to tell them what it's about.

So finally a new administration came into Warner Bros., the old people left and I went back to the new people. There was a guy named Arthur Manson, who'd been with Cinerama when Cinerama did a picture called *Willard*, and he'd come up with the *Willard* campaign, and he was now head of advertising for Warner Bros. He ran the picture and he thought it was a good picture. He called me up and told me, "I ran your picture like you asked me to, and I thought it was a very good picture. I looked at the original campaign and I thought it was terrible. I think you got the short end of the stick and I'm gonna see if I can help you."

Then Terry Semel, who was head of distribution and booking pictures, said this was a good picture, a good thriller. He looked at the previous history of the film and he thought that the picture hadn't really been released, so they test-marketed the picture with a new campaign and it did very well. Then they said to me, we're going out with the picture in six months because we want to hold it back. We have a specific time we want to open it. And that scared the hell out of me 'cause I figured in six month's time, these guys could be fired and I'd have to deal with another administration.

But that's the way it was. We waited, and we opened the picture in '77, and that was three years after the picture had originally opened, and the picture took off. For two weeks, it was the number one picture in America. It ended up doing about $36 million, a picture from nowhere. That was, of course, in the world market, U.S. and foreign. In the meantime, the picture had won the Avoirez Film Festival [Best SF Film], but that didn't impress Warner Bros. Nothing impressed the original people. It wasn't until after they'd left that I was able to get the picture brought back to life. That goes to show you, you never should give up on a picture.

Since the first *It's Alive* proved so successful, it was almost inevitable that it would spawn a sequel, which it did in 1978 with *It Lives Again* (aka *It's Alive, Part II*). The first film ended with a report that another murderous baby had been born, but this sequel offers three of the terrorizing tykes. John Ryan reappears as Frank Davies, now determined to save the kids and tame them. He joins forces with scientist-doctors Perry and Forest (Andrew Duggan and Eddie Constantine). Opposing them is Mallory (John Marley), a cop whose wife died on the operating table giving birth to her mutated baby.

Somewhere in the middle are the Scotts (Frederic Forrest and Kathleen Lloyd), who admit that their kid is not very well behaved but who are not ready to see it blown apart by the National Guard either.

Despite the good cast, the film suffers from showing too much of the killer infants, making their phoniness more apparent, and from having to set up situations where these relatively defenseless tykes can get close enough to their armed targets to attack.

Cohen agreed that "the less you saw, the better off you were":

> In the second pictures, we felt that if people came back and paid another five dollars, they had the right to see a little bit more, but I was wrong about that. It was much better if it was seen less. We saw more of the babies in the second picture and we should have had less.
>
> But I just kind of felt we couldn't have them come back and pay five dollars again and not show them the baby the second time. You see, the first time it was logical because the baby was born and escaped from the hospital, and the whole picture is the father looking for it and he never sees it until the end. So all right, that's OK. There's a logical reason not to show it.
>
> But in the second pictue, about a third of the way through the picture, they come to a house where the babies are kept in a basement in cages and are being raised. They're in captivity, and there's no reason in the world that you can justify not showing them, 'cause if I didn't show 'em, it would be a total cheat. So I was trapped into the fact that logically and dealing honestly with the audience, I would have to show them. I tried to keep it brief, but in showing the babies, you take some of the magic out of it because the great tease is what do they look like?

It Lives Again contains hints that the babies might be the next step up on the evolutionary ladder. The fact that two of them are named Adam and Eve gives them religious overtones as well as suggesting they may be the progenitors of a new race. But the religious conceits of *It Lives Again* pale in comparison to Cohen's earlier *God Told Me To* (aka *Demon*, 1976), in which aliens from outer space (where else?) impregnate two virgins and produce a hybrid race. This sort of situation was explored earlier in John Wyndham's *The Midwich Cuckoos*, which was filmed as *Village of the Damned*.

However unlike *Village of the Damned, God Told Me To* is plumbed for its religious significance. Said Cohen:

> My theory was that if a superbeing was born on earth, like Clark Kent, let's say the Superman story is treated realistically, so this kid is born, he can see through walls, he can fly, he has superpowers and everything. He goes to church every Sunday and he hears about Jesus Christ. He knows he can do all these things that no other human can do, so he has to figure *he's* Jesus Christ reincarnated, right? Reincarnated because we're waiting for him to come back. He's not going to think he's an alien from another planet. What is he going to think? The whole culture here, the whole of Western Civilization is waiting for the Messiah to show up. So an alien with superpowers becomes convinced in his own mind that he's God.
>
> His mother is a virgin, following the prophecy. She's convinced that he's God. We really didn't have time to explore all the details of it, but it's a very interesting theory that an alien being born on earth could very well mistake himself for Jesus because the prophecies of Jesus' coming tie in so closely with what an alien might end up being, looking like us and yet having all these superior powers.
>
> In this particular case, there were two of them. Tony LoBianco had all the recessive traits, and the other guy [Richard Lynch] had all the traits that were dominant because they were going to have a mating at the end; and that's really a crazy idea.

The character played by Lynch has a vagina in place of a male organ so that he can mate with his brother. However, Lynch is mentally disturbed and has been causing some people to turn into assassins who, when caught, can only explain their actions by saying, "God told me to."

The film did not perform well under its original title, so it was cut and released under the nonsensical title of *Demon.* (Another title, *Alien Encounter*, had to be scrapped when a film that later was released as *Starship Invasions* advertised with that title first. But then, the title would have given away the solution to the mystery behind the apparently motiveless killings too soon.) Among the scenes cut were scenes which more clearly explained Tony LoBianco's aversion to having children and a meeting between the would-be Messiah and twelve bankers on Wall Street.

Religious symbolism is incorporated throughout, even to having one of the twelve bankers betray the alien, Bernard Phillips, to the police and to Phillips having pentecostal flames above his head. A favorite scene of Cohen's was the one where the executives discuss whether to follow him or not. One of them says, "What kind of God is it that deals in murder?" Another guy replies, "Well, read the Bible. You'll know about a God that deals in murder. For crying out loud, He murdered almost the entire human race because He got angry one day and drowned everybody.... He killed the first-born of every Egyptian; He smote this one, He smote that one."

Said Cohen:

> They [the businessmen] also looked at all the gods in Greek mythol-
> ogy and all the gods going as far back as you can in all the different prim-
> itive cultures and everything. They always seem to have something
> tied up with virgin birth, raising from the dead, changing into some
> kind of an animal, changing into some kind of form. There's always a
> lot of killing and striking down anybody that doesn't believe in them.
> "You don't believe in me?! Pchew!" God is a very violent creature, and
> in *God Told Me To*, we said that.

Even before the outrageous climax, the showdown between the two
brothers, *God Told Me To* has some fairly interesting scenes amid its often
clumsy exposition. Two scenes stand out: a confrontation between Tony Lo-
Bianco and Sandy Williams as a sniper who commits suicide because "God"
told him to, and a chilling scene where a man explained why he had killed
his family, quietly stating: "He's done so much for us – I just thought it was
time we did something for Him."

Additionally, another subtext is added to the film because both these
characters come off as being gay. In fact, gay critic Robin Wood has interpreted the whole picture to be about "the repression of bisexuality within
Christian patriarchal culture," which seems to me to be a load of dingo's
kidneys. However, it is true that there is an obvious conflict between the repressed (LoBianco with his Catholic upbringing) and the unrepressed
(Lynch) in the film, though LoBianco's repression does not prevent him
from having both a wife (played by Sandy Dennis) and a lover (played by
Deborah Raffin).

Commented Cohen:

> I guess you can find a gay subtext in any movie you want to find it.
> Actually, when I was casting the picture, it occurred to me after cast-
> ing Sandy Williams in one part and another guy in another part – these
> were all well-known actors. Sandy Williams had won the Tony award
> for *A Chorus Line*; the other guy who played the guy who killed his
> children was a well-known Broadway and stage actor, and they were
> coming off gay. I said to myself, somebody's going to say that this pic-
> ture is all about homosexuals, and sure enough, just wait long enough
> and somebody said it. I thought that as long as I was going that way,
> we would leave it that way. Maybe that's why I put that thing in at the
> end about the alien wanting to mate with his brother.

It is interesting to note that LoBianco does not feel released until after
the destruction of his brother. Similarly, in *It Lives Again*, the relationship
between Eugene and Jody Scott is strained, largely because of Eugene

Scott's ambition. He has asked his wife to give up her career in favor of his and has been very demanding, which suggests that their mutant offspring might be a by-product of the tension in their marriage (something like the brood in Cronenberg's film being a manifestation of a person's rage). The couple cannot even bear to touch one another until they achieve catharsis at the end when they must kill their child to save another life. The sacrifice brings the pair together as they seek solace in each other's arms.

Again, both these films are about disruptions within families and about estrangement. LoBianco has a brother he never even knew about; then, having discovered him, he rejects him utterly. The Scotts find their own child frightening and repellent.

Q (originally titled *The Winged Serpent*) deals with a character, Quinn (played by Michael Moriarty), who has been estranged from society and finds in Quetzalcoatl, the giant winged serpent of the title, the means to gain power, wealth, and respect by threatening not to reveal the monster's whereabouts unless his demands are met.

"In general, I like to make a picture that is different, that hasn't been told before," Cohen said.

> I guess there have been movies about monsters in the city, maybe even flying monsters invading the Chrysler building, but in *Q*, we were more involved with the character that Michael Moriarty played. The monster itself was really secondary to him. His relationships, what happened to him, his relationship to the monster and to the police, his power trip. It was really more about a jailbird than a giant bird. They both have the initial Q.
>
> Actually, Q was the first title on the script when I wrote the script. Then I made the picture and other people said, "Well, Q doesn't sound right. People don't know what it means. Is it a cue like in pool cue, or is it a cue for an actor to go on stage, or is it a queue like you get on line?" They felt it was too ambiguous a title, so [Sam] Arkoff, who was one of the financiers of the picture, suggested we call it *The Winged Serpent*. Actually, we probably should have called it *The Sky Serpent*. The Winged Serpent is a hard thing to say.
>
> Anyway, Ira Teller, who was a guy in advertising, came up with that title and that's what they were going to call it at the Cannes Festival for foreign sales. Meanwhile, I made a deal for domestic distribution with the United Film Distribution Company and Sala Hasanon was president of the company, and he said he didn't like the title *The Winged Serpent*. He asked was that always the title? I said, "No, the first title I wrote was *Q*." He said, "I like that a lot better. Let's go back to that." So that's what happened. I think *Q* is a provocative title and lent us to that little ad, "Q is Coming."

The film received sneak previews in 1982, but was not officially released until 1983, when it became the first film Samuel Arkoff released after leaving

Filmways (who had bought AIP). As in *God Told Me To*, there are human sacrifices to a phony god; this time some mad Aztec is skinning people alive to revive his god, Quetzalcoatl, while Quinn dispenses with some annoying criminal types by leading them to the lair of the bird (actually, it is more like a lizard).

Moriarty gives a wonderful performance, almost making his sleazy, low-life character endearing, and the rest of the cast (including Candy Clark, David Carradine, and Richard Roundtree) are also quite good. The Winged Serpent itself seems like a stop-motion throwback to '50s style science fiction filmmaking and was animated by Dave Allen and Randy Cook.

Cohen stated that

the difference with *Q* [versus other effects pictures] was that the effects were done after the picture was shot, whereas a lot of times in a picture, the effects are done *before* the picture is shot. But what happened with *Q* was that I had been on *I, The Jury* and had not gotten along with the people, and we decided that we were not going to make the picture; we wanted to go our separate ways. I was feeling very depressed and I was still living at this hotel in New York City, and I was still seeing the people go to work everyday and come home. I thought, what am I going to do? Am I going to pack up my bags and go back to Los Angeles?

I had this script called *Q* which was about this bird and everything, and I said, "Jesus, I bet I could get this thing into production in a couple of weeks," which I did. So two weeks after I left *I, The Jury*, we were shooting *Q*. There was almost no preparation at all. I got Michael Moriarty and David Carradine and Candy Clark and Richard Round-tree, and inside of two weeks we were shooting the picture, and the *I, The Jury* people couldn't believe it. They were working in the same hotel shooting another picture and they were having terrible difficulties. They were shooting Saturdays and Sundays and having 20-hour days and the budget went over $11 million and the company went bankrupt. In the meantime, we were shooting our picture there, and we finished the same time they did, even though we started much later than they did. But, of course, we had no time to plan for proper special effects beforehand. We had to do that afterwards.

So then I brought the footage out and showed it to David Allen, and naturally, he and his people said, "Well, you know you shot this all wrong because you have all moving shots. We have to have stationary shots to do this model animation." I said, "I don't want stationary shots. I don't want the shot locked down, looking up a building, seeing a bird flying around the Chrysler building. I want the audience to be flying around with the bird. I want the shots to be in motion." He said he's never done anything like that before but he'd try, so basically I think it worked out better because it represented a challenge to him to do something a little bit different for a change. It worked out better.

There has almost always been a market for a good monster movie, but Cohen feels that the marketing department concentrated too much of their attention on the flying plesiosaur in the film's ad campaign:

> There were only six or seven minutes of special effects in the whole picture. I think the way the picture was advertised, you would have thought there was 30 minutes of special effects in the picture. They advertised it as a monster picture, so if you came expecting to see a monster like a *King Kong* movie and there was only six minutes of monster in the picture, then you'd be disappointed.
>
> I thought it was just the right amount (of special effects) for what the picture was and what it was intended to be. If they had sold the picture based on what it was rather than what they felt they could sell tickets the first day, I think it would have been more honest in what they were selling to the public.
>
> As it was, the picture did a lot of business. It made almost a million dollars the first week in New York City alone, so we did very nicely with the film and made a profit on it, but it wasn't a break-out picture like *It's Alive*. I think that's because it didn't have the proper campaign. A campaign of a giant bird flying over the Chrysler Building with a girl in its claw indicates to the audience that they are going to see a movie that was all special effects or a Japanese monster movie or something like that.

While Cohen often writes, produces, and directs his own films, there are some screenplays he worked on that he did not end up filming himself. One of these was the script for *'Salem's Lot*, the adaptation of the Stephen King novel which Tobe Hooper ended up directing. The project was scripted as a four-hour miniseries for television because it was decided that it was too expensive to do as a movie.

Cohen's script was later rewritten, and though he finds the results disappointing, he notes that some elements he added were retained. He mentioned what he feels were problems with the project:

> You wait a long time to see a creature that's supposed to be "Nosferatu" or something – it was basically my idea to use the same makeup as was used in the Murnau film, which was something they did do. I said, "Let's make it look like the monster in *Nosferatu*." The guy who played the creature, Reggie Nalder – he's the actor in *The Man Who Knew Too Much* – he's not much of an actor if you leave him on the screen too long, but he has a good [i.e., sinister] look to him. I thought it was dumb and I didn't think it was a successful version of *'Salem's Lot* 'cause it didn't have any New England atmosphere. One thing Stephen King's books have is a lot of atmosphere of the place, of the town, and I felt the adaptors lost all that.

Cohen eventually persuaded Warner Bros. to allow him to write and direct a sequel.

Cohen scripted the aforementioned *I, the Jury* with the intention of portraying Mike Hammer as an anti-heroic psychopath whom the CIA manipulates into killing the people they want killed. Cohen also scripted a film which became *Success* that was largely rewritten by the film's director. Cohen did manage to direct *The Private Files of J. Edgar Hoover* (1976) from his own script, a film which he considers to be "investigative filmmaking." In that film he makes what he considers an educated guess as to the identity of "Deep Throat," the informant who broke Watergate for the *Washington Post* reporters. It is his favorite of his films.

Unfortunately, the film prior to the success of *Q, Full Moon High,* was buried when Filmways was sold to Orion, despite the fact that it is one of Cohen's more entertaining efforts. The film was conceived as a sort of semi-sequel to *I Was a Teenage Werewolf,* and it constantly refers humorously to its own low budget. Adam Arkin is an ordinary high school student with a John Bircher (Ed McMahon) for a father. The father decides to go to Transylvania to fight communism first-hand. (The trip overseas includes a comical attempted hijacking and a shot of a toy plane jerkily making progress over a map to indicate the route, and then getting smashed by a fist to indicate the final destruction.)

Of course, poor Adam mixes with some gypsies and gets bitten by a werewolf. McMahon barricades himself in his bomb shelter and fires at his son only to have the bullet ricochet around the shelter so that he winds up shooting himself.

The years pass (indicated by different portraits of the President on the wall; Nixon's resignation is indicated by having his picture crash to the ground) and Adam returns to his hometown pretending to be his own son because, as a result of being a werewolf, he has not aged. He falls in love and tries to convince his newfound girlfriend that he is a werewolf by tying himself up and, with her help, filming the transformation, but she interprets this as indicating that he is into kinky sex (which is all right by her).

Alan Arkin comes in as a psychiatrist who is called in on the case, and he manages to have Adam locked up in jail. Comes the full moon, the transformation begins, but a stray bullet hits the cameraman and so the screen goes blank as we hear about the expensive special effects we are missing. The film ends in a send-up of the cliché climax at the big home football game.

Full Moon High is very silly but nonetheless has a certain charm and a sense of fun. Cohen inventively makes his biggest handicap, an inadequate budget, into a source of self-deprecating humor. The film is much funnier than the similarly budgeted *Teen Wolf,* which conveniently managed to cash in on *Back to the Future* star Michael J. Fox's popularity to great success. *Teen Wolf* replaced Cohen's crafty humor with TV movie moralizing and is a far less enjoyable film as a result.

Cohen had a banner year in 1985 with two films distributed by New Line Cinema, as well as *The Stuff* coming out from New World Pictures. His first film that year, *Perfect Strangers*, was originally titled *Blind Alley* until Columbia Pictures protested that they owned the rights to the title, which had appeared on an earlier film. *Perfect Strangers* centers around a two-year-old child who has witnessed a murder. The film happened to be released during time when the reliability of underage witnesses was being questioned in courts and in the media because of the events surrounding California's McMartin child abuse trial (where many of the charges were later dismissed because the allegations proved unfounded or unsubstantiated).

Said Cohen about the film:

> This picture is about a two-year-old who witnesses a murder but can't speak. He can't relate what he's seen, and nobody thinks he knows what he saw, but he knows exactly what he saw. He doesn't exactly know that it was bad; he just saw someone stabbing somebody. The killer is a person he happens to like, so he goes around trying to pick up knives and imitate the murder all the time, much to the killer's dismay because he has come to like the kid, kind of love him a little bit.
>
> This is an old-fashioned murder thriller. It's kind of a funny picture in its way. It's got a lot of humor in it too. There's a scene where the killer, who is a handsome young guy, has moved in with the little boy's mother – he becomes friends with the mother to try and see if the kid recognizes him. Naturally, the mother thinks he's interested in her, so they strike up an acquaintanceship which leads to romance, and he starts sleeping with her and taking care of the kid.
>
> She leaves him with the kid all the time because she is out doing her women's lib stuff and her militant feminism stuff, and he stays home and takes care of the kid. There's a scene where he's giving the boy a bath and he's reading him the E.T. storybook, relating to him about the E.T. He says to the child, "Remember what happend to E.T. when the police found out? He turned all white and he died. That's because mommy found out, remember when mommy found out what happened? Mommy must never find out. The police must never find out." This guy likens himself to E.T.

Once more Cohen is dealing with a threat to the family in an inventive way. What is most striking about *Perfect Strangers* is how the amoral child is affected by what he sees. The kid is too young really to understand the difference between good and evil, but he is perceptive enough to pick up on the actions of those around him and also on the things that come to him through the media.

"Murder is the ultimate special effect" is the premise of a down-on-his-luck movie director in the perversely titled *Special Effects*. Cohen realizes that while special effects can be attractive to the eye, they are not satisfying in and of themselves but merely serve to support story and characters.

Though his next film, *The Stuff*, is thus far his most effects-laden, Cohen daringly used *Special Effects* as the title of a movie that has none. The plot of the film is a bizarre combination of *Vertigo* and a snuff film as an egotistical director (Eric Bogosian, who went on to give a brilliant performance in Oliver Stone's *Talk Radio*) whose last effects-laden film bombed strangles an actress and films her while doing so. Deciding that this has given him some terrifically realistic and exciting footage, he then casts the woman's innocent husband in the role of the murderer and plans to make his scenario come true by leading the police to think that the husband is really the killer – the end result being that the director gets off scot-free and has a potentially big-grossing film about the case besides.

Borrowing a page or two from Michael Powell's *Peeping Tom* and Brian DePalma's *Hi Mom!*, the film is also about scoptophilia – the urge to look – and filmmaking and how they are related. Said Cohen:

The husband is a young guy who comes to New York to get his wife to come with him. They have a little baby, and he's bought a 16mm projector and has made home movies of the baby. He finds his wife working at a photographic salon where people take pictures of her naked – so the idea of people filming people is inherent from the beginning. He takes her home and shows her home movies of the baby, but she doesn't want to go home with him, so she makes up a story that she's close to getting a movie with this movie director, whose name she sees on the marquee across the street from the apartment window where they're running a retrospective. She says, "I'm going to be in his next picture. I'm going to meet him tonight and he's going to cast me in his picture." She's never met the guy. Subsequent to that, she goes to the director's house and tries to make her dreams come true, but instead she gets herself murdered.

Then, of course, when the police ask the husband, the husband says she was going to meet that director. They go to the movie director's house and the movie director denies everything and the husband gets arrested. While he's being arrested, the movie director goes up on the roof and photographs the arrest. He has the idea that he can make a film of this if only he can find someone who looks like the guy's wife. The husband is getting rid of all the wife's old clothes when the director insists that the husband gets the clothes back (so they can be used as wardrobe in the movie), and when the husband returns to the Salvation Army, he finds a brunette who looks like his late wife. The director transforms her into a replica of the wife and the husband falls in love with her. So we have transference of identity, a lot of twists, and I think it makes a statement about the movie business. I enjoyed making it up.

The film becomes a lightly amusing take on film-director-as-Svengali. However, it is Zöe Tamerlis, star of Abel Ferrara's *Ms. .45*, who really shines in the dual role of the untalented actress and the husband's new girl-friend.

Neither *Perfect Strangers* nor *Special Effects* was given much of a re-lease in the United States and both were quickly sold off to Embassy Home Video, who had put up money for their production, so that they could be re-leased to the burgeoning videocassette market (where profits now often ex-ceed those of most theatrical releases).

Cohen really pinned his hopes on *The Stuff* becoming a breakthrough film for him. As a horror film project, the film is bristling with ideas and is not the simple-minded *Blob* pastiche that some have made it out to be, but the ideas often step all over each other and many sequences were clumsily handled. I caught *The Stuff* at its disastrous sneak preview in Santa Monica where an audience mostly comprised of Westwood teenagers reviled the film. The film had ten more minutes trimmed and was quickly dumped into release by New World, who had lost faith in the film.

Most people consider their homes to be safe places, refuges from the terrors and problems of the outside world but in Cohen's films he has repeat-edly shown that horror often strikes in the home, which is also where we are the most vulnerable. In *The Stuff*, he decided to take this one step fur-ther by locating this unusual monster inside the refrigerator.

The Stuff opened with a parody of the "old man finds the menace" scene in which an old man sees something oozing out of the ground and foolishly decides to taste it. Cohen then plays on another commonplace fear – that of heartless and unscrupulous corporations exploiting the American public (remember the reason why the infant was destroyed at the end of *It's Alive*). The stuff in *The Stuff* becomes a metaphor for all the addictive, carcinogenic consumables that some corporations have foisted on the unsuspecting pub-lic.

"People eat it, not realizing they're eating a living creature," said Cohen, "but then yogurt is alive too. We eat a lot of living things, but very few of them think. The Stuff is a food that thinks. It doesn't get digested. It just accumulates and starves you. It dissolves part of you, so you don't gain any weight, and it takes the place of the part of you that it's dissolved until it takes you over." It has an appealing taste, and not many calories because it is indigestible, so the Stuff is marketed as the perfect dessert food. As a bonus for the people marketing it, it is also highly addictive and so soon con-sumers cannot get enough of the Stuff, as it is called. Cohen went on:

> The point of the story is that we live in a society where the powers that
> be will sell us anything, and people will buy anything. Even if they find
> out it's bad for them and will kill them, they will continue to buy it and
> it will be sold to them. With the proper amount of financing and public
> relations, with the proper slogans and advertising, people will work in

concert with people who don't have their best interests at heart. Even at the end of the picture when the Stuff is finally disposed of, there's still a black market for the Stuff, selling it at $75 a container, and people are buying it like they buy cocaine, in back alleys and under the table and everything. You can't stop it.

I'm glad I made the film, but I don't think it's going to get anyone to stop smoking or stop drinking Coke with cyclamates or anything else where it tells you it gives you cancer on the label. Most people go right on buying those things, which kind of makes me sad. Thinking about it caused me to look at all these fast food franchises and the fast food people are eating. I just thought people were being psychologically addicted to fast food by television commercials. They were being programmed into eating this food, which is an interesting idea that I decided to take to its extreme, so I came up with a food so good, you couldn't stop eating it until it finally controlled your mind and your body.

The moral ambiguity of the film extends into the main characters' professions. Michael Moriarty, the hero, plays an industrial spy who discovers the awful truth and decides to fight the onslaught of the Stuff. For most of his life, he has been totally unethical and even nicknames himself "Moe" because he always wants "a little mo'e." He falls in love with Andrea Marcovicci, who is the irresponsible mastermind behind marketing the Stuff to the American public. He must convince her that the product she's peddling is a threat to society's very existence.

There's also a subplot involving a boy named Jason (Scott Bloom), whose family comes to represent the typical American family. Jason sees the Stuff moving inside the family refrigerator and tries to warn his family, but it is too late. There's also Chocolate Chip Charlie (Garrett Morris), whose cookie chains have been bought out by the Stuff people (they plan to crumble his once famous cookies into the Stuff to create a new flavor). Their investigations into the Stuff lead these characters to come together and form a united front.

Finally Cohen pushes the satire too far by having Moriarty portray the Stuff as a communist plot to infiltrate America and deprive us of our essence in order to enlist the aid of a fanatical right-winger, Col. Spears (Paul Sorvino), who has a private army at his command. There are also some gruesome special effects as people and animals are revealed to be nothing more than shells now occupied by the Stuff, which starts to ooze from every orifice. (Morris' demise in a radio station is particularly unpleasant as his mouth becomes unnaturally elongated.)

The film features some delightful parodies of commercials and some wacky if interesting concepts, but it isn't technically polished, and as usual, Cohen sometimes has difficulty injecting his exposition smoothly into the narrative. Nevertheless, Cohen is almost a novelty in that he is one of the few

current horror filmmakers to make films that have ideas and to be concerned with how the events of the plot affect a character's personality.
Moriarty's character just like Tony LoBianco's in *God Told Me To* and John
Ryan's in *It's Alive*, must make a decision on what to do based on a problem
that has now changed his perception. Ryan has to come to terms with what
fatherhood means to him; LoBianco, with being a cop who is also the
brother of a dangerous and powerful psychotic; and Moriarty, with whether
his own interests or society's best interests are more important. Cohen may
work in the exploitation field, but he is not a simplistic exploitation filmmaker.

The non-success of *The Stuff* interrupted Cohen's plans to make *F.I.T.
to Kill*, a satire on the health club craze (though he intends to revive the film
eventually). Instead, realizing that sequels to popular films could generate
big bucks from the videocasette market, Cohen approached Warner Bros.
with the ideas of sequelizing or remaking Andre De Toth's *House of Wax*,
which had a successful rerelease during the 1983 3-D craze, or making *The
Exorcist Part III*, but he was unable to get the rights to do either. Instead,
he was offered sequels to *It Lives Again* and *'Salem's Lot*.

Island of the Alive, shot in four weeks on the island of Kauai, shows that
the mutant babies have grown up a bit. The film gets off to a good start with
a prologue in which a cabbie assists a woman who is about to give birth in
his cab only to discover to his dismay that "it's one of *them!*" Michael Moriarty, a Cohen regular ever since his highly acclaimed performance in *Q* as
Quinn, becomes the latest father who has to deal with his feelings about having a killer mutant baby for a son.

Playing a third-rate actor, Steven Jarvis, Moriarty goes to court to keep
these killer kids from being destroyed, and a compromise is reached. The
five mutant children that have been born are shipped to an island, where
they will be isolated and allowed to grow up in peace. (Still, as they lack
proper guidance, this does not seem like a very intelligent thing to have
done.) Jarvis and some scientists head out to the island to see how they are
doing, and soon the scientists are being picked off by the now larger and
stronger mutants.

Jarvis gives his ex-wife (Karen Black) the surprise of her life when the
mutants force him to take them back to Florida. Halfway there, the mutants
throw Jarvis off the boat and he is picked up by some Cubans who mistake
him for a spy.

The trouble is, Cohen tries to have things both ways in the movie: He
makes pleas for understanding, but the grown-up mutants are also truly
dangerous. Cohen also indicates how guilt by association can affect people
particularly in an amusing scene where a prostitute recoils from Jarvis after
having relations with him because she suddenly realizes who he is. "You
should tell people who you are before you have sex with them," she screams,

as if being the parent of a mutant child was as catching as AIDS. Still, while the film does have some topical humor, it is primarily created out of commercial considerations.

Return to Salem's Lot has very little to do with Tobe Hooper's TV miniseries of the Stephen King novel. Cohen simply used it as a commercially appealing title to tell a story about a town full of vampires in New England. Moriarty stars yet again, this time as an anthropologist who is trapped along with his son (Richard Addison Reed) in 'Salem's Lot. Perhaps the most delightful character in the film is a Jewish vampire hunter (played by director Sam Fuller) who goes after vampires with all the verve that the Jewish Nazi hunters demonstrate in tracking down their quarry. Judge Axel (Andrew Duggan) is the head of the town's vampire cult, a scoundrel who wraps himself in the American flag until he is trapped in sunlight and finally staked in the finale.

Unfortunately, because he was tied up making these films, Cohen did not direct his best script in years, *Best Seller*, which featured wonderful performances by Brian Dennehy and James Woods. Cohen had shopped the script around for 10 years until finally Orion decided to produce the film and let Joe Flynn direct. Cohen had come up with a very interesting story about a Joseph Wambaugh–type cop who has writer's block until a hit man, dissatisfied with the head of crime organization that he belongs to, offers to tell the cop his story while getting his revenge. Though it is important to the hit man (played by Woods) that the cop like and admire him, the cop is instead disgusted with the scummy crook – but nonetheless fascinated, and he cooperates in hopes of getting a best seller out of the deal. There are murders and convolutions aplenty, including some highly suspect corporate shenanigans, and the uneasy alliance between the differing personalities make this a good cut above the average thriller. Unfortunately, the film never managed to fulfill its potential, with distributor Orion burying it amongst an overcrowded season of suspense thrillers that were churned out after the success of *Lethal Weapon*.

Cohen also worked on another thriller, *Deadly Illusion*, for three weeks before hassles with the producers caused him to leave and let William Tannen (who had directed *Flashpoint*) to take over the direction of the film. Once more Cohen combines vicious murders and wry spoofery. The hero's name is Hamberger (Billy Dee Williams), a private dick whose office is set up at a local deli and who has to constantly fend off jokes about his name. (It is interesting to note that Cohen has consistently hired black actors for all his films and that he is just as willing to have them play unsympathetic characters as sympathetic ones.) Williams is very likable as Hamberger, as is Joe Cortese as the cop he keeps coming into contact with. Vanity and Morgan Fairchild make attractive female leads but demonstrate little in the way of ability, and the plot is a morass of hastily connected ideas.

Larry Cohen (right) with star Eric Roberts on the set of Cohen's latest opus, The
Ambulance, *in which an ambulance mysteriously whisks away unsuspecting victims, who are never seen again. (Photo courtesy of Larry Cohen.)*

For Shapiro-Glickenhaus Entertainment, Cohen combined the urban
cop thriller with a zombie from horror movies to produce and write *Maniac
Cop,* which William Lustig (*Maniac, The Vigilante*) directed. While the
opening of the film makes some interesting use of the nervous and intimidated reactions a cop can cause, exploiting people's fear of authority or the
way some cops play menacingly with their nightsticks, the basic conceit is
to place a Jason-like character (as in the *Friday the 13th* films) in the costume of a cop and set him loose in the city. As a result, the little originality
that the film has quickly dissipates.

The film establishes the maniac cop (Robert D'Zar) by having a mugging
victim run to him for help only to be attacked by her supposed savior. Next,
some other innocent citizens are stopped by a large cop, whose face we do
not see, and are then attacked by him.

Detective Tom McCrae (Tom Atkins) becomes concerned when he learns
that the killer's m.o. includes dressing as a cop, and he fears that the killer
may be someone on the force. His superior (Richard Roundtree) insists on
not releasing the information, but McCrae leaks it anyway to a female television news reporter, with the result that people start panicking and attacking innocent cops.

Embarrassed by the publicity, the department wants to put a lid on the matter quickly. The wife of officer Jack Forrest (Bruce Campbell of the *Evil Dead* films fame) is getting suspicious because he happened to be out on the nights of the murders. She follows him and finds that he has been fooling around with fellow officer Teresa Mallory (Laurene Landon); on her way back home, she gets murdered by the maniac cop. Learning that Forrest was at the scene of the crime that night and that he refuses to provide an alibi because he does not want to involve Mallory, the department decides to make him the scapegoat for the crimes.

However, McCrae is not convinced and seeks Mallory out, arriving in time to save her from the maniac cop, whom she has shot in the face. The fact that this does not stop or kill the maniac does not seem to sink in right away, but slowly McCrae puzzles out that the maniac is the revived and now demented form of an overenthusiastic cop who was put in prison for violating a criminal's rights and was then killed by inmates whom he had helped place there. Mysteriously returning to life, the maniac cop becomes the Terminator, wiping out an entire police station in a ridiculous climax.

McCrae frees Forrest and gets killed shortly afterwards, leaving Forrest the primary suspect for the massacre. He and Mallory go off in hot pursuit of the maniac (being banged around by zombies is now old hat for actor Campbell) until the maniac is at last destroyed and the charges against Forrest forgotten. But is that really the last we'll see of this implacable and seemingly unkillable maniac? No, for a sequel was filmed in 1989 and set for release in 1991 with Cohen writing and producing again.

Cohen brings to his films a quirkly and playful intelligence that establishes his films as different from the run-of-the-mill exploitation pictures that he competes with. Cohen does not go to the major studios because he wants to remain independent and make his films his way. While crime thrillers and horror films are typically safe commercial genres, Cohen is willing to take chances and experiment with unusual twists on his flamboyant ideas.

The people in his films are not designed as icons but as real people. He avoids the cliché of purely evil villains and saintly heroes because he knows that not only do such people not exist, they are not even very interesting. His villains typically are people who are out to get something and do not care who they hurt to get it; they are not so much evil as highly motivated and unethical. His heroes often face moral dilemmas and sometimes make the wrong decisions, leading to disastrous consequences.

This does not mean that Cohen is above commercial considerations, and the ability of almost all his films to turn a profit proves it. For example, during the filming of *God Told Me To*, he knew that the police were going to be out in force in a parade for St. Patrick's Day, so he injected this spectacle into his film in a memorable sequence, with Andy Kaufman playing a cop who suddenly goes mad and kills someone under the direction of the alien messiah. Later in *Maniac Cop*, the same parade shows up and is used as a distraction while the killer attempts to attack Mallory. Like many low-budget filmmakers, Cohen is capable of being inventive on the spot.

But his primary inventiveness comes when he delineates modern horrors such as the breakdown of the family, corporate greed at the expense of compassion, religious repression, or societal inability to assimilate those who are different and the violence that inevitably results. That these horrors are manifested as killer infants, deadly desserts, homicidal messiahs, teenaged werewolves, flying lizards and social pariahs does not change their essential message: We have to look out for and try to understand each other.

Roger Corman (1926–   )

Five Guns West; Apache Woman (1955); *The Day the World Ended; Swamp Women; The Oklahoma Woman; Gunslinger; It Conquered the World* (1956); *Naked Paradise* (aka *Thunder Over Hawaii*); *The Undead; Not of This Earth; Attack of the Crab Monsters; Rock All Night; Carnival Rock; Teenage Doll; Sorority Girl; The Saga of the Viking Women and Their Voyage to the Waters of the Great Sea Serpent* (1957); *War of the Satellites; Machine Gun Kelly; Teen-age Caveman; She Gods of Shark Reef* (1958); *I, Mobster; A Bucket of Blood; The Wasp Woman* (1959); *Ski Troop Attack; House of Usher; The Last Woman on Earth; Little Shop of Horrors* (1960); *Atlas; Creature from the Haunted Sea; The Pit and the Pendulum* (1961); *Premature Burial; The Intruder; Tales of Terror; Tower of London* (1962); *The Raven; The Young Racers; The Terror* (uncredited codirectors: Francis Ford Coppola, Jack Hill, and Monte Hellman); *The Haunted Palace; "X" – The Man with the X-Ray Eyes* (1963); *The Secret Invasion; The Masque of the Red Death; The Tomb of Ligeia* (1964); *The Wild Angels* (1966); *The St. Valentine's Day Massacre; The Trip* (1967); *Bloody Mama; Gas-s-s-s . . . Or It Became Necessary to Destroy the World in Order to Save It!* (1970); *Von Richthofen and Brown* (1971); *Target: Harry* (aka *What's in It for Harry?; How to Make It*) (1980 under the pseudonym Henry Neill); *Roger Corman's Frankenstein Unbound* (1990).

Roger Corman is a man of many hats, so any simple description of him is not apt to do him justice. Primarily, though, it can be said that he is a filmmaker and that making money by making films is his passion. Corman was one of the main suppliers of AIP in its early, formative years. He tried his hand at almost every exploitation genre and has been instrumental in creating a few subgenres of his own (e.g. motorcycle and nurse movies). He has been a prolific producer, the head of his own studio (New World, until he sold it) and his own distribution company (Concorde); he has released important foreign films profitably, helped start the careers of many top Hollywood talents (as well as given a chance to many whose careers did not take off), and in general has been an important cottage industry unto himself for the past three decades.

Not that all the material he produced was good – far from it. Many of his films, especially his earliest ones, were disposable exploitation flicks meant to give teenagers somewhere to go on a date, and later viewings and evaluations were never considered. Nonetheless, Corman's films often have an intelligence that other exploitation directors lack, and Corman proved more flexible than those other directors, willing to experiment and change with the times.

Corman learned early on that an exploitation filmmaker needed people he could trust to do their jobs well, or at least competently. Using television-style techniques, cranking out a different film first every week, then every month, he went through a large number of people. Those he liked stayed on to work on his next productions, forming a kind of talent pool or traveling company of dependable contributors. Corman himself admits that much of what he learned about film came from his frequent cameraman Floyd Crosby, who managed to give even some of Corman's cheapest productions a good look. Crosby had won an Academy Award in 1931 for his work on *Tabu*; he also cophotographed such films as *Of Men and Music* and *The Brave Bulls* and the wonderful sea scenes in *The Old Man and the Sea*. That he ended up working for Roger Corman after photographing *High Noon* is a bit strange, but may have been part of the anti–Communist fervor against the makers of that film, which in those days of blacklisting could have kept Crosby out of Hollywood productions until Corman started making use of him.

Corman did not give people chances to work in the film industry out of the goodness of his heart, but because he knew he could get them cheap. Still, many people are grateful for the opportunities Corman provided them and for his having prodded them to be inventive, because when time and budget are limited, invention may be all a filmmaker has. Corman got a reputation for being parsimonious, but the people who worked for him also considered him honest. He was at least up front about not giving you much, but you could count on him to hold up his end, unlike some others working in the low-budget field.

As a result of many shrewd deals, Corman has been one of the most successful figures in the film industry, making his money out of several small successes rather than just going for that one big blockbuster. As one associate put it, Corman has rarely lost money on a deal, giving him a record few Hollywood producers can equal and a longevity of career that few can match. Another associate charged that the reason Corman made films so cheaply was that he pocketed any difference between what the film actually cost and how much the distributor had paid for it.

Corman was born on April 2, 1926, in Detroit. He came out west when his father, an engineer, retired and moved to Beverly Hills. He went to Stanford University and graduated with an engineering degree and a conviction that he wanted to be something more artistic than an engineer. He did take an engineering job at U.S. Electric Motors, but it lasted a mere four days before he got so bored he could not stand it anymore. He tried finding work around the movie and television studios, taking jobs as a stagehand at KLAC-TV and as a messenger boy at 20th Century–Fox, graduating finally into being a story analyst for the story department there.

Getting nowhere, Corman joined the navy and served for three years. In Ed Naha's *The Films of Roger Corman: Brilliance on a Budget*, Corman relates:

> I then went to England and studied literature at Oxford on the G.I. Bill. . . . I returned to California and tried writing screenplays again. My first script was called *House by the Sea*. Allied Artists bought it and retitled it *Highway Dragnet*. They would have stuck the word "Dragnet" on the Bible back then to get some mileage off the hit TV show. As it turned out, the smartest thing about the Allied deal was my insisting that, as part of the contract, I get an associate producer's credit on the finished movie.

While Corman was not involved in the actual production of *Highway Dragnet*, the producer's credit did make it easier to borrow money to finance a picture of his own. He got together in 1954 with a writer named Wyott Ordung, who put up a majority of the money for a 20 percent stake. Corman then approached the Aerojet-General Company, convincing them that loaning him one of their one-man submarines for use in the film would give them plenty of free publicity.

A script was written to include the sub and credited to William Danch, (though it might have been Ordung, who took the directorial reins on the project). The plot concerns a woman (Anne Kimbell) who hears about and pursues a monster that has been killing people in Mexico. She shows a portion of it that she snags to Stuart Wade, who upon examining it postulates that it came from a colossal amoeba that was possibly irradiated. Stuart owns the one-man sub and in the film's climax, he takes it down and rams it into the octopus-like monster's cyclopian red eye.

Actually the Bob Baker–created octopus monster was not the original intended for the film. At a sneak preview for *The Monster from the Ocean Floor*, initially titled *It Stalked the Ocean Floor*, someone in the audience compared the original monster with his wife's diaphragm, and the resulting laughter convinced the duo that they needed a new monster pronto. Unfortunately, Baker was not able to work out how to create an underwater miniature set and so dabbed everything in glycerine, making the cheaply done scenes look even more ludicrous. Still, the laughter that this earnest ineptness creates is about the best thing in this exceedingly dull little film. Corman managed to sell it to the Robert Lippert organization sight unseen for a tidy $110,000 (the film itself cost between $12,000 to $17,000 to produce and looks it), and never looked back.

In an interview with Charles Flynn and Todd McCarthy in *Kings of the Bs* Corman explains:

I took the money from that and made a second picture [*Fast and Furious*], and realized that producing independently was a very slow process. You had to wait for the money to come back from one picture to put it in the other. That means you might do one picture a year. So I made a deal with Jim Nicholson and Sam Arkoff, who were starting a company called American Releasing. . . .

I made a proposition to Nicholson and Arkoff: that if they would take my picture and give me an advance, I would make a three-picture deal with them, getting money from franchise holders (that's kind of a states' rights operation throughout the country) in advance of each picture so that I would have financing.

After *Fast and Furious*, a race car movie, Corman embarked on a series of westerns and began assembling the people who would make the Corman team, including cinematographer Floyd Crosby, screenwriter R. Wright Campbell, actors Mike "Touch" Connors, Paul Birch, Jonathan Haze, Dick Miller and Beverly Garland, editor Ronald Sinclair, sound man Dick Rubin, and Chuck Hanawalt as the key grip.

In the midst of these westerns, Corman, a longtime reader of science fiction, decided to try his hand at his first science fiction horror film, *The Day the World Ended* from a script by Lou Rusoff. It was an after-the-bomb story made for just under $100,000.

The film begins in 1970 on TD Day – for Total Destruction. A few survivors make their way to an isolated valley where the radiation levels are comparatively low. The intruders disturb the valley's inhabitants, headed by Captain Jim Maddison (Paul Birch), who is concerned because his canned food supply is limited. Maddison explains the dangers of radiation by showing pictures he had sketched after an atomic blast on the island of Matsuo. Holding up a sketch of a six-legged furry creature with fangs, Maddison intones, "*That* was a chipmunk," in his most doom-laden voice.

An irradiated man (Jonathan Haze) stumbles into the valley and, before he dies of radiation poisoning, informs everyone that a small but strong number of mutants exist in the radioactive fog surrounding the valley and are fighting each other for supremacy. Meanwhile, one of the party, Radek (Paul Dubov), is slowly turning into a mutant himself, but is killed by a full-fledged "stage three" mutant who has been discreetly watching things, especially the women, from afar.

A gangster, Tony (Touch Connors), makes a play for Maddison's daughter Louise (Lori Nelson), who has been anxiously awaiting the return of her fiancé, Tommy, who could be the mutant (Paul Blaisdel) that is prowling around the house. Ruby (Adele Jurgens) tries to interfere, but Tony stabs her for her pains and dumps her over a cliff with the tender parting words, "Happy landings, sweetheart."

The mutant grabs Louise and makes off with her, with two-fisted geologist Rick (Richard Denning, of *Creature from the Black Lagoon* fame) in hot pursuit. Comments Bill Warren in his excellent *Keep Watching the Skies Vol. 1*:

> Corman's direction is perfunctory – he simply tells the story – until one sequence near the end. The camera is looking over Denning's shoulder as the mutant begins to advance on him and Denning fires the rifle. Without a cut, the monster turns toward the camera and advances, swatting angrily at the bullets. It almost reaches Denning before he turns aside. This imaginative staging was perhaps inspired by Harvey Kurtzman's typical action breakdowns in the comic books then being published by EC Publications; I've never seen this kind of action anywhere else before Kurtzman. The sequence still gets a strong reaction from an audience.

The monster is finally foiled by simple, uncontaminated rain which apparently dissolves the contaminated monster, freeing Louise for Rick's arms. Tony causes a bit of trouble when they return until he's dispatched by a dying Maddison, who informs Louise and Rick, "There was a voice on the radio while you were gone. There are others out there. There's a future out there for you two. You've got to go and find it." Rick and Louise are left to face what the end titles indicate is a new beginning.

The Day the World Ended is a modest, low-budget science fiction thriller deserving neither praise nor derision. The three-eyed mutant costume that Paul Blaisdel constructed and wore in the film almost proved his ultimate downfall: During the rain scene, he luxuriated in the cool water until he almost drowned when his costume became too waterlogged for him to sit upright again. Larry Buchanan directed and wrote an awful color remake, *In the Year 2889*. It was released only to television, but the original is a passable time waster, though far from one of Corman's best.

His next sf/horror project, *It Conquered the World* (a rather grandiose title for a modest but entertaining science fiction programmer), was a step up. While credited again to Rusoff, the final script was hastily rewritten by Charles B. Griffith, who also has a bit part as one of the scientists in the film.

The script was written in two days and the film itself was shot in ten. Originally, the fanged cucumber that plays the Venusian space visitor in the film was much shorter because Corman reasoned that Venus had a heavier gravity and so anything living on it would be squatter and very low to the ground. This design was changed during production when lead actress Beverly Garland allegedly kicked it contemptuously upon initial examination. (Despite its high cone-shaped head, the face on the front is still very low to the ground. Blaisdel, who built it, was told that the monster would be barely glimpsed in the shadows of the cave in which it dwells and gave it broad features so that something would register. Corman then decided to push the monster out of the cave into the light for the finale.)

Amazingly enough, *It Conquered the World* ties into many of the same themes as the classic *Invasion of the Body Snatchers*. Tom Anderson (Lee Van Cleef) is a brilliant but frustrated scientist who has established contact with a Venusian, whom he guides to Earth. The Venusian plans to do away with all emotion as part of a takeover plan, much to the delight of Anderson, who sees foolish emotions as blocking man's progress and causing him wars and strife.

The alien comes over on an abducted American satellite and soon turns off all power for everyone in the area except at the now smug Tom Anderson's house. Tom's wife, Claire (Beverly Garland), can appreciate that the opposition Tom has faced in his life has made him feel small, but she is furious with him for helping the invader and asks him whether it makes him feel like a big shot to have the only working equipment in the area.

Tom's scientist friend Paul Nelson (Peter Graves) realizes what Tom is up to and calls him the greatest traitor of all time. To make matters worse, Tom has supplied the creature the names of key people to be controlled, including various authority figures and Paul and his wife, Joan (Sally Fraser). Paul is able to destroy the bat-like "construct" before it can attach itself to him and control him; however, his wife is not so fortunate. When he discovers that his wife is permanently changed and will never be able to feel love or any other kind of emotion, Paul stoically shoots her before heading off to put a stop to Tom and the Venusian's plans.

Meanwhile, Claire confronts the monster in its cave, and over the radio Tom hears her death screams. He agrees to cooperate with Paul in destroying it. While Paul goes to a military base to prevent any more of the invaders from coming over, Tom heads out with a blowtorch and confronts the thing he had presumed would be the "savior" of all mankind. "I made it possible for you to come here. I welcomed you to this earth, and you have made it a charnel house!" he passionately exclaims before burning one of the creature's eyes out in a surprisingly gory scene for the time. (The blood was actually chocolate syrup ejected out of a hypodermic, which initially stuck and then released more "blood" than was probably intended. The British censor considered holding up release of the film until he was assured that monsters were not entitled to humane treatment.) Tom kills the monster but dies in the attempt. Paul stops to reflect that "if there is hope, it has to come from man himself."

The film gets by more on its snappy (and occasionally sappy) dialogue than on its visual invention, though Corman is good at staging the action during long takes, bringing the actors closer to the camera for emphasis and then having them back off to be part of the social milieu. The Venusian invader can even reasonably be read as a metaphor for the appeal and dangers of totalitarianism, a single controlling force that keeps the peace – or else. Considering the low expectations most rubber monster movies engender, *It Conquered the World* does have a modicum of ambition and a little something on its mind besides.

The same could also be said of *Attack of the Crab Monsters*, also scripted by Griffith. Said Griffith in an interview with this author, "Roger [Corman] came to me and said, 'I want to make a picture called *Attack of the Giant Crabs*,' and I asked, does it have to be atomic radiation? He responded yes. He said it as an experiment. 'I want suspense or action in every scene. No kind of scene without suspense or action.'"

A group of scientists land on an island in the Pacific and are alarmed to find that it is slowly crumbling into the sea. The scientist postulate the crumbling may be due to some undersea quakes but are alarmed to discover that the cause is actually a pair of giant crabs who are tunneling extensively under the island. (The crabs are an apparent by-product of recent nuclear testing.) The crabs are even more amazing in that they amputate the heads of their victims and assimilate their minds and personalities. The victims are then part of the crab, which uses their voices to lure other victims to their doom.

Corman establishes an ominous mood throughout the film, augmented by Griffith's dialogue and Ronald Stein's eerie score. Unfortunately, he occasionally blows it, as when Mel Welles pronounces (in an affected foreign accent) that there is no life on the island and Corman cuts to the squawking of seagulls flying in the air. The crab monsters themselves are hokey and silly-looking, with their eyes not on stalks but plastered on their shells. Also people in the film constantly refer to them as being black when they are in fact very light in color.

Aiding the film is the cynical sense of humor the characters demonstrate in their credulity-stretching situation. The mood Corman establishes helps, and the film moves at a good pace right up to the climax where the remaining crab creature is dispatched with electricity, à la James Arness in *The Thing*.

Attack of the Crab Monsters was doubled-billed with *Not of This Earth*, which was as good if not better. In that film, Griffith retells the opening of Stoker's *Dracula*, using a heroine instead of a hero (a typical Corman trick to spin off a variation of a successful film) and an alien instead of a vampire. However, like vampires, the alien needs blood; his planet is suffering from a disease in which the blood literally dries up in the inhabitants' veins.

A bulky, dark stranger wearing sunglasses (Paul Birch) pays a visit to a doctor (William Roerick) and promptly hypnotizes him. The stranger, whose name is Johnson, actually comes from the planet Davanna. On that planet, nuclear wars have led to a disastrous blood disease, and Johnson is investigating the possibility of using earth blood as a substitute by sending samples via a matter transmitter (a year before *The Fly* supposedly popularized the idea).

Nadine (Beverly Garland) is a nurse hired to look after Johnson in his home, but she finds herself a virtual prisoner there. Meanwhile, Johnson goes out to kill people – or, as in the film's most memorable scene with Dick Miller as a seedy hipster trying to sell vacuum cleaners, they come in to meet him. Miller's scene is classic for being at once humorous and scary. He is trying to hustle his way into Johnson's house, and Johnson, for a change from Miller's other customers, would like to have him come inside, ostensibly to demonstrate a special attachment he is selling. As Miller runs his patter, he looks back and catches a glimpse of Johnson without his sunglasses. He does a double take on Johnson's disturbing, pupilless eyes before having his brain seared.

While it is a very simple effect, it is nonetheless a very good one. Real people should not go around looking like Little Orphan Annie, and the sight of Birch's milky white eyes produces a shiver. Corman does some other visually inventive things in the film, including a shocking scene where Johnson cuts his wrist but it fails to bleed, and another in which the doctor is attacked by an umbrella-shaped creature which does something that causes a sudden pool of blood to form. Finally, Corman has an excellent dissolve between Johnson's eyes and the headlights of his car, equating the two in their pursuit of Nadine, who is saved when her boyfriend (Morgan Jones) turns on his siren and causes Johnson to crash.

The script has many clever touches. The aliens in it are telepathic, and so are unused to speech or even using their ears. High-pitched noises unnerve them (thus Johnson's death-by-siren). Johnson repeatedly demonstrates odd speaking patterns hinting at his "foreign" origin and unfamiliarity with earth culture. He even goes so far as to mistakenly give a messenger from Davanna blood from a rabid dog, which naturally kills her. The inventive film ends at Johnson's grave, marked "Here Lies a Man Who Was Not of This Earth" as a similarly business-suited alien shambles by in the background. It's a compact and memorable little film.

The Undead was Corman's first "straight" horror film, or at least the first without the science fiction angle for a change. According to Griffith:

> One day Roger said, "I want you to do a Bridey Murphy picture" because *Bridey Murphy* was being done at that time as a big budget picture, and the book was still relatively popular. [The book and film were about a woman, who when hypnotized, remembered her past lives.] I thought it would be dead by the time we could get anything out. I wrote this thing called *The Trance of Diana Love.* Curiously, I separated all the different things with sequences with the devil which were really elaborate and the dialogue in the past was all in iambic pentameter. Roger got very excited by that. He handed the script around

for everybody to read and nobody understood the dialogue, so he told me to translate it into English. It was really just ruined, but it was a fun picture to shoot because it was done in ten days at the Sunset Stage, which was a supermarket on Sunset Boulevard. We filled it with palm trees and fog and it was the first time Roger had used any of that stuff. He didn't like to rent anything.

Pamela Duncan plays Diana Love, a call girl who is accosted in the fog not by a john, but by a psychiatrist named Prentice (Val Dufour) who wants to prove to a skeptical colleague that he can bring out previous selves under hypnosis. The psychiatrist takes Diana back to an ancestor, Helene, who lived in eighth-century France and who is accused of being a witch, due to the machinations of a real witch, Lydia (played by that *Fifty Foot Woman*, Allison Hayes).

Diana's voice coming across the centuries distracts Helene's lecherous jailer long enough for her to escape, and she flees to the arms of her beloved, a knight named Pendragon (played by cowboy star Richard Garland, who gives the knight an anachronistic Texas drawl).

Lydia is a witch who performs real magic, such as turning into a cat, while her familiar (played by Billy Barty) turns into a spider or an iguana. They conjure up the devil (Richard Devon, who is also seen during the film's credits), who says that they must bring him a head if he is to grant their wishes.

Lydia contemplates the head of Smoukin (Mel Welles), the village idiot and grave digger, who is given to rhymes like, "Sing a song of graveyards / An acre full of germs / Four and twenty landlords / Dinner for the worms / And when the box was planted / The worms began to sing / Wasn't that a dainty dish to set before the Thing?" Smoukin is bright enough to convince them that an idiot's is not a top-quality head, so they go for the superstitious innkeeper's (Bruno VeSota) instead.

In Barry Brown's interview with Bruno VeSota in *Magick Theatre #8*, VeSota had this to say about the production:

> The studio where Corman shot the graveyard scenes and just about everything else in *The Undead* was so small. To do the smog scenes Corman wasn't going to spend any money on any sophisticated chemicals that you can act in. He took old smudgepots and put them on the stage. Every once in a while, the propman would send in some more smoke-pots, more fog. Everybody's eyes were running, everybody choked. The only person who didn't act like he was affected by all that smoke was Roger Corman. He was already counting the money the picture was going to make.

Prentice sends his soul back in time to see what is transpiring. Pendragon tries to barter with the devil to save Helene's life, and he kills Lydia, who has been not-so-secretly in love with the stalwart knight, when she tries to stop him. However, somehow Helene realizes that it is her fate to suffer the headsman's axe and that her descendants will suffer if she does not submit. Diana Love reawakens in the present and discovers that Prentice is trapped in the past; all that is left of him, in the hokey finish, are his clothes.

The film is minor Corman, but it is an obvious precursor to his later Poe films. It features two beautiful women and lively performances by Devon, as a pitchfork-carrying devil, and Welles as the poesy-spouting idiot.

Corman then tried his hand at a series of more conventional films until he reentered the fantastic genre by making a straightforward science fiction drama, *War of the Satellites*. Jack Rabin had promised him that he could have special effects for the film ready in two months' time to capitalize on the just-launched Soviet sputnik satellite (though Bill Warren points out it might have really been after the launching of the American satellite Explorer I in 1958, which suits the proclaimed time frame better). Corman himself turned in a brief cameo as a ground controller in the film.

War of the Satellites gave Dick Miller his first starring role as brave Dave Boyer, who realizes that fellow scientist Dr. Pol Van Ponder (Richard Devon) is occasionally being taken over by an alien intelligence. Boyer is also concerned because he is attracted to Sybil Carrington (Susan Cabot), who seems to have fallen in love with Van Ponder even if he is unresponsive since the change. Things get out of hand when Van Ponder begins splitting in two and killing fellow crew members aboard the American spaceship (dubbed a satellite in the film). Boyer kills Van Ponder and saves the day by yelling "Execute Plan A!" as they break the Sigma barrier, which supposedly has been destroying the previous unmanned satellites before this time. (There never really is a war between two or more satellites, as the title would indicate.)

In *Fangoria #19*, Dick Miller had this to say about the film:

> ...I don't know what kind of technical errors we had, but we had two of the best lounge chairs money could buy to take off for the moon in.... We had a lot of fun on those. I remember for the hallways on the spaceship ... we had four arches, that's all they were, the entire set was arches. You could set them close together to make a short hall or set them further apart and make a long hall. At the end of the hall was a flat – you made a turn. So on our spaceship, you always ran down to the end of the hall and made a turn. That was the entire ship.

The effects for *War of the Satellites* came out rather decently for a low-budget film under a rushed schedule, and so Corman listened when Rabin came back promising cheaply done, elaborate effects for a Viking fantasy film. That film was eventually titled *The Saga of the Viking Women and*

Their Voyage to the Waters of the Great Sea Serpent, though it is better known as simply *The Viking Women and the Sea Serpent.* A group of Viking women set off to rescue their husbands and lovers and encounter a whirlpool, a warrior race, and the Great Sea Serpent of the Vortex. According to Corman in Naha's book, the woman who was to play the lead female Viking was sick on the first day of shooting, so he simply promoted each actress up one notch to roles they had not prepared for and signed an extra to take over the additional part. *The Saga...,* like *War of the Satellites,* suffered from a poor script by Lawrence Louis Goldman, and this time the ambitious low-budget effects fall embarrassingly flat.

Corman made a couple of gangster films, *Machine Gun Kelly* played by a henpecked Charles Bronson and *I, Mobster* starring Steve Cochran, before returning to science fiction with *Teenage Caveman.*

Unfortunately, *Teenage Caveman* is a dull, stilted film full of recyclings (shots from *One Million B.C.* and *The Day the World Ended,* as well as the suit from *Night of the Blood Beast*). The lead, Robert Vaughn in one of his earliest roles, is obviously not a teenager and looks embarrassed by the part. He even has to shoot and carry a stuffed deer at one point.

Perhaps the most interesting and amusing aspect of the film is that it gave Corman regular Beach Dickerson a chance to play three death scenes. First he had to drown in some quicksand. According to Mark Thomas McGee in his delightful book on American International Pictures, *Fast and Furious,* Corman yelled, "I don't believe you're drowning. You're not convincing me." After having to sink and then float in the nauseating, brackish water, Dickerson decided to relax while Corman shot his funeral scene. Having a limited number of extras, Corman told Dickerson to join the crowd, insisting that no one would recognize him at his own funeral.

Next Dickerson had to fall from a horse onto granite and then die. The shot had to retaken because the cameraman, Floyd Crosby, casually commented that in taking the fall, he could see Dickerson's underwear. "You're wearing underwear," Corman cried, "how dare you!"

Finally, Dickerson was stuck in one of the all-time worst bear suits and was sent crawling along a rope down a steep hill before some extras came up and pounded him for his final death scene in the picture. "We were willing to do just about anything in those days," he told me with a shake of his head and a smile. "Roger really made you stretch and asked you to do things you never would have even considered before."

Though *Teenage Caveman* was uninspired, Corman's next film, *A Bucket of Blood,* has come to be considered a minor camp classic. Its beatnik setting helps make it a unique little film coupled with Charles B. Griffith's blackly humorous script and Dick Miller's marvelous performance as the schlub hero, Walter Paisley, a busboy and would-be artist.

The genesis for the film came when Corman showed Griffith around the

sets for *Diary of a High School Bride*, which included a squalid apartment and a coffeehouse, and asked Griffith to quickly write a script around those sets as he intended to use them before they were torn down.
Said Griffith:

> That had to be rushed through and that had to be a comedy. Roger asked me, "How do you shoot comedy?" and I told him, "Shoot it like you would anything else." That was that – instead of having him trying to shoot comedy and be funny.
> Well, that worked and we got applause on the set during the reading of the beatnik poetry. . . . The beatniks in the coffeehouse scenes were all my friends, I guess. I didn't know too many of the poets, but everybody went to coffeehouses in those days.

Griffith had written material for Lord Buckley, whose hep language was known for its amusing and colorful way with words. The poem which opens the film, uttered by Maxwell H. Brock (Julian Burton), is perfectly suited to the macabre plot, urging the artist to utilize anything, including living creatures, in the pursuit of the ultimate purpose: the creation of art. Griffith came up with such lines as "Burn gas buggies and whip your sour cream of circumstance and hope" and "Let them die, and by their miserable deaths, become clay within his hands that he might form an ashtry or an ark."

Paisley swallows all this guff and admires Brock. He, too, would like to be a great artist. Back home, his neighbor's cat gets stuck in his apartment wall, and in trying to get it out, he accidentally kills it. Coming up with the inspiration for covering the cat's cadaver in clay and passing it off as a statue, Paisley is proclaimed a genius. An admiring drug-user presses a packet of white powder as a "thank you" to Paisley, but the innocent busboy has no idea what "horse" really is.

A narcotics officer observes the action and comes to Walter's apartment to bust him, and in his panic, Walter clobbers him with a frying pan. Voilà! He has the material for another statue. His work gets praise for its lifelike realism and attention to detail. Later a man's sawed-off head becomes a bust. Things then go bust for Walter when, at a one-man exhibit, the nature of his statues is finally revealed. He dashes home to turn himself into his final masterpiece, "Hanged Man."

Comedy and horror can mix very well, one nicely offsetting the other, as Shakespeare himself demonstrated with the gatekeeper's scene in *Macbeth*. However, rarely does a feature sustain both throughout its length. Happily *A Bucket of Blood* is one of the exceptions. Corman's actors prove adept at putting just the right spin on the material, but photographically the film maintains the somber mood of a low-budget horror film.

Despite the fact that he's killing people, Paisley remains throughout the film a likable loser. He even gets to hear his hero Brock proclaim, "A master sculptor is in our midst. He is none other that Walter Paisley, our very own busboy, whose hands of genius have been carrying away the empty cups of your frustrations. His is the silent voice of creation within the dark, rich soil of humility, he blossoms as the hope of our nearly sterile century." Then Brock turns to him and says, "Bring me an *espresso*, Walter."

Without a doubt, this is Miller's best role, and he makes the most of it. *Bucket of Blood* opened Corman up to less conventional heroes and to adding more humor to his work. The film was originally advertised as an out-and-out comedy, but Corman quickly learned that simply promising that a film was funny was not as dependable a draw as simply sending it out as another horror film. As a result, most of the subsequent comedies that he made were almost never advertised as such; promotions concentrated on their generic elements instead.

Corman and Griffith were surprised by the favorable reaction on the set to *A Bucket of Blood*. "It was the first time anybody had ever liked anything," Griffith remembered, "so we had to do it again right away." In other words, Corman wanted a follow-up, which they discussed while *Bucket of Blood* was still filming:

> We sat down during the shooting, and he [Corman] insisted that it had to be the exact same picture, scene for scene, with just some of the names changed and so on. And I figured, oh well, I'll just go from satire to farce and he'll never know the difference.

The follow-up was originally to have been called *Gluttony* and centered on a clumsy chef who accidentally cooks customers, but that was rejected as cannibalism was against the production code. Griffith finally hit upon a florist with a man-eating plant and titled his screenplay *The Passionate People Eater*, though Corman released it via his Filmgroup Co. as *Little Shop of Horrors*. The main sequences were shot in two days at the tail end of 1959 to beat the new regulations requiring that actors be paid residuals for television showings of their films. While the interiors and the majority of the film were shot in that time, Griffith handled the second unit photography on a couple of the following weekends to shoot the remainder of the film for a pittance.

Miller was originally offered the role of Seymour Krelborn, but turned it down in favor of playing Vurson Fouch, a flower-eating man in the tale of a man-eating flower. Fouch serves as a kind of Greek chorus for the film, filling in the viewer on background between munching nasturtiums.

Playing the lead was Miller's frequent costar and long-time Corman collaborator Jonathan Haze, who makes Seymour a likable and memorable schlemiel. While Seymour is always apologetically saying, "I didn't mean it," he manages to foul up the simplest of tasks. One day while tossing stones, trying to figure out how to revive the flagging vitality of his unusual plant (grown from irradiated seeds, though that aspect is lost in a local in-joke about a cranberry farm, from a cross between a bloodwort and a Venus flytrap), he accidentally tosses a rock and knocks out a wino, who is then run over by a train. The frantic Seymour picks up the pieces and tries to find some place to stash them, finally returning to the florist shop in which he works, where he is startled by the plant requesting to be fed the bloody chunks of the wino's body. The plant grows bigger, attracts more attention and customers for shop owner Mushnik (Mel Welles), and requires some more "feedings."

The movie has a funny script and a certain no-budget charm about it that has made it a cult classic. More than twenty years later, Howard Ash-man emphasized the Faustian elements in the script (i.e., the terrible price for success) and changed it into a successful stage musical and then into a somewhat successful multi-million dollar film remake with beautifully photo-graphed, elaborate sets and an ingeniously manipulated talking flower puppet.

The original *Little Shop* gets by on the resources of $60,000 and a good cast, which in addition to Haze included Mel Welles' malaproping Mushnik, Jackie Joseph's comically innocent and sweet Audrey, and Jack Nicholson's standout bit part as a masochistic dental patient who loves going to the den-tist and has an orgasmically good time being maltreated by Seymour, shyly filling in for the skid row dentist he's just accidentally killed in a drill-bit duel. The whole film is bracketed by a straight-faced, tongue-in-cheek *Drag-net* parody, which only adds to the merriment. But most memorable of all is the plant, dubbed Audrey Jr. by Seymour, and its plaintive cries of "Feed me!" (voice supplied by screenwriter Griffith, who also plays a hold-up man who gets eaten by the plant). References to the plant have popped up in such films as *Eat My Dust* and *Saturday the 14th*, and its cry is second only to *The Fly*'s famous "help me" in fan popularity and recognition.

Just before *Little Shop*, Corman departed from AIP to form his own com-pany, Filmgroup, which produced the Curtis Harrington classic *Night Tide* and such Corman features as *The Last Woman on Earth, The Creature from the Haunted Sea, Ski Troop Attack, Atlas* and *The Beast from the Haunted Cave*. He abandoned the plan when the company proved not to be as pro-fitable as he had anticipated.

The Wasp Woman was a low-budget quickie seemingly designed to cash in on *The Fly*. While it features a good performance by Susan Cabot as a cos-metics manufacturer who overindulges in a scientist's "youth serum" made out of the royal jelly of wasps (I don't believe wasps have royal jelly, though bees do), the film is a jumbled mess with an exceedingly unconvincing

monster costume. The serum is supposed to make people youthful and prolong their lives, though just what is youthful about having a hairy face and
two bulging eyes I cannot understand for the life of me. Cabot kills a few
people before having acid thrown at her face and then being pushed out a
nearby window. (Apparently, wasp women cannot fly, despite what is depicted on the colorful but highly misleading poster for the film.)

In 1960, Corman left for Puerto Rico to film *Battle of Blood Island* and
Last Woman on Earth. The script for *Last Woman*, written by a young
Robert Towne, was not finished. There was no room in the budget to bring
an extra person along, so Corman recruited Towne to play one of the leads
in the film he was writing. Towne essayed the role of Martin Joyce under
the name of Edward Wain. Unfortunately, Towne's inexperience painfully
shows itself through this intelligent and somber, but talky and almost ac-
tionless, little B film.

Corman was getting more proficient at the technical aspects of filmmaking, but he never gave his actors much direction. Instead, he found good
people and gave them their head. If the person was not so good, little was
done to correct the situation. Luckily, in *Last Woman* the other leads, Antony Carbone and Betsy Jones-Moreland, were seasoned professionals, turning in capable acting jobs.

The primary plot centers around something causing all the world's oxygen to be suddenly withdrawn and then brought back again, killing nearly
everything. Our three heroes happen to be scuba-diving when the oxygen
disappears and so escape the catastrophe, though Martin pessimistically
assumes that they are the only people alive on earth. (Could not other people
have been receiving oxygen by artificial means at the same time, and would
they not also be alive? Strangely, this prospect never even seems to be considered.) There is a traditional love triangle as Harold (Carbone)'s girl Evelyn (Jones-Moreland) begins falling for the fatalistic Martin. But while Martin is more intelligent, he is prone to give up on everything, while the aggressive Harold eagerly fights to stay alive and has more vitality. In an
unusual twist for the genre, it is Harold who wins out in the final confrontation, but from Martin's death there is a hint that he has learned from past
mistakes and will defer to Evelyn more in the future.

The filming over, Corman found he still had a little more time and
money left over, so he contacted Charles Griffith in the states and asked him
to dash off a quick script he could film cheaply in Puerto Rico. To round out
the cast, Corman planned to take one of the roles, that of "Happy" Jack
Monahan, himself. Griffith wrote the script, *Creature from the Haunted Sea*,
in three days and sent it down in pieces, with the result that he could not
always remember what had gone on before.

Like *A Bucket of Blood* and *Little Shop of Horrors*, he decided to script
another outright comedy, but he made things difficult on Corman by having

the character of Jack go through the most extreme emotional variations in the script including falling in love and caving in to despair. Corman decided the part was too much for him and so gave it a young man named Robert Bean, who had paid his way to Puerto Rico to try to get involved. Corman had allowed him to act as boom man, and the very next week Bean was playing Jack, a major supporting character. It was perhaps one of the most rapid rises in screen history.

As *A Bucket of Blood* parodied beatniks, and *Little Shop* parodied *Dragnet*, Corman parodied spy stories in *Creature*, opening up with a silly shot of a man shining a tennis show and passing along a secret message. After a dull chase scene, Agent XK-150 (Towne acting under the Wain name again) eats the note and goes into a club to make contact with Agent XK-120. He spots her at a table playing chess. Conquering, her opponent's king, she philosophizes, "The king is dead, long live the king." "Is that supposed to be a political remark?" XK-150 returns from behind his patently phony mustache.

XK-150's mission is to recover the stolen Cuban treasury, which General Tostada and his men are giving over to Renzo Capeto (Antony Carbone) an American gangster and gambler, to transport because he would be less suspicious. (Though, naturally, the General and his men are going along to keep an eye on the gold, and what could be more suspicious than that?) They are pursued by machine gun–wielding revolutionaries in a Volkswagen convertible (well, I did say this was a *low*-budget film).

After the silly cartoon credits, we are introduced to the characters in the drama via voice-over by XK-150, who is posing as "Sparks" Morgan, notorious gum machine burglar from Chicago. He runs down the aliases for Renzo Capeto, which include Shirley Lamoore, while describing him as "the most trustworthy man ever to be deported from Sicily." Capeto's past achievements include trying to nominate Benito Mussolini for the Republican ticket and being rejected during World War II by the navy, the marines *and* the SS.

Sparks has the hots for Mary-Belle Monahan, Capeto's gun moll, who tolerates Sparks but is not interested in him. He describes her as being "nailed cold for pushing heroin in the laundry room in Boy's Town," but he is "willing to give anyone the benefit of the doubt, especially when they are as crazy-looking as Mary-Belle."

Happy Jack, so called because he developed a muscle spasm in his cheeks from watching too many Humphrey Bogart pictures, is Mary-Belle's kid brother, a former tennis bum and now a well-known dice loader and murderer. Rounding out the group is Pete Peterson, Jr. (Beach Dickerson), who blew his brain out of whack while imitating a whooping crane at an Elks convention in Oshkosh. Capeto tolerates his constant animal imitations in return for Pete's shining shoes and rubbing out Capeto's enemies.

They embark on what Sparks describes as "the most astounding adventure ever to be inflicted on man." Unfortunately, apart from the early off-the-wall humor, this description is fairly accurate as the film bogs down in a dull plot by Capeto to steal the Cuban treasury (to set up a home for aged hoodlums) by killing off the Cubans without making them suspicious. To do this, they devise a sea monster out of garden trowels, using a bathroom plunger for tracks and olive oil and seaweed for "evidence." Unbeknownst to them, there is already a monster who is happy to help with the plan, apparently created by a Mr. and Mrs. Monster.

The monster, one of the most pathetic ever to appear on film (remember, Corman had not planned on shooting a monster movie in the first place), was created by Beach Dickerson out of an army helmet and steel wool, with tennis and ping pong balls for eyes, at a cost of $150. The most remarkable thing about the final half of this monstrous mess is that the monster ends up living happily ever after with the treasure while XK-150 sails off into the sunset with a newfound love interest. It is definitely not up to Corman's comedic predecessors.

Corman realized that horror films needed to take a new turn. The B horror movie double bills he created for American International and Filmgroup were grossing less and less. AIP knew it would make more money if it could produce a successful leading film, which gets a percentage of the box office take, rather than a supporting feature, which receives a straight rental fee from the exhibitor—but would it be worth the gamble? For a change, Corman received $750,000, a fifteen-day schedule, and a name actor, Vincent Price, for one of his productions. Using Edgar Allan Poe's short story "The Fall of the House of Usher," Richard Matheson had written an intelligent script full of Poesque forebodings. Production designer Daniel Haller, finally having a bit of money, came up with some fairly moody sets that belied the film's still-lower-than-Hollywood-standard budget.

The *House of Usher* was filmed in bright and vibrant Pathecolor and CinemaScope. Corman even took advantage of a recent fire in the Hollywood Hills to present a properly blasted and bleak landscape for the hero, Philip Winthrop (Mark Damon), to ride through on his way to the Usher mansion.

Winthrop hopes to visit his fiancée, Madeline (Myrna Fahey), but is blocked by Roderick Usher (Vincent Price), who wishes the family line to die out and is given to muttering about the family's "foul thoughts and deeds." He is also hypersensitive so that he can only partake of the dullest food and sounds, otherwise the intensity becomes too painful for him to bear.

Corman even devised a strong color scheme for the picture in which Winthrop has bright blue clothes and seems lively, while the white-haired Roderick is dressed in dull red and seems to have the life bled out of him.

The crew on The House of Usher *(left to right): Chuck Hannawalt, Roger Corman (in coat), Harry Reif and Jack Bohrer.*

Madeline is subject to fits of catalepsy which leave her in a coma-like sleep. When she is presumed dead, Roderick orders her buried in the tomb, but she revives and claws her way out of her casket, being driven mad in the process. The hypersensitive Roderick could hear her struggles, and the sound has driven him mad as well. In the end, the house collapses as the now melancholy Philip departs.

The film does have a certain prestige lacking in the AIP product up to that time and garnered good reviews, though in retrospect, apart from Corman's subtle hints that Roderick has incestuous longings for his sister, the only interesting aspect of the film is Price's fine performance, one of his all-time best and far more restrained than he later came to be. Remarked Matheson in John Brosnan's *The Horror People*, "[I]n *The House of Usher* I think all three of the other cast people were not particularly good, and that was the whole cast!"

Corman took a break from Poe to make *Ski Troop Attack* and *Atlas*, his last projects for Filmgroup. *Atlas*, filmed in Greece, was supposed to be a parody of musclemen epics but failed to come off, while *Ski Troop Attack* was a lively, low-budget war movie.

House of Usher proved such a success that it seemed natural to try it again, though this time Price upped his price to $125,000 plus a percentage of the profits. In *Pit and the Pendulum,* once more with a Matheson script, Corman embellished on the good qualities of *Usher* with a better cast and more elaborate sets. He also began to experiment more with the camera, especially in the flashback scenes. Once more the film gets off to a slow start as a wooden young man, Francis Bernard (John Kerr), inquires about the health of a young woman, Elizabeth (Barbara Steele). He is put off by a bereaved man, Nicholas Medina (Price), who was Elizabeth's husband. However, something about Medina's story strikes him as wrong.

It turns out that Elizabeth is not dead but has conspired with Dr. Charles Leon (Antony Carbone) to drive her husband mad. The conspiracy succeeds, but Medina takes on the personality of his sadistic father, who was once a merry torturer for the Spanish Inquisition. The story picks up with the flashbacks and the plot begins to unravel as Medina tosses the perfidious physician into the pit and locks Elizabeth in a torture box. He sets the pendulum in action against Francis, who is rescued in time. But since Elizabeth is presumed dead, no one thinks to look for her when they permanently seal the torture chamber with her still trapped inside. (Barbara Steele gives a great frightened stare.)

Corman followed *The Pit and the Pendelum* with one of his best but least-seen movies, *The Intruder* (aka *I Hate Your Guts!*), about racism in the deep South. William Shatner gives one of his best performances as an agent provocateur who infiltrates organizations opposed to integration and blacks. Unfortunately, after Corman invested a lot of his own money, the film bombed, making it one of his few financial failures.

Hoping to copy AIP's success with Poe pictures on his own, Corman struck up a deal with color film processor Pathe, who hoped to start up their own distribution company. However, AIP, after warning Pathe that they were giving them a lot of business, bought the production out from them and Corman suddenly found himself working for AIP again on *The Premature Burial.*

This time the script was by Charles Beaumont and Ray Russell and the star was Ray Milland, who did not prove as effective as Price, though he later provided Corman with a fine performance in *"X."* Milland starred as Guy Carrell, who is cataleptic and deathly afraid of being buried alive.

Carrell combats this fear after marrying Emily (Hazel Court) by constructing a tomb which has several escape routes should he be prematurely buried. His friend Miles (Richard Ney) thinks he should combat his fears head-on and exhume his father's coffin in order to allay Carrell's fears that he was buried alive. However, upon opening the coffin, Carrell finds his suspicions confirmed and passes out. Mistaken for dead, he, too, is prematurely buried until two grave robbers fortuitously happen along. However, he is driven mad and turns into a murderer, causing Emily's scheme to scare him to death and take his money to backfire.

That some elements were becoming stock was readily apparent by the next entry in the series, an anthology film called *Tales of Terror*. As Mark Thomas McGee pointed out in *Fast and Furious*, Corman kept repeating certain elements in the films, in terms not only of plot but also of direction. There were frequently whip pans used to introduce a character in a "shock" moment. To build atmosphere, Corman often inserted the same shots of the ocean crashing against the rocks and clouds whizzing by a matte painting of a castle. In fact, having paid for the matte paintings, Corman was not satisfied until he had reused them at every opportunity, giving to them a striking air of familiarity. Frequently, running time seemed to have been consumed in having the characters keep wandering by the sets to show them off. And whenever there was a fire bringing the house down, Corman used the same shot of a chicken coop's flaming planks collapsing, even if the building burning were established as being made entirely of stone.

The first tale in *Tales of Terror* was based on Poe's "Morella," about a man, Locke (Vincent Price), who sends his child Lenora (Maggie Pierce) away because he blames the demise of his wife, Morella (Leona Gage), on Lenora's birth. After several years, Lenora comes back for a visit and finds Morella's corpse (there are suggestions of necrophilia). When Locke goes back to Morella's secret bedroom, Lenora is now mummified while Morella has been returned to the living, but Morella holds Locke responsible for her death. She strangles him while the house collapses amid burning (chicken coop) timbers.

The tale falls flat (the subject was handled better in Corman's later *Tomb of Ligeia*), though Price does give a professional performance. However, in the next tale, a combination of "The Cask of Amontillado" and "The Black Cat," Price is at his fruitiest and hammiest as the wine taster Fortunato, who seduces Annabel (Joyce Jameson), wife of the bleary and vulgar Montresor Herringbone (Peter Lorre). Though overdone, Fortunato's and Montresor's tasting contest is a comic highlight as Fortunato swishes small sips of wine delicately in his mouth to determine the vintage while Montresor swills great quaffs of wine to do the same, leaving him thoroughly plastered.

When Montresor recovers his wits, he figures out what has transpired and murders Annabel. Inviting Fortunato over for a drink, he gives him a spiked glass of Amontillado sherry. Montresor then handcuffs the unconscious Fortunato to the wall of his basement and builds a second wall, sealing him up alive. When the police come by to investigate the disappearance of Montresor's wife, he shows them around, but much to his chagrin, discovers that along with his two victims he had walled up a black cat, which wails and alerts the police.

A bloated and ailing Lorre manages to inject some genuine liveliness into the proceedings with his boorish characterization of Montresor, an alcoholic who loves wine more than his wife but still feels indignant when he finds himself betrayed. Thanks to Lorre's comic performance, the segment becomes the highlight of the film.

The final story, "The Case of M. Valdemar," features an aged Basil Rathbone as the evil mesmerist Carmichael who hypnotizes the ailing Valdemar (Price) so deeply that his soul remains trapped in his body even after it dies. His body in suspended animation, Valdemar finds this a horrible state. Complicating matters, his young wife, Helene (Debra Paget), is in love with Dr. Elliot James (David Frankham), but they refuse to wed each other until Valdemar is completely gone. This technicality does not deter Carmichael, who desires Helene for himself. Helene agrees to marry him if only he will release her husband from his perpetual trance. Carmichael releases him, and the vengeful Valdemar oozes his decayed body all over Carmichael in the film's most memorable shot, literally frightening him to death. Unfortunately, this story goes on for too long and Corman does not do enough with it before the effective climax.

Corman next essayed a remake of Rowland Lee's *Tower of London* for United Artists and Admiral Pictures, with Vincent Price playing the famous hunchbacked king of England whom Shakespeare had memorably besmirched in his play. (Basil Rathbone had played Richard III in the original, in which Price played Clarence, who is drowned in a butt of his favorite wine, Malmsey.)

The film marked a return to black-and-white photography for Corman, but it is not as moody as Corman's early black-and-white pictures. He does have some fluid camera work and there are delightful bits of macabre humor, such as when Richard adds a rat as an afterthought to the iron mask of an adversary. But while the film gets off to a good start, the limp script and far-from-rousing climax do it in.

However, the film is notable for its dialogue director: Francis Ford Coppola. Coppola, fresh from UCLA, was asked if he knew how to operate sound equipment, and Coppola answered in the affirmative, hoping to read the instruction booklet before having to operate the equipment. Corman took him to Europe for his next film, *The Young Racers*. That film is more famous for the people who worked on it than for its own sake. The star, Mark Damon, later became head of PSO, one of the biggest foreign film distributors. The location manager was Menahem Golan, later head of Cannon Films. Both Coppola and Charles Griffith worked on second unit photography, though Griffith totalled one of the cars in the race while driving it to a new location, causing it to mysteriously drop out of the race in the film. Cast members William Campbell, Luana Anders and Patrick Magee were kept around to make *Dementia-13* under the direction of Coppola afterwards.

Meanwhile, Richard Matheson decided to make his next Poe script a send-up. *The Raven* features Peter Lorre as the unfortunate Dr. Bedlo, who has been turned into a raven by the evil Dr. Scarabus (Boris Karloff). He goes for help to fellow magician Erasmus Craven (Vincent Price), who is still mourning the death of his lost wife, Lenore (Hazel Court).

Lorre has some marvelous ad libs in the film. He responded to Price's line that his wife's body "is buried in a crypt beneath the house" with a shrug and a "where else?" Going to the crypt set, he ran his hand along it and looked at Price, commenting, "Hard to keep clean, huh?"

Visiting the set of *The Raven*, film historian William K. Everson related the following amusing anecdote in *Castle of Frankenstein #5*:

> Corman shoots quickly, and there's no time wasted on his sets. I had little chance for prolonged conversation with Lorre that day. But we chatted for a few moments between takes. One of the supporting players, in grotesque makeup as a decaying corpse, came lumbering out of the men's room. My daughter Bambi, then three years old, was much impressed. . . . Used to King Kong, Dracula and the Franken-stein monster, and rather fond of them, she was quite excited at the prospect of seeing a real monster closeup. "Is that a *good* monster or a *bad* monster?" she asked. Looking around him to make sure that no one was listening – although I'm sure this was done for effect, as he cer-tainly never cared what he said or who heard him say it – Lorre informed her "Oh it's a *bad* monster. There are *no* good monsters at American-International."

After being returned to human form, Dr. Bedlo asks Craven why he keeps a picture of a woman he has seen wandering around Dr. Scarabus' house, little knowing the portrait is of Craven's lost Lenore. Deciding to in-vestigate, the pair make off for Scarabus' castle with their respective off-spring, Estelle (Olive Sturgess) and Rexford (Jack Nicholson with hair). Dr. Bedlo makes the mistake of challenging Scarabus to a display of magic, but while Bedlo toils over a spark-producing globe, the bored Scarabus un-leashes the heavens and Bedlo appears to be struck by a lightning bolt. In-vestigating the red spot left behind, Craven declares it to be raspberry jam.

Lenore makes an appearance. She never died but rather faked her demise to take up with Scarabus, who plans to torture Craven into revealing his magical secrets. Once more turned into a raven, the repentant Bedlo loosens Craven's fingers and the two magicians engage in a low-budget but imaginative and amusing duel of sorcery, casting spells at one another and achieving transformations with quick cuts. In execution, this is one of Cor-man's best brought off moments.

In Denis Gifford's *Karloff, the Man, the Monster, the Movies*, Karloff had this to say about Corman and his working methods:

James Whale was a brilliant technician with the camera and all the rest of it, just as Corman is. That, I think, is Corman's strong point. But I think Whale had the advantage because he was an older, more experienced man – Whale had a background in theatre and was used to directing actors. Corman expects an actor to get on with it himself. I've worked with him twice. The first time was on *The Raven* and I know that Vincent Price, Peter Lorre, and I had to find our own way, because Corman had all he wanted. He said, "You're experienced actors, get on with it. I've got the lighting and my angles. I know how I'm going to put this together." And if you asked him about advice on a scene he'd say, "That's your pigeon. Go on. I'm a busy with this."

This did not stop Karloff from getting involved in *The Terror*, a film made to utilize the leftover sets from *The Raven* before they were torn down to make way for something else. Corman told Leo Gordon to quickly write him some mysterioso scenes for Karloff and Jack Nicholson to play on the sets and then he would figure out how to shoot the rest of the film at a later date. The end result was naturally very erratic, talky, with plenty of pointless scenes of an ailing Karloff shambling through the castle corridors to pad out the running time. Later Francis Ford Coppola, Monte Hellman, and Jack Hill all shot material to make sense of the story and bring it up to the proper length. About the only thing in the whole production that does hang together is the wonderfully atmospheric musical score by Ronald Stein.

Nicholson plays Andre Duvalier, a French army officer who meets a strange and beautiful girl named Elaine (Sandra Knight), who suddenly disappears. A witch (Dorothy Neuman) comes to Andre's rescue, and when he revives, he starts catching glimpses of Elaine again. He is finally driven to the castle of Baron von Leppe (Karloff), where he catches sight of the portrait of the woman he has been following. However, the Baron explains that the portrait is of his late wife, Ilsa, and the Baron wants to be left alone in his grief. (For no apparent reason, after ordering Andre to leave, the Baron kills Andre's horse.) Outside the castle, Andre meets with Gustaf (Jonathan Haze), who tells him to rescue the girl back at the castle; later an eagle swoops down and scratches his eyes out, and he falls over a cliff.

Curiouser and curiouser, Andre catches sight of Elaine/Ilsa again, and the story really gets confusing. Finally, it is left up to Stefan, von Leppe's servant (played by Dick Miller), to explain what has really gone on. Miller was about the only actor to appear in the production throughout its length, though changes in the length of his sideburns, skin color and weight are readily apparent as the film was shot over a nine-month period. Recalled Miller when I spoke to him:

> The history of that picture was that the shooting schedule took eight, nine months. . . . We'd shoot a couple of days and stop, and then we'd

get a call and they'd say "Come back, we're shooting that picture."
What picture? "The one with Boris Karloff." Every time we'd go back
and shoot, somebody else would beat me up. Karloff had to hit me with
a chain, Sandra Knight beat the daylights out of me, a little old lady
beat the daylights out of me, and Jack Nicholson beat me up outside.
Somehow all these scenes fell into the last ten minutes of the picture.
It became like a game killing, everybody getting a shot at me, you
know. I went from one scene to the next. It's true. Karloff would hit
me with a chain, and I'd go through a door, and Nicholson's on the other
side of the door.

Beaten into a confession, Stefan reveals that the Baron is really the
witch's son who lost his mind after killing Ilsa and that Stefan accidentally
had killed the Baron himself and then encouraged the witch's son to think
of himself as the Baron. Meanwhile, the witch is seeking to take revenge on
"the Baron" for the killing of her son. The witch is arbitrarily struck down
by lightning, while everyone except Andre and Elaine/Ilsa perishes in a
flood rather than the traditional fire because, according to Corman in an interview in *Sight and Sound*:

> The primary forces – fire, water, the elements – symbolize certain
> natural powers and drives, and there may be a cleansing element in
> there as well. For instance, in the Poe pictures I used fire a number of
> times; so many times, in fact, for the necessary destruction of the
> house, that when I came to do *The Terror* I said, "We're going to *flood*
> this house." I don't think I've ever analyzed what these uses stand for,
> other than natural force, on the basis that (to quote certain religions)
> we are all *one*, and we come out of natural elements.

Footage from *The Terror* would later show up in both *Targets*, Peter
Bogdanovich's brilliantly conceived first film, and Joe Dante's *Hollywood
Boulevard*. On the former credit, Miller protested the use of film footage
from *The Terror* without pay and received a small dividend after taking the
case to the Screen Actors Guild.

From that muddled mess, *"X"* (better known as *"X" – The Man with
X-Ray Eyes* or simply *The Man with X-Ray Eyes*) is quite an improvement
and won the Best Picture award at the Trieste Science Fiction Film Festival. (The picture is actually only titled *"X"* but is better known by its advertising subtitle.)

"X" starts off with nothing more than an eyeball and Les Baxter's eerie
music. James Xavier (Ray Milland) is getting his eyes examined by his
friend Dr. Sam Brant (Harold Stone). Xavier complains that man can only
see from 4,000 to 7,800 angstrom units, a miniscule portion of the light spec-
trum. "My dear friend, only the gods see everything," Brant jocularly tells
him. "I'm closing in on the gods," Xavier returns.

Once more in Ray Russell and Robert Dillon's screenplay we have the cliché of the mad scientist who pursues his dream no matter what the consequences to himself or anyone else. Attractive Dr. Diane Fairfax (Diana Van Der Vlis) has been called in by the foundation that Xavier works for to find out what Xavier has been doing with the $27,000 he has extracted from them. Xavier provides a demonstration in which he puts a serum in a monkey's eye and the monkey flicks switches whenever he can see through colored screens to the screen behind. Dr. Fairfax is impressed until the monkey suddenly dies of heart failure. "What did he see?" she wonders aloud.

The pair go out to coffee, which Fairfax refers to as the "best experiment" Xavier's tried. Dr. Xavier hopes to perfect his serum to see inside sick people and cure them. He decides to experiment on himself, over Dr. Brant's objections. He initially takes just a few drops, and a colorful shot from his point of view shows how his perception has been altered. (Corman achieves many colorful, almost psychedelic shots, apparently with some kind of prism lens on the camera.) However, Xavier is overwhelmed by the amount of new light that he can see and is rendered unconscious.

Dr. Fairfax pleads with the foundation to allow Xavier to continue his work, though he has been irresponsible in experimenting on himself. She and Dr. Brant visit him at the hospital. He has bandages on his eyes but hardly notices because he can see right through them. Dr. Xavier is returned to regular duty, and he looks in on Stanton, a young girl whom the head doctor of the hospital (John Hoyt) is prepping for surgery in the morning. With his new vision, Xavier can see the doctor has misdiagnosed the girl's ailment, but he cannot convince the erring doctor that he knows what he is talking about.

Dr. Fairfax meets Xavier and offers to give him a cure for "intense doctors." We see a hypo being prepared, but then Corman pulls back to reveal that it is being used to inject vermouth into gin to make martinis at a party. While Dr. Fairfax is occupied, a blonde comes up to Xavier and coaxes him to dance, which he does uncomfortably. An attack of his X-ray vision comes and all the partiers suddenly appear naked to him. (Corman discreetly conveys this with only bare legs and backs.) Pleased, he goes over to Dr. Fairfax and tells her what is happening. Understandably, she is a little taken aback.

"Well, remember, I'm a doctor," he offers in an attempt to smooth the situation over.

"And you remember I'm a woman," she scolds him.

He looks her up and down appreciatively and comments, "I can hardly forget it."

The next day, Xavier asks the chief surgeon to reconsider and, when he refuses, slices the surgeon's wrist with a scalpel and takes over the operation. The operation is a success, but the surgeon intends to sue him for malpractice. With those magic words, Fairfax and Brant encourage him to go into hiding, though Xavier intends to carry on his research. He has discovered that the effect is cumulative, and so now has trouble seeing normally. People look like living dissections to him, he tells us. (Corman's effects budget was definitely limited on the film, though he makes inventive use of what he has.) "We can explore all the mysteries of creation," he gleefully asserts. Brant tries to sedate him and is accidentally knocked through a window to his death. Dr. Fairfax speculates that now Xavier will be considered insane, what with killing Brant, his strange experiment, and the occurrence in the operating room. Xavier flees.

Next Corman takes us to a carnival where two hecklers (Miller and Haze in their last appearance together in a Corman-directed film) go into the tent of Mr. Mentalo, the great seer. Crane (Don Rickles), a carnival barker, sets up Mentalo's act: Blindfolded, he reads messages that people write down. Of course, Mentalo is none other that Dr. Xavier, who always wears dark sunglasses when his blindfold is taken off. When he does not prove a fraud, the hecklers leave in disgust.

We get to see Crane from the point of view of Mentalo, who sees him as little more than a walking skull. Crane asks him what he wants, and he returns that he wants money and "to be able to open my eyes." When a girl at the carnival gets hurt, Mentalo can see her broken bones and helps set them before the doctor can finally arrive. Crane sees potential for big bucks and cons Mentalo into leaving the carnival and getting into the healing biz, giving "free healing" in return for donations.

Xavier cannot stop taking his X-ray serum, and as a result, cannot sleep in the daytime because he sees right through the roof and into the sun. When Crane brings in an old lady who cannot be cured, Xavier realizes that this is not going to be a pleasant task and simply tells her that the pain will go away. Corman indicates that Xavier is feeling more and more separated from humanity as time goes on and the effects of the serum accumulate. Eventually people appear as nothing but skeletons to him, hardly discernible as individuals.

Dr. Fairfax tracks him down, and he cannot even recognize her at first. She drags him away from Crane's operations. They take off in a car and, under his instructions, head for Las Vegas. There he can see when slot machines are set to win and makes a fortune at blackjack because he can see through the cards onto the other side. However, his special abilities and winnings attract attention from the casino managers, who are convinced he is cheating. He throws his winnings to the people as a diversion and escapes in a car.

However, his vision is so far from normal that he has trouble driving. A helicopter spots him by his erratic driving but before it can stop him,

Xavier drives through a tunnel and crashes on the other side. Surviving, he makes his way to a revival tent.

During the film his eyes have progressed from normal to bloodshot to silver. At the tent, we see his eyes have turned a particularly disturbing shade of ebony. He interrupts the proceedings to declare that he has seen the eye in the center of the universe that sees us all. The preacher insists that "if thy eye offends thee, pluck it out." He complies, leaving his eyes empty red sockets in the film's final shock scene.

"X" is a modestly made but imaginative science fiction thriller and a nice change from the Poe pictures. The gimmick of seeing through things was dubbed "Spectarama," though this mostly involved shooting half-completed buildings and things with a special filter on the camera. Milland gives a strong performance as the headstrong and ultimately pitiful Dr. Xavier. Corman was getting more visually inventive and perceptive in his use of color. (Eventually, he refined his technique to such an extent that his drug film about taking LSD, *The Trip*, which was scripted by Jack Nicholson, is little more than combination light show and leftover footage from other Corman productions which represent the hallucinations that the hero, Paul Groves [Peter Fonda], is having.)

Sadly, *The Haunted Palace*, based on H. P. Lovecraft's "The Resurrected" and given the title of a Poe poem, was a step backwards. Though scripted by an excellent fantasy writer, Charles Beaumont, and featuring some very atmospheric sets of the town of Arkham and some effective makeup of the mutants which wander its streets by Ted Coodley, the final film is mostly talky and dull.

In 1765, a warlock named Joseph Curwen (Vincent Price) is burned at the stake by angry villagers. When his great-great-grandson Charles Dexter Ward (Price again) comes into town, he is met with a frosty reception as well as by an alien (perhaps meant to be one of Lovecraft's Elder Gods) in his cellar. He becomes possessed by a painting of his ancestor who looks exactly like him, and he gets together with a pair of wizards played by Lon Chaney, Jr. and Cathy Merchant, but torch-wielding villagers put a stop to the planned villainy. Once the portrait burns, Ward returns to normal – or does he?

While a number of films have tried adapting Lovecraft, including Daniel Haller's *Die Monster Die* and Jesus Franco's *Necronomicon* (aka *Succubus*), none has succeeded in capturing Lovecraft's flavor, though Stuart Gordon's *Re-Animator* and *From Beyond* get points for outrageousness and enjoyableness.

Corman decided to return to Poe territory, but this time he decided to film in England using leftover sets from *Beckett*. With a strong script by Charles Beaumont and R. Wright Campbell, based on the Poe tales "Masque of the Red Death" and "Hop Toad," Corman fashioned *The Masque of the Red*

Death. The picture benefited from cameraman Nicolas Roeg's striking lensing. (Roeg would go on to become director of such films as the haunting *Don't Look Now* and the other worldly *Man Who Fell to Earth.*)

The film had a longer shooting schedule, five weeks, as well as top British craftsmen working on the film, though Corman complained that his British crew worked more slowly than his American ones. Unlike the previous Poe entries, *The Masque of the Red Death* wastes no time getting started and keeps a high level of incidents flowing, making it one of the most lively films in the series as well as one of the best.

Corman unquestionably borrowed the look of the Red Death itself from Bergman's *The Seventh Seal,* with his death being a robed figure in red. At the start of the film, the Red Death takes a white rose and turns it red, instructing an old woman to take it to her people and tell them that their day of deliverance is at hand. The people of the village have been suffering under the tyranny of Prince Prospero (Vincent Price), but rather than being delivered from him, the people of the village are "delivered" from all cares by way of the plague which the old woman brings to the village.

We see Prince Prospero in action when he stops off at his village to "thank" the villagers for turning over their harvest to him. A young man, Gino (David Weston), is very outspoken against the Prince, and when an older man, Ludovico (Nigel Green), joins him, Prospero orders them both garrotted. Francesca (Jane Asher) rushes forward and pleads for their lives. Prospero is taken with her innocence (he has dedicated a good part of his life to corrupting innocence) and replies that, very well, one will be spared and she must choose. She responds that she cannot since one is her father and the other is her lover.

The screams of the old woman from the beginning of the film and the revelation that she has the plague bring the proceedings to a standstill. Prospero orders that Gino, Ludovico and Francesca be taken to his castle and that the village be burned to the ground, leaving the rest of the poor villagers to fend for themselves without food and shelter before the approach of winter.

Once inside the castle, while Gino and Ludovico are sent to the dungeon, Prospero begins Francesca's "education." Prospero is a satanist who believes that God is dead and that mankind is little better than an animal. (He demonstrates this by asking guests at his castle to be pigs, worms, and jackasses before the whole crowd begins imitating animals.) His consort, Juliana (Hazel Court), is not thrilled with having to help bathe Francesca and give her one of her dresses, but she knows better than to cross the heartless Prospero.

A subplot also begins when one of Prince's guests, Duke Alfredo (Patrick Magee), becomes taken with the dancing abilities of the midget dancer Esmerelda (Vernia Greenlaw), but then slaps her when she accidentally knocks over his wine goblet. This offends her lover, Hop Toad (Skip Martin), who plots his revenge by persuading the Duke that he would like to leave the Prince's employ and that he can help make the Duke the hit of the masked ball with a special costume, that of a great ape.

Corman and Roeg make maximum use of special lighting to brighten the variously colored rooms of the castle. Francesca is taken on a tour of all the rooms save one. That night she wakes up to discover blood on the counter and, finally entering the black room that was forbidden to her before, she sees Juliana sitting on a throne and Prospero lying in a coffin. She checks to see if Prospero is dead, but he shocks her by opening his eyes and glaring at her, causing her to flee until she runs into a masked figure. That figure is revealed to be Alfredo, who expresses mock concern for startling her.

The next day, a nobleman who was late to the proceedings arrives at the castle asking for entry. Prospero spurns Scarlotti's pleas for sanctuary, so Scarlotti offers to him his "unobtainable" wife, but a smug Prospero says he has already had that dubious pleasure. When Scarlotti continues to beg to be spared from the Red Death, Prospero "saves" him by firing a crossbow bolt into him and throwing down a short sword for his wife to commit suicide with.

Meanwhile, he has not succeeded in persuading Gino and Ludovico to fight to the death for his entertainment, though a guard does provoke Gino into fighting with him. Prospero has contempt for the Christians and plots how he can force one to kill the other without their cooperation.

Juliana, concerned that Francesca is receiving more of Prospero's attention, consecrates herself as a handmaiden to Satan and burns the figure of an inverted cross into her ample bosom. She then plots to rid herself of her competition by giving Francesca a key with which to escape the castle with the help of a traitorous guard. Francesca goes, but not without first retrieving her father and lover, and the men and the guards end up in a skirmish in which three of the guards are killed. When they reach the battlements where the "friendly" guard was supposed to await them, the guard turns, revealing himself to be Prospero, who has caught on to Juliana's plan and has ordered his men to disarm the escapees.

At a banquet, parodying the Christian concept of one man laying down his life for another, Prospero drives five daggers into the table, one of which is coated in a fast-acting poison. For the amusement of the spectators, he forces Gino and Ludovico to take turns cutting themselves with the daggers. Finally only one dagger is left. Ludovico tries to take it and stab Prospero with it, but Prospero has anticiapted this and stabs him first. He decides that rather than kill Gino directly, he will release him outside where the Red Death will take him. Francesca pleads to be allowed to go as well, but Prospero refuses.

Corman plays around with distorted camera lens and angles again with a dream sequence in which Juliana dreams that she is being sacrificed through the ages by various high priests. She is confident that she has passed the test, but when she triumphantly strolls into the great hall, a raven swoops down and pecks her to death, which, Prospero announces to the startled guests who come out to investigate, completes her marriage to a friend of his (i.e., Satan).

Men from the village come to the castle pleading for shelter and once more Prospero kills, calling it a kindness. Gino finally scales the walls to get back into the castle, but discovers a guard dead of the Red Death. What is more, standing there is the figure of the Red Death himself, who instructs him to wait there for Francesca.

Meanwhile, Hop Toad tells Esmerelda not to go to the ball but to prepare to flee. While Alfredo goes through his rampaging gorilla act, Hop Toad lowers a chandelier and ties Alfredo to it, pulling him helplessly off the ground. Splashing the struggling Alfredo with brandy, Hop Toad completes his revenge by setting the unfortunate Duke on fire and he burns to death. As Hop Toad promised, he was the hit of the ball, and the stunt impresses Prospero, who orders that the body be removed and that Hop Toad be rewarded for such splendid "entertainment."

Prospero's attention, however, is distracted when he sees a figure wearing red in violation of his instructions. Propsero assumes it is either Satan or an emissary from him, and asks to see his face. "There is no face of death until your own death," the figure tells him. Back at the ball, the infected revelers are beginning to turn red and die. Prospero pleads that Francesca be spared, and the Red Death tells her to go to the battlements where Gino is waiting. The Red Death becomes annoyed with the honorifics Prospero piles on him and tells him so.

Then who is your master, Prospero asks. "Death has no master," is the response. "Each man creates his own heaven, his own hell." Snatching the mask off the Red Death, Prospero sees his own face looking intently back. Prospero tries to flee through the grasping throng, but the figure remains always before him. The Red Death finally confronts him, asking him, "Why should you be afraid to die? Your soul has been dead for a long time."

The film ends with the multi-colored deaths from all over Europe meeting. Only six – Esmerelda, Hop Toad, Gino and Francesca, a child and an old man – have been spared.

The Masque of the Red Death is generally acknowledged to be one of Corman's best films and the best of the Poe series, with its accomplished cast, intricate sets, and sometimes dazzling photography making it a good cut above the typical Corman programmer. Pleased with the value he was getting from the British craftsman, Corman had Robert Towne script his final Poe film, *Tomb of Ligeia*.

In John Brady's *The Craft of the Screenwriter*, Towne recalled the genesis of the script:

> Well, "Ligeia" was a *very* short story . . . and I felt the best thing to do would be to take Poe's themes and expand on them. There was a strong hint of mesmerism in the story. . . . Also in Poe there is a lot of necrophilia – implied if not expressed. So I took the combination of mesmerism, which was there, and necrophilia, which was sort of there (because the first wife was always in the background), and brought them together. It provided a natural explanation for this woman. She had hypnotized the protagonist, and he was making love to this body under posthypnotic suggestion, literally being controlled by someone who was dead – which is kind of a gruesome notion, but perfectly consistent with Poe. I was trying to use a theme consistent with him, even though it wasn't in the story.

Towne was not big on Vincent Price – he wanted an "almost unnaturally handsome guy" and felt that the audience would be inclined to suspect Price of any kind of depravity, taking away the intensity. Corman at first agreed, as Towne went on to tell Brady:

> At the outset, Corman told me he wouldn't cast Vincent Price in the film, but when it was done he called me in L.A. from London. He told me he had cast Vincent, and added, "It's OK, we've got Marlene Dietrich's makeup man." I've never been able to figure out what difference *that* made.

To be fair to Price, he gives one of his strongest performances in a Poe film since *House of Usher*. While *The Masque of the Red Death* called upon his talents for being flamboyant and larger-than-life, Price makes *Tomb of Ligeia*'s Verden Fell a romantic, distant, haunted and mysterious figure who speaks with a low-key intensity as though the dead wife he both loves and fears might overhear.

Price once supposedly claimed that he would like to work in a genuine architectural ruin, and if this is so, with *Tomb of Ligeia*, he got his wish. The exteriors were largely filmed around a scenic, ruined English abbey. The film opens with Ligeia's burial during which a cat jumps on Ligeia's coffin and her eyes spring open. A hopeful Fell checks the corpse, and then shuts its eyes, reporting, "A nervous contraction, nothing more."

The story picks up several years later during a fox hunt when Lady Rowena (Elizabeth Shepherd), bored with the chase, investigates the ruins of the churchyard. She comes across Ligeia's grave, when a cat snarls and startles her horse, sending Rowena flying. The estate's owner, Verden Fell, comes forward wearing dark glasses – because of a "morbid reaction to sunlight" he explains – and offers assistance. Fell carries her and she playfully pulls off his glasses, but the bright light proves too much for him. He takes her to his house and binds her ankles.

Shepherd is quite impressive in how effectively she manages the dual roles of Rowena and Ligeia, clearly limning that each has a different personality as well as different colored hair (black for Ligeia and red for Rowena). Though she does not seem to particularly like Fell, she nonetheless indicates that she is irresistibly drawn to him.

Fell is a mysterious character who makes continual references to the likes, obsession, and will of his first wife, Ligeia. The fox that was hunted by Rowena's father turns out to be Egyptian, one of Ligeia's former pets. While a discussion takes place, it mysteriously disappears, with Fell trying to explain that the cat (who continually seems to be under Ligeia's influence) must have dragged it off.

Things become even stranger when Rowena pays a surprise visit to Fell only to have him attempt to strangle her, mistaking her for Ligeia, who had planned to will herself back to life from the grave. A moment later, the madness passes and Fell cannot even remember the attack. Still, he seems a thoroughly morbid fellow, though Price does manage to inject a touch of Olivier's Heathcliff into the role.

When Rowena and Fell first begin to kiss, the cat jumps between them, as if Ligeia were trying to reestablish her hold on him. Fell orders the cat destroyed, but it still continues to pop up and plague Rowena, at one time making off with Fell's dark glasses and leading her on a chase up into the church bell tower where Fell must come to rescue her.

Fell falls in love with Rowena and weds her. Their honeymoon is apparently happy and he acts more human, but when they return to the abbey, he immediately dons his dark glasses again. Strange events begin to take place such as Rowena finding black hairs in her brush. She sees her husband going for late night walks by Ligeia's tomb, but he does not recall them the next day.

Additionally, one evening Fell decides to give an exhibition of hypnotism by taking Rowena back to a childhood memory, now long forgotten. He is successful when suddenly Ligeia's personality starts asserting herself within Rowena.

While the couple would like to sell the abbey, the estate was placed in Ligeia's name, and since the estate lies in two counties, when she died each county thought the other side had taken care of the paperwork. The result is that there was no death certificate and therefore no proof exists that the property is legally Vernon's. Rowena confesses to family friend, Christopher Gough (John Westbrook, who had played the Red Death in the previous film), that Ligeia seems to be more Vernon's wife than she is.

The film reaches a climax when one night Rowena sees light in the attic and a mirror breaks revealing a secret passageway. Upstairs she finds the still-preserved body of Ligeia being attended to by Vernon. (Moments earlier, Gough and Kendrick [Oliver Johnson], the family servant, had discovered that the body in Ligeia's tomb was a wax dummy.)

Rowena tries to free Fell from the hypnotic suggestion that Ligeia planted in him before she died by pretending to be Ligeia herself. Unfortunately, her plan almost works too well as the wrathful and tormented Fell, convinced that she is indeed Ligeia, starts strangling her. Luckily, Gough and Kendrick arrive and take her away before he can finish the job, but it is now apparent that Fell has gone quite mad.

Fell attacks the omnipresent black cat, believing it to be Ligeia's reincarnated spirit, and the cat retaliates by clawing his eyes out. The demented, frantic Fell sets his house on fire and perishes in the flames. Outside Rowena rests in Gough's arms, but her own hands have blood on them (suggesting some kind of connection to the cat's claws which dug out Fell's eyes) and she has a Ligeia-like expression on her face. Which is she? Corman leaves the ending ambiguous.

Tomb of Ligeia is definitely one of the best crafted of the Poe films, and Towne's script is far better than the one he turned in for *The Last Woman on Earth*, though his best work (doctoring *Bonnie and Clyde* and *The Godfather*, writing *The Last Detail* and *Chinatown*) was still ahead of him.

After working with this strong screenplay, Corman pretty much threw out the screenplay on his next project, *The Wild Angels*. While back in the '50s *The Wild One* with Marlon Brando had featured a motorcycle gang, the gang was depicted as being rowdy but mostly nice boys. The influx of Hell's Angels pictures stemmed largely from *The Wild Angels*, in which Peter Fonda plays an Angels leader with "nowhere to go." The film is also significant in that Peter Bogdanovich began schlepping for Corman on this movie, an association which led to Corman producing the Bogdanovich/Boris Karloff classic *Targets*.

Corman directed a couple more gangster films, *The St. Valentine's Day Massacre* and the particularly wild *Bloody Mama*, which starred Shelley Winters, Bruce Dern, Robert Walden, Don Stroud and Robert De Niro in a wonderfully outrageous script by Robert Thom (cowriter of *Death Race 2000* and writer of *Wild in the Streets*). In between was Corman's LSD movie, *The Trip*, with its arresting low-budget visuals (though one wonders who thought that Bruce Dern, in the middle of his psycho phase, would make a reassuring presence for Peter Fonda's first LSD experience).

Gas-s-s-s . . . Or It Became Necessary to Destroy the World in Order to Save It! was the last borderline horror/science fiction movie that Corman directed for AIP. The film is interesting as a bizarre tribute to Corman himself, with its stock of characters including bikers, cowboys, youth, gangsters, and even Edgar Allan Poe with a raven on his shoulder and Lenore behind him riding on a motorcycle. Such people as Bud Cort, Cindy Williams, and Talia Shire make early screen appearances in the film.

The plot revolves around the idea that some nerve gas has leaked and all people over 25 are doomed to die. A small group of people go on a quixotic quest for knowledge and truth. This George Armitrage–scripted satire seems broad and unfocused, but such segments as the group encountering a football team that plans to pursue the all–American dream of sacking and raping El Paso have a weird sort of logic to them.

The whole thing is very counterculture-oriented and, of course, very dated today. Corman became upset when distributor AIP recut the picture on him, removing the character of God, who apparently was given to divine wisecracks, so that God is left with little more than voiceover at a drive-in telling someone that his lights have been left on. The end of the film is no help either as a truck pulls up and out walk several people wearing masks representing Corman's heroes including Gandhi, John F. Kennedy, Martin Luther King, and Che Guevera.

Gas-s-s-s proved to be a disaster, but it can be fun for Corman fans and those into the decidedly odd. It also shows that Corman could try at making something other than the straightforward commercial films which have been his bread and butter. But most important, because of the recutting, Corman resolved to try setting up a company on his own. As a result, he started New World Pictures and had some successes starting up the "nurse" movie genre (featuring good-looking candy-stripers who took their clothes off), more motorcycle movies, and Filippino-women-in-prison pictures, before going on to tackle more ambitious things.

Corman directed one more feature film, *Von Richtofen and Brown*, for United Artists; a television movie, *What's in It for Harry*, which Corman directed under a pseudonym, was released later. *Von Richtofen and Brown* is a fictitious account of the famed Red Baron and the man who shot him down. It did not do very well and Corman complained that United Artists had the film redubbed with actors doing phony German accents.

After several years, Corman finally tired of the hassles of running a company as large as New World and shrewdly sold the company off while retaining its library of films. Corman started Millennium Pictures (perhaps an acknowledgment of a bizarre book titled *Roger Corman: The Millennic Vision* in which Paul Welleman proposes a pseudo-intellectualized timeline for Corman's pictures and how they relate to the millennium). Later this changed to Concorde Pictures, which has produced a number of sword-and-sorcery and South American–shot pictures. Unfortunately, where Corman was once a leader in the market, he now seems more of a follower, and his current productions lack the occasional brilliance of some of the films he produced for New World, many of whose filmmakers have gone on to greater success in Hollywood and elsewhere.

Corman has always been more of a businessman than an artist, but he is enthusiastic about movies and their creation, and his films show a guiding intelligence and occasional bits of experimentation and flair. He has also, partly because he worked in the low-budget field, been one of the most independent artists in the film industry, operating almost exclusively outside the major studios and their restrictions. Rather than continually gambling on a big hit, Corman was very successful at producing films that would attract a definite if small audience and accommodated himself to making a small but consistent profit on each film. Where things in Hollywood were tending towards the overblown, Corman managed to show that a small film can still be successful and concentrate on human dynamics and drama.

His work is also enjoyable because he decided not to take himself too seriously. The humor can give his best films a sense of fun that makes them memorable and enjoyable, leaving pleasant impressions in the audience's minds. In addition, Corman was savvy enough to deal with some serious themes, usually with a liberal slant, in most of his productions – everything from women's lib to the dangers of totalitarian influences to the effects of corruption on corrupt individuals.

Because these films were made and marketed as exploitation films, they have largely been downgraded by the keepers of the cultural flame or, conversely, overpraised by some aficionados who grew up with them as the exciting fodder of their childhood. Corman's cinematic achievements are modest, but they do deserve to be accorded as achievements. Also, Corman's influence apart from being a director has been extensive, often overshadowing notions that he helped demonstrate how science fiction could be accomplished without spending a fortune on special effects; how a gothic feeling could be returned to American movies after it had been lacking for many years; how horror pictures aimed at teens could be successful as double bills; and how horror films could finally be accorded A film status (with the Poe pictures in the '60s).

After a long hiatus from directing, Corman finally returned to helm his first picture in decades (though it is said he lent his directorial hand uncredited to Phil Karlson's *A Time for Killing*, Cy Enfield's *De Sade*, and Hector Olivera's *Wizards of the Lost Kingdom* as well as directing the TV movie *Target: Harry* under the pseudonym Henry Neill).

Adapted from Brian Aldiss' science fiction novel *Frankenstein Unbound*, the immodestly titled *Roger Corman's Frankenstein Unbound* is a fairly intelligent adaptation of Aldiss' ruminations on the Frankenstein legend – in fact, one of the more adult and intelligent variations on the Frankenstein theme, edited to a trim 85 minutes and with a superior cast overall. From the opening, Corman establishes a cosmic perspective – one reminiscent of a '50s film such as Byron Haskins' *War of the Worlds*. The script is by Corman himself in collaboration with film critic F. X. Feeney, and it retains some of Corman's liberal themes. Joe Buchanan (John Hurt) is a weapons expert living in America and ill-advisedly creates a devastating new weapon for the military that is ripping apart the space-time continuum (portrayed as a vagina-like cloud in the sky). Joe and his computerized car find themselves transported back to Geneva circa 1816. There he meets not only Mary Shelley (Bridget Fonda), Percy Shelley (Michael Hutchence of the rock group INXS) and Lord Byron (Jason Patric), but Dr. Frankenstein (Raul Julia) and his monster as well.

The monster demands that Frankenstein create for him a mate, and Frankenstein decides that with Buchanan's help, he can achieve it. Contemptuous of a God-created man, he has given his creature superhuman strength (but not, significantly, superhuman intelligence).

Dream sequences representing the guilt that haunts Buchanan retain the look of similar sequences in Corman's Poe films, complete with color filters and distorting lenses, though the film is far gorier than his '60s work. It all builds to a climax in which Buchanan, Frankenstein, and his creations are all transported to the future, now a frozen waste, where Buchanan confronts the fact that his invention is responsible for the end of civilization – that he is a greater Frankenstein than Dr. Frankenstein was.

While the film betrays its low budget, it is nonetheless an above-average effort, showing that Corman has lost none of his intelligence nor power in the intervening years. Sadly, the film was given scant release and even scanter promotion, and quickly sank without a trace except for the inevitable videocassette release.

There has long been a tendency to either over- or underestimate Corman as a director. While he has always been dependent on actors who can direct themselves, he has discovered imaginative ways to film on a low budget that make his works superior to others produced on a similar level. His protagonists are frequently unsavory and unpleasant people, locked in ruthless struggles for survival. His cynical view of humanity rings a little truer than that of many other exploitation directors. As in Edgar Ulmer films, the heroes must struggle with their fates, and how they handle that struggle is how they are judged. When a Corman hero is found wanting, his whole world will crumble around him like the House of Usher as the cosmic balance is once more restored by the end.

Corman may have helped to initiate some of the biggest and best careers in Hollywood, but he has secured his own lasting achievements in the world of cinema and shows great versatility, from the Griffith films where cliché is treated as grist for comedy to the Richard Matheson movies where decadence brings about its own destruction. Corman believes sincerely in making movies and making money – and however uneven the quality, he has been spectacularly successful at both.

Wes Craven (1949–   )

Last House on the Left (1972); The Hills Have Eyes (1977); Deadly Blessing
(1981); Swamp Thing (1982); A Nightmare on Elm Street (1984); The Hills Have
Eyes Part 2; Deadly Friend (1986); The Serpent and the Rainbow (1988); Shocker
(1989).
TELEVISION: Stranger in Our House (1978); Invitation to Hell (1984); Chiller
(1985); Twilight Zone (6 episodes); Casebusters.

Wes Craven, a man fascinated by dreams and the subconscious, originally intended to be an English professor at a small college on the East Coast.
Failing to get tenure, he caught the filmmaking bug after helping some
students make a film.
"I quit teaching," he recalled in an interview with this author, "and to
make a long story short, I spent about a year looking for work in New York
and ended up in a lower echelon job as a messenger. I worked my way up in
a post-production house, so I learned all of the post-production side of films."
Craven went on:

> One of the things I did on the side, sort of moonlighting, was the sync-
> ing of rushes for documentaries and various small films in the area. So
> there was this job syncing rushes for this guy Sean Cunningham [see
> chapter on Cunningham]. I went in and did that. They had just done a
> reshoot on this film that they were working on, Together, and then after
> doing that for about a week, he said, "Why don't you be an assistant
> editor to this guy?" There was one man who shot it, helped write it,
> helped direct it, and was cutting it, so I became Roger Murphy's assis-
> tant editor.
> Roger Murphy kept having fights with Sean and leaving. So then I
> said, "Well, let me try to do something." Sean and I would sit down, so
> by the end of the picture, I received credit for additional writing, addi-
> tional editing, and additional directing.
> When the film made money, the people who backed it gave us money
> to make a horror film of some kind. Sean suggested we do it together,
> so that's how Last House came about. I wrote it, directed it, and cut it.
> Sean produced it and provided the editing facility. He had a steam bin.
> We virtually made the film together. We taught each other how to
> make a film by making one. Together was much more of semi-documen-
> tary; Last House on the Left was our first feature film.

246

That accounts for its rough look. I didn't know what a master was or coverage. I didn't know any of that. It was shot much more like a documentary, a lot of continuous takes with multiple coverage. We'd stage a scene three times and cover it from three different angles. It was like reinventing the typewriter. It was after that that I read all the books on coverage and masters and work prints and all that. I hadn't studied film or anything. I was going into it as sort of a hobby. I had no formal training whatsoever, so *Last House* is a rudimentary film in some ways, but a very visceral film in other ways. Not knowing what the classic techniques were probably made it original in a way.

Last House on the Left started filming with a budget of $40,000. The people who backed the film were pleased with the rushes and the ante was upped to $90,000, which still was not a great deal of money. The film is very crudely put together. It contains some noticeable lapses in continuity, including a phone which stops working so often that it seems like the actors have to keep the audience constantly apprised of the phone's status.

On Mari's seventeenth birthday, she decides to go to a rock concert rather than stick around her parents' isolated country home, though her parents do not approve of her choice of companion, a low-life teenage girl from the wrong side of the tracks. Together the pair try to score some grass before the concert, and meet four more-than-slightly deranged escaped convicts.

The sheriffs try to warn Mari's parents, but the phones are not working. They spend the entire film–almost a day in the film's chronology–just to travel 20 miles (the squad car runs out of gas halfway there) and arrive too late. Their ineffectiveness and bumbling incompetence make them seem almost as contemptible as the killers in the film.

Craven's documentary approach does, however, accentuate the killers' nightmarish attack on the two girls. There is no style or flair given to the proceedings, leaving a feeling of absolute realism as the audience must helplessly watch the prolonged torture and demise of the young female victims. Part of Craven's premise is that it is tough to kill a human being, and so the horrors continue and continue as if they might never end. Mari's friend tries to escape and is finally trapped by three of the convicts in a cemetery. The scenes that follow were, in 1972, the grisliest, goriest scenes ever included in an American horror film. (I'm excepting Herschell Gordon Lewis' blood-splattered epics for the reasons that his films [a] never managed to be convincing, and [b] were defused by cornball humor and ineptness of execution.)

Commented Craven:

I think that without question that was the most powerful scene that I ever put on film. I think it was much too powerful for people to bear.

You did not see her actually being stabbed, but they [the killers] went into a frenzy of stabbing. At the end, they suddenly stop. Once they started stabbing the girl and holding her, it was very sexual and murderous. It was very upsetting and strange.

At the end, they lay her down, and the girl, Sadie, bends down and picks up a loop of intestine, and Fred says something like, "Well, we broke her" but he says it like a broken doll or something. And for a while, it looks like they're going to throw up, and they walk away. It just never stops. It's like walking into a real killing where people kill and they go into a frenzy, and then they suddenly realize what they've done, literally just broken the person open.

It was just too intense. Everybody just seized it. Projectionists would cut it and so did theater owners and distributors until there wasn't an intact print of the film left. It was really a very early telling lesson in the vulnerability of film. It's not like you print a book and there's an intact copy of it someplace. It is a series of physical objects that are printed and go out and are attacked by everybody from projectionists to theater owners. Some prints might have escaped pulverizing. I have a friend in New York that has a complete 16mm print. [A mostly complete version was released on video.]

And then Mari's death was more of a tragedy. The shooting was not, but the rape was crude and horrible. Krug carved his name on her chest. It was really horrendous. It really went on and on. A lot of it was based on things that I was reading that were going on in Vietnam, you know, cutting off the ears and carving the unit name into the dead Cong's chest, but it was just too intense, too much. The original concept was to make a film that broke barriers, and we broke too many.

Craven decided to reprise the plot of Ingmar Bergman's *Virgin Spring*, which itself was based on a violent folktale. After killing Mari, the killers go to her parents' house and claim to be friends of Mari's. Slowly, the parents discover just who their houseguests are and then take a revenge that is almost as gruesome and repulsive as the killers' own acts.

The film as shown lacks a key scene where the parents finally discover who their visitors are. The scene would have stretched the audience's credulity to the breaking point in that the audience is asked to believe that Mari, after being raped, having her chest carved up, shot, and drowned in the lake, was still living in the middle of the night when the parents run down to the lakeshore.

Said Craven:

The scene's still in where they [the parents] run down the drive-way, but in most prints, there is no following scene or it is very truncated, but originally what happened was they pulled her out of the water – she was half in the water and half out. There was a scene where the mother says, "Who did this, baby?" And she says, "Two men and a woman. I don't know why they did it." The father picks her up and starts carrying her back to the house, and they put her down on the couch. The father turns to the mother and says, "I'm going down into basement and get something to get them." But all the acting was so bad. That was the problem. It was impossible, and the acting was bad, the directing was bad. It just had to go.

The killers' deaths include a fellatio/castration and a chainsaw to the chest (a possible influence on Tobe Hooper?). Craven established what was to become one of his trademarks, the setting up of a complicated booby trap, this time of electrical leads wired up to a doorknob and under a wet rug to prevent the killers from escaping by the front door. There was also Craven's first effective nightmare sequence: Weasel dreams that the mother and father pry his mouth open and take a chisel to his teeth. Overall, the film is neither pleasant nor entertaining, and it is amateurishly made; yet it is unquestionably unsettling.

The title of the film remains a bit of a puzzle. The house is always on the right whenever anyone drives up, for example. It is ironic that the killers break down in front of Mari's and that she and her friend die only a few hundred yards from her door (and perhaps might have been saved if only they dared scream loud enough). Some people have seen the title as a reference to Kubrick's *A Clockwork Orange* where the writer F. Alexander (Patrick Magee) lives on the last house on the left of a dead end street, and that domicile is the one that Alex and his droogs attack, raping and killing Alexander's wife. But that is not how the title was chosen at all, according to Craven:

> The original title was *Night of Vengeance*, and when we came to release it, somebody said, "Well, that title doesn't really fit. What should we call it?" It was called *Grim Company* and *Sex Crime of the Century*. Broadway Frack, this guy who did publicity on little pictures, came up to us and said, *Last House on the Left*.
> We looked at him and said, "What's that got to do with anything? It's the only house on the road, but, well, we'll try it." So we opened the picture with three different titles, three different prints, and three geographically similar towns. The other two did so-so business, and the one with *The Last House on the Left* had lines around the block, so we all agreed that it would be *The Last House on the Left*.
> Everybody insists that it's a great title, but it means nothing. It was one of those cases where you realize that a title doesn't have to do anything but get people into the theater. Now interestingly enough, what this guy said was: "Titles with *house* in them are always hits." And it's true. A lot of very good films have the word *house* in the titles. There is something very relevant about the concept of house: *House of Usher*, *House Calls*. *Left* has always been used to signify the radical, the unusual, the side of death. The left side has always been a bit more suspect. And *last*, of course, implies death in the end, so it's a very canny combination of buzz words.

Despite the excesses that the film has been accused of, Craven considers the film to be moralistic in the sense of warning that one can get in over his or her head. The fact that the teens died because of people they tried to buy drugs off of also has a moralistic twinge. Said Craven:

> At the time, I happened to be doing every drug available, but I think at heart I felt that drugs were not such a great idea for kids to get into. I think it is very moralistic in a sense, but I'm not ashamed of that. I don't think the great, sort of libertarian opening of the floodgates of morality in the seventies has done the next generation a great amount of good. I think there was some sort of balance that had to be attained. The pendulum had to swing back the other way and come back. If nothing else, the film says be careful, the world is not all full of sweetness and light.

Craven's technical proficiency improved greatly with his next film five years later, *The Hills Have Eyes*. *The Last House on the Left* was shot on Super-16 and looks it, while *The Hills Have Eyes* was filmed using 16mm negative and lacks the telltale graininess that typically gives away films that have been blown up from 16mm. Still, *The Hills Have Eyes* is a very static picture as Craven's budget did not allow for the use of dollies or cranes.

Part of the inspiration for *The Hills Have Eyes* came from an account of the Sawney Bean family (recounted in *Historical and Traditional Tales Connected with the South of Scotland* by John Nicholson; it also appears in the "Human and Inhuman Stories" portion of *The Omnibus of Crime* by Dorothy L. Sayers). This was a family of robbers and cannibals that was perpetuated by incest. They waylaid unsuspecting passersby and took them to a secret cave where the victims were pickled for later consumption. Though it was estimated that over a thousand people had disappeared in the area, the family was not discovered until a man and his bride were attacked. The groom watched, horrified, as his bride's throat was slit and her body disemboweled. Fortunately for him, 20 or 30 men came upon them, and the Sawney Bean family made a hasty retreat, leaving their handiwork behind. The group went to Glasgow to notify the magistrates, who in turn summoned the king. With several hundred men and a large number of bloodhounds, the Beans' hideaway was discovered along with evidence of their ghastly crimes. Under strong guard, the men were taken to Leith, dismembered, and bled to death in a few hours. The women and children were afterwards burned to death.

Craven decided to combine a modern version of the Sawney Bean family with a dream he had had:

> I had a dream, a sort of Beauty and the Beast dream, and it ended with two dogs named Beauty and Beast, one very gentle and the other savage. There was the idea of the two families who mirrored each other

with parents and children on both sides, one civilized and the other not civilized. That was the genesis basically.

What I tried to do was start with civilized man and all the trappings of his civilization. It's mobile (i.e. they travel in a mobile home), but it's there. They have the dogs, they have the C.B.s, they have this and that. Then say, what happens when you destroy all that? What do they do with the remnants of that civilization and whatever is inside of them? It was a feeling like, well, this is the last days of American civilization, the decline and fall of Western civilization. What's going to come out of it? Will the generation that had to deal with the remnants of it be able to survive? Will they survive with their savageness and conquer, or will we just sort of go back into a dark ages? There was that sort of philosophical inquiry behind it, if you will.

In fact, the original draft had the family leaving New York in 1984. This was done in 1975, so it was set 10 years in the future. New York was uninhabitable and you had to have a passport to travel between states because states had become very territorial. The family was supposed to be stationed in Sun Valley, but they didn't have a passport to get into California, so they were trying to sneak in through the desert. That was the original premise.

The producers then decided that maybe that was too futuristic, so we had them go out for a silver mine. The basic notion was, and still is, what do you do with the pieces? How do you improvise with the pieces that are left of your civilization? And it answered the same thing. How tough are we or can we be if the chips are down? I think it was saying that the college generation has it in them. They can improvise with what they have, and they have the motivation to survive. It was also another way of saying we're not so gentle as we like to think we are. There is the savage in all of us, and there's the civilized in most savages too. I always try to show villains that are at least partially civilized. The wild family think about their family members and have things about them that are jealous or insecure or are humorous. In *Last House*, I have the scene where the killers don't know what utensils to use and they get embarrassed and talk about it later.

The Hills Have Eyes opens with a grizzled old gas station attendant (John Steadman) who mumbles something about, "Boy, they'd leave me belly up out here if they knew I was getting ready to run." Ruby (Janus Blythe), a savage girl, surprises him and expects to trade for whiskey and food supplies, but the old man has nothing to trade. Just then, a station wagon pulling a trailer pulls up, carrying a father, a mother, two brothers, a daughter, and a daughter-in-law with a baby. The family wants to buy some gas and check out a silver mine they inherited. The old man tells them they don't want to go back in there.

"Besides," he says, "there's nothing back in there but animals."

"Animals?" Ethel Carter (Virginia Vincent), the mother, responds. "You mean nobody lives back there?"

Horror Film Directors 252

"Nobody you'd want to meet, lady, believe me," the old man replies prophetically.

The ominous undertones build thick and fast. After being warned to stay on the main road, the family turns off. Rather than hit a rabbit, they even leave the dirt road on which they've been traveling at high speed, and the resulting accident breaks the station wagon's axle. "There'll be hell to pay now," someone comments.

We immediately suspect that person is right, because we hear the C.B. communication of the savage family regarding the invaders to their territory, which Russ Grieve, playing Mr. Carter, identifies as an Air Force nuclear testing site. That the area contains hidden threats is foreshadowed when Doug (Martin Speer) asks Lynn (Dee Wallace) for a jacket which turns out to have a tarantula crawling on it. The "white bread" family decides to stay together except for Doug, who will try to reach the military base while Mr. Carter backtracks to the gas station. After a quick prayer, the men leave, putting the younger son, Bobby (Robert Houston), in charge until they get back.

The family has two German shepherds named Beauty and Beast. Beauty becomes agitated and runs off with Bobby chasing after her. It is dark when Bobby returns, and he does not feel like talking. Beauty does not return with him.

Mr. Carter gets back to the gas station and tries to use the phone only to be shot at. Kicking down the door behind which his assailant has barricaded himself, he discovers the gas station attendant trying to hang himself. (His plans for escape were thwarted when someone blew up his pick-up truck.) The attendant explains that he mistook Carter for "somebody else." That somebody was his son, who probably burned the old man's house and wife years before and who has been living up in the hills with a prostitute for many years, raising a brood of savages. They live by scavenging things from the military and fencing them to the old man.

As the old man finishes telling his story, his son, Jupiter (James Whitworth), crashes through the window and drags the old man away before Carter can respond. Later, Carter finds the old man's remains and is waylaid by the savage family. Back at the savage family's hearth, Ruby is chained up for attempting to get away, but she is allowed to enjoy the remains of Beauty. She hears Beast howling for his lost companion and fears that it is Beauty's ghost come back to haunt her.

Doug returns to the trailer, having found a coil or steel cord, and prepares to sleep with Lynn out in the station wagon. When they are asleep, Pluto (Michael Berryman), Jupiter's bald-headed son, secretly drains gas out of the station wagon. He then creeps inside the trailer to raid it after Bobby leaves to check on Beast. Finding himself locked out of the trailer, Bobby disturbs Doug and Lynn and spills the beans about Beauty being dead.

Suddenly, there is an explosion, which the three check out. They find
Mr. Carter's blackened corpse crucified on a Yucca tree. Back in the trailer,
Pluto attacks Brenda (Susan Lanier), but his brother Mercury interferes,
and they fight. The noise and screams alert the people outside the trailer,
who come to the rescue. Pluto and Mercury are chased off, but Lynn is killed
in the fracas and the baby is kidnapped. The mother becomes almost catatonic, and Brenda is in shock.

Beast follows the savages back to camp and knocks Mercury over a cliff,
killing him. Papa Jupiter vows revenge.

By the next morning, Ethel Carter is dead and the family is panic-
stricken. They call for help and seem to reach the Air Force base. "What are
your defensive capabilities at this time?" says the voice over the C.B. after
being apprised of their situation. One gun with only two bullets, the family
replies, what do you recommend? The voice over the C.B. answers, "We
recommend that until we get to you, you stand on your heads with your
thumbs up your ass," and laughs. The voice that they've been hearing is actually Pluto's.

Doug sends Beast after the members of the savage family, while Bob
sets a tire on fire as a sort of distress signal, hoping to attract the attention
of the occasional low-flying Air Force jet that passes overhead. Brenda recovers from her shock and comes up with an idea involving the steel cable
Doug found.

Beast attacks Pluto and gnaws away at his foot, but Jupiter drives him
off. Meanwhile, back at the savage family's campsite, Ruby steals the baby
they were planning to eat, and Mars sets off in pursuit of her. Beast finally
kills Pluto, gnawing through his throat.

Back at the trailer, Brenda and Bobby use Ethel's corpse as a lure which
attracts Jupiter's attention. When he reaches the right place, Bob starts up
the station wagon. It is hard to start because it is now low on gas, but he
does manage to get the engine running, turning the wheels, which are used
as a winch for the steel cable. The cable whips around the back of Jupiter's
leg and drags him across the desert floor, but the car runs out of gas before
he is more than injured.

Luckily, Bobby has set up another booby trap in the trailer. He has
turned on the gas jets and rigged a match to ignite as soon as the door is
opened. The trailer explodes when Jupiter opens the door, but surprisingly
enough, Jupiter manages to survive and attacks Bobby, who returned to the
site in an effort to make sure Jupiter was dead. Brenda picks up a hatchet
and starts letting Jupiter have it, distracting him from noticing that Bobby
has picked up the family gun. Bobby then puts the two rounds into Jupiter,
finally killing the menacing father figure.

The climax has Ruby hiding with the baby as Doug tries to lure Mars
into a disadvantageous position from which he can kill him. Doug makes the

mistake of leaving his knife in a rattler's nest. Mars and Doug struggle to
the death, with Bobby gouging Mars' leg wound to gain an advantage while
Ruby resolves to pick up a rattler and have it bite Mars. Once bitten Mars
falls back as Doug stabs him repeatedly with an insane look on his face. Craven fades the scene to red.

In both of his first two features, Craven contrasts a normal family with
an abnormal one. In *Last House*, grief turns into a kind of vicious and cunning vengeance. Krug, Junior, Weasel and Sadie try to ape the manners of
normal society but fail miserably, making Mari's parents suspicious. In the
course of the film, Mari's parents are shown in the ritual of preparing for
Mari's birthday party; upon learning of Mari's death, they ritually slaughter
the guilty group.

But *Last House* is crudely made and poorly edited. *The Hills Have Eyes*
sets up a similar dichotomy but is far slicker in execution. Though the family
is motivated by vengeance, the message the film gives is more one of survival: When pushed to the wall, the "white bread" family are as capable of
ruthlessness and cunning (evidenced by the boobytraps) as the abnormal
family, although except for extreme situations, that is not their operative
mode. Still, the veneer of civilization proves thin.

Hills came about largely because Craven had managed to squander the
profit he made from *Last House*, but now he proceeded to pursue a film
career more avidly. He was hired by Sean Cunningham to do a small stunt
for *Here Come the Tigers*, in which Craven appeared as a man reading a
newspaper who leans against his car door just as the door is pulled off by
a prankster.

Craven was finally able to land a job for himself on the made-for-TV
movie *Stranger in Our House*, which allowed him to work with much better
equipment than he had used previously. Unfortunately, it wasn't a much
better script.

Stranger in Our House introduced Craven to Max Keller and Glenn
Benest, both of whom would work on *Deadly Blessing*, Craven's next
theatrical feature. *Stranger* was based on Lois Duncan's novel *Summer of
Fear* and was released under that title in Europe. Lee Purcell plays a teenaged witch who comes to live with her horse-riding cousin, played by Linda
Blair (of *The Exorcist* fame), and her family. She drives the whole family
into chaos until finally Blair figures out what is going on and has it out with
her at the end. Craven did some uncredited rewriting on the final screenplay, as a result of which he was called in to do a rewrite on *Deadly Blessing*.

Pleased with the rewrite, the producers offered Craven a chance to
direct *Deadly Blessing*, which he eagerly accepted. According to Craven,
the original film read like *Charlie's Angels Go to the Farm*, though Craven
was interested in doing a less "intense" type of horror film. Also, with

Universal supplying the equipment, Craven would have more of an opportunity to show what he could do with the proper equipment and backing, and the film does demonstrate increased technical proficiency.

Said Craven:

> I wanted to show, first of all, that I know how to do it, and second of all, it was a very different kind of picture. I wanted a big, smooth, sort of Philip Wylie look to it. We very consciously went in with that intention. Robert Jessup, the cinematographer, and I went through Philip Wylie's books and Van Gogh's paintings for the looks of the house down the lane and the young woman's paintings. I directed the artist to paint like a combination of Van Gogh and Walter Lantz [once head of Universal's cartoon department]. I wanted it very cartoony but sort of twisted, reflecting her mentality. That was the girl who was killed, who turned out to be a hermaphrodite painter whose paintings kept changing and getting more distorted.

Maren Jensen, whose Hittite farmer husband has been mysteriously crushed by a tractor, calls on her friends (Susan Buckner and Sharon Stone) for support, especially as the village elder (Ernest Borgnine) disapproves and warns of an incubus.

The isolated farm community begins to seem even more ominous, and the three women become terrified. Standout scenes include one where Sharon Stone dreams that a tarantula is dropped into her mouth; and one in which Maren Jensen gets an unexpected visitor while bathing—a snake that slithers up between her thighs. Also noteworthy is the scene in which Susan Buckner falls for one of the village lads (played by Jeff East) and initiates him into sex. For once, this sort of a scene is shot believably, with all the awkwardness and groping that such an initation would entail, as well as the caring. Unfortunately, East is dispatched at the end of the scene by an outside force, as if the director suddenly remembered this was a horror film and in a horror film, anyone who makes love is doomed.

Commented Craven:

> I've had a lot of people ask me if this is some sort of repressive sexuality or something, but I think the real reason is that in horror—if you look at the bald mechanics of it—in order to scare somebody or bring out fear or pity for victims, you put them in a very vulnerable, sort of "passed out" situation. One of the key places where we are totally preoccupied is when making love, where you drop your shield and become very unprotected. When people are sleeping, making love, in their bathtubs, listening to music through earphones, when their traditional defenses are down are the best times to strike. I probably should do one where somebody is on a toilet.

The film has many of the hallmarks of Craven's films: dream sequences, shocks piled on shocks, and Michael Berryman in a small but important role. The most peculiar thing about *Deadly Blessing* is that after the hermaphrodite killer is revealed and dispatched, a real incubus suddenly appears and carries Jensen away. It is the only supernatural element in the film, and it is a surprise since the audience assumed that the Hittite's claptrap about an "incubus" was meant to be a designation for Jensen and the outside evil of "sexuality" she was bringing into the community. Sometimes, this last ironic twist is omitted from the film by distributors or theater owners. The effects for it were originally to have been done by John Dykstra, but he had to bow out when *Firefox* had its schedule moved up, and so the effects were actually performed by Everett Alson and Ira Anderson with an assist from costumer Tony Masters.

Deadly Blessing works well in some of its segments, but overall, the plot just clunks and chugs along from incident to incident. While it is enjoyable, instead of being an explosive film which demonstrated what Craven could do with a bigger budget, it was more of a fizzle. It looked good for the money spent, but even with Craven's script surgery, the story was weak.

Unfortunately, the same thing could be said of Craven's next project, *Swamp Thing*. Originally, Swamp Thing was the creation of Len Wein and Berni Wrightson for D.C. Comics. It was a beautifully drawn, sensitively written, episodic series of stories about a scientist named Dr. Alec Holland who, in a lab accident, becomes a monstrous-looking half-man, half-plant creature. The Swamp Thing itself was a very sympathetic character, treated cruelly by the outside world because of his unprepossessing features. The character has much in common with Frankenstein's monster of Shelley's classic tale, and as such, seemed a good bet to translate well to the movies.

One of the film's central problems was that the producers decided to go with the lowest makeup bid, from Bill Munns, for $80,000. (The next highest bid was a more realistic $250,000.) Adding to Munns' headaches were the facts that (1) he was not given a full go-ahead until six weeks before production; (2) he had created one Swamp Thing body suit only to have a taller, thinner actor take over the role; and (3) the head intended for close-ups was discarded when it was felt that it did not match the body suit head well enough. (Actor Ray Wise, who played Dr. Holland in the film, was to have played the Swamp Thing in close-ups, but he had the wrong kind of nose and face to perfectly match up with the look of the Swamp Thing that had already been established. Dick Durock ended up playing the Swamp Thing throughout the movie with a head mask that was only intended to be seen in long shot.)

The Swamp Thing's face simply is not very expressive, and though Durock mimed the best he could, that limitations took away all the nuances that might have successfully brought the character to life. While the Swamp Thing suit was limited in its mobility and tended to disintegrate in the swampwater, it at least looked something like it was supposed to. Two other original makeups designed by Munns proved disastrous. One of of a "drowned rat"–type creature that Nicholas Worth turns into when given a sample of Dr. Holland's potion, and the other is the creature Arcane (Louis Jourdan) becomes after imbibing that fluid himself. In the comic book, Arcane turned into a fearsome werewolf by use of magic, but as *The Howling, The Wolfen,* and *American Werewolf in London* (in fact, the drawing of Arcane in the comic book looked remarkably like the werewolves in *The Howling*) were to come out soon, it was decided that another kind of monster should be employed. The result was a shaggy-haired lizard with an extended snout that looked ludicrous.

Said Craven:

> *Swamp Thing* had a lot of problems with the body and a rough schedule. The costume was a real problem. The designer was not given an adequate amount of lead time. He showed up on the set the day before we had to shoot it. It was virtually, "Well, do we stop production?" and there was no money to do that, so the attempt was to do something that would sort of transcend the costume.
>
> In a sense, it has. The film plays for kids all right, but it doesn't play for teenagers or adults. Because the technical abilities are so high these days, people have a hard time getting past that; but on the other hand, it does play for a lot of people – women like it, a lot of parents like it, a lot of young kids like it. It played very, very strongly on HBO and other cable and cassette releases. It's a Wes Craven movie which kids can enjoy and laugh at, you know?

Craven reworked the original story from the comic book, changing the person in charge of protecting Dr. Holland from Matt Cable to Alice Cable (played by Adrienne Barbeau) so that Craven could give the story a love interest and add a "Beauty and the Beast" overtone to the story.

> It was very much a Beauty and the Beast tale. It was clearly an attempt to do a variation on the Beauty and the Beast theme. You have a beast that you know inside is a handsome prince, but you see him as a toad. You've seen him before, and you know he was amorous and humorous and very, very scientifically brilliant, yet outwardly now he's a monster.
>
> On the other hand, you have Louis Jourdan's character, Arcane, who is someone who looks very nice on the outside, but when you see his true self, it's monstrous and ugly. Then there is the character of Bruno, who turns into a giant mouse. I like exploring the idea that there are antipathies to everything. Beneath the surface, there is another side. That theme has run through all of my films.

In addition, Craven added the character Jude (Reggie Batts), a young black kid who seems intended to act as spokesman for the kids in the audience:

> Jude was somebody that the kids could identify with. We wanted somebody that could ask the questions that only an uninformed person would ask, and who would add humor. That's basically it. He just came out of me, and we all liked him. Originally, he was an old man, but in the second or third draft [of the screenplay], he switched to being a kid. Overall, I kept the basic character names and sort of combined them, and then I created the kid and created the story. I would say up to the formula exploding in Holland's face, it was pretty much along the lines of the comic, and everything after that was just made up. It was a fun picture. I met my wife on it, so it was successful.

Swamp Thing does have a very dream-like feel to it, but it fails to evoke the same beauty and unease that Walter Hill was able to achieve with a similar location in the film *Southern Comfort*. Rather than a classic monster tale or an inspired adaptation of a very fine comic book, *Swamp Thing* is a kiddie matinee film, unlikely to attract audiences other than the younger set for whom it appears to have been intended.

Because of the success of *The Hills Have Eyes* on videotape, particularly in Europe, the European video distributors offered to finance a sequel to the original film, and so *The Hills Have Eyes Part 2* was born. However, since the video rights had already been sold, it became difficult for a distribution deal to be struck in the United States. Also, while Craven had mostly finished *The Hills Have Eyes 2*, the film was released unfinished, with Craven intending to go back and punch up the violence quotient but prevented from doing so. The results was a direct-to-video disaster, a fiasco of a follow-up to the original film.

The next Craven project was a telefeature called *Invitation to Hell*. Craven was called in after the script had been completed, but he ended up doing an uncredited polish job on it. The basic premise of *Invitation* (originally titled *The Club*) was that a family moves to a new location that is situated near the gates of hell. The family is lured into hell by a mysterious club comprised of the members of the local community. As luck and the screenwriter would have it, the father (Robert Urich) has been working on a special fireproof suit that allows him to enter hell to rescue his family. Any relationship to Greek mythology is purely coincidental.

Overall, the film is very tame. Said Craven:

> When television is dealing with me, they say, "We can't do violence, so we must be able to do witchcraft because that's something else, that's a little off-the-wall." Whenever I get approached by television, it

is usually for something supernatural. I think *Invitation* turned out well
for what it was. It was a very fast job. They were having to rush it to
make it because it was designed to fill a hole that suddenly opened up.
I think there were about two weeks pre-production and something like
three-and-a-half weeks post-production. We got the second highest ratings for the week, and swept the ratings for the night. I beat *Simon and
Simon* and *Magnum*, so for the time we had, we did very, very well.

However, Craven really hit his stride with *A Nightmare on Elm Street*.
In its original opening, the film did very well, climbing to a profit even before it reached wider release. More importantly, it was an unexpectedly
stylish and energetic film while Craven's last few films seemed to have
suffered from tired blood. Craven had a real dedication to the project and
had tried to get it made for years. Unlike his projects since the original *Hills
Have Eyes*, it was an effort he originated rather than coming in on something that somebody else had written and prepared. Craven had shown the
script of *Nightmare* around for several years without success. It had been
turned down virtually everywhere, but once it was released, it was evident
that his faith in the project was justified.

Despite the use of the overly prevalent "teenagers-in-peril" approach to
horror, the film did not descend to overused clichés, but rather used the
world of dreams to strike out into some fresh territory, resulting in some
first class horror filmmaking. The film recapitulated all of Craven's interests. It had dreams (long one of his fortes), clever boobytraps, and clearly
defined forces battling for survival. *Nightmare* gave ample evidence that
Craven had learned from his previous experiences and was refining his
craft.

He was still able to manage on a small budget. *A Nightmare on Elm
Street* was shot in 32 days on a budget of under $2 million. The film almost
did not come off when the financial backing fell out three days into shooting,
but fortunately a deal was struck and New Line Cinema agreed to distribute
the picture once it was completed. The actors and the crew were paid scale,
that is guild minimum. Said Craven:

> There were a lot of very talented people working on it. Nobody took
> much money on it. We improvised like mad. Our special effects guy, Jim
> Doyle, did a magnificent job. We had a very small crew. The entire
> special effects crew was somewhere around half a dozen people. They
> built an entire revolving room so that Tina could go up the walls and
> the ceiling. The room was revolving in that shot. We were strapped into
> chairs. The camera was strapped into a chair. We had to keep blood off
> the lens because it would totally ruin the shot.
> Actually, when it started to go sideways, it felt like the room was go-
> ing out of control. We started screaming. It was the best ride since Dis-
> neyland, strapped into a room with 250 gallons of blood flying around.

There were certain things that we were going to do with the revolving room that we couldn't afford. The fact was that the special effects people had so much to do, they needed to have control of the set, that we ended up having this room and not being able to do all as much with it as we could have done because we were so rushed. Towards the end, we were shooting in every corner of the set. I was literally running from one end of the stage to the other, shooting these little inserts. We'd have a camera crew over here shooting inserts and we'd have a camera crew over there shooting Rod being dragged across the floor, and a camera crew up here shooting where he went. It was just total insanity. It was like a test of how resourceful and resilient we could be. There were a lot of things we could have done with the special effects room, but we didn't have time to do them.

Craven feels that he was psychologically prepared for the film because it came at the tail end of what had been, so far, the busiest time ever in his career. He literally walked off of the soundstage of one project and onto the soundstage of another. He was also fortunate enough to find a cast largely composed of talented unknowns and beginners.

The story mostly focuses on the character of Nancy, who discovers that she and three of her friends all shared the same terrible dream one night. As one by one her friends begin to get murdered in the most bizarre and inexplicable fashion, she realizes that the razor-clawed horror that has been haunting her dreams will be after her next. To sleep is death, and so she must battle to stay awake. Meanwhile, the adults around her cannot believe her story and are all telling her to relax and go to sleep.

The part of Nancy is played by Heather Langenkamp in her first major role. In many ways, it is she who must carry the picture, and she does so, very well. Said Craven:

> I think she's fantastic. She was in *Rumblefish* before her part was cut.... She's a fine actress.
>
> As a director, you hope after you write a character you can find her. You make up somebody, and then you have to find that person in the real world, and then that person has to be able to act. I really felt that I'd found my Nancy. Heather's very talented, and she really has her head screwed on. She's a very serious actress.

The cloaked, rotting figure with the steel knives for fingers that is haunting the teens' dreams is Freddy Krueger (Robert Englund), a child molester who was the victim of some vigilante parents and who has now returned from the dreamworld to exact his revenge. Just who he was and why he was after these particular teens was clearer in the original cut of the film according to Craven:

...[I]t was much clearer that all the parents were in collusion, hiding this secret. It was the parents of these four kids who had killed Fred Krueger. There were scenes where various groups of parents talk about it and say they shouldn't have done it or that he couldn't possibly be hurting the children. There was even a line indicating that all the teenagers once had siblings who had been killed when Fred Krueger had originally terrorized the town, but nobody would believe that Nancy could not remember having siblings, so I cut it out.

Craven and his cinematographer, Jacques Haitkin, give a good look to the film which suggests the eerie wrongness of a dream, and it ably communicates the feeling that somehow reality has been skewed. There are a number of memorable sequences in the film including a girl who is lifted off her bed and onto the walls and ceiling while being attacked by an invisible adversary, a boy who gets sucked into his bed and becomes a torrent of blood, and a telephone mouthpiece that suddenly develops a slavering tongue which tries to french-kiss the heroine. "The tongue coming out the phone is one of my favorite scenes," said Craven, "simply because it cost about five dollars. It's very effective and very cinematic. Since I started off as a writer, I tend to be verbal, so I love it when I can get myself to do something totally visual like the bathtub scene. Tina's death is cinematic, the whole sequence going down the alley and all that. I feel good about the whole picture."

The only exception to the last statement that Craven makes is that he is not totally happy with the final shock at the end:

The ghost of *Carrie* haunts us all, unfortunately. There's hardly a producer alive that will allow a film to end classically – you must have that final shock. The script ended with her going out the door, getting into the car, driving off into the fog, and the mother seeing the girl leave before the credits.

That, more than any other scene, was fussed over by other people, especially the producer who felt we had to have a strong, "proper" end. So I said, OK, I'll pull the mother through the door, and they said, "Yeah!" I thought of that almost as a joke on the very last night before shooting had to stop. I said, OK, we'll put a cable on this dummy, and sure enough, we had eight people pulling in the other direction, and by God the thing went through the door like shot through a goose. It was just incredible. We looked at the shot and said we'll go with it. Some people love it; some hate it.

Producer Robert Shaye, president of New Line Cinema, wanted Freddy resurrected because he always kept the commercial consideration of sequels in mind. Therefore, the car that Nancy drives away in turns out to be Freddy in another guise as the dreamy shot of girls in white dresses skipping rope is reprised. Little did either man suspect the reaction they received.

In times past, horror fans "worshipped" the monsters in the movies, perhaps figuring it was best to be on the more powerful side. Kids identified with the Frankenstein monster because they were scared of him, and if you were on his side, it seemed less likely that the monster would come after you. Modern horror audiences strangely tend to identify with insane killers, spawning successful sequels to the *Halloween* films with successive portrayals of Michael Myers, the *Friday the 13th* movies with Jason every go round; but the most successful of all has been Freddy Krueger.

Craven named his creation after a child who had tormented him as a kid. Previously in horror, Craven had played on the idea that large was frightening, but small-statured actor Robert Englund convinced him that a small, fiendish but stylish killer could make an effective new approach. Part of what makes Freddy work is that he so thoroughly enjoys the mayhem he is creating, inviting the audience to appreciate his creativity and originality in manipulating reality.

A Nightmare on Elm Street helped initiate a cycle of "rubber reality" movies where anything and everything was possible. Dreams could intrude on reality; doors would lead to other dimensions; staircases could turn to marshmallow; nothing was dependable and all laws and rules were off. Freddy is a prime rulebreaker, and he gets away with pranks that other kids can only dream of.

Horror primarily appeals to an adolescent audience, and adults often forget what a scary time adolescence can be. The *Nightmare on Elm Street* films all play on these fears. The teens are mostly made sympathetic, unlike in some other stalk-and-slash horror films, but the adults tend to be alcoholics or simply unhelpful. They do not listen to the teens; they do not understand. Notice how much that parallels common teen complaints. In the first film, John Saxon, the square-jawed father, does eventually rush to the rescue, but only after the heroine has finally learned how she can deal with Krueger by herself. To triumph, the teens always have to win by themselves and not through the help of their parents or other adults.

Craven initially declined to work on *Nightmare 2*, and he found the script stupid and uninteresting, but Freddy Krueger's character proved to have enduring popularity with the audience. He did involve himself in *Nightmare 3*, sharing credit for the story, and probably supplied the basic concepts of bringing back Nancy and having a team of teens join forces to finally fight Freddy on his own turf – in dreams. Unfortunately, the series has not exploited this particular aspect of the Krueger myth too successfully. Instead, Krueger becomes more of a clown who utters vile jokes before killing off his hapless and helpless victims.

Krueger's depiction is full of iconography. First, his face has been forever scarred by his immolation by the angry parents of his victims. He wears a slouching fedora, like a vision of the famous pulp character, The

An example of Craven's nightmare imagery, simple but effective. Nancy Thompson (Heather Langenkamp) picks up the phone to warn a friend, only to have Freddy's tongue lick her in A Nightmare on Elm Street.

Shadow, gone mad. Typically, he sports a vivid red and grey sweater. His weapon of choice is a glove with a razor-sharp blade attached to the back of each finger. With Englund's performance, Freddy makes an unforgettable impression, and truly his only purpose is to torment and frighten both the audience and his victims. Perhaps most bizarre of all is that this creation is popular enough to have spun off a TV series: *Freddy's Nightmares*. But while audiences delight in his appearances, they still root for the human heroes.

Nightmare was followed by the release of the disastrous *Hills Have Eyes Part 2*, in which Bobby and Ruby, now known as Raquel, return to the desert with a racing team and encounter The Reaper (John Bloom), Papa Jupiter's brother and his gang. In a corny bit of manipulation, Craven has a blind girl save the day (because she can maneuver better in the dark) after the Reaper's gang has been tormenting the protagonists for some time. The film lacks the emphasis on families that the first *Hills* had and is totally bereft of power and effectiveness.

Deadly Friend, based on the book *Friend* and a script by Bruce Joel Rubin (*Ghost; Jacob's Ladder*), proved almost equally inept. At one time Craven had scripted a futuristic version of *Frankenstein* for Roger Corman, and *Deadly Friend* turns into little more than a *Frankenstein* rewrite. This time a brilliant young boy steals the body of a girl neighbor he is in love with and reanimates her by putting a computer chip into her brain. However, she lacks a soul and starts killing and rotting at the same time. A particularly ludicrous sequence has her killing Anne Ramsey by smashing her head with a basketball, the head exploding on impact.

The film does have a brief, effective sequence about the girl's dilemma as the victim of child molestation by her father, whom she simultaneously loves and abhors, but instead of making this thread pay off, Craven simply uses it as motivation for the revived corpse setting her house and father on fire.

Craven came back to form with his adaptation of Wade Davis' non-fiction book *The Serpent and the Rainbow*. While the film does add some trademark Craven dream sequences, it is largely based on ethnobotanist Davis' true-life adventures. Davis was sent to Haiti to discover the secret behind the powder that practitioners of *voudoun* use to turn people into zombies.

What Wade discovered was that the voodoo priests could give their victims a powder that was inhaled or absorbed through the skin, resulting in a kind of coma that closely resembles death. The victims would not respond to any stimulus and would consequently be pronounced dead and buried, all the while being still conscious and able to see and hear. The voodoo priest would then dig up the prospective zombie and through torture break its mind and will, resulting in a mindless, shambling slave that seemingly came back from the grave.

Craven does an excellent job of building up this milieu, as well as capturing the political background of the departure of Baby Doc Duvalier from Haiti. Unfortunately, Bill Pullman (*Spaceballs*) lacks charisma as the Davis-inspired Dennis Alan, never generating an interesting character or personality for him, which leaves the hero something of a cypher. Craven also added a corrupt, zombie-practicing police official as an antagonist as well as an effects-laden, metaphysical climax in which released zombie spirits (kept in jars) get their revenge on the corrupt police captain.

The result is an impressive but uneven horror film with a refreshingly different and authentic take on zombies, a welcome departure from the mindless cannibal movies that had become such a rage in Italy following *Dawn of the Dead*'s release there. In a scene guaranteed to have every male in the audience squirming, a police captain tries to frighten Alan out of the country by impaling his scrotum with an iron spike. There is also an effective dream sequence where Alan meets a bride in a Haitian procession; a zombie corpse is revealed beneath the veil, a snake lunging forward from its open jaws in a truly nightmarish image. Perhaps most impressive is a redo of the burial sequence from Carl Dreyer's *Vampyr* in which the hero is turned into a zombie and gets to watch himself get buried, an eerie and frightening sequence that produces shudders with its authenticity.

The film also benefits from good supporting performances by Cathy Tyson (as Alan's love interest), Paul Winfield (good priest) and especially Zakes Mokae as the unnerving copper whose smile has no humor in it and whose powers are more than they at first seem.

It is the first zombie film that was actually partially shot in Haiti, which created its own kind of problems, including a time when 2,000 extras forced the film crew to flee to the neighboring Dominican Republic. The extras revolted because they were paid $2 for three hours' work. The producers claimed this was twice the going rate in Haiti, but when the extras learned that the production company could have afforded more, they revolted with machetes in hand.

The movie does manage to capture some of the beauty of the country and of the ceremonies performed there. It also demonstrates that these people experience a different sense of ordinary, everyday reality. To them, it is not uncommon or surprising if a person is suddenly possessed by a spirit and does outrageous things, and the film fascinatingly captures this.

Craven worked on a few projects that did not go anywhere. One, called *Haunted*, was a combination of ghost story and love story. He also worked on the original screenplay adaptation of V.C. Andrews' *Flowers in the Attic*, which reached the screen in a much altered version. An idea for a TV series for the Fox network called *Dream Stalker* was shelved.

When Alive Films asked Craven to make a horror film that would "out-Freddy" Freddy, Craven dusted off *Dream Stalker* and came up with *Shocker: No More Mr. Nice Guy*. The villain this time around is Horace Pinker (Mitch Pileggi), a maniac TV repairman who is caught when Jonathan (Peter Berg) starts having visions of a serial killer and leads the police to Pinker. Unfortunately for Jonathan, and a great many other people, when Pinker gets fried in the electric chair, his spirit becomes one with electricity and he is able to invade any electrical system, from television to the body's nervous system, and create absolute havoc.

Craven claims that he was inspired to undertake this project because he

Wes Craven on the set of The Serpent and the Rainbow, *inspired by Wade Davis' book examining the chemical origins of zombism in Haiti. Craven's relaxed attitude belies the anxiety experienced during the film, which included passers-by becoming "possessed" by spirits and a revolt on the part of some angry extras who felt they were being underpaid.*

was looking for something as mysterious and pervasive as dreams, and he thinks he has found it in television, the viewing of which has been described as a dream-like state. Also, television defines reality for many people, most people receiving their news via the medium, but it can itself alter reality, even without a malevolent spirit behind it.

The formulaic and dramatically contorted *Shocker* was not destined to outpace the fantastically successful *Nightmare* series (which Craven created but does not own – New Line Cinema, who stepped in at the last moment to ensure that the film was made, owns the property), but it does show Craven trying new things and has moments of great creativity. Once more there are elaborate dream sequences which are important to the overall mood, even if they are not always important to the plot. However, plans for continuing the Pinker character in other films had to be scuttled when audiences were less than thrilled at the jumble Craven presented.

In general, Craven's films explore the utter helplessness and viciousness of all human beings. Characters beginning on one side of the equation can often end up on the other. His films offer no reassurances except that only the strong and resourceful will survive. Nancy defeated Krueger in the first *Nightmare* film by turning her back on him, denying his power over her, and grounding herself when she touched her bedroom doorknob, with the result that Freddy's energies were channeled elsewhere. Craven's energies, however, remain focused on developing new ways to surprise and shock audiences, creating some of the most visceral and dream-like imagery in the entire horror field. While his ouvre has almost exclusively been in exploitation, his films have been crafted with an intelligence that puts them above the ordinary horror fare. Pushing the boundaries of accepted reality, he explores the uses to which man's violent nature can be put – to harm or to save from harm – and acknowledges that we all have a darker side to our natures.

David Cronenberg (1943-   )

Transfer, From the Drain (shorts, 1966); *Stereo* (1969); *Crimes of the Future* (1970); *They Came from Within* (aka *The Parasite Murders; Shivers*, 1975); *Rabid* (1977); *Fast Company* (1978); *The Brood* (1979); *Scanners* (1981); *Videodrome; The Dead Zone* (1983); *The Fly* (1986); *Dead Ringers* (1988).
TELEVISION: *The Victim; The Lie Chair; The Italian Machine; Friday the 13th.*

David Cronenberg was dubbed by one critic as the "King of Venereal Horror," to which Cronenberg quipped something like, "Well, it's a small field but at least I'm king of it." On another occasion he declared, "I don't think there are any princes or knaves in that category, and I'm still looking for the queen." Typically, his films have been meditations on the horrors of aging or disease, cast as some kind of outlandish, usually science fictional peril that is threatening a small segment of mankind with the potential to spread unchecked.

Part of this obsession may have derived from the prolonged illnesses and deaths of Cronenberg's parents, which he remembers as being quite ghastly. One thing is certain: Cronenberg has few rivals when it comes to manufacturing genuinely disturbing horror films which deal with adult terrors and themes, as opposed to the childlike boogey men of other horror filmmakers.

Cronenberg was born in Toronto, Canada, on March 15, 1943, coming from a creative family where his mother was a pianist and his father a newspaperman. While a child, Cronenberg was drawn to the writing of Vladimir Nabokov, and as a result become a lepidopterist. His fascination with butterflies and other bugs led him to a fascination with the beauty of the unusual. He began to take a detached and scientific viewpoint to creatures in their habitat, something which has carried over into his films with regard to human beings.

Nonetheless, he had difficulty relating to other people in the sciences when he enrolled as a biochemistry student at the University of Toronto, so he dropped from that program to join an honors program in English after winning a short story contest put on by the English department. He graduated in 1967 with a degree in English, but before doing so he became interested in film production while watching some students setting up a project. Cronenberg decided to learn what he could by reading *American Cinematographer* and soon embarked on making his own short (the university did not offer any film courses). That short, a seven-minute 16mm color film known as *Transfer*, was about a psychiatric patient, desperate for any human contact, who follows his psychiatrist on a trip to the country. Cronenberg served as director, cameraman, sound man, and editor as well as writer on the film.

The same year he made another film, *From the Drain*, which was twice as long and more ambitious. In this one, a secret agent and a chemical and biological warfare scientist meet fully clothed in a tub and are strangled by stop-motion animated mutant slime that crawls up from the drain. Both films were donated to the University of Toronto's library.

In 1969 for a mere $3500, Cronenberg made his first 35mm feature, *Stereo*. It received a limited engagement in the United States in 1984, where it was played with *Crimes of the Future* and a 1976 short, *The Italian Machine*. The film was shot in black and white and without synchronized sound, making it seem very much like a student project. *Stereo*'s inspirations appear to be Chris Marker's *La Jetée*, the tale of a time traveler spoken over a series of still photographs, and George Lucas' student version of *THX 1138*. It features a narrator who drones on about the effects of an operation on eight individuals at the Canadian Academy for Erotic Inquiry who have been given enhanced powers of mental telepathy. While normal people receive information only "monoaurally," that is, through the single channels of sight and sound, these individuals can now receive in stereo information direct from other people's minds.

The final film runs 63 minutes and frankly is more than a trifle dull, with primitive techniques. It did show, however, that Cronenberg was developing a visual eye, and it involved ESP, which would be a major factor in his later effort *Scanners*. The film brought in $10,000 when it was bought by International Film Archives of New York, so financially it could be considered a modest success.

Cronenberg immediately started on a second film, *Crimes of the Future*, this time in 16mm and with a $20,000 budget. The film is an improvement on *Stereo* and shows many of Cronenberg's later obsessions in an early, undeveloped form. Cronenberg appears influenced by the New York underground film movement with his static camera setups, and once more there is a lack of sync sound.

Adrian Tripod (Ronald Mlodzik) searches for five-year-old Tania Zolty, who has been kidnapped by some pedophiles intent on impregnating her. The time is the future and all women of childbearing age have been wiped out by some contagion in their cosmetics. The disease, Rouge's Malady, causes them to ooze what is known as Rouge's Foam. Initially, this foam

excites males, causing them to lap it up, but finally it has left most men victims of sterile sexual obsessions such as foot and lingerie fetishes, the
"crimes" of the title.

Tripod goes from the House of Skin, where research is proceeding on
the disease, to the Institute of Neo-Venereal Disease, searching for answers.
He is a rather dull and uninvolving fellow, traveling across a future waste-
land of tall, largely empty and sterile buildings, the final legacy of mankind.
Cronenberg showed himself willing to experiment and played around with
feelings of revulsion, typically a strong element in his later horror films, but
the result was still not commercial.

Seeking to become involved in commercial filmmaking, Cronenberg approached Cinepix, a small distributor of soft-core pornography that was one
of the most successful film companies in Canada at the time. Screening
Stereo and *Crimes of the Future* for them, Cronenberg, to his surprise and
pleasure, garnered a favorable response, though Cinepix may have been
more impressed by how cheaply Cronenberg was able to realize his films
than by their actual quality. Cinepix was looking for new directors, and
those whose works were inexpensive were given a chance.

Cronenberg came up with a script he called *Orgy of the Blood Parasites*,
which Cinepix shopped around to other directors while Cronenberg hoped
for the chance to direct it himself. Finally, they decided to allow him to do
so. The resulting film was released as *The Parasite Murders* until Cinepix
realized that it was doing better under its French title, *Frissons*, so the
Canadian title was changed to *Shivers*. Finally, when it was picked up by
Trans-America for American release, the title was changed once more to
They Came from Within.

They Came from Within clearly establishes Cronenberg's theme of
bodies in revolt. Dr. Emil Hobbes (Fred Doederlein), probably named after
philosopher Thomas Hobbes, who argued for the primacy of the physical
nature of man in the universe, has created a parasite that he hopes will help
man reestablish contact with his physical nature and desires, and has implanted it in his teenage mistress (Cathy Graham). Unfortunately, possibly
because of the parasite, the mistress fools around and the parasite begins
to spread throughout the isolated community of Starliner Towers, a sterile
apartment complex "of the future."

In some ways, Cronenberg's film seems to be condemning a form of
hedonism. The film opens with a promotional film-within-a-film about the
advantages to living away from the hectic world outside and the joys of
residing in Starliner's apartments. The entire residence is a self-contained
environment designed to satisfy the appetites and needs of the residents.
Hobbes' parasites have needs too, and theirs are hinted at by a sign in
Hobbes' office: "Sex is the invention of a clever venereal disease."

What makes Cronenberg's film particularly disgusting, apart from the pulsing, fecal appearance of his phallic parasite (created by makeup man Joe Blasco), is how he manages to equate sexual lust and activity with disgust. The parasite causes anyone it affects to become intensely lustful, and the sight of senior citizens and little children in the throes of uncontrolled lust is profoundly disturbing because they are not usually figures associated with intense sexual activity.

The parasites are transmitted via sex or are simply coughed up, in which case they burrow their way into new victims. Some of the sequences cleverly manage to combine humor and horror, such as a man coughing up a parasite which lands with a splat on an old lady's transparent umbrella, or the famous scene where Betts (Barbara Steele) has a parasite crawl up her vagina while bathing in a tub and her lesbian tendencies take control.

In most science fictional invasions that have been filmed, the invaders want to kill mankind, but in *They Came from Within*, the parasites need humans to survive and want them to multiply. Soon everyone but the hero, Dr. Roger St. Luc (woodenly played by Paul Hampton), seems to have succumbed and is pursuing each other. St. Luc by contrast seems positively sexless and uninterested. For instance, when his nurse does an unexpected striptease in his office, he ignores her. His extreme lack of interest seems unnatural, though that is what allows him to survive for as long as he does.

They Came from Within suffers from some substandard photography and sound recording, and Cronenberg makes all his points in the first half of the picture, making the latter half little more than a series of scenes of people being infected or futilely running away from infection. He stops introducing new ideas, which bogs down the film. Nonetheless, the creation of the parasites and their ability to move under the skin of the host, chillingly realized with air bladders, is quite effective and imaginative for a low-budget film. (Dick Smith, duplicating these type of effects in *Altered States*, helped further the use of bladder effects until they have almost become a horror film staple for all transformation scenes.)

While Cronenberg was trying to get financing for *The Parasite Murders*, he wrote a similar script which became his next film for Cinepix, *Rabid*. In the meantime, Cronenberg threw in with *Shivers'* producer, Ivan Reitman (later to become the director of *Ghostbusters* and previously the director of *The Cannibal Girls*), who had Cronenberg help script a Doug Henning stage show called "Spellbound," a magic act with the novelty of characters and a plot.

Made for a mere $530,000, *Rabid* went on to gross more than $7 million at the box office, being distributed in the United States by New World Pictures. Once more a scientific experiment, meant to help mankind, goes awry. Unfortunately, the explanation for what happens in *Rabid* was partially cut and remains a bit obscure. A surgeon has created a tissue without specific characteristics which he hopes can be grafted into an area, read the genetic code of the surrounding cells, and turn itself into similar tissue, thereby replacing lost tissue. When a motorcyclist (played by Marilyn Chambers in her first non-porn role since the Ivory Snow Girl), has an accident and needs more intestinal tissue, the doctor operates, but the tissue does something unexpected—it turns Chambers into a kind of scientific vampire who drains her victims with a tiny, needle-like plunger that has mysteriously grown in her armpit.

Chambers means to be considerate. Normal food repulses and nauseates her, so she is driven to take a little blood. She tries to take cow's blood at one point, but that does not work. However, unbeknownst to her, her victims develop a mutated form of rabies and begin attacking other people, causing the disease to spread with great rapidity. Her blood sampling makes her a Typhoid Mary, spreading sickness and disarray wherever she goes.

Cronenberg had originally wanted to cast Sissy Spacek in the lead role after seeing her in *Badlands*, but his producer objected, saying that she had too many freckles. Shortly afterwards, she was on the cover of *Time* for her appearance in a horror film, *Carrie*, for which she received an Academy Award nomiantion. Chambers does a fair job playing the role; *Rabid*'s main drawback is that we never really get to know the Chambers character (or her boyfriend, who spends much of the picture tracking her down before the fateful motorcycle accident that sets all the events in motion).

Nevertheless, the film is energetic and contains such disturbing scenes as an infected surgeon amputating a nurse's finger in the middle of an operation so that he can suck up her blood. (Operations are associated with a feeling of helplessness which makes the feeling of horror all the more acute.) However, *Rabid* is essentially a retelling of *They Came from Within* over a less confined space. It shows Cronenberg improving in his filmmaking techniques, but the special makeup effects are not quite as elaborate and are mostly shot in close-up.

Some critics objected to the fact that Rose, the Chambers character, would attract her victims with a sexual come-on, portraying women as predators, luring and attacking unwary males. Such protests are silly, as it makes sense that Rose would make use of any means at her disposal to quench her uncontrollable appetite, and in some scenes, such as when she is picked up by a truck driver, it is obvious that the male of the species is already attracted to her. Films do reflect the sexual mores of society, but sometimes the search for subtexts in any particular film can be carried to ludicrous extremes.

Cronenberg had a change of pace, directing *Fast Company*, his only non–science fiction or -horror film, in 1977. The film starred William Smith as a drag racer who comes into conflict with John Saxon as an oil company baron. It took a while to find a release in the United States market. He followed this up with three films for television: *The Victim*, about an obscene phone caller; *The Lie Chair*, about two old ladies who become possessed by the spirit of their son; and *The Italian Machine*, about some motorcycle freaks who become obsessed by an expensive machine.

In his personal life, Cronenberg was going through turmoil as his wife decided to divorce him and fight for custody of their daughter. His feelings of helplessness and rage over these emotionally charged events were channeled into his screenplay for *The Brood*, a film that showed greater maturity and humanity than Cronenberg's previous films.

Cronenberg took his personal script to Pierre David and Victor Solnicki, whose Filmplan, in association with Mutual Films and the Canadian Film Development Corporation, put up $1.5 million to get the film made. For the first time, Cronenberg was able to afford such professional name actors as Samantha Eggar and Oliver Reed.

Dr. Hal Raglan (Oliver Reed) is pursuing a new line of therapy at his Somafree Institute of Psychoplasmatics. He insults a patient and then asks him to show what he is doing. The patients takes his shirt off and shows that he is manifesting his rage as spots on his body.

Frank Carveth (Art Hindle) takes his daughter Candice (Cindy Hinds) home from the Institute, where she has been visiting her mother and his estranged wife, Nola (Samantha Eggar). When he sees bruises on her body while bathing her, he assumes she is being abused by her mother. He goes to Raglan and demands to see his wife, but Raglan does not permit him to. Frank then accuses Raglan of being an "emotional opportunist."

Frank decides to drop Candice off at her grandmother's (Nuala Fitzgerald) while he sees what he can do about the situation legally. Unfortunately, Grandma is a borderline alcoholic. We hear Nola, in a session with Raglan, accusing her mother of being fucked up while Raglan responds, "Show me. Go all the way through it . . . to the end." Grandma's side of the story is that when she was young, Nola would wake up with big, ugly bumps, indicating that she had a previous susceptibility to this syndrome before undergoing psychoplasmatics.

Downstairs at Grandma's, there is a crash as something breaks the dumbwaiter. When Grandma goes downstairs, she is attacked by a dwarfish figure in a red raincoat (like the killer in Nicolas Roeg's *Don't Look Now*) and is beaten to death with a meat tenderizer. Candice walks in to find her grandmother dead and briefly sees the mysterious figure.

Obviously such a scene would have a traumatizing effect on a little girl. The police call Frank, and the police psychiatrist explains that Candice seems to be taking this too coolly and has forgotten what happened. For her to be well, she must remember and deal with what has occurred.

Partly, Cronenberg's film is about dealing with and confronting one's own rage and frustration. Nola is led into disaster when she is encouraged to manifest her rage without coming to terms with it, creating "children of rage" or the brood of the title, which are emotionally linked to her. When she becomes angry, they attack and kill the targets of her anger.

As Gary Svehla points out in his assessment of Cronenberg's films in *Midnight Marquee #32*, the film also deals with the paradoxes and difficulties inherent in many of today's disintegrating relationships. Throughout the film, Cronenberg takes great care to show that the individuals in the film *are* caring and concerned for each other. Juliana, Nola's mother, loves both her daughter and granddaughter, though there are plenty of hints that she abused one and neglects the other. Frank and Nola love each other despite their divorce. The insidious but well-meaning Raglan drives himself between them like a wedge because he, too, loves Nola, though it is not certain whether his love is perhaps partially inspired by her superior abilities in the realm of psychoplasmics. There is also a concerned schoolteacher who becomes a victim when Nola calls and mistakes her for Frank's mistress.

These people's love is not powerful enough to overcome their foibles and emotional frailties. By concentrating on her rage, Nola only increases and unleashes it, with disastrous results for everyone concerned. When her father comes to try and inform Nola of Juliana's death, Raglan prevents him from contacting her, and in his despondency he goes over to Juliana's house to recall the good aspects of their relationship (the good times they had together), only to be done in by the manifestations of Nola's rage.

Frank himself feels that Nola married him for his sanity, hoping it would rub off. Instead, it seems to be working the other way, her insanity rubbing off on him. In Cronenberg's dark and depressing view of the world, hatred and madness are driving out love and goodness, until at the end of the film, Frank is forced to strangle his wife (in a scene that Cronenberg called personally satisfying) in order to save his daughter. It is then revealed that Candice's experiences have infected her as well. Her arm has the telltale bumps, indicating that she too is a potential time bomb.

There is also a sidelight on ex-patients of Dr. Raglan who are suing him over psychoplasmics because the effects have caused their bodies to revolt, and they fear they are losing the revolution. Danny Peary noted this aspect of all of Cronenberg's Canadian-made horror films in his book *Cult Movies*, saying that these films are

> about our bodies in revolt; our bodies becoming our enemies by creating and, sometimes, transmitting "monsters" that literally destroy our flesh and our sanity. It is probably a morbid fascination for disease, as well as an awareness that nothing scares us more than sudden changes

in our physical composition, that makes Cronenberg fill his pictures with so many unpleasant images of bodies in open rebellion: open sores, lesions, bumps and bruises, malformations, abnormal growths, and quickly spreading infections that are embodied by living parasites working their way into our systems and moving about under the skin.

Deeply imbedded in Cronenberg's films are deep-seated fears of aging, death, and a disintegration of the relationships that are most important to us. But while most films on relationships are highly praised, this aspect of Cronenberg's films is typically overlooked and dismissed because they are horror films. Critics should realize that Cronenberg is using the horror genre to say things about the horror of personal rage and frustration in modern relationships in a cinematically innovative way.

Scanners, Cronenberg's biggest success, is also at its heart about a family in conflict. The hero, Vale (played with a lack of emotion by Stephen Lack), discovers that his father, Dr. Ruth (intelligently played by Patrick McGoohan), promoted the drug Empherol for pregnant women because fetuses would develop supertelepathic powers which Dr. Ruth hoped would be marshaled into a dominating force. His own sons, Vale and Revok (Michael Ironside), were to be the first of these *homo superiors*, but Revok revolted, forming his own group of militant Scanners (as the supertelepaths are called) who are intent on world domination. Vale, on the other hand, was left to become a derelict, unable to deal with all the voices in his head, until Dr. Ruth finally decides he needs him and trains him how to use his power in an effort to offset Revok's efforts.

The background information is rather confusingly presented, perhaps as a result of Cronenberg having to script much of the final product while filming was in progress. What makes the film click is the combination of spy-story action (the government agency Consec and Revok's rebels are intent on blowing each other away and disposing of any potential Scanners who might interfere) and science fiction psi elements, represented by the Scanners' various psychic powers.

The title *Scanners* was derived from Philip K. Dick's book *A Scanner Darkly*, which is more about a drug addict with a dual personality than telepaths, though it in turn derived from Cordwainer Smith's classic science fiction story "Scanners Live in Vain." Cronenberg also borrows the idea of a *homo gestalt*, that is, a group of telepaths who join their minds together to form a group which is greater than the sum of its parts, from Theodore Sturgeon's classic sf novel *More Than Human*.

Cronenberg gets the film off to a powerful start with an intense scene early on in which a scanner in a lecture unexpectedly comes across another scanner who proves so powerful that the first scanner's head literally explodes. The sight of this exploding head keeps the audience on edge for the rest of the film as the Scanners' abilities are graphically displayed. A budget of $4.5 million helped *Scanners* to look far more professional than Cronenberg's previous productions and allowed for the hiring of makeup ace Dick Smith to redo the film's climax in which Vale and Revok have a brain battle. Their veins bulge and pop, Vale's eyes blow out, and his body is eventually consumed by flame. However, in the final twist, we discover that he abandoned his own body to take over Revok's.

The film is filled with many memorable moments in between the confusion, though one may object to the disregard for logic and science in several scenes. For example, we see Empherol being transported from a factory in liquid tank trucks. Did expectant mothers drink it or bathe in it? Additionally, there is a ludicrous scene in which Vale links his nervous system to that of the Consec computer over a pay telephone connection which ends in the computer self-destructing (in an attempt to kill Vale by one of Revok's henchmen) and the telephone receiver melting. *Scanners* works well as a horror film, but it falls short as science fiction, which requires adherence to known physical laws unless a plausible explanation can be offered. Generally, science fiction requires more believability than this exciting but absurd tale of two evil agencies manipulating and killing innocent people between them in their paths to power.

Still, the film's success won Cronenberg an offer of *carte blanche* from a major studio, and the result was *Videodrome*, a far less commercial and more bizarrely personal film for the director, who explores the effect of media on human minds and expects his audience to have a familiarity with Marshall McLuhan and his theories (which he heavyhandedly parodies with the character of Brian O'Blivion). Additionally, Cronenberg blended fantasy and reality, making it hard to tell where one began and the other left off, always a bane to those who prefer that their movies depict all events as straightforwardly as possible.

Videodrome centers around cable station owner Max Renn (James Woods in a typically arresting and intense performance), who is looking for something new, something tough to put on his station, which typically shows hard-core violence and soft-core pornography. A video pirate at the station, Harlan (Peter Dvorsky), has picked up a program called "Videodrome," a torture show which he claims comes from Malaysia. It shows nothing more than men and women in front of a blood-red wall being tortured by people in hoods. Renn is fascinated, finding the show both attractive and repulsive, and he cannot take his eyes away from it. He immediately decides to track down the source of "videodrome" so he can show it on his station.

First he goes on the air on a talk show with pop radio psychologist Nicki Brand (Deborah Harry of the rock group Blondie) and Prof. Brian O'Blivion, whose video image appears on the program because he feels that since the medium is the message, the only way to appear on TV is appear on a TV screen, emphasizing that physical reality is not as important as broadcast reality.

The talk show host, Rena King (Lally Cadeau), feels that the sex and violence that Renn is broadcasting contribute to a climate of social malaise, but Renn explains they are just fantasy. Brand warns of the dangers of overstimulation, and Renn notes that her red dress is very stimulating. She smiles and admits that she too craves overstimulation even though she knows it is bad for her.

Afterwards Renn and Brand make a date, which ends up with her going back to his apartment. There he shows her "Videodrome," and she asks him to cut her shoulder with a pocket knife and burn her with a cigarette. Cronenberg is dealing with societal sickness on a direct level which is bound to make the average person uncomfortable. Renn and Brand are not interested in love; they seek only pleasure, and having become bored with the standard means of achieving it are seeking wilder and wilder means of satisfaction. Brand, upon seeing the torture of "Videodrome," loses herself in a masochistic fantasy, declaring that she was made to be on that program.

One of Cronenberg's theses in the film is that television is a drug. For Renn, "Videodrome" is habit forming. It is slowly altering his perception of reality. As a parallel, think of the fear generated by the six o'clock news that makes some people afraid to leave their houses. Cronenberg proposes that television can alter reality, perceptions, tastes, inclinations, and finally even affect the physical makeup of man himself.

On a lead to locate "Videodrome," Renn visits the Cathode Ray Mission, run by Prof. O'Blivion's daughter Bianca (Sonja Smits). Here, in a memorably surreal sequence, derelicts are exposed to television in an effort to prepare them to deal with and reenter society. Here, also, Renn becomes exposed to O'Blivion's philosophy that "the battle of the minds of North America will take place in the video arena" and "the video screen is the retina of the mind's eye." In other words, the hearts and minds of Americans are swayed most by what they see on television, and you are what you see.

Bianca reveals that O'Blivion has been dead for over a year, but can still make talk show appearances thanks to a large selection of videotapes that he prepared with generalized responses and bits of his philosophy. Thus, despite his death, he lives on in video, spreading his ideas and visions to the masses.

As Renn increasingly loses his grip on reality, Cronenberg reveals a sinister subtext. "Videodrome" does not come from Malaysia; it is being broadcast from Pittsburgh. Brand appears on the program and is killed, but her image continues to haunt Renn as his television set seems to become a living thing and her lips bulge from the screen to envelop Renn's head in a giant kiss.

Digging deeper, Renn finally discovers that "Videodrome" induces a lethal brain tumor in those who watch it. The Spectacular Optical Company, headed by Barry Convex (Les Carlson), makes "Videodrome" and wants Renn to distribute it. Convex hopes that the program will attract the sick elements of society, and the world will finally be purged of said elements because of the program's hidden and lethal nature. Additionally, in breaking down his mental defenses, "Videodrome" has caused Renn to develop a vaginal slit in his stomach in which is inserted a "living" videocassette which "programs" him to kill his "Videodrome"-resistant partners.

He is then sent to kill Bianca, whose father was also involved in the plot until "Videodrome" killed him. Bianca stops him and reprograms him, telling him, "You are the video word made flesh . . . death to Videodrome. Long live the new flesh!" Renn has evolved into a new kind of being, half-man, half-machine. Reaching into his stomach slit, his hand recovers a gun he placed there, and the gun sends out steel cables which burrow and attach themselves to his flesh. It also changes Harlan's hand into a hand grenade which explodes, killing Harlan. Renn tracks down Convex at an optical convention and shoots him. Great globs of cancer erupt from Convex's features and he dies a grisly death.

Videodrome is brimming with ideas, many of them crying out for explication which they never receive, and a convoluted plot which alienates most viewers. As a director, Cronenberg remains true to his obsessions rather than simply pursuing material that would be more conventional and commercial. In addition to the ofttimes interesting speculation on the nature of man and how video has affected him, the film features a strong performance from James Woods as the sleazy Renn (no easy audience identification here) and plenty of imaginatively conceived surrealistic imagery that is partly Renn's hallucinations as a result of being exposed to the ultrarealistic "Videodrome" (which Renn discovers does not fake its violence but is actually a video snuff program). We are shown video "snow" stretching from a television set in the image of Renn's handgun or an exploding, living TV set complete with human entrails (or as *Fangoria* put it, "At last, TV with guts!"). The imaginative makeup work was done by EFX, headed by Rick Baker, and many of the video effects were achieved by Michael Lennick. This is part of what makes Cronenberg's work so interesting: He goes beyond the conventional to create these hallucinatory images. Also, he is one of the few directors working in horror who actually manages to create stories which are genuinely disturbing, not simply disgusting or gory – stories with concepts behind them that simultaneously disturb and fascinate the viewer.

David Cronenberg tries on the "flesh gun" created by Rick Baker for Videodrome.

Naturally, this approach did not attract large audiences to *Videodrome*, and the film died a quick death at box office. As Gary Svehla observed in *Midnight Marquee*, gore fans "would rather see simplistic slasher movies than be induced to think about their gore," and others were so repulsed by the unwholesome characters and concepts that they could not even consider meeting the film halfway. Cronenberg needed a commercial hit to raise his stock with film companies, who considered his work too weird.

He found it in Stephen King's novel *The Dead Zone*. With a screenplay by Jeffrey Boam, Cronenberg fashioned one of the best screen adaptations of King's work. The novel, which is more science fiction than horror, poses

Horror Film Directors   280

the interesting question, what if a man who could see into the future discovered that a certain presidential candidate, if elected, will set off the missiles that will cause World War III out of an insane desire for glory? In the novel, King developed both the hero, Johnny Smith (played in the film by Christopher Walken), and his situation with great, page-turning effectiveness.

While *The Dead Zone* is less personal than other Cronenberg films, it is his most generally accessible work and features fine performances from the entire cast. Smith is a schoolteacher who sinks into a coma after an auto accident and wakes up five years later to find his fiancée married to another man, and himself possessed of the questionable gift of seeing into people's futures just by touching them.

This "gift" proves to be both a blessing and a curse, making him seem a freak. He opts to hide himself from the public eye, though in an important subplot, he must come to terms with the moral imperatives inherent in his gift when he helps Sheriff Bannerman (Tom Skerritt) track down a psychopath who has been killing young girls in a neighboring town. (This sequence leads to the most disturbing bit in the film, which truly seems a Cronenberg touch: the killer's suicide by driving his open mouth onto a pair of scissors as the police finally close in).

The "dead zone" of the title refers to the uncertain element in the futures that Smith sees. Smith finds that his predictions and visions are accurate, but there is a "dead zone" surrounding an aspect of the situation which could cause the future to change. The events are not inevitable. Cronenberg elects not to visually depict this dead zone.

Smith realizes that presidential candidate Greg Stillson (an appropriately smarmy performance by Martin Sheen) is power-mad and his election would lead to more deaths than those caused by Hitler, Stalin, or Mao. After discussing philosophy with his therapist, Dr. Sam Weizak (Herbert Lom), Smith resolves to assassinate Stillson before he can become elected. The attempt fails and Smith is fatally wounded, but Stillson ruins his chances when he grabs Smith's ex-girlfriend's baby to shield himself from the bullets and his photo is snapped and put on the cover of *Time* magazine. Thus the movie escapes condoning assassination and vigilantism, even under these specialized circumstances.

Cronenberg then worked for a time on *Total Recall*, a script by Dan O'Bannon and Ron Schusett based on Philip K. Dick's classic sf story "We Can Remember It for You Wholesale." In the story, memories of nonexistent adventures and vacations can be implanted in people too poor to have the real thing; however, things go awry when a man wants a spy memory and it is discovered that he actually is a spy whose memories of his experience have been erased. Despite reports that the original script was very exciting, Cronenberg was unable to come up with a rewrite that would satisfy producer Dino de Laurentiis, and the project eventually fell to *Robo-cop* director Paul Verhoeven.

At one point there was talk of Cronenberg doing his own version of the Frankenstein legend, but that never materialized. Along the way, people impressed with his handling of actors on *The Dead Zone* offered him such films as *Witness, Beverly Hills Cop, After Hours* and *Flashdance*. Cronenberg did get some exposure by playing a bit part in John Landis' *Into the Night*, which featured many film directors in supporting roles, and later starred in Clive Barker's *Nightbreed*, proving he should stick to directing.

After reading Charles Pogue's script for a remake of *The Fly*, Cronenberg found his new project. He rewrote Pogue's script without credit, changing much of the dialogue and characters to suit him while retaining the same basic situation. Based on Kurt Newmann's overrated '50s "classic," the new *Fly* is that ultra-rarity among remakes: a remake that surpassses the original film and is even original in its own way to boot. Unquestionably, Cronenberg added his personal touches to the film and made it his own.

The basic idea of a scientist who builds a matter transmitter and tries it out on himself only to have his DNA mixed with a fly's is retained from the original film. In Pogue's script, however, the scientist, Seth Brundle (Jeff Goldblum in an excellent and lively performance), slowly changes into a half-man, half-fly – unlike Al "David" Heddison who, in the original, gained a fly's head and arm and slowly lost his human consciousness. Neither film scores high for scientific accuracy, but Cronenberg sees his film as horror, not science fiction.

Brundle meets Veronica Quaife (played with intelligence by Geena Davis) at a Bartok Corporation party and promises to show her something really exciting back at his warehouse lab, not realizing that she is a journalist for *Particle* magazine. From Goldblum's performance, it is readily and amusingly apparent that Brundle does not leave his lab an awful lot, and he is awkward in social situations, though animated by his excitement at his project and his need to tell someone.

Brundle has built a matter transporter, and he demonstrates to a dubious Veronica its ability to transport inanimate objects from one chamber to another. She is impressed, but he is horrified to learn that she is a reporter and begs her to postpone doing a story on his work until he is further along.

A relationship develops between Brundle and Quaife. In addition, Cronenberg also brings in the strained relationship between Veronica and Stathis Borans (John Getz), her ex-lover and editor of *Particle* magazine. Getz gives an off-kilter performance that suggests he has not emotionally recovered from their breakup and is most desirious of getting back together with Quaife. Cronenberg decided that there should be no "bad guy" in

David Cronenberg directs Jeff Goldblum and his wife Geena Davis in a scene from The Fly. Goldblum's performance was so good that many Hollywood insiders felt he might receive an Academy Award nomination, but it was not to be.

conventional terms in the script, but this estranged relationship, typical of many Cronenberg films, does not have the dramatic payoffs that the ones in *The Brood* do.

During a period of emotional distress, Brundle decides to complete his experiment by transporting himself, but fails to notice that he is sharing the compartment with a fly. He appears to be all right when he emerges at the other end, and in fact, he believes that the trip has done him some good. (Once more there is some talk about the "new flesh," that is reintegrated by the matter transmission procedure.) Initially, Brundle discovers that he can perform acrobatics and make love for hours. He has gained new strength – so much that in one of the film's more disturbing scenes, he arm-wrestles someone and causes a compound fracture.

After this initial period of euphoria, disaster sets in. Brundle keeps changing and becomes more and more like a fly, losing body parts along the way. Another disturbing scene has Brundle losing his ear when he hugs Veronica, who has come by to check up on him. He even exhibits "Brundle's Museum of Natural History," a medicine cabinet in which he stores the body parts that he has lost (including what appears to be one of his testicles).

What takes the edge off the ludicrousness and grossness of the situation is that Brundle never loses his humanity completely nor his sense of humor about the strange and awful thing that is happening to him. He seems almost fascinated and delighted to demonstrate that he now eats like a fly by throwing up acid on his food to pre-digest it. Chris Walas' makeup is also remarkable for the amount of human expression it allows Goldblum, whose nervous mannerisms are perfect for the part.

Cronenberg gets some additional *frisson* from Quaife's fears because she is pregnant with Brundle's baby. In a memorable dream sequence, her gynecologist (a cameo by Cronenberg, who stepped in when producer Stuart Cornfeld got cold feet) delivers a maggot baby. This convinces her to get an abortion, tying in to women's fears about their unborn babies.

Actually, the main fear that Cronenberg is tying into once more is the betrayal of the body. *The Fly* can be seen as an elaborate metaphor for what happens when we age. In an interview with Ron Stringer, Cronenberg stated:

> [I]n a sense, what Seth Brundle is doing is dying. He's getting old and ugly, and I'm saying, "I feel about this the way you, the audience, do." I mean, we're *all* doomed to become monsters if we live long enough. We become diseased or senile. We lose our teeth, develop strange patches on our skin, do weird things – that's what *happens* when you live a long time. Everybody wants to live a long time but they also have to face what it really means.

Significantly, Brundle never gives up on his idea of matter transmission. Just because he was messed up, he does not blame the equipment. At the end there is an elaborate abduction of Veronica and attempted rescue by Borans, who is attacked by the "Brundlefly" monster and loses the use of a pair of limbs. In the final climax, one more transmission is made in which part of the machinery itself becomes part of Brundle, but the result cannot possibly live and does not, inadvertently taking Brundle's secrets with him. (Cronenberg found the original scene where the scientist destroys his own machine very unrealistic even for the '50s, arguing that the man who invented the car would not destroy his invention just because there was an accident or a car crash.)

Though it was expected to do well, *The Fly* became an unexpectedly big hit for 20th Century–Fox and managed to capture mainstream audiences while at the same time offering scenes that made even veteran horror fans cringe. The film spawned a Cronenberg-less sequel, helmed by Chris Walas, which demonstrated why effects are dependent on a good story by not having one. In it, Quaife's fast-growing prodigy follows in his father's footsteps after being manipulated by an unscrupulous corporation.

Perhaps the most astute comment about Cronenberg's films came from Marc Boyman, who stated, "David is continually fascinated . . . with the question of how long can you love someone who is changing." The crux of *The Fly* is the love relationship between Seth and Veronica and how Veronica's love turns to loathing as Seth continues to alter and disintegrate. A love relationship with a changing person is also the focus of Cronenberg's next, surprisingly subdued film, *Dead Ringers*.

Jeremy Irons does a fabulous job playing identical twin gynecologists with opposite personalities, a performance for which he won a "Genie," the Canadian equivalent to the Academy Award. The film is based on the book *Twins* by Bari Wood and Jack Geasland, which in turn was based on a real-life murder-suicide of a pair of twin doctors who died in 1975. (Cronenberg planned to call his film *Twins*, but Ivan Reitman registered the title first for a comedy with Arnold Schwarzenegger and Danny DeVito.)

As a horror film, *Dead Ringers* does not equal, for example, Brian De Palma's *Sisters* (one of De Palma's best, it must be admitted); but as a psychological study and as a Cronenberg film, it is fascinating. The idea of revulsion towards sex is established at the beginning as the nine-year-old Mantle twins, Beverly and Elliot (Jonathan Haley and Nicholas Haley), discuss the physical superiority of fish who do not have to have physical contact during sex. The bolder of the pair, Elliot, then proposes that he have sex with a young girl, who immediately turns him down.

The brothers grow up (into Jeremy Irons) and become respected gynecologists, promoting radical new techniques, applying for research grants, and running a chic clinic for a wealthy clientele of women who wish to have babies but cannot conceive. Cronenberg quickly establishes that Beverly is the harder working and more sensitive of the two, while Elliot is good at public relations—picking up awards and grants based on Beverly's research and picking up women who have been softened and made comfortable by Beverly's reticent but concerned attentions. Beverly is not too concerned about Elliott being a Lothario, and Elliot in turn allows Beverly to take to bed his discarded bedmates. Their relationship is established as being somewhat symbiotic in a decidedly odd fashion, and the brothers occasionally enjoy pretending to be each other, each possessing the qualities that his twin has but he lacks.

However, the balance of this relationship is disrupted when Beverly falls in love with Claire Niveau (Genevieve Bujold), a screen actress who desperately wants to have children but is unable to conceive because she is a medical freak—she has a "trifurcate uterus." Claire eventually catches on to the deception that the brothers have been practicing and leaves Beverly heartbroken, which creates something of a rift between the otherwise inseparable pair.

Claire and Beverly get together, but then Claire must take a part in a film that separates them, and Beverly turns to drugs. There is a slight suggestion of a "Corsican Brothers" relationship between the twins as Elliot empathetically starts feeling the ravages of his brother's drug addiction and becomes an addict himself. Elliott, seemingly the more confident of the two, finds he emotionally cannot do without his brother.

When Beverly in a psychotic rage instructs an avant-garde artist to make gynecological instruments for mutant women (a series of fearsome devices made in surgical steel designed to play on women's gynecological fears) and then tries to use these devices on a normal woman during an operation in which he goes beserk, his career is ruined. Because the pair have always been associated in the public mind, Elliot finds his career ruined along with his brother's.

Without each other as emotional anchors, they both become pathetic junkies, and the film finally comes to a conclusion when a spaced-out Beverly decides to operate on a heavily sedated Elliot to separate them once and for all, using his specially designed gynecological instruments on his brother and tearing open his chest. As a reflection of madness, it is not nearly as subtle as Polanski's *Repulsion* or *The Tenant*, but it is also far from the standard Hollywood film, horror or otherwise. Unfortunately, despite its weirdness and excellent central performance, it is not as interesting or inventive as *Videodrome* or Cronenberg's earlier films.

Stephen Lack from *Scanners* appears in a brief part as Anders Wolleck, but Bujold and Irons entirely dominate the proceedings. There is an amusing moment when Beverly calls Claire on location and suspecting that her gay assistant is really a lover, proceeds to gross the assistant out with a description of Claire's interior. Cronenberg collaborated on the script with Norman Snider, and it maintains an intelligent if uninvolving level. Peter Suschitzky, who worked on *The Rocky Horror Picture Show* and *The Empire Strikes Back*, does a fine job filming the movie, with no seams showing on the split-screen work. His shot of Dr. Mantel donning a red set of surgical garb as if he were about to sacrifice rather than operate on a patient is particularly striking. It makes for an image that is simple but unsettling, a description that is apt for the film as a whole.

Without a doubt, Cronenberg has some better work ahead of him, but it is interesting to note how he has managed to keep his cinematic obsessions intact while at the same time making the transition into more mainstream films. Cronenberg does have an artistic vision, and his films play on genuine fears far more effectively than any "maniac-on-the-loose" or slasher film, simply because he is dealing with a level on which we feel most vulnerable – that of our bodies betraying us (becoming diseased or dying) or our lovers altering their personalities into something hideous (such as the creator of *The Brood*). Finally, he reminds us that sex is not always viewed with joy and wonder, but sometimes with disgust and revulsion – that human beings can be repulsed as well as enticed by sex.

Sean S. Cunningham (1941–   )

Together (1971); *Case of the Full Moon Murders* (codirected with Brad Talbot; aka *Case of the Smiling Stiffs; Sex on the Groove Tube*, 1974); *Here Come the Tigers* (aka *Manny's Orphans*, 1978); *Friday the 13th* (1980); *A Stranger Is Watching* (1982); *Spring Break* (1983); *The New Kids* (1985); *Deep Star Six* (1989).

Sean S. Cunningham will best be remembered for creating the infamous *Friday the 13th* films and getting them marketed by a major studio (Paramount). But before he came up with Camp Blood, Jason Vorhees and his mother, he was the producer of another infamous horror film, *Last House on the Left*, directed by Wes Craven (see chapter on Craven) back in 1972.

Cunningham began his directorial career in 1971 with a film called *Together*, about which I have been unable to find anything. He followed this with the highly successful *Last House on the Left*, which made a tidy profit on a small investment. His next film, codirected with coscriptwriter Brad Talbot, was *Case of the Full Moon Murders* (aka *Case of the Smiling Stiffs, Sex on the Groove Tube*), about a female vampire who performs fellatio on men until they are killed by it. The vampiress (Cathy Walker) meets her end when the hugely endowed Harry Reems stakes her with his appendage. The film has been described as "hard-core smut about happy hard-ons."

Cunningham left sexploitation to try to cash in on a rip-off of *The Bad News Bears* called *Here Come the Tigers* (aka *Manny's Orphans*). The film followed the adventures of a kiddie baseball team and featured Cunningham's old friend Wes Craven in a bit part. According to the sometimes inaccurate Richard Meyers, Cunningham tried the formula again with a soccer team in a film called *Kick*.

With a screenplay by Victor Miller, Cunningham independently financed, produced and directed *Friday the 13th* for under a million dollars. The basic idea was to make a new riff inspired by John Carpenter's highly successful *Halloween*. It would be established that a killer who seemingly cannot be killed was murdering amorous teens with plenty of point-of-view shots to alert the audience that the killer was nearby. Cunningham made his film a little gorier than Carpenter's and, amazingly, was able to sell it to Paramount for distribution even though it was precisely the kind of film the majors would not have touched a few years previously. When an ad campaign promising to showcase spectacular murders proved an immense success, the ball began rolling as imitators quickly popped up and major studios began financing the kind of exploitation films that only the independent studios used to bankroll.

The film does not have a plot so much as a series of executions. It is established in the opening that two camp counselors were murdered in 1938 while making out, giving Camp Crystal Lake a bad reputation. Now, 22 years later, the camp is set to reopen when a new bunch of camp counselors arrive. Cunningham does not develop these people's personalities, giving them dull things to do like digging up stumps and taking a swim so that a bored and restless audience begins to hope for a murder just to liven things up.

Naturally, the audience is not disappointed. Ned (Mark Nelson) turns up dead in an upper bunk bed that Jack (Kevin Bacon, who has inexplicably gone on to have a rather successful acting career without ever becoming less wooden) and Marcie are making out in. Marcie leaves to go to the bathroom and Jack gets his throat cut. Marcie starts to come back and gets a hatchet in the face.

What are their friends doing while all this is happening? They are playing "strip monopoly." Brenda (Laurie Bartram) gets up to check outside. When Bill (Harry Crosby, Bing's son) gets an arrow in the eye, that only leaves Alice (Adrienne King), who meets Mrs. Voorhees (Betsy Palmer), a woman whose son was drowned in a canoeing accident these many years past.

Naturally, introducing this character so late into the film after giving Palmer top billing indicates that she is the murderess. Cunningham then prolongs things by having Alice knock out Mrs. Voorhees with a poker, then with her fist, then with a frying pan. Finally, disgusted that Mrs. Voorhees would not quit attacking her, she arranges for Voorhees' decapitation.

The obligatory, post–*Carrie* final jump comes when Alice has a dream that the young son of Mrs. Voorhees, Jason, has grown into manhood in the lake and springs up to pull her down from her canoe. It is nonsensical, but so is the rest of this film, the basic motivation of which is to do anything, no matter how illogical, to make the audience jump. One element that does create tension is Harry Manfredini's score, which seems to whisper, "Knife, knife, knife, kill, kill, kill," throughout the film.

Friday the 13th turned into something of a *cause célèbre* when critics Roger Ebert and Gene Siskel, who deplored the film, gave away its ending on television and asked viewers to write letters protesting it to star Betty Palmer. (Interestingly, this is the same Roger Ebert who championed *Last House on the Left* and wrote the grossly violent *Beyond the Valley of the*

Adrienne King discovers that one of her fellow campers has had an 'arrowing experience in Friday the 13th. *This is typical of the "body count" approach of Sean S. Cunningham's film. Written by Victor Miller and made for under a million dollars, it went on to become one of the summer's biggest sleepers and start a series which had gone down in horror movie history.*

Dolls *in which a woman performs mock fellatio on a gun before it blows her head off.) Naturally, such a protest only spurred more horror fans to go see the film.

Having made it big on the first film, Cunningham wisely turned over the sequels to other hands, beginning with his longtime associate Steve Miner (who also directed *Friday the 13th Part 3-D* and *House*). All the *Friday the 13th* films owe a thus-far-unacknowledged debt to Mario Bava's *Twitch of the Death Nerve*, which was more effective and had more style as well as black humor, but the series has proved itself durable and created an apparent demand for "dead teenager" movies, particularly those with gruesome makeup effects by Tom Savaini, who worked on *Friday the 13th* after just completing the more spectacular effects on George A. Romero's *Dawn of the Dead*. A new magazine from the *Starlog* group, *Fangoria*, capitalized on this gore craze and went on to help shape the tastes of young horror fans in the '80s.

Cunningham's next film, *A Stranger Is Watching*, based on a Mary Higgins Clark novel, is actually much better than *Friday the 13th* but did not fare nearly as well. Leaving painting the woods red to others, Cunningham had Victor Miller and Earl MacRauch (best known for scripting *Buckaroo Bonzai*) script an urban thriller with a creepy performance by Rip Torn as a nasty psychopath.

Torn's character, Artie Taggart, rapes and murders the mother of Julie Peterson (Shawn von Schreiber), but Julie identifies the wrong man to the police. A few years later, Julie's father, Steve (James Maughton), decides to remarry, selecting television news journalist Sharon Martin (Kate Mulgrew) to be his wife.

Apparently worried that Julie will realize her mistake, Artie plots to kidnap her. He manages to take both Julie and Sharon and secret them in an underground niche beneath Grand Central Station in New York, where he enjoys tormenting the two frightened females. Artie loves exerting control and dominance, but apparently he can only do it in his underground dwelling. He is almost stabbed in a mugging when he goes to the bathroom in Central Park, leaving the audience in the odd position of having to hope that this sadistic fiend will survive because otherwise no one will ever find Julie and Sharon before they starve to death.

The film definitely builds some visceral power, especially when Artie stabs Sharon with a screwdriver, but unlike the teenagers in *Friday the 13th*, Sharon is a character who invites our sympathy, and watching her writhe is very unpleasant. This is a disturbing horror film and by no means a fun one.

Cunningham took a break from horror films with *Spring Break*, an updated version of those beach movies from yesteryear, which uses its loose plot as an excuse to show off women in bikinis and young people having fun together. The film is all T & A and no mind, being neither more nor less distinguished than most other films of the same ilk.

The New Kids provided a return to terror thrillers as two young army brats, Loren (Shannon Presby) and Abby (Lori Loughlin), have to pull their lives together after their stern but loving military father (Chet Atkins in a short cameo) dies in a car crash. The kids are recruited by their Uncle Charlie (Eddie Jones in the Ned Beatty role) who needs their help to run a low-rent amusement park he has just purchased with his life savings. Called "Santatown," the park is located in sweltering Florida.

Sean S. Cunningham (center) directs Rip Torn (left) in a scene from A Stranger Is Watching, *based upon the novel by Mary Higgins Clark. This ugly thriller is actually much better than Cunningham's more famous films.*

They try to fit in at school, but they soon run afoul of blond-haired baddie Dutra (James Spader before his success in *Sex, Lies and Videotape* and *White Palace*) and his gang of toughs. Dutra and Gideon (John Philbin) even bet each other $50 over who can get into Abby's pants first and are shocked when Abby turns down their offers for a date.

Antagonism between the two groups escalates as Dutra's gang vandalizes the amusement park and Uncle Charlie's 1960 cherry red cadillac. The athletic Loren counters by invading Dutra's bedroom at night, tying him up and threatening him with a knife as Loren looks through Dutra's drug supply for some money to pay for damages to Charlie's car. When Loren goes on to beat up Gideon in a fist fight, he wins the admiration of Karen (Paige Lyn Price), the sheriff's attractive daughter. Dutra and Gideon retaliate first by beating up Loren in the bathroom and then planning the rape and torment of Abby at the school dance.

The protective Loren is distracted by Karen at the dance, while Abby's date, nice guy Mark (Eric Stoltz, later the star of *Mask, Haunted Summer* and *Some Kind of Wonderful*) is no match for Dutra and his gang. They kidnap Abby and take her out to an empty field. There Dutra pours lighter fluid all over her and Gideon threatens to light it with a match as a fat gang member takes down his trousers. The resourceful Abby kicks the fat gang member where it counts and makes an escape, heading back to the amusement park.

Meanwhile, Loren has noticed the absence of both Dutra and Abby at the dance and heads out looking for her. Dutra's gang now all have shotguns and have killed a goat, smearing the blood on Uncle Charlie's face and Abby's underpants with the intention of having them attacked by a pit bull that will relentlessly chew anything that smells of blood. Infuriated by Dutra's treatment of his niece, Uncle Charlie breaks free, knocking the bowl of blood all over the fat gang member, but is shot by Dutra while the pit bull chews through the fat member's jugular vein. Dutra shoots the dog and Abby escapes during the distraction.

Dutra sends one of his men to the top of the ferris wheel to shoot Abby when he sees her. Loren sneaks up from underneath and ties the chair so that it will not swivel as it goes down. When the power is turned back on, the thug is spilled out of the chair and breaks his neck. Loren also waters the electrical bumper car ride so that when the electricity is turned on, another member is electrocuted.

Gideon attacks Loren with his bare hands while Dutra shoots at them both until Abby can knock him off his perch with a two-by-four. Loren wins by forcing Gideon's head into the path of an oncoming rollercoaster, apparently decapitating him. (Like most of Cunningham's movies, the film is actually quite restrained in its use of blood.) The slightly dazed and certainly crazed Dutra recovers from Abby's blow and makes a flamethrower out of a gasoline pump, intending to incinerate Abby. Loren comes to the rescue and as they grapple, manages to turn Dutra into overdone toast.

The film ends with Uncle Charlie recovering from his wound and the amusement park a great success because of the notoriety of the local bloodbath. Loren and Abby affirm they have found a home, while Uncle Charlie leads spectators on a guided tour of where the thugs met their gory fates.

The New Kids is a cynical thriller, but fairly well made for what it is. Just before working on it, Cunningham helped his old friend Wes Craven complete *A Nightmare on Elm Street*, the film that would revitalize Craven's flagging career and create the most popular horror character since Jason, Freddy Krueger. Cunningham has since produced *House* and *House II: The Second Story*. Those films championed surrealistic nightmare horror, one of the developing forms of the '80s that was initiated by Don Coscarelli in *Phantasm* and has been a crucial element to the success of the *Nightmare on Elm Street* pictures.

Cunningham's most recent film, *Deep Star Six*, was one of numerous attempts at redoing the film *Alien* by setting it underwater. For a low-budget film, it has a rather professional look, but the story of a sea monster attacking an underwater base is all too familiar. Miguel Ferrer, who plays a continual screw-up named Snyder, is the only actor to provide much characterization; the others seem as sterile as their environment. Science is exploited when it can contribute to horror (e.g. use of explosive decompression) but then gets ignored so that the film can provide the requisite "unexpected" final shock.

The basic plot has this underwater crew, led by Marius Weyers, Taurean Blacque, Nancy Everhard and Greg McBride, trying to construct some underwater missile silos for the navy. They unleash a monster when an explosion blows up a long-sealed underwater cavern. The creature itself was created by makeup effects expert Mark Shostrom and features a pair of ludicrous yellow eyes atop its chitinous outer pate, which opens like a flower petal to reveal the monster's ravenous maw. Luckily, as in the film it is imitating, the monster is not shown very often.

The film appears quickly assembled to precede 1989's later underwater epics *Leviathan, The Abyss* and Mary Ann Fisher's *Lords of the Deep* at the cinemas, but audiences decided to deep-six it anyway.

Even worse, Cunningham appeared to cash in on old buddy Wes Craven's idea by ripping off some of *Shocker*'s basic concepts in *The Horror Show*, which was directed by James Isaac and written by Allyn Warner. Warner used the pseudonym Alan Smithee, usually reserved for directors in the guild who wish to have their names taken off of projects – for example, Michael Ritchie put the Smithee name on Mickey Rose's unfunny horror comedy *Student Bodies*. Cunningham was forced to direct *Deep Star Six* because he could not find anyone else he could trust who would take the job, but he relegated himself to the role of producer on *The Horror Show*.

The talented Lance Henriksen (*Aliens, Near Dark, Pumpkinhead*) is badly misused as a cop haunted by nightmares caused by the undying spirit of madman Brion James (*Crimewave, Blade Runner*), who gives an especially hammy and out-of-control performance. Cinematographer Mac Ahlburg did his usual job of making the film look better than it deserves, but James' trite quotations from other films and the stupidly ripped off "shock scenes" from other horror films make this one a strain to sit through.

Cunningham has shown in the past that as a director he knows how to build and pay off suspense and is able to convey some very original and disturbing notions on film, but his recent work suggests the ambitions of a quick-buck artist who is uninterested in quality. His devotion to screen surrealism seems based more on a desire to insert some easy "cheap shocks" than on an intention to display any artistic imagery or play with the idea of what happens when our foundations in reality break apart. Still, he has been a major force in '80s horror and may again be one in the '90s.

Joe D'Amato (1936–   )

Le Mille e una Notte da Boccaccio a Canterbury (1001 Nights from Boccaccio to Canterbury); Inginocchiate (Kneel Bastard); Eroi all Inferno (as Michael Wotruba) (1972); *Diario di una Vergine Romana (Diary of a Roman Virgin* as Michael Wotruba); *La Morte Sorride all 'Assassino (Death Smiles on the Murderer* as Aristide Massaccesi); *La Caduta dei Gladiatori (The Fall of the Gladiators); Pugni Pupe e Karate* (as Aristide Massaccesi) (1973); *Giubbe Rosse (Red Jackets); Novelle Licenziose di una Vergine Vogliosa* (as Aristide Massaccesi) (1974); *Voto di Castita (Vow of Chastity)* (1975); *Emanuelle e Françoise; Emanuelle in America; Il Ginecologo della Mutua* (aka *Ladies Doctor); Eva Nera* (aka *Black Eve; Black Cobra; Erotic Eva); Emanuelle Nera: Orient Reportage* (aka *Black Emanuelle 2); Emanuelle e gli Ultimi Cannibali* (aka *Emanuelle and the Last Cannibals; Trap Them and Kill Them); Emanuelle in Bangkok; Emanuelle, Perche Violenza alle Donne?* (aka *Confessions of Emanuelle)* (1977); *Papaya dei Caraibi* (aka *Die of Pleasure); Immagini di un Convento; Duri a Morire* (aka *Tough to Kill; Hard to Kill); Le Notti Porno nel Mondo n. 2; Crazy Nights; La Via della Prostituzione* (aka *The Street of Prostitution; Emanuelle and the White Slave Trade)* (1978); *Buio Omega* (aka *Blue Holocaust; Beyond the Darkness; Buried Alive); Blue Erotic Climax* (codirected by Claudio Bernabei); *Orgasmo Nero* (aka *Black Orgasm); Sesso Nero* (aka *Black Sex); Le Notti Erotiche dei Morti Viventi* (aka *Erotic Nights of the Living Dead; The Night of the Zombies; Sexy Nights of the Dead; Island of the Zombies); Paradiso Blu* (aka *Blue Paradise); Pornoshop della Settima Strada* (aka *The Pleasure Shop on 7th Avenue* as Aristide Massaccesi) (1979); *Anthropophagus* (aka *The Grim Reaper); Hard Sensations; Porno Erotic Love; Porno Video; Porno Holocaust; Super Climax; Sexy Erotic Love; Labbra Bagnate* (aka *Wet Lips)* (1980); *Rosso Sangue* (aka *Red Blood; Absurd* as Peter Newton); *Caligola . . . La Storia Mai Raccontata* (aka *Caligula . . . The Untold Story* as David Hills); *Caldo Profumo di Vergine* (aka *Hot Perfume of Virgins); Labbra Vogliose* (aka *Desirable Lips); Sesso Acerbo* (aka *Sour Sex); Stretta e Bagnata* (aka *Tight and Wet); La Voglia* (aka *The Desire); Voglia di Sesso* (1980); *Ator l'Invincibile* (aka *Ator the Invincible; Ator the Fighting Eagle* as David Hills); *Ator l'Invincibile II* (aka *Ator the Invincible; Ator, the Return; The Blade Master* as David Hills); *Delizie Erotiche* (aka *Erotic Delights); Super Hard Core* (1982); *Endgame–Bronx Lotta Finale* (aka *Endgame–Final Bronx Struggle,* as Steven Benson); *Anno 2020 i Gladiatori del Futuro* (aka *Year 2020–The Gladiators of the Future; 2020 Texas Gladiators; 2020 Freedom Fighters; Texas 2000* as Kevin Mancuso); *Orgasmo Infernale* (aka *Infernal Orgasm* codirected with Claudio Bernabei, 1983); *L'Alcova* (1984); *Il Piacere* (aka *The Pleasure)* (1985); *Voglia di Guardare; Lussuria* (aka *Luxury); Blue Erotic Animal Job* (1986); *Sharks; Top Model; Eleven Days,*

293

Eleven Nights; The Three Musketeers '87 (1987); *Color of Love* (1988); *Quest for the Mighty Squad* (1989).

Though extremely active, Joe D'Amato is considered by critics the Edward Wood, Jr., or the Herschel Gordon Lewis of Italian cinema. Actually, he is more akin to Jesus Franco and shares many of Franco's shortcomings as well as his predilections for tackling the sleaziest of cinema.

Born in Rome on December 15, 1936, D'Amato was another director who worked his way slowly through the filmmaking ranks. He was the son of a chief technician and was able to get jobs as a dubbing director, an editor, a camera operator, and finally as a director of photography. As a d.p., he photographed several films including *Bandit Skin, The Island of the Swedes, Desperately Last Summer, Django and Sartana Are Coming . . . It's the End; On Your Knees, Stranger . . . Corpses Cast No Shadows!; Arm Friends and Go!; Duck . . . Man* (aka *A Fistful of Death*); *For a Coffin Full of Dollars; The Families of the Victims Will Not Be Warned* (aka *The New Mafia Boss*); *Ben and Charlie* and others.

Perhaps William Connolly summed it up best when he wrote in *Spaghetti Cinema #23*, "*Spaghetti Cinema* fans who are unhappy with the present state of the Italian Action Film tend to use the films of director Joe D'Amato, whose real name is Aristide Massaccesi, as an example of everything that is wrong with the current product. His films sport miniscule budgets, uninteresting actors, haphazard if not unintelligible plotting, and the sort of pandering to the lowest common audience demoninator that could provide a definition for the term 'exploitation flick.'" D'Amato, though, has been incredibly prolific in a short amount of time. Among his other *noms de plume* are Steven Benson, David Hills, Michael Wotruba, J. Metheus, Kevin Mancuso, Peter Newton, and Peter McCoy.

His first horror film was *La Morte Sorride all'Assassino (Death Smiles on the Murderer)*, which was alternately known as *Sette Strani Cadaveri (Seven Strange Corpses)*. Klaus Kinski has a bit part as Dr. Sturges, a would-be Frankenstein who attempts to bring corpses back to life but is killed by an unseen killer. However, the main part of the story centers around a girl named Greta (Ewa Aulin of *Candy* fame) who was brought back to life by an Incan spell cast by her brother, whom she kills before eliminating several other people for no apparent reason throughout the course of the movie. There is a nice bit where a man gets into bed with Greta and makes sexual advances until he discovers that she is now a rotting corpse, but largely this movie is a nonsensical collection of supposedly atmospheric scenes.

D'Amato went on to direct a pirate film, a female gladiator film (which was cut in United States release by director Joe Dante, Jr.), a World War II prisoners-of-war movie, and a few sex films. He first used his D'Amato pseudonym on *Giubbe Rosse (Red Coat)*, a variation on Jack London's *Call of the Wild* and *White Fang* set in Canada. He also photographed a couple of horror films: Paolo Solvay's *The Devil's Wedding Night*, a variation on the Countess Bathory legend of a vampire that bathes in virgin's blood, and Alberto de Martino's *L'Anticristo* (aka *The Tempter*), an Italian *Exorcist* rip-off, which has been treated so shabbily that several reels are out of order in the United States version available in videotape.

D'Amato achieved a great success in *Emanuelle e Françoise*, which introduced the black Emanuelle Laura Gemser and set off a series of sequels that would keep D'Amato busy for a time. (D'Amato credits Bitto Albertini for bringing him and Gemser together. Gemser had appeared in the first sequel to *Emmanuelle, Emmanuelle: The Joys of a Woman* before becoming involved as the Black Emanuelle.)

Eventually, D'Amato made a horror entry in the series, *Emanuelle and the Last of the Cannibals* (aka *Trap Them and Kill Them*). The film has Emanuelle visiting an insane asylum where she sees a patient bite off a nurse's breast and eat it. Emanuelle interviews the patient and masturbates her, noticing a queer tattoo on her pubis and photographing it.

Someone at the newspaper Emanuelle works for identifies the tattoo as deriving from an Amazonian tribe. Emanuelle goes to Dr. Mark Lester (Gabrielle Tinti) and proposes an expedition to the Amazon as well as a little sex, not necessarily in that order. After giving her boyfriend a goodbye screw, Emanuelle is on her way.

The expedition meets up with some big-game hunters who are secretly looking for a planeload of diamonds that crashed in the jungle. Finding that their destination, a mission, was recently overrun by cannibals, the expedition turns back, but is picked off one by one by cannibals who like their meat raw. (Why do the cannibals in Italian movies never cook their food?) Emanuelle saves the day by painting the same tattoo above her pubis and posing as the local water god to frighten the natives.

The film does feature some rather gory effects of entrails being pulled out (courtesy of Fabrizio Sporza, an Italian Tom Savini), but for being part of an adult film series, it is most definitely unerotic. Nonethess, it started D'Amato working on gore films, which continued with his *Guio Omega* (United States title *Buried Alive*), in which a maniac dismembers women and dissolves body parts in a vat of acid. The maniac (Kieran Canter) is obsessed with giving his old lover the taxidermy treatment after a witch put a spell on her which killed her. The ex-lover's twin shows up near the end so that everyone can get confused and kill each other.

Even grimmer is *Anthropophagus* (aka *The Grim Reaper*), which is the story of a cannibal who eats his family before attacking tourists on a Greek island. At the end of the film, the cannibal has run out of people to eat and ends up eating his own intestines, a nasty twist given away by the film's poster. Particularly repellant is a scene where the cannibal rips a fetus from its mother's womb in order to feed on it like a delicacy. (These last gory scenes are trimmed from the United States video release.)

John Lamontagne and Michael Ferguson translated an interview with D'Amato from *Starfix* magazine in *Spaghetti Cinema #29* in which D'Amato responded to charges that his films were excessively violent:

> Are my films unhealthy? Certain scenes are too delirious to really shock. It's not unhealthy because they can not be imitated. My films, above all, provoke the imagination. Gore doesn't work well in Italy, but is okay in France, Germany, and America. I like to manipulate intestines, pieces of meat, vital organs. Is there a limit? Not at all! We can permit ourselves to go as far as we want. But with the fetus in *Anthropopagus*, I went beyond my own limits!

Le Notti Erotiche dei Morti Viventi (aka *Demonia; Island of the Zombies*) is another porno-gore film with George Eastman and Laura Gemser. There is a strange scene where Eastman makes love to a strange woman (Gemser) on a beach while zombies slowly approach. The woman suddenly disappears, but leaves a talisman that allows Eastman to drive the zombies away. When a researcher takes Gemser's picture, her image fails to register on film. This makes the researcher curious about her, but when he allows her to perform fellatio on him, ends up castrated instead and zombies eat the rest of him. Eastman falls in love with a nurse and is able to drive the zombies off. In the end, it is all revealed to be someone's fantasy – a pointless series of sex and living-dead scenes which have passed off as entertainment.

Not getting enough of cannibals, D'Amato decided to do *Anthropophagus 2* (aka *Absurd; Rosso Sangue; Red Blood; Monster Hunter*). George Eastman reappears as the cannibal, but this time without the scabrous makeup he had in the first film. The film turns into a rip-off of Carpenter's *Halloween* as the cannibal terrorizes an American town and a little boy decides that the cannibal is the boogey man. Also, this time the cannibal does not eat his victims, but rather dispatches them with drills, saws, pickaxes, etc. The cannibal survives disemboweling but is eventually dispatched by the boy's sister, who blinds him with a compass and chops off the fiend's head.

D'Amato made a back-to-back pair of awful heroic fantasy films starring Miles O'Keefe, *Ator, The Fighting Eagle* and *Ator, The Blademaster*, both of which understandably failed to catch on. He also did a pair of science fiction exploitation epics set in a decadent and depressed future, *Endgame* and *2020 Texas Gladiators* (of which *Endgame* is the better film).

The D'Amato filmography continues as Massaccesi becomes more involved with producing as well as directing, but with all the practice he has had, there seems to be little improvement in his technique. In most of his films, he shows an absolute unconcern for plot or characterization and is simply a yeoman delivering what he considers to be saleable goods to the cinematic marketplace. It is extremely doubtful we will ever see a work of art, or even a worthwhile film, from this Italian exploitation dynamo.

Joe Dante, Jr. (1946–   )

Hollywood Boulevard (codirected with Allan Arkush) (1975); *Piranha* (1978); *The Howling* (1980); *Twilight Zone – The Movie* (codirected with John Landis, Steven Spielberg & George Miller) (1983); *Gremlins* (1984); *Explorers* (1985); *Amazon Women on the Moon* (codirected with John Landis, Carl Gottlieb, Robert K. Weiss & Peter Horton); *Innerspace* (1987); *The 'Burbs* (1989); *Gremlins 2: The New Batch* (1990).

TELEVISION: *Police Squad* (2 episodes); *Amazing Stories; Twilight Zone* ("Shadowman").

Joe Dante, Jr., grew up in Parsippany, New Jersey, hooked on a steady diet of cartoons fed to him by his local movie theater. Not being into the kind of movies that interested adults, he would frequently leave before the main feature came on, but one day he stayed for *It Came from Outer Space* and was instantly hooked on movies as well. In his most successful film to date, *Gremlins*, he offers a scene of gremlins misbehaving in a movie theater as a sincere tribute to the kiddie matinees he endured as a child.

Dante, like many of his generation, cites the films of Walt Disney as one of his first influences. In an interview with this author, Dante said:

> During the '50s I had my mouse ears and my coonskin cap and my little Golden records and all my sort of infantile merchandising stuff that had gone on, and it was because the '50s were a great time to be a kid. I think they, judging from what I've heard, weren't a particularly good time for being an adult, but they had a lot of good stuff in the '50s for kids. They had Saturday matinees – the local theater was the Colony Theater and it cost 25 cents to get in, the first boy and girl in line got in free, so kids would line up and start fighting at 11 o'clock. Every Saturday they would run 10 cartoons and then maybe two features, maybe two Allied Artists features if you were really lucky.
> I didn't realize at the time that this was sort of the last gasp of cartoons. Disney at the time was actually phasing out the making of cartoons, and thinking back I think I realized that by the fact that there used to be a lot of Mickey Mouses and Donald Ducks mixed in with an occasional Woody Woodpecker and Bugs Bunny, but then they started phasing out the Disney cartoons and the Warners cartoons and replacing them with L'il Audrey and Baby Huey, so I guess I came in just about the right time.

I also remember going to a double bill of *Abbott and Costello Meet the Mummy* and *World Without End*, and it was such a great double bill I stayed through it twice. When I got home, my parents had called the police, so I didn't do that again, but it was great. The movies were so good I couldn't leave. And the other good thing was there was almost nothing you couldn't see if you were a kid. There wasn't a lot of questionable material on the screen since there was still a lot of supervision. If you happened to see a picture like *Executive Suite*, which is a good picture when you're 20 but not such a good picture when you're 8, you would just leave. You would go out and play ball.

Other influences included Carl Barks' episodic and entertaining comic book tales of the adventures of Donald Duck with his Uncle Scrooge and his three nephews, Huey, Dewey, and Louie. Also, Dante became addicted to watching horror movies on TV and discovered that there were other monster fans like him via *Famous Monsters of Filmland* magazine edited by Forry Ackerman. As a child, Dante won some notoriety when his list of the 50 worst horror films was published as "Dante's Inferno" in issue 18 of the magazine.

For a child of the '50s, *Famous Monsters* was easily accessible, open, warm, and filled with Forry's puns. It allowed children to see pictures of hundreds of other horror films they did not even know existed. However, as time went on, *FM* continued serving the pre-adolescent market while a portion of that market got older. In the '60s a more sophisticated magazine on horror films arrived, the erratic *Castle of Frankenstein*. Dante became a regular contributor to *CoF*, as it was otherwise known, and was a major reviewer and compiler of the magazine's famous "Movieguide" to fantastic films on television.

Dante studied art hoping to be a cartoonist, but no classes were available in cartooning, so he switched to filmmaking at the Philadelphia College of Art. He also took a job as a film reviewer and managing editor of *Film Bulletin*, where he worked from 1969 to 1974.

Then came the infamous *Schlitz Movie Orgy* project. Dante and his pal Jon Davison (himself now a movie producer of such films as *Robocop*) acquired a copy of the Bela Lugosi serial *The Phantom Creeps* and added footage from other titles in the public domain to make a lengthy, wacky feature. (For example, they would intercut Morris Ankrum from several different sf films in which he always seemed to be wearing the same general's suit.) Getting bookings on college campuses, they became sponsored by Schlitz to show their seven-hour movie marathon from campus to campus.

Davison was called out to California to work for Roger Corman, and Dante soon followed to work in the trailer department. There Dante edited some of New World Pictures' most infamous trailers, learning that it was more important to edit in good footage, no matter what the source, than it was to represent what the film was actually like. Dante's first trailer was for Jonathan Demme's cult classic *Caged Heat*. Working with Allan Arkush, he put together a number of the company's trailers until he and Arkush decided that they could make a better film than many of the ones they were cutting trailers for.

Corman indicated that he would allow them to make a film if it was the cheapest New World had ever made. Dante and Arkush, having a thorough knowledge of New World's stock footage and film library, thought that they could incorporate the best footage from a dozen films to bring the cost really down. (Corman was shrewd both as a filmmaker and as a businessman and loved to get extra mileage out of anything; see chapter on Corman.)

The pair decided to make a film about a movie company that was making a bunch of different movies so that the stock footage could be used for action sequences. In essence, the film, titled *Hollywood Boulevard*, would be a tribute to New World pictures and all the things that the young movie fans loved best. It would have Robby the Robot and Godzilla; it would have action and adventure and pretty, nubile young girls; and it would have Dick Miller, a character actor who has subsequently appeared in every Dante film (with the exception of *Amazon Women on the Moon*, where his sequence was cut).

Hollywood Boulevard was shot in ten days on a budget of $60,000, with Corman hoping for some foreign sales while not really planning to open it in the United States. However, he was surprised by the quality of the film, and it was able to achieve a limited release. It has now achieved a sort of cult status.

In addition to being one of the earliest pairings of the comedy team of Paul Bartel and Mary Woronov, *Hollywood Boulevard* features a number of future directors in bit parts. Paul Bartel, who had already made a couple of films, starred as director Eric Von Leppe (a combination Erich von Stroheim and beach movie in-joke), while Jonathan Kaplan (*Heart Like a Wheel*) played Scotty, a clumsy special effects man, and Joseph McBride (*The Big Easy*) played a drive-in rapist. Additionally, special effects artist Bill Malone contributed a cameo as Robby the Robot while Bob Short provided Godzina, a Godzilla clone. Additional movie in-jokes include Dick Miller reprising the role of Walter Paisley, the would-be beatnik artist from *Bucket of Blood*, and a pair of gangsters named Duke Mantee (*Petrified Forest*) and Rico (*Little Caesar*). The writing credit was given to Patrick Hobby, the subject of a series of stories on Hollywood by F. Scott Fitzgerald. (Hobby was in fact Dan Opatoshu, who also pseudonymously wrote *Massacre at Central High*, another cult film.) As a gag, Dante wrote up a phony but humorous "history" of Patrick Hobby for *Cinefantastique* magazine, claiming things like it was Hobby's tennis shoe that could be glimpsed under the giant crab in *Attack of the Giant Crabs* and that Hobby lost the expensive stop-motion footage for Bert I. Gordon's *King Dinosaur.*

Today Dante seems a bit embarrassed by *Hollywood Boulevard*, seeing it as a string of obscure cinematic in-jokes that very few people will get, and he is appalled by the movie's cheerful sexism. It is true that the movie is appallingly sexist. There is a running gag about the producer getting it on with would-be starlets hoping to further their career, two different rape scenes milked for humor, and gratuitous nudity – but then, part of what makes the movie funny is its direct satirization of how gratuitous most exploitation films are. For lovers of low-budget cinema, the movie is genuinely funny and on its own terms a success.

The setting is Miracle Pictures, which operates under the old vaudeville slogan, "If it's a good picture, it's a Miracle!" Von Leppe, the egotistical and pretentious exploitation director, is shooting a sky-diving sequence when the stunt woman's chute fails to open. This is all shot in a cartoony style with no violence shown. P.G. (Richard Doran), the insensitive producer, proclaims, "Don't worry, there are plenty of young girls in Hollywood who would die to make a picture."

We are then introduced to Candy Hope (Candice Ralston) as she tries to make the rounds in Hollywood only to be exploited. Finally, she enters the office of Walter Paisley, an agent, who immediately decides to change her name to Candy Wednesday because in Hollywood they change everything. He tells her, "You've got an agent, let me know when you get yourself a job." When she asks if that's possible, he tells her, "This town is crawling with producers, casting directors, little things" – making bug motions with his hand – "you know."

As a result, the gullible Candy is persuaded by Duke Mantee and Rico to be a getaway driver in a "film" they claim they are making, a *Bonnie and Clyde*-type project. This allows Dante and Arkush to use stock footage from *Crazy Mama* (Jonathan Demme, 1975, a funny picture in its own right) and gives Candy experience as a stunt driver which she uses to get her next job.

There on a real set she meets and instantly falls in love with screenwriter Patrick Hobby, after a "meet cute" scene which follows screen conventions. There is a nude audition scene in which P.G., to save time, simply has the T-shirted applicants sprayed with water while he dallies with some in the back of his van. This is followed up a musical interlude in which Commander Cody and His Lost Planet Airmen seranade Patrick and Candy on a picnic.

Miracle Pictures' B movie queen is Mary McQueen (Mary Woronov), an egotistical actress who is always bucking for larger parts and who despises her competition. When Paisley offers the lead in *Machete Maidens of Maro Tau* to Candy, she takes it instead despite her antipathy to shooting in the

Philippines. Joining them are Jill (Tara Strohmeier) and Bobby (Rita George), a pair of roller derby queens looking to meet a better crowd of people. Patrick informs Candy that two weeks previously, *Machete Maidens* was about Eskimo women fighting dinosaurs in Alaska but Miracle could not find any actresses willing to pose naked there.

Von Leppe explains to the actresses that their motivation "is to massacre 300 Asiatic soldiers," which they proceed to do to the tune of the "1812 Overture" and plentiful stock footage from previous Philippine New World epics. A gag has an extra eating lunch applying ketchup to both his burger and his wounds. Production assistant Mike Finnell later became Dante's regular line producer, but on this film he managed to lose a prop hand grenade, forcing an actress to fake throwing one.

In daringly bad taste, the romance between Patrick and Candy is developed by having him rescue her when, as she is being stripped in a rape scene, the extras ignore the director's instructions to cut. Before starting another scene, the director tells an actress, "You have the line that sums up the entire inner meaning, the core, the essence of the entire film. Are you ready? Action!"

The line emerges when a topless actress faces a naked man and says, "You're gonna get it up or I'll cut it off!"

Scotty, the clumsy effects man, destroys a nude scene of Jill's and breaks irreplaceable equipment. P.G. refuses to fire him, though, because Scotty's breakages prevent shooting 15 pages of the script and hence save P.G. money. However, Scotty's antics do not seem quite so amusing when Jill gets shot for real during a fight scene.

Back home, Paisley takes Candy and Pat to the world premiere of their film, which is showing as a supporting feature at a drive-in with *Zombie in the Attic* (a Fred Allen joke) and the ridiculously titled *Moonmen from Mars* as the top-billed features. Shots with Dick Miller from *The Terror* appear on the drive-in screen (this footage was also used in Peter Bogdanovich's brilliant horror film *Targets*) along with the sexually suggestive male and female aliens that Francis Ford Coppola had concocted and filmed "fighting" each other in *Battle Beyond the Sun,* a movie largely concocted out of stock footage from a Russian science fiction film that Corman had purchased and then padded out with American-shot footage.

Dante and Arkush have fun evoking the genuine pleasures of going to a drive-in. The group laugh and make jokes about the movie, drink Jack Daniels, and are treated to intermission come-ons to buy a meatball sandwich which looks moldy due to the discolored film.

However, the film lurches into bad taste again when an upset and drunk Candy approaches the projectionist while her rape scene is being played, demanding that he take it off. Confused as to fantasy and reality, he starts trying to undress her. A drive-in patron comes in to complain and stays to participate. Luckily, Paisley comes in and stops the rape, and together Candy and Walter fight the attackers off.

Why the film is titled *Hollywood Boulevard* is not made plain in the film, but the idea was that it would be one block sleazier than *Sunset Boulevard*. In addition to the sleaze, Dante and Arkush chronicle other problems of low-budget filmmaking – untalented people, lack of money for budgets, animosity on the set, clashing egos, last-minute major rewrites, etc. Hobby's next picture, begun as a 1950s film, is converted by the producer into a 2050s science fiction romp, *Atomic War Brides*, which Von Leppe describes as "a combination of the myth of Romeo and Juliet with high speed car action and a sincere plea for atomic controls in our time."

Footage from Bartel's *Death Race 2000* is cleverly incorporated as McQueen escapes an explosion, and top action footage from the previous film is combined in a sequence where Candy's brakes fail while "Ride of the Valkyries" blares on screen. Mutants in the film are played by actors in jumpsuits and cheap-looking Don Post masks. When McQueen objects to one wearing a simple gorilla mask, Von Leppe plops an astronaut helmet over it, an indirect reference to one of the all-time science fiction film baddies, *Robot Monster*. The director also tells Godzina what to project in the next scene: "Communicate that it's really love, and while you're at it, step on as many people as possible."

After this last act of sabotage, Bobby threatens to quit until P. G. talks her out of it, claiming to have all his money and his studio on the line for the making of this film. That night she gets a late call for retakes and is attacked by a cloaked and masked figure with a sharp knife who kills her in a Bavaesque sequence, the most stylish original footage in the film and the only real horror sequence. Later this footage was used as stock in Jim Wynorski's remake of *Not of This Earth*.

The police are working on a theory that Bobby was cleaning a knife and it went off accidentally. Candy is worried. Who could be behind the murders? Is Scotty fatally inept? Is it P. G., hoping for free publicity for his movies? Is it Patrick, who has a mysterious writing shack behind his house? Deciding to investigate Patrick's shack, she sees pictures of actresses including herself as Pat arrives and intones, "Looks like you're next." They have a car chase but she gets a flat. He goes back while she goes up to the Hollywood sign and asks to speak to Mary.

It turns out that the previous night's murder of Bobby has been accidentally filmed, and when it is shown in the dailies, Mary is revealed as the killer. Pat rushes off to rescue Candy, arriving just in time. Mary is accidentally rushed under the "Y" in the famous Hollywood sign, and the film ends with a party attended by Forrest J Ackerman, Todd McCarthy, and Robby the Robot, whom Paisley hopes to persuade to play Rhett Butler in a remake of *Gone with the Wind*.

While it does make references to some actual occurrences at New World, overall the film is just harmless silliness, and it certainly never set the world on fire. Dante was sent back to the editing room after he coedited this film with Arkush and Amy Jones. Dante tried his hand at editing someone else's feature, Ron Howard's directorial debut, *Grand Theft Auto* (written by Howard's father, Rance Howard). Dante also did a little work on the ending of *I Never Promised You a Rose Garden*, which had a disastrous preview when it was accidentally shown to some mental patients on a field trip.

It was not until 1978 that Corman offered Dante another movie to direct, but Dante did not want to do it. The movie was, of course, *Piranha*, which Corman intended as a *Jaws* rip-off to be released around the time of *Jaws 2*. Dante and Arkush had come up with a story for a film called *Rock 'n' Roll High School*, and so Arkush was assigned the high school film and Dante was given the fish story.

In an interview with Bill Warren for *Starburst* magazine, Dante explained:

> Initially, I had an incredibly poor script about mutant catranhas. Catfish and piranhas had interbred. It started out with them being delivered somewhere in a truck, and lightning strikes this truck, making it roll into a reservoir. Now these flesh-eating catfish will kill anybody that goes into the water. The original writer of the script couldn't figure out any way to get these people into the water once they knew there were horrible fish there, so he invented a bear that chased people into the water. After he got tired of the bear, he invented a forest fire that chased the whole cast into the water. It was godawful, it was a terrible idea, and was never going to work.

Luckily, Corman brought in a young short story writer, John Sayles, onto the project. Sayles, who respected Dante's ideas for turning the film into science fiction and making it more ambitious, turned in a good script, which he described as being like a rollercoaster ride – you bring the characters up and then shoot them down over and over again, taking them through twists and turns in the water. The film opens on a fence with a no trespassing sign, an homage to the opening of Welles' *Citizen Kane*, though moments later a girl and guy strip off their clothes and get eaten, assuring the audience that they are watching enjoyable schlock and not classic cinema.

Piranha still stands up today as one of Dante's most enjoyable movies, with a better-than-average performance by Bradford Dillman as Paul Grogan, a reclusive drunk whose wife has left him and who is unused to dealing with people. Heather Menzies gives a spunky, amusing performance as Maggie McKeown, a skip tracer on the lookout for the aforementioned and now deceased teenagers.

Piranha marks the first film to feature many Dante hallmarks. One of these is his astute use of character actors to make a brief but memorable impression. Dick Miller returns as Buck Gariner, an East Coast con man pretending to be a Texas good ol' boy who buys worn-out equipment for his "new" water resort. Paul Bartel plays an officious camp manager who pompously assures Susie, Grogan's frightened daughter, "People eat fish, fish don't eat people." Keenan Wynn plays a retiree who fetches Grogan's liquor for him and later gets his feet nibbled off by the piranha when Maggie unknowingly frees them into the river. Kevin McCarthy, a favorite actor of Dante's best known for his performances in *Invasion of the Body Snatchers* and *Death of a Salesman*, plays Dr. Robert "Bob" Hoak, the scientist responsible for creating these highly adaptive killer fish. Finally, scream queen Barbara Steele plays Dr. Mengers, Hoak's former lover and fish geneticist who is kowtowing to the military.

Another Dante hallmark is the use of a brief stop-motion animation shot. A shot of a piranha-type creature with legs walking through the laboratory was inserted at the last minute when Dante discovered that Phil Tippet, who had worked on *Star Wars* and would animate the scorpion in *Honey, I Shrunk the Kids*, was available to work cheaply. The delightful creature becomes something of a red herring as no other piranhas are shown having this capability and this one simply disappears from the film after a brief but delightful cameo.

The last Dante hallmark is a bit of animation, usually featured on a television and designed to correlate with the action. In *Piranha* he does this with a cartoon of a clever fish chasing after a worm just before a man prepares to open a dam spillway and let the piranha through. (In *The Howling*, Dante would employ a sequence in which a wolf is about to devour a little lamb on television before the first werewolf attack that is actually seen in the film. Dante's sequence in *Twilight Zone – The Movie* would be totally built around a cartoon world constructed by an omnipotent kid. In *Gremlins*, a Bugs Bunny cartoon would be shown briefly, then shut off by its creator, Chuck Jones.)

Roger Corman insisted that *Piranha* have two climaxes, but in the end that turned out to be a pretty good idea because it allowed Dante to do the unexpected. Throughout the film, we see Grogan worried about his little daughter Susie at a summer camp. He tries to warn people about the fish, but because of his reputation as a drunk, his warnings are ignored. Dante ignores the unwritten screen rules about not injuring little kids and has the piranhas make a bloody raid of the summer camp, something which movie-fed audiences expected would be averted at the last minute.

The film also touches briefly on some rich thematic material. Despite his designing fish which could survive poison and thrive not only in cold water but in salt water as well – piranhas which were intended to be released in

North Vietnamese waterways to attack soldiers and citizens alike – Dr. Hoak refuses to accept any responsibility for concocting such a dangerous weapon. He insists that he is a scientist and not a warrior, though perhaps a last-minute attack of guilt accounts for his sacrificing his life to save a boy stranded on an overturned canoe.

The military proves deceptive, powerful, and manipulative. After the report on the piranhas, they come in to check it out. Grogan is surprised that they have come fully prepared to poison the fish, making him suspicious. The military men refuse to accept the idea that the piranhas might survive poisoning by Rotinon-235 and could swing around the dam and reach the lower river by traveling through a side stream. Grogan and Maggie are locked up until they escape when she pulls off her blouse to distract a soldier (John Sayles in a cameo) while Grogan knocks him out.

The real concern of Colonel Waxman (Bruce Gordon) becomes apparent when we learn that he is a silent partner in Buck Gariner's water resort. A panic would hurt business at the park, and so he cold-bloodedly gambles with the lives of dozens of innocent people. His "me first" attitude is also apparent when the resort is attacked and injured swimmers start clambering onboard his party boat. He pushes them off until he falls in himself, providing a well-deserved feast for the fishes.

There is also a not-so-gentle poke at the media, whose representatives arrive to film the injured and dead, proclaiming, "Lost River Lake – terror, horror, death – film at 11." The distraught Gariner shoves a cameraman aside and asks him, what are you filming? This scene raises the question of whether people's genuine suffering is really appropriate material for exploitation by the news media.

To kill the piranhas, Grogan comes up with a clever idea: "We'll pollute the bastards to death!" Dante rigs up a suspenseful scene where Grogan must go into the water to open some controls which will release toxic materials into the water and kill the piranhas before they reach the ocean and are able to spread uncontrollably. Dante undercuts Dr. Mengers' final assurances that there is nothing to fear by reprising a shot of the rolling ocean tides while the title dissolves into red and spreads out over the sea.

While no great claims can be made for it, *Piranha* is more than a simple-minded though entertaining horror film. It has effective little touches, such as the fact that only the fish experts, Hoak and Mengers, pronounce the name of the fish correctly. What is particularly sharp about the film is its editing, by Dante and Mark Goldblatt. The faked piranha attacks are made more effective by quick cuts which suggest more than they show, and a sequence in which the piranhas gnaw through the ropes binding a raft are positively Eisensteinian.

While the special effects were handled by Jon Berg, this film introduced

Dante to two important special effects partners. Half the makeup chores were handled by Rob Bottin, who would become the key person involved in the werewolf transformations in *The Howling*, while Bob Short was assisted on special properties by Chris Walas, who would create the gremlins for *Gremlins*.

Piranha proved a hit with the audience, and though Universal considered suing, Steven Spielberg liked the film, which led to him executive-producing *Gremlins*. (Note: James Cameron, who directed *Terminator* and *Aliens*, started his directing career with a cheap sequel entitled *Piranha II: The Spawning*, which is left off his resume these days.)

Dante explained the attitude behind making these kinds of films:

> Roger had a wonderful formula, which was he had pictures that were made for a certain audience. He knew if he made them for a certain amount of money, they would always return a profit, and he was not adverse to hiring people who really wanted to make movies but didn't know a thing about them and [wanted to] learn how to do it. That's how I started and that's how a number of people who are currently working who have movies out this year started. The general rule seems to be that people who wanted to stay up late and literally kill themselves and go without eating and work for nothing to learn how to make a movie, if that's what they wanted to do, they would do that.
>
> The people who didn't would fall away. People who had attitudes about what they wanted to do – some people felt that all this was just a lot of trash, that this is not my great film, I'm just going to walk through on this, I'll just sort of do a slip-shod job on it, and I'll save my talent for my great epic that I will do, that they never got to make because their *Women in Chains* movie was so terrible that they couldn't get another job. It was a matter of attitude actually. If you looked down your nose at the material you were forced to work with, it usually showed in the movie. Even the undiscriminating audiences that these pictures were aimed at could see that this was a fake, that this wasn't the real thing.
>
> And so you had to try to galvanize yourself up into being enthusiastic about piranhas, for instance. It's not something I'd ever given much thought about. I thought it was a little late, two years after *Jaws*, to do a cheap rip-off of *Jaws*, but that was it. Roger offered me this job, and he said, "Here's a picture to direct. If you direct it and cut it, I will give you $8,000." Now you can't imagine how good an offer that was. . . . [T]he fact is I was making $100 a week as a trailer editor for Roger, and I managed to talk him into letting me have my $100 a week salary while I was shooting for four weeks, so it ended up being $8,400. I had to try to get the best of him somehow or other.
>
> The idea was that he had this deal with UA and he was going to make a picture that was a little more expensive than the usual Corman picture because he had a foreign distribution deal for it, and it was going to be about piranhas, and it was going to be about piranhas that ate

people. The budget was $600,000, which is quite a bit of money for Roger, and a big step up for me with my $60,000 picture that I'd made in ten days. And it was made in Texas and had real actors in it and Roger left us alone. Actually, he cancelled the movie after the first day's shooting because he said we'd gone over budget by hiring a stunt-man. But then he came to me and said, "Well, no, I may have been a bit hasty here, but no stuntman." So the actors had to do the stunts themselves.

Anyway, the point is it was not exactly a project that I ever wanted or hoped to make, but I did manage by giving one piranha attack per two reels or something – it was also John Sayles' first script – and John and I managed to come up with something that we kind of liked. We added a little science fiction and we added a little social comment – Roger likes social comment, so we tried to get some social comment. We added some prosthetic breasts, which was something for Roger so he would leave us alone. We had to imagine how to do these effects because nobody had ever shot any piranha effects, so we went down and got some people who had worked at ILM on *Star Wars* but were all working with us, and we went down to the Olympic swimming pool down at USC or UCLA, whichever one of those it was, and we went underwater with our wetsuits and we'd shoot these rubber fish, and change frame rates and go to the lab in the morning and it looked terrible, and we'd go back and try to shoot something else that would look good. Roger was actually not going to make the picture unless the effects were going to be OK, which was pretty smart. So we sort of cheated a little bit. We figured out a way to do them close up and they looked pretty good, but we knew that Roger was going to come in, so we got a mannequin and we had to make this raw frenzy, right? We had these prosthetic breasts and we put a lot of raw hamburger in them, and we had these plastic, rubber piranhas attack the breasts under-water with lots of Karo syrup and stuff.

So we figured surely this would get Roger to make the picture, so we ran all these special effects – endless, boring rolls for him Monday at the screening room, the same one that Howard Hughes locked himself in, but that's another story, and he sat through a whole bunch of it and said, "Fine, fine, fine" as he was watching and then left. And we said, "No, wait Roger, you have to stay. You have to see the breast scene." And he looked and he said, "Do I have to stay and see the breast scene?" We realized that he really didn't care much about that stuff at all. He trusted us to make a movie, and we got to make the movie just the way we wanted within the proper restrictions that we had. It turned out a good deal better than I imagined it would be. I was sure I would never work again while I was making it.

After the success of *Piranha*, Dante got typecast as a "fish movie" direc-tor, of all things. Dino de Laurentiis hired him to direct *Orca 2*, but he talked de Laurentiis out of making the film. He got his first experience working for a big studio when he was preparing *Jaws 3, People 0*, a comedy that was to be produced by the original producers of *Jaws* along with Matty Simmons of the National Lampoon. Finally, it was decided that a parody might kill the shark that laid the golden box office receipts, and so when a *Jaws 3* finally did arrive, it was a serious film shot in 3-D which had no relation to this one.

Dante did work on one last film for Corman and his friend Allan Arkush, which was *Rock 'n' Roll High School*. During filming, Arkush fell sick and so Dante shot a little second unit material (though claims that he codirected the film are inaccurate). He had never shot a musical before and was responsible for P. J. Soles' bouncy number in the gym. Working on the film, he met up again with Mike Finnell, who was producing.

Finnell was then going to produce *The Howling* with Daniel Blatt at Avco-Embassy. Avco-Embassy was filled with former New World executives, and for a time they produced a stream of high-class exploitation pictures before they started making serious films and proceeded to go out of business. Originally, *The Howling* was to have been directed by Jack Conrad, who had written a screen adaptation of Gary Bradner's novel, but A-E lost faith in him after reading his script.

The original concept had spirits leaving people's bodies and entering the bodies of wolves in the forest, which Dante found uninteresting and nonsensical. A wolf on screen is not innately scary; it just looks like a large dog. Dante brought in Sayles to concoct a new screenplay.

Said Sayles:

> Of the movies I've only written, *Alligator* and *The Howling* turned out the best. In the genre stuff, you know, you're trying to avoid giving people the usual ride. So you ask, "What would happen if people in a horror movie had *seen* horror movies?" What would a real werewolf today have to do? He'd have to *cope*. There aren't wolves around anymore. If somebody's been eaten by a wolf, people are going to *know*. That's the main difference we made between *The Howling* and the book Joe (Dante) inherited. Rather than put it in a small town, we said, "Let's set it in L.A. and see what these werewolves have to *deal with*."

Dante builds up a menacing atmosphere right from the titles that rip through the screen (courtesy of Pete Kuran and VCE). Dee Wallace is appealingly competent yet vulnerable as Karen White, a television newslady who is putting herself on the line in order to lure a serial killer known as Eddie out into the open. Eddie plays cat and mouse with her, drawing her to a porno shop where he shows her a "beaver" film loop while he stands behind her. When she turns, she sees something so horrible that her mind blocks it out and is saved by the overanxious firing of a rookie cop. (When a department official investigates and asks what happened – why they shot an unarmed man – Ken Tobey, one-time star of the original *The Thing*, here playing a humorously crusty older cop, responds, "I don't know. Ask Quick Draw McGraw here.")

In *Piranha*, subsidiary characters were named after baseball players in Sayles' script. For *The Howling*, they are named after horror film directors who have done werewolf movies. Karen's husband is named R. William "Bill" Neill (Christopher Stone) for the director of *Frankenstein Meets the Wolf Man*. White's fellow newsman is named Lew Landers (Jim McKnell) after the director of *Return of the Vampire*, which also featured a werewolf. The head of the station is Fred Francis (Kevin McCarthy), and Karen's best friend is Terry Fisher (Belinda Balaski, who was also in *Piranha*) after Terence Fisher.

The film makes fun of quirky California retreats and psychobabble as the werewolf group is fronted by a psychiatrist, Dr. George Waggner (Patrick Macnee), named after the director of *The Wolf Man*. Other characters named after werewolf film directors are Erle Kenton (John Carradine); Jerry Warren (James Murtaugk), director of *Face of the Screaming Werewolf*, Lon Chaney, Jr.'s last performance as the Wolf Man; Sam Neufield (Slim Pickins), director of *The Mad Monster*; Charlie Barton (Noble Willingman), director of *The Shaggy D.A.*; and Jock Molina, who has made numerous Spanish-language werewolf movies which he starred in under the name Paul Naschy.

The film also slyly chronicles the influence of wolf stories in our culture, showing drawings from fairy tales, a cartoon big bad wolf menacing a poor lamb, the movie *The Wolf Man* on TV, shots of Ginsberg's *Howl* and Wolf chili, and even a line in response to White's complaint that "dogs don't howl like that": "Honey, you were raised in L.A. The wildest thing you ever heard was Wolfman Jack."

Perhaps what is most remarkable about this fantasy-oriented horror film is how naturally and realistically it portrays White and Neill's troubled relationship. Vague memories of her traumatic experience keep Karen from wanting to have sex with her husband. Rather than comforting her, he insensitively turns his back on her, figuratively and literally, and goes to sleep. Later, after he has been bitten by a wolf, she tries to initiate sex when he does not want it, complains that they are out of sync and then does the same thing to him, turning away from him and going to sleep.

Complicating matters, Marsha Quist (a very sexy Elisabeth Brooks) looks at Bill with hungry, smoldering looks. When he tells her, "I'm looking for my wife," she responds, "Why?" creating one of those awkward but lifelike moments that the film excels in. After he has been bitten by this incarnation of lust, Bill leaves his marriage bed to consummate a relationship between them, with both turning into werewolves in the throes of passion (the film's least convincing special effect, done as a cartoon silhouette).

The most enjoyable werewolf movie thus far, *The Howling* distinguishes

Belinda Balaski has an important file snatched from her grasp by a huge, hirsute intruder, one of the imposing werewolves created by Rob Bottin for The Howling, *adapted by John Sayles from the Gary Brandner novel and directed by Joe Dante, Jr.*

itself from others in a number of ways. Apart from the in-jokes (which proved distracting to some, though I enjoyed them – they are far more obtrusive in Dante's later films), *The Howling* establishes werewolves that can change at will instead of waiting for the full moon. Also, these beings do not change into wolf men like Lon Chaney, nor into wolves, but rather into huge, commanding, upright Wile E. Coyote–type creatures that are unlike the wolves in any previous film. The film also cleverly uses shots of George Waggner's *The Wolf Man* to provide quick exposition, as well as using John Carradine as a horror icon. (After Karen expresses the hope that the people at the Colony are normal, Dante cuts to Carradine howling at the moon to immediately inform us that they are not.)

The Colony itself is an interesting idea. Hoping to find some way to coexist with the normal humans, the werewolves isolate themselves and breed cattle on which they feed. However, these are new ideas and the old-timers do not cotton to them very well. Setting themselves apart are the Quist family, dedicated to the old ways. Most prominent among them is Eddie Quist (Robert Picardo), a serial killer and maniac who also happens to be a werewolf. Only this family is responsible for all attacks upon humans throughout the movie until the final climax.

Dante perfects a blend of humor and horror in the film, juxtaposing the amusing and the awful in the manner of James Whale in *The Invisible Man*. This technique did throw some reviewers, who complained that they could not tell whether they were watching a horror film or a comedy. However, while the humorous touches do relieve tension, they never undercut the real menace.

Some inspired moments include Walter Paisley (Dick Miller again, naturally) running an occult bookshop and chasing Forry Ackerman out before turning to explain to Terry's news reporter boyfriend Chris (Dennis Dugan), "Silver bullets or fire – that's the only way to get rid of the damned things – they're worse than cockroaches. They come back from the dead if you don't kill them right. Plus they regenerate. You know what that is? Cut off an arm, cut off a leg, stick a knife in the heart – nothing. They may look dead but then three days later, they're as good as new."

The most outrageous moment occurs when Karen finally confronts Eddie again after he has transformed and killed Terry. He appears, grinning and obviously enjoyed being a werewolf, with a bullet hole still in his forehead from when the police had shot him. He tells her, "I want to give you a piece of my mind," before plunging his fingers into the bullet hole and digging the bullet out. However, she is able to stop his attack temporarily by throwing acid in his face, so that the next time we see him in human form, his face is heavily scarred.

Rob Bottin served as associate producer and created the special effects for the film. Initial attempts to make a full-sized werewolf turned out to look too much like a bear, so a more pronounced lupin snout was developed. The transformation began with air bladders, a technique in which bags under the makeup are inflated with air. A hydraulic snout extends as hair, fangs, and nails sprout. The werewolf itself was created by means of a giant puppet. There was an upperhalf with head, torso, and arms, and a lower half with wolf-like legs.

Dante wanted at least one shot in the movie when you see both halves together and so inserted a quick stop-motion animation shot created by David Allen. Another shot was filmed of the werewolves in the burning barn but was eliminated when it would not cut in with the other werewolf effects, especially as the design had changed.

Other elements that helped make the film effective were John Hora's atmospheric lighting, Pino Donaggio's evocative score, and Dante and Mark Goldblatt's editing. Hora became Dante's regular cinematographer until *Innerspace*, in which he played a cameo death scene. For fantasy scenes, he sometimes uses extreme saturations of color, principally orange and blue, which blend in with the unreality and help hide some of the seams.

Rick Baker was involved in the project as a consultant, but had promised his friend John Landis that he would do a werewolf transformation for him.

He did on *American Werewolf in London*, which won Baker an Academy Award. (As a non-union film, *The Howling* was not even considered.) It is interesting to compare the two transformations. Landis wanted to do his in broad daylight and not hide anything. As a result, the phoniness of some of the effects is more apparent and the shots lack atmosphere and power, although the transformation itself is a more elaborate one. Landis elected to have his werewolf turn into a giant killer dog, which proves less menacing than the upright and intelligent as well as powerful werewolves in Dante's film. (Additionally, Landis' film is more clearly a comedy until the sudden tragic ending.)

The film was a success and made money, though not for Dante. As he explained it:

> *The Howling* was $1.6 million, which was a lot of money, but they had to pay a lot for the book, which they owned, $50,000, and they had to pay off a number of other people who owned rights to things and there's a lot of money that didn't get up on the screen. . . . [I]t was an opportunity because it was a better project than we had been able to work with than to try to use all the things we had learned from Corman and really try to make them show up on the screen and really try to apply it to a picture we knew would be sold to a wider audience than the kind of pictures Roger made. Roger also had a very limited distribution set-up because he only distributed exploitation films and art films, like Bergman and Fellini. He got small bookings for those and he had his exploitation pictures in the drive-in market, but he didn't really crack the major market of mainstream pictures, whereas Embassy pictures were playing in the major markets and the advertising budgets were huge, which is why we never saw a dime from that picture.

The film ends on an interesting note, pointing up the ambivalent feelings that people have towards the television medium. Karen White, who has been a TV news reporter, sees television as a vehicle for disseminating the truth and is certain that in changing into a werewolf and being killed on camera, she will be sacrificing herself so that people will understand and believe. Instead, most people don't separate her noble sacrifice from the Alpo dog food commercial that follows it. They are convinced that it is just another special effect by a medium in which they long ago ceased to have faith. Reality is too often manipulated by this medium for the public to really regard it as trustworthy, making White's sacrifice ironically futile.

This ending was bizarrely reshot in a sequel, *The Howling II: Your Sister Is a Werewolf*, which was directed by Australian director Phillipe Mora with all the quality of a porno film with the sex cut out. Strangely enough, this did not discourage Mora from making *The Howling III: The Marsupials*, nor John Hough from making the equally execrable *The Howling IV*, which apparently was released directly to video.

Having been involved in advertising for Corman, Dante has some strong opinions on how his films are advertised, and admittedly at least three films – *Twilight Zone – The Movie, Explorers* and *Innerspace* – had very poor advertising campaigns. The *Twilight Zone* ad featured little more than a title and a quote of the show's opening by Rod Serling, telling viewers nothing about the movie. *Explorers* looked as if it were about skateboards as that was all it showed in its ad, while the campaign for *Innerspace* featured giant fingers crushing a miniaturized ship, again giving the audience no clue as to what the film was about.

The Howling almost suffered a similar fate. Said Dante:

> The studio one day brought in an ad which was a naked woman – naked women were a very popular way to sell a movie – it was a naked woman with her arms folded over her chest, and she was a werewolf on this side and she was a regular naked woman on the other. We were with Daniel Blatt, the executive producer, and Daniel is a guy who's done some good stuff. He did an Entebbe movie on TV and *I Never Promised You a Rose Garden*, and he's a guy who cares about what he's doing. And he pulled this ad out of the envelope it was in, and it wasn't really out of the envelope for more than I'd say half a second when he slammed it back down and was on the phone complaining about it. We tried to class this picture up a little bit, and here it was being classed down a bit.

Dante spent some time preparing to direct *The Philadelphia Experiment*, which originally was written by John Carpenter, but then abandoned it. It was later made into a movie by Stewart Raffill (*Ice Pirates; Mac and Me*). Despite all this directorial work, Dante did not get into the Directors Guild until he was called in to direct two episodes of the highly acclaimed but short-lived series *Police Squad*, which the writer-directors of *Airplane!* and *The Naked Gun* created. The series was famous for throwing in as many gags as it could while still keeping a coherent storyline, and Dante's next few projects began to take on the same anarchic construction, sometimes to the point where the in-joke gags got to be obtrusive and distracting, detracting from rather than adding to the overall ambiance.

Dante was called in by Steven Spielberg to work on *Twilight Zone – The Movie*. Spielberg's basic idea was to remake some of the best episodes from the original series into an anthology film with plenty of high-tech gloss, though his coproducer, John Landis, ended up directing an ill-fated *Twilight Zone*–like story of his own concoction. Dante did not really think redoing old episodes as a movie was such a hot idea, but he was excited at the prospect of working with Spielberg.

He took the opportunity to go back and reread Jerome Bixby's original story for his segment, "It's a *Good* Life," but while he liked the story, he thought that enough projects similar to it had already come down the pike. Instead, the basic idea was altered radically. In Dante's version a kid with omnipotent powers who can manipulate reality to his will is a cartoon fanatic, allowing the director free reign of his anarchic cartoon sensibility and enabling him to put a new twist on the thing.

He realized that the anything-can-happen world of animation was the perfect setting and has a natural affinity for a boy whose every selfish wish comes true. The house the boy inhabits wondrously recreates the cartoon houses of Tom and Jerry cartoons. A nonstop accompaniment of cartoons on television provides a collection of Carl Stalling cartoon scores to underlie all the scenes in the house, giving it a further cartoon feel. The upstairs is even done in the black-and-white surrealism of the early Fleischer cartoons, with some impressive lighting courtesy of John Hora.

The basic story follows Kathleen Quinlan, who meets Jeremy Licht when she almost runs him over outside of the bar owned by Walter Paisley (Dick Miller again). (Bill Mumy, the kid in the original *Twilight Zone* episode, makes a cameo in the bar.) She drives him home only to find his weird relatives all terrified and his power absolute. Tyranny has led to loneliness and Jeremy hopes to make friends with the teacher.

Dante adds a little genuine *frisson* to the film. One shiver comes in the depiction of a now mouthless sister forced to watch cartoons upstairs as a punishment. Another comes when Uncle Walt (Kevin McCarthy in a delightful, off-center performance) is forced to pull a terrifying, giant killer rabbit out of his hat in a magic act. And finally, through the makeup magic of Rob Bottin, a Tasmanian Devil–like creature with Big Daddy Roth–like features breaks forth from the television set with a whirlwind action. The creature, though goofy-looking, is also frightening because it is obviously powerful and obviously very insane.

The two aspects of the segment that do not quite work are when Licht sends one of his sisters to cartoon-land – created by Sally Cruickshank in a combination of her and Dave Fleischer's style, which is too ephemerally cute to be effective – and the hearts-and-flowers ending where Quinlan gets Licht to agree to limit his powers and they drive happily off into the sunset. Being trapped with an omnipotent boy who has already created a hellish house for his family might not seem the happiest of endings, but Dante makes the boy's conversion to sweetness and light seem complete. This tranformation seems at odds with the rest of the material, which is more imaginative and unnerving. Nevertheless, along with George Miller's "Nightmare at 20,000 Feet," Dante's was the best segment in the film.

Dante's most financially successful film to date (and once one of the top fifteen highest grossing films of all time) was *Gremlins* (though the director's own personal favorite from his own works is *Explorers*). Dante explained how he became involved on the project:

I found the script for *Gremlins* on my desk sometime after I'd made *The Howling* and during a period when a picture called *The Philadelphia Experiment* looked like it was never going to happen. It showed up and there was a note from Steven [Spielberg]'s office saying would I like to read this and meet with him about it, and I said sure. I read it, and it was certainly different from the version we made, but it had a lot of the same qualities to it, chief among them was a lot of special effects, more than I have ever counted in one movie, certainly more than in any movie that I had ever made, and more than in most pictures that I had seen. It did seem like it was going to be a monumental effort to do at all, but it was intriguing enough.

When I met with Steven, I said, "What do you have in mind for this kind of picture?" He wanted to do it comparatively low-budget, certainly lower than it is now. He was thinking of doing it non-union and filming it in some place like Utah, which may have been one of the reasons he decided to call on me and Mike Finnell. Things developed for varying reasons involving weather and the special effects and the fact that there were kids in it so that it was going to be impossible to make non-union, let alone on a real location. . . .

The gremlins weren't prankish in the original version; they just killed people. Period. The idea of them being prankish came more out of the idea that they were gremlins because gremlins have a reputation for being prankish and mischievous. Originally, it was pretty grim. It was kind of sweet too, and had this Capraesque tone. It was always *It's a Wonderful Life* meets *The Birds*, even in its old version, but as it went on into production, that just appeared to be too thin to justify all the time and expense that it was going to take just to do another picture where monsters come and bite people and get killed at the end. So to fill up the space, we decided to try to make a somewhat better movie out of it.

The original script for *Gremlins* was indeed far more of a horror film than the version released, which contained much more comedy. Another chief difference was that a sympathetic gremlin, Gizmo, was added to the final version (originally the idea was that the cute, cuddly gremlin turns into Stripe, the nasty one, forcing the [then much younger] boy hero to have to kill his once favorite pet). Also, there were originally some horror gags like gremlins attacking a McDonald's and eating the people but leaving the hamburgers. Dante decided that gory filmmaking had pretty much run its course and did not want to make a gory movie – though the scene of a fantasy creation like a gremlin exploding in a microwave did catch a lot of flak.

One of the first considerations on *Gremlins* was how the gremlins themselves would be manipulated. Dante briefly considered using stop-motion animation throughout the film, but there was too much character interaction for that, and it would have made *Gremlins* "the *Heaven's Gate* of effects films." Instead, the gremlins were created by Chris Walas mostly as cable-controlled puppets. Each gremlin required several people to operate, and with people lying on the floor and massive amounts of cables all over the place, moving the camera and getting a perfectly synchronized take proved difficult in the extreme.

Additionally, new ideas were always being funneled into the film. Dante said:

> *Gremlins* developed into a much more complicated thing than we ever imagined it would, simply because whenever we had one idea, it would lead to another idea and so on. We'd say, "We can't *not* do that, that'll be great!" Well, we don't have time and we never built on to do that, or we'd say we never planned it. So a whole lot of the latter stages of the movie had to be winged basically because of situations we'd gotten ourselves in where we never planned to have a puppet do one thing or another that it really didn't do as well as something different. And the thing it did well was great, but that wasn't in the script, so we changed the script so we could use the best part of what he did.
>
> In a script, you can change one thing and then two days later, that forces you to change another thing because it is all connected. It's a really dangerous thing to do to start winging a script because you can lose track of where you are. One of the reasons we didn't [lose track] was because Chris was so together about knowing what mechanisms could be stripped and used over and which kind of a puppet worked best in which scene.
>
> At a certain point, we had to throw away the storyboards because the story had changed so much, and the storyboards were planned around the mechanics of what we could see and how it needed to be operated. Storyboards are absolutely essential in a film like this. Luckily, by that time, we gained enough facility in the operation of the shooting of the effects that we could pretty much plan everything a shot ahead, and when people were working on one shot, a group would be working off on the next one while we were shooting. We were always behind.

The design of Gizmo itself, with its big round eyes, button nose, and overall cute and expressive face, is very much in the style of Chuck Jones' cartoon creations. Dante wanted Gizmo to have a wide range of expressions and a very reactive face. While Gizmo charmed the audience, he was a horror on the set. He was kept small, so as to remain cute, but his very smallness made the obstinately inanimate little furball extremely difficult to manipulate.

Said Dante:

> The only person on the crew that really liked Gizmo was the dog, who thought he was real. He was a little puzzled by the fact that Gizmo didn't smell real, but he was fascinated by Gizmo. He would stare at it,

and it was great. We'd rehearse the scenes and get it all ready, and we would get the dog and do the first couple of takes, and we could do as many as five takes and the dog would still remain fascinated and always look in the right place and react to it just as if it was an animal. The crew itself was not so lucky because on account of Gizmo, we would have to do many, many different takes at different speeds and different angles because we were never sure which would be best in any given situation. Sometimes the actors would have to act slow when we shot faster and sometimes they would have to be fast when we were shooting slower, and it was very difficult, which is one of the reasons why there was the scene of Gizmo getting darts thrown at him in this picture.

One day, even though we were behind, we were supposed to be shooting a scene where the gremlins are batting him around like a baseball, and they were hitting him behind books and he would roll up into a ball, and it really wasn't very interesting. So then I said, "OK, what else could we do?" And somebody said, "Well, let's throw darts at him!" So we found a dart board and we put him up on a phone cord, it was all made up on the spot, and they put a scared face on him and made him shake, and then gremlin hands came in and threw darts at him. It made everybody feel so good on the picture. The next day at the dailies, everybody would shout, "Run it again! Run it again!" It was just that every time we had to work with Gizmo, we knew it was going to take forever. Everybody would say, "Oh no, not him again!"

Dick Miller shows up in this film as Mr. Futterman, an out-of-work, gung ho American who detests all mechanical parts of foreign manufacture. Miller was selected for this part because he could talk fast, cramming a lot of exposition into very little time, and because he was able to inject an element of humor in almost everything he does. He was teamed up with Jackie Joseph, a commedienne who specializes in a type of charming innocence, who had costarred with him on Corman's *Little Shop of Horrors* and Allan Arkush's *Get Crazy*. Apart from the science teacher, they are the first townspeople to get attacked by gremlins as the gremlins begin their night of total anarchy.

Chris Columbus wrote the film as a sample script, not expecting it to get made until Steven Spielberg offered to buy it. He hoped to create a new kind of monster in the gremlins, inventing three simple rules for them: Do not expose them to bright light, for sunlight will kill them; do not expose them to water, for that makes them multiply; and don't ever feed them after midnight, for that will cause them to change. He even gave them a name suggesting an exotic origin: mogwai.

In working with Columbus on the screenplay, Dante added more humor and give the creatures more personality. Executive producer Steven Spielberg came up with the key concept of keeping Gizmo as a sympathetic gremlin all throughout the film. Said Dante:

He really took a liking to Gizmo, as you might imagine, and we sort of hedged our bets when we were showing him our original designs by making Gizmo the exact same color as Steven's dog, which he is very fond of. Luckily, [he was] also fond of our designs, which is a good thing because if he hadn't been, we wouldn't have been able to start the picture on time.

Originally I resisted Steve's suggestion that we keep Gizmo on all throughout the movie because I felt there was a certain verisimilitude to the fact that Gizmo became Stripe and that therefore when the kid has to have the confrontation with his former pet, that there's a moment when he can't kill it because it's his old former pet; however, it gets ruthless and takes advantage of this. That is interesting in the story; however, I can see that emotionally it is not as satisfying as having somebody to root for, especially given the fact that this is a totally fantastical, impossible movie, that the idea of having good supernatural forces opposed to the bad, a creature and its own id, in the same movie is really conceptually a lot better.

The other reason we resisted his suggestion was that Chris and Mike and I were always worried about Gizmo and whether or not we were going to be able to make him look very convincing. We were finally able to convince ourselves that we would be able to make him convincing for the requisite amount of time that he was onscreen, but then Steve said, "No, no, no, let's have him through the whole movie." And we went, "No, we can't do that. How are we going to do this?" That was one of the big reasons we resisted it, but in the end, I can't imagine the picture without him. I remember the way it was written, and I know it would not have been as satisfying as it is now.

Additionally, Spielberg was supportive of what Dante was doing and trusted him. Instead of being an active, hands-on producer, Spielberg, along with executive producers Frank Marshall and Kathleen Kennedy, were busy preparing *Indiana Jones and the Temple of Doom*. When it came time to preview the film, Spielberg allowed Dante to save Phoebe Cates' at once humorous and appalling story about how she hated Christmas because of the horrible way in which she discovered that there was no Santa Claus. (This is one of the things Dante kept from Columbus' original script and which has provoked a lot of negative comment. Spielberg protected Dante, saying it was his movie and he could keep it if he wanted.)

Dante presents the movie as if it were a tall tale being told by crackpot inventor Rand Peltzer (Hoyt Axton in a warm, avuncular performance). The opening scenes in Chinatown where he picks up Gizmo on the sly after a grandfatherly Oriental gentleman (Keye Luke, spoofing ancient clichés about Asians) refuses to sell him, have an unreal, fairy tale quality. Peltzer's own slogan is, "Fantastic ideas for a fantastic world; I make the illogical logical."

The rest of the movie takes place in Kingston Falls, your basic small-town American setting. There is a running gag throughout the film that Rand is a failed inventor whose inventions keep mucking up about his household. The family is actually supported by William "Billy" Peltzer (Zach Galligan) on his meager bank teller's salary. A subplot largely cut out of the film has the mean-spirited Mrs. Deagle (Polly Holiday) buying up property all over town to turn it into a chemical plant. Injected into this semirealistic setting is the story of Billy receiving a fantastic new pet but then getting careless with it and not following the very specific instructions that Rand passed along.

Though the gremlins hardly prove to be a force for good, most of their victims are punished for their inhumanity: Mrs. Deagle for her general unpleasantness; Mr. Hanson (Glynn Turman), the science teacher, for his objective, scientific approach that allows him to inflict pain when drawing blood from a gremlin; Sheriff Frank (Scott Brady, who has played a long line of sheriffs in B movies) and his deputy (Jonathan Banks), for callous disregard of Billy's warnings. Note that Lew Landers (Jim McKrell reprising his role from *The Howling*) reports that Mr. Futterman is still alive in the hospital.

Once more a number of character actors are employed in bit parts. In addition to the ones already mentioned, Dante had William Schallert in a bit as a priest, and Harry Carey, Jr., as a friendly townsperson. Ken Tobey was hired to improvise a comic scene with Hoyt Axton about a "smokeless" ashtray, a sequence which was largely cut as it unfortunately came in at the wrong time. John Williams, Jerry Goldsmith, Steven Spielberg, Robby the Robot, and the time machine from George Pal's *The Time Machine* (appearing in one scene and disappearing in the background in the next) all make cameo appearances.

Like many film buffs or fanatics, Dante says that movies played a big part in his life, and he pays tribute to their effect by making references to them in his films. In *Gremlins*, not only are *It's a Wonderful Life, To Please a Lady,* and *Invasion of the Body Snatchers* shown on television, but a theater advertises the films *A Boy's Life* and *Keep Watching the Skies!* (the original titles of *E.T.* and *Close Encounters of the Third Kind*). A radio personality has a *Raiders of the Lost Ark*–style ad. The local town doctor is Dr. Moreau. Deagle's last husband is Edward Arnold, Frank Capra's favorite heavy, who typically played grasping, greedy businessmen. The film even contains one of the first film references to *E.T.* as Stripe the nasty gremlin yanks out the phone line with the line, "Phone home – kaka!"

However, these references are not too obtrusive but mostly kept in the background. The least subtle aspect of the picture is Polly Holiday's Margaret-Hamilton-Wicked-Witch-of-the-West performance as the brash, unpleasant Mrs. Deagle. Heartless and arrogant, pushing her way to the head of every line as if it were her divine right, Holiday amusingly overplays the

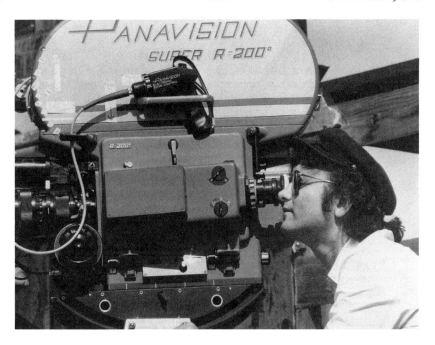

Joe Dante, Jr., lines up a shot on Gremlins, *his greatest box office success. More often he checks shots through a video monitor which reflects the framing of the film camera.*

part, even down to threatening Billy about his little dog Barney. She seems to have no friends except for her cats, whom she has named after kinds of money. But some aspects of her character, as well as much of Judge Reinhold's and Edward Andrews' parts, disappeared in the final editing.

One reason films cost so much is that almost every film will have shot an unneeded half-hour or more of footage in the making; there is no way to tell until it is assembled into a rough cut which footage needs to stay and which needs to go. All of Dante's films have originally run longer than released, and *Gremlins* was no exception. According to Dante:

> The two-hour version had a different beginning. Hoyt Axton went to an earlier store and met the kid who enticed him to the place, which we cut out because it's not so hot. It was a repeat, basically, of what happened in the second scene.
>
> There was some stuff in the back with Edward Andrews, which was pleasant but not particularly germane, and there was an earlier introductory scene with the teacher who was talking to the kids in school which was a very funny scene actually, and sort of cute, but the problem was there was no place to put it in the movie because every time you cut to the guy, the audience would go, "Who is this?" because there

were no main characters in the scene. You would think, why am I seeing this scene, so out it came.

There was a lot of stuff with Mrs. Deagle who used to go to the bank in the middle of the picture, and who was basically humiliated by the two kids and then she threatened to throw everybody out of the house the day after Christmas. Her line was that she would do it on Christmas, but everything's closed. That was taken out basically because it started to make her awfully sympathetic. They made fun of her and they made a paper airplane out of her check and threw it around, and the whole town was there and they all laughed at her. That was a rare occasion where an actress gave a performance that was too good for the part. You were starting to get to really see why this woman was the way she was and feel sorry for her. Maybe her husband made her do this? God knows what disappointment in her life turned her into this horrible person.

Which was not only not what the picture was about at that time, but seriously interfered with giving her any kind of comeuppance at the end of the movie. There was a little scene just before she gets killed where she goes down to the cats, and there's this picture of Edward Arnold on the piano. She says, "Oh, you've gotten kitty litter all over Daddy's picture." She looks down at this picture of her late husband, and she says, "Oh, Donald . . ." and in this one line she encapsulates this whole story which we haven't told about this character. It was a very nice moment, quite impressive, but it seriously affected the impact of what happened next because you thought oh, this poor lady, what a terrible way to go, which was not the point of what the scene was supposed to do. What the scene was supposed to do was on a very primal level, it's supposed to say here's the Wicked Witch being punished. And so all that stuff came out, and now she's more of a cartoon character than she was initially, but when you've got a three-hour movie, you've got to take stuff out.

You want every shot to be a masterpiece, and that scene started with a whole informational, biographical camera movement around her house which showed you all the stuff of her life, and that's another reason why you'd be so depressed by the time it was over. It had all these cats in it. I mean, thousands of cats, doing all sorts of things on cue, peeing and fighting, so where our shot starts, she's already coming down, but originally there was 90 seconds ahead of that of all cats, and these were the nastiest cats I'd ever seen.

First of all, they smelled terrible. They peed everywhere, and they sprayed which is worse. They fought. They all hated each other. It was almost impossible to get any useable dialogue because they were always screaming, and there's some growls in the picture right around the time that she hears the gremlin carolers outside and you hear [growls] and people think it's gremlins, but it's the cat in her lap, and he's making this unearthly, creepy noise that gives rise to why people must have thought that cats snatch babies' souls out of them because if they make noises like this, boy they can really scare you. They were horrible cats. Everybody got scratched.

Judge Reinhold's part was cut for two reasons. One was that when he reappeared in the story as Gerald, he had been off the screen so long that people had forgotten who he was. Also, the picture by then is building to a climax and the audience is more interested in what the gremlins are up to. Explained Dante:

> He was in the vault when they came back to the bank. They open up the vault and he's there, and he's not so tough anymore, and he's lost his mind. It was a good scene and he was good in it, but a lot of people didn't connect him again with the beginning of the picture. The same goes for Edward Andrews. He used to have a scene where they find him at the end of the movie, he used to have an obsession with time, and when they found him, he was covered with clocks and *Time* magazine. Those facets of the story didn't pay off, and the audience didn't want to spend time stopping the story for that stuff. The film was 111 minutes at the preview and 106 minutes when it was released. The reason you go to previews is to find out where you are slow and where you're fast, so we basically took some subplots out and just sped up the second half of the picture, but we didn't change much.

One of the most fondly remembered scenes in the movie is the bar scene where the gremlins are indulging in conspicious consumption. Here we have a paradigm for most basic human vices and overindulgence. Dante and Finnell drew up a list of things crew members would like to see the gremlins doing and culled the best suggestions. We see them smoking several cigarettes at once, drinking massive quantities of alcohol, overeating, and acting recklessly. Some gremlins conform to stereotypes, so there is a flasher gremlin, a blues gremlin, a gambler gremlin, a break-dancing gremlin, and even a masked robber gremlin. At one time there was even more, but the additional material veered toward the excessive and would have stopped the film cold, so the material was trimmed back to its present state.

As the gremlins get more prankish and puckish in the movie, the film changes its tone into something darker and more threatening. Some people felt that the film started to fall apart halfway through as it became overloaded with schtick , but it obviously pleased large sections of the national audience as the film went on to become a hit far beyond any of the creator's dreams.

Dante's later films suffer even more from this switching of gears where the film starts out as one kind of story and turns into another. *Explorers* starts out as a group of kids off on a marvelous adventure spurred on by visions and dreams of scientific wonders they make reality, but then it veers into a burlesque of space movies and television. *Innerspace* starts off as an adventure/comedy about a man being miniaturized and injected into another body and then turns into a spy thriller. *The 'Burbs* starts out as a comedy about suburbanites suspicious of their neighbors whom they fear are devil worshippers, and then towards the end, after being made to look foolish, their fears are suddenly confirmed and the film makes a last-second switch into being a horror movie.

Humor can be derived from both the expected and the incongruous, but Dante is not a filmmaker who makes straight comedies, though his films all contain humor. He is better when he keeps his narrative focus than when he tries throwing an unexpected twist at the audience, and the films that resist tweaking expectations have all tended to do better at the box office. (Paramount practically wrote off *Explorers* after its opening weekend, after having unmercifully rushed the film through all three phases of production to meet an expected opening date.)

Originally, *Gremlins* was to have ended when Rand Peltzer squirted Stripe with the bathroom buddy and then exposed it to light. Dante did not find the concept particularly thrilling. Then Speilberg insisted that Gizmo be kept throughout the whole film, and that meant he obviously needed to do something in the climax. Someone suggested that he drive around in a toy car, and Dante prepared for this by inserting a scene where Gizmo watches Clark Gable racing a car on TV. According to Dante:

> The idea of Gizmo driving the car came from looking at the set. He was supposed to run around a lot, but running around was not his best feature and it also wasn't very interesting. We were ending up spending an incredible amount of time to make some realistic effect of something that any animal can do. So, much like the idea of gremlins using guns and chainsaws, that was all added when we got to the department store because that was the last thing we shot, and we knew that this was the end of the picture and we knew we had to top what had gone on before. What was going on in the script was frankly not as good as the movie theater scene, so the idea of putting him in the car, well, Chris [Walas] sort of leapt at that because it was an easy thing to do.
>
> It was real hard in some ways, and there are some hysterical outtakes of him driving around in his little car, bumping into everything, which used to take up half a reel. I mean it used to be like *Raiders of the Lost Ark*. It was just him and giant basketballs chasing him down corridors and him bumping into things with his little remote control car. It was just hysterical on the set. It was literally like watching an animal who didn't know how to drive, drive into things.

Dante had inserted his trademark animation scene into the feature by having the gremlins watch *Snow White and the Seven Dwarfs* at the theater, while what is now Dreamquest provided one stop-motion shot of the gremlins invading the town after Stripe had jumped into the swimming pool at the YMCA. Like *Hollywood Boulevard* and *The Howling* (which featured a last shot from *The Wolf Man*), Dante wanted to include a post-credit bit of a picture of Stripe and Gizmo in a Buster-Brown-and-his-dog-Tige logo parody, but was forced to opt for gremlin laughter instead.

Also to wrap things up, Keye Luke is brought back to collect the mogwai from the Peltzers and issue a stern warning: Mankind is too irresponsible with nature's gift and is not ready to be entrusted with the mogwai as yet. This scene successfully brings the family together again after they have been separated during the course of the picture, and it adds a thin layer of social commentary. As Luke walks away with Gizmo under his arm, Axton gives a cheerful warning to look for gremlins whenever things start to mysteriously go wrong. (Note: Gremlins themselves originated during World War II as small creatures responsible for malfunctions on airplanes. Warner Bros. devoted two cartoons to this theme, "Falling Hare" and "Gremlins from the Kremlin," while Walt Disney had hired Raold Dahl to write a screenplay for an unfilmed movie about gremlins. Dante considered sticking a scene from "Falling Hare" into the film but discovered that Warner Bros. no longer owned the rights to it.)

Some people considered the film unfit for children, and it suffered some backlash from being given an original ad campaign similar to *E.T.*'s so that some parents expected a similarly non-violent movie. This led to the film industry adopting a new rating of "PG-13," warning parents that certain films might be unsuitable for pre-teens. However, most children I know who have seen the film regard it as a children's film and tend to delight in it unless they are exceedingly young, in which case it would definitely be irresponsible for parents to allow their children to see it in the first place. Strangely, adults mistakenly conceive of childhood as a safe and happy time, forgetting that children see a world in which they are surrounded by giants who give unfathomable commands. They are perfectly capable of dealing with a little uncertainty, and many people forget that the early Disney classics that they think are so sanitized and safe have this aspect as part of their mixture. The dark element is one of the reasons why the Disney films are so much more memorable and affecting than other "family" entertainments which are sugary sweet and quickly forgotten.

Dante is capable of being cute and cloying, but he is by no means a sugary sweet filmmaker, and his wild aspect helps give his movies their edge. *Gremlins* is certainly a departure from the exploitation nature of his previous films, and the most the hero and heroine (Phoebe Cates as Kate) exchange is a chaste kiss – far from the hop-in-the-sack mentality of most modern Hollywood movies, and this is to *Gremlins*' credit. Despite charges, it is not gratuitously violent, even if Lynn Peltzer (France Lee McCain) does grind a gremlin in a blender, knife another, and microwave a third. The gremlins are not pets but are fantasy creations who lose their lovableness when they lose their fur and turn into sadistic, reptilian creatures. Lynn's actions are heroic, defending her home against her attackers by using the weapons she knows best. Despite the widespread gremlin mayhem in Kingston Falls, no human blood is spilled anywhere in the film.

Unlike most modern horror directors, Dante is very restrained and achieves his tension-mounting effects largely through camera angles and editing. Sadly, modern audiences have taken today's gore epics as their standards of what a horror movie is and thereby predicated what future horror movies will be like, eschewing atmosphere and subtlety. This may account for Dante's largely leaving the horror field in favor of thrillers with a flavor of the fantastic which he loves so well.

At one time Dante was involved in what later turned out to be some of Hollywood's most successful movies, turning down directing *Batman* because of a bad original script and avoiding *Who Framed Roger Rabbit* simply because the film would take too long.

Instead he made a film very personal to him and his childhood – *Explorers*, which gently kidded the Spielberg-inspired notion that mankind will find its saviors in outer space. Dante has his pre-teen heroes meet television-routine-spouting alien children (including an inspired performance from Robert Picardo as Wak) who have stolen their father's spaceship when mankind finally makes its first extraterrestrial contact. Some viewers loved the first part of the movie but not the unexpected twist, and others loved the twist but not the semi-solemn buildup.

Because the film was rushed, Dante was not able to get a director's final cut into theatrical release – the theatrically released film had some buildup scenes, the payoffs for which had been trimmed – but was able to alter the film slightly to his satisfaction for the eventual video release. The film does have some charm, but too many film references in it are distracting or obscure (at one point there is a drive-in tribute to badly dubbed foreign science fiction films with a spaceship that looks like a special effects camera). The child actors (Ethan Hawke, River Phoenix and Jason Presson) are talented but don't seem terribly caught up in their wondrous experiments as they combine their talents and explore the frontiers of science, creating a force-field bubble that can defy gravity.

The blindness of the film industry to its past can be shown in the fact that the producers of *Innerspace* thought that shrinking a man and injecting him in a miniaturized submarine into another man's body was a hot new idea, not realizing it had been done in 1966 as *Fantastic Voyage* directed by Richard Fleischer. While Dante presents a somewhat more realistic look at the interior of the body, his film oddly lacks any sense of wonder at the achievement, preferring to concentrate on a puerile spy story that the miniaturized Dennis Quaid leads Martin Short to undertake in Jeffrey Boam's uninspiring story. The film won an Oscar for special effects.

In between these two features, Dante worked on an oddball project which came to be called *Amazon Women on the Moon*. John Landis' funniest film is *The Kentucky Fried Movie*, a series of blackout sketches written by the makers of *Airplane!* and *Police Squad* when they were performing as the Kentucky Fried Theater. Producer Robert K. Weiss hoped that lightning would strike again when he found a huge, unwieldy comedy screenplay by Michael Barrie and Jim Mulholland. John Landis stepped in to produce and direct some of the segments, and told Dante, Carl Gottlieb (*Caveman*), Peter Horton, and Weiss to look through the script for segments they would like to do.

Dante's segments were the hairlooming ad with Sy Swerdlow (Joe Pantoliano), in which bald men were literally given rugs; the very funny "Bullshit or Not" parody of TV's *In Search of* program with Henry Silva exploring the question of whether the Loch Ness monster was actually Jack the Ripper; the "Critics Corner" in which a Siskell and Ebert–like pair of critics critique a man's life, with its bad taste follow-up, "Roast Your Loved One" in which a eulogy turns into a celebrity roast with Slappy White, Rip Taylor, Jackie Vernon, Henny Youngman, Charlie Callas and Steve Allen all doing their patented and unfunny schticks (the widow becomes the comedy hit of the ceremony and it is held over for several weeks); and the wonderfully wacky but esoteric "Reckless Youth," a deliberately bad parody of Dwain Esper's exploitation films of the '30s with Paul Bartel as a doctor warning Mary Brown (Carrie Fisher) about her having a social disease in the hammiest and exploitative way possible. However, as the vast majority of the audience could not be expected to be familiar with these kinds of films, it's hard to determine for whom the film was geared.

The biggest liability of the film is its central segment of "Amazon Women on the Moon," Weiss' attempt to spoof cheap fifties sci-fi films like *Cat Women of the Moon* and *Queen of Outer Space* that ends up being as bad and as boring as the material it is spoofing. Additionally, the lame title drove people away rather than attracting an audience, though the film has achieved some popularity on video where people can speed through to the genuinely good segments.

Dante's next film, *The 'Burbs*, succeeded largely on the appeal of Tom Hanks, who plays another of his variations on the perpetual man-child. Here Hanks is on vacation and spends most of the film in his bathrobe as his paranoid neighbor (Bruce Dern) becomes increasingly suspicious of their Charles Addams–type neighbors. They go through elaborate ruses to find out the truth about these people, which provides some mild comedy, and eventually succeed in blowing up their neighbors' house. However, lest this be considered an especially cruel and thoughtless act, though accidental, the neighbors are revealed to be sick killers after all, and Hanks must save his own life for the happy ending.

The most impressive bit in the film is the wonderful opening shot, which begins with the Universal globe and then zooms down towards earth in a continuous take until through careful, seamless dissolves the camera lands in the neighborhood where the story takes place and travels down this exceedingly familiar Universal backlot street. However, overall *The 'Burbs* is a human cartoon with caricatures and all too many lame gags and will no doubt become a minor footnote in both Dante's and Hanks' careers.

Dante next struck with *Gremlins 2: The New Batch,* his most wildly anarchic movie yet, stuffed with more gags than plot and recalling the zany, anything-can-happen craziness of Ollie and Johnson's *Hellzapoppin'.* In this film, the narrative seems to have broken down completely in favor of setting up one gag after another. To Dante's credit, some of the gags do connect, but it does not make for a satisfying whole.

The film opens with some animation directed by Chuck Jones in which Daffy Duck makes a stink about Bugs Bunny taking precedence at the beginning of Merrie Melody cartoons. Just as the audience is set up to enjoy a full, new Warners cartoon, the real story starts, reintroducing Keye Luke as the old Oriental gentlemen who is the guardian of the Gizmo mogwai. He owns a plot of land that is blocking a development by Daniel Clamp (John Glover), an obvious satire of mulitmillionaire entrepreneur Donald Trump, whose Clamp Enterprises logo is a clamp squeezing the world out of shape. Luke dies and Gizmo gets loose, winding up in the Clamp Tower where Billy Peltzer (Zach Galligan) and Kate Beringer (Phoebe Cates) both work.

Dante has some fun decrying the sterility of the modern office environment. Naturally, the building becomes a perfect target for a new batch of gremlins (this time designed and created by Rick Baker) to wreak havoc in. The Clamp Tower encapsulates consumer-culture America with slick, vapid boutiques and yogurt bars, with the whole thing monitored by a crypto-fascist security organization run by Robert Picardo.

Additionally, the building houses a science laboratory, Splice O'Life (Designer Genes) run by a Dr. Catheter (Christopher Lee) who winds up capturing Gizmo in hopes of experimenting on him. Lee's part was specially written for his associations with past horror films, and he is delightful in the role. In fact, the movie could have used more of him and less of some of the subsequent gremlin desperation and desecration. The other delight in the film develops when one of the gremlins gets its brain enhanced in the laboratory and becomes known as Brain, with a voice by Tony Randall doing a quasi-parody of William F. Buckley, Jr. Interviewed by a horror movie host who is the only experienced television person left in the building, Brain explains, "We just want the good things in life," before blowing away another obnoxious gremlin. The gremlins have become symbols for hedonistic, amoral consumers who give no thought to the problems they create. They are cartoony caricatures without restraint, including a goofy gremlin who laughs crazily and rolls his eyes and a female, green-haired vamp gremlin with quivering red lips that long to kiss. There is even a sequence where one of the gremlins gets its revenge on a microwave.

Strangely, Daniel Clamp is portrayed by Glover as a kind of overgrown Boy Scout who also does not understand the havoc he creates. An overheard announcement proclaims that Clamp presents a colorized version of *Casablanca* with a new "happier ending." He listens to Billy Peltzer when Billy makes suggestions and is presented as redeemable, though not believable. Like cartoon characters, there are no real villains here; even the scheming Machiavellian Haviland Morris as Maria, who tries to get innocent Billy to bed, is too unreal to be genuinely dislikable.

Rather, the whole thing is somewhat like a live-action Tex Avery cartoon, and as in Avery's cartoons, there are even gags premised on the idea that you are watching a film (something which *Hellzapoppin'* did as well). For a climax, the gremlins all break into a chorus line of "New York, New York" simply because it seemed like a funny idea to scriptwriter Charles Haas at the time.

But Dante's comic inferno is disjointed and completely undisciplined, leaving no real lasting impression except cinematic and conceptual chaos. Even the continual trashing of popular culture becomes tiresome after a while. While one can respect Dante's refusal to play it safe, the time has come for this talented director to return to the fundamentals of storytelling and put his talents to the service of that. It almost seems as if Dante's endless "in-jokes" are his attempt to stave off boredom entailed by the shallow stories he is filming. It is time to grow up and move on.

Dante has a real commitment to fantasy and horror filmmaking, putting on the screen new and original visions the audience has not seen before. A devoted cineaste, he has the talent and technical expertise to be a really first-rate filmmaker. Somewhere between the slick exploitation filmmaking of *The Howling* and the nostalgic wonders of *Explorers* should be the kind of energetic, awe-inspiring movie magic that made the cinema the kind of place Dante and the rest of us returned to again and again, a place of make believe and thrills that enchanted our hearts and played on our emotions until we would eagerly look forward to a return. Dante has too much vim and vigor to be another Disney or a Spielberg, his narrative sense undercuts sanctimoniousness at every turn, and so one looks to him to provide the kind of sights which delighted our youth with the comic edge the appeals to our more experienced, adult selves.

Amando de Ossorio (1925–   )

Mi Ultimo Carnival (short); *El Miserio de la Endemoniada* (short) (1942);
La Bandera Negra (1956); *Escuelas de Enfermeras* (1963); *La Tumba del Patio*
(1967); *Malenka, la Nipote del Vampiro* (aka *Fangs of the Living Dead*) (1968);
La Noche del Terror Ciego (1971); *El Ataque de los Muertos Sin Ojos; Las Garras
de Lorelei* (aka *When the Screaming Stops*) (1972); *El Buqué Maldito* (aka *Horror
of the Zombies*); *La Noche de los Brujos* (aka *The Night of the Sorcerers*) (1973);
La Noche de las Gaviotas; La Endemoniada (aka *El Poder de las Tinieblas,
Demon Witch Child*) (1974); *Planeta Ciego* (aka *People Who Own the Dark*)
(1975).

Amando de Ossorio is one of Spain's few consistent horror practitioners.
In America, he is best known, if at all, for his Blind Dead series. These films
represent an unusual approach to the zombie genre. They are based on
myths about the Knights Templar and feature the mummies of dead knights
rising from their graves and terrorizing the country on horseback.

In Spain, the Knights Templar have an evil reputation because in the
late thirteenth century they were accused of sorcery and of torturing young
virgins to death and watering the ground with their victims' blood. Many
Templars were executed as witches. The knights in these films are blind
because they were buried in open graves where carrion eaters could pick at
their flesh and devour their eyes. When the Blind Dead rise, they retain their
intelligence, unlike many other movie zombies.

The first of de Ossorio's films that I am familiar with is *Malenka, la
Nipote del Vampiro* (aka *Malenka, la Sobrina del Vampiro; Malenka, the
Vampire; Fangs of the Living Dead*). Attractive Anita Ekberg stars as Silvia,
a young girl living in Rome. She receives word that she has inherited the castle of Waldrick (or Wolduck – with the dubbing it is hard to tell). Arriving in
Waldrick, Silvia discovers that the townspeople live in fear of vampires, and
they fear that the castle she is to inherit is the source of the undead.

Her uncle (Julian Ugarte) explains that she is the granddaughter of the
sorceress Malenka. When people die of a vampire's bite and the dead rise
from the grave, Silvia fears she is to blame. However, her fiancé (Gianni
Medici playing under the name John Hamilton) does not heed her protestations to leave her be. He is convinced of her innocence, and it turns out he
is right. Ugarte is actually a vampire who has gone to great lengths to get

A German still advertising Amando de Ossorio's The Blind Dead *(aka* Tombs of the Blind Dead). *This shows the look of the zombie Knights Templar which proved popular enough to create three sequels. (Photo courtesy of Donald Farmer.)*

Silvia to renounce her inheritance. (Ugarte had recently played a vampire as well in *La Marca del Hombre Lobo* aka *Frankenstein's Bloody Terror*.) The film is routine, receiving its major release in the United States as part of a horror triple bill (with *Revenge of the Living Dead* and *Curse of the Living Dead*). The film's primary asset are Ekberg's good looks, nice but not enough to keep an audience's interest for an hour and a half.

De Ossorio began his Blind Dead series with his next film, *La Noche del Terror Ciego (Night of the Blind Dead* aka *Tombs of the Blind Dead, Crypt of the Blind Dead,* and possibly even *Revenge of the Planet of the Apes*). The uncut version of the film starts out introducing the Knights Templar involved in some gory torture scenes back in the thirteenth century, but these have been cut out of most prints. The story picks up with a woman named Betty (Lone Fleming), who arrives in Lisbon and meets a couple of friends. She and Maria Elena Arpon vie for Cesar Burner's attention with some jealousy developing between them. They head by train to a little town, but Arpon gets left behind.

The town is in a shambles and looks uninhabited, but seeking shelter, Arpon goes to a dilapidated abbey where she intends to spend the night. The cadaverous Templars rise from the grave and, though sightless, can track her down by the sound of her screaming. They capture her and drain her blood.

Jose Luis Campos' makeup for these zombies is quite effective, detailing skeletal hands and wisps of facial hair on the sightless zombies. De Ossorio makes these scenes atmospheric, adding to the eeriness by filming the movements of the Blind Dead in slow motion.

Arpon rises from the dead the next night and kills the caretaker of the cemetery, but eventually she herself is dispatched when a woman she attacks throws a burning lamp at her and the dry husk that is left of her body goes up in flames. Meanwhile, Burner and Fleming look for their friend with some others, only for the Blind Dead to appear again and kill everyone except Fleming. She escapes and jumps onto a passing train, but the quick-riding knights catch up and kill everyone on the train. By quietly hiding, Betty escapes detection, but by the time she is discovered amidst the dead bodies, she appears to have gone quite mad.

The film is very bleak and sometimes dull in stretches, but it does contain some interesting visuals in the presentations of the Blind Dead and is atmospheric in a way that most similar low-budget efforts aren't.

Naturally enough, it lead to a sequel, *El Ataque de los Muertos Sin Ojos* (aka *Return of the Blind Dead, The Return of the Evil Dead*). Once again, the Blind Dead are on the prowl, this time during a festival celebrating how the Templars were massacred. A few survivors hole up in a church and try to figure a way out without being caught. Particularly suspenseful is a scene where the village idiot and a young woman try an underground passage to escape but, of course, find the Blind Dead waiting for them at the other end. Most of the escape attempts end in failure, but Luciano Stella and two women get free when the zombies crumble in the rays of the sun and they make their way gingerly through the zombies' ranks.

As in the first film, there is a connection made between the zombies and sex. In both films, they rise during an attempted rape and punish the promiscuous, particularly women. Their attacks become a metaphor for rape in that they assault their victims, penetrate them with swords, and drain them not only of desire (which seems to be what provokes them) but of life itself. The victim is left as cold, bloodthirsty and emotionless as they are.

De Ossorio took a break from the Blind Dead series to make *Las Garras de Lorelei* (aka *When the Screaming Stops*), loosely based on the German legend of the Lorelei. Here a Lorelei (Helga Line) lives in a cave near the Rhine river and occasionally turns into a reptilian creature that goes forth and lives off the hearts of young girls. Finally a girls' boarding school hires a young hunter (Luciano Stella acting as Tony Kendall) to rid them of this plague. With the help of a magic sword, he does.

While the removal of the hearts is gruesome and the cave is an interesting location, the dullness of the film overcomes any potential it might have had. It was enough to drive de Ossorio back to Blind Dead country.

For *El Buqué Maldito* (aka *Horror of the Zombies, The Ghost Galleon*), de Ossorio made some interesting changes in his tale. Back in the thirteenth century, some Templars board a galleon and go to sea, hoping to escape repercussions for their corrupt practices back home. However, the ship becomes a kind of "flying Dutchman," and while it continues to deteriorate, it remains sailing to the present day.

A pair of models get lost in a mist and suddenly find themselves aboard the ship, where they are promptly sacrificed in the traditional manner. Six of their friends back home get worried and decide to investigate. They too find themselves aboard the Templars' ship and are attacked, but quick-thinking Prof. Gruber (Carlos Lemos) holds up a small burning cross and keeps the Templars at bay.

At dawn, the Templars are forced to return to their coffins and the professor, being no dummy, tosses the coffins overboard. Unfortunately, before they can find treasure, the ship burns and sinks. Two survivors make it to shore, but so do the floating coffins and their deadly contents.

The ghostly galleon, decorated by art director Torre de la Fuente, is an atmospheric and spooky location. De Ossorio uses the nautical setting well and improves his pacing over his previous films, keeping this one fairly lively with shocks. Also, keeping up with the times, he made this one bloodier than before. The film benefits from the change of setting, becoming one of the better shipboard horror films, but some fans missed those slow-motion shots of the sightless knights on horseback.

Meantime, there was *La Noche de los Brujos* (aka *The Night of the Sorcerers*), an embarrassingly racist film in which eye-rolling African natives rip the clothes off a white woman and chop off her head as a sacrifice to a leopard god. The army comes in and massacres the blacks, and the head starts screaming.

A few years later, an expedition goes to the same area, where they encounter leopard-skin clad female vampires who have all previously been victims of the same bizarre ritual. (Talk about losing your head over religion.)

Despite dollops of gory violence and soft-core sex, *La Noche de los Brujos* is largely a tedious and uninspired exercise.

La Endemoniada (aka *El Poder de las Tinieblas, Demon Witch Child*) is an early attempt to cash in on *The Exorcist*'s success. An old hag gets revenge on the politician who imprisoned her by possessing the politician's daughter. Soon the daughter has gross fits, begins to preside over satanic rituals, and becomes promiscuous, disposing of opponents along the way by demonic means. Finally, an exorcist-priest does battle with her to save the day. All in all, a rather perfunctory and exploitative horror effort.

Returning to the old Blind Dead stomping ground, *La Noche de las Gaviotas* (aka *Night of the Seagulls*) was more in form. Victor Petit stars as a young doctor named Henry who visits a seaside village with his wife. After night falls, he hears the sounds of seagulls and some mysterious singing. When he asks about the singing and about the disappearance of a couple of young ladies, the villagers refuse to talk to him until the village idiot fills him in on the local background details.

To appease the marauding Templars, the village must sacrifice seven young people on seven successive nights. Henry listens to this tale, but he considers the source and refuses to believe it. However, that night the women of the village carry off a young girl and tie her to a rock by a cliff. Henry arrives just in time to save her from the Blind Dead. This causes the Blind Dead to retaliate by attacking the village. Amid the confusion, the doctor, the girl and his wife try to escape on the knights' horses, but the horses take them instead to a temple in which resides a hideous idol of a sea monster. The idol thrives on the hearts of its victims, but the threesome manage to destroy it, causing the Blind Dead to crumble once more.

Again, de Ossorio gets some atmospheric shots of his main locations – the haunting seashore, a depressing castle, and of course the temple of the idol. However, unlike *El Buqué Maldito, La Noche de las Gaviotas* fails to generate any tension, and the film begins to drag as if the whole thing were in slow motion. The most effective device is the tolling of a bell which signals time for another sacrifice and death for another unlucky victim. The three main characters had all been lured into town to become victims of the Blind Dead, an expedient way of keeping the village's population stable.

La Noche de las Gaviotas had an unofficial sequel of sorts, John Gilling's *La Cruz del Diablo,* which has never played in the United States and received scant distribution, reputedly because of bad feelings on the part of the Span-ish film industry about allowing an Englishman to direct the production. De Ossorio obviously cared about his Blind Dead films, frequently supervising the special effects and makeup himself. While they are basically typical low-budget exploitation fare, he is to be commended for creating an eerie en-vironment for his shocks and giving zombies a new and somewhat more in-teresting look.

Brian De Palma (1940–)

Icarus (short, 1960); *660124: The Story of an IBM Card* (short, 1961); *Wotan's Wake* (short, 1962); *The Wedding Party* (1966); *The Responsive Eye* (documentary, 1966); *Murder a la Mod* (1967); *Greetings* (1968); *Dionysus in '69* (codir. with Robert Fiore and Bruce Rubin); *Hi Mom!* (1970); *Get to Know Your Rabbit* (1972); *Sisters* (1973); *Phantom of the Paradise* (1974); *Obsession, Carrie* (1976); *The Fury* (1978); *Home Movies, Dressed to Kill* (1980); *Blow Out* (1981); *Scarface* (1983); *Body Double* (1984); *Wise Guys* (1986); *The Untouchables* (1987); *Casualties of War* (1989); *Bonfire of the Vanities* (1990).

Brian De Palma has been known for several years as the standard-bearer of Hitchcock, imitating the master in one stylish horror-suspense film after another, though recently he has renounced his intentions to make Hitchcock-style films and has produced an impressive body of work and demonstrated very capably his ability for cutting, developing suspense, camera movement, and sumptuous cinematography. Also, many players have given superior performances under De Palma's direction.

Hallmarks of De Palma's storytelling style include his penchant for exploring the uses of split screen, and his use of "doubles," in which each major figure has a corresponding duplicate or opposite in the drama. Voyeurism is a theme that he has pursued at length, as is the extremes to which people under duress will drive themselves.

De Palma, the son of a doctor, was born in 1940 in Philadelphia. He has attributed the amount of graphic violence in his films to the fact that his father was an orthopedic surgeon, saying in an interview with David Bartholomew in *Cinefantastique*, ". . . I have a high tolerance for blood, gore, I guess you'd call it. I've seen my father amputate legs and open people up. So I was used to it at a young age."

He initially majored in science at Columbia University, but as a sophomore was bitten by the film bug and began making shorts. He started out by buying a Bolex 16mm camera for $150 and used his allowance over a year and a half to finance his first film, *Icarus*. With his third short, *Wotan's Wake*, he won $1,000 and the Rosenthal Award.

He embarked on his first feature project, *The Wedding Party*, a collaboration with Cynthia Munroe and Wilford Leach, after attending Sarah Lawrence College on an MCA writing fellowship. The film was made in

335

35mm in black and white for $100,000. It failed to find a distributor until after the success of *Greetings*. De Palma dabbled in documentaries, making *The Responsive Eye* about the Op Art opening at the Museum of Modern Art, which managed to turn a tidy profit.

The *Wedding Party*, despite its obscurity, is an important film which launched the careers of Robert De Niro, Jill Clayburgh, Jennifer Salt and William Finley. It centered around a man who is getting married (the character was based on a friend of De Palma's), and like most of De Palma's earliest experimental films, was largely improvised by the cast.

The first De Palma film to use horror elements was *Murder a la Mod*, a murder mystery that plays with cinematic archtypes and styles. In the aforementioned *Cinefantastique* interview, De Palma explained:

> Basically, the idea is that we go through the same murder from three different points of view, the three principal characters. Each of the three sequences are shot in a different style to reflect the different natures and points of view of the same factors and events leading up to the murder. For instance, the girl who gets killed, her section is very much like a soap opera, because her life is like that. Then we go through the murder a second time, from the point of view of a guy, and we did that one like Hitchcock, very eerie, cinematic, suspenseful. The third one is done like a silent comedy because the character, a horror film actor (played by Bill Finley) is a deaf-mute. It's all action, gags, and pratfalls.

Despite the injections of Hitchcock and outrageousness, the primary influence on De Palma's early films was Jean-Luc Godard, particularly his film *Masculin Feminin*, though he also borrowed ideas from fellow film student and experimentalist Jim McBride, recently the director of *The Big Easy*. *Greetings*, titled after the first word in a '60s draft notice, was De Palma's initial breakthrough, made for $43,100 and turning a large profit for its distributor when it became a cult film in New York.

The film was originally the idea of Charles Hirsch, its producer, with De Palma acting as coscreenwriter. Initially, the film was shot in 16mm, but the footage came back from the lab all scratched, requiring that $4,000 worth be scrapped. De Palma and Hirsch decided to start all over again in 35mm and, using deferments, were able to get the film made. It became the first film to receive the newly created X rating – largely because of a scene where Gerrit Graham describes a sexual experience, for the film is definitely not pornographic.

The film's story centers around three obsessed characters: Jonathan Warden as Paul Shaw, who is obsessed with avoiding the draft and finding a girlfriend; Gerrit Graham as Lloyd Clay, who is obsessed with the Warren Report and its inaccuracies, becoming a target himself; and Robert De Niro as Jon Rubin, who creates the idea of "peep art," in which people are shown things through window frames to create an artificial outlook on "reality," a metaphor for the process of filmmaking itself.

An early, talky scene as the trio buy clothes in a boutique uses deliberate lack of continuity as a filmic in-joke – the actors inexplicably change attire and positions during a static conversation in the boutique. De Palma would later pay homage to himself by including a similarly silly scene in *Carrie* where William Katt and his friends try to find proper prom attire. Also, De Palma's interest in *Blow Up* is shown in the Gerrit Graham scenes, and the film is mentioned by name. (De Palma would later use the Antonioni film as the inspiration for *Blow Out*.) There's also a ludicrous tribute to "independent cinema" in the film-within-a-film porno movie, *The Errand Boy and the Bored Housewife*, that Paul gets involved in.

While the film does cover a great many anxieties that students had in the '60s – the draft, getting a girl, creating something meaningful, fearfulness of conspiracies and the people in power – it is a hodgepodge comedy that does not really hang together. Nonetheless, it was definitely an alternative to the standard Hollywood product that was being turned out at the time and was more attuned to student concerns. It also played around with its own limitations and with the possibilities of free-form cinema. The film proved a great success in New York and went on to gross over a million dollars, much to the bitterness of Hirsch and De Palma, who signed away most of the profits to the distributor in the effort to get it released.

Marty Ransohoff was so impressed by what the filmmakers had accomplished with *Greetings* that he put up $95,000 for a sequel. This film was eventually titled *Hi Mom!* and concentrated on the "peep art"–obsessed Jon Rubin character (played by De Niro again) after he has returned from Vietnam. (Ironically, it was Rubin rather than Shaw who was eventually shipped overseas. Apparently all Rubin's advice on how to evade the draft by pretending to be a Nazi or a homosexual was of no help to himself.)

Hi Mom! is more technically polished, and more importantly, much funnier than *Greetings*, but it proved an unfortunate flop. Once more, De Palma experimented with using different film styles for each of the three major characters in the film. While the Rubin section was shot in straightforward, 35mm color, he has a housewife shoot a film of her own dull life in a co-op in 16mm, and also includes a black-and-white pseudo-documentary section on the preparation and performance of a theater-of-cruelty piece known as "Be Black Baby."

The "Be Black Baby" scenes are some of the most powerful and horrific that De Palma has ever done and succeed in throwing the film off balance. The basic idea is that middle class white theatergoers are given the experience of what it is like to be black in America. The patrons are painted black and are harassed by blacks painted white. The film is shot in *cinéma vérité* style and has a high degree of realism which makes the events all the more disturbing. The blacks are particularly abusive to a white blond lady whom they apparently rape with a broom handle while harassing the cameraman who is trying to film the entire degrading experience. De Palma's lack of taste is shown when he immediately makes a joke out of this harrowing experience. He has the white participants interviewed after the performance, who insipidly babble on about how meaningful an experience it was and how the critics were "right" about it. De Palma then ends the film with Rubin becoming completely radicalized and blowing up the co-op in a Weatherman-like terrorist act. Interviewed on television at the scene of his crime, the only message he wants to communicate is a quick, "Hi, Mom!"

In between *Greetings* and *Hi Mom!* De Palma used split screen to record both the performance and the audience reaction to *Dionysus in '69*, an environmental theater piece based on Euripides' *The Bacchae* and performed by his friend William Finley with the Performance Group.

Despite the failure of *Hi Mom!* the success of *Greetings* encouraged Warner Brothers to hire De Palma to direct a comedy written by Jordan Crittenden. The comedy, *Get to Know Your Rabbit*, has Tom Smothers as a frustrated employee looking to escape from the rat race. De Palma uses a great overhead shot of Smothers traveling through his narrow apartment like a rat caught in a maze to give a wonderful pictorial depiction of the character's dilemma. The film starts out inventively as Smothers quits his job, visits Orson Welles who teaches him how to become a tap-dancing magician, and heads out on the road.

The comedy suffers, however, from the fact that Smothers' character is basically passive, never taking any action apart from dropping out. His career becomes exploited when his ex-boss, played by John Astin, learns of Smothers' happiness and becomes very successful creating a firm that invigorates executives by turning them into tap-dancing magicians.

De Palma originally wanted to end the film with Smothers taking action to destroy Astin's business by appearing on the Johnny Carson Show and messing up on a saw-the-rabbit-in-half trick, horrifying viewers from coast to coast. The movie would end with the viewer realizing that the rabbit's death was faked, and the Smothers character finally achieving the freedom that he has craved all along.

Warners blanched at De Palma's proposed ending, firing him and hiring Peter Nelson to shoot an upbeat happy ending with Smothers simply pulling a disappearing act again in order to find happiness.

De Palma did not like the interference of Warner Bros. on *Get to Know Your Rabbit* and so retreated to the relative freedom of working for one of Hollywood's independents. For American International Pictures, he created his first, and one of his best, pure horror films, *Sisters*. Dating Margot

Kidder at the time, he cast her in a breakthrough role as Danielle, one of a pair of Siamese twins who has developed a split personality after the death of her twin, Dominique. In becoming her twin, she develops murderous impulses.

Voyeurism remains a major theme throughout De Palma's entire career, from *Greetings* with its ideas of "peep art" to *Casualties of War*, in which Michael J. Fox as Erickson watches while his platoon kidnaps, rapes, and murders an innocent Vietnamese girl and feels himself a failure for not having prevented the sordid incident. *Sisters* begins with a satirical television game show that emphasizes society's moral dilemma regarding scopophilia, the desire to look.

Many of De Palma's movies show the influence of Hitchcock's famous film *Rear Window*, and De Palma develops Hitchcock's theme that looking can be an invasion of privacy (a bad thing) or can help to prevent or bring about retribution for a criminal act (a good thing). However, the act of looking can lead to manipulation by whoever is presenting what is being gazed upon, just as a director manipulates the elements that audiences see on the screen.

In the "Peeping Toms" show that opens *Sisters*, Philip (Lisle Wilson) is a black contestant in a kind of "Candid Camera" situation where the wall between a men's room and a women's room has been torn down. Danielle is a model pretending to be a blind girl who enters the women's room and starts stripping. She and the camera are in control of the situation for the purposes of the game show, in which panelists guess how Philip will react. Danielle's control is emphasized as Danielle is the one who suggests they go out to dinner afterwards.

But while the opening presents the theme of voyeurism and how it can be presented as entertainment, the key voyeuristic moment occurs slightly later in the film when we see Danielle (under the influence of Dominique's personality) take up a piece of cutlery that Philip won on the show and stab him with it. The dying Philip then goes to the window in a plea for help that is observed by the film's true protagonist, female journalist Grace Collier (Jennifer Salt). Despite her position as a truthteller (journalist), Grace cannot get the police to believe her, especially when they check the apartment after all telltale evidence has been cleaned away by Danielle's husband, Emil (William Finley), and Philip's body has been secreted in a fold-up couch.

Throughout much of his career, particularly in his horror films, De Palma has enjoyed throwing off the audience with his opening sequences. The supposedly real-life situation in *Sisters* proves to be a game show; the opening of *Obsession* omits crucial pieces of information; the shower rape in *Dressed to Kill* is only a masturbation fantasy recalled in a therapist's office; and the sleazy mad stalker sequence in *Blow Out* is simply a film that the main character, Jack Terri, is working on – as is the sleazy vampire movie that opens *Body Double*. Even *Casualties of War*, the story of a much-chronicled incident during the Vietnam War, is framed as a dream sequence set in 1974 so that De Palma can end the movie with an understanding Vietnamese student telling the hero, "It's over," indicating that the nightmare of the war has passed into history now.

But while De Palma developed as a film stylist and a master of suspense, he did not entirely abandon the social values that he displayed when he started working as a filmmaker. These are particularly evident in *Sisters*, one of the most feminist horror films ever made – from a man who has been decried by feminists for his exploitation of women in his films. The women in *Sisters* are ground down by the fact that society views women in terms of their relations to men.

Danielle is aggressive only when she flouts convention and picks up on Philip, a likable young black man who is quickly killed (which in recent years has become almost a cinematic convention and even appears in *Casualties of War*). Throughout the rest of the film she is manipulated by husband Emil, who covers up her homicide and tries to hypnotize her into accepting the death of her twin. Danielle's problems with her sister Dominique stem largely from her relationship to Emil, whom she loved but could share no privacy with.

Similarly, Grace Collier is aggressive in her pursuit of the story of what happened in Danielle's apartment and Danielle's background. However, the police are hostile to her (one of the stories on her wall is headlined, "Why We Call Them Pigs," indicating the source of their hostility); the detective she hires (Charles Durning) is condescending; and her mother belittles her profession as a "little job" and is more concerned that she get married, fulfilling the role that society and her mother expect of her.

Additionally, the film depicts society's condescension towards blacks as Philip's prize on the television show is tickets for dinner for two at The African Room, an embarrassing collection of clichés with black waiters in grass skirts, bowlers, and white shirts. When he has been murdered, the police express no great interest in solving the case, dismissing Collier's report out of hand when they can find no immediate evidence in Danielle's apartment.

While *Sisters* does borrow a few pages from Hitchcock's book of technique, De Palma also employs techniques that Hitchcock never used, such as effective use of split screen. In one scene, Philip presents Dominique with the knife and cake, telling her, "Surprise," and when she picks up the knife, "You're not supposed to cut the cake until you make a wish and blow out the candles." She slashes the candles out before plunging the knife twice into his groin and once into his mouth – a penetration to "avenge" the penetration of her other self the night before. De Palma then cuts to a split screen that simultaneously shows Philip's final struggles and Grace's awareness of his plight. De Palma continues to use the technique to build up suspense as we see Grace and the police arriving at the same time Emil and Danielle are removing the clues – clues which only the nosy Grace will spot – effectively keeping the audience guessing whether the murder will be discovered. To keep the sounds from overlapping on these simultaneous scenes, De Palma films the sequences in Danielle's apartment with minimal dialogue, eliminating crosscutting and making the sequence tighter and more compact. De Palma has shown himself to be one of the masters of this infrequently used and often annoying screen device, but even so, he uses it sparingly and when it will be most beneficial.

However, he is not above tricking his audience by not playing fair. In *Sisters*, when Danielle and Dominique argue, we see two shadows even though there is only one person there. (Note that in the split-screen scenes where Grace is watching, Dominique is only seen as a shadow.) Similarly, in the *Psycho*-derived film *Dressed to Kill*, to prevent the audience from guessing that Dr. Elliott (Michael Caine) is the killer, De Palma shows via split screen what appears to be the killer chasing the heroine at the same time that Caine tells his service that he is staying home all night. Mere seconds later, however, he will appear as his homicidal alter ego, Bobbi, and attack Elizabeth Blake on a subway train. (The initial pursuer is revealed to be a blonde cop named Betty Lou.)

Appropriate for a film about twins, *Sisters* is full of dualities and doubling up. Danielle acts as a lure, a decoy in the "Peeping Toms" show, and then lures Philip to her apartment. Philip gets rid of Emil twice. We get two views of the operation that separated the twins: one a realistic documentary, and the other a hallucination by Grace Collier filled with twins and doubles, in which Emil clearly intends not just to separate the twins but also to murder Dominique. Garden shears are seen threateningly at the institute, and we later learn what prompted the operations: Dominique attacked Danielle's unborn baby with garden shears. Emil murdered Dominique with a scalpel, and in trying to get Danielle to accept it, Dominique comes back and murders Emil with a scalpel.

The film depicts its male characters as being ineffective – none achieve the goals that they intend. However, Grace is active, intuitive, and intelligent, but ultimately regresses into the child that everyone has been treating her like throughout the film. The women, therefore, all end up victims of manipulation and subjugation.

Emil has Grace committed by calling her Margaret and pretending that she has a dual personality. He then hypnotizes her to say when questioned, "There was no body because there was no murder; it was all a ridiculous mistake" to cover up Danielle's guilt. He drugs Grace so that she will assume the role of Dominique in an effort to get Danielle to accept her sister's demise as real.

Unfortunately, his actions summon up Dominique, who kills him. When questioned, Danielle asserts, "My sister died last spring," indicating that she is possibly cured. Because of Emil's hypnotic command, Grace can tell the now believing police detective only what she has been ordered to say. In a final ironic and masterfully, blackly humorous touch, De Palma returns to Durning's detective hanging from a telephone pole and waiting for a nonexistent someone to pick up the coach with Philip's dead body in order to "solve" the mystery. The detective, like the characters in Beckett's *Godot*, waits patiently forever on a now pointless task, never realizing that he has pursued a dead end.

Though the excellent Bernard Herrmann score recalls Hitchcock's work, De Palma has done something that Hitchcock never did in films: He has the detectives and police ultimately foiled and lets the murderess get away clean. He also demonstrates not only a knack for entertainment, but clear mastery of cinematic *mise-en-scène*. The angles he chooses to shoot the characters from clearly indicate who is dominating in a particular scene, and he makes maximum usage of parallel actions to create rich resonances, in this fascinating film.

De Palma's next film is even more resonant and is, I think, his greatest work, a one-of-a-kind, stylish *tour de force* known as *Phantom of the Paradise*. In it, not only does he borrow plot elements from *Phantom of the Opera*, but he casually throws in references to the legend of Faust, Oscar Wilde's *Picture of Dorian Gray*, the James Whale version of *Frankenstein*, Frankenheimer's brilliant *The Manchurian Candidate*, and other elements of popular culture, combining them all into a bizarre and original melange of imaginative moviemaking.

Originally the film was to be entitled *Phantom of the Fillmore*, but Bill Graham, who owned the Fillmore name, refused its usage. Then the title was switched to *Phantom*, but the people who owned the comic strip "The Phantom" objected. Also, the villain's company was originally to have been Swan Song Enterprises, which explains why its label is Death Records, but the Led Zepplin–backed subsidiary Swan Song objected, and Swan Song had to be replaced in the film with the Death Records symbol of a dead bird. (However, the original logo can be glimpsed in the film above the factory Winslow goes into, as well as on the camera Swan uses to photograph his own lovemaking.)

Also, originally Jay Cocks concocted a *Citizen Kane*–type newsreel sequence to give the background of Swan, but this idea was scrapped in favor of a narration by Rod Serling, done shortly before his death, explaining Swan as the man who brought the blues to Britain and Liverpool to America, put folk and rock together, and launched the nostalgia wave of the '70s. The character of Swan was based on rock impresario Phil Spector, but not too closely. At one time, Gerrit Graham was going to play Swan while Paul

Williams took the role of Phantom and Peter Boyle was going to be hired to play Beef. Luckily, saner heads ruled.

American actor William Finley was very convincingly Canadian in *Sisters*, and in *Phantom of the Paradise* he portrays a gawky, gangling kid, one Winslow Leach, whom circumstances turn into the flamboyant Phantom. As the Phantom, Finley performs some very violent and reprehensible acts, but he never loses the audience's sympathy. Paul Williams is also quite good, delivering his best performance as Swan, a malevolent elf who occasionally can be glimpsed as a trapped soul behind a devilish facade.

The film is suffused with bird imagery, from the names of the major characters – Swan, Phoenix – to the costumes (the Phantom picks up an owl-like mask; Phoenix wears two different feather wraps or boas; Swan wears a shirt with birds on it), to the company symbols (a swan for Swan; dead bird for Death Records), to a finale with a giant swan onstage and women dancing in crazy crow costumes. The excellent design work is by Jack Fisk, husband of Sissy Spacek and director of such films as *The Raggedy Man*.

Like Tony Richardson in *Tom Jones*, De Palma adopts a number of styles to convey different moments in his film, but he does so more effectively than Richardson. (Richardson's use of silent film style is quite artificial, for example, where De Palma makes it amusing.) His shot of the Phantom planting a bomb in a stage car recalled Welles' famous opening shot in *Touch of Evil*, only here the potential victims get off the car before it explodes, a fact obscured by the use of split screen where we see Swan noticing the Phantom for the first time just as the car explodes, creating a rhythm that catches the audience off balance.

The film features a slashing satire of the music industry with song piracy, thug henchmen, men who create teen idols, sudden has-beens, and drugs unscrupulously served up to keep people working regardless of the consequences. Sha-Na-Na were originally to have played the nostalgia band The Juicy Fruits, but dissension as to who would play lead resulted in their dismissal from the project. They were replaced by Archie Hahn, Jeffrey Comanor, and Harold Oblong.

The film even opens with a song that satirizes the exploitation of dead rock stars, sending their memorial albums to the top of the charts (consider what the attention brought on by Roy Orbison's death did for his last two albums, *Traveling Wilburys* and *Mystery Girl*). The opening number also introduces the blending of fantasy and reality at a rock show as the backup singers mock an attack and a rape on audience members.

Winslow Leach is introduced playing an excerpt from his rock cantata of *Faust*, and while William Finley is not a professional singer, he sells the song by conveying how into his music this composer is and how enraptured he is to be playing it, even if only to a largely uninterested audience. However, he does attract the attention of Swan, who sends his henchman Philbin

(George Memmoli), named after the lead actress in the Chaney version of *Phantom of the Opera*, to acquire the music from Leach. A quick sequence demonstrates Leach's temper and power where his musical integrity is concerned: He pushes Philbin through a plate of glass after Philbin suggests that the Juicy Fruits might play a tune from the cantata on one of their records.

De Palma manages to condense a tremendous amount of exposition into a very short time. One month later, Winslow is ducking through a Swan-sized door to get into Swan's business office to find out what has become of his cantata. After being ejected roughly, he follows Swan to his home, the Swanage. There he finds a long line of females auditioning for parts in the cantata. Phoenix is there, but leaves because of the casting couch techniques. Winslow disguises himself as a girl to see Swan. When discovered, he is beaten up and a pair of corrupt cops plant dope on him.

There is an immediate cut to a distorted courtroom where a judge proclaims, "Life!" as Winslow proclaims, "But I'm innocent! Swan stole my music and framed me!" Following up, appropriately enough, is a shot of Sing Sing where Winslow is "voluntarily" enrolled in the Dental Health Research Program in which all his teeth are pulled and replaced with metal ones.

To indicate the changes in Winslow, De Palma has him go from long hair to a prison haircut, followed by longer hair and metal teeth. We have seen Winslow be very patient but persistent until he seems a crushed man. While working in a tiddly-winks factory, Winslow hears that the Juicy Fruits are going to play *Faust*. He goes berserk, escaping in the process via convenient outgoing toybox.

De Palma clearly shows that Winslow is not going to be a nice guy any longer, but his actions seem justified, given his provocations. He smashes up Swan's office and tries to blow up the record press, but gets his sleeve caught, slips on a loose record disk and falls into the machine, becoming the deformed phantom by having the grooves of the Juicy Fruits' *Faust* etched onto the right side of his face. (The makeup for this was designed by famous makeup artist John Chambers, who did makeups for the *Planet of the Apes*, and was executed by the late Rolf Miller.) When he stumbles out of the factory, he is also shot by a guard, but this sequence was omitted.

De Palma indulges in some in-jokes in the film. A girl madeup to resemble former paramour Margot Kidder is asked if she is kidding, to which she replies, "Do I look like a Kidder?" Newcomer Jessica Harper, who is very appealing as the innocent but hungry ingenue Phoenix, has an ad tacked up to her dressing room mirror captioned "Meet a Harper's freak."

Yet despite these attentions to details, the film has some visual gaffes as well. Swan is shown going into his private chamber behind a mirrored hallway in a beige suit. Inside the chamber he sits in a black coat with a red shirt, only to reemerge in the original beige suit when he leaves. The Phantom has a silver cape when he watches Swan and Phoenix make love, but this proved too reflective and was replaced by a crimson cape for the energetic finale.

Mirrors prove important. We see that Swan made a deal with the devil at an early age when he contemplated suicide rather than face the ravages of time. The devil appears as an image of himself in a mirror and promises him that as long as he protects a tape of their contract and watches it, *it* will grow old instead of him. (The idea of contracts is also used, very humorously but forbodingly, throughout the film.)

To gain Winslow's trust and compliance, Swan hired Phoenix to play a part in *Faust*, the rock opera with which he intends to open his new venue, the Paradise. However, as he cannot stand perfection in anything other than himself, he secretly plans to relegate Phoenix to the backup chorus, and looks about for a new means of debasing Winslow's music. Looking for something "heavy," he samples the key song in folk, duet, country & western, and soul style before settling on glam rock singer Beef (Gerrit Graham in a lisping, marvelously outrageous and funny performance). He promises that the concert will be recorded "live on the Death label" and tells Beef to make the music completely his.

De Palma shows how an industry can alter a creator's intentions. The song "Faust," which Winslow sings at the beginning, is next heard as a Beach Boys–style number which the Juicy Fruits play, the lyrics altered to proclaim, "Carburetors, man, that's what life is all about!" When Winslow loses his voice in the accident, Swan brings it back using electronic equipment and filters, but now when the Phantom sings, it is Swan's voice we hear. "Perfect," he purrs.

Swan puts Winslow under contract, a long and confusing document which Winslow is forced to sign, not being given another choice. He does not realize the agreement is diabolical in nature. When he tries committing suicide after seeing Phoenix making love to Swan, Swan points out that a clause in the contract says, "This contract terminates with Swan." Taking that for inspiration, the Phantom stabs Swan only for him to unexpectedly deliver the film's best line, "I'm under contract too!" Winslow cannot kill Swan until he destroys the tapes, and that will cause the gaping wound in his side to reopen, killing him along with his nemesis.

The film is sharply edited by Paul Hirsch, who has also put together some beautiful montages for it, indicating the passing of time and Winslow composing and rewriting while thoughts of Phoenix fill his head. Some parts of the film, particularly the climax, pile together so many kinds of visual excitement that they are almost literally breathtaking.

Still, one of the glories of the film is Graham's portrayal of a homosexual, lisping, frequently drugged glam rock star. When he hears the Phantom screaming over his stolen music, he gets nervous, telling Philbin, "That was something trying to get out of its premature grave." When Beef takes a shower, De Palma does a neat parody of the *Psycho* shower scene (before such parodies became commonplace), with the Phantom slitting open a plastic curtain with his knife and impaling Beef's mouth with the business end of a plumber's helper. Beef responds by trying to flee but is confronted by Philbin, whom he tells, "Look Philbin, I am a professional. I have been in this business a *long* time. If I don't want to do a show, it's not because I got stage fright, it's because some creature from *beyond* doesn't want me to do the show – now gang way!"

Still, Philbin forces Beef to ignore the Phantom's warning never to sing his music again. (The music, says the Phantom, is written only for Phoenix, and anyone else who tries to sing it will die.) The concert premiere wonderfully uses expressionism, both in a tower set that apes *Frankenstein*'s and in the makeup of the band, the Undead. (Prophetically, it resembles the makeup later adopted by the musical group *KISS*, though it was probably influenced by Alice Cooper.)

At the concert, fantasy and reality mix in the show as dummies in the audience are hacked apart and the pieces are assembled to produce Beef by the end of the song. Thus when the Phantom kills Beef with a neon thunderbolt, the audience assumes that it is just another part of the show. Phoenix goes out and becomes a big hit with "Old Souls," a song that is lovely but too low-key to really win over the highly excited crowd. From the energy onscreen, however, one can believe that the audience thought it was a great show.

Here De Palma introduces his last theme in the film: that death really has become a form of entertainment to the masses. Swan, wanting to exploit this and give the Paradise a really big send-off, decides to have Phoenix assassinated during a mock wedding ceremony the following evening. "An assassination live, on television, coast-to-coast – that's entertainment!" Swan crows to Philbin. The real significance of death has been lost in a media blitz, and Swan has apparently found too much perfection in Phoenix and must destroy her as well.

At the climax, the Phantom discovers Swan's secret and the assassination plans. He hits the assassin's rifle at the crucial moment so Philbin is shot instead. He then swings down to the stage onto which Swan has emerged masked from below (hinting at his hellish origin). The film offers a twin unmasking as the Phantom peels Swan's mask, revealing a now ravaged face, and stabs Swan with a pointed piece of costuming. Meanwhile, the crowd thinks it is all part of the show, Swan having played Faust, and they join the dancers up on stage, not comprehending the melodrama forming around them. The Phantom unmasks himself after preventing Swan from strangling Phoenix in an effort to collect her "voice," which he expected to gain from his contract with her. Phoenix recoils from the Phantom's visage. The dying Phantom crawls towards her until she recognizes that this "crazed freak," as she described him earlier when he had taken her aside as the Phantom, is in fact the long-presumed-dead composer Winslow. Saying his name low, she collapses on him in an embrace while the audience dances around them, oblivious.

The Phantom, with his superhuman strength (he is walled alive by Swan, à la Poe's "Cask of Amontillado," but bursts free) and flamboyant malevolence, is beautifully limned by Finley, who follows the part where it leads. His love of Phoenix does not seem to be motivated by anything more than his love of the way she sings his material (and she unquestionably does the best job singing it in the film). Both Swan and the Phantom are shown to have romantic natures and dark sides (the Phantom strangles a gaffer just to throw a spotlight on Phoenix), but the Phantom is motivated to protect innocence while Swan exploits it.

The result of the enterprise was an exciting and innovative approach to horror films that gave old ideas new energy. Unfortunately, it was not the breakthrough film De Palma hoped it would be. Twentieth Century–Fox, which distributed the film, initially gave it an advertising campaign that suggested it was a rock concert, almost guaranteeing that those who went to see it would be disappointed. A later, more horror-oriented approach to sell the film proved to be too little, too late. While its style and flair attracted some attention, audiences largely passed it by, though a few years later they would flock in great numbers to see another horror/rock musical, Richard O'Brien's B-movie-influenced *Rocky Horror Picture Show*. (The latter film inspired a unique phenomenon as audiences began supplying missing humor for this largely laughless production by supplying their own responses to the movie's silly B movie cliché lines. Jim Sherman provided an interestingly cluttered background, full of objets d'art, while O'Brien's rock score is catchy and appealing. However, though an inferior film, *Rocky Horror* was designed as a cult object and *Phantom of the Paradise* was not, leaving *Phantom* eclipsed on the midnight movie circuit.)

The name Phoenix implies life from death, and indeed her career arises out of the ashes of Beef's. She is obsessed with pleasing the crowd, ignoring the warnings of the Phantom who loves her. Swan is obsessed with his age and, like Phil Spector, a desire to be considered more important than the artists who record for him. He is the voyeur of the film, continuing De Palma's theme with his narcissistic obsession for watching himself. The pathetic Winslow is first seen adding his name to a banner of the Juicy Fruits, showing he has a narcissistic side as well, but he is obsessed with his own music, an idea De Palma conveys in a 360° pan around him as he performs on his piano.

This 360° pan became another De Palma visual trademark and particularly got a working out on his next film, *Obsession*. This aptly titled movie succinctly expresses another common De Palma theme, that of a character's obsession which goes beyond the healthful into the perverse. (Tony becomes obsessed with protecting his sister and having it all in *Scarface*. Elliott Ness is obsessed with getting Al Capone, not only for bootlegging but also for threatening his family and killing Malone – the Sean Connery character – in *The Untouchables*. Erickson is obsessed with court-martialing his squad after the heinous crime they commit despite his commander's discouragement in *Casualties of War*.)

To communicate delirium, De Palma relies on the 360° pan which appears three times in *Obsession*. The first is after Michael Courtland (Cliff Robertson) assumes that both his wife and daughter died when the kidnappers' car exploded. This brilliant shot marks a transition between 1959 to 1975, showing Michael older, with an ostentatious monument built to his dead wife and daughter. The device is reprised when Sandra/Amy goes through her mother's things, and finally when Michael and his now recognized daughter have their emotional confrontation at the airport.

(De Palma also used 360° pan scenes to indicate Carrie's transport into new realms of pleasure at the dance in *Carrie*, as well as Jack Terris' delirium in *Blow Out* when he puts on every tape he has and discovers that they have all been erased. The device signals that the character's world has been permanently altered, and it is a dizzying technique. De Palma executes these shots with split-second timing.)

Unfortunately, *Obsession* is too clearly patterned after Hitchcock's *Vertigo*. (The original titles for it were *Deja Vu* and *Double Ransom*.) Paul Schrader's screenplay presents Courtland as a man looking for redemption because he was dissuaded by the police from using his wealth to pay the kidnappers. He blames himself for his wife and daughter's deaths. Then, years later in Italy, he meets Sandra (Genevieve Bujold), the spit and image of his late wife, who unbeknownst to him is actually his daughter working in cahoots with his treacherous and money-obsessed business partner, Robert La Salle (John Lithgow), to defraud her father and get her revenge for not being properly rescued.

Courtland obviously has a morbid obsession with his late wife, and his building a monument – a replica of the church in which he first met her – on his grounds shows that he is a death-obsessed individual looking to atone. His relationship with Sandra is not healthy, but ironically, the scheme La Salle purposes of recreating the kidnapping to steal his money – an attempt that goes awry similarly to the first one – gives him an opportunity to recognize what has happened and achieve the longed-for redemption followed by a reconciliation with his suicidal daughter.

However, for a film whose plot is based on incest, *Obsession* skirts the question, implying that the good Christian Sandra would not go to bed with

Michael before their marriage. The film does feature a haunting score by
Bernard Herrmann but fails to get past a draggy middle and a feeling of
deja vu – it is so much like *Vertigo* that we feel we too have seen this before.

Though *Sisters* was successful, at this point De Palma still had not had
a mass market hit. That was to come with his next film, an adaptation of
Stephen King's *Carrie* which launched both their careers. As a hardcover
novel, *Carrie* had not been very successful, but when it sold to the movies,
the paperback rights went for $400,000, the publishers counting on a healthy
return from a future movie tie-in, and King has been writing his way to millions ever since. De Palma finally achieved the kind of success he was looking for, success that would make him a bankable director.

Carrie also launched the career of one of our finest actresses, Sissy Spacek, who garnered an Academy Award nomination for her performance, a
feat almost unheard of for a horror film. Actually, De Palma has an often
overlooked talent for getting excellent performances out of his actors and
has a real eye for discovering gifted performers. Robert De Niro who
started in De Palma movies went on to become one of America's most respected actors, returning to give De Palma a simultaneously humorous and
chilling portrait of Al Capone for *The Untouchables* (one of the hardest
things for an actor to do). John Lithgow went on to fame and fortune after
appearing in *Obsession* and *Blow Out*, achieving his first major success in
The World According to Garp and following it up with a major supporting
role in *Terms of Endearment*. Jessica Harper did her best work for De
Palma and has subsequently appeared in Argento's *Suspiria*, several
Woody Allen movies, Herbert Ross' unique *Pennies from Heaven*, and as the
replacement Janet in Sharman's sequel to *The Rocky Horror Picture Show* –
Shock Treatment, which showed she can still sing, charm and sizzle. Also
worth noting, Sean Connery won his only Oscar for his work in a De Palma
movie.

In *Obsession*, money was equated with death, while in *Sisters, Carrie*
and particularly *Dressed to Kill*, sex is equated with death. *Carrie* begins
with a steamy, lyric scene in a girls' locker room, the kind of scene many
boys would have cut their right nuts off to see during high school. Carrie
(Spacek) is isolated from this action. It is apparent she is a "plain jane" and
does not fit in. Her shower is shot slow and sensual as she feels her arising
sexuality. Unfortunately, she is traumatized by her first, long-delayed
period, which also coincides with the arrival of her telekinetic power,
brought on when the rest of the girls cruelly and unmercifully taunt her,
throwing tampons and yelling, "Plug it up!"

Carrie's mother, Mrs. White (Piper Laurie in her best performance), is
an evangelical religious fanatic obsessed with sex, considering it the primary source of sin and seeing in her own daughter a continual reminder of

the seeds of her own abandonment and misery. As a consequence, she forces the innocent Carrie to pray long hours locked up in a closet to atone for unnamed, unexpiated sins.

Carrie from the first equates the menstrual bleeding with death and mortality – not incorrectly, as it turns out. Her mother having kept her in ignorance of this very basic fact of life, Carrie feels she is bleeding to death internally. Her emotional upset causes the principal's ashtray to fly off the table and herself to be sent home. Her understanding gym teacher, Ms. Collins (Betty Buckley), has difficulty relating to Carrie's fears and discomfort, initially not realizing the extent of her ignorance. Though well-meaning, she only makes things worse when she punishes the other girls for making fun of Carrie, causing them to vent their anger and frustration on this all-too-convenient target.

Anyone who has had a difficult time in high school can relate easily to Carrie's problems and the feeling of being always looked down upon and tormented by one's classmates. Though her revenge is far too excessive to be morally condoned, it perfectly feeds the power fantasies of the helpless who would like to do something dramatic to get back at those pernicious fellow pupils, and this partially accounts for *Carrie*'s phenomenal success both as a book and film.

Blood is a motif all throughout the story beginning with Carrie's first menstrual cycle. This brings references to the "curse," or as her ultrareligious mother calls it, "the curse of blood" (one of a series of prophetic statements she utters) through which women brought sin into the world. Carrie's real curse is her mother, who has warped her into the outcast that she is. When Carrie tries to seek comfort in her mother's arms, Mrs. White hits her with a book instead, venting her righteous indignation at being asked why she did not tell her daughter about the "facts of life."

While Mrs. White sings about the "blood of the lamb," Carrie uses her power to crack and destroy a mirror. Later, Chris (Nancy Allen) goads her boyfriend, Billy (John Travolta), into slaughtering a pig for its blood to be used in a vengeful prank against Carrie. A baptism in this blood leads to the deaths of most of the student body of Bates (note *Psycho* reference) High School. Carrie tries to cleanse her soul by washing off the blood in the bathtub only to have her mother stab her in an attempt to sacrifice her to God. De Palma then has Carrie, after tumbling down the stairs, impale her mother with kitchen utensils in a gratuitous parody of the St. Sebastian statue that Carrie prayed to, emphasized by Piper Laurie's flowing hairdo and glowing eyes.

De Palma also sets up a dichotomy between the good couple, Tommy Ross (William Katt) and Sue (Amy Irving), and the bad couple, Chris and Billy. Both girls act equally reprehensibly towards Carrie at the start of the film, but Sue experiences guilt, which she tries to expiate by insisting that

A knife-wielding Piper Laurie is actually the scariest thing in Brian De Palma's memorable film adaptation of Stephen King's novel Carrie – *still one of the best movie adaptations of King's work. Laurie plays a religious fanatic who sees her daughter as a witch and decides she must be immolated.*

Tommy take Carrie to the prom, scuttling her own plans in the process. Chris, refusing to put up with Ms. Collins' detention, sets up the prank. Both girls manipulate their men using sex: Sue ignores Tommy, doing her homework until he agrees, while the cruder couple has Chris going down on Billy until he assents.

Tommy is a star athlete in the school and his head is wreathed in golden curls, proof of his goodness. His only connection to Carrie is that when a poem he plagiarized is read in class, Carrie describes it as beautiful, which brings down derision from the teacher (Sydney Lassick). It is not clear why he lets himself be persuaded so easily apart from Sue's sheer resolve, but when he takes Carrie to the prom, he is genuinely thoughtful and caring towards her, making their first time on the dance floor a magic moment with a sincere kiss.

Billy, by contrast, is never seen at school except at the dance and has dark greasy hair. He is almost caught drinking beer from an open can while driving, giving the police an all–American, aw-shucks grin that belies the truly sick person underneath. His sickness is indicated by the way he hits

Sue when she calls him a "dumb shit," the way he gets into hammering a pig in the head, and the way he so obviously enjoys the prank they are about to pull on Carrie.

The film, except for dreamy moments shot in slow motion and the artificially lit, split-screen apocalypse at the prom, is largely shot in a realistic style. An unfortunate exception is a scene intended to be amusing in which Tommy accompanies two friends going to pick up tuxes for the prom. The scene, which uses speeded-up motion and jump-cut lapses in time is a self-referential bit recalling the jokey, continuity-error clothing shop sequence in *Greetings*. It proves a short and unnecessary bit of self-indulgence.

De Palma precedes the prom with many portents of doom, allowing Carrie and her mother to have their last supper under a tapestry reproduction of Leonardo da Vinci's *Last Supper*. Mrs. White calls Carrie's light pink dress red, which is the color it will be when she gets home. She predicts that everyone will laugh at her, and this remains Carrie's greatest fear at the prom.

De Palma very effectively captures Carrie's nervousness and awkwardness when she and Tommy finally reach the prom. We see her slowly become acclimated and really begin to enjoy herself. By the time she and Tommy are chosen king and queen of the prom, she does look beautifully radiant – De Palma slowing down time to emphasize the radiance as well as draw out the suspense about the impending disaster that the audience knows will happen.

Ms. Collins has encouraged Carrie to go to the prom, but we discover that partially she wants to enjoy Carrie's pleasure vicariously watching the girl have the prom she never had (Collins had to walk half a mile in high heels to get to her prom, and her feet were too sore to dance). Sue shows up to see the results of her handiwork and discovers too late what Chris and Billy's plan is; she is roughly ejected by a suspicious Ms. Collins, an act which saves her life.

In the book, King has Carrie win the prom queen spot simply by the change in her personality coupled with Tommy's popularity. De Palma instead has the selection rigged by the villains, ensuring that Carrie would be onstage in the appropriate place, a more realistic though less romantic setup. When the blood falls over Carrie's dress and bouquet, and the bucket smashes Tommy in the head, the result is, appropriately enough, total shocked silence.

De Palma carefully eliminates any real sound as Carrie espies malicious Norma Watson (P. J. Soles), Chris' best friend, laughing and goading her date to laugh. By various techniques, including the use of a prism lens, De Palma suffuses the scene with unreality to clue us that Carrie's secret fear appears realized to her. She believes everyone is laughing at her even though this is not the case, and so unleashes her fury and her telekinetic power on everyone in the gym. Through the split screen, we see Chris and Billy escape, laughing, while Carrie animates a fire hose and sprays the crowd, knocking Norma off her feet. The water shorts out the lights and electrocutes Carrie's sarcastic English teacher and the principal who never gets her name right, causing the prom backdrop to burst into flames. Ms. Collins is practically cut in half by a descending basketball backboard. No one is spared, and Carrie exits the flaming gym by herself.

Obviously Chris and Billy are in for a cosmic comeuppance, and they receive it when Chris tries to run Carrie down in Billy's car, but Carrie causes it to swerve, turn over and burst into flame, the ultimate cleanser. At home, Carrie finds that her mother has lit every candle in the house (more flame) so that it appears like a shrine in preparation for her confession (relating to her self-hatred over her repressed sexual desires) and absolution (the planned murder of Carrie).

In the novel, King borrowed a page out of reports on telekinesis to have the Whites' house destroyed by falling rocks, but for the film this was abandoned as too expensive. De Palma instead has Carrie, in anguish over having murdered her mother, pull the house down around their heads while she seeks protection in her praying closet. Feeling cursed, she seeks self-immolation.

What really created word-of-mouth about *Carrie* was the final added shock in which Sue in a dream visits Carrie's grave only to have Carrie's bloody hand pull at her arm when she is placing flowers on it. De Palma wanted to create an air of unreality about this sequence, and so it was shot with a filter and filmed backwards (a car going backward can barely be glimpsed in the background) in order to give an otherworldly feeling to Sue's movements. With dreamy, peaceful music on the soundtrack, as if years had passed and a spiritually renewed Sue had returned, the sequence caught audiences off guard and provided a memorable shock.

Regrettably, this has led to what has been called the "Carrie Syndrome," where many subsequent horror filmmakers have felt the need to try to surprise the audience with a final shock. This has become such a cliché that audiences almost invariably spot the shock coming and are prepared for it, thereby making it ineffective. De Palma could not get the technique to work again when he tried it at the end of *Dressed to Kill*. Nevertheless, the tradition carries on, even if it frequently makes no sense in the context, or changes a satisfying upbeat ending into an unsatisfying downbeat one. Dream "shock" sequences began appearing in the middle of movies as well, where they are no less gratuitous but tend to be more effective.

De Palma finally had an unqualified success on his hands. Sadly, the same cannot be said for his next film, an adaptation of John Farris' novel *The Fury*. In typical Hollywood smart/dumb tradition, it was another story about people with telekinetic powers, though this time there was a sympathetic father, Peter Sandza, played by Kirk Douglas, and a spy story was meant to give added interest (though actually it detracts).

Once more De Palma is pairing things. Peter Sandza represents a good father, while Childress (John Cassavetes) becomes a bad father. Sandza shoots Childress in the arm during a guerrilla attack, but Childress manages to kidnap Sandza's psychically gifted son, Peter (Andrew Stevens), telling him that Arabs killed his father and developing Peter's power for his own perverted ends. In contrast to the bad psychic, Gillian Bellaver (Amy Irving) is a good psychic who helps Sandza track down his son. There is also a good woman (Carrie Snodgrass' Hester) and a deceptive one (Fiona Lewis' Susan), each of whom dies but while pursuing different means (noble for Hester; deceptive again for Susan).

We also have the blood motif again, this time represented by nosebleeds that people get when psychically probed and leading to gorier incidents. The violence becomes gratuitous, especially when a maddened Peter sends a pair of Arabs on a carousel flying through the air to land atop some others (indicating the success of Childress' indoctrination in developing Peter's powers and hatred), and most especially in Childress' own gorier demise in which we see his body exploding three different times.

Fortunately, excess is rarely the path to success, and *The Fury* did not become a hit and inspire a rash of imitations, though the horror film has become plenty gory on its own. Childress is a very deceptive character, but the narrative bogs down as Sandza tries to wend his way through the tissue of lies that are not terribly interesting in and of themselves. In the end, Sandza realizes his son is irredeemably corrupted and commits suicide to kill them both and prevent the spread of further corruption and power into the wrong hands. The typically peaceful Gillian responds by eliminating the threat of Childress forever. Perhaps the best thing the film brought us was Daryl Hannah in a bit part.

Next De Palma scaled back, going to his alma mater, Sarah Lawrence College, as a director in residence. He concocted a story and decided to teach low-budget filmmaking by having students complete the script and work on the film, though it would star professional actors and be professionally presented and released.

The result was *Home Movies*, a rarely screened but nonetheless interesting and outrageous film comedy that departed from Hollywood norms in a number of areas. Perhaps the most bizarre thing about it is that De Palma rewrote the basic plot to make his next horror film, *Dressed to Kill*, though I prefer the comedy version.

Home Movies contrasts real life with reel life, as the Maestro (Kirk Douglas at his comically hammy best), a director in residence at Now College, instructs his students not to be "extras" in their own lives. They are to make films of their lives just as he is making a film of his course.

The protagonist is Dennis Byrd (Keith Gordon), who is failing the Maestro's star therapy. His father (Vincent Gardenia) is a lecherous doctor, while his mother (Mary Davenport) is a neurotic who stages mock suicides whenever she learns of her husband's infidelities. Dennis hopes to catch him in the act on film so that his mother will achieve a peaceful and painless divorce. His brother, James (Gerrit Graham), is leading a troop of boys through a program he calls "Spartanetics," based on the ancient Greeks of Sparta, even down, it turns out, to their homosexual practices.

Adding to the complication is James' fiancée, Christina (Nancy Allen), who has a split personality, alternating between herself and a foul-mouthed puppet rabbit named Mr. Bunny that she talks to. Neglected by Spartanetics master James, she turns to Dennis for solace and later is given a cruel fate at odds with the film's comic tone. The film is unusual and entertaining enough to warrant more attention than it has so far received, and it carries out De Palma's voyeurism theme to a ludicrous degree, with everyone constantly watching and filming everyone else as the only way to bring out their true, inner selves.

Dennis in *Home Movies* becomes Peter in *Dressed to Kill*, both being obsessed with gadgets and both played by Keith Gordon. The lecherous doctor becomes Dr. Elliot (Michael Caine), who, like Danielle in *Sisters*, murders whenever he is sexually aroused owing to his alter ego's frustrated transsexualism. The concept behind the film seems to have been to create a De Palma version of *Psycho*, even down to killing the presumed lead, Kate Miller (Angie Dickinson), a third of the way through, and ending it on an unsatisfactory psychological explanation.

Kate's masturbatory rape fantasy in the shower which opens the film was considered too steamy by the MPAA for an R rating and so was slightly trimmed, but the unedited international edition was eventually released on video. The sequence begins with Kate's husband in the bathroom while Kate is stroking herself in the shower. The fantasy involves someone taking her from behind while her husband is watching, introducing the theme of voyeurism again. Kate's sex life is obviously unsatisfactory: We see the husband climax, pat his wife's cheek, and then turn away, leaving her unsatisfied. She reports these feelings to her therapist, Dr. Elliott, flirting with him and playing with the idea of having extramarital sex.

It is clear she has a loving relationship with her son Peter, who is a gadget lover and something of a computer nerd. When she asks what he calls his homemade computer, her son tells her, "It's a Peter," naming it after himself. She tells him that his grandmother will be disappointed not seeing him, but, "I'll explain that you're working on your Peter," the first of many sexual jokes and references.

Angie Dickinson's subsequent scenes are virtually without dialogue and very cinematic, using close-ups and reaction shots to convey the "story."

That story begins with an elaborate cat-and-mouse flirtation in a museum where Kate is sitting, watching people. When a strange man sits by her, she takes off her glove and shows her wedding ring, apparently driving him away. She drops her glove and pursues him, and then is pursued in turn. The strange man picks up the glove, puts it on, and touches her shoulder, she cannot find it or him, and so goes outside and throws her other glove away. Just then she sees the come-on of a hand holding her glove outside a taxi cab window.

In true Erica Jong style, she achieves her fantasized "zipless fuck" with an utter stranger who does not begin by telling her his name, but immediately starts kissing her and petting her, pulling her panties off in the cab while the cab driver – the voyeuristic element which excites her – looks on.

Back in his apartment, just from Dickinson's expression and movement, you can tell that she has had a good time. She now puts her clothes on and decides to write her unknown paramour a note. In the process she discovers that he has been notified that he has a venereal disease – something that is not going to be easy to explain to her husband.

There is a sense in the film of sex leading to punishment, and Kate's final punishment, meeting with the homicidal Bobbi in the elevator when she has to return to her lover's apartment to get her wedding ring, seems overly harsh and drawn out, causing many critics to object. The crude police lieutenant Marino (Dennis Franz) is of the opinion that she is looking to get killed by her behavior of picking up strangers in New York, though it is more likely that the sexually frustrated housewife was pursuing a fantasy and did not stop to consider the dangers.

Bobbi is dressed up in a getup that resembles Karen Black's disguise in *Family Plot*, another Hitchcock *hommage* in a film which is clearly a Hitchcock pastiche. Bobbi is really Dr. Elliott, who is portrayed as self-absorbed, constantly checking his looks in the mirror. He gets a call from Bobbi (actually himself) on the answering machine in his office. Bobbi gloats about the killing and using Elliott's straight razor to punish the woman. In a split-screen sequence, Bobbi tells Elliott, "You would have done the same thing yourself." After this call, Elliott watches a Phil Donahue show on transsexuals in which a transsexual asserts that transsexuals can be both macho and hetrosexual. Though later De Palma tries to throw us deliberately off scent, by the time Dr. Elliott goes to Dr. Levy (David Marguiles) to track down Bobbi, whom he has neglected to tell the police about, it is apparent that he is in fact the killer.

The protagonist of the film is Elizabeth Blake (Nancy Allen), a high-class call girl who caught a glimpse of Bobbi when the elevator Kate was on opened before her. Lt. Marino puts the screws to her, threatening to jail her unless she can turn up the John who might have been a cowitness; later

Nancy Allen witnesses the death of Angie Dickinson and gets a glimpse of Bobbi, the razor-wielding killer in Dressed to Kill, *De Palma's biggest horror hit.*

he blackmails her into illegally breaking into Ellott's office to steal his appointment book which Elliott has refused to turn over to the police. The guardians of the public trust are not depicted as being very moral, though they do save Blake's life in the end.

Elizabeth is resourceful, however, and teams up with Peter, who is anxious to find the killer of his mother, about whom the police have made disparaging remarks. Peter is able to rig up a device, à la *Home Movies*, in which he can photograph people coming in and out of Dr. Elliott's office over the period of a day. He is assuming that the killer is one of Dr. Elliott's patients.

No one in the film ever seems to make love to express love or simply to enjoy himself, except possibly Kate's self-centered husband and the venereally infected man Kate picks up. Liz uses sex to make money, pursuing it so avidly that she risks her life to take on one more call even when she knows she is in danger. Her relationship with Peter seems innocent and gives cause for hope, but the downbeat nightmare ending where she dreams that Elliott slashes her throat indicates a trauma from which she might not recover.

There simply is no wholesome sex in the film. Elliott turns into a murderer whenever his penis is engorged because it reminds his other self that he has not yet been transformed into a woman. Liz tries to exploit him by wearing sexy costuming in order to fluster him enough to snag a name out of his appointment book, but this manipulation backfires when it excites Elliott's uncontrolled homicidal tendencies.

The rash of explanations before the shock dream ending are a nasty clump of exposition that simply bogs the film down. *Dressed to Kill* portrays a corrupt world where "personal and professional ethics" mean nothing to most people, where women must always be on their guard against being victimized (in trying to avoid Bobbi, Liz stands next to some black toughs on a subway who immediately start to hassle her), where sex has become a series of power games, and where "justice" is a bullet from a gun used as a counterforce to the cutting violence of a razor blade.

Perhaps De Palma is capturing the unpleasantness of our times, but that does not keep *Dressed to Kill* from being a sometimes needlessly unpleasant movie. However, it did prove very effective with audiences and became one of De Palma's highest grossing films. In it and his two subsequent films, his camera mastery is unassailable, but his choice of subject matter is at times questionable. However, even so, *Blow Out* and *Body Double* are far less gory films than either *The Fury* or *Dressed to Kill*, though they provoked no less outrage.

The lack of success of *Blow Out* proved quite a blow to De Palma, though he should have known he was breaking cinema taboo by having his hero arrive too late to save the heroine after a prolonged buildup, and adding insult to injury with a callous and repellent ending.

The basic idea of this reworking of Antonioni's *Blowup* makes for a pretty good political thriller, and indeed the film features some of the most superb deep focus photography ever seen on screen. *Blow Out* is particularly canny in the way it exploits memories of Chappaquiddick, except this time the politician dies and the girl survives when the politician's car goes into the drink.

Most people are not too aware of how sound effects are added to motion pictures; De Palma, though his hero Jack Terri (John Travolta), shows a little of the process. When a scream in a cheap horror film shot in Philadelphia turns out to be pathetically inadequate, Terri must arrange to record new screams to overlay into the film. Also the producer is tired from hearing the same old library sound effects and wants Terri to record some new ones. This assignment puts him at the location on the fateful night where he rescues Sally (Nancy Allen), George McRyan's companion.

Under the credits, De Palma has a TV program blare necessary exposition, that Gov. George McRyan is ahead in the polls and could take the presidential nomination. De Palma even goes so far as to cue sound effects with the title credits, so that when Travolta's name is seen, the whine of sound recording equipment is heard; when Nancy Allen's name comes on, a scream, which at the end of the film will be associated with her; and when De Palma's name comes on, deep and heavy breathing.

In this era of "credible deniability," when the National Security Council can undertake to sell arms and perpetuate wars without approval of either the executive or legislative branches of government, the danger of a Burke, the assassin played by John Lithgow who not only murders the governor but successfully covers it up, is all too real. We know the man is sick when we realize that in his zeal he went beyond what the political Machiavellis for the other side intended for him to do (when he tells Mattes by telephone that he intends to secure the operation, Matters returns, *"What* operation?"").

Appropriate to a film which focuses on sound, Burke's presence at first is indicated only by sound at the scene of the crime, a strange clicking noise that Terri cannot account for. Later, when we see him for the first time, he makes the same strange noise, and we realize that he is nervously playing with a garrot wire that extends from his watch. To cover his planned murder of Sally, McRyan's companion, he initiates a series of serial sex murders in which he mutilates the victims by stabbing their lifeless bodies with an icepick and forming the shape of a liberty bell.

De Palma has had a character obsessed with a political assassination before – the Gerrit Graham character in *Greetings* – and Jack Terri is particularly a man with an obsession. He truly feels that if assassins are allowed to get away with the murder of a major politician, then nobody is safe, an argument often used since the Kennedy assassination. He also draws the parallel that the commission investigating McRyan's death has already come to a conclusion before they initiate their investigation.

Also, like Michael Courtland in *Obsession,* Terri has a key moment in his life which he must live over again. Before he became a sound man in movies, he worked in a department for ferreting out corrupt cops. One night he wired an undercover investigator for sound but did not take into account what would happen when the man sweated, which resulted in the battery shorting, his skin getting burned, and the undercover man giving himself away to some mobsters, who killed him. Terri repeats this horrible experience when he wires Sally, who is supposed to meet the television newsman Donohue (Curt May) and turn over the evidence that Terri has preserved concerning McRyan's investigation.

However, there is a problem with this idea of circularity – it does not make sense and it is not necessary, except as a means of putting Sally in jeopardy. Why should not Terri come along with Sally, especially as he was the one whom Donohue was going to meet with in the first place? However, the plot rules that he cannot come along because otherwise he would know immediately that Burke has taken Donohue's place and he would not get the scream De Palma wants for the ironic ending.

De Palma does convey society with skewed values. The cop heading the investigation does not like Terri because he "was responsible for putting a lot of good cops away," ignoring the idea that perhaps a corrupt cop is not a good one. Sally works with Manny Karp (a sleazy Dennis Franz) on a blackmail and extortion scheme as a way of making a living. Manny risks Sally's life in the McRyan setup without telling her, and then capitalizes on the incident by selling the film he makes of it everywhere to the highest bidder, though he refuses to relinquish it to the police. De Palma even includes a sailor who cheats a prostitute out of twenty dollars when he ejaculates too soon, commenting, "You blew it!"

Burke proves very effective in eliminating the evidence, wiping Jack's tapes, replacing the blown-out tire that he shot on McRyan's car, and finally throwing Karp's film into the river. Terri trusts in his sound equipment and what he has heard, even if he knows such equipment is usually used to fake reality. However, throughout the film his trust in machines is misplaced, and he forgets that reality can be shrewdly manipulated by the director of a conspiracy as easily as by the director of a film.

De Palma particularly manipulates reality in the cornball climax of the film. The all-too-trusting Sally is hustled off by Burke, who is foiled in his first attempt to kill her by the unexpected appearance of a witness. Burke and Sally hop a subway train, and Terri pursues over surface streets, driving recklessly through a building and a parade, endangering the lives of many to save Sally's life, emphasizing its worth to him. He crashes into a Nathan Hale window display and is knocked unconscious. A change in lighting indicates that many hours have passed before he wakes up again in an ambulance, but Burke still has not dispatched Sally. Terri arrives in time to kill Burke with his own icepick but too late to save Sally.

Where De Palma really errs is in having Terri use Sally's genuine death scream as the scream he needs in *Coed Frenzy*, the cheap horror film he is working on. It seems a really crummy and callous thing to do, even though De Palma shows that he is still tormented by the memory of his failure and her death. This cannot be judged a sacrifice of life for art, for clearly *Coed Frenzy* is not art. De Palma seems to like this unexpected solution to Terri's initial problem (recording a good scream), but while it provides a memorable ending, it is so emotionally insensitive that it often stuns audiences. In the end, even Terri is shown as corrupt.

Still, *Blow Out* is a well-made film and did not descend into the nonsensical. The same cannot be said of *Body Double*, an attempt to do another reworking on *Rear Window* and *Vertigo*. The plot hinges on the idea that claustrophobic actor Jake Scully (Craig Wasson), who loses a role in a vampire film because he cannot stand staying in the coffin, would become so obsessive a voyeur after watching a woman undress from the futuristic apartment of his friend Sam (Gregg Henry) that he would just happen to be

Brian De Palma on the set of Body Double, *which he cowrote with Robert J. Avrech. The film has plot holes galore, but De Palma does know how to cannily orchestrate an audience reponse. However, disappointing box office response to this film caused him to give up making horror movies and move on to more mainstream films.*

looking and provide an eyewitness account when a man murders his wife (Deborah Shelton). The man committing the murder is in disguise, which gives him an alibi despite the presence of the eyewitness.

Jake is another De Palma obsessive, but so much so that it is silly. He starts following Gloria (Shelton) everywhere she goes, going so far as to sniff her underwear when she discards it in the trash. Particularly dumb is a sequence when a strange man snatches Gloria's purse; Jake pursues him, but cannot overcome his claustrophobia when he goes into a tunnel. Gloria for no apparent reason gives him a passionate embrace while the camera swirls around them (De Palma's delirium trick again) and then just as mysteriously runs away.

Gloria is murdered by a man with a huge drill which has obvious phallic connotations. We never see the drill plunge into her, though Jake running to the rescue sees it coming through the ceiling as it goes out the other side; nevertheless, the sequence is very powerful and upsetting, particularly as De Palma prolongs it, building in the audience expectation that Jake will arrive just in time to rescue the woman.

The basic idea of the film was perhaps suggested by the use of a body double in the opening shower scene with Angie Dickinson in *Dressed to Kill*. The remorseful Jake watches a porno film with Holly Body (Melanie Griffith) and is surprised to see her do the same sexy, striptease dance he glimpsed in Gloria's apartment. He tracks the woman down and discovers that the first person he saw dancing was Holly and not Gloria, and that he was being set up to look.

De Palma had talked about getting genuine porno industry people to do the "dirty" parts in his movie, but that proved an idle threat. Jake is depicted as such a babe in the woods that he does not even know what a cum shot is, even though he is shown watching porno videos. Also dumb, Sam knocks Holly out and kidnaps her in full sight of a police blockade, counting on them not noticing anything (they do not). It is also very predictable that Jake will be shoved into a situation where he must overcome his claustrophobia and save the day.

Though the murder itself is very powerfully filmed and emotionally exhausting, *Body Double* is such a foolish and predictable copy of Hitchcock's films that it was clearly a dead end, and it did not do very well. De Palma then left the horror genre to inject blood into new fields.

His next three films were all in the now little filmed gangster genre, though they had the requisite violence that one could expect in a De Palma movie. The first one, a remake of Howard Hawks' *Scarface*, is bloated and overindulgent, with a vicious chainsaw murder in a shower and Al Pacino exploring new possibilities of excess – excess cursing, excess violence, excess drug taking. As filmmaking, it made an impact but lacked the sheer quality of the compact and impressively presented original, though De Palma does get some interesting material by updating the project: Present-day Cuban toughs become drug lords rather than Prohibition-era bootleggers and Roaring '20s gangsters.

Wise Guys is one of De Palma's least successful comedies, but *The Untouchables* proved a real return to form for the director with rich production design, a lush score by Ennio Morricone, an interesting plot based on actual events by David Mamet, and excellent acting by Sean Connery, Robert De Niro, Kevin Costner, Charles Martin Smith, and Andy Garcia. The scene where Al Capone "Reggie Jacksons" a fellow gangster to death with a baseball bat is based on fact and is horribly brutal in its suddenness. But De Palma indulges himself by turning a border raid into a pseudo-western and having Elliott Ness push Frank Nitti (played by a menacing Billy Drago) off a building; neither event happened in real life. Still, the film looks good and plays well, particularly Connery as the streetwise cop Malone, though some would argue with De Palma's contention that to fight crime, police need to resort to the same ruthless methods (i.e. the ends justify the means).

Based on a true incident, *Casualties of War* is likewise a powerful film, an indictment of irresponsible behavior regardless of the threat to one's personal safety. Elia Kazan shot a film about the events subsequent to what De Palma depicts in a 16mm art film called *The Visitors* that debuted actor James Woods. De Palma's Vietnam film is both well-made and harrowing. His next project was the social satire *Bonfire of the Vanities*, based on Tom Wolfe's book, but someday he may return to regain the title the Modern Master of Suspense.

Terence Fisher (1904–1980)

Colonel Bogey; To the Public Danger; Portrait from Life (aka *The Girl in the Painting*); *Song of Tomorrow* (1948); *Marry Me* (1949); *The Astonished Heart* (codirected with Anthony Darnborough); *So Long at the Fair* (codirected with Anthony Darnborough) (1950); *Home to Danger* (1951); *A Distant Trumpet; The Last Page; Stolen Face; Wings of Danger* (1952); *Four-Sided Triangle; Mantrap; Spaceways; Blood Orange* (1953); *Final Appointment; Mask of Dust; Face the Music; Children Galore; The Stranger Came Home* (aka *The Unholy Four*); *Murder by Proxy* (aka *Blackout*) (1954); *Stolen Assignment; The Flaw* (1955); *The Last Man to Hang* (1956); *The Curse of Frankenstein; Kill Me Tomorrow* (1957); *Horror of Dracula; The Revenge of Frankenstein* (1958); *The Hound of the Baskervilles; The Mummy; The Man Who Could Cheat Death; The Stranglers of Bombay* (1959); *The Brides of Dracula; The Sword of Sherwood Forest; The Two Faces of Dr. Jekyll* (aka *House of Fright*) (1960); *The Curse of the Werewolf* (1961); *The Phantom of the Opera; Sherlock Holmes und das Halsband des Todes* (*Sherlock Holmes and the Necklace of Death,* 1962); *The Horror of It All; The Earth Dies Screaming; The Gorgon* (1964); *Dracula – Prince of Darkness* (1965); *Island of Terror* (1966); *Frankenstein Created Woman; Night of the Big Heat* (1967); *The Devil Rides Out* (aka *The Devil's Bride*) (1968); *Frankenstein Must Be Destroyed!* (1969); *Frankenstein and the Monster from Hell* (1973).

The important contributions of Terence Fisher have frequently and easily been overlooked or downplayed. He was not a particularly daring director when it came to creating his visuals and so lacks the stylishness of his more esteemed comrades of the cinema. Nevertheless, during the period 1957–1962, he virtually redefined the genre and was the progenitor of modern horror cinema.

While he did not take a hand in his screenplays and pretty much directed whatever he was assigned, certain trends in handling are apparent in Fisher's work. One of his primary innovations was his concept of "the attractiveness of evil." Before his time, evil things, as a visual shorthand, were typically made to be ugly things. In an interview with G. R. Parfitt in *Little Shoppe of Horrors #3*, Fisher asserted, "This is the great strength of evil, to make itself attractive. Evil always tempts you – the promise of something you'll get, the attractiveness of evil. That's his great power – strength."

It is not far from attractiveness to sexuality, something in which

Hammer Films, the company Fisher primarily worked for, abounded, particularly with their many heroines who appear to have been hired on the basis of their ample bosoms rather than their thespian talents. Thus Peter Cushing's Frankenstein seduces male assistants into accepting his point of view; Christopher Lee's Dracula provides a sexual thrill for his victims; Paul Massie's Jekyll becomes more attractive when he is Mr. Hyde.

Fisher is also known for restarting the cycle of classic horror films with color remakes and his matter-of-face portrayal of body parts and vampire stakings – in effect, for early portrayal of gore onscreen. Though these depictions horrified contemporary critics when the films were released, viewed from today's perspective, they show quite a bit of British reserve and restraint. They did not shy away from the horrible or avoid depicting it the way horror films of the '30s and '40s did, but neither did Fisher indulge in such acts with Sadean glee. They were the shock scenes' punctuations, not their entire reason for being.

Fisher asserts a moral universe, one in which good inevitably triumphs because the egoism of evil continually causes it to trip over its own feet (something which is reflected in society as a whole by the way most criminals are finally caught and evil conquerors eventually fail in their grandiose plans). Evil may be attractive, and therefore tempting, but Fisher refuses to side with it. Interestingly, the evil forces present in his horror films are usually made part of the background; eventually they strike out and create a moral dilemma for the hero.

Despite his affinity for the horror film, Fisher was most interested in the emotions his fantastic stories stirred. The director whose work had the most influence on him was Frank Borzage, and he made no attempt to seek out or duplicate the achievements of a Browning or a Whale. He scorned the cold, unemotional approach of Powell's *Peeping Tom* and the cheap sensationalism of Friedkin's *The Exorcist*. Love, rather than lust, was often the pivot point of his films.

Fisher was relatively late in coming to the film industry. He was born in Maida Vale, London, in 1904 and was convinced by his mother to join the British navy as a teenager. Five years later, he left and became partners in the rag trade with John Lewis. He finally entered the film industry in 1933 as a clapper boy on *Falling for You*, and eventually worked his way up from teaboy to third assistant director to assistant editor and finally to editor.

In 1947, he was given the chance to direct his first feature, *Colonel Bogey*. He then tried his hand at a number of different genres including musicals, melodramas, suspense films and science fiction. Of these early films, Fisher is proudest of *To the Public Danger*, an obscure suspense film that has been stored in the British Film Institute's archives. Neither of his 1952 science fiction films for Hammer, *The Four-Sided Triangle* (about a scientist who makes a duplicate of a woman he is madly in love with only to discover that the duplicate loves his rival as well) and *Spaceways* (a thriller in which a rocket scientist is suspected of murdering a wife and her lover and secreting their bodies aboard a satellite), is very interesting.

Fisher found his forte and founded a horror renaissance with his break-through film, *The Curse of Frankenstein*, which marked the beginning of Hammer's most satisfying horror series. Hammer had made effective science fiction horror films with *The Quatermass Experiment* (aka *The Creeping Unknown*) and *Quatermass 2* (aka *Enemy from Space*), both directed by Val Guest and based on Nigel Kneale's television serials, and an often overlooked but also effective follow-up, *X – The Unknown*; however, *The Curse of Frankenstein* set the pattern of redoing period horror films in color and in a more graphic style than before.

Because many critics like the later pictures in Hammer's Frankenstein series better, the first one is often dismissed or unfairly compared to the James Whale *Frankenstein* where Karloff's monster proved the center of the film. Jimmy Sangster's script for *The Curse of Frankenstein* altered the focus to Baron Victor Frankenstein (superbly played by Peter Cushing), and it is around his unrelenting quest to create a perfect being that the series revolves. The Creature (played by Christopher Lee) appears late in the picture and does not have more than 15 minutes screen time, leaving many monster fans disappointed. These fans miss the point: Frankenstein is the primary monster himself.

Cushing portrays Baron Frankenstein as the consummate criminal, someone with a total disregard for anyone or anything but his own objectives. The film opens with Frankenstein sentenced to the guillotine and bringing a priest in for confession not because he believes in God, but because he needs to find someone who will listen to him while he brags about his achievements. (It is notable that in his confession, he confesses to a couple of carefully planned murders but hopes to get off at the end because he did not commit the crime he was sentenced for.)

The first part of the flashback shows the young baron (Melvyn Hayes) as arrogant and distant. When his father dies, he sends his aunt and cousin Elizabeth off and hires a tutor, Paul Kemp (Robert Uruquhart), to school him in the sciences. He proves brilliant at the work and the pupil soon surpasses the teacher, who then becomes his assistant.

As David Pirie describes the character in *Heritage of Horror*, the Baron is "a magnificently arrogant aristocratic rebel, in the direct Byronic tradition, who never relinquishes his explorations for one moment. . . ." Cushing's Frankenstein is cultured and highly intelligent, but his ego is enormous and he is ruthless in pursuit of his goals. His task of building a perfect specimen and bringing it to life is partly a rebellion against the scientific authorities of the day, intended to demonstrate his superiority to them.

Because the Baron is right about some things, his character would be a sympathetic one if only he were not so inhumane in pursuit of his goals. To get Paul's cooperation, he resorts to extortion; to get the brain he wants, he (not too wisely) pushes a mathematical genius over a railing and onto his head. He maintains an affair with Justine the maid (Valerie Gaunt) but violates his promise to marry her because she is below his class and he has decided to marry his cousin Elizabeth (Hazel Court) instead; when she protests, he first taunts her as a slut and then arranges for the Creature to kill her. Finally, at the end of the film when Paul threatens to go to the authorities, Victor threatens to hurt Elizabeth because he knows that Paul has fallen in love with her (ironically, just afterwards he shoots Elizabeth by accident as the Creature is about to attack her, which prevents her from ever seeing it).

Makeup man Phil Leaky could not repeat the Jack Pierce design for the monster because Universal had a copyright on it, so he gave Christopher Lee an appropriately corpse-like look as Frankenstein's Creature. The Creature had not been conceived with much personality, but as played by Lee he does convey animal ferocity combined with a certain pitiableness in this fierce, shambling hulk of a man. It is a shock when the camera rapidly tracks in to first reveal the Creature's face, and its first action upon coming to life is to strangle its creator, though Paul intervenes, perhaps to his later regret. The Creature kills an old blind man and a young boy, but it is nevertheless shocking to see the pathetically struggling Creature be easily dispatched when Paul shoots it in the eye. Later Frankenstein revives it to demonstrate his power over death (appropriately, a good portion of the Creature's hairline has been blasted off) and uses it to kill Justine. The Creature may not have a personality, but at least Lee gives it moments of confusion and pain to flesh out the minimal characterization.

Through careful camera placement, Fisher shows how the character of Frankenstein slowly builds in his passion and intensity, as well as his megalomania. He is shown to be nonchalant about the less savory aspects of his work when he wipes his bloody hands on his expensive frock, or immediately following the death of Justine when he pleasantly asks Elizabeth for the marmalade. He indulges himself in every whim, from fine clothes, food and wine, to finally marrying Elizabeth, to murder if that suits his ends. Increasingly, framing sets him apart from the other human figures, while two-shots of him and the Creature indicate that they are two aspects of the same being with a close association. He refuses to acknowledge that he failed, blaming Paul instead, and only loses his cool at the end of the film: first, when the monster prepares to attack him before it is doused in fire and then hurtles through a window into an acid bath, and second, when Paul refuses to corroborate his fantastic story. The closing shot is of Victor going to the guillotine, which is being raised.

Made on a fairly minuscule budget, *The Curse of Frankenstein* grossed over $7 million worldwide and became a great success. Naturally, Hammer Films wanted to revise another horror classic in hopes of repeating the success, and so they selected Bram Stoker's *Dracula* as the ideal project and Terence Fisher as the director. Originally, Fisher was hired on *Curse of Frankenstein* because he was still owed a film under his contract with Hammer, and while they had wanted him to finish *Curse* in four weeks, he insisted on and received five. For *Dracula* (the film's British title), all the key production people were reteamed: Anthony Hinds was the producer with Anthony Nelson Keys as his associate; the script once more was by Jimmy Sangster; the photography was by Jack Asher, who received an Academy Award nomination for his excellent work on *Horror of Dracula*; the makeup was again by Phil Leakey; and the exquisite low-budget sets were production-designed by the wondrous Bernard Robinson.

Shot in a mere 25 days on a budget of between $160,000 to $200,000, *Horror of Dracula* (the American title by which the film is best known) was long regarded by many fans as the finest horror film ever made. Certainly it remains one of the best renderings of the Dracula theme. While filming pacing has changed since the '50s, the film is impressively streamlined. Hardly a scene goes by that does not offer action or suspense, and the climax, though quick, is still quite rousing and unforgettable even today.

Like the Creature in *Curse of Frankenstein*, Dracula is not given much onscreen time in the film, but his presence and influence can be felt throughout. The film opens with Jonathan Harker (John Van Eyssen) arriving at Castle Dracula via a Swiss coach after the ominous opening (the camera pans down from a statue of an eagle against a troubled sky to the castle's crypt and dissolves into a shot of Dracula's sarcophagus that suddenly has blood dripped on it; it does not have a story point, but it does set the mood and establishes James Bernard's memorable 3-note Dracula theme). Once inside, he finds dinner and a note from his absent host. Suddenly a woman (Valerie Gaunt) appears to warn him that Dracula is holding her prisoner, but sensing Dracula's presence, she cuts off her pleas and runs away.

Fisher introduces Dracula as an imposing figure at the top of a staircase, part of the ornate background, just as he had introduced the Creature in *Curse of Frankenstein* as part of the library. Because of the woman's warning, there is a sense of menace in Dracula's arrival, though he is only polite and does nothing that could be interpreted as overtly menacing. However, in a subtle touch, the sound of Dracula's footsteps has been removed in all of the scenes in which he appears, giving him a supernatural quality, while Harker's footsteps still remain audible. Showing Harker to his room, Dracula takes a polite interest in a picture of his attractive fiancée, Lucy (Carol Marsh), then bids him good night. These are the last civilized words that the vampire is allowed to utter.

Dracula does not come onscreen again until the woman who appeared earlier is about to put the bite on Harker, having lured him into the library. With blazing red eyes and blood streaming from his fangs, Dracula makes a shocking appearance at the door and leaps across the room to chastize the woman, knocking Harker unconscious only when Harker remains determined to interfere. Lee portrays Dracula as a snarling animal, an impressive tower of strength from this point on. His Dracula is memorable and menacing because despite his suave and normal appearance, he is clearly capable of unrestrained ferocity and possessed of tremendous strength.

Harker survives the night but blows the chance to end the scourge the next day when he takes too much time to conceal the diary he has been keeping outside the castle and then disposes of the vampire woman first. The sun seems to set supernaturally fast, and Dracula is awakened by the vampire woman's first scream. To play upon Dracula's supernatural unpredictability, Fisher blocks the scene so that Harker turns to confront Dracula's coffin only to find it empty and Dracula nowhere in sight. On the staircase leading out of the crypt, we can see light shining through a grill, but suddenly the light disappears as a door closes and Dracula blocks the only exit. The camera approaches the unnerved Harker to quietly communicate his fate.

Considering that Harker has been narrating the film and is the focus of its first third, his demise is fairly surprising (and a departure from the book, like many others in this film). The film's real hero becomes apparent when Dr. (rather than Prof.) Van Helsing (Peter Cushing) shows up at an inn looking for his missing friend, but the traditional frightened villagers, with the exception of the innkeeper's daughter, refuse to cooperate or answer his inquiries. (The aforementioned daughter slips him Harker's diary, which her father intended for her to destroy.) Van Helsing heads off for the castle but arrives as a funeral coach speeds Dracula's white coffin off to some as yet unknown destination. Inside the crypt, he finds the staked vampire woman and his unfortunate friend, now vampirized. With a stake, he releases Harker's soul from its supposed torment.

In a subsequent scene where Van Helsing dictates his notes into a primitive dictaphone, Fisher has Van Helsing equate the vampire's victims with drug addicts. Visually, however, he associates them with lust, which we see on Lucy's face immediately afterwards as she expectantly prepares her bedroom for Dracula's approach and eagerly awaits his inevitable arrival, succumbing to his bite and caresses.

In perhaps the definitive article on the film in *Photon #27*, Ron Borst quotes Fisher as saying, "It's an off-shoot of the love situation because Dracula has the power, in a twisted way, to make Lucy and Mina give a sexual reaction."

Fisher's approach and intentions are made even more obvious by his comments in the same article regarding the depiction of Mina Holmwood

Christopher Lee as Dracula in Horror of Dracula *embodied a virile, sexual, attractive vampire to excellent effect. Here he has apparently bitten Mina Holmwood (Melissa Stribling) and she does not seem to mind a bit of necking from this tall, dark stranger. Terence Fisher directed this horror classic.*

(Melissa Stribling) just after she has first succumbed to Dracula's influence:

> Dracula preyed upon the sexual frustrations of his women victims. The [Holmwood] marriage was one in which she was not sexually satisfied and that was her weakness as far as Dracula's approach to her was concerned. When she arrived back after having been away all night she

said it all in one closeup at the door. She'd been done the whole night through, please! I remember Melissa saying, "Terry, how should I play the scene?" So I told her, "Listen, you should imagine you have had one whale of a sexual night, *the* one of your whole experience. Give me that in your face!" And she did, of course. I have a blow-up, a closeup I treasure. She was very good.

In the second part of the film, Van Helsing goes to tell Lucy that her fiancé has died. Although the English names of Holmwood and Seward have been retained from Stoker's novel, it becomes apparent that these English actors are not supposed to be in England, though from a comic sequence involving a border crossing, they are supposed to be in a nearby country – from the town names, presumably Germany or Austria. This is also borne out by the name of the Holmwood's maid, Gerda (Olga Dickie). Arthur Holmwood (Michael Gough) is not very receptive to Van Helsing's news or his presence when Van Helsing arrives at the Holmwood estate. (Gough is a talented actor who curiously tends towards one-note, hammy performances in his horror films. While *Horror of Dracula* has one of Gough's best horror performances, this weakness still applies here as he plays Arthur as constantly distrusting and angry.)

Mina goes to Van Helsing out of concern for Lucy's "anemia," and the good doctor immediately discovers the telltale teethmarks upon examining his patient. He orders that the room be filled with strong-smelling flowers and that the windows remain shut at night, but Gerda alters his plan at Lucy's insistence, leading to her death.

Cushing's performance as the heroic Van Helsing is one of *Horror of Dracula*'s greatest strengths. He is as dedicated in his pursuit of evil as Frankenstein is in pursuit of creating artficial life. However, while both characters project great learning and intelligence, Cushing's Van Helsing shows tenderness to other human beings (especially young Tania, the little girl the vampiric Lucy entices) and he is not unconscionable in pursuit of his ends. To get an index to Cushing's effectiveness in the part, one need only compare it to that of the more highly acclaimed actor Laurence Olivier in the same role in John Badham's 1979 adaptation of the stage play.

The scene where Arthur confronts his dead sister with Tania is quite effective. The vampire starts to ply her feminine charms on her own brother before Van Helsing steps out and forces her back with the power of the cross, putting an X (the standard rating of horror films in Great Britain) on her forehead which burns at the touch of the cross. Because it is a repeat of earlier action, Fisher makes this last staking far more graphic than the first, with blood welling around the white negligee that Lucy wears and Arthur's face registering pain as she screams; but Fisher is also careful to include a shot of her peaceful expression once she has permanently been put to rest.

The last section of the film entails the search for Dracula's whereabouts and his revenge upon Holmwood by seducing Mina. Arthur and Van Helsing set out but are turned back to where they came from, with Mina falling under Dracula's spell in their absence. Arthur and Van Helsing guard the outside of the Holmwood home, little suspecting that Dracula's coffin has been transferred to the basement, so that the vigilant guardians prove no obstacle.

The film becomes particularly dynamic as Van Helsing spots Dracula's empty coffin in the basement and places a cross there to prevent the vampire's return just as Dracula himself enters and then blocks the door. From that point on, the film becomes a frantic chase as Dracula must return to his native soil before daybreak (the dictaphone recording has made it plain that sunlight is fatal to vampires).

Arriving at Dracula's castle just as he is attempting to bury Mina alive to speed her transition into one of his vampire brides, Van Helsing pursues the dread Count into his library and distracts him from disappearing down a trapdoor. The two grapple with each other. Van Helsing plays dead to prevent Dracula from choking the life out of him (or perhaps he simply passed out); then, noticing sunlight streaming in the window, he runs across the table and pulls down the curtains with a mighty leap. Cushing came up with the additional idea of grabbing two candlesticks to form a cross and forcing Dracula into the sunlight, which turns his skin into ash the moment it touches him.

It has long been noted that some foreign versions of the final famous disintegration scene were longer than others, but there is no significant difference between them and the disintegration has always been entirely bloodless. Sangster had opted not to allow Dracula to turn into animals in an effort to take the film away from the realm of the fairy tale and make it seem more realistic.

Just as Dracula liberated repressed Victorian women into sensuality, *Horror of Dracula* liberated the horror film, allowing it to become more sensual as well as more graphic, with blood running red onscreen rather than remaining in black and white. *Horror of Dracula* proved a great success, Hammer Film found a new exploitable market, and the late '50s/early '60s horror renaissance was on.

Next Fisher tackled *The Revenge of Frankenstein*, which like *Bride of Frankenstein* before it, proved that sequels do not have to mean a drop in quality from the original film. Wisely, rather than making the Creature the returning character, Hammer knew its prime asset was Cushing's performance as the fanatical Baron. The sequel picked up immediately from its predecessor and devised a way for the Baron to escape the guillotine. In an ironic touch, at the last possible minute, the prison padre is placed under the blade while Frankenstein makes his escape with the aid of some handsomely bribed henchmen.

The Revenge of Frankenstein then turns into a study of contrasts. Frankenstein moves to Carlsbruck and sets up a medical practice among the lower classes under the name of Dr. Stein, which proves to be a great success. The hypocrisy of the time is revealed as Dr. Stein's success causes the town's medical board (composed of doctors who treat the upper class) to offer him membership because they are concerned he might take people away from their practices. (They had initially attempted to prevent him from practicing there in the first place.)

It becomes clear that the members of this board are not so much interested in saving people's lives as in saving face and that they are concerned that the competition is too good. Dr. Stein himself proves full of contrasts as he both helps the inmates of his charity hospital and takes limbs and other pieces to create an artificial body for his hunchback assistant, Karl (Oscar Quitak). He is shown to be at once compassionate (he truly helps most of his charity patients and is trying to help Karl by replacing his defective body with a new one) and ruthless (to create his perfect specimen, he has to hack perfectly good body parts off unwilling donors).

When a delegation from the medical board sees him at the hospital, Dr. Stein sees through them immediately. It is apparent that they are appalled at the idea of soiling their hands by working to help charity patients who cannot pay them. Stein rails against the stupidity of the town's medical establishment, clarifying his role as a rebel against society, but though he is correct in many of his theories, he is also blind to the misery he leaves in the wake of his pursuit, a sin that eventually strikes back at him.

His loyal and dedicated assistant, Dr. Hans Kleve (Francis Matthews), is also blind to the realities of human behavior. After Karl successfully has his brain transferred to a new body (Michael Gwynn), Kleve makes the mistake of telling Karl how he will become famous and will be exhibited before all the world's most famous scientists, doctors and universities. Because of his deformed body, Karl has been the object of attention since he was born. With his new body he desires only to find a wife and achieve the anonymity previously denied him, so Karl works to achieve his escape.

Frankenstein prepared for the operation by successfully transplanting a brain from one chimpanzee to another, but found that the new chimp had an unfortunate tendency towards cannibalism. He also experiments with constructing a mechanical brain, which he hooks up to a pair of eyes and hands, but realizes that the brain is far too complex an organ to be duplicated mechanically. (This establishes the Baron as supremely brilliant, but not a miracle worker. However, having invented a primitive computer, i.e., a mechanical brain, he does nothing with it, preferring to concentrate on the field of brain transplants.)

Unlike previous Frankensteinian creations, there is nothing monstrous about Karl's new body, and Karl gleefully disposes of his old body before anyone can get any ideas about transferring him back. However, things really begin to go awry when he is discovered by an abusive janitor (George Woodbridge) who bashes him over the head and damages Karl's brain. Karl begins to feel cannibalistic impulses and his healthy new body begins to assume the hunched and distorted form of his original body.

Margaret Conrad (Eunice Grayson) is one of Sangster's scheming, unscrupulous females who resorts to extortion to get a job at the hospital. She proves sympathetic but not very bright as she helps the restrained Karl to escape and hides him in a barn. Unfortunately, Karl's deteriorating condition causes him to murder a young girl. Meanwhile, Frankenstein and Kleve search for him frantically.

The film's climax is a fairly simple affair where Margaret's aunt, Countess Barzcynska, presents Dr. Stein and his assistant to "society," the rich, unsympathetic clods who run Carlsbruck. Suddenly, Karl crashes the party by smashing through the window and reveals Dr. Stein's identity by pleading, "Frankenstein, help me!" Naturally, proper society cannot have anything to do with the notorious Frankenstein, whom everyone had believed was dead, and Frankenstein soon finds himself abandoned, except by the vengeful inmates of the charity hospital who tear him to pieces.

In the film's final and ironic coda, Dr. Kleve proves himself to be a good pupil, succeeding where his teacher had failed by transferring Frankenstein's brain into a new body. Frankenstein then moves to England and sets up shop as Dr. Franck, with a scarred body, a mustache and a monocle. Despite his many subsequent attempts in the rest of the films of the series, only Dr. Kleve's creation of Frankenstein himself remains a successful experiment.

Though the film is very talky, Fisher keeps *Revenge* lively by injecting little bits of macabre humor into the proceedings. While Frankenstein retains his basic drive and goal, his presentation here is far more sympathetic, making him seem almost a martyr, killed because he defied society rather than for his cruel and needless amputations of helpless charity inmates. Despite his villainies, it is somehow reassuring that he has survived to practice again at the end of the film.

Fisher next tackled an adaptation of Arthur Conan Doyle's mystery classic *The Hound of the Baskervilles*, which is my favorite adaptation of this Sherlock Holmes story. Cushing played the famed detective in a manner reminiscent of his Van Helsing characterization, making Holmes a tireless fighter in the battle against evil.

In an effort to attract both horror and mystery audiences, the horrific elements of the tale were punched up and a prologue establishing the legend of the hellhound was added. In it, a cruel nobleman is utterly contemptuous of his servants, roasting one in a fireplace and attempting to rape his daughter besides. This unpleasant chap is then torn apart by an unseen hound from hell. The traditional Doyle tale follows, with excellent performances from the cast including Andre Morrell as a more intelligent than usual Dr. Watson and Christopher Lee as a stuffy but sympathetic Sir Henry Baskerville.

Fisher's direction keeps the story going at a good pace and generates some fine atmosphere out of Jack Asher's luscious photography and Bernard Robinson's detailed sets, with an added assist from James Bernard's moody score. While the hound itself proves not terribly effective, Fisher is able to invest the scenes before its climactic appearance with an eerie menace, and the whole film is very ably and intelligently conceived and executed.

Unfortunately, as a result of the attempt to capture two different audiences, most viewers were not sure if the film was fish or fowl, and it proved a box office disappointment to Hammer, who had hoped to generate a series of Holmes films as well.

Next Fisher tackled his much-maligned version of *The Mummy*. This film was unfairly and unfavorably compared to the Karl Freund version, which it is in no way a remake of. Rather, it is a compendium of the themes and devices of that film's sequels, the Universal mummy series, which the Fisher film is superior to, and is by far the best of all the Hammer mummy films.

The film opens in Egypt in 1895. The Banning expedition, led by Stephen (Sir Felix Aylmer) and John Banning (Peter Cushing), comes across the tomb of Ananka. While John is laid up with a broken leg, Stephen Banning enters the tomb after being warned away by a mysterious Egyptian, Mehemet (George Pastell). Inside, he discovers the sarcophagus of Ananka, as they had anticipated, as well as the scroll of life. What happens next drives him mad. We then see Mehemet, who has taken possession of the scroll, praying to Karnak that he will avenge the desecration of Princess Ananka's tomb.

In England three years later, Stephen Banning regains his sanity suddenly and tries to warn his son John that he had read the words on the scroll of life aloud, bringing to life a mummy that will implacably track them down. John is not convinced as to the veracity of his story.

Naturally, the opening of this film does not have the power of Freund's film, and the detail of the archeologist going mad is by and large thrown away without much in the way of dramatic effect. We do not see the mummy (Christopher Lee) until it comes out of a big swamp into which it had fallen while it was being transported to Mehemet's English address (passing by the asylum where Stephen is being kept, Stephen is suddenly aware of the mummy's nearby presence and screams, scaring the driver who is unknowingly transporting the mummy in a crate so that he drives recklessly and it ends up in the swamp).

The use of the swamp seems to have been borrowed from Leslie Goodwins' *The Mummy's Curse*, while the names of Stephen and John Banning are from Harold Young's *The Mummy's Tomb*, and the idea of a mummy named Kharis obeying a high priest started with Christy Cabanne's *The Mummy's Hand*. While Fisher's *Mummy* lacks the wonderful mystical atmosphere of Freund's, it greatly benefits from the sumptuous blues and golds of Jack Asher's cinematography and the incredibly rich detail and grandeur of the Egyptian artifacts that Bernard Robinson designed.

After Mehemet summons the mummy from the swamp to enter Stephen's room in the asylum and break his neck, John relates the history of Kharis and Ananka: Kharis was a high priest of Karnak who had fallen in love with the high priestess Ananka, despite the fact that she was a handmaiden of the god Karnak and that such love was forbidden. After much ceremony in which slaves and maidens are slain to accompany Ananka on her journey into the afterlife, Kharis commits blasphemy by reentering the tomb and attempting to revive Ananka using the sacred scroll of life, but he is caught in the act. As punishment, his tongue is cut out (despite rumors, never graphically filmed), and he is wrapped in bandages and buried alive to serve as a guard to Ananka's tomb.

The scenes depicting this historical background are the most beautiful and captivating in the film, giving this low-budget production the quality of a genuine spectacle. By comparison, the English scenes are rather drab as the mummy comes forth and strangles Joseph Whemple (Raymond Huntley), who accompanied Stephen into the tomb, and is shot by John Banning. The bullets have no effect apart from the mummy flinching at the impact.

Following Whemple's death, John relates what his father had told him, which calls to mind the missing "Egyptian artifacts" that Mehemet had sent for but never received. John then notices that his own wife, Isobel (Yvonne Furneaux) is the spit and image of Princess Ananka (and is probably her reincarnation, another lift from the Universal series).

Unable to convince the police, John prepares a shotgun to do battle with the mummy that is now stalking him. In the film's most famous scene, the mummy bursts through the glass doors of the Banning estate, is shot twice by John, lunges at him and misses. John takes a spear and drives it through the mummy to effect. The mummy is prevented from murdering John only by the appearance of Isobel, who commands him not to.

Christopher Lee is largely wasted in the role of the mummy, a mute and murderous automaton, though he does effectively convey a strong reaction to Isobel's appearance and manages to express a longing for the absent Ananka via his mime performance. George Pastell is suavely menacing as Mehemet, who is visited by John and is surprised to find out that the mummy failed to kill its intended victim.

Cushing makes for a good stalwart hero and is particularly delightful as he needles Mehemet about his outdated beliefs, trying to provoke a reaction. Mehemet in turn scolds him for presuming to violate sacred Egyptian tombs and not respecting Egyptian customs, conveying an underlying threat. All the while both men pretend to be polite and civilized.

Spying Ananka's seal in Mehemet's hallway, John is convinced that the strange Egyptian is connected with the deaths. He seeks and receives police protection, but this time Mehemet accompanies the mummy to see that the job is done correctly. Knocking out the police guards, the mummy attacks John and begins to strangle him. Again he is stopped by the appearance of Isobel, but then he continues strangling until she lowers her hair so that she looks more like Ananka.

This causes Mehemet to make his fatal mistake: He orders the mummy to kill Isobel. Regarding her as the woman he loves, the mummy breaks Mehemet's back instead and carries the swooning woman off in his arms. The finale has the mummy carrying Isobel into the swamp until she orders him to put her down. When he releases her, the police get a clear shot at the mummy, who, stunned by this betrayal, sinks with the scroll of life into the swamp, a tragic and forlorn figure.

The traditional mummy is not much of a menace, moving slowly with one hand extended. It would appear that most of its victims could get away easily if they did not let their fright get the better of them. However, Christopher Lee's interpretation was far more energetic and forceful. This mummy was quick, had superhuman strength, and could easily overpower his foes. In comparison to the Universal contract directors, Fisher's handling of the film is also more energetic, using the best elements of the series and discarding any dull spots that mar the originals.

To be able to utilize the elements of the Universal films in Jimmy Sangster's script, Hammer made a deal with Universal-International to release the film in the United States and elsewhere. However, the production did not please Nina Wilcox Putnam, coauthor of the original story of the Freund film, who sued and received a settlement for what she felt were unjustified appropriations from her story.

Although it also had a rich look, Fisher's first horror misstep was his remake of *The Man in Half-Moon Street*, which was retitled *The Man Who Could Cheat Death*. Anton Diffring starred as Dr. Georges Bonnet, a sculptor who keeps himself young and immortal by means of a special serum and a series of gland operations. When a woman who loves him, Margo (Delphi Lawrence), interrupts him before he has taken the serum, he begins to shrivel and his flesh sears hers.

To make matters worse, Dr. Ludwig Weiss (Arnold Marle) has become too old to perform the gland operation and so a new doctor must be trained. Bonnet decides on Dr. Pierre Gerrard (Christopher Lee), who bears him a grudge because Gerrard's girlfriend Janine (Hazel Court) has fallen for the talented but aloof sculptor.

While Gerrard agrees because of the information he might gleam from the operation, the tables turn when Weiss discovers that Bonnet has killed to get the replacement gland and retaliates by destroying the last of Bonnet's serum. In a fit of rage and going steadily insane, Bonnet kills Weiss, only to discover that Gerrard refuses to perform the operation without his guidance. Bonnet forces Gerrard to comply by threatening Janine, whom he plans to make his similarly immortal bride, but she has discovered the now demented Margo and no longer trusts him. Finally, after leaving the operating table to confront Janine, Bonnet discovers that Gerrard has tricked him and he begins turning into his true age. He plans to have Janine join him in death, but is foiled even in that when Margo gets her revenge by setting him and the whole basement on fire. Pierre and Margo escape to safety.

The script was based on a dull play by Barre Lyndon. Scriptwriter Jimmy Sangster, who also produced, failed in his attempt to make the film livelier. Lyndon had an interesting career which included another play, *The Amazing Dr. Clitterhouse* (also made into a film), and the screenplays of *The Lodger* (see chapter on John Brahm), *Hangover Square, Night Has a Thousand Eyes,* and *The War of the Worlds.*

The Stranglers of Bombay was a bit of a departure for Fisher as he shot it in black and white rather and used Arthur Grant as his cinematographer. Jimmy Sangster was also absent; the screenplay was by David S. Goodman. The film begins with the legend of Kali and depicts the rise of a Thuggee cult in India while smacking its lips over the violence that British Captain Lewis (Guy Rolfe) uncovers. Kali is personified by a mute Marie Devereux, who heaves her huge breasts and smiles in delight over various tortures including tongue amputations, hand amputations, blinding, etc. This is undoubtedly Fisher's most sadistic film, but it is not a traditional horror film, though the actions of the Thuggee cult are horrifying.

Whether the film may have partially inspired Steven Spielberg's *Indiana Jones and the Temple of Doom*, which depicts another Thuggee cult, is open to question, but there is no question what inspired Fisher's next film, *The Brides of Dracula*: the demand for a sequel to *Horror of Dracula*. Having killed Dracula off in the first film, Hammer decided to bring back Peter Cushing as Van Helsing and have him pursue some leftover vampires— Baron Meinster (David Peel) and a group of vampire brides.

Despite the fact that many of the same people worked on both films, and despite the handsome production and the rather fetching females of the title, *The Brides of Dracula* disappoints. The problem is not Peel's vampire, who received much of the blame, but simply a lackluster script by Sangster that was rewritten by Peter Bryan and Edward Percy.

Perhaps Baron Meinster seems less sinister and powerful a foe because the film begins with him chained with a silver chain by his mother (Martita Hunt), who feeds him on the blood of girls after he has been vampirized in his youth. A young woman, Marianne Danielle (Yvonne Montaur), who has been lured to the house by the Baroness, discovers the poor Baron, who convinces her that his mother is truly the monster. She frees him and he responds by vampirizing his mother and starting a harem of vampire women who follow him. Van Helsing learns of the cult and puts a stop to this scourge.

The tension and suspense, as well as the overall mood, fall far short of *Horror of Dracula*, but the film does feature three memorable sequences. In one, a servant, Greta (Freda Jackson), coaxes a newly formed vampire out of the grave. In another, Van Helsing suffers a bite and rids himself of the disease of vampirism by cauterizing the wound with a hot poker. In the finale Van Helsing destroys Meinster and his coven by shifting the fan of a great windmill so that it forms a cross and blasts the vampires. Overall, the pacing and the results are uneven.

Fisher took a short break from horror to make a swashbuckler, *The Sword of Sherwood Forest*, which continued the Robin Hood saga and starred Richard Green, Peter Cushing and Niall MacGinnis (who was so good in *Curse of the Demon*). He returned to horror with *The Two Faces of Dr. Jekyll* (United States title *House of Fright*), a ponderous adaptation of Robert Louis Stevenson's famous tale that at least offers some good dialogue courtesy of Wolf Mankowitz's screenplay.

Unfortunately, Paul Massie is uninteresting whether playing Dr. Jekyll or Mr. Hyde, though the fact that he becomes more handsome rather than less after the transformation is an interesting device and consistent with Fisher's other films. Dr. Jekyll seeks to find the "inner man" and thinks he has found it when he changes into Hyde. The film turns both on Jekyll's dual identity and on his jealousy as he discovers his wife, Kitty (Dawn Addams), dancing with Paul Allen (Christopher Lee), a rake and a gambler. Surprised by his wife's presumed infidelity, he makes a play for her as Hyde only to be rebuffed.

Continuing in his experiment, he returns and seduces Paul's mistress Maria (Norma Marla) and tries to make both her and Kitty Hyde's mistresses. Descending into depravity (represented by getting himself high on gin and opium), Hyde is finally beaten up by some toughs after Kitty continually spurns his intentions.

However, when he finally catches Kitty flirting again with Paul, whose gambling debts he has been making good on, he arranges for Paul to be crushed to death by Maria's python while he attempts to rape Kitty, who prefers to commit suicide rather than submit to the fabled "fate worse than death." Deciding to have a go at Maria again, Hyde only winds up strangling her. His passion and jealousy are now completely out of control. He kills a stable boy and passes off the body as that of Dr. Jekyll, but at the inquest, Hyde breaks down and transforms into Jekyll, who confesses to overpowering his inner nature at the cost of his own life.

Once more Fisher deals in hypocrisy. Jekyll's wife is not as good as she appears, nor is the sluttish Maria as bad as people perceive her to be. Hyde does not attempt to right wrongs to Dr. Jekyll. He even enables Allen to carry on his affair with Kitty as he becomes foolishly jealous of his other kinder and weaker self. Pursuing all pleasures with a callous and hedonistic glee, he finally becomes vengeful when his intentions are thwarted. Fisher consistently depicts sexuality as dangerous when it is separated from love, and *House of Fright* very explicitly illustrates this theme.

Contrariwise, the power of love is very important as a saving grace in *The Curse of the Werewolf*, set in Spain and based on Guy Endore's *The Werewolf of Paris*. Long highly regarded by horror fans, the film proves a bit of a disappointment when viewed today. It begins with a major gaffe in that the narrator, Don Alfredo Carido (Clifford Evans), not only relates events of which he could have no knowledge, but sets the early part of the story as being 200 years ago and then appears on the scene just after the death of the Marquis (Anthony Dawson) who appears in these scenes.

Fisher once more shows the cruelty of the aristocracy to those they considered their inferiors. The Marquis proves a holy terror and enjoys humiliating a beggar who arrives at his wedding feast to beg for food. He buys the beggar for himself and gives him as a gift to his bride. He then gets the man drunk and has him dance and scramble for table scraps. As the Marquis departs for the night to consummate his marriage, the drunken beggar makes the mistake of leering and loudly wishing the Marquis a very good night. The bride asks for mercy, and so the beggar is thrown into the dungeon and then forgotten.

The jailer's daughter who feeds him grows up to be Yvonne Romaine and attracts the eye of the Marquis, now a syphilitic old man whose wife has died long ago. Not understanding that the girl is mute as well as frightened, he punishes her when she spurns his advances by throwing her into the dungeon. There she is raped by the hairy beggar she once befriended. The attack exhausts the beggar and kills him, while the next day the abused girl is sent back to the Marquis, where she is expected to be more amiable. Repulsed by the hideous old man whose skin is flaking off of him, she stabs him dead and flees for her life.

Dawson gives such a powerful portrait of evil as the vile Marquis that he seems far more a monster than the werewolf. In discussing the makeup of his monsters, Fisher talked about the Marquis in an interview in *Films and Filming*:

The one case where I was afraid we'd gone too far was in *Werewolf* with the syphilitic old man who gets stabbed over the chessboard. It's horrid when you see those warts with the hairs growing out of them, isn't it? But his face had to be an image for his soul. He was evil, rotting away.

The censor allowed everything about the man's appearance, but for one little detail. On the set the actor was fiddling about, just getting into the part, and I saw him scratch a flake of skin off his nose and I said, "That's it – do that when we shoot," and he lifted a flake of skin off his nose and flicked it away with his fingers. And this one detail was not allowed to stand.

Don Alfredo finds the girl, pregnant from the rape by the beggar, and takes her in to be cared for. Because she gives birth to an unwanted child on Christmas Day, it is considered a mockery of Christ and the child is cursed with the taint of lycanthropy. To add to the misery, the poor woman dies giving birth to the child, whose name is Leon.

The film bogs down and loses momentum in its second portion which includes the childhood of Leon, who because of his ill-fated beginning is driven to attack sheep. However, with the love of his foster parents, Leon is able to keep his lycanthropy under control.

(Leon begins to attack goats after the distressing experience of seeing a friend kill a squirrel and then accidentally tasting its blood. When he is shot because he was mistaken for a wolf, his parents find out and control his impulses.)

The film depicts lycanthropy as a kind of Jekyll-and-Hydism, in which a man's body is inhabited by both a soul (representing the good side of his nature) and a spirit (that of a wolf, which represents the bad side, anything that could cause a man to lose control). By putting bars on Leon's window and giving him love, which raises man's soul, his foster parents keep him from turning into a wolf.

Oliver Reed shows definite hints of his fine acting ability playing the adult Leon, the first starring role of his career. He conveys Leon's moods from naivete to love to moroseness to torment very well. Reed's physique makes for an imposing werewolf in Roy Ashton's impressive makeup.

Leon as an adult leaves home to make his way in the world and gains employment filling and labeling wine bottles for Don Fernando (Ewen Solon). He makes friends with fellow bottler Jose, but he particularly has the eye for Fernando's daughter Christina (Catherine Feller). Fernando wants Christina to marry an arrogant rich fop who is introduced by callously splashing Leon when his coach passes him by on the road. Christina decides to fool her father and see Leon covertly and the pair fall in love. However, Christina knows that her father would never approve of their marriage and tells Leon so.

This leaves Leon depressed and he decides to stay home on Saturday night, but Jose urges him to go with him to a quiet and respectable place that proves to be neither. It is the night of a full moon and Leon is further troubled when a tavern tart persuades him to accompany her to her bedroom, where he begins kissing her. Once more, Fisher depicts lust as a force that creates evil as Leon changes suddenly into a werewolf, biting the woman and then killing her.

His animal nature unleashed, he next attacks and kills Jose and a villager whose dog was killed when shot with a silver bullet by a goatherd out to protect his flock from the rampages of the young Leon. When Leon wakes up, he does not remember what he has done, but he knows there is blood on his hands. He leaves his father's and returns to Don Fernando's house, where the police question him about his whereabouts the previous evening.

That night, Christina ignores his pleas to stay away from him, and Leon is surprised and pleased to find the next morning that he did not change. The sweet attentions of his true love prevented him from turning into a beast, and he vows to elope with her. However, the police decide to arrest him in connection with the murders. Convinced he is indeed responsible, he bribes a guard to send word to his father. Leon then begs his father to kill him before he kills again.

Meanwhile, Christina finds that Leon is in jail and shocks her father and the fop by stealing the fop's coach and running to him. Don Alfredo and the priest who baptized Leon try to persuade the authorities that Leon must either be freed to spend his life in a monastery or be killed either by burning him alive or shooting him with a silver bullet made from a silver crucifix. The authorities are not convinced and become even less so when Christina arrives on the scene and reveals she knows nothing of Leon's claims to be a werewolf.

The lovers are separated, and sure enough, that night Leon transforms once more. He kills his cellmate and when a guard comes forward to investigate, he smashes down the cell door on top of him. Don Alfredo obtains the silver bullet from the goatherd who fashioned it and sets off to look for his wayward son. Christina looks for Leon and narrowly escapes meeting him in the most unfortunate of circumstances when the werewolf hesitates as he is about to pounce on her from a rooftop.

While the villagers mill about the square, Leon leaps from rooftop to rooftop until Don Alfredo finally corners Leon in the bell tower of the local church. Stunned by the noise of the bells, Leon hesitates, allowing Alfredo enough time to shoot and kill him with the silver bullet, ending his tormented existence. The bell tower was the film's opening shot and now brings the film to a close.

The Curse of the Werewolf lacks some of the atmosphere of Fisher's earlier films, probably because of Arthur Grant's photography, which is flatter and more naturalistic than the more vivid and colorful photography of Jack Asher, who was dismissed from Hammer as an economy move. (Asher's careful attention to lighting placement and colored gels took more time than the more straightforward work of Grant.) The flaccid moments in the middle of the film hurt its overall pacing, and Reed's two appearances as the werewolf do not evoke the menace they might have as Fisher emphasizes the werewolf's power over building up atmosphere.

Hammer next decided to make a lavish remake of *The Phantom of the Opera*, which was based on Arthur Lubin's 1943 version starring Claude Raines rather than the classic version starring Lon Chaney or Gaston Leroux's fine fantasy novel. Christopher Lee was selected to play the phantom, but he turned it down and the part was offered to Herbert Lom instead. Rather than the tragic killer of previous *Phantoms*, Anthony Hinds' script made the phantom a figure of pathos and left the crimes to the phantom's overzealous henchmen.

Typically, a prima donna (Liane Aukin) is discouraged from singing when her aria is interrupted by the revelation of a hanged corpse. Christine (Heather Sears), a singer from the chorus, is recommended for promotion and comes to the attention of Lord Ambrose D'Arcy (Michael Gough). When Christine spurns his lecherous advances she is replaced by another singer, presumably a more cooperative one, called Yvonne (Sonya Cordeau).

It is revealed that Lord D'Arcy stole the opera from a Prof. Petrie (Lom). In attempting to destroy the manuscript rather than let it fall into D'Arcy's hands, Petrie has his face burned by acid. In the confusion of a fire and in pain, Petrie throws himself into the Thames. He is rescued by a dwarf (Ian Wilson), who protects this phantom's lair from any intruders. (The most grisly moment in the film has Patrick Troughton as a rat catcher who is stabbed in the eye by the fiendish dwarf, who is ruthless in looking after his master's interests, though his behavior is never clearly motivated.)

The Phantom becomes interested in Christine, who is kidnapped by the dwarf and taken to him. He feels she has the potential to become a great opera singer and begins giving her voice lessons. A mysterious figure who hides his visage behind a crudely fashioned mask, the phantom is not frightening but rather pathetic.

Bowing to the tradition of having an unveiling and a chandelier falling, the film leaves these events until the final moments when the dwarf brings the chandelier down and the phantom gallantly swoops down to knock Christine out of the way, saving her but fatally injuring himself and revealing at last his acid-scarred face.

Phantom of the Opera was one of Hammers' more expensive and elaborate efforts, and its failure must be counted as a setback for the company. Fisher then left Hammer for the first time in his long association with them to codirect a German film, *Sherlock Holmes und das Halsband des Todes (Sherlock Holmes and the Deadly Necklace)*. The screenplay was credited to Curt Siodmak and supposedly based on Conan Doyle's *The Valley of Fear*, but had been rewritten by the German producers. Christopher Lee starred as Holmes with Thorley Walters as his Watson, but Lee was horrified to discover that another actor had dubbed his voice over for the English version.

Next came *The Horror of It All*, a variation of *The Old Dark House* that Fisher directed for producer Robert Lippert from a script by Ray Russell. The film is little seen today and did not create much excitement when it was released. A houseful of eccentrics terrorize Pat Boone for 75 minutes.

The Earth Dies Screaming was also done for Lippert and 20th Century–Fox. Willard Parker stars as a test pilot who comes to London and finds that everyone has apparently been killed. Finding some more survivors (including Dennis Price, Thorley Walters, and Virginia Field), he discovers that earth has been invaded and that deadly robots are patrolling the countryside to wipe out the last few survivors. Somehow Parker concludes that all the robots must be controlled from one location, and if that location is wiped out, the robots will be disabled. He sets off in search of such a place and wipes it out in the nick of time. Fisher's handling is competent but undistinguished and the unthoughtout script dooms the overall project.

Fisher returned to Hammer for *The Gorgon*, which John Gilling scripted from a story by J. Llewellyn (with uncredited rewrites by producer Anthony Hinds) based on the myth of the Medusa. Sadly, the Gorgon herself, with snakes in her hair, is not as impressive as she ought to be; nevertheless, Fisher has crafted a moody and at times atmospheric film around Roy Ashton's creation.

Additionally, he set up his camera so that the relationship of Carla Hoffman (Barbara Shelley) to the Gorgon is apparent early on, drawing a visual parallel between Carla and the Gorgon (which is played by another actress because of scheduling difficulties). Once more the male stars are Peter Cushing and Christopher Lee, but this time Lee plays Prof. Meister, the hero, while Cushing plays Dr. Namaroff, the villain of the film.

Like *Curse of the Werewolf, The Gorgon* involves a family curse passed down from generation to generation. The story begins as Prof. Heitz (Michael Goodliffe) has seen the Gorgon and is slowly petrifying. He quickly writes a letter warning his son Paul (Richard Pasco) before the process is complete. Prof. Meister comes to investigate the mysterious deaths.

Meanwhile, Dr. Namaroff is hiding the fact that his assistant Carla is the Gorgon. Paul begins to fall in love with Carla, but Namaroff tries to discourage him. The film is set in a bleak and empty castle for much of its length and has a wistful and sad tone rather than a horrific one. Fisher treats it as the story of two doomed lovers which ends tragically – the Gorgon petrifies both Namaroff and Paul before Meister can lop its head off. The results are far less energetic than the classic Fisher films, but *The Gorgon* achieves its mood much more successfully than *The Phantom of the Opera*. (Regarding the latter film, when it was sold to television, the network added some unnecessary scenes of a pair of detectives who are not directly connected with the story to pad out the running time. Similar tactics were also employed on Don Sharp's *Kiss of the Vampire* and Freddie Francis' *Evil of Frankenstein*, the only one of the Cushing Frankenstein series not directed by Fisher.)

More successful was *Dracula – Prince of Darkness* which featured Christopher Lee's return as the fanged vampire count. However, Lee was so displeased with the dullness of Dracula's dialogue that he could not bring himself to utter it, preferring to emphasize Dracula's animal qualities by hissing and snarling his way through the role. Not having Dracula speak does make him more mysterious and something of a primal force, but it downplays Dracula's intelligence and cunning.

Dracula – Prince of Darkness was shot widescreen, presenting a difficulty when it came to reprising *Horror of Dracula*'s finale, which was shot in the standard 1.85 aspect ratio. Fisher solved this problem by opening the film with a magic mirror in which we see Dracula's destruction at Van Helsing's hands. Nothing in the film tops this opening, but then nothing in the original did either, and it does refresh the audience's memories and prepare them for Dracula's resurrection.

The film was scripted by Jimmy Sangster, but, unhappy with tampering by Anthony Hinds, he took the pseudonym John Samson instead. The story neatly contrasts the uptight prudery of Alan and Helen Kent (Barbara Shelley and Charles Tingwell) with the open lovingness of Charles and Diana Kent (Francis Matthew and Susan Farmer). In particular, the character of Helen is presented as fearful and disapproving, someone who has repressed her desires and is outraged at the idea of other people enjoying theirs.

The two couples are stranded in a forest and decide to take refuge in Dracula's castle, which mysteriously is prepared for a feast. A spooky servant, Klove (Philip Latham), appears and reassures them, "My Master's hospitality is renowned."

Helen and Alan are woken in the night by a strange sound outside their door, and despite Helen's misgivings, Alan goes to investigate. He is struck down by Klove, who hangs him up over his master's ashes and in ritualistic fashion slits his stomach so that the blood pours down on the ashes and resuscitates Dracula.

Klove then lures Helen down to Dracula and she becomes his first victim, transforming into a vampire herself. Suddenly, as a vampire, her repression is gone and she seems transformed into an alluring beauty, just as her husband has been transformed in a bizarre way into Dracula himself. Their fierce denial of sensuality causes their passion to boil over and create evil, which notably comes from this self-righteous couple rather than the more open one of Charles and Diana (the film couple, not the English royalty).

Helen in turn tries to infect Charles and Diana. They flee, but Klove manages to separate Diana from her husband, and it becomes obvious that Dracula has special plans for Diana as Klove drives away in a wagon with two coffins. Meanwhile, the now desperate Charles looks for help at a nearby monastery, where the local Van Hesting substitute, Father Sandor (Andrew Keir), is on hand to speak authoratively on vampires. There is also a lunatic named Ludwig (Thorley Walters), who is obviously based on the Renfield character of Stoker's novel, but he is only used to provide some weak comic relief and help Dracula get at his victims in the monastery.

The most striking scene in the film has the now voluptuous Helen undergoing a symbolic rape as the monks of the monastery hold her down and penetrate her heart with a stake. This attempt to subjugate the flesh takes on unpleasant sexual overtones as the once prim and proper woman is reduced to squirming and writhing and then finally released from her torment.

Charles and Father Sandor ride off to Dracula's castle to rescue Diana. Just when it looks as if Dracula might succeed in his evil designs, the ground gets shot out from under his feet courtesy of Father Sandor's marksmanship and the fact that Dracula has made the mistake of standing on his frozen moat. Running water will kill a vampire and it is not long before the old Count has slipped under, but not for the last time. (He was resurrected in Freddie Francis' *Dracula Has Risen from the Grave*, but *Prince of Darkness* was to be Fisher's last Dracula film.)

Dracula–Prince of Darkness was well made, but the lengthy period spent before the introduction of Dracula into the plot gets to be rather lethargic. Lee's onscreen time is quite small, which was also the case in the other Dracula films, but in this instance, because he is dead in the beginning, his influence is absent and there is no real menace until a good third of the way into the film. From this film on, things began to go downhill for the Dracula series, filmed on restrictive budgets, though both *Risen from the Grave* and *Scars of Dracula* have their moments.

Next came *Island of Terror* and *Night of the Big Heat* (aka *Island of the Burning Damned, Island of the Burning Doomed*), both of which proved to be minor films. These were done for a short-lived British studio called Planet. *Island of Terror* has a group of cancer researchers accidentally creating a creature called a silicate, which attaches itself to a human body and drains out all the bone marrow. Peter Cushing, Edward Judd and Eddie Byrne come to investigate and have a difficult time figuring out how to get rid of the pest until Cushing comes up with the successful plan of feeding it Strontium-90 and irradiating it to death (no one seems to think about what other possible consequences there could be to this).

Cushing turns up in *Night of the Big Heat* only to be burned to death early on when a secret experiment of Christopher Lee's goes awry. It turns out that Lee has been tending to some alien invaders from a dying planet who are used to living in tremendous heat and will devour any energy source to create heat for themselves. The alien blobs decimate the island's inhabitants, including Lee, before their heat creates a thunderstorm that cools them off, permanently. The film was based on a mediocre science fiction novel by John Lymington.

Far more interesting was Fisher's return to the Frankenstein series, *Frankenstein Created Woman*, which combined fantasy and science fiction. This time instead of transferring brains, the Baron has begun investigating the transference of souls. Also, establishing him as being on the cutting edge of science, his achievement is powered by a primitive atomic pile.

Perhaps the most interesting thing about *Frankenstein Created Woman* is its religious imagery. The Baron is equated with God, and even begins the film with a resurrection as he has tested his equipment on himself while his body was frozen and then discovered by his Watson-like assistant, Dr. Hertz (Thorley Walter), a doddering but capable surgeon whose hands are guided by the Baron. (As a possible link to Francis' *Evil of Frankenstein*, the Baron's hands are depicted as severely burned, leaving him to wear gloves and require an assistant for all delicate work.)

If the Baron is the Father, then Christina Kleve (Susan Denberg) is the Son (note the "Christ" in her name) and Hans (Robert Morris) provides the Holy Spirit. Given that at the time depicted in the story crucifixion had been abandoned as an instrument of human suffering, the film uses the guillotine as a substitute symbol. The film opens with a little boy rushing to the guillotine only to witness the execution of his father (who indicates that salvation has not reached him when he instructs the padre accompanying him on the gallows to speak up if the words are meant for his benefit). When we first see the adult Hans, the same guillotine is in the background, and it is upon that guillotine that Hans is murdered by society. Christina just happens to be returning to town in time to catch the sight of Hans being executed, leading to her own death and resurrection. (She drowns herself in water, another potent symbol of holiness and rebirth.) She will later put Hans' head atop a mirror that is visually reminiscent of a guillotine and use a sharp blade to administer "justice" to the three men responsible for the crime for which Hans was executed.

In addition to the trinity of the Baron-Christina-Hans, the film also has a trio of killers who murder Christina's father, Herr Kleve (Alan MacNaughton). These three then form the trio that Christina kills. We have three

A behind-the-scenes birthday party for Susan Denberg on the set of Fisher's Frankenstein Created Woman. The figures are (left to right): Denberg, Peter Cushing, Terence Fisher, Thorley Walters, and writer-producer Anthony Nelson-Keys.

major appearances of the guillotine. Additionally, as in the Last Supper, wine is equated with blood on several occasions. The three callow youths accidentally spill wine before they spill Herr Kleve's blood. When Christina kills Karl (Barry Warren), one of the killers of her father, she causes him to spill his wine first. In preparation for killing Johann (Derek Fowlds), she pours him some wine.

In his article on "The Symbolism in *Frankenstein Created Woman*" in *Little Shoppe of Horrors #7*, Daryl Coats goes on to notice that the wine is also used as a symbol of power. Initially, the three youths are in control of its distribution and they are the only ones allowed to pour wine. But as Christina grows more aggressive, she finally takes control of the wine and its pouring. Coats also notes the use of the biblical allusions to Christ as the conqueror of death in the Baron's boast, "I have conquered death."

The Baron becomes involved with Hans and Christina when he and Dr. Hertz decide to celebrate their initial success in using a forcefield to trap the soul in the body. They send Hans to buy some spirits at the local tavern, where his disfigured sweetheart works for her father. Christina has dark hair and an unfortunately scarred face, which she hides with her hair. Hans does not have enough money to pay for the wine, but offers to pawn his coat, knowing that Dr. Hertz will make good on the debt. Meanwhile, Christina is forced to wait on Anton (Peter Blythe), Karl and Johann, wastrel youths who owe a large bar tab but are catered to because the fathers of two of them are the mayor and the chief of police.

When they begin to mock and gibe Christina, Hans grows angry and lashes out at them in her defense, which sets up a motive for the crime he did not commit, and the police are forced to intervene to break it up. This also sets up the trio's motivation for coming back and breaking into Kleve's shop after hours, though Kleve's death itself is accidental.

Given that Hans' father was executed for his crime, Hans stands condemned in society's eyes, which is frequently shown to believe in the dictum, "Like father, like son." Despite the Baron's coming to Hans' defense at the trial, the lad is ordered to be executed. The focus of the film is on Hans and Christina, rather than on the Baron, but the injustice of society that Hans suffers reflects back on the Baron and his work – he also has suffered from society's prejudices and is regarded suspiciously as a sorcerer. The Baron's work, instead of being central to the story, is the key mechanism for exploring the consequences of putting a vengeful male soul into a previously passive female body.

For when Christina sees the death of her beloved, she commits suicide. The Baron has arranged for Hans' body to be brought to him so that he can trap Hans' soul (he has determined that a soul hangs around the body for an hour after death before moving on), and Christina's drowned body is sent to him also in the hope that the doctor may yet save her. The Baron forces Hans' soul into Christina's body – but, suggesting the biblical promises of life after death, Christina's body becomes new and improved thanks to Dr. Hertz operating under the Baron's guidance as the scar is removed and the hair is altered to blonde (representing Christina's initial purity). The new Christina also has no memory of her previous existence.

Unfortunately, the details of what it must be like for a male soul to find itself in a female body are never fully delineated, though it adds several intriguing layers of possibilities when, in pursit of Hans' revenge, the new Christina seduces young men to murder them, using her sexuality as a weapon to gratify Hans' urge to achieve an "eye for an eye" justice as the three men are murdered for Kleve's death, Christina's death, and Hans' own (another threesome).

To add another layer to her/his obsession, Christina carries around Hans' head in a hatbox and has conversations with it in which Christina has Hans' personality while the head has Christina's! Once Christina/Hans have achieved their goals, the new Christina is overwhelmed with remorse and commits suicide, ignoring the compassionate pleas of her creator, the Baron. She returns to the water and drowns herself, leaving him to shrug in disgust and wander off in the downbeat finale, a rather low-key moment on which to end this high-strung film.

Fisher gets good performances from his principal actors and concentrates on making the film more of an elaborate fairy tale than a horror story. The Baron is depicted as holding society in scorn and contempt, which except for the basically decent souls of Hans and Christina, it largely seems to deserve. This time while the Baron is bent on preserving life, society is hell-bent on destruction, and even the decent become uncompassionate killers as the actions of the new Christina prove. With the exception of the misnamed *Evil of Frankenstein*, this showed the Baron at his most compassionate, while Fisher's next Frankenstein film, *Frankenstein Must Be Destroyed*, would show him at his most ruthless.

Before then, however, Fisher created one of his and Hammer's all-time best films, *The Devil Rides Out* (United States title: *The Devil's Bride*) based on Dennis Wheatley's classic horror novel. The action of the book was beautifully condensed in Richard Matheson's terrific script. While the film could have used a larger budget to depict some of the satanic manifestations, it nevertheless remains the best screen portrayal of the powers of black magic and satanism.

The Devil Rides Out centers around the character of Duc de Richleau (ably played by Christopher Lee in one of his better roles), an occult specialist who learns to his dismay that a close friend, Simon Aron (Patrick Mower), is about to be initiated into a satanic circle. De Richleau is concerned when Simon does not show up for an expected reunion, and with mutual friend Rex Van Ryn (Leon Greene) he heads to Simon's house, which has had an observatory added recently.

Inside the house, a party is going on. Simon describes the guests as members of an astronomical society, but de Richleau becomes immediately suspicious when two more guests arrive and a woman they are talking to complains that there are now more than 13 people present. He guesses correctly that they will be asked to leave.

On the way out, he befuddles Simon by insisting on taking a quick look through Simon's telescope and then springing up the stairs. The observatory is filled with cabalistic symbols and when de Richleau hears a scratching sound, he discovers a wicker basket containing a black cockerel and a white hen, traditional sacrificial animals for a satanic sacrifice. He then turns and denounces Simon as a fool who can not realize the dangerous business he is meddling in.

This film treats the supernatural perfectly seriously. Rex plays the role of the skeptical observer who thinks that all black magic is only superstition, but whose extraordinary experiences in the film convince him that the dark powers are indeed real. With Lee's pompous authority, Fisher conveys that the danger is very real and from suspicion and unease, the film builds in intensity as the forces for good become increasingly desperate to save Simon's very soul. (As de Richleau observes, "I'd rather see you dead than meddling in black magic." The health of the body is not considered as important as the health of the inner soul.)

Indicative of the desperateness of the situation, de Richleau and Rex kidnap Simon to get him out of danger, but their problems have only begun. The head of the satanic circle is Morcata (Charles Gray, best known as the criminologist in *The Rocky Horror Picture Show* and as Blofeld in *Diamonds Are Forever*), a master of the black arts who can project his will across great distances. Morcata causes Simon to choke himself with a cross that de Richleau provided him, and once the butler removes it to save Simon's life, Mocata has Simon completely under his control and Simon escapes.

A strong contributing factor to the film's success is James Bernard's tense score that augments the feeling of oppressive forces in the air. It was one of Bernard's best and works very well in this context, giving the film a strong sense of intensity. Fisher also ably juxtaposes shots of the weary forces of good and the evil forces of the black art at work to show that evil can attack at any time and that it is difficult to be ever vigilant.

Dismayed by Simon's departure, Rex recalls that he knows how to contact one of the women he saw at Simon's party, Tanith (Nike Arrighi), and seeks her out. They know they must find Simon before he has received his satanic baptism and his soul is lost forever. Before this, they investigate Simon's home, breaking in to find it empty except for a minor demon which is guarding the house. (The appearance of the demon is not quite as effective as it might be as the black actor who was employed to play the part looks a bit cross-eyed, which is further called attention to when de Richleau insists that Rex not look in its eyes. However, its appearance is nicely presaged by smoke coming from the nostrils of a drawing of a satanic goat on the floor.)

Rex locates Tanith and tries to kidnap her by taking her out to the country. She reveals that she has not received her satanic baptism yet either, but is expected to that night because it is April 30, one of the major black sabbats. Rex takes her to Marie (Sarah Lawson) and Richard (Paul Eddington) for safekeeping, but she escapes in the car de Richleau has loaned him.

Pursuing in a separate car, Rex gets a taste of Mocata's powers as his windshield suddenly frosts over so that he cannot see through it and then a fog mysteriously covers Tanith's escape route, causing Rex to crash. (Steven Spielberg employed a similar effect in his TV movie *Something Evil*, though not as effectively.) Fisher indicates Mocata's control over Tanith by having her see Mocata's intense gaze in the rearview mirror looking back at her and issuing orders.

Luckily, Rex survives the car crash and finds the building which houses the satanists who are preparing for the night's ritual. He calls de Richleau to meet him, and together they witness the ritual of the black sabbat, beginning with the sacrifice of a goat and an orgy. In the midst of the revelry, the Goat of Mendes (the devil, a man with a goat's head) appears on a boulder to survey the festivities. De Richleau says, "If only there was some light," which gives Rex the idea of using one of the satanists' cars. While de Richleau turns on the headlights and drives the car through the crowd while reciting a psalm, Rex grabs Tanith and Simon and throws them into the car. By throwing a crucifix at the Goat of Mendes, de Richleau is able to disperse its image and the group escape.

Together they go to Marie and Richard's seeking sanctuary. However, de Richleau has to leave the next day to do some important research which will be of value to them, and as soon as de Richleau leaves, Mocata appears. He appears as a suave gentleman returning the car that de Richleau had loaned Rex and Tanith stole. However, there is an underlying menace to his steady, intense stare.

Fisher conveys Mocata's growing influence during their conversation with careful camera placement and editing. Initially, Mocata tries to explain that he is not the evil person that de Richleau no doubt made him out to be, that the sinister reputation of the supernatural arts is undeserved. Marie's nervousness is conveyed by her playing with her daugher's doll (a symbol of innocence and purity) and by her seating herself as far away from Mocata as she can. The two are kept in over-the-shoulder two-shots to show them relating as human beings. But when Mocata's hypnotic influence takes over, the crosscutting changes to one-shots as Mocata's will becomes the dominant and controlling one.

Added to this, Fisher juxtaposes Mocata's two acolytes, Tanith and Simon, suddenly waking and about to attack the people keeping watch over them under Mocata's baleful influence. Mocata's concentration is broken, however, when Marie's daughter Peggy comes in to request her doll, causing Tanith and Simon to wake up in midaction and realize what they have been doing. Mocata leaves with a threat, promising that he would not be back, but *something* will.

Fearful that Mocata can use her as an instrument to hurt these people that she has come to care for, Tanith decides to get herself as far away from them as possible. Rex, who has fallen in love with her, pursues and decides to restrain her at an inn, binding her hands and feet so that she can do no harm when Mocata takes her over again at sundown (the forces of evil are strongest in the nighttime).

When de Richleau returns, he draws a protective circle to guard Simon, Marie, Richard and himself, and within it they must wait without food while the forces of Mocata assault them. This onslaught of the forces of evil is one of the most memorable in any horror film despite *The Devil Rides Out*'s limited budget. While the special effects do not impress, the acting and sincere writing do.

The onslaught begins simply enough with Richard feeling that the whole thing is silly and preparing to leave the circle. De Richleau explains that it has begun, that Mocata begins his attack by exerting his influence over the group's weakest link, the person who is most skeptical. When that does not work, Mocata tries to trick them with the sound of Rex's voice outside the door, and Marie responds almost instinctively as a good hostess to leave the circle and open the door until de Richleau assures her that the voice is not Rex's and it disappears.

Meanwhile, Rex has his hands full with the struggling Tanith, who once more has become possessed by Mocata's power. Mocata plans to unleash great powers and, to avoid risk to himself, summons them through an intermediary, in this case Tanith. Tanith hypnotizes Rex into freeing her and the siege really begins.

The lights dim and the room grows colder. We hear the wind blowing strongly. Mocata keeps seeking ways to get someone to leave the circle. When Simon asks for a drink, the water tastes brackish and Richard offers to get some fresh water. The fireplace flames out and de Richleau offers a silent prayer.

Following the phony spirit who pretended to be Rex, a gigantic tarantula materializes in the room, terrorizing its four occupants, but the tarantula will not enter the circle. Trying a different tack, an apparition of Peggy walks into the room and is attacked by the tarantula. The anguished parents both rush forward to save their "daughter," but de Richleau restrains them and splashes water on the phantoms instead, which causes them to dissolve. Simon feels himself being drawn by Mocata's will outside the circle until Richard knocks him out.

Finally the angel of death himself arrives on a winged horse. While the upward shots of the angel's horse are rather imposing, its effectiveness is undercut by the patently phony wings and the use of repeated shots that jerk the horse back and forth through the same motions. De Richleau warns that if anyone sees the death angel's face, then someone will surely die – the angel of death cannot return empty-handed. Sure enough, a skeletal face is exposed, forcing de Richleau to recite his trump card, the Susamma ritual, a dangerous piece of magic that can "alter time and space."

As a result, the angel of death takes the one who summoned him, Tanith. Rex brings her dead body to Marie and Richard's home. But they have a second shock in store – Peggy has been kidnapped. De Richleau summons Tanith's spirit in hopes of getting her aid in finding the child. Tanith is prevented from revealing all, but reveals enough so that Rex can figure out where she might be.

Meanwhile, Simon blames himself for Peggy's disappearance and decides to return to Mocata in exchange for the child's life. Nothing could have worked better for Mocata's plans, for now he has Simon back and plans to exchange Peggy's innocent, unstained soul for that of Tanith. Richard, de Richleau and Marie follow in hot pursuit, arriving just in time to stop the ritual sacrifice of Peggy, and the forces of good are summoned to put an end to Mocata and his satanic followers, who go up in flames and then disappear from the desecrated church they inhabit.

Suddenly, Richard, Marie, de Richleau and Simon wake up back in the circle – the Susamma ritual has doubled back time so that Moccata, not Tanith, is now the one the angel of death has taken. A happy Rex and Tanith arrive, Peggy has now never been kidnapped, and de Richleau intones that God is the one they must thank.

As the horror film genre has grown increasingly pessimistic, it becomes refreshing to see a film in which the forces for good emerge triumphant. Fisher does not provide much preparation for de Richleau's "trump card," but that is what makes it so surprising and conceals the final twist. Because that twist conveniently arranges for the story to turn out the way the audience wants it to, the audience does not much question the mechanics of it. *The Devil Rides Out* has a certain dignity of bearing which commands respect, and it is certainly well researched. In all, it is a thrilling romance depicting the constant struggle between good and evil and serves as a warning of the dangers of practicing the "secret art," which with its promise of forbidden knowledge has intrigued mankind throughout the centuries.

Fisher unfortunately suffered two auto accidents, which prevented his being more active in making horror films at the end of the '60s. He would make only two more, both Frankenstein films, but his next, *Frankenstein Must Be Destroyed*, was the best of the series, the most consistently good horror series from any studio. (The initial Frankenstein films from Universal were classics and had a higher overall standard, but the series degenerated into B movie fodder of a relatively undistinguished sort. The same could be said of Hammer's Dracula series, as the later episodes in the series had inadequate budgets and relocated Dracula into modern times.)

Frankenstein Must Be Destroyed presented the Baron at his most fanatical and ruthless. The pursuit of his dream seems to have driven him mad so that he will resort to any extreme to accomplish his goal.

The mayhem begins at a rapid clip in the film's opening, featuring a mysterious man who uses a sickle to behead another man and then takes the head with him. Back at a laboratory, the mysterious man discovers a burglar at work and the two tussle, wreaking havoc. In the course of the fight, the mysterious man's bald-headed "monster" mask is pulled off to reveal him to be the ubiquitous Baron Frankenstein (Cushing once more) up to his old tricks, but the brawl puts an end to his current experiment and leaves the Baron having to seek new lodgings.

Frankenstein decides he needs some of the knowledge stored in the brains of his former colleague Dr. Brandt (George Pravda), who has been committed to an insane asylum. He discovers that a young doctor, Holst (Simon Ward), has been stealing drugs for the mother of his girlfriend, Anna (Veronica Carlson), and he blackmails the pair into giving him a place to stay and assisting him. This time the Baron is portrayed as an outright misogynist who only keeps Anna around to make coffee, by implication keeping her under his control.

In a controversial scene excised from American prints of the film, the Baron rapes Anna to demonstrate his absolute hold over her and keep her perpetually intimidated. Constantly, the film compares Frankenstein's outward civility with an inner brutality. When he overhears some gentlemen discussing derogatively the early activities of Frankenstein and Brandt, he goes out of his way to insult them and defend his position by saying, "It's fools like you that have blocked progress throughout the ages. You make pronouncements on half-facts that you don't even understand anyway. . . . I'll give you an analogy that you just may appreciate. Had men not been given to invention and experimentaion, then you, sir, would tonight have eaten your dinner in a cave. You would have strewn the bones all over the floor and then wiped your fingers on a coat of animal skin. In fact, your lapels do look rather greasy."

But while Frankenstein is right about the benefits of progress, his methods of securing it prove unsound. He kidnaps Brandt in hopes of making him better, but the good doctor is fatally injured in the escape attempt. To save him, he puts Brandt's brain into the body of Prof. Richter (Freddie Jones), curing Brandt of his illness in the process.

However, Mrs. Brandt (Maxine Audley) seeks out her husband, which brings her to Frankenstein's door. Because he is completely wrapped up in bandages, Mrs. Brandt does not realize that her husband's body is not his own when she comes to see him and communicate with him. As soon as Frankenstein hustles Mrs. Brandt out, he announces that they must pack and be leaving before the alteration is discovered.

To make matters worse, in one of the film's most macabre scenes, a water main breaks and pushes Brandt's original body to the surface of the flower bed. A panicked Anna has to hide the body in the bushes just as the police drop by so that she and her boyfriend will not be implicated in the crime. But while she keeps her head there, when she confronts the Baron's new creation (Jones), she stabs him out of panic. When the Baron discovers what she has done, he vents his fury by stabbing her in return and then seeks out his former friend.

Jones makes for one of the most sympathetic Frankenstein monsters ever created as he attempts to return to his wife and convince her to accept him; however, she cannot accept the idea that her husband's brain and personality are now in another man's body. Brandt's spirit is totally crushed and he resolves to get revenge on Frankenstein, who saved his life but at the cost of his happiness and peace of mind.

In *Bizarre #3*, Fisher remarked about the scene between the monster and his wife:

> I loved that scene very much. . . . Freddie Jones says, "Oh God, it's me! I'm here!" It is only on occasion that one gets a scene as great as that one to direct! I liked *Frankenstein Must Be Destroyed* better than some of the others for the very reason that one had a normal physical body with a new brain in it. This raises the whole basis of brain transplant if you want to call it that even though it is the wrong term. What happens to a person when he suddenly has a totally new body? Isn't he partly a stranger to her? . . . The possibilities are very exciting; wonderful!

Not only is the Brandt/Richter combination Frankenstein's most sympathetic creation (he did not ask to end up this way, though ironically he once worked in his career towards these same ends), he is also the only one to successfully (barring the escape for the sequel) attack and destroy his creator. The good doctor traps Frankenstein inside his own house, which he sets on fire. When Frankenstein escapes, he goes outside and carries the Baron back in to meet his well-deserved doom.

Nevertheless, Cushing's Frankenstein survived to make one more outing, *Frankenstein and the Monster from Hell*, which unfortunately proved the most mediocre of the Fisher Frankensteins, being largely a rehash and reshuffle of elements from the previous films. One of the things that gave the Frankenstein series a freshness was that while the Baron's basic goals were the same throughout, each film had its individual approach to the basic problem. Apart from the use of a monster and an assistant along with a few murders and body parts, the stories did not go through the same motions again and again, unlike many other horror series that tried to identically repeat successes, with diminishing returns.

As in *Revenge*, Cushing's Baron is once more found in charge of a lunatic asylum where he is hard at work on concocting another creature. (Fisher objected to how simian the monster appeared – David Prowse was covered in a suit that made him look like a gorilla in the process of shedding – so that it did not seem to have once had a human basis.) From his more demented inmates, the Baron takes body parts which he hopes will enable this particular creation to be an improvement over the others, but instead we have the traditional lumbering monster with the same murderous impulses as the Glenn Strange Frankenstein monsters.

Putting the manipulative Baron in charge of an asylum that he cannot leave (he was committed to the asylum and has been blackmailing the real head of the establishment, who prefers to while away his time with trollops rather than look after his patients) means that the Baron does not get to challenge the establishment in the mode of his previous excursions.

Also, his final goal here is not simply making a monster that is a perfect human specimen – his creation is far from that – but rather the more Dr. Moreau-like idea of mating his monster with a real human being, Sarah (Madeline Smith). Naturally, this does not sit too well with Simon (Shane Briant), his new assistant, who has developed a fondness for this "angel of the asylum" himself. Simon had long been an admirer of Frankenstein from afar, reading about his work in a rare tome by Frankenstein himself (though when Victor got the time to write it is never alluded to), but working in close proximity with him begins to create some doubts in Simon's mind that the Baron is entirely rational.

The reason given that the monster goes amiss is that its body is asserting itself over its brain – an old saw from many previous transplant films, most notably *Mad Love*. Given the Baron's plan, Simon decides to destroy the monster but nearly becomes its victim. This fate he escapes thanks to the timely intervention of Sarah, who is so shocked by the experience that she regains her voice (lost when she was attacked by her own father, the real head of the asylum). However, the monster is only temporarily quieted down, escaping from the Baron to kill Sarah's father and then going on a rampage until the inmates, protective of their angel, finally tear the jury-rigged monster into pieces.

Most of the film is fairly slow moving and not too interesting. The inmates are given quirks rather than fleshed-out personalities, and the guards are of the traditional sadistic variety. The most memorable scenes involve the operating room when Simon has to sew an eyeball into the monster, or especially when Victor removes the brain from a dead inmate's body only to let it plop into a bowl below him, which he proceeds to step in. Mayhap Frankenstein is getting senile; he has certainly gotten careless in his old age.

Still, despite its shortcomings, it is not a bad film, just a mediocre one. It also brought to a close Fisher's directorial career. Fisher crafted several horror classics which depended on good craftsmanship rather than flashy shock effects, and he virutally singlehandedly defined the British/Hammer style of horror filmmaking. He was certainly better at handling horror than many of Hammer's subsequent directors, having a better overall consistency to his work. That work left an indelible impression on a generation of horror filmgoers and filmmakers, many of whom acknowledge the debt of Fisher's influence. He was instrumental in resurrecting the classic monsters for their color retreads, and he took a moribund film genre and made it exciting again. Rest in peace, Terence.

Robert Florey (1900–1979)

One Hour of Love; The Romantic Age; Face Value (1927); Night Club (1928); The Hole in the Wall; The Cocoanuts (codir. with Joseph Santley); The Battle of Paris (aka The Gay Lady) (1929); La Route Est Belle; L'Amour Chante (French version); Kom zu mir zum Rendezvous (German version); El Professor de Mí Señora (Spanish version); Le Blanc et le Noir (codir. with Marc Allegret, 1930); Murders in the Rue Morgue; The Man Called Back; Those We Love (1932); Girl Missing; Ex-Lady; The House on 56th Street (1933); Bedside; Smarty; Registered Nurse; I Sell Anything (1934); I Am a Thief; The Woman in Red; The Florentine Dagger; Don't Bet on Blondes; Going Highbrow; The Pay-Off; Ship Cafe (1935); The Preview Murder Mystery; Till We Meet Again; Hollywood Boulevard (1936); Outcast; King of Gamblers; Mountain Music; This Way Please; Daughter of Shanghai; Dangerous to Know; King of Alcatraz (1938); Disbarred; Hotel Imperial; The Magnificent Fraud; Death of a Champion (1939); Parole Fixer; Women Without Names (1940); The Face Behind the Mask; Meet Boston Blackie; Two in a Taxi (1941); Dangerously They Live; Lady Gangster (under pseudonym Florian Roberts) (1942); The Desert Song (1943); Man From Frisco; Roger Touhy – Gangster (1944); God Is My Co-Pilot; Danger Signal (1945); The Beast with Five Fingers (1946); Tarzan and the Mermaids; Rogues' Regiment (1948); Outpost in Morocco; The Crooked Way (1949); The Vicious Years; Johnny One-Eye (1950).

TELEVISION: "Dante's Inferno," "The Man in the Box," "Sound Off, My Love," "No Identity," "The Last Voyage," "My Own Dear Dragon," "The Executioner," "Night at Lark Cottage," "Stuffed Shirt," Four Star Playhouse; A Letter to Loretta; Schlitz Playhouse of Stars; Disneyland; Wire Service; Jane Wyman Theater; Zane Grey Theater; M Squad; Wagon Train; Telephone Time; Frank Sinatra Show; The Texan; Desilu Playhouse; Markham; Joseph Cotten Theater; June Allyson Show; "Perchance to Dream," "The Long Morrow," Twilight Zone; Michael Shayne; Hong Kong; The Barbara Stanwyck Theater; Adventures in Paradise; "The Incredible Doctor Markesan," Thriller; "Face in the Window," Checkmate; The Untouchables; Alcoa Premiere; Going My Way; The Great Adventure; Dick Powell Theater, "The Moonstone," Outer Limits; "Repercussion," "Fast Break," "Midnight Kill," "Witness to Condemn," "Dara," Suspense.

Though he has worked in just about every genre under the sun, Robert Florey is best remembered as a horror director because his most memorable films, apart from codirecting the Marx Brothers' first comedy and launching the Boston Blackie series, were his horror films: Murders in the Rue Morgue,

The Face Behind the Mask, and *The Beast with Five Fingers.* He has also become well known as the man who worked on the script for and almost directed the original Universal *Frankenstein,* which James Whale, Colin Clive and Boris Karloff turned into a classic.

Florey was born in Paris, France, on September 14, 1900. As a child, he became interested in films while he was watching silent film special effects pioneer Georges Melies work on his trick films. By the age of 17, he was writing reviews and conducting interviews for *Cinemagazine,* France's first movie fan periodical.

He entered the film industry at 19 while studying in Geneva, working as an actor/screenwriter/assistant director in a series of Swiss one-reel short subjects, one of which, *Isidore à la Déveine,* he also directed. He returned to France and became an assistant to Louis Feuillade, working on the serial *L'Orpheline.* Florey talked *Cinemagazine* into sending him to Hollywood, where he managed to become hired as a technical director on *Monte Cristo* (1922). He also wrote comedy shorts for Al St. John and acted in a few productions.

According to Ephraim Katz in his *Film Encyclopedia,* Florey was a rapid success in Hollywood, in both a social and a business sense. Making friends with the likes of Douglas Fairbanks, he became foreign publicity director for that actor as well as for Mary Pickford. By 1923, in addition to his publicity work, he was directing his first American film, *Fifty-Fifty,* a two-reel comedy. He also began working as an assistant director for any number of Hollywood greats; Katz lists Louis J. Gasnier, Alfred Snatell, Josef von Sternberg, John M. Stahl, Edmund Goulding, Christy Cabanne, Robert Z. Leonard, and King Vidor among them. When Louis Gasnier proved unable to finish *That Model from Paris,* which Florey had written, Florey took over the direction. Among the films he directed following that project were his first feature, *One Hour of Love,* and four experimental shorts including *The Life and Death of 9413 – A Hollywood Extra.* "In addition," notes Katz, "he turned out numerous screen tests and short subjects at Paramount's Long Island City studios, including the three-reeler *The Pusher-in-the-Face* from a script by F. Scott Fitzgerald, and *Bonjour, New York,* featuring Maurice Chevalier."

Florey's first production of note was *The Hole in the Wall,* which was Edward G. Robinson's first sound film and his first appearance as a gangster (an image of him which was soon to be fixed in the public mind by his performance in *Little Caesar*). It was also an early film for Claudette Colbert.

Next came the Marx Brothers' feature film debut in *The Cocoanuts,* which Florey codirected with fellow Astoria director Joseph Santley. As with many early sound films, the film today is rather stagey, and its energy flags terribly whenever the Marx Brothers are off-screen. Florey's greatest problem, he claimed, was keeping the camera on the freewheeling and often improvising brothers. The film is blessed with a very humorous George Kaufman script and several classic comedy routines, but the awkwardly presented filler is less than routine and the overall production was not well photo graphed, something which has thus far prevented its release on video. (To be fair, the Marx Brothers' next film, *Animal Crackers*, is even more ineptly directed to the point where even the team's timing is affected.)

Florey went to England to make a French film (*La Route est Belle*) and then shot three different versions of the same story in different languages in Berlin. Finally he codirected another French film, *Le Blanc et le Noir*, with Marc Allegret.

After returning from Europe, Florey happened to become friends with Richard Schayer, who was head of the Universal story department. They discussed several ideas as possible topics for films including the Grand Guignol plays of France, H. G. Wells' *The Invisible Man*, Edgar Allan Poe's *Murders in the Rue Morgue*, and most especially Mary Shelley's *Frankenstein*.

Florey is quoted in Rudy Behlmer's *America's Favorite Movies: Behind the Scenes* as writing that "at first Schayer thought the . . . novel [*Frankenstein*] could not be adapted into a feature. However, I went home and typed a five- or six-page synopsis following, but taking liberties with the author's story. . . . I also learned later that John Balderston had adapted Peggy Webling's play *Frankenstein*—which I never saw nor read."

Behlmer goes on to quote Florey's assertion that he and Schayler "worked with Garrett Fort (who wrote Universal's *Dracula*) on the first screenplay following the lines of my synopsis treatment. . . . Fort wrote the dialogue. . . . My contribution . . . was its continuity of action and development."

When Florey wrote that he took liberties, he was not kidding. Little of Shelley's original concept seems to have been left in Florey's treatment, but Florey did contribute some key ideas to the final film. He came up with the concept of Frankenstein's assistant taking a criminal brain and having that brain be placed inside the monster, a simplistic explanation for the monster's murderous tendencies. He also changed the monster into a grunting, inarticulate brute from the eloquent and loquacious monster of Shelley's book and Webling's play. Finally, a Van de Kamp bakery's windmill that Florey lived near gave him the inspiration to set Frankenstein's laboratory and the climax in an old mill.

In an interview with Al Taylor for *Fangoria*, Florey revealed that he visualized casting Bela Lugosi, not as the monster, but as Doctor Frankenstein, a good follow-up role after Lugosi's success in *Dracula*. "Schayer agreed with my conception of the film and told me to go ahead with an extended and detailed adaptation," Florey related, "adding that the front office would insist on Lugosi playing the part of the monster."

Universal had purchased the rights to Webling's play and Balderston's adaptation of it on April 8, 1931, for $20,000 plus 1 percent of the worldwide gross. Schayer told Florey to go ahead with a full screenplay, but Florey insisted he be given a contract that promised him he could write and direct. This done, approval was given for a 20-minute film of test footage to be shot with Edward Van Sloan playing Dr. Waldman, Dwight Frye playing Fritz, and Bela Lugosi essaying the part of the monster, as well as two stock players filling in for roles yet to be cast.

The test film has long been lost, but it was shot on sets leftover from *Dracula*, and Florey related the contents to Rudy Behlmer, who reported:

> It was photographed by Paul Ivano, and it started in Dr. Waldman's study with a short conversation between Victor Moritz and Waldman leading to both going to the Frankenstein laboratory. Following a scene with Frankenstein and Fritz in the lab, there was the arrival of Waldman and Victor. According to Florey, the test lasted up to and including the initial awakening of the monster.

According to Edward Van Sloan in an interview conducted by Forrest J. Ackerman for *Famous Monsters of Filmland*, Lugosi's "head was about four times normal size, with a broad wig on it. He had a polished, clay-like skin." The description suggests that Florey took a similar approach to that of one of *Frankenstein*'s film predecessors, *The Golem*, which Paul Wegner filmed twice in Germany. But, according to Florey in *Fangoria*, "Lugosi kept exclaiming, 'Enough is enough'; that he was not going to be a grunting, babbling idiot for anybody and that any tall extra could be the monster. 'I was a star in my country and will not be a scarecrow over here,' he said repeatedly."

Lugosi, who perhaps had been told he was going to play Dr. Frankenstein and then discovered he was going to play the monster, was further angered when he learned that the monster had no lines. This, coupled with lengthy sessions in Jack Pierce's makeup chair (the two apparently did not get along) was too much. Though the film has been announced with Lugosi as the star, studio head Carl Laemmle, Jr., was happy to release him. Meanwhile, Laemmle had placed *Frankenstein* on a list of 30 possible projects for James Whale and had shown Whale the test footage. Whale thought *Frankenstein* was the most promising of the projects and expressed an interest. Having more confidence in Whale than in Florey, Laemmle handed the project over to him.

Florey discovered that his contract promised to allow him to write and direct a film but did not specify which film. Before completing his final draft of the *Frankenstein* script. Florey found himself shifted over to an adaptation of Poe's *Murders in the Rue Morgue*. Meanwhile, Whale took elements of Florey's screen adaptation and elements of Balderston's (e.g. the monster reacting to light for the first time; accidentally drowning the young girl) and had writer Francis Edwards Faragoh collaborate with Florey's partner, Garrett Fort, on the screenplay. To add insult to injury, Florey was not given any screen credit on the first prints of the film. (For more on Whale's version of *Frankenstein*, see the chapter on James Whale.)

An interesting aside on casting is that Leslie Howard was mentioned for the role of Frankenstein, though Whale later insisted on Colin Clive. Meanwhile, a young Bette Davis was briefly considered for the role of Elizabeth. When Florey was changed to *Murders in the Rue Morgue*, she went with it, testing for a role, but Carl Laemmle, Jr., was not happy with her and she was replaced by Sidney Fox.

For that matter, *Murders in the Rue Morgue* was originally to have been directed by George Melford until Universal handed the assignment over to Florey. However, the studio was suffering from financial difficulties at the time of production and wanted to modernize the story to cut costs. The studio relented but cut the budget by $40,000, causing Florey to temporarily walk off the production.

That film was budgeted at a mere $164,220, far less than the studio had spent on either *Frankenstein* or *Dracula*. The shooting took 23 days, including some retakes. The studio did agree to spend another $22,000 to add some action scenes to the film, including the rooftop chase at the end of the film as well as shots of a chimpanzee that were spliced ludicrously with shots of either Chalres Gemora (the first of many gorillas and monsters he was to play) or Joe Bonomo (who did most of the stunt work) as Dr. Mirakle's gorilla.

In Richard Bojarski's *The Films of Bela Lugosi*, Florey had this to say about the production:

> I wrote the *Rue Morgue* adaptation in a week and directed the film in four. That was during the fall of 1931. My association with Bela lasted for a month. He was habitually silent and not given to conversation. Between scenes he retired in his dressing room. I was very busy directing a number of players and spoke to Lugosi only to discuss scenes we were about to shoot and how I would want him to interpret them. It was at times difficult to control his tendency to chew the scenery. In *Rue Morgue*, I used the same device I employed in my *Frankenstein* adaptation. Bela Lugosi became Dr. Mirakle – a mad scientist desirous of creating a human being – not with body parts stolen from a graveyard and a brain from a lab, but by the mating of an ape with a woman.

While Florey got credit for the story's adaptation and his old friend Richard Schayer received credit as "Scenario Director," the actual screenplay is credited to Tom Reed and Dale van Every with additional dialogue by none other than John Huston. Huston went on to become a

From the set of Murders in the Rue Morgue: *Leon Ames (in cravat), the hero of the film; cameraman and future director Karl Freund (with pipe); and to right of the camera, holding the megaphone, is* Murders' *director Robert Florey. Given the bulkiness of the camera, Florey managed some amazing shots in this stylish, expressionistic film.*

great director, filming such classics as *The Maltese Falcon* and *The Treasure of the Sierra Madre*, but at this time he was under contract as a writer to Universal. In his autobiography, *An Open Book*, Huston recalled, "Next I worked on *Murders in the Rue Morgue*. I tried to bring Poe's prose style into the dialogue, but the director thought it sounded stilted, so he and his assistant rewrote scenes on the set. As a result, the picture was an odd mixture of nineteenth-century grammarian's prose and modern colloquialisms."

Originally the film was to have opened with a black carriage traveling down a fog-shrouded street and coming upon two men fighting each other. A streetwalker (Arlene Francis of television's *What's My Line?* making her film debut) looks on and screams. The men manage to fatally stab each other. The occupant of the carriage, Dr. Mirakle (Bela Lugosi with a curly-haired wig), approaches the woman and asks, "A lady ... in distress?" Claiming that he will help her, he demands she come along and pushes her into the carriage. The woman screams, moans, and cries no.

Next we see her shadow tied to the shadow of a great cross in Mirakle's laboratory. Mirakle approaches her and says, "Come! You're stubborn.

Hush. If you only last one more minute, we shall see. We shall know if you are to be the bride of science!" He then injects her with a blood sample, causing her to scream once more before passing out. Checking a blood sample under a primitive microscope, the furious Mirakle exclaims, "Your blood is rotten, black as your sins. You have cheated me. Your beauty was a lie!" Turning, he notices that she has died, and falls to his knees in defeat and remorse. He orders his servant Janos (famed black actor Noble Johnson in weird white makeup) to get rid of "it." Janos takes his hatchet to the ropes holding the woman's corpse, and Mirakle opens a trapdoor with his foot to plunge the body into the Seine down below. "Will my search never end?" he moans quietly to himself.

By comparison with Mirakle, Dr. Frankenstein seems positively sane. A large part of what makes *Murders in the Rue Morgue* such a memorable film is Lugosi's flamboyant and larger-than-life performance which helped set the form for dozens of B movie mad scientists to follow. Still early in his sound career, Lugosi was at the height of his acting powers, investing the richly morbid dialogue with memorable menace. The only other film of this period that gave Lugosi as much rich dialogue was *White Zombie*, which despite some handsome sets was not nearly so well made.

Unfortunately, this opening – one of the film's best sequences – was considered too downbeat, and a more upbeat series of scenes at a carnival, introducing the heroes of the tale, was placed before it. *Murders in the Rue Morgue* goes for strong contrasts, with Mirakle's secret, evil doings in the name of science sharply contrasted with the bright and innocent surroundings of medical student Pierre Dupin (Leon Waycoff, later Leon Ames, making his debut) and his friends. Dupin's roommate is fat and jolly Paul (Bert Roach), who supplies the tiresome "comedy relief" that was considered necessary to most films of the time, and who inanely ventures that visiting the carnival is "much nicer than visiting a morgue."

Together with their girlfriends, they are attracted, after looking at some Arabian belly dancers and some American Indians, to a tent that bears the legend "Erik: Le Gorille au Cerveau Humain" (The Gorilla with a Human Soul). They go inside, where the strange figure of Dr. Mirakle takes to the stage after directing the group to their seats. Behind him is a gorilla in a cage and a vast tapestry illustrating the evolution of life. Cinematographer Karl Freund shrewdly lit the scene with the lights pointed upward, giving Lugosi's face menacing shadows and highlights as he goes into his spiel about how he is not a "sideshow charleten" and then introduces Erik, the gorilla, talking to him and translating the story of Erik's capture to the audience.

Mirakle finishes with a lecture on evolution: "Here is the story of man," he says. "In the slime of chaos, there was a seed which rose and grew into the tree of life. Life was motion. Fins changed into wings; wings into ears;

crawling reptiles grew legs. Eons of ages passed. There came a time when a four-legged-thing walked upright. Behold," he finishes, pointing to Erik, "the first man!"

When a religious man in the largely unsympathetic crowd cries heresy, Mirakle responds, "Heresy? Heresy? Do they still burn men for heresy? Then burn me, Monsieur. Light the fire if you think your little candle will outshine the flames of truth! Do you think these walls and curtains are my whole life? They are only a trap to catch the pennies of fools. My life is consecrated to a great experiment. I tell you I will prove your kinship with the ape. Erik's blood shall be mixed with the blood of man!"

The crowd disperses, but Pierre and his friends decide to take a closer look at Erik. As Pierre's girlfriend, Camille (Sydney Fox), approaches, Erik extends his paw towards her bonnet. "Erik is only human, Mademoiselle," Mirakle comments. "He has an eye for beauty." It's readily apparent that Erik is not the ony one with "an eye for beauty," as Mirakle continues, "You have made a conquest, Mademoiselle." Erik quickly snatches away the bonnet, and when Pierre dashes forward to retrieve it, begins strangling Pierre. Mirakle drives back the beast, which sulks and teeths on the bonnet. Mirakle offers to replace it and tries to get Camille's name and address, but Pierre prevents him. They leave and Mirakle instructs Janos to follow them, turning to the ape and noting, "You liked her, didn't you, Erik?" as the ape murmurs something unintelligible back to him.

The problem with putting this sequence first is that following it with the pickup of the prostitute makes it seem like Mirakle was sidetracked in following Camille. There's a brief shot of Mirakle entering the coach with Erik already inside, suggesting that Erik was inside the coach when he picks up the hooker. The way the sequences ran originally would have made it clear that following his most recent disaster, Mirakle is attracted to Camille's purity in his megalomaniacal quest to mix human blood and Erik's blood. (Like Dracula, Mirakle is clearly fixated on blood, but this does not prevent him from being attracted to his victims as well.)

After the death of the prostitute, we see some gendarmes pulling a body from the river as some sewer rat character comments on how she is the third one this week. The man in charge of the morgue notes the new entrant, while Dupin arrives to purchase a cadaver for his medical studies. The man notes that there are three dead young women, each with the same marks on her arm. Dupin bribes him to bring the recent corpse to him.

Camille, staying with her mother (Betty Ross Clarke), unexpectedly receives a bonnet from Dr. Mirakle, who asks her to meet Erik and him at the carnival that night to read her fortune in the stars. Pierre shows up and escorts Camille to the park, where a montage reveals a series of students lying to their ladies. In an interesting shot, Camille swings back and forth on a swing and the camera swings with her while Pierre pushes. He asks about her new bonnet. Pierre insists that she not meet Mirakle and privately decides to meet him himself. (It has also been apparent that Dupin shares some of Mirakle's views on evolution.) That night, Mirakle tells Pierre that he is leaving with the carnival, and he curtly dismisses Pierre when he learns that Camille is not coming. Outside, however, Dupin overhears some men unloading Mirakle's things because he is staying behind.

Dr. Mirakle drives off, and Pierre jumps on the back of his carriage to keep an eye on him. He watches Mirakle and Erik get off at Mirakle's secret laboratory.

The next evening he goes to Camille's apartment and informs her of what has transpired as they look over the expressionistic housetops of the film's version of Paris. Meanwhile, Florey pans from Dr. Mirakle observing their balcony scene on the ground, to the two lovers, and back to Mirakle again, establishing that he has plans for Camille when Pierre leaves. Pierre asks that Camille bolt her door and bids goodnight. Mirakle arrives after Pierre leaves and tries to either stay in Camille's apartment or get her to come out with him to a cafe. When neither approach works, he leaves, but tells Erik that she is up there.

Back at Pierre's place, he discovers that the foreign substance in his cadaver's blood is the blood of a gorilla. Suddenly, Dr. Mirakle's horrible plans and intentions become clear to him, and he dashes back to Camille's. A scream is heard from outside Camille's door, and Florey employs an early shock cut as the shock registers on the bystanders' faces in ever tighter close-ups. The door is broken in, but they find no one inside and no money stolen.

The police come to interview everyone, and in a silly scene different nationalities identify the gorilla's noises as being in Italian, German, or Danish. (This scene may have influenced a similar scene in Charles Finney's *The Circus of Dr. Lao*.) Pierre insists he knows the solution to the perplexing mystery, and when the body of Camille's mother is found stuffed up the chimney, he asserts that they must make haste to Dr. Mirakle's lab before Camille is also killed.

The police agree to break into Mirakle's lab. Mirakle instructs Janos to hold them off so he can complete his experiment, but Erik, smitten with love for the unconscious Camille, attacks his master and kills him. Erik grabs Camille and carries her over the rooftops as the police succeed in breaking in after shooting Janos. Pierre follows them and finally shoots Erik when he sees an opportunity to do so without hitting Camille. Camille and Pierre embrace. Mirakle's body is taken to the morgue.

Like most of the films supposedly based on Poe's work, *Murders in the Rue Morgue* bears scant resemblance to Poe's original. In that story, C. Auguste Dupin solves a seemingly insoluble mystery by surmising that it was committed by an orangutan. To have followed this format faithfully would have led to a rather dull feature instead of the lively one that Florey concocted, which has more action and allows Lugosi to present himself at his villainous best.

The film's running time was originally given as 75 minutes, though most prints run about 62 minutes these days. Unfortunately, I have no way of knowing just what was trimmed. Carl Laemmle, Jr., did not have much faith in the film, and its receipts did not match those of its Universal predecessors. However, Florey was apparently delighted enough with his own work that he created a self-homage by aping a pursuit scene from the film in his later work, *The Preview Murder Mystery*.

While Florey went on to do many more murder and mystery stories, he was not to do another horror film until the borderline entry of *The Face Behind the Mask*, the best of a short series of films that Peter Lorre did for Columbia Pictures. In it, Lorre plays a criminal mastermind who is a "monster" by virtue of his face being irrevocably scarred in a hotel fire. Unemployable, he turns to a life of crime and a small-time crook named Dinky (George E. Stone) persuades him not to commit suicide but rather join his gang. Like many classic monsters, Lorre's Janos Szabo, a Hungarian immigrant watchmaker, is basically a sympathetic character.

The film features a terrific unmasking scene in which Florey builds up tension while showing very little. As a doctor begins to remove the bandage, Florey cuts to a shot from Janos' point of view. He sees a nurse who reacts to his ugly features and then regains her composure; however, another nurse walking into the room is unprepared for the sight she sees, causing her to scream. Janos struggles to get away while the doctor tries to have him sedated. Finally, Janos gets ahold of a mirror, much to his unending horror and dismay.

With the money from Janos' first robbery, he purchases a mask to cover his features. According to Youngkin, Bigwood and Cabana's *The Films of Peter Lorre*, "to achieve the effect of a mask without lessening the range of Lorre's acting, a degree of facial mobility was necessary. Thus, a mask was simulated by coating his face with a heavy white base. No highlights or lowlights were employed to emphasize his features, and in order to partially immobilize the muscles, the skin was drawn back toward the hairline with gauze strips glued to the actor's cheeks."

The look of the supposedly immobile face is fascinating, and possibly inspired the similarly fascinating "mask" in Franju's *Eyes Without a Face*. The gimmick of a horror figure hiding his burned and scarred face behind a mask was a key element in such subsequent horror classics as the Lubin *Phantom of the Opera* and Andre De Toth's *House of Wax*, though in the latter case it derived more from *Mystery of the Wax Museum*, the Curtiz film it remakes.

A touching undercurrent is added to the film when Janos falls in love with a blind woman, Helen Williams (Evelyn Keyes), and marries her. Only with her can he be himself again. Recalling his good side, he resolves to leave the gang forever, but this causes the gang to suspect that he plans to betray them to the police. They torture Dinky, and in a surprisingly cynical twist for an early '40s film, they plant a bomb in Janos' car, accidentally killing Helen instead.

The gangsters attempt to flee the country, but the pilot lands them in the desert and informs them he deliberately did not supply the plane with enough fuel. The pilot is revealed to be Janos, who is strapped to the plane and left to die of exposure. Those gangsters who do not die of thirst in the desert are finally caught by the police. (The ending is vaguely reminiscent of von Stroheim's classic *Greed*.)

Overall, this is a rather classy and entertaining little B movie, often overlooked. In addition to the horrible things that occur, the screenwriters wring some humor from Janos' malapropisms as he attempts to employ English. Don Beddoe plays O'Hara, the cop who initially recommends Janos stay in the hotel where he gets burned, and who later writes him a note and lends him some money because he feels guilty for recommending it. Like the important letters in films written by screenwriter Howard Koch, this letter becomes significant when it causes the gangsters to wrongly suspect that Janos has betrayed them and when, by the letter, O'Hara is finally able to identify Janos at the end.

Florey was faced with a difficult task in shooting *The Face Behind the Mask* in only 12 days. Further complicating everything was that Lorre was becoming an alcoholic at the time and tended to drink too much, causing him to be almost unusable for important scenes in the afternoons. His favorite drink was a bottle of Pernod.

When Florey and Lorre were reteamed on Florey's next and last horror film, *The Beast with Five Fingers*, neither of them liked the script. Lorre walked into Florey's office and told him, "I read it (the script). Don't worry — since you are in trouble I'll keep *two* Pernod bottles in my dressing room."

While *The Beast with Five Fingers* is considered a classic by many, it does indeed have a rather dull screenplay by Curt Siodmak based on the William Fryer Harvey short story. Lorre gives a rather dispirited performance until near the climax of the film, while Florey apparently had trouble figuring out where to focus the story and how to pace the film.

The main character is not Lorre's Hilary Cummins, but rather Robert Alda's Bruce Conrad, who is sometimes a con man, sometimes a sympathetic companion and chess opponent to disabled pianist Francis Ingram (Victor Francen), and sometimes a dashing romantic partner for Julie Holden (Andrea King) after Ingram's death. Cummins is merely a hanger-on whose only interest is Ingram's library of metaphysical books in which he hopes to discover great secrets.

Florey disliked the script and shooting schedule for *The Beast with Five Fingers* so much that he took a suspension from the studio for three months. However, when he returned, the project was still waiting for him. Lorre sympathized and together they vowed to do the best they could. They hit upon a plan of centering the story around the Cummins character and using expressionistic sets and angles as an indication of his madness, but producer William Jacobs nixed that approach.

As a result, the film is very dull until Ingram's death scene, in which the partially paralyzed pianist is startled out of bed by a banging window. Wheeling himself in a wheelchair, he begins to have a dizzy spell which results in a fatal tumble down a staircase that could have been engineered by frustrated Cummins. Julie Holden, his niece and nursemaid, stands to inherit everything when Ingram's brother-in-law and nephew bring in a lawyer to contest the will. The attorney dies while Bach's "Chaconne for the Left Hand" is played. Cummins blames it on Ingram's one good hand which has now taken on a life of its own. Sure enough, an investigation of Ingram's corpse reveals that his left hand is missing. However, wisecracking detective Ovido Castanio (J. Carrol Naish) is none too convinced. Something is rotten in the small town of San Stephano.

Unfortunately, it is Siodmak's plot as well as the awful "humorous" bits that Naish is forced to perform. It seems that Cummins, ever fearful of losing access to his precious archaic tomes, has devised a plot to convince everyone that there is a monstrous strangling, disembodied hand on the loose and then comes to believe it himself. The only classic scenes in the entire film are those in which Lorre battles the hand. He plays with Ingram's ring when guitar strings break, causing a sense of unease. A wind blows through the curtain and a spider-like hand crawls across the desk to get the ring. Later Lorre grabs the hand while it is playing the piano and throws it into the fire. It crawls out and strangles him, then vanishes because it was all in his mind.

The all-in-the-mind approach was also utilized on Oliver Stone's *The Hand*, while *The Crawling Hand* was a schlocky but amusing "killer hand" movie in which an astronaut's possessed hand is eventually eaten in a junkyard by common alley cats. These films are the most notable progeny of Florey's *Beast*. (Stories circulate that Luis Bunuel, who featured a severed hand in his famous *Un chien Andalou* and a crawling hand in *The Avenging Angel*, had wanted to film *The Beast with Five Fingers*, but he was never involved in the Florey version.)

Castanio reveals how Cummins faked the hand throughout the house and the lovers happily decide to depart at the finale, coming none too soon. The idea may have been suggested to Cummins when Ingram almost strangled him after telling him he planned to dismiss Cummins, shortly before Ingram's death.

During the reading-of-the-will scene, Lorre demonstrated his fondness for practical jokes by playing the first take of the solemn scene with a carrot in his ear. In some of the scenes, the hand employed was Florey's own. Upon completion, Lorre gave Florey a bottle of Pernod as a little something to remember him by.

Florey gave up films after completing six more and became one of the pioneering directors in the new medium of television. There he directed one of the few episodes of *Thriller* to actually star Boris Karloff, the moody and macabre "The Incredible Doctor Markesan," as well as "Perchance to Dream," the classic *Twilight Zone* episode in which Richard Conte plays a man with a heart condition who is afraid to go back to sleep because he has been dreaming that he was on a rollercoaster. The shock could kill him if he dreams it again, but if he does not sleep, the strain definitely will take his life. This episode is particularly effective due to Florey's carefully chosen, disorienting camera angles and Van Cleave's eerie music, plus the overall dream ambiance that imbues Charles Beaumont's script.

I have covered only a few of Florey's many films, but these are the films for which he is best remembered. He covered ground in many genres and was noted for his French charm, particularly when it came to soothing over actors' egos when they felt they were forced to take parts in the "lesser" medium of television. Florey was more of a craftsman than an artist with a unifying artistic vision, but at his best he could be memorably macabre with inventive camera work, stylish photography and art direction, and some rather foreboding and atmospheric set pieces. However, the fact he never had a runaway hit success kept him toiling in the more minor Hollywood vineyards without the resources to strut his stuff to the best advantage. He was another contract director for whom Hollywood was indeed a factory, churning out quaint, manufactured dreams that breezed into town one week and were whisked away by the end of the next. The French honored him in 1950 by making him a knight of the Legion d'Honneur for his contributions to film, but horror fans will never forget him for his important contributions to *Frankenstein* and his trio of horror movies.

Freddie Francis (1917–)

Two and Two Make Six (aka *A Change of Heart, The Girl Swappers*); *The Brain* (aka *Vengeance*) (1962); *Paranoiac* (1963); *Nightmare; Hysteria; Evil of Frankenstein; Traitor's Gate* (aka *Das Verräter*, 1964); *Dr. Terror's House of Horrors; The Skull* (1965); *The Psychopath* (1966); *The Deadly Bees; They Came from Beyond Space; Torture Garden* (1967); *Dracula Has Risen from the Grave* (1968); *Girly* (aka *Mumsy, Nanny, Sonny and Girly*) (1969); *Trog* (1970); *The Vampire Happening; The Intrepid Mr. Twig* (short); *Tales from the Crypt* (1971); *Son of Dracula; The Creeping Flesh* (1972); *Tales That Witness Madness; Craze* (1973); *The Ghoul* (1974); *Legend of the Werewolf* (1975); *Doctor and the Devils* (1985); *Dark Tower* (1987).

Freddie Francis was born in London in 1917 and began his film career as a clapper boy at the age of 17. He became a camera assistant and during World War II served as a director of photography with the British Army's Kinematographic Unit.

As a camera operator, he photographed such films as *Mine Own Executioner, Outcast of the Islands, Moulin Rouge, Knave of Hearts, Beat the Devil* and *Beau Brummell.* John Huston was pleased enough with his work on *Moulin Rouge* and *Beat the Devil* to hire him to handle second unit photography chores on *Moby Dick.*

He graduated to director of photography and became, for a short period (1955–1961), the top cinematographer in Great Britain. All the most interesting British films seemed to employ him, including *A Hill in Korea, Time Without Pity, Room at the Top, Saturday Night and Sunday Morning, Sons and Lovers* (for which Francis won the Academy Award), and *The Innocents.*

During this period, close friends urged Francis to try his hand at directing. His first film, *Two and Two Make Six,* was about the adventures of an AWOL soldier and his girlfriend, as George Chakiris falls in love with Janette Scott (of *Day of the Triffids* fame). The film proved little more than a pleasant diversion. From being an extraordinary cinematographer, Francis began shaping up into an ordinary and not particularly distinguished director.

Without credit, Francis helped pad out *The Day of the Triffids,* making his first excursion into horror, which he followed by directing *The Brain* (aka *Vengeance, ein Toter Sucht seiner Mörder*), a German/English collaboration based on Curt Siodmak's novel *Donovan's Brain* (previously filmed in 1944 as *The Lady and the Monster* and in 1953 as *Donovan's Brain*). Doctors Corrie (Peter van Eyck) and Shears (Bernard Lee) save the brain of industrialist Max Holt after his plane crashes near their laboratory. Because Holt was an extremely willful individual, his brain is able to exert an influence over Corrie using only thought waves. The brain has Corrie investigate the circumstances of the plane crash in an effort to track down Holt's murderer. Dr. Shears sees this influence as unhealthy and attempts to kill the brain.

Things get complicated when Corrie is set up when he goes to get information from Holt's chauffeur, who is shot before he can divulge anything. The police arrive. Corrie ducks out the back way and tries to evade them at a dance contest. There is a nice Hitchcockian scene where Corrie unexpectedly wins an impromptu dance contest, but must flee when it is discovered that he has left a blood-stained handprint on the back of his partner. Some men shuffle him into a car, but they turn out not to be the police.

They are representatives from Immerman, a monopolist who is seeking the formula to a wonder drug and the name of the chemist who invented it, which he planned to buy from Holt just before Holt's plane crashed. Immerman arranges to destroy the brain unless Corrie divulges the information to Holt's mistress. The mistress is shot by an unseen party and by her death gives the signal to have the brain destroyed.

However, when Corrie gets back to the lab, he discovers Shears had fooled them by destroying a monkey's brain and secreting Holt's brain away. Holt's daughter Ana (Anne Heywood) comes by to investigate; obviously, she has been tipped by someone as to what is going on and perhaps tipped the chauffeur. Holt takes over Corrie's body and he starts strangling his daughter until Shears finally destroys the brain.

Corrie still cannot let the mystery go, especially when he notices that the microphone Holt was clutching when he died has disappeared. He is able to track down that Holt was killed when Ana's lawyer, Stevenson (Cecil Parker), gave a tape recorder to the chauffeur to put a bomb in it. Corrie goes to accuse Stevenson, but Ana admits that the plot was her idea and she killed the others. (Unbeknownst to her, her confession is being tape recorded.) Her motivation? She discovers that the wonder drug developed by her father was perfected a year ago, but he waited to release it so he could sell it for the highest price to a monopolist like Immerman. Her own mother had died of the disease that the drug cured, and Ana plans to give the drug's secrets away. She offers Corrie the choice of taking her into custody or escorting her to the board meeting where she will disseminate information about the drug. He chooses the latter.

The film ends on the note of Corrie tapping his thumb as Holt's son reveals he knew what was happening all along and had warned his father. Francis had established the tapping thumb as a Holt mannerism and used it throughout the film to indicate Holt's influence. Perhaps Holt's grasping personality is still alive in Corrie.

The film plays more like a mystery than a horror film, but it does have its eerie moments and is efficient and involving. Francis gives the film a somber, low-key, black-and-white look that matches the intensity of Corrie's and Holt's ambitions and hints at the darker sides of the tale. The result is a moody and often gripping retelling of a by-now familiar tale, and the film features a fine cast of experienced players.

Hammer Films liked *The Brain* enough that they hired Francis to helm *Paranoiac*, which features strong performances by Janette Scott, who believes she is going mad when she sees and falls in love with her dead brother, and Oliver Reed, her living brother who is in reality a mad killer. The dead brother proves to be an imposter (played by Alexander Davion) who is trying to uncover the identity of a murderer. The script is full of red herrings and twists, and is about average as these tales go.

Next he did *Nightmare* for the same company; in it the old chestnut of people attempting to drive a woman insane is trotted out again. Jennie Linden fears for her sanity ever since she saw her mother kill her father. When her mother starts calling her name and a ghostly apparition shows up (played by Clytie Jessop, who served a similar function on *The Innocents* which Francis photographed), it is not long before she is headed around the bend, but then the schemers have the tables turned on them.

The film, though lackluster overall, does have a few creepy moments. This is more than can be said for *Hysteria*, which had yet another derivative Jimmy Sangster script. Robert Webber plays an amnesia victim who hires a detective (Maurice Denham) to solve the mystery of his identity. The film's strongest points are its hallucinations, and even these could use a bit more punch.

Based on his track record, Hammer decided to turn over the direction of *Evil of Frankenstein* to Francis. Said Francis about the film in an interview in *Little Shoppe of Horrors #4*:

> [T]his was really the first sort of monster/horror films that I had attempted and I was fairly worried about it because I did think the original Karloff *Frankenstein* was really a great film.... I did persuade Hammer to spend quite a large share of our rather low budget on the laboratory set, which I think was pretty good.... And obviously, there was no actor around of the caliber of Boris Karloff so I thought I'd take a chance on somebody like Kiwi Kingston, who you know was a wrestler, and a very nice, gentle soul, and to sort of have two ingredients in the film which I thought were completely right – which was

sort of a good-looking, interesting and exciting type of laboratory, and a gentle giant who one really felt sort of sorry for. But Karloff was so wonderful in the part, it's jolly hard to compete. . . . [M]ine was just a pale imitation.

Evil of Frankenstein represented a bit of a break from the previous two entries in the series, putting Peter Cushing as Dr. Frankenstein back in a Central European hamlet. There, he and his assistant, Hans (Sander Eles), are removing a heart from a stolen corpse when a local priest interrupts everything and begins smashing all the equipment, causing the Baron to flee back to Karlstadt.

The script by producer Anthony Hinds (written under the name of John Elder) borrows many devices from the Universal "Frankenstein" series, but unfortunately, it borrows the simplest aspects rather than the best. Instead of making the monster (which the film indicates in a flashback that Baron Frankenstein has previously built and lost to a hostile crowd of villagers) a character in its own right, Hinds chooses to follow the route of *Son of Frankenstein* and have the monster be an automaton that carries out the revenge scheme of another (Bela Lugosi's Ygor in *Son*, and Peter Woodthorpe as Zoltan the Hypnotist in *Evil*).

Kingston's makeup is obviously intended to recall Karloff's with its squarish head, but it looks like a badly applied mudpack with bits of straw sticking out of it. By emphasizing the creature's gentleness, Francis makes the monster sympathetic but not frightening or interesting. It just shambles through the dull plot of the film.

Cushing at least shines as Frankenstein, especially in the scene when he sees that Karlstadt's burgomaster has taken not only the Frankenstein family ring, but also most of the Baron's estate and possessions, confiscated after a previous monstrous debacle. Of all the Hammer Frankenstein series, he is at his most mellow in this film, quite a contrast to the ruthlessness which he would exhibit in *Frankenstein Must Be Destroyed*, the best film in the series.

Francis does little to enliven the proceedings, making this the weakest of the Cushing Frankensteins. The ending is also out of the latter part of the Universal series with the monster accidentally drinking a bottle of chloroform and setting the entire laboratory on fire, which purifies everything by burning it to the ground.

As tedious as this was, when the film was bought to be shown on network television, it was made more tedious with additional scenes of a mute girl's childhood and her first encounter with the monster. These scenes were added in the United States to pad out the running time to fill a two-hour prime time slot. (Don Sharp's *Kiss of the Vampire* suffered a similar fate and even had its title changed to *Kiss of Evil*.)

Francis broke off from Hammer to direct *Traitor's Gate*, based on an Edgar Wallace novel. It proved to be a decent thriller starring Gary Raymond, Albert Lieven, Klaus Kinski and Margot Trooger about two brothers who plan to steal the crown jewels.

Next, Francis showed up at Amicus Productions, Hammer's chief British competitor, to helm Amicus' first horror anthology film, *Dr. Terror's House of Horrors*. The anthology film, while it allows filmmakers to adapt horror stories which are not of sufficient length to justify a full-length feature, inevitably invites comparison on the relative merits of its stories and forces the audience to get acquainted with a new set of characters with each tale, slowing down the action and increasing the amount of exposition.

The most memorable aspect about this film is the framing story in which Peter Cushing as Dr. Schreck (German for terror) uses his tarot cards (the "House of Horrors" of the title) to tell the fortunes of five train passengers, and is revealed at the end of the film to be Death taking his victims to their final destination. The stories are an omnibus of familiar horror themes and monsters: Neil McCallum is killed by a female werewolf; a plant grows and envelops a couple's house; Roy Castle is punished for stealing music belonging to a voodoo ceremony in the most embarrassing and racist episode; Christopher Lee is a pompous art critic who accidentally runs over painter Michael Gough with his car and is then haunted by Gough's phony-looking hand; and Donald Sutherland kills his wife because she's a vampire and is convicted of murder because a vampire physician has plotted to eliminate all the competition.

The film was a modest success and led to Francis directing *The Skull* based on Robert Bloch's short story "The Skull of Marquis de Sade." Unfortunately, this story was uncomfortably and boringly padded to reach feature length as Professor Maitland (Cushing) acquires the dread skull despite warnings from a fellow collector (Christopher Lee) who asserts that it posseses evil powers. Does Maitland fall under the evil spell of the skull, or does it merely encourage him to indulge the Sadean aspects of his nature?

Francis' prime contribution was the unusual shots from the skull's point of view, which were accomplished by a roller-skating cameraman who put the skull's eyeholes in front of the camera lens. There are some good supporting performances by Patrick Wymark, Nigel Green, Michael Gough, Jill Bennett, George Coulouris, and Patrick Magee, whose finest role was portraying the Marquis de Sade in *Marat/Sade*.

Francis got to work from a Bloch script directly in his next film, *The Psychopath* (also released as *Schizoid*). The film is a passable thriller that was taken far too seriously by contemporary critics. Patrick Wymark investigates a series of murders in which a doll duplicate of the target is placed next to the victim. Obviously, the murderer was very clever in knowing ahead of time what each intended victim was going to wear down to the smallest detail. The victims are all part of a group who listens to chamber music and are all tied to investigating the records of a German business-man, leading to his downfall. Wheelchair-bound Mrs. Von Sturm (Margaret Johnston) and her son (John Standing) make for a suspicious pair, which is not helped by their being surrounded by an enormous collection of tiny dolls. Do you think Bloch was trying to tell us something about Momism? His hor-ror stories frequently have psychological undertones.

By contrast, *The Deadly Bees*, which Bloch also scripted, this time from H. F. Heard's novel *A Taste of Honey*, is a top competitor for the deadly dullest "bee" movie ever. Suzanna Leigh plays a pop singer who discovers that hives of bees can be even deadlier threats than flocks of birds. Despite the fluttering villains, the movie crawls along at a snail's pace, a fact that was still not helped when 40 minutes were chopped from the United States release.

Francis' next, *They Came from Beyond Space*, based on Joseph Millard's *The Gods Hate Kansas*, proved that Francis could take a science fiction film and make it just as boring, though an inadequate budget and script did not help matters. Particularly dreadful is the last-minute revelation of Michael Gough as the silver-clad leader of a group of friendly alien invaders. Said Francis in an interview with Chuck Wilson in *Cine Fan #2*, "We really did try very hard on this one, but there just wasn't enough money for better sets and better special effects. I think we could have had ourselves a very good science fiction film."

Torture Garden, a return to the anthology format, was a definite im-provement. This time Bloch adapted four of his own stories ("Enoch," "Ter-ror over Hollywood," "Mr. Steinway," and "The Man Who Collected Poe") involving killer cats, actors replaced by robot look-alikes, a jealous piano, and a man who not only collects Poe paraphernalia, but has managed to col-lect the spirit of Poe himself.

Said Bloch about the film in an interview with this author:

> I had my reservations about *Torture Garden*. First of all, it wasn't my title; there are no tortures in it, there is no garden – it's Octave Mir-beau's title from his novel of about 1900. It had nothing to do with that. I didn't particularly care for the way the framing story was handled [Burgess Meredith plays a fortune-telling devil in a carnival who reveals himself by the addition of plastic horns to his head at the end.] They saved a lot of money by handling it the way that they did, but I don't think it was well done.
>   I have heard that during the Edgar Allan Poe sequence the director decided to *improve* the ending, and I don't particularly think he did. It got a little murky. There was also a rather lengthy sequence that was

cut out of one of the other episodes in the interests of keeping the film to a certain length for theatrical release . . . [and] it changed the tempo and pace of that sequence considerably.

According to producer Milton Subotsky in John Brosnan's *The Horror People*, the endings of two Francis films were changed in the editing. *The Psychopath* was one: When audiences at preview showings easily guessed the murderer's identity, the dialogue of the last two scenes was completely overlaid with new dialogue to actually change the murderer. The other changed ending was for *The Torture Garden*, as Subotsky describes:

> [T]he last story . . . was the one about Poe that starred Jack Palance. In the scene with Palance when he discovers Poe in that room, every time that Palance starts talking we cut away from him and changed all the dialogue. What happened was that Freddie Francis changed the ending on the floor without telling me. Not that our original ending was that good but Freddie's version left us with no motivation for the whole place burning up. We had to do something before Palance went back to the States so that he could post-synch it, so I wrote a whole new ending in the cutting room, basing it on the footage we had.
>   Freddie Francis is a brilliant director pictorially. He is one of the world's great cameramen, he sets up the most beautiful and intricate shots, and his pictures are good to look at, but I don't think he has a very good story sense.

Francis replaced Terence Fisher, who had broken his leg, on *Dracula Has Risen from the Grave*. Francis in *Little Shoppe of Horrors* said that he did not enjoy doing this sort of movie, "because I do think they have been done to death." He claimed that he tried to "play about with the legend" to prevent every film from being "a remake of a remake of a remake."

This attitude may explain why *Dracula Has Risen from the Grave* contains one of the most surprising scenes for a horror film, in which Count Dracula survives being staked midway through the film and throws the stake at the people who were going to dispatch him, all because the would-be vampire killer was an atheist who had not prayed while performing this cleansing rite. Many horror purists howled in dismay, and the scene certainly raised quite a few eyebrows in the cinemas, but as Francis makes clear, he never was that concerned with vampiric lore. Instead, he got what he wanted: a scene that gave the audience a real jolt.

Dracula Has Risen from the Grave picks up where *Dracula — Prince of Darkness* left off, with Dracula trapped beneath the ice below his castle. There is an interesting pre-credit sequence that flashes back to a time when Dracula was on the rampage: A young boy goes to ring the church bells when he discovers blood on the rope, and going up into the belfry to investigate, he discovers the body of a young girl, her neck bitten, hanging upside down and muffling the bell's sound. Dracula has profaned even the sacred domain of the church.

Years later, a monsignor (Rupert Davies) comes to check on the parish and finds that people still fear to go inside the church. He insists that the priest (Ewan Hooper), a man of shattered nerves, accompany him on a trip to Dracula's castle to exorcise its demons and purify the place.

The frightened priest falls and cracks his head against the ice. His dripping blood falls on the lips of Dracula (Christoper Lee) and revives him. Francis immediately violates vampire lore by having the priest see in the water the reflection of the vampire standing over him. With the priest subservient to his will, Dracula finds his way back into the castle blocked by the monsignor's cross and demands to know who has done this. (After all the snarling and hissing in *Dracula – Prince of Darkness*, Lee's vampire is talking again, though he is not given much, or even much interesting, to say.)

According to Francis in *The Horror People*, he approached *Dracula Has Risen from the Grave* "as more of a love story than as a horror film. I was more interested in the love affair between the boy and the girl than with Dracula, he was just a fly in the ointment. Unfortunately a lot of that was cut out by Hammer and I never had a chance to put it back again." Sadly, this just is not an appropriate attitude to take on a Dracula picture, and it shows in the final product. Dracula is relegated to a peripheral menace, while the main story concerns a romance between Maria (Veronica Carlson), the monsignor's niece, and Paul (Barry Andrews), who is an unsuitable suitor because he is an avowed atheist. Dracula decides to get his revenge by targeting Maria as a victim, though he sinks his fangs into Zena (Barbara Ewing) first and then disposes of her when she fails in an attempt to lure Maria to him.

There are a few interesting confrontational scenes between Dracula and the other characters, and the idea that a priest would be Dracula's unwilling henchman seems vaguely blasphemous, but while it is better than the subsequent Lee Draculas, the story does not build much momentum or thrust as it goes along. The ending, where Dracula does a back flip and impales himself on a cross, also seems a bit weak, turning the super vampire into a super klutz. This pattern was only made worse in the sequel, *Taste the Blood of Dracula*, in which the vampire foolishly steps in front of a cross, cuts his hand by smashing a stained glass window at the end and then plummets to his death on an abandoned church altar.

However, Francis does put some drive and menace to the scenes where Dracula is whipping the horses of his carriage, urging them on to greater speed. The film's main problem is that it frequently fails to make Dracula a dynamic figure whose great power can only be overcome with wit, intelligence and luck.

Nonetheless, people all over the world were hungry for a good vampire film, and *Dracula Has Risen from the Grave* proved to be an unexpectedly huge success, sparking a vampire revival all over the world. Despite its scenes of blood and two women arguing about who is going to unzip Paul's pants, the film was rated G in the United States and reached a wide audience of filmgoers who were hoping for something fun. Horror films go in cycles, reaching and thrilling audiences until they tire of them and the inspiration goes out of the companies producing them. A new generation then pops up (every seven to ten years) and starts the ball rolling all over again. The '60s concentrated on psychological thrillers in the wake of *Psycho*, and classic monsters revived by Hammer were being used less and less until a new generation of *Famous Monsters* readers reached the age where they could take dates out to the movies.

Francis finished out the decade by filming *Mumsy, Nanny, Sonny and Girly*, the rather silly tale of a family whose specialty is kidnapping, murder, and game-playing. In *The Horror People*, Francis declared that *Mumsy, Nanny, Sonny and Girly* is one of his favorites of his own films, but distribution proved a problem:

> The distributors are all geared up to handle horror films or comedies, or musicals, et cetera, but when they get something that doesn't fall into one of their accepted categories they don't know what to do with it. With *Mumsy* they first tried to treat it as an outright horror film then they changed the title to just *Girly* as if it was a sex picture, which it certainly wasn't. I looked upon it as a black comedy. Slightly more black than comedy. But I would defend it against anything or anyone as a piece of *cinema*.

Francis followed this up with one of his biggest disasters, the Herman Cohen–produced *Trog*, Joan Crawford's ignobly awful last film. The story, concocted by Peter Bryan and director John Gilling, might have had some interesting possibilities as a rumination on the "noble savage" in its tale of a troglodyte or missing link (played by Joe Cornelius) who is discovered in a cave. (In fact, Fred Schepisi made a decent film, *Iceman*, on just this premise in 1984.) However, Charles Parker's makeup consisted of nothing more than an ape mask and some hair bunched around the troglodyte, making it appear as an ultra-cheap monster and showing contempt for the audience. Matters are not helped by having Sam Murdock (Michael Gough) as a developer who agitates that "Trog," as he gets to be called, be removed permanently, and then agitates him enough so that this will happen. The best bits in the film are some Ray Harryhausen dinosaurs taken from Irwin Allen's *The Animal World* which ludicrously are meant to be visual presentations of Trog's memories. (The producers of the film could not have cared less that dinosaurs and cavemen were thousands of years apart in time.)

Perhaps the most notable thing about *Trog* was that it helped launch the career of John Landis, who saw that in order to make a "sucessful" monster movie, one evidently did not even need much of a monster costume, and so started working on his first film *Schlock!* (aka *Banana Monster*), a comedy about a missing link (played by Landis himself in a Rick Baker–built ape suit) on the loose. On his low budget, he parodied the disregard that *Trog's* makers had for the same audience.

Next came *The Vampire Happening*, which does not appear to have received an English-language release. In an interview with Sam Irvin, Jr., in *Bizarre*, Francis had this to say about the film:

> I had gotten mixed up with this company in Germany I had never heard of and it was a sort of send-up horror film. I don't think send-up horror films work, so I decided to do it as a farce. . . . I told the producer I wanted it dubbed into English and released in England and America after we finished making it. He said all right, so I made it with all these second rate German actors with the idea that when I dubbed it, I would use first rate English actors and turn it into something really good. But after we finished, I never heard from the producer again about the film. . . . The story was about a blond Hollywood starlet who inherits this castle in Germany. She goes over there and would you believe it, this girl is the spitting image of her great-great-great grandmother except that her ancestor had brunette hair. Well, her ancestor was a vampire and now residing in this castle. The same actress plays both roles, and it follows those sorts of lines; need I say more? At the end, they have this big vampire ball where all the vampires in the area come. The hero sends his trusty manservant up to stop the clock so that the clock doesn't strike and the vampires all forget to get to their coffins in time and the dawn catches them. But Ferdy Mayne, who plays Dracula, hears a cock crow and he goes dashing out for his coffin with his trousers falling down. This is the sort of film it is.

Amicus decided to revive the anthology film, this time basing the stories on the famous E. C. horror comics of the '50s. The result, *Tales from the Crypt*, was directed by Francis and proved another unexpected success. In the *Bizarre* interview, Francis claimed that he was "still trying to figure and why. The script was rather bad and I had to do a lot of work on it."

Producer Milton Subotsky bought the rights to the E. C. stories and wrote the script himself, using panels from the original comics as storyboards. As a result, the film is remarkably faithful to the E. C. Comics originals. *Tales from the Crypt* begins when five tourists visiting some historical catacombs come upon the Crypt Keeper (Ralph Richardson), who tells them their potential future. The first, based on "All Through the Night" from *Vault of Horror #35*, has Joan Collins murdering her husband on Christmas Eve in order to collect on his insurance policy. Her daughter lets in an escaped lunatic because he is dressed as Santa Claus. The lunatic then proceeds to kill Collins, making this the first of the killer Santa Claus movies.

The second tale, "Reflection of Death" from *Tales from the Crypt #23*, has Ian Hendry returning after a car crash to find his wife terrified of him and his mistress blind. Looking into a mirror, he realizes that he is nothing more than the rotting corpse of a man who died in the crash. He wakes up, realizing that it was a dream, until he and his mistress go for a ride and it begins all over again, only this time for real.

Peter Cushing stars in the third story, "Poetic Justice" from *Haunt of Fear #12*, which many consider the best tale of the group largely due to Cushing's poignant performance. Originally he was to play Richard Greene's role in the fourth tale, "Wish You Were Here" from *Haunt of Fear #22*, but Cushing said he preferred the role of Grimsdyke, a kindly old man who loves dogs and children, and who wants to communicate with his dead wife. Cushing's own wife had just died at the time, and the pain that he felt can be see on screen. (In fact, Grimsdyke's wife's first name was changed to Helen, the same as Cushing's wife's.) Originally, the part did not include dialogue, but when Cushing agreed to play it, the role was expanded and Cushing was allowed to ad lib. In the story, Cushing's neighbors, the Elliots, want to drive the poor old man away, so they kill his dogs and send him hate messages instead of Valentine's Day cards. The old man's heart is broken and he hangs himself in despair, but on the following Valentine's Day, Grimsdyke emerges from the grave and delivers a grisly Valentine's gift of his own – the heart of the elder Elliot's son.

"Wish You Were Here" is a variation on and tribute to W. W. Jacob's classic story "The Monkey's Paw" (itself adapted as a film in 1915, 1923, 1932, and 1948). When Barbara Murray wishes on an Oriental idol for some money, her husband (Richard Greene) dies in a car crash (after seeing the figure of death riding a motorcycle in one of the film's niftier images), leaving her the insurance money. Heedless of the dangers of playing with fate, Murray then wishes that her husband be brought back as he was before the accident. Just then an autopsy reveals that Greene had died of a heart attack just before the car crash and his embalmed body is returned to her. With a final wish, Murray wishes him to be alive forever, and he comes alive with a burning sensation in his veins that will make his existence an eternal torture. Francis also altered the script on this story, so Subotsky added additional cut-aways to the idol and laid over some dialogue to bring the plot more into line with his original script.

The final story is "Blind Alleys" from *Tales from the Crypt #46*, in which the sadistic head of a home for the handicapped who fails to supply adequate heat and blankets for his patients is trapped in a narrow, razor-lined corridor with the lights turned out and his own starved mastiff in pursuit of him. Nigel Patrick scores as the callous director, and Patrick Magee is effective as an indignant and outraged blind man who helps plot the grim revenge.

While Francis' direction is rather pedestrian, *Tales from the Crypt* offered a tight little package of imaginative horror stories for those who were unfamiliar with the original comics versions, which were typically macabre little tales with black humor and shocking final twists. An excellent marketing campaign and saturation TV ads also helped bolster the film's box office.

After *Tales*, Francis received a telegram telling him to contact Ringo Starr of the Beatles, who, it turned out, was a fan of Francis and wanted him to direct a film. Francis looked at the original script and thought it was lousy, so he turned it down. Starr was insistent that they talk, and Francis admitted that the only idea he liked was that of a vampire who was seeking to become unvampirized, so the pair agreed to retain that idea and have another script written. Actress Jennifer Jay wrote the script under the name Jay Firbank. Then Starr had the brainstorm of making the film a musical and hired singer Harry Nilsson to play the lead, Count Downe, the son of Dracula. Nilsson wrote one new song, "Daybreak," and a medley of his old tunes made up the film's soundtrack, including his biggest hit, "Without You," and the sentimental "Remember (Christmas)."

According to Francis in his *Bizarre* interview, "I did not like this idea. But I said, 'Fine Ringo! That's a good idea.' So off we went to make a horror-musical-comedy. We were now faced with a 28 day picture which we had agreed upon before. We had a set budget and a set schedule, but we now had five musical numbers to do as well in the same amount of time and within the same budget."

The little-seen Francis version of the resulting film, *Son of Dracula*, is indeed a very strange work. At the beginning of the film, Dracula, king of the netherworld, has been killed, and Countess Dracula is discovered to have given birth to a male child by Merlin the Magician (Ringo Starr) and a loyal retainer. One hundred years later, when the child has grown, he will be crowned king of the netherworld.

Baron Frankenstein (Freddie Jones) looks forward to the coronation in hopes that it will unite the inhabitants of the underworld. However, Merlin sees something strange and unexpected in his astrological charts. Count Downe (Nilsson) falls in love with Amber (Suzanna Leigh), a human female, and resolves to make himself human with the help of Prof. Van Helsing (Dennis Price). The Baron worries about the effect of this and rallies the forces of the netherworld against it, but to no avail.

As one might expect, Francis plays havoc with the mythology. Van Helsing becomes the vampire's friend, the Baron has a pot-bellied monster, and zombies, mummies and werewolves all cavort together in this unruly film. The character of Merlin seems vastly out of place, and surrounded by professionals, Starr gives his worst acting performance. The idea of a musical vampire who wants to be humanized so he can feel human love is certainly different, and I really like Nilsson's songs, but Nilsson is more a singer than an actor and an inappropriate choice for a vampire. Still, at least it was something different.

For Tigon, Francis made *The Creeping Flesh*, a clichéd but interesting film about a serum gone awry. Prof. Emmanuel Hildren (Peter Cushing) comes across an ancient skeleton which "grows" flesh when exposed to water. Prof. Hildren injects some serum into his daughter, Penelope (Lorna Heilbron), who becomes consumed with a sexual hunger. This being Victorian England where overt sexuality is equated with evil and madness, she is shuttled off to her uncle's asylum, run by Dr. James Hildren (Christopher Lee). James Hildren learns of his brother's fossil find and resolves to steal it in the hopes that he can discover a cure for insanity and make himself famous. However, his plans are upset when, in a scene reminiscent of the climax of Robert Wise's *The Body Snatcher*, his carriage overturns and the fossil skeleton is exposed to rain, refleshing it completely. The resulting creature is Shish Kang, the very incarnation of evil, who begins stalking the countryside in a black hood, looking to find the good professor. It is an average horror film, but not bad as these things go.

Francis is prouder of *Tales That Witness Madness*, another anthology film which this time makes some weak stabs at black comedy. The film has a talented cast that is largely wasted on a tepid script, and the production was plagued by various problems. Rita Hayworth mysteriously left the production after a few days, never to return, and was quickly replaced by Kim Novak. Jack Hawkins died of throat cancer, and his part had to be dubbed by Charles Gray (of *The Devil's Bride* and *Rocky Horror Picture Show* fame).

Four inmates in an asylum tell their wacky stories. Young Russell Lewis has an invisible tiger kill his parents; Peter McEnery is sent into the past where he causes the death of Suzy Kendall; Joan Collins plays a bitchy wife who hates a tree and plans to dispose of it when it disposes of her; and the final story involves Kim Novak in a tale of virgin sacrifice and cannibalism at a Hawaiian luau.

The film was financed by Paramount Pictures, and they expected more of a horror film (having put money into it without reading the script) simply because Francis had directed *Tales from the Crypt*. Paramount insisted that he inject some more blood and gore, and Francis complied, but the whole thing still comes off as tepid as an average episode of Serling's *Night Gallery* series.

Francis' son, Kevin Francis, formed his own film company, Tyburn Productions, while he was still in his twenties. The company made *Persecution*,

Horror Film Directors 424

Lana Turner's last movie, directed by Don Chaffey, as their first production. It seemed only natural that the junior Francis would call on his father for the second production, *The Ghoul*. *The Ghoul* (aka *The Thing in the Attic*) was able to take advantage of leftover sets from *The Great Gatsby* and *Sleuth*, which gives it a look that belies its meager budget.

It also reunited Francis with Anthony Hinds, who wrote the script, and Roy Ashton, who devised the makeup, from their old days together at Hammer. Sadly, the film came off as being like a substandard Hammer production. Peter Cushing is trying desperately to cure his son (Don Henderson) whom he keeps locked away in the attic because he has a tendency to want to dine on human flesh, being the ghoul of the title. The film tries to be moody but ends up being just boring as Gwen Watford and John Hurt hack up some lost snobs for the son to dine on. However, there is a shockingly graphic scene at the end where a saw is pushed through a man's head that seems more like a concession to changing tastes in horror.

Francis' next film for Tyburn, *Legend of the Werewolf*, proved even worse despite some nice werewolf makeup by Graham Freeborn and above-average cinematography by John Wilcox, who had done a similarly fine job on *The Ghoul*. David Rintoul plays Etoile the werewolf who goes on the rampage when he discovers that the girl he loves is a whore working in a bordello. Cushing plays a police pathologist who tracks him down, and he is finally dispatched with the traditional silver bullets. The film does contain some humor, but not all of it seems intentional. Both this film and its predecessor suffered from being released when there was a glut on the horror film market; consequently they received very limited releases.

Francis left the directing field to go on a three-year sabbatical writing and developing his own projects. He then returned to work as a director of photography on David Lynch's *The Elephant Man*, on which he did a superb job, showing that he had not lost one whit of his talent since he had last worked as a cinematographer (on *Night Must Fall* in 1964) 15 years previously. Switching to color, he did another excellent job on Karel Reisz's *The French Lieutenant's Woman* and then collaborated again with Lynch on the epic *Dune*. He began work on Walter Murch's *Return to Oz*, but after some disagreements, left early in the production, being replaced by David Watkin. He then shot Jonathan Sanger's *Code Name: Emerald* before returning to directing with *The Doctor and the Devils*, based on Dylan Thomas' famous screenplay.

Thomas' script, about Burke and Hare and the ethics of medical doctors who rely on graverobbers for their cadavers, is highly reminiscent of Wise's classic *The Body Snatcher*, which went over much of the same ground. Still, the film has a sumptuous look, making it seem like the best film that Hammer never made, plus the cast is excellent with Timothy Dalton (who played James Bond in *The Living Daylights*) making a good, headstrong Dr.

David Rintoul as the werewolf in Freddie Francis' little-seen Legend of the Were-wolf. *Tyburn productions went bankrupt shortly after finishing the film.*

Thomas Rock, and Jonathan Pryce and Stephen Rea as Fallon and Broom, the scuzzy resurrectionists who are not above smothering derelicts in their efforts to get a body as fresh as Dr. Rock requires.

The sets designed by Brian Ackland-Snow evoke eighteenth-century London at its lowest very well and very effectively. Imogen Richardson does equally well with the period costumes as does production designer Robert Laing with the overall production. The result is a horror tale with the same high quality look as Carol Reed's production of *Oliver!* only with the sweetness and light cut out. Twiggy gives a surprisingly strong support-ing performance as a sympathetic prostitute, Jenny Bailey.

Still, while Ronald Harwood updates the script, he does not satisfactorily address the central moral questions. Is it right of Dr. Rock to look the other way because his research is valuable and he would not otherwise have the specimens that he needs because of Victorian "morality," or do the noble

Director Freddie Francis (left) instructs star Timothy Dalton on the set of The Doctor and the Devils, *based on the famous Dylan Thomas screenplay and very handsomely mounted by Francis. Definitely one of his best horror films.*

ends not justify the means by which he acquired them? How obligated is he to check into Fallon and Broom's techniques of acquisition, or should he perhaps have kowtowed to the conventions of society in the first place? These are the real issues of the story, and the film's failure to make them relevant to today's concerns kept *The Doctor and the Devils* from being a commercial success. Rather it appeared to be a well-made but anachronistic throwback to the films of another era, lovingly recreated by British craftsmen.

Still, this has not discouraged Francis, who recently finished working as both director and cinematographer on *Dark Tower*, produced by Sandy Howard. The dark tower of the title is the Unico Plaza, designed by Carolyn Page (Jenny Agutter). It is apparent that the building is cursed when at an open ceremony, a window washer is slammed repeatedly into a window and plummets to his death, killing an executive in the process. Investigator Dennis Randall (Michael Moriarty) checks into the incident, but Page insists that the washer was pushed by an invisible force. Meanwhile, the elevator takes on a life of its own, killing a security guard, and another security guard goes on a berserk killing spree.

To get an explanation for the mysterious events, Randall visits Dr. Max Gold (folksinger Theodore Bikel) at the Institute of Psychic Research, and Gold enlists the aid of Sergie (Kevin McCarthy), a psychic of amazing ability. They become convinced, because of an apparition that Randall sees, that the spirit of Page's late husband is responsible, and they attempt to contact him.

The film has a fine cast as well as a screenplay by Robert J. Avrech, Ken Blackwell, and Ken Wiederhorn (the last the director of *Shock Waves* and *The Return of the Living Dead Part 2*). The film was shot in Barcelona, Spain, where two bomb explosions occurred near the production, though no one connected with the film was injured. Mysteriously, Francis' directorial credit in the film was reassigned to Wiederhorn.

Karl Freund (1890-1969)

The Mummy (1932); *Moonlight and Pretzels* (1933); *Madame Spy; The Countess of Monte Cristo; Uncertain Lady, I Give My Love; Gift of Gab* (1934); *Mad Love* (1935).

Although primarily known as a lighting cameraman, Karl Freund also directed eight films, the two best (and best known) of which were the classic horror films *The Mummy* and *Mad Love*. Freund was born on January 16, 1890, in Königinhof, Bohemia (now a part of Czechslovakia), but later moved to Berlin. There, at the age of 16, he became an apprentice projectionist. By 17 he was an assistant cameraman and the following year he joined Pathe's staff as a full-fledged newsreel camerman. According to Ephraim Katz in his *Film Encyclopedia*, "A gifted innovator, [Freund] was experimenting with sound as early as 1908 and built his own camera to meet his high standards of quality. During the '20s he gained an international reputation as a master of daring camera angles, lighting effects and camera movement in such German film classics as Murnau's *The Last Laugh*, Dupont's *Variety* and Lang's *Metropolis*. He was once described by a film historian as 'the Giotto of the screen.'"

He shot his first feature as a cinematographer, *Der Liebling der Frauen*, in 1910. In 1919, he became involved with Murnau for whom he shot *Satanas; Der Bucklige und die Tänzerin; Der Januskopf; Marizza, Gennant die Schmuggler-Madonna; Der Brennende Acker; The Last Laugh*, and *Tartuff*. *Satanas* was a fantasy film involving Satan searching through the ages to find someone who can derive good from evil and thereby save Satan's soul, while *Der Januskopf* was an early adaptation of Robert Louis Stevenson's *The Strange Case of Dr. Jekyll and Mr. Hyde* starring Conrad Veidt as the troubled Dr. Warren and Bela Lugosi as his butler/manservant. The film apparently has been lost.

The Last Laugh was an important film for a number of reasons. It was one of the first silents to free the camera from the tripod. Murnau and Freund came up with the solution of placing it on a tricycle to get a primitive kind of dolly shot. Additionally, the film told its story purely cinematically. There were no intertitles, for everything was said with images. It was critically acclaimed and became an international hit.

Freund also worked on the 1920 version of *The Golem* with its memorable monster and weird, expressionistic sets and special effects. He was to imitate some of the look of this film in his work for Robert Florey on *Murders in the Rue Morgue*. He also cophotographed Part II of *Die Spinnen (The Spiders)* for Fritz Lang, which led to him later co-photographing the magnificent spectacle of *Metropolis*. After photographing a great many German films, he emigrated to the United States in 1929, where he resumed his career as a cameraman with *The Boudoir Diplomat*.

However, it was for his next assignment, teamed with Tod Browning, that Freund is particularly remembered: 1931's *Dracula*. He went on to do *Bad Sister, Murders in the Rue Morgue, Back Street,* and *Air Mail*. Executives at Universal were impressed with his work on *Dracula* and *Murders in the Rue Morgue* and allowed him to make his debut as a director with what they hoped would be their next horror hit, *The Mummy*.

The film was originally conceived by Nina Wilcom Putnam, who wrote a nine-page story called "Cagliostro," based on the Svengali-like hypnotist. Putnam's story was developed by Richard Schayer, head of the Universal story department, into a treatment. According to Paul Jensen in *Boris Karloff and His Films*, Cagliostro was

> an Egyptian magician who has, by injecting himself with nitrates, been able to stay alive for three thousand years. In revenge for a woman's betrayal, he seeks out over and over again women who resemble his love, and destroys them. In present-day San Francisco he poses as the blind uncle of Helen Dorrington, a movie-cashier who bears a fateful resemblance to the girl. Assisted by a Nubian servant, Cagliostro uses radio and television rays to commit robberies and murder. Also involved are Helen's boy-friend, and a professor of archaeology who learns the truth and helps to destroy Cagliostro.

John Lloyd Balderston, who cowrote the original stageplay that *Dracula* was based on, took this story, retained a few elements, and fashioned a new one designed to tie in with the idea of a mummy's curse, based on the sensationalized stories of the curse of King Tut's tomb which were rampant during the early 1920s. Unlike vampires and werewolves, which have a background of folk myth, the idea of walking mummies was never a part of Egyptian folklore and was a pure Hollywood fabrication. After having huge successes with vampires and stitched-together creations, Universal was looking for a new and exotic monster.

Significantly, as Ron Borst points out in his article "The Mummy Story" for *Photon* magazine, 1932's *The Mummy* was far from the first "mummy" film. That honor may be claimed by a 1911 film called *The Mummy* which concerns a female mummy brought to life when a high power line falls across her. There were also *When Souls Meet* (1921), *Dust of Egypt* (1915) and *The Eyes of the Mummy* (aka *Die Muma Ma*) directed by Ernest Lubitsch in 1918. But 1932's *The Mummy* was the first sound film about mummies on the loose, though in most respects it remains different from any subsequent mummy film.

Balderston seems to have looked back at *Dracula* to form the structure for his new screenplay. Again he includes a mysterious figure with hypnotic powers who has romantic designs on the heroine. Opposing him are an elder authority figure (once more played by Edward Van Sloan) and love-stricken young hero (once more played by David Manners). Again there is not much action but plenty of significant dialogue rife with possibilities and parlor room confrontations between the menace and the authority. There is even an amulet of Isis which protects from the mummy's influence much as the cross protects the wearer from the bite of the vampire.

The film opens with a shot of the Scroll of Thoth which contains the arcane spell by which Isis, the goddess of fertility, raised Osiris from the dead. A superimposed title translates the opening for us: "Oh Amon-Ra – Oh! God of Gods – Death is but the doorway to new life – We live today – We shall live again – In many forms shall we return – Oh, mighty one." In the background an adaptation of Tchaikovsky's "Swan Lake" music is heard fading into "Egyptian" music. (This particular snippet of "Swan Lake" was also heard at the beginning of *Dracula, Murders in the Rue Morgue* and *The Secret of the Blue Room*, apparently serving as Universal's "horror" theme for a time. It's gotten so that I can't hear this haunting piece of music without thinking of the old Universal horror films.)

Freund quickly sets up the locale as Egypt with a banner proclaiming a 1922 British expedition, a few exterior shots of diggings (probably shot in the California desert) and some bits of dialogue. Inside a newly discovered tomb Sir Joseph Whemple (Arthur Byron), occultist Dr. Muller (Edward Van Sloan) and Whemple's young assistant Norton (Bramwell Fletcher) are cataloging the finds of the day. Norton laments that they did not uncover any elaborate finds in the tomb, but Whemple cautions him that it is knowledge, not treasure, that they are after.

Norton is impatient to examine a box that they've found. Whemple tests it and discovers it is made out of gold. However, Dr. Muller warns them not to open the box, for there is a curse on it: "Death! Eternal punishment for anyone who opens this casket. In the name of Amon-Ra, King of the Gods." Whemple poo-poohs his notion that the power of the old Egyptian gods still exists. He whispers to Norton that they will open it later as he is escorted outdoors by Dr. Muller, who endeavors to convince him that they may have stumbled upon something both evil and dangerous.

Inside, the silence is oppressive. (While *The Mummy* was the first of the Universal horror films to actually have a score, Freund wisely chose to have the following sequence be absolutely silent.) Norton cannot wait until Whemple returns to open the small casket inside the box and extract the Scroll of Thoth. He immediately starts copying the hieroglyphs and mouths the sacred words. Freund cuts back to the mummy of Imhotep (the name has been variously given as Im-Ho-Tep and Im-ho-Tep, but the titles omit hyphens) who lies in his sarcophagus. With the silent utterance, a black eye dimly opens, and the 3700-year-old mummy's hands begin to move, first one and then the other.

Back at the desk, Norton is busy transcribing when he looks over and sees the mummy's hand take the scroll. Norton's mouth stretches back in a fearful grin as the camera pans past the empty mummy case to the sight of two bandages slowly trailing out the door. When his colleagues come rushing in, Norton can only babble, "He went for a little walk! You should have seen the look on his face!" while laughing hysterically. We know he has received a shock from which he will never recover.

Freund handles this scene brilliantly, knowing just which details to show and, even more important, which ones not to show. The change in Norton is quite pronounced as earlier we saw him as a nice chap with a sense of humor, asking mischievously if Imhotep, who according to Whemple and Muller had been buried alive without having his viscera removed, had been punished for fooling around with the vestal virgins. We can sympathize with his burning curiosity, and his insane laughter clearly indicates all that needs to be said. While we do not see Karloff in his mummy makeup for long, and unlike other mummy films, we never actually see him walk, the scene is unforgettable for the tone and atmosphere it builds up of an exotic location where supernatural spells work and there are things which could drive a man mad. Also, in its subtlety and suggestiveness, it shows that Freund was not looking for shocks but rather a strange and eerie kind of poetry. In fact, *The Mummy* is one of the most poetic horror films ever made.

The poetry is built on careful imagery, brilliantly lit by Charles Stumar (who also did *The Raven* and *Secret of the Blue Room*) and fluidly directed by Freund. That poetry is also reflected in Balderston's writing. Van Sloan does not simply ask Whemple to come outside; "Let us go and sit under the Egyptian stars," he says. Throughout the film's compact 72-minute running time Balderston tries to spice the dialogue with romantic references to the exotic location. Freund proves quite good at making the locations seem real.

The story resumes ten years later on another expedition headed by Whemple's son Frank (David Manners), from whom we quickly learn that his father has not been in Egypt for the past ten years despite loving the country and that Norton died still laughing while wrapped in a straitjacket. The mysterious figure of Ardath Bey (Karloff) comes in and, after ascertaining that the present expedition has not been successful, offers to show them

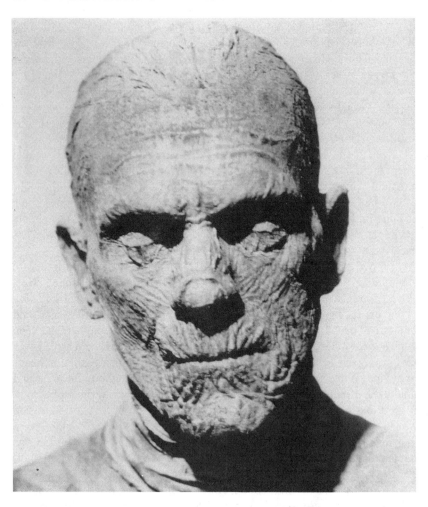

Boris Karloff as The Mummy, *buried under layers of clay and onion skin applied by the skilled hand of makeup artist Jack Pierce. Fortunately for Karloff, he only had to don the mummy makeup for a short time, appearing through most of the film as a wizened Egyptian (another brilliant makeup job by Pierce) with magical powers. Director Karl Freund showed he was the equal of Tod Browning in terms of style and performances in this magical movie.*

where he found an amulet bearing the name of the princess Ankhesenamon. He explains that only foreign governments are allowed to dig up the Egyptian dead. Quickly, some workers are hired and Ankhesenamon's tomb is found, but Bey disappears. Meanwhile, the expedition has an agreement to turn over whatever is found to the Cairo museum, where the contents of the tomb are put on display.

Balderston obviously did some research; not only does he throw in his knowledge of the practice of removing a mummy's viscera, he also takes his names from Egyptian history. Imhotep was a high priest under the Pharaoh Zoser who was the architect for the Step Pyramid at Sakkara, while Ankhesenamon was the name of King Tutankhamen's queen. (However, Imhotep and Ankhesenamon lived centuries apart and needless to say were never involved with each other.)

Karloff's makeup was by Universal's makeup genius Jack Pierce. Both makeups required that Karloff's skin have an extremely wrinkled appearance, which Pierce painstakingly achieved by stretching Karloff's skin and applying strip on strip of cotton dipped in collodion, which simulated wrinkles when the skin relaxed. Even when he poses as a living being, we can see there is something subtly wrong about Bey's alarming appearance. In addition, Karloff's performance emphasizes Bey's fragile and brittle qualities while nonetheless hinting at great psychic power. Bey is standoffish and his movement is very stiff and restrained but purposeful. Freund was particularly good at giving a smoldering intensity to Karloff's eyes: he adjusted a pair of baby spotlights, first to use Karloff's brow to cast a deep shadow over his eyes, then to direct light into the eyes so that they seemed to emanate from Karloff's skull with an unnatural intensity.

In fact, the whole film abounds with knowing photographic tricks that greatly enhance the image and the mood of the scenes. When Bey prays over a flickering oil lamp, Freund beautifully uses the below-the-face light source to cast creepy shadows on Karloff's wizened visage. Freund's use of Karloff as a horror icon is uncanny, and each of his close-ups is a beautiful horror image.

At the Cairo museum, Joseph Whemple meets Bey for the first time, but Bey refuses to shake hands, explaining a moment later, "I dislike to be touched – an Eastern prejudice." Because of his part in locating Ankhesenamon's tomb, Whemple offers to allow Bey to stay after hours in the museum. There he sets up the Scroll of Thoth and begins chanting the name of his beloved.

A quick pan across the rooftops of Cairo establishes a connection between Bey's spell and Helen Grosvenor (Zita Johann), the daughter of the English governor of Sudan and an Egyptian woman of long lineage. She is the reincarnation of Ankhesenamon in the present day and is also the patient of Dr. Muller, who is watching her at a dance as she gazes out over the rooftops at the Egyptian stars. We see her fall under Bey's spell and then in a trance proceed to the museum. However, before she can get inside, she is spotted by the Whemples, who drive her to their house in their car. Meanwhile, a museum guard discovers Bey at his prayers and takes the scroll. From an offscreen shout, we can surmise that Bey kills him, though when the body is finally found there is no apparent cause of death.

Meanwhile, back at the Whemples' parlor, Joseph is disturbed to hear Helen discoursing in a long-dead Egyptian language including the name of Imhotep, the mummy he had uncovered which subsequently disappeared. Frank keeps Helen company, explaining how he had almost fallen in love with Ankhesenamon after spending so much time around her personal things and so much time looking at her. Suddenly, subconsciously noticing the resemblance, he finds himself irresistibly attracted to Helen, who demurely asks him if he does not think she has had enough of a shock tonight without some strange man offering to make love to her.

Ardath Bey, realizing with the discovery of the museum guard that the Scroll of Thoth has fallen into Whemple's hands, suddenly decides to accept Whemple's earlier invitation to visit his home. When the front door is answered by a Nubian servant (Noble Johnson), Bey immediately hypnotizes him and the Nubian falls under his spell. However, he has a big shock when he sees Helen and finally realizes that she was the one who was answering his call for Ankhesenamon's soul. Bey announces that he is trying to recover a scroll he had bought and when Whemple lies about its whereabouts, Bey informs him of its exact location, giving proof of his supernatural powers. Dr. Muller threatens Bey but is powerless against the latter's occult forces. Bey, realizing he is not yet going to get the scroll he came for departs.

However, Dr. Muller quickly and accurately assesses the situation. He advises Joseph Whemple to burn the scroll as soon as he can. He sees that Frank and Helen are attracted to one another and that that will throw a monkey wrench into Bey's plans. Meanwhile, he gives Frank the amulet of Isis to protect him. When Frank protests that he should give it to Helen, Muller insists that Helen is not the one who is in danger from Bey.

Joseph goes to burn the scroll, but Bey sees him in his magic pool and with an outstretched hand and a spell manages to give Joseph a heart attack. Then the Nubian under his direction takes the scroll and burns some newspapers in its place. Muller examines the ashes and realizes that Bey has the scroll in his possession. Bey begins to cast his spell on Helen, attracting her and her dog to his hideout in the city.

There he uses his magic pool to reawaken memories in Helen's divided soul. The John Fulton–created swirling mist parts to reveal a flashback that details how Imhotep became a mummy because of his love for the Princess Ankhesenamon. When the princess died, he stole the Scroll of Thoth with the intention of reviving her but was caught in the act by the guards and priests "doing an unholy thing." He was sentenced to be buried alive. The slaves who buried him were killed, and the guards who did the killing were also killed, to keep his burial place a secret. To prevent such a thing from happening again, the Scroll of Thoth was buried with him. (These scenes were used again in *The Mummy's Hand* and *The Mummy's Ghost*.)

Karl Freund shoots this flashback in a silent film style, perhaps to emphasize how ancient these events were, though the sight of Karloff quickly
and furtively darting as if a few frames of film are missing is peculiar. Here
art director Willy Pogany shines in his Egyptian tableaux. We do not see
much of Zita Johann as Ankhesenamon; scenes showing her subsequent
reincarnations as an early Christian, a medieval princess, a Viking, and a
French noblewoman were filmed but later cut, perhaps because the actress
was proving difficult in contract negotiations.

The sounds of her dog dying rouse Helen from her trance, but Bey has
arranged it so that she remembers nothing of what she has seen, at least
not consciously. We learn later that her dog was killed by Bey's cat, a symbol of the Egyptian god that is the sender of bad spirits. Helen struggles
against Bey's influence, but when Frank discards his Isis amulet and is
almost crushed by Bey's psychic power before he can retrieve it (Bey
realizes that Helen is falling for the young man and so is set upon eliminating his rival), that is all the distraction Bey needs to get Helen completely
under his power.

In the museum, the soul of Ankhesenamon wakes up in Helen's body,
remembering nothing since her death 3700 years ago. Bey announces his intention to reunite them forever, showing her Ankhesenamon's mummy before burning it, explaining that he could have reanimated the mummy's
body but that it would have been a soulless thing under his command. He
loves Ankhesenamon's soul and has suffered for it through the centuries.

Ankhesenamon follows Imhotep/Bey into the museum's mock-up of an
embalming room, where the Nubian is preparing a vat of embalming fluid.
She protests that as a vestal virgin of Isis she should have no contact with
the dead and then notices the dead skin left behind from Imhotep's hands.
She learns that Imhotep plans to sacrifice her in her current body and give
her eternal life as a fellow mummy.

Seeing Helen gone, Muller and Frank hightail it to the museum just as
Imhotep is about to make his sacrifice. However, Imhotep holds up his ring
(Freund changing the focus from Karloff's face to his outstretched and be-
ringed hand holding the obsidian sacrificial blade) and stops them in their
tracks. Having nowhere else to turn, Ankhesenamon/Helen turns to the
statue of Isis and pleads: "I am Ankhesenamon, but I'm somebody else, too.
I want to live, even in this strange new world.... Save me from that
mummy – it's dead!" The statue swings its arm forward, the ankh on the end
of it glowing brilliantly white, and the Scroll of Thoth bursts into flames.
When it disintegrates, Imhotep disintegrates with it, leaving nothing but a
skeleton upon the floor. Helen's soul and personality return to her body as
she and Frank clinch.

Unlike most horror films of the period, *The Mummy* calls for a rather
matter-of-fact acceptance of the supernatural. The Scroll of Thoth is what

raises the mummy in the first place, and it is only the intervention of Isis at the end that puts an end to him. Unlike other mummies, Imhotep is able to shed his cumbersome wrappings and walk about in modern garb. He is not dependent on or controlled by a high priest, nor does he possess brute strength but rather an unfathomable supernatural power that is effective over great distances (such powers and associations being inherently cinematic). Also unlike subsequent mummies, Imhotep was buried with his tongue intact and can talk and communicate. These aspects were changed when Universal began its Kharis series in 1940 with Christy Cabanne's *The Mummy's Hand*.

As stated before, Karloff's performance is quite good. Observed Jensen:

> The pathos . . . is now achieved through a few graceful, formalized movements and a deep and burning gaze, combined with meaningful pauses, accented syllables, and the hollow, cultured tone of time and infinite sorrow. But dominating all, even a voice that echoes the desert's dry precision, is Karloff's quietly dynamic presence, which is threatening although he barely raises a hand.

Van Sloane brings the needed weight and dignity to the role of Dr. Muller. His dire warnings would seem risible were he not such a credible source, embodying the intelligent and learned man who has access to knowledge unknown to others. David Manners plays the stalwart hero in acceptable '30s fashion, though he seems to fall in love and start kissing Zita Johann much too quickly. Everyone does a credible job with none of the weak "comic relief" that disrupted other horror films of the period. Bramwell Fletcher's Ralph Norton is a standout.

Zita Johann recalled working with Freund in an interview with Delbert Winans in *Midnight Marquee*:

> Behind the camera Karl was great, but he couldn't deal with the actors. . . . He was a very nervous man, and he had to have a scapegoat. . . . [H]e told me I had to be photographed in a bathing suit because the costume had a similar design [that is, the costume to be worn in *The Mummy*]. I said all right, then later in the evening he told me he had to take some nude shots from the waist up. I thought for a moment, and with complete calmness, I told him okay if he could get it past the censors. He thought I was going to blow up top because I was Hungarian. Then he could blame different things on me during the filming. Freund never respected the actor's right of freedom to create, but at the time in Hollywood no one really did except men like King Vidor, Frank Capra, and such.

If there ever was any such nude scene filmed, it never made it past the censors. Johann went on to complain that her reincarnation scenes were cut and that "during the final stage of shooting, Freund worked me sixteen hours a day instead of the usual twelve." Not liking Hollywood, Johann spent most of her life in the theater. Her only other film credits are *The Struggle* (1932), *Tiger Shark* (1932) and *Luxury Liner* (1933).

Many critics have noted that *The Mummy* is a more fluid film than *Dracula*. Fruend was able to move the camera more, and this helps the film achieve a dream-like atmosphere. Unlike *Dracula* where all the action takes place within the confines of a single stage, in *The Mummy* Freund was able to suggest how unseen forces could stretch out over distances, relating actions that take place in differing locations. Freund does not dwell on static compositions the way Browning did but allows his camera to pick out choice details which are underscored by the effective lighting design. The result is not a horror thriller, but a moody, romantic piece of strange powers, immortal passions, undying love, and subliminated necrophilia. Imhotep is both fascinating and frightening, and with this slow-moving, suggestive presentation, Freund manages to suggest that there is something inexorable about it all.

I have not seen most of Freund's subsequent directorial efforts – *Moonlight and Pretzels, Madame Spy, The Countess of Monte Cristo, Uncertain Lady* and *I Give My Love* – nor do I think they are readily available. I did see a brief sequence from *The Gift of Gab*, a blackout musical comedy which had one notable sketch in which murder mysteries are burlesqued and both Karloff and Bela Lugosi make a token appearance.

Freund returned to the horror field to work on MGM's *Mad Love*, a remake of Robert Weine's (the director of *The Cabinet of Dr. Caligari*) *Orlacs Haende (The Hands of Orlac)* starring Conrad Veidt. The story was adapted by Guy Endore (who wrote *Werewolf of Paris* upon which *Curse of the Werewolf* is based) and Freund. They decided to emphasize not the tormented victim Orlac but rather the brilliant surgeon who grafted the hands of a murderer in place of Orlac's own. The final screenplay was written by John L. Balderston and P. J. Wolfson.

For the starring role of Dr. Gogol, Peter Lorre made his American debut while on loan from Columbia. Lorre had resisted early offers to come to America, but as European parts grew more difficult to come by with the rise of Hitler and Harry Cohn promised a greater variety of roles, Lorre made the transition to the United States and practiced his English. (He learned his part in *The Man Who Knew Too Much* largely phonetically, not having mastered the language yet.)

Freund could not have made a better choice for the lead. With his bulging eyes and expressive face, Lorre was just right to play a dedicated scientist who is driven mad by love for a woman who spurns him. To make him even more visually arresting (as well as somewhat repulsive), Lorre's head was completely shaved. Lorre's look in the film resembles that of the fat and balding Kane in *Citizen Kane*, and both the films include a large house with a white cockatoo. Since the films also share one of the great cinematographers, Gregg Toland, Pauline Kael and others have concluded that *Mad Love* was a definite influence on *Citizen Kane*.

The film opens in an appropriate if rarely utilized locale: a Grand Guignol theater in Paris, or more specifically, Le Theatre des Horreurs. Before the opening, we have a rather striking title sequence in which the titles are written on frosted glass overlooking a Parisian skyline before a shadow passes over them and a hand smashes through the glass (a witty and unexpected touch). Grand Guignol is a famed type of bloody melodrama noted for its sadism and ghoulishly realistic detail. The plots were filled with murders, stabbings, beheadings, and the like, all of which were performed onstage in gory detail. The violence allowed the audience the chance to scream, but often it was played so far over the top that the melodramas become blackly comic farces.

The star of this particular theater is Yvonne (Frances Drake), who after nightly being stretched on the rack (no gory scenes for 1935 movie audiences) receives a bouquet of flowers from a mysterious admirer. It is announced that Dr. Gogol, a surgeon famed for curing deformed children and mutilated soldiers, has a regular box in the theater. We see Gogol jealous of another man admiring Yvonne's wax effigy in the lobby. He finally screws up his courage to make a backstage visit.

"Every night I have watched you and tonight I felt I must come and thank you for what you have meant to me," he says, kissing her hand, oblivious to her obvious disgust and discomfort. She announces that her husband is famed pianist Stephen Orlac, who broadcast his concerto from the Fountainebleau that evening, and that she is retiring from the theater to devote herself to him. Gogol is beside himself. "But I have come to depend upon seeing you. I *must* see you; I *must!*" he shrieks.

Yvonne is surprised at Gogol's unlooked-for passion, but before she can react, the pair are swept up and herded into a farewell party being thrown for her by the cast. As the actors and friends line up to give her a farewell kiss, Gogol decides to get into the act, forcing her to kiss him on the forehead. She almost swoons. Leaving, Gogol buys the statue of Yvonne in the lobby for 100 francs, explaining to the manager about the legend of Galatea and Pygmalion and overtly expressing the desire that she come to life in his arms.

That night as Orlac boards the train to return to his wife, the train is stopped and a man in handcuffs is taken aboard. The man is identified as Rollo (Edward Brophy), the murderer who threw knives at the circus until one day he threw one into his father's back because of a woman. He is on his way to be guillotined. But then fate plays a hand and the train crashes.

When Yvonne arrives on the scene, a doctor (Charles Trowbridge) informs her that her husband will live but his hands will have to be amputated. She then remembers Gogol's reputation and orders the ambulance to take her husband to Gogol's clinic. Gogol is delighted at the chance to do something for the woman he loves. He remembers the execution he watched that morning (apparently he attends all executions regularly, another part of his morbid character) and decides to graft Rollo's hands onto Orlac's arms. Impossible, his associate Dr. Wong (Keye Luke) tells him. "*Impossible?*" returns Gogol, "Napoleon said that word was not *French!*" Gogol works feverishly but at last the operation is a success. He relaxes by playing the organ back at his house with a wax effigy of Yvonne positioned in a mirror over the keys.

Orlac's hands are finally released from their casts. They feel dead, he complains, but Gogol assures him they have merely atrophied from lack of use. "But they don't look like my hands," Orlac complains. "You forget they were badly crushed," Gogol reassures him. He accepts the grateful praise of Yvonne who proclaims that no one else could have performed this miracle. However, the "miracle" does not prevent the Orlacs from getting into financial difficulty over Stephen's prolonged recuperation. Orlac finds he has to build up his keyboard skill all over again. His hands do not seem to "know" how to play. The troubled couple go to visit Henry Orlac (Ian Wolfe), Stephen's father, who disapproved of his son's choice of career. When Stephen and Henry quarrel, Stephen takes up a display knife and expertly throws it into the wall.

Yvonne has noted this plus his apparent moodiness and lack of interest in playing the piano. (He throws a pen at the man who comes to repossess it; the pen buries itself into the woodwork.) She goes to Gogol to ask if Orlac will ever be able to play again. Mournfully, Gogol inquires, "Your thoughts are only for him, is there no room in your heart – even pity – for a man who has never known the love of a woman, but who has worshipped you ever since the day he walked past that absurd little theater?" Yvonne breaks down, confessing that there is something about Gogol that she finds frightening.

A few days later, Orlac himself comes to visit Gogol, demanding to know, "Whose hands are these? They seem to have a life of their own. They feel for knives . . . and know how to throw them. They want to *kill!*" However, Gogol assures him that his hands are his own, that he is merely suffering from shock after the accident.

A mad plot begins to brew in Gogol's mind. While in surgery, he can see a dapper version of himself in the surgical mirrors urging him to use the power of suggestion. Henry Orlac is found dead, and a frantic Stephen receives a phone call from a mysterious stranger who requests a meeting. Orlac agrees to meet him in a dark room on a back alley. There the cloaked figure tells him, "Your hands . . . they throw knives. Your hands were once mine. I have no hands," he says, revealing a set of artificial hands made out of tubular steel that the figure says Dr. Gogol gave him.

The figure tells him that he killed his own father and tells Orlac to use a knife, which he drives into the table, when the police come for him. "Who are you?" demands Orlac.

"I am Rollo."

"But Rollo died on the guillotine!"

"Yes, they cut off my head, but Dr. Gogol put it back," the dark figure gloats. Taking his steel fingers, he pulls away more of the cloak to reveal an elaborate chin and neck brace which seems to hold the figure's head to his body.

This unforgettable moment is beautifully realized. The audience understands that the figure is Dr. Gogol impersonating Rollo, but nervewracked Orlac is too agitated to see through the bold deception. The lighting is suitably low-key and shadowy, adding to the overall creepiness, and Lorre's costume is consummately designed.

Orlac departs and is arrested. Yvonne decides to spy on Gogol while he is at the clinic and see if she can find anything out. Unfortunately, her plans go awry when Gogol returns unexpectedly in his wild outfit (cluing in the slower members of the audience). He exalts to himself, "The power of suggestion – it worked! They will put him away . . . while it is *I* who am mad!" Thinking quickly, Yvonne decides to hide by taking the place of the wax figure of herself in Gogol's bedroom; however, Gogol notices her breathing and in his madness thinks that the statue has come to life. He starts strangling Yvonne with her own braids. Meanwhile, the police and Stephen are just outside of Gogol's locked door and trying to get in. Instinctively, Stephen hurls a knife through a narrow slit in the door and into Gogol's back before he can strangle Yvonne in his wild delusion. Yvonne, ironically, is saved by the unexpected gift that Orlac gained when Gogol grafted his hands.

Gogol was one of Lorre's meatiest roles, and he makes the most of it. His appetite for Grand Guignol horrors and executions are indications of his disturbed personality, but Lorre is also able to suggest the tender and pathetic side of the man. Unlike most mad doctors, he is very compassionate towards his patients and is involved in no mad scientific research. Despite any malice he might harbor for Stephen, his intentions in grafting on the hands are pure. After all, the thought that a part of a murderer's soul and skill might linger on in a pair of hands is more than faintly ridiculous and could be, as in Oliver Stone's *The Hand*, just a delusion that the neurotic patient has – except that we find out that it is to be taken seriously, though it also turns out that Orlac did not kill his father. Colin Clive shines as Orlac, but then he was always best when he could play tortured souls. Clive would

Cameraman turned director, the great Karl Freund, whose innovations include putting a camera on wheels for Murnau's The Last Laugh *to setting up the three camera sitcom for* I Love Lucy. *He was known as a meticulous perfectionist.*

take only four more film roles, none of them horror, before dying of pneumonia on July 25, 1937.

Most of the rest of the cast performs well, except for Ted Healy as a snooping reporter who supplies some dull exposition and "comic relief." Mercifully, his scenes are kept to a minimum. The photography by Toland

and Chester Lyons is good with numerous scenes shot from low angles and inventively using shadows. Once again, Freund called on his own photographic background to add visual interest to the film, though the result is not as fluid as in *The Mummy* and the pacing occasionally becomes erratic. Nonetheless, while a cult film, it is rarely shown and deserves resurrecting for its excellent acting and the superior treatment of its bizarre and macabre tale. The story has been filmed at least once more in 1960 as *Hands of a Strangler* aka *Hands of Orlac* (with Mel Ferrer and Christopher Lee), though it did not prove as interesting as *Mad Love* and was rather flat. (Directed by Edmond T. Greville, it adds the novel twist that the murderer was found to be innocent.)

Freund resumed his director of photography career, doing an excellent job photographing *Camille* and winning an Academy Award for his work on *The Good Earth* (with the photographic effects of a locust swarm being particularly notable). According to Ron Borst, it was Freund who photographed and conceived the famous ending for Lewis Millestone's *All Quiet on the Western Front* where Lew Ayres is shot while reaching for a butterfly. Freund proved extremely versatile in a number of photographic styles, doing excellent work on such films as *Golden Boy, Pride and Prejudice, A Guy Named Joe, The Seventh Cross, Tortilla Flat,* and *Key Largo*. After working on *South of St. Louis, Montana,* and *Bright Leaf,* he left the cinema to work in the new field of television, pioneering the three-camera system of filming sitcoms on the *I Love Lucy Show*, for which he was the head cinematographer for many, many years. He passed away on May 3, 1969, ending a long and illustrious career in film. That he was the director of two fine horror films in which the two top horror actors gave excellent performances certainly warrants more than a footnote in the annals of film history.

Robert Fuest (1927–   )

Just Like a Woman (1967); *And Soon the Darkness, Wuthering Heights* (1970); *The Abominable Dr. Phibes* (1971); *Dr. Phibes Rises Again* (1972); *The Final Programme* (aka *Last Days of Man on Earth*) (1973); *The Devil's Rain* (1975); *Aphrodite* (1982 – French).

TELEVISION: "Game," "They Keep Killing Steed," "The Rotters," "Take Me to Your Leader," "Pandora," "Take-over," "My Wildest Dream" *The Avengers; The Gold Bug; Return of the Stepford Wives* (1980).

Born in London in 1927, Robert Fuest started out to be a painter, studying art in school before going into the army. At one time, he wrote liner notes for Decca Records, but his big break came when he became a production designer for the inventive and sometimes fantastic British television series *The Avengers* at its inception (i.e., the early British episodes which have never appeared on American television).

While on the show, Richard Lester, who became famous as the director of the Beatles' *A Hard Day's Night,* hired him away from the show. After six months, Fuest decided he wanted to try his hand at directing and made his first film, *Just Like a Woman* in 16mm. The film starred Wendy Craig, Dennis Price, and Francis Matthews and abounded with in-jokes about British television. The situation centered around a TV producer and his wife breaking up their marriage.

Though the film received some very good notices from the British press, it was not a big success and Fuest did not work for a year. He finally returned to *The Avengers,* but this time as a director, directing nine episodes with Linda Thorson after Diana Rigg had left the series.

Fuest commented in an interview with Sam L. Irvin, Jr., for *Bizarre*:

> To do a series is marvelous training. You learn so much discipline. You cannot flub up or else you don't do the next episode. You get ten days to do an hour show. You learn more about lenses, and how to deal with actors on a short term basis. Everything has to be spontaneous. There just simply is no time to sit down and analyse anything. Pressure forces some nice results that might never have come about otherwise.

The producers of *The Avengers,* Brian Clemens and Albert Fennell, asked Fuest to direct a feature for them, *And Soon the Darkness,* based on a script by Clemens and Terry Nation. The film starred Pamela Franklin as a young English girl who is on a bicycle trip through France with a blonde friend. When her friend wants to hang around to check out a mysterious Frenchman in sunglasses, the pair have a fight and Franklin heads on. Up the road, she waits, but her friend never arrives. Heading back, she can find neither hide nor hair of her friend.

Meanwhile, the man with the sunglasses offers to take her back to the previous town to investigate. There she meets an Englishwoman who explains that a girl with long blond hair had been murdered in the vicinity just a few years ago. Suddenly, Franklin becomes more and more paranoid as she cannot understand the French-speaking natives and does not know whom to trust.

Inventively staged upon occasion – the film cleverly arranges its lighting so that all the early morning scenes have the right kind of lighting, with the sun casting fewer shadows during midday and longer shadows in the evening, every detail carefully worked out and kept within the unity of occurring during a single day – nevertheless, the film never quite takes off as a suspense thriller and lacks Fuest's trademark humor that has made most of his other horror work so delightful.

Nonetheless, the film impressed Sam Arkoff of AIP enough that he decided to entrust Fuest with the company's intended high-class production of *Wuthering Heights*. Timothy Dalton, who has recently become well known for playing James Bond in *The Living Daylights*, made a respectable Heathcliff, though Anna Calder-Marshall was unfortunately lackluster as Cathy. Though fairly low-budget, the film was handsomely made and showed that Fuest had a good eye when it came to the pictorial elements.

Fuest, however, found himself with one difficulty regarding the film. He delivered a 140-minute final cut which was deemed too long to play at the drive-ins that most AIP product played, so the film was reduced to 105 minutes, with some versions ending up as short as 90 minutes, leaving some glaring gaps in the story. Still, the film did prove a success for AIP, which led to Fuest's breakthrough for horror audiences, *The Abominable Dr. Phibes*.

Recalled Fuest in the Irvin interview:

> This time they told me that they wanted a 90 minute film. They sent me the script by James Whiton and William Goldstein. It was 275 pages long! The average script only has about 100! It was dynamite, but totally serious. . . . I decided that it would work much better as a send-up. . . . The ending was wild. It had a confrontation at Wembly Stadium between Phibes and the whole of the Metropolitan police. He went up in a balloon or something like that. All this was great, but we had a budget to watch and I wanted to make it campy.

However, Fuest decided to keep this decision a secret from AIP, who thought he would be delivering a straight horror film rather than a black comedy. Fuest was afraid that if they knew his intention, they might stop him. Happily, the result turned out fine, pleasing not only AIP's execs, but also much of the horror film–going public, which responded to seeing a fresh approach to the genre. The film set the pattern for others involving a series of imaginative and macabrely humorous murders as well as a tongue-in-cheek tone which easily took the edge off the gruesomeness.

The Abominable Dr. Phibes opens with an organ/elevator rising in the middle of a tremendous art deco set, designed by Brian Eatwell, who would go on to do the superb sets for Richard Lester's *The Three Musketeers*. Vincent Price plays Phibes with tremendous theatrical flourish, accentuating his gestures while keeping his voice urgent though fairly monotone, since Phibes has had to recreate his vocal cords after his body was burned in a car crash. He also keeps his expressions subtle, appropriate to Phibes, who wears a mask throughout the film. (Near the beginning, there is a brief scene where we see Phibes assembling the portions of the mask, a plastic ear and nose and a sandy-haired wig, but we do not see his face.) Phibes is assisted by a mysterious beauty, Vulnavia (Virginia North), as they travel forth in a '30s automobile.

Their nefarious purpose is the demise of a physician on whom they unleash a flock of bats. Inspector Trout (Peter Jeffrey) comes to investigate the crime, while his assistant, Crow (Derek Godfrey), recalls that another physician had died a week earlier as a result of a hive of bees being unleashed on him, leaving him covered in boils. Meanwhile, we see Phibes at a masked ball giving a frog mask to Dr. Hargreaves (Alex Scott), who introduces himself and says, "I'm a psychiatrist actually – headshrinker," with wry amusement.

Typical of Fuest's humor, Hargreaves dies because the mask is set to become ever tighter, finally crushing or shrinking his head. He films this flamboyantly by having Dr. Hargreaves ascending the staircase at the masked ball while the mask clicks off notch after notch. At last, a shot from the Hargreaves' point of view turns blood red as his head is crushed.

The next victim is Dr. Longstreet (Terry-Thomas in a memorable bit), who is dispatched while watching the '30s silent equivalent of a porn movie. After finally getting rid of his housekeeper for the night, he is interrupted in his voyeuristic pleasures by the appearance of Vulnavia, who straps him to a chair while Phibes bleeds him to death. Terry-Thomas plays the scene so outrageously, joyously partaking of forbidden pleasures, that it never loses its comic flavor. However, Phibes loses a medallion at the site where he has been putting wax busts of each victim before melting them with a blow torch. (Obviously, whatever Phibes is up to, it is quite premeditated.)

While the police are shown to be fairly, though amusingly, fatuous in the film, even they cannot overlook this vital clue. Inspector Trout takes it to a goldsmith who recognizes it as his work, a part of a set, and identifies the character on it as Hebrew. Naturally, Trout follows this up by taking it to a rabbi (Hugh Griffith), who identifies it as one of the symbols of the *Haggadah*, which is the story of the Ten Plagues that afflicted the Egyptians as God persuaded the Pharaoh to let His people go. (Those who've seen *The Ten Commandments* are at least somewhat familiar with this story.) The rabbi shows him a pictograph of the ten plagues, including a plague of boils, another of bats, one of frogs and one of blood.

Crow uncovers that all the victims were at one time associates of one Dr. Vesalius (Joseph Cotten in the only horror role he seems to remember with pride). Vesalius explains that the only common element among all the men who have thus far been murdered is that they all had strived to save the life of Victoria Regina Phibes (whose likeness Phibes offers poetic soliloquies to and who is portrayed in portrait by Caroline Munro, a future horror queen herself), Phibes' late, lamented wife. However, reports Vesalius, Phibes died when racing back; his car went off a cliff and he was burned to death. This dashes Trout's hope for a quick and easy solution to the crimes.

Meanwhile, Phibes' car is by a roadside, a shade pulled down the side window with a likeness of the car's owner on it. The chaffeur of the other car gets out and is rendered unconscious by Phibes, who squeezes the back of his neck. Naturally, the car's owner is another victim, this time suffering from a machine which creates a hailstorm in his car.

Vesalius' son Lem (Sean Bury) mentions a clue which helps Vesalius and Trout along. A music shop owner, said Lem, knew all the great organists, including Phibes. Vesalius visits the blind owner who insists that Phibes has been his patron for years. He and Trout decide to investigate the Phibes burial site.

Fuest helps set the scene by having a strange graveyard caretaker mumble something about, "Fools! Fools! They'll have worms soon enough," while he leads them to the Phibes tomb. Vesalius inquires if anyone visits the tomb, and the caretaker shakes his head no even though there are fresh roses on Victoria's plot. Inside Phibes' grave, they find ashes, but, speculates Trout, are they really Phibes? Inside Victoria's grave, the coffin is completely empty. Phibes has taken the body.

Dr. Phibes is not a medical doctor and does not have a high degree of respect for the profession, members of which he holds responsible for his wife's death, hence this bizarre revenge scheme. He has two degrees, one in music from Heidelberg and the other a Ph.D. in theology. Judging from the clockwork musicians he has created and ingenious methods of murder he pulls off, he is even more clever than his degrees suggest.

In short order, a Dr. Kitaj (Peter Gilmore) is gnawed to death by rats while flying an areoplane, despite Crow's valiant attempts to reach him first, and then a brass unicorn's head impales another doctor just as the police are leading him to safety. Fuest uses the latter scene for another bit of ghoulish humor. Since the horn which impaled the victim to a wall has a left-hand screw, they have to twist the whole body around and around to unscrew it and free it, much to the annoyance of members of the exclusive club where the victim was killed.

In the final credits, both Dr. Vesalius and Dr. Phibes are listed as protagonists (other designations include the Girl, the Victims, the Law, and interested parties). Phibes is not motivated by personal gain, but purely by revenge. Once his mission is completed, he looks forward to joining his beloved wife in a secluded corner of the Elysium fields in the Great Beyond. There are only three curses to go, and the last, the plague of darkness, he has reserved for himself.

Meanwhile, he prepares the plague of the locusts for Nurse Allan (Susan Travers). Fuest does not allow the preparation scenes to simply set up her eventual demise, but rather continually inserts short, pungent jabs of humor such as Phibes inspecting vegetables he is throwing into his locust-attracting concoction, rejecting those that do not meet with his standard of quality. When preparing to unleash the locust fluid from the room above the nurse, he expertly pulls out an outline of a female form and lays it down on the floor where Nurse Allan's bed below should be in order to determine the proper place to begin drilling. Given a sedative, the nurse sleeps through the greenish fluid pouring down and encasing her body, which is subsequently consumed by locusts while a policeman guards the door, oblivious to what is happening to his charge.

Brian Clemens suggested the curse of the first-born in which Vesalius' son is kidnapped and placed on an operating table, a key in his heart needed to unlock him from the table. Phibes calls Vesalius and tells him where to find his son. Unfortunately, in six minutes, acid will pour down on the poor boy's head if Vesalius cannot extract the key and free the boy in time. (The time element is based on how long Victoria has lasted on the operating table. The fact that Phibes is not a medical doctor and would have had a difficult time setting up this particularly fiendish torture without hurting the boy is completely glossed over. It does, however, make for a suspenseful finale as the police rush to arrive as well.)

Vesalius is succcessful, Vulnavia is pushed under the acid at just the wrong moment, and Phibes embalms himself next to Victoria under a crypt depicting the night sky as, in the great tradition of classical horror movies, Fuest disposes of the mad doctor and reestablishes the basic normalcy of the world. Fuest gets some mileage out of Phibes' unmasking scene in which he removes his Vincent Price visage to reveal his true, skull-like face which lacks such appendages as lips and ears, its teeth in a permanent grimace. (Earlier, we were shown that Phibes has a mouth opening in the back of his neck somewhere.) Unfortunately, the effect was somewhat dissipated when a shot of the unveiled Phibes kissing Vulnavia in a parody of the *Love Story* poster was used to advertise the film – hence the audience would already know what he looked like. All in all, the film seemed like a fresh new approach to horror at the time, with the audience invited to delight in the protagonist's fiendish machinations and the comedy never dissipating the horrific aspects.

Deciding that they had struck a vein of gold with Phibes and his ghoulish humor, AIP immediately set up a sequel which Fuest cowrote with Robert Blees, *Dr. Phibes Rises Again.* Fuest told Irvin:

> They had one of their writers change a few things, and the sequence of events was re-arranged. I got it back and was relatively pleased. I made the film, pushing for more comedy than before. In fact, it was a send-up of the first one. I loved the film I made, but you have not seen it. AIP violently cut it up and subdued the comedy to a great extent. I guess it was because it was full of subtle "British Humor," but contrary to what AIP thinks, I feel that Americans not only understand, but enjoy British humor.

Rises Again picks up three years after the original film (though still in a period setting). After a brief rundown of the previous film, we see a reversed shot of the blood going out of Phibes and the embalming fluid going in. He rises again because the time is right to take Victoria to the Egyptian River of Life in the Temple of Hibiscus and restore his late beloved to life. Once more he calls on Vulnavia (this time played by Valli Kemp, a former Miss Australia who, though attractive, has less of an otherworldly beauty than North, possibly because her expressions are more human and her actions more animated) to help him.

However, when they ascend on the organ/elevator, they discover that their house has been leveled and the contents of their safe, which held a papyrus map of the River of Life's location, have been stolen. Phibes (once more played by Price) quickly deduces that the map's recipient is none other than Biederbeck (Robert Quarry, fresh from his success as *Count Yorga*), who has been able to sustain himself through the ages with an elixir of life that has almost run out.

Phibes spies on Biederbeck and Ambrose (Hugh Griffith) as they make plans for an archeological expedition to Egypt. Biederbeck's fiancée, Diana (Fiona Lewis), comes in and ushers them off to a party. Their hulking, bald manservant (Milton Reid) stays behind by the billiard table to keep an eye on things. Fuest establishes the tone for the sequel early as Vulnavia unleashes a windup snake in the billiard room. When the manservant discovers the reptile is a fake, his suspicions are temporarily allayed, but then he is bitten by a real snake. Rushing to the phone, he picks up a phony receiver which delivers the *coup de grâce* with a gold spike that enters one ear and goes out the other.

Who would be called in on a bizarre case but our old friend Inspector Trout (Peter Jeffrey again), who asserts that no common thief would have indulged in such an elaborate plan – only someone who knew the value of Biederbeck's map. Still, the death of his manservant does not dissuade Biederbeck and party from sailing, despite the inevitable inquiries, much to the displeasure of Waverly (once more played by John Cater), the head of police.

On shipboard, Biederbeck decides to reveal some of his secrets to Ambrose, who, hungry to learn more, heads down into the hold for a model of the Egyptian tomb they plan to invade. Also stored in the hold are Victoria and some of Phibes' clockwork creations which Ambrose comes across. Feeling that Victoria's resting place has been desecrated, Phibes arranges for Ambrose to be stuffed in a 7-foot-tall gin bottle and thrown overboard, where he is washed ashore and brought to the attention of the local authorities.

Meanwhile, the ship's captain (a brief cameo by Peter Cushing) tries to allay Biederbeck's fears about his friend (asking if he indulged in the bottle), but Biederbeck surprises him by being impatient to get on with his journey. Back in England, the police have contacted the shipping agent, Lombardo (Terry-Thomas), who is asked if there is anyone odd on board. They are all odd to Lombardo, but he does let slip that one passenger wanted an organ in his suite and was also transporting several life-sized clockwork musicians. Deciding that Phibes is back, Trout and Waverly contact Ambrose's widow to find where the party is going and make off for Egypt.

Having landed, Phibes enjoys the local cuisine, though in a fine bit of Fuestian humor, he almost chokes on a fishbone lodged in the back of his throat, which is where he ingests food. Phibes has already been to this temple and has constructed an elaborate secret chamber for himself, which he unveils. Once more art deco is the predominant influence, but it also has some colorful Egyptian touches as well. Phibes swears those who violate the sacred mountain will die, and sure enough, an archeologist who does is clawed to death by an eagle. Phibes, meanwhile, finds a sarcophagus which contains the key to the River of Life, which can only be obtained once a century during a full moon.

Back at camp, Diana finds the dead archeologist's body, though how it got there is never cleared up. Another bit of clever humor has Phibes secreting himself among a group of skulls to keep an eye on Biederbeck's expedition. The team does not seem to notice that one of the skulls has a bloodshot pair of eyes. Other odd touches include a Rolls-Royce grill and

Robert Fuest on the set of Dr. Phibes Rises Again starring Vincent Price as Dr. Phibes (exiting from tomb with Fuest). This time out, Fuest cowrote the screenplay with Robert Blees.

figurine on either end of Victoria's glass coffin, which Phibes puts in the sarcophagus for safekeeping.

A horny expedition member who has been watching the silhouette of Diana undressing in her tent is lured away into the night by Vulnavia, who seats him in a strange couch the shape of a giant scorpion. Once he is there, Phibes flicks a switch and the hapless member finds himself trapped. Phibes takes the key for his release and puts it in a ceramic statue of Nipper, the dog in the famous RCA symbol. The trap proves even more fiendish when in breaking the dog to get the key, the victim finds he has unleashed a swarm of scorpions which crawl all over him and sting him. (Fuest even has shots of them entering his shirt and pants before he begins screaming.) The whole scene is played like a parody of the vamp movies of the late '20s with an Arabic setting, à la *The Shiek.*

Meanwhile, the Law makes its appearance in the desert, as it tries to locate the Biederbeck expedition. When Trout asks his superior if he thinks he knows where they are, Waverly replies, "I don't think – I know," to which Trout responds sardonically, "I don't think you know either, sir."

The expedition, rather than getting scared away, comes across the sarcophagus in which both the key and Victoria are hidden and takes it away, enraging Phibes further. Biederbeck discovers and takes the key. Having discovered what he has truly been seeking, he decides that Diana should be escorted to safety by the police and the other members of the party while he finishes up a few things. While Biederbeck is shown as apparently callous to the deaths of the other members of his party, Fuest establishes that he truly loves Diana, who is becoming increasingly puzzled by this other side her fiancé is exhibiting. Biederbeck assigns Baker (Lewis Flander) to guard the sarcophagus.

Fuest dares to play with our awareness that this is a movie by having Phibes create a desert sandstorm using a movie wind machine. Vulnavia straps the unfortunate Baker to his cot while he is asleep and Phibes sets up a device which squeezes together, crushing everything but Baker's astonished head.

In the morning, the expedition finds what remains of Baker, but both the sarcophagus and their Arab workers are gone. Scotsman Hackett (Gerald Sim) discovers a truck by the temple and uses it to try and drive Diana to safety. En route, he sees a British flag and hears the bagpipes and drums of the Scottish Highlanders on the other side of the huge sand dune. Stopping the car to seek aid, he discovers instead some of Phibes' clockwork figures. Returning to the car, he finds Diana is gone. He is then sandblasted from a hole in the dashboard that Phibes somehow managed to rig up.

Hackett's truck comes crashing back into camp with Hackett's skull blasted clean. When Waverly, unaware of Hackett's demise, wants to know what Hackett has to say for himself, Trout offers, "He has nothing to say, sir."

As in the previous film, the stylish and preposterous execution methods coupled with an undercutting absurdity help keep the Phibes films enjoyable romps, in contrast to the somewhat inventive but unpleasantly grim deaths manufactured in the *Friday the 13th* series, which replaces Fuest's wit with simple gore. Nevertheless, both types of films offer a body count and promise numerous inventive murders will be depicted, making the Phibes films precursors to the far less stylish slasher films of the '80s.

Biederbeck, Trout and Waverly all rush to the ruined temple, but only Biederbeck makes it through Phibes' secret entrance, where he discovers that Phibes has set up a fiendish bargain. Biederbeck must give up the key to the gate to the River of Life or his beloved Diana, who, strapped down to a wooden raft, will rise on the waters of the tide and be impaled on the prong-like tongues of a dozen serpent figures in the trap's ceiling (an eye-

catching and beautifully surreal touch). Biederbeck is able to stop the onslaught of the deadly serpents with a board from the raft used as a wedge
but ultimately has to give up the key to save Diana while Phibes paddles Victoria down to the River of Life like the figure of Charon on the River Styx
(yet another piece of iconography that Fuest wittily uses in the film).

Having saved Diana in the nick of time, Biederbeck rushes back as the
gates closed and he is locked out. Without a refill of his elixir of life, he rapidly
ages before the astonished eyes of Trout, Waverly and Diana. Phibes happily
paddles off into the darkness while "Somewhere Over the Rainbow" swells
on the soundtrack. (Unfortunately, the videocasette version apparently
could not secure rights for the song, though it is still used briefly at the end
of *Abominable*, and has music from elsewhere in the film substituted in its
place, ruining Fuest's final comic coda for the film. Phibes literally has gone
off to the other side where his dream will come true.)

AIP had planned to make a third Phibes film, but plans did not go very
far, as the second film's box office proved disappointing. For the third film,
Fuest recalled in the Irvin interview "one of the ideas was to have Phibes
fight Adolf Hitler; now that would have been really interesting!"

Fuest was offered *Theater of Blood* but turned it down, not wanting to
be typed as a director of Vincent Price movies in which nine people died.
The film, directed by Douglas Hickox, turned out to be one of Price's best,
giving him a chance to show off all his strengths as a hammy actor who tries
to commit suicide when he is not given an acting award. He then becomes
a god to a cult of freaks who help him track down and murder his critics,
each death done as a variation on a scene from Shakespeare. The witty
screenplay was by Anthony Greville-Bell, and Shakespearean scholars will
discover some delightful foreshadowing buried in the dialogue. In addition
to Price's fine performance, the film has a sterling cast of fine British performers including Diana Rigg, Coral Browne (Mrs. Price), Jack Hawkins,
Arthur Lowe, Robert Morley and Dennis Price. The plot has long been a
favorite of filmmakers.

For his next project, Fuest selected an adaptation of Michael Moorcock's *The Final Programme*, released in the United States as *The Last
Days of Man on Earth*. In an interview in *Cinefantastique* with Tim Lucas,
Fuest said that he chose the project because, while he didn't want to do
another horror film right away, he was attracted to fantasy of the sort found
in *Phibes*. *The Final Programme* seemed to have the right elements, even
though, as Fuest said,

> The film is nothing to do with the novel. I read the script treatment
> of the novel, 286 pages, and I couldn't understand it. Then I found *The
> Nature of Castastrophe*, which is a book of other people's interpretations
> of a Cornelius saga. There is a marvelous story among them called "The

Last Hurrah of the Golden Horde" and, upon reading it, I suddenly saw a way in which we could actually scythe through the script, because both Moorcock's book and all the scripts that were coming in had no dramatic thrust. They were too extraordinary, unfilmic and untheatrical. Out of sheer desperation, I elected to do the script myself. So I just sat down and began with Cornelius' father being buried, which allowed us to know where we were and went from there–playing my cards like in a poker game. Up to that moment in time, I had just bumbled along until I read this *kitsch* of a thing that was so outrageous and written in such a way that the story cuts were like cinema cuts. It was these that showed me how to make the film.

The Final Programme was the first of a series of novels about Jerry Cornelius, one of the incarnations of Moorcock's the Eternal Champion, a heroic figure who has a special weapon and is constantly embroiled in a struggle with an evil brother over his sister. "The Last Hurrah of the Golden Horde" was a humorous *pastiche* of the series by fellow science fiction writer Norman Spinrad and it sends up the character. Fuest was obviously attracted to the idea of doing another send-up and followed suit in his screenplay, much to the displeasure of the story's original author, Moorcock.

Moorcock originally sold the rights to the novel and its sequels to Sandy Lieberson of Goodtimes Enterprises because he had been impressed with *Performance*, which Lieberson produced. After others had attempted to do so, Fuest wrote a script which Nat Cohen, the head of EMI, liked, and that got the film financing. Moorcock did not like Fuest's script and concocted one of his own, inserting a clearer plot than the book had. However, Fuest rejected Moorcock's script and when filming went back to using his own.

Said Moorcock in John Brunas' *Future Tense*:

> The result was that he ended up with about three hours of film, two hours of which were primarily reaction shots–all of the stuff that I'd crossed out with a pen was back in there. When it came to editing it, of course, it was all out again but by then they'd spent thousands of quid shooting it.... None of the actors knew what they were supposed to be doing–and they had a lot of good actors in it. By the time the film was halfway through the actors were all coming up to me and saying: "Look, what the hell is it all about because *he's* not telling us." And the emphasis of the film kept shifting all the time, because the actors didn't know if it was supposed to be serious or a James Bond type of film or a take-off or what. The final sequences were, by and large, the best ones–they certainly had a lot more of the spirit of the book largely because they gave up. Most of the good bits in it were the little cameo parts that the actors did themselves. For instance, that joke-fight sequence in the underground cavern between Finch and the villain where Jerry shouts: "Miss Brunner, I'm losing!" and all that sort of stuff–that all came about after Jon Finch and I talked about it."

Fuest himself tells a very surreal story about the meeting he took to get the film financed in his interview with Sam Irvin in *Bizarre*. Faced by a huge group of reserved men in conservative attire, Fuest began describing the plot. Though he was very excited, acting out the parts and "jumping all over the room," he got little reaction. But then came the breakthrough:

> After a while, I came to the subject of the needle gun which is in the picture. Suddenly another man said, "Ah, a needle gun!" He was involved with toy manufacturing, and he was envisioning a toy needle gun to merchandise in connection with the release of the picture. He then said, "What sort of noise does it make when you shoot it?" I said, "I suppose it goes something like "pphhiittt." Then he said, "Oh no, it should go more like "chheewwww." All of a sudden, this entire table that had been completely inanimate, began making gun noises; each man had a different one, and each thought they had the best. All they were interested in was the wretched noise! I just smiled and stood there in awe.

Part of the reason that Fuest was able to get financing was that by designing his own sets, he promised that he could deliver the final film for only $600,000. Fuest accomplished this by constructing sets out of huge building blocks which could be reordered and used again and again throughout the film. Often times, as in the scene where Jon Finch playing Jerry Cornelius is in a hospital, an entire set could be suggested by only a few objects, much as Welles did in *Citizen Kane*. The hospital set, for example, has nothing more than a window, a bed, Cornelius, a nurse, a nightstand and a screen in front of a nondescript background.

The book, one of Moorcock's earliest, is a hodgepodge of various material, and the film reflects this quality with its fractured narrative. As a result, there are many imaginative scenes and bits, but the film fails to build or generate much excitement. Nevertheless, it has become a cult film and has a unique flavor quite different from the typical science fiction programmer as well as dollops of Fuest's quirky sense of humor.

The film opens up by cutting between what seems like Eskimos preparing a body (Jerry's father) for cremation and Jerry Cornelius (Jon Finch, who has given excellent performances in such films as Hitchcock's *Frenzy* and Polanski's *Macbeth*) listening to a Brahmin doctor, Professor Hira (Fuest stalwart Hugh Griffith), who predicts the end of the world as we know it when the 2,000-year-old dark age comes to an end. Dr. Smiles (Graham Crowden) at the funeral asks what Cornelius' future plans are. He responds that he plans to blow up his father's house.

"What about your brother Frank?" asks Smiles. "I understand he never leaves the place."

"That's why the idea appeals to me so much," returns Cornelius with a slight smile.

Fuest's film plays like a parody of the spy genre, with Cornelius as a combination of a brilliant special agent and a simple Everyman. Cornelius wears only black (except for a white frilly shirt), eats only chocolate biscuits (British for cookies), has black fingernails, and is a former Nobel Prize winner.

Fuest adds a great deal of background information on this decadent future world from time to time. For example, as Cornelius sets off a flare to attract the attention of John (Harry Andrews), the faithful family retainer, the radio blares the news that $600 million has been paid to the five remaining survivors of America's accidental bombing of Amsterdam. John shows up in a boat and informs Jerry that his sister Catherine has been drugged and asleep for seven weeks and is being held prisoner in the family's island estate.

As Cornelius makes his way through London to a weapons dealer, Major Lindberg (Sterling Hayden, who was instructed to play his character like a "used car dealer in a Hieronymus Bosch painting"), he passes a huge pile of car hulks that help suggest the overall decay of the landscape. Cornelius schemes with Lindberg to buy an F-14 to take his sister Catherine to safety in Cambodia.

From there he goes to Emmett's Coin Casino which resembles a giant pinball table. There he is approached by and kisses a Miss Dazzle (Julie Ege in a cameo) and meets with top assassin Shades (Ron Lacey, later memorable as one of the main Nazis in *Raiders of the Lost Ark*) from whom he wishes to buy some napalm. "For what purpose?" asks Shades. "Matters domestic," Cornelius cryptically replies. Originally, author Moorcock was to have a cameo in this scene as well, but it was cut from the final print. Neither Shades nor Miss Dazzle is heard from again either.

A meeting is arranged between Cornelius and Miss Brunner (Jenny Runacre in a striking performance) and her scientist friends, Dr. Smiles and his associates (George Coulouis and Basil Henson), who were all former associates of Cornelius' father. Miss Brunner is a computer specialist who is working on "the final programme," an attempt to fuse all human knowledge into one individual. The scientists are all desperately seeking a piece of microfilm that was left in Cornelius' father's safe, and they need Jerry to help them get past the house's defenses and to this safe. Cornelius arrives to instruct them where they are all to meet later that evening.

The scientists arrive, leaving behind Dimitri (Gilles Milinaire), who is an important part of their immortality programme. Approaching the house on foot, they set off some lights designed to cause epilepsy while a sound is emitted which destroys the inner ear. Cornelius turns it off before any damage is done and opens a door with his fingerprint. Turning to the others, he adds cryptically, "Just a thought. By the time we get there, he'll have activated the whole house."

While he and Miss Brunner take an elevator to the house's control room in hopes that Frank (Derrick O'Connor) might be passed out in a drug-induced haze and make their job simple, the scientists are instructed to remain behind and not move. Of course, they begin exploring, setting off some colored gas which drives them into another room. They find a door made out of a vertical chess set and a clue on the piano as to how to open the door. However, when they move one of the pieces, one of the scientists is pricked by a long steel needle which pops out, though the door does open. They find themselves in a series of brightly colored balloon-like corridors, from which Cornelius finally rescues them. These scenes seem almost like a surreal *hommage* to the Patrick McGoohan series *The Prisoner*.

John was supposed to have taken Catherine to safety before the invasion, but Jerry finds John on the floor. It seems Frank has taken Catherine and shot John, putting Catherine "back to bed." Cornelius finds her in the bedroom with needle marks on her arm. He takes out his needle gun, suspecting that Frank must be nearby. He is, and the pair begin to fire at each other. "Throw out your needle and come out with your veins clear," instructs Jerry as Frank fights back. Unfortunately, the skirmish ends disastrously when Jerry shoots what he thinks to be Frank only to kill Catherine (there are overtones that their relationship is not only obsessive but also incestuous).

"I'll see you in the next time phase," Frank calls out. "Sorry the family reunion has not been a great success."

However, Frank reckons without Miss Brunner, who proves more than his match, tossing him gamely about the room and threatening to deprive him of his drug supply if he does not turn over the needed microfilm. Frank retrieves the microfilm, but makes off with it himself when he shuts Miss Brunner and the scientists out on the other side of the transparent impenetrable sliding door.

Cornelius wakes up in a hospital, still grieved by the loss of Catherine. From a nurse, he discovers that he's in the Sunnydale Nursing Home, but the nurse insists that he go back to sleep over Cornelius' objections. "It's much easier to run a hospital with all the patients sleeping," she says sensibly.

Miss Brunner picks him up and they go out to an elegant dinner at the ringside of a mud wrestling palace. A waitress doing a Judy Holiday imitation comes by and offers them some drinks. Cornelius selects some industrial waste to drink but asks if it is from the right bank. The waitress complains she does not know what side the factory is on. They are met by a girl named Jenny, whom Cornelius asks, "Hello darling, how are you fixed destinywise?" Jenny has a preference for Miss Brunner's company, and they go back to Jerry's flat.

As Jerry prepares to go to sleep, he sees a naked Jenny playing the piano for Miss Brunner and assumes they are about to engage in a lesbian relationship. Instead, Miss Brunner gestures Jenny over and absorbs her. The next morning when Cornelius asks what happened to Jenny, Brunner replies, "She got absorbed in somebody else."

"How did you find her?" Cornelius politely inquires.

"Delicious."

Tracking down Baxter (Patrick Magee), an old associate of Jerry's father who had stolen his secrets and sold them, Cornelius and Brunner see Frank meet with Baxter. Frank wants to sell Baxter the microfilm, though he does not know what is on it. He simply figures that if so many people took so much trouble to get it, it must be valuable. While Jerry and Frank get involved in a shootout chase scene, Miss Brunner absorbs Dr. Baxter. Fuest comically cuts to a lemon squeezer to indicate that the life force has been squeezed out of him. (When Miss Brunner absorbs someone, she takes possession of his knowledge and talents.)

Jerry finally kills Frank and Brunner retrieves the microfilm. Looking for Baxter, Cornelius asks where he is. "Oh, he's somewhere inside," Brunner nonchalantly replies. "Inside who?" Jerry asks, catching on. "It's the way I have of getting the best out of people," Miss Brunner replies. "What do you do with the bones?" asks an annoyed Cornelius, who then takes a swig of wine and adds, "I hate long goodbyes – so piss off!"

Instead, Cornelius finds himself accompanying Miss Brunner on a balloon trip to Lapland. They land at his father's secret laboratory there, much to the relief of the scientists who declare that there are only 45 minutes left. (To what?) Jerry admires their German K class submarine, possibly left over from *The Land That Time Forgot*, which Moorcock had scripted for AIP based on the Edgar Rice Burroughs novel. (The excuse is that the laboratory was an old Nazi base left over from when the Nazis were trying to find a polar entrance to the center of the world.)

Regarding the sub, Cornelius says, "I had one a few years ago."

"What happened to it?" asks Miss Brunner.

"It sank."

"I thought it was supposed to," she returns.

The Germanic background is also called to mind when someone mentions the concept of Götterdämmerung, that is, the Twilight of the Gods.

Fuest keeps the jokes coming thick and fast. A sign on a computer reads: "The Most Complex Computer in the World – Do Not Touch." Jerry, upon being asked about a brain suspended in a fish tank à la *Donovan's Brain*, replies, "It's going to be a brain-washing machine," while casually feeding it bits of chocolate biscuit.

The brain in the fish tank is only one of several. The scientists have assembled all the best brains in Europe (sans the rest of their bodies) to compile the sum of human knowledge which they have fed into the computer, and now they want to feed it into a human brain. For the requisite energy this process will take, they have been storing solar energy over the past six weeks in a special chamber. (Lapland was chosen as a location because the sun does not set there for long periods of time.) The microfilm was the link between the two purposes of the final programme, to create the all-purpose human being, a hermaphrodite that perpetuates itself into immortality to be the new messiah.

Knowing that one brain alone could not hold this knowledge, they planned to use two by combining Miss Brunner with Dimitri; however, the microfilm indicates that Jerry Cornelius should merge with Miss Brunner to create this "perfect" being. Miss Brunner responds by writing "Goodbye" in lipstick on Dimitri's glass cage and turning up the heat, but Dimitri escapes and attacks his rival Cornelius, who, when he realizes he is losing, calls for help from Miss Brunner. She shoots Dimitri, but not before Cornelius receives a grappling hook in the arm. He passes out and then awakes in the chamber with Miss Brunner preparing to make love to him as the power is unleashed and they are combined.

From here, Fuest gives us a distorted point-of-view shot from the new "messiah," which surveys the laboratory in a wreckage. It is the end of an age; time to start building anew. The "perfect" being turns out to be a Neanderthal man with Cornelius' features and Brunner's fingernails who addresses the last remaining scientist in a Bogart accent – "See you around, sweetheart" – before walking on water into the sunset, observing that it is "a very tasty world."

The ending is a total send-up of Moorcock's ending and a subtle *hommage* to the apes in *2001* as well. As this rundown of the plot indicates, the film is suffused with incongruity and absurdity, including such throwaway bits as Cornelius' complaint that Rome is not the same without the Vatican. The film, however, proved too different to succeed with audiences in either England or America. Roger Corman's New World Pictures, which released it as *The Last Days of Man on Earth*, did an excellent job of cutting seven minutes out of the British version, mostly speeding up transitions, without removing any essential footage. There are reports that the trimming was done so that Corman could save on postage by having one less reel of film to mail around to theaters running it.

While the quirky final product displeased Moorcock and many cinemagoers as well, I find *The Final Programme* an inventive and sometimes almost endearing excursion into low-budget science fiction, with some marvelous clipped dialogue that gives the proceedings a flippant, zesty, though human flavor. Fuest is better with caricatures, but he does have a talent for creating ingenious eccentrics and adding both comic and visual flair.

Unfortunately, both were sadly lacking in Fuest's next film, the disastrous *The Devil's Rain*. Sandy Howard, the film's producer, had originally approached Fuest to do *The Neptune Factor*, a colossal turkey starring Ernest Borgnine, Ben Gazzara and Walter Pidgeon. Fuest pointed out that if Howard went ahead with his plan to create the special effects in an aquarium using normal fish blown up to huge size, it would be a disaster, and in fact it was. (The film was even appropriately retitled *The Neptune Disaster* in some engagements.)

Howard next offered Fuest *The Devil's Rain*, promising a bigger effects budget. Borgnine was again to be featured, along with other "name" actors. Fuest accepted, and shooting began in Mexico with a $1.5 millon budget. At 29 days for shooting, it was one of Fuest's shortest projects; even on lower-budget films he generally had at least six weeks. The higher budget did not help the film, as Fuest noted in the Irvin interview:

> I, unfortunately, am not very proud of the film. . . . The only thing better about it is that my salary was larger. . . . I really did not understand the script. . . . The whole film is far too commercial; nothing really happens except the spectacular melting scene at the end.

Sadly, Fuest's criticisms are on target. *The Devil's Rain* proved to be an unappetizing mess, though the sequence at the end where the demons' faces melt into a pizza-like ooze is fun in a bad-film sort of way. However, gone is the Fuestian humor that had enlivened his productions since *And Now the Darkness*, and the result is largely tedium.

The film opens appropriately enough on a painting by Fuest's favorite, Hieronymous Bosch, but flags quickly downhill from there. It unfolds the tale of a satanic cult which has systemically destroyed the descendants of one family line for generations because an ancestor had stolen a book with the names of the members of the coven inscribed in blood. Mark Preston (William Shatner) comes seeking his mother (Ida Lupino), who has been kidnapped by the devil cult, tracking it down and finally confronting the cult's leader, Corbis (Ernest Borgnine in a memorably bad performance; others who are wasted in the cast include Eddie Albert, Keenan Wynn, Tom Skerritt and, in a bit part, John Travolta, who had his participation played up when the film was rereleased following the success of *Saturday Night Fever*). Sadly, this sodden disaster has been, apart from a French film unreleased in this country, Fuest's last theatrical outing.

Fuest seems to have vanished into oblivion. Too bad, as he made a trio of quite enjoyable films and showed promise for making more, establishing a personal style he could truly call his own.

Lucio Fulci (1927–   )

I Ladri; Ragazzi del Juke-Box (1959); *Urlatori alla Sbarra* (1960); *Colpo Gobbo all'Italiana; I Due della Legione Straniera; Le Massaggiatrici* (1962); *Gli Imbroglioni; Uno Strano Tipo* (1963); *Secret Agents 002; I Due Evasi di Sing Sing; The Maniacs* (1964); *002: Moon Mission* (aka *Operazione Luna*); *I Due Pericoli Pubblici; Come Inguainiammo l'Esercito* (1965); *Come Svaligiammo la Banca d'Italia; I Due Para; Tempo di Massacro* (aka *The Brute and the Beast*) (1966); *Come Rubammo la Bomba Atomica; Il Lungo, il Corto, il Gatto* (1967); *Perversion Story; Operazione: San Pietro* (1968); *Una sull'Altra; Beatrice Cenci* (1969); *Schizoid* (aka *Lizard in a Woman's Skin, Una Lucertola con la Pelle di Donna,* 1970); *All' Onorevole Piacciono le Donne* (1971); *The Long Night of Exorcism; Zanna Bianca* (aka *White Fang*); *Non Si Sevizia un Paperino* (aka *Don't Torture the Duckling*) (1972); *Il Ritorno di Zanna Bianca* (1974); *Dracula in the Provinces; Four for the Apocalypse* (1975); *The Psychic* (1976); *Sella d'Argento* (1978); *Zombi 2* (1979); *City of the Living Dead* (aka *Twilight of the Dead*); *The Beyond; The Black Cat* (1980); *The House by the Cemetery* (1981); *The New York Ripper; Contraband; Manhattan Baby* (1982); Conquest (aka *Mace the Outcast*); *I Guerrieri dell'Anno 2072* (1983); *Murderock Uccide a Passo di Danza* (aka *Murder Rock,* 1984); *Il Miele del Diavolo* (aka *The Devil's Honey,* 1986); *Aenigma* (1987); *Zombi 3; Quando Alice Ruppe lo Specchio* (aka *Touch of Death*); *I Fantasmi di Sodoma* (aka *Ghosts of Sodom*); *Demonia* (1988); *Un Gatto nel Cervello; Voci del Profondo* (aka *Voices from Beyond,* 1990).

TELEVISION: *La Dolce Casa degli Orrori; La Casa del Tempo* (1990).

Lucio Fulci spearheaded the growth of the Italian zombie-cannibal movie by whipping up a quick sequel to Romero's *Dawn of the Dead,* titled *Zombi* in Italy, with a gross-out low-budget sequel titled *Zombi 2* (aka *Zombie Flesheaters* or simply *Zombie* in the United States). Fulci had been grinding out low-budget films in Italy for years before hitting paydirt. *Schizoid* was the first horror film of his to receive any extensive release here in the United States.

Schizoid (aka *A Lizard in a Woman's Skin*) exploits nudity and horror in its tale of a strange woman (played by Florinda Bolkan, aka José Soara Bulco) who is haunted by dreams where she pushes her way past naked couples to stab a woman who caresses her. When her father (Leo Genn) receives a blackmail threat, she begins to wonder if the dream could have been a reality, only to be arrested for a crime similar to the one in her dream. Is it all part of a plot on the part of her cheating husband (Jean Sorel)?

Long-time horror film fans will easily guess, having been down these corridors before. The film is chiefly notable for its dream-like quality and for
the explicitness of some of its images. There are some impressive dream images involving dogs with their stomachs sliced open, bats with blood-
dripping fangs, and sightless zombies roaming about. The ending, however,
is conventional, as Carol is revealed to have killed the woman to cover up
the fact that they had a lesbian relationship, and Fulci's penchant for zooming and panning rapidly causes more stomach distress than Rambaldi's
effects.

    Though Fulci has become a busy practicioner in the horror field and oc-
casionally shows a flair for setting up suspense scenes, he never really has
become a good director. Perhaps his most notable directorial trait is that he
will linger on an unpleasant event much longer than most directors, until
the audience gets beside itself wondering just when a particularly unpleasant bit of business is going to end. (Most American horror films have their
moments of extreme violence trimmed due to MPAA restrictions, so they
will set up a quick shock and then move on. Not Fulci; he will take a horrific
situation and continue milking it long after it has reached the apex of its
effectiveness.)

    Bolkan also appeared in *Long Night of Exorcism* (aka *Don't Torture the
Duckling*) as a gypsy woman who is killed because she is blamed for a series
of killings actually perpetrated by a young priest with homosexual urges.
The film is filled with unpleasant stereotypes and scenes of horrendous
violence. The Italian *giallo* films had started competing for how bloody they
could get, and this was one of Fulci's entries in the competition.

    With Pupi Avati, who also coscripted Lamberto Bava's *Macabre* and
went on to direct horror films of his own, Fulci cowrote *Dracula in the Provinces* (aka *Il Cavaliere Costante Nicosia Demoniaco ovvero Dracula in
Brianza*) and directed this Dracula spoof. When Lando Buzzanca is bitten
by Dragulescu (John Steiner), he fears he might catch not vampirism but
homosexuality, and en route finds that drinking blood cures what ails him.
Then, in an elaborate political metaphor, he becomes the rich capitalist who
lives off the blood of his workers, who are compelled to donate to a blood
bank near his factory.

    The Psychic (filmed as *Sette Note in Nero*) proved an exceedingly dull
horror thriller with frequent and repetitive zooms into Jennifer O'Neill's
eyes whenever she experiences a psychic vision of someone's death. The
scene of her mother's suicide, jumping off a cliff and smashing her head on
the way down, is the most effective, but from there on, the viewer is likely
to head to slumberland as O'Neill tries convincing the authorities and
warding off her own death. The film's dialogue is minimal, but O'Neill wandering around a villa just is not inherently cinematic.

    Fulci's biggest breakthrough came with *Zombie* (aka *Island of the Living*

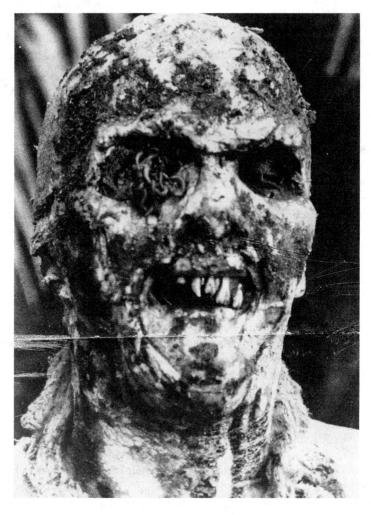

This worm-faced zombie was the poster boy for Lucio Fulci's Zombie, *an example of Fulci's heavy-handed and unsubtle approach to gory zombie films. "We Are Going to Eat You" the ads promised; "Disgust You" is more likely.*

Dead; Zombie Flesh Eaters). It was filmed as *Zombi 2* to cash in on the huge success of *Dawn of the Dead* in Italy, and it helped open the floodgates for a whole passel of imitation films about cannibalistic zombies.

When a sailboat returns to New York with only zombies onboard, Tisa Farrow sails to the island of Matul in search of her father, accompanied by a reporter (Ian McCulloch) and another couple. Technical credits are not very good on the film, which was mainly noted for its stomach-turning gore including a prolonged shot where a woman's eye is impaled on a long splinter and a ridiculous sequence where a zombie attacks a great white shark. The film may have lacked finesse, but it was an almost guaranteed gross-out, and because it became a hit, it established that there was an audience out there for these kind of splatter movies.

Fulci first studied film at the Experimental Film Center in Rome with teachers like Antonioni and Visconti. He claims he passed the oral exam to be admited to the center by being brave enough to tell Visconti to his face that he had borrowed shots in *Ossessione* from Jean Renoir films.

He later became an assistant director on Marcel Lherbier's *Last Days of Pompeii* before becoming a writer of comedy scripts. (He claims to have worked with Stefano Steno on *Tempi Duri per i Vampiri*, aka *Uncle Was a Vampire* or *Hard Times for Vampires* with Christopher Lee.)

Fulci's first film was about a thief and it flopped. He would try his hand at comedies, westerns, and rock 'n' roll movies before venturing into the horror field with the *giallo* film *Perversion Story*, which did not have any fantastic elements, making *Schizoid* his first film of note. (Fulci claims that Rambaldi's disemboweled dogs were so realistic that he would have gone to jail for cruelty to animals if Rambaldi had not been able to produce artificial ones.) Fulci formed his basic crew while working on *The Psychic*, and with the success of *Zombie*, he was off and running.

Said Fulci in an interview with Robert Schlockoff published in *Starburst*:

> For a fantastic film, you need not only a strong team, but also people who know everything about technique, as it is particularly difficult to do special effects. My associates and myself get along together very well and work in a totally relaxed atmosphere. When we finished shooting *Zombi 2*, I said we had just made a horror film classic, without knowing it, and, to some extent, having fun like a circle of friends. I say that in reaction to those who think a film can't be successful if it is not made under some tension.

Fulci claims to be more interested in sensations and tension than horror scenes in and of themselves, and his films bear this out. However, this does not exempt them from containing a good deal of gratuitous violence, though Fulci denies this charge, saying in *Starburst*, "[C]ensorship is wrong about my films being an incentive to violence. Far from participating in this violence, the spectator, on the contrary, is rid of it, freed from horrors he holds within himself, the film being the catalyst for this liberation."

Fulci followed up *Zombie* with *City of the Dead* (aka *The Gates of Hell, Twilight of the Dead, Paura nella Città dei Morti Viventi*), which is set in Lovecraftian Dunwich. A priest commits suicide and as a result the gates of hell open up and brain-eating zombies emerge.

The film does feature a rather intense scene where Peter Bell

(Christopher George) realizes that a woman named Mary (Katriona Mac-Coll) has been buried alive and attempts to dig up her grave with a pickaxe. What makes the scene intense is the fact that the pickaxe keeps penetrating Mary's coffin, missing her forehead by inches. Fulci sadistically plays with his audience as we do not know if Bell will be her rescuer or put the final nail in her coffin, figuratively speaking. Bell later heads off to investigate what is happening in Dunwich. The main setpieces include a woman who vomits up her intestines and a father who drills a hole through the head of a retarded boy he is fearful and suspicious of (which Fulci claims is a commentary on fascism).

Regarding the scenes where worms rain down or the woman expunges her insides, Fulci commented in the *Starburst* interview:

> It was not easy; actors would not quite accept all those worms stuck on their faces – we used thousands of them, over twenty pounds! As for the bowel vomiting sequence, we had to use the tripe of a freshly slashed lamb (for after ten minutes, it dries up and becomes unusable), which the actress actually swallowed, and vomited afterwards. For close-ups where the bowels rush out, it was of course a doll containing a pump.

The Gates of Hell was followed up with *The Beyond*, which even the director describes as a plotless film containing nothing more than a hotel, people, and zombies coming from the beyond. The extremely gross makeups are by Gianetto de Rossi; Katherine MacColl and David Warbeck are the nominal stars. The basic concept echoes Michael Winner's *The Sentinel* in that a particular hotel stands at one of the seven entrances to hell.

Fulci acknowledges that his films are "pessimistic," but said in the *Starburst* interview that "humor and tragedy always join, anyway. If one emphasizes the tragic side of things, it may have a comical effect. Everthing considered, having directed so many comedies when I started my film career turns out to be very useful for my true cinema, the cinema of the Fantastic."

The Black Cat, which Fulci describes as a tribute to Roger Corman, was at least a respite from his zombie epics. Mr. Miles (Patrick Magee) is trying to tape record messages from the dead, while Inspector Gorley (David Warbeck) is investigating a series of mysterious deaths. Visiting tourist Jill Travers (Mimsy Farmer) solves the ridiculous mystery by establishing that the murders were committed by Miles' cat. Miles and the cat battle for mental supremacy and then the cat claims its next victim, Travers, who foolishly assumed that Miles must have been behind it all.

This was followed by *The House by the Cemetery* in which the innocence of a young boy (Giovanni Frezza) is contrasted with the evil of Dr. Freudstein (Giovanni de Nari), a zombie mad scientist who sustains himself on victims that have stumbled upon or rented his house. The boy keeps seeing the

This is Dr. Freudstein in House by the Cemetery *(1982). From the makeup, you can see why he spends the entire film down in a dark basement as director Fulci veers between suspense and tedium once again.*

apparition of a girl who beckons him to come and play until he finally uncovers Dr. Freudstein and his terrible secret. Bats attack, floors crack open and crush people, and there is even a scene where the boy's father takes an axe to the cellar door while Dr. Freudstein presses the boy's head against it so that the axe just barely misses him.

The bizarre ending, in which the boy ends up in limbo with the girl, leaves us wondering if everything might not have just been the boy's imagination. While the audience may want the boy saved and spared, living in limbo is not much of an existence and Freudstein is not dispatched, so if he does exist, he will merely have to wait for the next victims to come ambling along. The film ends on a quotation from Henry James: "Are children monsters, or would monsters be children?" which does nothing to clarify things.

Fulci apparently cares nothing for story, seeing his films as little more than a succession of often repulsive images. His films have the illogic of a nightmare, but considering their uneven nature, Fulci seems to be breaking every rule of coherent narrative more out of ignorance than in any way which would accentuate a meaning. He knows his audience requires shock and gore, so these he gives them, but little else.

Fulci departed from horror to make the equally nonsensical sword and sorcery film *Conquest* in which a pair of warriors have endless and tedious battles with furry monsters sent out by the sorceress Ocron (Sabina Siani, star of several Italian fantasy films). The film does contain such horror touches as various monsters, a crucifixion, and Ocron eating the brains of her victims. Siani is attractive and looks appealing in the nude, but she can do nothing with this role, which climaxes when she is killed and then turns into a wolf and runs off into the sunset with a mate. (Say what?)

Unfortunately, the final result is more exasperating than amusing, if amusement indeed was Fulci's intent. The last Fulci films that I have seen were *The New York Ripper* and *The Possessed* (aka *Manhattan Baby*). *The Possessed* has a young woman possessed by an Egyptian deity after her father invades a tomb and is struck blind. For a Fulci movie, it is surprisingly goreless, but typically befuddling. In *The New York Ripper*, any woman who dresses in a remotely sexy manner has some portion (eyes, breasts) slashed, and a detective warns a husband that sexually free women are just asking for it. The film is nauseating in more ways than one, but especially in its "moralistic" tone and misogynist treatment of women. This is the kind of movie which can almost make a Jesus Franco film look good. Despite occasional flashes of talent, Fulci remains one of the worst and most repulsive horror directors ever.

John Gilling (1912–1984)

Escape from Broadmoor (1948); *A Matter of Murder* (1949); *No Trace; Blackout* (1950); *The Quiet Woman* (1951); *The Frightened Man; Mother Riley Meets the Vampire* (aka *My Son, the Vampire); The Voice of Merrill* (aka *Murder Will Out*) (1952); *Recoil; Three Steps to the Gallows; Escape by Night; The Deadly Nightshade* (1953); *White Fire; Double Exposure; The Embezzler* (1954); *Tiger by the Tail; The Gilded Cage* (1955); *The Gamma People; Odongo* (1956); *High Flight; Interpol* (1957); *The Man Inside* (1958); *Bandit of Zhobe; Idle on Parade* (1959); *The Flesh and the Fiends* (aka *Mania; Psycho Killers; The Fiendish Ghouls); The Challenge* (aka *It Takes a Thief*) (1960); *Fury at Smuggler's Bay; The Shadow of the Cat* (1961); *The Pirates of Blood River* (1962); *The Scarlet Blade* (aka *The Crimson Blade*) (1963); *Panic; The Brigand of Kandahar* (1965); *The Plague of the Zombies; The Reptile; Where the Bullets Fly; The Night Caller* (aka *Blood Beast from Outer Space*) (1966); *The Mummy's Shroud* (1967); *Cruz del Diablo* (1970).
TELEVISION: *Douglas Fairbanks Presents; The Saint, Department S; Gideon.*

A director and a screenwriter, John Gilling had a long but not particularly distinguished career that included its share of horror films, most of which had their offbeat aspects or moments, but which nevertheless were not terribly different from the run-of-the-mill horror films being exhibited at the time. He is perhaps best remembered as the director of *The Plague of the Zombies* and *The Reptile*, both of which received reputations that were not warranted by the films themselves.

Born on May 29, 1912, in Great Britain, Gilling entered the British film industry as an assistant director in 1933. He had left school at the age of 15 and spent three miserable years as a clerk for the Asiatic Petroleum Company. He traveled to the United States for a brief period where he worked at whatever he could, including extra work, singing and acting. On his return to England, his uncle W. P. Kellino was able to get him a job as his assistant. He began to try his hand at scriptwriting in 1938 but was not too successful at it initially.

In 1946, Gilling wrote a film called *Black Memory*, which he did not think was very good; nevertheless it managed to be a fairly successful support feature and launched the career of actor Sid James. Scripting *The House of Darkness*, Laurence Harvey's first movie, led to scripting *Escape*

From Broadmoor, the first film Gilling was also to direct. According to an interview with Gilling in *Little Shoppe of Horrors #4*, "The film starred Victoria Hopper and John Lemusier and cost 6,000 pounds to produce."

Gilling's first horror film was *Mother Riley Meets the Vampire*, one of a series of films starring comedian Arthur Lucan as Mother Riley. Alex Gordon tried to distribute the film in the United States under the title *Vampire Over London* and eventually it was released in reedited form in 1964 as *My Son, the Vampire*, a title taken from a comic ditty by Alan Sherman which was added to the beginning of the film. The prime reason for interest in the film (as a comedy it is very unfunny) is that it gave Bela Lugosi one of his rare roles as a vampire, or at least a man who thinks he is a vampire.

The plot concerns Scotland Yard's attempts to locate a man called Von Housen, who is also known as the Vampire. Von Housen thinks himself the "earthly reproduction" of his ancestor Baron Von Housen, whom legend has immortalized as a vampire. Von Housen (Lugosi) wears a cape and sleeps in a coffin, sending his minions forth in an effort to dominate the world.

Julia Loretti (Maria Mercedes) is kidnapped so that Von Housen can discover the whereabouts of some uranium mines in South America that he needs to manufacture the atomic weapons which will allow him to achieve his goal. He tells Julia that he intends to build 50,000 robots, but when she asks him how many he has constructed so far, the abashed Von Housen has to admit he has only manufactured a single tin man.

Von Housen makes a fatal mistake when he has his robot fetch Mother Riley and tries to convince her he loves her. The film's best joke comes when Mother Riley asks him why he always wears formal evening clothes and Von Housen reasonably explains, "I was buried in them." Mother Riley brings in the police and foils the madman's plans.

In the aforementined interview with Gilling, he recalled:

> Bela Lugosi was a charming person who I think actually believed he was a vampire. He slept in a coffin and, surprisingly, possessed a keen sense of humour. He was great to work with. Arthur Lucan, his co-star in *Old Mother Riley Meets the Vampire* was, in my view, one of the greatest clowns ever to emerge from Vaudeville. Kitty, his ghastly wife, actually had him under personal contract and alas, ruined him. She left him for an ancient concert juvenile and lived unhappily ever after. She died bankrupt and I am afraid Arthur died in poverty.

Giling proved better with murder mysteries such as *Murder Will Out* (aka *The Voice of Merrill*) and managed to make quite a number of them before creating one of the oddest science fiction/horror films ever made, *The Gamma People*. The film is a comedy which combines elements of Graustarkian romance with a nefarious scientist conducting sinister experiments in a small village in Eastern Europe.

The story begins as an American journalist (Paul Douglas, who definitely looks out of place) and a British photographer (Leslie Phillips) banter in a railroad car that comes unhooked and rolls into the restrictive country of Gudavia. This is all very dull. The pair know that something odd is happening, but it seems to take them forever to find out what – namely that mad scientist and dictator Boronski (Walter Rilla) has been experimenting with subjecting his subjects to gamma radiation with the result that they either become geniuses, like one small boy they meet, or mindless goons that do Boronski's bidding. (Boronski has apparently been far more successful at producing the latter than the former.) With the help of Eva Bartok, Douglas and Phillips are able to destroy Boronski and his lab and thus save the country.

Despite the film's relative obscurity, Columbia Pictures' video branch released it on videocassette where it no doubt met with a bewildered response. The film remains a hodgepodge that never jells, and the threatening goons, who look only semi-human, consistently fail to frighten in their awkwardly and unimaginatively staged scenes. Gilling was apparently more able to throw out wild ideas in his screenplay along with producer John Gossage than to figure out a way to execute them effectively.

Gilling's first important horror film was the variously titled *The Flesh and the Fiends* (aka *Mania*, *The Fiendish Ghouls* and *Psycho Killers*). Blessed with a reasonably decent cast, the film is an effective retelling of the Burke and Hare story with Peter Cushing as Dr. Knox and George Rose and Donald Pleasence as Burke and Hare. (The pair were also the inspiration for *The Body Snatcher* and Freddie Francis' *The Doctor and the Devils*, both of which were a bit better than *The Flesh and the Fiends*.)

Cushing's performance as Dr. Knox is reminiscent of his performances as Frankenstein in Terry Fisher's films as he turns a blind eye to Burke and Hare's doings in the interests of furthering science. However, Hare is caught after killing a prostitute (Billie Whitelaw) and offers to turn King's evidence, resulting in Dr. Knox having to make some hasty explanations to his colleagues. However, all turns out well for him, while Burke is hanged and Hare has his eyes burned out by an angry mob.

John Gilling came up with the idea of making the story of Burke and Hare into a film and took it to Robert Baker and Monty Berman, who had produced a couple of relatively high quality horror films the year before (*Blood of the Vampire* and *Jack the Ripper*). The three of them formed a company called Triad to make the film.

The Shadow of the Cat, Gilling's next horror film, has become known as the Hammer film that is not a Hammer film. Although it used many of Hammer's regular crew including art director Bernard Robinson and cinematographer Arthur Grant and was filmed at Bray Studios, the film nevertheless was released by a company known as BHP (for British Hammer Production, according to one wag).

The film has some interesting cat's-eye-view shots as a cat watches its owner (Catherine Lacey) being murdered by her husband (Andre Morell) and two servants (Freda Jackson and Andrew Crawford). The murderers spot the cat watching them and whenever they see it, it reminds them of their guilt, so they conspire to get rid of it. However, their efforts in tracking it down only lead to their own deaths, leaving the inheritance to the nice niece of the owner (Barbara Shelley). Gilling actively uses the cat as a symbol of guilt and retribution and indicates that it possesses a malevolent spirit. It is an average, not-too-exciting film that does have a few interesting camera setups.

Gilling was hired by Hammer to write *The Gorgon* (see chapter on Terence Fisher), but it did not prove to be a happy experience as Anthony Hinds altered the beginning and ending of the film and much of the dialogue in between. Hinds also insisted that the villain in the film be completely unredeemable and that the hero be pristine in his goodness, while Gilling wanted more subtle characterizations with more moral ambiguity.

Nevertheless, he accepted when Hammer offered him a back-to-back film deal to make *Plague of the Zombies* and *The Reptile*, which have become known by some horror fans as the "Cornwall Classics." Anthony Hinds wrote the scripts and both films utilized the same basic sets, carefully redressed by Bernard Robinson. Gilling decided to do partial rewrites on the scripts of both films as he "went along." The final screenplay for *Plague* was credited to Peter Bryan.

Viewed today, *Plague of the Zombies* is not nearly as impressive as it must have been in 1966, before the appearance of George A. Romero's *Night of the Living Dead*. Though the film does have a few very evocative shots, overall there is an absence of action and interesting dialogue. The zombies themselves make only brief appearances, the best remembered of which proves to be a nightmare.

The getups of the zombie masters are interesting, and the film opens on them performing some kind of mysterious rite. A small nineteenth century Cornish village has been suffering from a mysterious plague, and the local doctor, Peter Thompson (Brook Williams), sends for his former professor Sir James Forbes (Andre Morell), who is accompanied by daughter Sylvia (Diane Clark). On their way to the village, Sylvia diverts some hunters on horseback who are chasing after a fox.

Once in town, Sir James and Sylvia come across a funeral procession. The angry hunters get revenge for being sent on a wild goose chase instead of a fox hunt by sending the carriage forward into the procession, knocking the dead man out of his coffin.

Sir James and Peter decide to conduct some autopsies, but when they dig up coffins, they are surprised to find them empty. Peter's wife, Alice, who suffers from a mysterious cut on her arm, strangely wanders off. Sylvia

John Gilling (right) gets input from writer-producer Anthony Nelson Keys on the set of Plague of the Zombies.

later sees her in the arms of the man who had been spilled out of his coffin, now a pallid zombie. In between, she pays a visit to the squire of the town, Clive Hamilton (John Carson), who has returned from Haiti after the death of his father and has somehow managed to make the bankrupt estate quite profitable, despite the fact that no one seems to be working the mine that the family owns. (It is easy to guess what workers Hamilton is using.)

The police recover Alice's body and she is buried. Hamilton drops by to pay his respects and offer his condolences, and in the process cuts Sylvia's finger on a wine glass and secretly stores a drop of her blood in a vial.

That night, Peter is shocked to see Alice as a zombie and Sir James ends her undead existence by cutting off her head. Peter falls down and has a terrible nightmare in which zombie hands claw at the grave and dig themselves out of the ground. Gilling gives this scene a sickly green tint, and though its conception is very similar to a shot in Mario Bava's *Black Sunday*, it was much praised and frequently shown as a sterling example of horror. A large group of zombies, one carrying Alice's head, converge on Peter just as he wakes up.

Sir James sees what must be done and invades Hamilton's house, killing one of his minions. Meanwhile, Sylvia is put in a trance and is drawn to the mine where Hamilton plans to kill her to make a zombie out of her. Peter tries to stop her but is cut off by the elevator gate. Sir James finds the secret passage into the mine and sets the controlling zombie doll aflame, which sets fire to all the zombies and kills Hamilton and his minions in the process.

The zombies and the costumes of the zombie masters have an interesting look to them, and the famous nightmare sequence has an appropriately eerie and uneasy feel, but most of this film concerns a mystery that the audience can easily guess and is rather dull. Gilling does not do much to build an atmosphere of menace, and the zombies themselves are used far too sparingly.

Jacqueline Pearce, who played Alice in *Plague of the Zombies*, starred as Anna Franklyn, the title character, in Gilling's *The Reptile*, which was filmed just before *Plague of the Zombies* but was released just afterwards. *The Reptile* represented Hammer's attempt to make an original monster, rather than borrowing a classic Universal monster or a mythological one as in *The Gorgon*. It was also one of the rare female monsters. In most earlier films where a woman is suspected of being a monster (e.g. Edgar Ulmer's *Daughter of Dr. Jekyll* and Jean Yarborough's *She-Wolf of London*), the film often revealed that she only thought she was a monster and that someone else was committing the murders.

The most interesting thing about *The Reptile* was Roy Ashton's monster makeup of a woman turned into a snake-person, a sort of giant cobra, which was featured prominently in ads for the film. The same kind of a creature was less effectively done in Sidney J. Furie's *The Snake Woman* and in Bernard Kowalski's *SSSSSSS*.

Gilling does set up a moody opening where Eastern music is played on a flute while the camera prowls about a Cornish mansion in the year 1902. Charles Spalding (David Baron) has been found dead and his brother Harry (Ray Barret) and his wife Valerie (Jennifer Daniel) are summoned. Arriving in town, the couple find the place almost deserted and the people in the pub seem unfriendly towards strangers. Innkeeper Tom Bailey (Hammer stalwart Michael Ripper) explains that people are uneasy over some mysterious deaths from unknown causes.

One night, Dr. Franklyn (Noel Willman) drops by looking for his daughter Anna. Meanwhile, Harry comes across a local eccentric known as "Mad Peter" (John Laurie) and invites him home for supper. "Mad Peter" talks about a mysterious "they" who came and spread evil. Harry tries to find out more about the death of his brother, but Peter hears a sound that was similar to the one he heard when Charles died and so leaves, apparently to track it down. Later, he reappears at the door with his face all blackened and swollen, infected with the "black death."

Harry immediately seeks out his neighbor Dr. Franklyn to see if he can help the poor man. However, he discovers that Franklyn is not a medical doctor and can do nothing, though he does send by a Malaysian servant (Marne Maitland) to pick up "Mad Peter's" corpse.

Valerie finally meets Anna, a comely girl who appears to be heavily restricted by her overbearing and overly protective father. Pearce makes Anna a seductive figure, one who becomes easily entranced by music and is given to sinuous writhing and swaying. Though her onscreen appearances are few, Gilling gives them maximum impact.

Tom aids Harry in exhuming some of the bodies of the recently departed to accurately determine the cause of death. They find marks that would indicate that the victims had all suffered some sort of snake bite. Harry receives an urgent summons from Anna and goes to help her, but instead encounters the Reptile, a snake-woman, which bites him on the shoulder. Breaking away from the Reptile's deadly embrace, Harry makes it back home where he has Valerie cut out the poison with a knife.

While her husband recovers, Valerie worries that Anna might still be in danger and so goes to the Franklyn house to investigate. In one of the film's most *outré* scenes, she discovers Anna's discarded skin in her bed – like a snake, Anna has shed her skin and is recovering next to a hot sulphur spring in the cavernous cellar. Dr. Franklyn prepares to take a sword to his daughter but is prevented by the Malaysian servant until he finally throws the servant into the sulphur pit and then notices Valerie. He explains that he had once been researching the magical practices of the Snake People of Borneo and that in punishment for his prying, they kidnapped his daughter and turned her into a human reptile that sheds her skin each winter and feeds.

Returning to the cellar where his daughter is, Franklyn is finally killed by the Reptile and the whole house begins to catch on fire. Expecting Dr. Franklyn to return through the door, Valerie is instead surprised by the Reptile, which attacks and bites her. However, its venom was used up on the attack on Dr. Franklyn, and Harry arrives in time to break a window and let in the cold night air, which paralyzes the Reptile into inaction. Apparently, it is cold-blooded and can only function well in heat. Valerie and Harry escape while the Reptile perishes in the flames.

The Reptile, while no classic, can be considered Gilling's best film and at least manages to find a balance between atmosphere, suggestiveness, and action. It was hampered by a low budget, but Ashton's venom-dripping monster is unusual.

Next Gilling tackled *Blood Beast from Outer Space*, an adaptation of Frank Crisp's novel *The Night Callers*, which is an alternate title for the film. Made in black and white for a small British company, the film chronicles the efforts of an alien mutant (Robert Crewsdon) to find beautiful women to kidnap and take back to the third moon of Jupiter by placing ads in *Bikini Girl* magazine. The mutant's moon had recently suffered a nuclear war and they need women who have not been irradiated to produce non-mutant offspring so that the population will not die out.

John Saxon gives a typically wooden performance as a young scientist named Jack Costain whose investigations of a strange transmitting orb begin to unravel the mystery. His partner, Prof. Morley (Maurice Denham), becomes the monster's first victim as it tries to cover its tracks. A fellow scientist named Ann (Patricia Haines) offers to pose as a model to find out what is going on.

Perhaps the most daring thing about the film is that it sets up for a showdown with the army or the police but becomes philosophical instead as the alien mutant puts forth its case. Gilling does build up an atmosphere of suspense in the first half, but this dissipates as the film gets simultaneously sillier and more pretentious. Still, the film is not so bad that it deserves the almost total obscurity to which it has been consigned.

A film that *is* that bad is Gilling's last Hammer project, *The Mummy's Shroud*, which features some very interesting camera angles and some of the dullest acting and one of the dullest plots of any mummy movie – and that is going some way.

The film does have one in-joke in that Dickie Owen, who had appeared as the mummy in Hammer's previous mummy film, *Curse of the Mummy's Tomb*, appears as Prem, the faithful servant to the boy Pharaoh Kah-to-bey, in the pre-credit sequence set in ancient Egypt. The mummy itself was played by stunt man Eddie Powell.

Gilling brings on yet another expedition headed by businessman Stanley Preston (John Phillips) and archaeologist Sir Basil Walden (Andre Morell), who face yet another sinister Egyptian, Masmid (Roger Delgado), who warns them of yet another curse. Sir Basil is soon bitten by a viper and sent to an insane asylum as the curse begins to take effect, leaving Stanley's son Paul Preston (David Buck) to take charge of the exploration of the tomb. Clare de Sangre (Maggie Kimberley) notices some horrifying inscriptions on the shroud of a mummy that they find.

The shroud is stolen and Sir Basil escapes from the asylum, seeking out an Egyptian fortuneteller who happens to be the mother of Hasmid, the self-appointed keeper of the tomb, who intones the sacred words to summon the mummy back to life.

The one inventive thing Gilling does in the film is present each murder in an oddly refracted reflection. We see the mummy crushing Sir Basil's head in the fortune-teller's crystal ball. A photographer (Tim Barrett) sees the mummy in the chemical solution for developing photographs, throwing acid at the mummy, which has no effect, before he himself gets an acid bath. Longbarrow, a nervous, bespectacled little man, spots the mummy through his broken spectacles just before he is thrown to his death through an upper-story window. Stanley Preston rushes to meet a boat to get him out of Egypt and knocks over a wine barrel, catching a glimpse of the mummy in the spilled wine before his brains are dashed out on the cobblestone sidewalk.

But Anthony Hinds' dialogue between these scenes is so dull that it robs the film of any power. Clare finally seeks out the mummy and hopes to appease it by praying for its forgiveness, but Hasmid is not so forgiving. Paul shows up in time to embed an axe in the mummy and Police Inspector Barrani (Richard Warner), who has been trying to get to the bottom of this murder spree, arrives in time to shoot Hasmid and watch the mummy crumble into dust.

Gilling found himself becoming more of a factory director, particularly from working in television where he worked on such series as *The Saint, Department S*, and *Gideon*. He came up with the script that eventually became *Trog*, a Herman Cohen disaster starring Joan Crawford as a scientist who tries to save a violent Neanderthal Man, which was to prove the most embarrassing film Freddie Francis ever made (it even inspired John Landis to make *Schlock*, an ineptly humorous send-up of the film that parodies its contempt for its audience).

Wanting a change of scenery and climate, Gilling moved to Spain in 1970. He tried to continue his career in Spain but was able to make only one film, *La Cruz del Diablo (The Devil's Cross)*. The film was a semi-follow-up to Amando de Ossorio's "Blind Dead" series in which the Templar Knights turn up once again. The plot was derived from three stories by Gustavo Adolfo Becquer, a highly respected nineteenth century Spanish writer. Adolfo Marsillac starred as a writer who loses his grip on reality and comes to believe that he is possessed by the devil. He turns to the love of a woman, played by Carmen Sevilla, hoping to break the spell. The film has only rarely been screened outside of Spain and I have had to rely on the reports of others for my information.

Gilling died in Spain in 1984. While by no means a director of great horror films, even his worst films did have their interesting moments and unusual approaches. He always seemed willing to try something different, and those who knew him personally have described him as a charming man. His work in swashbucklers shows him to be one of Britain's best action directors, and films like *The Flesh and the Fiends* and *The Reptile* will always have their adherents.

William Girdler, Jr. (1947–1978)

Asylum of Satan (1972); *Three on a Meathook* (1973); *Abby* (1974); *The Zebra Killer, Sheba Baby* (1975); *Grizzly* (1976); *Day of the Animals* (1977); *The Manitou* (1978).

If it were not for *The Manitou*, director William Girdler would not rate much more than a footnote for his career of highly derivative low-budget efforts. But *The Manitou* – surprisingly enough, given Girdler's track record – turned out to be one of the most outrageous and visually inventive horror films ever made. It boded well for Girdler's future, but tragically, that future was never to be. In January of 1978 while he was scouting locations for his next film in Manila, Girdler's helicopter hit a powerline and crashed into the underbrush below, killing all passengers including Girdler, Patrick Allan Kelly, Dennis Jovan and Jess Garcia.

Girdler's directorial career got off to an inauspicious start when at the age of 24 he directed his first film, *Asylum of Satan*. The story concerns Dr. Spector, the director of an insane asylum who is practicing devil worship on the side. Practicing is the operative word, for when he decides to offer up one of his patients to Satan, his master, he makes the mistake of selecting a woman who is not a virgin. Satan is not pleased and makes an ineptly staged appearance as literally all hell breaks loose.

Asylum of Satan is, unfortunately, a hopelessly amateurish effort. Dr. Spector's asylum is not even vaguely believable; Girdler has all orderlies dressing up in black cloaks as if they are expected to be on call for a black mass at any moment. Furthermore, there is an exasperating subplot about one girl's boyfriend who tries to convince the people in the nearby town that his beloved is in danger, but no one will listen. (At least there are no angry villagers here.) He finally returns to the asylum just in time to find that it has gone up in a puff of smoke. The cast and crew obviously had little experience and it painfully shows.

Charles Kissinger, the star of *Asylum of Satan*, returned to star in Girdler's next production, *Three on a Meathook*. Like *Psycho* and the later films *Deranged* and *The Texas Chainsaw Massacre*, *Three on a Meathook* is based on the deeds of Ed Gein, the infamous Wisconsin farmer who dug up graves and eviscerated unwary travelers in a quiet little town. Girdler adds a somewhat interesting twist by having the maniac's innocent son be the one blamed for the murders. For the early seventies, it was a rather gory production intended for grindhouses and drive-ins.

Three on a Meathook represented the start of a mini–film industry in Louisville, Kentucky, where Girdler would shoot his next film, *Abby*, for Mid-America Pictures. Compared to his previous two features, *Abby* was more ambitious, but Girdler bit off a little more than he could chew. The blaxploitation genre was picking up some easy cash for low-budget features, and *The Exorcist* had recently become the top-grossing (in more ways than one) film of all-time. Girdler and screenwriter G. Cornell Layne decided that a blaxploitation version of *The Exorcist* would be a natural.

While Girdler assembled some decent actors for a change – including William Marshall, Carol Speed, Austin Stoker (of *Assault on Precinct 13*), and Juanita Moore – the script didn't just borrow from *The Exorcist*, it wholeheartedly stole. In fact, whole scenes and bits of dialogue are reprised from the earlier film. Warner Bros., *The Exorcist*'s distributor, filed a successful lawsuit against Mid-America Pictures, who made the film, and American International Pictures, who distributed it. As a result, *Abby* has been pulled from circulation and is difficult to see. More to the point, it is not worth the effort. It even imitates the original *Exorcist* by starting off the story in Africa.

In Nigeria, Bishop Garnett Williams (Shakespearean actor William Marshall, who, sadly, is still best known to the public as the star of those AIP successes *Blacula* and *Scream, Blacula, Scream*) is seeking evidence of a link between African and Christian religions. Instead, he finds a box of ashes containing the demon Eshu, whom he inadvertently unleashes.

Meanwhile, back in Louisville, Kentucky, the Bishop's son Emmett (Terry Carter) moves into a new home with his wife Abby (Carol Speed). Somehow Eshu makes it across the world and finds Abby to possess while she's in the shower. Her features puff out in some very obvious makeup that is supposed to do for her what possession did to Linda Blair. Instead, it makes her look like an old black woman with the mumps. Naturally, this preacher's wife also begins to talk dirty and sleep around. Williams comes back and, following her to a bar, does the first disco exorcism on record. It is a success and Abby returns to normal, much to the relief of her family and theatergoers who had enough of this idiocy.

If played for laughs, *Abby* could have been amusing, but it was done with a straight face and its attempts to shock are feeble at best. Marshall is a fine actor, but there is not much he can do in the part as written. (To this day he has not been placed in a vehicle suitable to his talents.) Juanita Moore is trapped in an Aunt Jemima role in this, her last film. Carol Speed had shown some promise in *The Mack* and particularly *The New Centurions*, but buried beneath the laughable makeup she does not appear to be able to do much more than scream and flail about.

In an interview in *Monsters of the Movies*, Speed declared that the production appeared to be cursed. Whenever she appeared before the camera, the generators stopped. Louisville was hit by its first tornado in 80 years. A crew member had to be rushed off to the hospital when a small scrape suddenly became seriously infected. On top of all this, the film was being made in the heart of the Bible belt. Fearing that residents might not approve of a film on demonic possession, Speed was instructed to tell anyone who might ask that she did not know what the film she was starring in was about – causing her to withdraw and avoid talking to anyone. Perhaps somebody up there was trying to tell them something.

According to Richard Meyers in *For One Week Only*, *The Zebra Killers* was "based on a real-life series of murders in San Francisco. *Sheba Baby* was a Pam Grier vehicle in which she played a Second City private eye who comes home to protect her father in Louisville, Kentucky."

For his next horror film, Girdler decided to rip off *Jaws*, replacing the famed shark with a grizzly bear. Once again, the structure of the original is somewhat closely followed. *Grizzly* (aka *Killer Grizzly*) opens with the 15-foot carnivorous bear eviscerating several tourists (most of them scantily clad females, a staple of the genre).

This sets a determined forest ranger, Kelly (Christopher George), on the killer bear's trail. Like *Jaws*, we are not treated to the sight of the menace until the movie is almost half over. Instead, we are given a "bear's eye view" of a Georgia forest. Instead of a grizzled boat captain, we get Dan (Andrew Prine) a helicopter pilot, and instead of ichthyologist Richard Dreyfuss, we get eccentric naturalist Scott (Richard Jaeckel).

When we do finally see the grizzly, it is only an average, everyday bear, and there just is not anything scary-looking about your average bear, dangerous though he may be. In fact, the lumbering behemoth looks almost cuddly upon occasion and certainly delivers a better performance than most of the actors in the film. Even the normally professional Jaeckel has trouble putting his lines across believably, and he is the best of a bad lot. Add to this the fact that much of the photography appears to be underlit and murky and that Girdler seems to have no idea how to build suspense and you have a boring rip off. When Kelly blows up the bear with a bazooka it comes none too soon, but one gets the impression he was aiming that thing at the wrong target.

Evidently impressed by the absurd sight of a grizzly pulling a helicopter out of the sky, distributor Film Ventures decided that Girdler was just the man to handle animal horror features and put him in charge of *Day of the Animals*, once more starring Christopher George and Richard Jaeckel. The screenplay by William and Eleanor Norton (I do not know if they are any relation to B. W. L. Norton, who wrote and directed *Baby: Secret of the Lost Legend*) blames the animals' actions on damage caused to the ozone layer by aerosol spray cans. I guess the animals sense that humans are to blame for destroying their environment and all beasts residing over 5000 feet above sea level become hostile including tarantulas, wildcats, wolves, German Shepherds, eagles, rattlesnakes, and need we say it, a bear.

The characters all have recognizable faces and are assigned job titles – this is apparently considered to be characterization by the filmmakers. We have got Leslie Nielsen as Mr. Jenson, the ad executive; Richard Jaeckel as Prof. MacGregor; Lynda Day George as newslady Terry Marsh; Paul Mantee as football star Ray Moore; Michael Ansara as an Indian named Santee; and Ruth Roman as a Beverly Hills dowager, Mrs. Shirley Goodwin. When Mrs. Goodwin mutters, "I don't know what I'm doing here," we can certainly be sympathetic. The other members of the cast and the audience must be wondering the same thing.

Perhaps to compensate for the underlit photography of *Grizzly*, this film is overexposed. However, the shots of animals are better executed than previously. The inspiration for the film appears to have been Hitchcock's *The Birds*, but at least this film is not a slavish imitation. While not very well done, the film is kept lively by a few chuckles in between the carnage. It is an improvement, but nothing to write home about.

Then one day Girdler was in the London airport and he noticed a book on the rack, *The Manitou* by Graham Masterson. A minor paperback best seller, the property in Girdler's opinion was a cross between *The Exorcist* and *Star Wars* with plenty of potential for shock. Together with Jon Cedar and Tom Pope he wrote a screenplay, and forsaking low-budget outfit Film Ventures for medium-budget and more respectable Avco-Embassy, he became the producer-director of *The Manitou*.

A manitou is a spirit which inhabits some aspect of nature. Every natural object has its own manitou, or dominating spirit. Author Masterson based his book on the legends of the Algonquin Indians. The book contained such grisly sequences as a man being turned inside out and an elevator being filled with the dismembered bodies of a squad of police officers, but Girdler elected to cut the gore and try for a more class production. He also decided to switch the locale of the book from New York to San Francisco because he thought that San Francisco was more moody and he could take advantage of the fog and the architecture. With a $3 million budget, this was Girdler's bid at class, and he went with it.

The story is bizarre beyond belief, but keeping tongue slightly in cheek and the visuals lively, the film will carry you along if you let it. Tony Curtis stars as Harry Erskine, a medium who is more than a bit of a fake. Curtis' career had been going downhill ever since he made *The Boston Strangler*, though he had proven that he actually was a good actor in such films as

Trapeze, Mister Cory, Sweet Smell of Success, Some Like It Hot and *The Great Race*. Curtis appears to be enjoying having a meaty role. Sadly he was not to get another until *Insignificance* (Nicolas Roeg, 1985).

The way Curtis plays the role, it is obvious that Harry knows himself to be a fake, but he also realizes the value of paying attention to and charming the largely elderly ladies who come to his establishment to have their fortunes told. It is apparent they like coming to him because he treats them kindly and with respect, making them beautiful promises about the future and eliminating their loneliness if only for a short time. It is a mutually beneficial relationship, though it is just as obvious Harry is not performing the services out of the goodness of his heart.

When an old flame and true believer, Karen Tandy (Susan Stransberg), comes to him, things begin to get out of hand. A young woman with a problem, she has a lump on her neck which is growing and she is mumbling strange things in her sleep.

Next Girdler daringly combines humor, horror and pathos in a bizarre and toucing scene in which Harry is reading the fortune of an elder client and they are both enjoying the charade, Harry as a spiritualist and the client as an intent seeker. We can see that they enjoy each other's company.

Then the tenor of the scene changes suddenly as the old woman becomes possessed. She starts speaking in a foreign language and her body lifts off the ground. Her body rigidly vertical, her feet not touching the ground, the poor woman is being controlled by a malevolent outside force. As a fake medium, Harry is utterly dumbfounded by this demonstration of genuine occult powers. The woman's body floats to the head of a staircase and then is released to be flung down the stairs. Harry is cleary horrified, and he rushes to his client and cradles her bleeding body in his arms. The surprise, shock and concern of this scene really register, indicating that Girdler was learning enough about directing to take chances and get them to pay off.

Realizing that he is in over his head, Harry looks for outside help, which he finds in the form of an Indian medicine man, John Singingrock (Michael Ansara playing another Indian). But before that, Karen goes to the hospital to find out what is wrong with her. The lump on her neck is growing.

The doctors naturally decide to X-ray the lump, but that only makes it bigger. When they decide to cut into it, a doctor is forced to cut his own hand and a surgical laser goes wild. The doctors inform Harry that the lump is a form of pregnancy, that she is giving birth to something. "In her *neck*?!" asks an incredulous Harry. Soon, in a séance with two geniune mediums, Harry gets a look at what exactly is in Karen's neck as the spirit of Misquamacus, a 400-year-old evil medicine man who is attempting to resurrect himself, makes an appearance as an evilly grinning head over the séance table.

While Harry seeks out Singingrock, Karen finally gives birth to Misquamacus in a stunning scene. The skin on Tandy's back stretches and a deformed arm and a head with long black hair pop out. (Misquamacus is played by two dwarfs, Felix Silla and Joe Gleb, in elaborate makeup courtesy of Tom Burman of the Burman Studios. The deformity is an unfortunate side effect of being X-rayed.) By the time Harry and Singingrock can get back Misquamacus has taken over the hospital. According to Singingrock, the spirit is one of the most powerful and evil in Indian lore.

Misquamacus demonstrates his power by causing an earthquake, conjuring a "dragon" and freezing the entire floor of the hospital that he is housed in. (Unfortunately, the "ice" on the walls looks rather synthetic, but it is a wild change in the commonplace scenery and a weird idea.) He becomes positively cosmic as Karen's hospital room dissolves into a kind of limbo, leaving just Karen, Misquamacus, and the bed over an elaborate field of stars which whiz by at rapid speed. (This is a particularly arresting visual image which was later borrowed in the Japanese animated film *Lupin III: The Castle of Cagliostro*). How does one combat this powerful creature?

Singingrock mentions something about all things having manitous, and that the white man's special manitou is the spirit of his computers and other machines. Harry immediately decides to use these powerful forces to offset the dread powers of Misquamacus, ordering, "Get me more of this complicated stuff." (Realistically and amusingly, Harry is no expert on computers and so makes his request simply. He may not be technically educated, but he is deeply concerned.) By switching on the machines, the pair set up a counter force, but Misquamacus laughs. It is not enough.

What is there left but – you guessed it – the power of love. Channeled through the power of love (Harry's love for Karen), power rays emanate from Karen's fingers and drive Misquamacus back until he is blasted into nothingness. Once more love triumphs and everything is restored to normal. Said Girdler about this finale in *Starlog*:

> Suffice to say, the Great Old One is a total optical effect. What happens when they step into Karen's room for that last time took seven months to film. In the last reel, during 180 feet, we have 87 opticals. A month before release, we were still working on them.

(The effects in the film were achieved by Dale Tate and Frank Van Der Veer, who worked on *Star Wars*.)

The film is audacious and even silly, but as such, it does succeed in doing what the best horror films of yore always did: It shows you something that you have never seen before and gives you a new perspective. This quality is rare, but a B movie like *The Manitou* has it. Not all the conceptions and conceits come off as well as might be hoped, but at times they suggest amazing possibilities and allow your imagination to sketch in the rest. Besides, the film is fun and designed to be entertaining. It is eager to please with its visual inventiveness.

After years of very derivative movies, Girdler finally made something that can truly be said to be original. How tragic and unfortunate that he never got the opportunity to follow it up. Meanwhile, for those who can appreciate it in all of its glorious absurdities, *The Manitou* is a minor gem.

Stuart Gordon (1946–   )

H. P. Lovecraft's Re-Animator (1985); *From Beyond* (1986); *The Dolls* (1987);
Robot Jox (1989); *The Pit and the Pendulum* (1991).
TELEVISION: *Daughter of Darkness* (1990).

Stuart Gordon is that rarity among rarities, an intelligent man who truly loves horror and horror movies. With an independently financed film, *Re-Animator*, which was picked up by Empire Pictures and has gone on to become one of the biggest cult favorites of the '80s, Gordon established himself as a major new horror director who delighted in the idea of scaring people and putting perverse twists of humor into his projects.

He was born in Chicago in 1946. His father interested him in art at an early age, and Gordon became an art major at the prestigious Lane Technical High School. After trying his hand at commercial art for half a year upon graduation, he decided to try college and so went off to the University of Winconsin at Madison. Unable to get into a film course, he tried a theater course instead. Gordon managed to get cast in a bit part in *Marat/Sade* and got bitten by the theater bug.

Moving off campus, Gordon started the Organic Theater and produced a version of *Richard III*. Hearing rumors that there was nudity in the play, the police shut down the production on building code violations, but the Organic Theater simply moved elsewhere, eventually winding up in Chicago.

The first piece of writing Gordon produced was a play called *The Gameshow*, which was intended to take *Marat/Sade* a step further. The play had uncanny echoes of living theater and Grand Guignol. "Audience members" (actually plants) were brought up on stage where they were beaten, raped and even murdered. Another play Gordon tackled was a mute version of *Titus Andronicus* with the violence intact, called *Vis* (the Latin word for violence or viscera). Grunting like extras from *One Million Years B.C.*, the actors would simulate the rape and mutilation (amputating tongue and hands) of a girl.

Gordon was interested in trying all kinds of new ideas for theater. He had a production of Albee's *Who's Afraid of Virginia Woolf?* which did not begin until two o'clock in the morning – the time setting of the play – and

483

which had the audience following the actors from room to room as the play progressed. He tried a western version of *Hamlet* in which the audience sat on bleachers that were moved around (the bleachers being set on rollers). He was finally arrested on an obscenities charge (later dropped) for his production of J. M. Barrie's *Peter Pan*, in which the Lost Boys were all hippies and the players "flew" by dropping acid.

Following a disastrous attempt to take a *commedia dell'arte* version of *Candide* to an unrenovated theater in New York, Gordon began *Poe*, covering a mysterious 48-hour period in Edgar Allan Poe's life during which he disappeared before being found delirious and in someone else's clothes in a pauper's hospital. *Poe* was Gordon's first direct attempt at horror, and his continuing interest is evidenced by his current production of an adaptation of Poe's "The Pit and the Pendulum."

The Organic Theater's first hit was *Warp*, a comic bookish science fiction play about a bank teller who is revealed to be Lord Cumulus, Avenger of the Universe. Another success was a production of Ray Bradbury's play *The Wonderful Ice Cream Suit*, which had a successful United States tour. Another science fiction writer with whom Gordon worked was Joe Haldeman, for whom he did a play adaptation of the Hugo Award–winning novel *The Forever War*. Additionally, Kurt Vonnegut worked with Gordon on a stage adaptation of *The Sirens of Titan*.

The Organic Theater's biggest successes were *Sexual Perversity in Chicago*, *Bleacher Bums*, and *E/R*. *Sexual Perversity* established playwright David Mamet and has become a modern dramatic staple, but it was originally two different one-act plays that Gordon combined with great success. *Bleacher Bums* was largely improvised and eventually was filmed by WTTW, Chicago's Public Television station; that program won an Emmy for direction. Gordon sent a tape of *E/R* (for *Emergency Room*) to Norman Lear and managed to sell Lear on the idea of a spin-off series, which starred Elliott Gould and ran for a short while.

Gordon had thought about breaking into films and had developed a couple of screenplays, including one based on the Karen Silkwood story, but he did not meet with much success. Someone turned him onto H. P. Lovecraft's early and rarely reprinted first serial "Herbert West – Re-Animator," and Gordon thought it might make a good basis for a wild television series. Gordon scripted a one-hour pilot with ideas for 12 additional episodes and shopped the package around. While there was some interest from Tribune Entertainment, they decided to back George Romero's *Tales from the Darkside* series instead.

Bob Greenberg, one of the special effects people behind Carpenter's *Dark Star*, had told Gordon repeatedly to come out to California and convinced him that the only way to market the Herbert West material was as a horror feature. He introduced Gordon to Brian Yuzna, an energetic young

producer who was enthusiastic about the project. Yuzna insisted that the
only way to go was an all-stops-out approach. (In fact, he was constantly
looking for ideas and even asked my input on the film when I was covering
Re-Animator for *Fangoria* magazine. Perhaps the one influence I had was
when Yuzna asked me what I thought was the greatest horror film score,
and I told him without hesitation that I thought Bernard Herrmann's for
Psycho was the best that the field had produced. I learned later that Yuzna
went to Richard Band, *Re-Animator* composer, and asked for a score just
like *Psycho*, and indeed the score is a pastiche with only minor variations
on Herrmann's string score.)

I talked to Gordon for the first time on the set of *Re-Animator*, where
he explained to me:

> First of all, I'm an H. P. Lovecraft fan, and somebody once started
> describing to me a story called "Herbert West – Re-Animator," and I'd
> never heard of it, and I thought I knew H. P. Lovecraft pretty well. He
> told me it was a kind of modern-day Frankenstein story, which in-
> trigued me because there'd been all of this stuff done about Dracula and
> vampires, but no one has really gone back to Frankenstein.
>
> So what I did was I went to the library to look it up. I found that the
> story was not in any of the published anthologies. It was really kind of
> a lost story. So I put in a call slip and it took them over a year to locate
> the story for me.
>
> It appeared in a hardcover collection called *Dagon* which had never
> been reprinted. It turned out that Lovecraft had written the story as
> a serial for a magazine. He'd written it as six tiny stories, six two-page
> stories in serial form, and he recaps each of the stories. It's about Her-
> bert West and it's written from the point of view of his assistant who
> is never named in the story, talking about these horrible experiments,
> and each one ends with this big pay-off.
>
> They struck me as being awful and funny at the same time because
> the recurring theme is that every time Herbert West has a failed ex-
> periment, he just says, "Well, he just wasn't fresh enough." That's his
> solution to find fresher and fresher specimens until eventually he's kill-
> ing people just to bring them back to life.
>
> We started developing it. Originally, I do a lot of theater work, and
> I was thinking of it as a play, but then I got more into it, I realized it
> was more something for TV or film. The first idea was to do it as a pilot
> for a TV show. Since it was done as a serial, we thought about doing
> it as a miniseries, six short half-hour shows. We did a half an hour script
> based on the first show, but we found that no one was interested in a
> half hour for dramatic or horror things on television; it had to be an
> hour. That's what we were told. So we went back and added the second
> story to it and had an hour version and we were trying to sell that, but
> we found we had a real hard time because the material was so explicit
> that the only people who were interested at all were something like
> HBO or the pay TV kind of thing. Horror is a genre that they've

Top: Herbert West (Jeffrey Combs) has a good head on his shoulders . . . and one on his desk (that of Dr. Carl Hill played by David Gale), according to the witty ads for H. P. Lovecraft's Re-Animator, *directed by Stuart Gordon. Bottom: Stuart Gordon with the torso of Dr. Hill on the set of* Re-Animator. *The film's casual outrageousness won it a large following and much critical praise. Gordon had nothing to do with the sequel,* Bride of Re-Animator, *and unfortunately that made a tremendous difference.*

never gotten into, so they were leery of it. At that point, it seemed like the project had dead-ended.

That was around the time I got introduced to Brian Yuzna through Bob Greenberg, and Brian is a real horror buff, and said this really should be a feature film. And then instead of adapting just the first two or three stories, tell the whole thing.

One of the early decisions was to update it from its turn-of-the-century origins to the modern day because the period sets and costumes would have added tremendously to the budget. Gordon prepared himself by taking visits to morgues. Additionally, he brought in some outside expert help:

> We have a Dr. Ron Burman who is a friend of mine, and we worked together on a play called *E/R*, which [was] a TV series. He [was] the medical consultant for the TV series and he [was] also our medical consultant, so all of the medicine that's practiced in the movie is going to be accurate. I think it's important when you're dealing with something like fantasy that you have some sort of basis in reality built, so all the early scenes before we get into all the way out stuff are going to be very almost documentary-like in feeling. We're going to establish that these are real doctors and these are real medical students, and pathologists and so forth, and that this is a real world, a real hospital we're living in, so when things start getting crazy, it's going to be grounded in some sort of reality.

Despite his lack of experience as a film director, from his theater background Gordon realized the value of preparation. The most difficult point turned out to be the need to have coverage in order to protect oneself in the editing room – i.e., to have alternate shots and angles to cut to so that the pacing could be adjusted or story elements could be rearranged.

Gordon explained his preparation for *Re-Animator*:

> What I did . . . and it was real helpful to me, was to storyboard this. I'm lucky in that when I was in high school, I majored in commercial art, so I can draw, and I ended up drawing up all the special effects sequences shot by shot, so they were able to know exactly what was needed. The effects themselves, although many of them were kind of simple effects, the kinds of effects that could be done live onstage because we're not going to do any real optical effects on this picture, they're all really practical, floor effects they call them. We did one sequence which employed half a dozen techniques to create the illusion of a headless body moving its head around the room and so forth. When we are done with it, I think the results will be very believable.
>
> The thing I hate the most in a horror film is when the audience starts sitting there thinking, "How did they do that?" To me, what I like to have happen is for them to get involved in the characters and the story and then for the effects to work with that story, and really I think that

that's when you get the big pay-offs. . . . I've seen so many horror films where you don't care about anybody, and that to me sort of sinks the film. If you're not afraid for someone, you're not afraid. It's important. I think that one of the things that we've really got going for us is that we really have some wonderful actors in this film who are doing spectacular performances and are making these characters live for the audience, and so when things happen to them, I think the audience is going to really care, and they're going to really feel bad about a lot of it and horrified.

In examining the appeal of horror films, Gordon commented:

I agree with the thing that Stephen King wrote about horror – it is basically dealing with the fear of death, and I think *Re-Animator* does that to a large degree. What this film is about is conquering death. I mean Herbert West's dream is something that all doctors have shared, and that is to prolong life as long as you possibly can. They used to believe that when your heart stopped, you were dead. Now they have drugs like epinephrine, which is like an adrenalin derivative which can make the heart start after it has stopped, so now stopping the heart does not necessarily mean you're dead. Now what they're calling death is defined as "brain death," which happens six to 12 minutes after the heart stops.

West is trying to conquer brain death. What he is trying to do is prolong that six to 12 minutes as long as he possibly can so that a person who has died, even though their brain has never received any blood or oxygen . . . can be brought back. His attitude is the same as any doctor, that it's better to save a life even if it means the person is going to be debilitated than it is to let the person die, so that even if there is brain damage, it's still better to have that person living than dead. So his approach is medically correct.

In many ways, *Re-Animator* took '30s clichés (the obsessed, even mad scientist) and updated them with an '80s sensibility (outrageous humor, gore). Jeffrey Combs comes off like a man possessed as hardworking Herbert West, whose reanimating agent causes his Zurich professor's eyes to burst from his head in the opening sequence (courtesy of a John Buechler special effect). Expelled, he enrolls in the mythic Miskatonic University in New England (site of numerous H. P. Lovecraft tales) and becomes the roommate of Dan Cain (Bruce Abbott).

Gordon makes the film a study of ethics and responsibility. For Herbert West, the ends justify any means, no matter how extreme. He blackmails Cain into allowing him to use Cain's basement as a laboratory to continue his experiments. (Cain is afraid of the dean [Robert Sampson] discovering that he has been fooling around with the dean's daughter.)

Even less ethical is Dr. Carl Hill (David Gale), who steals other doctors'

ideas and who succeeds in getting West expelled when he has the bad form
to point this out and to disagree with his instructor on the permanence of
brain death. When West is caught pursuing his studies, both he and Cain
are expelled. This does not deter West from continuing and forcing Cain to
participate in a disastrous experiment which winds up accidentally turning
Dean Halsey into a zombie.

Gordon delights in simultaneously sending up his material while pretending to treat it seriously. He uses a Talking Heads poster as a bit of fore-
shadowing. Later West will decapitate Dr. Hill and reanimate Hill's body
and head separately as an additional experiment, but the head keeps falling
over until West resourcefully impales it on a bill spike. Hill is not discouraged
by having his head separate from his body (somehow one still controls the
other) and has his body carry his head in a tray, continuing his plans to usurp
West's work, undaunted by his less-than-presentable condition.

The actors give the kind of arch, hammy horror performances that horror fans have grown accustomed to and love, giving a stylized spin to the
material. There is even a slight poignance when the zombified dean is shown
battering his head against a one-way mirror behind which stand his nemesis
(Dr. Hill) and his daughter, as if the brain-dead dean can sense his daughter's peril. And indeed, Gordon uses the decapitated Hill to give a whole new
literal meaning to the phrase "giving head." For a climax, Cain and West
must fight reanimated cadavers, and when West overdoses Hill with his
reagent, intestines spew forth and attack like tendrils until both irresponsible doctors are snuffed out.

The black humor of the film caught on very well with audiences, despite
the film's limited run. While *Dawn of the Dead* had managed very well as an
unrated film, it has become harder to book unrated films in mainstream
theaters. *Re-Animator* found most of its success on videotape, where it was
released in both an R-rated and an unrated version.

Next Gordon began preparing *The Dolls* with scripter Ed Naha (who
would also write *Troll* for John Buechler), but the first cut was missing
something in the way of excitement and was temporarily shelved while some
additional effects sequences (including some excellent stop-motion animation from David Allen) were worked up to insert into the film. Filming in
Italy, Gordon went right into his next project, *H. P. Lovecraft's From Beyond*, using the same sets as before.

Gordon had plans to make "The Lurking Fear" and "Shadow over Inns-
mouth" as well, but as yet those projects have not materialized. He did note
that audience's applauded Lovecraft's name, but previous Lovecraft adaptations (including Roger Corman's *The Haunted Palace* based on "Charles
Dexter Ward," Daniel Haller's *Die, Monster, Die,* based on "The Colour Out
of Space," and *The Dunwich Horror* starring Sandra Dee and Dean

Stockwell) had proved spectacularly unsuccessful and ineffective. Using the Lovecraft stories only as a framework and giving them a bit more zip proved far more acceptable to modern horror audiences.

In discussing the appeal of Lovecraft, Gordon said:

> He has a strange sense of humor. I mean, it's a very wry one, too, and I think you have to kind of read a lot of Lovecraft and learn some of the in-jokes of his group. There's references to his friends and there are little gags in his stories, though it is definitely true there very few knee-slappers in an H. P. Lovecraft story.
>
> The reason I was drawn to *Re-Animator* was that I felt it was, for Lovecraft, a very explicit story. It was written as a serial and he never really liked it much himself. Lovecraft always has this tendency when things start getting really scary to kind of have his main character faint or talk about these things that are so horrible that he can't describe them – unspeakable, unnamable, unmentionable – it's all left up to your imagination, whereas in *Re-Animator*, everything is very clearly laid out there, so I felt it was an excellent story in terms of dramatizing.
>
> *From Beyond* was based on an even earlier work than *Re-Animator*. It was no more than a five-page story, it was a much shorter piece, so that really was (only) a jumping off point. The story is our opening scene and then what happens next? Although, we tried to incorporate Lovecraftian notions into the thing, borrowed things from other stories and so forth.

One aspect of both of these Gordon films that is different from Lovecraft's prim and proper work is that Gordon has emphasized the sexuality, giving his films a kinky subtext. Said Gordon, "One of the things that Brian Yuzna [who was also *From Beyond*'s producer] and I felt is that there is an intertwining of horror and sex. I guess it is life and death is really what we are talking about here. Monsters in all the old movies were always dragging the heroine off and she was in her negligee. In our movies, we just find out what happens when they get home."

In each era, horror movies have reflected something of the current fears of the society of that age. Some critics have noticed a trend in "venereal horror" that was started by David Cronenberg with *They Came from Within* (aka *Shivers*) and has continued in his films through his remake of *The Fly*. According to Gordon:

> I think *From Beyond* was definitely about AIDS. The best I could figure from reading the story was that it was kind of an outgrowth of Lovecraft's fear of germs. Lovecraft was very much a hypochondriac and was constantly worried about his health. The idea of these things that are in the air and are invisible to us that can kills us are germs. I mean the way he describes them in the story – these jellyfish things

that swim around in the air – is like a giant amobea or something. So my first reaction to that was, well, it's kind of an awfully wimpy fear, to be afraid of germs. But then you just have to look at a newspaper and the fears of AIDS is just such a powerful force running through society right now, that you just tap into that. I think it is sort of a Lovecraftian disease.

Due to the limited success of *Re-Animator* theatrically, Empire decreed that *From Beyond* would have an R-rating. After four trips to the MPAA for additional trimming, an R-rating was secured without any significant changes according to Gordon. In addition to the makeup artists that had worked on *Re-Animator* (John Naulin, Anthony Doublin, John Buechler), Gordon also brought in Mark Shostrom for the elaborate makeups for *From Beyond*.

A Doctor Pretorious (Ted Sorel) had constructed a "resonator" which is designed to stimulate the pineal gland. The seventeenth century French philosopher René Descartes believed that the pineal gland enabled man to see the devil, while other scientists maintained until recently that the pineal gland influenced sexual function. When the resonator is switched on, eel-like entities can be perceived swimming in the air. Unfortunately, these entities can also see humans if they move, and will attack them as well. A disastrous first experiment ends up with Pretorious headless and the only survivor his lab assistant Crawford Tillinghast (Jeffrey Combs).

Barbara Crampton, Gordon's wife, who played the dean's daughter in *Re-Animator*, here plays Dr. Katherine McMichaels, who is determined to cure Tillinghast of his apparent delusions, despite the warnings of other hospital staff. To assist her in this endeavor, she relies on ex-cop Bubba Brownlee (Ken Foree of *Dawn of the Dead* fame).

Taking Tillinghast out of the hospital, she brings him back to Pretorious' mansion and the resonator. Restoring the resonator and activating it, McMichaels discovers that the machine provides a kind of sexual stimulation while enlarging the pineal gland. Eventually it is revealed that Pretorious, in a much altered form, is trapped in the unseen world that the resonator reveals, and that each time it is switched on, he grows more menacing and more powerful. Meanwhile, Tillinghast's pineal has received so much stimulation that it pops out of his forehead like an asparagus stalk or a phallic symbol. Dr. McMichaels becomes more obsessed with the idea of taking part in the sadomasochistic loveplay that Dr. Pretorious amused himself with while playing his power games, and eventually the house of cards comes tumbling down as all the characters realize that they are dealing with forces beyond their control.

The screenplay does have it wild moments, but fails to reach the giddy heights of *Re-Animator*. Nevertheless, its sex-horror combination, with ultimate pleasure supposedly coming out of a threatening alternate dimension, seems a likely inspiration for horror-author-turned-director Clive Barker's film *Hellraiser*, a horror hit for New World, which has already spawned one sequel, *Hellbound: Hellraiser II*. Barker made his proceedings a bit more stylish and mysterious, but apart from centering it around a betrayal (in *Hellbound*, a wife will do anything to resurrect her lover from the hellish half-world he's trapped in), adds very little to the basic idea.

Gordon's main theme is that the more freedom one tries to acquire, the more important it becomes to be responsible. Dr. McMichaels takes many unnecessary risks in reactivating the resonator and puts all the main characters' lives in danger. Dr. Pretorious proceeded without regard for anyone's desires but his own, but while his ruthlessness gave him power, it also led to his own destruction. The message in this nuclear age of ours is that mankind must be very careful with the powers he unleashes, thinking of consequences rather than blindly acting.

The Dolls deals with the responsibilities of parenthood and plays like a dark fairy tale. The film centers around the innocent young girl Judy Bowers (Carrie Lorraine), whose irresponsible father, David (Ian Patrick Williams), has married an evil stepmother named Rosemary (Carolyn Purdy-Gordon). Caught in a rainstorm and having almost run over some teens with their car, the trio seek refuge in the house of a pair of old dollmakers, the Hartwickes (Guy Rolfe from Castle's *Mr. Sardonicus* and Hilary Mason).

Some teens and a timid businessman also show up at the house. The teens prove an avaricious and thieving lot, and it is not long before they awake the wrath of the magical dolls that guard the Hartwickes' place. The dolls kill or transform every human being after they reveal themselves to be vile except for the innocent Judy and the bumbling businessman (Stephen Lee) who takes on the responsibility of being Judy's new daddy. At the end, the Hartwickes look smilingly on in approval, magical beings that reward the good and punish the bad very severely.

The film does have its interesting and creepy moments (I particularly like one shot where all the dolls in a room turn their head the same way and glower at an intruder) as well as some heart, but the characters and the plot, which merely involves one killing after another, are not very interesting and fail to lift the film much above the routine.

At best, *The Dolls* is about maintaining the child inside, with childhood representing the ultimate freedom. Responsibility comes with maintaining the childlike aspect of one's life (something that Judy and the businessman have not lost) despite the pressure from society to grow up and conform to expectations.

As one becomes an adult, the world tells people to put aside their childish things, such as dolls. As Gordon puts it:

What *Dolls* is saying is you cannot do that. You have responsibilities to the child within, and . . . as soon as you murder the child within you or let him die within you, then you are dead as well.

There's a line in there that almost every reviewer picked up on, which was [when] the old toymaker, when he is turning the father into a doll, says, "Being a parent is a privilege, not a right." That, in a nutshell, is what the movie is about. As a parent you have to remember what it is like to be a child.

Thinking about children got Gordon involved in a project called *Teeny Weenies*, in which some children would be shrunk down below the size of ants and have a wondrous adventure in their own backyard. The idea was to present a film he could take his own kids to and revive the kind of family film that has almost faded from sight. Gordon was going to begin production right after he finished his next project, *Robot Jox*, but he fell ill and exhausted as sets were being constructed in Mexico and was forced to bow out. Former ILM effects director Joe Johnston took over directing the project which has since been released as *Honey, I Shrunk the Kids*.

A number of other planned projects fell by the wayside as well. There was one called *Cops*, written by Terry Curtis Fox for the Organic Theater back in 1976, which Tri-Star considered making into a movie starring Jim Belushi. There was another called *Gris Gris*, a voodoo story set in Haiti, which was cancelled when a spate of voodoo-oriented pictures (Parker's *Angel Heart*, Craven's *The Serpent and the Rainbow*, and others) came out that repeated elements of *Gris Gris*' screenplay.

With the sinking of Empire films, such projects as *Bloody Bess*, based on a play about a female pirate; *Beserker*, about a wrestler who finds that steroids are turning him into a killing machine (sort of a variation on *The Terminal Man*); and *Bride of Re-Animator* were also sunk for the time being.

One film that did not sink was the elaborate *Robot Jox*. Scripted by ace science fiction writer Joe Haldeman and, according to Gordon, inspired by Homer's *Iliad, Robot Jox* is the futuristic story about a time when war has been replaced with hand-to-hand combat between giant fighting machines. The machines are manipulated by individuals whose physical reactions a robot will precisely duplicate. These individuals, called robojox, are international heroes who supply the "bread and circuses" that keep the masses occupied. The basic idea of a future world captivated and controlled through a sport had been explored previously in Jewison's *Rollerball* (which pitted the individual against corporate non-identity) and Paul Bartel's satiric *Death Race 2000*, but in *Robot Jox* men inside of robots are representing confrontations of all kinds, both big and small, between the governmental and marketing forces that control our lives.

Gordon is a strong believer that war will always be a part of man's existence, but for the sake of civilization, less destructive means of fighting will be found. The battle between these titanic technical marvels is, in effect, war by proxy, a popular concept in an age where the United States government can send money to counter-revolutionaries to attack governments the United States is opposed to.

For the basic story, Gordon took from *The Iliad* the idea of the Greek hero Achilles who did not want to fight in the Trojan War. Haldeman fleshed this out with a character named Achilles (Gary Graham), a robojock whose robot has fallen on a stadium of people during one of these epic battles, resulting in the deaths of hundreds of people. Conscience-stricken and consumed with guilt, Achilles declines to participate when the Common Market (read Western Democracy) sets up a contest between Achilles' robot and the champion of the Confederation (read the Eastern/Soviet bloc), Alexander (Paul Koslo), an undefeated pilot.

Launching herself into the breach is Athena (Anne Marie Johnson), a friend of Achilles and a robojock of some reputation herself. (Robojox are people who have been genetically engineered for quick thinking and fast reflexes.) Achilles' strong personal feelings towards Athena cause him to reconsider his position about taking the responsibility onto himself.

The film took an exceptionally long time to produce, largely due to problems in financing which held up money for the production and due to an elaborate special effects process employed where the miniature "giant robots" were shot against desert skies to avoid the blue-screen look of many modern effects.

Today, Gordon has resumed his relationship with Charles Band, the former head of Empire Pictures, and started his version of Edgar Allan Poe's "The Pit and the Pendulum." As with his adaptations of Lovecraft stories, Gordon is simply using the Poe story as a framework to build on and from. Gordon's story is about a monk involved with Torquemada's infamous Inquisition who falls in love with a woman and is unable to reconcile his feelings with his beliefs. He decides that she must have "bewitched" him and so condemns her and her husband as witches. The husband must suffer the torture of the pit and the pendulum.

Gordon seems fascinated by the idea that the torturers of the Inquisition grew increasingly less concerned with the damage they were inflicting on a person's body the more they tortured their victims, reasoning that "saving" the immortal soul justified crushing the temporal body that soul was housed in. Still, paradoxically, it was the torturers' job to keep the victims alive so that they might confess and be saved – they were not intended to be executioners.

The film also projects the callousness of a bureaucracy in the form of a scribe who is employed to take down the confessions and see that proper procedures are followed. Gordon also adds an ironic angle with the wife accused of being a witch finally becoming one in an effort to save herself (similar to the bleak idea in Michael Reeves' *Witchfinder General* wherein a soldier pursues a madman and eventually goes mad in his effort to destroy him). Finally, Gordon intends the film not only to entertain, but also to attack what he perceives to be the "moral majority" attitude in which one group imposes a single "correct" way of thinking on all other groups by any means which come to hand or mind.

Gordon attacks the complicity of people who turn their backs on other's sufferings, those who refuse to get involved, by having the husband initially go to the witch burnings as a prime location to sell his wares to hungry passersby. After experiencing the suffering first-hand, the husband understands the danger of letting such monomaniacal thinking go unchecked or unexamined.

Gordon has also directed an obscure made-for-television movie called *Daughter of Darkness*, which appeared late-night on the CBS network in January, 1990. The story centered around Cathy (Mia Sara), who seeks out her father in Romania. Her father turns out to be Tony Perkins, who appears as a kindly vampire who saves her from a band of blood-swilling fiends. Unfortunately, the whole thing was rather uninspired and so is deservedly forgotten.

From his output, it is apparent that Gordon is content to continue working in the horror field. But unlike many other toilers in this vineyard, he uses the genre intelligently to comment on issues that have constantly plagued mankind. He understands there is a difference between showing someone being tortured and passing it off as entertainment, and coming to grips with what it means – namely, that some humans are capable of inflicting great and unnecessary pain on other human beings for their own twisted ends. The horror genre needs more directors like Gordon who can not only be visceral but can engage the intelligence of the audience as well, using the horror film as a forum to address uncomfortable issues and fears.

Piers Haggard (1939–)

Wedding Night (aka *I Can't . . . I Can't*, 1969); *The Blood on Satan's Claw* (aka *Satan's Skin*, 1971); *The Fiendish Plot of Dr. Fu Manchu* (1980); *Venom* (1982); *A Summer Story* (1988).

TELEVISION: *The Quatermass Conclusion* (1979); *Pennies from Heaven* (19??); *Mrs. Reinhardt* (1981); *Rolling Home; Marks* (1982); *Desert of Lies; Waters of the Moon* (1983); *Return to Treasure Island* (1986); *Visitors* (1987); *The Fulfillment of Mary Gray* (1989); *Back Home* 1990).

Piers Haggard, a British director, burst onto the horror scene with *Blood on Satan's Claw* (aka *Satan's Skin*), a little sleeper of a film from a small company called Tigon. In style and tone, *Satan's Claw* was reminiscent of *Conqueror Worm*, but while it lacked that film's deeper symbolic significance, *Claw* featured good atmosphere and a rather intriguing storyline in which a demon is plowed up and resurrects itself piece by piece by infecting a variety of innocent villagers.

During the reign of James III, a young farm lad, Ralph Gower (Barry Andrews), plows up what appears to him to be the face of a fiend. He runs to report the event to a judge (Patrick Wymark) who is visiting from the city. Meanwhile, the household is in an uproar because young Peter Edmonton (Simon Williams) has brought back a farm girl to be his bride; his mother clearly does not approve.

Unlike many horror films of the time, *Blood on Satan's Claw* wastes little time on romantic subplots. In short order, Ralph returns to the plowed field with the judge, but they fail to find the "anatomical remains" that Ralph dug up, encountering Reverend Fallowfield (Anthony Ainley) playing with a snake instead. A portion of the remains, a claw, is in the possession of Angel Blake (Linda Hayden), a mischievous friend of Cathy Vespers (Wendy Padbury), Ralph's beloved but underaged bride-to-be.

That night Peter begs that his fiancée be allowed to sleep at the house despite the impropriety, and so his aunt offers the poor girl a room in the attic that has been unused for five years. The lovers promise to rendezvous at eleven, but when eleven strikes, Peter is still listening to the judge warn him about the wiles of women. When he makes it upstairs, his fiancée lets out a scream. When his aunt enters her room to investigate, she is scratched across the face. Ralph is sent for to nail the deranged young woman in her

496

room until the people from Bedlam can pick her up the next day. Peter is shocked to see the girl leave her room with a demented and bestial expression on her face and a set of claws where her fingers used to be. Haggard sets up his last shock beautifully as we go from the shock on Peter's face to the clawed hand suddenly resting on the stair railing in the foreground.

With crisp photography by Dick Bush, Haggard directs the film so that it develops an atmosphere of growing evil and madness. We see the village children in church passing around a bag containing a claw rather than paying attention to the reverend's lessons, and we know there is going to be trouble. Peter's aunt becomes ill and the doctor (Howard Goorney) is sent for, but the only thing he can think of to do is open a vein and hope that the bad humor will pass out of her body.

In short order, the aunt disappears into the woods, never to be seen again. The troubled Peter spends a night in the room where his fiancée went mad and hears noises from under a trapdoor in the room. Reaching in, he is clutched by a hairy, clawed hand. Later the same hand seems to be choking him, but when he takes a knife and cuts it away, we discover that he has amputated his own hand.

The judge is skeptical concerning rumors of witchcraft, but these odd events give him pause. The doctor shows him a book with the image of a devil or demon from a saint's vision, and the judge decides to borrow it. He has to return to the city, but as he leaves, he mysteriously warns Squire Middleton (James Hayter) that sometimes evil must be allowed to grow before you can destroy it completely.

Young Mark Vespers (Robin Davies) discovers that he has a mysterious pain his side. His friends have taken to wearing woodland garlands and they insist on playing a game of blindman's bluff with him that ends in his getting garroted. Ellen, Marks' kind-hearted mother, returns along a forest path bringing Mark some medicine when a prankster smashes the bottle with a stone and informs her that "Mark don't need it no more. . . . We put 'im in the woodshed." There in the woodshed, the distraught Ellen finds Mark's ravaged body, a portion of it missing.

That night, Angel comes to the reverend in the church. Taking her clothes off she tries to seduce him and enjoins him to play in their games. The reverend casts her out of the church, but after Marks' funeral services, discovers that Angel has accused him of raping her and killing Mark, which the Squire believes despite Fallowfield's protests of innocence.

A pair of Angel's cohorts kidnap Cathy and take her to the ruins of an old church where a hideous furry figure hobbles in the background. As Angel's followers chant Cathy's name, she feels a pain in her backside. Her clothes are ripped off to reveal a furry patch of skin on her back. A youth starts raping her as Angel takes some shears and removes the skin, leaving her dead. Ralph finds her body and brings it to the Squire, who realizes that the reverend could not have been responsible for this crime and that Angel Blake seems to be behind these evil doings.

The screenplay by Robert Wynne Simmons with additional material by Haggard keeps up a steady stream of bizarre events that suggest things without explaining them. The fact that their children and a few old folks seem to have gone off to worship the devil has not left the villagers unaffected, but they do not want to kill their own loved ones. Haggard includes a segment on the dangers of superstition when some villagers throw Margaret (Michele Dotrice) into a lake to see if she is a witch. If she floats, she will be pronounced a witch, but if she does not, Ralph says, "You've done her murder." When she sinks, the villagers turn dejectedly away, while Ralph finally dives in and saves the girl.

He takes her to Ellen, and they decide to nurse Margaret back to health, but they notice she has a hairy bit of skin on her leg. The doctor is called and they persuade him to remove Satan's mark, which he then preserves in a glass jar. Margaret recovers from her near-drowning and operation and tries to seduce Ralph, who is disgusted by her admitted Satan worship. Margaret then escapes as the judge returns.

Using the skin taken off Margaret's leg, he has hunting dogs sent after her trail. Margaret goes to Angel to plead for help, getting her foot caught in a trap, but when Angel finds that her master's skin has been removed, she leaves Margaret to the mercy of the dogs and the judge.

Strangely, one key scene is omitted from the videocassette release of the film (which runs 100 minutes in its uncut form), and that is when Ralph swings his axe and hits his own foot. Looking at the wound, he discovers that he is now growing the creature's foot in place of his own. He decides to hide out in the infamous upstairs spare room, but footsteps are heard and he is whisked away to the ruined church.

The judge leads the villagers to the church and brandishes a holy sword. They watch as Angel and her followers begin a strange rite where a naked woman dances in front of Ralph and offers him a knife to cut off his own foot. (Some of the followers are missing other body parts.) However, before he does so, the judge springs into action, which causes Angel to flee right onto the prongs of a pitchfork. Confronting the demon figure, the judge impales it, holds it aloft, and then thrusts it into a bonfire, ending its evil spell.

The film suggests that evil takes many forms and can grow from peer pressure and other sources as well. The key figure of the judge is depicted as an intelligent, practical and sensible man who overcomes his skepticism once he is provided with proof and does what must be done. Meanwhile, poor Ellen has her offspring killed and other families are obviously affected as well. (The plights of Ellen and Ralph give the story a personal and emotional depth as they are both very likable characters who are directly affected by the growing contagion.)

The period setting works to the story's advantage, adding interesting de-tails, and the lush, green countryside makes a nice contrast to the paganistic horrors it hides. Haggard proves a capable director by his ability to create tension and then release with an unexpected shock, so the film never becomes wearying or predictable in the way so many horror films do.

After this promising beginning, Haggard worked mostly in television during the '70s, directing the disappointing *Quatermass Conclusion,* Nigel Kneale's final film about Bernard Quatermass. It centers around how old druid circles are calling young people to them only for the possessed adoles-cents to be vaporized by aliens once they reached their goal. The episodes of this serial were hastily and ineffectively cut together, excluding many im-portant plot points, for an eventual videocassette release that was even more disappointing.

Far better but rarely seen is Haggard's miniseries of Dennis Potter's *Pennies from Heaven* starring Bob Hopkins, which was remade as a big-budget musical by Herbert Ross starring Steve Martin. *Pennies from Hea-ven* contrasted harsh Depression reality with the cheery fantasies evoked by the era's songs as a song salesman (Hopkins) pursues his dream.

Haggard returned to the big screen with Peter Sellers' last film, a pathetic parody of Sax Rohmer's *Fu Manchu* series called *The Fiendish Dr. Fu Manchu.* The film was a terrible misfire from beginning to end and was said to be plagued with problems throughout production. There were even rumors that Sellers himself took over writing and directing parts of the film, but if so, it was to no avail.

The film was set in the 1930s as Fu Manchu is celebrating his 168th birth-day (with minions surrounding an enormous cake, chanting, "Happy Birth-day to Fu"). Fu Manchu has masterminded a series of robberies, including the Crown Jewels, to get the ingredients for an elixir which will restore his youth.

Sellers plays both Fu Manchu and his English arch-nemesis Nayland Smith, but does not manage to essay either role very well (which is especially disappointing as he had just finished giving one of the best performances of his career in *Being There*). Particularly embarrassing is when Manchu finally gets his hands on the elixir and transforms into an Elvis Presley imitator who belts out, "Rock a Fu," an incredibly dumb ditty. Of the cast, which in-clude David Tomlinson and Sid Caesar, the only one not to embarrass her-self was Helen Mirren as an undercover agent.

Haggard was to do much better with another problem-plagued film, *Venom.* Taking the reins after Tobe Hooper and his crew were dismissed, Haggard crafted a rather suspenseful tale of a kidnapping and a black mamba snake with an especially good cast. The snake was intended for toxicologist Dr. Stowe (Sarah Miles) but through a mix-up winds up in the posession of Philip Hopkins (Lance Holcomb) an asthmatic young boy living in London.

Everything starts to go amiss when a German terrorist, Jacmel (Klaus Kinski), conspires with the boy's servants, Dave (Oliver Reed) and Louise (Susan George), to kidnap the boy. In the process of the abduction, the brutish Dave kills a British bobby, which leads to a standoff with the police while the mamba gets loose and terrorizes everyone within the house. (Haggard makes interesting use of angles that provide a snake's-eye-view of the proceedings.)

Helping the boy on the inside is his grandfather, Howard Anderson (Sterling Hayden), while Commander William Bulloch (Nicol Williamson) holds the criminals at bay on the outside. The cast is uniformly good, and Kinski and Reed make their warped characters particularly interesting, with Kinski projecting a cool-headed menace while Reed seems barely able to keep his inner violence contained and appears ready to explode at any moment. The basic tense situation is set up and interest is maintained as the snake strikes at unpredictable moments.

Overall, *Venom* proved a surprisingly good thriller even if some of the performances are a bit arch and the story stretches credulity at times. However, Haggard seems to have left the horror field behind, working more readily in television in Great Britain. Haggard's most recent film, *A Summer Story*, is an adaptation of John Galsworthy's "The Apple Tree" and has received good critical notices, but it has that "Masterpiece Theater" shine that effectively embalms a story rather than enlivening it. The result is respectable, but far from the unpredictable liveliness that sparked *Blood on Satan's Claw* or *Venom* and made them offbeat gems. Haggard can put together a great horror thriller if only he's willing to get his hands soiled and get a little disreputable again. Perhaps we will have to wait and see.

Curtis Harrington (1928–   )

Night Tide (1961); *Voyage to the Prehistoric Planet* (as John Sebastian, 1965); *Queen of Blood* (1966); *Games* (1967); *What's the Matter with Helen?; Whoever Slew Auntie Roo?* (1971); *The Killing Kind* (1973); *Ruby* (1977); *Mata Hari* (1985).

TELEVISION: "A Lonely Place," "A Burying Place for Rosie," *Legend of Jessie James* (1966); *How Awful About Allan* (1970); *The Cat Creature* (1973); *The Killer Bees; The Dead Don't Die* (1974); "Set-Up City," "Murder for Me" *Baretta* (1975); "A Hand for Sonny Blue" *Tales of the Unexpected* (1976); "Stargate" *Logan's Run;* "Pariah" *Lucan* (1977); *Devil Dog: The Hound of Hell* (1978); *Glitter; Dynasty* (multiples).

Genteel, rather than gentle, describes the macabre movies of Curtis Harrington. Harrington's films betray a fondness for moody atmosphere and disturbed personalities. Harrington evokes a feeling of horror by creating an atmosphere of impending doom about to come down on his leading characters (the sailor and Mora in *Night Tide;* Katherine Ross' character in *Games;* Debbie Reynolds and Shelley Winters in *What's the Matter with Helen?*). His best films tend to be the ones in which he was involved in the scripting. His personal vision then shapes his films into what the advertising for *Night Tide* called "a unique experience in the weird and terrifying!"

Recently, Harrington has been laboring in the fields of episodic television, working on such shows as *Glitter* and *Dynasty,* and has directed a feature version of *Mata Hari* starring Sylvia Kristal. He has not, however, forsaken his love of the *outré* and the macabre. For years, he has been pushing to make a film of Iris Murdoch's classic gothic novel *The Unicorn.* As Harrington told me in an interview:

> I've tried to get financing for it in every way I can think of and I've come close to it. It's been announced by Fox Classics, and they will partially finance it and release it, but I still haven't been able to get the financing needed even with their offer. I have a new producer who is eager to do it, and he may have some avenues of financing that he's going to explore that we haven't tried before. That's a producer named Kenneth Hyman, who was the executive producer of *What Ever Happened to Baby Jane?*
> The script of *The Unicorn* was given to Kenneth Hyman by someone

and he liked it. He contacted me and said, "I see you like the script so much, well, I'd like to produce it." Since my last producer didn't seem to be able to find a dime to help finance it, I'm working on it now with him and we'll see what we can do. It's in the tradition of *Rebecca*, a neo-gothic thriller. It's quite a cut above the usual paperback gothic. Murdoch's a much more complex and sophisticated writer. She wrote it in the '60s, and it's a very interesting, offbeat novel.

According to Harrington, he has long had an interest in the macabre:

> There's a saying that when you are born into this world, you come in with something. My interest in the macabre is so deep in my nature that there is no way to explain it except by something in my psyche that I came into this world with. One of the earliest memories that I can remember is seeing some poster from *The Bride of Frankenstein*. This must have been in 1935. I was very young, and I couldn't even read then. I was so fascinated by it, and then I asked my mother to take me to see it, but she wouldn't.
>
> Somehow I became aware of horror films and I begged and begged and begged. Finally, a couple of years later, she took me to see *The Raven* with Karloff and Lugosi. I saw it at the old Majestic Theater in Santa Monica. I remember she said that I climbed out of my seat and got under it because I was scared. She grabbed me and took me out of the theater and said, "That's the last horror film I'm going to take you to." I didn't get to see any more until I finally got my father to take me to see one of those revival double bills of *Frankenstein* and *Dracula* that played in the late '30s. Those were the first two genuine horror films I got to see in their entirety.
>
> There was always an overwhelming interest. It would take a psychiatrist to figure it out. I remember when I was five years old, I began to make puppets, and I was already into macabre things like making a puppet that was a phantom, so it is very hard to explain all that. It was the macabre aspect of fairy tales that fascinated me as a child. I was interested in witches and goblins and things like that, the whole concept of the macabre.
>
> When I was a teenager, I began to read the short stories of Edgar Allan Poe, which I devoured with intense interest. Then, shortly afterward, I discovered in the newsstands *Weird Tales* and the old *Unknown* magazine, which I have almost a complete collection of.

At the age of 14, Harrington made his first film, an adaptation of "The Fall of the House of Usher." His interest in film brought him to the USC film school, which was quite different in his day – a long way from the one that George Lucas and John Carpenter attended in the late '60s and early '70s. Recalled Harrington, "At that tme, they hadn't gotten around to having students make student films. They had courses in film history, screenwriting, and film editing. The idea of really making student films, though it had been done at points in the history of the USC cinema school . . . wasn't the standard part of the curriculum." Nevertheless, Harrington made several short films outside of the university and started developing his skills as a filmmaker.

Harrington studied acting under Robert Gist and played Cesare in Kenneth Anger's *Inauguration of the Pleasure Dome*. Later he became an assistant to Jerry Wald, a dynamic producer who made such films as *Peyton Place* and *The Stripper*. He left Wald's organization for a time to direct his first feature, *Night Tide*:

> I wrote the script myself. It was based on an unpublished short story I wrote called "The Secrets of the Sea" and I adapted it myself, so it was an original screenplay. From the time it was made to the time it was released, it was somewhat delayed. It was released by Roger Corman's company, the Filmgroup, and was distributed by American International for the Filmgroup. It was finished in 1961, but it wasn't released until 1963.
>
> The reason that it was held up in the laboratory had to do with the way the film was financed. It was one of those things that low-budget films sometimes get involved in. The guy who financed it wanted some kind of guarantee before he would give the money to get it out of the lab.
>
> Roger Corman is so well known now as being the patron saint of filmmakers over the last 20 years. I went to him with my *Night Tide* project, and what he did was he gave me some distributor guarantees. He didn't hand me any money, but he gave me those distributor guarantees which helped me raise money. He also helped me get a lab [film-processing] deferral deal at the film laboratory, which they were giving in those days. As I remember, the lab gave part of the financing, maybe $10,000 worth or something.

Night Tide was very consciously made in the tradition of the Val Lewton films, *The Cat People* in particular. The film is about a girl named Mora (Linda Lawson) who thinks she is a mermaid and fears that like mermaids in fairy tales, she will lure anyone who loves her to his doom. There is even a strange woman who approaches her and says something unintelligible (played by painter Cameron Parsons), much like Elizabeth Russell approaching Simone Simon and addressing her as a sister.

The main character is a sailor, Johnny Drake (played by Dennis Hopper), who comes from Colorado and who is fascinated by the sea. He quickly falls in love with the aloof Mora and seeks to learn more about her. He learns that her two previous boyfriends were both found drowned, and he is warned off by her employer, Captain Murdock (Gavin Muir). Mora stars as a mermaid in a sideshow exhibit, where she is exhibited complete with tail under a water-filled glass tank. The getup is just a fake – or is it?

The film was largely shot on the Santa Monica pier and along the weed-choked canals of Venice, California. Harrington uses these locations to evoke decay and despair. The pier, once the source of amusement, now seems forlorn and barren, a shadow of the joys it once offered. Dennis Hopper's sailor is an achingly lonely man, haunted by a mysterious woman who fears growing close to any man. Their relationship is always uneasy and uncertain.

The film is moody, recalling Herk Harvey's *Carnival of Souls*, and some would even call it ponderous, but it does have several memorably eerie moments. In one scene, the sailor goes to Murdock's house to try to find out more about Mora. He is shocked to find a human hand floating in a jar of formaldehyde in one of Murdock's cabinets. Later, he dreams about Mora being a mermaid and the dream turns into a nightmare where he is struggling in the tentacles of an octopus on Mora's couch. When he sees the strange woman addressing Mora, he pursues her, only to have her disappear inexplicably while in plain sight. Finally, Mora, driven mad by her sexual repression and the tales of the sea's sirens, pulls the sailor into the moonlit surf, laughing hysterically. Diving, she makes an attempt on his life and then disappears. The sailor finds her dead, killed by Murdock and placed in the mermaid's tank.

Said Harrington:

> The ending of the film is intentionally ambiguous. In other words, the ending allows the audience to have one of two interpretations as they wish. What happened to Mora? Was she really what she thought she was after all? Or was it all just a hoax perpetrated by the sea captain? ... [If] you have a very realistic frame of mind, you'll accept the captain's story [that Murdock told Mora these tales to keep her close to him and not see other men] and let it go at that, and if you don't, you can entertain a measure of doubt.

Night Tide is a mermaid film far from the lighthearted tone of Ron Howard's *Splash*. Vilis Lapenieks' cinematography is subtle and low-keyed, but it beautifully communicates the despairing mood that Harrington was aiming for. This is one of the finest low-budget chillers of the '60s.

Harrington's next directorial effort was *Queen of Blood*, which also bears the television title *Planet of Blood*. Said Harrington:

> *Queen of Blood* came about sometime after I finished *Night Tide*. As I remember, Roger Corman contacted me at some point and said, "I have this footage from a Soviet science fiction movie which I have the rights to." He simply asked me if I could devise a new storyline. He said I could write it and direct it and he would finance it and pay me to do

Rare shot of Curtis Harrington (left) with star John Saxon on the set of Queen of Blood. *Notice that Saxon's spacesuit is more a mechanic's overalls with an overlay around the neck. The films was shot in seven and a half days for a mere $65,000 and designed to utilize special effects from a Russian film that Roger Corman had picked up the rights to.*

it. I devised a storyline, which had nothing to do with the storyline of the Soviet film other than just the physical effects which we used.

It's interesting to me that it has the formula of more recent, spectacular movies like *Alien*. It's exactly the same plot, except the alien is different and the incidents are different, but it's the same basic idea.

Queen of Blood is a mildly enjoyable science fiction/horror thriller about some astronauts who discover a beautiful alien (Florence Marly) and decide to bring her back to earth. En route, they discover she is a vampire and so the crew take turns donating blood for her to drink. Unfortunately, this only whets her appetite, and she starts draining the crew members of all their blood. While her form is human, her green skin and iridescent eyes, not to mention her vampiric tendencies, mark her as being of an alien race. Marly may not be the most convincing alien, but she is definitely one of the most attractive. Despite the film's low budget, the rest of the cast was also fairly solid. Basil Rathbone played Dr. Farraday, one of the head scientists back home; other cast members included John Saxon, Judi Meredith, Dennis Hopper, and Forrest J Ackerman in a small but memorable cameo. Said Harrington:

> This was towards the end of Basil's career, but he was still a name. We paid him quite a bit of money to work for two days on the film. He came out there and did it. We got John Saxon and Dennis Hopper for a bit. It was my idea to put Florence Marly in it because I had known her socially, and she had been in a famous Czechoslovakian science fiction film called *Krakatit*, which to this day I've never seen. I think she was quite good in the part. Forry, who has been a friend of mine for many years, I wanted. I thought it was perfect and I asked him to be in it, to be the scientist in the end so that all of his fans could see him.

Harrington next worked on *Voyage to the Prehistoric Planet* under the pseudonym John Sebastian. The film was basically an English-language version of the Russian science fiction film *Planeta Burg* directed by Pavel Klushantsev. Harrington's recollections:

> *Voyage to the Prehistoric Planet* doesn't even have my name on it because all I did for that was some reshooting. They had some scenes that took place in a spacecraft hovering over the planet Venus. In the original Soviet film, there were a couple of Russian actors, and I redid all those scenes almost verbatim with Basil Rathbone and Faith Domergue so that there would be some American names in the film. But 90 percent of the film is just a dub job on a Soviet science fiction film. I had so completely adapted *Queen of Blood* that it was just like using some stock footage, whereas this film was all the Soviet film. I wouldn't have wanted the credit.

Harrington's next film was one of his finest, *Games*. Primarily a suspense thriller, the film does have some supernatural and horrific overtones and is an extremely effective portrayal of three personalities in conflict. Katherine Ross plays a rich heiress who has married James Caan, a layabout with a love of games. Their home becomes a shrine to pop art and game-playing. Enter Simone Signoret as a mysterious traveling saleslady who works her way into the couple's household and who is interested in far more serious (and deadly) games.

A connection with the occult is established early on during a mock black mass. Later, James Caan has his wife seduce the delivery boy as part of an elaborate game; then, playing the enraged husband, he shoots the delivery boy with a gun loaded with blanks. Unfortunately, it seems a live cartridge was mixed in with the blank shells, and now there is a body to be disposed of. Ross starts fearing that the soul of the delivery boy is coming back to haunt her. Meanwhile, the couple must try to keep their secret away from

Signoret, their house guest, who in turn makes Ross uneasy with her tarot cards (depicting calamity striking a house and death) and her crystal ball (from which springs an image of the delivery boy bleeding from his right eye).

Caan dismisses Signoret for disturbing his wife and disposes of the body by disguising it as one of sculptor George Segal's plaster statues (reminiscent of the way Dick Miller covers people in clay in *Bucket of Blood*) and then having it "accidentally" fall into the water while transporting it to a friend. However, there are still a few more twists and turns to come. Left alone, Ross sees the delivery boy once more and shoots him, only to have her husband appear and reveal that the delivery boy had not died, his death had been faked, and that Ross has just murdered him. He calls up the police and reports the homicide. Dumbstruck, Ross is led away to prison. Apparently, Caan lost an old flame to a rich man and married Ross to get her money so that he could court the old flame again. Simone Signoret was in on the plot and comments that professionals keep their games simple. "Oh," returns Caan, sipping his poisoned wine, "you wouldn't call my plan simple." "That is exactly the point," Signoret observes, watching him die.

The plot is extremely well constructed with each of the elaborate games designed to keep the audience guessing and to reveal something about the characters. The film is top notch from the script to the cast to the set decorations to Bill Fraker's cinematography to Harrington's superb direction. It is everything a good thriller should be: interesting, intriguing, lush in its visuals, with complex characters involved in a fascinating plot.

There is no doubt that *Games* is a tribute to Harrington's abilities as a director and reflects his Sternbergian influences. Josef Sternberg, famous for his films with Marlene Dietrich such as *The Blue Angel, The Scarlet Empress*, and *The Devil Is a Woman*, is the director that Harrington feels the greatest affinity with and admiration for. In fact, Harrington's first scholarly work was an annotated filmography of Sternberg's films which later led to a reassessment of the man's work by modern critics. Like Sternberg, Harrington carefully controls the elements in his frame (i.e., his *mise en scène*) with particular attention paid to careful and beautiful lighting, detailed backgrounds with various kinds of artwork in evidence, and the performances of the actors themselves. They also share a fondness for throwing in a bit of uncontrolled madness amidst their meticulous settings.

Harrington recalled how *Games* evolved:

> I started *Games*. George Edwards was the producer of the film, he also produced *Queen of Blood*, and he and I collaborated on the original story. It was basically my idea, but from the idea of this woman visiting this young couple, we evolved the story over a few days so it is very hard for me to say what precisely was his contribution and what was

mine. Although the basic idea was mine, he contributed a lot of twists and turns. It was one of those things that evolved out of mutual conversation, and then we put it down on paper and we sold it to the studio. Then we worked with George Kearney, who developed it into a script and who contributed more twists and turns to the plot.

It was intended to be a *Diabolique* kind of thriller. It was purely coincidental, however, that the star of *Diabolique* ended up being the star of our movie. The film was conceived as a vehicle for Marlene Dietrich. She would have played the Simone Signoret role, but the head of the studio didn't feel that she was, at this point in her career, sufficient box office interest, so that's why we got Simone Signoret instead.

After *Games*, Harrington began an association with Henry Farrell, the screenwriter and author of *What Ever Happened to Baby Jane?* The first project Farrell wrote for Harrington was a made-for-TV movie called *How Awful About Allan*. In it, Tony Perkins, noted for playing psychos in *Psycho* and *Pretty Poison*, plays a semi-sighted man just getting out of a mental institution. He is racked with guilt over a fire he feels responsible for which killed his father and scarred his sister (Julie Harris of *The Haunting* fame). Slowly, while staying at his sister's, Perkins begins to suspect that the new boarder in the house is his sister's old boyfriend who is trying to trick Perkins into killing himself. He confesses his troubles to his old girlfriend, Joan Hackett, but she does not believe him. Said Harrington:

> *How Awful About Allan* was also produced by George Edward. That was an idea he had. He had been interested in trying to make a film because of our association with Henry Farrell, and by that time we were developing *What's the Matter with Helen?* which was based on an original outline by Henry Farrell. *How Awful About Allan* was, I think, a novel he had published either before or after *Baby Jane*. George thought it would make a good movie. At first I couldn't see the possibility of it because it dealt with someone who was blind. If you read the novel, so much of the novel is from the subjective point of view of someone who can't see. How can you do that? You can't just show a lot of black on the screen.
>
> George was the one who came up with an idea of how to do that [Perkins' sight partially returns, so everything he sees is blue.] He really was the mover and shaker behind that. We did it for Aaron Spelling Productions for ABC, I think. I think it was the only TV movie that Tony Perkins has ever made. He was perfect for the part. He was very interesting, and he was such a conscientious actor. He wears contact lenses, so to my surprise, by the time he arrived to work on the film, he had had his optometrist make him opaque contact lenses, so in all the scenes in which he appears, he is actually blind. He had to be led onto the set because he couldn't see what he was doing.

In *What's the Matter with Helen?* Debbie Reynolds and Shelley Winters play the mothers of a Leopold and Loeb–type murder team. After their sons'

convictions, the mothers flee to Hollywood, where they set up a dance studio
for would-be Shirley Temples. While Adele (Reynolds) starts falling in love
with a Texas millionaire (Dennis Weaver), Helen (Winters) turns to religion
in the form of Sister Alma (Agnes Moorehead), an Aimee Semple MacPher-
son–type evangelist. Adele has a resilient spirit and she looks forward to life
with hope, while Helen is consumed with guilt which she hopes to expiate
by serving Sister Alma. She is as frightened a creature as the rabbit she likes
to carry around with her and is slowly going mad.

The film is full of odd touches and homages. There are bizarre midgets,
little girls acting much older than they are, and revolting stage mothers
who act younger. The most disturbing moment of all occurs when Adele discovers Helen has butchered all her rabbits. The portrait of Hollywood depicts
a rather pathetic town with tarnished dreams, yet we see echoes of what
the characters are aspiring to in visual references to *Singin' in the Rain,*
Sunset Boulevard, Mae West, and others.

Unfortunately, the climactic murder is only a shadow of what Harrington had intended because the producer Martin Ransohoff insisted on a PG
rating rather than an R. Nevertheless, the final image of the dead Debbie
Reynolds dressed in a drum majorette outfit and propped against a wall as
if prepared to perform, followed by a shot of the completely deranged Shelley Winters, presented an unhappy ending counter to the times and was a
particularly effective depiction of a final descent into madness and death.

Harrington was able to find a champion for *What's the Matter with
Helen?* when he brought it to the attention of Debbie Reynolds. Said he:

> Again, George Edwards developed it at Universal, and we couldn't
> cast it. It was the same old problem. We had all these people who tried
> to get a couple of people the studio wanted, and we didn't succeed.
> Later it turned out Debbie Reynolds, who had just done a TV series,
> had a deal with NBC to finance a couple of pictures starring her. When
> we got her interested in it, that's how it got made. We got it made inde-
> pendently through Martin Ransohoff and it was released through United
> Artists. It was mostly financed by NBC. They had the first rights to
> show it on television.
>
> We originally tried to do it at Univeral as a follow-up to *Games,* but
> they decided not to make it because we couldn't cast it to their satisfac-
> tion. We also developed another interesting script while we were there
> that was never made called *The Guests.* Oddly enough, I had never read
> Agatha Christie. I've just been seeing the movies these recent years.
> I've never been interested in the detective story *per se.* I never read
> Hercule Poirot stories; I had never read *Murder on the Orient Express,*
> so when I saw the movie, I realized that quite unwittingly, we had used
> the basic gimmick of *Murder on the Orient Express* in . . . *The Guests,*
> which was written by Joseph Stefano who had written the screenplay
> for *Psycho.*

We sort of collaborated on the story with Joseph Stefano. The basic idea was – I can't remember, I guess it was mine – I wanted to do a story about a group of people who are invited to an isolated mansion for a weekend and all the mad things that happen. The gimmick we had was . . . these people . . . are invited to this weekend, and everybody when they arrive in their room, they find an identical gun laid on the dresser or whatever, like a gift for their weekend. Then they go down to the shooting range and learn how to shoot the gun. As the story evolves, one by one, all of these guests learn that the host of the party has something on each guest which he threatens to reveal.

It was made, of course, when certain things were considered to be more shocking than they are now. With one girl, he threatens to reveal she was a prostitute. Another guest used to be involved in some shady financial dealings. They all had things they don't want revealed about their past, and this guy threatens to reveal everything. All the guests get together and decide that if they kill him together, then nobody would be to blame. It was a different version but the same basic gimmick as *Murder on the Orient Express*. Once again, we couldn't cast it to the satisfaction of the head of the studios, so it was never made. I think it would have been a very entertaining movie.

It's much harder to do now. You see things have changed. This was in 1970. By 1984, these kinds of secrets don't mean much. Nobody gives a damn. If somebody is gay, nobody cares if it gets revealed. If somebody used to be a whore, they say, "So?" Big deal. The mores of society have changed to such a degree that it's no longer such a shocking secret. It's very hard to think of things that people don't really want revealed, unless, on a certain level naturally, if you're a minister of the cloth and it's going to be revealed you murdered somebody or something. That's pretty shocking. But generally it's harder to work it out. We'd have to revamp the whole thing.

Shelley Winters was so pleased with *What's the Matter with Helen?* that she asked Harrington to direct her in her next feature, *Whoever Slew Auntie Roo?* The script went through a number of changes in the process of being made. It started out as a short story by David Osborn which was adapted into a screenplay by Robert Blees and Jimmy Sangster (the latter was one of Hammer Films' top screenwriters). Harrington was not too happy with the initial script and had Gavin Lambert make a few changes. Originally, the project was to be called *The Gingerbread House* and was about two orphans and a more-than-eccentric Auntie Roo who become the figures in a non-supernatural retelling of "Hansel and Gretel."

As the film opens, Auntie Roo (Shelley Winters) has lost her daughter Kathryn, whose mummified body she walks around with and talks to. It is quite apparent that Auntie is a few bricks shy of a load. Not wishing to accept her daughter's death, she visits a phony medium, Mr. Benton (another one of Sir Ralph Richardson's marvelous performances), but the séances seeking to contact the other side simply does not help ease the pain of her loss.

Each Christmas, kindhearted Auntie Roo gives a party for children from the local orphanage, and during the course of one such party, she develops a fondness for Katy (Chloe Franks), whose name and appearance remind her of her own daughter. Auntie decides to kidnap the young innocent and does so successfully; however, Christopher (Mark Lester), the little girl's older brother, arrives on the scene and convinces Katy that Auntie Roo is in reality the wicked witch from the famous "Hansel and Gretel" fairy tale.

Given this perspective, every time Auntie picks up a knife or a meat cleaver, she seems menacing, and the children's belief that she really is a witch becomes credible. Harrington takes advantage of the '20s setting and several fine character actors (in addition to Richardson, there are also appearances by Hugh Griffith and Lionel Jeffries to perk things up) to give the film a pleasantly unreal feeling that persuades the viewer to accept its fairy-tale interpretations of real life. Unfortunately, we all know the ending of "Hansel and Gretel," so the ending of the film becomes quite predictable. Curtis Harrington has been quoted as saying he found Winters' "mad behavior vastly amusing." Unfortunately, that air of humor does not carry over into the film itself where she merely seems befuddled and eccentric. One feels too much pity to laugh at her.

Strangely enough, the film has two similar titles. Harrington explained what happened:

> The title on the screen is *Whoever Slew Auntie Roo?* That was the title it had in England. In America, they called it *Who Slew Auntie Roo,* I guess because AIP, being such a lowbrow organization, thought that the word "whoever" was too fancy for people to understand. I thought it gave it an edge of poetry to say *whoever.* It's like *Whatever* is quite different than *What Happened to Baby Jane.* . . . It changes. With *Who Slew Auntie Roo,* who cares who slew Auntie Roo? But *Whoever Slew Auntie Roo* makes it more poetic. That's the real title for the film, despite whatever the distributors labeled it.
>
> I originally wanted it to be called *The Gingerbread House,* but they opposed the title. I thought as long as they opposed that title, it might as well be as good as it can be. I think one of the reasons they changed it was that there was a play called *The Gingerbread Lady.* They thought it might, especially if a film was made of it . . . cause confusion.

The characters of the children are fairly complex as they seem, by turns, to be innocent, then knowing; aware of reality, then caught up in fantasy. Harrington clarified his intentions:

> I think I made it pretty clear I had two levels with the children. The boy was not innocent. The little girl was innocent. The little boy put all

those ideas into the little girl's head. If you remember the film, you see he is not innocent because of the way he smiles at Auntie Roo when she is locked in there, but nevertheless, the boy is still trading off his – from the point of view of the adults – his childhood innocence, so that the irony at the end was that these adults were saying, "Oh these poor children. They'll never forget this horror." You go back and the children on two different levels have gotten away with it. The little girl, completely innocent about the whole thing, is just delighted that the wicked witch is dead. [The little boy saves his sister's teddy bear into which he deposited Auntie Roo's jewelry.] They smile and are very happy. They are not scarred at all by the incident.

The Killing Kind, Harrington's next film, was not so much released as buried, and unfortunately so, as it again is an interesting study of disturbed personalities. John Savage plays Terry, a young man who was accused and convicted of a rape he didn't commit. After serving two years, he goes to live with his mother (Ann Southern), who wants to take over his life and whose loving care seems suffocating to him. Troubled to begin with, he goes over the deep end and murders the trollop who charged him with rape and later dispatches his lawyer for having done such a poor job. However, he goes beyond revenge when he turns on a female boarder (Cindy Williams in an early role) whom he finds pushy.

The material borders on the familiar (after *Psycho* there were several films about mama's boys going on killing rampages), but there are fine performances by Savage, Southern, and Luana Anders as Terry's female counterpart who is saddled with a handicapped, overbearing father.

Said Harrington:

> That film I'm quite proud of, even though it had virtually no release. I found John Savage. He had appeared in a couple of films in small roles, but this was his first major role and he's very good in it.
>
> It played in the South. It only played regionally. It was unfortunate, but again it was one of those things that [was] independently financed. A man who is long gone from Los Angeles had a company that produced TV commercials which he also distributed. He wanted to have his own distribution organization. He convinced these financiers in Texas that they should give him the distribution rights to the film and that he would guarantee them a return on their money. They fell for it, being inexperienced in this business.
>
> While they would be getting his personal guarantee, they would also be getting unbelievably terrible distribution. I mean it was like giving the film to my grandmother to distribute. They had no organization. Nothing, it was just a fantasy.
>
> I know Sammy Fuller [director of several great B movies] loves the film and he tried to help me get another distributor later, but he couldn't do it because once a film has been semi-distributed or partially

distributed, it's got to have something very, very special to try again with it.

During this time in the '70s, Harrington also did some noteworthy TV movies. Two of them, *The Cat Creature* and *The Dead Don't Die*, were written by famed horror writer Robert Bloch. Bloch credits Harrington with the idea of changing the main character in *The Cat Creature* from male to female so that Harrington could use the wonderful Gale Sondergaard (famous for her portrayals of "the Spider Woman" and her performance as the Cat in the Shirley Temple version of *The Blue Bird*) as Bast, the Egyptian cat goddess who is seeking a sacred amulet. As a kind of in-joke, Kent Smith (hero in *The Cat People* and *Curse of the Cat People*) makes a brief appearance. The film has some of the feel of a '40s horror story and abounds with many delightful B movie actors: John Carradine, Key Luke, John Abbott, Stuart Whitman, and David Hedison. A problem occured when, after the script was trimmed at the insistence of the producers, the film came out 12 minutes short. Quickly Bloch had to cobble some inserts together to fill out the time using new sets (the old ones had been struck), and Harrington was able to mesh the results into the final film fairly well.

Bloch credits Harrington with doing the best he can within the limitations of time and budget as well as being a helpful collaborator rather than a dictatorial *auteur* on their mutual projects. *The Dead Don't Die* also had many fine supporting actors but they were let down by the leads, George Hamilton (in a typically hammy performance as a man trying to clear his executed brother's name) and Ray Milland (who stumbles through his role and makes a shambles out of it). The plot concerns a group of West Indians led by a voodoo master who plans to raise up a zombie army to rule the world. Bloch's original story was set in the '50s at a carnival, but the producers, perhaps under the influence of *They Shoot Horses, Don't They?* decided that a Depression-style dance marathon would make for a less expensive location.

Made between the TV movies, *The Killer Bees* has only a fine performance by Gloria Swanson, as a wine-grower who sends out swarms of bees to attack her enemies, to recommend it. Still Harrington cannot be faulted terribly as no one else has been able to make a good movie out of the killer bee premise, and the other films do not even have a good performance to keep one's mind off the inanities of the plot.

For his last three excursions in horror, Curtis Harrington experienced some unfortunate interference, and as a result he considers them "absolute travesties of my intentions." The first of these was an episode of the short-lived *Tales of the Unexpected* TV series called "A Hand for Sonny Blue." This was a "Hands of Orlac"–type piece about a major league pitcher who receives an arm transplant from a vicious young hoodlum.

Said Harrington of the experience:

> In my opinion, absolutely nothing is left of me in that show. That was completely recut by the producer, and he took out every element that I tried to get in. He systematically took them out. Not only that, but he had whole sections reshot by another director, so despite the fact that my name is on it, it does not in any way have my endorsement.
>
> First of all, working quite apart from what it might have been, at least it would have been my version, but the project was doomed from the moment that the producers decided to cast Ricky Nelson in the leading role because Ricky Nelson can't act. He's a sweet boy, and I don't mean to speak ill of him, but the project was doomed from the moment they cast him. The irony is, I said to the producers that the one thing that will make this thing work is we have to have a really superb actor. It really requires an absolutely first rate actor to do this part because it's a very difficult part. They said, "Yes, of course, you're absolutely right!" Two days later, they came to me and said, "We cast Ricky Nelson."

Devil Dog: The Hound of Hell, about a family menaced by a satanically possessed dog, was a hopeless project from the start, though Harrington did the best he could with it as he had with his other television projects, most of which have fine casts and cameramen. However, the worst blow came with the 1977 film *Ruby.*

Despite its clichés, *Ruby* had the potential to be a really fine horror film. The story was about a gangster who returns from the dead to possess his daughter and avenge his murder by several gang associates who are now running a drive-in (showing scenes from the absurdly surreal *Attack of the 50 Foot Woman*). Unfortunately, Piper Laurie as the gangster's moll overplays her role and the film was highly altered in post-production, making it both confusing and absurd. There are a few memorable touches. One great moment of macabre humor has a mob member killed and hooked up inside a soda machine. A woman puts her quarter in to get a cup of Coke and gets a cup of blood instead. The other memorable moment occurs at the end where, in a twist on Shelley Winters' demise in *Night of the Hunter*, Piper Laurie embraces the skeletal remains of her lover at the bottom of the lake. It's a moment worth remembering for its beautiful eeriness in a film that is not.

So what happened?

> Steve Krantz [*Ruby*'s executive producer] is a monster. It was just a nightmare to work with him. He completely recut the film. He didn't even allow me to shoot certain things in the story, important things, and he stuck in some additional scenes later that were shot by somebody else. The film is just a travesty of my intentions. I just disavow it.

The television version had even less of my work, so in the case of the
TV version, I went to the Director's Guild and asked them to take my
name off of it. I've never seen it on TV, so I don't know if they actually
went through all the prints and took my name off of it or not, but they
were supposed to have done so. It's not supposed to have my name on
it when it's shown on television, so if you ever see it with my name on
it, please let me know.

Harrington is definitely one of the more talented aficionados of the horror field. However, even with several good films behind him (particularly
Night Tide, Games, and *What's the Matter with Helen?*), it seems as if his
potential has not fully been tapped. Perhaps his intended adaptation of Irish
Murdoch's *The Unicorn* will provide him with the proper tapestry to create
an exquisitely realized horror project utilizing all of his assets as a fine director: an ability to create and sustain a mood, good handling of actors, careful
but not contrived attention to decor and photography, and a rich visual
style.

Gordon Hessler (1930–   )

The Woman Who Wouldn't Die (aka *Catacombs*, 1965); *The Oblong Box; The Last Shot You Hear* (1969); *Scream and Scream Again; Cry of the Banshee* (1970); *Murders in the Rue Morgue* (1971); *Embassy* (1973); *The Golden Voyage of Sinbad* (1974); *Traccia di Veleno in una Coppa di Champagne* (1975); *Escape from El Diablo* (1983); *Pray for Death* (1985); *Rage of Honor* (1986); *Wheels of Terror* (aka *The Misfit Brigade*, 1987); *The Girl in a Swing; Out on Bail* (1989); *Shogun Mayeda* (1990).

TELEVISION: *Alfred Hitchcock Hour* (as producer, '63–'65); *Convoy* (series, producer, '66); *Scream Pretty Peggy* (1973); *Skyway to Death; Hitchhike!; A Cry in the Wilderness; Betrayal* (1974); *The Strange Possession of Mrs. Oliver* (1977); *Puzzle; Secrets of Three Hungry Wives; KISS Meets the Phantom of the Park* (1978); *Beggerman, Thief; The Secret War of Jackie's Girls* (1980).

The popularity of Gordon Hessler as a horror film director is rather hard to explain given that his films show almost no affinity for the genre and, apart from a few shocks in *Scream and Scream Again*, are rather tepid and unexciting besides. Perhaps it is just a result of enthusiasm for some new blood in the field. Perhaps it was expected that with practice, Hessler would churn out better thrillers. But the fact of the matter is that Hessler's earliest horror films are his best, and he appears to have found a much more comfortable niche working in American television.

Born in Berlin in 1930, Hessler started his screen career as a story editor for *Alfred Hitchcock Presents* and graduated to producer of *The Alfred Hitchcock Hour* prior to his directorial debut, *The Woman Who Wouldn't Die* (British title: *Catacombs*). Based on a novel by Jay Bennett and scripted by Daniel Mainwaring (best known for scripting the 1956 *Invasion of the Body Snatchers*), this is another of those "two people conspire to dupe a third into thinking that someone has come back to haunt him" films that were so popular following the success of Clouzot's *Diabolique*. This time a gigolo (played by Gary Merrill) who has killed his wife (Georgina Cookson) is tricked by a mistress (Jane Merrow) and the wife's male secretary (Neil McCallum). It proved to be a very routine thriller.

Hessler returned to the horror film four years later with *The Oblong Box*, originally to have been directed by Michael Reeves, who died shortly after it commenced production. The amount of Reeves' involvement has sparked some debate, but those who should be in the know say the film is all Hessler's. The script by Lawrence Huntingdon was supposedly based on "The Oblong Box" by Edgar Allan Poe but is actually much closer to Rudyard Kipling's "The Mark of the Beast" and was rewritten slightly by Christopher Wicking. In an interview in the *Kine Weekly*, Hessler was quoted as saying, "I agree with Hitchcock that logic in thriller and horror movies is not that important. If audiences are continuously keyed up to a full pitch, as they should be, then the logic of a scene or a character's behavior does not matter a bit." Hessler's work reflects that philosophy, as some of his films are flagrantly illogical, but unfortunately they never get the audience so keyed up that it doesn't notice.

The Oblong Box centers around a curse that black African natives inflict on Sir Edward Markham (Alistair Williamson) as punishment for riding down a small black child with his horse. Unfortunately, they cannot tell whites apart, and the cruel act was actually committed by Markham's brother, Sir Julian (Vincent Price).

The curse has left Edward horribly scarred and quite deranged, and so Julian chains him up in the attic of the Markham mansion. However, Edward arranges to ingest a drug that will simulate death, and a pair of confederates are hired to dig him up so he can escape. The first part of the plan works beautifully, but the confederates decide to abandon Edward to his fate, take the money and run. Fortunately for Edward, some resurrectionists come along and transport him and his coffin to the house of Dr. Neuhartt (Christopher Lee), who finds a more lively cadaver on his hands than he anticipated.

While Julian looks forward to having a good time with his wife, Elizabeth (Hilary Dwyer, Sara of *The Conqueror Worm*), Edward plots his revenge on his brother, the witch doctor who made the drug he took and the two men who abandoned him. He blackmails Dr. Neuhartt with exposing his resurrection activities unless he is provided lodgings. Donning a red mask to disguise his hideous features, he goes out murdering his victims one by one, as well as anyone curious enough to take a peek behind the mask.

Meanwhile, the body from Edward's coffin (Edward thoughtfully procured one to cover his tracks) is washed downriver where it is sketched by Joshua Kemp (Rupert Davies), who ends up showing it to Julian. From the sketch Julian knows that the body is not Edward's. He thus anticipates Edward's attempt at revenge and shoots him, but not before Edward has a chance to bite him and pass along the infection. The final shock reveals that Julian has caught the disfiguring disease that should have been his in the first place as the circumstances under which it was initially contracted are now finally revealed.

While the script does manage to mix together such horror elements as premature burial, grave robbers, a Jack the Ripper–type killer, madness, horrible disfigurement and a curse, the results were not particularly horrific

Director Gordon Hessler discusses a scene with Vincent Price and Hilary Dwyer on The Oblong Box, *which borrows its plot from Rudyard Kipling's "The Mark of the Beast" but nevertheless was marketed as a Poe picture. Hessler was called in to helm the production when Michael Reeves died shortly before he was to have begun it.*

but rather routine, though John Coquillon's cinematography gives a nice sheen. None of the characters have any real depth; they are only supplied with motivations as to why they would want to kill or what caused them to become victims of a killer.

Nevertheless, the results were more coherent than *Scream and Scream Again*, which has some good shock sequences thanks to Wicking's script, but fails to hang together as any kind of a story. It is notable as a teaming of Vincent Price, Christopher Lee and Peter Cushing, but only Price receives a significant amount of screen time, while Lee is shunted off into a minor role and Cushing is entirely wasted in a cameo appearance.

Scream and Scream Again was based on Peter Saxon's novel *The Disoriented Man*, but it is the disoriented viewer who will have trouble making heads or tails of Hessler's fractured narrative scheme. The film opens memorably enough, intercutting between a healthy jogger and the same man waking up in a hospital bed and finding one of his limbs removed. Each time

Hessler cuts back to him, he has lost another limb, which does suggest the chilling mood.

However, from there things get confusing as a police detective, Bellaver (Alfred Marks), investigates a pair of mutilation killings that leave the victims drained of blood, much to the surprise of pathologist David Sorel (Christopher Matthews). The police seem to spend a lot of time in British discothèques listening to music by The Amen Corner, but they finally come across the man they believe to be the killer (Michael Gothard).

In the film's most effective sequence, the killer displays superhuman strength in leading the police on a rapid chase, often eluding them until he is captured in a rock quarry. Handcuffed to the back of a police car while the officers have a look around, the killer frees himself by pulling his own hand off and makes for the house of Dr. Browning (Vincent Price), where he disposes of himself by flinging himself into a convenient vat of acid.

Meanwhile, there is a lot of obscure political maneuvering going on, and Bellaver has been ordered to drop the case. When he persists, he is murdered by a powerful foreigner named Konratz (Marshall Jones), who has governmental connections. Considering that Bellaver appeared to be what passed for a main character in this film, this proves a big surprise.

Sorel takes up the gauntlet and pursues the investigation to Browning's house, where he discovers that Browning has been grafting the limbs and organs of human beings onto emotionless androids in his quest to perfect a race of superhumans, using the acid bath to dispose of leftover evidence. Just as Browning is about to dispose of Sorel, Konratz appears and reveals himself to be one of these new superhumans, but one who is opposed to Browning. He too ends up in the acid bath.

Then Fremont (Christopher Lee), head of the British Secret Service, arrives and reveals that he is also a superhuman and that Browning's muddling must come to an end, which is achieved by disposing of him you-know-where.

What is behind all this ridiculous mess is anybody's guess, as *Scream and Scream Again* is played for sensation, not storytelling or logic. The machinations and hints of a secret police state are never made clear enough to be threatening (though that aspect impressed famed director Fritz Lang and film critic David Pirie), and the only time the film has any life is when mayhem is depicted or threatened. In between, it is unforgivably dull and talky with the talk making little sense and clarifying nothing. Mysteriously, possibly because of problems with music rights, the film was given an entirely new score when released on videocassette. *Scream and Scream Again* proves that wild ideas and a few good shock scenes do not a good film make.

This was followed by *Cry of the Banshee*, the boring tale of a sixteenth century magistrate (Vincent Price again) who persecutes the followers of an old Celtic religion. The high priestess Oona (Elisabeth Bergner, a famous European actress in the '30s) unleashes a *sidhe*, an evil spirit, that decimates the magistrate's household, but Oona gets her throat cut for her troubles. While the film is rife with violence, it remains uninvolving, uninteresting, and downright cheap in appearance.

Alas, many of the same adjectives could be applied to *Murders in the Rue Morgue*, Hessler's remake of Robert Florey's 1932 classic, though despite the title and the famous Poe story as a basis, the two films have little in common. Filmed in Spain with an ultra-cheap-looking monkey suit, this modern *Murders* follows an acting troupe (led by Jason Robards) who while performing Poe's work on stage are plagued by attacks from an acid-scarred maniac (played by Herbert Lom). The blending of reality, play-acting, and dreaming, with each reflecting another, is ambitious but not entirely successful.

Next came a spy thriller, *Embassy*, in which hero Richard Roundtree must smuggle Russian defector Max von Sydow past a KGB agent played by Chuck Connors. *The Golden Voyage of Sinbad* was a bit better thanks to Ray Harryhausen's stop-motion models, and Tom Baker (of "Dr. Who" fame) makes an interesting villain who visibly ages each time he casts a magic spell. Unfortunately, the effects for the finale, in which a centaur fights a griffin, are below Harryhausen's usual high standard, and star John Phillip Law affects an unsuccessful exotic accent which greatly mars his performance as Sinbad. However, overall Hessler does convey a mood of jaunty adventure appropriate to a children's tale, along with a bit of humor and the right touch of menace, and he is to be commended for making a film that almost matches the magical *Seventh Voyage of Sinbad*.

Before *Golden Voyage*, Hessler took time out for *Scream Pretty Peggy*, a feeble imitation *Psycho* movie for TV, primarily notable for its casting of Bette Davis as the over-protective mother of *That Girl* costar Ted Bessell. Bessell plays a mad sculptor who thinks he is his fictitious murderous sister. While Peggy screamed, the viewers were more apt to yawn.

While Hessler did more TV thrillers, such as *Skyway to Death* and *Hitch-hike!* he did not really return to horror, except for the appalling *KISS Meets the Phantom of the Park*, until his adaptation of Richard Adams' peculiar ghost story *The Girl in a Swing*. The *KISS* TV movie featured Anthony Zerbe as a mad scientist who plans to make "evil" clones of the infamous third-rate rock group *KISS*. Perhaps it was a terrifying idea for music lovers, but it would hardly quicken the pulse of any other person.

The Girl in a Swing tries for something more delicate, and while it is a better piece of pabulum, it too fails. Adams' ethereal Käthe becomes Meg Tilly's German-accented Karin, the strange and mysterious young girl whom an English antique dealer (Rupert Frazer) falls in love with. However, there is something melancholy about his new bride, which she tries to block out by indulging in rambunctious sex on the lawn. It turns out that because the stiff-necked Englishman could not stand the idea of marrying a person who already had a child, Karin, desperately in love, has strangled her own child to be with him. However, the guilt torments her until she eventually kills herself.

Hessler does evoke an offbeat atmosphere and convey the unspoken guilt and psychic forces at work, but the film has a bit too much of that old English reserve and so feels a bit stultifying, as well as proceeding at a deadly, lugubrious pace. The most touching moment comes when Karin's spirit returns to help her lover lie convincingly at the inquest, ensuring that he will not wrongly be accused of her murder.

While Hessler does at times seem devoted to the horror genre, he has a consistent inability to generate much excitement or entertainment in his plodding, disjointed films. With no strong themes or artistic desires to express, he is simply a yeoman director who has descended into a justly deserved obscurity.

Seth Holt (1923-1971)

Nowhere to Go (1958); *Taste of Fear* (aka *Scream of Fear*, 1961); *Station Six –
Sahara* (1964); *The Nanny* (1965); *Danger Route* (1967); *Blood from the Mummy's
Tomb* (completed by Michael Carreras after Holt's death, 1971).
TELEVISION: "Savior of Vladik," "La Belle France," *Court Martial* (1968);
(credits for his work in British television are unfortunately unavailable).

The death of Seth Holt at 48 from alcoholism represents a tragic loss
that was mostly ignored by the press and the public alike. David Thomson
in *A Biographical Dictionary of Film* said he was "the most gifted British
director working in Britain." Those who knew him all agree about his genius,
but unfortunately that gift for filmmaking only shows up sporadically in the
handful of films that he directed.

Holt was born in Palestine of British parents and was converted to filmmaking by seeing *Citizen Kane* a dozen times when he was 19. He was able
to land a job at the highly regarded Ealing Studios as an assistant film editor
and proceeded to work his way up. His contributions there include being the
voice of the blizzard in *Scott of the Antarctic* and assisting in the cutting of
such classics as *Dead of Night, Kind Hearts and Coronets, The Lavender Hill
Mob*, and *The Titfield Thunderbolt*.

I have not seen his first film, *Nowhere to Go*, which was also Ealing's
last. He did receive a sort of quiet renown for saving Karel Reisz's *Saturday
Night and Sunday Morning* and Tony Richardson's *The Entertainer*, which
were initially regarded as unreleaseable messes, but through Holt's judici-
ous and audacious "new wave" cutting they came to be hailed as avant-garde
critical successes that heralded a new age in British cinema.

Holt himself held such respected British directors as David Lean, Carol
Reed and Anthony Asquith in contempt because of their desire to enshrine
or even embalm classic works of the past rather than tackle something truly
new or original.

He achieved that originality – though with a nod to Clouzot's classic *Les
Diaboliques* – with his next directorial assignment and Hammer's most
effective psychological thriller, *Taste of Fear* (better known in the United
States as *Scream of Fear*). Featuring one of Jimmy Sangster's most ingenious screenplays, the film begins with the mysterious retrieval of a body

being pulled from some water. We are then introduced to Penny Appleby (Susan Strasberg), a crippled heiress on her way to her father's house in France.

In time-honored fashion, Penny begins to become unnerved by her vaguely menacing stepmother (Ann Todd) and becomes anxious for her father's return. That night she has a vision of her father as a dead spirit. Naturally, viewers used to this genre suspect that a plot is afoot, particularly when the stepmother brings in Dr. Gerrard (Christopher Lee), who assures her that her vision was all in her mind. Nonetheless, the father fails to return, but his apparent spirit continues to pop up, even frightening Penny causing her to fall into a swimming pool from which she must be rescued by the chauffeur (Ronald Lewis).

The original twist in the production lay with the revelation that rather than everyone in the family conspiring to drive Penny insane, she and Dr. Gerrard arranged to investigate Mr. Appleby's disappearance after the death of the actual Penny by suicide (which finally clarifies the opening of the picture). Against them is the conspiracy on the part of the chauffeur and the stepmother to try to do away with "Penny," which is finally fouled in a poetically appropriate way when the chauffeur kills the stepmother when he mistakes her for "Penny," and pushes the wheelchair she is sitting in over the cliff.

Holt pulls off the whole concoction with much suspense and aplomb, getting excellent performances form his cast. The result is an often overlooked fright classic, worthy of comparison to *Psycho* and *Games* or *Les Diaboliques* (which Holt at one time hoped to remake but was unable to get the project off the ground).

Still, the film was only a moderate success financially, and directing jobs were hard to come by. *Station Six–Sahara* proved to be something of a misfire despite an excellent cast and a script by Bryan Forbes and Brian Clemens. In it, Carroll Baker crash-lands at a desert oasis with her husband and five sex-starved men.

Holt returned to Hammer with *The Nanny*, which Jimmy Sangster adapted from Evelyn Piper's novel for Bette Davis, who had recently revived her career with *What Ever Happened to Baby Jane?* and *Hush . . . Hush, Sweet Charlotte* (both with Robert Aldrich).

Davis plays the nanny of young Joey (William Dix), a ten-year-old boy who has been kept at home after attending a school for disturbed children. The boy's mother (Wendy Craig) worries that he might not have recovered from the shock of being involved in the death of his younger sister, who drowned in the bathtub. Joey refuses to let his nanny anywhere near him and tensions begin to mount.

Joey's father (James Villiers) is called away on business, while his mother finds out that she must look after her sister who has a medical problem. Thus the boy is left with no one to depend on but . . . you guessed it, the stern nanny.

Joey befriends a neighbor (Pamela Franklin) and explains that his sister died in the bathtub due to the nanny's neglect – the nanny had left the water on and little sis fell and knocked herself unconscious. Unable and unwilling to take the blame, the nanny pointed the finger at Joey.

When Joey's mother becomes ill and poisoning is suspected, the others fear that Joey is up to his old tricks again. Holt cannily plays this with Joey acting suspiciously enough that the audience can suspect he is capable of killing his sister and poisoning his mother, no matter what he says. This added bit of ambiguity works well in this small scale thriller's favor.

We also know that something is not right with nanny when she steadfastly refuses to give a visiting guest (Jill Bennett) her medicine when she has a heart attack and finally dies. The guest's death uncorks the nanny's repressed guilt; she confesses to being responsible for the death of the little girl and blaming Joey because she feared losing her cushy job. However, she begins to fear that Joey might one day be believed and decides to go after him, knocking him unconscious and preparing to drown him. Suddenly, this repetition of her crime snaps her out of her psychotic state and she relents, rescuing the boy rather than perpetrate another ghastly crime. She faces up to the fact that she is not serving the household properly, packs her bags, and leaves.

Overall, the film is quiet and understated, with Holt effective at evoking an uneasy mood. As an added benefit, Bette Davis gives one of her better and more restrained performances as the malevolent ("This is for your own good") nanny. However, this cannot hide the fact that the film is merely a better-than-average programmer.

After a double-crossing spy yarn, *Danger Route*, Holt was consigned to the relative oblivion of directing sporadic television episodes. His alcoholism increased and did not help to make him more employable. While brilliant at times, his work had an unfortunate tendency to be rather erratic. He started his last project, *Blood from the Mummy's Tomb*, in 1970 but did not live to see its finish. *Blood* is an adaptation of Bram Stoker's novel *Jewel of the Seven Stars*, which was also filmed in 1980 as *The Awakening* by director Mike Newell.

Holt died a mere three weeks into production and Michael Carreras, Hammer's head of production, took over. Unfortunately, Carreras found the script confusing, and some of what Holt had intended to do had been kept in his head, not on paper. Carreras filmed several pickups and some additional scenes and tried to patch the thing together, but the result was a disappointing hodgepodge, though the film does still contain some wonderfully mysterious moments. To compound problems, the role of Dr. Fuchs was originally to have gone to Peter Cushing, but he had to bow out and it was taken over by Andrew Keir, who did an acceptable job. The plot centers around the less adequate Valerie Leon who plays a woman taken over by the spirit of an Egyptian princess from time to time. Luckily, the film is not your standard shambling mummy romp, which at least made for a slightly interesting departure from the formula as Queen Tera tries to reincarnate herself in the body of Fuchs' daughter, who was born the moment that Fuchs invaded Tera's tomb. However, the house-collapsing finale seems like something out of a Roger Corman Poe film, a disappointingly predictable outcome after the film's interesting buildup.

Sadly, much of the same may be said of Holt's life and work. Holt held great promise for British cinema, but like one of his tormented characters, succumbed to fate because of his own weakness. Still there is much to appreciate and learn from in the work he left behind, as he showed himself to have a good eye for visual dynamics and appreciable talent at directing a wide variety of actors and actresses.

Inoshiro Honda (1911–   )

The Blue Pearl (195?); *Eagle of the Pacific* (1953); Gojira (aka *Godzilla, King of Monsters*, 1954); *Love Tide; Mother and Son; Jujin Yukiotako* (aka *Abominable Snowman; Half Human*); *Gojira no Gyakushu* (1955); *Sorano Daikaijyu Radon* (aka, *Rodan*, 1956); *Chikyu Boeigun* (aka *The Mysterians*, 1957); *Bjo to Ekitainingen* (aka *H Man*); *Hanayome Sanjuso; Daikaijyu Baran* (aka *Varan the Unbelievable*) (1958); *Kodama Wa Yondeiru; Tetsuwan Tosho Inao Monogatori; Uawayake Shitayaka Godoyaku; Uchyu Daisenso* (aka *Battle in Outer Space*) (1959); *Gasu Ningen Daiichigo* (aka *Human Vapor*, 1960); *Mosura* (aka *Mothra*, 1961); *Yosei Gorasu* (aka *Golath; Gorath*); *Kingu Kongu tai Gojira* (aka *King Kong vs. Godzilla*) (1962); *Matango* (aka *Attack of the Mushroom People*); *Kaitei Gunkan* (aka *Atragon*) (1963); *Mosura tai Gojira* (aka *Godzilla vs. the Thing*); *Uchu Daikaiju Dogora* (aka *Dogora the Space Monster*); *Sandai Kaiju Chikyu Saidai no Kessen* (*Ghidrah, the Three-Headed Monster*) (1964); *Frankenstein tai Baragon* (aka *Frankenstein Conquers the World*); *Kaiju Daisenso* (aka *Invasion of the Astro Monsters*) (1965); *Come Marry Me; Sanda tai Gaira* (aka *War of the Gargantuas*) (1966); *Kingukongu no Gyakushu* (aka *King Kong Escapes*, 1967); *Kaiju Sosingeki* (aka *Destroy All Monsters*, 1968); *Ido o dai Sakusen* (aka *Latitude Zero*); *Oru Kaiju Daishingeki* (aka *Godzilla's Revenge*) (1969); *Yog–Monster from Space* (1970); *Meka-Gojira no Gyakushu* (aka *The Terror of Godzilla; Terror of Mecha-Godzilla*) (1975).

While Honda was not the best Japanese director of horror films, he is certainly the most prolific, and in creating the figure of Godzilla, as well as other gigantic nuclear-spawned monsters in rubber suits, has added a permanent legacy to horror films. While his initial horror films were seriously intended for adult consumption, eventually, the cinema-going public in Japan changed, as did the perception of these monster mashes, resulting in the films catering to an ever younger audience. Thus, Honda became the first horror director whose specialty was Japanese-made children's films. While he was eventually replaced by Jan Fukuda (who created the character of Minya, the son of Godzilla, as a monster personality that small children could identify with), Yoshimitu Banno, and Kohji Hashimoto, there is no question of the superiority of Honda's work. His films are a delight to small children, lovers of vast miniatures (courtesy of ace Japanese special effects technician Eiji Tsuburaya, with whom Honda collaborated on most of his films), and playful scenes of mass destruction. Made on relatively low budgets, Honda's work sometimes shows a strong visual sense, one that would bring the wildest scenes of science fiction magazine illustrations to life (witness *The Mysterians, Monster Zero* and *Gorath*).

The downside is that these films became so predominant on American air waves that for many Americans, they represented the totality of Japanese cinema, whereas Japan has left the world with a very rich cinematic legacy. As mentioned before, Honda's work does not even represent the best Japanese horror films, which often combine sex, death, and spirits in unusual ways. The masterpiece of Japanese horror cinema is Kenji Mizoguchi's *Ugetsu* (1953) (see appendix), but there are other films such as Kaneto Dhindo's beautifully visual and atmospheric *Onibaba* (aka *The Hole*) about a mother and her daughter living during a massive war who survive by killing wounded soldiers and selling their armor for food. When a neighbor returns from the war with the news that the daughter's husband has been killed, he and the daughter enter into a passionate sexual relationship that worries the mother, who fears she will be left behind to starve. As a result, she conjures up a demon to keep her daughter home with disasterous results. The film very effectively uses its soundtrack and claustrophobic setting (amid wind-swept reeds by the shores of a lake) to build up an atmosphere of unease and it paints a very bleak view of human worth and dignity as all ethics and morals are discarded or used to try to manipulate and keep the subservient under control. Shohei Imamura's *The Ballad of Narayama* is equally harrowing and disturbing in its depicting of human beings as basically bestial. This time the story deals with the elderly people of a tribe being abandoned to die on a mountain top, while one of them, a 70-year-old widow, tries to set her life in order before making the final sojourn. Also unforgettable is Nagaisa Oshima's *Empire of Passion* in which two lovers conspire to kill the woman's husband, only for the husband's spirit to return and haunt them to their gruesome deaths. The film is distinguished by its beautiful photography and the feeling of an all-consuming passion followed by an equally all-consuming guilt, of lust leading to the lovers' inevitable demise and destruction. Also worth mentioning is Akira Kurosawa's classic *Rashomon*, the famous film where the tale of a woman being raped by a bandit and the death of the husband is told from four points of view, one of which is the husband's dead spirit who communicates through a medium. Ultimately, each tale presents contradicting testimony and favors whomever is telling the tale, indicating that our personalities color our perceptions of reality which is ultimately unknowable.

Getting back to Honda, *Godzilla* was deliberately designed to be a Japanese version of Eugene Lourie's dinosaur-on-the-loose tale *The Beast from 20,000 Fathoms*. The Japanese name for the famed green scaly one is Gojira, a combination of the Japanese words for gorilla and whale. Unlike the more child-like successors, the original *Godzilla* was a very grim film and Honda is to be credited with coming up with a properly melancholic mood for it. Honda contributed ideas to the screenplay along with screenwriter Takeo Murata and Tsuburaya. The film definitely reflects the mourning mood of post-war Japan, and the attribution of Godzilla's creation to atomic power is far from accidental, as Godzilla is created after an atomic test.

The scenes of Raymond Burr in Japan were all added exclusively for the American film version months after the original film's completion and were directed by Terrell O. Morse, though their insertion is relatively seamless. The film played on various fears, from atomic power to fear of the sea and what might come from it. The military, which had not prevailed against the West, proves useless against the menace. Godzilla's onslaught of the cities comes on like a bombing raid, leaving only death and destruction in its wake.

An important subplot has a scientist inventing a weapon, an oxygen-destroyer, which he feels is too dreadful ever to be used, and he hides its discovery for fear that it might fall into the wrong hands. The weapon is finally used to dispatch the monster, but all knowledge of the weapon's construction dies with the scientist. (The subsequent Godzillas had a different design and were obviously intended to be similar but different beasts.) There is a haunting, ethereal quality to Honda's scenes of the two divers submerging to set the trap for Godzilla, which includes movement that Jon Inouye has compared to Kabuki theater.

Next Honda made an oddball abominable snowman picture that was released in the United States three years later as *Half Human* with additional scenes featuring John Carradine and Morris Ankrum directed by Kenneth G. Crane. It is impossible for U.S. audiences to judge Honda's film as the dialogue was replaced by Carradine narrating the events of the movie to cut down on dubbing costs.

Next Honda went on to the original *Rodan*, which actually features two prehistoric pterodactyls and was one of the last of Honda's films to attempt to build up mood and anticipation. Once more atomic testing is to blame, this time releasing larvae from underground chambers near a mine. The larvae in turn are eaten by Rodan, who quickly grows to such enormous size that he can achieve supersonic speeds in flight and a sweep of his wings can create typhoons, a tsunami of tsuris, a titantic tidal wave of terror and trouble. If that were not enough, another one of the beasts shows up and blows miniature military hardware all over the scenery. Unlike *Godzilla, Rodan* was filmed in color, and as a result some of the moodiness dissipates. Also, the film fails to maintain the tension of its opening scenes, hinting at further degeneration yet to come.

The Mysterians features gigantic forest fires (these Japanese monster movies are among the first well-defined disaster movies, later a significant trend in the '70s following the success of Ronald Neame's *The Poseidon*

Adventure and Mark Robson's *Earthquake!*), a Godzilla-like robot, and aliens who seek to mate with Japanese women and take over the Earth in order to perpetuate their sterile civilization. Honda throws in a mass of animation as alien rays are projected hither and yon, but they are not enough to distract from the thinness of the story, though they do make for quite an eyeful.

The H Man, H for hydrogen, has the atomic bomb turning people into green radioactive slime which eats people in turn. That basic idea is very similar to Irvin S. Yeaworthy's *The Blob*, also released in 1958, though this time the police are battling the underworld and not local teenagers. Unfortunately, while Honda's work remained lively it became steadily less interesting. *Gorath* attempts to be a serious science fiction picture with a *When Worlds Collide* premise, but it was ultimately a bore. *Attack of the Mushroom People* features castaways eating and then becoming mushrooms, which became something of a regular joke on horror host programs.

The best of the latterday Honda films is *War of the Gargantuas*, originally a sequel to *Frankenstein Conquers the World* in which a Japanese boy eats the heart of Frankenstein's monster and mutates into a superhuge replica of same. In *War of the Gargantuas*, the flat-topped gigantic Frankenstein is split into green and brown selves which are alternately good and bad. These selves battle each other physically, wreaking havoc all over Tokyo, which gets destroyed for the nth time. The film represents a kind of mindless, dumb fun. Russ Tamblyn is appealing as an American who is helping out and develops an interest in a local Japanese girl, giving the film a bit more heart than the usual run-of-the-mill monster wrestling marathons. Also above average was *Monster Zero*, in which brainwashing aliens persuade Earth to lend them Godzilla and Rodan so that the Japanese supermonsters can rid their planet of Ghidrah, a three-headed dragon codenamed Monster Zero. However, the sinister aliens soon turn all three monsters loose to wreak havoc on Earth until the now relatively benign Godzilla and Rodan can be freed from mind control and send the aliens and Ghidrah packing.

Honda's films will never be regarded as masterpieces of fantasy film art, but many who watched them while growing up have a soft place in the heart for their vividly colorful comic book antics. In terms of direct sequels featuring the same character, Godzilla, that big grey-green galoot, may well be the most successful monster of them all, mostly because he has won the hearts of children. Godzilla developed something no reptile ever does – a personality, something akin to a big brother who would beat up on bullies for his kid brother and who enjoyed showing off his sumo wrestling moves before a captive audience. The unconvincing special effects never give parents cause for alarm, and dubbing in dirty dialogue would be unthinkable. Somehow it is appropriate that Honda took the world's biggest fear, atomic destruction, and sanitized it into something loveable.

Tobe Hooper (1943–   )

Heisters (short; 1963); *Down Friday Street* (?); *Eggshells* (1970); *The Texas Chainsaw Massacre* (1974); *Eaten Alive* (aka *Death Trap; Starlight Slaughter; Horror Hotel Massacre; Legend of the Bayou*, 1977); *The Funhouse* (1981); *Poltergeist* (1982); *Lifeforce* (1985); *Invaders from Mars; The Texas Chainsaw Massacre 2* (1986); *Spontaneous Combustion* (1990).

TELEVISION: *Peter, Paul & Mary Special; 'Salem's Lot* (1979); *The Equalizer; Freddy's Nightmares* (pilot, 1989); *I'm Dangerous Tonight; Haunted Lives; True Ghost Stories* (1990).

Tobe Hooper is a cigar-smoking, cinema-obsessed Texan who has slowly gained respect as the director of a horror film with the unlikely title of *The Texas Chainsaw Massacre*. By combining the wonder of a *Close Encounters* with the horrors of a haunted house, he created his most successful film, *Poltergeist*, for producer Steven Spielberg. His films often have an outrageous, unreal, comic-book feel to them that Hooper attributes to the influence of E. C. Comics, which he avidly read when he was growing up in the '50s.

In an interview with Michael Ventura, Hooper explained:

> I started watching movies at a very early age – like 3. Even earlier. My memories from childhood are mostly memories of movies rather than my own life because I spent a lot of time in a movie theatre. My dad had a hotel, and he had a movie theatre in San Angelo, Texas, so I stayed in the movie theatre when they went out to dinner. I probably learned to talk there, actually. It wasn't until San Francisco in the '60s that I realized that life wasn't a movie. I was standing on a cliff, looking over the ocean one day and the aperture went away.

Hooper began his directorial career with a theatrically distributed ten minute short called *Heisters* in 1963. A film about conserving old houses, *Down Friday Street*, went on to win an award at the New York Film and TV Festival, and a documentary about the famous folk group Peter, Paul & Mary became a perennial favorite for a time on public television stations.

Hooper's almost entirely forgotten first feature is the little seen *Eggshells*, which Hooper described to me as being about hippies in a haunted house. In an interview with director Donald G. Jackson (*The Demon Lover*) for Bill George's fanzine *The Late Show*, Hooper explained that

> some sort of strange presence enters the house and embeds itself in the walls of the basement and grows into this big bulb, half electronic, half organic. Almost like an eye but it's like a big light. It comes out of the wall. It manipulates the house. Animates the walls. Anyway, that's sort of what it is. I think that the film is a mixture really. It has sort of a Paul Morrissey look at times, like *Trash* and other times it has a *Fantasia* look.

Eggshells received very limited distribution as an art film and has virtually disappeared. Four years later, Hooper succeeded in making the film that would make him famous. His coscripter on the sequel, L. M. "Kit" Carson, told me:

> I talked with Tobe while we were making [*Chainsaw 2*]. He told me how [the first] movie came about for him. . . . [I]t happened at Christmas time. He went into a Montgomery Ward and got kind of stampeded into a heavy equipment department and looked up and saw a wall full of chainsaws with Christmas bulbs and tinsel hanging from them, and said to himself, if I want to get out of here, I'm going to have to take one of these things down, yank-start it, and cut my way out. He drove home where he was working on a script about hippies in a haunted house, and when he was a kid his relatives used to tell him Ed Gein stories because they knew people from the same town as Ed Gein – booger stories to scare him – and so all of a sudden it just happened like that. He took the hippies and ran them into Ed Gein and handed that sucker a chainsaw and he had the story right there.

Hooper got together with Kim Henkel to put a story together. In *Fangoria #23*, he told Bob Martin:

> I had no money to speak of at the start. . . . All I had was seed money for Bob Burns and myself to start working on the design of the picture, and the props, so I could show something to the potential investors. I had been in business as a documentary and commercial filmmaker, so I had some equipment, but I had no idea at the time who I would go to for money. I started just piecemealing the thing together; after Bob Burns had built bone furniture, and after Kim and I had finished the screenplay, I had something to show, and the money came together very rapidly – within about six weeks. But it was "do it or bust." I *had* to do it. . . .

The film started with a budget of about $60,000 and that went up to about $93,000. Hooper shot at a 10-to-1 (that is, ten feet of film exposed to each foot actually used) shooting ratio. The film proved an uncomfortable ordeal for everyone who made it, and according to art director Bob Burns, production was delayed because Hooper was often indecisive, ill-prepared, and looking for inspiration. The animal remains seen in the film were soaked in formaldehyde, which gave off a terrific stench, and Marilyn Burns received several injuries in the course of playing the film's main survivor who has to jump out of an upstairs window twice. Gunnar Hansen, who played the famed "Leatherface" (so-called because he wears a mask made of human skin), also received several injuries as the result of running into things because with the mask on he lacked peripheral vision.

The film was initially released by the now defunct Bryanston Pictures and apparently made a lot of money (it proved a perennial favorite at southern drive-ins), but the people who made the film never participated in the profit and for a long time there was a great deal of acrimonious feeling. (New Line Cinema owns the rights to *Chainsaw* now.)

It is true that despite the film's gory and lurid reputation, it is relatively goreless (the only really bloody scenes are when Ed Neal as the hitchhiker cuts himself with a knife and at the end of the film when Leatherface falls and cuts his own leg with his chainsaw). The film depends a lot on suggestion and its lurid title which makes people cringe even before they have seen anything. It is also, once it gets under way, a relentless descent into madness and achieves a uniquely horrific atmosphere of fear and dread. It can truly be said that there is not another horror film like it, even though many have similar plotlines and subject matter.

The advertising come-on almost dared the viewer to sit through the film: "Who will survive and what will be left of them?" Hooper himself photographed the *outré* opening in which flashbulb flashes reveal a couple of corpses that have been dug up and jury-rigged together for God knows what purpose. An offscreen narrator gives a news report about the incident. What follows is a film unique in its horrifying and unsparing bleakness.

Hooper then cuts to a dead armadillo on the road, communicating that this is a film about slaughter and death. We are introduced to a van full of teenagers, including Sally (Burns) and her wheelchair-bound brother Franklin (Paul A. Partain), Kirk (William Vail), Pam (Teri McMinn) and Jerry (Allen Danziger). They stop by the cemetery to see if Sally and Franklin's grandfather's grave has been disturbed and meet a drunk old man who claims to have seen strange, unspecified things. As they travel along, amateur astrologer Pam explains that Saturn is in retrograde, an evil omen for everyone, while Franklin disgusts the van's passengers with tales of what happens in a slaughterhouse.

They pick up an oddball hitchhiker (Neal) who claims to have worked in the slaughterhouse back when they killed cattle with ball-peen hammers. The young man is obviously deranged and delights in revolting everyone by gouging the palm of his hand with a knife. He then takes out a polaroid and snaps an awful picture for which he demands two dollars. When refused, he burns the picture and slashes Franklin's arm with a razor. Everyone screams and they throw the hitchhiker off the van, but he smears his blood on the side, marking it for some mysterious purpose.

The puzzled and bleeding Franklin persuades everyone to stop by his grandfather's old deserted house when it turns out that they cannot get anymore gas for a while, as they have run low and the cook (Jim Siedow) who runs the combination gas station and barbeque explains that the truck will not be by for a while. Naturally expectations are built up that something terrible will happen at the deserted house, but nothing does. It is a red herring.

Instead, Kirk and Pam go to a nearby farmhouse where they hear a generator running, hoping to borrow some gas. They find several rusted automobiles around the house, but that does not suggest anything to them. Finally, Kirk barges indoors, hoping to find somebody there. His prayers are answered in the worst possible way when a door suddenly opens and Leatherface brains Kirk with his hammer, pulling Kirk's twitching body into the corridor and rapidly shutting the door before Pam, who is outside on the porch, is even aware that something has gone on.

It is important that the killers in *The Texas Chainsaw Massacre* are never sympathetic and that their attacks seem completely unmotivated. The audience's sympathy is always with the unfortunate victims, whose demise we are not meant to cheer on, making the film different from many modern horror flicks. *Chainsaw* is not interested in delivering any deep, psychological insights into its maniacs; rather it concentrates on building as intense and horrifying an experience as possible. The killers are outsiders, a family who once worked at the slaughterhouse but has been displaced by modern methods. Undaunted, they continue to ply their trade with the occasional human being who comes along, and their house is nightmarishly decorated with bones and animal remains, littering the floor and often hanging like a mobile from the ceiling.

Pam naturally comes inside to find out what has happened to Kirk and becomes shocked at what she sees of the house's interior. As she rushes out, she is intercepted by Leatherface, who drags her into the kitchen and hangs her on a meathook. Having put her in her place, Leatherface then proceeds to pick up a chainsaw and divide the body of Kirk into sections. Neither the impaling on the hook nor the cutting up of Kirk is actually shown, but there is no question as to what is happening.

Meanwhile, back at the van, Sally, Jerry and Franklin begin to wonder what has happened to Pam and Kirk, who said they were going to the old swimming hole. It has gotten dark and Jerry leaves to investigate only to be done in by Leatherface. Sally decides it is her turn to find out, especially as

Kirk has the keys to the van; however, Franklin insists on coming with her despite making slow progress in his wheelchair. Suddenly, Leatherface appears and disembowels the frequently obnoxious Franklin on the spot, causing Sally to run to the farmhouse in search of help.

Inside the house, she hears a strange thumping noise from inside the deep freezer. Suddenly, Pam's corpse pops up in one of those post-death body contractions. Upstairs she sees what appears to be a pair of corpses that have had the benefit of a little taxidermy. Leatherface meanwhile is taking his chainsaw to the front door and cutting his way through. Jumping from the upstairs window, Sally runs back to the gas station and babbles incoherently to the cook. The cook goes outside to investigate.

When he comes back, he picks up a burlap sack and some rope and tries to calm the hysterical Sally, but his actions are none too soothing. He throws her in his truck and delights in poking her with a broomstick as they drive along. The cook meets up with the hitchhiker, picking him up and heading back to the farmhouse. We realize that he is "one of them." The cook is pissed off over the damage that Leatherface has done to the door. Meanwhile, the hitchhiker and Leatherface bring their aged grandfather (a young man in unconvincing old age makeup) downstairs and give him Sally's pricked finger to suck. The taste of blood revives some semblance of life in the corpse-like old man.

The hitchhiker decides it would be a good idea to let Grandpa kill the young woman, but the feeble old man can barely manage the weight of the hammer. Holding the trussed-up Sally over the edge of a bucket, Grandpa drops the hammer on her head time after time in the film's most prolonged and unpleasant scene.

When Leatherface is distracted, Sally manages to break loose and head off towards the main highway with a chainsaw-toting Leatherface and the hitchhiker in hot pursuit. She reaches the highway and tries to wave a diesel truck to stop. The hitchhiker runs out on the highway and is run over by the huge truck. Sally swings through the cabin of the puzzled truck-driver while Leatherface attacks the door of the cab with his trusty chainsaw.

Running down the road again, Sally flags down a pickup truck and is driven away to safety just in time, leaving the mad Leatherface, holding his chainsaw aloft, twirling round and round in the morning sun.

According to Ron Borst, the basic conception of the film owes much to James Landis' far inferior film *The Sadist*, which features Arch Hall, Jr., as a maniac who kills people for no good reason one by one until the fleeing heroine is the only one left. (The film was shown on television as *The Face of Terror* or *Profile of Terror* and has been released on video by Rhino Video.) The revulsion that *Texas Chainsaw Massacre* engenders is the result of how senseless the murders are and how the victims die, rather than any graphic bloodletting or grisly special effects.

The success of *The Texas Chainsaw Massacre* still did not lead any immediate job offers for Hooper. Finally producer Marti Rustam, who had been making a number of low-budget productions, cowrote a story with Alvin Fast that they felt would be perfect for Hooper's talents. Filmed as *Eaten Alive*, it has been shown under numerous titles including *Death Trap* and *Starlight Slaughter*. The result was a sleazy albeit interesting production that once more was unlike any other horror film ever made.

The entire film was shot on a soundstage and employs a striking lighting style that Hooper concocted with director of photography Robert Caramier. Often the lighting is eerie and unnatural, but not annoyingly so. It gives the film an appropriately surreal quality and adds to its overall effectiveness. Unfortunately, the use of fog machines gave the cast infinite problems. Everyone had to wear masks between takes, and the film has been described as a rough shoot.

According to Rustam, Hooper was not too interested in coming to Hollywood; he wanted to stay in Texas. Rustam convinced Hooper that *Eaten Alive* would be an independent production and therefore he would not be "going Hollywood." Hooper and the producers did not get along. The producers say that was because they wanted a comedy while he wanted a more serious film. According to Hooper, it was because they insisted he add some gratuitous nudity (which was shot over Hooper's objections by Rustam when Hooper took sick). The film had a mere $600,000 budget, and the producers were concerned because they felt that Hooper was used to taking his time.

Just as Bob Burns' designs for *Chainsaw* included a setting with such macabre accoutrements as a couch covered with human bones for backing and an armchair that uses human arms, *Eaten Alive*'s seedy hotel has a similarly bizarre set design with Nazi flags draping chairs and sawdust floors.

The biggest feature of the film was Neville Brand's marvelous performance as a muttering psycho who runs the Starliner Motel, a run-down, bottom-of-the-barrel joint with a "zoo" that consists of a crocodile in an underwater corral. Brand is quite believable as an old coot who has gone crazy from loneliness and isolation and is also quite amusing, though it is hard to make out his stream-of-consciousness mutterings as he gives a running commentary on his feelings to himself.

The film opens with Roberta Collins, a young runaway who in desperation winds up in a whorehouse. She is introduced to her first trick, Buck (Robert Englund), who is gruff and crude and frightens her into leaving the house of ill repute and seeking safety at the Starliner. Unfortunately, hotel owner Judd (Brand) recognizes her as one of those "hoors" and attacks her with a scythe and feeds her to his crocodile. (Most folk think it is a large alligator, but Judd swears he got it from Frank "Bring 'em back alive" Buck.)

A young couple arrives (played by William Finley – of *Sisters* and *Phantom of the Paradise* – and Marilyn Burns) with their young daughter and her dog, Snoopy. Snoopy pokes his head where he should not and is eaten by the croc, upsetting the daughter and driving Finley into a neurotic frenzy which climaxes with his trying to take a shotgun to the beast. Judd intervenes and Finley becomes croc food. (Finley, an underrated actor, gives a splendidly off-the-wall performance that is all too short.) Marilyn Burns seems fated to be the perennial victim as she gets slapped around and tied to a bed by Judd while her daughter crawls to safety under the house.

Meanwhile, Collins' estranged father (Mel Ferrer) and his other daughter show up looking for Roberta. Since Judd identifies her as a prostitute, they seek out Stuart Whitman, playing another in a long line of sheriffs, who takes them to see the local madame, played by a mummified Carolyn Jones. Jones lies and claims never to have seen the girl. Before long, Ferrer is confronted with the business end of Judd's scythe on the one hand and the croc's mouth on the other. (I guess that means he was between a croc and a hard place.)

Buck shows up again, tries to make the moves on Roberta's sister, and meets a well-deserved end of his own. Since the taboo against killing cute animals onscreen has already been broken, the audience now develops a genuine anxiety as to whether Hooper will also break the taboo against harming innocent children as Judd pursues the young child.

Perhaps the problem with the film is that it is sometimes too powerful for its own good, killing sympathetic characters like Ferrer's and unpleasantly torturing Burns' character. It wavers between blackly humorous comedy and the kind of relentless power that *Texas Chainsaw Massacre* has. As L. M. "Kit" Carson would put it, Hooper is always trying to take the audience beyond where it wants to go, creating genuinely disturbing and bizarre cinematic moments. His *Texas Chainsaw Massacre 2* shares many of the variances of tone that *Eaten Alive* has.

One of the most effective bits of atmosphere that *Eaten Alive* has going for it are the preposterous country & western songs that are constantly featured on the soundtrack. (My favorite is one about a man who shoots his wife's brother because he thought the man was her lover.) This is a picture that is willing to get down and dirty, unlike most of the Hollywood and independent product of the time, and as a result seems more than a bit crazed and doesn't always make for comfortable viewing.

Hooper went through a period where he had trouble picking up or keeping projects, starting such films as *The Dark* (which was taken over by John "Bud" Cardos) and *Venom* (which was taken over by Piers Haggard) without finishing them. His most fortuitous opportunity occurred when Warner Bros., after approaching directors from Larry Cohen to George Romero to film an adaptation of Stephen King's horror epic *'Salem's Lot*, turned to

David Soul (right) and Lance Kerwin try their hand at vampire hunting in 'Salem's Lot, *Tobe Hooper's adaptation of Stephen King's novel. The 200-minute original was later whittled down to 150 minutes for later showings and appears in a 112-minute version as* 'Salem's Lot: The Movie *overseas.*

Hooper to get the job done. Even condensing the book into a four-hour television miniseries resulted in a number of omissions, but within the boundaries of network standards and practices, Hooper managed to craft a few memorable scenes for his version of *'Salem's Lot.*

   Strangely it is not Reggie Nalder as the *Nosferatu*-inspired vampire that dominates the film, but rather sinister James Mason as the conniving Barlow who brings the vampire into a small Maine town and helps it spread. David Soul makes a stalwart hero as the novelist who perceives what is going on, but Lance Kerwin seems too old to be playing a monster-obsessed adolescent whose friends are slowly becoming vampirized as the evil spreads.

Still, one of 'Salem's Lot's best moments occurs when Kerwin's friends, floating in midair, come scratching at his window pane and beg to be invited in. The scene is effectively eerie and has influenced later vampire films such as *The Lost Boys*. The cast, which includes Lew Ayres, Elisha Cook, Jr., Fred Willard, Kenneth McMillan, Marie Windsor and Clarissa Kaye, is uniformly good, but Hooper seems bogged down in the large number of characters and the restraints that filming for television put on him. (A shortened version, released theatrically overseas, adds a graphic impalement and a little extra violence, but apart from drastically shortening the story, it does not make a big difference in the overall feel of the film.)

The result is that the full potential for the project was not reached, though 'Salem's Lot remains an entertaining film with a few eerie moments and has proven itself to be better than most attempts at adapting King's work.

Hooper moved on to *The Funhouse*, one of his best films, though many horror fans have expressed disappointment that the film is half over before the mayhem really begins. Hooper takes his time exploring the seedy atmosphere of a traveling carnival, delighting in the grotesque figurines inside the funhouse and the promise of illicit thrills. He begins with an *hommage* to Carpenter's *Halloween*: We see a point-of-view shot in a monster-obsessed young boy's room where hands select a small machete and a mask which is donned over the camera. This unknown figure then goes into the bathroom where Amy (Elizabeth Berridge) is taking a shower.

There is a quick parody of the shower scene from *Psycho* as the "killer" is revealed to be Joey (Shawn Carson), Amy's younger brother, who plunges his rubber knife into sis' navel. Amy is naturally a bit outraged at having her shower disturbed in this manner and threatens to get even if it is the last thing she does.

While her parents watch *The Bride of Frankenstein* on TV, Amy waits to be picked up by Buzz (Cooper Huckabe), a gas station attendant her father does not approve of. He insists Amy stay away from the carnival because a couple of kids died near it when it was visiting a nearby town. But when Buzz picks her up, she agrees with his suggestion of going there with their friends Liz (Largo Woodruff) and Richie (Miles Chapin).

Berridge plays the heroine very sympathetically, bringing out the character's vulnerability. She is the virgin of the group, embarrassed by Liz's teasing but enjoying necking with Buzz. She is the only one reluctant to puff a joint which the others pass around. On a whim, the group decides to spend the night inside the funhouse after the carnival closes, and once more Amy goes along.

Before then, they visit a freak show with live animals. There is a cow with a cleft palate and another with two heads. There is also the preserved embryo of an infant with a cleft forehead. Madame Zena (Sylvia Miles), the fortuneteller, tells Amy she will meet a "tall, dark stranger," and gets angry at the laughter and derision of the others, throwing them all out of her tent. William Finley has a memorable cameo as Marco the Magnificent, a seedy, alcohol-swilling magician in clown makeup who makes it look like a magic trick has gone awry when a girl from the audience appears to have actually been staked in the course of a trick.

These sequences help set up an atmosphere of foreboding and delirious surprises. Finally secreting themselves in the funhouse, the group observes as Madame Zena visits a man (Wayne Doba) who has been parading around the funhouse in a Frankenstein's monster mask (tying in both to what Amy's parents were watching and Madame Zena's prediction). Zena refuses the man's offers of money for sex until the figure offers a hundred dollars, and then she begins stroking him with her hand until he climaxes prematurely. In his rage, the man kills her.

When the man leaves, the teens look for a way out, but find themselves locked in. Rickie makes the mistake of helping himself to a cache of cash, so that when the man returns with one of the carnival barkers (all the barkers in the film are played by Kevin Conway, each with a different accent and look, suggesting that they are brothers), the barker notices the money is missing. Richie compounds his mistake by dropping his automatic lighter, alerting the barker to their presence.

The man in the Frankenstein monster mask is revealed to be a hideous freak with a cleft forehead, albino skin and red eyes (the makeup was designed by Rick Baker and executed by Craig Reardon). He refers to the barker as his "father," enraging him. Earlier the teens overheard a dirty joke about a man making it with a cow, and there is a reference to the Creature's "twin brother Tad" as the embryo in the freak show, suggesting that the Creature was part-man, part-cow and all freak. The barker also reveals that he has had to cover up for the Creature in the past and since the teens know that it killed Madame Zena, he exhorts the Creature to begin dispatching these witnesses.

The teens get unnerved as the power in the funhouse gets switched on and off. Then, in the middle of telling a story about how he once scared himself while preparing to scare someone else, Richie is garrotted from above and disappears. A figure approaches in one of the funhouse electric carts and Buzz embeds an axe into its head before they discover that it is simply the now-dead Richie.

Hooper plays with horror conventions in The Funhouse. *The opening parodies the obligatory masked killer, in this case the diminutive Joey (Shawn Carson) attacking the woman (Elizabeth Berridge) in the shower.*

In short order, Liz disappears down a trapdoor and when the Creature approaches, attempts to come on to it. However, she proves treacherous as she stabs it in the back, and it viciously retaliates by forcing her head towards a large rotating fan.

Joey has followed Amy and her friends to the carnival and knows they are trapped inside the funhouse. However, when he is caught prowling around after hours and his parents are summoned, he remembers Amy's threat and decides not to tell them that Amy is spending the night at the carnival against her father's order. (She had phoned and claimed that she was spending the night at Liz's.)

Buzz and Amy finally confront the barker directly and Buzz and the barker get into a scuffle that leaves the barker impaled on a prop sword. When Buzz goes to get the keys off the barker's body, the barker tries to impale Buzz on the same sword until Buzz shoots him with the barker's own gun. Just then the Creature drops down and Buzz is out of bullets.

Amy escapes, but a figure of a clown bears Buzz's dead body in. Amy tries to hide herself in the machinery that runs the funhouse, but the Creature eventually discovers her. In the film's tautest scene, the pair play cat-and-mouse around the machinery's grinding gears until the Creature nearly

The monster (Wayne Doba) in The Funhouse *disguises himself as Frankenstein's Monster while his father (the highly versatile Kevin Conway) berates him.*

electrocutes itself by hitting a powerbox. It then gets caught on one of a series of hooks running along a chain overhead. It wakes up and tries to attack Amy, but is unable to disentangle itself before being cut in half by the huge grinding gears, leaving the hysterical Amy sobbing but alive.

Despite the added time at the beginning of the story, none of the characters are well-developed, perhaps to avoid alienating the audience when they appear in their future role as corpses. The Creature seems tragic when negotiating for sex with Madame Zena, but then proves an inhuman monster thereafter. Hooper works well developing an atmosphere and makes the final confrontation very suspenseful as poor Amy is almost petrified with fear, but he does not show how the events affect the characters in the story (written by Larry Block) because they are not really individuals in the first place. The audience roots for Amy only because she is "good" and vulnerable, and is appealingly played by Berridge.

This kind of approach to characters is typical in '80s horror films, of which *The Funhouse* did prove to be an above-average example, and can be partly traced to Hooper's similar use of characters in *The Texas Chainsaw Massacre*. The result was the "body count" movie as typified by Sean Cunningham's *Friday the 13th* and its ilk.

Following *Funhouse*, Hooper was approached to direct *Night Skies*, Steven Spielberg's intended follow-up to *Close Encounters of the Third Kind*, in which a nasty extra-terrestrial landed and wreaked havoc. (This project eventually became *E.T.*) Hooper declined, saying he wanted to do something about poltergeists, and Spielberg proved very receptive to that idea. Initially they had trouble licking the script (the film had no ending) until they thought of hanging everything around a child's kidnapping, just as the actions in *Close Encounters* were set off by the kidnapping of Cary Guffey.

Interestingly, many of the special effects featured in the film were remarkably similar to those in a script that actor Paul Clemens had submitted to Spielberg's organization, the result being that there was out-of-court settlement for an undisclosed sum. Others noted similarities between the basic plot of *Poltergeist* and Richard Matheson's classic *Twilight Zone* episode "Little Girl Lost," in which a small girl finds herself trapped inside another dimension until her father can get her out. Soon after *Poltergeist*, Spielberg began making *Twilight Zone – The Movie*, and he gave Matheson a lucrative contract to script three of the film's four segments.

Poltergeist proved an effective combining of two talents, but the end product looked more like a Spielberg movie than a Hooper movie, with the result that stories circulated that Spielberg had "ghost"-directed the film, though Spielberg himself took an ad out in the trades to compliment Hooper on his fine direction. There is no question that producer and coscripter Spielberg had a profound effect on the overall film and that he took an active role in its complicated production, but it would also be unfair not to give Hooper any credit.

The film proved a tremendous financial success, spawning two sequels so far, but neither of the follow-ups has matched the power and appeal of the original. *Poltergeist* is not a scary film, but it is a dazzling one that combines as much supernatural "lore" from the supermarket tabloids as it can in one movie. The setting is the type of new suburban community that Spielberg grew up in and loves so well (exploiting it in his other movies, notably *E.T.*).

The family, Steve (Craig T. Nelson), Diane (Jobeth Williams), Dana (Dominique Dunne), Robbie (Oliver Robbins) and Carol Anne (Heather O'Rourke), are basically clean-cut and decent people. Their remote control may interfere with their neighbors' television set and Steve and Diane may smoke pot on the sly, but they are clearly meant to represent the decent, average American family.

Things become disrupted when Carol Anne complains that there are people inside the television screen and paranormal forces begin to manifest themselves. Rather than being frightening, the film becomes a procession of interesting paranormal events created by colorful effects, though a giant cyclone has the disturbing effect of smashing a pair of arm-like branches (reminiscent of the living trees in *The Wizard of Oz*) into the kids' bedroom and snatching Robbie away. Poor Robbie almost gets eaten by the maw of the tree until Steve saves him. Not long afterwards, Carol Anne is kidnapped by the spirits from inside the television and things begin to go really wonky.

Enter a group of paranormal investigators led by Dr. Lesh (Beatrice Straight) who think they know what they are doing, and they find phenomena beyond their wildest dreams. In fact, all the film's inventiveness seems to have been lavished on creating spirits, floating objects, a giant living throat in a closet, a steak that moves like an inchworm, a man who imagines that he has torn the flesh off his face, an invisible spirit that knocks Dana up a wall and onto the ceiling, an imploding house, corpses that pop up in swimming pools, horror heads and such-like manifestations from "the other side."

Things are only temporarily brought under control when a psychic named Tangina (Zelda Rubinstein in her most memorable role) explains what they must do to bring Carol Anne back from the other side. Based on reports of people who claim to have died and then come back, Carol Anne is warned not to go into a bright light that signals the final crossover into death. The skeptical Steve becomes convinced and rescues his daughter by entering one dimensional porthole and exiting another.

The cause of all this psychic disturbance is revealed when Steve discovers that his boss (James Karen) built the housing tract over a cemetery but did not trouble himself to relocate the bodies, moving just the headstones instead. As a result, the spirits of the deceased have sprung up in a unique show of strength and the family is forced to flee the neighborhood permanently.

The film just piles one effect on top of another so that while it is dazzling, it fails to be credible. It is also odd that nobody in the neighborhood seems to notice the odd things going on at the house. Nevertheless, the acting is very good and Hooper manages to inject humor very well so that the film seems to have a constant "human" element among its amazing manifestations. There are also some offbeat bits here and there that add to the overall impact, from a toy clown that becomes menacing as it changes expression to Tangina being a little person who talks sonorously and authoritatively, indicating that she can read Steve's mind but prefers to converse like a person. Even the end, when Steve wheels a television set out of the motel room the family stays in after it has escaped, plays like a macabre joke (the film pokes constant fun at television being the banal source of the evil).

Hooper became involved with *The Return of the Living Dead*, which producer Tom Fox had optioned from John Russo, cowriter of the original *Night of the Living Dead*, and then turned over to Dan O'Bannon for scripting. The film was announced as being filmed in 3-D (*Friday the 13th Part 3-D* had been a tremendous success) and directed by Hooper, but Hooper backed out and O'Bannon took over as director. According to Hooper in an interview with this author:

> The producers had let me down, and I was no longer under contract to them. I was trying to get them to make a "pay or play" commitment to me so I could stay with them because of other projects available. It took them a long time to get their deal together, to get financing. Actually, when I left the project, I didn't expect the project was even going to continue.

Instead, Hooper signed up for a three-picture deal with Cannon Films. The first film was to be an adaptation of Colin Wilson's novel *Space Vampires*, and for a long time the project carried that title. However, Cannon saw they could make a tidy profit by selling the film to Tri-Star, who would release it and changed the title to *Lifeforce*.

The screenplay was by the team of O'Bannon and Jakoby, who had worked together on John Badham's *Blue Thunder*. They ended up unhappy with how Hooper had treated their material, with O'Bannon referring to it derisively as "another Hooper special." The special effects by John Dykstra and his company, Apogee, were elaborate but often unconvincing, and Dykstra blamed poor and rushed film processing for some of the shabby look.

According to Hooper in our interview, *Lifeforce* is "about destiny, and it's about the genesis of the vampire legend. These aliens have visited us in the past, maybe many times, and it's even possible that we are partly kin to them, that they were part of the makeup of our coming to be on this planet as a lifeform, so that in the future, they could pay us a visit." These sorts of ideas were derivative of Nigel Kneale's *Quatermass and the Pit* which Roy Ward Baker filmed beautifully as *5 Million Years to Earth* (see chapter on Baker).

While the basic concepts could provide the foundation for a good epic science fiction thriller, audiences began to laugh at the hysterical tone of *Lifeforce*, which caused Hooper to step forward and say that he meant it to be funny all along. He claimed that the lovely Mathilda May, the lead female space vampire who parades around in the nude throughout the film, represents male fears of female domination because of her ability to drain the life out of males while sexually stimulating them. Drive-in critic Joe-Bob Briggs probably said it best when he exclaimed that the film has "electric-lip-space vampires. Some of the best ones I ever seen."

Hooper came up with what he calls the "lynchpin" of making the film a contemporary piece: tying in the film to the approach of Halley's Comet. The English spaceshuttle *Churchill* winds up dead in space and Captain

Tobe Hooper lines up a shot for Lifeforce, *a reworking of Colin Wilson's book* Space Vampires *with a screenplay by Dan O'Bannon and Don Jakoby.*

Tom Carlsen (Steve Railsback) of the United States shuttle comes over to find out why. He discovers that inside the head of the comet is an enormous alien spacecraft. Investigating with a team of astronauts, they find that all of the inhabitants of that craft are dead, but there are also three glass sarcophagi that contain human forms, which the astronauts decide to take back to their spaceship.

When the shuttle returns to earth, a rescue mission discovers the crew dead and the inside of the shuttle burned out. They also discover the three human forms in their sarcophagi and decide to bring them for study to the European Space Research Centre in London. Things go from bad to worse when the female of the group (May) gets up and drains the "lifeforce" out of a guard by kissing him, not so much sucking face as sucking the life right out of him.

To make matters worse, SAS Col. Colin Caine (Peter Firth) discovers that anyone who has had the lifeforce sucked out of him becomes undead and has to drain off another person's lifeforce every two hours or explode and disintegrate into fine dust. Caine discovers that Carlsen escaped in a one-man escape pod before the destruction of the American shuttle and summons him to London for debriefing at once. Carlsen reveals that he is psionically linked with the female space vampire as it was she who seduced him while she drained the life of his shipmates one by one.

Frank Finlay does an interesting job with Dr. Hans Fallada, a scientist who is involved in the study of death phenomena. He gives Caine and Carlsen the vital information that the space vampires can be killed if stabbed through their centers with steel, which will release their stored-up electrical energy. As more and more people become infected, the contagion quickly spreads and all of London starts going up in flames. Overall, the film is plotlight but incident-heavy as Hooper keeps incredible events happening constantly.

What the film lacks, though, is a genuinely human perspective. Everyone seems so excited by what is happening that no one seems to stop and consider the cost in terms of human lives and personalities. No one seems terribly upset whenever anyone else is killed. Even worse, after enough lines like "You're not going to believe this, but. . ." or "It's incredible but true that. . ." the dialogue starts becoming unintentionally risible. Rather than evoking a sense of wonder, the film constantly reminds us of how preposterous the whole thing is.

Hooper tries to cram too much into too short a time, never taking the time to build up characterization or tension. There is always something happening and the pace never lags, but the end result is like getting the bum's rush through the story. Railsback, who has shown that he is a very talented actor with *Helter Skelter* and *The Stunt Man*, plays his role in perpetual hysteria so that he never seems normal and becomes hilariously funny instead. The rest of the actors likewise overplay their parts. The only calm and sedate character is that of the female space vampire herself, bewitchingly attractive but sadly mute, unable to convey anything about her race's intentions, which seem largely devoted to gathering up unleashed souls into the giant alien spacecraft which unfolds like some cosmic umbrella to catch them.

The film did not recoup its cost at the box office, though it initially attracted a good crowd. Still, it is enjoyable on a kind of disreputable, gonzo level, which is more than could be said for Hooper's next misfire, a remake of the beloved William Cameron Menzies '50s science fiction classic *Invaders from Mars*. To be fair to Hooper, many people did not understand that his approach to this film was to tell it from the point of view of a child's dream and so its offbeat element were not mean to be realistic.

When I asked Hooper why he wanted to remake a classic film, he replied:

> I hear this question a lot about why remake a picture. Well, if you don't remake it, you can see the original on television or on video, but a picture made in the early '50s isn't going to play on the circuit and get wide distribution. So we can have the opportunity to see it in a motion picture house in 70mm and six-track stereo. I'm remaking it

because it was one of my favorites and I hope not to fall into a situation
where I don't do the remake justice or I do an injustice to the original
by the remake, so I am remaking it with respect because I am fond of
it. . . . I think it would be interesting to see an alien come to earth in
the '80s that isn't so friendly.

In Menzies' original, everything was designed to be seen from the little
boy's point of view, but the designs are subtle so that this is not immediately
obvious. Particularly noticeable is when, after his parents have been taken
over by the invaders, he runs into a police station that consists only of an
incredibly high desk behind which sits a sergeant with a large clock on the
wall behind him. These emphasize the things a young boy would notice in
a police station and so nothing else is shown.

The script was again by O'Bannon and Jakoby, who claim it was insensitively rewritten. Nevertheless it slavishly follows much of the original
story. Regrettably, Hooper's strange dream-style never makes credible the
concept that David (Hunter Carson) has had his friends and parents
(Timothy Bottoms, Laraine Newman) taken over by alien invaders. Hooper
adds to the air of unreality by having a threatening school teacher (Louise
Fletcher) swallow a dissecting frog and a general (genially played by James
Karen) listen to and believe the young boy's story about an invasion, immediately mobilizing his forces.

David is a boy absorbed in the worlds of science fiction and astronomy.
One night he thinks he sees a flying saucer land over the hill in his backyard.
(In this colorful remake, the "saucer" looks like a combination of a meteor
and a multicolored dance-floor ball.) His dad goes out to check and starts
behaving strangely when he returns, arousing David's suspicions. It is not
long before his mother is taken over as well and David figures out what is
going on.

The only person he can turn to is the sympathetic school nurse (Karen
Black, Carson's real-life mother), who spends the first half of the film wondering what she is doing and why, and the second half either constantly terrified or awaiting a Martian conversion herself. Finally, David reaches the
general and the battle against the Martians begins in earnest.

The film is not without a sense of humor, particularly of the tongue-in-
cheek kind. David's dad makes a joking reference to a recently taken-over
neighbor as working in the "switching" department; Jimmy Hunt, who had
played David in the original, returns as a cop who goes up the hill where the
Martians have landed and casually remarks, "I haven't been here since I was
a little kid"; even the original head Martian makes a brief reappearance in
the basement of the Menzies Elementary School which David attends.

However, the film could have used more humor and inventiveness.
While it has a much larger budget than the original, even accounting for

inflation, the film has a tacky look about it with its pantomime horse Martians and their toothy smiles, the plaster-of-paris underground tunnels that the Martians dig, and their Supreme Martian Intelligence, which is a brain that appears to be situated on the end of a giant tongue that is sticking out at the audience.

Additionally, the performances in the film all have an unrehearsed quality about them, as if the actors were rushed through their lines before they had a chance to practice them, internalize them, or get a handle on their characters. As a result, they frequently end up looking unprofessional and foolish. This slapdash remake sank quickly and almost without a trace.

Hooper was scheduled to direct a film version of the comic character *Spider-Man*, but that was put on hold and later handed to another director. Hooper also promised to write and produce a sequel to *The Texas Chainsaw Massacre* and so was quickly assigned to direct that. His basic idea was that the Chainsaw family would attack yuppies (young urban professionals, a term that became an '80s byword). To script the film, he brought in Hunter Carson's father, L. M. "Kit" Carson, who had recently been highly praised for his script for Wim Wender's *Paris, Texas*. Carson had worked with Hooper once before, back in 1978, on a project that William Friedkin (*The Exorcist*) was developing called *Dead and Alive*. Carson enjoyed exploring the possibilities of madness and working with Hooper.

Carson gave me his own perspective of the Chainsaw family as he envisioned them for the sequel:

> They were ordinary human beings. The cook is a small businessman, an entrepreneur, who's caught the spirit of the '80s. Leatherface is actually sort of a Baby Huey, a 10-year-old child caught in a 28-year-old body . . . who comes upon sex for the first time in his life. S-E-E-X as the cook spells it. And this other character, Chop Top, is someone who is stuck back in the '60s, and there's a lot of those people around. Chop Top happened to be in Vietnam during the '60s and he missed it, and he came back and they weren't playing Iron Butterfly and Humble Pie anymore, and he wants to bring the '60s back. What he wants to do is take this big, abandoned amusement park outside of Dallas that they live under what was called "Texas Battleland" . . . and turn it into "'Namland." He thinks people . . . just want to go back and kick some Cong butt and hose down those hippie demonstrators, bust dopers, and do all the great, fun things that he misses from the '60s.

Another dimension was added to the film with Dennis Hopper's character Lt. "Lefty" Enright, a Texas Ranger who is seeking out the Chainsaw family for killing members of his family. Commented Carson, "What was interesting about this family is that there was no mother or father in the [Chainsaw] family; there was a patriarchal grandfather who handed down his skill, but [the rest] were orphans. Hopper comes in as the punishing father who has been absent all these years and says, 'You boys shouldn't be doing this.'"

However, *The Texas Chainsaw Massacre 2* encountered some severe problems, including expectations that the gore previously avoided would now be depicted (with the king of splatter, Tom Savini, hired to do the special effects makeup); an overly tight production schedule; and a large amount of second unit footage that was simply botched and never used, screwing up the overall structure of the film and diminishing some of its impact. (The primary scene dropped was an all-out attack on yuppies by the Chain Saw family in Dallas during Super Bowl weekend.)

Unlike the first film, *Chainsaw 2* encourages its audience to be on the side of the maniacs by making the first victims, a pair of obnoxious yuppies in a Mercedes, so unlikable. The audience roots for Leatherface (Bill Johnson) to take out his giant chainsaw and split their heads wide open. Thanks to a cellular phone, radio deejay "Stretch" Brock (Caroline Williams) unintentionally records an "earwitness" account of the murder. The murder also attracts the attention of Enright, who has been waiting for the family to come out of hiding.

Meanwhile, Drayton Sawyer the cook (Jim Siedow, back from the original), has been winning awards with his chili, the secret ingredient of which is obvious when he has to remove a toenail from a chili cook-off judge's bowl. He sends Chop Top and Leatherface after Stretch so that they will eliminate any clues that might lead to their discovery.

Bill Moseley does a marvelous job of making Chop Top a truly demented character and is the best thing in the film. He plays Chop Top as pure sleaze and scum who enjoys touching the metal plate in his head (a war injury he received in 'Nam and then proceeded to scrape the skin off of it because it itched) with heated metal objects. With his warped sense of humor, Chop Top is one frightening freak.

Deciding that Stretch must be eliminated, he sends Leatherface in to do the job, and Hooper has some fun parodying "first love" attraction scenes as Stretch pretends to be attracted by the bigness of Leatherface's nonoperating chainsaw and puts his instrument of death suggestively between her legs. The implications are both outrageous and uncomfortable. Leatherface is so taken aback by this unique response to him that he fails to kill Stretch and simply leaves, but not before a would-be boyfriend of Stretch's has his skull smashed and his body taken by the maniacs.

Lefty meets with Stretch and prepares for the final onslaught with chainsaws strapped to his arms and guns at the ready. Cary White's and Daniel Miller's art direction of the abandoned Texas Battleground park is genuinely weird and interesting, particularly with the caves lit up by chandeliers and lamps stolen from hundreds of now-dead victims, which gives the film an interesting, surreal quality.

Top: An example of puckish humor, this pose of the Saw family from The Texas Chainsaw Massacre 2 *parodies the poster of John Hughes'* The Breakfast Club. *The members are (clockwise) Grandpa (Ken Evert); Leatherface (Bill Johnson); Cook (Jim Siedow); Chop Top (Bill Moseley, center); and the mummified Hitchhiker lying down at the bottom. Bottom: Here's Hooper (right) with the rest of the cast of* Chainsaw 2: *Lefty Enright (Dennis Hopper) and disk jockette Stretch (Caroline Williams).*

Stretch winds up recaptured by the family, and the most gruesome scene has her tied up next to her previously bashed coworker as Leatherface uses an electric knife to remove the flesh from his face and put it on hers (to make her like him). Topping this bit of gruesomeness is the idea that the coworker, while in shock, is not quite dead and gets up after parts of him have been stripped away so that he can free Stretch.

Sadly, the inventiveness stops here and the end of the film is simply a replay of the end of the original, with Stretch taking the place of Sally at the dinner table while Grandpa fumbles with the hammer once more. The only difference is Lefty shows up and sets chainsaws a-swinging, with the result that Leatherface's chainsaw hits Cook in the behind ("The small businessman always gets it in the ass," he moans). There is a confrontation with an altar made out of the bones of the family's long-lost mother, and Lefty and Stretch escape while Leatherface does another *danse macabre* in the sun, holding his chainsaw aloft and reminding us that we have been there before.

While its sick humor is outrageous, *Chainsaw 2* in no way matches the mood of the original film to which it is supposed to be a companion piece. It has more in common with *Eaten Alive*, which in turn had been inspired by the prologue of Martin Scoresese's *Alice Doesn't Live Here Anymore*. In Hooper's worldview, the maniacs seem to have taken over the circus.

Hooper's most recent film, *Spontaneous Combustion*, continues the downward trend of the Cannon films and frankly is a mess. The basic idea deals with a young couple who are bribed by the government to participate in a dangerous experiment. In exchange for $10,000 and a new house, they submit to being exposed to the heavy radiation of a nuclear bomb blast. Not long after giving birth to their son, they both spontaneously combust, that is, the fat in the bodies bursts into flames and melts them.

Years later, their son, Sam Kramer (Brad Dourif), discovers that he can make people erupt into flame whenever he is angered. He works with his girlfriend Lisa (Cynthia Bain) to discover the reason for this incandescent ability. Hooper cowrote *Spontaneous Combustion*'s script with Howard Goldberg, but the whole thing plays like a warmed-over version of Stephen King's novel *Firestarter*, which director Mark Lester had ineptly adapted into a film some years before.

Produced for a mere $7 million, the film received scant release in this country before being released on videocassette; however, it is said to have made its money in foreign sales. As with *Lifeforce* and *Invaders from Mars*, once more Hooper blamed the film's inadequacies on post-production tampering; however, the fact that he kept trying to rewrite the script while he was filming it also must have added to the confusion. The film ended up being an embarrassment to its star, Dourif, but he need not have worried—almost nobody saw this turkey.

Hooper's career is a puzzle, filled with some genuine achievements and messy disasters. He wisely separated himself from *Leatherface: Chainsaw Massacre 3*, directed by Jeff Burr and scripted by splatterpunk David Schow, but he has had a hard time getting away from the tinkering that is making his movies fiascos. What he needs to do is settle himself down to a good horror project, concentrate on the directing, and leave the writing to the writers.

John Hough (1941–   )

Wolf's Head (1970); *Sudden Terror* (aka *Eyewitness); The Practice* (1971); *Twins of Evil; Treasure Island* (1972); *The Legend of Hell House; Dirty Mary, Crazy Larry* (1974); *Escape from Witch Mountain* (1975); *Return to Witch Mountain; Brass Target* (1978); *The Watcher in the Woods* (1980); *The Incubus* (1982); *Triumphs of a Man Called Horse* (1983); *Biggles* (1986); *American Gothic; Biggles–Adventures in Time* (1988); *The Howling IV* (1989).

TELEVISION: "The Super Secret Cypher Snatch," "The Morning After," "Fog," "Homicide and Old Lace," *The Avengers; The New Avengers; Black Arrow* (1985); *A Hazard of Hearts* (1987); *Dangerous Love* (1988); *The Lady and the Highwayman* (1989); *A Ghost in Monte Carlo* (1990).

John Hough makes lively adventure and horror films that are occasionally possessed of some interesting and offbeat aspects. In the '80s, he seems to have concentrated on television, where detailed credits are hard to come by, but his film work shows a good sense of pacing and style.

Hough was born on November 21, 1941, in London, England. In an interview with Bob Martin in *Fangoria* magazine, he claimed that his interest in the films of Ingmar Bergman led him to seek a career in filmmaking. After sending off letters of inquiry to several studios, he was accepted for an apprenticeship at Elstree Studios in 1960. He worked his way up, becoming a second unit director on *The Saint* TV series and, finally, a director on the classic *The Avengers* series. His first film, *Wolf's Head*, was a non-mythic treatment of the Robin Hood legend. Robin and his men secreted themselves in caves rather than Sherwood Forest. The distributor of the film soon went out of business and the film has practically vanished.

Hough's second film, *Eyewitness*, has become better known by its second title *Sudden Terror*. It starred Mark Lester, Susan George and Lionel Jeffries. The film is basically a variation on *The Window*, Ted Tetzlaff's suspense classic. This time Lester sees the murder of a black president of an African nation but nobody believes him.

Hough's first horror film and my favorite from among his works is *Twins of Evil*, the last of the Karnstein trilogy supposedly based on J. Sheridan Le Fanu's "Carmilla." (The other films were Baker's *The Vampire Lovers* and Jimmy Sangster's *Lust for a Vampire*. There was also an interesting semifollow-up, Robert Young's *Vampire Circus*.)

553

In the Martin interview, Hough said:

> As soon as I read the script, I knew that one of our main difficulties
> would be finding identical twins for the title role. . . . There were twins
> who sang professionally, but not many twins who were acting, and
> would do the nude scenes required. We were lucky to find the Collinson
> twins, who had just previously appeared in a *Playboy* centerfold. I was
> fairly pleased with their performances though I rather wish that I had
> more time; at Hammer a director never was given more than six weeks
> of preparation, and, in this instance, it had taken so long to cast the title
> roles that over half of that time was gone.

Twins of Evil proves to be a bit of a misnomer as a title, as only one of
the twins turns out to be evil and becomes transformed into a vampire. Still,
Tudor Gates' script is interesting in that while it allows the antagonists to
be purely evil, the protagonists of the tale are morally ambiguous upon occasion. Peter Cushing stars as Gustav Weil (the name even sound like "vile"),
the leader of Karnstein's puritan Brotherhood. At the start of the film, the
Brotherhood drags out a woman who lives in an isolated house in the woods,
tears her cross off her, and burns her as a supposed vampire. We realize
later that the woman was indeed innocent and that the vigilante Brotherhood has been picking on the unprotected in futile effort to root out the evil
in its midst. There has been a rash of victims that have had the blood drained
from them, but the Brotherhood dares not attack the decadent Count Karnstein (Damien Thomas) for fear of harsh reprisals from the emperor.

Into this mess comes Maria and Frieda (Mary and Madeline Collinson),
Weil's nieces, whose parents have just died. In true horror film fashion, one
of these identical twins, Frieda, is attracted to evil, while the other is good.
Hough establishes the difference: Frieda as aggressive and defiant while
Maria is demure and submissive.

Thomas does a good job playing the loathsome Count Karnstein. When
the Brotherhood surprises him in bed with one of its chosen victims, he is
saucy with the group and even tempts Weil to shoot him, though his black
servant Joachim intervenes. (Each film in the series features a mysterious
"Man in Black," though this time the character is actually a black man.) Karnstein lets the Brotherhood burn his innocent bedmate while he returns to
the castle.

There Dietrich (Dennis Price) has prepared a black mass to summon up
the devil for the Count's amusement including a veiled village virgin as a
sacrifice. However, this is not original enough to please the bored Count,
who dismisses everyone before sacrificing the peasant girl himself. Her
blood runs into the crypt housing Mircalla, and in one of the film's most
effective and atmospheric shots, a rising mist turns into a hooded figure that

approaches the occupied Count. This figure turns out to be the spirit of Mircalla, who explains that when evil people are bitten by a vampire, they turn into vampires themselves. To answer the Count's call to Satan so that he can experience undreamt-of pleasures, she vampirizes him.

While this is one of the best sequences in the film, it does create some plot holes that are never explained. From this point on, the Count is a vampire, but then who was draining the earlier victims of blood? Mircalla? She promptly disappears from the story, never to be heard from again. There are also slight but inoffensive departures from the vampire myths. These vampires can travel about in sunlight; if they are burned they merely assume another form; and they can only be dispatched by a stake through the heart *or* decapitation.

It is not long before Frieda is drawn to the castle after seeing Count Karnstein in the village and seeing him being warned away from her by her uncle. The Count quickly vampirizes her and bids her feast upon a buxom village beauty as her first victim (the obligatory "lesbian" scene in the series, which is done tastefully and cut away from quickly).

The hero of the story is the town's choirmaster and historian, Anton Hoffer (David Warbeck), who initially regards vampires as superstition (though a superstition he apparently regards as interesting enough to have several books on the subject). In accordance with the Hammer tradition of playing up the attractivenss of evil, Hough and Gates have Anton immediately falling for Frieda over her twin sister because there is something about Frieda that fascinates him.

Speaking of attractiveness, Hough does play up the story's erotic aspects. In a lovely bit of film symbolism, one scene features the Count making love to the bewitching Mircalla, stroking her all over, and Hough then concentrates on her stroking a lit candle up and down as the Count goes down on her. The twins are very attractive, with Frieda having a nice nude scene with Hoffer when she tries to seduce him (he gives in initially and then realizes this is the vampirish sister). The only thing missing is the candle wax overflowing when the lovers climax.

Frieda kills Dietrich and then gets caught with her fangs bared by the Brotherhood. Weil is dissuaded by his wife from also attempting to execute the innocent Maria, while the Count comes and steals Maria away to the jail holding Frieda, and the twins are switched so that Maria will be burned and Frieda can continue her reign of terror. However, Hoffer sees through the ruse and stops Weil from killing Maria just in time.

The Brotherhood then storms the castle, violently staking Joachim. Weil decapitates Frieda, whom the Count had sent on ahead to see if it was safe. Trapped in the castle, the Count kidnaps Maria and holds her hostage. Weil tries to kill him but gets an axe in his back and pushed over the railing for his pains. Finally Hoffer takes a trident and hurls it into the heart of the

Count, who suddenly ages and decays into a corpse (though he has been a vampire for only a very short time).

All in all, *Twins of Evil* was an entertaining, lively horror film deserving of a better reputation than it has thus far received, and it demonstrated that Hough was a horror director of some promise. The sets look better at Pinewood than the Elstree locations of the other two films in the series, and the whole thing was nicely photographed by Dick Bush. Hough made some attempt at creating atmosphere with some effective lighting and fog without overdoing it or bogging the spritely-paced story down.

Next Hough tackled an interesting version of *Treasure Island*, co-scripted by Orson Welles, who also played Long John Silver in a menacing, unlovable fashion, contrary to tradition. Unfortunately, it still did not hold a candle to the Victor Fleming or Byron Haskin versions. After the film, Hough left England for Hollywood.

James H. Nicholson, cohead of American International Pictures, decided to split from his old partner Sam Z. Arkoff and form his own production company. The first and, because of Nicholson's untimely demise, only venture of the company was an adaptation of Richard Matheson's book *Hell House*.

Though it has something in common with both William Castle's *House on Haunted Hill* and Robert Wise's *The Haunting*, Hough's *The Legend of Hell House* was not as good as either of those. Matheson's novel went through the standard paces of surviving a night in a haunted house coupled with an attempt by a physicist to take a scientific approach to spook-hunting, which the movie also follows. But Matheson's novel also went into detail about the sexual escapades that had given the house an evil reputation and the effect of repressed sexuality on the psychology of the physicist's wife in particular, as she undergoes the experiment with her husband along with a medium and the sole survivor of a previous expedition into Hell House.

With Roddy McDowall playing the previous survivor, Pamela Franklin playing the medium, Clive Revill playing the physicist and Gayle Hunnicutt playing his wife, the cast is a fairly good one, but the movie itself is uninspiring and not particularly frightening or horrifying. Michael Gough, who had become known for his wooden acting in horror films, has an amusing, unbilled cameo as the corpse of the mad millionaire, Emeric Belasco, who built the house and whose unquiet and overcompensating spirit is creating a rash of psychic phenomena and ectoplasmic sightings.

The sex scenes in Matheson's novel were shocking for their time (the early '60s), but Nicholson wanted his film to appeal to the family trade, so they were eliminated and no particular character insights or shocks were generated in the film to take their place. The film is obviously a serious-minded venture that wants to be a quality horror film, but good intentions do not a great film make. There is an interesting scene where Franklin is molested by an unseen spirit and McDowall is suitably frantic, but Franklin was much better in *The Innocents* and McDowall gave his best horror performance in Tom Holland's *Fright Night*.

Hough's next fantasy films were for Disney. The first two were the *Witch Mountain* pictures, about alien children who have telekinetic powers. In the first film, *Escape to Witch Mountain*, the children (Kim Richards and Ike Eisenmann) are trying to discover who their parents were while a rich tycoon (Ray Milland) and a psychic researcher (Donald Pleasence) plan to exploit the tykes. Along comes Eddie Albert in his Winnebago and the kids escape to rendezvous with a flying saucer.

The sequel, *Return to Witch Mountain*, exploits the same basic formula. The kids are dropped off for a vacation on earth by their Uncle Bene (Denver Pyle) and save a man (Anthony James) from falling off a building under the direction of a mind control device manipulated by mad scientist Victor (Christopher Lee) and his accomplice Letha (Bette Davis). Having revealed himself to this nefarious pair, Eisenmann is kidnapped by them and sis Richards enlists the local angels with dirty faces to help seek out her brother. As in the previous film, there are some cheap laughs and lively special effects of things being telekinetically lifted and floated all over the place. Both films were appealing, lightweight family entertainment and managed to do reasonably well.

Unfortunately, *The Watcher in the Woods*, an adaptation of Florence Engel Randall's young adult novel, was far more troubled. The film starred Lynn-Holly Johnson as Jan Curtis, a young girl who suspects that there is a mysterious something watching in the woods next to the house her family rented from the dying Mrs. Aylwood (Bette Davis). It builds up to a climax where the Watcher and its dimension were supposed to be finally explained and revealed. However, the special effects turned out looking like something out of a cheap Japanese film, and Disney quickly pulled the movie to tinker with it. They eventually decided to lop off the ending almost entirely, so that the audience never received the expected payoff and ended up being puzzled as to what the film was all about.

Costars David McCallum and Carroll Baker are in the film so little they practically phone in their performances. This just leaves the puzzled kids and the enigmatic Mrs. Aylwood as main, Disney-style characters. Perhaps the film was supposed to be about Jan coming to grips with the idea of death, particularly the death of a friend, as Mrs. Aylwood knows her time is near to pass on to "the other side." However, this concept is obscure in the mysterious occurrences that make up this slick movie. Hough generates some atmosphere and what we have is not bad, but neither is it fish nor fowl. It is not a family film, not a science fiction film, not a horror film, but some mixed-up combination of the three. The result was unsatisfying and unfortunate, though there are some nicely atmospheric scenes.

In the fall of 1980, Hough traveled to Canada to make *The Incubus* as part of a Canadian tax shelter scheme. Based on Ray Russell's novel, the film took a couple of years to get released, and the wait was not worth it. A Wisconsin kid (Duncan McIntosh) has a nightmare that convinces him he is a demon (shown only briefly) who has been killing several of his friends. Film director John Cassavetes stars as Dr. Cordell, who has been having similar nightmares and decides to investigate the case. Also on the case is John Ireland as a local sheriff, and there's the mysterious appearance of Laura Kincaid (Kerrie Keane), who looks just like Cordell's wife who was killed in a car crash.

Much of the picture is taken up with tracking down the demonic killer who sexually assaults his victims and fills them with "red sperm," in between attacks in which the aggressor is not glimpsed. Hough does his best to inject some style with some unusual camera angles, and Albert J. Dunk's camera work is not bad. Too bad the same cannot be said for George Franklin's awful script or the actors wretched performances.

Sadly, *Biggles – Adventures in Time* is almost equally exasperating. Based on an endless series of British novels about a World War I flying ace named Biggles, whose chums are called Algy, Bertie and Ginger, *Biggles* has a modern-day would-be frozen food tycoon, Jim Ferguson (Alex Hyde-White), suddenly slipping back and forth to and from the time of Biggles. The film is so busy whipping Ferguson back and forth in time that it never really gets anywhere, though Peter Cushing has a nice supporting role as the mysterious Col. Raymond. Perhaps the saddest thing about *Biggles* is that it will reportedly be Cushing's final film role, an inauspicious exit to a fine film career. This film is not just disappointing from time to time, it's disappointing all the time.

A bit better is Hough's most recent horror film, *Amerian Gothic*, another mad family epic where they "slice and dice" members of three stranded couples. The demented family includes Ma (Yvonne De Carlo), who stuffs her guests with food and urges them to dance the Charleston; Pa (Rod Steiger really chewing the scenery), who is given to waving his shotgun around and lecturing on the necessity of abstaining from sex; Fanny (Janet Wright), who plays with her mummified baby; and Woody and Teddy (Michael J. Pollard and William Hootkins), who have an interesting idea of what constitutes fun and games.

Though the film recaptures some of the energy of Hough's earlier efforts, the heavy-handed satire is no more effective here than it was in Charles Kaufman's *Mother's Day*, a particularly repellent attempt to do a variation of Tobe Hooper's *The Texas Chainsaw Massacre* theme. Hough, as he has amply demonstrated in his adventure pictures, his *Avengers* episodes, and his earlier films, is capable of better things. What he needs now is to stop accepting assignments with inferior scripts.

Erle C. Kenton (1896–1980)

Trial Marriage; Father and Son; Song of Love (1929); Mexicali Rose; A Royal Romance (1930); The Last Parade; Lover Come Back; Leftover Ladies; X Marks the Spot (1931); Stranger in Town; Guilty as Hell (1932); Island of Lost Souls; From Hell to Heaven; Disgraced!; Big Executive (1933); Search for Beauty; You're Telling Me (1934); The Best Man Wins; Party Wire; The Public Menace; Grand Exit (1935); Devil's Squadron; Counterfeit; End of the Trial (1936); Devil's Playground; Racketeers in Exile; She Asked for It (1937); The Lady Objects; Little Tough Guys in Society (1938); Everything's on Ice; Escape to Paradise (1939); Remedy for Riches (1940); Petticoat Politics; Melody for Three; Naval Academy; They Meet Again; Flying Cadets (1941); Frisco Lil; North to the Klondike; The Ghost of Frankenstein; Pardon My Sarong; Who Done It? (1942); How's About It?; It Ain't Hay; Always a Bridesmaid (1944); House of Frankenstein; She Gets Her Man; House of Dracula (1945); The Cat Creeps; Little Miss Big (1946); Bob and Sally (1948); One Too Many (1950).

TELEVISION: Racket Squad (1950–53); Public Defender (1954); The Texan (1958–62).

Erle C. Kenton is a largely forgotten director, best known for his few horror films and work on some Abbott and Costello comedies. He was born in Norboro, Montana, in 1896 and began working in film as a writer for Mack Sennett in 1914. He began as a director in the silent era with A Small Town Idol in 1921. (I have omitted his silent film credits.)

His first important film was Paramount's 1932 production of Island of Lost Souls, which was not only his best horror film, but also one of the best of the '30s. Paramount entered into the horror field after the enormous successes of Dracula and Frankenstein, but when subsequent films failed to match those classics' grosses, reportedly Paramount got nervous about their property, an adaptation of H. G. Wells' Island of Dr. Moreau.

They need not have been. The film is an exciting and wonderfully crafted horror thriller featuring excellent performances (particularly from Charles Laughton as Moreau), an intelligent and suggestive script by Waldemar Young and Philip Wylie, scrumptuous photography by Karl Struss, and wonderful makeups from Wally Westmore. Though there have been two remakes (Terror Is a Man and The Island of Dr. Moreau), both were greatly inferior, and Island of Lost Souls remains the definitive screen version of this classic tale.

559

Wells, like George Bernard Shaw, was suspicious of medical doctors and was an anti-vivisectionist and wrote his book partly as an anti-vivisectionist tract. The scriptwriters alter the basic story to emphasize its overtones of sexuality, perversity, and eroticism as well as to lampoon religion (typical of Wylie who was very much a free thinker). Wells, however, did not approve of the changes wrought in his work and condemned the film publicly. It was not shown in Great Britain until many years after its release because of its suggestions of bestiality and daring.

The film begins simply enough with Edward Parker (Richard Arlen) being picked up after being shipwrecked. He sends a cablegram ahead to his fiancée who has been awaiting him anxiously at Apia, and then explores the ship which is carrying a cargo of animals. He sees a strange man named M'ling (Tetsu Komai), who has a fur-covered ear, prowling on the deck.

Captain Davies (Stanley Fields), the skipper of the boat, is a crude drunkard who resents having taken Parker aboard. When he viciously slugs M'ling for no reason, the outraged Parker makes the mistake of knocking the captain out. Strangely, M'ling shakes off the blow to his head as if he were a dog rather than a man.

When the ship makes a rendezvous with Dr. Moreau's ship and unloads its cargo, Captain Davies suddenly remembers the blow he received and decides to heave Parker overboard onto Moreau's ship, deciding that he has fulfilled his obligation by dropping Parker off at the first "port." Moreau protests, but Davies simply sails away.

Helping Moreau on shipboard are Montgomery (Arthur Hohl) and several beast-like men. Unlike other early sound films, the jungle scenes in *Island of Lost Souls* were filmed on location on nearby Catalina Island, and cinematographer Struss makes the most of the opportunity, showing how sunlight and shadow blend over the foliage. Adding to the atmosphere are scenes filmed in California fog, giving the location a misty, mysterious quality.

Struss and Kenton worked well together, and Struss praised him highly in *Hollywood Cameramen*:

> Erle C. Kenton . . . had been a pictorial photographer, and I met him when I was exhibiting stills in the early twenties. We actually went on a steamer to Catalina and shot the picture on it, with the half-human animals whimpering on board before you get to the island where Charlie Laughton was the mad scientist. . . . I admired Kenton; he had a greater command of the English language than anyone I ever worked with. He played every scene through for the actor, even for Laughton, who was superb as Dr. Moreau.

In early sound films, directing was often a split chore with the director handling the performances while the director of photography worried about

Taking a break on the set of Island of Lost Souls *are, from left to right, Charles Laughton, Erle C. Kenton, and Richard Arlen. Note the enormity of the 1930s style 35mm cameras behind them.*

the visuals. That *Island of Lost Souls* benefited from Struss' involvement in ways other than its excellent cinematography and lighting can be seen when one compares it to other Kenton projects. The fluid use of camera movement was far more typical of Struss' other work than Kenton's, but both men deserve high praise for their work on the film.

Kenton proves very adept at building an atmosphere of unease and never letting it falter. From the strangeness of the cargo to the oddness of the "natives" of Moreau's island, the visuals present one intriguing image after another. As they approach Moreau's home, Parker becomes aware of the eerie shapes that scamper through the underbrush, things which are not distinctly seen but are clearly there.

Also, Parker and Moreau are dressed in white suits which are given almost a luminescence by Struss' lighting, giving the impression that they are gods wandering through a dark domain. This fits in perfectly with the plot motif of the film as we learn that the Beast-Men of the island do regard human beings as gods initially. In fact, the scriptwriters are daring enough to include the line that had been cut out of *Frankenstein* the year before as Moreau turns to Parker after showing him his "House of Pain" and says, "Parker, do you know what it feels like to be God?"

Laughton gives a brilliantly malevolent performance as Moreau, a man whose constant smugness and self-assuredness never allow him to question the morality of what he is doing. That Moreau himself is brilliant is obvious in his successes. Moreau has found a way to speed up the process of evolution in living things. (He begins with plants, which he proudly shows off to Parker.)

The film presupposes that evolution is a natural force constantly taking place and that all animals are slowly evolving into a man-like state. Through his vivisection techniques, Moreau has been able to speed up the evolution of the animals he imports onto his island until they are nearly human. He forces his alcoholic assistant to assist him because Montgomery was run out of England for a "violation of his medical ethics" (probably performing an abortion) and Moreau has given him drink and shelter.

There is a strong undercurrent of eroticism throughout the film as it is very apparent that Moreau hopes his most successful creation, Lota (Kathleen Burke), will fall in love and mate with the handsome Parker. Though Parker has a fiancée and initially resists Lota's charms, it becomes obvious that he is attracted to this strange, cat-like woman. Moreau promises to loan Parker his boat to sail to Apia but arranges to have the boat sunk when they get to it the next morning. Moreau expects that time and the monotony will take care of the rest.

And indeed, despite learning what Moreau has been doing in his "House of Pain," Parker does not suspect Lota until he sees she has panther-like claws instead of fingernails and realizes with horror what Moreau's intentions have been. Moreau himself is depressed that his creations seem to regress back into their animal states, but rejoices when Lota sheds tears over her rejection by Parker, a growing indication of her humanity.

The lighting of Moreau's house, with its slats and blinds that cast thin shadows, suggests a giant prison or cage. When Parker suspects that Moreau is experimenting on human beings, thinking the natives were once human beings that Moreau has deformed, he tries to escape to Lota by running into the jungle where from a rise he espies the village of the Beast-Men. Visually, the higher and lower orders of man are clearly defined.

This is further reinforced when Laughton arrives to snap his whip and have the hairy-faced Sayer of the Law (Bela Lugosi) recite the Beast-Men's laws ("Not to run on all fours, that is the law! Are we not men? Not to eat meat. . . . Not to spill blood. . . .") Though it is only a small part, Lugosi's performance is quite extraordinary in how well it suggests an animal in pain, particularly when he raises his hand to Moreau and declaims, "*His* is the hand that makes! *His* is the hand that heals! *His* is the House . . . of . . . *Pain!*"

Meanwhile, Parker's fiancée, Ruth Walker (Leila Hyams), confronts Captain Davis and forces him to reveal where he dropped Parker off. Given aid by Captain Donahue (Paul Hurst), she arrives with the captain at Moreau's island. Ruth's arrival excites the interest and lust of Outan (Hans Steinke), a fact that does not escape Moreau's notice. Perhaps, he muses, he does not need Parker to prove his theories. He puts up Donahue and Ruth for the night, but Outan breaks the bars of Ruth's window and intends to abduct her until Parker drives him off with his pistol.

This spurs Donahue to action; he decides to return to his ship and bring back his men. Moreau gives Outan instructions to overtake Donahue, put his hands around Donahue's neck and squeeze, which Outan does. Amazed that one of the human "gods" can die, Outan takes the body back to the Beast-Men's village, where the alarmed Sayer of the Law puzzles out that if Donahue can die, so could Moreau – that these humans are not God and the law restraining the Beast-Men has been broken.

Montgomery tries to warn Moreau, but Moreau remains arrogant. He is used to the natives being "restless," and he goes to the Beast-Men's village to restore order. However, they do not respond to his commands or his lashings, and as the others escape, Moreau is driven back to his own House of Pain, while Montgomery, Ruth and Parker escape out the back way. The Beast-Men break into the glass cabinets containing the scalpels and face Moreau with a forest of steel. His fate is made clear by a prolonged groan of pain.

For its time, *Island of Lost Souls* was quite horrific and quite daring, and it still impresses even today. It was obviously made before the revised Hollywood Code of 1935, with its overt suggestions of not only sexuality but mating with animals. Laughton, a homosexual, does not restrain his foppish mannerisms and makes those an effective part of his characterization. The film itself is a poke in the eye at assertions of godliness. And what is more, it is a damn fine horror film besides.

However, Kenton was not to return to horror until *The Ghost of Frankenstein* in 1942. En route, he directed one of W. C. Fields' best films, *You're Telling Me*, a remake of the silent *So's Your Old Man* which includes Fields' classic golf routine. He also handled *Pardon My Sarong, Who Done It?* and *It Ain't Hay* for Abbott and Costello, and directed Lugosi in *The Best Man Wins*.

Universal had returned in 1939 to make a new installment of their Frankenstein saga. This time it was *Son of Frankenstein*, produced and directed by Roland V. Lee, who had concocted the memorable *Tower of London* for *Son of Frankenstein* stars Basil Rathbone and Boris Karloff. Amazingly, Karloff's monster was reduced to an automaton with virtually none of the personality that Karloff had exhibited in the Whale films, and it was Bela Lugosi who stole the show as a malevolent hunchbacked shepherd named Ygor. This handsomely produced but overrated horror film proved another box office bonanza for Universal, so a sequel was ordered.

Eric Taylor, who had worked on *Black Friday* and the 1941 version of *The Black Cat*, came up with a story involving the return of Frankenstein's son Wolf. This story was largely thrown out, but elements were retained in the *Ghost of Frankenstein* script by W. Scott Darling. Kenton, who had been churning out B films for the studio, was selected to direct with Sir Cedric Hardwicke taking on the role of Dr. Ludwig Frankenstein, Wolf's brother, and new horror star Lon Chaney, Jr., who was allergic to the makeup, taking the role of the monster (Karloff was busy on Broadway, where he was enjoying a huge success with *Arsenic and Old Lace*).

Ghost of Frankenstein begins with villagers urging the burgomaster (Lawrence Grant) to blow up Frankenstein's castle, which the villagers proceed to do. They become alarmed at the spectacle of Ygor, believed to have been killed by Wolf in the last film, still alive and taunting them with laughter and rocks. Setting off charges around the old castle tower, Ygor plummets inside and discovers that the Frankenstein Monster is still alive in the hardened sulphur of the pit into which he had been cast.

Ygor takes his old "friend" for a walk to escape the villagers, and there is a weird scene where a lightning bolt hits the Monster and recharges its energies. "Your father was Frankenstein, but your mother was the light-n-ing!" Ygor proudly proclaims.

Things were not going too well in Europe in 1942, and this is reflected in *The Ghost of Frankenstein* when gloomy villagers complain about hunger and a lack of bread even before the Monster makes his appearance. In the village of Vasaria, Ludwig Frankenstein is a respectable medical doctor who specializes in "Diseases of the Mind." With the aid of Dr. Kettering (Barton Yarborough) and Dr. Bohmer (Lionel Atwill), he has successfully operated on a brain after removing it from the skull and then replacing it. Dr. Bohmer, who used to be Frankenstein's teacher before he was disgraced over what he describes as "a slight miscalculation," is clearly jealous and envious of Ludwig's success. Interestingly enough, in *Ghost* the mad scientist is not Frankenstein but Bohmer, and Atwill plays the part with a superbly suave menace, always appearing as if he is keeping his raging emotions carefully in check.

Once more the Monster develops a relationship with a small child, Cloestine (Janet Ann Gallow), whom it helps to retrieve a ball off the roof. A crowd regards its actions as threatening, which results in a death and the monster being overpowered and hauled off to jail again. At expressing any tenderness towards the young girl, Chaney proves to be a complete washout, but with the aid of Kenton's low angles, he does make an imposing monster with a definite suggestion of inhuman strength.

Ralph Bellamy appears as Erik Ernst, the love interest of Frankenstein's daughter Elsa (Evelyn Ankers) as well as the town prosecutor who calls Dr. Frankenstein to the inquest concerning the Monster. Ludwig is about to go when he is surprised by an unexpected visit from Ygor, who wants him to recharge the Monster's power. Ludwig wisely refuses, explaining that he regards the Monster as a curse upon his family. Ygor then blackmails him into accepting custody of the Monster at the inquest.

The Monster becomes very upset when Frankenstein enters the courtroom and claims to know nothing about him, but is calmed by a tune from Ygor's shepherd's horn, which impels him to escape the courtroom. Ygor is waiting in a carriage and the pair escape.

Some shots of the original *Frankenstein* and *Bride of Frankenstein* are included as flashback material as Elsa reads the notebook compiled by her grandfather entitled *The Secrets of Life and Death*. A lightning flash reveals that she is being observed by the Monster and Ygor, which causes her to scream. The Monster smashes down the door and kills Dr. Kettering, who has come to Elsa's assistance. Frankenstein saves his daughter by unleasing a knock-out gas and then summons Dr. Bohmer in an effort to save Kettering's life, but they fail.

Frankenstein reiterates what Dr. Waldeman had said: The only way to kill the Monster is to dissect it. As he is preparing to do this, he sees the ghost of his father (thereby justifying the title) who suggests that rather than destroying the Monster he give it another brain, a better brain than the criminal one it had accidentally received. This inspires Frankenstein to want to transplant the brain of the learned Dr. Kettering into the Monster, though a learned monster seems a rather odd idea.

Ygor has another idea. Tired of his crippled body, he insists that Frankenstein put *his* brain into the Monster's body. "That would be a monster indeed!" observes Frankenstein. Thwarted, Ygor plots with Dr. Bohmer to insure his cooperation, promising to aid Bohmer in his medical career. The dim-witted Monster also seems pleased by the idea of getting a new brain, but it does not want Ygor's brain, it wants Cloestine's!

In kidnapping the child, the monster burns Cloestine's house to the ground so that she is not immediately missed, the villagers assuming she perished in the blaze. When Ygor insists, "You will have the brain of your friend Ygor! Tonight, Ygor will die for you!" The Monster accidentally crushes him behind a heavy door. Seeing that Ygor's body is dying gives added impetus for Bohmer to switch brains on Frankenstein.

The operation is a success and the Monster slowly recovers. However, villagers are beginning to wonder why the giant maniac that had escaped from them cannot be found. Believing that Frankenstein is sheltering the monster, an angry mob goes to Frankenstein's sanitarium, but Erik arrives and placates them, promising to confront Frankenstein himself.

Frankenstein admits that he has been protecting the Frankenstein Monster and explains how he hoped to use the Monster to atone for Kettering's death. Unfortunately, the revived monster announces that it is not Dr. Kettering but Ygor. "I've created a hundred times the monster that my father made!" exclaims Frankenstein in dismay. The gloating Bohmer smiles a cruel smile which causes Frankenstein to attack him, but the Monster intervenes.

Despite the many instances of mad scientists conducting experiments with transplants, *The Ghost of Frankenstein* remains one of the few that actually addresses the problem of matching blood types. It turns out that Ygor lacks the same blood type as the Monster and is thus rendered blind. (The sequel, *Frankenstein Meets the Wolf Man*, depicted the monster as blind, walking along with his arms outstretched ahead of him so as to not bump into things, but dialogue to this effect was omitted, causing further confusion and establishing an image of the Frankenstein Monster that was not true of earlier depictions.) The enraged Monster kills both Bohmer and Frankenstein. Meanwhile, the angry village mob has filled the house with gas, which catches fire and leaves the Monster in the midst of the burning wreckage as it crashes around him. Elsa, Erik and Cloestine all escape to safety and future happiness.

In an interview in the *Film Fan Monthly*, Ralph Bellamy provided this amusing look into Erle C. Kenton's working methods:

> Cedric and I had a pleasant hour, two hours, and finally decided to go down to see how they are doing. There was a lot of hollering and running around, and the assistant director finally went to this little director and said, "We're ready." He picked up the megaphone and almost bumped the assistant as he turned it around. He said, "Get Evelyn Ankers at the top of the stairway." He started to pace, back and forth, with the megaphone, and said, "Now Evelyn, you're all alone in this dim, dark, dank, dingy, ancient, oozing, slimey castle at four o'clock in the morning. Your mother's been carried off by the Frankenstein Monster, your father's been killed by the wolf man, the servants have fled, your lover is being chased across the moors by dogs. I want to get the feeling from you as you come down this stairway, that you're fed up with it all!"
>
> Anytime, Cedric and I saw each other anywhere in the world after that – and it was a lot of places – we'd say, "You fed up with it all?"

The Ghost of Frankenstein was undoubtedly the best of the post–Karloff Frankenstein films, featuring a strong cast and a good number of thrills, so

Erle C. Kenton

it was not surprising when Kenton was selected to helm *House of Franken-stein*. After having teamed the Frankenstein Monster and the Wolf Man, Universal decided to pile together as many monsters as possible for *House of Frankenstein*, adding Dracula, a hunchback, and a mad doctor to the Monster and the Wolf Man, to create an uneven hodgepodge of a film.

Universal believed that audiences liked to see familiar faces in their horror films and so constantly reused actors in their Frankenstein series, with the result that villagers killed in *Son of Frankenstein* would reappear in *The Ghost of Frankenstein* in different roles. Able to secure the services of Boris Karloff again, they gave him the film's leading role, Dr. Gustav Niemann, while Lon Chaney would recreate his role of Larry Talbot, the Wolf Man. Lionel Atwill was given yet another role as Inspector Arnz, but though he was considered, Bela Lugosi was not asked back to play Count Dracula. Lugosi had other commitments, plus the studio had been unhappy with his portrayal of the Frankenstein Monster in *Frankenstein Meets the Wolf Man*. Instead his part went to popular villain John Carradine, who adopted the white mustache that Bram Stoker described in the original book. The Monster was given a largely inactive role in this segment of the series and cowboy star Glenn Strange was cast based on height, strength, and a strong brow that could be made up to resemble Karloff's as the Monster.

The monsters never really all come together in the episodic film, but this never troubled young, monster-loving fans and the film did prove a financial success. The film begins with Dr. Niemann, who has been attempting to follow in Frankenstein's footsteps and has apparently been placed in an insane asylum for attempting to transplant a man's brain into a dog's body. He tells Daniel, a sympathetic hunchback, that with Frankenstein's records, he could give Daniel a perfect body. Then, as if ordained by God, lightning strikes the walls of the asylum and the pair escape.

In the rain they find Prof. Bruno Lampini (George Zucco) and his Chamber of Horrors, which includes the skeleton of Count Dracula. Under Niemann's direction, Daniel strangles Lampini and Niemann assumes the late professor's identity. Heading back to the town where he had practiced, Niemann plots his revenge against those that had imprisoned him. He removes the stake from Dracula's skeleton, thereby reviving him, and coerces him into helping carry out his revenge by attacking the burgomaster (Sig Rumann) and his daughter-in-law Rita (Anne Gwynne).

However, Dracula's abduction of Rita leads to a pursuit by her husband (Peter Coe), and when Niemann sees that the pursuit might lead back to him, he abandons Dracula's coffin and refuge by the side of the road. Dracula is burned by the sun's rays before he can reach the safety of his coffin, and Rita and her husband are happily reunited.

Still searching for Frankenstein's records, Niemann receives a frosty welcome from the village where the Monster and the Wolf Man were supposedly destroyed when the dam was destroyed (at the end of *Franken-stein Meets the Wolf Man*). Meanwhile, Daniel sees a gypsy beating a pretty gypsy girl, Ilonka (Elena Verdugo), and whips her beater in return, taking the wounded Ilonka with him.

The discovery of the bodies of the Monster and the Wolf Man, encased in ice, leads to their being thawed out. Larry Talbot revives and offers to assist Niemann in exchange for Niemann's promise to cure him of lycanthropy. Meanwhile, a love triangle forms; Daniel loves Ilonka, who begins to fall for Larry and refuses to believe when Daniel tells her that Larry is a werewolf.

Niemann begins concocting various mad schemes, starting with the removal of the brains of two of the people who had testified against him. He plans to give one brain to the Frankenstein Monster and use the other body to house Talbot's brain while he gives the Wolf Man the Frankenstein Monster's brain. Somehow, Daniel senses in this game of musical brains, Niemann's promises to him have gotten lost in the schuffle.

Talbot changes into the Wolf Man in the full moon and kills a villager so that the rest of the villagers begin to go out and look for the Wolf Man. Meanwhile, Ilonka becomes convinced that Daniel was telling the truth and fashions a silver bullet. The Wolf Man comes for her next, but she manages to shoot him with the silver bullet, and the romantic pair die in each other's arms.

However, the loss of Ilonka, the only thing he ever loved, enrages Daniel, who confronts Niemann as he reenergizes the Monster. When Daniel attacks Niemann, the Monster breaks its straps and kills Daniel by throwing him out of a window. The flashes of electricity emanating from the ruins have alerted the villagers, who storm the place. The Monster takes Niemann's body and wanders off into some quicksand despite the dying Niemann's protests.

Somehow, when Ygor's brain was transferred to the Monster, it not only lost its sight (though the monster regains it in this film, laughing cruelly at the sight of the unfortunate hunchback), but apparently all of Ygor's cunning as well. *House of Frankenstein* is largely uninspired horror hokum, but Kenton does manage to enliven the proceedings occasionally by bringing out the pathos of Daniel's situation or adding atmosphere to Talbot's transformation by panning from Talbot running to his footprints which change to animals tracks and back up to the Wolf Man now fully revealed. The actors are all old troupers, but their roles are too short or erratic to create much of a lingering impression.

Perhaps the main impression that *House of Frankenstein* leaves was that it was not so foolish nor so funny as its sequel, also directed by Kenton, *House of Dracula*. The last of the serious Universal Frankenstein films, *House of Dracula* centers around Onslow Stevens as Dr. Franz Edelmann,

Erle C. Kenton (center) explains the workings of a camera distortion screen to John Carradine (left) and cameraman Frank Heisler (right) on the set of House of Dracula.

who apparently specializes in curing monsters of their afflictions. In short order, both Dracula and the Wolf Man come to his door seeking cures, while his pretty hunchbacked nurse Nina (Jane Adams) waits patiently on the sidelines for the doctor to get around to his promise of curing her with the aid of Clavaria Formosa, a fungus which softens the bones.

Edelman's diagnosis of Dracula is that he has a parasite in his blood and that an injection of a pure culture of this parasite might cause it to destroy itself and cure Dracula in the process. Edelman diagnoses Lawrence Talbot as being the victim of self-hypnosis brought on by too much pressure on the brain, something he could cure with his bone-softening drug once he had sufficient quantities.

Chaney makes the most of playing Talbot yet again, as he has himself locked in prison rather than risk killing anyone as the Wolf Man. When he learns that Edelman cannot kill him right away, he attempts suicide by jumping off a cliff. Edelman risks his life by being lowered over the cliff, hoping to recapture Talbot in mid-transformation. In doing so, he discovers: (1) a cave that is perfect for growing his fungus; (2) the Frankenstein

Monster, still holding Niemann's skeleton; and (3) a secret stairway back up to his castle! How convenient!

Things go awry when Dracula repumps some of his blood into Edelman's body, causing him to behave like a Jekyll-and-Hyde while his reflection disappears from the mirror. The film maintains its delirious content throughout, but at least it seems more original than *House of Frankenstein*, though it overly relies on stock footage for a dream sequence in which Dracula rises from the dead and the Frankenstein Monster goes on the rampage (mostly from Whale's *Bride of Frankenstein*).

Edelman saves Miliza (Martha O'Driscoll) from becoming Dracula's next victim by waving a cross at the Count and then dragging his corpse out into the sunlight where it disintegrates, leaving Miliza to fall in love with the troubled Talbot. (It must have been his animal nature that caused so many attractive women to fall for a guy who looks like Lon Chaney, Jr.) Meanwhile, infected with Dracula's parasite, Edelmann goes mad and kills a villager, though he regains his sanity long enough to convince Inspector Holtz (Lionel Atwill in his last horror role) that Talbot, recovering from an operation, was not responsible. While Talbot is revealed as finally cured when he does not change as the full moon rises, Edelmann sinks back into madness and recharges the Frankenstein Monster, killing the sympathetic Nina when she tries to intervene.

Investigating the death of the villager that Edelmann killed, Inspector Holtz and the villages arrives at Edelmann's castle in time to see him unleash the Monster. Suddenly, stock footage from *The Ghost of Frankenstein* is intercut: Lionel Atwill is once more thrown into an electric dynamo, and when Talbot knocks over a shelf of chemicals, the whole place catches on fire. Talbot kills the insane Edelmann, who finds peace in death, and escapes with Miliza as stock footage shows the Lon Chaney Frankenstein Monster being beaned by a burning beam from *The Ghost of Frankenstein*. By the miracle of stock footage, Chaney gets to fight himself as two different monsters.

While it is undoubtedly a mess, *House of Dracula* at least is a lively one. Both Edelmann and Nina arouse our sympathy before their deaths; Larry Talbot is granted a happy ending for a change (though this might have been partially due to the fact that makeup artist Jack Pierce had just about run out of the yak hair he used to create the Wolf Man); and the fraudulent scientific rationalizations of the monsters' ailments are amusing. Whatever its logical shortcomings, Kenton did craft a concoction that was never dull.

However, Kenton's last horror film, the 1946 remake of *The Cat Creeps*, was sabotaged by its atrocious attempts at comedy. Fred Brady, Lois Collier, Noah Beery, Jr., and Douglas Dumbrille gather at a deserted old house on an island to determine whether a suicide 15 years ago had really been murder. People die, and a cat supposedly possessed by a spirit leads the group to the treasure that inspired the mayhem. A creaky, uninspired film, *The Cat Creeps* is little seen and quickly forgotten.

Kenton would make only a few more B movies before turning his talents to television, where he worked steadily into the '60s. Kenton will always be remembered for the classic *Island of Lost Souls* and his monster match-up combinations which epitomized non–Lewtonian horror in the '40s and which continue to delight young monster fans everywhere.

Harry Kumel (1940–   )

Monsieur Hawarden (1968); *Le Rouge aux Lèvres* (aka *Daughters of Darkness*, 1971); *Malpertuis* (1972); *Verloren Paradijs* (aka *Lost Paradise*, 1978).

Though he has primarily worked in television, Harry Kumel remains Belgium's premier horror filmmaker. Kumel developed his experience by working on television projects in Holland and Belgium, as well as teaching in a Dutch film school. Though he has been called gothic, he thinks of himself as being a disciple of Sternberg much as Curtis Harrington is.

The primary themes in his films seem to be the difference between appearance and reality and the nature of sexuality. His most famous, best-known, and most easily accessible film is *Daughters of Darkness*, famous as a lesbian vampire movie. His *Malpertuis*, one of Orson Welles' last film appearances, is worth a great deal of attention but has thus far received little, probably due to its inaccessibility. Perhaps someone will revive it at a major film festival.

Kumel was born in Antwerp, Belgium, on January 27, 1940, to wealthy Jewish parents. He developed an early interest in cinema, something akin to Truffaut's or Bogdanovich's, two other critics who went on to become filmmakers.

His first excursion into horror was a television adaptation of Franz Kafka's *The Gravedigger* (1965), about a gravedigger who must confront the ghosts of the dead every night. Kumel keeps the viewer guessing whether the ghosts are real or just a figment of the old man's imagination, but one thing is certain: To the old gravedigger, these ghosts are very real.

In 1968, he directed his first feature-length film, *Monsieur Hawarden*, starring Ellen Vogel and Hilde Utterlinden. Vogel plays Hawarden, a woman who goes around posing as a man. When her female valet falls in love with a man, she becomes jealous and cuts open the valet's head with a hatchet. She then proceeds to make love to a man and then kill herself in this brooding, sensitive film. The film, written by Jan Blokker, purportedly was based on a true story.

Monsieur Hawarden went on to win awards, and initially 20th Century–Fox agreed to finance a film to be titled *Le Rouge aux Lèvres (Blood on Red Lips)* about a modern-day Countess Bathory, a mad woman who tried to keep her beauty by bathing in the blood of virgins. However, after a disagreement, Fox pulled out and Kumel went to Gemini Films for backing. Gemini agreed, but only if Kumel would make the "arty" film more "commercial" by including more nudity and violence than Kumel had originally intended. Additionally, Gemini head J. J. Amiel made contributions to the script by Kumel and Pierre Drouot and received coscreenplay credit.

The result, finally titled *Daughters of Darkness*, was an odd mix indeed – part art film and part exploitation vehicle with kinky underpinnings. Kumel is a master of *mise-en-scène*, setting up his lighting, players, and sets with the utmost care, and he is especially good at conveying the sexual tension that might underlie a scene.

The film focuses on the character of Valerie Tardieu (Daniele Ouimet), who has married a handsome young man named Stefan (John Karlen), about whom she actually knows very little. We begin to fear for Valerie when Stefan makes a call to his "mother" (played by Dutch director Fons Rademakers, who directed the Academy Award–winning *The Assault* and *The Rosegarden*), an orchid-sniffing, large gay man who says impatiently, "I can't wait to see our new flower." What could this diabolical pair be up to?

The film opens with Valerie and Stefan making love on a train. Valerie then asks Stefan playfully if he loves her, and he responds in the negative. After the phone call, this takes the nefarious aspect of truth – he merely wants to use her – a point that is underscored when he beats his new bride with a belt for no apparent reason and is shown viewing the corpse of a young girl whose body has been drained of blood in Bruges. It is not too difficult to peg him as a sadist.

Meanwhile, they meet the mysterious Countess Elisabeth Bathory (the exquisite Delphine Seyrig), who when asked what keeps her looking so youthful, replies, "Diet . . . and plenty of rest." Kumel plays with the audience's awareness that Bathory is a vampire without making anything overt.

Kumel adds another element to this sexual stew by making Bathory's female valet, Ilona Harczy (Andrea Rau), a jealous lesbian who does not care for the way her mistress looks at Valerie with pleasure and approval. Ilona is full of conflicting desires of all types, for sex, death, release, and satiation.

Ironically, Elisabeth sees that Stefan wants Valerie to be his slave – ironic because Bathory has similar intentions for Valerie herself, but with her caring and compassion, we are shown that they make a better match than the supposedly "normal" relationship that Valerie already has.

Matters are further complicated when Elisabeth, trying to show Valerie how worthless her husband is, orders Ilona to seduce Stefan. When the turned-on Stefan pulls Ilona into the shower, she falls on an open razor blade and is killed – an act witnessed by Elisabeth and Valerie, who bury Ilona and become lovers themselves.

The trio have a dinner together, and Valerie reveals the change in her feelings when Elisabeth orders her to kiss Stefan and she does so with obvious displeasure, causing him to strike her. The two women then kill him by bashing him over the head and drinking his blood. They hide Stefan's body in Bathory's car trunk and drive off, but the rising sun temporarily blinds Valerie. She crashes the car, impaling it and Elisabeth on a large tree branch, the traditional "staking" death of a vampire. There is a brief suggestion that Valerie has become like Elisabeth.

The film is particularly scathing in its treatment of men, for whom Elisabeth indicates she has no use, a fairly radical idea for an early '70s film where lesbian characters were primarily consigned to providing cheap thrills to porno filmgoers. But there is no sense of taboos being broken here, or even of an illicit thrill. Instead *Daughters of Darkness* is rather stately paced with the emphasis on character relationships rather than action. The film is also striking in being the only film I can recall that fades to *red* after a sequence is over rather than the traditional fade to black, or even the non-traditional white. Kumel reminds us that blood is at the heart of the drama, though the fangless Elisabeth is far from a traditional vampire. Kumel keeps her exact nature so nebulous that it is hard to say exactly what she is supposed to be.

Moody, sometimes alienating, dreamlike and sometimes outrageous, *Daughters of Darkness* is a curiosity in the horror cinema, and an interesting one. Nevertheless, while the characters Elisabeth and Valerie rejoice in the idea of tasting life to the fullest, it remains a carefully studied film that lacks genuine vitality. Or perhaps that is Kumel's point: that the outsider (lesbian vampiress) can never really experience life's vitality.

Kumel has been anything but a prolific filmmaker and has created only one more major film thus far, the little-seen *Malpertuis* based on Jean Ray's book. Made for a mere $800,000 with a cast of international stars (Orson Welles, Susan Hampshire, Michel Bouquet, Mathieu Carrière, Sylvie Vartan and Jean-Pierre Cassel), the film's limited release ensured its failure.

A sailor named Yann (Carrière) has a feeling of deja vu when he enters a deserted village and eventually comes to a ruined chateau where Kronos (Orson Welles) shouts from his deathbed. Like M. Hawarden and Elisabeth Bathory, Yann is another of Kumel's androgynous leading characters, but with a difference: He slowly realizes that he is part of a race of immortals that were once the gods of the Greeks and Romans.

The film is heavily influenced by Sternbergian cinema and the Belgian Symbolist movement, and in fact was scripted by Jean Ferry, a member of that movement. Any pretenses to reality break down early as Yann goes seeking absolutes like God, Love, Truth, and Beauty. The result is very dreamlike and confusing. It did not help when the film was drastically recut by Richard Marden and was rendered in Kumel's opinion virtually unintelligible, but those who have seen its bizarre imagery (including a god nailed through the head to the wall, reciting Solomon's "Song of Songs") will not soon forget it. Meanwhile, Kumel remains an uncompromised artist who challenges audiences to look beyond the conventional.

Reginald LeBorg (1902–1989)

She's for Me; Calling Dr. Death (1943); *Adventure in Music* (codirector);
*Weird Woman; The Mummy's Ghost; Jungle Woman; San Diego, I Love You;
Dead Man's Eyes; Destiny* (1944); *Honeymoon Ahead* (1945); *Joe Palooka –
Champ; Little Iodine; Susie Steps Out* (1946); *Fall Guy; The Adventures of Don
Coyote; Philo Vance's Secret Mission; Joe Palooka in the Knockout* (1947); *Port
Said; Joe Palooka in Winner Take All; Fighting Mad; Trouble Makers* (1948);
Fighting Fools; Hold That Baby; Joe Palooka in the Counterpunch (1949); *Young
Daniel Boone; Wyoming Mail; Joe Palooka in the Squared Circle; G.I. Jane; Joe
Palooka in Triple Cross* (1950); *Models, Inc.; Bad Blonde* (aka *The Flanagan Boy*)
(1951); *The Great Jesse James Raid; Sins of Jezebel* (1953); *The White Orchid*
(1954); *The Black Sleep* (1956); *Voodoo Island; The Dalton Girls* (1957); *The
Flight That Disappeared* (1961); *Deadly Duo* (1962); *Diary of a Madman* (1963);
The Eyes of Annie Jones (1964); *So Evil My Sister* (1973).

Reginald LeBorg is one of those contract directors who is frequently
overlooked in histories of Hollywood or the film medium. His work has been
generally good, but is rarely distinguished. Nonetheless, he has made
enough interesting films in the horror genre that his work there is worthy
of some note, though he himself admits that he never felt a great affinity
for his horror material and prefers works like his comedy *San Diego, I Love
You.*

LeBorg was born in Vienna, Austria, in 1902. While there, he assisted
his father in banking, but the Great Depression brought an end to his banking career. He had always loved the theater and successfully endeavored to
become a playwright and a director.

"Then I went to New York," he told me in an interview. He went on:

> I met some friends of mine who were in the motion picture business
> whom I had helped to get their start. I was given parts as an actor,
> though I only did a few bits. I learned directing by going to the cinema
> in the morning and staying until 6 o'clock at night. I sat through the
> same film four or five times, so by the end of the day, I could forsee
> every cut. That was my education.
>
> Then I received some engagements and made some contacts working
> in a cutting room for a few months. I worked as an assistant to a direc-
> tor, and then to a couple of others. Finally, it was very clear that I had
> to get an agent, and he got me a break at Metro working in the shorts

576

department. Incidentally, I wrote a short *(Heavenly Music)* which later won an Academy Award.

When sound came to Hollywood in the late '20s, many theater directors were hired to be directors for films on the theory that they knew about using actors with spoken dialogue. Sometimes the theater directors would work side by side with one of the pre-sound film directors. However, after the initial glut, the chances for becoming a film director were drastically reduced. LeBorg found that in order to get anywhere, he needed to make a number of contacts, and the only way to do that was to take any job that would get him on the studio lot.

He received his first break with a semicomedic drama called *She's for Me*. This came about because of his work on the second-unit direction of bigger features such as *Intermezzo*. Said LeBorg:

> I worked on *Intermezzo* with Ingrid Bergman and did all the musical numbers there. Actually, I started on that picture. Selznick had engaged Willie Wyler, and William Wyler called me into do the musical scenes because I had assisted him on the Goldwyn pictures. He had a fight with Selznick and walked off the set, and Selznick needed someone to start the picture, so he asked me, which I did with inserts and action shots and shots of the girl, et cetera. At the same time, I coached Ingrid Bergman on the piano. She did an A minor Grieg concerto.
>
> On *A Day at the Races*, I handled the full second unit. I did the musical dances, I did the songs with Alan Jones, and the Marx Brothers musical numbers – Harpo on the harp and Chico on the piano.

The scene with Harpo in a black shantytown is one of the most impressive in the picture, but is often excised on television prints of this semiclassic film because of its use of ethnic stereotypes. While the stereotypes are undeniably there and undeniably dated, it is unfortunate that this scene, which exhibits some dazzling performances by black dancers, is often totally done away with, as it injects energy into the film at a point when the pace begins to flag and is the liveliest non–Marx brother dominated scene in the film. Ivy Anderson does a spirited rendition of "Who Dat Man?" and a pair of unknown jitterbuggers are nothing short of incredible.

Having proven his ability to handle a full B movie feature and not just a musical sequence with *She's for Me*, LeBorg was entrusted with directing the first of a series of mystery-horror films known as the "Inner Sanctum" series. Each film in the series began with the disembodied head of actor David Hoffman in a crystal ball reciting the following invocation: "This is the Inner Sanctum, a strange, fantastic world controlled by a mass of living, pulsating flesh: the mind. It destroys, distorts, creates monsters, commits murder. Yes, even you, without knowing, can commit murder...."

The Inner Sanctum name had long been famous as a radio series which specialized in fright stories and as a series of mystery novels from Simon and Schuster. Universal bought the rights to the title and decided to use the series to showcase their current horror star, Lon Chaney, Jr., who starred in each of the six films produced. As Anthony Tate and George Turner's article on the series in the August 1986 *American Cinematographer* points out:

> The series is memorable more for the high standard of cinematography achieved in all the entries than as a showcase for actors, directors or writers. However variable the results achieved by the other major contributors – and they were extremely uneven – the photography was invariably top drawer. In fact, the series was predicated in part on the fact that 20th Century–Fox was willing to loan them their mystery film virtuoso, Virgil Miller, ASC. Miller had earned acclaim for his work in Fox's *Charlie Chan* and *Mr. Moto* mystery films. In the silent era he had been a favorite photographer of Lon Chaney, who often requested that Miller be assigned to his films at Universal.

Miller and LeBorg worked together on the first two films of the series, *Calling Dr. Death* and *Weird Woman*, which are also the two most interesting films in the series. *Calling Dr. Death* was scripted by Edward Dein, who later directed such films as *Shack Out on 101* and *The Leech Woman*, and concerns a Doctor Steele (Chaney) who is being tormented by his unfaithful wife (Ramsay Ames). According to Tate and Turner's article, Chaney requested that Dein script a large amount of his dialogue as a stream-of-consciousness voiceover because of his difficulties in having to master the technical terms that his character, a neurologist, would employ.

Dr. Steele suffers a blackout when his wife runs off with another man (David Bruce), and when he recovers, he learns that his wife has been murdered and the other man arrested for the crime. Steele is tormented by the idea that the other man is innocent and that he himself might have been responsible during this blackout.

J. Carrol Naish costars as a police detective who suspects that Steele is guilty and plays on Steele's feelings of guilt. LeBorg comes up with a memorable nightmarish point-of-view shot as the camera becomes Steele who has to confront the distorted faces of reporters and policemen as he walks through the morgue. Using hypnosis, he finally exposes the killer as his own secretary (Patricia Morrison), who has secretly been in love with him.

Calling Dr. Death was followed by an even better film, *Weird Woman*, based on Fritz Leiber's classic horror novel *Conjure Wife* (later filmed by Sidney Hayers as *Night of the Eagle* aka *Burn Witch Burn*). When Prof. Norman Reed (Chaney) brings back Paula (Anne Gwynne) as his new wife after a South Seas expedition, he raises the ire of Ilona Carr (Evelyn Ankers), the college librarian he had flirted with and a secret practitioner of the black arts.

Ilona decides to spread the word that Paula is practicing voodoo in order to put pressure on their marriage. Ilona herself resorts to voodoo and causes Prof. Sawtelle (Ralph Morgan) to commit suicide under circumstances unfavorable to Paula's reputation. However, this raises the ire of Sawtelle's wife, Evelyn (Elizabeth Russell, best known as the mysterious woman addressed the heroine of *Cat People* as her sister), who links up with Reed to convince Ilona that black arts are being used against her.

Thrown in for good measure is a student who tries to kill Reed when he suspects that Reed has been fooling around with his fiancée and is himself killed in the attempt. Paula tries to use voodoo to strike back and Reed and Evelyn convince Ilona that it's working. Ilona panics, falling off a roof and hanging herself on the ivy of the university's ivy-covered walls (depicted by LeBorg with shadows).

LeBorg is able to give the story some atmosphere, using such devices as trees rustling in the night wind. The story is fast-paced, energetic and intriguing. One of the things LeBorg was proudest of was a knock-down, drag-out catfight between the two attractive female costars. He explained to me how he set it up:

> The two women had to fight and I didn't want to choreograph it because it would have been too stagey, so I used a trick. The day before, I told one girl, "You know that your co-star talked about you, and she hates you, so be careful." Then I took the other one for lunch and told her the same thing about her. I got them ired up, so to say.
>
> Then I made room in a certain apartment and got a second camera and told the cameraman to light the whole thing and just follow them. The dialogue was that they started to insult each other, and one hits the other and the other takes her by the hair, and then it's a free-for-all. They really hit each other. It was one of the best fights ever made.

However, LeBorg really preferred working on films like his *Adventure in Music*, a film intended to introduce classical music to the masses, and *Destiny*, in which Alan Curtis escapes from prison after being convicted of a homicide and hides out on a farm, becoming interested in the owner's blind daughter (Gloria Jean). The latter story was originally intended as part of the anthology film *Flesh and Fantasy*, directed by Jules Duvivier in 1943, and was expanded for its presentation as a separate film.

Still, after his first "Inner Sanctum" films, the studio assigned LeBorg to direct more horror films, starting with *The Mummy's Ghost*, a sequel to *The Mummy's Tomb*. Of the Universal Kharis mummy films, *The Mummy's Ghost* certainly was the best with its absence of lowbrow comedy and its attempts at atmosphere and pathos. These are particularly apparent in the finale when Kharis (Chaney) carries off Ramsay Ames because he believes her to be the reincarnation of Ananka, his dear, departed princess, and they both sink into a swamp, united in death at last.

After being killed twice, high priest Andoheb (George Zucco) makes another appearance, passing his knowledge down to a new acolyte, Youssef Bey (John Carradine), who tends to Kharis' needs and lusts after Amina Mansouri (Ames). Prof. Norman (Frank Reicher) returns from *The Mummy's Tomb*, contradicting a speech about tana leaves being extinct by producing a plentiful supply, which he boils in an unfortunate experiment to summon Kharis. Indeed, Kharis is summoned, but he quickly disposes of his "benefactor" because of previous desecrations. (With *The Mummy's Tomb*, Kharis was relocated in America.)

There is a touching scene where Kharis visits the mummy of Ananka in a museum and reaches out to the lifeless body only to have it crumble in his hands. To make the connection between them, LeBorg cuts to Amina waking from her sleep and screaming. Her hair begins to turn silver, lock by lock, as Ananka's spirit takes over her body. Kharis takes Amina to Youssef so that he might mummify her and make her Kharis' bride, but Youssef decides that Amina is something of a looker and tries to keep her for himself. Kharis kills him and Amina rapidly ages into Ananka in the most original twist in the series, having the heroine die with the monster.

Chaney did not like playing the mummy, but he was under contract and had no choice. Still, that is no excuse for his sloppy performance as he alternates from dragging one foot behind him to simply limping with it. It is Ames in her white satin evening gown who really steals the show, becoming the icon of the beautiful female victim who is loved tenderly and faithfully by the monster and embraces him in death, the final consummation of their mutual passion.

Next Universal gave LeBorg the sequel to Edward Dmytryk's *Captive Wild Woman*, entitled *Jungle Woman*. This film revives the character of Paula the Ape Woman, a gorilla who has been transformed by John Carradine via gland grafts into Acquanetta. LeBorg's film begins with the shadows of a man and a woman struggling and then settles down for a recap of *Captive Wild Woman* as Dr. Fletcher (J. Carrol Naish) explains what happened in response to accusations that he killed the woman.

Dr. Fletcher has bought Crestview Sanatorium and finds Paula wandering around aimlessly (despite having changed back into a gorilla at the end of the previous film). Paula falls in love with Dr. Fletcher's daughter's fiancé (Richard Davis) and begins suffering from a broken heart. Unlike the first film where Acquanetta was mute, scriptwriters Bernard Schubert and Henry Sucher gave her dialogue this time, which proved an unfortunate mistake as Acquanetta was clearly more a model than an actress. Even more

Reginald LeBorg (left) with star Lon Chaney, Jr., on the set of The Mummy's Ghost *(1944). LeBorg had mixed feelings about his alcoholic costar, but they did work together frequently.*

frustrating for monster fans, Paula is not shown in her ape woman makeup until the final few minutes after she has died.

The film seems strangely incoherent; nothing really connects. LeBorg obviously took no interest in what was going on and just churned this one out. The film spawned a final sequel, *Jungle Captive*, with Vicki Lane taking over the role of Paula Dupree, Otto Kruger playing the mad scientist and Harold Young directing. While none too good, it proved marginally more interesting than the incredibly dull *Jungle Woman*, LeBorg's worst horror film.

LeBorg returned for one more "Inner Sanctum" mystery, *Dead Man's Eyes*, this time photographed by Paul Ivano and starring Lon Chaney, Acquanetta and Jean Parker. Chaney is Dave Stuart, an artist rendered blind when Tanya (Acquanetta), his model, puts acid in his eyewash in a jealous rage over Stuart's affections for Heather (Parker).

Heather's father (Edward Fielding) donates his eyes in his will to Stuart and is soon murdered, with Stuart caught standing redhanded over the body. Nevertheless, a transplant operation proceeds with Stuart getting the father's eyes but pretending that he still can't see in an effort to draw out the real murderer. The guilt-ridden Tanya is murdered when she tries to expose him, but nevertheless Stuart is finally able to reveal that the murderer is a friend (Paul Kelly) whom no one thought to suspect. He can see after all, and he and Heather plan to live happily ever after.

The film shows Acquanetta at her most attractive, and one feels sympathetic for the panicked Stuart when he blindly stumbles on the dead body, but this is mostly standard mystery fare enlivened only by the bizarreness of the storyline.

LeBorg switched from Universal to Monogram when he was offered the Joe Palooka series despite his lack of knowledge about boxing. After the success of the first film, *Joe Palooka – Champ*, LeBorg directed five more sequels among other assignments. He finally returned to horror with *The Black Sleep*, notable for being a mediocre film starring most of the greatest horror actors in Hollywood.

When asked how he had handled them all, LeBorg replied:

> It wasn't easy. They all wanted to shine. Somehow I got them to cooperate. They are, in a way, like children. I had to hold them down until the very end of the picture, then I let them loose and you'll probably notice just where.
>
> Bela Lugosi played the part of a deaf and dumb [actually, Lugosi played a mute who could hear perfectly well] in the picture. He used to be a great star who somehow deteriorated. He came to me and said, "I want some lines! I want some lines!" I said, I can't give you any, you're playing a deaf and dumb. He said, "Well, give me something to do." I said, you're the servant of Basil Rathbone, and you have to serve him. He was very unhappy.
>
> In order to placate him, I said, I'll give you enough closeups. So I placed him behind Basil Rathbone quite often and then shot. He then reacted too much to Basil's dialogue and, of course, spoiled the shot. So I couldn't do anything. I couldn't use two-shots of him or closeups of him, so I just shot Basil with Bela out of camera range.

The film took 12 days to shoot and cost less than a half million dollars. Basil Rathbone is quite good as a doctor engaged in a series of experiments to save his sleeping wife. Unfortunately, ruthless chap that he is, the victims of his experiments are left living but in an awfully poor and brain-damaged condition. (My favorite is John Carradine, who imagines he is fighting the Saracens in the twelfth century and jumps about shouting, "Kill the Infidels!") When the doctor gets his comeuppance from his creations at the end of the film, Rathbone has a brief shot where he gazes at his "never-to-be-saved" wife with a look of sad, tender resignation that is quite touching.

An overweight Lon Chaney shambles about as Mungo, supposedly once a great scientist who is now a hulking brute. Chaney, who was beginning to suffer from alcoholism during his earlier pictures with LeBorg, was in particularly sad shape for this one. Akim Tamiroff manages to twinkle and be energetic if more than a bit hammy as a gypsy peasant involved in shady dealings with Rathbone.

The "Black Sheep" itself turns out to be an eastern potion that puts the user into a trance that resembles death and is used to save young doctor Gordon Ramsay (Herbert Rudley) from the hangman's noose as well as to anesthetize Rathbone's experimental subjects before operating on their brains. Rathbone has arranged for Rudley to aid him in his diabolical research. The best scenes feature Rudley watching Rathbone cut into a brain and Rudley discovering Tor Johnson, John Carradine and others as unsuccessful experiments stored in the doctor's dungeon.

The Black Sheep was Bela Lugosi's last film appearance except for the footage of him that was added to *Plan 9 from Outer Space*. It was also his first appearance after recovering from his addiction to drugs (mainly morphine). Unfortunately, he looks wasted and is given little to do, though he does have a peculiar scene where he stops in his duties, looks off in the distance for no apparent reason, grimaces, and then moves on. The scene was apparently a character bit to placate Lugosi and has nothing to do with the rest of the film.

Despite the fact that it was made in the '50s, *The Black Sleep* seems a throwback to an earlier time when mad scientist movies were more common. LeBorg manages to make a few scenes creepy and Rathbone gives a fine performance, but the film frequently sags and drags, and is lacking in both excitement and inventiveness.

Nevertheless, it certainly outshone *Voodoo Island*, which has the distinction of being one of Boris Karloff's dullest films and features one of his most uninspired performances as Phillip Knight, a famous writer who exposes fraudulent attempts at creating the supernatural. Knight is hired to head an expedition to a tropical island in the Pacific where a rich man hopes to build a new hotel. On the island is a giant man-eating plant which can change people into zombies. Knight is forced to admit that the supernatural does exist after all. The film is later issued as *Silent Death*, but under any title this film was a stinker.

LeBorg turned his talents to working in the television medium for a while, doing such shows as *77 Sunset Strip, Bronco, Bourbon Street* and *The Alaskans*. I do not know anything about the films *Deadly Duo* or *So Evil My Sister*; the last horror film that I know for certain LeBorg was connected with was *Diary of a Madman*, based on Guy de Maupassant's story "The Horla." (The Horla is an evil spirit.) Vincent Price starred as Simon Cordier, a French magistrate who finds himself possessed by an evil spirit after killing a condemned murderer. Soon Cordier begins going on killing sprees under the spirit's malign influence. Nancy Kovack has a nice bit as Odette Duclasse, a sculptor's model whom Cordier turns to and later kills as he seeks respite from his torment. Just why the project was given the title of a Gogol novel remains unknown, though Cordier does eventually write a diary which explains what has happened to him before he immolates himself in an effort to rid the world of Horla.

LeBorg also crafted an offbeat film about a young girl with ESP who helps solve murders called *Eyes of Annie Jones*, but despite Francesca Annis' performance as the young girl, the film is uninvolvingly dull.

LeBorg's career is that of a man who sought to deliver what was expected of him but no more. His heart was not in horror films, despite his frequent assignments in that genre; as a result, his horror films have no heart except for the oddball touching moments in *The Mummy's Ghost, The Black Sleep* and the wilder wonders of *Weird Woman*.

Ulli Lommel (1945–)

Haytabo (1970); *Royal Flush* (1971); *Sergeant Rahn* (1972); *Who So Loves* (1973); *Tenderness of the Wolves* (1974); *Der Mann von Oberzalzberg; Monkey Business* (1976); *Adolph and Marlene* (1977); *Blank Generation; Cocaine Cowboys* (1979); *The Boogey Man* (1980); *A Taste of Sin; Brainwaves; Double Jeopardy; The Devonsville Terror* (1983); *Strangers in Paradise* (1984); *Revenge of the Stolen Stars* (1985); *Defense Play; IFO* (1986); *Overkill; A Year of Lincoln Plains* (1987); *War Birds; Cold Heat* (1989); *The Big Sweat; Destination Unknown* (1990).

Born in the American sector of West Berlin in 1945, Ulli Lommel began acting at the age of four. As one of Germany's most popular teenage stars, he appeared in over 60 films, 13 of them under the direction of Rainer Werner Fassbinder. However, by 1970, he was frustrated with acting and decided to try his hand at directing, making his directorial debut with *Haytabo* starring Eddie Constantine.

A couple of police dramas and a comedy later, Lommel began to attract real attention with his first horror film, *Tenderness of the Wolves*, based on the life of Fritz Haarman, the infamous "Vampire of Düsseldorf" that served as the inspiration for the killer in Fritz Lang's *M* (1931). Fassbinder himself produced the film and played the part of Wittkowski. Haarman (Kurt Raab) was a homosexual tortured by Catholic guilt who lured young boys into his apartment and chopped them to pieces, drinking their blood. Yet by portraying him as sensitive, intelligent, and charming, Lommel makes Haarman the most sympathetic character in the film, a victim caught in a world full of nastiness whose friends prove false to him and are only after his money and whose wretched victims are simply "cured" of their incredible stupidity. Given the greediness and grubbiness of the environment, Haarman almost seems justified in selling the leftover flesh of his victims on the black market.

Raab with his bald head and bloody mouth comes across as a cross between Peter Lorre in *Mad Love* and Max Schreck in *Nosferatu*, and Lommel uses him as an icon more than a performer. The focus of the film is primarily on the dreariness of Depression-era Germany. The film depicts alienation with a vengeance.

Coming to America, Lommel began again by making the horror film *The*

Boogey Man, which he produced and wrote as well as directed. It starts out with a mother whose kinky boyfriend likes to make the mother's son watch while they make love. The boy's sister comes out and frees him, watching in a mirror while he murders the pair. Years later, the sister, Lacy (Suzanna Love, Lommel's wife and frequent star) has grown up and married Jake (Ron James) and is still haunted by that horrible night. So too, apparently, is the little brother, who keeps a collection of spiders and snakes and refuses to talk to anyone. Jake suggests Lacy see a doctor, played by John Carradine, who tells her that after visiting her old house, her fears will be banished.

The old doc proves consummately wrong; when Lacy looks in the old mirror again, she sees the reflection of the murdered boyfriend, so she picks up a chair and smashes it. Oddly enough, Jake decides that the best way to prove there was no evil image in the mirror is to glue the whole thing back together again.

However, he misses a piece, which starts glowing and breathing heavily. Soon a series of mysterious murders starts, including a woman stabbing herself with her scissors, a man choked by a window, a boy and girl spiked into an eternal kiss, and a man and a woman hayforked to death. Lacy gets a piece of mirror in her eye, turns green and attacks her husband and a priest.

All these events finally lead the long-silent brother to suddenly shout a sage piece of advice: "Throw the mirror down the well." What do you know – it works. Lommel obviously was not interested in concocting a believable plot, but rather tried to come up with as many creative deaths as he could in the 79-minute running time. The result was a solid piece of exploitation released by the Jerry Gross Organization.

Bizarrely, a sequel appeared, *Boogeyman II*, which was directed and co-produced by a Bruce Starr but consisted of footage from *The Boogey Man* for half its length. Stranger still, Ulli Lommel appears in the new footage as Mickey Lombard, a Hollywood director who is listening to Lacy (Suzanna Love again, though the character's name is spelled differently) tell what happened to her. Also strange is that there is no screenplay credit.

Lommel appears to be having a good time taking pot shots at Hollywood excesses. Lombard is forced to insert some nude scenes into his art film which he calls *Nathalie and the Age of Diminishing Expectations*, but which his producer has retitled *Kiss and Tell*. Looking at a photo of von Stroheim in Kenneth Anger's *Hollywood Babylon*, he comments caustically about the "good old days when Hollywood destroyed real people instead of toys."

Naturally, the glass shard is back, possessing people and using offbeat devices for mayhem including a garden hose, hedge clippers, corkscrew, barbecue tongs, an electric toothbrush, and even shaving cream, which smothers a woman. Because of the success of *The Boogey Man* on videocassette, *Boogeyman II* was rushed into video rather than theatrical release.

587 *Ulli Lommel*

Suzanna Love in an atmospheric still from The Boogey Man *which belies the cheap quality of the film. Actress Love is the wife of director Ulli Lommel, who got an unexpected hit with this fractured film.*

Lommel returned to working behind the camera with *Brain Waves*, which appears to have been made to cash in on the publicity surrounding Douglas Trumbull's film *Brainstorm*. *Brain Waves* may well be Lommel's most entertaining film as it deals with the intriguing science fictional concept of transferring thought processes and memories via machinery.

Suzanna Love returns as Kaylie Bedford, wife of Julian Bedford (Keir Dullea). Kaylie has a horrible auto accident which leaves her in a coma. Julian and mother Marian (Vera Miles) agree to let Dr. Clavius (Tony Curtis) try an experimental medical procedure. The procedure involves fixing damaged brain tissue by transferring corrective patterns from a donor brain.

Unfortunately, the donor, Lelia Adams (Corinne Alphen), proves to have been murdered, and when Kaylie recovers, she is plagued by first-person memories of the murder. The murderer, frightened of exposure, begins to seek her out. Julian must discover the killer's identity before it's too late.

Brain Waves certainly has the best cast of any Lommel film, including the likes of Percy Rodrigues and Paul Willson, but only Love, Dullea and Ryan Seitz (who plays the Bedfords' son) have significant parts. Unlike earlier Lommel films, *Brain Waves* keeps a spritely pace and does not get too draggy. For a low-budget thriller, it is pretty slick, and Lommel keeps his occasional film *hommages* to a minimum.

I have not seen *A Taste of Sin*, but Lommel's other 1983 release, *The Devonsville Terror*, has Suzanna Love as Jenny Scanion, an elementary school teacher caught up in a web of witchcraft. The movie opens with three witches being tortured and burned at the stake in 1683 and vowing to return 300 years later. Naturally, when Jenny and two other women, Monica (Deanna Haas), a disk jockette, and Chris (Mary Walden), an environmentalist, come into town, the long-memoried townsfolk's tongues start to wagging.

Jenny does not win any friends among the strict townsfolk when she tells their children that in early religions, God was supposed to be a woman. However, Matthew Pendleton (Robert Walker) does break from the rest of the townsfolk to befriend her. Though she is not exactly a witch, Jenny does have supernatural powers and is in town for a purpose: to wreak vengeance on Walter Gibbs (Paul Willson) for murdering his wife.

Lommel adds nods to *Halloween* by casting Donald Pleasence as a worm-infested victim of the 300-year-old curse and by having Love made up to resemble Jamie Lee Curtis. He borrows his finale partly out of *Raiders of the Lost Ark* as supernatural agents prevent Scanton from being burned at the stake. Giving the film a better look, Lommel handled the cinemagraphic chores himself.

Lommel definitely shows some potential, but most of his films are judged to be too offbeat for the mainstream theatrical market and are shunted into video release, if released at all. Nevertheless, he is a director who bears investigating.

David Lynch (1946–   )

Eraserhead (1978); *The Elephant Man* (1980); *Dune* (1984); *Blue Velvet* (1986); *Wild at Heart* (1990).
TELEVISION: *Twin Peaks* (series, 1990).

David Lynch's first love is painting, and his approach to filmmaking has been centered on textures, lighting, and unusual compositions. His first work in film began as an attempt to explore painting techniques. Lynch's work is noted for its creative use of sound as well as its imagery, and for its obsessions – Lynch seems fascinated by machinery, by the quirky, by the seemingly unknowable.

Born in Missoula, Montana, on January 20, 1946, Lynch had a happy childhood. Later he moved, and growing up in Virginia, he met Jack Fisk, who later designed some of Brian De Palma's films and later still became a director in his own right, and the pair shared a studio. Fisk would appear as the Man in the Planet in Lynch's first feature-length film, *Eraserhead*, a definite *sui generis* movie. Lynch studied painting at the Corcoran School of Art and after high school went on to the Boston Museum School, which he attended for a year before dropping out and planning to go to Europe to paint. However, Lynch discovered that he was uncomfortable in Europe and returned home rather quickly.

It was on his way to his draft physical that Fisk told Lynch about the Pennsylvania Academy of Fine Arts. Lynch enrolled in the school in 1965. There he experimented with a number of different styles and made his first animated film based on his paintings. Accompanied by the sound of a siren, the film was intended as a loop showing six figures catching fire, getting headaches, expanding their bodies. After making the film for $200, Lynch lost interest in the process of filmmaking, declaring it "too expensive."

However, a rich painter named H. Barton Wasserman gave Lynch almost a thousand dollars to make one of his "film-paintings," as they were called. Lynch purchased some new equipment and tried something new. Unfortunately, the film came back from the lab all blurred. Lynch contacted Wasserman, who told him to do whatever he wanted with the rest of the money, so with additional money from his father, Lynch made his first titled short subject, called *The Alphabet*. An abstract film, it centered on the

589

fear of learning. Letters go in and out of a mechanical head as a young student thrashes around.

Lynch learned about the American Film Institute and, devising a script, sent it with a copy of *The Alphabet* to AFI to receive a grant. At this time, Lynch was living in Philadelphia with his recent bride, Peggy; there he had a job printing engravings. AFI called him and offered him $5,000 to make his film, saying that after they had sorted their other submissions into categories, there was Lynch's work by itself, steadfastly uncategorizable, and so they just had to give him a chance.

So Lynch began work on *The Grandmother*, a 34-minute film that combined live action with animation, black and white with color, the surreal with the realistic. When the budget proved insufficient, AFI even kicked in another $2200 to complete the project. The plot of this dialogueless film concerns a young boy craving attention but receiving only anger from his parents. He plants a seed, which grows into a tree, which in turn becomes a grandmother who gives the boy the attention he craves – only to wither away and die. Many of the seeds of *Eraserhead* are apparent in the film, including the central character's feelings of isolation and the plaintive appeal of his charge.

In his early filmmaking years, Lynch concentrated on building a mood and creating his own nightmarish world of unreality. He described the film *Eraserhead* itself as a "dream of dark and troubling things," and indeed there are few cinematic experiences which come closer to the feeling of being trapped inside somebody else's nightmare than *Eraserhead*. There is no doubt in watching the film that one is experiencing a unique artistic vision with the recognizeable and the *outré* linked side by side.

Initially while at AFI, Lynch tried to make a film called *Gardenback*, revolving around a physical manifestation of what grows inside a man's head when he desires a woman he sees, a manifestation that metamorphoses into a monster. Unfortunately, there were script problems that Lynch never managed to lick, so he abandoned the project to make *Eraserhead*. (For a detailed discussion of the making of Lynch's early films and *Eraserhead*, see K. George Godwin's excellent article in the September 1984 issue of *Cinefantastique*.)

The script for *Eraserhead* was only 21 pages long, but it was written in a compressed style that relied heavily on images. The AFI's first attempt at a feature had been a disaster, so feature projects were discouraged. With Lynch's short script, however, the head honchos decided that the project would be manageable and agreed to give him a go-ahead.

Eraserhead reflects in some ways Lynch's feelings of confusion when he left rural areas and entered urban ones. It portrays a bleak industrial landscape from which its central figure, Henry (Jack Nance), is trying to escape. He has had a relationship with Mary X (Charlotte Stewart) and the result is a deformed, living fetus which Mary foists off on Henry as she seeks her own escape. The actions of Mary's parents are completely incomprehensible to Henry (or anyone else for that matter), and the scene where Henry is served a chicken dinner at their house is one of the film's high points in uncomfortableness and weirdness. (Henry is served a chicken which twitches on his plate and bleeds thick black blood when he tries to carve it.)

The film chronicles Henry's frustrations – he cannot leave because the "baby" keeps crying. Later it becomes sick and spotted. The film follows Henry's dreams, especially of a better world inside his radiator where Laura Near dances and sings, stepping sometimes on what seem to be giant spermatozoa. Across the hall, a prostitute (Judith Anna Roberts) escorts strange men in her room and equates the bizarrely coifed Henry with his deformed offspring. The baby itself is one of the film's most remarkable creations, achieved on a minuscule budget. It is astonishingly expressive and lifelike, and yet undeniably alien and unreal. The title of the film comes from a dream Henry has where his head pops off his body and people drill holes into his brain to use the soft bits inside for pencil erasers.

The film was started for a mere $10,000, but it took over four years to complete. It received some attention at Filmex and later traveled the midnight movie circuit. It played successfully for years at the Nuart Theatre. The film plays oddly to audiences, who find in its characters no clues as to how they should take anything in the film. It prompts diverse responses, from laughter to repulsion. Filled with sexual symbolism, the film seems to view sex itself with repugnance. Throughout it all, an industrial hum plus clicks and clanking make the world seem a very threatening place indeed. All problems assume a level of difficulty beyond their appropriate scope, and Henry achieves a release only when he tries to remove the infant's bandages and a strange foamy substance spews all over the room.

Eraserhead is very artistic and avant-garde, while Lynch's next film, *The Elephant Man*, proved he could bring his sensibility to a far more conventional approach. The film came about when producer Jonathan Sanger optioned an early draft of a screenplay by Christopher DeVore and Eric Bergren about John Merrick, a deformed man better known as the Elephant Man. Near the end of his life, Merrick met a brilliant young surgeon named Frederick Treves who gave him the chance to live his remaining years with dignity and grace.

Sanger brought the project to Mel Brooks and Brooksfilms Ltd. Brooks was enthusiastic about the project and gave it a go-ahead. Sanger brought in Lynch based upon seeing *Eraserhead* and persuaded Brooks to do the same. Both agreed that Lynch would make an excellent choice for the project. Lynch proceeded to write the final draft of the screenplay in collaboration with DeVore and Bergren.

For the background of the film, Lynch concentrated on the sights and sounds of Victorian England in the midst of the Industrial Revolution. There are gaslights and steam-driven machinery, with the poor huddled along cobblestone streets. The first patient we see of Dr. Treves (Anthony Hopkins) is "another machine accident" which Treves observes to be growing more common. There is a real sense of hostility about the environment.

This atmosphere is augmented by Freddie Francis' brilliant black-and-white cinematography. It catches the seediness of the outside world very clearly, as well as the wonder of the theater in the later scenes and the antiseptic world of the hospital to which Treves confines Merrick (brilliantly played by John Hurt).

The opening of the film is very surrealistic; a picture of a young woman seems to come to life. There are gauzy shots of elephants and finally one attacks, evoking the fable of the Elephant Man's creation. John Morris' musical theme hints of a polyphone or mechanical music box, suggesting a memory as well as an ironic bit of cheerfulness amid the tragedy.

Overall, the movie is magnificently executed in every detail, from Lynch's direction to Christopher Tucker's elaborate makeup, which took between six and nine hours to apply each time. Freddie Jones does a superb job playing Merrick's "owner," a portrait of malicious venality incarnate. Both John Gielgud as Mr. Carr Gomm, chairman of the London Hospital, and Dame Wendy Hiller as Mothershead, the London Hospital's head matron, bring a distinguished respectability to the project, while Anne Bancroft as Mrs. Kendal, considered to be one of the finest actresses of the Victorian Theater, gives a liveliness to her part that demonstrates the theater's ability to be transporting.

The film bespeaks Lynch's fascination with the hidden. Various characters are drawn to John Merick because of the extremity of his deformity. Lynch depicts how crowds come to leer, jeer, upset or shock their partners, or indulge in lewd loveplay before the eyes of the freak that they have come to view. But if Lynch shows mankind in its ugliness, he is also willing to show the saintly side. Treves, learning that Bytes has beaten the Elephant Man, takes over his care and slowly discovers that there is a mind and a personality buried under that deformed tissue. He fights to get Merrick accepted and to help Merrick learn and express himself. The film's primary theme is Merrick's search for dignity and the redeeming qualities it brings. In the emotional climax, the disguised Merrick is pursued by a crowd which strips off his attire only for him to proclaim through his malformed lips, "I am not an animal, I am a human being!"

The film was a success, earning many glowing reviews. Lynch had shown himself to be a master of moods, acting and artistic vision. As with all Lynch films, the human and inhuman are carefully juxtaposed and contrasting visions of the world are given between those that intend to uplift and those that prefer to exploit.

The biggest monster in The Elephant Man *proves to be this circus sideshow owner played by Freddie Jones. This remains Lynch's most accessible, though not best loved, film.*

Lynch took on this latter theme in his next film, an adaptation of Frank Herbert's science fiction classic *Dune*. Given an extravagantly high budget (estimates are between $40 and $60 million), the film turned into a visual feast and was for the most part very faithful to Herbert's epic tale, but crammed down to 140 minutes, it plays more like highlights from *Dune* rather than the story itself. The principal conflict in the film is between two families, the Atreides and the Harkonnens. The Harkonnens are from a foul industrial world and have been administering the planet Arrakis, also known as Dune. The emperor of the galaxy, in a bit of political maneuvering, has placed the Atreides family in charge of Arrakis, which provides the spice drug that allows for interplanetary travel. The Harkonnens have placed a traitor, Dr. Yueh (Dean Stockwell), in the Atreides household to betray them and allow the Harkonnens to consolidate all the power that Arrakis provides.

Herbert wrote the book to explore the messiah complex in societies, where socially troubled people will turn to someone to become a messiah and lead them out of a metaphoric wilderness. In *Dune*, the messiah is Paul Atreides (Kyle MacLachlan), who escapes with his mother, the Lady Jessica (Francesca Annis), into the desert. There they meet up with the Fremen, the native inhabitants of Arrakis, who end up looking to Paul to form a revolutionary army against the Harkonnens and free Arrakis for them.

Dune as a film had trouble with audiences and critics alike because it required that an audience digest a large amount of exposition at the very beginning to set up the long and complex story. Also, the condensation often meant that many characters were given little in the way of screen time and never quite came to life. The effort was akin to taking a Cadillac and trying to squeeze it into the shape of a Volkswagen bug.

Still, the film featured an excellent cast including Brad Dourif, Jose Ferrer, Linda Hunt, Freddie Jones, Richard Jordan, Virginia Madsen, Kenneth McMillan, Jack Nance, Sian Phillips, Jurgen Prochnow, Paul Smith, Sting, Max von Sydow and Sean Young. Freddie Francis' cinematography is once again very rich, and the production designs of Anthony Masters are magnificent. The film was not the wash-out that some accused it of being, but it failed to win over the uninitiated to its grandiose vision.

Dune was executive-produced by Dino De Laurentiis, who was impressed with Lynch's talents and decided to back Lynch in one of his personal projects. The result was *Blue Velvet*, a quirky mystery about the hidden terrors that can exist beneath the bland surfaces of society. The film helped consolidate the career of Lynch's discovery, Kyle MacLachlan, who stars as Jeffrey Beaumont, as well as boosting the careers of Laura Dern (playing Sandy, the girl who falls in love with Jeffrey), Isabella Rossellini (as Dorothy Valens, a persecuted mother who is forced to become the sex slave of Frank [Dennis Hopper]), and Dean Stockwell (whose turn as the bizarre Ben, who runs a sleazy cathouse and lip-syncs Roy Orbison's "In Dreams," helped bring him once again to the attention of casting directors all over Hollywood). Many people believe that Dennis Hopper's Oscar nomination for *Hoosiers* had more to do with Hopper's electric performance as the foul-mouthed Frank than with the film he was nominated for.

After credits across a blue velvet curtain, the film opens up with a crystal blue sky and a pan down to bright white picket fence with blazing red roses in front of it. Here are the American colors in postcard-perfect vividness. This is followed by Norman Rockwell–type scenes of a halcyon American small town, a nostalgic, romanticized, "perfect" environment.

Lynch hints at the rottenness underneath by showing a man watering his lawn and then suddenly collapsing. His dog nips playfully at the water spouting from the hose, oblivious to his master's danger. The camera descends into the fresh, green grass and uncovers the gnawing and rumbling of scurrying black bugs, the ugliness below the surface. This in turn is a visual metaphor for the entire film as Jeffrey discovers the ugliness hidden beneath the quiet surface of Lumbertown where he dwells.

Jeffrey visits his father in the hospital, hooked up to machines so that he hardly looks human any more and seems unable to communicate.

One-time Time *magazine cover boy David Lynch directs* Blue Velvet, *one of the most critically acclaimed films of the '80s. It typifies Lynch's view that there is evil under the normal-seeming exterior of the world.*

Returning, he discovers a human ear and brings it to the police, who tell him to not mention it to anyone and to restrain his curiosity. But Sandy, the daughter of the detective, starts filling in some pieces of information and Jeff discovers that he wants to know more.

The central idea that Lynch had for the film was that of a young man hiding in a woman's closet and learning terrible secrets. Jeffrey arranges to hide in Dorothy's closet and sees her sexually abused by Frank. He is later discovered by Dorothy herself, who forces him to take his pants off and comes on to him sexually. Perversity and danger pile up quickly as Jeffrey becomes more embroiled in the mystery.

It is all presented very stylishly, with Lynch's personal obsessions coming through. There is, as in his other films, a complex sound scheme worked out with Alan Splet, whom Lynch had worked with since *Eraserhead*. The cinematography and lighting this time are by Frederick Elmes, but they match the quality of other Lynch pictures. Mostly, there is a fascination with the quirky ways that people will behave, a quest for understanding why we have evil. There is also a comic sensibility behind the whole project which gives it an oddball humor.

Lynch's most recent projects include the television series *Twin Peaks* and the film *Wild at Heart*. *Twin Peaks* is an extended and involved *Blue Velvet* kind of story, in which a young girl is murdered, causing an entire town to mourn. Kyle MacLachlan stars as a peculiar FBI agent who comes in to take over the investigation. Dark secrets start being uncovered about all the town's inhabitants. The series' stylish qualities made it unique television and garnered a high amount of interest and praise at its inception.

Wild at Heart is a delirious road film starring Nicolas Cage and Laura Dern as a couple on the run, trying to escape mother Diane Ladd who is equated with the Wicked Witch of the West. Such quirky performers as Harry Dean Stanton, Willem Dafoe and Crispin Glover add to the film's passionate eccentricity. It's both very funny and very disturbing.

Throughout his career, Lynch has maintained the status of an artist, someone who truly brings a personal vision to what he is doing. He is unique enough that it may be unfair to classify him as a "horror director," but his works consistently deal with aspects of the horrific, with the ways that people are horribly exploited and abused by an increasingly mechanical and inhuman society. Lynch, along with David Cronenberg, is one of the few modern directors who seems truly in touch with the disturbing and indeed is fascinated with it. The result is an *oeuvre* of films that are fascinating themselves. Lynch is a director who will risk looking ridiculous in order to achieve the sublime. He is truly an artist who pushes at the boundaries of the possible.

Roman Polanski (1933–)

Two Men and a Wardrobe (short, 1958); *When Angels Fall; The Lamp* (shorts, 1959); *The Fat and the Lean* (short, 1961); *Mammals* (short); *Knife in the Water* (1962); "A River of Diamonds" segment of *Les Plus Belles Escroqueries du Monde* (aka *The Best Swindles in the World*, 1963); *Repulsion* (1965); *Cul-de-Sac* (1966); *Dance of the Vampires* (aka *The Fearless Vampire Killers (or Pardon Me But Your Teeth Are in My Neck*, 1967); *Rosemary's Baby* (1968); *Macbeth* (1971); *What?* (1973); *Chinatown* (1974); *The Tenant* (1976); *Tess* (1979); *Pirates* (1987); *Frantic* (1988).

A gifted filmmaker whose private life has been constantly shrouded in tragedy, Polanski is in danger of becoming more notorious for the sensational scandals that have surrounded his life than for his genuine cinematic achievements. He was born on August 18, 1933, to Polish-Jewish parents in Paris. His parents returned to Cracow when he was three and by the time he was eight, they had been taken to a Nazi concentration camp where his mother died. Polanski himself managed to escape, but he witnessed many horrors along the way and was even used for target practice by German soldiers.

His wife, Sharon Tate, was murdered by the Charles Manson family. Polanski himself was brought up on charges of drugging and raping a 13-year-old girl whom he was giving shelter from a father who had raped and abused her. Sensing that he could not expect a fair hearing, he fled the United States and has resided in exile in Paris.

Is it any wonder that his films all have downbeat endings and tend to maintain a rather bleak view of humanity? While he has divided his attention between "entertainments" and more serious projects, even his entertaining films feature interesting themes and a definite psychological insight that put them above the run-of-the-mill time-wasters that the film industry produces. Polanski has not restricted himself to horror films, but it was as a horror film director that he first achieved international prominence, and his return to the genre is eagerly awaited by aficionados who appreciate the subtleties and sophistication of his work.

When Polanski was 14, he began a career as an actor in the theater and later began to work in Polish films including Andrzej Wajda's first film, *A Generation*. He also attended an art school in Cracow and studied painting,

597

sculpture and graphics. He attempted his first film, *The Bike*, in 1955, but it was never finished. He worked on the screenplays for *Break Up the Dance* and *The Lamp*, though these films are almost never screened outside their country of origin. Polanski attended film college and his graduate project was a short entitled *Two Men and a Wardrobe*, a surrealistic and symbolic comedy about two men burdened with a wardrobe cabinet that has risen out of a lake. It was typical of the early Polanski shorts, which featured only a few characters engaged in absurd and symbolic actions. *When Angels Fall* concerns a woman longing for her dead lover, who returns at the end of the film as the angel of death come to take her away. *The Fat and the Lean* satirizes the relationship between masters and servants as a master presents a servant (Polanski) with a present – a goat – that only makes things more difficult for the servant. Consequently the servant is ecstatically grateful when the master takes the present back and works harder to please him than ever before. Polanski's absurd film *Mammals*, which won prizes at a few film festivals, has two men on a snowy landscape constantly plotting to exploit each other and get the other person to drag a sled across the frozen landscape.

Polanski really began to draw attention with his first feature, *Knife in the Water*, an art film that is still popular on the circuit. Coscripted by Polanski with Jerzy Skolimowski (himself a talented director) and Jakub Goldberg, it chronicles the efforts of a sports writer (Leon Niemczyk) to prove to his wife, Christine (Jolantte Umecka), that he is more capable than a hitchhiker (Zygmunt Malanowicz) that he picked up and takes sailing. The two men are forever showing off and competing. The sports writer gets jealous of the younger man's facility with a switchblade knife (an obvious phallic symbol) and takes it when the young man cavorts on deck with the writer's wife. In a scuffle over the knife, the boy falls into the lake and the writer remembers that earlier the boy confessed that he could not swim. Panicked, he begins to search for the boy.

Meanwhile, the boy crawls on board and makes love to the writer's wife. The boy leaves and the writer returns and the pair head back to the car. The writer discovers that somebody has stolen the windshield wipers (a symbol of lost potency? cuckoldry?). The writer is nervous about going to the police. The wife tells him what happened, but he claims he does not believe her. The film ends on his indecision: Will he go to the police and admit his culpability in the boy's supposed demise, or accept his previously browbeaten wife's word as to what transpired and admit that he has been disgraced?

The film was widely regarded and popular in critical circles and allowed Polanski to contribute a segment to an anthology film, *The Best Swindles in the World*. The segment, about a girl who steals a necklace, was scripted by Gerard Brach, who would become Polanski's frequent contributor. The other segments were by such directors as Chabrol, Gregoretti and Horikawa.

Polanski then went to England, where he and Gerard Brach scripted *Repulsion* for producer Gene Gutowski. The film slowly takes the viewer into the private world of a pretty, repressed psychotic (played by Catherine Deneuve). Catherine (Deneuve) is a near-catatonic blond Belgian girl who lives with her sister Helen (Yvonne Furneaux) and Helen's lover, Michael (Ian Hendry). She does not relate well to other people and seems both attracted and repulsed by Michael.

Catherine works in a beauty shop where all day she hears the aging matrons complain about what beasts men are. Helen and Michael make plans to go away by themselves and Catherine meets a nice young man named Colin (John Fraser), who mistakes her passivity for acquiescence. As she withdraws further into her apartment, he finally breaks in on her in desperation. She responds by refusing to look at him and then hitting him over the head with a candlestick, killing him.

Most striking about the film are Catherine's hallucinations, which begin to impinge more and more on her world as she gets more frantic and disturbed. These begin simply with the sounds of cracking and the sudden appearances of cracks in the walls. She begins to imagine strange men in her bedroom and one of them finally attacks her, but only in her imagination.

Her neglect of reality is suggested by her leaving a skinned rabbit for dinner out to rot, as well as her increasing neglect of work. Surrounded by what she perceives as the strangeness of the world, she becomes increasingly oblivious to what is actually there. In perhaps the most imitated of the film's images, Catherine imagines hands popping out of the walls to grab at her (which, following the utilization of the same device in Romero's *Night of the Living Dead*, became a frequent shock tactic in subsequent horror films).

Following Colin's death, Catherine barricades herself inside her apartment and cuts the telephone cord with Michael's straight razor, which had earlier fascinated and repulsed her. The overweight landlord, angry that the rent has been neglected, pushes his way past the barricade and starts to chastize Catherine; however, his manner softens when he notices that she is dressed in a negligee. When he attempts to embrace her, she picks up the razor and slashes repeatedly at his face.

Helen and Michael return home to find two dead bodies, their apartment a shambles, and Catherine completely out of her mind. When Michael cradles Catherine in his arms, she begins to look peaceful at last, as if this were what she had wanted all along. The final famous shot, which must have influenced Kubrick's last shot in *The Shining*, has the camera moving in on an early photograph of Catherine as a child, showing that she was "different" even then, before losing the frame in her dark, staring eyes.

Repulsion is an oddly compelling film, a descent into madness that lingers with the viewer. However, the unrelieved loneliness, alienation, and ennui of Catherine's existence become wearying, making it a film that is more respected than enjoyed. Polanski would later return to depicting alienation and the disintegration of a personality with *The Tenant*, a blackly humorous film that covers much of the ground of *Repulsion* but in a more entertaining fashion.

With another *succès d'estime* under his belt, Polanski tackled an outright absurdist comedy with his next film, *Cul-de-Sac*. *Cul-de-Sac* means dead end, and all the characters in the story are trapped in a dead-end situation. A pair of robbers, Richard (Lionel Stander) and Albert (Jack MacGowran), have both been shot and their car runs out of gas in the middle of a causeway. Richard goes to get help, passing a couple making love in the sand, and ends up at a castle owned by George (Donald Pleasence), a bald, middle-aged man who sold his business to live out the fantasy of living in castle with a young, new wife, Teresa (Françoise Dorleac).

The castle proves to be a dead end, not only for the robbers, but for George as well. Cut off from society, his visiting friends convince George that he can never return, while his assertive wife humiliates him by dressing him in women's clothes and applying eyeliner and by taking lovers on the outside. Teresa feels trapped by this boring and lonely existence, but although she is the only character that really has any life in her, she is also the least likable character in the film.

Richard comes and insults George and holds both George and Teresa under gunpoint, forcing them to try and help his mortally wounded friend Albie, who dies and must be buried. While Richard bullies George, he likes him better than he likes Teresa, whom he regards with utter contempt.

The film is a compilation of odd moments and much of the dialogue is unfortunately improvised, depriving it of pertinent thrust. The movie ebbs and flows like the tides which surround and isolate the castle. The robbers keep hoping that their boss, Katelbach, will save them, but it becomes clear that Katelbach has abandoned them. George tries to hang onto his fantasy existence, but it all crumbles around him while he keeps insisting that he does not want to cause trouble or make waves. Only Teresa escapes by abandoning her husband and returning to society with another man.

The film has some remarkable moments, as might be expected of a Polanski film, but I find it far too meandering for its own good, and its score by Krysztof Komeda is a positive liability rather than an asset, a grating, annoying concoction that makes the film even harder to sit through. Stander and Pleasance both turn in wonderful performances, but this is a dead-end film.

Dance of the Vampires (better known by its inane United States title *The Fearless Vampire Killers, or Pardon Me But Your Teeth Are in My Neck*) is a farce than seems far less funny or original now than it did when it was first released. In a way, it represents Polanski's *hommage* to Hammer

Films, the British company that produced quite a number of vampire movies from the late '50s to the early '70s. The film received some notoriety because American producers lopped off nine minutes of footage, changed the title and some of the sound effects, and redubbed many of the voices in the film so that Polanski asked unsuccessfully to have his name removed from the credits.

There is not a tremendous difference between the two versions – the primary deletions are some slapstick sequences centered around Alfie Bass after he has become a vampire and his endless pursuit of Fiona Lewis – but Polanski's version does have a slight edge. The film is notable as the work in which Polanski starred and fell in love with his costar Sharon Tate, who plays Polanski's love interest in the film. It was to be the only Polanski movie she appeared in before her unfortunate and untimely demise.

Polanski wanted to shoot the film in Panavision, a wide-screen format, but MGM insisted that it be shot in the standard 1.85 aspect ratio. The few outdoor scenes were shot in this format, but Polanski switched to Panavision once he began to film his interiors. As a result, the exteriors seem a bit grainy as they were blown up to Panavision. Additionally, the many outdoor scenes shot on a soundstage are obviously artificial, giving the film a general air of unreality.

The film follows the quest of Prof. Abronsius (Jack MacGowran) and his assistant Alfred (Polanski) to wipe out the scourge of vampirism. Arriving at an inn in Transylvania, Abronsius is pleased to note all the proper clichés – garlic hanging up, reticent villagers, anxious and nervous denials. The primitiveness of the professor's knowledge is indicated sublimely by having him read to his assistant from a tome on vampire lore as Alfred applies heated glass jars to his back (creating a vacuum – an ancient medical technique for drawing out foul spirits).

Dance of the Vampires features two outstanding sequences and two memorable jokes. The first sequence is one in which compulsive bather Sarah (Sharon Tate) is taking one of her innumerable baths when she notices snowflakes slowly swirling down into her tub. Looking up, she sees Count von Krolock (Ferdy Mayne) floating down towards her from a skylight amidst falling snow. The shot has a great lyrical beauty to it.

Also very lyrical is the sequence whence the British title derives. In an effort to rescue Sarah from Count von Krolock, Abronsius and Alfred go to Krolock's castle, where a vampire ball is about to take place and Sarah is presented as a debutante in a blood-red dress. The professor and assistant disguise themselves in period costumes and mingle with the vampires, but their presence is revealed in a huge mirror that shows their reflections, but not the vampires'.

In Ivan Butler's *The Cinema of Roman Polanski*, *Dance*'s cinematographer Douglas Slocombe remarks on the sequence:

It was, I think a *tour-de-force*, and entirely Polanski's conception. The whole thing took two days to shoot, working out all the camera movements, picking out a line here and a line there, then timing the dance to a glance between Alfred, the Professor or Sarah, and interlinking with the others. The success of the plan depended a lot on the intelligence of our crowd artists – we were fortunate enough to have an excellent bunch. The climax, with the whole assembly stepping towards the large mirror but only the three of them being visible, was worked by building a duplicate set in reverse behind the "mirror" and substituting doubles for the Professor, Alfred and Sarah. When they start dancing round one another, of course, the doubles were out of camera.

The once-original jokes include the Jewish innkeeper Shagal (Bass), now a vampire, saying to his former mistress, who is trying to fend him off with a crucifix: "Oy veh, have *you* got the wrong vampire"; and Iain Quarrier as Herbert, Krolock's sensitive vampire son, as a gay vampire who tries to put the bite on Alfred but ends up sinking his fangs into a book of lovemaking techniques instead. The ideas of homosexual vampires and vampires that would not react to a cross were then new but have been mined extensively since.

The theme of the film is Abronsius and Alfred's total failure to achieve their quest, ironically escalating the tragedy they work so hard to prevent. The traditional accoutrements of vampire killers are useless in these do-gooders' hands, as Alfred becomes too nervous to tell one end of a stake from another, and the bag of hammers and stakes keeps getting dropped on their feet, doing more damage to them than they ever do to any of the film's vampires. Some critics have chosen to see this as an oblique commentary on the general uselessness of weapons and the disasters that well-intentioned bunglers can create when they come in as outsiders to rectify a situation they do not fully understand.

Like all Polanski films, *Dance of the Vampires* ends very pessimistically as Sarah is revealed to be a vampire and puts the bite on Alfred. Instead of escaping to safety, the unknowing and self-absorbed Prof. Abronsius is spreading throughout the world the very plague he endeavored to prevent. Throughout the film, he has been portrayed as a dreamer with his head in the clouds, absolutely heedless of the needs or desires of his assistant or anyone else – constantly leaving Alfred to do the work while he contemplates "higher things." A message about how self-absorbed authority leads from exploitation to disaster is inescapable.

Rosemary's Baby lacks most of the humor and abstractions of *Dance of the Vampires*, but in every way it was a far more successful film, Polanski's first for Hollywood, and was the movie that brought him to recognition with mainstream audiences across the globe. Based on a bestseller by Ira Levin,

Alfred (actor-director Roman Polanski, right) wards off the attentions of Herbert (Iain Quarrier), the screen's first gay male vampire in Dance of the Vampires. *The quick-thinking Alfred uses the Bible to ward off a supposed fate worse than death. The vampire ball in the film is a more elaborate version of the one in Don Sharp's* Kiss of Evil.

Rosemary's Baby cannily exploits the fears that pregnant women undergo before giving birth, but this time the neurotic mother, Rosemary (Mia Farrow), finds that her fears are justified—she really is caught up in a conspiracy which involves a coven of satanists in New York.

An agent named Martin Birdt had brought the galleys of Levin's book to the attention of film director William Castle in hopes of selling the rights for a quarter of a million dollars. (He had previously tried to sell the rights to Alfred Hitchcock.) This was as much as Castle had spent on many of his films, but he decided it was a dynamite property and made a counter-offer of $100,000 plus another $50,000 if the book became a best seller (it did) and 5 percent of the net profits, which Birdt accepted.

Now that Castle owned the rights to *Rosemary's Baby*, he needed to find financing. Luckily Robert Evans of Paramount called to indicate that they were interested in making a film of the book. A meeting was arranged with company head Charles Bluhdorn and Castle settled for making the film for

$250,000 plus 50 percent of the profits. Castle intended to direct the film himself, but Bluhdorn suggested using Roman Polanski, with Castle's approval.

Initially, Castle took a dislike to Polanski, but he found that Polanski's ideas so coincided with his own that he capitulated and agreed to allow Polanski to both script and direct. As to casting, Polanski wanted Tuesday Weld to play Rosemary and Robert Redford to play Guy and initially hated the idea of using Ruth Gordon to play Minnie Castevet.

Castle pushed for Mia Farrow and Ruth Gordon and got them. Robert Redford declined the part of Guy when he was served with a subpoena by a Paramount lawyer while discussing the part (Redford and Paramount were involved in a lawsuit). Polanski wanted Castle to play the part of Dr. Sapirstein, but Castle refused, opting for Ralph Bellamy instead. John Cassavetes volunteered himself for the part of Guy and eventually was given the part since Redford was out of the picture.

The location selected for the film to substitute for the Bramford Building was the Dakota. Castle found Polanski to be a perfectionist who took his time and looked out for every detail. (Castle himself was used to shooting his films quickly and cheaply – see chapter on him – and as producer was responsible for keeping the production running smoothly, on time and on budget.)

The film begins with a panoramic shot of the most fashionable part of New York, finally ending on the Bramford Building while a lullaby plays in the background, an ironically soothing element to prepare the viewer for Rosemary's terrifying journey of discovery. Rosemary looks over an apartment in the building, the former tenant having recently died, and is puzzled to discover that a chest of drawers is blocking a small closet at the end of a corridor. Depsite its irregularities, Rosemary is enchanted with the flat and decides to take it, over the objections of her friend Hutch (Maurice Evans). Hutch tells her the building has long had a bad reputation, that women who were reputed to eat babies and a satanist named Adrian Marcato had lived there. Rosemary and her husband, Guy, move in.

Polanski included some in-jokes, one of which was having the character Terry Gionoffrio (played by playmate Angela Dorian) claim that people kept mistaking her for that Italian actress, "Victoria Vetri." Dorian's real name was Victoria Vetri, and she would later return to acting under that name. Terry befriends Rosemary and shows her a charm filled with tannis that an elderly couple in the building, the Castevets, gave her.

Rosemary begins to get uneasy when a short time later she discovers that Terry has leaped to her death from the top of their building. At the scene of the suicide, they first meet the Castevets (Ruth Gordon and Sidney Blackmer), and that night she hears Minnie Castevet chastizing husband Roman, saying, "Sometimes I wonder how come you're the leader of *anything."* Rosemary falls asleep and has a troubling dream about her Catholic childhood.

Rosemary is a lapsed Catholic who has alienated her family by marrying Guy, an atheist, and leaving home to live with the young actor in New York. However, she does not have any friends in the big city and is lonely as Guy doggedly pursues the acting parts. (Loneliness and alienation are common themes in Polanski's work.)

Guy and Rosemary have dinner with Minnie and Roman and they get to talking about the Pope's upcoming visit. Roman and Guy dismiss the hoopla as mere "show business," but Rosemary becomes defensive and says, "Well, he *is* the Pope." Roman takes an interest in Guy's acting career, while Rosemary remains quietly puzzled by the fact that the Castevets apparently took down their pictures before the dinner – what did they not want their guests to see?

However, she is gradually won over by Minnie, who gives her a charm identical to the one Terry had. Meanwhile, another actor's misfortune becomes Guy's good luck when the actor selected for a part Guy wanted suddenly is struck blind and Guy gets the part. News of his success, however, troubles Guy and causes him to go out for a walk by himself. Rosemary notes the change and begins to wonder why.

Then one day she comes home to roses and a happier Guy, who immediately suggests that they have a baby. The prepare a romantic evening, but it is interruped by Minnie, who drops off a gift of a "chocolate mouse," a mousse that Rosemary finds has a "chalky undertaste." She pretends to finish it but is suddenly overcome with dizziness which propels her into a strange dream.

It starts off on a yacht with a Kennedy-like captain, but it alters so that Rosemary finds herself in some kind of a church where she is surrounded by naked men and women. There is some strange chanting, and then Guy approaches and begins to make love to her, but he starts transforming into some kind of devil. Rosemary grows frightened and calls out, "This isn't a dream, this is really happening!"

Next morning she wakes up and finds scratches on her back. Guy is apologetic but explains that he did not want to miss baby night. She goes to a doctor on the recommendation of a girlfriend and discovers she is pregnant. When the Castevets hear of it, they insist she switch from Dr. Hill to Dr. Sapirstein, who changes her medicine from a modern prescription to a special herbal mixture, which Minnie prepares for her. The fearful Rosemary begins wearing the charm Minnie gave her. She finds that she succumbs to desires to eat raw meat.

Though the Castevets may be nothing more than a dotty couple, Polanski plants the seeds of suspicion early while denying confirmation. Throughout most of the film there is not any positive proof that anything sinister or untoward is going on, but there are plenty of troubling dreams and suspicions that play on Rosemary's growing paranoia. *Rosemary's Baby* is very much an adult horror film, lacking the thrills that attract the horror genre's primarily adolescent audience; they do not have the patience or reference points needed to appreciate it, preferring action to unease. However, anyone who has known or been an expectant mother can readily understand Rosemary's concern for her child, her fear of the hostile world around herself and it, and even her growing fear that the changes taking place within her are somehow not normal. The ever-anxious Rosemary perceives threats and betrayal everywhere, even in the most innocuous sources. With Farrow's short locks shortened even further, she begins to look like some form of persecuted penitent.

When Rosemary's friend Hutch slips into a coma after losing a glove, and Rosemary discovers that Guy had switched ties with the actor who was struck blind, she begins to grow really scared. A New Year's toast by the Castevets and Dr. Sapirstein – "to 1966, the Year One" – is even less reassuring, and Rosemary begins to try to break away from their influence. Rosemary wants to change back to Dr. Hill, but Guy refuses, and suddenly Rosemary's pains go away.

Hutch dies and leaves her a book, *All of Them Witches* by Adrian Marcato, and a message that "the name is an anagram." Adrian's son was Steven, and Rosemary figures out that Steven Marcato is an anagram for Roman Castevet. This convinces her that the Castevets are part of a witch's coven that plans to sacrifice her child. Guy ridicules the idea and Dr. Sapirstein tries to convince her it has no basis, but she becomes obsessed with the subject, reading book after book.

Becoming frantic, she decides to contact Dr. Hill and give him the information she has. In the film's most famous in-joke, Rosemary is trapped inside a phone booth when she sees a man who looks like Dr. Sapirstein outside the booth. Screwing up her courage, she leaves, only for the man to turn around and reveal himself to be William Castle, who made the cameo at Polanski's insistence.

Naturally, Dr. Hill does not put much stock in her suspicions and decides to summon her personal physician, Dr. Sapirstein, to take over the case. She tries to flee but ends up in labor, and Sapirstein delivers her baby.

When she wakes up, she is told that the baby has died, but she hears an infant crying and is convinced that the baby still lives. She also becomes suspicious as her breasts are milked, and she hides the sleeping pills she is given. Taking a large kitchen knife, she begins exploring and discovers the coven celebrating, proclaiming both the death of God and the birth of the son of Satan, Rosemary's baby. Rosemary realizes she has been betrayed by her husband in exchange for furthering his career. The question is whether she will accept the child.

Significantly, many people feel they have actually glimpsed the baby in the film, but that is not so. The only clue we get, apart from the black cradle and an upside-down crucifix over it, is Rosemary exclaiming about what they have done to its eyes (with the response that the child has its father's eyes). Polanski builds such a sense of expectation that audience's imaginations fill in the missing image.

Rosemary accepts the child as her own, but it is not so much a triumph of mother love as the triumph of evil's plan. God is absent in Polanski's world, leaving the satanists with their dark powers to triumph. Naturally, the film stirred up some religious controversy and was condemned by the Catholic church. However, the popularity of the book proved enormous and carried over to the film, which was a tremendous success, breaking box office records in many areas.

Interestingly, Frank Sinatra had tried to scuttle the film because delays in production were holding up a film he planned to make costarring Farrow, then his wife. However, Farrow insisted on finishing *Rosemary's Baby*. Afterwards, Castle claimed the film had a curse when he suffered from uremic poisoning and had to undergo a series of painful kidney stone operations; composer Krysztof Komeda injured his head in a ski accident, went into a coma and died; and Polanski's pregnant wife Tate was killed by the Manson family. Ever the showman, Castle found a way to get additional publicity for the film out of various tragedies that were in no way connected with it.

Following the Tate tragedy Polanski left the United States and returned to Europe, undergoing a period of inactivity and mourning. He returned to the screen in 1971 with an even more powerful and often underrated horror film, his adaptation of William Shakespeare's *Macbeth*. Some critics might blanch at *Macbeth* being called a horror film, but what else would you call a work that involves witches, ghosts, prophecies, and several rather gory murders? Given that Shakespeare was one of the most poetic and incisive writers in the English language, the dialogue and story of *Macbeth* are particularly rich and luxuriant.

There had been some notable previous film adaptations of this Shakespearean masterwork, including Orson Welles', which was filmed on Republic's western sets and delivered with a Scots accent, and Akira Kurosawa's beautiful *Throne of Blood*, which altered all the dialogue and set the story in feudal Japan; thus far, however, Polanski's must be considered the definitive screen version.

At the time of the film's release, several critics complained that Polanski depicted onscreen all the murders and violence that Shakespeare either had happen off stage or merely discussed in his dialogue. Some even attributed this to the Tate tragedy; however, Polanski was merely being cinematic. None of the violence is overdone or gratuitous, but it does emphasize the horror both of the times and of Macbeth's ruthless actions. There were also complaints about the witches being in the nude, but there is nothing prurient in their portrayal.

Polanski gets very good performances out of his actors, abandoning the typical florid stage style for a more natural and realistic delivery of the dialogue. Jon Finch and Francesca Annis make for a young but particularly good couple as Macbeth and his lady.

The entire production is suffused in class from the participation of Kenneth Tynan on the screenplay to Gil Taylor's fine cinematography. Polanski crams the frame with detail, communicating the violence and splendor of the times while simultaneously propelling the plot forward. (For example, as Macbeth talks with Banquo [Martin Shaw] about the prophecy that he will be king, we see prisoners of war being hanged in the background.)

As in most of his other films, Polanski in *Macbeth* uses his camera to capture the "truth" of the situation rather than to be flashy and call attention to itself. We see and can understand the characters' actions and motivations without approving or disapproving. Still, the film does have one brilliant shot that is splendidly cinematic in which Macbeth returns to the witches to find out why Banquo's heirs will be king instead of his own. The witches show him a mirror which shows a long line of Banquo's descendants, each holding a mirror reflecting another descendant, to represent the long line of kings that will spring from Banquo's progeny.

Perhaps the only visual that Polanski seems to fumble is the movement of Birnam Wood, though the preparation for its progress is made credible, and this is more than made up for by the exciting battle than ends in Macbeth's beheading. However, in accordance with Polanski's fondness for circularity, he ends the film with Donalbain (Paul Shelley) going to visit the witches to learn of his future, suggesting that there is a pattern here that will repeat itself endlessly.

Next Polanski went to Italy and tackled *What?*, a ribald comedy about the excitement that gorgeous Sydne Rome leaves in her wake, unaware of the effect her beauty has on men. The film was later recut and released on video as *Roman Polanski's Diary of Forbidden Dreams*.

Polanski's greatest success and his best film followed with *Chinatown*, a modern *noir*-ish film classic based on the San Fernando land-grab scandal in Southern California's history. The film boasted a wonderfully well-written screenplay by Robert Towne and a terrific performance by Jack Nicholson as private detective Jack Gittes, who gets his nose slit by Roman Polanski as a punk in the course of the movie. While not a horror film, it features possibly the screen's greatest villain in the person of Noah Cross (superbly played by film director John Huston), an evil and lecherous old man who has raped his own daughter and will stop at nothing to get millions of extra dollars by cheating the farmers of San Fernando Valley.

Interestingly, Chinatown was meant by Towne to represent a state of mind, one in which the forces are stacked against you and you can't win, as well as a place where Gittes once worked as a police officer. It was never intended to be shown onscreen. However, studio executives became alarmed that there were no scenes set in Chinatown in a film called *Chinatown* and demanded changes.

The film ends as it presently does because of Polanski. Towne intended to have the Faye Dunaway character cover up for her child who murders Cross, and he claims that Polanski was emotionally incapable of ending the film without having the blonde Dunaway get shot. However, Polanski's instincts seem to have been correct, as the ending is far more powerful with Dunaway being shot and killed by Cross as she tries to escape and then Cross comforting his "granddaughter," leaving evil once more triumphant and Jake being admonished to "Forget it, Jake, it's Chinatown."

Paramount acquired the rights to *The Tenant*, a novel by Roland Topor, and Bob Evans was interested in knowing if Polanski wanted to direct it. Polanski was familiar with the book, having been offered it after *Repulsion*, but he was more interested in playing the book's lead character, Trelkovsky, a Pole who has become a French citizen but is nonetheless an outsider (a part which Polanski could easily identify with). When deals to make *Pirates* fell through and another director could not be found to helm the project, Polanski relented and agreed to both star and direct in *The Tenant*.

However, the subject was not geared towards mainstream audiences, which had been attracted to both *Rosemary's Baby* and *Chinatown* in large numbers, and the resulting film was vilified by the press and ignored by the public. It is unfortunate as *The Tenant* was worth seeing – a blackly comic but nevertheless unsettling portrait of a man's mental breakdown, driven by the paranoid delusion that he is being forced into a role he does not wish to play.

The film's brilliant opening shot is atypical of Polanski's work – a long continuous take that begins with a dimly seen figure by a window. The camera then peers downward where there is a hole in a glass awning, then back to the window, along the inner courtyard of an apartment building, past another window which has Simone Choule (Dominique Poulange) and then suddenly Trelkovsky (Polanski) in it, past the office of the concierge to the outer gate, into which Trelkovsky enters for the first time to inquire about a newly vacant apartment. Trelkovsky is a perennial victim, a meek, timid, inoffensive man who spends his time constantly trying to appease the anger of others.

Trelkovsky has heard about Simone Choule's apartment from some unspecified person. Choule had attemped suicide by jumping out of her window and now lies in a hospital where she is not expected to recover. Desperate for the apartment, Trelkovsky does his best to assure the owner, the cantankerous Mr. Zy (Melvyn Douglas), that he is the kind of quiet tenant that Zy prefers to have in his apartment building.

Trelkovsky goes to visit Simone to check on her progress and meets Stella (Isabelle Adjani), a friend of Simone's. He passes himself off as a friend who only knew Stella slightly, and the heavily bandaged Simone suddenly howls at him in wide-mouthed horror.

Everywhere around him, Trelkovsky sees what seems to him a threatening and crazy world. He walks off with Stella only to be accosted by a bum who deprives him of a few bills on the theory that he would not want to seem cheap in front of his girlfriend. Immediately, Stella chastizes him for giving the beggar any money. Trelkovsky then steps in some animal excrement. Stella and Trelkovsky go on a date to see *Enter the Dragon* together, and the sight of Bruce Lee crushing a man's balls seems to turn Stella on and she starts stroking Trelkovksy's crotch. However, as he begins kissing her, he notices a woebegone and interested party in the seat behind him and cannot bring himself to continue to neck in the theater.

Philippe Sarde's music sets a somber mood, equally captured by Sven Nykvist's depressing photography. Trelkovsky seems incapable of having a good time. When he invites some friends over to his new apartment, he does not relax, he fears that the neighbors will complain about the noise. When they do complain of the noise, it confirms his fears and begins to drive him into defensiveness and paranoia.

The film neatly divides its characters into the meek and the oppressive. One of Trelkovsky's bombastic friends, the obnoxious and obstreperous Scope (Bernard Freeson), falls into the latter category, being overly aggressive and self-assertive. He takes Trelkovksy to his apartment and plays military music very loudly, marching smugly in time to the music and smiling. When a neighbor comes to complain, he immediately intimidates him.

Similarly, Trelkovsky begins to see the owner of a cafe that Simone used to frequent as forcing him to accept Simone's usual order of hot chocolate and Marlboro cigarettes. He sees Mme. Dioz (Jo Van Fleet), a woman who asks him to sign a petition against a neighbor that has never caused Trelkovsky any trouble, in a tramp who was taking a nap inside the courtyard. The concierge (Shelley Winters) and Mr. Zy are constantly berating him for his shortcomings.

Instead of feeling safe in his apartment, he begins to notice oddities here, like a human tooth embedded in some gauze in a hole in the wall. He sees people standing in the bathroom opposite his window and staring at him for hours. (Later, he has the experience of going to the bathroom himself and seeing himself staring at the bathroom and raising his opera glasses for a better look.) When he is robbed, he is berated for the amount of noise the robbers made, and he loses his personal possession (representing his identity) while the robbers leave Simone's things behind (an indication of the dominating influence she is beginning to have on Trelkovsky's mind).

When he is robbed, Mr. Zy requests that he not go to the police because it would hurt the apartment and might put Trelkovsky himself under suspicion since he would not be considered French. Finally, the police summon him in response to complaints they have had about the amount of noise he supposedly makes and intimidate him as well.

At the same time, there are victims. A mother with a crippled daughter comes to see if Trelkovsky was the one who complained about her, and when she is kicked out of the apartment building, she leaves a puddle of diarrhea in front of every door except Trelkovsky's. (Trelkovksy complains that this will make the neighbors think that he did it, so he is forced to scoop up some from one of her puddles and put it on his own doorstep.)

Another obvious victim is a man who secretly loved Simone but never had the courage to tell her. He shows up on Trelkovsky's doorstep one evening. When he learns that Simone is dead, his sounds of mourning are so loud, they frighten Trelkovsky and he escorts him out of the apartment so they can talk and commiserate with one another. At one bar, a drunken man comes in and offers free drinks on the house except for Trelkovsky's companion, singling him out for misery.

Alienation is very basic to the story and Trelkovsky's mental breakdown. He has no real friends, only acquaintances at work. He reunites with Stella and she takes him home to have sex with him, but he gets too drunk and engages on a rambling discussion as to what comprises the essential self. ("If you cut my head from my body, is it me and my body or me and my head?" he muses. "By what right is my head considered me?") He falls asleep before Stella can finish undressing him.

Trelkovsky is constantly trying to placate people, even if it means telling lies. In the absence of any relationship which would develop a stronger sense of self, he begins to see people surrounding him as being engaged in a conspiracy to force him to adopt Simone Choule's personality. He begins to succumb by resorting to transvestism, dressing up in Simone's makeup and outfits.

Polanski demonstrates how this inner angst leads to acts of violence and cruelty. The normally mild-mannered Trelkovsky smacks a puffy-faced child with a tooth missing for no apparent reason other than the child had been crying about a missing boat. Seeking shelter at Stella's, he begins to imagine that she is part of the plot to drive him nuts as well, and so he destroys her apartment and steals her money so that he can rent a new apartment, get drunk, and buy a gun.

The film comes to a delirious finish when Trelkovsky is struck by a car as he crosses the street and imagines the car is being driven by Zy and Mme. Dioz instead of an inoffensive Claude Daphin and his wife. He attempts to choke the wife and accuses them both of attempting to kill him. He is given a sedative, and the kindly couple take him home where the disgusted concierge can only shake her head. Imagining the entire courtyard as if it were an opera house packed with spectators, Trelkovsky finally dons Simone's makeup and clothing and recreates her suicide attempt. Then, declaring his individuality ("It may not have been as good as last time, but I'm not Simone Choule, I'm *Trelkovsky*"), he crawls his way back up to his apartment and hurtles himself over a second time, driven by images of the apartment dwellers as evil demons goading him on.

The whole film has a very Kafkaesque feel to it, with Trelkovsky as a doomed and despairing character. Like the slow building of paranoia in *Repulsion* and *Rosemary's Baby*, Polanski creates his haunting mood not by bombast, but by the careful application of detail upon inventive detail so that we come to know and understand the madness into which the central character has descended. The modern urban world does not deal kindly with weak-minded and suggestible outsiders.

One of the film's subtleties is the idea that perhaps Simone has been reincarnated in Trelkovsky. It is established that Simone worked for a museum department that studied ancient Egypt, lent a friend a book on Egypt, and was sent a postcard of an Egyptian sarcophagus. When Trelkovsky sees her in the hospital, she looks like a mummy herself, and later Trelkovsky has a vision of her in the bathroom slowly and joyously unwrapping herself, an indication that her spirit is unleashed and is becoming dominant in Trelkovsky's mind. Finally, the film ends with the twist that the same figure is lying in a hospital bed, only now it is Trelkovsky, and peering out, he sees Stella and himself visiting him as Simone. The film ends abruptly as the camera descends into his screaming mouth.

Just as Trelkovsky would lose his identity, so Polanski would soon lose his as an American filmmaker. He was preparing to shoot *The First Deadly Sin* for Columbia when he was arrested for drugging and having sex with a 13-year-old girl. During his arraignment, he was assigned Dino De Laurentiis' remake of *Hurricane* instead and was released on bail. Instead of directing the project, he fled the country and finally sought asylum in France.

He returned to filmmaking with a brilliant adaptation of Thomas Hardy's frankly dull book *Tess of the D'Urbervilles* and succeeded in making an international star out of Nastassja Kinski for her portrayal of the title role in *Tess*. The beautifully crafted film showed that Polanski had lost none of his ability, but funding for other projects proved hard to come by outside of Hollywood.

He finally raised the money to make his pet project, *Pirates*, which starred Walter Matthau, but his attempt to revive the swashbuckler genre met with ill favor from vindictive critics. It is a handsome-looking film, but its bleak and circular ending (in the tradition of *Repulsion*, which opens and closes on Denevue's eye, or *Dance of the Vampires*, which opens and closes on a sled in a snow-covered landscape) made the adventure pointless.

Pirates opens and closes on Captain Red (Walter Matthau) and his partner Frog (the handsome Cris Campion) trapped on a small raft in a shark-infested sea. While the film is handsomely staged and photographed and Red and Frog undergo a number of adventures, the film fails to be the kind of rousing fun one expects from old pirate pictures and ended up being treated harshly.

Frantic is Polanski's most recent film, a thriller in which a luggage mix-up causes the wife of an American doctor to be kidnapped. Though the doctor (Harrison Ford) becomes involved with an attractive Parisian girl, he remains faithful to his wife, for whom he frantically searches, imperiling himself in the process. It was a slick, well-crafted thriller, but it was not excitingly different – nor was it a hit, perhaps in part because of its European-style editing and pacing.

Polanski has not worked in the horror genre since *The Tenant*, but his psychologically probing films show him to be a major talent, and his return with a good property could go a good ways towards enlivening a now moribund genre. Meanwhile, he has created a number of timeless classics which stand up to repeated viewings, and he deserves respect for his obvious artistic achievements.

Michael Reeves (1944–1969)

Castle of the Living Dead (codirector with Luciano Rici and Warren Keifer, uncredited, 1964); *Revenge of the Blood Beast* (aka *The She Beast*, 1965); *The Sorcerers* (1967); *Conqueror Worm* (aka *The Witchfinder General*, 1968).

Born in 1944, Michael Leith Reeves was educated at the Radley School in England. While visiting his parents in the United States, he flew to Los Angeles and visited the home of one of his favorite directors, Don Siegel, who, impressed with Reeves' chutzpah, gave him a job on the spot as a dialogue director for some tests he was filming.

Reeves was a passionate movie fan and a real hustler. He managed to get work as a gofer on *The Long Ships* and *Genghis Kahn* before becoming an assistant director on television commercials, all before the age of 20.

Paul Maslansky gave him his first big break by inviting him to be assistant director on *Castle of the Living Dead*, which was to be directed by Warren Kiefer but credited to "Herbert Wise" (Luciano Ricci) for quota purposes. The amount of Reeves' participation remains in question, but producer Maslansky maintains that he mainly shot second unit material. However, his second unit material was so good that it was given an expanded role in the film, allowing for the introduction of Antonio de Martino as an energetic dwarf who protects Gaia Germani, the film's heroine.

Christopher Lee stars as Count Drago, who transforms people into motionless effigies. Donald Sutherland has two memorable bit parts, as a policeman and later as a witch. Though beautifully photographed by Aldo Tonti, the most memorable part of the film has the dwarf fending off a scythe-wielding henchman (Mirlo Vanlentin) of Drago's who seeks to kill Germani. In *A Heritage of Horror*, David Pirie calls the film "a collector's item for its uncharacteristically authentic flavour of medievalism which derives largely from the bizarre collection of minor characters like the dwarf and Donald Sutherland's highly grotesque witch."

Maslansky was pleased enough with Reeves' footage to offer him his own film to direct, from a screenplay called *Vardella* with an 18-day shooting schedule and a budget of a mere 13,000 pounds. Reeves collaborated on a new script with Charles B. Griffith, scriptwriter for Corman's film *Little Shop of Horrors*, under the pseudonym of Michael Byron. The result,

Revenge of the Blood Beast (better known in the United States as *The She Beast*), is an amalgam of horror scenes and facile jokes. Griffith was assigned to handle the second unit to bring the film in on time and added some non sequitur jokes, such as a constantly reappearing motorcyclist during an overlong and dull chase scene, or the She Beast throwing a scythe atop a hammer to form the Communist symbol after she has murdered a lecherous Transylvanian innkeeper played by Mel Welles.

The film differs from most low-budget European productions of the time in that it constantly pokes fun at the way present-day Transylvania is being run. Von Helsing, a former aristocrat, has been kicked out of his castle and now lives in a cave where he reads about a witch named Vardella. This witch, as we see in a flashback, was captured by the townspeople, stabbed with an iron stake, and drowned before an exorcism could be performed to prevent her from returning. She placed a curse on the town and vowed to return.

Meanwhile, in the present day, a honeymooning couple, Philip (Ian Ogilvy, best known as *The New Saint* and the star of all Reeves' subsequent films) and Veronica (Barbara Steele, who was only available for a short time), are touring Transylvania and stop at Welles' hotel, where they are served English tea with garlic cloves and meet the oddball Von Helsing (John Karlsen). During the night, Welles' innkeeper proves to be a peeping tom (earlier he had busted into their room and, when Philip complained, answered that "privacy leads to con-spy-racy"). Philip smashes his face with the window, goes outside and beats him up.

By way of revenge, the innkeeper steals the distributor cap from the couple's Volkswagen, but an angry Philip detects the ruse and gets it back. Driving away, he loses control of the car and plunges into the same lake that Vardella had been drowned in. A helpful truck driver fishes both bodies out and returns them to the innkeeper.

When Philip wakes up, he finds Vardella's body lying next to him rather than Veronica's. Von Helsing promises to help save Veronica, but takes Philip back to his cave rather than to the lake as Philip expected. Von Helsing tries to explain that Vardella's spirit has taken possession of Veronica's body and must be exorcised at the proper time to get her back, but Philip merely becomes convinced that the man is mad, and heads back towards the inn. Von Helsing beats him there and awakens Vardella, who strangles him and escapes. A frightened girl stops by the inn and the innkeeper tries to molest her after he has been drinking heavily. When Philip arrives just after the girl runs away, he surprises the innkeeper, who brains him with a bottle and assumes he has killed him. Frightened that the police will get hold of him, he places Philip's body in the road so that it will get run over and look like an accident. The helpful truck driver from earlier just misses him, and Von Helsing discovers and revives him before he can be injured.

Meanwhile, Vardella takes her revenge upon the innkeeper, one of whose ancestors was clearly glimpsed during the flashback. Von Helsing and Philip go through town looking for Vardella, mistaking drunks and the like for possible victims. Finally, they catch her assaulting a boy and Von Helsing injects her with a drug to knock her out. If they kill her, they will kill Veronica as well.

Pretty soon the police get hold of Vardella's body and plan an autopsy. This procedure would kill Veronica but still leave Vardella's spirit around to do further harm, so Von Helsing and the now-convinced Philip steal the body back and set off the lengthy chase scene that was mentioned earlier. The final exorcism, once it is achieved, apparently amounts to no more than dunking Vardella's body in the lake again. The film ends with Veronica returned and helping Philip spirit Von Helsing out of the country to avoid the wrath of the police commissar. As they depart, Philip comments how miserable a place it was, but Veronica smiles and says, "I'll be back," echoing the words of Vardella.

While by no means a horror classic, the film is interesting in two respects. First, the destruction of the witch at the opening is reminiscent of similar but superior scenes in *The Conqueror Worm*. Second, it develops a trend in Reeves' work where the evil deeds of others help unleash additional evil forces. In a resurrection obviously based upon the one in Bava's *Black Sunday*, Vardella's maggoty face comes back to full life while the innkeeper is attempting to rape the young girl, representing a corresponding evil. Later, she kills the innkeeper after he has tried to dispose of Philip and attacks a young boy after he had disobeyed his parents to sneak out to see a cockfight.

Reeves' next production, *The Sorcerors*, proves far more interesting. In it, Boris Karloff plays Professor Monserrat, a hypnotist who invents a machine that will allow others to control a person's body and experience the sensations that the subject experiences. He selects as a test subject an angry youth named Mike (Ian Ogilvy) and promises him undreamed-of excitement without penalties.

Monserrat's wife, Estelle (Catherine Lacey), becomes involved and soon they have Mike under their control. When he is made to crush an egg in his hand, they are delighted to experience the same sensations. The prospect of living vicariously really excites Estelle, who spurs her husband on to more and more risky things, from plunging into cold water for a midnight swim to robbing a store for a fur for herself. Prof. Monserrat becomes appalled, but he cannot help admitting that the thrill of the robbery was exciting for him as well. Estelle becomes a thrill junkie, forcing Mike to beat up his friend Alan (Victor Henry), and after restraining her husband to prevent him from interfering, enjoys the sensations of Mike murdering two young women. As Mike escapes by car, Prof. Monserrat summons the last of his will and causes the car to crash, bursting into flames. Back at their apartment, the Monserrats also experience the sensation of burning to death, and their charred bodies are left for the police to find.

The film covers its simple but interesting idea very well and very convincingly. People have found in the central concept a metaphor for going to the cinema to experience vicariously the lives of the heroes and villains on the screen. Others see it as depicting the Reeves theme of decent people giving in to their worst impulses. Some proclaimed that the film parodied the depiction of modern youth in the tabloids, fulfilling the public's worst nightmares about young people living merely for thrills and sensations, ignoring possible consequences, and showing that the older generation is in fact behind this behavior. The beauty of the film is that it manages to be all that and more. However, the best was yet to come.

Reeves' masterpiece was *The Conqueror Worm*, based on the novel *Witchfinder General* by Ronald Bassett, though Reeves and coscriptwriter Tom Baker threw out most of Bassett's book. The film was known by Bassett's title in Europe, where it received some acclaim, but in America a prologue and epilogue of star Vincent Price's voice was added of him reading extracts from Edgar Allan Poe's poem "The Conqueror Worm." The result was that American critics treated it as another routine Poe picture from AIP, which advertised it as a "science fiction shocker"! The film was rarely screened at revival theaters and was mostly known through a butchered version on television which made mincemeat of the plot until a recent video version was released. Sadly, this video release lacks Paul Ferris' fine score which helps evoke the seventeenth century setting of the film and plays a wonderful counterpoint to its grisly violence.

The major theme of the film is that violence begets violence, and evil begets evil. There is also a running thread about how some men are not what they appear to be, and another about how honor is perverted. The film has a much richer look than Reeves' other films, partly due to John Coquillion's cinematography, and partly due to excellent use made of the English countryside. The costumes, props and settings all expertly recall the year 1645.

The film opens simply and powerfully as a screaming woman is hauled up a hillside and then hanged for being a witch. The camera moves from the excited faces of the townspeople to the impassive one of Matthew Hopkins (Vincent Price), who, in his Puritan garb astride a black horse, looks like the angel of death. (The full title on the American print of the film is *Matthew Hopkins – The Conqueror Worm*.)

The film then cuts after the credits to Richard Marshall (Ian Ogilvy), a young soldier in Cromwell's army. His company is ambushed by some Royalist snipers, and Marshall fires his pistol in time to save his captain's life. We see from the shock and surprise on his face that this is the first man

Rare shot of Michael Reeves (squatting left) conferring with producer Tony Tenser (squatting right) on the set of The Conqueror Worm.

Marshall has killed, and he stammers to the captain that the man was trying to kill him, as if he has only just caught on what the war was all about.

For his act of valor, he is given a promotion and leave. Marshall heads to Brandiston, where his girlfriend, Sara (Hilary Dwyer), lives under the watchful eye of her uncle, John Lowes (Rupert Davies), a priest. Because Catholics are being persecuted at the time, Lowes has become concerned for Sara's safety and volunteers that he is willing for Marshall to marry Sara if he will take her away from danger, though the priest obviously dislikes Marshall's profession of, as he sees it, "killing good Christians."

Marshall takes Sara to bed, they make love, and he promises to keep her from harm. On his way out of town to rejoin the regiment, he encounters Hopkins and his partner, John Stearne (Robert Russell), riding into it. He asks who Hopkins is and what he wants, to which Hopkins replies that he is a lawyer and wants "a man who is not what he seems to be."

In many ways, this is certainly true of Hopkins himself, who cloaks himself in righteousness while committing foul deeds. Price plays Hopkins (who is based on a real person) to perfection in one of his best performances, suggesting repressed anger and scorn without the hamminess that marred many of the later Poe films. We see a man who has a contempt for mankind and a special hatred for women, whom he coerces into having sex with him, then tortures and kills for money. The tortures are carried out by his saucy companion, Stearne, who, as Hopkins observes, enjoys his work. Stearne notes that Hopkins enjoys Stearne's work himself.

The man accused of witchcraft is none other than John Lowes, and the fact that he is Catholic is sufficient to have him branded an idolator and put to Stearne's test. The test consists of pricking him in search of the devil's mark (which is a mark put on by Satan to bind a witch to him; when pricked, it does not cause the witch to cry out or bleed. However, as this mark can be hidden anywhere on the body, frequently numerous pokes are required to divulge its location.)

Sara comes forward to try to stop the torture and save her uncle. She claims that her uncle is a good man and that she is a foundling her uncle adopted. She offers herself to Hopkins in exchange for Lowes' life, to which Hopkins agrees. The cease-and-desist order short of a confession surprises Stearne, who is deprived of his sadistic thrills. That night Hopkins goes to Sara, telling her that some men "have strange motives for doing what they do" and he only wants to get at "the Truth" as he unbuttons her blouse.

Stearne finds another victim, a woman, whom he can torture "in the prescribed method," but he is still curious about Hopkins' absences and his reluctance to pursue conviction of the priest. That night he observes as Hopkins goes up to Sara's bedroom, and using a ladder, he listens in on their lovemaking. The next day, Hopkins announces that he has business elsewhere for a time and puts Stearne in charge. Stearne interprets this as meaning that he can take Sara, proceeding to rape her in a field.

A crony of Hopkins observes this and informs Hopkins that Stearne has had her, which causes Hopkins to approach Stearne and announce that he has changed his mind about the priest.

Lowes and two beaten women who have been accused of witchcraft are taken to a bridge. The older of the women pleads for mercy, claiming that she is with child, but Stearne ridicules the suggestion. The trio are bound and lowered into the water. If they float or appear to swim, they are judged to be guilty. One of them drowns and she is declared innocent. Lowes and the other woman are hanged and Hopkins is paid for his efforts by the magistrate.

Marshall returns to Brandiston and discovers the church ravaged and the word "Witch" written on the walls. He finds a cowering Sara, who confesses what Hopkins has done to her and her uncle. Angry that Hopkins has violated his oath that he would protect Sara, he pledges his troth to Sara and considers himself married to her without benefit of clergy, and then utters a separate oath to bring Hopkins and his assistant before God's judgment.

As the film progresses, we see the violence welling in Marshall, which is first indicated when he returns to Sara the first time. Marshall kisses her tenderly and then more and more passionately, digging his hands into her shoulder. She thrusts him away for a moment and charges that the army has taught him rough manners. Seeing the corruption in the social institutions, he "marries" without their involvement. It becomes clear that he has appointed himself as a vigilante and has no intention of bringing Hopkins to society's justice, but rather his own. His only evidence is Sara's word, but that is sufficient for him.

Charging off in his search for Hopkins after instructing Sara to go to Lavenham, Marshall comes across Stearne in a bar and, upon learning his identity, immediately assaults him. The barman clubs Marshall over the head with a wooden mallet, allowing Stearne to escape, and attempts to bring Marshall to the attention of the magistrate, but Marshall ignores him and gives chase.

Stearne has a rendezvous with Hopkins and the pair hide behind some trees while a hard-riding Marshall passes them by. Stearne is frightened because he knows that Marshall is out after their blood, but Hopkins is unconcerned. You forget your power, he says; we can charge him with being a witch and it is he who will die. Despite his pretense that he is doing God's work in ferreting out witches, this sentiment clearly indicates how cynically Hopkins will use the power of his office.

Meanwhile, Marshall must return to his regiment and is almost charged with desertion. After a successful campaign, Marshall is promoted to captain and is assigned by Cromwell (Patrick Wymark) to take three men and seek out the fleeing King Charles. Meanwhile, it has been established that horses are scarce, and some of Marshall's army buddies stop Hopkins and Stearne with the intent of confiscating their horses. Hopkins successfully flees, shooting his pursuer's horse in the process, but Stearne's horse is taken and the soldiers express their intent to draft him. Abandoned by Hopkins, Stearne uses his dirk to stab two of the soldiers but is shot in the arm in the process and must painfully dig out the pellet.

At the next town, Hopkins finds a very cooperative magistrate who has three women charged with witchcraft for him, two young ones and an old one. He has the two young women sent up to his bedroom because it takes longer for them to confess. After commenting on the perfidy of women, he mentions that he has developed a new method of disposing of witches, which is revealed to be a public burning in which a convicted witch is tied onto a ladder and then lowered onto a burning pyre. We see this done the next day before the agonized eyes of one of the victim's lovers.

Meanwhile, Marshall discovers that the king has made good his escape and that Hopkins is in Lavenham prosecuting witches. Knowing that Sara is there, he speeds towards the town. Stearne appears and Hopkins offers to split all the money after doing the work. Together they see Sara, and Hopkins realizes that Marshall will not be far behind. Marshall and Sara have a passionate reunion, but it is cut short by the appearance of Hopkins, who charges them with witchcraft and takes them to the magistrate's keep where their confessions can be tortured out of them. The burned woman's lover makes an appearance to stop Hopkins but is shot for his pains; however, he lives long enough to tell the soldiers accompanying Marshall where Hopkins has taken him.

Stearne begins torturing Sara by pricking her and then Hopkins prepares to brand her with a brand in the shape of a cross. He promises to stop the torture if Marshall will confess that he is a witch, but Marshall merely repeats his vow that he will kill Hopkins. Hopkins orders Stearne to bring Marshall closer to observe the agonies of his wife, but Stearne is distracted when Marshall's solider friends start a melee above them, trying to break into the torture chamber.

Marshall, now loose, kicks Stearne, knocking him to the floor, and then gouges an eye out with his spur. Picking up an ax, he begins hacking at Hopkins. Marshall's friend, Trooper Swallow (Nicky Henson), is horrified at what he sees and shoots Hopkins to put him out of his misery. A mad and enraged Marshall screams, "You've taken him from me!" Sara observes the violent madness in her husband and simply screams. On the soundtrack, Price's voice intones the last stanza of Poe's poem: "The play is the tragedy Man, and its hero, the Conqueror Worm."

Reeves' *Conqueror Worm* is a powerful and impressive film. It depicts not only how men of power can exploit their positions to satisfy their debauched and depraved tastes, but also how a once innocent man can be driven to become just what he despises. From a brief lovemaking interlude at the beginning of the film, we see that Marshall has not been deprived of tenderness, but as the film progresses, he becomes increasingly insensitive to anything except the satisfaction of exacting his revenge upon Hopkins and Stearne. We see him rejecting the institutions of his day (the church and the law, even strict obedience to his army unit) in his pursuit. Finally, at the end of the film he is even oblivious to the torture of his sweetheart, single-mindedly concentrating on his oath to kill Hopkins personally. When even this is foiled by Swallow's bullet, he becomes completely deranged. He was relishing his torture as much as Hopkins or Stearne ever relished theirs, and his frustrations know no bounds.

The film keeps closing the circle upon itself. The action is set in motion by Marshall's vow to keep Sara safe, which he fails to do, and ends with Marshall unable to keep his final oath – which has become the only thing that matters to him. The film opens with the scream of a condemned witch and ends in the scream of Sara. At the beginning, Hopkins was a man who was not what he appeared to be – a high-minded lawyer – and at the end, it is

Marshall, who is no longer gallant and dashing but a depraved lunatic hell-bent on revenge.

At the time, many criticized the violence in the movie as being extreme, but it remains important because violence is the force that creates this change. In Reeves' view of the world, there is no counterforce to evil; evil merely promotes more evil until the foul deeds finally consume the evildoer himself. Also the accurate lore on the treatment of witches is fascinating in its own right, plus Reeves clearly shows that even the idiotic prescribed methods are exceeded by the villainous Stearne and Hopkins.

Sadly, *Conqueror Worm* was to be Reeves' last film. He was preparing pre-production for *The Oblong Box*, later directed by Gordon Hessler, when he died unexpectedly of an overdose of barbituates. That he was capable of fashioning a stunning horror film out of a Jacobean revenge plot with philosophical overtones demonstrates that the 25-year-old director was one of great promise, and one whose genuine achievements deserve an honored place along with the best that the horror cinema has produced.

Mark Robson (1913-1978)

The Seventh Victim; The Ghost Ship (1943); *Youth Runs Wild* (1944); *Isle of the Dead* (1945); *Bedlam* (1946); *Champion; Home of the Brave; Roughshod; My Foolish Heart* (1949); *Edge of Doom* (1950); *Bright Victory; I Want You* (1951); *Return to Paradise* (1953); *Hell Below Zero; Phffft; The Bridges at Toko-Ri* (1954); *A Prize of Gold; Trial* (1955); *The Harder They Fall* (1956); *The Little Hut; Peyton Place* (1957); *The Inn of the Sixth Happiness* (1958); *From the Terrace* (1960); *Nine Hours to Rama; The Prize* (1963); *Von Ryan's Express* (1965); *Lost Command* (1966); *Valley of the Dolls* (1967); *Daddy's Gone a-Hunting* (1969); *Happy Birthday, Wanda June* (1971); *Limbo* (1972); *Earthquake* (1974); *Avalanche Express* (1979).

Born on December 4 in Montreal, Mark Robson was still studying political science and economics when he first started working for the film industry as a property boy at Fox, later becoming an assistant at the studio's art department. He joined RKO in 1935 and four years later was assigned to assist Robert Wise on editing Orson Welles' first film, which was to be an adaptation of Joseph Conrad's "Heart of Darkness." The project turned into *Citizen Kane*, and the rest is history.

Robson was promoted to coeditor with Wise for *The Magnificent Ambersons*, a film that was drastically recut while Welles was out of the country because it had received an unsuccessful test screening. Nevertheless, Robson was selected as editor for the next Welles project, *Journey into Fear*, which Norman Foster directed in a flamboyant style similar to Welles', making excellent use of light, shadow and sound.

When Welles was kicked off the RKO lot, Lew Ostrow, executive producer in charge of B films at RKO, assigned Robson to the newly developing Val Lewton unit. Lewton, a very talented producer and scriptwriter, had been a story editor for David Selznick and was offered a chance by Ostrow to show what he could do by producing low-budget films to coincide with audience-tested titles.

According to Robson in *The Celluloid Muse*: "I was assigned to Val's unit as an editor: to show him something about film and to help guide that department involved with his films. He thought of his unit – and he had his own little horror unit – in terms of the producer, the writer, the director, and the editor; a kind of team on which we all worked extremely closely together."

After Jacques Tourneur (whose films will be covered in a separate chapter) directed three very successful low-budget films, he was promoted to A film status with *Days of Glory*. Lewton had worked very closely with Robson and was rather fond of him, respecting his knowledge and talent. When Robson wanted to become a director, Lewton backed him for the job. Initially Lewton wanted to make a comedy out of the title given him, *The Amorous Ghost*, in which the ghost of Casanova takes a modern girl to an eighteenth century concept of heaven. However, the studio put their support behind a story called *The Seventh Victim*, scripted by DeWitt Bodeen, about an orphan girl who has been marked as the seventh victim of a murderer and her attempt to discover the murderer's identity before he commits the crime.

The studio bosses were pleased with Lewton's work and were willing that Lewton's next project be an A-budgeted picture, but not with an unknown and untried director like Robson at the helm. Ever loyal to his people, Lewton insisted on Robson and turned down the promotion to continue making B features with the autonomy that he was accustomed to.

Said Robson in *The Celluloid Muse*:

> I was signed as a director at RKO at two hundred dollars per week and my first picture was *The Seventh Victim*. That picture achieved some kind of notoriety in England after the war, as I discovered when John and Roy Boulting came out here about that time, wanting to meet the fellow who had directed it. They used to bicycle a print of *The Seventh Victim* around London, among them Carol Reed and Cavalcanti and people like that, thinking it an advanced, weird form of film-making. . . .
>
> *The Seventh Victim* was a very low-budget film for those days; I think it cost about $100,000. I don't remember much about it now. I do remember however that it had a rather sinister quality, of something intangible but horribly real; it had an atmosphere. . . . We had the characters speak throughout in a deliberately quiet, polite, and subdued manner, engendering a very calculated undercurrent of *possible* disaster. That technique, which I guess today appears rather funny, was very daring in its time.

In bringing *The Seventh Victim* to the screen, Lewton brought in Charles O'Neal to write the script and altered the story quite a bit, replacing the murderer with a devil-worshipping cult. The result is one of Lewton's most personal films and one of the subtlest horror films ever made, pervaded with a sense of gloom and despair around every corner, with a very literate script (that Lewton no doubt worked on himself), a talented cast, and beautiful design, photography and direction. Robson fully justified the trust that Lewton had placed in him.

Not only did Lewton have a debuting director, he also placed his trust
in a debuting star. Kim Hunter made an impressive debut as Mary Gibson,
the film's troubled heroine. Mary is very uncertain and fearful about life outside the Highcliffe Academy for Girls, which is where she grew up. She is
summoned by the headmistress, who informs her that her only living relative, a sister named Jacqueline, has disappeared. As she leaves, she is warned
by a strange woman (Eve March) not to come back to the academy: "I left,
as you are leaving, but I didn't have courage – one must have courage to
really live in the world. I came back." There is the implication that having
lost her nerve, the woman will never leave the world of the academy.

When Mary arrives in New York, she discovers that her sister has sold
her cosmetics company to a Mrs. Redi (Mary Newton) and is directed to Jacqueline's old apartment above Dante's Restaurant in Greenwich Village.
Getting access to the empty apartment, Mary finds nothing in the room except a noose and a chair. Apparently, Jacqueline is a morbid person who can
only enjoy life by knowing that she has the power to end it.

In her search for her sister, Mary comes across Irving August (Lou
Lubin), a small-time private detective who has taken an interest in the case
and suggests that Jacqueline might be being held captive at the offices of
La Sagesse Cosmetics Company. Mary follows August as he investigates,
but at one point he goes through a door with a frosted glass window and is
murdered. Mary panics and experiences a second severe shock when she
sees two men on the subway propping up the body of August between them,
passing him off as a drunk. She goes to another car for help, but when she
returns the men are gone.

Meanwhile, Jacqueline's psychoanalyst, Dr. Judd (Tom Conway, the
brother of George Sanders, who played a similar role in *The Cat People*),
goes to Jacqueline's old boyfriend, Gregory Ward (Hugh Beaumont, best
known as the father on *Leave It to Beaver*), and tells him that he knows
where Jacqueline is and that she is in need of money. Gregory agrees to pay
the money but Judd refuses to divulge her whereabouts. Judd than finds
Mary and promises a rendezvous with her sister back at Jacqueline's empty
apartment. Initially, the apartment remains empty when Mary arrives, but
Jacqueline (Jean Brooks) makes a brief appearance before fleeing, and two
detectives turn up who claim they are working for Jacqueline's husband.

Said husband is Ward, who obviously begins to fall for the attractive
Mary but remains faithful to his missing spouse. His friend Jason Hoag (Er-
ford Gage), a failed poet, also begins to fall for Mary and offers to help find
Jacqueline. He takes them to a party of seemingly ordinary people who turn
out to be a group of Palladists, a society of satan worshippers whose symbol
of a rectangle enclosing a triangle is identical to the logo of the La Sagesse
Company.

In one of the film's most famous sequences, Mrs. Redi surprises Mary while she is in the shower. Her black outline on the shower curtain strongly resembles, and possibly influenced, Norman Bates' shadow before the infamous shower scene in *Psycho*. (Lewton and Hitchcock knew and were mutual admirers of each other.) She tells Mary to get out of town, that Jacqueline killed August and might be found out if Mary continues her meddling.

Surprisingly, after Jason's romantic interest in Mary is established, he deems himself unworthy and decides to play "Cyrano" for his best friend, the already attached Gregory. This romantic plot alternates with the Palladists kidnapping Jacqueline and urging her to commit suicide by drinking poison rather than endanger their society. A frightened Jacqueline refuses.

Though there is a palpable tension in these scenes, the Palladists seem very passive and make no overt motions to have their wishes acceded to. In fact, apart from a one-armed woman who plays the piano and shuffles cards, they do not appear the slightest bit out of the ordinary, and only the seriousness of their request and their anxious delivery of it indicate that there is something deadly and dangerous about them.

Jacqueline flees and, in the film's biggest horror set piece, heads homeward ever wary of a possible attack, frightened by the sounds of the noisy street. Six previous members of the Palladists have met their fates for betraying their group, but Jacqueline resists being thrust into the role of the seventh victim. A young man with a switchblade chases her, but she manages to enclose herself in a group of celebrating actors and make her escape.

An odd character, Mimi (Elizabeth Russell), who seems consumptive and has made odd appearances throughout the narrative, finally approaches Jacqueline in a scene which ties together the life and death themes of the film. After explaining that she is dying, Mimi says, "I've been quiet, oh, ever so quiet. I hardly move yet it keeps coming all the time . . . closer and closer. I rest and rest and yet I am dying."

"And you don't want to die," says Jacqueline. "I've always wanted to die. Always."

"I'm afraid," says Mimi. "I'm tired of being afraid . . . of waiting."

"Why wait?" Jacqueline rejoins.

This exchange settles each character on a different course of action. Mimi suddenly resolves that she might as well go out, have fun and enjoy life because one day she will die anyway, but what is the point waiting for death to overtake her? Jacqueline decides that rather than torture herself waiting for the Palladists to finally catch up with her, she will take her own life.

A classic shot deftly puts together these dichotomous resolutions without a word, showing a well-dressed, happier, healthier Mimi leaving to go out and passing Jacqueline's door, behind which we hear the sound of a chair falling over. Robson's shot is simplicity itself and all the more chillingly effective for it.

The death of Jacqueline allows Mary and Gregory to happily get together as they have become enamored of each other. The film ends with the John Donne quote that begins it: "I run to Death and Death meets me as fast, and all my Pleasures are like Yesterday."

The film is very quiet and understated, a poetic rumination on not letting the loneliness and indifference of life in a big city lead to despair. There is something restrained but intelligent about it, and as a portrait of a woman's growing unease it compares favorably with Polanski's *Rosemary's Baby*. Still, the poetry and romanticism left some viewers cold, and the film does suffer a bit from some post-production editing in which story points about minor characters were trimmed. Yet the resulting ambiguity makes parts of the film all the more intriguing.

In addition to Robson's sensitive direction, the film benefits from its evocative script, Nicholas Musuraca's moody photography, and the excellent production design of Albert S. D'Agostino and Walter E. Keller, who go a great way toward disguising the small budget and creating suitably claustrophobic rooms.

Robson's next project for Lewton, *The Ghost Ship*, must be considered something of a "lost" film, the result of an unexpectedly successful plagiarism suit brought against it which resulted in the film being withdrawn from circulation. Fortunately, a few 16mm television prints were struck, but the film itself is rarely viewed.

The plot of *The Ghost Ship* concerns a homicidal ship captain and has been compared to Jack London's *The Sea Wolf*, but in fact the script was not based on that work. The film centers around Tom Merriam (Russell Wade), a young man who signs on as third officer of the *Altair*. He is warned against going aboard the ship by a mute sailor (Skelton Knaggs) who spends a lot of time sharpening a knife. From time to time we hear the mute sailor's poetic thoughts on the situation. (In one particularly memorable speech, the sailor muses, "I see the white steel thirsting for blood and the blood running to meet it. I am a Finn and my soul is in my hand here, white and cold and knowing all things." It was just such beautifully wrought lines that got Lewton dubbed as being overly literary.)

The danger aboard the ship is Captain Stone (Richard Dix), a strong man who commands the respect of the crew. A man turns up dead, but no one thinks anything of it. Tom warns Stone about a hook that needs to be secured and in the film's tautest sequence, the hook comes loose during a storm and wreaks havoc, but luckily no one is seriously injured. The captain, who will not admit to anything that might weaken his men's faith in him, passes the blame for the incident onto Tom. Tom also has to help the captain when he is unable to perform an appendectomy following instructions over the radio because of his fear of failure.

A sailor named Louie (Lawrence Tierney) makes some complaints to the captain, who obviously does not relish the criticism. Tom discovers that Stone has jammed a door that Louie needs to get out through after scrubbing the chain lock, where the anchor chain is stored. When the anchor is released, Louie is crushed because his cries for help cannot be heard over the rattling of the descending chain. (Robert Wise used an almost identical bit in his film *The Sand Pebbles*.)

When the ship docks, Tom complains, but he lacks evidence and the crew support the captain, having no knowledge of Tom's helpful actions. That night he is shanghaied back aboard and practically made a prisoner in his own cabin. The captain becomes increasingly psychotic, killing Tom's friend (Edmund Glover) because he refuses to broadcast that Tom is not aboard. Finally, the mute sailor and his knife come to Tom's rescue at a crucial and climactic moment.

The film is not really a horror film as it is sometimes classified, but it is an intelligent thriller about a psychotic and is expertly directed by Robson, who shows his Welles influence in the use of low angle shots, steam and mist, and in fluid movements of the camera. In some ways, the film is reminiscent of *Journey into Fear*. It is aided by an able cast that includes Lewton regulars Sir Lancelot and Ben Bard.

Robson's next Lewton film was *Youth Runs Wild*, a sanctimonious piece about the problem of juvenile delinquency due to the disruption of family life caused by World War II with fathers fighting overseas and mothers working in factories. It is interesting in that it faced a genuine American social problem at a time when all Hollywood films promoted only how wonderful America was and how its goodnesss meant that it was destined to win the big one. The film suffers, however, from a weak script and never pleased Lewton, though esteemed critic James Agee accorded it accolades as one of the best pictures of its year because of its daring.

Robson returned to horror with *Isle of the Dead*, a film that came about because RKO had signed a contract to do three films with Boris Karloff. Initially, this worried Lewton because he wanted his films to be naturalistic while Karloff was associated with flamboyant horror, but he found Karloff to be a sophisticated gentleman and the pair hit it off splendidly, so much so that Karloff once referred to Lewton as the man who had rescued him from the living dead and restored his soul.

Meanwhile, the head of RKO's B film production unit became Jack Gross, who, perhaps after the dismal showing of *Youth Runs Wild*, insisted that Lewton's next film have no messages. Lewton or Robson – the stories differ – called back to say that their new film based on the Boecklin painting "Isle of the Dead" did have a message – "Death is good."

Robson also turned to Goya's drawings of the Iberian campaign from his "Disasters of War" for visual inspiration on how to depict the ravaged battlefield that opens the film. A large cyclorama was borrowed from *The Enchanted Cottage*, and a few extras are positioned as corpses amid wreckage that a general (Karloff) wanders through, implicitly commenting on the awful waste of war.

Unfortunately, after this brief scene, the first half of the film becomes an utter bore, partly because a longer and more complex and poetic screenplay was junked just prior to shooting. The hastily assembled one meant to take its place gives its main characters very little to do after the general, a reporter, a British consul and his wife and some others are trapped on a Greek island in an effort to avoid spreading a windblown plague. Meanwhile, they while away the time and hear of a peasant legend concerning *vorvolakas*, demons that possess the dead. The natives suspect that the vorvolakas are responsible for the graves that have been rifled, but the general knows that it is simply greedy men who are responsible and vows that he will find them and punish them. People begin dying of the plague, but a superstitious old woman insists once more that a vorvolaka is responsible.

When the consul's wife (Katherine Emery) lapses into catalepsy, it is assumed that she too has died of the plague and so she is promptly entombed. Suddenly the dull film comes to life in an effectively eerie set piece where water dropping on the coffin lid revives the woman, who is driven mad by her premature entombment. Wandering about somnambulistically in a white nightgown, she is easily mistaken for a vorvolaka come back from the grave.

In the meantime, the superstitious crone has convinced the general that an ailing Ellen Drew is in fact a vorvolaka and responsible for the deaths. Emery shows up and kills the old woman and Karloff just in time to save Drew from death and then commits suicide (murder could not go unpunished in old Hollywood films). The threat of the plague ends and the survivors go home.

It is indeed unfortunate that *Isle of the Dead* is so dull for most of its length as the finale ranks with the best moments of horror cinema. The last portion is cinematic, poetic, exciting, atmospheric—but it comes too late to save the film from a general tediousness.

Luckily, the same cannot be said for the next Robson/Karloff combination, *Bedlam*. Once more inspired by a painting, this time William Hogarth's engraving "Bedlam" that was one of the plates from "A Rake's Progress," the resulting film comes close to matching the excellence of Robert Wise's *The Body Snatcher*, though it is less well known.

The film is a beautifully put together historical work that serves as an indictment of the treatment of the insane during the so-called "Age of

Reason." It has its modern applications as well (today's asylum inhabitants tend to be drugged rather than beaten). The story also serves to promote a view of compassion for all mankind versus the view that men are sometimes beasts and must be treated brutally by necessity.

The compassionate side of this dichotomy is represented by a Quaker named Hannay (Richard Fraser), while the opposite view is expounded articulately by Master Sims (Boris Karloff), the Apothecary General of the Hospital of St. Mary of Bethlehem, better known as Bedlam, the insane asylum. In between is the heroine Nell Bowen (Anna Lee in a feisty and spirited performance), who at first lives only for her own pleasure, but after a sign of compassion for the unfortunates, comes to be convinced by Hannay's philosophy.

Karloff gives a superb performance as Master Sims, full of subtle shadings as we see him alternately toadying to the buffoonish Lord Mortimer (Billy House) or menacing Bowen. Sims is a proud and intelligent man who prizes wit and curries the favor of the gentry as a means of achieving what little esteem he can be granted. Time and again, he shows himself to be quick-witted and cunning, and if his position is threatened, capable of being absolutely ruthless.

The lively Nell is an interesting character because initially she is shown to be rather flawed, exhibiting capriciousness and ill-mannered enough to call Master Sims ugly to his face, even striking him with a riding crop when her fury takes the better of her. Because she vacillates between selfishness and altruism, she is more complex and interesting than the typical, impossibly "pure" Hollywood heroine.

The screenplay by Robson and Carlos Keith (Lewton's pseudonym) has the qualities of a good Restoration play with its intellectual arguments neatly crafted to be proved in the action of the film. The performances are uniformly excellent; Karloff and Lee are standouts, though Fraser deserves praise for keeping his portrayal of the Quaker human rather than stuffy and House enacts a fatuous Lord perfectly. Also Ian Wolfe deserves special kudos for his portrayal of Sidney Long, the seemingly most rational of the asylum inmates who every once in a while betrays an inner indignation that his "many enemies" have been able to commit him, "the greatest of all!"

Robson and Lewton obviously strove hard to present a class production on a minimal budget, and they succeeded admirably. It is interesting to note certain economy measures, such as reusing the church from *The Bells of St. Mary's* as Bedlam and Lee wearing one of Vivien Leigh's dresses from *Gone with the Wind*. Robson himself was particularly proud of having found a building with leaded glass and putting a candle behind each panel, converting the interior into a barber shop for one attractive shot. Also interesting is his device of dissolving to and from a Hogarth engraving between sequences to set the mood for the following scene.

The film establishes Bedlam as a place of danger from its opening scene in which a man trying to escape has his fingers stepped on by a guard and falls to his death. Because the man was a poet who owed Lord Mortimer several verses when he died, the incensed Mortimer summons Master Sims to see him the next morning.

Kept waiting for hours and all but forgotten, Sims craftily manages to restore Mortimer's good spirits by offering to write the verses himself and put on a play for his upcoming party by using inmates from his asylum as actors, which strikes Mortimer as a capital jest. Nell is none too taken with the idea, but Mortimer insists that she must go down to Bedlam and see the "funny" things the inmates do. (Sims has been charging an admission of tuppence for the "entertainment.")

Nell goes, but rather than laughing at the pitiful spectacle of lunatics who are treated as animals and lack proper beds and clothings, she is appalled and moved to pity. A Quaker, Hannay, whom Sims offered to employ in exchange for a kickback, observes her distress and suggests she could do something to improve these wretches' lot. Nell denies feeling pity, but hating Sims, decides to persuade Lord Mortimer to makes changes in order to annoy Sims.

Sims manages to counter the implied criticism of how he has been running the establishment by pointing out that such changes will require a great increase in taxes and end up costing Lord Mortimer a lot of money. When Mortimer backs down, Nell becomes incensed and lets slip the contempt she really feels for Mortimer, who in turn kicks her out and sends his men to reclaim all the furniture he has given her.

A previous scene illustrated how cruelly the inmates were treated even out of their prison. For Mortimer's Tory party Sims has an inmate painted over with gold portray Reason and deliver lines which Sims had "beat into" him all morning. The frightened, confused and suffocating inmate dies (the gold paint has covered his pores) before he can finish the recitation praising Mortimer (the same unusual method of death was later used in the film *Goldfinger*). The guests who attend see nothing tragic in the youth's demise and laugh as other inmates are brought on to perform a play, but Nell finds herself appalled and deeply disgusted with this lack of humanity.

Nell decides to get back at Mortimer by putting up "for sale" her parrot which has been taught an insulting rhyme in the marketplace so that everyone in town will hear of it. She refuses Master Sims' offer of 20 pounds and Lord Mortimer's offer of 100 guineas for it. Sims brings his niece (Elizabeth Russell) by to find favor with Mortimer, warning her to drink only wine, but before long she's helping herself to some good English gin.

After the pair try to bribe Nell to keep her from causing additional embarrassment (to which she responds by putting the bribe between two pieces of bread and taking a bite out of it), Sims convinces Mortimer that to save face, he must have her committed to Bedlam, even though they both know she is sane. (It is suggested that it was not an uncommon practice for a man to dispose of an unwanted wife in this fashion.) Sims railroads a board of inquiry into committing her when she cannot explain to their satisfaction why she refuses 100 guineas for a parrot worth five shillings and why she ate the bribe.

Her late-night entry into this world of madness is truly terrifying. She cannot make out the shapes that move in the darkness and never knows when hands will thrust out of a cage at her. Equally maddening is that some of the inmates will pick up and imitate any name which is called out on the street, and Nell hears her name when outside. Hannay seeks to find out what happened to her.

Finally, after helping some workmen who are building a wall inside the asylum, Hannay finds Nell, who insists that he give her a weapon for her protection. As a Quaker, he keeps no such weapon, but he does have a mason's trowel which he reluctantly grants her. Hannay then departs to seek out Nell's lawyer friend (Leyland Hidgson) to free her, but the lawyer is presently out of town.

Feeling lonely, Nell befriends Sidney Long, a former lawyer himself, and his associates who desire a fourth hand in playing faro. However, Nell finds she cannot play because one inmate is moaning due to his chains biting in to his skin. She goes to the inmate and puts clothing between him and his chains, but her trowel is mysteriously stolen in the process.

Sims comes the next day and berates her for not attempting any of the reforms for the asylum once she is on the inside. He notes that she congregates only with a few of the lunatics, those from the middle and upper classes. She responds to his taunts by becoming a ministering angel in the place, even going so far as to enter the cage of a vicious brute man that she is afraid of rather than conceding to Sims' perception of some of mankind being fit only for treatment as beasts.

The film reaches a climax when Hannay finally reaches the lawyer who arranges for Nell to have a new hearing. Fearing the worst, Sims enters the asylum intending to torture her so that she will not be able to stand up under the inquest. The inmates, remembering her many acts of kindness, fly to her aid, banding together and overcoming their jailer. Because of his barbarous treatment of them, they decide to try him for his sanity. Long volunteers to be the judge and inquisitor.

During the melee, Nell is able to escape with the help of the brute she befriended who lifts her out an unguarded window. Meanwhile, Sims pleads in his defense that he acted cruelly towards the inmates because he was frightened of displeasing the men who put him in charge and expected him to maintain control by beating the lunatics and spending as little money on them as possible. As a result of Sims' pitiable portrait of himself as a cringing toady and an intelligent man forced to make a mockery of himself, they pardon his fear without condoning it and judge him sane.

However, while they agree to let him go, a strangely staring woman whom Sims had patted suggestively on the cheek and called his "dove" suddenly removes the missing trowel from under her cloak and stabs him. Believing Sims to be dead and fearing reprisals, the lunatics band together and decide to hide the body behind a brick wall which they build in a narrow alcove. Sims revives from the shock of his wound only to see the last brick put in place and is thereby walled in alive!

The next day Hannay and Nell visit the asylum and Hannay notices the change and the fresh mortar between the bricks. Nell, finally won over to feeling compassion for her fellow man, begs him not to say anything to the authorities. Hannay assures her that he will not add to the burden of the lunatics by volunteering any information about Sims' murder. The film ends noting that conditions for the insane subsequently improved.

Shot in a mere month, the film is beautifully photographed by Nicholas Musuraca, who does wonders inside the asylum with light and shadow. *Bedlam* represents the last flowering of Lewton's talent at RKO and the last time he was given relative autonomy over the production with his hand-picked team of craftsmen. Lewton would have only one more film of note, the underrated *Apache Drums*, before dying of a heart attack at the age of 46.

On the other hand, Robson's star was rising, and his next films, *Champion* and *Home of the Brave*, received A budgets and were highly acclaimed. (*Home of the Brave* is a particularly powerful little film about a black soldier driven insane because of racism and remained one of Robson's favorites of his films. The film was a financial success and opened the way for more films starring blacks in major roles.)

At this point, Robson pretty much left horror behind him, though *Edge of Doom* is worthy of note. In that film, Farley Granger plays an impoverished young man who becomes embittered by the Catholic church when it refuses to grant services for his father because he was a suicide, and really loses his marbles and kills a priest (Harold Vermilyea) when he cannot come to terms over his mother's death. Perhaps in an effort to keep the Catholic church from seeming too unfeeling in the film, Charles Vidor shot some additional scenes which serve as a framing story in which Father Roth (Dana Andrews) is telling the story of the film to a novice priest in order to demonstrate by Granger's confession at the end of the film that conscience has triumphed over fear and despair—though that interpretation does not quite jibe with the way in which Robson shot it. (Granger only confesses because he knows that Andrews knows he is guilty, and he begs to be allowed to attend his mother's funeral.)

Also of note was Robson's famed anti-boxing story, *The Harder They*

Director Mark Robson gives instructions to Ava Gardner in Earthquake, *a bloated epic that is a long way from the tight little thrillers Robson used to direct for Val Lewton, though equally as uneven.*

Fall, starring Humphrey Bogart. Based on the career of Primo Carnera, that film, after showing how the mob has exploited a would-be pugilist and ends up giving him a pittance, ends with a plea to outlaw boxing. Robson was not afraid to be controversial and was one of the most outspoken opponents of HUAC and the blacklist among directors in the '50s.

While Robson came to be associated with big-budget, risqué productions like *Peyton Place* and *Valley of the Dolls*, he also crafted some nifty thrillers like *Nine Hours to Rama* (about the events that led to the assassination of Mahatma Gandhi) and *Daddy's Gone a-Hunting* (in which a psychopath kidnaps his ex-lover's daughter and leads the police on a tension-filled chase throughout San Francisco).

His last four films were an unexciting, anti–Vietnam piece centering on

three wives waiting for their husbands (*Limbo*); two science fiction films—
one an unsatisfying adaptation of Kurt Vonnegut's play *Happy Birthday,
Wanda June* and the other a what-if disaster film with a memorable finale,
Earthquake; and *Avalanche Express*, a dull spy thriller about CIA agents
hoping to get information from the KGB about a biological warfare scheme.
Robson had just finished filming this last work when he suffered his fatal
heart attack.

Robson was a versatile and talented filmmaker who never tied himself
down to a single genre or theme. As a result, many critics proved as blind
to his virtues as the hero in *Bright Victory* (in which Arthur Kennedy plays
a soldier who can only perceive some people as human after he has been
blinded). Robson may not have been an important artist, but he was a gifted
craftsman who was knowledgeable both about the technical end of shooting
a film and about guiding his actors through some excellent performances.
He deserves respect for the many fine films that he did create, and only his
Goldwyn period, with the exception of *Edge of Doom*, lacks something of interest to the discerning cineaste.

George A. Romero (1940–   )

Night of the Living Dead (1968); *There's Always Vanilla* (1972); *Jack's Wife* (aka *Hungry Wives; Season of the Witch*); *The Crazies* (aka *Code Name; Trixie*) (1973); *Martin* (1978); *Dawn of the Dead* (1979); *Knightriders* (1981); *Creepshow* (1982); *Day of the Dead* (1985); *Monkey Shines* (1988); *Two Evil Eyes* (codirected with Dario Argento, 1990).

TELEVISION: "Lou Brock: The Thief," "Franco Harris: Good Luck on Sunday," "Reggie Jackson: One-Man Wild Bunch," "NFL Films: The 27th Team," "Johnny Rutherford: The Eleven Year Odyssey," "Bruno Sammartino: Strong Man," "O. J. Simpson: Juice on the Loose," "Willie Stargell: What If I Didn't Play Baseball?," "Tom Weiskoff: On Tour," "The WFL Story," *The Winners* (1973–76).

In its own quiet way, George A. Romero's first feature film, *Night of the Living Dead*, revolutionized the modern horror film. The film was initially distributed by the Walter Reade Organization and was largely ignored except for a scathing review in *Variety*. Gradually word of mouth spread from people who had seen it at a drive-in or a 42nd Street theatre. Roger Ebert wrote a famed *Reader's Digest* article attacking parents for irresponsibly leaving children at a theater playing the film without checking out the film's gruesome (for that time) contents. Slowly, this whetted the appetite of horror fans until *Night of the Living Dead* became *the* horror film to check out in the early '70s.

The film was interesting for a number of reasons. For one, it had a unique and somber mood – this was not an energetic jaunt in Transylvania, it smacked of real-life despair and depression. The heroine, Barbara (Judith O'Dea), goes into shock and becomes catatonic after the half-humorous, half-horrific assault by a cemetery zombie (Bill Hinzman) which attacks her after her brother Johnny (Russell Streiner) jokingly warns, "He's coming to get you, Barbara," in mocking, Karloffian tones. Then the zombie winds up murdering Johnny instead. Not content with Johnny's death, the zombie relentlessly follows a very frightened Barbara to her car and tries to smash it open. In trying to escape, she smashes the car herself and seeks refuge in a nearby farmhouse where she meets a newcomer, Ben (Duane Jones), a black pickup truck driver.

Qualities which make the film different from the run-of-the-mill horror

636

Publicity still of an introspective George A. Romero, Pittsburgh's most famous artistic export.

film of the time include the absence of a love story and the sheer relentlessness of the plot. Even if the zombies are not always attacking, they are always out there ready to attack, while tensions inside the farmhouse start to build as a young and an old couple are discovered in the house's cellar. While Romero makes use of Hitchcockian angles and cutting, the overall tone of the film is like a matter-of-fact documentary, a "you are there" quality that helps viewers identify with the protagonists' plight. In terms of graphicness, the scenes of the zombies chowing down on human meat were unparalleled for the time; Romero obviously was not pulling any of his punches.

It is obvious that Romero's primary intention was to concoct the toughest zombie film ever made. A lot of nonsense has been written about how the zombie hordes represent everything from the silent majority to returning Vietnam vets in attempts to explain the film's incredible popularity. While the film does have its interesting, intriguing and well-thought-out aspects, it was obviously popular because *Night of the Living Dead* was one of the few horror films that really delivered the goods in terms of giving the audience a memorable fright.

Romero and scriptwriter John Russo based their premise on Richard Matheson's classic horror novel *I Am Legend*, about a man trapped in a world of vampires, which has been flaccidly filmed twice (with Vincent Price as *The Last Man on Earth* by Sidney Salkow and with Charlton Heston and Christ imagery in Boris Segal's *The Omega Man*). In looks, the zombies resembled those in Edward L. Cahn's *Invisible Invaders*, and they are not harder to get away from than your average movie mummy.

Which brings about one of the film's points: These characters die largely because of their own fear. The zombie menaces are neither quick-witted nor quick-moving, and only their sheer numbers make them dangerous; nevertheless, time and again the protagonists do not take elementary precautions and die because of actions derived from panic and fear.

One way in which the film is cannily of its time is that its seeming main hero is black and very much his own man. Frequently opposing him is Harry Cooper (Karl Hardman, one of the film's producers), a loudmouthed white man who resents Ben taking charge and whose first priority is to save his own neck. Because of these cross-racial arguments, many critics assumed that Cooper was a bigot, though at no time does he use racial epithets. In fact, Ben's race was not specified by the script and Jones was cast simply because he gave the best audition; the arguments between the characters are not racially motivated. (However, it should be noted that subsequently, Romero has been very good about giving heroic major roles to black performers, especially in the other two films of the *Dead* trilogy.)

The film also launches Romero's major theme, that of the dangers of a lack of communication. Ben and Harry argue, but they do not really listen to each other; rather they end up trading insults. If they had worked together, they might have survived, but Ben becomes firmly convinced that Harry is wrong and "stupid." Their bickering only ends up endangering them more until Ben becomes so fed up with Harry that he kills him.

Ironically, while Ben wins our sympathy with his apparent clearheadedness and his ability to take charge, viewed objectively he makes one critical blunder after another. He refuses to barricade himself in the cellar from which there would be no escape (but where there would be only one entrance to defend) and insists on trying to defend the entire house, which could be attacked from a number of points. Almost everyone dies by trying to follow Ben's plan of action. He stupidly leaves a flame near gasoline which results in the immolation of Tom (Keith Wayne) and Judy (Judith Ridley) as they try to steal a truck to escape in. Finally, Ben himself survives by following Harry's advice to hide in the cellar as the ghouls overrun the house.

Romero subverts the normal order by having the dead come back to life. Respect for the dead must be replaced by respect for the living. Still, when the Coopers' daughter Karen (Kyra Schon) dies, mother Helen (Marilyn Eastman) does not handle the situation properly according to the instructions they hear on the television and is stabbed to death by her zombified daughter who uses a garden trowel. Not even the American family is sacred as children attack their parents.

Standard horror devices abound, from dramatic lighting of tense faces to the use of trapped characters in a restricted environment as well as assorted shocks and "busses." There are even black humorous moments to relieve the horror, particularly a television interview with Sheriff McClelland (George Kosana) in which he matter-of-factly describes how the flesh-eating ghouls will be dealt with. "Beat 'em or burn 'em," he says, "they go up pretty easy. . . . They're dead. They're all messed up."

One of the longest lasting of Romero's innovations is that his zombies are flesh-eaters. This was even more played upon after the success of *Dawn of the Dead*, the European success of which spawned an entire industry of Italian imitators. The other is the film's downbeat ending, which came almost as a surprise in a period where most horror films ended with a hopeful restoring of the natural order. The ironic twist of having Ben mistaken for a zombie and shot in the head had a definite impact as the film ended with still shots of the redneck posse piling up the bodies of zombies they have shot in the head (the only way of killing the dead) and setting them on fire. American International had been offered the film but had refused to distribute it with the downbeat ending that Romero insisted upon.

Some people complain about the acting in the early Romero films, and with some justification, but while many thought that Karl Hardman overplayed his part, he does capture the feeling of an overwrought man who has not come to grips with his world falling apart, and he makes a good counterpoint to Duane Jones beautifully underplaying his. Jones' Ben is more appealing because he has a cooler head and is more in control, but when Harry steals his gun rather than help him fight off the zombie attackers, Jones reveals the rage his character keeps contained by blasting Harry in front of his wife's horrified eyes.

George Andrew Romero was born on February 4, 1940, and as a child grew up in the Bronx. His secret passions were E. C. horror comics and movies, and he worked as a gofer on Hitchcock's *North by Northwest*. In 1954, he made an 8mm movie, *The Man from the Meteor*, based on Edgar

Ulmer's *The Man from Planet X*, followed by a would-be jungle epic called *Gorilla*.

Romero had his first real taste of freedom after he left home and started attending Carnegie-Mellon University in Pittsburgh. There, with a group of friends, he founded Latent Image, a production company that specialized in commercials. Romero developed his knowledge of filmmaking skills, serving as a cinematographer or editor on Latent's productions.

Saving up money from commercial assignments, Latent Image began to plot its first feature by forming a group of ten people who called themselves Image Ten. Filming the black-and-white feature on weekends and deferring lab bills of about $60,000, they made *Night of the Living Dead* for a total of $114,000. The film collected millions on the distribution circuits through drive-in and midnight screenings.

However, very little of that money made its way back to the film's creators as the Walter Reade Organization ended up bankrupt. Due to an oversight, a copyright line was not added to the picture, leaving many video companies to assume that the film was in the public domain. Innumerable copies were thus issued on videocassette. Recently, the film's copyright was established in court, but it was too late to recoup the losses on the film. Romero had old friend Tom Savini remake the film in 1990 to reimburse the original investors.

Nevertheless, the film succeeded in establishing Romero, and he proceeded with plans to make other kinds of independently produced films. Romero wanted to show how versatile he was by making *There's Always Vanilla* (aka *The Affair*), a formless film about modern aimless youth. The project proved a disaster; perhaps a clue to the reason lies in Romero's admission that there really was no script during shooting.

Romero followed this with *Jack's Wife* (aka *Hungry Wives*, released on video as *Season of the Witch* after the Donovan Leitch song), a film about a frustrated housewife who ends up involved with witchcraft. (The same kind of premise led to an excellent film, *Burn Witch Burn*, based on Fritz Leiber's classic novel *Conjure Wife*.) Joan Mitchell stars as a woman who fears that the magic has gone out of her life – she cannot communicate with her husband, her daughter, or even her religion (Catholicism). Her dreams emphasize her feelings of frustration and helplessness.

After going with a fellow housewife to see a witch, she becomes intrigued with witchcraft. This interest increases with the appearance of her daughter's suitor, a young college professor that Mitchell takes an interest in. She starts casting spells in an effort to secure him for herself. However, as she becomes more involved, she becomes less able to distinguish fantasy from reality, and Romero leaves the effectiveness of her spells clouded in ambiguity. The film ends with her killing her dull husband and then exchanging one label, "Jack's wife," for another, "witch."

Jack's Wife is a film with ideas, but they are not excitingly presented. Additionally, Romero suffered the frustration of losing a major portion of his financing right before production. This early feminist film failed to catch on and has been largely forgotten.

More success from an artistic standpoint was Romero's next film, *The Crazies* (aka *Code Name: Trixie*). The film is a fairly intelligent though not fully fleshed-out treatment of the effects of a biochemical disaster on a small town. Once more, Romero's theme of the lack of communication is very much to the fore. In order to keep a lid on the disaster, the Pentagon tries cover-up after cover-up, without seeming to realize that if you put a lid on a volatile situation, it will begin to boil.

Following a plane crash that released a disease that causes carriers to go crazy, the army informs a few authority figures in a small town to look out for people who might be running mysteriously high temperatures. When the problem is revealed to be more serious than that (the film opens with a man killing his wife, attacking his children, and setting his house on fire), the whole town is quarantined and martial law is instituted.

Time after time, vital information is not transmitted because of blocks set up by military procedure. In one of the film's most effective ironies, a scientist finally discovers a possible vaccine but is fed up with having to wait for "voice print identification" before he can get his message through. He decides to attempt to leave the high school where the townspeople are heavily guarded by the military to the military base set up across the street. Just as he leaves the laboratory without telling his assistant what his discovery is, the crowd breaks through the guards and pandemonium reigns until the soldiers quell the crowd. In the process, the scientist is killed, dropping the test samples of blood that held the secret.

With their gas masks and protective clothing, the soldiers do not look like anything human and have been instructed to keep order no matter what the cost. The increasingly infected populace grows more irritated at being kept in the dark (as many of the soldiers themselves are, not having been briefed by their higher-ups – Romero does not conveniently paint anyone connected with the army as being in the wrong, as the soldiers are just as much victims of the system as the townspeople). Eventually, the populace begins to retaliate with guns and force.

The basic story was concocted by Paul McCollough as an allegory questioning the basic level of sanity in the world. Romero refashioned the script to focus the situation around some basic points of view and to provide plenty of action. Primarily, we follow a young nurse named Judy (Lane Carroll) and her boyfriend, David (W. G. McMillan), whom she hopes to inoculate. (This later proves unnecessary as David turns out to be naturally immune to the disease, called "Trixie" for some unknown but possibly significant reason.) They are joined in their attempt to escape the unexpected quarantine by their friends Clank (Harold Wayne Jones), Artie (Richard Liberty) and his daughter Kathie (Lynn Lowry). Both Artie and Kathie begin to exhibit signs of the disease, with Kathie becoming more "out of it" and Artie starting to come on to and then attack his daughter. Stopped before he rapes her, he hangs himself in remorse. Clank's head proves not too tightly screwed on when he viciously obliterates an inoffensive group of soldiers waiting in a farmhouse.

Meanwhile, the soldiers are having difficulty herding up the seemingly ordinary townfolk, many of whom are infected but show no outward signs until approached. Perhaps the most remembered moment in the film is when a soldier comes to escort a kindly looking grandmother to the high school only for her to stab him with her knitting needles, smiling sweetly all the while.

The local invasion force is headed by Col. Peckham (Lloyd Hollar), a take-charge black in the mode of Ben from *Night of the Living Dead*, but he is only able to exert control, not to solve or fully contain the problem. In many ways, military snafus tie his hands before he has even begun, and the film ends with his being reassigned to a new town where the same infection pattern has started all over again. There is even talk of bombing the town (and thereby the infection) out of existence with an atomic weapon (the same kind of a device that Dan O'Bannon proposed and used later in *Return of the Living Dead*).

The film effectively makes its points about the potential danger of such a situation and how it could be mishandled. However, with the constantly shifting points of view, we never get to know any of the characters terribly well, and this lack of characterization keeps the film from becoming as powerful as it might have been. Still, while not on the level of a *Night of the Living Dead*, the film is above average for a science fiction/horror thriller.

Nevertheless, the film did not succeed in attracting an audience due to unsuccessful marketing by its small-time distributor, Cambist Films. The film did lead to Romero being introduced to Richard P. Rubinstein, and together the pair formed a production company called Laurel that initially produced sports documentaries for ABC.

This work kept Romero busy, but by 1976, he was anxious to get back into doing feature films. His next film became one of his favorites, *Martin*, which made an unsuccessful bid at capturing the cult/midnight film crowd in 1978 and was given only a limited release by its distributor, Libra Films.

Martin is a troubling, interesting and unusual although not entirely successful work. Romero derived his premise from the idea of the difficulties that a modern-day vampire would face coupled with the report of a murderer who believed he was a vampire.

It is a film about suffocated lives. Martin is a troubled teen who dreams of being a genuine gothic vampire and who is unable to communicate well with other people. He lives with his grandfather Cuda (Lincoln Maazel), who believes he really is a vampire and who laments that things are not the same as they were in "the old country." Cuda's granddaughter Christina (Christine Forrest, later Romero's wife) is desperate to get out of the suffocating household and pins her hopes on her boyfriend, Arthur (Tom Savini, who also did the film's makeup effects).

In many ways, the film is like *Jack's Wife* only with a male lead. Whether Martin has any supernatural powers is kept ambiguous, but it is easy to believe that he does. (Possessing no hypnotic powers or fangs, he injects his victims with a knockout drug and then uses a razor to slice their wrists to get at their blood.) Martin is also sexually repressed, indicated by his having necrophiliac-style sex with his unconscious female victims.

He is a very complex character for a horror film, but by and large not a sympathetic one, especially at the film's opening where we see him attack one of his victims aboard a train. The film, shot in 16mm and then blown up, is ugly and often slowly paced. Martin's only contact with the outside world is as a caller on a late-night talk show, where he is dubbed "the Count" and relates his vampiric experiences to the amusement of the deejay.

The performances in the film are often amateurish and uneven, which also reduces its power. Nonetheless, Romero does not lose his humorous or ironic touches entirely. There is a prolonged and amusing sequence where Martin waits at a house for a husband to leave, planning to attack the wife, only to surprise the wife and her lover in bed. Martin is finally done in when, after being seduced by Mrs. Santini (Elayne Nadeau) and having normal sex for the first time, he discovers that she committed suicide. His grandfather also discovers this and vows to put a stop to the plague, staking Martin in the tragic finale (though Romero adds a strange coda where the "Count" can be heard talking on the airwaves once more – is Martin really dead?).

There is no question that Romero has taken an offbeat approach to the horror genre, but while it may be possible to feel sorry for Martin, as played by John Amplas he is a sullen character who only brightens when he displays parlor-room magic for Christine. (In a reversal on *Jack's Wife*, Cuda believes in real magic, while Martin dons a phony cape and fangs at one point to convince him that magic is basically fake, that there is no magic.) The result is somber and depressing, not horrifying or exciting.

Romero's big break came when he decided to do a sequel to *Night of the Living Dead*, something long anticipated after the enormous success of the first film. While visiting a potential backer at a shopping mall in Monroeville, Pennsylvania, Romero had the idea of setting the sequel in such a mall. He wrote half a script and started looking for financing for a projected $1.5 million picture.

The half-completed script was looked at by an Italian producer named Alfredo Cuomo, who passed it along to Dario Argento. Argento, along with his brother Claudio and Cuomo, agreed to put up half of the film's budget in exchange for all foreign rights in non–English-speaking parts of the world excepting South America. Romero then revised the script while his partner Rubinstein finished raising the financing.

The result was quite a departure from *Night of the Living Dead* in overall style and tone. The tenseness generated from the small, enclosed surroundings of the farmhouse was replaced by the sprawling openness of the mall. Rather than film one particularly memorable revolting scene, Romero and his makeup artist Tom Savini decided to devise the most graphic "splatter" effects they could imagine and scattered them all throughout the script.

The use of these effects had two results. One, it ensured that if the film were rated, it would be given an X for its violence, but X had long since been associated exclusively with pornographic sex films, which the new film, *Dawn of the Dead*, certainly was not. As a result, the decision was made to release the film without an MPAA rating. This decision, while courageous, was also a necessity if the film was to be distributed, as many newspapers across the country refused to advertise X-rated films, and newspapers still are the primary means by which theater information is given to the public. *Dawn of the Dead* certainly was not going to appeal to everyone in the public, but it did have to be advertised widely so that its selected audience could find it.

Secondly, the effects launched the new vogue of "splatter" movies that carried over into the '80s, with *Day of the Dead* ironically being one of the last examples. There had been gruesome, gore-oriented films in the United States before, most notably those of Herschel Gordon Lewis, but they had played only in small regional markets and were not offered to the mainstream. Potentially very gruesome films like *The Texas Chainsaw Massacre* and *Halloween* were, in fact, rather restrained in their depiction of onscreen gore. *Dawn of the Dead* was the first American horror film with a substantial budget to really paint the walls red and show a graphic disemboweling as one of the film's "highlights."

The blood Tom Savini chose was a particularly bright and not very convincing shade of red and the victims were more often zombies than human beings; nevertheless, the film made a powerful impact when first viewed and turned many a stomach that had laughed through such horror extravaganzas as *The Exorcist*. I must admit that when I first saw the uncut version at Filmex in 1979, I was repelled by the constant violence, and while a scene of a zombie getting the top of its head sliced neatly off by a helicopter rotor can be fascinating on a "gosh, how did they do that?" level, the nonstop shooting of very human-looking people was both revolting and deadening. In a SWAT team attack on a tenement building, a bigoted cop goes berserk and blows one man's head into a million red fragments that look like the insides of an exploded watermelon. As the rather lengthy film progresses, we see people shot in the head so frequently that we begin to get used to it and it loses its shock value. However, some things should no doubt remain shocking, and perhaps some of the callousness that some of today's generation exhibit towards extreme acts of violence can be attributed to films like *Dawn of the Dead*, where watching a living biker have his intestines ripped from him is not an important dramatic point, but just part of the "entertainment."

Naturally, Romero is careful to present his tale as an absurdist fantasy with dollops of broad humor (my favorite being a Hare Krishna zombie that seems indistinguishable from a living Krishna member), and the audience realizes that it is only an elaborate and impressively staged form of make-believe, but *Dawn of the Dead* is a clear illustration of the dawning trend in which the makeup effects would replace the story as the show.

As a story, *Dawn of the Dead* is not impressively constructed, though unlike many of the imitators that followed the same path, it does have something on its mind. The posse at the end of *Night of the Living Dead* suggested that perhaps there was a good chance to control this plague which revives the dead and sends them after the living. *Dawn of the Dead* opens at a TV station where it is apparent that the plague is out of control and has spread worldwide. Society definitely appears to be doomed.

Fran (Gaylen Ross) works at the station and becomes annoyed that a director (played by Romero himself with his wife by his side) risks sending people to inoperative rescue stations. Her boyfriend, Steve (David Emge), explains to Fran that he plans to steal the traffic-report helicopter that night and tells her to join him on the roof.

Dawn of the Dead is framed by two action sequences which demonstrate that supposedly normal human beings are just as capable, if not more so, of the awful violence that the zombies inflict. In an incredible sequence of gruesome action we have the SWAT team storming the tenement at the beginning of the film, a scene which also shows a zombie graphically putting the bite on somebody and explains why the team goes to such extremes; and there is a marauder biker gang that plays macabre jokes on the zombies at the end of the film (jokes against which the zombies effectively retaliate, once the bikers' attention is divided between them and the film's protagonists).

In *Night of the Living Dead*, in imitation of Hitchcock's *The Birds*, it was intended that there be a number of explanations for the phenomenon of the dead coming back to life so that the audience would never know the real cause. However, in editing the film, only an explanation about how a NASA space probe brought back a germ was actually retained, making that the "official" explanation. In *Dawn of the Dead*, Romero rejects that explanation in place of a more "religious" one. A heroic black cop, Peter (Ken Foree), relates this apocalyptic disaster to what his voodoo priest grandfather had told him: "When there's no room left in hell, the dead will walk the earth." Mankind's evil has become so pervasive that even hell can no longer contain it, and it strikes back at mankind all over the world.

In one amusing *hommage* to the original film, the only spot on earth that does not seem overrun with the undead is Georgia, where gun-happy rednecks treat the zombies wandering the countryside as part of their own life-sized shooting gallery. The shambling zombies keeling over in longshot and the absurdity of the situation make this brief segment one of the film's most effective uses of black humor.

Peter learns from fellow cop Roger (Scott Reineger) about the rooftop helicopter escape and joins Fran, Steve and Roger in their escape attempt. They end up setting down on a mall which they decide to make their home. Here Romero lays on some heavy-handed satire about how zombies represent the new mass consumers. One character speculates that they come to the mall because of "memory, instinct . . . this place was important in their lives." Peter comments, "They don't know why – they just remember . . . remember they want to be here. They're after the *place*."

There are signs that the zombies are beginning to remember a faint bit and possibly are able to learn, signs of intelligence that they have not exhibited previously. Due to their numerical superiority, they have become the new society, the new norm.

The foursome work together, cleverly arranging trucks to block the entrances and securing the mall for themselves by eliminating the zombies still wandering there. However, the fact that the riches of the mall have little value now that society has disintegrated takes a long time to sink in for these four, who cavort and enjoy their newfound spoils as much as they can, becoming a pathetic picture of greed run rampant.

The foursome's halcyon existence is first disrupted by Roger becoming a zombie after being infected from a bite while maneuvering the trucks. He slowly and painfully dies while declaring his intention to do his best not to return as one of "them," but it is no use and Peter must put a bullet through his former friend. This is interspersed with a plea from a scientist for everyone to remain rational or everyone will be dead. The underlying theme of the film is that human foibles – bigotry, greed, jealousy, hatred, contempt – will always surface at some time and prevent people from being rational, that in effect humans will become the victims of their own instincts (a theme Romero also utilized in *Monkey Shines*).

The temporary balance in the remaining three people's lives is finally upset by the appearance of the aforementioned motorcycle gang (led by Tom Savini), which breaks into the mall and raises havoc in a series of kinetically edited gore shots and stunts. In the melee, Steve suffers a serious injury and is overtaken by the zombies before he can activate an elevator to get him to safety. With memory of Fran and Peter's hiding place intact, he leads the other zombies that have reentered the mall to the once-secret location that had served as their home base.

Peter sends Fran off to take the helicopter while he "takes care" of Steve by putting a bullet into his brain. Depressed, he contemplates suicide, but at the last moment opts for life and joins Frank aboard the helicopter while they sail off into a very uncertain future.

Perhaps as befits the middle film of a trilogy, nothing is resolved here. The living dead are still a plague and a pestilence on the land and there is not much to hope for in the couple's bleak future. The only point, apart from the entertainment of wild gore effects and seeing zombies clumping through malls to piped-in muzak, is that man must use cold-blooded reason to prevent the utter destruction of his world, a rather revisionist sentiment in light of '50s science fiction films where the unemotional, intelligent man was always suspect because of his lack of "normal" emotions and basic human drives.

The film proved a tremendous success in Europe as well as in the United States, where it is acclaimed as one of the biggest grossing independently made and released features of all time. Unquestionably, it was a breakthrough film in many ways, and its success led to Romero being able to do my personal favorite of all his films, *Knightriders*.

While not a horror film, *Knightriders* is consistently offbeat and different. It is a bit overlong at 145 minutes, but that is due to Romero trying to cram too much into a single film which is based on the Arthurian romances. The film died in the shadow of John Boorman's *Excalibur*, a beautifully realized and visually rich retelling of the Arthurian legends, which is unfortunate as both films have much to offer and are in reality quite different from each other. The problem with the Arthurian legends is that they are not one story but many which have been interconnected over the years.

Basing his ideas on the Society for Creative Anachronism and various traveling Renaissance fairs which tour the United States and recreate times past, Romero came up with a group that tries to live up to the ideals of Arthurian chivalry while raising money by performing jousts on motorcycles, rather than horses, for the tourists. The image of knights on motorcycles left the impression that it was simply another "Hell's Angels" type of film, and attendance in the opening weeks was very poor. The East Coast critics, perhaps unused to the oddball cults that spring up around California and places west, thought that the film was some sort of Aryan call to law and order and detested the film, completely missing the real points that it made.

The film centers around King Billy (Ed Harris, who is particularly charismatic in his first starring role and gives indications of his later great performances), a romantic who is fanatically devoted to the ideals that the troupe represents. He is guided in his wisdom by a mysterious black man named Merlin (Brother Blue in a mesmerizing performance) as they try to keep the troupe aware of the ideals that are their foundation in the face of difficulties they face in securing places to camp and making enough money to keep the whole thing going.

The temptation to succumb to the lure of publicity and commercialism to make some easy money is always out there and eventually becomes too much for Morgan, the Black Knight (engagingly well played by Tom Savini). The group's dream begins to fall apart after he goes off on his own.

The troupe itself is a microcosm of misfits who do not fit in regular society but as part of this roadie Camelot can be true to themsevles. These include a gay master of ceremonies (Warner Shook), a tough female knight named Rocky (Cynthia Adler), and Morgan's girlfriend, Angie (Chris Romero), the grease monkey who keeps the bikes in repair and the show going. Together they grant each other the dignity and respect they deserve but which they could not find in society at large due to their not conforming to prescribed roles.

The motorcycle jousts that Romero stages are action-packed and exciting, good come-on for a story with deeper intentions and significance. Horror author Stephen King made his screen debut playing an obnoxious boor in the audience who speculates on how contrived and faked everything is (which it pointedly is not).

Eventually, Morgan finds that "selling out" was not as fun as he thought it was going to be and returns to the troupe to accomplish his dream of challenging Billy and becoming the new king. While always a good jouster, by discovering how shallow and unfulfilling life in the fast lane outside the troupe could be, Morgan learns the value of the ideals that Billy has been trying to instill in him. Morgan beats Billy's champions and finally Billy himself, and true to the code, becomes the new king and a better person than he was before.

Satisfied that all is as it should be, Billy leaves the troupe to take care of some unfinished business (in the form of humiliating a deputy sheriff who went out of his way to make things rough for the troupe), and then rides off into the oncoming grill of a truck, having fulfilled his destiny. This last sequence is beautifully shot and bizarrely moving.

Knightriders is very refreshing in its look at the people who fall outside the normal scope of society and also outside the scope of those usually featured in motion pictures. The film is not afraid to be mystical and different – working on its own terms rather than within the conventions of Hollywood. Romero even gives Billy a speech to indicate that he is not a messianic leader, a nutcase, or a would-be hero, but simply someone fighting to live according to a code of honor that was abandoned by society long ago.

Despite its death in the theaters, the film continues to be discovered on cable or on videocasette, where it delights and surprises new viewers. While filmically it is not as successful in doing what it is trying to do as *Night of the Living Dead*, it is a far more amibitous film and is very representative of Romero as a fiercely independent filmmaker, not bowing to outside temptations or constraints, but struggling on diminishing resources to follow his own muse.

However, *Knightriders'* lack of financial success undoubtedly made things difficult for Romero. Luckily, he had an ally in Stephen King, whose books were achieving astronomical sales levels, with the movies based on those books initially proving to be big box office. (Both *Carrie* and *The Shining* were financial successes, but there was not another major hit from a King story until Rob Reiner so beautifully directed an adaptation of King's "The Body" under the title *Stand by Me*.)

Warner Bros. had offered Romero a chance to film *'Salem's Lot* as a theatrical feature, but then changed their mind as a slew of vampire films (John Badham's *Dracula*, Herzog's *Nosferatu, Love at First Bite*) came out. They decided to change the lengthy novel into a television miniseries, which resulted in Romero bowing out and Tobe Hooper taking over the job.

Romero then considered an adaptation of *The Stand*, an even lengthier work, but a usuable script and proper financing were not forthcoming. Instead, King offered to script a series of revenge tales that would pay tribute the E. C. Comics of both Romero's and King's youth. Romero also liked the idea that he would be able to employ some broad comedy in the anthology film that came to be known as *Creepshow*.

Creepshow represents Romero's experiment in trying to perfect a "comic bookish" style, with garish backgrounds of the type that might actually be found in a horror comic. The film's stories are linked together by the device that the tales are being read from a comic book by a small boy, and some scenes are linked by having illustrations "come to life," or using moving comic strip borders rather than the usual wipes. The lighting style is reminiscent of some Italian cinema of the '60s and '70s that aped comic book styles (cf. Bava's *Black Sabbath* and *Diabolique*, Elio Petri's *The Tenth Victim*, and Dario Argento's *Suspiria*). Also, for the first time Romero used a cast of well-known and experienced actors who managed to keep their stereotyped and caricatured roles humorous without straying into camp.

The opening segment, "Father's Day," is also one of the weakest, centering around a highly inebriated Aunt Bedelia (Viveca Lindfors) visiting her family while overcome with guilt for having allowed her sick father to die while demanding a father's day cake and then being overcome by the rotted father who uses her head to form the basis of his long-delayed tribute.

The second segment, "Weeds," was a humorous send-up of the original *The Blob*, only this time instead of turning people into blobs, the mass of protoplasm inside a meteor turns them into giant weeds. Author King shines as Jordy Verrill, a dumb-as-a-box-of-rocks hick who suffers weedification in an outrageous and comic turn.

"Something to Tide You Over" is the most E. C.–like of the segments. Leslie Nielsen sadistically kills his wife and her lover, burying each of them up to their necks and positioning a television set and a camera in front of each so that they can watch each other drown as they die. Proud of his technical expertise, Nielsen gloats, "Just look at that picture," a humorous indication of his lack of compassion and humanity. The drowned corpses return from the dead to exact an appropriate revenge.

This is followed by "The Crate," a story King had previously published in *Gallery*. The story is a slight one about a thing in a crate that eats people and how a henpecked milquetoast (Hal Holbrook) lures his obnoxious wife, Billie (Adrienne Barbeau), to become one of its victims while mouthing her favorite catchphrase, "Just tell it to call you 'Billie.'" Romero enlivens this segment with a couple of memorable daydreams of Holbrook disposing of his wife that are done in an absurdist, black comedy style. Apart from the humor, however, there is no substance to the tale.

Finally, "They're Creeping Up on You" features E. G. Marshall as a Howard Hughes–type recluse who demands an absolutely germ-free environment and who spares no sympathy for the unfortunate tenants in his slums, or anyone else for that matter. King exploits people's fear and disgust of cockroaches as Marshall's virginally white and sterile interior becomes overrun with the critters and finally the business tycoon himself is revealed to be infested with nothing but thousands of roaches, consumed in his own vileness (which obviously the roaches represent).

Creepshow is an enjoyable romp, but it is marred by the slightness of the stories and, stylistically, by an overemphasis of comic book devices employed, such as shots of people shrieking with garishly colored backgrounds and bolts of lightning emanating from around their heads as might be glimpsed in a comic book panel. The film is unnaturalistic enough without overemphasizing the fact and distancing the viewer further.

Romero scripted a sequel, *Creepshow 2*, which was also based on King stories and was directed by his longtime cameraman Mike Gornick. Unfortunately, the film was far less successful both artistically and financially, with a dull first story, a dreadfully botched job of adapting the second (King's "The Raft"), and an overlong joke for the third of a zombie hitchhiker who keeps trying to thumb a ride no matter how many ways he has been mutilated or run over.

Creepshow proved a moderate success and led to Romero working on developing a low-budget horror anthology series called *Tales from the Darkside*, for which he wrote the teleplays for the opening episode, "Trick or Treat," as well as a few other ("The Devil's Advocate," "Baker's Dozen," and "Circus"). Mostly shoved into late-night slots on independent stations, the series was a moderate success though it rarely had the kind of first-class stories that one associates with anthology series of the past such as *Twilight Zone* or *Thriller*. Romero never directed for the series and left halfway through the first season as story editor to concentrate on fulfilling his obligation to write and direct *Day of the Dead*.

After the completion of *Creepshow*, Romero began planning *Day of the Dead*, which he intended to be the most elaborate zombie film yet, involving action and gory special effects on an unprecedented scale. Originally, he intended that a group of survivors find a military outfit on an island that has trained the zombies and is keeping them under control using refrigerated chunks of human beings as their food. A depraved group of humans is kept on hand to be a food supply. Underground scientists work on ways to control the zombies, leaving the moral decisions to the decidedly amoral military group that runs the place. The whole thing was to be a satire on the levels of society with the deprived "lower" classes being nothing but fodder to the people in power who live luxuriously off the livelihood of the oppressed. Even more ironically, there are indications that the masses of zombies are little different from society as it exists today, with the same fascination with violence.

Estimates placed the budget of the initial script at $6.5 million, but United Film was unwilling to put up that kind of money unless the film was brought in for an R rating, a concession that *Dawn of the Dead*'s fans were unlikely to accept. If Romero insisted in making the film unrated, United Film was only willing to finance it for $3.5 million, which meant that the script was going to have to be drastically altered – and so it was, much to Romero's disappointment.

The altered script retained many of the basic ideas but was scaled down and emphases were shifted. The story now centered around Sarah (Lori Cardille), a scientific researcher; her lover, Miguel (Antone DiLeo); McDermott (Jarlath Conroy), an electronics whiz; and John (Terry Alexander), a Jamaican helicopter pilot. After Sarah has an initial nightmare where zombie arms thrust through a wall and grab her on Halloween, we see the group flying in a helicopter and scouting Florida cities for survivors but finding only the dead.

The group is part of a research team that the government assigned to an underground installation and is presided over by a military outfit headed by Captain Rhodes (Joseph Pilato), who indicates that he will be quick to shoot anyone who so much as challenges his authority.

However, the most interesting character in the film is Dr. Logan (Richard Liberty), nicknamed "Frankenstein," who proves to be just as crazy as Rhodes. Logan represents the amoral scientist so caught up in his work that he never even considers the moral implications of what he is doing. He hopes to deal with the dead by training them and keeping them under control. His prime experiment is Bub (Howard Sherman in an expressive mime performance), a zombie who clearly shows glimmerings of intelligence and who seems fascinated by objects such as razors and a paperback copy of King's 'Salem's Lot.

Logan's experiments with Bub disgust Rhodes, who sees extermination as the only answer to the problem of the living dead. When Bub unpredictably salutes him, Rhodes refuses to return the gesture, commenting, "You want me to *salute* that pile of walking pus?" However useful his efforts may seem, Logan is also conducting gruesome experiments in which he tries to determine how much of a zombie's body can be lost before it is killed. (In a couple of effectively gory scenes, everything but the brain is stripped away and the zombie is still "alive," even if the guts may have a tendency to slip out.)

The film is filled with tense confrontations, but the tone becomes rather strident as Romero's characters continually shout at one another. The totalitarianism of Rhodes is vile. Dr. Logan is killed when it is discovered that he has been storing parts of dead comrades to feed to Bub and the other zombies he has been experimenting with. The film is filled with unpleasantness, and the only character, apart from Logan, who seems to have a measure of inner peace is John, who believes that the scientists should give up their endeavor and start the world over by having babies in some idyllic setting. He believes the zombie plague was brought on by God: "We been punished by the creator, punished for our sins. He visited a curse on us so we might get a look at what hell was like. Maybe He didn't wanna see us blow ourselves up and put a big hole in His sky. Maybe He wanted to show us He was still the boss man. Maybe He figured we was gettin' too big for our britches tryin' to figure His shit out."

Things begin to come unhinged when Miguel becomes infected after being bitten by a zombie that is part of the group's underground corral of experimental zombie subjects. Discovering Logan's perfidy, Rhodes demands that John fly only the military men off the base, and when John initially refuses, Rhodes has one of the scientists, Ted Fisher (John Aplas), shot and locks Sarah and McDermott in the zombie corral.

A pain-wracked Miguel decides to end the base once and for all by leading the zombies inside the compound and onto the elevator platform before they tear him to pieces. The zombies kill the sadistic Rhodes and his men, with Bub being instrumental in taking revenge for Rhodes' snub and putting him in the eager hands of a hungry horde. Sarah, McDermott and

John all make it to a helicopter and finally find an isolated island where it is suggested that they could put John's laid-back plan of action to work, if they can get over being haunted by the horrors that they have left behind.

The film is generally despairing in tone, and the only solution it offers is to drop out of society entirely. There is and will be no cure for the zombie plague. Mankind will continue to be pestered by evil and petty people who will exploit other people and situations to their own advantage. Overall, *Day of the Dead* presents an ugly and bitter view. Once more Romero decries the lack of communication and understanding as well as its disastrous consequences.

Unlike *Dawn of the Dead*, where the audience wants the protagonists to succeed in securing a safe home for themselves, there are no heroes in *Day of the Dead*. Romero's worldview has become too bleak to believe in heroes, so even the likable characters are involved in a dubious undertaking. The film is imaginative in its concocting of revolting special effects, but apart from the sequences with Bub, lacks a sense of humor that would help relieve the grimness.

The story is rather diffuse and spread over several characters, none of whom we get to know too well. While the film proved very pleasing to splatter fans who enjoyed Savini's special effects mini-miracles, it was too nauseating to attract a mainstream audience and was given a very limited release, with a small number of prints touring from market to market, resulting in an overall disappointing box office take for the film.

While it has its interesting and inventive aspects, Romero's *Day of the Dead* probably misjudged the kind of horror film most aficionados want to see. Released the same summer was Dan O'Bannon's semi-sequel to *Night of the Living Dead*, *Return of the Living Dead*, which proved far more successful. *Return* had some memorably conceived scare, suspense, and simply outrageous scenes served with style and humor. Most of the zombie makeup was vastly inferior to Savini's as were many of the special effects, but *Return* was a fun and entertaining film, which *Day* was not. Plus, *Return* did not take itself too seriously, which *Day of the Dead*, with its hyped-up conflicts, did. Both films use stereotypes, but *Return* does so more effectively by giving the characters larger-than-life turns and reveling in special effects that elicit a response of "Oh my God, you've go to be kidding!" Romero's characters have less personality and his effects are more realistic and disgusting. In both films the zombies remain threatening, something which *Return*'s pathetic sequel failed to achieve, but *Return*'s outrageous humor makes for a better time in a movie theater than *Day*'s grimness.

Monkey Shines disappointed many of the ardent Romero fans in that it forsook the use of gore to concentrate on story and character instead. As a result, it actually was one of Romero's better films, though a stupid fake-out ending was tacked onto the film by Orion over Romero's objections because his original ending did not go over well at one test screening.

The film centers around Allan Mann (Jason Beghe), an athlete who becomes a quadriplegic because of an auto accident. Romero builds up sympathy for the character as we see the difficulties he has in adjusting to his new condition and the effect it has on his relationships: his girlfriend (Janine Turner) decides to leave him; his mother (Joyce Van Patten) smothers him with compassion and guilt; the surgeon (Stanley Tucci) who operated on him smugly walks off with his ex; the nurse (Christine Forrest, Romero's wife, who was forced by the studio to test for the role) hired to take care of him regards him as an unending burden, from whom she is always trying to take a break; and his best friend, Geoffrey Fisher (John Pankow), is developing a drug problem in his fight against exhaustion. Geoffrey gives Allan one of his experimental capuchin monkeys to be trained by Melanie Parker (Kate McNeil) as a "helping hand." (The relationship is similar to the one between the monkey and Donald Pleasence in *Phenomena*.)

What the monkey can be trained to do is one of the most fascinating parts of the film. Called Ella, Allan's monkey helps to feed, groom, play music, and even make phone calls for her "master." However, things go awry when she starts picking up on his inner rage and starts killing for him as well because of a serum that Geoffrey injected into Ella. Romero creates some interesting, scurrying shots from Ella's point of view as she goes about her nightmarish nocturnal missions of mayhem.

Making a quadriplegic murderer credible is something that even Agatha Christie would have problems pulling off, but Romero manages to get the audience to suspend their disbelief for the sake of the story. The film becomes a metaphor for man's animal nature and the danger of its being allowed to free itself from civilized restraints. Romero has done an interesting job of adapting Michael Stewart's novel.

The film presents no clear-cut villains, only flawed humans and a murderous monkey acting out the frustration and anger of a helpless cripple. The film asks whether this violent side is an essential component of man, or simply something we share with the animals—just as *Day of the Dead* asks us to consider at what point flesh-eating zombies like Bub become human. However, most modern horror audiences were not there to ponder such questions but rather to be excited by some gore scenes. When Romero offered suspense instead, the film quickly trailed off into oblivion.

Romero's most recent film is an anthology he did in collaboration with Dario Argento, *Two Evil Eyes*, which took some time to receive a release in the United States via a minor distributor. Argento directed the second and better episode, an adaptation of Edgar Allan Poe's "The Black Cat," replete with his stylish camera moves. Romero's segment, an adaptation of "The Strange Case of M. Valdemar," also by Poe, is somewhat off-kilter, too simple and straightforward in its approach. Filmed previously by Roger Corman as one of the segments of *Tales of Terror*, Corman's version proved the superior. Romero does build some tension with a voice beyond the grave, but Valdemar's appearance after death proves anti-climactic.

Romero is a rather uneven but maverick filmmaker. He will surely continue to follow his muse, and his contributions have already earned him a permanent place in the horror hall of fame. As a wild card, we will never know quite what to expect from him next, but he has shown he is willing to break any taboos, to go unsparingly for the gut, or even to throw in some intelligence as well. He is not the most accomplished horror filmmaker, but he remains one of the most personal, and when he really cares about a subject, it shines through in his films. Because he is not content to follow Hollywood conventions and has retained his artistic independence, Romero remains one of the most consistently interesting modern filmmakers.

Don Sharp (1922–   )

The Golden Airliner (1955); *The Adventures of Hal 5; The In-Between Age* (aka *The Golden Disc*) (1958); *The Professionals* (1960); *Linda* (1961); *It's All Happening* (aka *The Dream Maker*); *Kiss of the Vampire* (1963); *The Devil-Ship Pirates; Witchcraft* (1964); *The Face of Fu Manchu; Curse of the Fly* (1965); *Rasputin – The Mad Monk* (aka *I Killed Rasputin*); *Bang, Bang, You're Dead* (aka *Our Man in Marrakesh*); *Bride of Fu Manchu* (1966); *Those Fantastic Flying Fools* (aka *Jules Verne's Rocket to the Moon*, 1967); *Taste of Excitement* (1968); *The Violent Enemy* (1969); *Puppet on a Chain* (1972); *Psychomania* (aka *The Death Wheelers*, 1973); *Dark Places* (1974); *Hennessy; Callan* (1975); *The 39 Steps* (1978); *Bear Island* (1980); *What Waits Below* (aka *Secrets of the Phantom Caverns*, 1984).

TELEVISION: *The Avengers; The Champions; Ghost Squad; The Four Feathers* (1978); *A Woman of Substance* (1984); *Tusitala; Hold the Dream* (1986); *Tears in the Rain* (1988).

Don Sharp was born in Hobart, Tasmania, in April 1922. His parents wanted him to be an accountant; this he avoided by becoming involved as an actor in amateur theater. Hobart, a small community of about 64,000 people, did not provide much of a living for actors, but Sharp struggled along and eventually got into directing plays.

He volunteered for the Royal Australian Air Force in 1940 and served in the Far East. He decided not to return to Hobart after his stint, but instead headed for Melbourne, Australia, where he landed a major role in the comedy *Kiss and Tell* when the person he was understudying for suddenly got sick with laryngitis.

However, he was more interested in films than theater and decided, in the absence of any kind of major film industry in Australia at the time, to strike out for England. Unable to get a job acting, Sharp collaborated with his roommate, an assistant director, on the film *Ha'Penny Breeze*, on which Sharp cowrote the screenplay, coproduced, and starred. The experience enabled Sharp to start working as a producer's assistant on the films that he wrote, which include *Child's Play* and *Robbery Under Arms*.

I don't know anything about his first film, *The Golden Airliner*, but *The Adventures of Hal 5*, his second film, was a children's movie about a car with a mind of its own. Other early features he would direct included a caper film called *The Professionals* and a look at the British music scene starring

656

Tommy Steele called *It's All Happening*. He also worked quite a bit shooting second unit material for other directors' films, including segments of *Carve Her Name with Pride* and *Those Magnificent Men in Their Flying Machines*. However, his big break came when Hammer offered him the horror film *Kiss of the Vampire* (which was horribly mangled when released to American television and retitled *Kiss of Evil*).

In an interview in *Fangoria* magazine, Sharp recalls:

> [M]y agent told me that Hammer . . . were seeking out some new blood to direct horror. And I had no idea what a horror movie was! I had actually never gone to a horror movie. They sent me a script, and it was good. I said, "That's fine, but I must know what it's about, and how these things are treated," and they decided to show me three or four of their best. So I was stepping into a totally new world.

Sharp observed that horror films seemed to work best as period pieces because the stories required that audiences be removed from their everyday surroundings. He felt that the period settings called for a "certain theatricality." He also observed that Hammer seemed to be making each film a little bloodier than the last, a progression of which he disapproved:

> I felt it might work better if, instead we suggested [the blood]. I went and discussed my ideas with Tony Hinds, and I must say he was a bit aghast, because I wanted to take a lot of the horror elements out.
> We talked and talked, and eventually he came around. So, in the finished film, the audience is hit with a big scare in the beginning, then suggestion and more suggestion, another small scare in the middle – and the rest is reserved for the climax.

Sharp opens the film very effectively with a funeral of a young girl being interrupted by Prof. Zimmer (Clifford Evans), who throws holy water on the casket and then drives a shovel through the center of the lid, causing blood to well forth. Thus this town's infection by vampires is strikingly and immediately established. (Sadly, this sequence and the climax of the film were omitted when it was shown on American television, with new, dull footage added to pad out the running time.)

Unfortunately, Anthony Hinds' script is largely a compendium of familiar clichés as a honeymooning couple, Gerald and Marianne Harcourt (Edward De Souza and Jennifer Daniel), are stranded in Bavaria and have to take shelter in an inn full of unfriendly natives and a mysterious stranger (who resides in Room 13, no less). The couple are befriended by Dr. Ravna (Noel Williams), who invites them to a masked ball, which turns out to be full of Ravna's vampire followers. During the course of the ball, Ravna puts the bite on Marianne. Sharp gives the masque a pictorial beauty, but it falls short of what Polanski accomplished in *Dance of the Vampires*. Sharp also does not seem to have Fisher's facility at giving an impression of space, so that the sets seem more cramped here than they do in Fisher's Hammer films.

Perhaps the oddest thing about *Kiss of the Vampire* is that Hinds decided to do a typical *Twilight Zone*/*The Lady Vanishes* twist: When Gerald wakens the next day, everyone denies knowing his wife and pretends she never existed, driving the poor man to distraction. Finally, he takes Prof. Zimmer's dire warnings seriously and begins to believe that Ravna is holding Marianne captive in the castle.

Gerald becomes trapped in the midst of his rescue attempt, but Prof. Zimmer conjures up the forces of darkness in the form of vampire bats and unleashes the bats on Ravna's vampires so that they are torn to bits by their mistakes. It is a pretty spectacular idea (though *Brides of Dracula* was originally to have ended in the same way), but the rubber bats hooked up by Les Bowie are not as impressive as they ought to be. The shot of hundreds of animated bats circling the castle is quite good, though.

Sharp's best contributions to the film is adding an erotic tone as the vampire coven are given sexy white costumes to slink around in. The film has some subtlety, preferring not to bludgeon the viewer, and as a result builds some atmosphere lacking in some of Hammer's other vampire productions. (*Kiss of the Vampire* was undoubtedly one of the best of these, though it falls short of *Horror of Dracula*'s classic status.)

Unlike many previous vampires, Sharp's are able to walk about in limited light, making their activities as real people seem more believeable. Also, Sharp is constantly at pains to equate vampirism with a disease. Prof. Zimmer even explains how his daughter caught the disease from Dr. Ravna and was a vampire *before* she died.

With Sharp's first horror film a success, he then turned out a period swashbuckler for Hammer, *The Devil-Ship Pirates*. He followed this up with the little-known horror film *Witchcraft* starring Lon Chaney, Jr., for the Robert Lippert organization. The plot has the descendant of a family that persecuted witches, Bill Lanier (Jack Hedley), plowing up a cemetery and releasing the spirit of Vanesa Whitlock (Yvette Rees), who had been buried alive while the Laniers stole her family's property. Vanessa seeks revenge and causes fatal accidents by popping up unexpectedly in the back of people's cars. Chaney played the elderly head of the Whitlock family who intends to sacrifice Lanier's wife (Jill Dixon) at a black mass, but the tables turn and the Whitlock clan gets inundated with boiling oil.

Witchcraft, which had a short, four-week shooting schedule, proved to be an above-average programmer and demonstrated that Sharp could be inventive with limited resources. Sharp proved even more inventive with his next film, one of his best, *The Face of Fu Manchu*, which spawned a series of Fu Manchu films, all starring Christopher Lee as the insidious Oriental doctor and all produced by the penny-pinching Harry Alan Towers. Perhaps one of the most inventive ideas that Sharp came up with was using an Irish jail, Kilmainham, to serve as a Tibetan monastary. The film gets off to an intriguing start as we see what appears to be the execution of Fu Manchu by beheading, which Sharp builds atmospherically with sounds of thunder and wind coupled with images of stately order and procedure surrounding the grim task. It is quickly revealed that Fu Manchu had a hypnotized double take his place and is still on the loose, plotting a form of gas warfare derived from the seeds of a black poppy.

Nigel Green gives a good performance as the strongly determined but reservedly British detective Sir Denis Nayland Smith. Tsai Chin provides able support as Fah Le Suee, Fu Manchu's nefarious daughter, who aids her father in his plans, while Howard Marion-Crawford lends his support to Smith as Dr. Petrie. Corpses begin turning up in bizarre fashion and then Fu Manchu makes a radio announcement (the series is set in the '30s) about his plans for world conquest and demonstrates his power by wiping out an English village. The most memorable sequence in the film has Fu Manchu killing a treacherous female helper by drowning her in a glass cage in his secret fortress under the Thames. Smith chases Fu Manchu out of the country and succeeds in blowing him and his daughter up in their Tibetan lair while a now famous superimposition appears and announces, "The world will hear of me again!"

And indeed, Sharp directed the first of the sequels, *The Brides of Fu Manchu*, in 1966. This film reportedly had a racier version for the European continent. The plot had Fu Manchu kidnapping an industrialist's daughter (Marie Versini) and planning to unleash a death ray, with which he intends to disrupt an arms convention in London. Douglas Wilmer took over the role of Nayland Smith, and more time was accorded to Fu Manchu's daughter, Lin Tang (again played by Tsai Chin), than to Fu Manchu. The scripting and action were weaker than before, but it proved far better than any of the subsequent, non–Sharp directed sequels (*Vengeance of Fu Manchu, Kiss and Kill,* and *Castle of Fu Manchu* aka *Assignment: Istanbul*).

Before *Brides*, Sharp first worked on a sequel to *Return of the Fly* called *Curse of the Fly*. The film, scripted by Harry Spaulding, is decidedly an odd one. Its heroine, Patricia Stanley (Carole Gray), begins the film by escaping from an insane asylum, walking through a window in only her bra and panties (a touch of the famed Sharp eroticism). While she feels she is liberated, she becomes the figurative unwary fly in the trap of Henri Delambre (Brian Donlevy) as she marries his son Martin (George Baker) and is slowly introduced to Henri's menagerie of horror.

Sharp knew he ws revamping an old idea, and his means of distinguishing it was to make Henri the most ruthless of the Delambres. He keeps

Martin's first wife and two other unfortunate results of his teleportation experiments locked in the cellar. Periodically, the housekeeper releases the first Mrs. Delambre to play the piano, leading to the odd image of a giant fly's claw trying to play the keys.

Henri thinks he has finally mastered the technique of breaking down solid matter and teleporting it elsewhere, namely the teleporter manned by his son Albert in London. When two of his previous experiments end up dead, he transports them to Albert where they reassemble as pulsating blobs of flesh. The police are now suspicious and Henri makes the mistake of using his teleporter on himself without checking with Albert to see if the receiving chamber is hooked up at the other end, with the result that his atoms are permanently scattered.

Patricia almost suffers the same fate but is rescued by Martin, who as the result of his father's machinations is aging rapidly and dies after setting her free. Predictably, Patricia finally seems cured of her insanity now that the oppressive parental authority figure is gone (her over-demanding mother was the one who sent her to the asylum in the first place).

Overall, the film is cheap and disappointing, but Sharp does occasionally add some interesting visual touches, especially in the memorably offbeat opening. However, most of the film's excitement level runs about even with *The Alligator People* or *The Beast with Five Fingers* as the lonely heroine tries to figure out the deep, dark, terrible secret that everyone in the house is trying to keep from her.

Far more thrilling was *Rasputin – The Mad Monk*, which featured one of the Christopher Lee's best performances in the title role. The film was far from historically accurate and was mainly served up to titillate the audience, particularly in the scenes where Rasputin tries to degrade Sonia (the rather fetching Barbara Shelley), the tsarina's lady-in-waiting, whom he ravishes, hypnotizes and drives to suicide. However, the script by Anthony Hinds lacks scope, setting up Rasputin as a demonic character with almost Draculean powers of hypnotism and lust, and then finally having him killed by Dr. Zargo (Richard Pasco) in an overly drawn-out death scene. (The actual demise of Rasputin was very drawn out as well, proving that he was extremely difficult to kill, but Hinds departs from both the facts and the legend.)

Next Sharp tried his hand at a gangster spoof starring Tony Randall known as *Bang Bang* or *Bang, Bang, You're Dead!* There was a dull '60s science ficton picture, *Those Fantastic Flying Fools*, starring Troy Donahue and Burl Ives, which was based on a Jules Verne work. (It is also known as *Jules Verne's Rocket to the Moon* and *Blastoff*.) I have never seen *Taste of Excitement* or *The Violent Enemy*. Sharp codirected an adaptation of Alistair MacLean's *Puppet on a Chain* and is said to be responsible for the exciting speedboat chase (Sharp is one of Britain's few accomplished directors of action), though the rest of the film has little to recommend it.

Between scenes on the exterior set of Hammer Films Rasputin–The Mad Monk
*(1965) are director Don Sharp (coffee cup in hand), producer Anthony Nelson-
Keys (center) and director of photography Arthur Grant (right). This same ex-
terior set was also used for* Dracula–Prince of Darkness, The Reptile *and*
Plague of the Zombies. *(Photo courtesy of Richard Klemensen and Hammer
Films.)*

Perhaps Sharp's oddest film was the exploitation vehicle *Psychomania*
(aka *The Death Wheelers*), in which the head of a motorcycle gang commits
suicide, after making a pact with the devil in order to conquer death. The
young lad returns from the grave, persuades his gang to do likewise, and
leads a troop of similarly clad leather-attired motorpsychos across the country wreaking havoc everywhere they go. It was films like this one that drove
star George Sanders (who plays a devil worshipper) to commit suicide out

of "boredom," though Sharp has noted that Sanders was going deaf and feeling isolated at the time. The whole production has tongue-in-cheek flair that makes it outrageous.

Sharp's *Dark Places* has Christopher Lee, Joan Collins and Herbert Lom trying to scare Robin Hardy away from an old house that hides a huge inheritance. Hardy seems to become possessed by the spirit of the previous owner of the house, who had murdered his wife and children, but is revealed to be an inmate from the asylum of Dr. Mandeville (Lee) who kills Dr. Mandeville and his sister (Collins). He then tears down the wall hiding the money and the corpses of his original victims, whom he had killed for killing his mistress. Though Sharp handles the film well, the thriller elements are all standard and could have been enlivened by some real wit or thrills.

From here on Sharp left horror to concentrate on some undistinguished thrillers, finally returning to the genre with the limp *What Waits Below* (originally filmed as *Secrets of the Phantom Caverns*), a romp down some caverns to discover the lost tribe of Lummeria. The film starred Timothy Hutton, who had won an Oscar for *Ordinary People*. Filmed on a limited budget with a dull script, it went almost immediately to video and is best forgotten as an undistinguished footnote to an interesting career.

Jacques Tourneur (1904–1977)

Un Vieux Garçon (short); *La Fusée* (short); *Tout Ça Ne Vaut Pas l'Amour* (1931); *Toto; Pour Etre Aimé* (1933); *Les Filles de la Concierge* (1934); *They All Come Out; Nick Carter, Master Detective* (1939); *Phantom Raiders* (1940); *Doctors Don't Tell* (1941); *Cat People* (1942); *I Walked with a Zombie; The Leopard Man* (1943); *Days of Glory; Experiment Perilous* (1944); *Canyon Passage* (1946); *Out of the Past* (1947); *Berlin Express* (1948); *Easy Living* (1949); *Stars in My Crown; The Flame and the Arrow* (1950); *Circle of Danger; Anne of the Indies* (1951); *Way of a Gaucho* (1952); *Appointment in Honduras* (1953); *Stranger on Horseback; Wichita* (1955); *Great Day in the Morning; Nightfall* (1956); *Curse of the Demon; The Fearmakers* (1958); *Timbuktu* (1959); *The Giant of Marathon* (1960); *The Comedy of Terrors* (1963); *War Gods of the Deep* (aka *The City Under the Sea,* 1965).

TELEVISION: *Jane Wyman Theatre; General Electric Theatre* (1956); *Northwest Passage; Walter Winchell File* (1958); *Northwest Passage; The Californians; Bonanza* (1959); "The Devil Makers," *The Alaskans; Barbara Stanwyck Theater; Follow the Sun* (1960); *Adventures in Paradise;* "Night Calls," *Twilight Zone* (1961).

Jacques Tourneur has been hailed as one of the cinema's supreme stylists, mostly of the basis of his horror films and one *film noir* classic, *Out of the Past*. Like his father, director Maurice Tourneur, he never really showed himself to be good with action; his forte was mood and atmosphere, and he excelled in his ability to create them. He was a subtle director who never underlined his points by calling obvious attention to them; rather he effectively manipulated light and shadow, camera movement and sound to build a sense of place and a character's unease in a given situation.

Tourneur was born in Paris in 1904 and emigrated to America with his father in 1913. He started working for his father as a script clerk and later made some forays into acting for some other directors (*Scaramouche, The Fair Co-ed, Love* and *The Trail of '98*). When his father returned to Paris, Jacques returned with him, working as an assistant and then an editor. He made his first films in France but then returned to America where he hoped to be allowed to make features at MGM. Instead, they assigned him to make short films for the studio (about 20 in all) and loaned him out as a second unit director on *The Winning Ticket*. David Selznick planned a glossy version of the Dickens classic *Tale of Two Cities* and needed some second unit

663

work done which depicted the storming of the Bastille and the beginning of the French Revolution. He picked Tourneur because he thought the French name would look good in the credits.

This assignment proved a fortuitous one as the line producer Tourneur was assigned to work with was none other than Val Lewton, who had been toiling for the studio as a story editor and was hoping to be promoted to producer. The pair shared a love of boating and often went sailing together. Their sequences for the film worked beautifully, and Lewton was to remember Tourneur when he set up his unit at RKO.

Tourneur's first screen project was a dull semi-documentary about prisons called *They All Came Out*. Next came *Nick Carter – Master Detective*, a slickly done but unremarkable B film in which Walter Pidgeon tracks down an industrial spy. I am afraid I do not know anything about *Phantom Raiders* or *Doctors Don't Tell*, but it is generally acknowledged that Tourneur's first major film was *Cat People* for Lewton.

When Lewton set up shop at RKO, he began by hiring DeWitt Bodeen to be his writer. Meanwhile, looking for a new horror angle, Charles Koerner, who was head of production at RKO, noted that a lot had been done with vampires, werewolves and man-made monsters. Deciding that nobody had done much with cats, he audience-tested the title *Cat People*, which tested well. He then assigned Lewton and Bodeen to come up with a story that would fit that title. Combing around for material, Lewton decided to base the plot on Algernon Blackwood's story "Ancient Sorceries" and began negotiating for the rights when he changed his mind. Initially, Bodeen had given the screen story a period setting after the fashion of most horror films of the day. According to Tourneur in an interview in *Cinefantastique*, he argued against that approach, saying the film would be far more effective in a modern setting that the audience could relate to.

Lewton was almost unique among producers in allowing his director and his editor (Mark Robson for the first film) to sit in on the story-planning sessions and toss ideas back and forth. Recalled Tourneur in *The Celluloid Muse*:

> We started talking, and a young man called DeWitt Bodeen – he's a writer, a very talented playwright today – suggested ideas and we suggested others. The whole film, including the scoring, the cutting and everything, cost $130,000. And I got three thousand dollars flat fee for it. We made it very quickly.
>
> We worked out the story of a girl who is obsessed with the idea of cats, who herself turns into a cat. . . . We believed in suggesting horror rather than showing it.

From these elements, Tourneur and Lewton produced not only *Cat People*, but a whole new approach to making horror films. Lewton deliberately avoided the old-fashioned monsters and shocking sequences – sometimes much to the annoyance of the front office – opting instead to build a mood of unease and anticipation, to leave a certain amount of information ambiguous, and to let the audience's imagination fill in the horrific details that are only hinted at. Tourneur's style and approach realized all these ambitions beautifully.

The title *Cat People* alone builds up certain expectations in an audience, but the story is structured so that the horrific scenes do not really begin until the last half of the film, leaving the audience primed for something to happen but unable to anticipate when.

Lewton had been impressed with Simone Simon because of her sexy bit part in Wilhelm Dieterle's *All That Money Can Buy* (aka *Daniel and the Devil*, an adaptation of Stephen Vincent Benét's "The Devil and Daniel Webster") and discovered that he could bring her back over from France to work on the film relatively inexpensively. Kent Smith, the male lead, was cast because Lewton noticed him riding his bicycle to the studio every day waiting to be assigned to a film. (Smith had been an actor on Broadway and waited nine months before he was cast in *Cat People*.)

The film begins simply with Irena Dubrovna (Simone Simon) making sketches at the local zoo. One of the sketches falls to the ground and is picked up by Oliver Reed (Kent Smith), who becomes interested in the girl and escorts her home. (The staircase from Welles' *The Magnificent Ambersons* shows up as the entrance to her apartment.)

As the pair begin courting, Reed notices that Irene is obsessed with cats, which is reflected in the decor of her apartment. He also notes that her presence has a disturbing influence on animals when he takes her to a pet shop, but unfazed, he buys her a canary anyway.

Tourneur and cinematographer Nicholas Musuraca do a marvelous job of suggesting Irena's cat-like nature in a short sequence in her apartment. While she works at designing a dress, we see a screen with a large panther painted on it. The shadow of the canary in a cage falls near the mouth of the panther on the screen, visually suggesting not only Irena's predatory nature, but also how she feels trapped by her fate. The shot also visually echoes the animals we saw at the zoo. Irena gets up and goes to the cage, which excites the canary. She playfully extends her arm into the cage, and a strange expression on her face suggests that of a cat playing with its prey. The result is that the canary becomes frightened to death, and Irena feeds its body to the panther at the zoo. Nothing is overtly stated, but this scene visually depicts much of the underlying tension in the story.

Oliver finally gets to the bottom of what is troubling Irena. She is haunted by the fear that she is descended from a race of Serbian cat-women who turn into cats whenever they are emotionally aroused. As a result, Irena has done her best to repress and deny her emotions. Oliver has fallen in love with her and convinces her that her fears are groundless. They marry, but at the reception a strange woman (Elizabeth Russell) approaches Irena and addresses her as "my sister" in Irena's voice (dubbed in by Simon) before moving on (leaving a hint of lesbianism to explain the following scenes).

This so unnerves Irena that she refuses to consummate the marriage in fear that doing so will cause her to turn into a cat. Naturally, the sexless marriage begins to drive the initially understanding Oliver to distraction, and he takes her to see a psychiatrist, Dr. Judd (Tom Conway), who, it becomes apparent, has lecherous designs on Irena of his own.

Oliver turns to coworker Alice (Jane Randolph) for sympathy, and we clearly see that Alice has a definite interest in Oliver and is jealous of his marriage to Irena. There is a clear-cut antagonism between the two women. In one of the film's most famous scenes, Alice walks beside the wall of the zoo on her way home. Though there are streetlights, there are large patches of darkness between them, and her way alternates from dark to light and back. The wind brushes the branches of the tree against the tops of the wall and we begin to hear the growling sound of a cat on the prowl. Suddenly, there is the sound of a snarl, like a cat about to strike, which resolves itself as the hiss of the pneumatic brakes of a bus that unexpectedly lurches into frame. (This type of scene with a slow buildup and sudden release became known as a "bus," and was a component in many horror films thereafter. The idea was to get the audience to expect something and then catch them totally off guard from another direction. The canny use of sounds makes this sequence doubly effective.)

This sequence is followed by a shot of savaged sheep, the first clear evidence that Irena is indeed a cat woman and has taken out her fury on the innocent animal. There is also a tracking shot of panther paw marks transforming themselves into the marks left by a woman in high heels, though one might be skeptical about the idea that Irena's clothes magically transform with her. We then cut to Irena sitting in her bathtub weeping uncontrollably while the camera pans to the end of the tub which rests on feet shaped like animal claws, suggesting the animal nature which is the basis of Irena's problem.

That night Irena has a very evocative dream with cartoon black panthers slithering along the bottom of the frame and Dr. Judd as King John of Serbia (Irena has a statue of King John spearing a panther on a sword in her apartment) representing the fears of her subconscious. Pictorially, the dream suggests that Irena's problems are Freudian (a quote from Freud is attributed to Dr. Judd at the beginning of the film) and furthers the idea that we are seeing things as Irena perceives them. Perhaps she does not turn into a cat after all, but uses that as an explanation for her repressed hostility and guilt. (She is afraid that she cannot satisfy her husband and is losing him to another woman and that her animal nature, once unleashed, would be uncontrollable.) The best-remembered sequence in the film is pure Tourneur. Alice goes for a swim alone in a pool. Light is reflected off the water, hitting the ceiling and we hear water dripping. As Alice is swimming, she becomes aware of the sound of a panther and sees a large shadow reflected on the wall. Terrified, she must wait in the water until the panther has gone away; then she recovers her bathrobe, only to discover that it has been torn to tatters.

Tourneur based this sequence on an occurrence that had happened to him at a friend's house: The friend kept two pet cheetahs and one of them got loose while Tourneur was in the pool. To get a feeling of claustrophobia, Tourneur chose a pool at an existing apartment building which had white walls and a low ceiling, so that it generates the feeling of an enclosed place, emphasizing how trapped the character is. After trying several ways to get a convincing shadow on the wall, Tourneur finally used his own fist to represent the shadow of the killer cat passing by the light source.

We never see the panther itself in that sequence and originally were not intended to see it anywhere in the film, but the RKO front office insisted that some scenes showing a panther be shot. Tourneur added one to a later sequence where Alice and Oliver are trapped at their work with only the light of drafting tables to illuminate the office while a panther prowled underneath the tables. There is even a small parody of conventional horror films when Oliver picks up a set square to use as a cross, holding it up and commanding Irena to leave them alone as if she were some form of vampire. Between Tourneur's shooting the panther in the darkest corners of the set and Robson's editing, only a brief glimpse and the flavor of the panther's presence remain.

The distraught Irena goes to Dr. Judd for solace, but he attempts to rape her to convince her that her fears are foolish. We see his shocked face as Irena apparently transforms before his eyes and the two battle—Judd knocks the lamp over and removes a sword from his cane, and we see the shadows fighting on the wall. Judd is killed and the wounded Irena just makes it to the zoo where she intends to free the panther before she too expires, leaving Oliver free to wed Alice.

Things did not go smoothly for Tourneur initially; after seeing the third day's rushes, Lew Ostrow wanted to fire Tourneur and replace him with a contract director. However, Lewton had faith in his protégé and was able to have the decision postponed until Koerner could see the footage, which was approved and Tourneur was retained.

Upon completion, the studio's reaction to the film was lukewarm to hostile, until it started doing business in theaters. Then Lewton and Tourneur turned into the studio's fair-haired boys. Tourneur was promised a promotion to A budget features after completing two more films for Lewton (as was Lewton; see chapter on Mark Robson). *Cat People* proved a tremendous success for a B film, but Tourneur and Lewton were already caught up in the rigors of their next project, which Koerner insisted be based on an article by Inez Wallace called "I Walked with a Zombie."

Initially, this concept depressed Lewton until he came up with the idea of doing *Jane Eyre* in the tropics. Using the Brontë classic as the basis for his storyline, he set Curt Siodmak (scriptwriter of *The Wolf Man*) and Adel Wray to work on the script.

The result was Tourneur's and Lewton's greatest work, *I Walked with a Zombie*. One of the most poetic and mournful horror films ever made, the film elegantly mines its locale for its exoticism and its background in pain and misery. The pure heroine, Betsy (Frances Dee), finds herself falling in love with brooding, Byronic hero Paul Holland (Tom Conway, whom Lewton considered "the nice George Sanders"), who is troubled by the suspicion that he drove his wife mad.

Betsy meets Paul on the boat over to the island of St. Sebastian, where he informs her that the beauty she sees surrounding her is all based on death (underscored by the mournful chant "O Marie Congo" that black sailors are chanting with their dinner). A black coachman fills her in on how the blacks on the island were originally brought over as slaves, and this event has colored the entire island's society.

Betsy discovers what seems to her a topsy-turvy world in which people cry at births (because in slavery times, babies were entering a life of misery) and rejoice at death (because through death they were freed). The sound of a mother crying is what leads Betsy to leave her room the first night and investigate a stone tower near the house where she first meets Jessica (Christine Gordon), Paul's wife, who is now a zombie.

Tourneur, with the help of J. Roy Hunt as cinematographer and Albert S. D'Agostino and Walter E. Keller as art directors, elegantly disguises the film's B movie budget and gives it a rich look. In the dark, there is a brightness to the light images, and shadows are constantly employed to show how a character can feel enclosed or entrapped. A mood is quickly established and wonderfully maintained as we slowly learn of Holland's sorrow.

Paul's half-brother Wesley Rand (James Ellison) casts some doubt as to Paul's motives. Wesley shirks work and drinks too heavily, a borderline alcoholic. It is quickly apparent that he too loved Jessica and had intended to take her away before she became ill with a fever and ended up a zombie. The rational Paul refuses to believe in the local folk superstition. Judging his wife a mental case, he mourns the loss of her mind and her vitality.

Betsy learns some of the background of the divided family from the song a calypso singer (Sir Lancelot) sings, set to the tune of "Shame and Scandal (in the Family)" with lyrics tailored to fit the present story. Blacks in this film, and in all of Lewton's films, were given a measure of respect and dignity not found in most other films of the '40s. The calypso singer acts as a Greek chorus, supplying background exposition, but it is notable that he is allowed implicitly to criticize the ruling whites on the island without retribution.

Betsy finds that she loves Paul when he softens towards her as they begin to speak of the family's troubles, but his mood changes dramatically when the voodoo drums begin. The natives are troubled, ostensibly by the lack of rain, but also by the discord sown by the zombified Jessica, who represents an ill omen.

Because of her love for Paul, Betsy suggests that insulin shock therapy be tried, which could result in death or a cure for Jessica. (It is notable that Betsy does not suggest this before she falls in love with Paul. While she believes she is suggesting it to give Paul what he most desires, it can also be interpreted that she wants the question of Paul's eligibility resolved. Should Jessica die under the treatment, then Paul would be free to love Betsy; should she be cured, then Paul would have what Betsy thinks he wants.) However, the treatment fails to provoke any change in Jessica's condition despite the best efforts of Dr. Maxwell (James Bell).

The black house servant Alma (Teresa Harris) then suggests that there are better doctors at the Houmfort, the location of the island's voodoo ceremonies. Betsy resolves to take Jessica there in her search for a cure. Alma quietly outlines the way in some cornmeal she spills on the floor and pins contrasting triangular patches to Betsy's and Jessica's clothes so that they will be able to pass by the zombie who guards the entrance to the Houmfort.

There follows one of the most beautiful and sustained sequences in the history of the horror genre. Betsy leads Jessica through the sugar cane to the accompaniment of the howling wind (which proves far more effective than any musical underscoring could have been), past various zombie talismans and the carcass of a goat hung from a tree, to reach Carre-Four (Darby Jones), the zombie guard who lets the pair pass and then silently follows them. When Betsy's flashlight beam hits Carre-Four's face, the sound of the voodoo drums comes up to prepare us for the ceremony. (Before that, we hear only the occasional sound of a conch being blown to call the faithful.)

Despite the fact that there is no big dramatic payoff, the sequence carries a simple elegance all its own. The movement is slow, languid and purposeful. We know these women are about to have some fateful encounter, but we cannot tell the shape or form it will take. The result is hypnotic and unforgettable.

By contrast, the voodoo ceremony is quiet and respectful. There is drumming and dancing, but there is nothing frightening in this alternate form of worship. With the women's arrival at the Houmfort, all feeling of menace is dissipated, though Tourneur does extend the mood when Betsy is taken inside the witch doctor's hut in her search for answers, showing a curious native testing Jessica's state by stabbing her in the arm with a sword and drawing no blood.

Inside the hut, Betsy discovers that Mrs. Rand (Edith Barrett), Paul and Wesley's mother, is the voodoo high priest. A former missionary's daughter, she explains that after her husband's death, she had to resort to voodoo in order to convince the natives to follow her medical advice, which they had ignored otherwise.

In some ways this is the culmination of the dual roles theme that runs throughout this and many other Tourneur films. The motivations and roles of all the main characters in the film are a little obscure. In a subsequent scene, Mrs. Rand chides a child for wearing both a cross and a voodoo amulet, but she exposes herself to be not much different. She initially pooh-poohs Betsy's belief that voodoo might help effect a cure, proclaiming her background as a Christian and a medical assistant herself, but then shortly afterwards she confesses that it was she who put a zombie spell on Jessica during a voodoo ceremony because Jessica was "pulling her family apart" by planning to run off with Wesley. (There are even elements of a Jocasta complex here, as despite his drunkness, Mrs. Rand dotes on Wesley and was perhaps jealous that he wanted to run away with another woman.)

Meanwhile, there are hints that Paul's brooding personality and his tendency toward pessimism might have existed before Jessica developed into her current state and may well have been the cause of it. We cannot tell whether Jessica deserved her fate or not, or whether Wesley was a scoundrel or Jessica's failed savior. Finally, even the seemingly innocent Betsy has dual motives for her actions, which bespeak different intents.

The natives are upset about Jessica and decide that the matter must be resolved. They pray night and day, and one of their shamans makes a voodoo doll resembling Jessica. Meanwhile, Wesley sees that Paul has fallen in love with Betsy and goes to Betsy to persuade her that she should end Jessica's half-life, but Betsy refuses to break the code of her profession.

Ironically, Wesley is made the instrument of Jessica's death. After Carre-Four makes an unsuccessful attempt to fetch her, the voodoo shaman causes both the doll and Jessica to move towards him. Betsy blocks her way temporarily by closing the gate, but Wesley later opens it and takes an arrow from a figure of St. Sebastian. When the voodoo shaman plunges a needle into the doll, Wesley apparently stabs the arrow into Jessica, possibly while under the influence of a voodoo spell. Carre-Four once more approaches as Wesley scoops up Jessica's fallen body and carries her out to sea where he drowns himself.

Tourneur makes this wordless sequence haunting, adding the poetic touch that the bodies are discovered by torch-bearing fishermen who take

Wesley's body back while Carre-Four carries Jessica's. The film closes on the image of the arrow-pierced St. Sebastian, the saint after whom the island was named and who is a symbol of the pain and suffering that was caused to the natives there. A voiceover proclaims that death has claimed the evil and asks God to bring joy and happiness to the living. The film has rightfully been proclaimed a minor masterpiece.

Tourneur's next film, *The Leopard Man*, did not achieve the same greatness, but sometimes it is too quickly dismissed by horror enthusiasts, for it is certainly far better than the average '40s horror film. Based on Cornell Woolrich's novel *Black Alibi*, it was once more scripted by Ardel Wray (with polishes by Lewton himself).

Perhaps what is most peculiar about *The Leopard Man* is the way the narrative is fragmented, dropping one character's story to pick up another, so that the film really does not have a main character or focal point except for the series of murders it depicts. As a result, tension does not build around one protagonist.

The film opens with a publicity stunt that goes awry. We see a ball balanced precariously on a fountain while a dancer, Clo-Clo (Margo), dances around it clicking castanets. Enter Kiki Walker (Jean Brooks) leading a black panther on a leash, a gimmick thought up by her companion and press agent Jerry Manning (Dennis O'Keefe). However, before long, the leopard escapes, leading to disaster.

There follows one of the most accomplished shock sequences ever filmed. A frightened Mexican girl (Margaret Landry) is forced to go out into the night and buy flour for the evening meal. Under a train trestle, she is further frightened by the sudden appearance of a tumbleweed, but she manages to make it to the store without incident. Now she must go home, and her terror mounts. Once more under the trestle, she thinks she sees a pair of glowing eyes and then hears a shocking sound, but it proves to be just a train passing overhead. However, after the train is gone, the camera reveals a waiting panther. The girl flees.

Having established sympathy for the girl and concern for her immediate safety, Tourneur then cuts to the interior of her house, where her mother is preparing supper. Outside we hear the daughter's cries for help and she begins pounding the door, but at first the mother thinks it is no more than her fear of the dark. Then, she realizes that something is seriously wrong and frantically tries to open the door, but the sudden appearance of blood seeping under the doorway indicates that she is too late. Without showing the least bit of violence, Tourneur has fashioned one of the most evocative and memorable terror pieces ever committed to film. It is so powerful, it threatens to overwhelm the rest of the film.

Later, a young girl goes to the cemetery to meet her boyfriend on a date (of all romantic spots), but arrives too late. To her horror, she discovers that she has been locked in for the night. She screams to try and attract the attention of a passing motorist, but instead her screams attract something else – something that moves in the branches of a tree overhanging the cemetery wall.

The final victim is Clo-Clo, who is told by a fortuneteller that she will meet a rich man, accept money and die. She spends some time in a nervous walk along the streets to get back home, with the accompanying sound of castanets on the soundtrack. She meets a rich man who gives her money, and the audience is led to suspect that this is the killer, but she arrives home safely – only to discover that she lost the money that was given to her. When she goes out to seek it, she meets her doom at the hands of Dr. Galbraith (James Bell), a psychopathic professor compelled by forces beyond his control to murder women in such a manner that the authorities will think that the escaped leopard is responsible.

However, Galbraith makes the mistake of sending Kiki flowers, which puts Jerry onto him. In the finale, the killer is apprehended at a funeral mass, as black-hooded mourners (who look like refugees from the Inquisition) escort a casket among the Joshua trees. It is a macabre setting to be sure, but its potential is barely tapped in the rapidly resolved climax of the film. Still, while the film as a whole does not hang together, its terror set pieces are among Tourneur's – and indeed, horror filmdom's – most accomplished.

Tourner received his promotion and began working on *Days of Glory*, a tribute to the Russians fighting the Nazis which served as Gregory Peck's screen debut. Better was *Experiment Perilous*, a melodrama about a frightened wife who begins to wonder if a wealthy philanthropist is what he seems. This was followed by *Canyon Passage*, a western involving a romantic triangle where Dana Andrews is in love with Susan Hayward who is Brian Donlevy's fiancée.

Tourneur then began one of his most important films, *Out of the Past*, based on Daniel Mainwaring's novel *Build My Gallows High*. (Mainwaring is perhaps best known to horror fans for scripting *Invasion of the Body Snatchers*.) *Out of the Past* proved one of the definitive *noir* films as it traced the story of a decent man destroyed by a combination of fate and a femme fatale. The plot is overcomplicated but involves Robert Mitchum as a filling station owner whose past as a detective catches up with him. He was hired by a big mobster (Kirk Douglas) to track down the mobster's ex-girlfriend (the beautiful and bad Jane Greer) who made off with $40,000. Finding her in Mexico, Mitchum is manipulated into believing her story that she did not do it. He falls in love with her, but sees her true colors when she kills Steve Brodie, Mitchum's former partner, who was sent after the wayward pair.

Tourneur delineates a world of light and shadow, (gorgeously shot by

Nicholas Musuraca), of constant turnabout and intrigue where nobody can be counted on to be what he seems. From the quiet ordered world he left behind with a mute assistant and a lovely girlfriend, Mitchum becomes enmeshed once more in Greer's and Douglas' deadly world, much to his disgust. While not a horror film, this is undoubtedly one of Tourneur's major works, with corrupt evil taking the place of the supernatural element in Tourneur's horror thrillers.

Berlin Express followed, another *noir* film. This time the plot concerned the attempts of a Nazi underground group to eliminate a Dr. H. Bernhardt (Paul Lukas) after World War II in order to thwart his plans to reunify Germany. Bernhardt's character was based on Thomas Mann and is even given some Mann sayings to quote. Particularly memorable were a scene of an assassination attempt through the windows of a passing train and another sequence where a clown keeps performing after he has been shot, though we see what the audience applauding him does not – the blood seeping from his costume.

However, Tourneur was not always lucky in the assignments given him, as *Easy Living*, a film about football, attests. Nevertheless, *Flame and the Arrow* deserves acclaim as a flashy and entertaining swashbuckler that makes good use of star Burt Lancaster's acrobatic talents as he plays with buddy Nick Cravat. Lancaster is a rebel leader in medieval Italy who is out to rescue his young son in bits of derring-do that easily rival those of *The Crimson Pirate*.

Also worthy of special note is *Nightfall*, an engaging B movie starring Aldo Ray as a man hunted down by two desperate criminals (Brian Keith and Rudy Bond). Ray was present when the pair of bank robbers shot and killed a doctor that he was hunting with and was shot and left for dead himself. However, the killers mistake the doctor's black bag for their own, leaving Ray with the loot. He decides to hide it, otherwise he might be accused of the crime. At the beginning of the movie, Ray befriends Anne Bancroft, but is abducted by the criminals shortly afterwards, leaving him to wonder if he has been betrayed. There is a memorable sequence where he escapes death beside a deserted oil derrick and a grand finale in the snow where Ray triumphs with the help of a convenient tractor-snowplow.

Tourneur triumphantly returned to the horror genre with *Curse of the Demon* (United Kingdom title *Night of the Demon*), scripted by Charles Bennett, who wrote the story or screenplay for many of Alfred Hitchcock's early suspense films. Indeed, a number of Hitchcockian elements appear in the film (ordinary man in extraordinary circumstances; intellectual, diabolical villain; a dotty old woman; dangerous strangers; feelings of paranoia).

Bennett bought the rights to Montague R. James' story "Casting the Runes" for the purpose of converting it into a screen story for himself to direct. Unable to find financing in Hollywood, he allowed producer Hal E.

Chester to option the rights only to discover too late that RKO now expressed an interest. At least the producer had the foresight to hire Tourneur to direct.

Although Chester has been much criticized for his inclusion of a demon both at the beginning and the end of the film, far more damaging to the feature was the excision of 13 minutes when it was released in America in order to bring it down to second-feature length. According to Bennett, the title was changed from *Night of the Demon* to *Curse of the Demon* so that it would not be confused with *Night of the Iguana*, though this is unlikely as the latter film was not released until several years later. American distributors frequently felt that British film should have more lurid titles (for example, *Night of the Eagle* was changed to *Burn Witch Burn*).

Luckily, the preferred British version is the one most often shown now, though oddly the version that I have seen is missing any change-over marks (those small white circles that appear in the upper right part of the frame that are used to alert projectionists when it will be time to change over from one projector to another).

The film establishes a tense atmosphere right at the beginning as Prof. Harrington (Maurice Denham) begs Dr. Julian Karswell (Niall MacGinnis, who is simply excellent) to call off his demon as Harrington will now call off the investigation of Karswell's devil cult. But it is too late—the spell has been set in motion, and the parchment which marks Harrington for death has been destroyed. Harrington flees, but finds a ball of fire pursuing him. In backing up his car, he smashes into a pole which crashes down on his car and electrocutes him. (A controversial shot of a demon and the demon's foot crushing the car were added over Tourneur's objections.)

The film then cuts to the plane flight of Dr. John Holden (Dana Andrews), who is arriving in London to attend a paranormal convention and help Harrington with his investigations. Holden is a skeptic who does not believe in the devil or supernatural powers. He vows to continue the investigation of Karswell, though Harrington's niece Joanna (Peggy Cummins) tries to warn him that Karswell is indeed dangerous.

While researching witchcraft in the British Museum, Holden meets the mysterious Karswell, who determines that Holden will not call off the investigation. Dropping some books, Karswell secretly passes a parchment with runic writing on it to Holden. Joanna, reading from Harrington's diary, reveals that Harrington had been passed the same kind of parchment just before he died, and that it tried to immolate itself in the fireplace.

Tourneur beautifully contrasts the sinister and the innocent. Holden and Joanna decide to visit Karswell's estate where he is throwing a party for a group of orphan children and has dressed himself up as a clown. "I used to make my living like this years ago," he tells Holden. "You see before you Dr. Bobo the Magnificent!" Apparently, Karswell has gained immensely in power and position since his days of playing Dr. Bobo, and he gives Holden a demonstration of his powers by creating a small storm which scatters the party and its accoutrements. (Tourneur was proud to have created a powerful windstorm by using tied-down aircraft rather than meager wind machines, and the result is definitely impressive.)

During the storm, Mrs. Karswell (Athene Seyler), Karswell's frightened mother, shows Joanna a copy of *The True Discoveries of the Witches and Demons*, a very rare *grimoire* which has been stolen from the British Museum that contains a woodcut similar to the demon glimpsed at the opening of the film. Karswell comes in and after bidding Joanna good-bye, scolds his mother and then warns her: "You believe in the supernatural. I've shown you some of its power and some of its danger. Then believe this also. You get nothing for nothing. This house, this land, the way we live . . . nothing for nothing. My followers, who pay for all this, do it out of fear. And I do what I do out of fear also. That's part of the price." He has revealed to Holden that Holden has three days to live, but when his mother asks if he cannot stop it, Karswell explains that if it is not somebody else's life, then it will be his that will be taken. What has been started cannot be stopped.

Unfortunately, this revealing exchange was trimmed out of the American version, though it goes a good way towards establishing why Karswell became involved in black magic and that he is dealing with powers beyond even his control. It also establishes that the often foolish-seeming Mrs. Karswell is worried about her son, that their relationship is strained, and that she knows that if she attempts to stop this thing, her own son's life will be forfeit. The pair talk quietly but forcefully, lending credence to their utterances. That Karswell entertains orphan children also suggests that he is trying, in some small way, to hold onto his humanity as well as maintain a link with his pathetic past.

Even though a skeptic, Holden becomes nervous enough that when his parchment flies into the fireplace grill just as Harrington's had, he stops it from catching fire. Despite the fact that he knows he should not believe in spells, he becomes nervous and decides to get permission to hypnotize a man named Hobart, a former member of Karswell's group who has gone insane.

The sequence at the Hobart farm, also cut from the American release print, shows Holden slowly discovering that the farm is run by Karswell's satanists. Hobart has been accused of murder, and the farmers reveal that he "made the killing happen" by "passing it to a brother." When Holden's parchment flies out of his wallet, Mrs. Hobart (Janet Barrow) exclaims, "He has been chosen. . . . Let no arm be raised to defend him." The group stare at him as if at a condemned man, and, frightened and confused, Holden leaves the farm, noting runic symbols on the door.

Joanna takes Holden to a séance arranged by Mrs. Karswell and conducted by Mr. Meek (Reginald Beckwith). During the séance, Meek suddenly speaks with Harrington's voice and urges that Holden give up the investigation. "Karswell has the key, he's translated the old book, the answer is there," Harrington's voice insists. Holden becomes disgusted, believing that the whole thing has been staged for his benefit. Mrs. Karswell runs after him, pleading that he must believe, when Karswell suddenly shows up in a parked car and demands that she come along with him.

There follows the best sequence in the film, which shows that Tourneur had lost none of his power since his Lewton films. Holden makes a nervous trip through the forest and breaks into Karswell's house, Lufford Hall. After a quick look upstairs, he goes to the study, but there are two quick shots of a hand on the railing that indicate the presence of Karswell, though in a full shot revealing the staircase there is apparently nobody there. Suddenly, Holden finds himself attacked by a panther, which when Karswell snaps on the lights becomes nothing more than a house cat, though Karswell describes it as a minor "house demon" that he has arranged to protect his belongings. Karswell offers to show Holden the door, but Holden insists on going out the way he came. There is a classic Lewton "bus" as Holden walks back through the forest. A branch suddenly snaps into frame, startling him. However, even more startling is the appearance of a distant fireball, which from the opening of the film we have learned to associate with the demon. Holden runs for his life and makes it to safety, but he does not have much time left.

He finally reaches Hobart, who explains that the only way to save himself is to return the parchment to the one who passed it to him. Worried that Holden might try passing the parchment to him, Hobart commits suicide by jumping out a window.

Convinced that the danger is real, Holden discovers that Karswell has kidnapped Joanna and that they are on the train headed for Southampton. It is Karswell's turn to panic when Holden enters his compartment and the fidgety Karswell is ever on the alert not to accept the parchment while Holden tries ruse after ruse. When the police stop by, Holden slips the runes into Karswell's coat pocket and when Karswell picks up the coat, he knows that the parchment has been successfully passed with only minutes to go before the 10 o'clock deadline.

The train stops and the parchment blows out of Karswell's hands and along the train tracks. Before Karswell, who chases frantically after it, can retrieve it, it bursts into flame and the demon reappears and mangles Karswell's body. The police discover the body and assume it was run over by a train. Holden leaves with Joanna, declaring that some things are better left unknown.

There has been much debate about the insertion of the demon into the film, some critics feeling that the murders would be best left ambiguous–

Jacques Tourneur (in bow tie) on the set of War Gods of the Deep *(aka* The City Under the Sea*), his final feature but sadly not one of his finer moments.*

were they caused by a demon or were they not? – while others felt it was better to leave the demon to the imagination. The existence of the woodcut in the book indicates that the demon was meant to be shown, and indeed it presents an unforgettable image in the film, though luckily it is not shown doing much. It might have been more effective if its appearances were cut back – there is an unfortunate shot of the demon picking up and throwing down an obvious doll representing Karswell – but it is such a splendidly ugly monstrosity that I would prefer not to imagine the movie without it.

With *Night of the Demon,* Tourneur created one of the finest horror films of the '50s, a film whose atmosphere is palpably thrilling and chilling. Dana Andrews gives one of his best performances as John Holden, a modern man whose faith is in science but who slowly becomes convinced of the power of the supernatural world. Niall MacGinnis is superb as Karswell, a ruthless villain who nevertheless retains his humanity and whose evil doings have succeeded in making a victim of himself.

Sadly, Tourneur was not to match this level of quality horror again in motion pictures, though he came close in the classic *Twilight Zone* episode "Night Calls" about a young girl who receives phone calls on her toy phone from her dead grandmother. However, by and large, Tourneur despised working in television.

The Fearmakers offered a witchhunt of a different kind as Dana Andrews sought out Communist subversives in Washington, D.C. This was followed by some unfortunate films including *Timbuktu*, *Frontier Rangers*, and two films he worked on but did not receive credit for, *Mission of Danger* and *Fury River*. Tourneur received credit for *The Giant of Marathon*, an historical epic about the battle of Marathon with Steve Reeves as the "giant" of the title, though Mario Bava is often credited with the action scenes and the producer was said to have taken a hand. Tourneur was not happy that each member of his cast spoke a different language and refused to do the underwater scenes.

Tourneur returned to horror with *The Comedy of Terrors*, which featured an excellent cast (Vincent Price, Peter Lorre, Boris Karloff and Basil Rathbone) but a sub-par script by Richard Matheson, hot off of writing his comedic version of *The Raven*. Karloff was so ill during production that he switched roles with Rathbone.

The premise has promise as Vincent Price plays a poor undertaker who, with his clumsy assistant, sets out to dig up some business by killing someone. Price also plots to poison his father-in-law, played by Karloff, and after a bungled first attempt settles on offing his persistent landlord, played by Rathbone, who keeps falling into cataleptic fits and then reviving. However, rather than the outrageous black comedy that the premise calls for, Matheson's script relies mostly on slapstick, which the talented cast did not quite pull off on the rushed 15-day schedule the film was given. Matheson was associate producer and wanted Tourneur, but did not seem to realize that the material was not geared towards Tourneur's forte, i.e., fluid and moody atmospheric set pieces that create a feeling of unease and impending disaster.

War Gods of the Deep (aka *City Under the Sea*) starts off more promisingly. Vincent Price stars as the ruler of a submerged kingdom off the British coast and has some of the poetic feel associated with Tourneur's earlier films in the first half. But as the heroes reach the kingdom itself, with its weak gill monsters and Price's attempts to win Susan Hart for himself because he is convinced that she is the reincarnation of his wife, the film falls apart. Once more, Tourneur refused to film the underwater scenes, leaving them to John Lamb.

Sadly, that was the last film that Tourneur was to direct, and he died in 1977. Tourneur will be remembered for the fine work he produced, particularly his qualities as a visual stylist and his ability to create scenes where the audience empathizes with the character on the screen in tense and quiet moments. He worked notably with the theme that good and evil are in conflict in the world and that evil may pop up in the most unexpected places –

a quiet girl who transforms into a vicious animal when aroused, a clown who unleashes a demon from hell, a beautiful woman who has torn a family apart with her beauty and is transformed into a zombie, a professor who uses a leopard as the black alibi for his killings, and a femme fatale who is innocent one minute and a vicious killer the next. All are memorable characters who demonstrate the uncertainty of a world where duplicity can hide danger and it is difficult to know whom to turn to or trust. This is the world Tourneur outlines so poetically in his films.

Edgar G. Ulmer (1904-1972)

Menschen am Sonntag (*People on Sunday*, codir. with Robert Siodmak, 1929); *Damaged Lives; Mr. Broadway* (1933); *The Black Cat; Thunder Over Texas* (1934); *From Nine to Nine* (1935); *Natalka Poltavka* (in Ukrainian); *Greene Felde* (*Green Fields* in Yiddish; codir. with Jacob Ben-Ami, 1937); *Yankel dem Schmidt* (*The Singing Blacksmith* in Yiddish, 1938); *Zaprosh za Dunayem* (*Cossacks in Exile* in Ukrainian); *Die Klatsche* (*The Light Ahead* in Yiddish); *Fishke der Drume* (*Fishke the Lame One* in Yiddish); *Moon over Harlem; Americaner Schadchen* (*American Matchmaker* in Yiddish); *Cloud in the Sky* (documentary) (1940); *Another to Conquer* (documentary, 1941); *Let My People Live* (documentary); *Tomorrow We Live* (1942); *My Son the Hero; Girls in Chains; Isle of Forgotten Sins* (aka *Monsoon*); *Jive Junction* (1943); *Bluebeard* (1944); *Strange Illusion* (aka *Out of the Night*); *Club Havana* (1945); *Detour; The Wife of Monte Cristo; Her Sister's Secret; The Strange Woman* (1946); *Carnegie Hall* (1947); *Ruthless* (1948); *I Pirati de Capri* (aka *The Pirates of Capri; Captain Sirocco*, 1949); *St. Benny the Dip; The Man from Planet X* (1951); *Babes in Bagdad* (1952); *Murder Is My Beat* (aka *Dynamite Anchorage*); *The Naked Dawn* (1955); *The Daughter of Dr. Jekyll* (1957); *Hannibal; The Amazing Transparent Man; Beyond the Time Barrier* (1960); *L'Atlantide* (aka *Queen of Atlantis; Journey Beneath the Desert;* codir. with Giuseppe Masini, 1961); *The Cavern* (1965).

TELEVISION: *Swiss Family Robinson* (pilot).

By his own count, Edgar G. Ulmer directed 128 films in countries as diverse as the United States, Mexico, Italy, Spain, and Germany, and it seems unlikely that a complete filmography will ever be known. Though thought of by many as a horror specialist, Ulmer was in fact nothing of the kind; he was instead a highly diverse individual who attempted low-budget films in every conceivable genre – mysteries, westerns, musicals, animated films, public service documentaries, regionally released foreign language movies, you name it. He became celebrated by French film critics with film-maker François Truffaut giving high praise to his western *The Naked Dawn*. Throughout his film career he was forced to work on the most minuscule of budgets and shooting schedules but even so managed to imbue most of his projects with some integrity and flair.

In all this variety, it is hard to imagine a unifying theme in Ulmer's work, especially since he seemed to ignore plot in many of his films to concentrate

680

on establishing attractive visuals and building particular moods. However, one story trend that follows much of Ulmer's work is the "detour," in which fate lays out a wrong turn that plunges the protagonists into a kind of nightmare world, where people make mistakes and then have to pay heavily for them.

This theme is probably given its best workout by Ulmer in the cult classic *Detour*, a fatalistically *noir* tale of a grifter who is trying to hitchhike his way back to his fiancée when he is picked up for a ride by a rich man who happens to die on him. Afraid the police will think he murdered the gentleman, the wanderer steals the man's car only to pick up a ruthless female who knew the dead man and threatens to "expose" the protagonist. She cows him into going along with her schemes until he accidentally murders her in a cheap Los Angeles hotel room by pulling on a telephone cord from under a doorway that happens to be wrapped around her neck on the other side.

Detour is a shining example of how an artistically interesting film can be made out of virtually nothing. Ulmer uses sophisticated silent film techniques to set up his narrator and create a bleak mood, having him stumble into a coffee shop and hear music that makes him remember what he has left behind (and will now have to forsake forever). While actor Tom Neal, looking and acting like an emotional zombie, provides the key narration, Ulmer's camera does some telling tracking shots that take us into the man's pain.

How many directors would have the audacity or the imagination to create a nightclub scene with nothing more than a singer on a stage and three shadows of musicians on the wall, as Ulmer does? Or to keep a film griping and emotionally involving while playing out most of the action using nothing more than a dingy motel set or a car mockup and a process screen, as Ulmer does here?

Born in Vienna, Austria, Ulmer studied architecture at Vienna's Academy of Art and Sciences and philosophy at the University of Vienna. He used his architecture background extensively in his films, often designing key costumes, sets, models and background paintings himself.

His first work in the dramatic arts was as an actor and assistant set designer for the famous Burg theater. He got his start in the moviemaking business when Rochus Gliese asked him to be a silhouette cutter for Paul Wegener's *The Golem*. During the silent era, silhouettes were used to provide an additional context for a scene. For example, a love scene was often shot through a silhouette of a heart, or if the director wanted to shoot some scenery outside of a window, a silhouette of a window was placed next to the camera lens. After two weeks, Ulmer started working on set construction under Hans Poelzig, whom he named a character after in his most famous horror film, *The Black Cat*.

Ulmer was involved in a number of notable silent features in Germany, working with Murnau on *Nosferatu* and *Faust*, with Lang on *Metropolis, Die Nebelungen* and *Spione (Spies)*. The influence of these directors figure heavily in his work with his careful attention to *mise-en-scène* à la Murnau and his doomed characters à la Lang. Finally, he codirected the film that would presage the French *nouvelle vague* or "New Wave" cinema by 30 years, *Menschen am Sonntag (People on Sunday)*, which he directed with Robert Siodmak.

Coming to the United States with Murnau, Ulmer worked on *Sunrise* (1927) and *Tabu* (1929), designed sets for Universal, MGM, and Broadway productions before directing his first sound film, *Damaged Lives*, which was a remarkably early treatment of the subject of venereal disease. This was followed by *Mr. Broadway*, one of Ulmer's many obscure films that I have not seen.

Ulmer became friends with Carl Laemmle, Jr., who regarded him as something of an intellectual. When Ulmer came up with the idea of teaming Boris Karloff and Bela Lugosi in *The Black Cat*, Laemmle jumped at it.

An early script was written by Stanley Bergerman and Jack Cunningham, which was titled *The Brain Never Dies* and combined Edgar Allan Poe's "The Black Cat" and elements from "The Fall of the House of Usher" with the tale of a brain surgeon who transplants a portion of a human brain into a cat. This was followed by another script closer to the original Poe story about a man who gouges out the eye of a cat and accidentally walls it up when he buries his wife's body in the cellar.

Both these approaches were junked when Ulmer collaborated with George Sims who wrote books and short stories (as Paul Cain) and film scripts (as Peter Ruric). Sims' other films include *Gambling Ship* (based on his own novel *Fast One*), *Affairs of a Gentleman, Dark Sands, Twelve Crowded Hours, The Night of January 16*, and *Grand Central Murder*, and he is said to have worked with von Sternberg on *The Salvation Hunters*. He worked on *Mademoiselle Fifi* for Val Lewton and Robert Wise. His last screen credit was *Alias a Gentleman*, released in 1948, though he did go on to write *The Lady in Yellow* for television in 1960 before dying the same year.

Sims' real reputation, however, rests on his work for *Black Mask* magazine writing as Paul Cain. His novel *Fast One* is considered to be the progenitor of the hard-boiled school of writing with tough-talking heroes who take their lumps and dish out plenty of violence. His only other book, *Seven Slayers*, is a collection of his shorter works.

It was Sims, writing as Ruric, who did the screenplay for *The Black Cat*, and his peculiar style accounts for many of the film's oddities. By no means a great stylist, his writing was nonetheless quick, sharp, and to the point, though at times the motivations of the characters and the plot points are hard to follow. However, his work was praised by no less a writer than

Raymond Chandler, and some still refer to *Fast One* as the ultimate hard-boiled novel.

There is also no doubt that one of Ulmer and Sims' influences in writing *The Black Cat* was the sensational trial of Aleister Crowley, a satanist who described himself as "the wickedest man in the world," who took artist Nina Hammett to court over what she revealed about his devil-worship practices in her autobiography. Crowley became the inspiration for Karloff's character of Hjalmar Poelzig, while Sims patterned nominal hero Peter Allison, who describes himself as "the world's greatest writer . . . of unimportant books," after himself.

Like many of Ulmer's most important movies, the film begins with a journey. This time, Allison (David Manners, at the time a specialist at Universal in playing the handsome if bland hero in horror movies) and his bride, Joan, have just left their wedding reception to begin their honeymoon, boarding a train. There they encounter the curious character of Dr. Vitus Werdegast (Bela Lugosi), a Hungarian psychiatrist recently released from prison, who has accidentally been assigned the same train compartment as they have.

While many critics have complained about or disdained Lugosi's acting ability, and there is no question his range was limited, *The Black Cat* contains one of his best parts and he plays it with flamboyant flair, conveying quite a lot in his odd phrasings of the script lines. When a bag almost falls on top of Mrs. Allison (Jacqueline Wells, later known as Julie Bishop), he observes, "It is better to be scared than to be crushed," with a smile. Lugosi is playing a good guy in the film, but Ulmer uses his oddness to good effect – we frequently see him being helpful, but there is always the possibility that he might also be crazy, which adds to the atmosphere of gloom and misery that the film builds up.

Atmosphere is very important to appreciating *The Black Cat*. There are no real onscreen shocks and not a tremendous amount of action, though things are constantly happening. Rather, it is designed to be a mystery in which two innocents (the Allisons) are thrust into a deadly situation they cannot comprehend and there are sinister implications and dark forebodings everywhere.

Ulmer seems to have directed his actors to move as though sleepwalking, giving the film a very eerie dream-like quality as first one character and then another seems to fall victim to the "mediumistic" vibrations in the air. This might also help explain all the little pieces in the film that do not quite tie together – in fact, the film ends on a joke about Allison's previous book being too fantastic to be believed, and the couple laugh at how much more fantastic real life has been.

In addition to Ulmer's themes of the vagaries of fate and the interrupted journey, *The Black Cat* also includes his theme of the battle of wills:

Very rare shot of Edgar G. Ulmer (left) with star Bela Lugosi on the set of The Black Cat. *Little did these novices know that they were already at the apex of their respective careers, though much fine work followed.*

Poelzig and Werdegast are constantly in conflict, but try to keep their enmity hidden under a civilized veneer when the Allisons are around. (Other examples of this theme in Ulmer's work include Tom Neal vs. Ann Savage in *Detour*; Zachary Scott against the world in *Ruthless*; Ricardo Cortez vs. Jena Parker in *Tomorrow We Live*; and Arthur Kennedy vs. Roy Engel in *Naked Dawn*.)

There are many trance-like performances, beginning with the pained expression of Lugosi as he first hears how, in the words of their driver, "all this countryside was one of the greatest battlefields of the war. Tens of thousands have died here. That ravine was piled twelve deep with dead and wounded men. A stream of blood ran here. And that hill yonder, where Engineer Poelzig now lives, was the site of Fort Marmaros. He built his home on its very foundations. Marmaros, the greatest graveyard in the world." With a slow close of his eyes, Lugosi conveys that he can picture this grisly scene from his past all too clearly.

Karloff is trance-like when he first rises in silhouette in a stiff and unnatural manner, and initially he hardly speaks to his unexpected guests, warming his frosty facade only after he has seen the couple kissing and begins to make plans for them. The servants of Poelzig and Werdegast, the Thamal and the Majordomo, rarely speak and seem to be under a hypnotic influence. Finally, Joan Allison herself walks in a trance after her car accident that brings the group to Poelzig's manor.

These trance performances Ulmer uses not only to add a dream-like quality to the film, but also to convey a visual metaphor for death. The war (World War I, obviously) has destroyed the souls of Poelzig and Werdegast and those associated with them. Werdegast explains to the couple, "Have you ever heard of Kurgaal? It is a prison below Amsk. Many men have gone there. Few have returned. *I* have returned . . . after fifteen years." Werdegast has been pursuing Poelzig from country to country in search of his missing wife and daughter, his one aim to rescue them and murder Poelzig.

In Poelzig's past, we find he once commanded Fort Marmaros, but betrayed the fort to the Russians, thereby insuring the deaths of thousands of men, so that he might escape. He has become the leader of a satanic cult and in one of the film's most memorable touches, has preserved the bodies of several beautiful young women in glass coffins which are suspended vertically along the walls of the now barren fort which still remains below his house. It is not too great a jump to speculate that these women are Poelzig's former victims, preserved as trophies for their beauty and his enjoyment.

In a fascinating interview conducted by Peter Bogdanovich in *Film Culture* and later reprinted in the book *King of the B's*, Ulmer explained some of the background that went into his thinking:

> I had been in Prague . . . and had worked on *The Golem* (1920). I met at that time Gustav Meyrinck, the man who wrote *Golem* as a novel. Meyrinck was one of these strange Prague Jews, like Kafka, who was very tied up in the mystic Talmudic background. We had a lot of discussions, and Meyrinck at that time was contemplating a play based upon Doumont, which was a French fortress the Germans had shelled to pieces during the First World War. There were some survivors who didn't come out for years. And the commander was a strange Euripides figure who went crazy three years later when he was brought back to Paris, because he had walked on that mountain of bodies. And I thought it was a subject that was quite important. And that feeling was in the air in the twenties. . . .

The black cat of the title itself is proclaimed by Poelzig to be an ancient symbol of evil, and is deathless in the way that evil is deathless. In one of the more bizarre scenes, Werdegast experiences a severe anxiety attack at the sight of a black cat and throws a knife into it, which strangely does not cause Poelzig, the cat's owner, even to blink an eye. Later, Poelzig will pick up a living black cat – whether the same one or a different one is never clear, but the implication of deathless evil is there as well as a suggestion that Poelzig is a warlock petting his familiar. The cat's other significant moment comes when Poelzig has placed it in a chamber with the glass coffins before showing them to Werdegast. Just as Werdegast is about to shoot and kill Poelzig, he is startled by the black cat's shadow and crashes into a glass chart instead. Poelzig simply smiles, leads the way out and suggests that they play a game – a game of death.

As in Bergman's classic *The Seventh Seal*, two figures play a game of life or death. Ulmer expertly uses it as a metaphor for the situation (Poelzig, the former military commander, gambles only with other people's lives; Werdegast is honor-bound to find some means of protecting the innocent couple that he has escorted to Poelzig's house) and as a means of building suspense. While they play, they are interrupted by some comical gendarmes who have come to investigate the previous night's car crash. As the gendarmes ride bicycles, they cannot transport the Allisons back to the train station. Poelzig offers the use of his car, which his servant then explains needs repairs, and his telephone, which is dead. As Peter frantically tries to find a way to leave Poelzig's house immediately, Poelzig and Werdegast calmly play for their lives.

Poelzig predicted Werdegast would lose, and he is right. Poelzig announces "checkmate." (Executives at Universal were afraid that a large number of people in the audience would not be familiar with chess and it was decided that the line, "You lose, Vitus," be dubbed in to clarify matters. However, Karloff was not available for this last bit of post-production and so, strangely, another actor delivers Poelzig's line in that one shot.) That also becomes a signal for Thalmal to cooperate with Poelzig and prevent Peter and Joan from leaving. Thalmal knocks Peter out and places him in a revolving room beneath the house while Joan is taken upstairs to her room.

Mention should be made of the setting for this film, designed in Bauhaus style by Ulmer himself. Unlike the typical rotting mansion in most horror thrillers and murder mysteries, Poelzig's house is extremely modern for the time. It is filled with peculiar touches – a front door that slides open, a radio that looks like a clock, lights that automatically turn themselves on and off in some parts, a bright, austere design that is attractive to the eye. Though the underground fort is quite barren, the film amply demonstrates Ulmer's good visual eye for interesting compositions and designs. John Mescall's dramatic and fluid camerawork are a big asset to this design as well.

Some people, like Danny Peary in his article on the film in *Cult Movies #3*, would have you believe that the house is even odder than it actually is.

Peary presents a theory that "the story we are watching unfold is indeed meant to be a weird manifestation of the postwar delirium shared by Poelzig and Werdegast, then Ulmer can get away with any inconsistency, any break in continuity. Joan's door can, logically, slide open one moment yet need to be pushed open the next."

While the film does suffer from some continuity errors, the door is not one of them, as more careful observation of the film shows. That there are in fact *two* doors to Allison's bedroom, one sliding and one not, is demonstrated in long shots of the room and the relative positions of the doors to the bed. Peary also errs in claiming the film has two mute servants (the Majordomo can talk, though he has few lines), and while he complains that no two actors pronounce some names the same way, this is not atypical in Europe, where differing nationalities have differing pronunciations of person and place names. Poelzig is supposed to be Austrian, and so pronounced Karen differently from Werdegast or Joan, who Americanizes the name.

Peary also questioned why Poelzig would choose to sacrifice Joan instead of his own wife, Karen, whom he kills after Karen reveals her identity to Joan – she is Werdegast's daughter. Joan in turn informs her that Poelzig has been lying all these years, her father is alive and has come looking for her. However, Peary has overlooked the passage from the *Rites of Lucifer* book that we see Poelzig reading in bed with his sleeping wife which demands a maiden (i.e. a virgin) be sacrificed. Married to Poelzig for several years, Karen is obviously not a virgin, but Joan had just started on her honeymoon when she was injured in the car accident, and so her marriage has not been consummated. Significantly, Poelzig gives Joan and Peter separate rooms.

Peary does, though, make some valid points in his interesting critique of the film. Werdegast does provide us with the information that Poelzig's house is built on a cache of dynamite, but there is never any indication of how he knows this or why Poelzig would want it done in the first place, though since the controls are in the fort area and not up in the house, perhaps it has been rigged that way since the war. Peary complains that the revolving room is too easy for Peter to get out of, but perhaps it is not meant as a permanent prison, just simply a place to get him out of the way for a while. (Also, Peter can only see the controls because he fortuitously brought some matches with him.) It is true, as Peary points out, that the only real action Peter takes, shooting Werdegast as he is skinning Poelzig alive, is the wrong one, but a shot Ulmer inserts makes it clear that when Werdegast and Joan struggle to retrieve a key from the dead Thamal's hand, from Peter's angle it looks like the two are struggling with each other.

The fact that Poelzig is portrayed as a satanist made censors nervous in England, where the nonsensical description of "sun worshippers" was looped in instead and the film retitled *The House of Doom*. The scenes of Karloff leading his congregation by some tilted crosses, reciting in Latin while his followers don their robes and bring down Joan to be sacrificed, are exquisite compositions. Notable, too, is John Carradine in one of his earliest film roles as an organist whom we see only from the top of his head in these scenes. When a cult member screams before the sacrifice, that gives Thamal and Werdegast sufficient time to unbind Joan and carry her to safety.

At this point, Poelzig loses the superb control that he has demonstrated throughout the film and becomes frantic in his efforts to stop Werdegast and regain the intended victim. In the frenzied climax, the Majordomo knocks out Peter as he is about to escape and shoots Thamal, who nonetheless retains enough strength to strangle him. Poelzig attacks Werdegast, but with Thamal's help, they are able to overpower him and tie him to his own embalming rack.

Having discovered that Poelzig has married and killed both Werdegast's wife and daughter drives Werdegast to an almost insane level of violence to get his revenge, namely stripping the flesh from Poelzig's body while he is still alive to torture his soul. (The glass coffins also hint at necrophilia, but that is never made explicit.) Poelzig has taken everything from Werdegast that Werdegast could care about. Shot by Peter, Werdegast tells the young couple to go and sets off the dynamite (which has a five-minute delay) in order to destroy the fortress and Poelzig's devil cult with it.

While lines like Lugosi's retort, "Superstition, perhaps; baloney, perhaps not," may seem campy and risible to modern audiences, the film does retain its dignity and is much more than a battle of the odd accents between Karloff and Lugosi. The two represent the "living dead," people who have survived a tremendous tragedy and have either given in to or become obsessed by the horrors that they find or manufacture around them. The Allisons represent the danger to innocent people when ensnared by forces they can neither comprehend nor control, forces intent on dread and death.

In the Bogdanovich interview, Ulmer said that Karloff was

> very charming. And he never took himself seriously. My biggest job was to keep him in the part, because he laughed at himself. . . . One of the nicest scenes I had with [Karloff], he lies in the bed next to the daughter of Lugosi, and the young couple rings him down at the door, and he gets up and you see him the first time in costume, in that modernistic set. I explained the scene to him and he said, "Aren't you ashamed to do a thing like that – that has nothing to do with acting?" So I told him to be nice and do it, and he never took himself seriously – he got into bed, we got ready to shoot, and he got up, he turned to the camera, after he put his shoes on, and said, "Boo!" Every time I had him come in by the door, he would open the door and say, "Here comes the heavy . . ." He was a very, very lovely man.

What Karloff did not understand as having to do with acting did have a lot to do with making good cinema. He smiles in the role, but only to be ingratiating, and delivers a fine performance as the sinister Poelzig. His wardrobe consisted largely of bathrobes and pajamas, reinforcing the sleep or death imagery, and his hair is cut into a memorably severe widow's peak. As a last sinister touch, he has black lipstick in some of his scenes, but this apparently comes and goes.

Of their six screen appearances together, this one was Karloff and Lugosi's first and most evenly matched film. Lugosi had the better role in *The Raven* and, surprisingly, *Son of Frankenstein*, where his performance as the vindictive hunchbacked shepherd Ygor was one of his best while Karloff's lumbering performance as the monster was the poorest in the series; and Karloff clearly took the major roles and all acting honors in *The Invisible Ray, Black Friday* and *The Body Snatcher*.

The film, though cut down by Universal, proved far more successful than Florey's *Murders in the Rue Morgue*, which had flopped financially. However, the success did Ulmer little good. On the set he fell in love with his wife to be, and script girl on many of his films, Shirley Castle. Unfortunately, she was married to a high-ranking executive at the studio, who had Ulmer blacklisted for taking his wife away from him. Unable to get studio work, he had to start working for independents under the pseudonym John Warner and later left to make Yiddish and other foreign language films in New York.

Ulmer did not return to work in Hollywood until he came back in 1942 to work for Producers Releasing Corporation, or PRC, one of the most impoverished studios on poverty row, but one which would give him freedom provided he kept a film under budget and would only shoot for six days. To achieve these minor miracles, Ulmer would spend weeks in pre-production and preparation, even going so far as to rehearse the actors without the camera, a technique uncommon on poverty row.

Bluebeard was Ulmer's second horror film, and while *The Black Cat* is relatively well known, *Bluebeard* is often neglected or overlooked despite the fact that it was John Carradine's first leading role in a horror film. Perhaps the reason for this neglect had to do with *Bluebeard* being made in 1944, and in the '40s the horror films that garnered all the attention were either the Universal monster marathons or Val Lewton's subtle RKO chillers (see chapters on Jacques Tourneur, Mark Robson and Robert Wise). *Bluebeard* was not from a major studio and its story of a psychotic killer makes it a borderline horror film, albeit a good one. It is also one of Ulmer's finer films and features a solid performance by John Carradine; he even considered it one of his best film performances.

Ulmer considered Carradine one of America's finest actors and had starred him in *Isle of Forgotten Sins* (aka *Monsoon*), a South Seas adventure quickly assembled to make use of the vast miniature palm tree set leftover from John Ford's *Hurricane*. To give *Bluebeard* a richer feel, Ulmer created his own matte paintings and model work to give this six-day epic scope, as well as pouring six weeks of preparation into it.

For the story of the film, Ulmer departs from the Charles Perrault tale of a man who married several wives and tells each one not to open a secret door which conceals a room containing the corpses of the unfortunate wives who did not follow Bluebeard's advice. Arnold Phillips and Werner H. Furst's story eliminates the marriages and the secret room and leaves only a man who kills women.

The film opens and closes on the waters of the Seine, where bodies have been fished out by policemen. A sign clues us into what has been going on: "Warning! Citizens of Paris! A murderer is in your midst! A criminal who strangles young women! Any person having information concerning this Bluebeard, please communicate with the Police at once!" The warning is signed by the prefect of police, and from its message and the fact that Carradine plays a character named Gaston Morel, it is apparent that the story is about *a* Bluebeard rather than *the* Bluebeard.

Morel is a puppeteer and a painter caught up in forces he cannot control. He strangles a model played by Sonia Sorel (who became engaged to Carradine during the filming of *Bluebeard* and later married him). Carradine is a necktie murderer, slipping off his cravat to strangle his victims before dumping their bodies into the river below his apartment. As there is no mystery as to who the killer is, Ulmer's challenge was to make him interesting and sympathetic. The real mystery becomes, why does he do this and when will he get caught? Ulmer uses the character's being a puppeteer as a visual metaphor. Morel manipulates people according to his grand scheme, but is himself a helpless puppet, the victim of impulses he cannot control, as well as of his partner in crime, an art dealer (Ludwig Stossel) who sells Morel's paintings.

Ulmer was a very cultured man who liked to use classical music in his scores (which he did on both *The Black Cat* and *Bluebeard*). He also used Morel's profession of puppeteer to make an allusion to the story of *Faust*, introducing us to the character as he is presenting a puppet version of Gounod's opera. *Faust* parallels *Bluebeard* in that they are both stories of men who have given in to evil and who are tormented by love. (Also, it is worth noting that Gounod himself originally staged *Faust* as a puppet show to interest opera impresario Meyerbeer into producing it for the stage.) Morel is shown manipulating the character of Mephistopheles, the cunning seducer, which metaphorically reveals his secret nature. Carradine wanted to sing the role himself but was overruled by Ulmer, who insisted he lip-sync it with the other actors.

Ulmer's camera work and sharp close-ups focus our attention on this show, giving it force, power and meaning as a dramatic device to under-score the rest of the film. We see it sparking the interest of Lucille (Jean Parker), who watches it with her two companions. Lucille will be Morel's Marguerite while Stossel, who demands paintings to see to pay Morel's rent, becomes his Mephistopheles. Morel asks to paint Lucille and she assents, but because he has fallen in love with her, he cannot bring himself to paint her because he knows he would be driven to kill her.

Ulmer heightens the tension by allowing us a view of Morel's precarious state of mind, then showing Lucille noticing something wrong with his cravat and offering to sew it for him. The cravat represents an instrument of pas-sion, both love and death, the uncontrollable urges that Morel feels.

Naturally, the police begin to notice a connection between women who have had their portraits painted and the dead bodies turning up in the Seine. They try to track down the artist responsible for the paintings in hopes of getting a clue to the mystery which has baffled them for so long. They per-suade Lucille's sister (played by Teala Loring) to act as a decoy to trap the killer. Tracking the paintings of Stossel, they offer him 75,000 then 150,000 francs if the particular artist they have in mind will paint Loring.

The offer proves too tempting to Stossel's greed, and so he arranges for a sitting in his own gallery, adding the proviso that the artist must be al-lowed to conceal himself behind a canvas when painting. The scene where Carradine paints the overly curious sister is very suspenseful, and Ulmer makes effective use of Modest Mussorgsky's "Pictures at an Exhibition" for the scenes in the art gallery below. Loring no more than catches sight of Morel before he strangles her. The art dealer clubs the police accomplice who was supposed to have rescued her. Morel catches Stossel trying to escape and kills him, leaving by Stossel's own secret passage but leaving behind a crucial clue – the cravat that Lucille had repaired earlier.

Showing an equal degree of bravery and foolhardiness, Lucille decides to confront Morel while the police are still on their way. Ulmer stages the scene so that the puppets in Morel's studio resemble hanged men, giving a feeling of final judgment to the scene. This leads to the most impressive se-quence in the film, an extensive flashback wherein Morel relates the origin of his obsession.

For the only time in the film, tilted camera angles are used to suggest a mind out of kilter. The sets were specifically designed to play up the strangeness of these skewed scenes. We find that Morel once saved a woman's life and nursed her back to health. He fell in love with her and made a great painting of her, but one day she disappeared. Later, he dis-covered that she was a whore, and when he confronted her, she laughed at him and offered him money, shattering his idealized image of her. The broad playing by the woman enacting this role plus the unusual camera angles reinforce the idea that this experience has had a profound and traumatizing effect on Morel, and that his obsession with it has exaggerated and distorted what actually happened, has caused him to lose touch with reality, leaving him with a compulsion to kill all whom he paints in an effort to purge himself from his feelings of shame and purge the world from what he conceives of as deceitful women.

Carradine asked Ulmer to allow him to direct part of the following scene where Lucille looks on Morel with a combination of horror and compassion. Ulmer agreed, and this marked Carradine's only experience directing a film. Recalling this memory and seeing the shadows of the suspended puppets remind Morel of strangulation, driving him to remove his cravat and commence strangling Lucille. His love for her and his desire to end his fatal cycle prove not to be stronger than his compulsion.

Fortunately for the heroine, the police break in and chase Morel to the roof, whence he dives to his death in the same river that opened the film. Just before this climax, there is a short scene that suggests Lucille will live happily ever after and marry the captain of the Surete. The ending is remarkably similar to the one used by John Brahm in *The Lodger* the same year.

While Jockey Feindel received the director of photography credit on *Bluebeard*, the true cinematographer was Eugene Schüfftan, who has shot *Menschen am Sonntag*, Ulmer's first directorial effort. Schüfftan, while a much-acclaimed German cameraman, was forbidden from receiving a credit because he was not a member of the cinematographers' guild (ASC). In fact, he became the first non-member ever to win an Academy Award, for his work on *The Hustler*. Schüfftan invented the Schuefftan process, which used mirrors to composite miniature sets with live-action ones and was first employed on *Metropolis*. (The process involves scraping the backing from a mirror which reflects the miniature while a live-action sequence is filmed through the scraped-away area.) Schüfftan also provided the lovely cinematography in Georges Franju's horror classic *Les Yeux sans Visage* (aka *Eyes Without a Face* or *The Horror Chamber of Dr. Faustus*).

On *Bluebeard*, Ulmer served as his own art director and designed all of the sets. The results were very stylish and effective despite what must have been severe limitations. In fact, PRC was initially unhappy with the film, but it later proved to be a big moneymaker for them, particularly in France. Additionally, Ulmer had a fight with Charlie Chaplain over the title – Chaplain originally wanted to use it for his picture *Monsieur Verdoux*, or so Ulmer claimed. Overall, *Bluebeard* is a tightly and artistically constructed little B picture which has received all too scant attention and is far superior to the Edward Dymtryk/Richard Burton *Bluebeard* of the '70s.

Ulmer had a borderline return to the horror field with *The Man from Planet X*, a rather gothic-feeling horror film that was inexpensively produced by scriptwriters Aubrey Wisberg and Jack Pollexfen in the '50s. The film is a superior piece of ultra-low-budget science fiction heavy on the atmosphere, and is notable for reusing leftover sets from the 1948 *Joan of Arc* and for its interesting treatment of the title alien.

Unlike many science fiction films of the '50s, *Planet X* features an alien who is neither hostile nor an invader. Played by an unidentified five-foot actor in a mask and space suit, the alien gathers sympathy throughout the film by refraining from aggression, even going so far as to turn off its own air supply in a gesture of goodwill to the hero of the film, Robert Clarke (who appeared in a number of later '50s sci-fi films).

The film does bog down for a time about halfway through its short running length, but is interesting for the eerie mood it generates. The setting is Scotland, with lots of fog, used to conceal the sparseness of the set but also to add to that atmosphere. The alien's spaceship is deliberately designed to resemble a diving bell, with the suggestion that it has been lowered into our atmosphere from a passing planet, designated Planet X.

When confronted by the avarice of an unscrupulous scientist who tries to manipulate the visitor by turning down his air supply, the alien only takes over human beings to build up a defensive bulwark until he can get away. William Schallert does a good job of playing the heavy, but most of the other characters are wooden and uninteresting. The basic idea may have influenced Ray Bradbury's script for Jack Arnold's *It Came from Outer Space*, which has a similar general plot, though it offers superior writing and story.

Bill Warren in his excellent book *Keep Watching the Skies!* opines from reading the script that the writer-producers "apparently thought that simply having come from outer space was enough reason for the alien to be killed" and credits Ulmer with portraying the alien more sympathetically and interestingly. Jack Pollexfen, in Tom Weaver's *Interviews with B Science Fiction and Horror Movie Makers*, insists that "making the Earthlings – or some of them – the heavies was a key part of the script from the first," though again, this is not evident from the script alone.

The film *Tomorrow We Live* has sometimes been credited as a horror film because it has a character who is called "The Living Ghost." He actually is a gangster kingpin who earned his nickname because he had been shot in the head and heart and left in the desert to die and somehow managed to survive. It is most definitely a gangster melodrama and not a horror film.

Ulmer's next horror was also for Pollexfen, though it was a far less happy one. *Daughter of Dr. Jekyll* has rightly been described as a mess, and while it too made use of tilted angles for flashbacks and once more dealt with a tormented mind, it is far less effective than his other horror projects. The film is not only a horror, it is also lame – crippled in almost every department starting with a wretched script, uninspired direction and acting, and finishing up with a budget that must have been more "no" than "low."

The story is so garbled that it seems to have been concocted by someone who had never actually seen a horror film. Thus, Dr. Jekyll becomes a werewolf who slept in a coffin and was dispatched by a stake through the heart. It takes half the film to establish that Janet Smith (Gloria Talbot) is indeed Dr. Jekyll's daughter, who has come to claim her inheritance.

She is engaged to George Hastings (John Agar), but Dr. Lomas (Arthur Shields) tries to discourage her by revealing that her father, Dr. Jekyll, was suspected of being the werewolf Mr. Hyde, a piece of news which a servant overhears and which is soon spread throughout the village. When a series of murders begin where the victims appear to have been clawed, Janet soon fears that her father's curse has overtaken her as well, but her fiance George discovers that it is all a plot of Dr. Lomas', who has been hypnotizing Janet and then assuming a hirsute disguise to eliminate some villagers. George stops Janet from committing suicide while the villagers discover and dispatch Dr. Lomas. We are assured in the final stupid twist that the monster will never prowl again, only to have the werewolf turn to the camera, grin, and say, "Are you sure?" with a laugh.

According to Don Glut in *Classic Movie Monsters*, "When *Daughter of Dr. Jekyll's* 71 minute running time proved too short for television, some of the frames were double-printed to stretch out the action, while Janet's nightmare sequence was augmented by stock footage from Allied Artists' *Frankenstein 1970* made in 1958. Strangely, the Frankenstein's Monster of the one film became the Mr. Hyde of the other."

In 1960, Ulmer simultaneously directed two science fiction epics on extremely low budgets, *The Amazing Transparent Man* and *Beyond the Time Barrier*. *Transparent Man* stars Douglas Kennedy as a small-time thief coerced into becoming invisible to aid megalomaniacal James Griffith. Kennedy robs a power plant and a bank but starts becoming visible again. He learns that the treatment is fatal. Griffith kills his girl friend, and the pair battle it out in an exploding laboratory. The film is fast-paced and fairly daring for its low budget but remains a minor programmer.

Beyond the Time Barrier is even worse. Producer-star Robert Clarke travels via a jet plane forward in time after the ionosphere and most of mankind have been destroyed. Almost everyone on earth is mute or a mutant. This tale was quickly assembled to take advantage of a futuristic display in a Texas mall and never survives Arthur Pierce's dull screenplay. The only action comes from three men in bald wigs who represent a mutant revolt. Universal's makeup genius Jack Pierce provided the old man makeup on Clarke for the surprise twist when he returns to his own time.

Ulmer's last films, *L'Atlantide* (aka *Queen of Atlantis; Journey Beneath the Desert*) about engineers finding the lost city of Atlantis, and *The Cavern*, a Pirandelloesque tale of seven characters trapped in a cavern during wartime, were equally doomed. Ulmer's life had become like one of his films, playing out a dull existence under restrictive and limited circumstances, his journey to greatness never completed.

George Waggner (1894–1984)

Western Trails; Outlaw Express; Guilty Trails; Prairie Justice; Black Bandit; Ghost Town Riders (1938); *The Mystery Plane, Wolf Call; Stunt Pilot* (1939); *Drums of the Desert* (1940); *Man Made Monster; Horror Island; South of Tahiti; Sealed Lips; The Wolf Man* (1941); *The Climax* (1944); *Frisco Sal; Shady Lady* (1945); *Tangier* (1946); *The Gunfighters* (1947); *The Fighting Kentuckian* (1949); *Operation Pacific* (1951); *Destination 60,000* (1957); *Fury River* (codirector with Jacques Tourneur, Alan Crosland, Jr. & Otto Lang); *Mission of Danger* (1959).

TELEVISION: "The Magic Box," *Colt .45* (1957); The Girl Who Couldn't Remember," *77 Sunset Strip; Cheyenne; Colt .45; Wagon Train* (1958); "The Sheriff of Duck 'n' Shoot," "You Can't Beat the Percentage," *Maverick; The Alaskans; Cheyenne; 77 Sunset Trip* (1959); *Maverick; The Alaskans; The Roaring '20s; Cheyenne; 77 Sunset Strip; Surfside 6* (1960); *The Roaring '20s; 77 Sunset Strip; Hawaiian Eye* (1961); *Bronco; 77 Sunset Strip* (1962); *Cheyenne* (1963); *Batman*: "An Egg Grows in Gotham – The Yegg Foes in Gotham," "Green Ice – Deep Ice," "Pop Goes the Joker – Flop Goes the Joker," "The Wait of the Siren" (1966).

Born George Waggoner in New York on September 7, 1894, George Waggner will best be remembered as the director and associate producer of *The Wolf Man* (one of the last of the great Universal monsters) and as a producer of other horror films in the '40s (including *The Ghost of Frankenstein, Frankenstein Meets the Wolf Man, The Phantom of the Opera, Cobra Woman,* and *The Climax*), just as Herman Cohen and Milton Subotsky were regular horror producers in the '60s.

He studied at the Philadelphia College of Pharmacy before serving in World War I. After the war, he went to Hollywood and got work as an actor, and even tried his hand as a songwriter and a scriptwriter. His most famous parts as an actor include an appearance in *The Sheik* (starring Rudolph Valentino) and the role of Buffalo Bill in *The Iron Horse*. As a scriptwriter, he worked on *City Limits, The Line-Up, The Nut Farm, The Keeper of the Bees, I Cover the War, Idol of the Crowd* and *The Spy Ring*.

He began his career as a director by working in westerns. When it came time for his first horror film, Waggner turned to western actor Creighton Chaney, who had been forced to change his name to Lon Chaney, Jr., to play the monster when an old property originally titled *The Electric Man* and meant for either Karloff and Lugosi was dusted off. Chaney had proved that

695

he had some acting ability, or at least the ability to play redoubtable big, stupid lugs, with his classic portrayal of Lennie in Lewis Milestone's film adaptation of Steinbeck's *Of Mice and Men*.

Chaney starred as a man who bills himself as an "electric man" at carnival sideshows and demonstrates his ability for tolerating unusually high amounts of electricity. News of his ability intrigues Dr. Regas (Lionel Atwill, who was especially adept at playing suave, mad scientists), who wishes to turn him into a *Man Made Monster*, the final title for the film.

Chaney's character, Dan McCormick, is the sole survivor when a bus crashes into some electric wires because of his high tolerance for electricity. Dr. Lawrence (Samuel S. Hinds) takes him to Dr. Regas in order to study him and find out why he survived. With increasing amounts of electricity being administered to him, McCormick finds that not only does he electrocute his goldfish but he is increasingly falling under the dominion of Regas.

As in the *Frankenstein* films, Joseph West's script equates electricity with the life force itself. Regas' plan is to create a race of zombies, "men (that) could be motivated and controlled by electrical impulse supplied by the radioactivities of the electron ... eventually, a race of superior men could be developed; men whose only wants are electricity."

When Dr. Lawrence discovers what is going on, Regas has McCormick murder him and take the rap. He is sentenced to the electric chair, but naturally that does not do any good. He breaks out of the electric chair, murders the warden, and wanders around the countryside glowing in the dark. To keep him from frying things inadvertently, Regas gives him a strange rubber suit, which also keeps McCormick's energy from being drained away.

However, Regas makes the mistake of threatening to turn Lawrence's daughter (Anne Nagel) into an electric woman. McCormick turns on Regas and electrocutes him. Then, despondently, he wanders out into the countryside where barbed wire tears into his rubber suit and drains the electricity and life right out of him.

The film benefited from an atmospheric score by Hans J. Salter, whom Waggner would employ to score many of his later horror entries. It ended up being released in England under its original title and was later reissued in the United States as *The Atomic Monster*. Overall, Waggner showed he could make an energetic B horror film, making good use of Atwill's ability to play madmen and tapping into some pathos in Chaney's portrayal of a good-hearted boob who loses his will and is turned into a monster.

Waggner followed it up with *Horror Island*, another fast-paced and diverting B horror thriller but far less memorable, largely due to the umpteenth retelling of an "old dark house" story where visitors are murdered one by one. The plot is very forgettable; the stars were Dick Foran, Leo Carrillo and Peggy Moran.

Waggner's real success came with his next horror film, one of the classic B movie gems, *The Wolf Man*. Universal had experimented with werewolves before in the lackluster *WereWolf of London* where a not-so-indomitable Henry Hull has his face break out with isolated hairs as the result of exposure to the mariphasa lumina lupina plant in Tibet and an attack by Warner Oland when he transformed into a werewolf. Hull's character, Dr. Glendon, lacked personality, and though well produced and full of the quality touches that Universal was capable of at the time, *WereWolf of London* failed to excite much interest.

Even before that, in 1915, Reliance-Mutual had made a silent film entitled *The Wolf Man*, though Don Glut reports that there was no werewolf in the storyline. The Wolf Man that everybody knows and loves was actually created by scriptwriter and horror specialist Curt Siodmak. Siodmak remembers the genesis of the film as George Waggner coming to him and saying, "We have a title called *The Wolf Man*, it comes from Boris Karloff, but Boris has no time. He is working on another picture, so we have Lon Chaney and we have Madame Ouspenskaya, Warren William, Ralph Bellamy, Evelyn Ankers and Claude Rains, and we have $180,000 and we start in ten weeks. Goodbye."

Said Siodmak in an interview with this author:

> After seven weeks, I gave him the screenplay and we discussed it some. I don't think they made many changes. . . . There is a parallel between *The Wolf Man* and Aristotle's *Poetics*, which was pointed out to me by a Prof. Evans from Augusta College in Georgia. In the Greek plays, the gods tell man his fate – he cannot escape it. In *The Wolf Man*, when the moon comes up, he knows he's going to kill. The influence of the gods over the man is very strong, and there's the domineering father he had in *The Wolf Man*. It was constructed like a Greek tragedy, without my knowledge at the time, but it fell into place and that's why it's run for 48 years.

Siodmak wrote such horror films as *The Invisible Man Returns, Son of Dracula, I Walked with a Zombie,* and *The Beast with Five Fingers* and is probably most famous as the author of the novel *Donovan's Brain*, which has spawned at least three official film adaptations and influenced countless others. He researched lycanthropy (the belief that a man can turn into an animal) back into the stone ages, and *The Wolf Man*, while an original concept, was based on these legends. The famous and oft-quoted ditty, "Even a man who's pure in heart and says his prayers by night, may become a wolf when the wolfbane blooms and the autumn moon is bright," is not a piece of folklore but simply something Siodmak made up for the film.

Chaney was finally able to establish himself as a horror actor with his portrayal of the doomed and tormented Lawrence Talbot. He begins the film innocently enough by returning to Talbot Castle in Wales where his father, Sir John Talbot (Claude Rains), resides. Looking through a telescope (a device with connections to the stars and fate), he espies Gwen Conliffe (Evelyn Ankers, soon to be Universal's premier scream queen) and decides to make her acquaintance. She tries to interest him in a cane with a pentagram and a wolf's head etched into it (more foreshadowing).

Larry asks Gwen out and, accompanied by Gwen's friend Jennie (Fay Helm), they go to a nearby gypsy encampment which is having a kind of carnival. At the camp, a gypsy named Bela (Bela Lugosi, who else?) sees a pentagram in Jennie's palm and is horrified. Later, Larry responds to Jennie's screams; with the silver wolfshead cane he purchased from Gwen, he kills a wolf that is attacking her.

Apparently, Talbot is bitten by the wolf during the struggle and as a result becomes infected with lycanthropy himself. He is taken back to his ancestral castle to recover and wakes up to discover a pentagram-shaped wound on his chest. He is further alarmed when Sir John informs him that rather than the body of a wolf, he found the body of Bela the gypsy at the site where Lawrence was attacked. Though Talbot is not arrested, he gains a reputation as a murderer among the disapproving townspeople.

Like the other classic monsters (the Frankenstein monster, Dracula), the Wolf Man engenders our sympathy because he is a monster through no fault of his own. He does not wish to become a beast when the moon is full, but he cannot help it. Fate has turned against him and he must play out his role until fate decrees that he can die. He embodies the basic good/evil dichotomy of a Jekyll-and-Hyde character with the personalities altering without his consent or control.

Talbot goes to the gypsy queen Maleva (Maria Ouspenskaya in her most memorable bit), who confides to him that her son had been a werewolf and that whoever is bitten by a werewolf and lives becomes a werewolf himself. Maleva gives Talbot a pentagram for his protection, but he gives it to Gwen so that she will be safe. Meanwhile, Maleva quickly spreads the word that there is a werewolf near the camp, so the gypsies break camp and go quickly.

Waggner is constantly equating Talbot with dogs, showing that Talbot's dog no longer responds warmly to its master. When Talbot goes to a gypsy camp and tries to relax by firing a few rounds at a shooting gallery, he becomes unaccountably horrified at the image of a wolf as one of the targets. Finally, after leaving Maleva, the transformation becomes complete (thanks to Jack Pierce's makeup and John Fulton's special effects) as Talbot sprouts hair all over his body and becomes not a wolf like Bela but a Wolf Man. (Chaney's makeup is much hairier than Hull's but his entire face does not sprout hair. His nose becomes bestial, not hairy, nor is there hair around his eyes or on his cheeks apart from where a beard might grow. His hands are made hairier and given claws and his feet become giant paws to complete the transformation of this manbeast.)

While the appearance of the Wolf Man is very memorable, Waggner does not provide too many glimpses of him in this first film of what later proved to be a series. He saved a good look for times when he wanted a scene to have a particular impact, though Chaney's silhouette could often be seen traipsing through the woods in the moonlight.

Talbot's first victim is a gravedigger (Tom Stevenson), and he follows his kill with a howl that can be heard through the village. In the morning, Talbot is horrified to see the tracks of the Wolf Man leading from the window to his bed. He has no recollection of the previous night but quickly learns about the gravedigger's death. The next night he prowls again only to be caught in a trap and transformed back into a man. Maleva the gypsy woman comes along and frees him before the police catch him with his foot in their trap.

Seeking out Gwen, he is horrified to see the image of a pentagram in her palm. He knows that a werewolf can only be killed with silver. He insists that his father carry his silverheaded walking stick. His father agrees but tries to prove Larry's fears are groundless by strapping him into a chair and locking the room. This sets the stage for the one prolonged and detailed information in the film, which according to Chaney involved 21 makeup changes in 22 hours while his hands were held in place by tiny nails driven through the skin on his fingers and his head kept in place by positioning it according to a target on an opposite wall.

Maleva warns Gwen that she must avoid meeting Larry, but she looks for him anyway, encountering the Wolf Man in the fog. Her screams attract the attention of Sir John, who batters the Wolf Man into the ground with the wolfshead cane. Talbot transforms back to normal while the chief constable (Ralph Bellamy in a bit part) comes up and concludes, "The wolf must have attacked her and Larry came to the rescue. I'm sorry, Sir John."

Larry's final and fittingly poetic eulogy is delivered by Maleva, who said the same thing when her son died: "The way you walk was thorny, through no fault of your own. But as the rain enters the soil, the river enters the sea, so tears surround your predestined end. Your suffering is over, my son. Now you will find peace."

In addition to the special effects and the classical Greek tragedy elements of the story, *The Wolf Man* benefits from an excellent cast, with Lon Chaney truly making Lawrence Talbot his own creation and Evelyn Ankers establishing herself as the best and most beautiful screamer on the Universal lot. Claude Rains could give almost any role authority and firmly establishes himself as Talbot's domineering, no-nonsense but still loving father. Despite her many other roles in other films, Maria Ouspenskaya is still best known for her role as the wise Maleva. Bela Lugosi has only a small but important role, as do Ralph Bellamy, Patric Knowles and Warren William, all of whom acquit themselves well.

Waggner in addition to guiding his cast does an excellent job of pacing the film. One of the things that is distinctive about *The Wolf Man* was the way it used fog to create atmosphere. Tod Browning and James Wong Howe has used fog atmospherically in *Mark of the Vampire*, but Waggner really poured it on, using massive amounts in some scenes, to create a new look. Additionally, it was given an almost luminous glow by cameraman Joseph Valentine. Also, it helped hide the patent phoniness of the film's forest sets, and so Waggner, who produced as well as directed, was able to make this B film resemble an A-class production.

Universal was pleased with the success of *The Wolf Man* and pleased with Waggner's abilities as a producer, immediately assigning him as head of their horror unit, for which he would produce their follow-up to the successful *Son of Frankenstein*, Erle C. Kenton's *Ghost of Frankenstein*. (See chapter on Kenton.) He also began to work with writer and future director Richard Brooks on a film called *Sin Town*, which he produced.

According to Curt Siodmak in our interview, *Frankenstein Meets the Wolf Man* came about as a joke:

> I was sitting in the commissary and a friend of mine – this was during the war – was drafted and went to the war and had an automobile. You couldn't get an automobile in those days. I wanted to buy it, but I didn't have the money. I asked George Waggner if I could get a job. I needed to buy a car.
>
> First he was sitting there and I made a joke – *Frankenstein Wolfs the Meat Man*, I mean *Meets the Wolf Man*. He didn't laugh. He came back a couple of days later and asked, did you buy the automobile? I said no, I don't have a job. He said, you'll get a job – go buy the automobile. Finally I left and bought the automobile. He said, OK, you have a job – *Frankenstein Wolfs the Meat Man*, er, *Meets the Wolf Man*. I give you two hours to accept.

Waggner assigned Roy William Neill, a B film specialist who had done quite a number of films (he even started *The Lady Vanishes* before Hitchcock took over) and would become known for his work in the Sherlock Holmes series, to direct. Siodmak originally scripted the Frankenstein monster as being blind, to tie in with *The Ghost of Frankenstein*, and able to talk, but the Frankenstein monster, played by Bela Lugosi, jeers at Lawrence Talbot's protestations about changing into a wolf in Lugosi's distinctive Hungarian accent and so these elements were cut from the picture. Waggner originally wanted Chaney to play both the Monster and the Wolf Man, which would be a big public relations coup for his friend Chaney, but it was decided that it would be too difficult to maintain the illusion and

*Director-producer George Waggner (right) with star Boris Karloff on the set of
The Climax, a quickie follow-up to the Claude Rains version of Phantom of the
Opera which Waggner also produced but did not direct, using the same female
star (Susanna Foster) and the same sets as well as a similar story.*

stunt doubles would have to be used anyway when the monsters finally battle at the climax of the tale.

The follow-up films in the Frankenstein saga were produced by Paul
Malvern and directed by Erle C. Kenton. Meanwhile, Waggner turned his
hand to producing *White Savage* and the expensive Claude Rains version of
The Phantom of the Opera directed by Arthur Lubin as a showcase for so-
prano Susanna Foster. (The film has long held an overly inflated reputation,

being unfortunately dull through most of its length and not really able to compare with the superior silent version starring Lon Chaney for atmospherics and theatricality. Though short in stature, Rains makes for a sympathetic and yet commanding Phantom, but he is not given too many interesting things to do and he is the only really interesting character in the film.)

Having the sets for *The Phantom of the Opera* at his disposal, Waggner decided to make a follow-up, *The Climax*, which he himself would direct. For his star, he chose Boris Karloff to play Dr. Hohner, the resident physician at the Continental Opera House. Hohner falls in love with Marcellina (June Vincent), a talented singer, and strangles her when he finds that she does not return his love. Enter Angela (Susanna Foster) with a voice very much like Marcellina's, and Hohner objects to her singing his lost love's material. He hypnotizes her to break down when commanded to perform and then decides to murder her when her fiancé, Franz (Turhan Bey taking a break from mummy movies), becomes suspicious.

Luise (Gale Sondergaard) becomes aware of Dr. Hohner's influence and has a great success while Hohner accidentally knocks over a lit lamp by a shrine he has made to his beloved Marcellina and immolates himself.

The Climax is a pretty hokey melodrama in which Karloff gives a dull performance. It is mostly notable as being his first color film. Though very similar to *The Phantom of the Opera* that Lubin directed, it is in no way an improvement on it, proving even duller without even the tepid excitement of a chandelier dropping or an acid-scarred face being unmasked.

The last horror film that Waggner was associated with was *Cobra Woman*, which Richard Brooks scripted and Robert Siodmak directed. *Cobra Woman* is a delirious Maria Montez pseudo-spectacle with Montez as the queen of a South Seas kingdom. She is kidnapped just as she is about to marry Jon Hall, while the high priestess Nadja, her evil twin sister (also Montez), takes over the tribe of snake worshippers on Cobra Island. Montez's acting is the worst, making this a camp classic which also features Lon Chaney as a mute captain of the guards, Edgar Barrier as a bad guy who becomes impaled on some spikes, large numbers of handmaidens in high-heeled pumps, sublimely ridiculous demonic dancing, human sacrifices, a woman who is immune to cobra venom – you name the South Seas cliché and it is probably here done in an absurb style.

Waggner finished his career making westerns for both film and television, though the last series he worked on was the highly tongue-in-cheek *Batman* series. His name has never been synonymous with great horror films, but the ones he directed are mostly lively and memorable affairs produced under modest means. He deserves some kudos for giving the world *The Wolf Man* if nothing else, one of the most beloved horror films of all time and one of the few non–Lewton-produced horror highspots of the '40s.

Peter Walker (1938–   )

Hot Girls (1961); *I Like Birds* (1967); *Strip Poker* (1968); *School for Sex; Man of Violence* (1969); *Cool It Carol!* (1970); *Die Screaming, Marianne* (1971); *The Four Dimensions of Greta; The Flesh and Blood Show* (1972); *Tiffany Jones* (1974); *House of Whipcord, Frightmare* (1974); *The Confessional* (aka *House of Mortal Sin*, 1975); *Schizo* (1976); *The Comeback* (1977); *Home Before Midnight, House of the Long Shadows* (1983); *Blind Shot* (1988).

Peter Walker is another case, like Herschell Gordon Lewis, of nudie filmmaker turned horror/exploitation director, but with the difference that Walker has talent for making his films something other than laughably bad. In fact, such efforts as *House of Whipcord* and *House of the Long Shadows* show evidence that Walker could become a top English horror director if he were given the proper resources, but meanwhile he seems content in eking out a marginal career on the fringes of the British independent scene.

Walker is the son of British radio and music hall comic Syd Walker, who made a few forgotten British comedies (*I Killed the Count; What Would You Do, Chums?*) and died in 1945, leaving Walker an orphan at the age of seven. Walker was sent to an actors' orphanage and plans were made for him to follow in his father's footsteps, though he had no particular ambitions towards acting. He was, however, an inveterate filmgoer, finally being thrown out of Brighton Grammar School for perpetually sneaking off to the cinema.

At the age of 15 he began doing standup comedy at a few nightclubs and burlesques. Walker met many elderly British comedians through these associations, and he would put some of them in bit parts in his later sex films. Walker switched from music halls to rep theaters, but confessed that he was a terrible, dreadful actor. In between his stage work, he began working at Brighton Studios, a bottom-of-the-ladder independent film outfit where he worked his way from third assistant film director to first.

He then went to work for Michael Winner on such films as *Shoot to Kill, Climb Up the Wall,* and *Out of the Shadow,* telling scriptwriter David McGillivray in *Films and Filming* that Winner would call him up to his office and say, "I'm writing this comedy script, Walker. Tell me some jokes." In between assignments, Walker would make a living any way he could, as a laborer, a vacuum cleaner salesman, and anything else that came along. In 1960 he went to America, where his general knowledge of film production helped him secure jobs, as an actor and factotum.

He got a bit part on *The Dick Powell Show* that except for some on-camera cameos in his own production was his farewell to acting. He worked briefly with Otto Preminger and was introduced to a man who made nudies. Walker made his first 35mm feature, *Hot Girls*, in America about the same time that Russ Meyer was pioneering the field with *The Immoral Mr. Teas*.

Returning to England, Walker found that working in America had given him confidence. From 1962 to 1963, he made 470 16mm girlie films for Heritage, each shot in about a half-hour. Said Walker in *Films and Filming*:

> I didn't want to be known as a tit man, didn't want to be Harrison Marks, never have done. I hate tits. Horrible things. Except when they're in bed next to you. I hate it in the business, I think it's a terrible slant the business has taken. So for every girlie film I produced, I also distributed a feature or a cartoon. I was the first person to bring in 8mm sound features on the market.

When the bottom fell out of the market, Walker sold out to Mountain, but by 1966, he managed to get enough money together to make *I Like Birds* (English slang for women). Made in six days and costing 6,740 pounds, it is reputedly an ugly sex comedy about a sex magazine editor who is also the head of an East Grinstead Puritan Group. Somehow it was bought by Rank who released it on a double bill with *Pretty Polly* starring Hayley Mills.

Copping an idea from *His Kind of Woman* (a gangster spoof with an absolutely delightful Vincent Price performance as an egocentric movie star), Walker's next film, *Strip Poker*, featured a gangster who sought to re-enter the country by giving himself someone else's face with the aid of plastic surgery. This was followed by *School for Sex* in which Derek Aylward teaches girls to swindle rich men in return for 10 percent of their earnings.

Walker decided to change his approach and made *Man of Violence*, a thriller "with the necessary ingredients: Luan Peters with her 42″ bust and a bit of blood." For the first time, Walker allowed someone else other than himelf to do the screenplay, reputedly to its improvement. However, he had yet to receive good notices for a film, something which was to change with his next film, *Cool It Carol!*

Cool It Carol! caused a bit of a sensation, based on the story of a young girl and her boyfriend who come to the big city and make money in modeling, prostitution and vice. Later the pair returned to their old village and when the girl told of what she had done, the boy was arrested for living off her immoral earnings and was sent to prison for two years. The look of Walker's films improved with the acquisition of Peter Jessop as cameraman, but they still were obviously made on the cheap. The story got some play on *News of the World* and some critics complained that Walker had made an immoral film, but it was obviously a setup.

Walker decided to try and make a thriller without sex scenes and came up with *Die Screaming, Marianne*, starring Susan George. The story concerns a dancer, Marianne, whom a number of individuals are trying to convince to reveal the number of a Swiss bank account, the contents of which she is to inherit on her twenty-first birthday.

Walker followed this with the first British-made 3-D film, *The Four Dimensions of Greta*, in which a German reporter looks for Greta and interviews people who tell lurid stories about her. Only the four flashbacks are in 3-D, amounting to about 20 minutes of the final film. And while it is amusing that Walker borrows the old Universal catchphrase at the end of his film (a good cast is worth repeating), a good cast is exactly what his film did not have.

Explained Walker, in McGillivray's piece on him in *Films and Filming*:

> You really can't make silk purses out of sow's ears. And unfortunately, if you have an inexperienced leading player, as we had with this particular person, they drag the performance of everyone else down. I certainly could have used a better actor. But one doesn't have the heart really to con sombody into doing a picture that you know isn't going to do anything for them, and when you want them for their pubes and very little else.

The film is little more than an attempt to cash in on the success of *The Stewardesses*, the first 3-D porno movie, which was a phenomenal success. Walker quickly followed *Four Dimensions* up with *The Flesh and Blood Show* (aka *Asylum of the Insane*) in which he diluted the sex scenes with horror scenes. *Show* follows some people into an Old Dark Theater where they are to audition and a hooded figure begins killing them off. The killer (Patrick Barr) turns out to be their unseen employer (he has hired them to rehearse a grand guignol play) who has hated the acting profession ever since he found his wife was cheating on him while she was playing Desdemona in *Othello*. Only the conclusion was filmed in 3-D.

I do not know anything about Walker's next film, *Tiffany Jones*, except that it is an adaptation of a strip cartoon, and like *The Flesh and Blood Show* was scripted by Alfred Shaughnessy. However, after *The Flesh and Blood Show*, Walker made a conscious effort to invade the horror market, collaborating with ex-critic David McGillivray on four horror scripts: *House of Whipcord*, *Frightmare*, *The Confessional*, and *Schizo*.

House of Whipcord is a pseudo–women's prison film in which a blind man and his mad wife decide to set up their own "correctional" facility to punish young women whom they perceive as being immoral. The film has an archly moral tone that is risible (not to mention such touches as a son called Mark E. Desade and a wonderfully over-the-top performance by Sheila Keith as a sadistic warden). Well photographed for a low-budget film, it also has its grim side with the young ladies being placed in solitary with rats, whipped, or even hanged. There is not so much a plot as a series of gruesome incidents strung together all centering around the excesses of this particular "institution," which is set up because the couple believe the courts have been letting immoral youngsters off with light sentences. The film maintains an ironic tone, noting how the self-righteous villains are given to greater moral excesses than their victimized charges.

Frightmare followed, a gory piece of hokum about an elderly couple (Rupert Davies and Sheila Keith) who have been released from a mental institution. They were put there 15 years ago for unspecified "sickening crimes." We quickly discover that mother is reverting to cannibalism and is given to mutilating her victims with an electric drill before eating the raw flesh. (Like Romero's and the subsequent Italian cannibals, Keith's character never bothers with cooking her victims.) Hubby helps and soon daughter Debbi (Kim Butcher) becomes a homicidal maniac and follows suit, helping kill a psychiatrist (Paui Greenwood) who has come to investigate, and then turning on her half-sister (Deborah Fairfax).

The daughters' boyfriends get involved and there is a grisly climax at the farmhouse. Like *The Texas Chainsaw Massacre* released the same year, *Frightmare* indicated that horror was taking a turn away from maniacs who killed people out of sexual repression or confusion toward those who killed because they wanted to see their victims reduced to quivering slabs of flesh. (Or as John McCarthy put it in *Splatter Movies*: "In splatter movies, mutilation is indeed the message – many times the only one.") While the emphasis in *House of Whipcord* was on the main characters' sadism, here we have straight gore photographed starkly and drearily with a forceful performance by Keith who dominates the cast. (The film is not to be confused with Norman Thaddeus Vane's 1981 effort also titled *Frightmare*, which had Ferdy Mayne as a horror actor who comes back from the dead to kill off the fan club teens who stole his body. On video, Walker's film was retitled *Frightmare II*, though there is no connection between the two.)

Having tackled prisons and families, Walker and McGillivray next went after the Catholic church in *The Confessional* (aka *House of Mortal Sin*). It is the brutal tale of a sex-obsessed, homicidal priest (Anthony Sharp) who uses the confessional to blackmail women by tape-recording their confessions. The traditional paraphernalia of salvation is turned on its head in this topsy-turvy movie with the priest using rosaries to strangle people and holy communion wafers to poison them. (Some people may remember Sharp as the minister in *A Clockwork Orange*.) One man is even killed by being bashed with a smoking incense burner. Subtlety is not one of the film's strong points.

A priest who is curious about Sharp sets him off, but we also see that he had an abnormal mother-son relationship (*Psycho hommage?*) and an unsatisfactory love life (his attempts at sexual liaisons are not only blasphemous, they are disastrous). Susan Penhaligon plays his prime target, but the film abruptly cuts off just after the priest rids himself of his final impediment, perhaps hinting that evil dominates and will inevitably win out. There is a strange side bit where a woman with a glass eye who skulks around turns out to be a jilted girlfriend of Sharp from 30 years before. Stranger still, the film was often advertised as *Death's Door*, though that never seems to have been a title on the film itself. Naturally, it was condemned by the Catholic church.

Schizo (aka *Amok; Blood of the Undead*) stars Lynne Frederick as a famous ice skater who is hunted by a strange man (John Leyton) and haunted by the memory of a maniac killing her mother following some sadomasochistic sexual experience. Naturally, she is puzzled and becomes frantic when more and more of her friends are found with knitting needles shoved through their heads and their faces pounded in. Actually, Walker tries for a more conventional approach to horror in this film, toning down the violence and using such old standbys as lurking shadows, creaking doorknobs, and a séance.

In the shock ending, it is revealed that Leyton has been trying to scare her into confessing that it is she who killed her mother, with the unfortunate side effect that her mind shifts the blame onto an alternate personality which has been doing the killing. There is one particularly nasty scene in which a knitting needle emerges from an eyeball.

Nothing so gross appears in *The Comeback* (aka *The Day the Screaming Stopped*), Walker's first PG-rated horror film. Jack Jones plays a singer who decides to record his next album in a creepy mansion, an attempt to get away from it all after his wife's recent death. Imagine his consternation when he comes across her putrefying corpse in a cobwebby room and her head in a hatbox in the cellar. He also finds his new lover, Pamela Stephenson (who later became a TV star on Britain's *Not the Nine o'Clock News*), walled up with another cadaver, and his manager (David Doyle) has an outrageous scene in drag.

For a novel twist, those old red herrings the sinister caretakers (Sheila Keith and Bill Owen) are in fact the culprits. It seems their daughter committed suicide when Jones got married and they are out for revenge. However, they are such an inept couple that Owens accidentally manages to axe his wife to death.

Walker often manages to include some lowbrow humor and tongue-in-cheek elements in his productions, and *The Comeback* is no exception. What is surprising is how lively Walker makes the film using familiar plotting and settings. We have seen many of these kinds of scenes of a man frightened in an old dark house, but Walker handles them with more verve than most horror hacks including some of the rather tired treatments the theme had back in the so-called classic '30s and '40s. However, Jack Jones' rock songs are not as appealing as those in other horror rock musicals (*Phantom of the Paradise, The Rocky Horror Picture Show,* Freddie Francis' *Son of Dracula*) and are something of a drawback.

Walker went through a bit of a dry spell for the next six years. Among other projects he tried to get off the group were a remake of PRC's *The Enchanted Cottage*; a remake of *Svengali; Cats,* a sequel to Burt Brinckerhoff's *Dogs* (1981) in which man's best friend turns on him with David McCullum trying to keep the pack at bay; and a proposed film for the short-lived Sex Pistols called *A Star Is Dead.* He finally got behind the cameras in 1983 for another sex film, *Home Before Midnight.* Then Cannon Films offered him what one hoped would be the chance of a lifetime – to come up with a script that would feature all four of the top horror stars living today: Vincent Price, Peter Cushing, Christopher Lee and John Carradine.

The script was tailor-made for the stars by Michael Armstrong, himself the director of *Mark of the Devil* (1970) and *Horror House* (1969), and was loosely based on Earl Derr Biggers' novel *Seven Keys to Baldpate* which had been turned into a play by George M. Cohan and filmed six times previously. (Biggers is best known for having created the character of Charlie Chan.) The result was called *House of the Long Shadows.*

In a lunch with his publisher, writer Kenneth Magee (Desi Arnaz, Jr.) accepts his publisher's bet that he can write a *Wuthering Heights*–like gothic novel in a mere 24 hours. Magee is brash, confident, and cares only about the money he could win (though the time period allotted for this achievement is ridiculously short; however, that is only the first unbelievable thing that crops up, an indication that we should not take this whole endeavor too seriously). Naturally, he needs an isolated place with plenty of atmosphere, and the publisher, Sam Allyson (Richard Todd), just happens to know of the perfect location, Bllydpactwr Manor in Wales. (The closest anyone can come to the Welsh name is Baldpate, hence the original title.)

Before long, the clichés are flying thick and fast, with Walker delighting in each one. There is a woman who mysteriously vanishes in the steam at the train station; the house which has supposedly remained empty for 40 years has two elderly and mysterious caretakers (John Carradine and Sheila Keith again); and soon, far from being isolated, Bllydpactwr Manor begins to resemble Grand Central Station as the tragic members of the Grisbone family all come home to roost – Sebastian Rand (Peter Cushing), Lionel Grisbone (Vincent Price), Corrigan (Christopher Lee) and an unknown personage who has remained locked up in the attic for years.

At 3 million pounds, this is the biggest budgeted and handsomest Walker production to date. It benefits from being largely filmed on location at an old Hampshire manor, and Norman Langley's photography is clean, with plenty of dark shadows and deep recesses to give the place atmosphere. The film is mainly notable for this first-time teaming of the titans of terror, and they come through for it. While the aging and ailing Carradine is not given much to do, taking little advantage of his still magnificent voice, Price brings just the right kind of hammy flair to the role of Lionel Grisbone, getting laughs by telling Magee not to interrupt him while he is soliloquizing, and commenting on the death of his sister Victoria (Keith) after she has given an abominable performance of a Verdi aria and attracted the killer's attention that "he must have heard her singing." Lee plays Corrigan as an arrogant and uptight outsider who demands authority, something he commands very well, while Cushing plays Sebastian as a frightened, Elmer Fudd type, an odd change for the usually clear-dictioned thespian.

The violence is quite minimal for a Walker film as it tries to get by on the performances of its main stars and the affectionate use of horror clichés. Adding to the group are a young couple getting in out of the rain, and everything finally comes to a head in an axe murder climax only for Magee to discover that the whole thing has been a ruse on the part of his publisher to inspire him to write a new book. Magee gleefully tears up his check while Price and Lee ad lib barbs about overplaying their parts. All in all, it is a fun film, but one that goes against the trend of horror films in the '80s.

In that trend, horror films no longer seemed to require actors to play the various florid parts. Instead, the special effects makeup man seemed to have become the new star. Where people once went to horror films because they starred a Karloff or Lugosi or Price, now all that mattered was sufficient scares, however illogically derived, to reduce the audience into a state of shocked disbelief. The low-budget shocker had become king, and *The House of the Long Shadows* looked like an attempt to return to past days of glory which was out of step with what was in the marketplace. Hence, the film received scant distribution and was quickly sold to cable and videocassettes.

Most of Walker's films have received poor distribution in the United States; however, videocassettes do allow for a new assessment of his lively and often grotesque work. He has made enormous improvements from his days as a porno filmmaker, and his last films have a handsomeness that belies their low budget. While his sense of humor can be crude, it helps make his films fun, and he has devoted himself to horror, showing a knowledge of the previous achievements in the genre lacking in many recent directors' work. I would expect that given the opportunity, he will continue to improve as a director and add to the genre. Meanwhile, he has accomplished enough that his body of work should not be ignored.

James Whale (1889–1957)

Hell's Angels (codirected with Howard Hughes); *Journey's End* (1930); *Waterloo Bridge; Frankenstein* (1931); *Impatient Maiden; The Old Dark House* (1932); *The Kiss Before the Mirror; The Invisible Man* (1933); *By Candlelight; One More River* (1934); *Bride of Frankenstein; Remember Last Night?* (1935); *Show Boat* (1936); *The Road Back; The Great Garrick* (1937); *Port of Seven Seas; Sinners in Paradise; Wives Under Suspicion* (1938); *The Man in the Iron Mask* (1939); *Green Hell* (1940); *They Dare Not Love* (1941); *Hello Out There* (unreleased, 1949).

Although James Whale is best known for his four famous horror features – films which practically defined the genre for several decades – he was a talented and versatile director who worked with many genres. In fact, before embarking on his horror period, he had been typed as a director of war films due to his work on *Hell's Angels, Journey's End* and *Waterloo Bridge*. While they do not fall within the scope of this work, these films are noteworthy along with *One More River*, an adaptation of John Galsworthy's last novel about an overbearing husband (Colin Clive in his fourth great performance for Whale) who accuses his wife (Diana Wynyard) of having an affair; the 1936 (and best) version of *Show Boat*, the Jerome Kern-Oscar Hammerstein musical with a magnificent performance by the great Paul Robeson; the overlooked gem *The Great Garrick* in which a French acting troupe, having heard that the famous English actor David Garrick (Brian Aherne) has boasted of the superiority of English actors to French, decides to pull a hoax on the egotistical thespian by impersonating the inhabitants of an inn along Garrick's way; and the highly entertaining swashbuckler *The Man in the Iron Mask* based on Alexandre Dumas' classic novel. These films demonstrate that Whale was one of the most talented directors in the Hollywood of the '30s and is long overdue for a major reevaluation.

However, Whale was initially ignored by *auteur*-ist critics for much the same reasons that John Huston was. Rather than concentrating over and over again on a particular theme or type of story, Whale dedicated his skills to bringing the best he could out of various literary and stage properties which he selected with care. At the height of his films' popularity, Whale was considered the top director at Universal Studios and had a good deal of power. Unfortunately for his career, he was also a homosexual when such behavior was not socially acceptable and his parties were considered minor scandals. When the box office takes of his films declined, he was virtually shut out of the film industry, and his last film, *Hello Out There*, a 41-minute adaptation of William Saroyan's play, was never released. (It might have been intended to be combined with the two other shorts that comprised the Huntington Hartford production *Face to Face*. For the record, that film contained an adaptation of Joseph Conrad's "The Secret Sharer" by the talented John Brahm and a memorable version of "The Bride Comes to Yellow Sky" by Stephen Crane directed by Bretaigne Windust.)

Whale was born in the English Midlands on July 22, 1889, to relatively poor parents. He disdained the idea of a life of manual labor and delighted in drawing and painting. After the outbreak of World War I, he was a volunteer and enrolled in the Cadet Corps to become an officer. Commissioned a second lieutenant, he fought in France and was captured by the Germans in Belgium. To keep himself occupied, he drew and he also organized a theatrical company.

While in a POW camp, Whale gambled a lot with young men from wealthy families, winning checks and promissory notes by wagering nonexistent wealth. After the war was over, he quickly returned to England and cashed the checks before payment could be stopped and proceeded to get a job as a staff cartoonist with *The Bystander*. Now solvent, Whale devoted more time to theater, occasionlly undertaking to perform spear-carrier roles. It was while performing in Shakespeare's *The Merry Wives of Windsor* that Whale first met Ernest Thesiger, who would perform so memorably for him in *The Old Dark House* and *The Bride of Frankenstein*. When working on *The Insect Play*, he met Elsa Lanchester, who was to be the title character in *Bride* as well as Mary Shelley, while she was making her stage debut.

Working in English theater, Whale became more and more involved in designing the scenery for various productions. Reportedly, Whale was very conscious of his lower class accent at the time and worked very hard to eradicate it, developing the manners and speech of a gentleman. Whale also began taking larger acting roles in Oxford and London, managing to make a decent living for himself on the stage. By about 1927, Whale started actively seeking directing assignments, having gained skill and confidence from performing and designing other shows as well as assisting various directors. Whale finally landed a chance to act in and direct the Spanish play *Fortunato* by Serafin and Joaquin Alvarez Quintero. However, Whale suffered a blow to his ego when Harley Granville-Barker, the translator of the play, came in and removed Whale from the lead and changed around much of the staging.

Fortunato, cobilled with *The Lady from Alfaqueque*, was not a great success, nor was the next play Whale directed, *The Dreamers*, which Whale directed while concurrently appearing in another play. However, the next production offered him was ideally suited to the World War I veteran and proved his big chance, R. C. Sheriff's *Journey End.*

Journey's End is a play about the difficulties and pressures of living in the trenches in World War I. It centers around the character of Captain Stanhope, an alcoholic commander whose best friend is Lt. Osborne. When Second Lt. Raleigh, an old school chum, arrives, it throws Stanhope into a tizzy because it reminds him that he has fallen short of his own dreams of glory and he fears that Raleigh will report his inadequacies back to the woman he loves–Raleigh's sister. The original play production starred a then unknown Laurence Olivier as Stanhope with Maurice Evans as Raleigh and George Zucco as Osborne, Stanhope's good friend who dies on the battlefield.

Olivier only stayed with the production for its initial test dates and then landed a part in *Beau Geste* and left the play. Whale and Sheriff, who worked together on the final version of the script in an effort to keep it from getting too sentimental, decided to take a chance on another unknown, Colin Clive, despite Clive's initially bad audition and rehearsals. Clive carried with him the right ragged and agonized air that they wanted Stanhope to have, and after getting over his case of nerves with a stiff drink, Clive proved that their instincts were right.

Despite the fact that plays about the wars were considered uncommercial, Whale and Sheriff were able to find a backer for a longer production. The play connected with both audiences and critics and enjoyed a spectacular run. A deal was cut to take the play to Broadway where it enjoyed a similar success, despite fears that it might be considered too British. Film rights to the play were purchased by two small British companies as a joint venture; however, talkies had just come in and neither company had the facilities for making a sound picture. A deal was cut in America with the small independent company Tiffany-Stahl to produce the film and distribute it in the United States.

Whale's associates stuck up for him as the only man who should be allowed to direct *Journey's End.* Whale was taken out to Paramount to see how picturemaking was done and received his first screen credit as "Dialogue Director" on the Richard Dix vehicle *The Love Doctor.* While he was out there, his name was brought to the attention of Howard Hughes as a hot, new British director.

Hughes had sunk over $600,000 of his money into making a silent picture called *Hell's Angels* about World War I flying aces. Unfortunately, despite some highly impressive aerial photography directed by Hughes, the film was considered unreleaseable. Hughes hit on the plan of scrapping the ground footage and shooting a new story incorporating the aerial footage which would be dubbed for sound. Though he took full directing credit himself, Hughes hired Whale to direct these ground scenes concocted by writer Joseph March.

This erratic and fragmented footage unfortunately remained dull and Whale found the eccentric Hughes a trial to work for, though Hughes was pleased enough with Whale's work to give him a $5,000 bonus. The Whale footage is notable for the screen debut of Jean Harlow and for the snappy and quick way many of the scenes are edited. Whale wanted to go for naturalism and not waste a moment in establishing the point of a scene, which ran contrary to the more theatrical sense of most '30s directors. One brief scene consists of nothing more than Roy running in to tell his best friend, "I've enlisted, Monte – Royal Flying Corps!" To which Monte curtly replies, "You're a fool, Roy." Snap, end of scene, personalities established, emotional point made, on to the next scene. As Paul Jensen puts it in *Film Comment*:

> In this fashion Whale goes to the heart of a narrative without wasting time or space. And yet, this ability is combined with his obvious pleasure in a leisurely pace, and a fondness for observing the small details of person and place that might not be needed to tell a story, but which do give social and psychological texture to it. By saving time on the narrative, Whale is able to provide these "extras" while still making an efficient, short film that encompasses a great deal of character interaction.

Far more significant than *Hell's Angels* was the film version of *Journey's End*. While nowhere as well known as *The Big Parade* or *All Quiet on the Western Front*, I believe *Journey's End* has dated better and stands up today as the best World War I film ever (with the exception of Kubrick's *Paths of Glory* which was filmed much later). Unfortunately, coming from a small company, the film did not get a big push. It came out the same month as *All Quiet on the Western Front*, which went on to win the Best Picture Oscar, and was left forgotten in its wake. Nowadays it is seldom revived and a hard film to get to see, but well worth the effort for Clive's magnificent performance and for the feelings of pressure and despair that Whale brings to bear on these characters, most of them trapped in a war they no longer wish to fight.

Whale returned to England to direct more plays while Tiffany hoped to get him involved on another project, but soon the studio was dead. Meanwhile, Carl Laemmle, Jr., had bought the rights to a Robert Sherwood play, *Waterloo Bridge*, about how a chance encounter between a soldier and a prostitute develops into a failed relationship, each going to his separate fate. Laemmel wanted John Stahl, who was busy, but was persuaded to talk with Whale and the two hit it off well. Whale was still under contract for two pictures to Tiffany, but when he threatened to sue them for additional post-production time on *Journey's End* for which he had not been paid, they agreed to let him go.

Waterloo Bridge was not as good as *Journey's End*, but it did make some improvements on the Sherwood play. Its reputation has been eclipsed by the more frequently seen Mervyn LeRoy version (1940) in which the prostitute was changed to a ballet dancer when Vivien Leigh took the lead. Bette Davis, under contract to Universal, had a small part in *Waterloo Bridge* and was considered to play the female lead in Whale's next production, *Frankenstein*, but was passed over in favor of *Waterloo Bridge*'s star, Mae Clarke. *Bridge* also united Whale with Arthur Edeson as cinematographer, Clarence Kolster as editor, and Joe McDonough as assistant editor, and Whale took these people with him to work on *Frankenstein*.

There can be no question that the original *Frankenstein* is one of the most important horror films ever made and was for its time a fantastic success. The director Robert Florey remained bitter for the rest of his life that the project was taken away from him (see chapter on Florey), but I'm convinced that Whale's peculiar touches were what made the film as great as it is. This is not to downplay the superb performance of Boris Karloff which made that actor's career, but that performance would not have existed had not Whale decided to give the Monster a personality, one that suggests an innocent alternately hurt by and attacking a cruel, uncaring world.

The simple idea of providing the character with pathos and sympathy was somehow overlooked by many of the film's imitators who often would treat their Frankensteinian creations as unreasoning brutes, and the difference is enormous. But there are other touches as well that make Whale's film particularly memorable.

Universal got interested in the property when they purchased the rights to the Peggy Webling stage adaptation of Mary Shelley's classic novel (the novel itself was in the public domain, but there is no evidence that anyone went back to consult it). The play switched the monster creator's name, Victor Frankenstein, with the name of his best friend, Henry, and the film does likewise. The play had been performed in Great Britain, along with *Dracula*, which Universal had had a success with, but was never performed in the United States. Screenwriter John Balderston managed to sell an adaptation of the play and rights for $20,000 plus 1 percent of the gross of the film. A number of different hands labored on different screenplays with Robert Florey conceiving of the criminal brain episode and the burning windmill at the end. Garrett Fort came up with Frankenstein being thrown off the windmill. When Florey was forced off the project, Francis Edward Faragoh took over as Fort's collaborator. Faragoh, who had written *Little Caesar*, changed Fritz from a mute into a character with dialogue, and Frankenstein's laboratory was switched from an old windmill to an old watchtower. (However, in a continuity gaffe, there is still a scene in the film where Baron Frankenstein, Henry Frankenstein's father, wonders what his son is doing messing around in an old windmill when he has a pretty fiancée.)

Obvious cinematic influences on the film include *The Magician*, the 1926 Rex Ingram film, and *The Cabinet of Dr. Caligari*, a film that Whale specifically sought out. *The Magician* contained a similar tower and also involved the creation of human life by lightning by a sorceror and his dwarfish assistant. *The Cabinet of Dr. Caligari* has an abduction scene similar to the one in which the monster attacks Elizabeth and then leaves her behind, plus the film has a toned-down expressionistic look.

Colin Clive's angular face was particularly exploited to give the film some expressionist shots. Universal originally considered the low-key Leslie Howard for the role, but Whale insisted on and got Clive, who was equally good projecting warmth and hysteria. Clive's performance as Frankenstein is one of the anchors of the film, suggesting an intelligent man who is frantically driving himself to the breaking point in the search for his ideal. It is significant that both he and his creation remain sympathetic throughout the course of the film.

After seeing Boris Karloff in Howard Hawks' *The Criminal Code*, David Lewis suggested that Whale check the actor out for the part of the Monster. In the Hawks film, Karloff plays a kind of angel of death who stalks and kills a prison stoolie with the kind of silent menace and power that Whale was looking for in his Monster. Karloff was on the Universal lot working on *Graft* when he was approached by Whale in the studio commissary. Karloff gave interviews saying that he worked as a truck driver when he was not working as an actor, and so some publicity was released which suggested that Whale cast Karloff after seeing him as a truck driver, but this is pure fiction. Karloff had been acting in films since 1919, mostly in bit roles.

Of course, a key part of making the Frankenstein Monster the unforgettable horror icon that it is the makeup of Jack Pierce. In preparing for the film, a number of sketches of what the Monster should look like were prepared, but none of them resemble the final result. Pierce worked for some time with Karloff on a way to best accentuate his features while allowing the highest latitude of expressions and emotions. The result is a far cry from the rubber-and-latex monsters of later, more technically advanced pictures, evincing the painstaking care that Pierce put into his work. Making Karloff up was a daily four-hour task.

In a rare interview with the *New York Times* around the time of making *Son of Frankenstein* (Rowland Lee, 1939), Pierce explained his design:

> My anatomical studies taught me that there are six ways a surgeon can cut the skull in order to take out or put in a brain. I figured Frankenstein, who was a scientist but no practical surgeon, would

take the simplest surgical way. We would cut the top of the skull off straight across like a pot-lid, hinge it, pop the brain in and then clamp it on tight. That is the reason I decided to make the Monster's head square and flat like a shoe box and dig that big scar across his forehead with the metal clamps holding it together....

Here's another thing. I read that the Egyptians used to bind some criminals hand and foot and bury them alive. When their blood turned to water after death, it flowed to their extremities, stretched their arms to gorilla length and swelled their hands, feet and faces to abnormal proportions. I thought this would make a nice touch for the Monster, since he was supposed to be made from the corpses of executed felons. So I fixed Karloff up that way. Those lizard eyes of his are rubber, like his false head, I made his arms look longer by shortening the sleeves of his coat, stiffened his legs with two pairs of pants over steel struts.

A blue-green greasepaint was applied so that the Monster would have a deathly gray pallor, with black shoe polish applied to its nails to further the impression of something dead. The shambling walk was necessitated by a pair of asphalt spreader's boots which weighed a total of 25 pounds. Pierce inserted bolts into the sides of the neck to further suggest the Monster's electrical origin. The whole thing weighed a staggering 48 pounds, and under hot studio lights, it is not hard to imagine the suffering Karloff put in for his art. Karloff claimed he requested mortician's wax on the Monster's eyelids because otherwise he looked too aware and awake, while what they wanted was a puzzled and confused creature.

Like many early '30s films, *Frankenstein* has no underscoring music, just a strange "mysterioso" theme (composed by David Broekman) under the odd opening credits which show a face and a swirl of staring eyes in the background. There is no other music until the closing credits. An added measure of suspense was built up by not listing Karloff in the opening credits, which read "The Monster?" However, Karloff's name does appear in the closing credits and on the film's poster.

Whale sets the mood right off with a clanking bell accompanying a funeral that Frankenstein and his hunchbacked assistant, Fritz (a memorably wigged-out performance from Dwight Frye), are observing. The story wastes no time in getting under way, but Whale still takes time out for the quick character bits which help distinguish his work. Though afraid, Fritz does his master's bidding, whether it is cutting down hanged men or ascending the laboratory's electrical equipment in a storm. When Victor, his fiancée, and Dr. Waldman show up, Fritz is dispatched to get rid of them. His hobbling gait down the steps, supported by a too-small cane, encapsules his pathetic nature, and he seems to delight in having the power to turn the visitors away. However, his frailty is instantly suggested as he stops while returning up the stairs to pull up his garterless socks.

Fritz does not get much screen time, being the Monster's first victim, but in a very short amount of time his character has been established. We understand why he sadistically delights in torturing the Monster with a whip or a flaming torch, finally having found a creature more pathetic than himself. When Frankenstein sets up the creation scene, he says, "Quite a good scene, isn't it? One man, crazy; three very sane spectators," omitting reference to Fritz, also present, entirely. In Frankenstein's view of things, Fritz simply does not count, and Fritz longs to assert himself, though he is so nervous that a simple gong sound causes him to drop the normal brain he originally snatched from Waldman's laboratory.

Some people have criticized the fact that the Monster is given a criminal brain, explaining his propensity towards rage, violence, and murder, and that Frankenstein does not recognize that Fritz has given him an abnormal brain. However, what if the brilliant Dr. Waldman's theory about criminal brains is just so much poppycock? There is little medically to support it, nor does the film itself support that as the reason for the Monster's actions, giving him different motivations. It could be considered a device to build up dread in the audience and yet another example of Waldman being wrong. (Waldman is also incorrect about Frankenstein's ambition, thinking Henry wanted to murder people and then revive them, and ignorant of the secret light "above ultraviolet" that Frankenstein has discovered.)

The creation scene shows that Whale had a clear understanding of showmanship. Paul Jensen quotes Whale in his *Film Comment* article:

> [Frankenstein] deliberately tells his plan of action. By this time the audience [in the laboratory and in the movie theatre] must at least believe something is going to happen; it might be disaster, but at least they will settle down to see the show. Frankenstein puts the spectators in their position, he gives final orders to Fritz, he turns levers and sends the diabolic machine soaring upward to the roof, into the storm. He is now in a state of feverish excitement calculated to carry both the spectators in the windmill and the spectators in the theatre with him.

Thus economically Whale sets up the required exposition and builds interest in what is happening in the scene. Adding to the interest are Herman Rosse's set designs and Kenneth Strickfaden's odd electrical devices which arc, clack and spark all over the lab. (These devices were put in storage and successfully rescued for the film *Young Frankenstein*, Mel Brooks' loving tribute to the series and his funniest and most artistically successful film.) There is even a parallel setup, with Henry commanding Victor to sit down several times, just as he will later do to the Monster. Throughout the scene he is in command and commands our attention until the final discovery where the Monster's hand moves and he ecstatically proclaims it alive.

It is at this point that one of the most famous excisions from *Franken-*

stein was made. Originally, after Henry shouted "It's alive!" several times, Victor responded, "Henry, in the name of God!" However, this was later considered too blasphemous as Hollywood tightened its moral code in the mid–'30s and so was replaced by an obvious jumpcut with the sound being covered over by a peal of thunder just as the scene fades out and Henry collapses.

Some have criticized that the moving hand does not make much of a climax to the scene, but the focus here is on Frankenstein's reactions, not the Monster. Certainly, there have been enough subsequent movies where the Monster gets off the slab to show that perhaps Whale was right in not showing this action, just as Browning did not show Dracula leaving his coffin. Instead, the Monster's entrance is given a beautiful buildup and development.

But first there is an excellent scene where Henry, talking to Dr. Waldman (Edward Van Sloan), is questioned about doing something so dangerous and explains what it is that drives him: "Dangerous? Poor old Waldman! Have you never wanted to do anything that was dangerous? Have you never wanted to look beyond the cloud and stars, or to know what causes the trees to bud and what changes the darkness into light? But if you talk like that, people call you crazy. Well, if I could discover just one of these things – what eternity is, for example – I wouldn't care if they did think I was crazy." Clive's quiet delivery of this scene is a marked contrast to the frenzy of his previous one. Suddenly Frankenstein is not a mad scientist, but a fevered seeker of knowledge revealing both his motivations and his human side.

The Monster too is portrayed as a seeker of knowledge, symbolized by light, which is cruelly denied him by his creator. Whale builds the Monster's entrance beautifully, beginning with shambling footsteps, a slowly turning dark figure in a doorway, and a series of increasingly closer shock cuts to Karloff's face. This is simply one of the loveliest scenes in the film.

Frankenstein explains that his creation has been kept in darkness. By a commanding tone and gestures, he makes clear to the Monster that he wants it to sit down, which it does. Frankenstein then pulls open a skylight, revealing light to the Monster for the first time. We see the character as a total innocent, a *tabula rasa* on which anything can be written. The Monster slowly stands up and reaches out, trying to touch the light. When Frankenstein arbitrarily shuts it out again, the Monster's face conveys a questioning and pleading expression. He reaches out to his creator for understanding. It is clear that the Monster is a child in a man's body.

And like a child, it learns from the environment around it. When Fritz carelessly arrives and sends his torch in the Monster's direction, we see it experiencing unwarranted cruelty. Fritz then torments it whenever Frankenstein, now disappointed in his creation, keeps himself occupied elsewhere. In retaliation, the Monster hangs his tormentor, earning a death sentence from Dr. Waldman. Frankenstein and Waldman successfully drug the uncomprehending creature, but it wakes up as Waldman is about to dissect it, strangling the good surgeon and achieving his freedom. Whale effectively contrasts the village of Goldstadt celebrating the coming nuptials of Victor and Elizabeth with the later scenes of the angry mob pouring through the village (a set that remained standing from *All Quiet on the Western Front*) in search of the Monster. For years, fans have sought the missing footage of Frankenstein tossing the little girl into the pond after he runs out of flowers to throw, and recently MCA has released some videocassettes and discs with the long-sought footage. Despite Karloff's expressed misgivings, the scene remains a touching one.

In it we see two innocents meeting. The child is not afraid of the Monster and immediately treats him as a playmate, evoking a smile on the Monster's visage. However, only moments after discovering joy, the Monster experiences loss when he tosses his newfound friend into the water and she unexpectedly drowns. We see that the event at first perplexes the Monster — he slaps at the water as if scolding it or summoning his playmate back, and as the realization dawns on him, he leaves the scene emotionally devastated.

However, with the last part of this scene cut, there is the unwanted suggestion that the Monster molested the child when we see her father carrying her drowned body through the midst of the village celebration.

Regarding the classic scene where the Monster starts to abduct Elizabeth on her wedding night, Mae Clarke told me the following story:

> I . . . had known Boris because we'd all been together, more or less, like a play, rehearsing and meeting each other and becoming familiar with each other. Mr. Whale managed all of this in his own wonderful way, so that we all knew each other almost like a family excepting it wasn't a gooey family, it was a professional understanding of each other's motivations, etc. So we had a very pleasant association that way.
>
> When it came to the day . . . I'd been watching as we all had – taken little trips down to see how Jack Pierce was creating this marvelous makeup, and they spent hours and hours and weeks. They spent hours doing it every day; in getting it created, they worked for many hours, and we'd all go down and watch the progression, so I should have been familiar with it. I knew that it was gray, and I knew that this went on, and then the hat, which was his head – there was this hat like a pillbox with hair coming down, and then his knob things which they pasted on, well, I knew they weren't coming through his neck. I knew all these things. I knew this enormous thing in the corner was what he would put his arms into . . . and these enormous shoes that not only added to his height but were so heavy he could lean his weight against them, you see, because he always walked forward.

So when the day came for the scene and I knew he was going to come in that window, we didn't have a playing scene, but I saw a visual effect of him coming in through the window. I said, "Boris, I can't do it. I'm not going to be able to control myself. When you're that far away, I know it's the Monster, I don't know it's you." He said, "I'll tell you what I'll do. You know the camera will be over there, I'll be coming in there, and you're standing here. My left hand is my upcamera hand, and I'll just take my little finger and wiggle it, so when you turn and see me coming, don't look at me at all. Just look right for my hand, and when you see that wiggling, I just hope you don't laugh." And that's what happened. I remember it distinctly. Here's this incongruous little finger going, and there's this whole body and head and everything else. I nearly laughed.

The mountain chase and windmill fight proved less happy occasions. Carrying Clive up the hill and through the windmill several times resulted in a painful back injury for Karloff, while the increasing aggressiveness that Whale asked for in their fight scene resulted in Clive dislocating his shoulder. The film was budgeted for $262,000 and given a 30-day shooting schedule, but it went five days and $30,000 over budget.

For the time period, it was an adequate budget but not an overly large one. Whale seems to have liked the control he could get in a studio and filmed many of the outdoor locations on a stage. He was also fond of vistas where the horizon disappears quickly as if the participants in the scene were framed on on the top of the hilltop. This can be seen in the opening funeral scene and the later mountain chase scenes, including some scenes where the background is particularly phony, and appeared in some of Whale's other films as well.

One final peculiarity about the film is that it was originally intended that the Monster and his creator both be destroyed at the end, but Frankenstein was given a last-second reprieve after a disastrous preview that alarmed Universal executives with a large number of walk-outs. Throughout the film, Victor is set up in traditional Hollywood fashion to take Henry's place with Elizabeth after Henry's death, and Henry even gives a speech to that effect before undertaking his pursuit of the monster in the mountains. However, after he is thrown off the windmill, a voice was dubbed in saying, "He's alive," just before the burgomaster calls his name, gets no response, and says, "Take him to the village." Finally, a scene was tacked on with Baron Frankenstein drinking a toast outside his son's sickroom to "a son to the house of Frankenstein."

Additionally, Edward Van Sloan, who played Dr. Waldman, was recalled to provide a curtain speech at the start of the film warning the audience that the subsequent film would thrill, might shock, and might even horrify them. The advertisements played up how horrifying the film was, unlike *Dracula*, which promoted itself as a "strange love story." This led to even greater receipts than the Browning film and so a new sound genre was born: the horror film.

Whale was quickly assigned to a floundering comedy, *The Impatient Maiden*, which he directed in a perfunctory manner and which has become deservedly obscure. Meanwhile, Whale developed an interest in J. B. Priestley's short novel *Benighted*, which was titled *The Old Dark House* in America. Universal acquired it for him while assigning him to tackle Eric Remarque's sequel to *All Quiet on the Western Front*, *The Road Back*. Benn Levy was assigned to write the script for *The Old Dark House*.

The Old Dark House is an odd film in many respects. The Priestley novel was largely an allegory about the precarious position of post-war England with disillusionment running rampant. The character of Roger Penderel (played by Melvyn Douglas) has been battered by the war but puts on a cheerful facade. He cannot see much point in doing anything until he falls in love with Gladys DuCane (nee Perkins, played by Lillian Bond), an inebriated chorus girl who is the weekend companion of Sir William Porterhouse (Charles Laughton in his first American film performance). Porterhouse is a hard-working industrialist who is driven to destroy his competitors and earn money after his late wife died of a broken heart when society had snubbed them for being too poor.

Much of this introspection remains in the film, but mostly it concentrates on the eccentric characters and a kind of black comedy. The story is also a parody of a series of Broadway mystery plays in which characters would enter an old dark house on a rainy night and find a family full of murderers and dark secrets. Despite the horror scene setting, *The Old Dark House* is a film where something keeps threatening to happen but very little does.

The film begins with Penderel riding with Mr. and Mrs. Waverton (Raymond Massey and Gloria Stuart), who are lost in the Welsh countryside during a storm. They trade amusing banter and seek shelter in a convenient nearby mansion belonging to the Femm family. They are met at the door by Morgan (Boris Karloff), the family's mad mute butler, who growls at them and lets them in.

After achieving stardom with *Frankenstein*, Karloff was used as a major draw by Universal, though he has one of the least interesting characters in this film and is primarily used to provide the few action scenes that exist. Because his makeup here is so different from the one in *Frankenstein*, a prefatory note assures the audience that the Karloff in the film is the same one who "played the mechanical monster in *Frankenstein*."

The real star of the film is Ernest Thesiger, whom Whale had specially imported from England to perform the role of Horace Femm. Horace is a delightfully eccentric character who is at once civilized, fearful, greedy, haughty, and pathetic. His hatred for his sister Rebecca (Eva Moore) is peculiarly established in one of Whale's most offbeat touches. Horace picks up a bouquet of flowers, says, "My sister was on the point of arranging these flowers," and then unceremoniously dumps them on top of the fire in the fireplace.

Rebecca proves a little deaf, chanting over and over again that there are no beds available for the guests to sleep in. She is a religious fanatic and head of the household; it is apparent that Femm is afraid of her. One of the most effective scenes in the film has Rebecca describing the family history to Mrs. Waverton in her bedroom, talking about her late sister's screams while being oddly reflected in a distorted mirror, climaxing with her gesturing to Waverton's dress and saying, "That's fine stuff, but it'll rot," and then touching Waverton's breast and adding, "This is fine stuff, too, but it'll rot too in time." After this lecture on the evils of vanity, she stops to check her hair in the mirror on the way out.

Whale did not evince much humor in *Frankenstein*, though there is an odd touch near the beginning where Frankenstein's first shovelful of grave dirt gets tossed in the face of a cemetery idol. There were a few scenes with a pompous Frederick Kerr as Baron Frankenstein that were designed to relieve tension but which were not too amusing. In contrast, *The Old Dark House* shows Whale a master of the humor of the unexpected.

One of the best examples comes during the dinner scene where Horace explains that his sister is about to embark on one of her "strange tribal rights," as she is about to say grace. When she chastises him for it, he explains to the guests that she feels that the food will be better if she prays "to her gods" first and gives thanks for all the many blessings that have been bestowed upon the family. This last statement drips with sarcasm.

The guests watch Horace cutting into some roast beef and expectantly wait for their portion, which never arrives. Instead, Horace turns to each and says, "Have a po-ta-to," which apart from some vinegar and pickled onions is all they are offered. It is at this point that Porterhouse and DuCane arrive and are reluctantly let in. Porterhouse sees the roast beef and sings about roast beef in expectation only to have Femm's peculiar rite and offer of a potato repeated. When Porterhouse tries to lighten the mood, observing that they are all together, friendly, and yet know nothing about each other, Horace immediately dampens their spirits with a quick, "How reassuring!"

Throughout, Whale develops a mood of menace. The house is in danger of being swept away by a flood; it makes its own electricity, but Horace observes, "We aren't very good at it"; Morgan is described as dangerous when he is drunk and he starts getting drunk; and finally Rebecca goads her brother into going upstairs to get the lamp, though clearly he is afraid of what is up there.

Mr. Waverton is finally persuaded to go in his stead. Upstairs the Wavertons meet the other members of the Femm household. Sir Roderick Femm, the elderly invalid father, believes himself the only sane member of the family in between mad cackles, and warns against Saul (Brember Wills). Roderick is played by the oldest female actress that Whale could find, Elspeth Dudgeon, in chin whiskers. She is credited as John Dudgeon.

Saul is the last and most dangerous member of the family, a pyromaniac who is dedicated to killing. In a drunken rage, Morgan frees him and he is introduced as a hand on the stairwell, but at first Morgan unexpectedly appears instead of him. He feigns timidity at first, but Saul develops an evil leer when Penderel is not looking. Finding a carving knife, Saul threatens Penderel and compares fire to knives. He makes an unsuccessful knife attack and proceeds to start setting fire to the house, but he is stopped by Penderel, and both of them tumble over a stairwell railing.

The result is that Saul is killed, cradled in Morgan's arms (the claim that Morgan used to beat him adds an odd touch to their relationship) and carried away never to be seen again. The surviving Penderel waits for an ambulance and proposes to DuCane, having found in love a reason for striving again.

Arthur Edeson in photographing *The Old Dark House* took the "dark" part very seriously, and the film does indeed have a dark look with heavy shadows. Unfortunately, many copies of the film today are not too clear for that reason. Ownership fell into private hands which has kept the film off television and videocassette for years, making it a hard film to find. Those who do see it and expect an exciting, Karlovian horrorfest like *Frankenstein* are inevitably disappointed, as were audiences when the film was first released.

As in *Frankenstein*, there is an introduction of the dangerously drunken Morgan in a series of three jump cuts, each coming closer to his face, but Whale's direction here is not as effective as it was in *Frankenstein*. The film acknowledges the implication of DuCane's relationship with Porterhouse, but then skirts around it by indicating that they are just good friends and he is still in love with his dead wife, leaving DuCane virginal enough to go away and marry Penderel at the end.

The comedy is not broad here, but subtle and offbeat. No doubt it left many audiences perplexed, though Whale does evince a good scene sense. Highlights include Thesiger's performance throughout, stealing the film from his better known fellow cast members; the oddball scene in Rebecca's bedroom, at once atmospheric, comic and unnerving; and the development of the genuinely dangerous Saul's madness into a crescendo. Following this film, peculiar characters became the main delight and focus of many subsequent Whale films.

The Road Back was temporarily shelved and numerous other projects were discussed, especially as Universal wanted to develop some new properties for their new star, Karloff. In keeping with his reputation for working on play adaptations, Whale was given *The Kiss Before the Mirror* to complete in the interim. He obviously enjoyed developing the irony of the film, which concerns a defense attorney with an unfaithful wife defending a friend who murdered his wife for being unfaithful.

Like *Frankenstein*, *The Invisible Man* started off as a proposed project for Robert Florey, but with *Murders in the Rue Morgue*'s lack of success, the project was taken away from him and eventually fell into the hands of James Whale. Both Garrett Fort and Preston Sturges took a whack at a screenplay adaptation of Wells' famous science fiction novel, with the Sturges version being set in Russia, but these attempts got further and further away from the book.

Whale suggested that his old friend R. C. Sherriff be given a chance. Meanwhile, Universal also bought the rights to Philip Wylie's *The Murderer Invisible*, a variation on the idea of the Wells novel, to plumb for ideas and to protect themselves against any possible lawsuit. Sherriff, however, insisted on sticking solely to the Wells original.

The project was originally developed for Boris Karloff to star in, but the actor had just temporarily left the studio when, after he had agreed to one salary reduction, the studio balked at paying him the agreed-upon salary increase when it came time to renew his option. Initially, Whale approached his old friend Colin Clive to take over the role, but Clive turned down the part in favor of returning to England.

Whale then saw possibilities in a screen test for Claude Rains for *A Bill of Divorcement*. Rains was a prominent actor on the London and New York stages, but he had never appeared in films. After performing a test involving the scene where Griffin outlines his plan for taking over the world, Whale was convinced he had his man. Now all he had to do was convince the studio.

Given that it was the leading role, Rains insisted on star billing, which caused costar Chester Morris, a one-time box office idol, to leave the cast. Universal agreed to have Rains head the cast when Whale convinced them that the real draw of the film would be its spectacular special effects.

These effects would be accomplished by the new head of Universal's special effects department, John P. Fulton, who assured Whale that the shots could be done. Shooting on the film took two months, a long time for a '30s film only 70 minutes in length, and the final lab work took even longer.

In the June 1934 issue of *American Cinematographer*, Fulton explained how the effects of *The Invisible Man* were accomplished:

> We used a completely black set – walled and floored with black velvet to be as nearly non-reflective as possible. Our actor was garbed from head to foot in black velvet tights, with black gloves, and a black

headpiece rather like a diver's helmet. Over this, he wore whatever clothes might be required. This gave us a picture of the unsupported clothes moving around on a dead black field. From this negative, we made a print and a duplicate negative, which we then intensified to serve as mattes for printing. Then, with an ordinary printer, we proceeded to make our composite: first we printed from the positive of the background and normal action, using the intensified, negative matte to mask off the area where our invisible man's clothing was to move. Then we printed again, using the positive matte to shield the already printed area, and printing in the moving clothes from our "trick" negative. This printing operation made our duplicate, composite negative to be used in printing the final master prints of the picture.

The chief difficulty we encountered in these scenes was not primarily photographic, but had to do with acting and direction – getting the player to move naturally, yet in a manner which did not present, for example, an open sleeve end to the camera. This required endless rehearsal, endless patience – and many "takes." In many scenes, too, we had to figure out ways of getting natural-looking movement without having our "invisible" actor pass his hands in front of himself.

In several sequences, the player had to be shown unwrapping the concealing bandages from about his head; and in another, pulling off a false nose, revealing the absolute emptiness of the head-swatchings, the back of which showed through when the nose was removed. This latter scene was made by using a dummy, an exact replica of the player's makeup, and with a chest ingeniously contrived to move as though breathing. The unwrapping action was handled in the same fashion as the other half-clad scenes – that is, by multiple printing with travelling mattes. . . .

Fulton's effects have stood the test of time superbly, largely due to the inordinate amount of detail and time he spent on the project. To cover up any imperfections (e.g. hidden eyeholes that should not be seen), Fulton had the negative retouched on 4,000 feet of film in which each frame was individually worked on by hand. The most difficult effects shot in the film had the invisible man unwrapping his head in front of a mirror, which required four separate takes to be perfectly matched and combined so that one simultaneously sees his head unwrapped from front and back in the mirror.

But while *The Invisible Man* remains an effects marvel, there is more to the picture than that. Whale wanted Griffin, the man who is invisible throughout the film, to remain sympathetic, though he does some rather horrific things, so a bit was added to the script in which the drug that makes him invisible also renders him partially insane. (Actually, without anything to reflect light off the retina, an invisible man would also be blind, but this problem has been ignored in virtually every movie involving invisibility.)

One way Whale kept the film fresh during the effects scenes was by frequent cutting, rather than locking down the camera in one or two positions for a given effects sequence. The movie is shot as if the special effects could be taken for granted, and the number of different angles from which we can see them adds to their believability.

Another important aspect is the lively characters that have been injected throughout the storyline. For the first time, Whale used Irish actress Una O'Connor to be an oddball innkeeper's wife, and she gives a broad and amusing performance that builds up interest and tension in the opening scenes of the film.

The film begins like Wells' novel with a stranger wrapped in bandages checking into a snow-covered country inn. The innkeeper's wife continually gets more suspicious of and interested in her alarming new guest, who hides his features and speaks to everyone in a contemptuous manner. She finally badgers her husband into turning him out for cursing, spilling chemicals and being a week behind in the rent, which unleashes Griffin's fury.

The humor is sometimes broad but nonetheless funny. The atmosphere in the inn is established by a character taking bows for his piano playing only to have his compatriot insert another coin in what proves to be a player piano. The astonished constable (E. E. Clive) tells patrons of the bar, "'E's invisible, that's what the matter with him is," before leading them on back to the room. In a bit of risqué humor, Griffin turns his back and unzips his fly just as he delivers the line, "Now they'll see something really shocking!" My favorite bit of oddball humor comes near the end of the film as Griffin frightens a woman by donning only a pair of pants and singing gaily, "Here we go gathering nuts in May, nuts in May, nuts in May, on a chill and frosty morning."

The film has interesting small turns by people such as Walter Brennan (who gets his bicycle stolen), John Carradine (who calls the police with a suggestion on how they might capture the invisible man) and Dwight Frye (as a newspaper reporter asking the police what techniques they thought of). Gloria Stuart does not have a large part as Flora, the love interest, but she is appealingly sympathetic.

The largest role other than Rains' is William Harrigan's as Dr. Kemp, who wants to take Griffin's place in Flora's affections. When Griffin reappears at his house Kemp is utterly terrified and his pusillanimous behavior quickly loses him any sympathy from the audience as he deceives and betrays his former, though admittedly mad, friend.

Rains' physical gestures are a trifle overly theatrical, though some of this is for the benefit of frightening his spectators, putting on a mad act. The film allows the audience to live out prankish fantasies vicariously, and it is obvious that Griffin enjoys his invisible antics, and the audience does with him.

Rains' voice is quite commanding though, switching from feverish arrogance to frantic pleading to gentle wooing of Flora that builds as madness replaces Flora in his mind. The best speech amply demonstrates the horror and Griffin's growing megalomania: "Just a scientific experiment at first. That's all – to do something no other man in the world had done. Kemp, I know now! It came to me suddenly. The drugs I took seemed to light up my brain, suddenly I realized the power I held – the power to rule, to make the world grovel at my feet. Ha, ha! We'll soon put the world to right now, Kemp.... We'll begin with a reign of terror. A few murders, here and there. Murders of great men, murders of little men, just to show we make no distinction. We might even wreck a train or two. Just these fingers 'round a signalman's throat."

In a departure from the book, Griffin succeeds in killing Kemp, which becomes the dramatic climax of the movie. (Griffin's eventual shooting and capture seem perfunctory by comparison, given little in the way of buildup by Whale.) Kemp performs the function of an antagonist, with the police being a secondary force opposed to Griffin. Additionally, Griffin is given some murders and a train derailment which allow him to relish his powers, as well as outwitting the police who are trying to protect Kemp through elaborate measures.

Whale's seemingly simple style is actually quite meticulous. He knows when to use a series of quick cuts to imply a broad range of action (people locking their doors after being warned about an invisible man; the police searching everywhere). There are smooth tracking shots that focus the audience's attention. One of his most effective techniques is to provide a slightly different angle when cutting from a close-up to a two-shot and then back again, moving his camera fractionally closer as if the audience is bending forward with interest to catch every syllable that a character utters. He also shoots Rains from a low angle when he wants him to appear more commanding, and while deprived of facial expression for obvious reasons, Rains commutes his character's feelings through inflection and body language quite effectively.

There may have been something more elaborate intended for the climax; Fulton revealed that he had been instructed to devise a method for producing footprints in the snow that was not stop-motion – that is, taking some frames without a footprint, then adding one, taking some more frames, then adding another and so on – because the shot would have people in it. However, no such shot appears in the film with the footprints appearing by themselves. Fulton's technique involved laying a trench under the snow with secret wooden doors. When a footprint needed to appear, the door was pulled away and the snow fell into a pit in the shape of a footprint.

As Griffin dies, he slowly becomes visible again, allowing us our only look at Claude Rains. To accomplish this effect, Rains lay under some sheets made of papier-mâché (to keep their shape and not move from shot to shot).

In a slow dissolve, the invisible figure becomes a skeleton, which was then replaced by a sculpted figure resembling Rains and finally by the actor himself before the camera pulls away to end the film.

Universal needed a big success and it got one in *The Invisible Man*, which helped Rains become established in Hollywood. While primarily designed as an entertainment, the film also touches on wish fulfillment, power fantasies, brutal violence, arrogance, aspirations and some humorous absurdities. It helped establish that big horror cliché of "there are some things in which mankind was not meant to meddle" by stating it overtly (but unselfconsciously). It shows the wisdom of the old Chinese proverb, "Be careful what you wish for, you might get it." All told, *The Invisible Man* remains one of horror's greatest classics.

However, Whale's greatest horror film would prove to be his next and last one, *The Bride of Frankenstein*, a film he had long resisted doing, feeling he had used up his ideas on the initial film. Following *The Invisible Man*, he planned to make *A Trip to Mars*, with Boris Karloff, who had been loaned to John Ford and RKO for *The Lost Patrol*. Instead, he was asked to assume direction of *By Candlelight*, which had been started by Robert Wyler, William Wyler's brother. The film is a typical romantic comedy about a butler who is mistaken for a prince falling in love with a maid whom he mistakes for a grand dame.

A Trip to Mars was eventually canceled because Carl Laemmle, Jr., decided it would be too costly for the financially strapped studio to film and because he did not like the script. Meanwhile, Whale, concerned over the financial situation at the studio and receiving offers from others, considered getting out of his contract. But as he left for his vacation, he did find a property which interested him, John Galsworthy's novel *Over the River*.

This led to the film *One More River*, one of Whale's better efforts, though it ignores half of the novel it is based on, concentrating on the story of a woman, Diana Wynyard, who, having been beaten by her husband (Colin Clive in one of his best performances), finds herself named as correspondent in a court case in which Clive accuses her of having an affair with Frank Lawton. The film also featured the debut of Jane Wyatt as Wynyard's sister and such delightful English actors as C. Aubrey Smith, Mrs. Patrick Campbell, Alan Mowbray, Lionel Atwill and E. E. Clive.

Given Whale's insistence that he did not want to do *The Return of Frankenstein*, the studio temporarily handed *Bride of Frankenstein* over to Kurt Neumann, but it languished until Whale agreed to make the film if guaranteed complete artistic freedom. Desperately in need of more hits, Universal readily agreed.

Whale consulted with writers John L. Balderston and William Hurlbut on working out a treatment for the sequel. Several ideas from the original novel were incorporated: the Monster trying to save a drowning girl,

A delicious behind-the-scenes shot from Bride of Frankenstein *shows the Monster (Karloff) confronting his artistic creator, director James Whale. Whale resented that Karloff had received more publicity on the first film than he had.*

meeting with a blind man in the woods, learning to speak and demanding a mate. Balderston reportedly grew unhappy with the amount of horror injected into the story and so the final screenplay was the work of Hurlbut alone.

Most of the original cast returned along with some regular Whale performers with the exception of Mae Clarke, who had departed Universal and was replaced by Universal contract player Valerie Hobson. Frederick Kerr, the original Baron Frankenstein, had died and so was not included in the script, while E. E. Clive took over the officious role of burgomaster, proving more amusing than Lionel Belmore. To the lamentation of some critics who considered her role an injection of camp, Una O'Connor was given a major supporting part as Minnie, the Frankenstein's housekeeper and general village busybody.

For the key role of Dr. Septimus Pretorius, who persuades Henry Frankenstein to resume his work and build a mate, Whale wanted to use Claude Rains again. However, Rains proved unavailable, so Whale substituted Ernest Thesiger, who once more practically stole the show whenever he was onscreen with his odd personification of a demented doctor.

As in *The Invisible Man,* both John Carradine and Walter Brennan were given bit parts, while Dwight Frye was given the role of Karl, combining two characters from the script – Pretorius' assistant and a village idiot who takes advantage of the Monster's rampage to murder his miserly uncle, a subplot that was eliminated after initial previews of the film because it turned attention away from major characters to minor ones. All told, 15 minutes were removed from *Bride of Frankenstein* before general release.

Some of the missing footage expanded the prologue that Whale insisted on and that film editor Ted Kent recommended be cut entirely. In the prologue, we are introduced to Mary Shelley, author of the tale, and her companions Percy Shelley and Lord Byron. Whale agreed to some cuts but was very insistent on retaining this opening as being important to his conception.

One can see that he took a great deal of effort in crafting it, setting up a separate angle for each line of dialogue, showing the speaker or what is being spoken of or simply reaction shots. Gavin Gordon makes a delightful Lord Byron, who loves horror and delights in shocks. Whale wanted this sequence for a number of reasons. First, it obviously made it easy to show flashbacks and encapsulate the plot of the preceding film to prepare audiences for the current one (though note one quick shot of the Monster strangling E. E. Clive as the burgomaster among the flashbacks, a sequence cut out of *Bride of Frankenstein* rather than the original film). Second, it takes the tale from being "real" to being a story that Mary Shelley is telling her friends (and us). Finally, it allows Whale to contrast the seemingly innocent and demure Mary Shelley with the monster that Elsa Lanchester will later play in the film, demonstrating a proposition that terrible things can spring from the most seemingly ordinary people.

Some have been bothered that the characters in *Bride of Frankenstein* largely wear modern dress and that it contains such devices as a telephone. Originally, this was explained in the script by giving Mary Shelley the line: "I've taken the rest of the story into the future – and made use of developments which science will someday know – a hundred years to come. I think you will find the new horrors far more entertaining, Lord Byron." However, this line was excised and we must suppose that either Pretorius or Frankenstein invented the telephone, called an electrical device, far ahead of Alexander Graham Bell.

The film itself is suffused with cinematic references and oddball humor. However, the story itself begins on a properly horrific note. Having fallen through the floor of the mill and into a pit of water below it (providing the only plausible survival of the Monster from one film into the next in the entire series), the Monster waits angrily below for the villagers to depart. A relative of Maria, Hans (Reginald Barlow), insists on seeing the charred remains for himself so that he can sleep at night. (Maria's father was Ludwig, played by Michael Mark in the original film.) Falling into the underground pond himself, he encounters the Monster, who quicky kills him and then climbs up the stairs to the top where Hans' wife (Mary Gordon) waits to give him a hand up. In a bit of macabre humor, she helps rescue the Monster only to be thrown to her death for her pains. The ubiquitous Minnie sees the Monster, gives a shriek and runs off while the perplexed Monster looks on in bewilderment, making no attempt to harm her.

In carting away Henry, a reference is made to taking him to his father. In a scene cut from release, it is revealed that the Baron died of shock after hearing what happened to his son, making Henry the new Baron Frankenstein (and so he is addressed when Dr. Pretorius pays a call). In order to accommodate the new continuity, Universal cut the sequence of the Baron toasting a son to the house of Frankenstein from the re-release prints of the original film, and said scene was not shown again until the film's television sale in the late '50s.

In *Bride of Frankenstein*, the Monster and the creator switch places in many ways. While the first film concentrated on Frankenstein's dream and its dissolution and consequences (his crime being not so much creating the Monster but ignoring him and not raising him properly), *Bride* concerns itself more with the Monster and his development. While Henry is a divinely created human soul who rejects the company of others, the Monster is portrayed as a humanly created being who seeks the company of others but is continually rejected.

Henry is presumed dead until, in a parody of the original creation scene, he moves his hand and Elizabeth screams, "He's alive!" When the Monster and Henry first meet again late in the film, the Monster has taken over Henry's role, instructing Frankenstein to sit down, and he uses the same hand gestures that Frankenstein used.

Whale gives a big buildup to the entrance of Dr. Pretorius into the story, beginning with Elizabeth trying to comfort Henry after his delirium and then going into a kind of delirium herself as she proclaims that there is a figure of death coming to take Henry away from her. Indeed, with his swirling cloak, Dr. Pretorius could easily be a death figure as he knocks at the door, his face fully revealed only when the light from inside hits it as Minnie opens the door to this unexpected guest. He explains that he has come "on a secret matter of *grave* importance."

Frankenstein and Pretorius are left alone as Pretorius alternately tries to intrigue, cajole and threaten Frankenstein. He has been booted out of the university in which he had once taught Henry but proclaims he has succeeded in creating artificial life on his own. He threatens to expose Henry as the creator of the Monster and lay the blame for the deaths the Monster has caused at his door. (While it is not clear in the first film if the villagers connect Frankenstein with the Monster, later in this film when the huntsmen come upon the Monster in the blind man's hut, they obviously know all about who the Monster is and who made him, making Pretorius' threat here seem rather empty.) Somehow he has knowledge that the Monster did not die in the mill fire but still lives, and he desires that Henry become partners with him to create a female Monster and hence start an artificial race. "A woman," he leers, "that should be really interesting."

Rather than reanimating dead corpses, Pretorius has been growing miniature human beings from cultures, and in a delightful effects sequence, he displays the results of his work. Originally, there were to have been seven bottles, the last with Billy Barty portraying a baby in monster make-up pulling a flower apart while Pretorius promises, "I think this baby will grow into something worth watching," but the last bottle was cut and only a brief glimpse of it remains in long shot and in a publicity still.

Echoing his line from *The Old Dark House*, Pretorius proclaims that gin is his only weakness before drinking a toast, "To a new world of gods and monsters." (Later, Pretorius offers the Monster a cigar, proclaiming *them* his only weakness.) One of his creations is a little king, patterned after Henry VIII from the film *The Private Life of King Henry VIII* which won an Academy Award for Elsa Lanchester's husband, Charles Laughton.

Pretorius proclaims himself a doctor of philosophy and his personal philosophy seems to be based on the Marquis de Sade's. He wants to eliminate the concept of good and evil, and thinks it would be so much more "amusing" if everyone did what he or she wanted to. However, as the film develops, we find Pretorius is unscrupulous and is only interested in getting people to do what *he* wants them to. One of his figures is of the devil (played by Peter Shaw, Thesiger's double), in whom Pretorius sees a certain resemblance to himself – "Or do I flatter myself?"

With the mechanics of the plot set up, the film then concentrates on the chronicle of the Monster. Espying a young shepherdess who screams and falls into a stream at the sight of him, the Monster tries to rescue her (apparently learning from his experience with Maria the danger of water). Here the Monster is humanized, even heroic. But when his visage still provokes screams, despite his overtures of tenderness, he simply waves his arms above her, indicating "no."

The screams attract the attention of nearby villagers, who shoot at him, wounding him in the arm. While he rolls a boulder on a pair of his pursuers, he is soon overpowered and trussed up in a parody of Christ imagery. (A bit cut from the script had the Monster trying to rescue a figure of Christ from its cross.) The angry villagers throw rocks and pillory him, placing him in a chair in the town jail that is peculiarly just the right size and shape.

The comic character of the burgomaster proclaims the Monster an escaped lunatic ("Monster, indeed," he repeatedly sniffs) but with his great strength the Monster almost immediately breaks his chains and goes on the rampage through town. Whale shows an anxious mother looking for her missing child, who is found dead in a graveyard, and a married couple are found dead in their beds but never shown. By not showing us the victims themselves, Whale is able to keep the audience's sympathies with the much-persecuted Monster.

Additional scenes were shot here but later removed in which the burgo-master conducts an inquiry, dismissing the charges of a Monster because of a lack of eyewitnesses – though he himself has seen the Monster, having had it helpfully pointed out to him by Karl in the earlier forest scene. (Whale provides a suitably bleak atmosphere for the forest scene by showing only the bare trunks of trees and leafless or needleless trees in the background, giving the impression of desolation.) The burgomaster is subsequently strangled by the Monster he has declared nonexistent. Observing this, Karl then murders his uncle in the previously mentioned subplot, exclaiming, "Very convenient to have a Monster around. This is quite a nice cottage – I shouldn't be surprised if he visited auntie too!"

However, these scenes take too much time away from the story of the Monster and make the Monster more unsympathetic, particularly in an un-provoked attack on a comic character. The Karl bit makes a worthwhile point about copycat murderers, but it fails to provide a coherent portrait of his character, later shown to be nervous following Dr. Pretorius into a crypt ("If there's much more like this, what you say, pal, we give ourselves up and let 'em hang us? This is no life for murderers!") though subsequently he mur-ders a young girl for her heart under instructions from Dr. Pretorius and the promise of 1000 crowns from Frankenstein, who assumes he acquired it from an accident victim.

An additional bit of filming was ordered, showing the monster stumbl-ing on some gypsies in an effort to get food. This connects up well with the scenes in which the Monster first experiences friendship in the film as he enters the hut of a blind man (Australian actor O. P. Heggie in his most famous role) who is playing "Ave Maria" on his violin.

The scenes with the blind hermit are some of the best beloved in horror cinema. Though they venture on the maudlin, they remain very effective and even moving. Karloff was against having the Monster talk, feeling it would detract from the mystique of the character, but he did a superb job with the Monster's vocalizations. As it turned out, the delight in having the Monster express his joy in good food, good music, and good fellowship outweigh the possible disadvantages. While he proves far from a consum-mate grammarian, the Monster's expression makes it clear that he has in-telligence, reacts well to kindness and is not a brutish, unthinking thing.

The religious symbolism in *Bride of Frankenstein* has given many critics pause. With his resurrection and his being pilloried by the mob, the Monster does draw some parallels to Christ. Dr. Pretorius is openly contemptuous of religion, commenting in an aside that he is following the lead of nature, ". . . or of God, if you like your Bible stories. . . ." The Monster will later knock down the statue of a bishop and rail at an unkind creator in the heavens, while Frankenstein wonders if death is sacred and he has profaned it or if his discovery is part of God's divine plan.

While there are amusing religious jabs in the film, Whale is never contemptuous of the hermit's deeply religious faith nor of his following the commandment to love thy neighbor. Instead, he is portrayed as an extremely lonely man who gives thanks to God for the companionship of the Monster, moving the Monster himself to tears. Whale fades out on scene of the Monster comforting the hermit with an after-image of Christ on a crucifix lingering on momentarily after the rest of the scene has faded. Perhaps the point is that religion should not be used to excuse intolerance, something which Whale himself experienced in his own life, as did Colin Clive, who was an alcoholic bisexual married to a lesbian and a close friend of Whale's.

The point is further driven home when a pair of huntsmen, trying to help the old man, succeed merely in burning his hut down and chasing his companion away. They are doing what they "know" is right, not stopping to inquire and learn about the situation, and the results are tragic. Alone again, the Monster realizes he has lost his only friend.

The "inhuman" Monster having achieved speech and humanity now meets up with the human but not humane Dr. Pretorius, who is delighted to have discovered the skeleton of a woman properly firm for his proposed artificial woman and is enjoying a macabre picnic in the crypt. Selling the Monster on the idea of persuading Frankenstein to make a friend and mate for him, Pretorius takes the Monster to Frankenstein's castle where he is preparing to leave for his belated honeymoon, having recovered from his bad fall.

While Pretorius cajoles him, the Monster has been instructed to kidnap Elizabeth, which he does successfully. The house is in an uproar, but Pretorius smashes a vase to get everyone's attention and announces that Elizabeth will be returned unharmed, so long as Henry cooperates. Pretorius will clearly do anything and use anyone to achieve his aims. When Frankenstein needs a heart, Pretorius has no compunctions about sending Karl out to murder someone. He even betrays the Monster by feeding him a drink with knock-out drops in it which he makes no effort to disguise.

The creation scene for the "Bride" is a vast improvement on the old one, as Whale builds up tension and makes use of more elaborate equipment. Frankenstein is depicted as suspicious of his "partner," but he gets caught up in the excitement of the experiment. Cameraman John Mescall, who did a superb job photographing the film although he was frequently reported to have been drunk, uses some dutch tilt angles very effectively to suggest that in performing the experiment, the scientists are out of kilter. This experiment requires two assistants, Karl and Ludwig, who release kites to catch the life-giving lightning that will be transferred to the Bride, who looks like a mummy swathed in bandages.

It has long been rumored that the original idea was for Elizabeth's heart to be placed within the Bride for the Monster, combining Frankenstein's and the Monster's bride into one, but there is no indication of this in the shooting script. Cut out of the film is a brief scene where Ludwig releases the kidnapped Elizabeth from her cave, explaining why she is able to run to the door of the watch tower just after the Bride is brought to life.

Franz Waxman's musical score, which even includes such amusing touches as wedding bells when the Bride first steps forth from her platform and expertly uses tympani to suggest the beating of the Bride's heart and to build tension, is a masterpiece, one of the best of his long and varied career, and was one of the first Hollywood scores to use leitmotifs for the characters. Waxman later sued Oscar Hammerstein for stealing his three-note, eerie "Bride's Theme" for the song "Bali Hai" in *South Pacific* and received a generous settlement.

Elsa Lanchester based her performance of the Bride on swans that she had seen while in England. Whale himself designed the Nefertiti hairstyle employed so memorably, made to stick up and out to suggest the electricity that had shocked her to life. Lanchester makes quick, darting, bird-like movements and easily conveys her preference for Frankenstein rather than her intended, whom she avoids and then screams and hisses at.

Originally when the Monster said, "We belong dead," his remarks were to have included Elizabeth and Frankenstein, as well as Pretorius, the Bride and himself. In the laboratory destruction sequence, the figure of Frankenstein can be briefly glimpsed standing next to the door after the Monster pulls the deadly switch, but at the last moment in filming, it was decided to let Frankenstein and Elizabeth live and let the Monster nobly spare their lives (though his reasons for doing so are unclear).

With its humor, whimsy, vivid characterizations, moving moments, and offbeat fairy-tale quality, *The Bride of Frankenstein* remains one of the best horror films ever made. Karloff gave unquestionably his best performance as the Monster, conveying a complexity in the creature as well as a soul. While the passage of over half a century has dated the film somewhat, in many ways the direction is still surprisingly modern with its quick cuts and artistic visual compositions.

How sad that *Bride* was a flop on initial release, that Whale's homosexuality caused him to be driven out of show business years later and he died a suicide in 1957. Like his Monster, Whale railed against a world that made no place for him.

Robert Wise (1914–)

The Curse of the Cat People (codirected with Gunther von Fritsch); *Mademoiselle Fifi* (1944); *The Body Snatcher; A Game of Death* (1945); *Criminal Court* (1946); *Born to Kill* (1947); *Mystery in Mexico; Blood on the Moon* (1948); *The Set-Up* (1949); *Two Flags West; Three Secrets* (1950); *The House on Telegraph Hill; The Day the Earth Stood Still* (1951); *The Captive City; Something for the Birds* (1952); *The Desert Rats; Destination Gobi; So Big* (1953); *Executive Suite* (1954); *Helen of Troy* (1955); *Tribute to a Bad Man; Somebody Up There Likes Me* (1956); *This Could Be the Night; Until They Sail* (1957); *Run Silent Run Deep; I Want to Live* (1958); *Odds Against Tomorrow* (1959); *West Side Story* (Codirected with Jerome Robbins, 1961); *Two for the Seesaw* (1962); *The Haunting* (1963); *The Sound of Music* (1965); *The Sand Pebbles* (1966); *Star!* (1968); *The Andromeda Strain* (1971); *Two People* (1973); *The Hindenburg* (1975); *Audrey Rose* (1977); *Star Trek – The Motion Picture* (1979); *Rooftops* (1989).

Robert Wise is a talented director who has achieved success in a number of genres including two of the biggest musicals of all time, *West Side Story* and *The Sound of Music*; two of the best boxing pictures, *The Set-Up* and *Somebody Up There Likes Me*; a suspenseful submarine thriller, *Run Silent Run Deep*; a melodrama with Susan Hayward, the memorable *I Want to Live*; and three important science fiction features, *The Day the Earth Stood Still* (one of the most intelligent such features from the '50s), *Andromeda Strain*, and *Star Trek – The Motion Picture*. However, for the purposes of this book, we will simply concentrate on his few but vivid horror films.

Wise was born on September 10, 1914, in Winchester, Indiana. Forced to quit college during the Depression, he became an assistant film cutter at RKO, a job secured by his brother David who worked as an accountant for the studio. Becoming a full-fledged editor, he cut such films as *The Hunchback of Notre Dame, All That Money Can Buy, Citizen Kane* and *The Magnificent Ambersons*.

Wise was hired to cut a sequel to RKO's highly successful *Cat People*, which Charles Koerner dubbed *Curse of the Cat People*. However, perversely, producer Val Lewton decided to come up with a film that featured no "curses" nor even any "Cat People," though it is definitely a sequel to the original. Instead, he decided to make a film about the difficulties of

736

childhood, drawing on his own difficult childhood which he populated with imaginary playmates. He also patterned the film on his own problems in raising his daughter whom he had great trouble relating to. (Associates who knew Lewton well indicate that this was the main flaw of an otherwise exemplary man.)

Busy working on *The Ghost Ship* with Mark Robson, Lewton selected former documentary filmmaker Gunther von Fritsch to direct, but after the 18 days of the schedule had passed, von Fritsch had only filmed half the script. The head of the B film unit at the time, Sid Rogell, decided to replace him with Robert Wise; he liked Wise's second unit work and knew that Wise was pushing for a shot at directing. Wise was uncomfortable with taking over from a man he had been working for, but Lewton urged him to go ahead as von Fritsch was being replaced with or without him.

Naturally, this arrangement makes it hard to assess exactly what Wise's contributions to the film were; nevertheless, *Curse of the Cat People* is an interesting and rare look into a child's world from a child's point of view. The child in question is Amy (Ann Carter), the daughter of the now married Oliver Reed (Kent Smith) and Alice (Jane Randolph) from *Cat People*. Amy is an imaginative but lonely child.

While the original *Cat People* ended with Reed opining that Irena never lied to him, in *Curse* it is readily apparent that he considers Irena (Simone Simon) to have died as a result of her delusions and is uneasy with all kinds of make-believe. He is especially troubled by Amy's apparent inability to distinguish fact from fantasy when after being told that a tree trunk was a magic mailbox, she deposited birthday party invitations that needed to be mailed there rather than in a mailbox, with the result that no one received them and no one attended her party.

Upset and feeling unloved because of the harshness she detects in her stern and stuffy father, Amy gazes into a wishing well and wishes for a friend. She hears the modulated tones of a French accent of an invisible playmate. Later, when she glimpses a photograph of Reed's first wife, the playmate takes shape and form as Irena.

Amy made her wish on a ring which was thrown out of a nearby old house, and her father's kindly black servant Edward (Sir Lancelot) tells her it is a Jamaican wishing ring. However, when her parents find out about it, they insist that she must return it to its owners. Amy goes to the strange old house and meets a senile old woman, Julia Farren (Julia Dean), and her "caretaker," actually her daughter, Barbara (Elizabeth Russell).

Barbara is bitter over the fact that her mother, the elderly Mrs. Farren, refuses to recognize her as her daughter, and she resents it when Mrs. Farren befriends the young girl Amy. She desperately wants to regain her mother's love, but her best efforts fail as Mrs. Farren is afraid of her.

While there is a small element of fear in the film, *Curse of the Cat People*

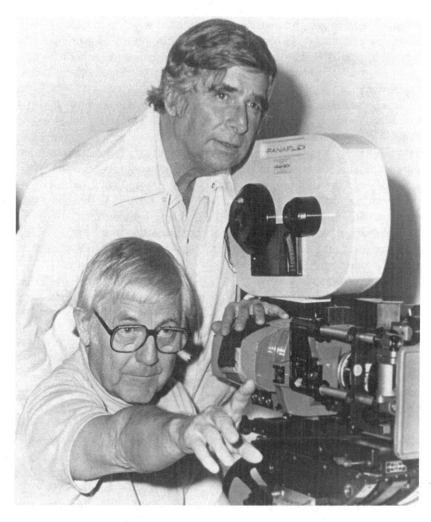

Robert Wise (bottom) with Star Trek *creator/producer Gene Roddenberry on the set of* Star Trek – The Motion Picture, *an unwieldy project that gave Wise several production headaches while needing to be completed on a tight schedule to make its release deadline. It may not have been Wise's finest hour, but he did get the job done.*

is no ordinary horror film. The few terrors it has to offer are the kinds of things that frighten only very young children – the dark, nightmares, old people, strange old houses. In fact, the only really frightening moment is gratuitously grafted onto the film: Mrs. Farren retells the tale of Washington Irving's "The Legend of Sleepy Hollow," to which Wise has added some very good sound effects that greatly enhance the spookiness of this time-honored classic. Through the wind there builds a sound that resembles the hoofbeats of the Headless Horseman; then the sound is revealed to be a tarpaulin flapping loose on an approaching truck.

A surprising aspect by today's standards is how willing father Reed is to beat poor Amy because she refuses to deny the existence of her imaginary playmate, though it is indicated that he is frightened that his daughter might be becoming infected with the same kind of "delusions" that resulted in his first wife's demise. Predictably, a beating does not prove the best way of dealing with the situation.

The frightened Amy flees to Mrs. Farren's house. Mrs. Farren picks up on how upset the child is and interprets it that Barbara is planning to get at her somehow, and so the old lady rushes up the stairs, but it is too much for her heart and she dies in Amy's arms. Barbara, distressed at the sight of her now dead and reconciled mother on the stairs with the child she has come to hate, approaches Amy menacingly. Amy calls on help and protection from Irena, but her pleas for "my friend" are misinterpreted by Barbara as referring to her. The lonely woman is grateful for any sign of friendship and suddenly softens towards the child, befriending her as Amy's father and the police arrive in search of the missing girl. (Significantly, the name Amy derives from the French word meaning "friend.")

The film ends with Reed pretending that he sees Irena, reconciling with his estranged daughter, at which point the imaginary playmate no longer is necessary and the ghostly Irena promptly disappears. The entire film is played ambiguously so that the audience can interpret it in two ways: Either Irena really was there, a ghost who befriended the nearly friendless little girl, or she was simply a figment of that child's imagination.

Apart from the unusual subject matter, the film's principal virtues are those that are manifest in every Lewton production: sensitive handling, excellent black-and-white cinematography (this time provided by Nicholas Musuraca), richly detailed production designs achieved on a miniscule budget, a moody musical score by Roy Webb, and basically an overall exemplarily crafted movie. What is particularly striking about *Curse of the Cat People* is the way the changing of the seasons is depicted on the same basic set, with leaves or snow falling at appropriate times to create indelible images, plus the playfulness of Irena's ghostly appearances.

Lewton next selected Wise to helm *Mademoiselle Fifi*, a costume drama based on two stories, "Boule de Suif" and "Mademoiselle Fifi" by Guy de Maupassant. Once more Simone Simon starred, this time as a dignified lower class French woman traveling by coach who is coerced into compromising herself by spending the night with a Prussian officer only to be scorned by her fellow passengers after having acceded to their wishes. Made during World War II, the film has been perceived as a subtle criticism of the middle class French who became collaborators with the Germans during the war, showing that the bourgeoisie were all too willing to accept subjugation as long as the status quo could be maintained. Wise did a decent job directing, but he was hampered by an inadequate budget and allowed John Emery to ham outrageously, making this one of Lewton's lesser films.

By contrast, Wise's next production for Lewton, *The Body Snatcher*, was one of the best, with beautiful performances that capture many subtle nuances and a rich period flavor. The film was based on Robert Louis Stevenson's story, which in turn was based on the activities of Burke and Hare, resurrectionists who dug up graves and sold the bodies to medical students. Eventually the pair decided that all that spade work was too much trouble and simply killed the victims to provide the requisite bodies.

Philip MacDonald was initially hired to come up with a screenplay, but when Lewton totally rewrote him, he insisted that Lewton take cocredit, which Lewton did under his pseudonym Carlos Keith. The film was made during a break in *Isle of the Dead*, which had to shut down because Karloff was suffering from a leg injury. He recovered to star in *The Body Snatcher* and then finished *Isle of the Dead*. Bela Lugosi was signed up for *The Body Snatcher* to add to the marquee value, and there are rumors that Lugosi was originally considered for the major role of Dr. MacFarlane, but his accent would have been out of place for a Scotsman and he was in the throes of drug addiction at the time. Thus, despite his costar billing, he was relegated to the minor role of Joseph, MacFarlane's servant. The years were not kind to Lugosi and he was in dilapidated condition when he made the film, though his "out of it" look was appropriate for the character. Henry Daniell, however, shone in what was possibly his best performance as MacFarlane, a role perfectly suited to Daniell's cold personality.

As *Mademoiselle Fifi* reused sets from *The Hunchback of Notre Dame*, *The Body Snatcher* revamped sets from Tourneur's *Experiment Perilous* to good effect. Considering the low budget, Wise expertly evokes 1821 Edinburgh with vivid detail. Adding to the overall ambience is a blind street singer (Donna Lee) who sings Scottish songs and halfway through the film becomes involved in the story proper.

The story opens as a young medical student named Fettes (Russell Wade) sits in a cemetery and eats his lunch, preparing to leave MacFarlane's school because his family has run out of money for his tuition. An older woman comes up and feeds a dog that remains in the cemetery mourning its dead master. The woman explains that the dog can guard his master's body from being taken by graverobbers as she cannot afford to pay guard to watch over the body.

A coach driven by John Gray (Karloff) pulls up in front of MacFarlane's house and the coachman assists a mother and her handicapped daughter onto the porch, taking the daughter to his white horse and promising her that the horse will nod at her when next he meets her. Gray is a servile, friendly character, but an exchange of looks with the housekeeper Meg (Edith Atwater) indicates she has had some dark dealings in the past with Gray and does not approve of him.

MacFarlane agrees to see the mother and child, but his cold manner frightens the small girl who refuses to cooperate and explain to MacFarlane about her pain. MacFarlane drafts Fettes, who has come to resign, to see if he can do better, and the little girl quickly takes to him. The examination proves that the girl has a malignant tumor on her spine and could soon be permanently paralyzed. The mother looks to MacFarlane as her only hope, but he declines, saying he has given up active medicine to devote his full attention to preparing students for becoming doctors.

MacFarlane is convinced that Fettes will make an excellent doctor and refuses to accept his resignation. Instead, he gives Fettes a job as his assistant so that he can meet his expenses. That night, Fettes becomes acquainted with Gray, who has killed the small dog at the opening and robbed the grave, bringing the corpse to MacFarlane's so that it may be used for medical experiments in exchange for 10 pounds, which he advises Fettes to record in MacFarlane's bookkeeping log.

In a very economical fashion, all the major threads of the plot have been set up. MacFarlane is a man haunted by his past; he was an assistant to the infamous Dr. Knox, who had bought bodies from Burke and Hare, but he paid Gray to shield him in court, for which Gray went to jail. Another peculiar thread reveals that his pride is so great that he refuses to acknowledge that Meg is not really his housekeeper but his wife. His life has been poisoned by his refusal to accept responsibility.

However, MacFarlane is a very knowledgeable and gifted man, and the audience sympathizes with him when, because of social constrictions that will only allow him cadavers of paupers on which to study human anatomy and teach his students, he is forced in the interests of science to associate with Gray and other resurrectionists. Because of a misguided respect for the dead, many of the living have needlessly died because important knowledge could not be acquired given the lack of specimens. Lewton's script underlines this point with the mawkish subplot about the crippled young girl, whom MacFarlane will eventually make well.

Initially, MacFarlane is opposed to the project and the mother turns to Fettes to plead on her behalf. Fettes broaches the subject in a tavern while sitting with Gray and MacFarlane, and Gray seizes upon MacFarlane's proclaimed reluctance as a way to demonstrate his power over MacFarlane. He insists that MacFarlane do the operation, "for old times' sake," to which MacFarlane reluctantly agrees. Gray also insists on addressing MacFarlane as "Toddy," despite his protests, rather than giving him the respect that would have been expected from one of his station.

Wise guides the actors well, and Lewton's script provides plenty of psychological motivation, making the characters in *The Body Snatcher* far more interesting and memorable than those in the average horror film, which typically are stereotypes rather than characters. Karloff gives Gray a very full and rounded characterization, one that combines a certain sweetness and good cheer with an inextricable menace and evil.

Gray is indeed a complex and contradictory character. He spends most of the movie smiling sweetly, so when he loses that smile, it is highly significant and makes more of an impact. Thanks to his intervention, MacFarlane is forced to save the young crippled girl, but Gray does not exert his influence out of compassion but rather to demonstrate his control over MacFarlane, which is the only thing in life that truly gives him pleasure. As he says to MacFarlane near the end of the film, it helps his pride "to know I can force you to my will. I am a small man, a humble man, and being poor I have had to do much that I did not want to do. And so long as the great Dr. MacFarlane jumps to my whistle, that long am I a man. And if I have not that, I have nothing. Then I'm only a cabman and a graverobber. You'll never get rid of me, Toddy."

But while Gray is genuinely sweet with the crippled girl, and genuinely honored when Fettes pays him a call in hopes that Gray can dig up a corpse that MacFarlane can study to prepare for tackling the crippled girl's spinal problem, we see he is quite capable of being inhumanly ruthless as well. This is best illustrated in the classic sequence that follows Fettes' request. Watching Fettes go, Gray looks out and sees the street singer go by. Because of his most recent grave robbery, the kirkyards are being heavily guarded, but in a dialogueless close-up, we can see that Gray has come up with an alternative way of acquiring a corpse. The street singer, traveling up a dark alley, is followed by the coachman in his coach. Suddenly her singing is abruptly cut off in mid-verse. The camera lingers on the darkened alley for a moment or two to confirm our suspicions before dissolving into the next scene. This sequence is remarkable for its simple economy – nothing is really shown, there is only one camera setup, but the sudden absence of a sound where there should be one tells the whole story in a way that is more memorable than most far more explicit murder scenes.

Fettes is shocked to discover Gray has delivered the body of the street singer and has an attack of conscience, but MacFarlane persuades him that he cannot be sure that Gray murdered the girl and that Fettes could become implicated in the murder for having gone to Gray and asked for a body in the first place. Joseph overhears this exchange and decides to use it to blackmail Gray for money.

Wise wisely films this confrontation between Gray and Joseph with backlighting from a fire, giving their faces menacing dark shadows. Gray reacts jovially to Joseph's demands and quickly gets him drunk, making references to Burke and Hare, whom Joseph has not heard of. His wits are too dulled by the drink to understand the significance of the Burke and Hare story that Gray tells him, and in response to his pleas that he does not understand, Gray smiles and offers, "I'll show you how they did it, Joseph. I'll show you how they Burked them." He proceeds to smother Joseph with his hand and then deposit the body in a water barrel in MacFarlane's cellar so that if there is any trouble, he can spread the story that MacFarlane, running out of "specimens," had turned on his own household staff.

MacFarlane is tormented by Gray's hold over him, his own conscience, and his apparent failure to cure the crippled girl, who refuses to walk after the tumor has been removed. The addition of Joseph's death is the final straw and he prepares to rid himself of Gray forever, either by bribing him to spend the rest of his days away from Edinburgh or by killing him. When Gray rejects the first offer, MacFarlane attacks him, and though Gray gets the upper hand twice and obviously does not want to do in his "old friend," MacFarlane persists until he succeeds in bashing Gray's head in. (Presaged by an earlier scene where he took a poker to a large lump of coal, to which Meg observed that he wished that were Gray's head.) MacFarlane then takes the body to the medical school where it is dissected until it is unidentifiable (which is presaged in an earlier scene where Fettes jokes about Burke and Hare doing just that).

When Fettes is discussing the child's problem with her mother, the crippled girl is driven by her desire to see Gray's white horse nod at her to leave her wheelchair and finally walk. Overjoyed, Fettes rushes to find Mac-Farlane, who has just disposed of MacFarlane's horse and is convinced that the girl can walk because Gray's evil influence is gone.

However, on the ride back, it is readily apparent that Gray's evil influence has not dissipated. Learning of a newly buried body, MacFarlane resolves to dig it up, doing his "own dirty work" as he calls it, and to pursue his studies with renewed vigor. Traveling through the rain in a one-horse carriage with Fettes, the body of an elderly women between them, Mac-Farlane begins to hear the voice of Gray calling, "Toddy," over and over again in the wind. The drum of the horse's hoofbeats reminds him of Gray's threat, "You'll never be rid of me," which echoes over and over in his mind.

Consumed with guilt for murdering Gray, MacFarlane becomes convinced that the body they are transporting is actually Gray's. He knocks Fettes out of the carriage in his fright when he takes a look and the carriage surges forward, out of control. In MacFarlane's mind, the body has become that of Gray, and jostling over the mountainside, the carriage breaks loose from the horse and plunges over the side (fulfilling a prophecy of Meg's that she sees MacFarlane and Gray plunging into a great pit) and kills Mac-Farlane. Checking on his mentor, Fettes finds him dead alongside the body of the old woman they had dug up. A closing title indicates that knowledge must journey from the darkness into the light.

The Body Snatcher is an expertly crafted film that wastes none of its short running time, and it proved a tremendous success for RKO. The intelligent performances of Daniell and Karloff, the ambiguous way that we can see good in the evil Gray and bad in the gifted and well-intentioned MacFarlane, and the psychological underpinnings make this a fascinating film that is fondly remembered. Unfortunately, it also marked Wise's departure from the horror film for a long time, though he regards it as his best film from this early period.

Wise left the umbrella of Lewton's productions and next directed *A Game of Death*, one of the many remakes of the classic story "The Most Dangerous Game," though despite a few thrilling scenes, it is an average film populated by largely uninteresting actors. Of more interest was *Born to Kill* in which the sleazy Lawrence Tierney kills his girlfriend when he sees her out with another man. Based on a novel by science fiction writer James Gunn, the film benefits from the moody photography of Robert de Grasse (as did *The Body Snatcher* which de Grasse also worked on). Tierney plays a fascinatingly evil man who brings out the worst in others while causing two women, Claire Trevor and Audrey Long, to fall hopelessly in love with him. He ends up killing his only friend and perennial patsy, played by Elisha Cook, Jr.

Wise gets some menace out of the robot Gort in *The Day the Earth Stood Still*, but the primary plea of that film was one in which Michael Rennie, playing a highly intelligent and Christ-like visitor from outer space, urges people not to let fear replace reason. *The Captive City* generated an atmosphere of fear, but in that case it is John Forsythe who fears for his life because organized crime might rub him out before he has a chance to tell his story to the Kefauver Committee. Wise was not to return to horror until *The Haunting* in 1963.

But what a return! *The Haunting* remains one of the most frightening and effective horror films of all time, based on Shirley Jackson's classic novel *The Haunting of Hill House*. Robert Wise projects an atmosphere of palpable evil and menace in the claustrophobic locale of the sinister Hill House without so much as showing one of the noisy poltergeists that boom across the soundtrack and create such a fine *frisson* of terror. In addition to being a superbly crafted scare film, *The Haunting* also contains a superb psychological profile of its heroine, Eleanor Vance, played to perfection by Julie Harris.

The film opens with a shot of Hill House and the suggestive lines that open Shirley Jackson's novel: "Hill House had stood so for 90 years and might stand for 90 more. Within, walls continued upright, bricks met neatly, floors were firm, and doors were sensibly shut; silence lay steadily against the wood and stone of Hill House, and whatever walked there, walked alone."

This passage beautifully evokes a feeling that Hill House has a history, contains dark and evil things, is somehow not quite right, is silent as the tomb, and is almost a living thing that contains some prowling force. Wise follows this effectively with a series of scenes that reflect the voiceover narration of the history of the house by Dr. Markway (Richard Johnson). With the aid of David Boulton's atmospheric and moody cinematography and a variety of distorting lenses, Wise presents a capsule portrait of the evils and tragedy that have surrounded the house's history: from the death of the first wife of Hugh Crain, its architect and owner and an avowed misanthrope, just as she was to enter the house for the first time, to the unexplained tumble down a spiral staircase by the second wife, to Crain's daughter Abigail's death while calling her companion who has been dallying with a village lad instead of tending to her duties, to the companion's suicide by hanging herself from a balcony in the library (presented as a chilling point-of-view shot).

Dr. Markway intends to lease the house in order to do some psychic research on it with a hand-picked team of people who have had previous psychic experiences. The owner of the house agrees with the proviso that her nephew Luke (Russ Tamblyn), who expects to inherit the house, accompany the misguided expedition. As an old lady, she hopes they will discover some definite proof of an afterlife.

However, all this material has been prefatory to introducing the main character of Eleanor Vance, a lonely, frustrated and sexually repressed young woman who had been nursing her mother for 11 years until her recent death (in circumstances that echo the death of the companion in Hill House). She lives with her sister and brother-in-law when she receives an invitation to come to Hill House, but despite the fact that they are obviously uncomfortable living together, they are reluctant to let her go. Eleanor virtually steals the car she half-paid for to escape to Hill House, where she hopes to find romance and a better life for herself.

Instead she finds an oppressively odd old house and the creepy Mrs. Dudley, who repeatedly harps on the idea that no one will be around when it gets dark. "No one lives any closer than town; no one will come any closer than that. So no one will hear you if you scream. In the night. In the dark," she says, and then departs with a disturbing smile.

Her fear and gloom dissipate somewhat when she meets a psychic named Theo (Claire Bloom) and Dr. Markway, with whom she begins to fall in love. They join the recently arrived Luke for dinner and Markway explains that they are what is left of all the people he had invited to come to the house. The others, investigating the history of the house, have decided not to show up.

Markway also mentions that Eleanor, who prefers the nickname of Nell, was invited because as a young girl a rain of rocks had fallen on her house, an indication of telekinetic powers. The repressed and guilt-ridden Eleanor tries to deny it ever happened. Interestingly, it is quite possible to believe that the subsequent supposedly supernatural events in the film were actually caused by subconscious telekinesis on the part of Eleanor rather than real ghosts, making this a borderline science-fiction film. No ghosts actually appear, and there is much to suggest that many of Eleanor's experiences are products of her fertile imagination and her obviously agitated state of mind rather than the presence of some outraged spook.

The film carefully and almost scientifically takes stock of the many oddities of the house, including the idea that Crain deliberately avoided using right angles and that all the wrong angles add up to one big distortion, thereby explaining the doors that open and shut by themselves. Just as obviously, Eleanor's mind is full of distortions. She vacillates from loathing the house to loving it. She is shown to feel guilty and bitter about her past, sometimes covering it up with lies. She takes to these strangers as newfound friends and as a form of salvation. She mistakes Dr. Markway's tender concern for an expression of love. Eleanor is clearly presented as a woman who has fled from life and seeks sanctuary behind the forbidding doors of the house.

The film indulges in numerous foreshadowings and circularities; for example, a statue of a saint healing the lepers that was modeled on members of the Crain household includes the figure of a young girl that looks like Eleanor. After the first night, when Theo and Eleanor hear a mysterious and threatening booming sound, the message "Help Eleanor Come Home" is found chalked on the wall. Obviously, this message could be interpreted a number of different ways, including that Hill House is Eleanor's home – she later expresses a desire to make it so – and someone is asking for assistance in making her a permanent resident there.

Eleanor is contrasted with the more worldly Theo, whose psychic powers enable her to partially read Eleanor's mind and to rip away veils of pretense. The character is subtly, sympathetically, and daringly for the time presented as a lesbian who is sexually attracted to the fragile Eleanor. However, Theo's refusal to allow Eleanor her fantasies causes Eleanor to finally lash out at her, turning a comment on the "unnaturalness" of the house back on her. (The line is presented so that the unnaturalness that Eleanor refers to could be either Theo's psychic abilities or her being a lesbian or both. Naturally, given Eleanor's Midwestern upbringing, she is a bit prejudiced and does not know how to react to her strangely different companion, though by the end of the film it is clear she accepts her when she calls Theo over to say good-bye.)

The film comes to an emotional climax followed by a story climax when with the appearance of Mrs. Markway (Lois Maxwell), Eleanor discovers that Dr. Markway is married and in her resentment spitefully suggests that Mrs. Markway sleep in the nursery, which has been identified as the "evil heart of the house." Almost immediately Eleanor is apologetic and tries to rescind her suggestion, but Mrs. Markway is determined to flaunt her disbelief in the supernatural by spending the night there. The doctor's wife is then spirited away when Luke leaves his post for a drink in a parlor and the parlor itself is assaulted by poltergeist phenomena, including the famous shots of the wooden door that bulges maddeningly inward. (The mere fact that we know doors should not do that makes this shot particularly horrifying.)

In the trauma that follows it becomes obvious that Eleanor has descended into madness and her actions echo her earlier activities. She pretends to dance with Hugh Crain; she goes into the library where she previously refused to go; she ascends the spiral staircase, from which Marway must rescue her; she almost plunges off the balcony; and she is shocked by the sudden appearance of Mrs. Markway's face above a trapdoor.

Perhaps most significantly, she feels that Mrs. Markway has "taken her place," that the house had singled her out and chosen her as the special someone it wants, but ended up with Mrs. Markway by accident. Thus, in her mind, the house becomes equated with her would-be lover (Markway) and she resents the idea that she has been usurped, particularly since she has lived a life of self-denial for so long. With Markway ineligible as a lover, the house has become a substitute, as well as representing a haven from the hateful and stifling life she left behind.

Markway sees that the house would be dangerous for her and insists that she be driven away. However, she becomes convinced that if the house intends to have her, it will use its power to prevent her from escaping, so she gets behind the wheel of her car and drives recklessly away from the house. Eleanor feels as if something were fighting for control of the vehicle and then feels joy at the idea that something is finally happening to her. (One of the underpinnings of her character is that she secretly wants to be the center of attention and then denies the gratification it gives her. She denies the previous psychic episode that made her the center of attention when she was young. She changes her appearance to attract Markway's attention, but when Theo calls her on it, she says it was Theo's idea. It is Eleanor who is singled out by the "ghosts" of Hill House, but when Theo mentions that she might subconsciously want her name on the wall, Eleanor becomes flustered. When Eleanor paints her toenails, another way of calling attention to herself, she associates it tellingly with "wickedness" while Theo assures her that she is mixing wickedness with foolishness.)

Eleanor's car crashes into a tree just as she sees a white figure dart through the woods (the tree coincidentally proves to be the same one that the first Mrs. Crain was killed by when her carriage ran into it). The scene is ambiguously filmed, leaving it to the audience to decide whether Eleanor was subconsciously trying to commit suicide or was startled by the white figure's sudden appearance, the white figure being revealed to be the dazed Mrs. Markway, who unexpectedly finds herself released from the house. Theo puts a happy interpretation on Eleanor's death, suggesting rightly that in a way, it was what she wanted, to be permanently a part of Hill House. However, a reprise of the opening narration, this time read by Eleanor, ends with, "We who walk there, walk alone," suggesting that in death Eleanor was as she was in life – solitary and separated from everyone and everything.

The Haunting is one of those rare horror films that is as notable for its character interactions and revelations as for its shocks, both of which are supremely well handled. Harris gives one of the finest performances ever in a horror film with her frightened, mousy, anxious, and soft-spoken portrait of Eleanor, while the rest of the cast is also excellent, from Claire Bloom's intuitive Theo to Russ Tamblyn's lively Luke (who goes from looking at the house as a source of huge personal profit to seeing it as a source of evil that should be utterly destroyed) to Richard Johnson's quietly authoritative psychic researcher who emphasizes the seriousness of their undertaking and induces the audience to take it seriously as well.

Some of the credit for *The Haunting*'s strength of characterization must go both to Jackson's book and to Nelson Gidding's screenplay which makes the most of its source material. Sadly, these qualities were largely lacking in Wise's last horror film, the lackluster *Audrey Rose*.

In between the two films, Wise did a science fiction thriller that is certainly worth mentioning, *Andromeda Strain*, which in some ways is a frightening, convincing portrait of what could happen if a probe from outer space unleashed a rapidly spreading disease that mankind has no immunity against. Particularly pertinent to today's world is the way that the audience is manipulated into thinking that technology will save mankind from the disaster as scientists struggle against the clock hoping for some solution. However, it is technology which created the problem in the first place, and most of technology's attempts to solve the problem either have no effect or worsen the situation. In the end, nothing that technology does solves the problem of this new strain of disease; it simply works itself out via a natural evolution.

But while *Andromeda Strain* had the strong source material of Michael Crichton's convincing if contrived novel, *Audrey Rose* is based on a dull novel by Frank de Felitta that expects the public to find the concept of reincarnation an exciting, new idea. Reincarnation has been a staple of horror films for years, and usually a very minor element at that, but de Felitta makes it the entire basis of this ponderous story.

Anthony Hopkins stars as a man who tries to convince a couple (Marsha Mason and John Beck) that their daughter Ivy (Susan Swift) is the reincarnation of Hopkins' daughter Audrey Rose, explaining her mysterious screaming fits as her soul reliving the car accident that burned her to death. (Wise does an effective job of cutting between a trapped child in the car and Swift pounding on a rain-washed window pane, but that is about the only effective imagery in the movie.)

Rather than having interesting characters or exciting events, the film spends its running time doing nothing more than presenting the case for the existence of reincarnation, something that the audience was willing to grant in the first place if it had been attached to an interesting story. The endless lectures and the slow conviction of the anguished parents make for very poor drama and a snooze of a horror film from Wise, who previously had done such an outstanding job handling his material.

However, an artist should be judged by his best works, not his worst, and Wise has certainly made some valuable and important contributions to the horror cinema. His horror films are notable for their subtle characterizations and for Wise's ability to create *frisson* without explicitness, adding a sense of terrible things lurking just beyond the camera's view and an ambiguity about the existence of ghosts and ghouls and things that go bump in the night which piques the interest of viewers. His complex characters and their ambiguous relationships take horror films away from their adolescent appeal and provide them with the possibilities of a more literate and adult approach. It is this quality of reconciling the imaginative and the demonic within his characters that puts Wise at the forefront of horror movie makers.

Jean Yarbrough (1900–)

Rebellious Daughters (1938); *The Devil Bat; Caught in the Act; South of Panama; King of the Zombies; The Gang's All Here; Father Steps Out; Let's Go Collegiate; Top Sergeant Mulligan* (1941); *Freckles Comes Home; Man from Headquarters; Law of the Jungle; So's Your Aunt Emma!; She's in the Army; Police Bullets; Criminal Investigator; Lure of the Islands; Silent Witness* (1942); *Follow the Band; Good Morning, Judge; Get Going; Hi'ya, Sailor; So's Your Uncle* (1943); *Weekend Pass; Moon Over Las Vegas; South of Dixie; In Society; Twilight of the Prairie* (1944); *Under Western Skies; Here Come the Co-eds; The Naughty Nineties; On Stage Everybody* (1945); *She-Wolf of London; House of Horrors; Inside Job; Cuban Pete; The Brute Man* (1946); *The Challenge; Shed No Tears; The Creeper; Triple Threat* (1948); *Henry, the Rainmaker; The Mutineers; Leave It to Henry; Angels in Disguise; Holiday in Havanna; Master Minds* (1949); *Joe Palooka Meets Humphrey; Square Dance Katy; Father Makes Good; Joe Palooka in Humphrey Takes a Chance; Sideshow; Triple Trouble; Big Timber* (1950); *Casa Manana* (1951); *Jack and the Beanstalk; Lost in Alaska* (1952); *Night Freight* (1955); *Crashing Las Vegas; Yaqui Drums; The Women of Pitcairn Island; Hot Shots* (1956); *Footsteps in the Night* (1957); *Saintly Sinners* (1962); *Hillbillys in a Haunted House* (1967).

There is not much known about Jean Yarbrough. He was born on August 22, 1900, and started working in films in 1922 as a prop man on Hal Roach comedies. He worked as an assistant director and finally became another of those faceless men who crank out one undistinguished B picture after another.

His first horror credit was *The Devil Bat*, Bela Lugosi's first film for PRC. Lugosi played Dr. Paul Carruthers, who has been cheated by his ex-business partners. To get revenge, he develops a special brand of shaving lotion that will attract a giant killer bat that he has been developing in his laboratory. The film is now considered a sort of camp classic, a poorly made but nonetheless fun feature with Lugosi delivering one of his riper performances. Especially remembered are the scenes in which Lugosi's partner bids Dr. Carruthers, "Good night," after receiving the gift of the shaving lotion, and Lugosi returns a meaningful, "Good-*bye!*"

Frank Wysbar, who made PRC's best horror film, *Strangler of the Swamp*, directed a strange sequel several years later called *Devil Bat's Daughter* in which Carruthers' daughter succeeds in exonerating her father

750

of the crimes with which he has been charged. An identical plot to *Devil Bat* turned up in PRC's *The Flying Serpent* with George Zucco in the Lugosi role, a living Quetzalcoatl instead of a devil bat, and feathers instead of shaving lotion. That film was directed by Sherman Scott and certainly was not an improvement on Yarbrough's original.

Yarbrough did not immediately become a horror specialist, though in the following year he made *King of the Zombies*, Monogram's first zombie film. (John Stanley's *Creature Features* perversely suggests that George Zucco stars in this film, though he is nowhere to be found.) The plot concerns a small group who intercept a strange message in German and then crash-land on a jungle island. Making their way through the undergrowth, the survivors find their way to the abode of Dr. Miklos Sangre (Henry Victor) who offers them his hospitality. The black valet (Mantan Moreland) discovers that there are zombies on the island who march on into Dr. Sangre's house for dinner at the clap of the cook's hands. The black servant, Jefferson Jackson, cannot convince his cohorts of the zombies' existence and becomes increasingly frustrated.

The film is basically a farce in which Jackson becomes convinced that he too is a zombie (telling a group of them to "Move over boys, I'm one of the gang now") while heroes Bill Summers (John Archer) and "Mac" McCarthy discover that Dr. Sangre is holding Admiral Wainwright (Guy Usher) prisoner in an underground dungeon and plans to extract military secrets from him. To do so, he intends to use the voodoo "Rite of Transmigration," in which Wainwright's thoughts would migrate to the mind of Madame Sangre (Patricia Stacy), whence they can be more easily extracted.

When Mac starts acting strange, Bill locates another doctor (Lawrence Criner) who explains that Mac has been dead since morning and apparently is now a zombie. Meanwhile, Jackson learns he is not a zombie when he discovers he cannot stomach the zombie brew being fed the others and seeks out his friends. Summers and Jackson arrive just as Dr. Sangre is forcing his innocent niece to complete his "Rite of Transmigration." Bill leads the zombies to attack their former master and throw him into a fiery pit. Despite being pronounced dead and being shot as a zombie, Mac makes a miraculous recovery and returns to normal.

Perhaps the most amazing thing about this zombie comedy is that its musical score by Edward Kay was actually nominated for an Academy Award, and it is certainly one of the film's few pluses. Yarbrough's direction is barely competent, but Henry Victor, best known for playing the strongman in *Freaks*, does give an interesting performance as the heavy, and Mantan Moreland shows himself to have good comic timing even with lame material. The scares are negligible, but the film does have a few laughs.

Yarbrough's next really notable film was the Abbott and Costello comedy *In Society* in which several classic vaudeville actors appeared, along with some classic vaudeville routines borrowed by Abbott and Costello. While not the best of the comic duo's work, it does have the memorable and nightmarish sequence in which whenever Costello mentions the name of a particular street, the person he is chatting with suddenly explodes with rage and attacks whatever is at hand (usually the wares the boys are selling).

Yarbrough also helmed *The Naughty Nineties*, a dull Abbott and Costello comedy set on a riverboat which nonetheless preserves the classic "Who's on First" routine on film.

He returned to horror with the obscure *She-Wolf of London* (aka *The Curse of the Allenbys*), an imitation *Undying Monster* which is also a cheat as the She-Wolf turns out not to be a werewolf but merely an insane murderess. The She-Wolf is none other than June Lockhart, the famous TV mom from the series *Lassie* and *Lost in Space*, who has nightmares and believes she has been infected by the Allenby Curse. As a child, she had dreams about running with a wolf pack and as an adult, she wakes up with blood on her hands and reports of a beast-woman skulking through the countryside. Naturally, this is all a red herring to cover up the misdeeds of her aunt (Sara Haden) who must have seen *The Scarlet Claw* too many times and has taken to killing people with a garden trowel. Yarbrough's attempts at atmosphere and suspense prove deadly dull.

Probably Yarbrough's most memorable film is *House of Horrors*, which revived the character of "The Creeper" from *The Pearl of Death*, one of Universal's Sherlock Holmes series. The Creeper was played by Rando Hatton, one of the most pitiable horror stars of all time in that he was afflicted with acromegaly, a disease which enlarged his once handsome features into grotesque proportions. He was the first monster who did not need makeup and apart from Lon Chaney, Jr., the only new horror star to be introduced in the '40s.

Sadly, acromegaly puts pressure on the brain, diminishing the intelligence of the afflicted. Hatton plays a touching, pathetic character who has been exploited, not only in films but in real life. Perhaps that is part of the fascination horror fans have with the Creeper series.

The true star of *House of Horrors* is Martin Kosleck, playing a demented artist named Marcel de Lange who, after hearing a viciously critical assessment of his work, decides to commit suicide, but then discovers the Creeper. Fascinated by the Creeper's features, he decides to use him as inspiration for a new statue and makes friends with the taciturn brute.

The Creeper proves a habitual criminal, despite de Lange's compassionate treatment, and he slips out to crack the back of a prostitute, his consistent m.o. When de Lange complains of his treatment at the hands of famed art critic F. Holmes Harmon (Alan Napier), the Creeper goes out on an expedition to "help" his newfound friend by going out and strangling Holmes.

Meanwhile, an inquiring female art critic, Joan Medford (Virginia Grey), starts poking around and sneaks a peak at de Lange's bust of the Creeper, which alerts her that de Lange may be involved with this deadly assassin. Her own boyfriend, Steve Morrow, has been implicated in Harmon's murder and she naturally wishes to clear him.

To lure the killer out, the police persuade another art critic to savage both de Lange and Morrow in the press, with the result that Morrow is caught with his hands on the neck of the critic (Howard Freeman). While the police hold him, the Creeper sneaks in and dispatches the critic when he goes into the kitchen for a drink, finally providing Morrow with an alibi.

Joan goes back to de Lange's and steals a sketch of the Creeper which her newspaper identifies for her. De Lange for some reason becomes enraged with Morrow and sends the Creeper out after him, but the Creeper merely finds a model in Morrow's studio and quickly kills her instead. Knowing the identity of the man in de Lange's sketch, Joan decides to confront de Lange, telling him she only stole the sketch to give him publicity. He returns that she must die, a conversation overheard by the now returning Creeper, who also hears that de Lange expects the Creeper to be blamed for the murders he has done on de Lange's behalf. Enraged, he decides to kill them both, starting with de Lange, but the Creeper is shot down before he can kill Joan when the police and Morrow arrive in the nick of time.

The plot, as you can see, is rather standard, though it affords far more pathos for Hatton's role than his other films. One thing that makes it stand out above other films in this short series is the Greenwich Village studio with its bizarre bust of Hatton that forms an unforgettable image in the film.

Yarbrough and Hatton made one more film together, *The Brute Man*, before Hatton died of his disease. Produced by Universal, the film was sold to PRC in Universal's effort to wash their hands of the whole affair. Seldom screened, *The Brute Man*, while last in the series, shows the Creeper's origin: He was a handsome, young football player who had acid splashed on his face during an accident in the chemistry lab. The old bit of hokum about his best friend being a beautiful blind girl (Jan Wiley) who is not afraid of his awful looks but touches his heart is dragged out. Nonetheless, he remains a homicidal brute intent on revenge. Tom Neal of *Detour* fame was the costar.

To add to the confusion, in 1948 Yarbrough made *The Creeper* which did not feature the Hatton character, but rather a shape-changing cat creature. This is a listless melodrama that seems designed to cash in on the famed Val Lewton films. Janis Wilson has nightmares about being clawed by cats

Director Jean Yarbrough (right) with Rando Hatton and JaNelle Johnson on the set of The Brute Man.

while in the West Indies with her father (Ralph Morgan), who is collecting one of those special serums for his experiments. The serum is what changes a man into a cat-like killer, but Morgan's creation manages to kill him and almost kills his daughter before meeting its end.

At this point, the horror cycle had pretty much died. It would be revived by the science fiction films of the '50s adding alien menaces to all the old-time monsters. Meanwhile, Yarbrough squeezed out one more brutish killer in the execrable Bowery Boys comedy *Master Minds*, in which Huntz Hall can predict the future whenever his tooth aches, and Alan Napier plays a mad scientist who creates a man out of an ape, played by former Franken-stein monster Glenn Strange with makeup by a down-on-his-luck Jack Pierce. It is about as stupid as you would expect.

In 1952, Yarbrough directed *Jack and the Beanstalk*, one of Abbott and Costello's more minor productions in which Lou dreams that he and Bud are the heroes of the famous fairy tale. Like *The Wizard of Oz*, the film starts off in black and white and then switches to color, but when the giant is played by Buddy Baer (star of the absolutely awful *Giant from the Unknown*), you know the results are not going to be too special.

Yarbrough's final film and his final shot at the fantasy/horror genre was *Hillbillys in a Haunted House*, a sequel to *Las Vegas Hillbillys* directed by Arthur C. Pierce. Ferlin Husky returns as Woody, the hillbilly who inherited a casino in Las Vegas, who joins pal Joi Lansing in a haunted house that is being used by spies. George Barrows, the Ro-Man from *Robot Monster*, plays another ape, while Lon Chaney, Jr., is a body guard, John Carradine is a mad scientist, and Basil Rathbone is a henchman who try to frighten away nosy people with fake spirits in order to cover up a spy ring. The horror stars are absolutely wasted, and you can see the same kind of plot done better on your average episode of *Scooby-Doo*. It was a fittingly undistinguished finale to Yarbrough's consummately undistinguished career.

II
The Hopeless and the Hopeful:
Promising Directors,
Obscurities,
and Horror Hacks

Al Adamson

Two Tickets to Terror (1964); *The Female Bunch; Gun Riders; Blood of Dracula's Castle* (1969); *Satan's Sadists; Hell's Bloody Devils* (aka *The Fakers*) (1970); *Five Bloody Graves; Horror of the Blood Monsters* (aka *Vampire Men of the Lost Planet*); *Last of the Comancheros* (1971); *Blood of Ghastly Horror; The Brain of Blood; Doomsday Voyage* (1972); *Dracula vs. Frankenstein* (1973); *The Dynamite Brothers; Girls for Rent* (1974); *The Naughty Stewardesses; Stud Brown; Blazing Stewardesses* (1975); *Jessie's Girl; Black Heat* (1976); *Cinderella 2000; Black Samurai* (1977); *Sunset Cove; Death Dimension; Nurse Sherri* (1978); *Freeze Bomb* (1980); *Black Heat* (1981); *Carnival Magic* (1982).

Al Adamson is the son of Australian producer-director-actor Denver Dixon, whose real name is Victor Adamson and who is best known for his early western films. Al ran nightclubs and looked for a break making movies. His first film, *Two Tickets to Terror*, faded into utter obscurity.

Adamson's breakthrough came when he collaborated with would-be ex-ploitation showman Samuel Sherman, though his first horror film, *Blood of Dracula's Castle*, was coproduced by Rex Carlton and Adamson himself. While the film's star, John Carradine, had played Dracula before and was to play it again, he was here relegated to the role of butler while Alex D'Arcy took over the role of the sanguinary count. Future science fiction and action director John "Bud" Cardos played a bit part in this forgettable film about the deadly count and his countess feasting on modern-day New Yorkers.

Adamson's best film, and possibly his most famous, was his next, *Satan's Sadists*, a motorcycle drama so outrageous and over-the-top that it almost cannot help entertaining on a very crude level. Russ Tamblyn runs around putting LSD in young girls' drinks in order to later rape and kill them. Another future science fiction director, Greydon Clark, joined Cardos on acting chores this time around. Regina Carrol, who played the "Freak-Out Girl," later became Adamson's wife.

Adamson's exploitation films all follow overused formulas and are generally uninteresting and ineptly made. The best known is the miserable *Dracula vs. Frankenstein*, and that only became known because of the title characters and because Adamson and Sherman offered Forrest J Ackerman a bit part in hopes that he would plug the film in his *Famous Monsters of Filmland* magazine. Originally, the film was titled *The Blood Seekers* and starred the ailing actors Lon Chaney, Jr., and J. Carrol Naish. The results were so abysmal, the film almost became permanently shelved. However, in an effort to "rescue" the project, Sherman came up with the idea of injecting the characters of the Frankenstein monster and Dracula into the story with J. Carrol Naish's Dr. Duryea revealed to be the infamous Dr. Frankenstein. The whole thing was packaged under a misleading ad campaign and went on to pick up dollars from unwary cinematic patrons. The film also managed to secure the talents of Anthony Eisley, Jim Davis, Russ Tamblyn, Angelo Rossitto (the famous dwarf actor who has been in scores of films from *Freaks* to *Mad Max 3: Beyond Thunderdome*), and of course Regina Carrol, but to little avail. Later it was re-released under the titles *Blood of Frankenstein* and *They're Coming to Get You.*

What's notable about *Horror of the Blood Monsters* (aka *Vampire Men of the Lost Planet*) and *Brain of Blood* is that they are both so badly done in the Filipino style that many assumed they had been filmed in the Philippines.

Adamson has branched out into other exploitation ventures but still not honed his craft. His independent productions are decidedly minor and he will remain a mere footnote in the history of the horror genre, deservedly untouted and forgotten.

Clive Barker

Hellraiser (1987); *Nightbreed* (1990).

Clive Barker is one of the major writers and stylists in the horror field, having written some critically well-received works not to mention several best sellers. Unlike competitor Stephen King, whose directorial debut *Maximum Overdrive* is accounted a disaster, Barker had a success with his first attempt at directing, *Hellraiser*. The film even spawned a sequel, *Hellbound: Hellraiser 2*, which Barker wrote the story for and helped British director Tony Randel produce.

In an era when the short story has practically died as a form, British writer Barker came to notoriety via his collections of original short stories called *The Books of Blood*, which notes that books are like bodies: Whenever they are opened, they are *red*. George Pavlou directed *Underworld* (released by Empire as *Transmutations*), a strange and little-seen thriller about underground mutants that was based on a Barker story and represented his first dealings with the film world. Charles Band's Empire pictures adapted Barker's story *Rawhead Rex* into a cheap horror movie centered around the unearthing of a demon.

Neither of these adaptations was as impressive as when New World allowed Barker himself to adapt his story "The Hellbound Heart" into

Writer/director Clive Barker playing with his favorite boa constrictor on the set of Hellraiser, *his first film. Barker claims to have attended autopsies not just for background information but also for fun.*

Hellraiser. The look of the film is, like Barker's prose style, very ornate and oddly compelling, though the narrative itself is quite simple. Stuart Gordon's *From Beyond* appears to have been an influence on Barker's approach with its hints of S & M torture and upstairs depravity.

Peculiarly, New World was concerned about the cast's British accents, and so many of the characters in the film were unfortunately dubbed into "American." As the lead, Andrew Robinson, best remembered as the crazed killer from *Dirty Harry*, is quite good as the decent Larry Cotton. In fact, it was Robinson who came up with the line "Jesus wept" when his character is torn apart by his treacherous new wife, Julia (Clare Higgins), who meticulously sets about murdering people in order to resurrect her old lover Frank (Sean Chapman), Larry's brother. Frank, in trying to seek out undreamed-of pleasures, opens up a magical Oriental puzzle box which sends him to a hellish dimension that provides him instead with undreamed-of pain and strips the flesh from his bones while leaving him alive. The bizarre denizens of that dimension are the Cenobites, mysterious corruptions of the human form with altered features such as nails driven through the skull in a regular pattern. One woman with an exposed voice box looks like a living dissection.

Blood spilled in the attic returns Frank to our dimension, but he lacks a body. Julia goes out to lure men to the attic where their flesh and blood can be transformed into Frank's. Meanwhile, Kirsty (Ashley Laurence), Larry's daughter by his first marriage, begins to suspect what is going on and gets caught up in the nightmare world of the Cenobites.

While perverse, Barker's story is not very rich in significance, but he does manage to do wonders with a mere $2.5 million budget, and his film has that frightening, anything-can-happen nightmare feeling that became popular in '80s horror filmmaking. Robin Vidgeon's cinematography is both good and atmospheric, and uses light and shadow to suggest we are discovering things in the dark which would be better off hidden. The film is both repulsive and effective.

Not so for Barker's second feature, however. This time adapted from Barker's novel *Cabal, Nightbreed* tries a different take on monsters, one in which they are the sympathetic characters and the real villains are a super-rational psychiatrist (David Cronenberg, the famed horror director who gives a very "off" performance) intent on eliminating the deviant and a super-macho police chief who aids him.

Unfortunately, the normal hero (Craig Sheffer) and heroine (Anne Bobby) are not very interesting, and though there are a number of very creative monster makeups, the nightbreed themselves are not given much in the way of characterization either. Barker shows a remarkable visual eye, creating the monstrous designs himself, but his dialogue and plot sense are dull here. He tries to make the ugly lyrical, a unique quality in itself, and shows the forces of "normality" as being hypocritical and more murderous than the supposed forces of darkness. But it is still all style and no substance. Nevertheless, Barker remains a major name and talent.

Lamberto Bava (1944–   )

Macabre (1980); *House of the Dark Stairway* (aka *A Blade in the Dark*, 1983); *Blastfighter* (as John Old, Jr.); *Monstershark* (aka *Devouring Waves* as John Old, Jr.) (1984); *Demons* (1985); *Demons 2; Carroll Will Die at Midnight* (1986); *Delirium; Graveyard Disturbance; Demons 3* (aka *The Ogre; Until Death*) (1987); *Dinner with a Vampire; Per Sempre, Fino alla Morte* (aka *The Changeling 2: The Return*) (1988).

TELEVISION: *Venus of the Isle* (codirected with Mario Bava, 1978); *Per Sempre, Fino alla Morte* (*Forever*, 1988); *High Tension* (1989).

Son of famed horror director Mario Bava, Lamberto decided to follow in his father's footsteps, but sadly, he lacks his father's talent. Lamberto began his film career as an assistant director on Mario's 1965 film *Planet of the Vampires* and served the same position on many subsequent films, as well as being Dario Argento's assistant director on *Inferno* and *Tenebrae.*

Bava, Jr.'s, first feature film, *Macabro (Macabre)*, was cowritten with Roberto Gandus and Pupi Avati (the latter later directed and scripted *Revenge of the Living Dead*). Bernice Stegers, who was also in *Xtro*, plays a very peculiar young woman who keeps the head of her ex-lover around for company and who is eventually killed by an obsessive, blind next door neighbor (Robert Posse). The head gets its revenge.

Bava proceeded to direct a couple of films under the pseudonym of John M. Old, Jr., as a tribute to his father. He scored big with *Demons*, produced by Argento, though the film definitely lacks the visual polish typical of Argento's films. It has a rather way out concept of innocent theater patrons lured into a horror movie and then trapped there while their numbers are decimated by demons which have been unleashed. A quickie follow-up with an almost identical story was prepared, this time with the demons emanating from TV sets in an apartment complex.

Unlike his father, Lamberto seems to have quickly run out of fresh ideas, though he occasionally can produce an effective twist on an old one. Without the lushness of his father's style or his father's sense of humor, he will continue to be regarded as at best second-rate.

Larry Buchanan (1924–   )

The Naked Witch (aka *Common Law Wife*); *Apache Gold* (1960); *Free, White and 21* (1963); *Naughty Dallas; Under Age; The Trial of Lee Harvey Oswald* (1964); *High Yellow; Strawberries Need Rain* (1965); *The Eye Creatures; Curse of the Swamp Creature; Mars Needs Women* (1966); *In the Year 2889; Zontar: The Thing from Venus; It's Alive; Creature of Destruction* (1967); *Hell Raiders; The Other Side of Bonnie and Clyde* (1968); *Commanche Crossing* (1969); *Down on Us; A Bullet for Pretty Boy* (1970); *The Rebel Jesus* (1971); *Goodbye, Norma Jean* (1977); *Hughes and Harlow: Angels in Hell* (1978); *Mistress of the Apes* (1981); *The Loch Ness Horror* (aka *Nessie*, 1982); *Down on Us* (1984); *Good Night, Sweet Marilyn* (1989).

Larry Buchanan began his career in movies by making documentaries for Oral Roberts back in 1951, and unfortunately, it has been all downhill from there. He worked as an assistant for George Cukor on *The Marrying Kind* and appeared in films as an actor in the '50s including *The Ox-Bow Incident, The Gunfighter* and *Comin' In on the Wing of a Prayer*, mostly very small cameos.

Buchanan's films are beloved by the sleepless everywhere. They usually appear on television in the late night slots where they are almost guaranteed to put even the most hardened insomniac fast asleep, so I suppose one could say that Buchanan has performed a public service. Not only is Buchanan one of the worst directors who has ever lived, he multiplies the crime by being one of the most boring. His films are uniformly dully scripted, ineptly acted, with static camera placement and no pacing. Naturally, a special cult has formed around his uniquely and perversely bad films.

Buchanan's filmmaking philosophy can be summed up by this quote from an interview with Jeffrey Frentzen in *Fangoria #41*: "If they're only willing to spend $30,000 . . . you grab it while it's there. You run with it. Find a way to make it work." Unfortunately for Buchanan, while he got the films made, he almost never found a way to make them work.

Buchanan's best-known films among horror fans are those that he made between 1966 and 1968 for AIP. AIP sold a film package to television, and television wanted some color films, so AIP had Buchanan shoot remakes of several AIP pictures in color in 16mm for around $22,000 a picture. They were not too concerned about quality; they simply needed titles, and it showed. Buchanan does not seem to have been interested in shooting master scenes, so the films cut together very poorly, but as they seem to be indifferently done to begin with, it does not appear to make much difference.

The first of these pictures was *The Eye Creatures*, which is practically a scene-for-scene remake of *Invasion of the Saucer Men*, and as a result is the most entertaining of the group. Later, AIP decided to save bucks by not sending Buchanan the original scripts, instead reading plot synopses over the phone from which he would have to fashion quick screenplays. The infamous *Zontar: The Thing from Venus*, one of actor James Woods' all-time guilty pleasures, is a remake of Corman's *It Conquered the World*, while *In the Year 2889* remade *The Day the World Ended*.

Mars Needs Women featured Tommy Kirk of the Mouse Club, who had seen better days at Disney. Strangely, the film plays like a serious remake of *Pajama Party*, in which Kirk also played a Martian teenager. Buchanan also directed Kirk in the 1968 version of *It's Alive* (not to be confused with the Larry Cohen film) which is supposedly based on the Richard Matheson story "Being," but is mostly about a monster that lurks in a cave and eats somnambulistic actors.

The monster from *It's Alive* also shows up in *Creature of Destruction*, which featured poor Les Tremayne as a hypnotist who predicts that a sea monster will murder people, and then finds a girl who is the monster's reincarnation, hypnotizes her, and has her carry out the murders. Finally there was *Curse of the Swamp Creature* in which John Agar is involved with the creation of a half-man, half-crocodile monster which does not look reptilian, though it does look silly.

Needless to say, Buchanan has not improved with age, as one glance at

The Loch Ness Horror, a $40,000 horror film done as a tax write-off, will show. Buchanan remains the king of horror *ennui*. Once you start one of his films, you will tremble at the thought of watching it to the end, and be horrified at how your time has been wasted if you do.

John Carl Buechler

Dungeonmaster (codirector with Rosemarie Turko, Charles Band, David Allen, Steve Ford, Peter Manoogian, and Ted Nicholaou, 1985); *Troll* (1986); *Cellar Dweller* (1987); *Friday the 13th Part VII: The New Blood* (1988); *Ghoulies Go to College* (1990).

John Carl Buechler is one of the busiest makeup men in the business, for years being a prime supplier to Roger Corman's New World Pictures and then moving on to Charles Band's Empire Pictures. His work is noted for its quickness, though the work itself varies in quality from mediocre puppetry to some quite good and effective makeups. (One of the best of these was his cover for John Fogerty's album *Eye of the Zombie*.) So far, he is the only makeup man to have worked on the Shape from *Halloween*, Jason from *Friday the 13th* and Freddy Krueger from the *Nightmare on Elm Street* series – the three big horror stars of the '80s.

He has worked on films as varied as *Forbidden World* and *Re-Animator*. In exchange for his extensive duties on Empire Pictures' exploitation movies, he was granted a chance to pursue his primary ambition – to become a director. As an experiment, Charles Band came up with the film *Dungeonmaster*, originally intended as a direct-to-video release, which was to combine several episodic tales, each segment directed by a would-be first time director to see how they would do under stringent conditions. The segments were only allowed a few days of production each, creating severe time restrictions, meaning that the neophyte directors really had to be prepared and quick. Buechler came though with a brief segment in an ice cave.

With that successfully completed, he was given the go-ahead for his first feature, *Troll*. Buechler's idea was to take the simple plot of your basic *Friday the 13th* film, but instead of a maniac hacking up one teen after another, there would be a troll who would turn people into cocoons that would split open and reveal magic, fairy kingdoms.

Ed Naha's script supplied the film with some heart, particularly the character of a dwarf played by Phil Fondacaro. The cast itself was quite accomplished, beginning with Michael Moriarty and Shelly Hack. June Lockhart and her daughter Anne together play a local witch who can grow older and younger at will. Sonny Bono has a memorable cameo as a kid-hating neighbor who is the first to be changed into a blob of foliage.

However, the overall project is both stiff and a bit tame. The budget was small and so restricted the extent to which the fairy kingdoms could be portrayed, plus much of Naha's dialogue was rather pedestrian. Still, it made for a promising debut, attempting something a little different.

Cellar Dweller was the unpromising and unsatisfying follow-up. *Re-Animator* star Jeffrey Combs appears as a cartoonist who is inspired by some curses of the Ancient Dead and proceeds to render some rather satanic cartoons which come to life. Years later, Deborah Mullowney comes to the house and starts to follow in Combs' footsteps, returning the dreaded Cellar Dweller to life. Once more, the film is small and limited in scope and the writing is not particularly inspired.

After working on creating a new, more ravaged, corpse-like appearance for Jason in *Jason Lives: Friday the 13th Part VI*, Buechler was approached about directing *Friday the 13th Part VII: The New Blood. New Blood* tries to combine Jason with an "unusual" adversary, a small girl who has *Carrie*-like telekinetic powers. Buechler tries to experiment with the *Friday the 13th* formula, but almost all the carnage in the film was trimmed by the MPAA before release and some of Buechler's more interesting ideas were nixed by the producers. What is left is one of the more uninspiring entries in this ridiculously long-lived series, satisfying neither its long-term fans nor any newcomers looking for fresh thrills.

Buechler's most recent directorial effort is *Ghoulies Go to College*, a soon-to-be-released entry in the wretched *Ghoulies* series, for which Buechler has done the makeups. The Ghoulies were an obvious cash-in on the popularity of *Gremlins* without the humor, and the first two films were lousy. Buechler promises to upgrade the series with some zany humor and more elaborate Ghoulie creatures. We wish him luck.

Kevin Connor (1940–   )

From Beyond the Grave (1973); *The Land That Time Forgot* (1975); *At the Earth's Core; Dirty Knight's Work* (aka *A Choice of Weapons*) (1976); *The People that Time Forgot* (1977); *Warlords of Atlantis* (1978); *Arabian Adventure* (1979); *Motel Hell* (1980); *The House Where Evil Dwells* (1982).

TELEVISION: *Goliath Awaits* (1981); *Master of the Game* (codirected with Harvey Hart); *Mistral's Daughter* (codirected with Douglas Hickox, 1984); *North and South Book II* (1986); *The Return of Sherlock Holmes* (1987).

Connor is a horror hack whose best films are *From Beyond the Grave*, a horror anthology which is a little above the generally mediocre quality of most anthology films, and *Motel Hell*, a cannibalist, chainsaw-wielding outrageous comedy, though *The House Where Evil Dwells* with its talking crabs possessed by the spirits of the dead is good for a few laughs.

Connor began his film career as an assistant editor and later edited such pictures as *Oh! What a Lovely War, Young Winston,* and *Hitler: The Last Ten Days.* Sad to say, his first film represented something of a peak for him, though it must be admitted his later Edgar Rice Burroughs–based films were saddled with woefully inadequate budgets and unconvincing costumes and effects. Like Baker's *The Monster Club, From Beyond the Grave* was based on the stories of British horror writer R. Chetwynd-Hayes, and the linking story involves the much-loved Peter Cushing as the proprietor of a sinister antique shop. The film features an above-average cast as a whole, with David Warner making an impression as a man who becomes trapped within a mirror, Donald Pleasence as a sinister match-seller, who's daughter uses voodoo, Ian Carmichael and Nyree Dawn Porter becoming victims of an elemental spirit; and finally Ian Ogilvy as a man who gets most unpleasant results from a magical wooden door that he has purchased.

Motel Hell proves engaging mostly because it is so willing to go over the top. As Robert Jaffe's screenplay puts it, "It takes all kinds of critters to make Farmer Vincent's fritters." Vincent (Rory Calhoun) and his sister Ida (Nancy Parsons) think they have found a way to solve the world hunger problem and make some money in the bargain – they will rid the world of "undesirables" by planting them in the ground, fattening them up, and grinding them into sausages. Vincent attracts victims to his "Motel Hello," which, of course, has the neon "O" in its title burned out. The result is some very black comedy capped by the infamous chainsaw duel at the end. The film owes a debt to the films of Peter Walker in its conception but has a level of outrageousness that is all its own.

Don Cascarelli (1954–   )

Jim – The World's Greatest; Kenny and Company (1976); *Phantasm* (1979); *The Beastmaster* (1982); *Survival Quest* (1987); *Phantasm II* (1988).

Coscarelli's is a prime example of a career which stalled out after a promising debut. *Phantasm,* with its dream-logic nightmare world, presaged the popular "rubber reality" horror of the '80s such as the *Nightmare on Elm Street* and *House* movies.

Don Coscarelli started his love affair with photography at an early age, graduating to 8mm films, making a short documentary for his science class while still in school. At the age of 18, he completed his first feature, *Jim – The World's Greatest,* by convincing his father, D. A. Coscarelli, an investment counselor, to put up the financing. Projected at a cost of $35,000, the film ran over $100,000, though the pair still managed to make a profit by selling the completed film to Universal for $200,000.

Top: *Director Don Coscarelli preps* Phantasm II. Bottom: *The ball was back, along with the Tall Man (Angus Scrimm) in* Phantasm II, *but it seemed more like a polished but less spirited remake than a sequel and failed to ignite at the box office.*

Moving from melodrama, Coscarelli next tried his hand at a comedy, *Kenny and Company* for 20th Century–Fox, centering around Halloween. The film sported normal kids surrounded by antic and crazy adults. The film did poorly everywhere except in Japan; there it proved a surprise hit, possibly because the sassiness of Michael Baldwin, a kid who regularly tells adults off, goes against the Japanese tradition of family honor and so made Baldwin into an instant juvenile hero.

Coscarelli decided to try his hand at an all-out horror film, *Phantasm*, with Baldwin as the likable young hero and Angus Scrimm, who had appeared in *Jim*, as a tall, malevolent menace. The film would have a small budget and so needed to rely more on ingenuity than anything else. Luckily, Coscarelli had some talented people helping him, including special effects designer Paul Pepperman and production designer S. Tyler who were instrumental along with Coscarelli in designing the film's impressive effects.

Baldwin plays Mike Pearson, a boy who has recently lost his parents and must depend on his brother Jody (Bill Thornbury). His cousin Tommy (Bill Cone) goes out to the Morningside Mortuary for a late-night date, but does not return, causing Mike to get suspicious and do some investigating. While there he encounters a creepy person known only as The Tall Man (Angus Scrimm) who is in charge of the mortuary.

The film is largely devoted to creating an atmosphere of the uncanny, which it achieves through some memorable visuals. Mike, for example, sees a photograph of Morningside which is decades old and still has the same Tall Man. Then, to add a macabre and magical touch, the photograph comes to life with the Tall Man gazing at Mike malevolently. Guarding the mortuary in the film's most famed sequence is a little flying silver ball, which has spikes that jut out and embed themselves into the forehead of one of the mortuary's caretakers. This is followed by a gruesome scene which almost caused the film to be given an X rating in which a drill protrudes and burrows into the man's skull, emitting a stream of blood from the other side which becomes so excessive that the scene veers from the appalling to the merely silly.

Additional pieces of the puzzle are provided when it is discovered that the Tall Man drips embalming fluid instead of blood, and after Mike severs the Tall Man's finger, the finger later changes into an attacking bug (portrayed by a simple mechanical toy that helps betray the film's paltry budget). The Tall Man's henchmen are mysterious cowled dwarves, resembling the Jawas in *Star Wars*. Slowly, Mike discovers that the Tall Man is reviving dead bodies and shipping them to another planet or dimension which has incredibly powerful gravity, necessitating that human beings be crushed into a compact size to survive there.

The film proved an independent success, and as a horror film which showed some real imagination and effective scare pieces, it deserved the minor acclaim it was accorded.

Next Coscarelli ended up tackling an adaptation of Andre Norton's juvenile novel *The Beast Master*, which proved so embarrassing to Norton that she had her name removed from the film's credits. The film was beautifully shot by John Alcott in Simi Valley and fits into the general sword-and-sorcery, beauty-and-beast mold. Marc Singer plays the well-muscled title character who makes his way through a fantasy kingdom aided by an eagle, whose vision he shares, a black panther (played by a painted tiger), and a pair of mischievous ferrets. Rip Torn displays a large slice of ham as the evil sorcerer who ends up Singer's antagonist as he tries to save Tanya Roberts' kingdom from Torn's tyranny and avenge the death of his father. The cinematography is quite good for a low-budget feature, and the plot itself is no worse than mediocre, yet the film's failure helped sink Coscarelli's career. He next tried another sword-and-sorcery epic at New World, but political infighting caused him to be removed from the production before completion. *Survival Quest*, a dull film about a group of people who have to band together to survive in a hostile mountain environment, sat on the shelf a few years before receiving a spotty release.

Coscarelli finally returned to his original success with *Phantasm II*, but rather than displaying some inventiveness, the new film seemed a rehash of the elements of the old one on a bigger budget. For audiences who missed the original film, Coscarelli clues them in by having a woman named Liz (Paula Irvine) have strange dreams which include generous helpings of footage both new and old to explain who Mike (this time played by James Le Gros) and the Tall Man (Angus Scrimm again) are. Mike is released from the Morningside Psychiatric Hospital and sets off in search of the Tall Man accompanied by his old friend Reggie (Reggie Bannister), who drove an ice cream truck and was a friend of his brother's in the first film. The Tall Man succeeded in blowing up Mike's house awhile back, and now Mike senses a telepathic connection with Liz. Realizing that she is in danger, he tries to rush to her before it is too late.

Generally there is not much attention paid to plot. Rather the film is a series of set-pieces designed to unsettle audiences and catch them off guard with odd pieces of surrealism. Missing from this second film, much to its detriment, is the profound sense of mystery that unified the first. Once more, however, the cinematography is quite good (this time by Daryn Okada), and Kenneth Tigar is memorably hammy as an alcoholic priest trying to make sense of the Tall Man's doings.

Coscarelli has demonstrated some talent, but he still has to show he is on the ball. Now that *Phantasm II* has failed to clean up, perhaps he will launch an attack in a new direction. What other wonders might he have up his sleeve?

Richard E. Cunha

Giant from the Unknown; She Demons (1958); *Frankenstein's Daughter; Missile to the Moon* (1959); *Girl in Room 13* (1961).
TELEVISION: *Adventures of Marshal O'Dell; Captain Bob Steele and the Border Patrol.*

What can one say about a director dumb enough to remake *Cat Women of the Moon*, one of the worst science fiction films of all time, and actually manage to make it duller and worse? Each one of his horribly inept science fiction/horror films is an incredible time waster, inviting laughter without deserving anything more than contempt, and displaying in turn an astonishing contempt for the audience.

Perhaps the saddest thing about a film like *Giant from the Unknown*, about a giant conquistador (played by wrestler Buddy Baer) who is brought back to life via a lightning bolt and disturbs townspeople who think a spirit has come to haunt them, is that it was among the last films of actor Morris Ankrum and once makeup artist par excellence Jack P. Pierce. Horror writer John Stanley assumed that the Arthur Jacobs who produced the film was the same one who did *Planet of the Apes*, but this simply is not so. The *Giant* producer is Arthur A. Jacobs, while the producer of the *Apes* films was the late Arthur P. Jacobs.

She Demons, about Nazis in the jungle and a mad scientist trying to transfer the beauty of young women to his wife, was not any better an exercise in tedium, making *Frankenstein's Daughter* Cunha's "best" film, and a very relative "best" at that. Like the others, *Daughter* is completely wretched, with a man playing the female monster of the title, but at least it is a little bit amusing.

In a career move not to be lamented, Cunha turned to making commercials and later operating a video rental place. He is no doubt much better at renting films than making them.

Dan Curtis (1928–   )

House of Dark Shadows (1970); *Night of Dark Shadows* (1971); *Burnt Offerings* (1976).
TELEVISION: *The Night Strangler; The Norliss Tapes* (1973); *Scream of the Wolf; Dracula; Melvin Purvis: G-Man; The Great Ice Rip-Off* (1974); *Trilogy of Terror; The Kansas City Massacre* (1975); *Curse of the Black Widow* (1977); *When Every Day Was the Fourth of July* (1978); *The Last Ride of the Dalton Gang; Mrs. R's Daughter* (1979); *The Long Days of Summer* (1980); *The Winds of War* (1983); *War and Remembrance* (1987); *Dark Shadows* (1990).

It is ironic that one of the biggest television director-producers of all time should have three horror films as his only feature credits, but so it goes. Curtis was the one who managed to package horror as a soap opera and sell it successfully as the *Dark Shadows* TV series with Jonathan Frid playing the initially evil then later benign vampire Barnabas Collins.

The cheaply produced series was so successful that it spun off a film, *House of Dark Shadows*, which Curtis helmed as his directorial debut, and the result was a better-than-average horror film with Frid trying to find a way to get together with the lovely Kathryn Leigh Scott. The film contained some *frisson* and played everything straight, with far more action than the slow-moving soap series that it was based on. The result was a vampire film comparable to the Robert Kelljan Count Yorga series starring Robert Quarry, though with more authentically gothic atmosphere.

However, *Night of Dark Shadows*, the follow-up, proved to be a disaster. Quentin Collins (David Selby) becomes the focus as he inherits the decrepit New England manse Collinwood and feels himself possessed by the spirit of his ancestor Charles. The film was thoroughly dull and uninvolving.

Curtis' last feature, *Burnt Offerings*, was not much better wasting the talents of Oliver Reed, Karen Black, Bette Davis, Lee Montgomery and Burgess Meredith with a story of spirits in an old house taking over people's bodies and killing them.

His horror television work is much better, including *The Night Strangler*, the Richard Matheson–scripted sequel to John Llewellyn Moxey's (*Horror Hotel*) highly entertaining made-for-TV movie *The Night Stalker*; a Jack Palance version of *Dracula*; and Karen Black in *Trilogy of Terror* (all scripted by Matheson).

The Night Strangler continued the story of monster hunter and newspaper reporter Carl Kolshak (played by a very engaging Darren McGavin) who once again must contend with his unsympathetic and cantankerous editor (Simon Oakland) only to find an immortal killer living in a separate city beneath Seattle (a sort of variation on Ralph Murphy's *The Man in Half Moon Street* scripted by Barre Lyndon). There are some amusing character bits for the actors with appearances by John Carradine, Wally Cox, Jo Ann Pflug, Margaret Hamilton, and Richard Anderson.

The Jack Palance version of *Dracula* (1973) does feature some fine cinematography from Oswald Morris, but apart from Palance's interesting performance, was rather a pedestrian telling of Bram Stoker's famous tale. It needed a larger budget to encompass the elaborate scope, though Matheson's script is refreshingly faithful to the book, unlike most cinematic adaptations.

Trilogy of Terror had Karen Black starring in three terror tales. After dull tales about witchcraft and schizophrenia, this telefeature comes alive in the Matheson-scripted "Prey" about a Zuñi fetish that comes to life and attacks Karen Black. Here Curtis has the camera zooming along at ankle height to give a fetish-eye-view of an attack, and he cleverly builds up anticipation where the seemingly unstoppable wooden idol could be hiding. Much imitated, it is a neat little model for building up and releasing tension and suspense with the fetish playing "cat and mouse" with its human prey.

Ray Danton (1931–   )

The Deathmaster (1972); *Crypt of the Living Dead* (1973); *Psychic Killer* (1975).
TELEVISION: *The Return of Mickey Spillane's Mike Hammer* (1986); *Vietnam War Story* (codir. with Georg Stanford Brown & Kevin Hooks, 1987).

One-time actor turned horror hack director, Danton first helmed *The Deathmaster*, an offshoot of the Robert Quarry *Count Yorga* films. This time Quarry was the vampire head of a hippie cult. Only slightly less forgettable and inept was *Crypt of the Living Dead* in which Gimpera, the wife of Louis VII who was buried alive in 1269, comes back to life as a zombie and kills everyone in her way. *Psychic Killer* is the best of the lot, possibly because it comes closest to having a fresh idea and has some interesting cameos by Aldo Ray, Della Reese, Neville Brand, and Rod Cameron. In this one, actor Jim Hutton is wrongly accused of murder and is placed in a mental institution where he learns how to project himself astrally to commit murder and revenge. Still, Danton's horror film work remains steadfastly below average and there is no reason to suspect any surprises from him.

Fred Dekker (1959–   )

Night of the Creeps (1985); *The Monster Squad* (1987).

Fred Dekker is a very young filmmaker who shows some definite promise based on his first two features. *Night of the Creeps* has the same basic premise as Jack Shoulder's *The Hidden* but without the police procedural material. Instead, it was a loving tribute to '50s-style, invasion-of-mind-controlling-things-from-space movies with a not-bad visual look for a low-budget film.

In many ways, *Monster Squad* was less successsful, resurrecting old horror icons like Frankenstein's Monster, Count Dracula, the Mummy and the Creature from the Black Lagoon, giving them little personality and less motivation, and then sending them into modern-day suburbia to interact with a group of heroic kids. Still, it does have moments when it connects – as in the wonderful scene in Dracula's tomb at the opening of the film, which

manages to capture the mood and look of Browning's *Dracula* in color, complete with armadillos scampering about. There is also a bit about the protagonists being afraid of a scary old man who, when they finally have a chance to meet him, proves more tragic than frightening – a reclusive concentration camp victim who had shut out the world and invited unwarranted suspicion and mistrust.

The Monster Squad has a good look and showcases some Richard Edlund effects at its monster-dispensing climax, but scenes of the sort where a little girl teaches the Frankenstein's Monster to say "bogus" are just that – bogus. The film could have used less daydreaming and kiddie wish fulfillment and more *frisson*, but there is definitely some promise here and Dekker should be a director to watch out for when he matures.

Abel Ferrara

Driller Killer (1979); *Ms. .45* (1981); *Fear City* (1985); *China Girl* (1987); *Cat Chaser; King of New York* (1990).
TELEVISION: *The Gladiator; Crime Story* (1986).

Abel Ferrara got his start with *Driller Killer*, an undeniably unpleasant and disturbing film. It become the center of some controversy in England where its appearance on video tape caused an outcry against "video nasties." Ferrara starred under the pseudonym of Jimmy Laine as a man who becomes unbalanced, partially because of a punk rock group which has moved in next door and partially because he fears he will end up a derelict like his father. This causes him to start roaming around the city killing derelicts with his electric drill. It is not as grisly as its reputation suggests, though it was obviously influenced by the previous year's *The Tool Box Murders*, directed by Dennis Donnelly.

What distinguishes it from the previous film is that, first of all, there is some obvious social commentary intended. Additionally, the victims are largely male rather than the traditional nubile females. Ferrara even manages to wring a few laughs out of the main character's frustrations, particularly those dealing with his attempt to have an art career. Though very cheaply made, the film has gritty, realistic quality and does pack some power into its simple premise.

Opposite Top: *Young writer/director Fred Dekker with even younger actress Ashley Bank on the set of* The Monster Squad. Bottom: *A new look for the classic monsters designed by Stan Winston for* The Monster Squad. *The monsters are (left to right): Gill-Man (Tom Woodruff, Jr.), Count Dracula (Duncan Regehr), Frankenstein's Monster (Tom Noonan), the Mummy (Michael Mackay) and the Wolf Man (Carl Thibault).*

Ms. .45 was a considerable improvement and remains Ferrara's best film to date. The premise is somewhat similar to the execrable *I Spit on Your Grave*, but much more accomplished and disturbing. The attractive Zoë Tamerlis stars as Thana, a mute seamstress in New York's garment district who is raped on the way home from work and returns to her apartment only to be raped again by a robber, whom she kills. Emotionally dead inside, Thana decides to cover up her murder by cutting up the robber's body into little pieces and disposing of them in plastic garbage bags. When a man tries to return one of the discarded bags, Thana blows him away with a .45 pistol, initiating a killing spree. To lure more victims, Thana begins dressing up like a hooker or a nun.

Ferrara claims that Polanski is a major influence, and indeed there are some significant parallels between *Ms. .45* and *Repulsion* in terms of plot, character, and mood. Thana certainly is a symbol of the silent victim finally giving a comeuppance to those who exploit her, but what is also significant is that while we understand her actions the audience is never expected to condone them. This is not a pro-vigilante film.

Ferrara's direction of the film is quite good, making effective use of surreal images and wide-angle lenses. Throughout, the mute Thana remains both dangerous and sexy, while men are consistently portrayed in obnoxious, repulsive ways to underscore the battle of the sexes taking place and explain why this "Angel of Vengeance" (as the film was titled in foreign countries) has decided to catatonically carry out her own vision of justice.

Ferrara's subsequent films have remained fascinated by violence but have failed to provide interesting themes or plotlines. Ferrara also spent some time working on TV's *Crime Story* series, but his narrative sensibilities seem to have gone awry, particularly in the somnambulant *Cat Chaser*, an adaptation of an Elmore Leonard novel that intersperses some extreme violence between long stretches of tedium. However, Ferrara shows too much talent to be written off completely.

Jesus Franco (1930–   )

Arbol de España (O'Olivier, 1957); *L'Exil du Cid* (1958); *Tenemos Dieciocho Años* (1959); *Labios Rojos (Operation Lèvres Rouges); Reina del Tabarin (La Belle de Tabarin)* (1960); *The Awful Dr. Orlof* (1961); *La Muerte Silba un Blue* (aka *077 Operation Sexy); Vampiressa 1930 (Certains l'Aiment Noire)* (1962); *Rififi en la Ciudad (Chasse à la Mafia); La Mano de un Hombre Muerte (Le Sadique Baron von Klaus); El Llanero (Le Jaguar)* (1963); *Dr. Orloff's Monster* (aka *El Secreto del Doctor Orloff*, 1964); *The Diabolical* (aka *Miss Muerte*, 1965); *Cartas Boca Arriba (Cartes sur Table*, 1966); *Residencia para Espias; Lucky el Intrepido; El Case de las Dos Bellezas* (aka *Sadisterotica); Kiss Me Monster* (aka *Castle of the*

Doomed; Besame, Monstruo); Necronomicon–Getraumte Sunden (aka *Succubus, Delirium*) (1967); *Castle of Fu Manchu; Blood of Fu Manchu* (aka *Kiss and Kill, The Deathkiss of Fu Manchu*); *Sumuru; 99 Mujeres; Justine* (1968); *Black Angel* (aka *Paroximus, Venus in Furs*); *De Sade '70; Count Dracula* (aka *El Conde Dracula*); *Il Trono di Fuoco; X 312 Flug zur Holle; Fierno Tuya Es la Victoria* (1969); *Las Vampiras* (aka *Die Erbin des Dracula, Vampyros Lesbos, Sexualité Speciale*); *Eugenie de Sade; Der Teufel Kam aus Akasawa; Dr. M. Schlagt zu* (aka *El Doctor Mabuse, Mabuse '70*); *Les Yeux de la Nuit; Sex Charade; Sie Totete in Ekstase (Mrs. Hyde; Night of the Blood Monster); Der Todesracher von Soho* (aka *El Muerto Hace las Malestas*) (1970); *3 Filles Nues dans l'Ile de Robinson; Christina, Princesse de l'Érotisme (Une Vierge chez les Morts-Vivants); Jungfrauen Report* (1971); *Dracula Contra Frankenstein* (aka *Dracula Prisonnier de Frankenstein*); *A Filha de Dracula (La Fille de Dracula); La Maledicción de Frankenstein (Les Expériences Érotiques de Frankenstein); Los Demonios (Les Démons); Un Capitaine de Quinze Ans; Les Ébranlées (La Maison du Vice); Le Journal Intime d'une Nymphomane; El Misterio del Castillo Rojo; Un Silencio de Tomba* (1972); *Los Ojos Siniestros del Doctor Orloff (Los Ojos del Doctor Orloff); Relax Baby; Plaisir à 3; La Comtesse Perverse; Al Oltro Lado del Espejo (Le Miroir Obscene); Les Amazones de la Luxure (Maciste Contre la Reine des Amazones); Les Exploits Érotiques de Maciste dans l'Atlantide; La Noche de los Assesinos; Le Chemin Solitaire (Frissons sous la Peau); Sexy Blues; Les Nuits Brûlantes de Linda* (aka *Le Plaisir Solitaire*); *Los Amantes del Isla del Diablo (Violences Érotiques dans une Prison de Femmes); Les Avaleuses* (aka *La Comtesse aux Seins Nus, The Bare Breasted Countess*) (1973); *Exorcisme et Messes Noires (Sexorcisme); Celestine, Bonne à Tout Faire; Lorna ... L'Exorciste (Les Possédées du Diable); Les Chatouilleuses (Les Nonnes en Folie); Le Jouisseur (L'Homme le Plus Sexy du Monde); Les Emmerdeuses (Les Grandes Emmerdeuses)* (1974); *De Sade's Juliette; Shining Sex (Le Sexe Brilliant); Midnight Party; Frauengefangnis; Down Town; Lèvres Rouges et Bottes Noires* (1975); *Jack the Ripper; Dirty Dracula* (aka *Ejaculations, Le Portrait de Doriana Gray*); *Lettre d'Amour d'une Nonne Portugaise* (1976); *Greta, Haus Ohne Männer; Das Frauenhaus; Frauen ohne Unschuld; Frauen für Zellen Block 9; Die Teuflischen Schwestern (La Cabaret des Filles Perverses!); Die Sklavinnen; Camp Érotique; Passions et Voluptés Vaudoués (Le gri d'Amour de la Déesse Blonde; Ruf de Blonden Gottin* (1977); *Cocktail Special; Elles Font Tout; Je Brûle de Partout; Symphonie Érotique* (1978); *El Escarbajo de Oro; Mondo Cannibale* (1979); *Le Corps et le Fouet (Il Cacciatore di Uomini); Les Bourgeoises et l'Amour (Die Nichten der Frau Oberst); Sadomania; Bloody Moon; Linda; Gefangene Frauen* (1980); *Eugenie–Historia de una Perversione (De Sade 2000); Orgía de Ninfomanas; Las Chicas de Copacabana; Aberraciones Sexuales de una Mujer Casada; La Chica de las Bragas Transparentes; Girls Pick Up; El Sexo Esta Logo; El Lago de las Vergines; La Tumba de los Muertos Vivientes* (1981); *Porno Dama (Lady Porno); El Siniestro Dr. Orloff; Nevrose (El Hundimiento de la Casa Usher); Botas Negras, Latigo de Cuero; Confesiones Intimas de una Exhibicionista; El Hotel de los Ligues; Historia Sexual de O (The Story of O); La Casa de las Mujeres Perdidas; La Mansión de los Muertos Vivientes; Germidos de Placer; La Noche de los Sexos Abiertos; Las Orgías Inconfesables de Emmanuelle; Macumba Sexual* (1982); *Sangre en los Zapatos; Los Monstruous de Fiske Manor; El Tesoro de la Diosa Blanca* (aka *The Treasure of the White Goddess*) (1983); *Viaje a Bangkok, Ataúd Incluido* (aka *Trip to Bangkok, Coffin Included*, 1985); *Sida, la Peste del Siglo XX* (1986); *El Ojete de Lulu; El Chupete de Lulu* (1985); *Predateurs de la Nuit* (aka *Faceless*, 1988).

Jesus Franco is at once the most prolific and the worst horror director of all time. His films are so quickly made that sometimes he does not even bother to make sure the camera was in focus throughout a whole shot. Said camera work is very eccentric and perhaps personal as well, to say the least, but then so might be your Uncle Marty's. For some strange reason – perhaps it is Franco's complete absence of a sense of taste, which allows him to show anything, no matter how exploitative or depraved – Franco has suddenly developed a rabid following among the farther fringes of horror fans seeking new thrills.

I have seen only a fraction of his output, but those two dozen or so films were more than enough for me, thank you. What makes Franco particularly hard to assess apart from the sheer size of his output is that his films are constantly undergoing title changes from country to country, and often the same film can be packaged under many different titles as a video. Needless to say, the poor qualities of his productions have kept his work off of mainstream American cinema screens, but apparently he is still able to sell his enormous backlog of titles to foreign countries. The hallmark of Franco's major films are their sheer perversity – he unabashedly will combine sex and horror to create a new kind of pornography.

Franco's major films are *Miss Muerte* (1965), *Necronomicon* (1967), *Venus in Furs* (1969); *De Sade 70* and *Count Dracula* (both 1970), *Les Possédées du Diable* (1974); and the gruesome *Jack the Ripper* (1976). Few directors are so willing to revel in sadism on camera, so perhaps that is the attraction. For cinematic masochists only.

Richard Franklin (1949–   )

The True Story of Eskimo Nell (1975); *Fantasm* (1976); *Patrick* (1978); *Road Games* (1980); *Psycho II* (1983); *Cloak and Dagger* (1984); *Link* (1986); *F/X 2* (1990).
TELEVISION: *Beauty and the Beast* (pilot); *A Fine Romance* (pilot, 1988).

Australian-born Richard Franklin started making 8mm films when he was only ten years old. He came to the United States in 1967 to study film at USC, where he persuaded Alfred Hitchcock to show and give a talk about *Rope* for other USC students. That led to him being invited on the set of *Topaz*. Unquestionably, the master of suspense's work had an effect on Franklin.

Director Richard Franklin. This shot was taken when he was directing Road Games *in Australia.*

However, Franklin began his directorial career not in horror but in sex films which were financed with Australian money. These were *The True Story of Eskimo Nell*, based on the bawdiest ballad ever written, and *Fantasm*, a soft core film about people's erotic fantasies.

Franklin went back to Australia and taught film at Melbourne's Hawthorne College. While there, he was able to raise $600,000 to finance *Patrick*, based on a script by Everett De Roche, who went on to become Australia's premier screenwriter of fantastic films (including *The Long Weekend, Harlequin* aka *Dark Forces*, and *Razorback*).

Patrick is the story of a man who is confined to his hospital bed but has great telekinetic powers. Franklin tried for years to get financing, but it was only when *Carrie*, another film about telekinetic powers, became a hit that he was able to get financing from Antony I. Ginnane.

Patrick (Robert Thompson) has murdered his mother and her lover by throwing something into their tub and collapsed into a semi-comatose state. Everyone assumes that he is a mental vegetable. However, with his mental powers he begins to move things around him, threatening his doctor (Robert Helpmann) and his nurse (Susan Penhaligon).

Unfortunately, the script is largely talky and dull, and the uncommunicative Patrick is simply a cypher – we never know what he is thinking. Matters are not helped by the fact that this Australian picture was dubbed into "American," making the line readings seem even duller.

Road Games, a kind of *Rear Window* on the road, was a definite improvement and showed that Franklin was capable of creating an effective Hitchcock-like thriller. Stacy Keach plays Pat Quid, a lonely, poetry-spouting trucker who picks up a hitchhiker, Pamela (Jamie Lee Curtis), while transporting a load of pork to Perth. Before this, Franklin has fun with Quid, who whiles away the time by talking to his dog and fantasizing about the people in the surrounding cars. However, a driver of a green van begins to arouse his suspicion, and Quid eventually convinces himself that the driver is the killer of young women that the police have been hunting for.

Naturally, no one will listen to Quid, suspecting that he has an overactive imagination. Scriptwriter Edward De Roche gives Quid's character plenty of interesting and amusing quirks and dialogue. Pamela, an heiress on the run, befriends the lonely Quid and keeps him company. As one might expect, the killer becomes aware of Quid's accusation and kidnaps Pamela. Now Quid must save her.

Franklin manages to milk some good suspense out of the situation and shows a deft touch handling the characterization, making this a good cut above the average imitation Hitchcock suspense thriller. A particularly grisly point is that the killer chops up his victims, and some of the carcasses that Quid is hauling might not be porcine in origin. Franklin also gets some mileage out of Quid drawing attention and suspicion to himself.

Road Games impressed producer Hilton Green enough that he offered Franklin the plum assignment of directing the sequel to Hitchcock's *Psycho*. *Psycho* is a horror masterpiece that did not need a sequel, but Franklin did a reasonable job that certainly was better than most of the "psychos"-on-the-loose pictures, losing its relative restraint in only a couple of scenes and benefiting from the performance of Anthony Perkins, who once more played Norman Bates.

The film opens with the horror highpoint of the original film, the infamous shower sequence designed by Saul Bass, and nothing else in *Psycho II* comes close to it in quality, but the same can be said of the original film, despite its many fine touches. However, where Hitchcock milked humor out of the characters and the macabre situation, Franklin derives most of his humor from knowing tributes to Hitchcock and the original. (There is even a "cameo" Hitchcock appearance in which the outlines of Hitchcock's shadow appear in one quick scene.)

Franklin does a nice blending of changing the film from black and white to color. Norman has been released from the insane asylum, now pronounced cured, though there are those who have their doubts. Meg Tilly plays a young waif who comes to stay and keep Norman company, but an unfortunate twist in the script has Vera Miles, the surviving sister, involved in a plot to drive Norman insane again. Frankly, after building up so much sympathy for Norman Bates' plight, it seems a little pointless to come full circle and drive him mad all over again. Then for the sake of a shock finish, a woman (Claudia Bryar) shows up and claims to be Norman's real mother (it was the killing of his mother and her lover, unshown but mentioned in the first film, that drove Norman around the bend in the first place). Norman asks if she would not like a sandwich and then brains her with a shovel in order to keep control of the situation.

Psycho II benefits more from Dean Cundey's lensing than Tom Holland's respectful script. (Holland scripted *The Beast Within* based on *Curse of the Werewolf* for Australian director Phillipe Mora and went on to write and direct *Fright Night*, a flashy and occasionally exciting compendium of vampire clichés.) The film does have fluid camera work and makes excellent use of its gothic location, and the efforts of the talented cast are not to be sneered at. (Unfortunately, Perkins was unable to keep up the quality when directing himself in *Psycho III* from a Charles Edward Pogue screenplay.)

Holland also scripted Franklin's *Cloak and Dagger*, an espionage thriller in which a little boy (Henry Thomas of *E.T.* fame) witnesses some secret agents trying to steal government secrets in a videocassette of a "Cloak and Dagger" game. As in the suspense classic *The Window* in which a young boy witnesses a murder and nobody but the murderer believes him, the boy, Davey Osborne, is soon on the run, getting help only from a young girl named Kim (Christina Nigra) and an imaginary superheroic playmate, fearless Jack Flack (played by Dabney Coleman, who also plays the boy's father).

Unfortunately, the whole project seems overly contrived, leaning more toward a Disneyesque fantasy than a straightforward and exciting suspense thriller. Michael Murphy makes for a convincing villain and Thomas is an appealing kid, but the almost tongue-in-cheek approach does not really work when a palpable sense of menace is needed to give the suspense scenes an extra edge. Also, a great many scenes stretch credulity to the breaking point. Understandably, the film did not take off at the box office.

Back in 1980, Franklin came up with the idea of a movie about a killer chimp, and in 1984 he finally got funding for it from Thorn EMI. The resultant film was *Link*, scripted by Franklin, De Roche, and Linda La Plante. However, not since the original *King Kong* have simian menaces been big box office, and the miscalculated *Link* was no exception, though it did introduce the attractive Elizabeth Shue, who began receiving real notice after her appearance in Chris Columbus' *Adventures in Babysitting*. Terence Stamp is the supposed star of the film as Dr. Steven Phillip, a scientist investigating the intelligence of apes, but the orangutan who plays Link truly steals what little there is of the show. The whole project is singularly lacking in thrills or even any interesting ideas.

Franklin had better luck with the hairy, violent Vincent (Ronald Lacey), star of the television series *Beauty and the Beast* for which Franklin directed the successful and offbeat pilot. Franklin has shown some facility for making thrillers, though he is not the stylist De Palma is, but while he likes taking things to the extreme, he should do fewer homages and more original thinking.

William Fruet (1933–   )

Wedding in White (1973); *The House by the Lake* (aka *Death Weekend*, 1977); *Search and Destroy* (aka *Striking Back*, 1979); *Funeral Home* (aka *Cries in the Night*, 1981); *Baker County USA* (aka *Trapped*, 1982); *Spasms* (1983); *Bedroom Eyes* (1984); *Killer Party* (1986); *Blue Monkey* (1987).

TELEVISION: *Full Circle Again* (1984); *Chasing Rainbows* (codir. with Mark Blanford, Bruce Pittman & Susan Martin, 1986).

William Fruet is the "other" Canadian horror film director, totally eclipsed in David Cronenberg's shadow. His films are standard exploitation fare. *Funeral Home* did show some promise for building a creepy atmosphere, though the ending appears ripped off from Paul Bartel's little-seen gem *Private Parts*. It concerns a young girl (Lesleh Donaldson) who moves in with her grandmother (Kay Hawtrey). She begins to hear threats from a murderer and guests start mysteriously disappearing.

Spasms is a rather bizarre feature about how a big game hunter (Oliver Reed) finds himself in telepathic contact with a giant poisonous snake, which he has captured after it has killed his brother. Peter Fonda plays a scientist who is hired by Reed to investigate the link and who must save the day when the snake escapes and starts biting people. Mainly, the film becomes an excuse to show some silly makeup effects of people's skin and faces swelling and exploding as the snake poison invades their system. Don Enright's plot itself is fairly dull.

Killer Party is your standard dead-teenager movie in which a vengeful killer uses the standard creative methods for dispatching various victims, though Paul Bartel is delightful as always as a stuffy professor who gets it in the neck. Fruet's last film has the really strange title of *Blue Monkey* (it was originally to have been called *Green Monkey*, but since it is about a killer bug, that seems equally inappropriate). Steve Railsback finds himself in the midst of some weird goings-on at County Memorial Hospital as an insect turns into a superbug when fed some steroids and proceeds to suck all the calcium out of people.

Fruet's films provide very standard horror fare based on tried-and-true formulas. Perhaps sometime he will let his oddball sensibilities lead him into something really original, but in the meantime his *ouvre* can be noted only for its mediocrity.

Sidney Hayers (1921–   )

Violent Moment; The White Trap (1959); *Circus of Horrors; The Malpas Mystery* (1960); *Echo of Barbara* (1961); *Night of the Eagle* (aka *Burn Witch Burn*, 1961); *This Is My Street; Three Hats for Lisa* (1963); *The Trap* (1966); *Finders Keepers* (1967); *The Southern Star* (1969); *In the Devil's Garden* (aka *Assault*); *The Firechasers* (1971); *All Coppers Are . . .* (1972); *Inn of the Frightened People* (aka *Terror from Under the House; Revenge*, 1973); *Deadly Strangers* (1974); *What Changed Charley Farthing?; One Way* (1976).

TELEVISION: "The Cybernauts,"; "A Surfeit of H₂O," The Man-Eater of Surrey Green," "The Hidden Tiger," "The Superlative Seven," "The Joker," "Death's Door," *The Avengers; Mister Jericho* (1970); *Diagnosis: Murder* (1974); *The Seekers* (1978); *The Last Convertible* (codirected with Jo Swerling Jr. & Gus Trikonis, 1979); *Condominium* (1980); *Philip Marlowe–Private Eye* (aka *Chandlertown*, codirected with Bryan Forbes, Peter Hunt & David Wickes, 1983).

One of the most overlooked British directors of thrillers is Sidney Hayers. He has not only directed two minor horror classics, *Circus of Horrors* and *Burn Witch Burn* (aka *Night of the Eagle*), but he was also responsible for some of the most atmospheric and enjoyable episodes of *The Avengers* TV series, his work for which was consistently high quality.

Circus of Horrors was one of the earliest horror films to revel in its own luridness. Anton Diffring is Dr. Schuller, a brilliant German plastic surgeon who is forced to flee after one of his patients removes her bandages too early, resulting in permanent scarring. For some reason, he thinks it is a good idea to hide his identity by running a circus that travels all over Europe. He populates his circus with deformed women whom he cures of their deformities, in exchange for which they agree to perform as aerialists, lion tamers, and the like. If any of these lovely ladies give him trouble, he arranges for them to meet with an unfortunate accident, which in turn draws larger crowds to the circus. (The film is every bit as cynical as Billy Wilder's classic *Ace in the Hole*, but lacks the Wilder film's sense of outraged morality.)

Special effects assistant Mark Williams becomes a leaning post for the monster he created (played by Ivan Roth) for William Fruet's Blue Monkey. *The film was originally titled the equally meaningless* Green Monkey.

Unlike the more frequently shown *Berserk!* (Jim O'Connolly, 1967), *Circus of Horrors* uses its setting well and does build up anticipation with typical dangerous circus stunts. In addition, Schuller's palpable sexual attraction to deformity adds an interesting if perverse edge to the film, and it is notable that Schuller tries to create his "most beautiful circus in the world" out of deviants, being one himself.

Burn Witch Burn is an even better film, though the Abe Merritt title is highly misleading as the film is an adaptation of Fritz Leiber's classic horror novel *Conjure Wife*, which had previously been adapted as *Weird Woman* (see chapter on Reginald Leborg). *Burn Witch Burn* is better than its predecessor, slowly building up an atmosphere of absolute menace as a professor played by Peter Wyngarde finds his complacent world suddenly falling about his ears after he uncovers various talismans that his wife, Tansy (Janet Blair), has been secreting about their home.

The professor starts the movie by discussing rationalist beliefs, an idea he underscores by writing "I do not believe" on his chalkboard. (At the climax of the film, he will back against the chalkboard and eliminate that "not.") There are frequent references to superstition threaded throughout the dialogue, particularly at a dinner party Tansy throws. However, she becomes alarmed when she discovers a bad luck charm left behind by one of her guests, and we can see her panic growing as she tries to cover it in front of her unbelieving husband. Hayers is very good at setting up compositions that suggest the isolation of a character in a frame, though it should also be admitted that some close-ups of Wyngarde were necessitated simply by the actor's insistence on wearing extremely tight trousers to the set.

The professor finds his luck turning consistently from bad to worse as a student accuses him unjustly of abuse, his position is threatened, and ultimately, his wife is put into a trance and almost killed. The premise of the film is that all women have magical powers that can aid their men or retard the progress of others. Soon the other witches on a spiteful, small college board are scheming by sending spells via tape recordings and telephone wires.

The British title, *Night of the Eagle*, comes from a stone eagle which (as suggested by Hayers' camera work) comes to life and attacks the professor in the tension-filled climax of the film. The taut script is by two of the genre's masters, Richard Matheson and Charles Beaumont, and builds credibly from the world we know into one of the supernatural. (The story was remade a final time by Richard Shorr as *Witches' Brew*, but the Hayers version remains definitive.)

Hayers' films, some of which have not made their way across the Atlantic, are usually at least interesting. *The Trap*, for example, is one of Oliver Reed's better movies, in which he plays a fur trapper who settles on taking a mute woman for his wife. *In the Devil's Garden* (aka *Assault* and *Tower of Terror*) follows the story of a psycho rapist terrorizing a girls' school. Hayers turns the tables in *Terror from Under the House* in which two men track down the recently released man who was suspected of murdering and molesting their daughters. In *Deadly Strangers*, Hayley Mills offers a recent escaped mental patient a ride with some thrilling results. And in *Diagnosis: Murder*, a psychiatrist is suspected of murdering his wife after she disappears.

None of these films are classics, but they all have their interesting moments and are the work of an above-average craftsman. There are enough dull "thrillers" about that anyone who can direct ones that are interesting without being derivative is surely worthy of more notice than Hayers has received. And, as mentioned before, given the restraints of television, his *Avengers* work is outstanding and includes many of that acclaimed series' most memorable episodes.

Frank Henenlotter

Slash of the Knife (short); *Basket Case* (1982); *Brain Damage* (1988); *Frankenhooker*; *Basket Case 2* (1990).

Henenlotter started out by shooting sound 8mm movies with his friends in which he enjoyed juxtaposing jokes and bloodshed in order to give them an out-of-control feeling. He finally tried his first feature with *Basket Case*, shot extremely cheaply on 16mm with a very limited budget. (One take scenes were not unusual). The film started off with a $7,000 budget, though Henenlotter was able to get investors and a video company to put more money into it, so by the end of production it cost a total of $160,000.

The story of the film is very simple. Duane Bradley (Kevin VanHententryck) wanders around the sleazy, downtown New York area with a wicker basket, inside of which is Belial, his hideously deformed Siamese twin brother. Henenlotter builds up a vivid portrait of the area as well as sympathy for this alienated outsider with his strange burden. Belial is arranging to avenge their separation years before in a makeshift operation at his parents' house. Belial communicates with Duane telepathically, sending him instruction to take care of his needs. Meanwhile, the lonely Duane meets Sharon (Terri Susan Smith), a nurse in a nearby doctor's office. The awkward pair slowly become friends and she agrees to show him around New York. The pair begin to fall in love, but brother Belial resents losing his hold over Duane and starts to interfere with their relationship.

While the film is very crudely made, it is interestingly offbeat, has an unusual sense of humor, and builds up some sympathy for the poor down-and-outers. A bit overpraised in some quarters when it first came out, it was more often ignored, except by the MPAA who demanded several cuts which were restored in the video version. The deadly Belial, who enjoys using his claws to rip out people's throats and who looks like some kind of bizarre sculpture of a head and arms come to life, is even rendered sympathetic despite his viciousness, no mean accomplishment.

After the minor success of *Basket Case*, Henenlotter found that he was offered formula slasher films to do, a prospect that did not interest him. He instead ended up working as a graphic designer for a New York ad agency

This is Belial, the deformed twin puppet monster from Frank Henenlotter's twisted Basket Case 2. *Henenlotter deliberately seeks the outrageous with varying success.*

and it was several years before he made his next film, the equally looney and delightful *Brain Damage*.

Brain Damage saw scant theatrical release before going to video, but it was a horror film worthy of more attention. This time there is another symbiotic relationship between a confused human being and a monster. However, Henenlotter used the storyline as a parable about the dangers of drug addiction. (Rick Herbst) stars as Brian, a young man who is taken over by a queer, Japanese monster–looking critter called the Aylmer (voice, uncredited, is by horror host Zacherle), who persuades Brian to help him murder prostitutes. The Aylmer has an all-consuming appetite for brains. Naturally, Brian is repulsed by this suggestion, but the Aylmer injects him with a strange narcotic that gives him psychedelic visions. Eventually Brian's brains and whole world begin to unravel as he becomes caught in a horrible addiction.

With two solid cult favorites behind him, it is disappointing to relate that Henenlotter had a major misfire with *Basket Case 2*. VanHententryck's acting was adequate for the first film, but the follow-up makes greater demands that he is not up to. The film picks up where the first one left off with Duane and Belial hitting the ground. The hapless pair are spirited to a hospital where they are rescued by a woman who runs an institute for freaks. There are a number of outrageous makeups involved and a parallel love story, in which Belial finds Eve, an equally deformed female thing, while Duane is attracted to a seemingly normal girl who helps the elderly lady take care of her "special" charges; however, the characters are not presented as sympathetically this time around and the weird, unfleshed out freaks detract from the focus of the story. The film is obviously influenced by Tod Browning's *Freaks*—the freaks are meant to be both sympathetic and menacing to outsiders—but is nowhere near as effective. The villains this time around are a nosy tabloid newspaper reporter and photographer, plus anyone else who seeks to exploit the freaks or disturb their halcyon retreat. It may be outrageous, but genuine humor and feeling are absent from this poorly formed sequel.

Frankenhooker pushes up the outrageousness quotient with its super-crack-smoking exploding prostitutes (who caused the MPAA to give the film an X rating despite the phoniness of the effects) and lovers shredded by lawnmowers while Dr. Jeffrey Franken (James Lorinz) eases the pain of existence by drilling holes in his head. Louise Lasser has a bit part as Franken's mother but she appears sadly overweight and underused. Franken is an electric plant worker who has been thrown out of three medical schools. For his father's birthday, he invents a radio-controlled lawnmower that his fiancée demonstrates—while standing in front of it. Jeffrey has an estrogen blood bath in which he preserves his girl's head. Hoping to find a new body to go with it, he tracks down some New York prostitutes who assume he wants to play doctor with them. Jeffrey whips up some supercrack which speeds up the addiction process, causing the victims to explode into little pieces. He plots to conduct a beauty contest and use the winner to supply his finacée's new body; however, things get out of control when all the tarts start smoking his stash.

Picking up the pieces, he reassembles his girl, but the parts retain memories of their former thoughts and profession. He's created a Frankenhooker who takes to the street and asks strangers, "Wanna date?" Meanwhile, the whores' pimp, Zorro, wants a piece of the person responsible for blowing up his bitches.

The film has some of the sleazy quality of previous Henenlotter opuses, but Franken is an unfortunately charmless character, full of strange quirks that add up to nothing. Coscripting the film with former *Fangoria* editor Robert Martin, Henenlotter smirks at his characters more than he reveals them. Most are stereotypes bereft of any human qualities.

Henenlotter has shown himself capable of making oddball films with people you could care about. His first films are stronger because they revolve around a central theme that is part and parcel of the story. His is a unique vision in horror cinema, one that shows us the seedier side of town, but he is in danger of becoming a maker of miscalculated madcap monster movies rather than one who presents the horrific poignancy present on skid row.

Tom Holland

Fright Night (1985); *Fatal Beauty* (1987); *Child's Play* (1988).

Tom Holland started out as a screenwriter, scripting *The Beast Within*, a Philippe Mora horror epic that was patterned after Terence Fisher's *Curse of the Werewolf*. Holland had daring, a good background in horror films, and not a bad way with setting up climaxes. His script for Richard Franklin's *Psycho 2* was much better than what one would have expected.

When it came time for Holland to direct his first film, he demonstrated a definite sense of style, along with a willingness to set up big climaxes, to exploit vampires for their sexuality, and to borrow outright from several sources. The basic premise was a variation on *The Window* in which Charley Brewster (William Ragsdale) discovers that his next-door neighbor, Jerry Dandridge (Chris Sarandon), is a vampire. A faithful watcher of the horror show *Fright Night*, he goes to see its down-and-out star Peter Vincent (Roddy McDowall in a hammy and endearing performance), who had once appeared in a series of vampire epics, to help him out. However, the perturbed Vincent wants nothing to do with Charley and his outrageous claims. More helpful is Charley's geeky friend "Evil" Ed (Stephen Geoffreys) who hips him to the requisite vampire lore that the audience might have forgotten or not been familiar with.

While the film is devoid of any real originality, at least it knows how to use the old horror clichés well. Bisexual vampire Dandridge develops an interest in Charley's girlfriend, Amy (Amanda Bearse), because he believes her to be a reincarnation of a past love. Social misfit "Evil" Ed ends up accepting vampirism as an improvement; at least now he is a social outcast with supernatural powers. Best of all, the hard-to-convince Vincent is delightful when he is convinced by Charley that the threat is real and proceeds to tackle the problem with false bravado. Holland shows that he has a lively visual sense and makes good use of his performers.

Fatal Beauty proved to be a major misfire for Holland and stars Whoopi Goldberg and Sam Elliott. (It does say something of the times that a love scene between Goldberg and Elliott was omitted after initial previews proved disastrous.)

Child's Play is in its own way a very antic, hyped up, and silly film, though enjoyable if not taken seriously. Once more Chris Sarandon stars, this time as a cop Mike Norris who tracks down a baddie named Charles Ray (Brad Dourif) and traps him in a toy store. But Charles Ray has been

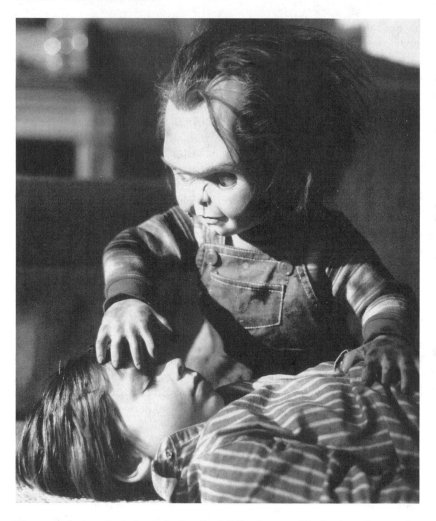

The soul of a psychotic in the body of a child's playtoy, Chucky practices voodoo on six-year-old Andy Barclay (Alex Vincent) in Tom Holland's Child's Play. *The character proved popular enough to inspire two sequels.*

brushing up on his voodoo, and before he dies, he transfers his soul into a "Chucky" doll, meant to be a young child's best friend and playmate.

The doll is given to young Andy Barclay (Alex Vincent) by his mother (Catherine Hicks), and it is not long before he realizes that there is something a little bit different about his "Chucky," especially after it manages to kill a babysitter. The doll comes to life and starts a campaign of mayhem, which is made even sillier when he starts cursing à la Linda Blair in *The Exorcist*. Rarely do people do things that make sense in the film, preferring to heighten the tension by doing something stupid. The result could have been a terrifically funny horror comedy, but Holland tries to play it all straight. As a result, it is a highly charged and highly silly movie. (Holland's rewrites were not welcomed by the script's original writers, Don Mancini and John Lafia.)

Holland has talent and a dynamic visual sense, but he will need to carefully select his material. One need only compare *Fright Night* to the thoroughly mediocre *Fright Night Part 2* directed by Tommy Lee Wallace to see how Holland has more style and energy than a run-of-the-mill horror hack. He can get an audience's blood running; now if only he will try something less derivative and more original.

Neil Jordan

Angel (1983); The Company of Wolves (1984); *Mona Lisa* (1986); *High Spirits* (1988); *We're No Angels* (1989).

Irishman Neil Jordan is an artistic director in an era where artistic directors are less and less in demand. His first horror film, *The Company of Wolves*, is based on the highly literary work of Angela Carter, and it recasts various famous myths about wolves, including centrally the "Little Red Riding Hood" myth, in terms of the sexual symbolism they present. His visual style is highly dense with some beautiful production design abounding. Chris Tucker's werewolf transformations all go for the unusual, attempting what has never been seen before, and they are just fine for the film although they are less than convincing.

The whole film has a deliberate artificial air about it that many reviewers found offputting, but that is partially because Jordan is closer in temperament to Carl Th. Dreyer than the horror hackwork that was anticipated. This film did not deliver expected gore thrills but rather presented werewolf tales as metaphors for the awakening sexuality of a young girl who discovers that men have begun to prowl after her.

The Company of Wolves does not present a linear story, but something more scattershot, full of dream-like, Freudian interpretations, and is therefore one of the strangest and most daring cinematic fairy tales ever filmed. The story is full of the fear of sex, with Red Riding's "hood" possibly symbolizing her maidenhead, and wolves symbolizing the lust in all men. The forest is full of phallic images from tall trees to strange mushrooms. What is at work here is a dream sense rather than a literal sense. The film invites you to immerse yourself in its rich imagery and make your own sense of these retellings of Angela Carter's *Bloody Chamber* stories.

Mona Lisa is not a horror film, but it is a superb piece of work with terrific performances from both Bob Hoskins, as an ex-con given the job of chauffeuring a callgirl, and Cathy Tyson as the woman he is driving around who manipulates him to her own ends.

Jordan returned to the horror genre with the more conventional but disappointing *High Spirits*, in which Peter O'Toole is the hammy head of Castle Plunket and decides to fake the presence of ghosts to attract trade from lunatic-fringe Americans. Unfortunately, his plans go awry when the real ghosts of the castle do not take to his and his staff's shenanigans. There is the usual collection of oddball characters who come to the old dark house, including a would-be priest who is nervous about forgoing pleasures of the flesh, a young woman looking for love, and Steve Guttenberg as a man trapped in an unhappy marriage who begins to fall in love with Daryl Hannah, a comely ghost trapped into repeating the same actions night after night. Liam Neeson (later *Darkman*) plays the ghostly lover of Hannah who falls for Guttenberg's wife, Beverly D'Angelo. The entire production was intended to be whimsical, but was rendered frantic at the producers' insistence, and as a result flies off into too many different directions at once to ever satisfy. Nevertheless, it does have some striking designs for the castle and ghosts and some colorful special effects. The humor is largely hit-and-miss, but it is not the total disaster that some corners have made it out to be.

Jordan is a talented director with a very strong visual sense. Attempts to turn him into a simple Hollywood craftsman are bound to fail. What he can do is present us with visual poetry – beautiful things never before seen – and bring a long-missing artistic intelligence to the horror field. One can only hope he will pass this way again.

Frank LaLoggia (1955–   )

Fear No Evil (1981); *Lady in White* (1988).

Frank LaLoggia got his start making 8mm movies in his teens. Graduating to 16mm, he made several short films, the first of which, *Gabriel*, was an award-winning study of autism and schizophrenia. After receiving a degree in acting, he found work on pilots which, unfortunately for him, did not sell.

His first feature film, *Fear No Evil*, was produced by his cousin, Charles M. LaLoggia. Made on a minuscule budget, the film had severe narrative problems; however, it did show a striking visual imagination and had several ambitious and impressive qualities. LaLoggia, for example attempted a *Citizen Kane*–type montage depicting the passing of the years at one particular household. The film as a whole had a colorful visual design,

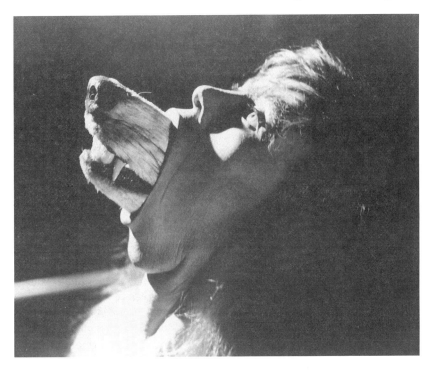

An example of Christopher Tucker's startlingly different transformations from Neil Jordan's The Company of Wolves, *based on stories by Angela Carter, who cowrote the screenplay with Jordan.*

practically the only thing holding it together, and was produced for a mere $840,000. (To be fair, it should be noted that the film was tampered with by its releasing company, Avco-Embassy.)

The story centers around Andrew (Stefan Arngrim), who slowly realizes that he is the fabled anti–Christ, and that some of the people he knows are actually angels who have been sent out to destroy him. The alienated high schooler eventually turns into Lucifer (now played by Richard Jay Silverthorn) and mischievously causes a performance of the Passion Play to turn real, with the actor playing Christ really getting crucified. Meanwhile, he also summons the dead from their graves at a nearby cemetery as the forces for good slowly close in.

Angry at having rock music imposed upon *Fear No Evil*, LaLoggia went a different route when it came to making his second film seven years later. Rather than taking financing from a major film company, he sold shares of the film to several different investors, allowing him to retain creative control. Between the two films, LaLoggia worked on shooting inserts for troubled projects. One of the projects he worked on was Jeff Obrow's *The*

Power and another was called *The Splits*. Another project for Universal, *Somewhere Is Calling*, simply fell through.

Lady in White in many ways is a charming and gentle film, which makes it unusual for a horror movie. The family situation in the film was based on LaLoggia's own Italian-American background, and it provides some extra warmth. It has echoes of *To Kill a Mockingbird* in that a writer (cameo by LaLoggia) goes back to his old town and remembers what it was like in 1962. Lukas Haas, the young boy who was so impressive in Peter Weir's *Witness*, stars as Frankie Scarlatti, youngest son of Angelo Scarlatti (Alex Rocco, cast against type and doing a marvelous job). After establishing the family and millieu, the story really begins.

One day Frankie is locked in the school cloakroom by some pranksters. He sees a vision of the spirit of a young girl who had been murdered there. Suddenly, the man who murdered her returns to the scene of the crime to recover a bit of lost evidence. Frankie sees the killer without seeing his face, and the intruder spots Frankie and tries to strangle him.

There is a subplot where a black janitor is wrongly accused and jailed, but while it is a touching reminder of the terrible race prejudice of the time, it detracts from the main thrust of the story. Hoping to resolve his troubled conscience and the mystery, Frankie goes to the reputedly haunted house of the Lady in White, the dead child's mother, Amanda (Katherine Helmond). He discovers her secret and, finally, who the murderer is.

The characterizations in the film are very strong, and the cinematography by Russell Carpenter is excellent. While some critics were distracted by the attractive special effects, they are subservient to the story itself. An unusual ghost story, *Lady in White* is easily one of the best horror films of the '80s and bodes well for LaLoggia's promising future.

Jeff Lieberman

Squirm; Blue Sunshine (1976); *Just Before Dawn* (1982); *Remote Control* (1988).

TELEVISION: *Doctor Franken* (codir. with Marvin J. Chomsky, 1980).

Jeff Lieberman made an above-average horror film with his debut, *Squirm*. Unlike most horror films, this one did live up to its title and caused audiences to squirm across the country, connecting with some primal fears. An electrical storm creates some man-eating worms that go on the rampage. Lieberman shows not only an ability to create an atmosphere of fear and disgust, but also a tongue-in-cheek sense of humor which makes this film fun to watch, unlike many of its dreary counterparts. (Frank Marshall's recent *Arachnophobia* is similarly effective and features an even slicker presentation.)

Lieberman's next film starred Zalman King, who went on to produce *9¹/₂ Weeks, Wild Orchid,* and other steamy adult films. *Blue Sunshine* showed the Lieberman had lost none of his sense of humor. The film's premise is that back in the '60s a form of LSD called Blue Sunshine was created that caused a hormonal imbalance ten years later so that those who ingested the drug suddenly lose all their hair and become homicidal maniacs. The result is both outrageous and fun for a run-of-the-mill low budget horror film.

Sadly, *Just Before Dawn* seems to indicate that Lieberman may have lost his touch. It is an uninspired imitation of Wes Craven's *The Hills Have Eyes* with none of the redeeming humor of Lieberman's previous efforts. The performances by George Kennedy, Chris Lemmon, and John Hunsaker in the dual role as a pair of mutant twins are all perfunctory.

His most recent film, *Remote Control,* contains like his first two the germ of a good idea that has, unfortunately, been poorly carried out. However, it is the first horror film to really deal with the popularity of renting films on cassette, as a particular cassette plays a movie that inspires a rash of killings.

While certainly no artist, Lieberman can be a low-budget craftsman with a sense of humor, but whether he will be a Larry Cohen for the '90s remains to be seen.

Herschell Gordon Lewis (1926–   )

Living Venus (1960); *The Adventures of Lucky Pierre* (1961); *Daughter of the Sun; Nature's Playmates* (1962); *Boin-n-g; Blood Feast; Goldilocks and the Three Bares; Bell, Bare and Beautiful; Scum of the Earth* (1963); *2000 Maniacs; Moonshine Mountain* (1964); *Color Me Blood Red; Monster A-Go-Go* (codirected with Bill Rebane); *Sin, Suffer and Repent* (codirected, 1965); *Jimmy, the Boy Wonder; Alley Tramp; An Eye for an Eye* (1966); *The Magic Land of Mother Goose; Suburban Roulette; Something Weird; A Taste of Blood; The Gruesome Twosome; The Girl, the Body and the Pill; Blast-off Girls* (1967); *She-Devils on Wheels; Just for the Hell of It; How to Make a Doll* (1968); *The Ecstasies of Women; Linda and Abilene* (1969); *Miss Nymphet's Zap-In; The Wizard of Gore* (1970); *This Stuff'll Kill Ya!* (1971); *Year of the Yahoo!; The Gore-Gore Girls* (1972).

One of the film world's most distressing events of the '80s was the virtual canonization of the gore films of Herschell Gordon Lewis. While Lewis was not the first to use gore in a movie, he created an exploitation type of motion picture that dispensed with such niceties as coherence and story and simply strung a series of ineptly staged gore scenes together, and passing them off as entertainment.

Lewis was born on June 15, 1926, in Pittsburgh, Pennsylvania, and was reputedly an English teacher with a Ph.D. before entering into the film business with the notorious David Friedman, one of porno's biggest pioneers. Lewis initially partnered with him and produced his first film, *The Prime Time*, a supposed exposé of the modern, fast-living youth of the time. He became a director with his second film, *Living Venus*, one of the early nudie films, and opted to be a cinematographer as well with his third, *The Adventures of Lucky Pierre*. The nudies were very cheap to shoot and proved very successful on the exploitation circuit.

However, Lewis could see that the nudie era was coming to an end and did not want to risk censorship problems by shooting soft core then. Trying to figure out what he could provide that the major studios would refuse to do, he came up with the idea for the first gore epic, *Blood Feast*. Almost alone of Lewis' films, *Blood Feast* was so bad that it could be considered good in a perverse way. The dialogue is clumsy beyond belief, the outpourings of blood on bodies are ludicrously overdone, and the awful cello-trombone-piano-tympani score clues the audience in that the whole thing was meant to be taken as a gag.

However, in its own small way, the awful film was a success. Lewis himself admits that *Blood Feast* was not any good, though along with the unbelievably bad *Gore-Gore Girls*, which starred Vicki Lawrence and Henny Youngman, it is certainly the most viewable film he ever made. Lewis is fond of saying that *Blood Feast* is like a Walt Whitman poem: It may not be any good, but it is the first of its kind.

However, rather than improving, Lewis' films simply became progressively duller. *2000 Maniacs* is perhaps the only genuinely disturbing of his horror films, thanks largely to a sick scene where a maniac suddenly decides to amputate a girl's thumb, and not satisfied with that, goes for the whole arm. The basic concept of *2000 Maniacs* is openly borrowed from the Broadway musical *Brigadoon* in which a village in the mist becomes accessible once every 100 years. This time it is a Confederate town of depraved maniacs who are out to get revenge on Yankee tourists that happen to drop by. *Color Me Blood Red*, a simple revamping of *Bucket of Blood*, is an incredibly dull film about a painter who finds that only blood provides him with just the "right" shade of red and goes about finding victims to keep him supplied.

Lewis went on to make country-boy pictures, soft core porn, biker epics, even an animated children's film, *The Magic Land of Mother Goose*. He also did an ultra-low-budget vampire epic, *A Taste of Blood*; a tale of two crazies who scalp their victims to sell wigs, *The Gruesome Twosome*; another of a magician whose gory magic tricks come undone half an hour after the performance, *The Wizard of Gore*; and a comedy about a sadistic killer that reached new levels of bad taste, *Gore-Gore Girls*.

These gory no-budget epics are produced and directed without an iota of style or wit and are merely exercises in unrelieved sadism. That they have found a ready market on videocassette probably says more about the expectations and lack of taste of today's gore-saturated horror audiences than anything else. Lewis allegedly ended his career after being arrested in a scandal involving an abortion clinic, but today he is free and revered by the gorehounds for pioneering outrageous splatter films. There have been attempts to lure him behind the camera again, but there has not been sufficient financing, and I for one am not rooting for them to succeed. That Lewis' execrable films were not quietly forgotten as might be expected indicates that any kind of garbage can be dug up and passed off as entertainment.

Armand Mastroianni

He Knows You're Alone (1980); *The Clairvoyant* (aka *The Killing Hour*, 1982); *The Supernaturals* (1986); *Distortions* (1987); *Cameron's Closet; Double Revenge* (1989).

Cousin of the famous Italian actor Marcello Mastroianni, Armand has yet to show a similar talent in his field. In the early '80s, he jumped on the slasher film bandwagon with *He Knows You're Alone*, about a jilted man who is out to get young brides-to-be. *The Clairvoyant* (also released as *The Killing Hour*) is a variation on John Carpenter's story for *The Eyes of Laura Mars* in which a woman gets premonitions of a serial killer's murders and starts drawing them for talk show host Perry King.

Writer-producers Michael S. Murphy and Joel Soisson wanted to concoct a Howard Hawks–like horror film about an ensemble of recruits in a difficult situation. Mastroianni took on *The Supernaturals* with a good cast including Nichelle Nichols (Lt. Uhura of *Star Trek*), LeVar Burton (Geordie LeForge on *Star Trek: The Next Generation* and Kunte Kinte on *Roots*), Maxwell Caulfield, Scott Jacoby, and Bobbi Di Ciccio. Unfortunately, the characterizations simply are not that well fleshed out, though they are certainly superior to the level found in many horror films. The menace this time are a legion of Confederate zombie soldiers, forced to walk across a mine field during the Civil War and now raised by a local witch to wreak revenge. Despite the ambitions, the film fails to rise about the level of adequate.

Cameron's Closet, in which a boy's fears actually create a monster in his closet, does not even achieve that level. If Mastroianni has not learned how to build excitement and suspense by now, perhaps he should try working in some other genre.

Ted V. Mikels

The Black Klansman (aka *I Cross the Color Line*); *The Undertaker and His Pals* (1966); *Up Your Teddy Bear; The Girl in Gold Boots* (1968); *The Astro-Zombies* (1969); *The Corpse Grinders* (1972); *Blood Orgy of the She-Devils* (1973); *The Doll Squad* (1974); *The Worm Eaters* (1975); *Ten Violent Women* (1982); *Space Angels* (1985); *Naked Vengeance* (1986); *Angel of Vengeance* (1987).

Andy Milligan

The Naked Witch (1964); *The Degenerates* (1967); *The Ghastly Ones* (1968); *Bloodthirsty Butchers* (1969); *The Body Beneath; Torture Dungeon* (1970); *Guru, The Mad Monk* (1971); *The Rats Are Coming, the Werewolves Are Here!* (1972); *Blood!* (1974); *Legacy of Blood* (1978); *Carnage* (1983); *Weirdo, the Beginning* (1988).

These gentlemen directed ultra-low-budget horror films for between $7,500 and $35,000 for the most part. They only played in selected parts of the country, typically drive-ins in the deep South to help fill out a triple bill. What is unique about them is their sheer perversity as they have no other purpose and are at best crudely made. (The lack of budget shows.)

Mikels did have an unexpectedly huge hit with *The Corpse Grinders*, the tale of how corpses ground into cat food spawned a series of lethal attacks by kitties all over the city. It grossed several million dollars, not bad for a paltry budget in the tens of thousands. However, these films have no artistically or socially redeeming value. *Astro-Zombies* may be a weird footnote in the careers of John Carradine and actor Wayne Rogers, who co-wrote and produced, but that does not make it worth seeing.

Mikels is only marginally better than Milligan, whose films are absolutely mind-numbing trash. The basic appeal is towards those who watch films for sadistic acts and nothing else, in essence, badly faked snuff movies.

Steve Miner (1951–   )

Friday the 13th Part 2 (1981); *Friday the 13th Part 3-D* (1982); *House; Soul Man* (1986); *Warlock* (1989); *Wild Hearts Can't Be Broken* (1991).
TELEVISION: *The Wonder Years* (pilot); *Elvis* (pilot + 4 episodes, 1988–89).

Connecticut born Steve Miner began his professional career as a production assistant and soon began working in all facets of production and post–production. He started a relationship with Sean S. Cunningham by co-producing and editing *Here Come the Tigers* and *Manny's Orphans*. This led to his helping Cunningham on the original *Friday the 13th.*

Significantly, Miner was given the sequel to direct and it was in that film that the character of Jason as an adult zombie in a hockey mask who spends his time hacking away at amorous teenagers was first formed. The film surprised audiences by beginning with Jason killing Adrienne King, who had played the sole survivor from the previous film. (Miner also shows Jason keeping Mrs. Voorhees' head as a souvenir.) It was also the first *Friday the 13th* to run afoul of the MPAA who insisted that some of the graphic violence be cut; sadly, with these films, once the inventive violence is cut, there is little in them to sustain interest, though Tom McLoughlin does give it a game try in *Jason Lives: Friday the 13th Part VI*, the best of the long-lived series. As in the first film, the emphasis in Miner's films is on the body count and the variety of execution methods, mostly involving impalement.

Friday the 13th Part 3-D was a slight improvement and benefitted at the box office from a brief 3-D revival as a whole new generation queued up to put on the stereoptic glasses and watching things fly out of the screen at them while they tended to develop headaches. The gruesome highlights include severing a torso in half and an eyeball popping out of a head towards the audience.

House at least was a step up, capitalizing on the concept of rubber reality movies. Here mystery writer Roger Cobb (William Katt), seeking peace from his broken marriage, his absent son, and his troubling Vietnam memories, moves into a haunted house where any room can suddenly open up on another dimension. Richard Moll plays a very tall ex–G.I. buddy who appears to terrorize Cobb while George Wendt provides comic relief as the nosy next-door neighbor. The whole movie is played for laughs more than thrills; however, Ethan Wiley's script does not provide too many of either. (Wiley would later direct *House II: The Second Story* which managed to be even worse.) At least Miner's film does have some inventive visuals and effects, but the whole thing comes across like a low budget *Poltergeist* movie.

Soul Man, a comedy about a would-be college student who pretends to be a black man in order to take advantage of affirmative action to get into exclusive Havard Law School, was a small step up, though it provided only weak satire while trodding on some sensitive toes. That Miner's affinities lie outside of the horror field became readily apparent with his fine work for the nostalgic TV series *The Wonder Years* for which he won a Director's Guild of America Award for his work on the pilot. The show possessed much of the charm of Jean Shepherd's best work.

So far, Miner's final horror film is the cornball *Warlock*, released in England almost two years before finally appearing in the United States. Julian Sands stars as a warlock condemned in the seventeenth century who is rescued by Satan and sent 300 years into the future where he encounters a beauty-obsessed young waitress named Kassandra (Lori Singer). Unfortunately, for him, his nemesis, Giles Redferne (Richard E. Grant) has made the trip to the future and continues his pursuit. Some of screenwriter D. T. Twohy's lines are hoots and the warlock indulges in some malicious violence, including chopping off a child's finger, gouging out the eyes and skinning it, but that is not enough to keep audiences interested while the warlock searches for his Grand Grimoire and Kassandra looks for him to end a spell he cast where she ages 20 years every day. Nicholas Meyer's wonderful *Time After Time* demonstrates how much better a pursuit through time combined with a love story can be.

Miner remains a minor horror director, but his films are getting slicker and he has gotten some fine performances from his actors. Still, his mainstream work remains by far his best.

Jacinto Molina (1936–   )

La Inquisición (1976); *El Huerto del Frances* (1977); *Madrid al Desnudo; El Caminante* (aka *Four Faces of the Devil; The Traveller*) (1978); *Los Cántabros; El Retorno del Hombre Lobo* (aka *The Craving*); *El Carnaval de las Bestias* (aka *Human Beasts; Cannibal Killers*, 1980); *Latidos de Pánico; La Bestia y la Espada Mágica* (aka *La Bestia y los Samurais; The Beast and the Magic Sword; The Werewolf and the Magic Sword*, 1983); *El Último Kamikaze; Mí Amigo el Vagabundo; Operación Mantis* (1984); *El Aullido del Diablo* (aka *Howl of the Devil*, 1987).
TELEVISION: *El Museo del Prado* (1980); *Palacio Real de Madrid* (1981).

Little known in the United States, under the name of Paul Naschy the pudgy Molina has long been Spain's greatest horror star. He is most associated with the part of Waldemar Daninsky, El Hombre Lobo (Wolf Man), which he has played in 11 features starting with E. L. Equiluz's *La Marca del Hombre Lobo* in 1968 (which was released in the United States under the misleading title *Frankenstein's Bloody Terror* because the distributor had contracted to release a film of that name). For the United States release, 43 of the film's 133 minutes were brutally chopped away, but the fact that it was filmed in 70mm and 3-D still makes it more than somewhat unique.

Molina was born Jacinto Molina Alvarez in 1936 and claims to have been an extra in Nicholas Ray's *King of Kings* and *55 Days at Peking*. His acting work occasionally pops up on Spanish-language stations across the United States, and several of his films are now available on Spanish-language videocassettes. His most accessible films in America have been *Dracula vs. Frankenstein* (aka *Assignment Terror*), which has Michael Rennie in his last film appearance resurrecting monsters on earth; *Dracula's Great Love* (aka

Actor-director Jacinto Molina as Waldemar Daninsky about to turn into El Hombre Lobo, a part he's played in 11 Spanish horror films, making it one of the longest-running horror series extant.

Dracula's Virgin Lovers; Cemetery Girls, and *El Gran Amore del Count Dracula*), in which Molina played a playboy vampire who commits suicide; *House of Psychotic Women* in which Molina plays a handyman who investigates some eye gougings in a house owned by three mad sisters; and *Night of the Howling Beast*. He worked for such Spanish horror directors as Leon Klimovsky, José Luis Madrid, Javier Aguirre, and Carlos Aured.

With the death of Spanish dictator Francisco Franco, Molina decided to try his hand at directing, beginning with a film about the Inquisition. He attempted to revive the El Hombre Lobo character in 1980's *El Retorno del Hombre Lobo*, but that type of filmmaking had fallen from favor with the public and the film was a resounding flop. (The "Hombre Lobo" films were highly influenced by the Universal classics of the '30s, and while they often benefited from good photography that emphasized atmosphere, the stories tended to be on the dull side.)

As a result of this setback, Molina traveled to Japan, where he made *Human Beasts* and two documentaries for Japanese TV. Still, roles became fewer and fewer. For Molina's last film, *Howl of the Devil*, he attempted to play ten different roles, including, of course, El Hombre Lobo. However, prolonged legal problems have prevented the film's release and Molina's moribund career now resides in the kind of limbo that his doomed characters frequently find themselves trapped in.

Philippe Mora

Trouble in Molopolis (1972); *Swastika* (1974); *Brother, Can You Spare a Dime?* (1975); *Mad Dog* (aka *Mad Dog Morgan*, 1976); *The Beast Within* (1982); *The Return of Captain Invincible* (aka *Legend in Leotards*); *A Breed Apart* (1983); *The Howling 2 . . . Your Sister Is a Werewolf* (1985); *Death of a Soldier* (1986); *The Howling 3: The Marsupials* (1987); *Communion* (1989).

Australian director Philippe Mora definitely has a dogged persistence despite discouraging results. He first drew attention on American shores for *The Beast Within*, scripted by Tom Holland and starring Paul Clemens as the boy with the beast within. It seems his mother (Bibi Besch) was raped on her honeymoon by some hairy-legged thing, and after 17 years, the bestial strain comes out in Clemens. The film is cheerfully rapacious and gory, though the gore was trimmed somewhat over Mora's objections. The supporting cast, including Ronny Cox, R. G. Armstrong, L. Q. Jones, and Luke Askew, contributes strongly to making the derivative semi-remake of Terence Fisher's *Curse of the Werewolf* fun though not significant.

The Return of Captain Invincible also has a few funny moments amid vast puerile stretches with Alan Arkin as a down-and-out superhero who is persuaded to come out of retirement. The highpoints are an attack by killer vacuum-cleaners and the Richard O'Brien–penned song "Name Your Poison" that evil Mr. Midnight (Christopher Lee) sings to Captain Invincible to tempt him back to alcoholism. The plot centers around Midnight stealing a top secret hypno-ray in a nefarious scheme to rid the United States of all its minorities. (The three songs by the *Rocky Horror Show* writer are the only decent ones in this musical's wretched score.) The film was not so much released as escaped, and for Mora it was all downhill from there.

The Howling 2, shot largely in Prague, suffers from an extremely poor budget, script and effects. The werewolves here look like mop-faced mongrels, and even the presence of Christopher Lee as a lycanthropic expert whose sister (Sybil Danning) turns out to be queen of the werewolves is not able to add much class to the film. The whole thing is forgettable except for the ridiculous end credits, where the same shot of Danning exposing her bosom is shown over and over again while other characters from the film move their eyes in apparent reaction to the exposed ovoids.

The Howling 3: The Marsupials is even further into loony-tunes land, this time establishing a connection between werewolves and kangaroos.

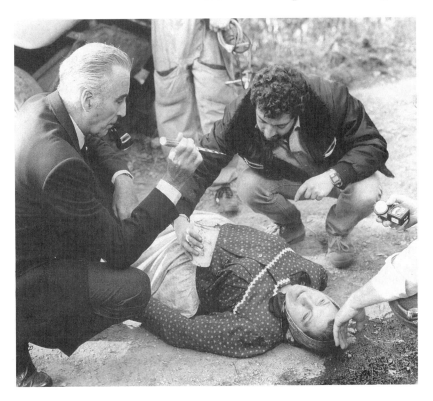

Director Philippe Mora adds some blood to an extra on the Transylvanian set of
The Howling 2 . . . Your Sister Is a Werewolf *while star Christopher Lee looks
on.*

Actually, it was marginally better than its predecessor, but that is not saying much. Somehow it is not surprising that Mora then became involved
with *Communion*, a wonky retelling of the supposed experiences of Whitley
Strieber (author of *The Hunger*) and his alleged anal rape by a curious group
of aliens in a UFO. While Christopher Walken gives an interesting performance as Strieber, who cooperated with the film adaptation of his bestsell-
ing novel *Communion*, Mora simply cannot make this patently ludicrous
tale believable and renders it more of a low-budget riff on *Close Encounters
of the Third Kind.*

Dan O'Bannon (1946–   )

Bloodbath (short, 197?); *The Return of the Living Dead* (1985); *The Horror
of Charles Dexter Ward* (1991).

Dan O'Bannon has made his mark thus far by being the premier American horror screenwriter of the '80s, writing or cowriting the scripts for such films as Ridley Scott's *Alien* (1979), Gerald Potterton's *Heavy Metal* (1981), John Badham's *Blue Thunder* (1983), Tobe Hooper's *Lifeforce* (1985) and *Invaders from Mars* (1986). His cowriter on the last three films, Dan Jakoby, went on to script the Frank Marshall gem *Arachnophobia* (1990), while O'Bannon wrote the original screen play for Paul Verhoeven's 1990 superhit *Total Recall*. Still, his directorial feature debut, *The Return of the Living Dead* (1985) must be accorded one of the major and most successful horror films of the '80s, and while O'Bannon would rather not be typecast as a horror director, his return in the 1990s with *The Horror of Charles Dexter Ward*, based on the Lovecraft novella, promises great things in his future.

O'Bannon originally started out in college as an art student in Missouri, planning a career as a commercial artist, but by the age of 21 he felt he did not fit in with the other people at the art school. He tried different majors, including psychology, architecture, and philosophy, but decided that his one genuine enthusiasm was for making movies, so he signed up for the film school at USC.

There he created his first film, a short called *Bloodbath*, which was a black comedy about a man committing suicide in a bathtub. He also put some time in on a never-to-be-finished parody called *Attack of the 30 Foot Chicken* when he met John Carpenter, who wanted him to act in a student film which was to be called *The Electric Dutchman* about four seedy astronauts who drop bombs that cause suns to go supernova and must deal with the consequences when one of these bombs get stuck.

O'Bannon's parents had stopped sending him money and he was desperate for a way to showcase his talents, hoping to achieve his ambition of becoming a director. In exchange for Carpenter putting him up, he offered to help Carpenter not only by acting but also by helping with the script, doing the effects for the film, and numerous other chores. O'Bannon added such ideas as having the bombs talk, making the captain be already dead and constantly referred to as a kind of *Waiting for Godot* in outer space, and the character of the starstruck Talby (played by Andreijah Pahich but dubbed by Carpenter himself).

For a time, the project was called *Planetfall*, but it ended up being completed as *Dark Star*. Future director Jonathan Kaplan arranged to give the pair $10,000 to expand their 50-minute student short into a low-budget feature, but while they were able to finish filming, adding a subplot about a beachball alien on board that terrorizes O'Bannon's Pinback character, there was no more money left for finishing the post-production and blow-up from 16mm to 35mm. Eventually, Bob Greenberg brought in Jack Harris who provided the money for finishing the film and then took over complete ownership of it, leaving Carpenter and O'Bannon with a credit but no profit.

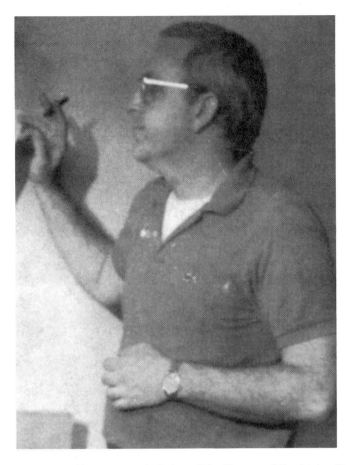

Writer-director O'Bannon at the helm of The Return of the Living Dead.

Meantime, the three-year gestation period that creating the film entailed led to flared tempers and so Carpenter and O'Bannon broke up. O'Bannon had planned another science fiction project called *They Bite*, about alien creatures that can take on the appearance of ordinary objects (shades of Carpenter's later *The Thing*) and another called *Alien*, which O'Bannon pictured as a low-budget, Roger Corman–style science fiction thriller. *Alien* would take the malevolent alien loose on a spaceship concept from *Dark Star* and play it straight for chills instead of laughs.

Star Wars came and borrowed O'Bannon's effect of a ship entering hyperspace and hired O'Bannon to do a minor bit of animation in the film. Because of *Dark Star*, O'Bannon was hired to head special effects for Alexandro Jodorowsky's proposed film adaptation of Frank Herbert's *Dune*, but that project ran out of money before pre-production could be completed.

However, by working on that project, O'Bannon met H. R. Giger, the Swiss surrealist whose impressively alien work gave the film *Alien* its distinctive look. Together with producer Ron Shusett, O'Bannon was able to sell *Alien* to David Giler, Walter Hill and 20th Century–Fox, who decided to make a big budget effects extravaganza out of it filmed by top English film technicians. O'Bannon worked closely with director Ridley Scott, brought Ron Cobb and H. R. Giger onto the project, and when Giler and Hill had rewritten his script, did a last minute rewrite in an effort to bring it more in line with his original conception, which owes something to Chris Nyby's *The Thing* (1951) and Edward L. Cahn's *It! The Terror from Beyond Space* (1958) (though there was an eventual lawsuit over story similarities to A. E. Van-Vogt's classic science fiction story "Discord in Scarlet," which also had an alien menace planting eggs inside of human victims aboard a starship).

Needless to say, the film was a tremendous success, and Scott's smoky interiors would prove to be a very influential look on films of the '80s while *Alien* itself produced a rash of imitation space horrors. O'Bannon was somewhat embittered when Giler and Hill tried to remove his screenplay credit and take it for themselves. A Writers' Guild arbitration ended up giving O'Bannon sole screenplay credit, though the foolishness by which the evil corporation which owns the spaceship *Nostromo* places an android aboard to safeguard the alien lifeform when no human is even aware of its existence was added by other hands. O'Bannon declined to write a sequel, claiming to have exhausted all of his ideas on the first film, so that had to wait until James Cameron's *Aliens* (1986) which was closely structured on the original film.

At the time that *Alien* was getting off the ground, O'Bannon was working with Ron Shusett on writing another screenplay based on a Philip K. Dick story, "We Can Remember It for You Wholesale" that Shusett had purchased the rights to. O'Bannon felt that the story was a good first act for a film that needed expanding. He proposed that it be a big budget, James Bond–like feature, with the hero going to Mars and discovering the secret of his identity – that he is an invincible, synthetic human with God–like powers created by the Martians. The script for *Total Recall* was declared one of the ten hottest unproduced scripts in Hollywood by *American Film* magazine. Shusett disagreed with O'Bannon on the ending and the project went through several other hands, though many of Dick's and O'Bannon's ideas were retained through the final draft, resulting in O'Bannon being awarded co-screenplay credit on the final film.

O'Bannon broke with Shusett after Shusett set up a cheap horror film called *Dead and Buried* and paid O'Bannon to put his name on it to help sell the project. According to O'Bannon, Shusett promised to keep the quality up but failed to do so and that O'Bannon never actually worked on the screenplay.

For a time O'Bannon worked with the makers of *Heavy Metal*, scripting two of the film's episodes, albeit minor ones, and for a time was considered as a possible director of a follow-up feature. He later began a collaboration with writer Dan Jakoby, who later scripted *Arachnophobia* for Frank Marshall, and together they wrote *Blue Thunder, Lifeforce* (originally named *Space Vampires* after Colin Wilson's book) and the remake of *Invaders from Mars*. Each project suffered from directorial changes. Director John Badham did not like a bad guy cop being the main character and so changed Roy Scheider's part to make him more heroic and he proceeded to take the sting out of the finale so that it became ludicrous (helicopters battle over L.A. shooting at each other and no one gets hurt). Tobe Hooper kept performing impromptu rewrites on the scripts written for him with disastrous results.

O'Bannon's directorial debut, *Return of the Living Dead*, was also originally designed as a project for Tobe Hooper which Hooper was going to direct in 3-D. Said O'Bannon, "I had been holding off so that my first directing project could be something of quality, and while I was holding off, I saw one bum after another direct a cheap horror movie and quickly escalate up to a position of power in the industry doing a big movie, and finally my nerve broke. I said, 'All right, the next shitty horror movie that comes along, I'll take it, I don't care how rotten it is.' It was an entry level position.

"It was difficult (directing the film). It was not uplifting. I had to uplift the entire production on my shoulders. It was very low budget and the people who put it together did so in a fairly scattered way. All films come about by a series of accidents, but this one ended up being not well organized. I had to do a lot more than I think a director should be obliged to do, especially if they are trying to achieve some sort of artistic result on the screen. A person only has so much attention. You really come to realize that when the demands that are made upon your attention exceed those of any human being, you have to start cutting corners as to where you should give you attention."

O'Bannon emphasizes that it is the writer's job to give his attention to the script, which ideally should be in satisfactory shape before the start of production, and not the director's. The director has enough to occupy his attention in simply dealing with placing the cameras and getting the performances that he desires. However, because of the low budget nature of the film, O'Bannon found himself involved in everything from setting up the production schedule to renting a warehouse for it to be filmed in, from finding new makeup artists to replace the original when his work proved unsatisfactory to helping production designer Bill Stout dress up the set to his satisfaction. The result was a very draining experience.

O'Bannon is the first to admit that brain-eating zombies is not the richest dramatic concept in the world, but his script delighted the producers who accurately predicted that it would be a hit. (It even spawned a moronic sequel by Ken Wiederhorn that was totally lacking O'Bannon's caustic wit and failed to make much of an impression as a result.) O'Bannon's film depicts a world relentlessly on the road to an apocalypse, one where disaster occurs because of the average human being's efforts to duck responsibility and where the American military is so numbed to humanity that nuking a city seems like a reasonable way of "containment."

Return of the Living Dead remains one of the best horror films of the '80s. It begins with the premise that everything in Romero's *Night of the Living Dead* was true, or at least based on a true incident, but the army who created the havoc forced the filmmakers to alter the facts slightly. Exploiting the audience's distrust of all inefficient bureaucracies, O'Bannon has cannisters containing zombies stored in the Uneeda Medical Supply Warehouse and forgotten about. Supervisor Frank (James Karen, who is delightful) decides to show the new worker Freddy (Thom Mathews), and as a result releases the gas that creates the zombies. Immediately, O'Bannon ups the stakes. These zombies cannot be killed by a shot to the head, it requires incineration or complete dismemberment.

The pair become sick and call on their boss Burt (Clu Gulagher) to help solve the situation. Burt helps them chop up a reanimated corpse and take the pieces to Ernie (Don Calfa) who runs the incinerator next door, but in burning up the pieces, the gas goes up into the clouds and a quick rainstorm brings the local cemetery to life. To complicate matters further, a group of punks have decided to use the cemetery as a hang-out and soon find themselves hip deep in brain-eating corpses (eating brains is the only thing that eases the pain of being dead you see).

O'Bannon wanted to show what he could do as a director, and so the film showcases strong character performances, is loaded with some rather funny humor, but the situation itself is taken very seriously. O'Bannon knows how to generate suspense and really put the screws on. Because the characters are likable, the audience keeps expecting them to figure a way out of their dilemma, but it only becomes increasingly more hopeless, becoming a grim warning not to let any autonomous agency experiment with building unstoppable weapons that they might be unable to control.

The film has a bright and colorful look, thanks to production designer Bill Stout, though the original makeup artist delivered rather anemic and inadequate zombie masks. However, during filming Tony Gardner appeared as a replacement and perfected some effectively gruesome effects, including a zombie half-woman who helps explain just where the dead are coming from. The soundtrack became popular with punks due to its inclusion of tracks from many of the top local punk bands including the Cramps and the Damned. (Punks were used primarily because they offered a colorful look to their characters, and unlike many modern films, they are presented sympathetically as well as humorously.)

While not everything works in the film (the special effects finale obviously could have used a larger budget), the film is more engrossing than gross and invites the viewer to have fun while the writer-director goes wild with the most far-out things he can think of. After a long break, O'Bannon plans to get behind the camera again, and from his entertaining and promising debut, he could well turn out to be one of the most powerful horror film directors of the '90s.

Sam Raimi

Evil Dead (1983); *Crimewave* (1985); *Evil Dead 2* (1987); *Darkman* (1990).

Evil Dead was ferociously heralded by Stephen King in *Twilight Zone Magazine* as a film to watch for, and so horror fans waited with bated breath for its appearance. It was made on a shoestring by some college students who had initially filmed an 8mm version in order to interest financial backers. Eventually, the result was hailed in both the United States and Europe, but United States distributor New Line had problems booking the picture, leaving Raimi without any real profit for all the effort he and his crew put in (a familiar story with popular horror films).

The film does not really have a plot, centering around a group of teens who come to a cabin and listen to a tape recording of forbidden phrases from the Book of the Dead that releases evil invisible spirits, causing the teens to die and turn into practically unkillable zombies. The intention was to pile shock upon shock, showing great inventiveness on minimal resources, as well as a lot of cinematic verve and style.

Perhaps the most successful element of the film is what has been labeled "unsteadicam." This involves nailing the camera to a two-by-four and, with someone at either end of the two-by-four, running it quickly over rough terrain, creating dizzying "tracking" shots. It does give the film plenty of energy and movement.

There is not much in the way of characterization, though Bruce Campbell, who plays Ash, became a Sam Raimi regular. The film borrows from all kinds of other horror films, but the borrowings are judiciously selected and do not detract from the film, which is fun in its sheer outrageousness.

Raimi has formed a friendship and worked with those other cinematic tyros, the Coen brothers (Ethan and Joel, who created *Blood Simple* and *Raising Arizona*). He worked on a comedy, *Crimewave*, which was equally outrageous and which simply misfired all over the place with its cartoon humor. It involves a pair of bumbling hit men who electrocute their victims and a hapless hero who runs afoul of them. Raimi was further dismayed when the film was taken away from him, and the new editing did not help the package became any more palatable.

Luckily, with *Evil Dead 2*, Raimi was back in form and even funnier than before, though this time the film ran into problems with both the ratings board and its distributor, DEG Films, which was having serious financial problems at the time. The film was actually released under a pseudonym of DEG, Rosebud Releasing. It featured the subtitle *Dead by Dawn* and resurrected the Ash character.

Peculiarly, the sequel chooses to do a mini-remake of the original film in its opening sequences in which Ash once more has a girlfriend (Denise Bixler this time) become possessed by the evil demons and then be murdered by Ash himself when she comes back from the dead. This time, however, Ash becomes semi-possessed himself as another group of intrepid adventurers find their way to the cabin of evil.

There are plenty of blackly humorous, outrageous moments. Ash tries to reassure himself in a mirror with the old "it's all a dream" gambit only to be assured by his reflection that it is not. In a hilarious cartoony segment, Ash's hand becomes possessed and tries to kill him almost *Dr. Strangelove* fashion, and so he is forced to retaliate, finally using a chainsaw to cut it off while shouting, "Who's laughing now, eh?" (To cap off the joke, the severed hand is trapped under a bucket with a copy of Hemingway's *A Farewell to Arms* on top of it.)

The special effects of all kinds are very ambitious and often take over the film for long stretches at a time. There are also some wild shots, such as the camera panning with Ash's body as he is forced through the tops of a forest of trees while being spun around. The film ends with our hapless hero, still minus his arm, with a chainsaw affixed to the stump and homemade armor over his body, popping through a dimensional doorway and back in medieval times where obviously a special destiny awaits him. This second film is less atmospheric – the comedy undercuts the feeling of dread – but its non-stop inventiveness keeps it from ever being boring.

Darkman, Raimi's latest feature, is also inventive but ultimately unsuccessful. For the first time, Raimi really has to worry about a plot and getting an audience involved with a character, and he simply does not succeed. This is one film that stretches credibility far past the breaking point. The intention was to go back and create a sympathetic horror figure along the classic Universal lines (with *Phantom of the Opera* and *Fantomas* being particular inspirations).

The film follows the fortunes of Dr. Peyton Westlake (Liam Neeson), a scientist who unrealistically seems to be pursuing on his own the dream of manufacturing permanent synthetic skin, without any outside funding or

Top: Director Sam Raimi on the set of Evil Dead 2. *Bottom: Actress Kassie Wesley is attacked by Richard Domeier, one of the demonically possessed zombies from* Evil Dead 2.

interference. Unfortunately for him, his synthetic skin will only last 99 minutes before dissolving into nothing, though by accident he discovers that if the skin is not exposed to light, it may last longer.

The film opens when a psychopath (Larry Drake) has his small gang of thugs wipe out a veritable army put together by a dockyard boss. Not only are the psycho's men terrific shots, eliminating the opposition without sustaining a single injury, but their chief loves collecting victim's fingers, cutting them off with his cigar trimmer. When he learns that Westlake's girlfriend (Frances McDormand) possesses a very incriminating document, he pays Dr. Westlake a visit, killing his assistant in cold blood and then shoving Dr. Westlake into his own artificial skin mixture. Leaving him for dead, the psychopath arranges for the entire lab to explode after he has left, which presumably kills Westlake.

Instead, he is found floating in a nearby lake and sent to a county hospital with terrific resources. There, he undergoes a radical technique which eliminates all his feelings of pain but leaves him with an empowering sense of rage. With superhuman strength, Westlake escapes, discovers that most of the skin on his face has been permanently burned away, recovers most of his equipment – which miraculously he is able to get working again – and then sets about accomplishing his revenge.

His primary gimmick is the artificial flesh he can create, which allows him to look like anybody he chooses to, but only for a limited amount of time before the skin begins to bubble and boil away, leaving his true features exposed. (Even more unbelievable, his body changes height and bulk according to whomever he is impersonating.) Meanwhile, he has to come to terms with his feeling of being a freak and his desire to reconcile himself with his girlfriend.

Raimi and his scripters, including Jim Jacks, Ivan Raimi, Chuck Pfarrer, and Joshua and Daniel Goldin, spin several threads but cannot convincingly weave them together, which is unfortunate as *Darkman* has some honestly interesting potential. However, there must come a time when filmmakers realize there is a limit to how cavalier they can be with reality before the willing suspension of disbelief is not so willing anymore. Raimi evidently does not mind taking some outrageous chances, but he will have to recognize when those chances just are not paying off.

Meanwhile, his warped, energetic sensibility promises more lively horror films in his future if only he can get his story sense under control.

Fred Olen Ray

Alien Dead (aka *It Fell from the Sky*, 1979); *The Brain Leeches* (1982); *Biohazard* (1983); *Scalps* (1984); *The Tomb* (1985); *Commando Squad; Prison Ship: The*

Adventures of Taura; Armed Response (1986); *Phantom Empire; Cyclone; Demented Death Farm Massacre* (codir. with Donn Davison) (1987); *Hollywood Chainsaw Hookers; Deep Space* (1987); *Beverly Hills Vampire* (1988); *Demon Sword; Haunting Fears; Mob Boss; Alienator; Bad Girls from Mars* (1990).

Fred Olen Ray is a horror fan turned filmmaker. He has boundless enthusiasm and an ability to churn out several features in a short time for a minimal amount of money. Sadly, what he really lacks is talent and a sense of pacing. His first "major" feature was *Scalps*, which was shot for a mere $15,000. *The Tomb* was made because he had free access to an imitation *Raiders of the Lost Ark* hidden tomb set built for a blue jeans commercial.

Prison Ship was shot in two days using uniforms from B. D. Clark's *Galaxy of Terror* which was produced by Roger Corman. The film also has popped up under the title *Star Slammer*, but either way, watching it is like being imprisoned for an hour and a half.

Ray does manage to attract some professionals to his casts and has used such people as Carol Borland, Aldo Ray, Martine Beswicke, Robert Quarry, Heather Thomas, David Carradine and Lee Van Cleef, but there is not much they can do with atrocious scripts, sometimes scribbled together in as little as ten days. Ray's films rarely appear in theaters and so patrons should beware of them appearing at their local video store.

Stephanie Rothman

Blood Bath (codirected with Jack Hill, 1966); *It's a Bikini World* (1967); *The Student Nurses* (1970); *The Velvet Vampire* (1971); *Group Marriage* (1972); *Terminal Island* (1973); *The Working Girls* (1974).

Female directors have always been in short supply, and female horror directors in even shorter supply. Feminist Amy Jones made the repellent *Slumber Party Massacre* while Deborah Brock made *Slumber Party Massacre II*, but they are no different from and no less sexist than the horrible slasher films they imitate. Barbara Peeters made the campy *Humanoids from the Deep*, which had scenes of nudity added to it over her objections, but at best the film was no more than an amusing piece of exploitation trash, with a willingness to be comically outrageous demonstrated by its woman-raping fish monsters and silly save-the-environment posturing that is typical of New World under Corman. Only Kathryn Bigelow's *Near Dark*, about a group of vampires who rampage across Texas like the Wild Bunch, shows a directorial talent that could lead to a regular film career.

And so director and screenwriter Stephanie Rothman has been something of an anomaly. She graduated as a sociology major from Berkeley in 1957 and then studied filmmaking at USC. She got her start working on

Curtis Harrington's *Queen of Blood* as an associate producer and then serving the same function on *Voyage to a Prehistoric Planet*.

Rothman made her inauspicious debut when she was hired by Roger Corman to rescue a troubled film project. The footage originally filmed in Yugoslavia as *Operation Tician* proved unusable, so Corman hired Jack Hill to shoot some extra footage of the star, William Campbell, as an insane painter who murders his models. Corman was still dissatisfied, so he hired Rothman to film still more footage and turn it into a vampire film to be called *Blood Bath*. Rothman's material added a character played by Sandra Knight as well as a chase sequence in Venice, California. Her shot of the vampire killing a victim while passers-by assume they are a couple making out in a car presages her similar juxtapositions in *The Velvet Vampire*.

It's a Bikini World was Rothman's first solo credit, and it satirized how adults exploit the youth market. It has the same low quality as other beach pictures of the period, but at least the heroine, Deborah Walley, demands that the boyfriend be intelligent for a change, and the group The Animals appear and do "We Gotta Get Out of This Place." Rothman made her next film, *The Student Nurses*, with her husband, Charles Schwartz, who served as producer (just as Jackie Kong's lame movies are produced by her husband, former porno moviemaker Bill Osco). The film led to a popular series of "nurse" films by other hands.

More interesting is *The Velvet Vampire*, in which Rothman endeavors to stand the old vampire clichés on their heads. The vampire is portrayed sympathetically, a dune-buggy-loving girl named Diane (Celeste Yarnall) who seeks to seduce a young couple, Susan (Sherry Miles) and Lee (Michael Blodgett). (She is introduced to them by an art gallery owner named Stoker after the writer of *Dracula*.) Instead of the typical Gothic setting, Diane lives out in the Mojave desert and actually enjoys the sun.

Once at Diane's place, Susan and Lee get the feeling that something peculiar is going on. They hear a scream in the night (that of a mechanic whom Diane summoned to fix her dune buggy and then feasted on) and have strange dreams (out in the desert on a brass bed with a red scarf with Diane) that are full of sexual connotations. Susan sees Lee making love to Diane and starts wanting to make love to Diane herself, while Lee wants to leave. The uptight couple seem to slowly leave their repressions and inhibitions behind and enter a dangerous new world. Later released as *Cemetery Girls*, this little-seen movie has garnered a cult reputation like Kumel's *Daughters of Darkness*, but its ruminations on sexuality and vampirism (the need for a submissive other) are not as interesting. Still, if occasionally boring, it showed promise and a willingness to tackle subjects previous horror films had ignored.

Rothman also wrote but did not direct such exploitation pictures as *Sweet Sugar* and *Beyond Atlantis*. Her last film that falls into the scope of this work is *Terminal Island*, an interesting speculation on what might develop if all criminals were exiled to a particular island and forced to make their own way. The women on the island are treated as slaves and the whole thing has come to be run by a psychotic overseer (Sean David Kenney).

The film ran into some problems when the proposed lead, Ena Hartman, pulled a tendon, necessitating some last-minute rewriting to work around her central role. Hartman plays Carmen, a woman convicted of murder and sentenced to Terminal Island, where since the death penalty was declared unconstitutional all murderers are sent. Right from the beginning she is exploited by the news media, though she lashes out. On the island, she finds herself on the bottom of the pecking order along with the other women who must work during the day and sexually service the men during the night. (The film is full of metaphors for social repression.)

However, a group led by A. J. (Don Marshall) have split off from the others and represent the dangerous idea of freedom. A. J. and his followers kidnap some of the women on the island, and Carmen proclaims she would rather kill someone than be enslaved again. Instead, the group decides that each must pull his own weight. When Bobby (Kenney) and Monk (Roger E. Mosley) attack, the women fight alongside the men, and unlike elsewhere on the island where apathy prevails, this group mourns their dead. Slowly the members of the group form a more ideal society where labor is based on interest and ability rather than strength and gender. Having discovered the benefit and necessity of working together, the group overthrow Bobby and Monk and set up a more pacifistic society. The film ends with a doctor (TV star Tom Selleck in a minor role) electing to stay with the island society he fought for rather than return to the corrupt society on the mainland. Rothman has fashioned a thought-provoking fable on the needs for companionship and cooperation that exist within us all while decrying sexism and providing the type of action an exploitation film requires. It is a subversive and interesting fairy tale about what is and what could be.

Joseph Ruben

The Sister-in-Law (1975); *The Pom-Pom Girls* (1976); *Joyride* (1977); *Our Winning Season* (1978); *Gorp* (1980); *Dreamscape* (1984); *The Stepfather* (1986); *True Believer* (1989); *Sleeping with the Enemy* (1990).
TELEVISION: *Breaking Away* (pilot).

Early in Ruben's career it would have been possible to dismiss him as a lightweight maker of exploitation fluff. *The Pom-Pom Girls* received a good reputation in exploitation circles for being more good-natured than most such films, but it was not until Ruben tackled the horror-science fiction field with *Dreamscape* that he truly began to impress.

In an age of dumb, nonsensical movies, *Dreamscape* impressed with both its style and its intelligence. Here at last was an imaginative movie which made interesting use of dreams. The film is premised on the idea that the President of the United States (Eddie Albert) has been having a series of nightmares about the horrors of nuclear destruction. His close adviser and friend (Christopher Plummer) is concerned that because of his dreams the President will make dangerous concessions to the Russians, and he has diverted money to a special research project run by Max von Sydow to discover ways of getting inside people's dreams. Von Sydow arranges to have Dennis Quaid, who plays a former patient of his with genuine telepathic abilities, brought to him. Quaid has been wasting his talents betting money at the race track and has raised the ire of the local bookies who want to know the secret of his success. Falling for von Sydow's assistant (Kate Capshaw), he allows himself to be persuaded to be hooked up into a machine that allows him to enter other people's dreams.

The dreams he enters are mostly nightmares that give clues about a patient's fears and psychological problems. Particularly vivid are a young boy's fears about a snakeman that attacks him in his dreams. Ruben uses an expressionistic style to convey these dreams' off-kilter world. Adding spice to the mixture is David Patrick Kelly, doing an excellent job as a psychopath who discovers that he can alter the reality inside people's dreams and literally scare them to death. Plummer plans to use Kelly as a dream assassin as a last resort.

Ruben shows a highly developed sense of camera movement and placement, drawing us into the action and the ideas of the film. He also uses the dreams to show facility in a number of styles and creates some indelible images on a low budget. The performers are all quite good and the performances themselves quite polished. Twentieth Century–Fox had high hopes that they would have a hit on their hands, but *Dreamscape* got buried amidst the more highly publicized summer features when it came out, leading most people to discover it on cable or videocassette. Still, it is a very entertaining and thrilling yarn, one with a believable villain who has what he feels are sound reasons for his extreme actions. Quaid reveals the star quality that made him a delight in *The Right Stuff* and *The Big Easy*, and Kate Capshaw has never been more attractive.

Next Ruben went to New Century Vista, where Donald Westlake scripted another drama about a psychopath on the loose. However, *The Stepfather* proved to be quite a cut above the run-of-the-mill slasher film, thanks largely to Ruben's direction and Terry O'Quinn's performance as the beguiling psychopath in search of the "perfect" family. O'Quinn's character inevitably finds imperfections in his idealized version of the American family, murders them, changes his identity, and moves on.

The film follows him from the scene of his latest carnage to his new

Director Joseph Ruben, taken after the completion of his recent hit Sleeping with the Enemy *in which Julia Roberts faces the horror of an abusive husband.*

family where his stepdaughter (Jill Schoelen) soon begins to suspect that all is not quite right with her new stepfather, though on the surface he appears blandly normal to everyone else. What distinguishes the film is the emphasis on character rather than gore. As a result, the film won a number of critical kudos, but the ad campaigns could not lure large audiences into the theaters, though once again the film did fairly well on videocassette, which led to the filming of a highly inferior sequel.

Meanwhile, Ruben abandoned plans to do another horror film and went onwards and upwards with *True Believer*, based on a San Francisco radical lawyer famed for getting his drug-dealing clients off. Dynamic actor James Wood is riveting as the lawyer who regains his lost scruples and investigates a murder case at the behest of an idealistic young partner played by Robert Downey, Jr. Ruben is now established as a talent. One hopes that he will continue to use his intelligence and skill and bring it back to the horror field sometime in the future. He is a very promising up-and-coming director of whom one can expect big things.

Jimmy Sangster (1927–   )

The Horror of Frankenstein (1970); *Lust for a Vampire* (1971); *Fear in the Night* (1972).

Jimmy Sangster's contributions to the horror film have been more as Hammer's main horror screenwriter during its formative horror period in the late '50s than as a director. In fact, his directorial efforts have been quite disappointing. *The Horror of Frankenstein* was an unusual attempt to update the Frankenstein myth for more modern audiences, with Ralph Bates taking over the Peter Cushing role and David Prowse as the monster. Unfortunately, this is a duller remake of *Curse of Frankenstein*, with added unconventional bits like Dr. Frankenstein making a disembodied hand give someone the finger. It is unusual in that Dr. Frankenstein accidentally has his creation destroyed and gets off scot-free at the end, and it maintains a jaunty, amoral tone, but it is nowhere near as funny as it thinks it is.

Lust for a Vampire is the middle film in the Karnstein trilogy, and a thoroughly misguided one. Yutte Stensgaard made an extremely attractive, big-bosomed vampire as Mircalla but proved to be utterly without acting talent. She is happily seducing her female students and drinking their blood when Giles Barton (Ralph Bates), the school's headmaster, confronts her with his suspicions. Naturally, he becomes her next victim, to the awful strains of a pop song "Strange Love." Sangster's attempt at generating an erotic atmosphere falls miserably flat, and the film simply marks time waiting for the old standby angry villagers to come and put an end to the whole dreary mess.

Fear in the Night also fails to generate any effective atmosphere. It simply follows the psychological thriller formula of a man (Ralph Bates) and woman (Joan Collins) plotting to drive his wife (Judy Geeson) insane while encouraging her to murder Peter Cushing, who plays a one-armed school headmaster. It proves drearily predictable in every department, and Sangster went on to write for *Believe It or Not*.

Cirio H. Santiago

Women in Cages (1972); *Bamboo Gods and Iron Men* (1974); *TNT Jackson; Cover Girl Models* (1975); *The Muthers; Ebony, Ivory, and Jade* (aka *American Beauty Hostage*) (1976); *Vampire Hookers; Death Force* (1978); *Firecracker* (1981); *Caged Fury* (1984); *Desert Warrior; The Destroyers* (1985); *Naked Vengeance; Silk* (1986); *Demon of Paradise; Equalizer 2000; Fast Gun* (1987); *The Sisterhood; The Expendables* (1988); *Last Stand at Lang Mei; Future Hunters; Silk 2; Nam Angels* (1989); *Full Battle Gear; Dune Warriors; Behind Enemy Lines* (1990).

Cirio Santiago is the Filipino and South American king of the drive-in movie. He has long been a dependable associate of Roger Corman, turning out cheap exploitation pictures with clockwork regularity. His films have no discernible style or personality, though scriptwriter Howard Cohen (*Saturday the 14th*) does bring his infantile level of humor to *Vampire Hookers* (aka *Sensuous Vampires*) with some outrageous though embarrassing results. (It may be notable for containing the first fart vampire, though it is difficult to understand why that would be a milestone anybody would want to reach.) And Santiago's *Desert Warrior* was certainly no worse than most of the other *Road Warrior* knock-offs from around that time. His more recent films have had only scant theatrical play in this country, though no doubt they are clogging up video store shelves somewhere.

Peter Sasdy (1934–   )

Taste the Blood of Dracula (1970); *Countess Dracula; Hands of the Ripper; Doomwatch* (1972); *Nothing But the Night* (1975); *The Devil Within Her* (aka *I Don't Want to Be Born*, 1976); *Welcome to Blood City* (1977); *The Lonely Lady* (1983).
TELEVISION: *The Stone Tape* (1973); *Murder at the Wedding* (1979); *The Secret Diary of Adrian Mole* (1985); *The Growing Pains of Adrian Mole; Imaginary Friends* (1987); *Ending Up* (1989).

Hammer Films imported Peter Sasdy to be an exciting new talent and inject some new blood into the old Hammer formula, but while *Countess Dracula* proved diverting, with Ingrid Pitt both exotic and fetching as the Bathory clone who tries to maintain her youth by bathing in the blood of young girls, Sasdy's overtly sexual handling of his stories made them more sleazy than erotic.
Sasdy was born in Budapest, Hungary, and after emigrating to England, became involved in the television industry. His first film for Hammer in 1970 was *Taste the Blood of Dracula*, Hammer's follow-up to Freddie Francis' highly successful *Dracula Has Risen from the Grave*. However, the focus this time is more on three corrupt old men (Geoffrey Keen, John Carson, Peter Sallis) who go to Lord Courtley (Ralph Bates, whom Hammer was grooming for horror stardom that never came) looking for new illicit thrills. In the process of resurrecting Count Dracula, Courtley is killed, and Dracula vows revenge on those who destroyed his disciple. He decides to do this by attacking the children of these old men (including attractive actresses Linda Hayden and Isla Blair). However, Dracula is not an active participation in much of the film and the other characters were not particularly interesting; nor was the nth repetition of the revenge plot. This contributed to the continuing downward spiral of Hammer's Dracula series.

Countess Dracula is much easier on the eyes, but then the shapely Ms. Pitt is fun for most men to look at. Unfortunately, as a piece of filmmaking, it is at best merely adequate, as is the sometimes overrated *Hands of the Ripper*, in which Angharad Rees is the daughter of Jack the Ripper who has seen her dad slice up her mum and understandably has not been the same since. As a result, whenever she becomes sexually aroused, she is filled with a homicidal impulse – much to her lovers' dismay. The film was made worse when shown on American television by some unnecessary additional footage of a psychiatrist who lamely tries to explain things to the presumably befuddled audience. (Actually, the intention was more to simply pad out the running time so that it would fill a two-hour slot; the original film was a mere 85 minutes.)

Sasdy continued working as a horror specialist for other companies. He tackled a film version of the British miniseries *Doomwatch* about radioactivity creating an isle of mutants. The film starred Ian Bannen and George Sanders in one of the latter's final performances and proved to be slow-moving and dull. Distributor Tigon folded up shop shortly afterwards.

Nothing But the Night was the first and last production of Christopher Lee's Charlemagne Productions, which sadly depended on a hit that it did not get. Lee plays a chief inspector who investigates a murder at an orphanage. Gwyneth Strong plays a child from that orphanage who has some surprisingly adult memories, and so pathologist Sir Mark Ashley (Peter Cushing) is called in. There is a fight over the child by a prostitute named Anna Harb (Diana Dors) who claims to be her mother. There are some additional murders and eventually it is discovered that the children become possessed, and kill while under the influence of the possession. The film got into trouble with the Catholic church and received scant bookings.

The Devil Within Her has Joan Collins giving birth to a homicidal infant; *Welcome to Blood City* was an imitation of Michael Crichton's *Westworld*; and *The Lonely Lady* has Pia Zadora in an adaptation of a Harold Robbins novel that is bad beyond belief. Sasdy has since returned to working in television after a mediocre and undistinguished career as a film director.

David Schmoeller

Tourist Trap (1979); *The Seduction* (1981); *Crawlspace* (1986); *Catacombs* (1988); *Puppet Master* (1989).

David Schmoeller can be counted on to add interesting touches to the same basic dumb and dull plot. His first film, *Tourist Trap*, was your typical dead-teenager movie except for the unusual m.o. of villain Chuck Connors, who uses some oddball mannikins to kill for him. This gave the film an odd atmosphere as people went to Connors' tourist attraction and viewed the strange life-sized dolls that Connors set up. The victims ended up looking like dolls themselves.

The Seduction offered Morgan Fairchild as a TV newswoman whose most ardent fan is a voyeuristic psychopath. It's a typical "cat-and-mouse" tale with Fairchild showcasing her ability with makeup more than her acting talents.

Crawlspace is simply an unpleasant variation on the voyeur-killer theme, this time with Klaus Kinski playing yet another homicidal maniac, Dr. Karl Gunther. Gunther runs a boarding house for starlets, whom he likes to scare and eventually kill. Talia Balsam is a Nazi hunter who begins to have some suspicions about him. Kinski has real talent as an actor, but he is squandering it here, though he remains compelling and watchable even when the film is not.

Puppet Master has a magician's puppets coming to life and killing people in an isolated hotel. A knock-off of Stuart Gordon's *Dolls*, *Puppet Master* features some fine stop-motion animation of the deadly dolls, but like most of Schmoeller's movies, its only purpose is to provide mayhem for entertainment. Apart from the consistent use of voyeuristic killers, there do not seem to be any real thematic concerns in Schmoeller's work. All characters are dolls to be pulled apart or killed in Schmoeller's playful, sadistic universe.

Jim Sharman

Shirley Thompson vs. the Aliens (1972); *The Rocky Horror Picture Show* (1975); *Summer of Secrets* (1976); *The Night of the Prowler* (1978); *Shock Treatment* (1981).

Jim Sharman, most famous for directing the cult hit *The Rocky Horror Picture Show* in both its theatrical and cinematic versions, first thought of the idea of combining rock-and-roll and science fiction with his cheaply made debut movie in his native Australia, *Shirley Thompson vs. the Aliens*. It was a compendium of B movie clichés shot in 16mm for $17,000 Australian dollars. The story dealt with Shirley Thompson (Jane Harders) who had seen some aliens in the Tunnel of Love back in 1956. She becomes convinced several years later that they have taken over the statute of the Duke of Edinburgh and are now plotting to take over the world. It is a rarely screened, rather bizarre little film, cowritten by Sharman and Helmut Makaitsi.

Sharman went on to direct theatrical productions of *Hair* and *Jesus Christ Superstar* in Australia, and then came to England to do the same.

While working on *Jesus Christ Superstar*, he got to know Richard O'Brien, who was playing Herod. When O'Brien's son Linus was born, he left the show to work on a musical he called *They Came from Denton High*, which eventually turned into *The Rocky Horror Picture Show*. After getting financial backing from Michael White, O'Brien and Sharman managed to put the show on cheaply, and with Tim Curry as its star, it became an unexpected hit.

Record producer Lou Adler caught the show and thought it was worth the risk of trying it in America. The show had a successful run at the Roxy Theater in Los Angeles, but an attempted New York opening proved a disaster. Still, during the Los Angeles run, Adler had persuaded 20th Century–Fox that a movie could be made for a million dollars. The film itself was shot at the old Bray Studios, one-time home of Hammer horror movies. Fox ran off an initial 200 prints to give the film a regional release, but it played poorly in its initial opening everywhere except in Westwood, the student village near UCLA. As a result, it was decided to open the film in New York as a midnight movie, saving tremendously on the cost of promotion.

The film inspired a unique and astonishing phenomenon. The people who responded to the film really responded and came back again and again. They began singing along with the catchy score by Richard O'Brien, and they even started yelling straight lines to which the next line onscreen would be a joke response. This was happening in places as different as Los Angeles, Texas, and New York. Soon going to *Rocky Horror* became almost a "coming of age" ritual. Certainly the screenings became very ritualized. Regulars came dressed as characters from the film. When it rained on-screen, some people raised umbrellas while others squirted water over the audience. During the song "There's a Light," people flicked Bic lighters. Rice was thrown during the wedding scene, toasted bread when Frank N. Furter offered a "toast," and toilet paper when Brad exclaimed, "Great Scott!" The audience became key participants in the movie, rendering the whole thing a definitely different cinematic experience.

Apart from its audience, *Rocky Horror Picture Show* was still an unusual film. It opens with the song "Science Fiction Double Feature," a paen to the joys of watching B science fiction movies while making out in the back row of the theater. The film opens on Patricia Quinn's lipstick-reddened lips on a black background, articulating the words with great care, though the voice is supplied by O'Brien himself. Here indeed was a different kind of *Jaws*, as well as a different *Rocky*.

Sharman piles on lots of visual details that come out on repeated viewings. At the church wedding that begins the plot, the wedding guests are played by the same group who will play the crazed Transylvanians later in the film. The preacher is played by Tim Curry, who will later appear as Frank N. Furter, the mad alien scientist behind it all, flacked by his hench-people, Riff Raff (O'Brien) and Magenta (Quinn).

The main cast of The Rocky Horror Picture Show, *king of the midnight movies, which has now grossed over $100 million in midnight showings across the country. These aliens from the planet Transylvania are: Frank N. Furter (Tim Curry, center); Columbia (Little Nell, left); Magenta (Patricia Quinn, above); and Riff Raff (writer Richard O'Brien). Curry gives a brilliant performance, and director Jim Sharman makes his nefarious actions seem liberating and positively heroic.*

The film plays out the cliché of two people going to an old dark house in the rain. (Nixon's resignation speech is heard over the radio to set the time.) Hoping to phone a mechanic, Brad Majors (Barry Bostwick) and Janet Weiss (Susan Sarandon) find themselves in the midst of some unconventional conventionists. Escorted inside, they are stripped of their outer garments and invited to join the "Time Warp."

The story itself is presented as a case history by a narrator (Charles Gray), and as a comic touch during the "Time Warp" dance sequence, he pulls down a dance chart and demonstrates the steps of the dance.

Brad and Janet slowly lose their inhibitions along with their clothes as the film tries to be knowingly wicked and naughty, though never really as naughty as it thinks. The bisexual Frank N. Furter has murdered his ex-lover Eddie (rock star Meat Loaf) and used part of his brain to create the "perfect man," Rocky (Peter Haines), who in time-honored fashioned is tormented by the hunchbacked Riff Raff. Meanwhile, Frank seduces both Janet and Brad, using exactly the same type of arguments and deception with each (namely, that it will feel nice and he will not tell). Janet discovers Frank with Brad after sex on a viewscreen; her libido inflamed, she now seeks relief from Rocky. Meanwhile, Eddie's uncle and Brad's science teacher, Dr. Scott (Jonathan Adams), shows up looking for his nephew and reveals that Frank N. Furter and his gang are all aliens, Transsexuals from the planet Transylvania.

Sharman festoons the decor with objets d'art. In various corners, he puts Leonardo da Vinci's *Last Supper*, the RKO radio tower, the Sistine Chapel ceiling, a copy of *Weird Science* comics, Michelangelo's David and other art masterpieces. The whole enterprise is presented with verve and flair, with corny old-fashioned wipes and other cinematic techniques of a bygone era. Curry gives a thoroughly delightful performance, remaining likeable despite his propensity to use people simply for his pleasure without a thought to their feelings. Yet despite its preaching, "Don't dream it; be it!" the film ends moralistically, with Frank N. Further punished for his excesses and Brad and Janet devastated by their loss of innocence. This was underscored by the song "Superheroes," which was cut from the American release of the film, where a reprise of the popular "Time Warp" was included instead.

The film's phenomenon was even celebrated in the film *Fame*, in which a character attends a *Rocky* screening with all its madness. O'Brien's B movie lines have some real flavor, though the film never really delivers on the promised laffs. However, *Rocky* was cheerfully devoted to being different and having a good time at it, which made it fun to watch even if it was not as slick as De Palma's *Phantom of the Paradise*.

Regrettably, Sharman was not able to do it again. He directed a couple of minor films, *Summer of Secrets* and *The Night of the Prowler*, before finally tackling the long-awaited sequel to *Rocky Horror*. O'Brien originally conceived the film as a very direct sequel, in which Janet seeks Dr. Scott's help because Brad has turned gay after his night with Frank N. Furter. Rocky was not killed, having the same immortality as Frankenstein's Monster, and he too seeks out Dr. Scott to try and resurrect Frank. They succeed, and Frank was to sing "Little Black Dress" to indicate what to wear to one's resurrection. However, Curry refused to reprise the role of Frank, having already played it on stage and on film several times. He was hoping to launch a credible, independent rock career and did not want to be too closely associated with *Rocky Horror*, which might lead to typecasting that was not in his favor. (Curry appeared in minor roles in such films as *The Shout* and *Clue*.)

Additionally, 20th Century–Fox had some objections to the plotlines, but O'Brien had already written the songs. Rather than rewrite his tunes, he fashioned a new story to fit them. The story was to be a satire on the effect of television in our lives, with the town of Denton, Ohio, transformed into a giant television studio. The resulting film was *Shock Treatment*. Cliff De Young took over the role of Brad, as well as playing Farley Flavors, Brad's identical twin brother, who is the biggest sponsor in Denton. Jessica Harper took over the role of Janet as Sarandon's salary demands were too high. Charles Gray, Patricia Quinn, Richard O'Brien, and Nell Campbell were all given new characters to play, while Barry Humphries adopted a German accent to take on what was to be the Dr. Scott role, that of a blind television show host.

The story is a bit of a downer after the good spirits of *Rocky Horror*. Brad is locked up in a mental hospital run by Cosmo McKinley (O'Brien) and his sister (Quinn) while Farley tries to seduce Janet away from her loyalty to Brad by making her a star. The film was unusual and often a bit surreal, and O'Brien's toe-tapping songs showed he had lost none of his songwriting ability, but it was an experiment that fell flat, bombing as a midnight movie release and quickly disappearing forever. It simply did not offer to television affectionate tribute the first film had offered to B monster movies.

Gary Sherman

Raw Meat (aka *Death Line*, 1973); *Dead and Buried* (1981); *Vice Squad* (1982); *Wanted: Dead or Alive* (1986); *Poltergeist III* (1988); *Lisa* (1990). TELEVISION: *Mysterious Two* (1982); *Island of Women; The Helping Relationship; Sable* (TV series).

Gary Sherman studied design and photography at the renowned Illinois Institute of Technology, eventually becoming an associate professor there in animation and optical effects. Later he began directing TV commercials and moved to London, where he cowrote and directed *Raw Meat*, his first feature.

Filmed in England as *Death Line*, the story concerns the discovery of a man and a woman in a disused portion of the London Underground. It is slowly revealed, as Inspector Calhoun (Donald Pleasence) keeps probing, that in 1892 when the tube was first being built, eight men and four women were trapped by a cave-in and left to die because there was not sufficient money and it was felt that the effort to rescue them was not worthwhile.

Director Gary Sherman (left) discusses filming with producer Frank Yablans on location for Lisa.

Throughout, the film attacks the callousness and hypocrisy of the upper class, showing how they are accustomed to privilege and licentiousness while condemning others for consorting with the same whores they dally with. There is also a contrast between the British (as demonstrated by Sharon Gurney) and American (demonstrated by David Ladd) reactions to violence. Gurney's character is far more sympathetic when the survivor (Hugh Armstrong) is found, but later, when she is kidnapped, she has trouble relating to him. (His only vocabulary is, "Mind the doors," a phrase he must have inherited from his cannibalistic forebears who had survived the cave-in by living off their fellows.)

The basic theme of the consuming aspects of violence repelled some and attracted others, and as the years pased, the film has gained quite a cult reputation. It may, along with his Emmy Award–winning PBS documentary *The Helping Relationship*, be considered Sherman's best film. It is certainly his most atmospheric.

Sherman returned to Los Angeles, where he started writing TV-movies-of-the-week and television pilots. In 1981 he returned to the horror field with the repugnant effort *Dead and Buried*, which featured some gruesome effects by Stan Winston. The plot centers around some mysterious murders. The sheriff (James Farentino) notes some suspicious doings at Dobbs', the mortician's place. It seems Dobbs (Jack Albertson in his final role) has been experimenting with reanimating corpses. There are some interesting twists along the way to the final revelation. One of the most shocking is when the sheriff sees some film of his wife (Melody Anderson) copulating with a large man and then killing him. The sheriff gradually realizes that the town is populated with immoral – or perhaps amoral is more accurate – zombies.

Sherman went on to direct a couple of regular exploitation films, with *Vice Squad* doing particularly well. His other work includes a one-hour documentary on the life of Bo Diddley and the TV series, *Sable*, which he produced, directed, and wrote. He returned to horror with the ill-fated *Poltergeist III*, whose youthful star, Heather O'Rourke, died before the film was even released.

In this segment of the *Poltergeist* saga, little Carol Anne (O'Rourke) moves in with her Aunt Trish (Nancy Allen) and Uncle Bruce (Tom Skerritt) in a large high-rise. The evil Reverend Kane (Nathan Davis taking over the role from Julian Beck, who had died after the previous film) returns from the land of the dead to continue tormenting Carol Anne. With Brian Taggert, Sherman cowrote the hodgepodge and uninvolving screenplay, which is simply an excuse to showcase a few effects. The public lost interest and the film did poorly.

Most recently, Sherman has tried his hand in the psycho-killer genre with *Lisa*, the story of an adventurous teen who starts phoning a mysterious handsome stranger (D. W. Moffett) who turns out to be a serial killer.

Staci Keanan plays a very believable 14-year-old who chafes under the restrictions of her overprotective mother (Cheryl Ladd), but while the performances are good, the film is simply a thriller that fails to thrill and is rather formulaic to boot.

At least here the focus and sympathy are on the victim rather than the killer. Sherman refrains from showing any of the actual killings or violence until the final showdown.

Coscreenwriter Karen Clark seems to have contributed a believable mother-daughter relationship, but the film does little to distinguish itself from the mass of other psychological thrillers with maniacs on the loose.

Sherman needs to get away from the standard, formula plotlines which are dulling his work and return to more fresh, original, and thematic material.

While his films do contain some interesting ideas, his strengths are more as a director than as a writer. He seems willing to explore relationships interestingly, but his efforts at being more commercial have immersed his material in insufferable blandness.

Jack Sholder

Alone in the Dark (1982); *A Nightmare on Elm Street 2: Freddy's Revenge* (1985); *The Hidden* (1987); *Renegades* (1989).
TELEVISION: *The Garden Party* (?); *Grand Tour* (1989); *By Dawn's Early Light* (1990).

Jack Sholder started his film career as an editor, editing such projects as the Emmy award-winning series *Lifeline*, the documentary *King: From Montgomery to Memphis*, and the feature *The Burning* (aka *Cropsy*), a *Friday the 13th* imitation directed by Tony Maylam that served as Holly Hunter's screen debut. He then turned to writing and directing, later scripting an adaptation of Mary Higgins' thriller *Where Are the Children?* for Bruce Malmuth.

His first film, *Alone in the Dark*, was an above-par maniacs on the loose film which benefited from the actors playing the main three maniacs: Martin Landau, who uses his creepy smile to particularly good effect; Jack Palance as the type of man who is evil and loving it; and Erland Van Lidth, the enormous man-mountain from *The Wanderers* and *Stir Crazy*. When there is an electric failure at Donald Pleasence's insane asylum, the creepy threesome make their way to a new doctor's (Dwight Schultz) house where they terrorize his family until he can take the nuts on and rescue his family from their nefarious clutches. The film is overtly melodramatic and revels in its excess, making it enjoyable if you can get into the spirit of the proceedings. *Straw Dogs* it is not, but good casting can make a difference.

A Nightmare on Elm Street 2: Freddy's Revenge turned out to be the most disappointing of the Freddy Krueger films, with Robert Englund scarcely appearing in it. Krueger takes over the body of an innocent teen, and in the film's most successful visual, we see Freddy's features poking through Jesse Walsh's (Mark Patton) stomach. *Nightmare* creator Wes Craven refused to have anything to do with the sequel as he was squabbling with Robert Shaye over payment of profits from the first *Nightmare* film. The film concentrates on Jesse's tortured sensibilities, lacking in the wild nightmare visions and malicous mayhem that marked the other entries in the series. The buildup and payoff of the film are fairly lame, but it managed to be successful enough to ensure the continuation of the series.

Much better was *The Hidden*, a buddy-cop variation of Fred Dekker's *Night of the Creeps* that benefits from some well-directed action sequences and an otherworldly performance from David Lynch favorite Kyle MacLachlan as the FBI agent from Altair (a *Forbidden Planet* reference). The alien he is pursuing takes over people's bodies by invading their mouths and then taking over, making it difficult to track down as it keeps switching hosts and indulging its penchants for loud music, fast cars, and powerful weaponry. Michael Nouri plays the cop MacLachlan is teamed with and provides a good straight man. There is not much to the plot, but Sholder keeps the action moving well and manages to make it entertaining. Despite the disappointing action flick *Renegades*, teaming a cop and a native American, *The Hidden* bodes well for Sholder's directorial future provided he is supplied with strong, witty, and fast-moving screenplays.

By *Dawn's Early Light*, for example, is a gripping examination of a snafu where an order to launch America's missiles has been given while the president's (Martin Landau) plane has crashed, leaving the decision in the hands of a minor functionary (Darren McGavin) who finds himself under pressure from gung-ho generals. As with Sidney Lumet's *Fail-Safe*, Kubrick's *Dr. Strangelove* or even John Badham's *Wargames*, the film argues that our state of preparedness just might bring about the very catastrophe that it is supposed to avert because fate and human beings will always be throwing unexpected twists into the delicate balance.

By *Dawn's Early Light* is a made-for-cable feature, showing that opportunities can pop up anywhere and its shows the viability of that form. Sholder shows talent, but the most important thing for a director to do is tell a good story, and he needs to pick his projects with care.

Alfred Sole (1943–   )

Alice, Sweet Alice (aka *Communion; Holy Terror*, 1977); *Tanya's Island* (1981); *Pandemonium* (1982).

Alice, Sweet Alice stirred quite a bit of comment from horror fans when first released. It created even more of a stir when it was re-released because Brooke Shields, by the time of the re-release a superstar model, appeared as the first murder victim. The film is set in Paterson, New Jersey, in the 1960s and concerns a series of murders in and around a local Catholic church. The prime suspect is a quiet and strange girl named Alice (Paula Sheppard). Her family is unable to deal with her alienation; the Catholic church provides guilt but no real help; and the local police seem useless. Alphonso De-Noble is particularly memorable as the disgusting, overweight landlord who gets graphically knifed midway through the film. The killer hides behind a plastic, smiling mask, long blond hair, and a white dress, presenting a picture of innocence on the one hand and perversity on the other.

While *Alice, Sweet Alice* has an effective decadent atmosphere of corruption and decay, *Tanya's Island* proves to be a rather ridiculous, though sexy, retelling of "Beauty and the Beast." D. D. Winters, a gorgeous black woman, has dreams of a tall, dark and handsome gorilla for a lover. There is a very realistic-looking ape costume courtesy of Rick Baker and Rob Bottin.

However, the whole thing tells us more about producer-writer Pierre Brousseau's sexual fantasies than anything else.

Sole's last film was originally to be titled *Thursday the 12th*, a parody of slasher films, but received scant release as *Pandemonium*. There is an amusing cheerleader shishkabob when the killer throws a javelin through some cheerleaders carrying giant vegetables. The plot has to do with a mad killer at a revived cheerleading school. The hero is Tom Smothers as a Canadian mountie, and Carol Kane appears as an imitation *Carrie*. The film is chockful of dumb gags along the lines of Mickey Rose and Michael Ritchie's *Student Bodies* and Mike Miller's *National Lampoon's Class Reunion*. Not surprisingly, this sophomoric mess has disappeared without a trace.

Ray Dennis Steckler (1939–   )

Drivers in Hell (1961); *Wild Guitar* (1962); *The Incredibly Strange Creatures Who Stopped Living and Became Mixed-Up Zombies* (1962); *The Thrill Killers; Rat Pfink a Boo-Boo* (1964); *Scream of the Butterfly* (1965); *Lemon Grove Kids Meet the Monsters* (1966); *Sinthia, the Devil's Doll* (1968); *Super Cool* (1969); *The Chooper* (aka *Blood Shack*, 1971); *Body Fever* (1972); *The Hollywood Strangler Meets the Skid Row Slasher* (1984).

Ray Dennis Steckler deserves a place in the Motion Picture Hall of Infamy as one of the most inept directors of all time. His greatest legitimate claim to fame was coining one of the longest and goofiest horror titles ever: *The Incredibly Strange Creatures Who Stopped Living and Became Mixed-Up Zombies*. But the film itself, like all of Steckler's work, in no way matched up to the creativity of its title.

Steckler began his film career as an assistant cameraman and became a cinematographer much to his surprise when visiting the set of Timothy Carey's *World's Greatest Sinner* with a friend. When Steckler's friend left, Carey turned to Steckler to continue photographing the film.

Steckler convinced Arch Hall, Sr., to let him direct Arch Hall, Jr., in *Wild Guitar* and thus began his directorial career. It also proved to be the beginning of an acting career when Hall had second thoughts about casting a black actor, Eddie Roland, in the part of the sadistic villain. Worried that a black villain might make the film a difficult sale in the South, he convinced Steckler to essay the part under a pseudonym. Using the name Cash Flagg, Steckler proved himself as abysmal an actor as he was a director. Notably, "Flagg" was never hired to appear in a non–Steckler movie except for Hall's *Eegah!* but he would keep on trotting out his Huntz Hall imitations in his own films.

Steckler came up with the idea of doing *The Incredibly Strange Creatures* when he got his hands on some leftover costumes from a Las

Vegas revue. The most remarkable thing about *Creatures* is that some of Hollywood's top cinematographers, who were just breaking into the business, worked on it including Vilmos Zsigmond, Laszlo Kovacs, and Joe Mascelli. Despite having talented men behind the camera, Steckler did not have any money to put anything interesting in front of the camera, coming up with a story about a gypsy fortuneteller, Madame Estrella (Brett O'Hara), who hypnotizes customers, changes them into zombies by throwing acid in their faces, and keeps them in cages.

Made on a mere $38,000, the film largely involves various dance numbers which are interrupted by the mixed-up zombies, led by Cash Flagg himself, going on a murder spree. The most inventive bit about the movie, apart from being the first horror musical since *Phantom of the Opera*, was that Steckler got the idea of planting monsters in his audience to rampage through the theater when the film was shown for added matinee excitement. Years later, he added a new beginning and released the same film as *Teenage Psycho Meets Bloody Mary*. Later he used the identical gimmicks on *The Thrill Killers* (released years later as *Maniacs on the Loose*).

These films were independently distributed. Often there would be only one print which Steckler would follow around from town to town, making a profit by what is called "four-walling"; that is, he would rent the theater for a limited engagement and then take all box office receipts on the film. When his time was up, he would move on to the next town.

I have not seen *The Thrill Killers*, but according to Michael Weldon in his *Psychotronic Encyclopedia of Film*, it has a prologue in which a hypnotist pretends to hypnotize an audience to convince them that characters can actually come off the screen (actually ushers in masks). The plot apparently is something about three maniacs who escape from an insane asylum and decapitate people.

Unfortunately, I have seen the execrable *Rat Pfink a Boo-Boo*, a definite cinematic "boo-boo" if there ever was one. Made to cash in on TV's *Batman* craze, it features two crime crusaders that are literally clad in long-johns, "Rat Pfink and Boo-Boo" (the title accidentally left off a couple letters, but Steckler did not bother to fix it, figuring "a-boo-boo" sounded like "a-go-go.") The film's biggest expense appears to have been the rental of a Kogar the Gorilla costume in quite shaggy old age, and it features one of the most interminable chase sequences ever put to film.

Steckler also kept busy by photographing *Scream of the Butterfly*, about a loose woman who is murdered by her lover, for director Ebar Lobato. According to Johnny Legend, the film was unsalable until a few second of accidental nudity were reinstated. (There are some who feel that Lobato may be a pseudonym for Steckler, who began to fear that his name was turning people away from his films; given his reputation, it would not be very surprising if that were true.)

Sinthia, the Devil's Doll is supposedly Steckler's favorite and is reportedly a lost film. Steckler then churned out three 30-minute shorts about a pseudo–Bowery Boys group he called The Lemon Grove Kids, and their misadventures were compiled in *The Lemon Grove Kids Meet the Monsters*. The first episode features Carolyn Brandt as a vampire lady and David Miles as "the Green Grasshopper from Outer Space." In the second episode, Flagg foils an attempt to kidnap actress C. B. Beaumont (also played by Carolyn Brandt). The last episode is a plotless ramble into which a mummy and a gorilla are somehow injected (both played by Bob Burns, who starred as the gorilla in the original *Ghostbusters* TV series in the '60s).

Body Fever proved to be an attempt at film noir and was Steckler's last production to actually be credited to him. He decided to revive his career and try again under the name Wolfgang Schmidt, making the films *Blood Shack* and *The Hollywood Strangler Meets the Skid Row Slasher*, which were improvised on the spot without scripted dialogue. Needless to say, they were fully as atrocious as Steckler's other films. Steckler admitted that he did not even think of adding dialogue to *The Hollywood Strangler* until after the film had ostensibly been completed, when backers begged him to add it. Steckler solves the problem by having the killer give a stream-of-consciousness narration throughout the film.

There are rumors of other films including *Revenge of the Ripper, Warning: No Trespassing!; Goof on the Loose; Bloody Jack; The Chickenhawks* and *Terror at Girls' Ranch*, but even if these titles never surface, rest assured you will not be missing much.

Tibor Takacs (1954–   )

Metal Messiah (1977); *The Tomorrow Man* (aka *Prisoner 984*, 1979); *The Gate* (1987); *Hardcover* (1988); *I, Madman* (1989).

Canada's most recent horror director is Tibor Takacs, whose early work shows promise. *The Gate* proved to be a small sleeper, delighting horror fans with some good special effects pulled off on a small budget. The not-so-gory tale revolves around a gate to hell which opens up in a suburban backyard, out of which a demon lord and his minions emerge to wreak some havoc. Two young boys, Glen (Stephen Dorff) and Terry (Louis Tripp), dig open a hole to get some unusual rocks and inadvertently set free the restrained evil thereunder. With their parents gone on vacation, they have no one to turn to to help them out except older sister Al (Christie Denton). Luckily, a heavy metal album provides them with the needed background information on the demon lord when supernatural events start occurring.

Canadian director Tibor Takacs sets up camera placement for a Hell effects shot in Gate II, *completed in 1990 but postponed until 1991 for release.*

While the film lacks originality and takes its time getting things going, it does benefit from Randall Cook's imaginative effects and Takacs' sensitive handling. Though they remain stereotypes, the characters at least become persons the audience can care about. The result was one of the more entertaining if minor horror films of recent years.

I, Madman proved that *The Gate's* success was no fluke. This is the first horror film to deal with an occurrence common to horror readers – that of reading a scary novel that disturbs you but you simply cannot put it down. Virginia (Jenny Wright) is hooked on the trashy horror novels of Malcolm Brand, and in a nice touch imagines herself as the heroine in one of Brand's stories. After enjoying Brand's first book, she comes across a copy of *I, Madman* and to her horror, the events of the book begin to start happening in real life. This leads her to anticipate the next move of a mad killer (Randall William Cook); however, as much as she wants to use her knowledge to prevent the next murder, she cannot convince the police, not even her boyfriend, Richard (Clayton Rohner), who is on the force himself. The murderer is trying to make-over his misshapen features by lopping off parts of his victims and sewing them to his own torso. However, the gruesomeness is kept to a minimum and Cook has a couple of opportunities to showcase his stop-motion technique with a neat subsidiary monster.

Takacs smartly allows for close audience identification without making his film in the least pretentious—this is just smartly directed trash.

Gate 2 is a more ambitious follow-up to the original. The nerdish Terry has now grown up into a typical troubled teen who after the death of his mother is now in the care of an alcoholic father (a typical device to emphasize that the hero must rely on him or herself). Instead of a heavy metal record, Terry unleashes dark forces through the use of a computer in the second go-round, in which he hopes to use their power in a good way. However, it is soon apparent that these are forces beyond his control.

One of Randall Cook's demon minions helps give the film personality by having more of a personality of its own. The minion is something of a gleeful trickster who gets Terry to make a sort of Faustian bargain. Rather than use time-consuming stop-motion, Cook elected to create this film's minion by applying varous foam latex pieces to a ballerina.

Takacs may never turn into a real film artist, but there is always room for a movie-making entertainer who knows how to thrill audiences.

Lewis Teague (1941–)

Dirty O'Neil (codirected with Howard Freen, 1974); *The Lady in Red* (1979); *Alligator* (1980); *Fighting Back* (1982); *Cujo* (1983); *Stephen King's Cat's Eye; The Jewel of the Nile* (1985); *Collision Course* (1988); *Navy Seals* (1990). TELEVISION: *Shannon's Deal (?)*.

Lewis Teague came to the attention of horror film fans with *Alligator*, a surprisingly enjoyable low-budget effort with an amusing script by John Sayles. The whole thing is premised on the old apocryphal story about pet baby alligators growing up in the sewers after being flushed down toilets. In this particular case, the baby alligator also feeds on animal bodies that have been injected with illegal growth hormones and so grows to humongous size.

Policeman David Madison (Robert Forster) and scientist Marisa Kendall (Robin Riker) discover the presence of the menace as it eats its way uptown. They join forces to combat it while the city hires big game hunter Col. Brock (Henry Silva in a hilarious performance) to track down and kill the oversized gator. There are in-joke gags like having a sewer worker alternately addressed as either Ed or Norton. One bizarre sequence has a newspaper photographer who tries to film the monster ending up shooting a roll of the monster devouring him. It is an unpretentious movie with a good sense of humor and of fun.

Teague returned to the horror genre with *Cujo*, a good adaptation of one of Stephen King's weakest works. The novel's most interesting moments were the soap operatic character relationships, but the central menace is nothing more than a rabid St. Bernard, hardly the most terrifying or interesting of menaces. Teague is able to convey a truly claustrophobic feel in a prolonged scene where the dog's owners, mother Donna (Dee Wallace) and son Tad (Danny Pintauro), are trapped in the family Pinto while the giant dog slavers over the outside, and the movie does make a surprising departure from the book for the ending, but the main story itself simply is not that interesting. Still, Teague does carefully build an atmosphere of unease.

Cat's Eye, an anthology film with three stories by Stephen King, unfortunately never quite gels. The film does get off to a good start with its first episode, "Quitters Inc.," which postulates what would happen if the Mafia got involved in quit-smoking programs. James Woods plays an inveterate chain-smoker who seeks help from Dr. Donatti (Alan King), but discovers that Quitters Inc.'s technique involves torturing a loved one by putting her in a room with an electrified floor while Question Mark and the Mysterians play "96 Tears."

The second story does not build up the requisite tension. In it, a gambler named Cressner (Kenneth McMillan) forces his wife's lover, Norris (Robert Hays), to circumnavigate a six-inch ledge around the twentieth story of a building, fighting off strong winds and pecking pigeons.

The whole thing is connected by a cat who wanders from place to place, observing the stories. (As an in-joke, the cat passes by a Fury with a *Christine* bumper sticker in the opening.) The cat itself is involved in the final tale, in which Drew Barrymore is threatened by a soul-sucking troll but is saved thanks to her cat. The film is competently made, but unfortunately King is not the best screen adaptor of his own work.

Since then, Teague has been concentrating on more mainstream movies. He does not seem to have a particular affinity for scare films, but he is versatile enough to handle them when he gets them. He specializes more generally in action films and is best when coupled with a strong screenwriter like John Sayles.

Kevin S. Tenney

Witchboard (1985); *Night of the Demons* (1988); *Peacemaker* (1990).

Kevin S. Tenney is an up-and-coming exploitation director whose films will never be acclaimed as art, but they at least deliver the exploitation values promised (bare-breasted babes and grisly gory deaths).

His first film, *Witchboard,* had Tawney Kitaen making contact via a Ouija board with a dead 11-year-old named David who was killed in a boating accident. In the process of continuing to contact him, Kitaen unwittingly unleashes the spirit of a mass murderer. That spirit dispatches any of Kitaen's friends who try to help her in her predicament as she becomes increasingly possessed by the power of the board. The film helped showcase Tenney's strengths, which include a sense of humor (Kathleen Wilhoite is very funny as a wigged-out punk medium) and performances by the actors that create believable characters whom the audience could conceivably be concerned about.

Night of the Demons has no connection with Tourneur's classic *Night of the Demon* (aka *Curse of the Demon*), but it is another high-energy exploitation film, though this time Tenney also creates some repellent characters whose comeuppance the audience enjoys. The plot resurrects the old chestnut about partying teens spending the night in a haunted house.

The teens make merry in an abandoned funeral home that was once owned by a necrophiliac and is now possessed by evil spirits. The spirits take possession of the party's hostesses, Angela (Mimi Kennkade) and Suzanne (Linnea Quigley, who in the film's most memorable moment injects a stick of lipstick into her nipple — courtesy of her husband, makeup man Steve Johnson).

The good teens are a sweet blonde named Judy (Cathy Podewell) and a frightened black named Rodger (Alexis Alvins). Leading the list of obnoxious teens is Stooge (Hal Havins), whose posturing in a "Pigman" costume suits him. Tenney relies on all the tried-and-true methods of scaring an audience and trying to catch them off guard, as well as adding modern unpleasantries such as tongues bitten off, eyes gouged out, hands burnt, and the usual detritus of the genre. It is far from a memorable horror film and fails to capture even the persuasive imagery of a *Nightmare on Elm Street* film, but it does show some verve on a low budget and evinces a love for and commitment to the genre that puts it above the usual by-the-numbers formula fright film.

Peacemaker, Tenney's next film, is a definite improvement and bodes well for his future even if it did not make much of a splash at the box office. The plot is a variation on Jack Sholder's *The Hidden* and Stephen Herek's *Critters*, with an intergalactic police officer or peacemaker tracking down an intergalactic serial killer on modern-day earth. The twist is that both claim to be the cop, making it difficult for outsiders to know whom to believe. The pair are looking for the last functioning space rover, and each tries to enlist the aid of medical examiner Dori Caisson (Hilary Shepard). Like the zombies in a Romero film, the extraterrestrials can only be killed by massive brain damage, meaning they are able to take enormous amounts of punishment to their torsos with hardly any ill effect. (In a borrowing from one of the few effective moments of Hessler's *Scream and Scream Again*, one of them severs an arm to escape from handcuffs.)

Tenney keeps the action at a relentless high level and shows himself an effective action director. Thomas Jewett's cinematography is also above par for a low-budget feature. Robert Forster and Lance Edwards both deserve kudos for their performances as aliens. Having gained some good experience, Tenney should now attempt something more original, but there is something to be said for someone who can deliver the goods expected from a modest genre film, especially when there are so few directors who can achieve even that much.

Fred Walton

When a Stranger Calls (1979); *Hadley's Rebellion* (1984); *April Fool's Day* (1986); *The Rosary Murders* (1987).
TELEVISION: *Alfred Hitchcock Presents* (codirector with Steve DeJarnatt, Randa Haines and Joel Oliansky, 1985); *I Saw What You Did* (1988); *Trapped* (1989); *Murder in Paradise* (1990).

Walton's *When a Stranger Calls* is for its first third the most effective retelling ever of the old "babysitter murders" urban legend, in which a killer keeps calling a babysitter until she slowly realizes that he is calling from inside the house she is in. Carol Kane is dynamite as Jill Johnson, the babysitter in question, and the film packs some real thrills as Walton builds tension with the persistent calls asking Jill, "Have you checked the children?"

Unfortunately, the middle third of the film takes a bizarre wrong turn and follows the fortunes of Curt Duncan (Tony Beckley) after he gets out of prison several years later. He is hounded by police detective John Clifford (Charles Durning), and so strangely becomes the object of sympathy during this middle third.

The film recovers in its final third as Duncan returns to his old tricks, calling Jill while she is out on a date with her husband. Running home, she finds herself trapped in a deadly game of cat-and-mouse. I do not think I have ever heard a theater scream louder than in the scene where Jill crawls into bed with what she thinks is her husband only for it to turn out to be the killer, an all-time classic "jump." The peculiar structure sabotages the overall effectiveness of the film, originally expanded from a short Walton directed, but there is no denying the tension he was able to create with this little sleeper.

Walton did not return to the horror genre until *April Fool's Day*, a Canadian-made dead-teenager movie in which a mysterious killer knocks off the guests at the island home of Muffy (Deborah Foreman). The twist to this

Producer Frank Mancuso, Jr. (on ladder) and director Fred Walton share a laugh with actors Leah King Pinsent and Griffin O'Neal during a break in filming April Fool's Day. *The film pulls an April Fool's joke on its audience.*

imitation *Friday the 13th* feature is that the whole thing is an elaborate prank which has been perfectly pulled off – as dissatisfying an explanation as has ever been foisted on an audience. The result was bad word of mouth advertising and audiences consequently staying away in droves. It is not badly made for a formulaic little film, but the twist proves a total turn-off and nothing before it is much of a turn-on. It tries to be, of all things, a slasher film in good taste.

Walton's next film, *The Rosary Murders*, was more interesting. A variation on Hitchcock's *I Confess* scripted by Elmore Leonard, it features Donald Sutherland as a priest who discovers through confession who has been killing other Detroit priests. Religious law, unfortunately, forbids him to reveal his information.

Well acted, but slow-going and short on thrills, the film had the misfortune of being released the same week as *A Prayer for the Dying*, another thriller about a priest involved in criminal activities.

Walton has also been active in television, doing a remake of a classic *Alfred Hitchcock Presents* episode for the short-lived revived remake series as well as a not-bad remake of William Castle's *I Saw What You Did*. Walton has shown himself to be able, but he needs to connect with some better material.

Edward D. Wood, Jr. (1924-1978)

Glen or Glenda? (aka *I Led Two Lives; I Changed My Sex; He or She?; The Transvestite*, 1953); *Jail Bait* (1954); *Bride of the Monster* (1955); *Plan 9 from Outer Space* (1959); *The Sinister Urge* (aka *The Young and the Immoral; Hellborn*, 1961); *Take It Out in Trade* (1971); *Necromania; Encyclopedia of Sex* (19??).
TELEVISION: *Crossroads Avenger* (pilot).

Edward Davis Wood, Jr., was born October 10, 1924, in Poughkeepsie, New York the second son of Edward Senior, a postal clerk, and Lillian, a jewelry buyer. Wood developed an early interest in both the theater and movies, directing his first school play at the age of 11. He studied drama in Philadelphia after high school, but then enlisted in the Marines at the start of World War II. He was wounded on Tarawa and again in Guam. After the service, he joined a carnival and ended up in California, where he decided to stay. He wrote, produced, directed and starred in an unsucccessful play called *The Casual Company*, and he tried to launch his first film, a western called *The Streets of Loredo*, shortly afterwards.

While Wood will never be a household word, he gained a certain notoriety when shortly after his death he started to be touted as the worst director of all time. Though his films do raise incompetence almost to a high art, their sheer watchableness refutes the claim. Undoubtedly, Ed Wood was one of the worst scriptwriters filmdom has ever produced or encouraged, as amply demonstrated not only by the scripts he wrote for his own films but also those he did for others, which include such deathless cinematic classics as *The Violent Years, The Bride and the Beast, The Shotgun Wedding*, and *Orgy of the Dead*. He had a positively wooden ear for dialogue, leading to many amusing malapropisms and lines such as, "I'm not nervous – I'm just bubbling over with perspiring enthusiasm."

Enthusiasm is one thing Wood did not lack, leading him to tackle ambitious, often very malformed projects. Nor did he try to hide his oddities of personality, which were exploited after his death for the amusement of snide cineastes. He eventually persuaded exploitation film producer George Weiss to front the money for his first film, *Glen or Glenda?*, a proposed documentary about transvestism. The film is to some extent autobiographical – Wood enjoyed donning women's clothes throughout his life and had a particular fixation on angora sweaters. Wood himself starred in the film as the transvestite under the pseudonym of Daniel Davis.

However, the film changed when Wood befriended a down-and-out Bela Lugosi, who was a recovering drug addict at the time and was eventually hospitalized for the problem in 1954. Wood cast Lugosi as a presiding "Spirit," and gave him odd and often incoherent bits of poetry to spout

The star at the bottom of the picture, "Daniel Davis," is actually director Edward G. Wood, Jr., working under a pseudonym in the infamous Glen or Glenda *(aka* He or She; I Changed My Sex; I Led Two Lives*). This is from a nightmare sequence in the film, but it readily suggests the off-kilter quality of all of Wood's product.*

("Beware big green dragons that sit on your doorstep and eat little boys"). As if that were not strange enough, Wood makes the film seem even more deranged by interspersing stock footage of a steel foundry, a battle from World War II, some buffalo, and shots of lightning between the dull, talky scenes that constitute the heart of the film, a plea for understanding of transvestism. In 1981, Paramount Pictures purchased the rights to the film, hoping to generate a popular cult item, but it received scant bookings or attention. Still, scenes from it appeared as a major portion of *It Came from Hollywood*, a poorly put together compilation of footage from bad movies with even worse comedy filler from Dan Aykroyd, John Candy, Gilda Radner, and Cheech and Chong.

Wood's next film, *Jail Bait*, is a simple crime thriller premised on a puerile "ironic" twist. A gangster involves the son of a plastic surgeon in crime, which gets the son killed. The hood then goes to the boy's father for a new face, and the father obligingly gives him his son's face, insuring that the police will apprehend him.

Wood returned to horror with *Bride of the Monster* (aka *Bride of the Atom; Monster of the Marshes*) which once more starred Bela Lugosi. The story came from American International producer Alex Gordon, who was unable to get financing and turned it over to Wood, who did a rewrite. The financing finally came from Arizona rancher Donald E. McCoy, whose son became the leading man and associate producer. The film ends with a shot of an atomic explosion in order to comply with a request of a backing minister who wanted the film to warn mankind against the dangers of nuclear weaponry.

While the film is more coherent than most of Wood's other work, it is also more boring and no less inept. A leftover prop octopus from *Wake of the Red Witch* becomes the means by which mad scientist Lugosi disposes of his victims. The film marks the first appearance of Wood's continuing character of Kelton the Cop as well as the first time for Tor Johnson, a Swedish wrestler who played the moronic menace Lobo. Harvey B. Dunn, who plays the police captain, had a bird act and insisted on including his feathered friend on his shoulder in all his scenes, which adds an extra level of surrealism.

If that were not enough, the continuity errors are horrendous, with interiors never matching exteriors. Of particular note is Lugosi's lab with its fake rock walls, neon tubes, telephone dial in a control panel, spaghetti strainer helmet, photo enlarger ray gun, and an ever present bottle of Pepto-Bismol among the test tubes.

After the film was completed, Wood worked on four more screenplays for Lugosi: *The Vampire's Tomb, The Ghoul Goes West, The Final Curtain,* and *Revenge of the Dead.* He had shot a few preliminary scenes for *The Vampire's Tomb* when the aging star died. The footage found its way into *Plan 9 from Outer Space,* which became Lugosi's official final film.

The plot of *Plan 9* centers around some humanlike aliens who are desperate to have the earth people "accept their existence" while they are equally anxious to avoid being observed at "the scene of operations." The aliens' secret plan is to resurrect the dead, and they end up terrorizing one small family. *Plan 9* features a remarkable number of non-actors in speaking roles. John Breckinridge and his traveling secretary, David DeMering, found their way into the film by being Paul Marco's houseguests when the film was being made. Because Lugosi was dead, additional scenes with his vampire character were filmed with Tom Mason, Lugosi's chiropractor, who holds a cape over his face to disguise the fact that he really did not resemble the aging actor at all. Businessman J. Edward Reynolds put up financing for the film on the condition that the cast and crew be baptized.

The flying saucers in the film were made out of hubcaps (some say Chevy, others Cadillac) suspended from strings. Wood did not have enough money to get his "day-for-night" shots darkened in the lab, so one chase sequence appears to last several days. The shabbiness of *Plan 9* is evident everywhere, from the cheap cemetery set, built in someone's garage with cardboard crosses that keep falling over, to the airplane cockpit that is no more than a doorway with a curtain, to the reappearance of the lawn furniture inside the main characters' house, to the spaceship set replete with two wooden tables, a cardboard box, a desk and chair. An establishing shot of a general's office in the Pentagon has a Sante Fe Railroad map in the background, which was noticed when it came time to shoot close-ups. The map was kept up, but the Sante Fe logo was removed, so that when the scene plays, it constantly disappears and reappears.

The footage of Bela Lugosi was very meagre, with one shot of Lugosi – walking out of the woods in his Dracula outfit, looking around, and then turning back – being used three separate times. The only other footage of Lugosi was a brief shot Wood had of him leaving Tor Johnson's house with a pained expression. Wood freezes this shot while Lugosi's shadow is still on the lawn, then overdubs the sound of a car crash to indicate the character's death.

The film was a fiasco from start to finish and does deserve its infamous reputation. Wood actually helps matters by including such laughable lines as, "Inspector Clay's been murdered and one thing is for sure – somebody's responsible!" When one character observes, "This is the twentieth century," another counters, "Don't count on it." One really could not be certain in the crazed world of Wood's films. His aliens are especially stilted, as if unfamilar with English ("Life is not so expansive on my planet. We do not cling to it as you do"). However, his earthling dialogue is equally inept.

Other filmmakers have worked with extremely low budgets and done some credible work; however, Wood had no training and no inborn feel for writing and directing. His scenes are consistently static and heavy with dialogue, and he has no real flair for using the visual medium.

Wood filmed a sequel to *Bride of the Monster* called *Revenge of the Dead* (aka *Night of the Ghouls*), involving a con man who pretends to raise the dead and who unexpectedly succeeds with disastrous consequences. It was the last film to feature Paul Marco's characterization of Kelton the Clumsy Cop, but the film was never officially released because Wood was unable to raise the money to pay for the film's developing, though there was a brief sneak preview showing in 1959 for the cast and crew. After the appearance of a Wood cult, the film finally found its way to a video release.

Wood directed the sleazy *The Sinister Urge*, which involved a man seeing explicit photographs of a young woman, tracking her down, raping and killing her, and being tracked down by the police. Wood had a small part in the film. Unable to make regular features, Wood drifted into the world of pornography, where he wrote several porno novels under the pseudonyms Dick Trent and Angora Peters. (The titles include *Devil Girls, TV Lust,*

Killer in Drag, 69 Rue Pigalle, Naked Bones, It Takes One to Know One, Diary of a Transvestite Hooker, And He Rode All Night and *Hollywood Rat Race*.) He directed some porno shorts including *The Final Curtain* and *The Sun Also Sets*, as well as the features *Take It Out in Trade* and *Necromania*. He also worked on Pendulum Publications' *Encyclopedia of Sex* series.

However, Wood's brand of soft-core pornography lost favor and he was unable to continue in the field. In addition, he began having problems with alcoholism and was unable to find work. He died shortly after being evicted from his home on December 10, 1978.

One does have to give Wood credit. Despite his lack of talent, he did get things made, and his friends all spoke of his charm, enthusiasm, and intelligence. No one else is likely to have scripted as wonky a picture as *The Bride and the Beast*, where a woman who is drawn to angora sweaters discovers she was a gorilla in her previous life and goes off to live contentedly with the gorillas in the jungle. One can laugh derisively, but Wood shows that if you are willing to work hard enough, there is still a place for the weird in the world of moviemaking.

Jim Wynorski (1950–   )

The Lost Empire (1984); *Chopping Mall* (aka *Killbots*, 1986); *Deathstalker II; Big Bad Mama 2* (1987); *Not of This Earth* (1988); *The Return of Swamp Thing* (1989); *The Haunting of Maurella; Transylvania Twist* (1990).
DIRECT-TO-CABLE FILMS: *Nighty Nightmares; Tower of Terror* (1989).

Jim Wynorski is a longtime horror film fan, but unlike many other fans turned filmmakers, Wynorski has managed to keep his sense of humor about the exploitation field while delivering the kind of material exploitation audiences expect. Like many other filmmakers, Wynorksi got his start working for Roger Corman, for whom he would quickly script knock-off imitations of popular films. When *Sword and the Sorcerer* proved that "sword and sorcery" films could be popular, and *Conan the Barbarian* was about to come out, Wynorski came up with the outrageous script for *Sorceress* to be directed by Jack Hill, who did the cult classic *Spider Baby*. Wynorski's *Porky's* rip-off, *Screwballs*, was actually funnier than the film it was imitating and was one of the better teen sex comedies of the period.

Wynorski finally got his chance to write and direct and feature with *The Lost Empire*, which sent up several type of exploitation films with a straight face and utilized stock footage from *Our Man Flint*. The film showed that Wynorski was no Orson Welles, but he did have a lively sense of action and humor.

Killbots followed, in which Wynorski hoped to cash in on the popularity

Actor Dick Durok once more becomes a big green plant man in Jim Wynorski's Return of Swamp Thing, *complete with typical Wynorski cornball dialogue.*

of Japanese robot toys which had taken the kiddie market by storm. He resurrects the Paul and Mary Bland characters from the cult comedy *Eating Raoul* (played by Paul Bartel and Mary Woronov) for his opening scenes, and has Corman character actors like Dick Miller help pad out the sequences between those starring his teen leads. The film failed initially, though it did better with a revised ad campaign and a new title, *Chopping Mall*. The plot concerned security robots who malfunction and become overzealous at their job, killing some teens and janitors trapped inside a shopping mall after hours.

At that time, Wynorski became a specialist in sequels, particularly to those films that had performed well on videotape, making cheapie follow-ups that would likely be ordered from the same video rental places that the initial films had done well in. This is what led to Wynorski's filming *Death-stalker II, Big Bad Mama 2,* and *The Return of Swamp Thing,* all of which are studded with examples of Wynorski's sophomoric sense of humor, though admittedly they are not boring.

Not of This Earth was a surprise mini-hit in which Wynorski cannily exploited the fact that it was underage porn star Traci Lords' first legitimate movie. The film was practically a scene-by-scene remake of Roger Corman's original *Not of This Earth* with the bums written out and top-heavy hookers put in their places. The opening credit sequence is a compilation of stock footage of Corman's New World science fiction pictures, and an entire sequence is lifted out of Joe Dante and Allan Arkush's *Hollywood Boulevard* to help pad out cheaply the scant running time.

According to the not always accurate Wynorski, the film was created as part of a bet Wynorski had with Corman that he could produce a movie as quickly and as cheaply as Corman had done back in the '50s. Corman felt it could not be done, but while Corman was on vacation, Wynorski pulled off the feat. Faced with a *fait accompli,* Corman released the film to general critical disdain but definite profit, though the original Corman version is still superior.

Except for *The Haunting of Maurella,* which is a serious attempt at making a period Poe-style picture, Wynorski's most recent projects have all been exploitation horror-comedies, designed to feature attractive female heroines and get them into negligees as quickly as possible. Both *Nighty Nightmares* and *Tower of Terror,* directed under the pseudonym Arch Stanton after a character in *The Good, the Bad, and the Ugly,* were inexpensively shot for the direct to video and cable market.

Wynorski obviously loves sleazy movies with plenty of action and good-looking females prancing about naked as often as possible. He always seems to have his tongue planted firmly in his cheek, which makes his films more palatable. While he will never be a cinematic stylist, at least there is an exploitation filmmaker left with a sense of pacing and of fun.

Appendix:
Classic Horror Films
by Non-Horror Directors

While most of the significant horror films have been made by the directors covered in this book, there have been a few classics which were the solo
flight into the genre by some major directors and which should not be overlooked. In fact, some of the genre's best works were created by the one- or
two-excursion directors. They include the following:

Carl Theodor Dreyer's *Vampyr* (1931) is a pictorially beautiful, nearly
silent and highly atmospheric film centering around a traveler who encounters a female vampire and a doctor henchman. The film contains some
indelible images: a scythe-carrying figure which looks like death ringing a
bell; a man whose shadow walks away from him; a man who looks helplessly
on while he is buried alive; and the final destruction of the vampire in a cloud
of white flour which buries her. The film has a hazy, hypnotic, dream-like
quality that is unforgettable.

Rouben Mamoulian's *Dr. Jekyll and Mr. Hyde* (1931) is still the
definitive representation of this classic Robert Louis Stevenson story. Fredric March won the Best Actor Oscar for his portrayal of Dr. Jekyll, making
him the only actor to win that distinction for a horror film, though Linda
Blair was nominated for *The Exorcist*, as was Sigourney Weaver for *Aliens*.
The film is visually quite inventive, with a long, subjective camera shot opening; the famous transformation without dissolves (created by using colored
makeup and filters by Karl Struss); a 360° pan around Dr. Jekyll's laboratory; and creative use of wipes to split the screen and suggest dominating
influences. Mamoulian saw Jekyll as a conflict not between good and evil,
as was traditional, but between man's civilized and primitive sides. He insisted that Hyde be given a Neanderthal appearance to suggest his regres-
sion. Miriam Hopkins shines as a coquettish prostitute who uses her leg to
lure Dr. Jekyll only to have Hyde come back and force himself upon her as
her lover. Ultimately, we see that the brutish Hyde is the result of Jekyll's
repressed sexuality, which he had hoped to unleash using his formula. Unquestionably an intelligent film and a classic in the genre.

Alberto Cavalcanti's sequence in *Dead of Night* (1945) with Michael Redgrave as a ventriloquist who develops a dual personality, presuming his mechanical dummy has come to life, is another cinematic highpoint, though the story has been retold so often by lesser hands that much of its impact has dissipated. *Dead of Night* was one of the earliest horror anthology films, and not all of its parts hold up equally well, but its tricky framing story did a wonderful job of conveying the idea of a nightmare replaying itself endlessly, and it evokes a comfortable British drawing room where ghost stories, both amusing and frightening, are told until the terrors talked about seem to start intruding on the real world. People will also remember the hokey joke about "room for one more," and while a Christmas episode also directed by Cavalcanti about a young girl who discovers she has been consoling the spirit of a dead child at a party does not come off with the proper *frisson*, Robert Hamer's sketch about a haunted mirror that looks out on another time and draws a man into strangling his wife does. The film does not scare anymore, and it shows a kind of British reserve in its approach for most of its length, but it is undeniably a class act and has been an important film in the development of the horror genre.

Henri-Georges Clouzot's *Les Diaboliques* or simply *Diabolique* (1955) was highly influential on a vast number of '50s and '60s chillers, particularly the films of William Castle and all those films about someone trying to drive another person insane or scare him to death which cropped up in the '60s. *Diabolique* builds slowly as a wife and a schoolteacher murder the wife's husband by drowning him in a tub only to have his body mysteriously disappear. The climax is one of the scariest things in the history of cinema, utterly unforgettable, and consequently has been much imitated, most recently in Adrian Lyne's *Fatal Attraction* (1987). Clouzot is a vastly underrated French director who made several brilliant films including the classic suspense thriller *The Wages of Fear*; a look at the web of hatred and complicity created by a poison pen writer in *Le Corbeau (The Crow)*; a daring interpretation of Claude Pagnol's *Manon of the Springs* in *Manon*; and the one-of-a-kind creation of *The Mystery of Picasso*, a photographic exploration of how Picasso painted, using time lapse photography to show all the changes, blind alleys, etc., that Picasso went through in the process of creating. (The pictures seen are available only on film per an agreement with Picasso, which stipulated that all canvases were burnt after filming.)

Andre de Toth's *House of Wax* (1953) is not only significant for being the best of the color 3-D horror films and for signaling a change in the course of Vincent Price's career; it is also one of the most feminist of horror films, with Phyllis Kirk as the strong female hero who struggles against male condescension to solve the mystery of what Price's vengeful sculptor has been doing to get his wax figures. As in all of de Toth's work the film features quiet acting, sudden violence, and moral corruption rendered with clear-eyed sophistication. Amazingly, de Toth has only one eye and could not even see the 3-D process he was shooting in.

Charles Laughton's *Night of the Hunter* (1955), based on Dennis Grubb's novel, is a flawed American masterpiece, which makes it all the more unfortunate that Laughton never directed another film, though he was scheduled to do the adaptation of Norman Mailer's *The Naked and the Dead* before Raoul Walsh took over. The film is brilliantly photographed by Stanley Cortez (*Magnificent Ambersons*) and is a compendium of filmmaking styles from Griffith-style naturalism to German expressionism. Rich with imagery, inventive with cinematic approaches and angles, meaningful in the way it conveys its story visually, it also features Robert Mitchum's most daring performance as the memorable mad preacher with "love" tattooed on one hand and "hate" on the other. Mitchum's character is both comic and menacing at the same time, a daring feat which Mitchum and Laughton pull off brilliantly.

Kenji Mizoguchi's *Ugetsu Monogatari* (1953) is a masterpiece from one of Japan's top directors. The film brilliantly fuses reality and fantasy in a tale of poor Japanese potters who forsake their wives to seek their fortunes. One potter falls in love with the ghost of a deceased Japanese Lady Wakasa. They enjoy an enchanted idyll, but reality obtrudes, bursting the man's bubble forever. By the time he returns home to his wife, she has died as well and is a ghost too. Mizoguchi is known as a feminist filmmaker for the way he portrayed women paying for men's negligent sins, and this film certainly supports that claim. It is haunting, beautiful, moving and unforgettable – a rare combination in a horror film or any other effort.

Alfred Hitchcock directed only two horror films, *Psycho* (1960) and *The Birds* (1963), but the first of these is a masterpiece and one of the most written-about films of all time. Hitchcock established himself as the premier director in the suspense field, and a great many horror directors owe him a debt of gratitude for helping establish various suspense conventions which they have appropriated. Though the famous shower scene was designed shot-for-shot by the brilliant Saul Bass, the film is still Hitchcock's in its manipulation of characters, motivations, and events. *The Birds* was far less successful, a fatty film that dragged on too long, but it too has moments of brilliance – especially the scenes of the birds gathering outside the schoolyard and the actual bird attacks which are beautifully cut together for maximal impact. It launched a spate of imitative animal attack movies.

Robert Aldrich is a director who deserves more attention than he has received, having created a near masterpiece in *Kiss Me Deadly*, executed some excellent action films (*Attack!; Vera Cruz; Ulzana's Raid*), and directed two very influential horror films, *What Ever Happened to Baby Jane?* and *Hush . . . Hush, Sweet Charlotte*. Each of these latter two films features a fevered performance by Bette Davis and has moments of true hysterical poetry. Sparks flew between Davis and costar Joan Crawford on the set of *Baby Jane*, causing the sisters' hatred of each other to seem all the more deep and real. Each film relies wonderfully on Gothic atmosphere and turns on a battle of nerves. Each ended up being far superior to its numerous imitators.

Michael Powell's *Peeping Tom* (1960) has been called one of the supreme achievements of the British cinema, and while that is a trifle hyperbolic, it is certainly one of the most reflexive movies ever made. The subject is voyeurism, the human "need" to look, an apt metaphor for cinemagoing itself. The story focuses around a repressed young man (Carl Boehm), who as a child was constantly filmed while subjected to cruel psychological tests by his father. The young man has grown up to be a cameraman who has a similar desire to capture intense emotions on film, causing him to rape his victims with his camera in a figurative sense while impaling their bodies with a tripod spike effecting penetration in a literal sense. *Peeping Tom* has plenty to make the intelligent viewer uncomfortable, and that worked against the film when it opened, as it was almost universally reviled despite Powell's reputation as one of Britain's premier filmmakers who has co-directed such classics as *Thief of Bagdad, The Red Shoes, Black Narcissus* and *A Matter of Life and Death*.

Herk Harvey's *Carnival of Souls* (1962) is worth mentioning if only to show what a haunting and disturbing little movie can be made for almost no budget. Candace Hilligoss plays a church organist who suffers an auto accident but appears to have emerged unscathed. Only slowly does she recognize that she is dead and walking in a dream world, haunted by the sinister appearance of the Strange Man (Harvey himself). Scenes shot at a derelict amusement park are particularly moody, atmospheric, and memorable. It's a film that plays like a dream turned into a nightmare.

Georges Franju's *Les Yeux Sans Visage* (aka *Eyes Without a Face* or *The Horror Chamber of Dr. Faustus*, 1959), is another horror film with un-forgettable imagery and a bleak, despairing mood. It tells the story of a mad surgeon (Pierre Brasseur) intent on using skin grafts to restore the beauty of his daughter (Edith Scob), whose face was destroyed in a car crash. Scob wanders through the film like a wistful spirit in an immobile but nonetheless incredibly expressive mask, watching with pained eyes as her father destroys the beauty of one woman after another to accomplish his goal.

While horror fans cringe at the memory of the surgeon graphically peel-ing the skin off one of his victim's faces, what I will always carry away from the film is its eerie and poetic beauty, particularly in the last shots after Scob has killed her father and frees the dogs and birds he kept locked up, ex-pressing visually her own feelings of having escaped a horrible cage. The result is extraordinary and mesmerizing.

851 *Appendix*

Masaki Kobayashi's *Kwaidan* (1964) with its artificiality did not inspire many imitators, but its virtues are quite apparent – strong imagery, haunting atmosphere, memorable moments. Particularly strong are the tales about a "Snow Maiden" who lures men to their death and, especially, an elaborate tale called "Hoichi the Earless" about a blind biwa player who is summoned by spirits to recite his saga of the ill-fated Heike clan's defeat at the hands of the Taira clan. Hoichi has been protected by a monk who painted protective symbols all over his body, but the monk overlooked Hoichi's ears, which are ripped off by the emotionally stirred-up spirits. The movie is both highly stylized and extremely colorful, rich and exotic.

Another classic but perhaps underappreciated film is Peter Bogdanovich's *Targets* (1968), which came about because Boris Karloff owed Roger Corman a few days' more work. Corman told Bogdanovich that he could incorporate footage from *The Terror* and make a cheap new film, but Bogdanovich did something clever and quite unexpected. He decided to contrast the old-fashioned type of horror film represented by Karloff with the modern-day horrors of a Charlie Starkweather, the lone gunman who shoots people from an isolated tower. The film gave Karloff his last meaty role as old-time horror star Byron Orlok, who has been persuaded to attend the drive-in premiere of his latest horror epic. Meanwhile, Bobby Thompson (Tim O'Kelly) is an alienated youth living in his parents' home with his young wife, Ilene (Tanya Morgan). His father is a gun nut, and there is some repressed hostility between the two. Something snaps in Bobby's personality and he shoots his family and heads to a nearby freeway to snipe at others. The results are suitably horrifying. Eventually Bobby ends up at the drive-in where Orlok is appearing. In the memorable climax, the confused Bobby sees Orlok both on the screen and in real life as the courageous horror star puts an end to the slaughter by confronting him. The film is an indictment of America's capacity for violence and the easy accessibility of guns and ammunition, so that all of us are targets. Bogdanovich cannily sets up how helpless people are before a sniper as we observe Bobby lining up his sites time and time again while his victims are oblivious to their danger.

Clint Eastwood starred in *Tightrope*, which was a horror film of the mad stalker genre disguised as a police thriller while aping most of the clichés of the genre. It received some surprising critical acclaim, but his main horror film still is the classic he directed as well as starred in, *Play Misty for Me* (1971), which obviously exercised a strong influence on 1987's *Fatal Attraction*. Jessica Walter plays a harridan whose grasp of reality is tenuous at best and who does not understand that the disc jockey she is in love with (Eastwood) does not return her obsessive love. This film is a virtual compendium of male fears about out-of-control females who can switch from loving to hateful in an instant and are capable of the most excessive acts upon the slightest provocation. Eastwood has also dabbled in supernatural themes in his *Pale Rider*, a pale imitation of the classic *Shane*, and in the Leone-inspired *High Plains Drifter* in which a vengeful spirit literally paints a town red and turns it into Hell on earth.

Robin Hardy's *The Wicker Man* (1972) is another one-of-a-kind film, this time with a highly intelligent script by Anthony Schaffer (*Sleuth*) and sterling performances from Edward Woodward and Christopher Lee. Woodward plays an extremely repressed and religious policeman searching for a missing girl on what he discovers to be a pagan island, while Lee is the sardonic lord of that isle. The film became something of a *cause célèbre* because its distributor hacked it up and virtually buried it on initial release, but eventually an almost uncut version was released. The film is not intended to be frightening, but rather vividly contrasts pagan and Christian ideologies, giving demonstrations of ancient pagan practices and beliefs, culminating in different attitudes to human sacrifice. It is a religious treatise presented as a cunningly conceived mystery.

Another often overlooked film is Robert Mulligan's *The Other* (1972), based on the Thomas Tryon best seller. It is the story of twins, one of whom (Chris Udvarnoky) feels that his identical brother (Martin Udvarnoky) is doing terrible things. The film is a lush piece of nostalgia with twinning images and incidents throughout. The twins' grandmother (Uta Hagen) has taught them how to project their thoughts onto other things and suddenly realizes that the game is not so innocent as it appears. The film is limned with beautiful parallels, the most memorable being a deformed fetus the twins see at a freak show and the later appearance of a baby drowned in a wine casket. Mulligan has finely crafted an eerie, disturbing, and very atmospheric fright film.

Nicolas Roeg crafted a classic psychic thriller with *Don't Look Now* (1973), based on the Daphne Du Maurier short story (Du Maurier also supplied the story for *The Birds*). The film is very rich in imagery and is very sensual and senuous – the love scenes between Donald Sutherland and Julie Christie became famous for the time. The film begins when the world of Laura and John Baxter (Christie and Sutherland) is shattered by the unexpected death of their daughter, which John had a premonition of but arrived too late to prevent. Later, by again ignoring his premonitions, John insures his own immolation. It is a wondrously detailed and realized film, fully deserving of classic status.

Douglas Hickox's *Theatre of Blood* (1973) has become a favorite of anyone who hates critics, with its story of hammy Shakespearean actor Edward Lionheart (Vincent Price), who murders the critics who denied him a best actor award after the fashion of murders in Shakespeare's plays. Anthony Greville-Bell's script is full of subtle and obvious Shakespearean references and some very funny lines, delivered by an extremely able cast of British players, including Diana Rigg, Ian Hendry, Coral Browne, Robert Coote,

Jack Hawkins, Arthur Lowe, and Robert Morley. The excessive gore of the uncut version becomes part of the joke, and the film is patterned after the stylishness of Robert Fuest's films (see chapter on Fuest).

Werner Herzog's remake of *Nosferatu: Phantom der Nacht* (1979) was a stylish retelling of the Murnau original that in many ways was superior to the original. An attempt was made to film it in English as well as German, but most of the cast was not up to it, so the only available English verison is a subtitled one. Klaus Kinski pays the monstrous vampire in makeup clearly patterned after Max Schreck's with huge malformed ears, blue skin, and rodent-like teeth. Yet despite his vampire's power, he limns the most pitiable vampire to hit the screen, one operating under a terrible ravaging disease that is most definitely a curse. Vampirism becomes equated with the plague in the film, and it spreads the way plague-bearing rodents invade the town of Bremen. Sadly, despite its wonderful use of shadows, mood, and atmosphere, the film was largely spurned and ridiculed.

Another important horror film, the quality of which was not appreciated upon initial release, was Stanley Kubrick's adaptation of Stephen King's novel *The Shining* (1980). Star Jack Nicholson gave more to Kubrick than any other director had ever asked of him, and it is a performance that some say goes over the top. However, there is no denying that it is also a classic, smartass, funny performance in which Nicholson clearly shows his mental disintegration in an entertaining fashion while retaining his menace. The film thwarted the expectations of those who had read the book, but Kubrick and coscreenwrter Diane Johnson were after a less conventional tale. The subject of the film is the disintegration of an American family, with Jack Torrance's wife, Wendy (Shelley Duvall), never quite trusting Jack again after he hurt the arm of their son, Danny (Danny Lloyd), while in a drunken stupor. Consumed by guilt and by anger at being made to feel guilty, Torrance falls under the eternal evil influences present at the Overlook Hotel, where he had been hired as caretaker. The film stands up to repeat viewings with very stylish camera work, some unforgettable imagery (those elevators full of blood), and several blackly comic performances. Kubrick explodes the conventions of claustrophobic horror with a huge, opulent setting where mirrors reveal the ghostly influences and even little Danny's psychic power, the "shining" of the title, exposes him to the horror as much as it helps save him and his mother.

In 1990, two major directors that had hits in the horror genre tried again. William Friedkin, whose film *The Exorcist* is still one of the biggest horror hits of all-time, spawning two unsuccessful sequels to the original film (John Boorman's beautiful but erratic *Exorcist II: The Heretic* [1977] which gambled with appearing ludicrous and lost; and the novel's originator, William Peter Blatty's own *Exorcist III* [1990], based on his novel *Legion*, which was hastily given some added footage when it was realized that the film Blatty delivered did not have a single exorcism in it). Friedkin also directed "Nightcrawlers," perhaps the most intense episode of the new *Twilight Zone* TV series based on Robert McCammon's story about a Vietnam veteran who brings the ghosts of the war with him wherever he goes, so expectations were high when it was announced that he was adapting Dan Greenberg's horror story "The Nanny." Unfortunately, the resulting film, *The Guardian* (1990), proved to be a somewhat stylish exercise about a dryad or tree spirit (played by Jenny Seagrove) who plans to sacrifice the young child of a yuppie couple. There are some impressive baby's eye view perspectives executed by John Alonzo, but the whole enterprise never recovers from the ludicrousness of being about a killer tree that absorbs babies' souls.

Better by far was Nicolas Roeg's return to the genre with his delightful adaptation of the Roald Dahl's children's book *The Witches*. Featuring an absolutely delightful performance by Anjelica Huston as the Grand High Witch who is intent on changing all young children into mice courtesy of the makeup wizardry of Jim Henson (his final film before he died of pneumonia), the film plays with the mythology of witchcraft and demonstrates that children's films do not have to be unsophisticated and uninteresting for adults. Jasen Fisher is also great as the nine-year-old who slowly uncovers the witches' nefarious plan to poison Britain's chocolates, and who must survive being turned into a mouse to thwart these hags' heinous plot.

Annotated Bibliography

Books

Anderson, Craig W. *Science Fiction Films of the Seventies*. Jefferson, North Carolina: McFarland, 1985.
   A picture-by-picture look at the major films. Useful for its section on Larry Cohen's first two *It's Alive* films.
Balun, Chas., ed. *The Deep Red Horror Handbook*. Albany, New York: Fantaco, 1989.
   A hodgepodge of information about modern horror films with primary focus on gory and peripheral films. Balun and his fellow writers seem primarily concerned with films that are either gory or provoke queasiness rather than other considerations of quality, but they offer a cornucopia of information. Balun has also written *The Gore Score: Ultraviolent Horror in the '80s* and *Horror Holocaust*.
Bare, Richard L. *The Film Director: A Practical Guide to Motion Picture and Television Techniques*. New York: Collier Books, 1971.
   Bare is a working film and television director whose work is more craftsmanlike than artistic. However, he presents a clear, straightforward account of a director's responsibilities on a film and how to achieve them.
Beck, Calvin Thomas. *Heroes of the Horrors*. New York: Macmillan, 1975.
_____, with Robert Stewart. *Scream Queens: Heroines of the Horrors*. New York: Macmillan, 1978.
   These books cover the major horror stars' filmographies film by film. Though only six male horror stars are covered, the companion volume recounts the careers of 28 actresses and one female director, Stephanie Rothman. The writers of these volumes (Stewart worked on both but is credited only on the second) were writer/editors of *Castle of Frankenstein* magazine and generally know their material.
Behlmer, Rudy. *America's Favorite Movies: Behind the Scenes*. New York: Ungar, 1982.
   Has interesting chapter on the making of Whale's *Frankenstein*.
Belton, John. *The Hollywood Professionals. Vol. 3: Howard Hawks, Frank Borzage, Edgar G. Ulmer*. New York: Tantivy, 1974.
   Has excellent chapter on the films of Edgar G. Ulmer.
Bliss, Michael. *Brian De Palma*. Metuchen, New Jersey: Scarecrow, 1983.
   Good book-length overview of De Palma's horror films.
Bojarski, Richard. *The Films of Bela Lugosi*. Secaucus, New Jersey: Citadel, 1980.

855

Some interesting tidbits and one of the few books to cover some of the more obscure horror films that Lugosi appeared in.

Bouzereau, Laurent. *The DePalma Cut: The Films of America's Most Controversial Director*. New York: Dembner Books, 1988.
Less pretentious and more straightforward look at De Palma's films than the Bliss book with well-researched behind-the-scenes information; however, does not do the early De Palma films justice in its limited coverage.

Briggs, Joe Bob. *Joe Bob Goes to the Drive-In*. New York: Delacorte, 1987.
Joe Bob Briggs is the pseudonym for film reviewer John Bloom. This book is primarily intended as humor but contains plenty of information in a series of tongue-in-cheek, redneck-style reviews written for the *Dallas Times Herald*.

———. *Joe Bob Goes Back to the Drive-In*. New York: Delacorte Press, 1990.
More jokey drive-in reviews, but less valuable than the original collection as writer John Bloom concentrates more on the mythical background for his infamous drive-in critic.

Brosnan, John. *The Horror People*. New York: New American Library, 1976.
A hodgepode, cut-and-paste book with interesting material on Tod Browning, Roy Ward Baker, William Castle, Roger Corman, Freddie Francis, Karl Freund and James Whale.

Butler, Ivan. *The Cinema of Roman Polanski*. New York: Barnes, 1970.
———. *Horror in the Cinema*. New York: Warner Paperback Library, 1970.
Both of these Butler books are worthwhile. The first is an indispensable look at Roman Polanski's early, horror-influenced career, and the second is an early look at the development of the horror field.

Castle, William. *Step Right Up, I'm Gonna Scare the Pants Off America*. New York: Putnam, 1976.
Castle's anecdote-filled autobiography was invaluable for his chapter.

Clarens, Carlos. *An Illustrated History of the Horror Film*. New York: Capricorn, 1968.
A seminal work, the first serious and scholarly look at the horror film genre. The book is flawed in that it contains descriptions of films that Clarens never saw (particularly in the silent section), gives most films superficial coverage, and seems uninterested in post-'40s horror films. Nevertheless, it is an important early work.

Coursodon, Jean-Pierre, with Pierre Sauvage. *American Directors. Vols. I & II*. New York: McGraw-Hill, 1983.
Intelligent assessments of the careers of most major American directors, far more thought-out and detailed than Sarris' more famous volume.

Curtis, James. *James Whale*. Metuchen, New Jersey: Scarecrow, 1982.
An excellent and thus far the only book-length look at Whale and his career.

Daniels, Les. *Fear: A History of Horror in the Mass Media*. London: Granada, 1977.
A book on horror in general reprinting several short stories, with a longish chapter on horror films.

Derry, Charles. *Dark Dreams: A Psychological History of the Modern Horror Film*. Cranbury, New Jersey: Barnes, 1977.
A good account of how horror changed in the '60s and early '70s, concentrating on the horror subgenres of the psycho film and *The Exorcist* spin-offs. Has useful material on the films of Castle and Harrington.

Dillard, R. H. W. *Horror Films.* New York: Monarch, 1976.

From the screenwriter of *Frankenstein Meets the Space Monster,* a peculiar book on horror films detailing only four movies: *Frankenstein, The Wolf Man, Night of the Living Dead* and *Satyricon.* Limited by fuzzy photos and short length, Dillard does make a case for the poetry of horror movies.

Dunn, Linwood G., and George E. Turner. *The ASC Treasury of Visual Effects.* Hollywood: American Society of Cinematographers, 1983.

Wonderful collection of articles from the pages of *American Cinematographer.* The chapter on *The Invisible Man* was very useful. Turner is also the coauthor of the excellent *Making of King Kong* and *Forgotten Horrors.*

Everson, William K. *Classics of the Horror Film.* Secaucus, New Jersey: Citadel, 1974.

_____. *More Classics of the Horror Film.* Secaucus, New Jersey: Citadel, 1986.

Everson is one of the world's premier film historians and gives an informed look at many classic horror films, several of which have been relatively overlooked and forgotten. He does not care much for post-'40s horror films, however, and is strongest on films from the '30s and '40s.

Frank, Alan G. *Horror Movies.* London: Octopus, 1976(?).

_____. *Monsters and Vampires.* London: Cathay, 1976.

Both of these volumes are primarily intended as picture books, though Frank clearly knows the field. The second is thunderingly literal in its title, the first is better, but both are hampered by limited space.

Gagne, Paul R. *The Zombies That Ate Pittsburgh: The Films of George A. Romero.* New York: Dodd, Mead, 1987.

A well-researched, very detailed, and fairly uncritical look at Romero's films and how they got made.

Gifford, Denis. *Karloff: The Man, the Monster, the Movies.* New York: Curtis, 1973.

_____. *Movie Monsters.* New York: Studio Vista/Dutton, 1969.

_____. *A Pictorial History of Horror Movies.* London: Hamlyn, 1973.

Gifford is a very careful film researcher, as evidenced by the Karloff book, which contains complete credits on all of Karloff's films as well as summaries and reviews. The other two books are primarily pictures, though *Movie Monsters* does feature fairly complete filmographies on variations of the basic monster theme for the time, and *Pictorial History* pays attention to several otherwise neglected B films. However Gifford hates Hammer movies and has very little to say about post-'50s movies.

Glut, Don. *Classic Movie Monsters.* Metuchen, New Jersey: Scarecrow, 1978.

_____. *The Frankenstein Legend.* Metuchen, New Jersey: Scarecrow, 1973.

Both of these tomes are excellent and thoroughly researched presentations on their respective subjects, following how different media have treated the different monsters, but concentrating on film. These are genuine treasure troves for any horror movie fan.

Grant, Barry Keith, ed. *Planks of Reason: Essays on the Horror Film.* Metuchen, New Jersey: Scarecrow, 1984.

Probably the most pretentious volume on the horror film genre ever concocted. Frequently reads things in that the filmmakers never intended. It is hard to know whether to describe this as a semiotic reading or a semi-idiotic one.

Greenberg, Harvey R. *The Movies on Your Mind*. New York: E. P. Dutton, 1975.
Psychoanalyzes the world's most popular movies, including *Psycho, Dracula, Frankenstein* and *King Kong* with a pop psychology approach.

Halliwell, Leslie. *The Dead That Walk*. London: Paladin/Grafton, 1986.
Famed compiler of the *Filmgoer's Companion* does a poor job of covering the horror genre in this ultimate cut-and-paste book. Large sections of public domain writings are reprinted, numerous errors crop up, and Halliwell obviously relied on scripts rather than films for his synopses. Still, it does contain material edited out of *Bride of Frankenstein*.

Hardy, Phil, ed. *The Encyclopedia of Horror Movies*. New York: Harper & Row, 1986.
Has far more extensive information on foreign horror films than any other publication, but it is also flawed by relying on inaccurate pressbooks and borrowing materials uncredited from numerous sources. Still, despite the errors, it is a highly worthwhile and major work on the genre.

Higham, Charles, and Joel Greenberg. *The Celluloid Muse: Hollywood Directors Speak*. New York: New American Library/Signet, 1969.
An excellent collection of interviews with various directors. Useful for the chapters on Mark Robson and Jacques Tourneur.

Hoberman, J., and Jonathan Rosenbaum. *Midnight Movies*. New York: Harper & Row, 1983.
Good survey of the major cult films including sections on *Rocky Horror Picture Show, El Topo, Night of the Living Dead, Martin*, John Waters' films, and *Eraserhead*.

Hogan, David. *Dark Romance: Sexuality in the Horror Film*. Jefferson, North Carolina: McFarland, 1986.
Though one wishes at times the book would go further, this is a knowledgeable and intelligent look at how sex has been combined with horror.

Jensen, Paul M. *Boris Karloff and His Films*. Cranbury, New Jersey: Barnes, 1974.
Jensen is a sharp and incisive critic who gives the films of Karloff their due. Offers some very perceptive comments on the work of Whale and Freund.

Katz, Ephraim. *The Film Encyclopedia*. New York: Perigee, 1982.
Simply put, the best single-volume film encyclopedia ever. Invaluable.

King, Stephen. *Stephen King's Danse Macabre*. New York: Berkley, 1981.
King's book is not well-organized but simply a hodgepodge of whatever King felt like writing about at the time; however, some of his remarks on horror films do offer perceptive insights.

Leaming, Barbara. *Polanski: The Filmmaker as Voyeur*. New York: Simon and Schuster, 1981.
Leaming relates Polanski's films to her personal life in this semi-biography which traces the theme of voyeurism throughout his films.

Lee, Walt. *Reference Guide to Fantastic Films: Science Fiction, Fantasy & Horror*. 3 vols. Los Angeles: Chelsea-Lee, 1972.
A highly impressive and accurate collection of credits on 40,000 fantasy films from the beginning to 1972. Capsule descriptions provided by Bill Warren explain why each film was included. Excellent, but overdue for an update.

McCarthy, John. *The Official Splatter Movie Guide.* New York: St. Martin's, 1989.

———. *Psychos: Eighty Years of Mad Movies, Maniacs, and Murderous Deeds.* New York: St. Martin's, 1986.

———. *Splatter Movies: Breaking the Last Taboo of the Screen.* New York: St. Martin's, 1984.

———. *Video Screams.* Albany, New York FantaCo, 1983.

McCarthy is an author who knows the field, with assessments from the on-target to the superficial. The first and last works are books of capsule reviews with *Movie Guide* far outweighing *Video Screams* in quality. *Splatter Movies* was important in defining the genre for the '80s, and *Psychos* does a decent job of defining its subgenre. Neither is a brilliant work, but both contain material of interest.

McCarthy, Todd, and Charles Flynn, eds. *Kings of the Bs: Working Within the Hollywood System.* New York: Dutton, 1975.

An excellent and indispensable volume on Hollywood B movie directors.

McGee, Mark Thomas. *Fast and Furious: The Story of American International Pictures.* Jefferson, North Carolina: McFarland, 1984.

———. *Roger Corman: The Best of the Cheap Acts.* Jefferson, North Carolina: McFarland, 1988.

Both these books cover some of the same territory and both are delightful collections of anecdotes and information, impeccably researched, of an often neglected section of American filmmaking – the B movie factory. McGee avoids any detailed critical appraisal of his subject but wallows in how these mini "epics" were cobbled together on a shoestring, which makes for delightful reading.

Mank, Gregory William. *The Hollywood Hissables.* Metuchen, New Jersey: Scarecrow, 1989.

Wonderfully detailed looks at the careers of Hollywood's top nine heavies, including John Carradine, Lionel Atwill, Lon Chaney, Jr., Basil Rathbone, and Laird Cregar.

———. *It's Alive! The Classic Cinema Saga of Frankenstein.* San Diego: Barnes, 1981.

Wonderfully written and exhaustively researched look at Universal's complete *Frankenstein* series, with plenty of behind-the-scenes material.

Marrero, Robert. *Nightmare Theater.* Key West, Florida: RGM, 1986.

Poorly written series of capsule reviews.

Meyers, Richard. *For One Week Only: The World of Exploitation Films.* Piscataway, New Jersey: New Century, 1983.

Seems more a collection of pressbook clippings than a coherent book, but does cover a number of cinematic obscurities and profile some major figures.

Moore, Darrell. *The Best, Worst, and Most Unusual Horror Films.* New York: Beekman House, 1983.

A hodgepodge of uninteresting short reviews of horror films.

Mulay, James J. *The Horror Film.* Evanston, Illinois: CineBooks, 1989.

Above-average capsule reviews with credits on 700 horror films available on video.

Naha, Ed. *The Films of Roger Corman: Brilliance on a Budget.* New York: Arco, 1982.

_____. *Horrors! From Screen to Scream*. New York: Avon, 1975.
The Corman book gives synopses of all films directed by Corman and comments from him on them, but fails to match the McGee book in going to additional sources. *Horrors!* is one of the earliest capsule review books and one of the better ones in this proliferating approach to genre filmmaking.

Newman, Kim. *Nightmare Movies*. New York: Proteus, 1984.
A look at how the horror genre has developed after *Night of the Living Dead*.

Nicholls, Peter. *The World of Fantastic Films: An Illustrated Survey*. New York: Dodd, Mead, 1984.
An intelligent look at how the genre has developed after 1968, including sections on Carpenter, Cohen, Cronenberg, De Palma, and Romero.

Parish, James Robert, and Steven Whitney. *Vincent Price Unmasked*. New York: Drake, 1974.
An unauthorized biography of Vincent Price that culls information from numerous sources. Done without cooperation or input from Price himself.

Pattison, Barrie. *The Seal of Dracula*. New York: Bounty, 1975.
Best of the Bounty horror book series, it briefly looks at vampire movies from all over the world.

Peary, Danny. *Cult Movies*. New York: Dell, 1981.
_____. *Cult Movies 2*. New York: Dell, 1983.
_____. *Cult Movies 3*. New York: Dell, 1988.
_____. ed. *Omni's Screen Flights/Screen Fantasies: The Future According to Science Fiction Cinema*. Garden City, New York: Doubleday, 1984.
Peary has given in-depth and perceptive coverage of cult films, and his work on selected horror films in the *Cult Movies* series is excellent. *Screen Flights/Screen Fantasies* is a collection of miscellaneous pieces which has a useful interview with Roger Corman plus contributions from Dan O'Bannon and Stephanie Rothman.

Pirie, David. *A Heritage of Horror: The English Gothic Cinema, 1946-1972*. New York: Avon, 1973.
_____. *The Vampire Cinema*. New York: Crescent, 1977.
Pirie is one of the most intelligent writers on the genre, and he offers the most astutely critical look at the output of the Hammer studios, tracing the film's literary antecedents and intentions. *The Vampire Cinema* is mostly a picture book, but one accompanied by accurate and intelligently written copy.

Pohle, Robert W., Jr., and Douglas C. Hart, with Christopher Lee. *The Films of Christopher Lee*. Metuchen, New Jersey: Scarecrow, 1983.
Extensive credits with some films given much better coverage than others, what particularly distinguishes this book is that Lee has written comments on each of his own films. A valuable look at an actor's varied career.

Russo, John. *Making Movies: The Inside Guide to Independent Movie Production*. New York: Dell, 1989.
Russo worked on *Night of the Living Dead* and has done his own subsequent horror films. What makes this book noteworthy is the inclusion of comments from filmmakers such as George A. Romero, Sam Raimi, and Tobe Hooper.

Sarris, Andrew. *The American Cinema: Directors and Directions 1929-1968*. New York: Dutton, 1968.
The seminal work in terms of the *auteur* theory and studying directors. Some

people have taken some of Sarris' comments too seriously, but he does not do
a bad job of briefly tracing several directors' careers and pointing out some of
the best of American cinema. Undoubtedly, this remains an important work.
Schoell, William. *Stay Out of the Shower: 25 Years of Shocker Films Beginning
with Psycho*. New York: Dembner, 1985.
    Another look at the maniac-on-the-loose subgenre. Not bad.
Siegel, Joel E. *Val Lewton: The Reality of Terror*. New York: Viking, 1973.
    Terrifically perceptive and well-researched look at the Lewton films of the
'40s. Essential for material on Tourneur, Wise and Robson.
Skal, David J. *Hollywood Gothic: The Tangled Web of Dracula from Novel to
Stage to Screen*. New York: Norton, 1990.
    An excellently researched and detailed account of the history of *Dracula*
from its conception on the part of Bram Stoker, to the first unofficial adaptation, Murnau's *Nosferatu*, Stoker's widow's attempts to suppress that film, the
various stage versions and the first official adaptation. Skal obviously prefers
the Melford-directed Spanish version and makes a good case. The book also
features several lovely and rare photographs plus a listing of all the best-
known vampire films ever produced.
Stanley, John. *Revenge of the Creature Features Movie Guide*. Pacifica, California: Creatures at Large, 1988.
    Four thousand joky capsule reviews of varying quality, better on recent
films than on older ones. This third edition does clean up some previous errors.
Steinbrunner, Chris, and Burt Goldblatt. *Cinema of the Fantastic*. New York:
Galahad, 1972.
    In-depth look at 15 films including *Freaks, The Black Cat* and *Mad Love*.
Taylor, Al, and Sue Roy. *Making a Monster*. New York: Crown, 1980.
    Fascinating look at Hollywood's most famous makeup men and their crea-
tions during the era prior to makeup dominating the horror field, i.e., before
Savini, Bottin, Baker, Fullerton, et al.
Vale, V., and Andrea Juno, eds. *RE/Search #10: Incredibly Strange Films*. San
Francisco: RE/Search, 1986.
    Interestingly skims over the marginalia of cinema.
Van Hise, James. *Nightmares on Elm Street: The Freddy Krueger Story*. Las
Vegas: Pop Cult, 1988.
    A look at the most popular horror figure of the '80s.
Warren, Bill. *Keep Watching the Skies! Vols. I & II*. Jefferson, North Carolina:
McFarland, 1982 and 1986.
    The best books on the science fiction film genre yet written, with detailed
and loving looks at every science fiction film released in the United States be-
tween 1950 and 1962. During this period, the horror field was mostly con-
sumed by the science fiction field, resulting in some hybrids. This is a must-
have tome for any science fiction film aficionado.
Weaver, Tom. *Interviews with B Science Fiction and Horror Movie Makers:
Writers, Producers, Directors, Actors, Moguls and Makeup*. Jefferson, North
Carolina: McFarland, 1989.
    Weaver and his occasional cointerviewers John and Michael Brunas do a
wonderful job of catching up with the B movie people others have overlooked
and getting many fascinating behind-the-scenes stories. A must for the B movie
lover and anyone interested in low-budget filmmaking and its problems.

Weldon, Michael. *The Psychotronic Encyclopedia of Film.* New York: Ballantine, 1983.

    Probably the best book of capsule reviews of exploitation movies, with accurate plot synopses and credits, some unusual still selections, and (most important) a sense of fun. Truly a delightful and valuable work.

Willis, Donald C. *Horror and Science Fiction Films II.* Metuchen, New Jersey: Scarecrow, 1982.

    Willis is one of the pioneers in tracking down obscure horror credits and revealing their horror element. Makes an excellent supplement to Walt Lee's quintessential guide.

Youngkin, Stephen D.; James Bigwood; and Raymond G. Cabana, Jr. *The Films of Peter Lorre.* Secaucus, New Jersey: Citadel, 1982.

    One of the best *Films of* . . . books ever written about an actor who is often sorely underappreciated. Includes detailed looks at all of Lorre's films.

Periodicals

American Cinematographer

    This journal of the American Society of Cinematographers has provided some of the best behind-the-scenes coverage of making classic American films for the past 50 years. It is a constant treasure trove of cinematic lore.

Bewilderbeast

    Short-lived magazine by the author which was highly praised for its interviews and insights.

Bizarre

    A fanzine originally published by Sam Irvin, Jr., as a teenager. The third and fourth issues were huge and had impressive interviews with some top horror filmmakers. The magazine started at the press kit level and then got much better.

Black Oracle

    George Stover's little horror fanzine with its miniscule print, sometimes packed a lot into its pages. It lasted for ten issues and then became the slick *Cinemacabre*, q.v.

Bleeder's Digest

    Paul Higson's fanzine from England keeps track of the careers of horror stars past and present with numerous capsule reviews and some interviews as well.

Castle of Frankenstein

    Was published sporadically throughout the '60s and into the early '70s and offered a more adult view of contemporary horror films than its professional competitors.

Cine Fan

    Randall Larson puts out a huge issue every half-decade, offering a cornucopia of information and background material on all kinds of fantastic-oriented films.

Cinefantastique

    Went slick and quickly became the premier magazine on fantastic films in the '70s. Published by Fredrick E. Clarke, it has always had superior layouts, courted the friendly and attacked the difficult, with the result that it has alienated some of the major filmmakers and studios in the '80s. It dares to print stories on issues that other magazines will not address, with the result that sometimes the information is more rumor than fact. The magazine has made some enemies, but when it covers something well, there are few film magazines that can compare.

Cinemacabre
Geroge Stover and John E. Parnum put this slickly formatted horror fanzine out with some sharp reviews and interesting articles on major horror film-makers.

Daily Variety
The green-sheeted "bible of show business" has been an inexhaustible source of reviews and sundry pieces of information for more than 60 years.

Deep Red
Chas. Ballun's approach is uncritically glorifying the gore film, but never-theless, he does cover some foreign filmmakers who are often neglected and overlooked. This one is definitely oriented to the modern-day horror fan and gives fans what they want.

Famous Monsters of Filmland
The horror magazine that started horror film criticism and horror film fan-dom. Edited by the incomparable Forry Ackerman, it provided extensive tid-bits and stills on all manner of horror films and did much to revive and con-solidate the horror field, as well as being written on a simple, fun level that acquired new converts.

Famous Monsters of Movieland
Forry Ackerman left by the fourth issue of this attempted revival in the '80s, but it did have occasional worthwhile pieces however poorly printed it was.

Fangoria
Quickly became the premier horror film magazine of the '80s. It also did much to glorify overlooked and forgotten filmmakers of the past. It is still tops in its field.

Fantastic Films
Michael Stein published this now-defunct *Starlog* (q.v.) competitor and now does the more interesting and specialized magazine *Filmfax*, q.v.

Film Comment
One of the major American film journals. Occasionally features an intel-ligent look at a horror filmmaker and has done some wonderful coverage of exploitation films.

Filmfax
Specializes in getting the stories on nostalgic B movies of the '50s and before.

Films and Filming
One of the major British film magazines. Features extensive pictorials and reviews, and some excellent articles on the genre as a whole have appeared.

Gore Creatures
Juvenile title of Gary Svehla's horror fanzine, now known as *Midnight Mar-quee*, q.v. Despite the title, the contents offered some very well-researched,

intelligent, and informed commentary on various horror films. One of the best of the fanzines.

Gorezone
A *Fangoria* (q.v.) spin-off cynically designed to push competitors off the rack at the newsstands. Occasional interesting features do not make up for skimpy, picture-heavy presentations, though it has already spawned another spin-off, *Toxic Horror*.

Hi-Tech Terror
Video review magazine edited by Craig Ledbetter. Specialized in reviewing the hard-to-find and little-seen foreign film productions. Has now been replaced by Ledbetter's new reviewzine *European Trash Cinema*.

The Hollywood Reporter
The film community's other major paper (besides *Daily Variety*, q.v.) is also an excellent source of news, information and reviews on films going back to the beginning of the sound era.

Horrorfan
Bruce Schoengood's shortlived horror film magazine was well intentioned but suffered from squeezed presentation and a difficulty in establishing credibility.

Japanese Fantasy Film Journal
Greg Shoemaker's impressively designed magazine was the best English-language source of information on Japanese fantasy films.

Little Shoppe of Horrors
Richard Klemensen's fanzine started covering all British horror films but then quickly specialized in the products of Britain's major horror studio – Hammer. There is still no better source of information on Hammer films than the back issues of his sporadically published magazine.

Magick Theatre
With a sense of graphics, design and fun that owed something to *Castle of Frankenstein* (q.v.), Raymond Young's magazine became one of the fan favorites of the '80s.

Midnight Marquee
Gary Svehla has set and maintained a high standard of film scholarship and criticism for his magazine, which looks at horror films both past and present. It is the longest-lived publication devoted exclusively to horror films.

Photon
The premier magazine of horror films past, edited by Mark Frank. With a terrific staff that included Ron Borst, Bill Warren, Paul Jensen, and Scott MacQueen, the horror film genre has not seen its like in impeccably well-researched, thorough presentation on film from the '30s to the '60s. A treasure.

Psychotronic Video
Michael Weldon, author of the *Psychotronic Encyclopedia of Film*, has launched this interesting and oddball video review magazine with a plethora of information for the lover of exploitation films and schlock rock.

Sam Hain
Named after the Celtic celebration that inspired Halloween, this has become the horror magazine of Great Britain, calling attention to quality horror films in the present and recent past.

SF Movieland
   Bob Straus and James Van Hise edited this informative but often overlooked magazine on the science fiction and horror film field. Featured some fine interviews.
Shock Xpress
   An iconoclastic and sometimes amusing horror film fanzine from Stefan Jaworzyn. It knows when it is covering trash but delights in covering it anyway. This is a good source of information on obscure foreign horror filmmakers.
Slaughterhouse
   A nationally distributed joke, now defunct, that comically covered the horror film field with a unique (to say the least) approach. Sometimes delightfully informal, it could also be frustratingly misleading or even a waste of time, depending on the article in question. Would sometimes have articles on films which ended up having nothing to do with the film in question. Edited by the Cleaver.
Spaghetti Cinema
   Bill Connolly's fanzine sometimes relies heavily on plot synopses, but no one has done a more thorough job of covering the Italian film field in English than he has.
Splatter Times
   Once a newsletter of the gore film field which featured info on the obscure. Its editor, Donald Farmer, has gone on to become a low-budget horror film director himself.
Starburst
   A British magazine that showed some promise and had some good articles in the early '80s but has now degenerated into a series of short puff pieces.
Starlog
   Specializes in celebrities of science fiction film and television, but there is occasionally some overlap with the horror field. Quality and interest of material range widely – it's become the *People* magazine of visual science fiction – but each issue has at least one article of genuine interest for those serious about the genre.
Take One
   Lamented Canadian film magazine featured insightful reviewers and some terrific articles on Hollywood's up-and-comers, as well as Harry Ringel's famous piece on the films of Terence Fisher. Too bad there is not something like it around today.
Video Watchdog
   The brainchild of Tim and Donna Lucas, *Video Watchdog* specializes in tracking down obscure foreign video releases, notifying consumers about title changes, trims, various versions, and providing in-depth articles on overlooked European exploitation directors.
Wet Paint
   Jeff Smith puts together an oddball hodgepodge, the interests of which vary widely, but there should always be a place for an eclectic fanzine and it has featured some interesting surprises from time to time.

Index of Film Titles

A

Abbott and Costello Meet Franken-
   stein 99, 105
Abbott and Costello Meet the
   Mummy 299
Abby 477–78
The Abominable Dr. Phibes 444–48,
   452
Absurd 296
Alice, Sweet Alice 829–30
Alien 118, 805, 806
Aliens 806, 847
Alligator 309, 834
The Alligator People 660
Alone in the Dark 828
The Amazing Transparent Man 694
Amazon Women on the Moon 300,
   327
American Gothic 558
American Werewolf in London 257,
   313
And Now the Screaming Starts 56–
   57
And Soon the Darkness 443–44
Angel Heart 493
The Anniversary 46–47, 60
April Fool's Day 837–38
Arachnophobia 794, 807
Assault on Precinct 13 119–20
Astro-Zombies 798
Asylum 54–55, 60
Asylum of Satan 476
Atom Age Vampire 69
Attack of the Crab Monsters 216
Attack of the 50 Foot Woman xiv,
   218, 514
Audrey Rose 748–49
The Awakening 524
The Aztec Mummy 3

B

Baron Blood 78
Basket Case 786
Basket Case 2 787
The Bat Whispers 1, 98
The Beast from 20,000 Fathoms 527
The Beast Master 770
The Beast with Five Fingers 399,
   408–10, 660, 697
The Beast Within 781, 789, 802
Bedlam 629–33
Beetle Juice 7
Before I Hang 3
The Beyond 464
Beyond the Door 81
Beyond the Time Barrier 694
Big Trouble in Little China 138–39,
   140
Biggles – Adventures in Time 558
The Bird with the Crystal Plumage
   11–12, 13, 17
The Birds 5, 316, 479, 645, 849,
   852
The Black Cat (1934) 22, 681, 682–89
The Black Cat (1941) 564
The Black Cat (1980) 464
Black Christmas 174
Black Friday 564, 689
The Black Room 2
Black Sabbath 22, 72–74
The Black Sleep 162, 582–83, 584
Black Sunday 61, 62–69, 72, 471
Blacula 477
The Blob (1958) 650
Blood and Black Lace 74
Blood Bath 813
Blood Feast 796
Blood from the Mummy's Tomb˙
   524–25

867